HAMMOND

CONTEMPORARY

WORLD ATLAS

NEW CENSUS EDITION

INCLUDING ZIP CODES

DOUBLEDAY and COMPANY, Inc.   GARDEN CITY, NEW YORK

GAZETTEER-INDEX OF THE WORLD

This alphabetical list of grand divisions, countries, states colonial possessions, etc., gives page numbers and index references on which they shown on the largest scale as well as area and population of each unit. The index reference shows the square on the respective map in wh the name of the entry may be located.

Country	Page No.	Index Ref.	Area (Sq. Miles)	Population
Afars and Issas, Terr. of the..	55	P 9	8,498	125,050
*Afghanistan	70	A 2	250,000	17,078,263
Africa	54, 57	......	11,682,000	345,000,000
Alabama, U.S.A.	130		51,609	3,444,165
Alaska, U.S.A.	133	......	586,412	302,173
*Albania	43	E 5	11,100	2,126,000
Alberta, Canada	114	E 5	255,285	1,614,000
*Algeria	54	F 6	919,595	13,547,000
American Samoa	89	J 7	76	27,769
Andorra	31	G 1	175	19,000
Angola	57	K14	481,351	5,430,000
Antarctica	88		5,500,000	....
Antigua & Dependencies	125	G 3	171	63,000
*Argentina	111	......	1,072,070	23,983,000
Arizona, U.S.A.	134	......	113,909	1,772,482
Arkansas, U.S.A.	139		53,104	1,923,295
Ascension	5	G 8	34	1,486
Asia	58	......	17,032,000	2,043,997,000
*Australia	86	......	2,967,741	12,630,000
*Austria	38	B 3	32,374	7,419,341
Bahama Islands	124	C 1	4,404	168,838
Bahrein	60	F 4	231	207,000
*Barbados	125	G 4	166	253,620
*Belgium	25	......	11,779	9,660,154
Bermuda	125	H 3	21	52,000
Bhutan	70	G 3	18,000	770,000
*Bolivia	102	......	424,163	4,804,000
*Botswana	57	L16	219,815	629,000

Country	Page No.	Index Ref.	Area (Sq. Miles)	Populat
*Brazil	99	......	3,284,426	90,840,
British Columbia, Canada	114	D 5	366,255	2,161,
British Honduras	122	C 2	8,867	122
British Solomon Is. Prot.	89	G 6	11,500	161,
Brunei	83	E 4	2,226	130
*Bulgaria	43	G 4	42,829	8,501,
*Burma	81	B 2	261,789	27,000,
*Burundi	57	M12	10,747	3,475,
California, U.S.A.	140	......	158,693	19,953,
*Cambodia	81	E 4	69,898	6,701,
*Cameroon	54	J10	183,568	5,836,
*Canada	114-115	......	3,851,809	21,489,
Canal Zone	123	H 6	647	44
Cape Verde Islands	5	F 9	1,557	250
Cayman Islands	124	B 3	100	10
*Central African Republic	54	K10	240,534	1,518,
Central America	122-123	......	196,928	16,090,
*Ceylon	70	E 7	25,332	12,300,
*Chad	54	K 8	495,753	3,510,
Channel Islands	11	E 8	75	117,
*Chile	106	......	292,257	8,834,
China (mainland)	77	......	3,691,506	740,000,
*China (Taiwan)	77	K 7	13,948	14,577,
*Colombia	94	......	439,513	21,117,
Colorado, U.S.A.	145	......	104,247	2,207,
Comoro Is.	57	P14	838	270,
*Congo, Dem. Rep. of the	57	L12	905,563	21,637,
*Congo, Rep. of	57	J12	175,676	915,

* Members of the United Nations.

Country	Page No.	Index Ref.	Area (Sq. Miles)	Population
onnecticut, U.S.A.	146	......	5,009	3,032,217
ook Islands	89	K 7	93	20,000
osta Rica	122	E 5	19,575	1,800,000
uba	124	B 2	44,206	8,553,395
yprus	64	E 5	3,473	649,000
zechoslovakia	39	C 2	49,370	14,497,000
ahomey	54	G10	44,290	2,640,000
elaware, U.S.A.	181	R 3	2,057	548,104
enmark	19	......	16,614	4,910,000
istrict of Columbia, U.S.A.	180	F 5	67	756,510
ominica	125	G 4	290	70,302
ominican Republic	124	D 3	18,704	4,011,589
cuador	100	C 3	109,483	6,144,000
gypt (U.A.R.)	54	M 6	386,100	33,329,000
l Salvador	122	C 4	8,260	3,418,455
ngland, U.K.	11	......	50,327	46,102,300
quatorial Guinea	57	H11	10,832	286,000
thiopia	54, 55	O 9	471,776	24,764,000
urope	6	......	4,063,000	644,574,000
aerøe Islands, Denmark	19	B 2	540	38,000
alkland Islands	90	E 8	4,618	2,000
iji	89	H 8	7,015	519,000
inland	16	......	130,128	4,706,000
lorida, U.S.A.	148	......	58,560	6,789,443
rance	26	......	212,841	50,770,000
rench Guiana	96	E 3	35,135	48,000
rench Polynesia	89	L 8	1,544	109,000
abon	57	J12	103,346	500,000
ambia	54	C 9	4,003	357,000
eorgia, U.S.A.	152	......	58,876	4,589,575
ermany, East (German Democratic Republic)	20	......	41,814	17,117,000
ermany, West (Federal Republic of)	20	......	95,959	61,194,600
hana	54	F10	91,843	8,545,561
ibraltar	31	D 4	2	27,000
ilbert and Ellice Is.	89	J 6	369	55,185
reat Britain and Northern Ireland (United Kingdom)	8	......	94,214	55,534,000
reece	43	F 6	50,548	8,838,000
reenland	112	O 2	840,000	47,000
renada	125	G 4	133	105,000
uadeloupe and Dependencies	124	F 3	687	324,000
uam	89	E 4	212	86,926
uatemala	122	B 3	42,042	5,200,000
uinea	54	D 9	94,925	3,890,000
uyana	96	B 3	83,000	763,000
aiti	124	D 3	10,694	4,867,190
awaii, U.S.A.	155	......	6,450	769,913
olland (Netherlands)	25	......	13,958	13,077,000
onduras	122	D 3	43,277	2,495,000
ong Kong	77	J 7	398	4,089,000
ungary	39	E 3	35,915	10,315,597
celand	19	B 1	39,768	203,000
daho, U.S.A.	156	......	83,557	713,008
llinois, U.S.A.	158	......	56,400	11,113,976
ndia	70	......	1,261,483	546,955,945
ndiana, U.S.A.	163	......	36,291	5,193,669
ndonesia	83	......	735,264	119,572,000
owa, U.S.A.	164	......	56,290	2,825,041
ran	68	......	636,293	28,448,000
raq	68	......	167,924	9,431,000
reland	15	......	26,600	2,944,000
reland, Northern, U.K.	15	G 2	5,459	1,512,500

Country	Page No.	Index Ref.	Area (Sq. Miles)	Population
Isle of Man, U.K.	11	C 3	227	50,000
*Israel	67	......	7,993	2,911,000
*Italy	32	......	116,303	54,504,000
*Ivory Coast	54	E10	124,503	4,800,000
*Jamaica	124	C 3	4,411	1,972,000
*Japan	75	......	142,774	103,540,000
*Jordan	67	......	37,297	2,300,000
Kansas, U.S.A.	168	......	82,264	2,249,071
Kentucky, U.S.A.	173	.....	40,395	3,219,311
*Kenya	57	O11	224,960	10,880,200
Korea, North	74	D 3	46,540	13,300,000
Korea, South	74	E 5	38,452	31,683,000
*Kuwait	60	E 4	8,000	733,196
*Laos	81	E 3	91,459	2,900,000
*Lebanon	64	F 6	4,015	2,800,000
*Lesotho	57	M17	11,716	930,000
*Liberia	54	E10	43,000	1,200,000
*Libya	54	J 6	679,359	1,900,000
Liechtenstein	37	J 2	61	21,000
Louisiana, U.S.A.	175	......	48,523	3,643,180
*Luxembourg	25	J 9	999	339,000
Macao	77	H 7	6.2	292,000
Madeira, Portugal	30	A 2	308	268,700
Maine, U.S.A.	178	......	33,215	993,663
*Malagasy Republic	57	R16	226,657	7,011,563
*Malawi	57	N14	45,483	4,530,000
Malaya, Malaysia	81	D 6	50,670	9,000,000
*Malaysia	81, 83	......	128,308	10,583,000
*Maldives	58	L 9	115	110,770
*Mali	54	F 8	463,948	4,929,000
*Malta	32	E 7	122	321,000
Man, Isle of, U.K.	11	C 3	227	50,000
Manitoba, Canada	114	G 3	251,000	979,000
Martinique	125	G 4	425	332,000
Maryland, U.S.A.	181	......	10,577	3,922,399
Massachusetts, U.S.A.	184	......	8,257	5,689,170
*Mauritania	54	D 8	397,954	1,140,000
*Mauritius	57	S19	709	823,000
*Mexico	119	......	761,601	48,313,438
Michigan, U.S.A.	186	......	58,216	8,875,083
Midway Islands	154	A 5	2	2,356
Minnesota, U.S.A.	190	......	84,068	3,805,069
Mississippi, U.S.A.	192	......	47,716	2,216,912
Missouri, U.S.A.	197	......	69,686	4,677,399
Monaco	26	G 6	368 Acres	23,035
*Mongolia	77	F 2	604,247	1,300,000
Montana, U.S.A.	198	......	147,138	694,409
Montserrat	125	G 3	38	12,300
*Morocco	54	E 5	172,413	15,577,000
Mozambique	57	N16	302,328	7,376,000
Nauru	89	G 6	8.2	7,000
Nebraska, U.S.A.	201	......	77,227	1,483,791
*Nepal	70	E 3	54,362	10,845,000
*Netherlands	25	......	13,958	13,077,000
Netherlands Antilles	124	D 4,F 3	390	220,000
Nevada, U.S.A.	202	......	110,540	488,738
New Brunswick, Canada	115	K 6	28,354	624,000
New Caledonia and Dependencies	89	G 8	7,335	100,579
Newfoundland, Canada	115	L 5	156,185	520,000
New Guinea, Terr. of (Aust. Trust.)	89	E 6	92,160	1,722,572
New Hampshire, U.S.A.	204	......	9,304	737,681
New Hebrides	89	G 7	5,700	80,000
New Jersey, U.S.A.	209	......	7,836	7,168,164

Members of the United Nations.

Country	Page No.	Index Ref.	Area (Sq. Miles)	Population
New Mexico, U.S.A.	210	......	121,666	1,016,000
New York, U.S.A.	212	......	49,576	18,190,740
*New Zealand	87	......	103,736	2,815,000
*Nicaragua	122	D 4	45,698	1,984,000
*Niger	54	H 8	489,189	4,016,000
*Nigeria	54	H10	356,669	66,174,000
Niue	89	K 7	100	5,323
North America	112	......	9,363,000	314,000,000
North Carolina, U.S.A.	217	......	52,586	5,082,059
North Dakota, U.S.A.	218	......	70,665	617,761
Northern Ireland, U.K.	15	G 2	5,459	1,512,500
Northwest Territories, Canada	114	E 2	1,304,903	34,000
*Norway	16	......	125,181	3,893,000
Nova Scotia, Canada	115	K 7	21,425	767,000
Oceania	88-89	......	3,291,138	19,649,000
Ohio, U.S.A.	220	......	41,222	10,652,017
Oklahoma, U.S.A.	225	......	69,919	2,559,253
Oman	60	G 6	82,000	565,000
Ontario, Canada	114	H 5	412,582	7,707,000
Oregon, U.S.A.	226	......	96,981	2,091,385
Pacific Islands, U.S. Trust Terr. of the	88-89	E, F 5	700	98,009
*Pakistan	70	B, F 3	365,527	112,600,000
*Panama	122	G 6	29,209	1,425,343
Papua, Australia	82	B 7	86,100	648,000
*Paraguay	104	......	157,047	2,314,000
Pennsylvania, U.S.A.	230	......	45,333	11,793,909
*Persia (Iran)	68	......	636,293	28,448,000
*Peru	100	......	496,222	13,586,300
*Philippines	83	H 4	115,707	39,079,000
Pitcairn Islands	89	O 8	1.8	74
*Poland	45	......	120,664	32,889,000
*Portugal	30	......	35,510	9,560,000
Portuguese Guinea	54	C 9	13,948	530,000
Portuguese Timor	83	H 7	5,762	590,000
Prince Edward Island, Canada	115	K 6	2,184	110,000
Puerto Rico	124-125	G 1	3,435	2,689,932
Qatar	60	F 4	8,500	100,000
Québec, Canada	114	J 5	594,860	6,023,000
Réunion	57	R20	969	436,000
Rhode Island, U.S.A.	184	H 5	1,214	949,723
Rhodesia	57	M15	150,332	5,310,000
*Rumania	43	F 3	91,699	20,394,000
*Rwanda	57	N12	10,169	3,500,000
Ryukyu Islands	75	L 7	848	989,000
Sabah, Malaysia	83	F 4	29,388	633,000
St. Christopher-Nevis-Anguilla	124	F 3	138	56,000
St. Helena and Dependencies	5	H 8	47	6,462
St. Lucia	125	G 4	238	40,000
St-Pierre and Miquelon	115	L 6	93.5	5,235
St. Vincent	125	F 4	150	95,000
San Marino	32	D 3	23.4	19,000
São Tomé e Príncipe	57	G11	372	66,000
Sarawak, Malaysia	83	E 5	48,250	950,000
Saskatchewan, Canada	114	F 5	251,700	933,000
*Saudi Arabia	60	D 4	920,000	7,200,000
Scotland, U.K.	13	......	30,411	5,194,700
*Senegal	54	D 9	75,750	3,780,000
Seychelles	58	J10	109	51,396
*Siam (Thailand)	81	D 3	198,456	35,448,000
*Sierra Leone	54	C10	27,925	2,512,000
*Singapore	81	F 6	226	2,034,000
Solomon Islands Prot.	89	G 6	11,500	161,525

Country	Page No.	Index Ref.	Area (Sq. Miles)	Populati
*Somalia	55	R10	246,200	2,730,0
*South Africa	57	L18	471,663	21,282,0
South America	90	......	6,875,000	186,000,0
South Carolina, U.S.A.	232	......	31,055	2,590,5
South Dakota, U.S.A.	234	......	77,047	666,2
South-West Africa	57	K16	317,838	615,0
*Spain	31	......	194,896	33,290,0
Spanish Sahara, Spain	54	D 7	102,702	63,0
*Sudan	54	M 9	967,495	15,312,0
Surinam	96	C 3	55,144	389,0
*Swaziland	57	N17	6,704	411,8
*Sweden	16	......	173,665	7,978,0
Switzerland	37	......	15,941	6,230,0
*Syria	64	G 5	71,498	5,866,0
*Tanzania	57	N13	362,819	12,896,0
Tennessee, U.S.A.	173	......	42,244	3,924,1
Texas, U.S.A.	238	......	267,339	11,196,7
*Thailand	81	D 3	198,456	35,448,0
*Togo	54	G10	21,853	2,004,7
Tokelau Islands	89	J 6	3.9	2,0
Tonga	89	J 8	270	83,0
*Trinidad and Tobago	125	G 5	1,980	1,040,0
Tristan da Cunha	5	J 8	40	2
Trucial States	60	F 5	32,278	179,1
*Tunisia	54	H 5	63,378	5,027,0
*Turkey	64	......	301,381	34,375,0
Turks and Caicos Is.	124	D 2	166	6,0
*Uganda	57	N11	92,674	9,764,0
*Ukrainian S.S.R., U.S.S.R.	50	C 5	232,046	47,136,0
*Union of Soviet Socialist Republics	46, 50	......	8,649,498	241,748,0
*United Arab Republic (Egypt)	54	M 6	386,100	33,329,0
*United Kingdom	8	......	94,214	55,534,0
*United States of America	126-127	......	3,615,123	203,184,7
*Upper Volta	54	F 9	105,841	5,330,0
*Uruguay	105	......	72,172	2,900,0
Utah, U.S.A.	240	......	84,916	1,059,2
Vatican City	32	B 6	109 Acres	1,0
*Venezuela	92	......	352,143	10,398,9
Vermont, U.S.A.	204	......	9,609	444,7
Vietnam, North	81	E 3	61,293	21,340,0
Vietnam, South	81	F 4	66,263	16,543,4
Virginia, U.S.A.	243	......	40,817	4,648,4
Virgin Islands, British	125	H 1	59	10,4
Virgin Islands, U.S.A.	125	H 1	133	63,2
Wake Island, U.S.A.	89	G 4	3	1,0
Wales (incl. Monmouthshire), U.K.	11	D 5	8,017	2,724,5
Washington, U.S.A.	246	......	68,192	3,409,1
West Indies	124-125	......	91,118	24,843,0
Western Samoa	89	J 7	1,097	139,8
West Virginia, U.S.A.	248	......	24,181	1,744,2
*White Russian S.S.R. (Byelorussian S.S.R.), U.S.S.R.	50	C 4	80,154	9,003,0
Wisconsin, U.S.A.	253	......	56,154	4,417,9
World	5	......	57,491,000	3,632,000,0
Wyoming, U.S.A.	254	......	97,914	332,4
*Yemen Arab Republic	60	D 7	75,000	5,000,0
*Yemen, Peoples Democratic Republic of	60	E 7	111,075	1,220,0
*Yugoslavia	43	C 3	98,766	20,586,0
Yukon Territory, Canada	114	C 3	207,076	17,0
*Zambia	57	M14	290,586	4,056,9

* Members of the United Nations.

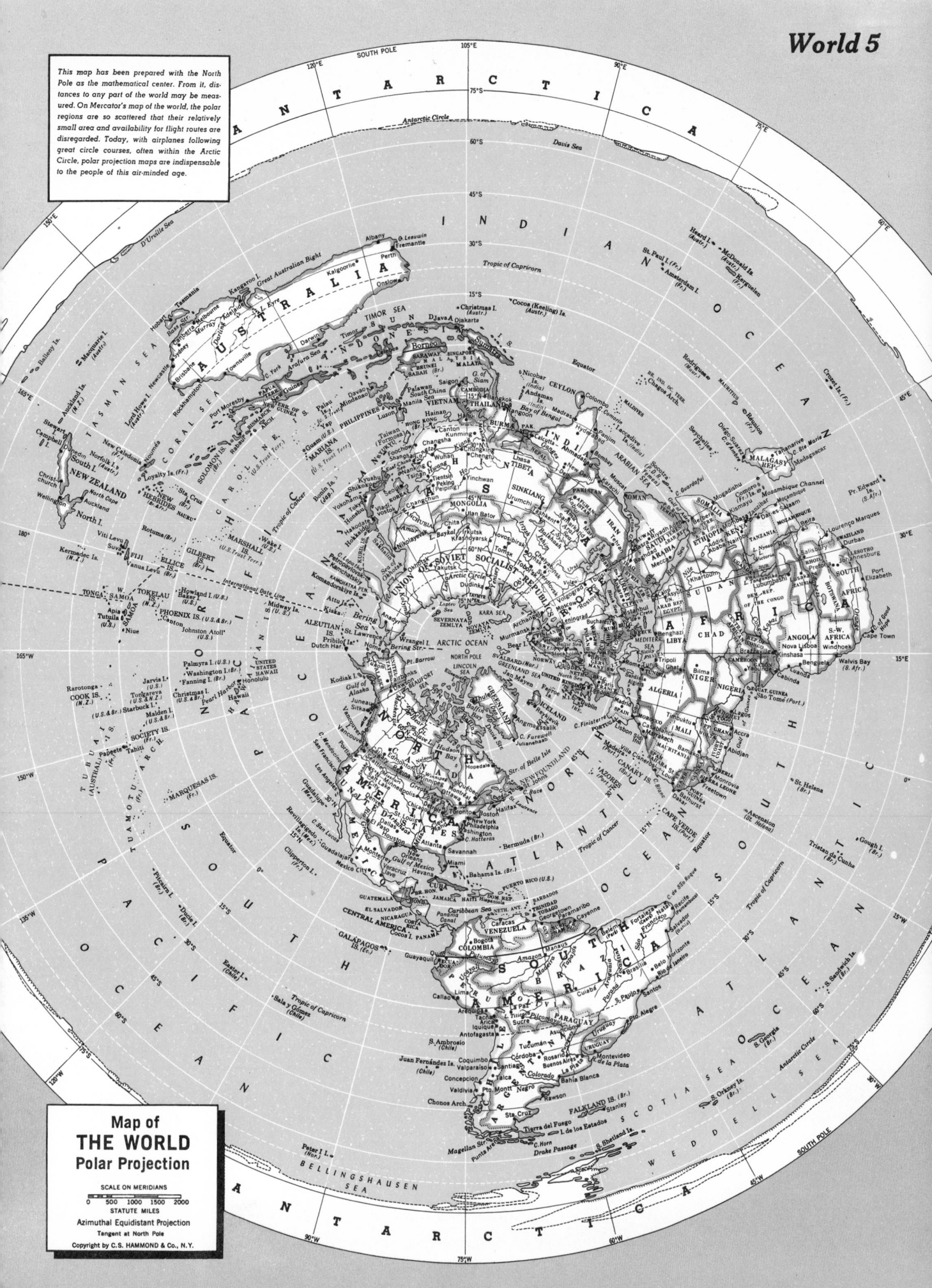

World 5

This map has been prepared with the North Pole as the mathematical center. From it, distances to any part of the world may be measured. On Mercator's map of the world, the polar regions are so scattered that their relatively small area and availability for flight routes are disregarded. Today, with airplanes following great circle courses, often within the Arctic Circle, polar projection maps are indispensable to the people of this air-minded age.

Map of
THE WORLD
Polar Projection

SCALE ON MERIDIANS

0   500   1000   1500   2000
STATUTE MILES

Azimuthal Equidistant Projection
Tangent at North Pole

Copyright by C.S. HAMMOND & Co., N.Y.

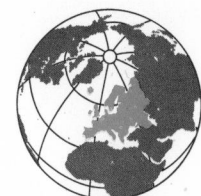

AREA 4,063,000 sq. mi.
POPULATION 644,574,000
LARGEST CITY London
HIGHEST POINT El'brus 18,481 ft.
LOWEST POINT Caspian Sea -92 ft.

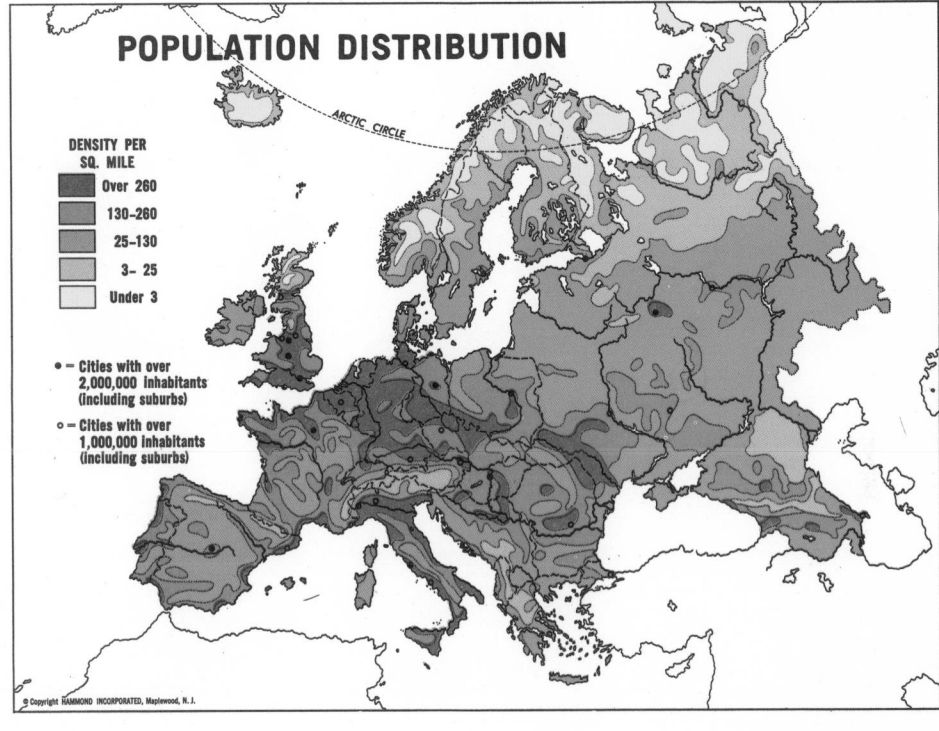

POPULATION DISTRIBUTION

DENSITY PER SQ. MILE

- Over 260
- 130–260
- 25–130
- 3– 25
- Under 3

● – Cities with over 2,000,000 inhabitants (including suburbs)

○ – Cities with over 1,000,000 inhabitants (including suburbs)

© Copyright HAMMOND INCORPORATED, Maplewood, N.J.

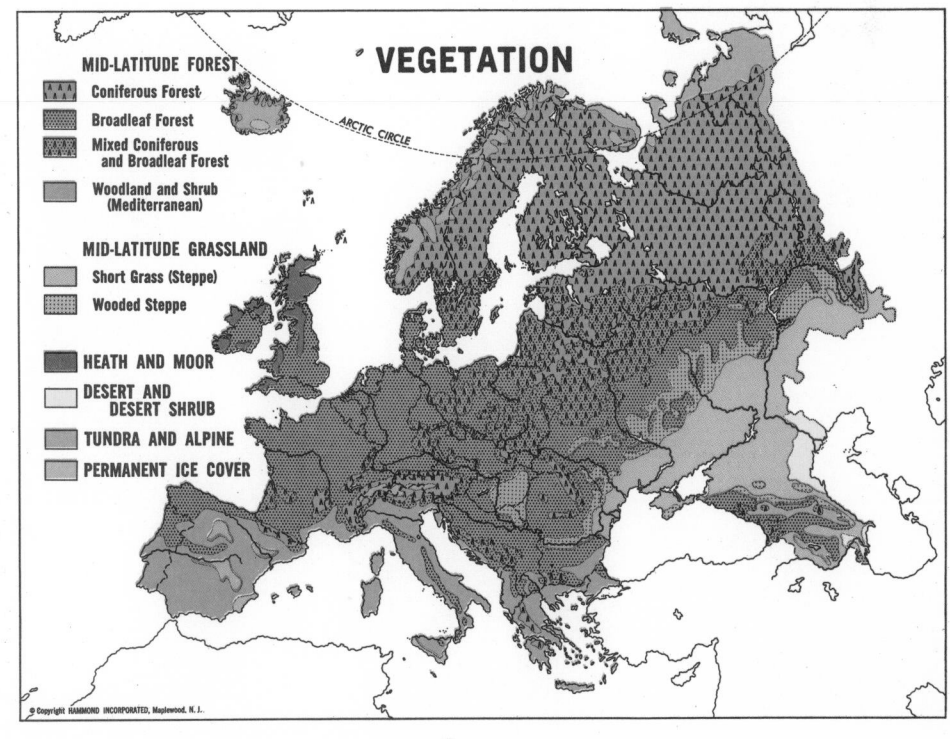

VEGETATION

MID-LATITUDE FOREST

- Coniferous Forest
- Broadleaf Forest
- Mixed Coniferous and Broadleaf Forest
- Woodland and Shrub (Mediterranean)

MID-LATITUDE GRASSLAND

- Short Grass (Steppe)
- Wooded Steppe

HEATH AND MOOR

DESERT AND DESERT SHRUB

TUNDRA AND ALPINE

PERMANENT ICE COVER

© Copyright HAMMOND INCORPORATED, Maplewood, N.J.

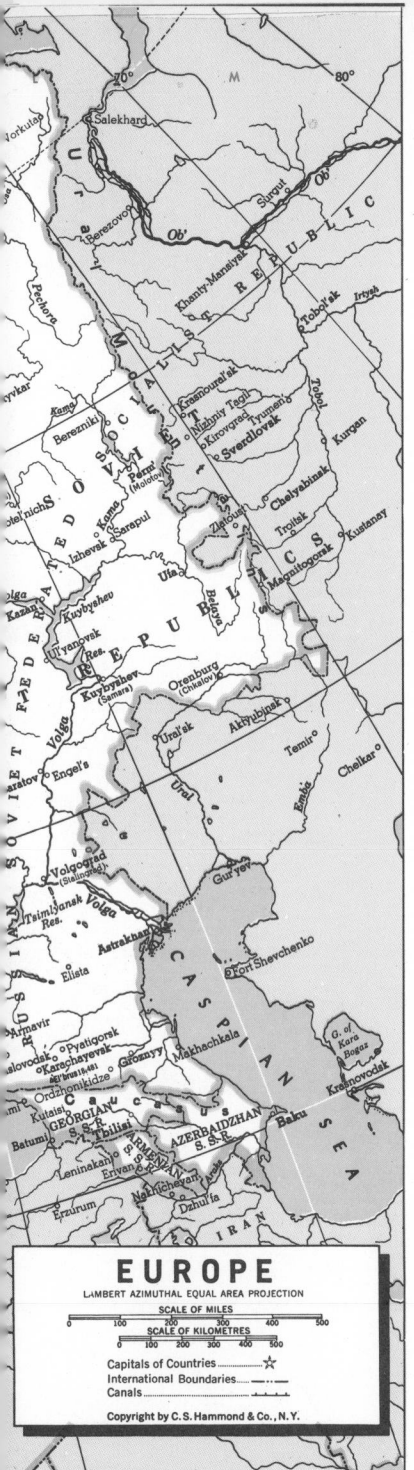

EUROPE

LAMBERT AZIMUTHAL EQUAL AREA PROJECTION

SCALE OF MILES
100   200   300   400   500

SCALE OF KILOMETRES
0   100   200   300   400

Capitals of Countries .... ☆
International Boundaries .... — · —
Canals ....

Copyright by C. S. Hammond & Co., N.Y.

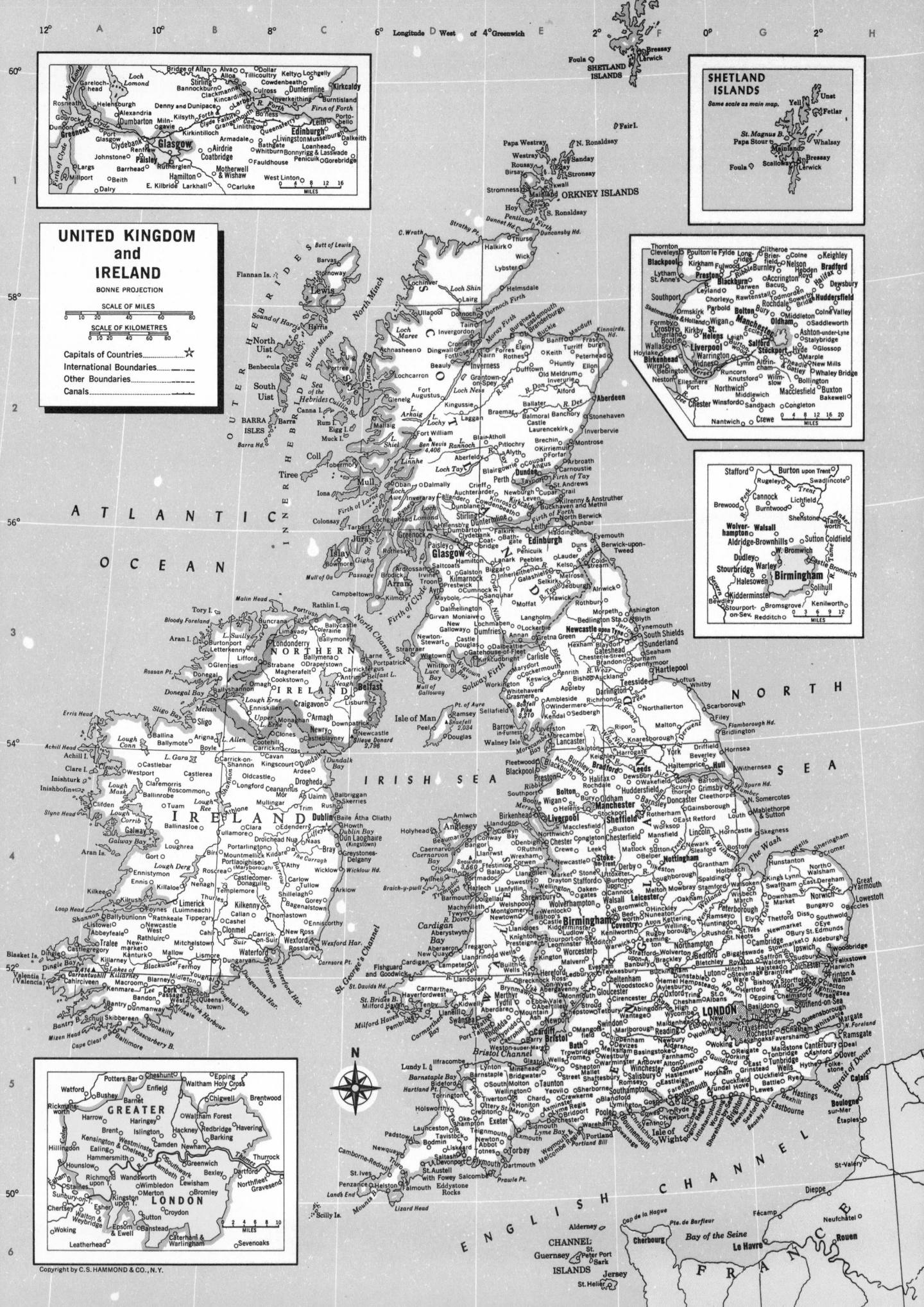

UNITED KINGDOM
and
IRELAND

BONNE PROJECTION

SCALE OF MILES

SCALE OF KILOMETRES

Capitals of Countries............☆
International Boundaries_____
Other Boundaries ___ ___
Canals ___ ___

SHETLAND
ISLANDS

Same scale as main map.

GREATER

LONDON

ORKNEY ISLANDS

ATLANTIC

OCEAN

IRISH SEA

NORTH

SEA

IRELAND

NORTHERN

IRELAND

SCOTLAND

ENGLISH CHANNEL

FRANCE

UNITED KINGDOM
AREA 94,214 sq. mi.
POPULATION 55,534,000
CAPITAL London
LARGEST CITY London
HIGHEST POINT Ben Nevis 4,406 ft.
MONETARY UNIT pound sterling
MAJOR LANGUAGES English, Gaelic, Welsh
MAJOR RELIGIONS Protestantism, Roman Catholicism

IRELAND
AREA 26,600 sq. mi.
POPULATION 2,944,000
CAPITAL Dublin
LARGEST CITY Dublin
HIGHEST POINT Carrantuohill 3,414 ft.
MONETARY UNIT Irish pound
MAJOR LANGUAGES English, Gaelic
MAJOR RELIGION Roman Catholicism

UNITED KINGDOM

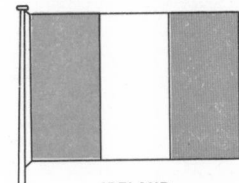
IRELAND

GREATER LONDON

CITIES and TOWNS

Banstead, 44,790 ......B 6
Barking, 167,960 ......B 5
Barnet, 314,530 ......C 5
Bexley, 215,610 ......C 5
Brent, 281,530 ......B 5
Brentwood, 58,250 ......C 5
Bromley, 303,550 ......C 5
Bushey, 25,290 ......B 5
Camden, 228,080 ......B 5
Caterham and Warlingham, 37,760 ......B 6
Chertsey, 45,250 ......B 6
Cheshunt, 43,890 ......B 5
Chigwell, 56,030 ......C 5
Croydon, 327,130 ......B 6
Dartford, 46,280 ......C 5
Ealing, 297,910 ......B 5
Egham, 30,800 ......B 5
Enfield, 265,600 ......B 5
Epping, 11,380 ......C 5
Epsom and Ewell, 72,190 ......B 6
Esher, 63,190 ......B 6
Gravesend, 55,310 ......C 5
Greenwich, 228,030 ......C 5
Hackney, 238,530 ......B 5
Hammersmith, 192,810 ......B 5
Haringey, 242,300 ......B 5
Harrow, 207,700 ......B 5
Havering, 252,860 ......C 5
Hillingdon, 237,050 ......B 5
Hounslow, 205,060 ......B 5
Islington, 235,990 ......B 5
Kensington and Chelsea, 208,480 ......B 5
Kingston-upon-Thames, 143,670 ......B 6
Lambeth, 325,070 ......B 5
Leatherhead, 39,200 ......B 6
Lewisham, 282,080 ......B 5
London (cap.), 7,703,410 ......B 5
Merton, 183,570 ......B 5
Newham, 252,090 ......C 5
Northfleet, 25,450 ......C 5
Potters Bar, 25,240 ......B 5
Redbridge, 244,800 ......C 5
Richmond-upon-Thames, 176,600 ......B 5
Rickmansworth, 30,360 ......A 5
Sevenoaks, 18,150 ......C 6
Southwark, 290,530 ......B 5
Staines, 56,610 ......B 5
Sunbury-on-Thames, 40,120 ......B 6
Sutton, 166,430 ......B 6
Thurrock, 124,830 ......C 5
Waltham Forest, 235,880 ......B 5
Waltham Holy Cross, 13,670 ......B 5
Walton and Weybridge, 52,530 ......B 6
Wandsworth, 319,190 ......B 5
Watford, 76,700 ......B 5
Westminster, 240,360 ......B 5
Wimbledon, 57,312 ......B 5
Woking, 78,180 ......B 6

OTHER FEATURES

Colne (river) ......A 5
Thames (river) ......C 5

BIRMINGHAM AREA

CITIES and TOWNS

Aldridge-Brownhills, 87,530 ......G 3
Bewdley, 6,400 ......F 3
Birmingham, 1,086,400 ......G 3
Birmingham, *2,440,540 ......G 3
Brewood, 5,751 ......G 2
Bromsgrove, 39,440 ......F 3
Burntwood, 112,085 ......G 2
Burton-upon-Trent, 50,850 ......G 2
Cannock, 54,540 ......G 2
Castle Bromwich, 9,205 ......G 3
Dudley, 181,380 ......G 3
Halesowen, 51,930 ......G 3
Kenilworth, 21,000 ......G 3
Kidderminster, 46,740 ......F 3
Lichfield, 22,530 ......G 2
Redditch, 37,910 ......G 3
Rugeley, 19,320 ......G 2
Shenstone, 5,174 ......G 3
Solihull, 110,350 ......G 3
Stafford, 54,200 ......G 2
Stourbridge, 52,290 ......G 3
Stourport-on-Severn, 16,090 ......G 3
Sutton Coldfield, 82,220 ......G 3
Swadlincote, 20,130 ......G 2

Tamworth, 37,360 ......G 3
Walsall, 184,260 ......G 3
Warley, 167,810 ......G 3
West Bromwich, 171,850 ......G 3
Wolverhampton, 264,520 ......G 3

OTHER FEATURES

Anker (river) ......G 3
Penk (river) ......F 3
Severn (river) ......F 3
Tame (river) ......G 3
Trent (river) ......G 2

LIVERPOOL-MANCHESTER AREA

CITIES and TOWNS

Accrington, 36,340 ......G 1
Altrincham, 41,000 ......G 2
Ashton-under-Lyne, 48,180 ......G 2
Bacup, 16,270 ......G 1
Bakewell, 4,170 ......G 2
Bebington, 57,060 ......F 2
Birkenhead, 141,950 ......F 2
Blackburn, 100,010 ......G 1
Blackpool, 146,700 ......F 1
Bollington, 6,150 ......G 2
Bolton, 152,500 ......G 2
Bootle, 79,950 ......F 2
Bradford, 293,210 ......H 1
Brierfield, 7,290 ......G 1
Burnley, 76,610 ......G 1
Burtonwood, 12,766 ......G 2
Bury, 67,070 ......G 2
Buxton, 20,100 ......G 2
Cheadle and Gatley, 57,290 ......G 2
Chester, 60,880 ......F 2
Chorley, 30,990 ......G 2
Clitheroe, 12,910 ......G 1
Colne, 18,890 ......G 1
Colne Valley, 21,000 ......G 2
Congleton, 19,610 ......G 2
Crewe, 51,960 ......F 2
Crosby, 58,580 ......F 2
Darwen, 28,500 ......G 1
Dewsbury, 51,560 ......H 2
Eccles, 39,830 ......G 2
Ellesmere Port, 56,750 ......F 2
Formby, 21,730 ......F 2
Fulwood, 19,880 ......G 1
Glossop, 21,830 ......G 2
Halifax, 93,570 ......G 1
Hebden Royd, 8,800 ......G 1
Hoylake, 32,190 ......F 2
Huddersfield, 130,600 ......G 2
Hyde, 38,710 ......G 2
Keighley, 55,400 ......H 1
Kirkby, 65,260 ......F 2
Kirkham, 6,380 ......F 1
Knutsford, 14,000 ......G 2
Leigh, 46,200 ......G 2
Leyland, 23,100 ......G 1
Litherland, 24,540 ......F 2
Liverpool, 677,450 ......F 2
Liverpool, *1,341,660 ......F 2
Longridge, 6,170 ......G 1
Lymm, 9,380 ......G 2
Lytham Saint Anne's, 37,000 ......F 1
Macclesfield, 41,870 ......G 2
Manchester, 593,770 ......G 2
Manchester, *2,433,370 ......G 2
Marple, 24,100 ......G 2
Middleton, 57,510 ......G 2
Middlewich, 8,000 ......G 2
Nantwich, 11,200 ......G 2
Nelson, 31,230 ......G 1
Neston, 16,940 ......F 2
New Mills, 8,880 ......G 2
Northwich, 18,940 ......G 2
Oldham, 108,280 ......G 2
Ormskirk, 25,900 ......F 2
Parbold, 1976 ......G 2
Poulton le Fylde, 16,150 ......F 1
Preston, 102,100 ......G 1
Rawtenstall, 21,640 ......G 1
Rochdale, 86,600 ......G 2
Runcorn, 31,560 ......G 2
Saddleworth, 19,620 ......G 2
Saint Helens, 102,770 ......F 2
Salford, 137,750 ......G 2
Sandbach, 12,160 ......G 2
Skelmersdale and Holland, 23,640 ......F 2
Southport, 79,430 ......F 2
Sowerby Bridge, 16,610 ......G 2
Stalybridge, 21,620 ......G 2
Stockport, 140,030 ......G 2
Thornton Cleveleys, 26,250 ......F 1
Todmorden, 15,430 ......G 1
Wallasey, 101,360 ......F 2
Warrington, 70,870 ......G 2
Whaley Bridge, 5,390 ......G 2
Widnes, 55,120 ......F 2
Wigan, 79,780 ......G 2
Wilmslow, 28,790 ......G 2
Winsford, 22,040 ......G 2
Wirral, 26,000 ......F 2

OTHER FEATURES

Dee (river) ......F 2
Irish (sea) ......F 2
Mersey (river) ......F 2
Ribble (river) ......G 1

ENGLAND
(map on page 13)

COUNTIES

Bedfordshire, 443,960 ......G 5
Berkshire, 623,540 ......F 6
Buckinghamshire, 578,210 ......G 6
Cambridgeshire and the Isle of Ely, 302,560 ......H 5
Cheshire, 1,512,820 ......E 4
Cornwall, 362,180 ......C 7
Cumberland, 295,530 ......D 3
Derbyshire, 891,570 ......F 4
Devonshire, 881,590 ......D 6
Dorsetshire, 348,840 ......E 7
Durham, 1,433,990 ......F 3
Essex, 1,314,680 ......H 6
Gloucestershire, 1,078,050 ......E 6
Hampshire (Hants), 1,551,900 ......F 6
Herefordshire, 142,060 ......E 5
Hertfordshire, 903,390 ......G 6
Huntingdon and Peterborough, 196,670 ......G 5
Isle of Wight, 102,100 ......F 7
Kent, 1,388,820 ......H 6
Lancashire, 5,182,380 ......E 4
Leicestershire, 740,170 ......F 5
Lincolnshire-Holland, 105,170 ......G 5
Lincolnshire-Kesteven, 233,040 ......G 5
Lincolnshire-Lindsey, 464,350 ......G 4

London (greater), 7,703,410 ......G 6
Norfolk, 609,930 ......H 5
Northamptonshire, 453,920 ......G 5
Northumberland, 823,030 ......E 2
Nottinghamshire, 969,730 ......F 4
Oxfordshire, 374,610 ......F 6
Rutlandshire, 29,860 ......G 5
Shropshire (Salop), 332,330 ......E 5
Somersetshire, 664,690 ......E 6
Southampton (Hampshire), 1,551,900 ......F 6
Staffordshire, 1,846,970 ......E 5
Suffolk, East, 384,210 ......J 5
Suffolk, West, 163,760 ......J 5
Surrey, 1,002,140 ......G 6
Sussex, East, 736,050 ......H 7
Sussex, West, 469,900 ......G 7
Warwickshire, 2,139,640 ......F 5
Westmorland, 71,710 ......E 3
Wight, Isle of, 102,100 ......F 7
Wiltshire, 496,930 ......F 6
Worcestershire, 683,820 ......E 5
Yorkshire-East Riding, 545,430 ......G 4
Yorkshire-North Riding, 721,870 ......F 3
Yorkshire-West Riding, 3,800,750 ......F 4

CITIES and TOWNS

Abingdon, 17,820 ......F 6
Accrington, 36,340 ......E 4
Aldershot, 38,120 ......G 6
Alfreton, 22,440 ......F 4
Andover, 24,780 ......F 6
Arnold, 31,780 ......F 4
Ashford, 35,360 ......H 6
Ashington, 25,830 ......F 2
Aylesbury, 36,730 ......G 6
Banbury, 27,900 ......F 5
Barnet, 314,530 ......G 6
Barnsley, 74,880 ......F 4
Barnstaple, 16,850 ......D 6
Barrow-in-Furness, 63,460 ......D 3
Basildon, 122,760 ......H 6
Basingstoke, 43,570 ......F 6
Bath, 84,760 ......E 6
Batley, 40,276 ......F 4
Bedford, 68,650 ......G 5
Bedlington Station (Bedlingtonshire), 30,040 ......F 2

Bedworth, 40,700 ......F 5
Beeston and Stapleford, 63,600 ......F 5
Belper, 16,360 ......F 4
Benfleet, 46,270 ......H 6
Berwick-upon-Tweed, 11,530 ......E 2
Beverley, 17,320 ......G 4
Bexhill, 33,470 ......H 7
Bideford, 11,240 ......C 6
Birkenhead, 141,950 ......D 4
Birmingham, 1,086,400 ......F 5
Birmingham, *2,440,540 ......F 5
Bishop Auckland, 34,480 ......F 3
Bishop's Stortford, 21,270 ......H 6
Blackburn, 100,010 ......E 4
Blackpool, 146,700 ......D 4
Blaydon, 32,000 ......F 3
Bletchley, 28,300 ......G 5
Blyth, 35,130 ......F 2
Bognor Regis, 31,710 ......G 7
Bolsover, 11,770 ......F 4
Bolton, 152,500 ......E 4
Bootle, 79,950 ......H 5
Boston, 25,260 ......G 5
Bournemouth, 149,820 ......F 7
Bracknell, 20,378 ......G 6
Bradford, 293,210 ......F 4
Braintree and Bocking, 23,380 ......H 6
Brandon and Byshottles, 18,490 ......F 3
Brentwood, 58,250 ......H 6
Bridgwater, 26,800 ......D 6
Bridlington, 26,430 ......G 3
Brighouse, 33,130 ......F 4
Brighton, 163,600 ......G 7
Bristol, 427,230 ......E 6
Broadstairs and St. Peter's, 20,900 ......J 6
Bromsgrove, 39,440 ......E 5
Burgess Hill, 17,980 ......G 7
Burnham-on-Sea, 11,530 ......D 6
Burnley, 76,610 ......E 4
Burton-upon-Trent, 50,850 ......F 5
Bury, 67,070 ......E 4
Bury Saint Edmunds, 25,140 ......H 5
Buxton, 20,100 ......F 4
Camborne-Redruth, 38,380 ......B 7
Cambridge, 100,200 ......H 5
Cannock, 54,540 ......E 5
Canterbury, 33,140 ......J 6
Carlisle, 71,090 ......D 3
Carlton, 42,640 ......F 4
Castleford, 39,160 ......F 4

(continued on following page)

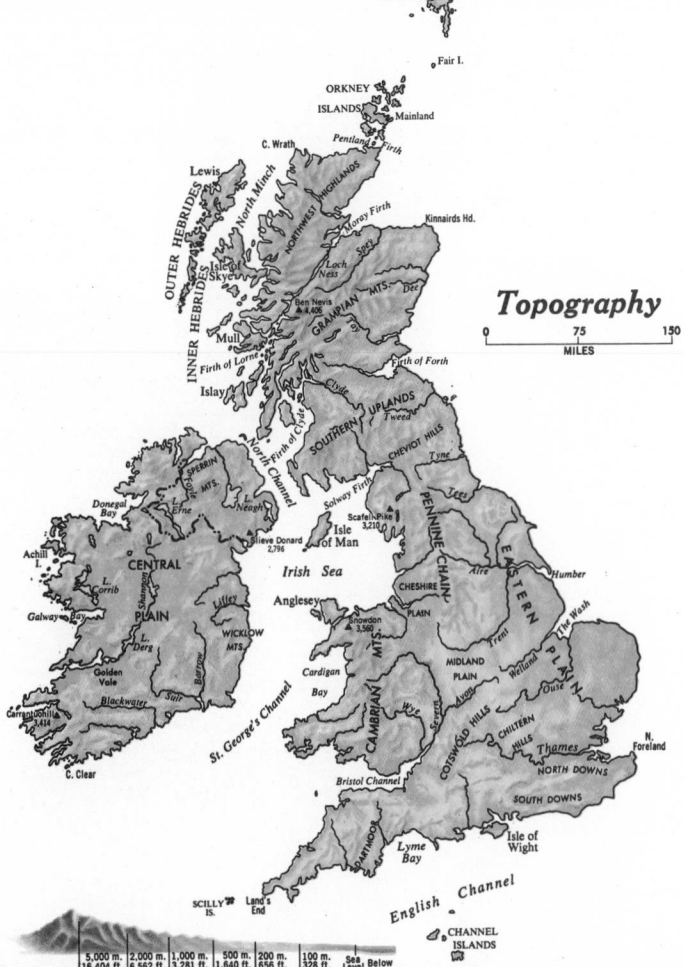

Topography

0   75   150
MILES

5,000 m. / 16,404 ft.   2,000 m. / 6,562 ft.   1,000 m. / 3,281 ft.   500 m. / 1,640 ft.   200 m. / 656 ft.   100 m. / 328 ft.   Sea Level   Below

ENGLAND
AREA 50,327 sq. mi.
POPULATION 46,102,300
CAPITAL London
LARGEST CITY London
HIGHEST POINT Scafell Pike 3,210 ft.

WALES
AREA 8,017 sq. mi.
POPULATION 2,724,540
LARGEST CITY Cardiff
HIGHEST POINT Snowdon 3,560 ft.

SCOTLAND
AREA 30,411 sq. mi.
POPULATION 5,194,700
CAPITAL Edinburgh
LARGEST CITY Glasgow
HIGHEST POINT Ben Nevis 4,406 ft.

NORTHERN IRELAND
AREA 5,459 sq. mi.
POPULATION 1,512,500
CAPITAL Belfast
LARGEST CITY Belfast
HIGHEST POINT Slieve Donard 2,796 ft.

10 United Kingdom and Ireland

(continued)

ENGLAND (continued)

Caterham and Warlingham, 37,760 .. G 6
Chatham, 55,460 .. H 6
Cheadle and Gatley, 57,290 .. F 5
Chelmsford, 56,900 .. H 6
Cheltenham, 76,000 .. F 6
Chesham, 20,750 .. G 6
Cheshunt, 43,890 .. G 6
Chester, 60,880 .. E 4
Chesterfield, 70,420 .. F 4
Chester-le-Street, 20,800 .. F 3
Chichester, 20,740 .. G 7
Chippenham, 18,970 .. F 6
Chorley, 30,990 .. E 4
Christchurch, 31,780 .. F 7
Cirencester, 13,080 .. F 6
Clacton, 35,730 .. J 6
Cleethorpes, 35,370 .. H 4
Clevedon, 13,980 .. E 6
Clitheroe, 12,910 .. E 4
Coalville, 28,470 .. F 5
Colchester, 75,210 .. H 6
Colne, 18,890 .. E 4
Congleton, 19,610 .. F 4
Consett, 37,010 .. F 3
Corby, 49,210 .. G 5
Coventry, 335,650 .. F 5
Cowes, 18,000 .. F 7
Crawley, 64,520 .. G 6
Crewe, 51,960 .. E 4
Crook and Willington, 23,050 .. F 3
Croydon, 327,130 .. G 6
Cuckfield, 24,640 .. G 6
Dalton-in-Furness, 11,000 .. D 3
Darlington, 84,700 .. F 3
Dawley, 24,240 .. E 5
Deal, 27,130 .. J 6
Derby, 221,240 .. F 5
Dewsbury, 51,560 .. F 4
Doncaster, 84,050 .. G 4
Dorchester, 13,660 .. E 7
Dorking, 22,850 .. G 6
Dover, 35,640 .. J 6
Dunstable, 29,780 .. G 6
Durham, 25,780 .. F 3
Ealing, 297,910 .. G 6
East Grinstead, 8,390 .. G 6
East Retford, 18,860 .. G 4
Eastbourne, 69,290 .. H 7
Eastleigh, 45,100 .. F 7
Ellesmere Port, 56,750 .. E 4
Ely, 10,020 .. H 5
Epping, 11,380 .. H 6
Evesham, 13,170 .. F 5
Exeter, 92,880 .. D 7
Exmouth, 23,630 .. D 7
Falmouth, 17,350 .. C 7
Fareham, 79,740 .. F 7
Farnborough, 42,060 .. G 6
Farnham, 30,150 .. G 6
Faversham, 14,610 .. J 6
Felixstowe, 19,310 .. J 6
Fleet, 21,900 .. G 6
Fleetwood, 28,970 .. D 4
Folkestone, 45,270 .. J 6
Frinton and Walton, 12,060 .. J 6
Frome, 12,600 .. E 6
Gainsborough, 17,680 .. G 4
Gateshead, 100,060 .. F 3
Gillingham, 90,840 .. H 6
Glossop, 21,830 .. F 4
Gloucester, 90,530 .. E 6
Godalming, 18,230 .. G 6
Goole, 18,430 .. G 4
Gosport, 76,160 .. F 7
Grantham, 26,630 .. G 5
Gravesend, 55,310 .. H 6
Great Yarmouth, 50,760 .. J 5
Greenwich, 228,030 .. H 6
Grimsby, 96,500 .. H 4
Guildford, 55,890 .. G 6
Guisborough, 13,000 .. G 3
Halifax, 93,570 .. F 4
Haltemprice, 51,790 .. G 4
Harlow, 76,240 .. H 6
Harrogate, 62,680 .. F 4
Hartlepool, 98,710 .. F 3
Harwich, 14,870 .. J 6
Haslemere, 13,560 .. G 6
Haslingden, 14,280 .. E 4
Hastings, 69,020 .. H 7
Heanor, 24,470 .. F 5
Hemel Hempstead, 66,200 .. G 6
Hereford, 47,170 .. E 5
Herne Bay, 24,510 .. J 6
Hertford, 19,180 .. G 6
Hetton, 17,250 .. F 3
Heysham (Morecambe and Heysham), 40,880 .. D 3
High Wycombe, 57,360 .. G 6
Hinckley, 45,070 .. F 5
Hitchin, 27,410 .. G 6
Horsham, 26,360 .. G 6
Hove, 71,190 .. G 7
Hoylake, 32,190 .. D 4
Hucknall, 26,440 .. F 4
Huddersfield, 130,600 .. F 4
Hull (Kingston-upon-Hull), 292,600 .. G 4
Huntingdon and Godmanchester, 15,650 .. G 5
Hythe, 11,700 .. H 6
Ilkeston, 35,400 .. F 5
Ilkely, 19,820 .. F 4
Ipswich, 122,050 .. J 5
Jarrow, 29,370 .. F 3
Keighley, 55,400 .. F 4
Kendal, 20,160 .. E 3
Kenilworth, 21,000 .. F 5
Kettering, 40,040 .. G 5
Keynsham, 18,670 .. E 6
Kidderminster, 46,740 .. E 5
King's Lynn, 30,650 .. H 5
Kingston-upon-Hull (Hull), 292,600 .. G 4
Kingston-upon-Thames, 143,670 .. G 6
Kingswood, 29,340 .. E 6
Kirkby-in-Ashfield, 22,610 .. F 4
Knottingley, 17,010 .. F 4
Knutsford, 11,900 .. E 4
Lancaster, 48,170 .. E 3
Leamington (Royal Leamington Spa), 45,090 .. F 5
Leatherhead, 39,200 .. G 6
Leeds, 503,720 .. F 4
Leeds, *1,727,300 .. F 4
Leek, 19,180 .. E 4
Leicester, 278,470 .. G 5
Leigh, 46,200 .. G 6
Leighton-Linslade, 19,370 .. G 6
Letchworth, 29,870 .. G 6
Lewes, 14,030 .. H 7
Leyland, 23,100 .. E 4
Lichfield, 22,930 .. F 5
Lincoln, 75,570 .. G 4
Littlehampton, 18,200 .. G 7
Liverpool, 677,450 .. D 4
Liverpool, *1,341,660 .. D 4
London (cap.), 7,703,410 .. G 6
London, ‡12,956,440 .. G 6
Long Eaton, 33,170 .. F 5
Loughborough, 40,190 .. F 5
Louth, 11,480 .. H 4
Lowestoft, 50,730 .. J 5
Luton, 156,690 .. G 6
Lymington, 33,510 .. F 7
Lytham Saint Anne's, 37,000 .. D 4
Macclesfield, 41,870 .. F 4
Maidenhead, 46,050 .. G 6
Maidstone, 67,400 .. H 6
Maldon, 12,920 .. H 6
Malvern, 29,810 .. E 5
Manchester, 593,770 .. E 4
Manchester, *2,433,370 .. E 4
Mangotsfield, 23,530 .. E 6
Mansfield, 56,210 .. F 4
March, 14,080 .. H 5
Margate, 49,080 .. J 6
Maryport, 12,000 .. D 3
Matlock, 20,240 .. F 4
Melton Mowbray, 18,440 .. G 5
Morecambe and Heysham, 40,880 .. E 3
Morley, 44,120 .. F 4
Morpeth, 14,620 .. F 2
Nantwich, 11,200 .. E 4
Nelson, 31,230 .. E 4
New Windsor, 31,270 .. G 6
Newark, 24,580 .. G 4
Newbury, 22,170 .. F 6
Newcastle (Newcastle-under-Lyme), 76,570 .. E 5
Newcastle upon Tyne, 240,340 .. F 2
Newcastle upon Tyne, *839,910 .. F 2
Newham, 252,090 .. H 6
Newmarket, 12,190 .. H 5
Newport, 21,440 .. F 7
Newquay, 12,420 .. B 7
Newton Abbot, 18,660 .. D 7
Northampton, 123,800 .. G 5
Northfleet, 25,450 .. H 6
Northwich, 18,940 .. E 4
Norton-Radstock, 14,540 .. E 6
Norwich, 118,800 .. J 5
Nottingham, 303,090 .. F 5
Nuneaton, 64,650 .. F 5
Oakengates, 15,770 .. E 5
Old Fletton, 13,330 .. G 5
Oldham, 108,280 .. E 4
Ormskirk, 25,900 .. E 4
Otley, 13,090 .. F 4
Oxfored, 109,720 .. F 6
Penrith, 11,170 .. E 3
Penzance, 18,790 .. B 7
Peterborough, 66,800 .. G 5
Plymouth, 248,470 .. D 7
Pontefract, 30,820 .. F 4
Poole, 101,930 .. E 7
Portland, 12,780 .. E 7
Portslade-by-Sea, 18,420 .. G 7
Portsmouth, 214,800 .. G 7
Preston, 102,100 .. E 4
Prudhoe, 10,930 .. F 3
Queensborough-in-Sheppey, 28,790 .. G 5
Ramsgate, 39,140 .. J 6
Rawmarsh, 19,740 .. F 4
Reading, 127,530 .. F 6
Redditch, 37,910 .. F 5
Reigate, 57,830 .. G 6
Ripley, 17,910 .. F 4
Ripon, 11,840 .. F 3
Rochdale, 86,600 .. E 4
Rochester, 55,810 .. H 6
Rotherham, 86,450 .. F 4
Rugby, 57,700 .. F 5
Rugeley, 19,320 .. E 5
Runcorn, 31,560 .. E 4
Rushden, 18,130 .. G 5
Ryde, 22,290 .. F 7
Saint Albans, 52,680 .. G 6
Saint Austell with Fowey, 29,900 .. C 7
Saint Helens, 102,770 .. E 4
Salisbury, 36,440 .. F 6
Saltburn and Marske-by-the-Sea, 17,820 .. G 3
Sandbach, 12,160 .. E 4
Sandown-Shanklin, 14,030 .. F 7
Scarborough, 42,500 .. G 3
Scunthorpe, 69,720 .. G 4
Seaford, 15,600 .. H 7
Seaham, 24,800 .. F 3
Selby, 11,340 .. F 4
Sevenoaks, 18,150 .. H 6
Sheffield, 528,860 .. F 4
Shildon, 13,660 .. F 3
Shipley, 29,010 .. F 4
Shoreham-by-Sea, 18,050 .. G 7
Shrewsbury, 54,190 .. E 5
Sidmouth, 12,180 .. D 7
Sittingbourne and Milton, 30,820 .. H 6
Skegness, 12,680 .. H 4
Skelton and Brotton, 14,270 .. G 3
Skipton, 12,940 .. E 3
Slough, 92,750 .. G 6
South Shields, 106,150 .. F 3
Southampton, 210,000 .. F 7
Southend-on-Sea, 164,700 .. H 6
Southport, 79,430 .. D 4
Southwick, 11,360 .. G 7
Spalding, 16,300 .. G 5
Spennymoor, 18,400 .. F 3
Stafford, 54,200 .. F 5
Stalybridge, 21,620 .. F 4
Stamford, 14,000 .. G 5
Stockport, 140,030 .. E 4
Stoke-on-Trent, 272,260 .. E 4
Stourbridge, 52,290 .. E 5
Stourport-on-Severn, 16,090 .. E 5
Stratford-upon-Avon, 19,110 .. F 5
Stretford, 58,820 .. E 4
Stroud, 18,970 .. E 6
Sunderland, 218,970 .. F 3
Sutton-in-Ashfield, 40,570 .. F 4
Swindon, 98,290 .. F 6
Tamworth, 37,360 .. F 5
Taunton, 37,420 .. D 6
Teesside, 393,810 .. F 3
Teignmouth, 12,260 .. D 7
Thurrock, 124,830 .. H 6
Tiverton, 14,810 .. D 7
Tonbridge, 28,970 .. H 6
Torbay, 100,820 .. D 7
Trowbridge, 17,940 .. E 6
Truro, 14,590 .. C 7
Tunbridge Wells (Royal Tunbridge Wells), 44,930 .. H 6
Tynemouth, 72,390 .. F 2
Ulverston, 10,850 .. D 3
Wakefield, 59,630 .. F 4
Wallasey, 101,360 .. D 4
Wallsend, 47,120 .. F 2
Walsall, 184,260 .. F 5
Ware, 14,240 .. H 6
Warminster, 12,710 .. F 6
Warrington, 70,870 .. E 4
Warwick, 18,720 .. F 5
Watford, 76,700 .. G 6
Wellingborough, 35,680 .. G 5
Wellington, 16,890 .. E 5
Welwyn (Welwyn Garden City), 41,230 .. G 6
West Bromwich, 171,850 .. F 5
Weston-super-Mare, 47,960 .. E 6
Weymouth and Melcombe Regis, 42,120 .. E 7
Whitby, 12,130 .. G 3
Whitehaven, 26,760 .. D 3
Whitley Bay, 38,040 .. F 2
Whitstable, 23,780 .. J 6
Widnes, 55,120 .. E 4
Wigan, 79,780 .. E 4
Wigston, 28,130 .. G 5
Wilmslow, 28,790 .. E 4
Winchester, 31,070 .. F 6
Windsor (New Windsor), 31,270 .. G 6
Winsford, 22,050 .. E 4
Wisbech, 17,510 .. G 5
Witham, 13,080 .. H 6
Woking, 78,180 .. G 6
Wokingham, 19,580 .. F 6
Wolverhampton, 264,520 .. E 5
Wolverton, 13,600 .. G 5
Wombwell, 18,970 .. F 4
Worcester, 71,540 .. F 5
Workington, 29,710 .. D 3
Worksop, 35,660 .. F 4
Worthing, 83,100 .. G 7
Yeovil, 25,740 .. E 7
York, 107,940 .. F 4

OTHER FEATURES

Aire (river) .. F 4
Avon (river) .. F 5
Avon (river) .. F 6
Axe Edge (mt.) .. F 4
Beachy (head) .. H 7
Bigbury (bay) .. C 7
Blackwater (river) .. J 6
Bridlington (bay) .. G 3
Bristol (channel) .. C 6
Brown Willy (mt.) .. C 7
Carter Fell (mt.) .. E 2
Cheviot (hills) .. E 2
Cornish Heights (hills) .. B 7
Cotswold (hills) .. E 6
Cross Fell (mt.) .. E 3
Cumbrian (mts.) .. D 3
Dartmoor (forest) .. C 7
Dee (river) .. D 4
Derwent (river) .. G 4
Don (river) .. F 4
Dorset Heights (hills) .. E 7
Dover (strait) .. J 6
Dukeries, The (dist.) .. F 4
Dungeness (prom.) .. J 7
East Anglian Heights (hills) .. H 5
Eddystone (rocks) .. C 7
Eden (river) .. E 3
English (channel) .. D 8
Esk (river) .. D 2
Exmoor (forest) .. D 6
Flamborough (head) .. H 3
Formby (head) .. D 4
Foulness (isl.), 316 .. J 6
Hartland (point) .. C 6
High Willhays (mt.) .. C 7
Holy (Lindisfarne) (isl.), 190 .. F 2
Humber (river) .. H 4
Isle of Purbeck (pen.) .. F 7
Land's End (prom.) .. B 7
Liddel Water (river) .. F 2
Lincoln Wolds (hills) .. G 4
Lindisfarne (Holy) (isl.), 190 .. F 2
Little Ouse (river) .. H 5
Lizard (head) .. B 8
Lundy (isl.), 32 .. C 6
Lune (river) .. E 3
Lyme (bay) .. E 7
Manacles, The (rocks) .. C 7
Mendip (hills) .. E 6
Mersea (isl.), 3,840 .. J 6
Morte (point) .. C 6
Mounts (bay) .. B 8
Naze, The (prom.) .. J 6
Nene (river) .. H 5
New Forest (dist.) .. F 7
Nidd (river) .. F 3
North Foreland (prom.) .. J 6
North Tyne (river) .. E 2
Orfordness (prom.) .. J 5
Ouse (river) .. F 3
Ouse (river) .. H 5
Parrett (river) .. E 6
Peak, The (mt.) .. F 4
Peel Fell (mt.) .. E 2
Pennine (range) .. E 3
Portland (pen.) .. E 7
Prawle (point) .. D 7
Ribble (river) .. D 4
Saint Austell (bay) .. C 7
Saint Bees (head) .. D 3
Saint Mary's (isl.), 1,736 .. A 8
Scafell Pike (mt.) .. D 3
Scilly (isls.), 1,980 .. A 8
Selsey Bill (point) .. G 7
Severn (river) .. E 6
Sheppey (isl.), 28,790 .. H 6
Skiddaw (mt.) .. D 3
Solent (channel) .. F 7
Solway (firth) .. D 3
South Downs (hills) .. G 7
South Tyne (river) .. E 3
Spithead (channel) .. F 7
Spurn (head) .. H 4
Swale (river) .. F 3
Tamar (river) .. C 7
Tees (river) .. F 3
Thames (river) .. H 6
Till (river) .. F 2
Trent (river) .. G 4
Tresco (isl.), 283 .. A 7
Trevose (head) .. B 7
Tweed (river) .. E 2
Tyne (river) .. F 3
Ure (river) .. F 3
Walney (isl.), 9,811 .. D 3
Wash, The (bay) .. H 4
Waveney (river) .. J 5
Wear (river) .. F 3
Wharfe (river) .. F 4
Widemouth (bay) .. C 7
Wight (isl.), 102,100 .. F 7
Witham (river) .. G 4
Wye (river) .. D 5
Yare (river) .. J 5

WALES

COUNTIES

Anglesey, 58,210 .. C 4
Breconshire, 54,940 .. D 6
Caernarvonshire, 120,620 .. C 5
Cardiganshire, 53,500 .. C 5
Carmarthenshire, 163,600 .. C 6
Denbighshire, 182,050 .. D 4
Flintshire, 169,210 .. D 4
Glamorganshire, 1,258,450 .. D 6
Merionethshire, 37,700 .. D 5
Monmouthshire, 463,990 .. E 6
Montgomeryshire, 42,870 .. D 5
Pembrokeshire, 101,150 .. C 6
Radnorshire, 18,250 .. D 5

CITIES and TOWNS

Aberaeron, 1,220 .. C 5
Aberdare, 38,210 .. D 6
Abergavenny, 9,600 .. E 6
Abergele, 11,520 .. D 4
Abertillery, 22,610 .. E 6
Aberystwyth, 10,420 .. C 5
Amlwch, 3,890 .. C 4
Ammanford, 5,940 .. C 6
Bala, 1,600 .. D 5
Bangor, 14,930 .. C 4
Barmouth, 2,210 .. C 5
Barry, 42,500 .. D 6
Beaumaris, 2,060 .. C 4
Bethesda, 4,210 .. C 4
Betwys-y-Coed, 800 .. C 4
Brecknock, 6,380 .. D 6
Bridgend, 15,260 .. D 6
Brynmawr, 6,530 .. D 6
Builth Wells, 1,560 .. D 5
Burry Port, 5,900 .. C 6
Caerleon, 6,030 .. E 6
Caernarvon, 9,130 .. C 4
Caerphilly, 39,890 .. D 6
Cardiff, 285,860 .. E 6
Cardigan, 3,830 .. C 5
Carmarthen, 12,820 .. C 6
Chepstow, 7,840 .. E 6
Colwyn Bay, 25,060 .. D 4
Conway, 11,910 .. D 4
Cowbridge, 1,430 .. D 6
Criccieth, 1,580 .. C 5
Cwmamman, 4,050 .. D 6
Denbigh, 8,600 .. D 4
Dolgellau, 2,670 .. D 5
Ebbw Vale, 26,470 .. D 6
Ffestiniog, 6,350 .. D 5
Fishguard and Goodwick, 4,940 .. B 6
Flint, 14,650 .. D 4
Haverfordwest, 10,490 .. C 6
Hay, 1,340 .. D 5
Holyhead, 10,970 .. C 4
Holywell, 8,750 .. D 4
Kidwelly, 2,950 .. C 6
Knighton, 2,120 .. D 5
Lampeter, 2,120 .. C 5
Llandeilo, 1,880 .. C 6
Llandovery, 2,090 .. D 6
Llandrindod Wells, 3,240 .. D 5
Llandudno, 16,610 .. D 4
Llanelli, 27,570 .. C 6
Llanfairfechan, 3,230 .. C 4
Llanfyllin, 1,110 .. D 5
Llangefni, 3,580 .. C 4
Llangollen, 3,030 .. D 5
Llanidloes, 2,320 .. D 5
Llanrwst, 2,590 .. D 4
Llwchwr, 26,030 .. D 6
Machynlleth, 1,760 .. D 5
Menai Bridge, 2,390 .. C 4
Merthyr Tydfil, 56,360 .. D 6
Milford Haven, 13,670 .. B 6
Mold, 8,040 .. D 4
Monmouth, 6,280 .. E 6
Montgomery, 1,000 .. D 5
Mountain Ash, 28,130 .. D 6
Narberth, 1,040 .. C 6
Neath, 29,690 .. D 6
New Quay, 870 .. C 5
Newcastle Emlyn, 670 .. C 6
Newport, 112,000 .. E 6
Newtown, 5,590 .. D 5
Neyland, 2,410 .. C 6
Pembroke, 14,200 .. B 6
Penarth, 23,120 .. D 6
Penmaenmawr, 3,970 .. C 4
Pontypool, 36.600 .. E 6
Pontypridd, 35,010 .. D 6
Port Talbot, 50,970 .. D 6
Porthcawl, 13,410 .. D 6
Portmadoc, 3,840 .. C 5
Prestatyn, 13,670 .. D 4
Presteigne, 1,300 .. D 5
Pwllheli, 3,790 .. C 5
Rhondda, 94,300 .. D 6
Rhyl, 21,510 .. D 4
Risca, 16,030 .. D 6
Ruthin, 4,180 .. D 4
Swansea, 171,320 .. C 6
Tenby, 4,580 .. C 6
Tywyn, 4,440 .. C 5
Welshpool, 6,820 .. D 5
Wrexham, 37,620 .. E 4

OTHER FEATURES

Bardsey (isl.), 17 .. C 5
Berwyn (mts.) .. D 5
Braich-y-Pwll (prom.) .. C 5
Bristol (channel) .. E 5
Cader Idris (mts.) .. D 5
Caldy (isl.), 61 .. C 6
Cambrian (mts.) .. D 5
Cardigan (bay) .. C 5
Carmel (head) .. C 4
Clwyd (river) .. D 4
Dee (river) .. D 4
Gower (pen.), 16,100 .. C 6
Great Ormes (head) .. C 4
Holyhead (Holy) (isl.), 12,550 .. C 4
Lleyn (pen.), 19,840 .. C 5
Menai (strait) .. C 4
Pencilan (head) .. C 5
Plynlimon (mt.) .. D 5
Ramsey (isl.) .. B 6
Saint Brides (bay) .. B 6
Saint David's (head) .. B 6
Saint George's (channel) .. B 5
Saint Gowans (head) .. B 6
Severn (river) .. D 5
Skerries (isls.) .. C 4
Skomer (isl.) .. B 6
Snowdon (mt.) .. D 4
Snowdonia Nat'l Park .. D 5
Swansea (bay) .. C 6
Teifi (river) .. C 5
Towy (river) .. D 6
Tremadoc (bay) .. C 5
Usk (river) .. D 6
Wye (river) .. D 5

ISLE OF MAN

Total Population 50,000

CITIES and TOWNS

Douglas (cap.), 19,517 .. C 3
Michael, 353 .. C 3
Onchan, 3,609 .. C 3
Peel, 2,739 .. C 3
Ramsey, 3,880 .. C 3

OTHER FEATURES

Ayre (point) .. C 3
Calf of Man (isl.) .. B 3
Langness (prom.) .. C 3
Snaefell (mt.) .. C 3
Spanish (head) .. C 4

CHANNEL ISLANDS

Total Population 117,000

CITIES and TOWNS

Saint Anne, Alderney, †1,472 .. E 8
Saint Helier (cap.), Jersey, 19,661 .. E 8
Saint Peter Port (cap.), Guernsey, 15,804 .. E 8
Saint Sampson's, Guernsey, †5,916 .. E 8

OTHER FEATURES

Alderney (isl.), 1,472 .. E 8
Guernsey (isl.), 48,000 .. E 8
Herm (isl.), 90 .. E 8
Jersey (isl.), 68,000 .. E 8
Sark (isl.), 550 .. E 8

*City and suburbs.
†Population of parish.
‡Population of metropolitan area.

SCOTLAND

(map on page 15)

COUNTIES

Aberdeen, 317,803 .. L 5
Angus, 277,279 .. K 6
Argyll, 58,360 .. F 7
Ayr, 354,005 .. H 9
Banff, 43,753 .. K 5
Berwick, 20,499 .. L 8
Bute, 12,465 .. F 8
Caithness, 28,202 .. J 3
Clackmannan, 44,084 .. J 7
Dumfries, 87,276 .. J 9
Dunbarton, 277,635 .. G 7
East Lothian, 55,070 .. L 8
Fife, 325,139 .. K 7
Forfar (Angus), 277,279 .. K 6
Inverness, 84,786 .. G 5
Kincardine, 25,694 .. M 6
Kinross, 6,347 .. K 7
Kirkcudbright, 27,899 .. H 9
Lanark, 1,541,455 .. J 8
Midlothian, 595,590 .. K 8
Moray, 52,241 .. K 5
Nairn, 7,991 .. J 5
Orkney, 17,264 .. K 1
Peebles, 13,339 .. K 8
Perth, 124,199 .. H 7
Renfrew, 359,090 .. G 8
Ross and Cromarty, 56,641 .. F 4
Roxburgh, 42,619 .. L 9
Selkirk, 20,273 .. K 9
Stirling, 203,977 .. H 7
Sutherland, 12,995 .. G 3
West Lothian, 106,030 .. J 8
Wigtown, 27,611 .. G10
Zetland, 17,089 .. M 3

CITIES and TOWNS

Abbotsford, 15 .. L 8
Aberchirder, 838 .. L 4
Aberdeen, 181,089 .. N 5
Aberfeldy, 1,542 .. J 6
Aberfoyle, 853 .. H 7
Aberlour, 801 .. K 5
Abernethy, 772 .. K 7
Aboyne, 1,012 .. L 5
Acharacle, 93 .. E 6
Achiltibuie, 49 .. F 3
Achmore, 158 .. C 3
Achnasheen, 50 .. F 4
Airdrie, 36,188 .. D 2
Alexandria, 8,229 .. B 2
Alford, 758 .. L 5
Alloa, 14,205 .. E 1
Alness, 1,177 .. H 4
Alva, 4,100 .. J 7
Alyth, 1,705 .. K 6
Annan, 6,019 .. K10
Applecross, 25 .. E 5
Arbroath, 21,632 .. L 6
Ardcharnich, 16 .. F 4
Ardgour, 21 .. F 6
Ardrishaig, 1,047 .. F 8
Ardrossan, 9,946 .. G 8
Arinagour, 54 .. C 6
Arisaig, 174 .. E 6
Armadale, 6,384 .. E 2
Arrochar, 100 .. G 7
Auchinleck, 5,694 .. H 9
Auchterarder, 2,343 .. J 7
Auchtermuchty, 1,331 .. K 7
Auldearn, 359 .. J 4
Aultbea, 99 .. E 4
Aviemore, 635 .. J 5
Avoch, 899 .. H 4
Ayr, 47,635 .. G 9
Ayton, 425 .. M 8
Badachro, 35 .. E 4
Badcall, 17 .. F 3
Ballachulish, 381 .. F 6
Ballantrae, 420 .. F 9
Ballater, 1,076 .. K 5
Balmaha, 40 .. C 1
Balmoral Castle, 66 .. K 5
Balquhidder, 38 .. H 7
Baltasound, 240 .. M 2
Banavie, 197 .. F 6
Banchory, 2,066 .. M 5
Banff, 3,492 .. L 4
Bannockburn, 3,887 .. D 1
Barr, 224 .. G 9
Barrhead, 17,560 .. C 2
Barvas, 378 .. D 3
Bathgate, 14,763 .. J 8
Bearsden, 23,143 .. C 2
Beauly, 1,386 .. G 5
Beith, 4,993 .. B 2
Bellshill, 16,527 .. D 2
Berriedale, 30 .. K 3
Bettyhill, 99 .. H 3
Biggar, 1,668 .. J 8
Bishopbriggs, 19,779 .. D 2
Blair-Atholl, 509 .. J 6
Blairgowrie and Rattray, 5,071 .. J 6
Blantyre, 16,288 .. D 2
Boddam, 854 .. N 5
Bonar Bridge, 437 .. H 4
Bo'ness, 13,493 .. J 7
Bonhill, 4,024 .. B 2
Bonnybridge, 5,742 .. D 2
Bonnyrigg and Lasswade, 7,017 .. K 8
Bowmore, 840 .. D 8
Bracadale, 246 .. D 5
Braemar, 468 .. K 5
Brechin, 6,775 .. L 6
Bridge of Allan, 4,285 .. D 1
Broadford, 293 .. E 5
Brodick, 647 .. F 8
Brora, 1,256 .. J 3
Buckhaven and Methil, 18,815 .. L 7
Buckie, 7,697 .. L 4
Bunessan, 107 .. D 7
Burghead, 1,368 .. J 4
Burntisland, 5,451 .. K 7
Burravoe, 136 .. N 2
Cairnryan, 167 .. G10
Callander, 1,777 .. H 7
Cambuslang, 18,868 .. D 2
Campbeltown, 6,285 .. E 9
Cannich, 197 .. G 5
Canonbie, 194 .. K 9
Carbost, 118 .. C 5
Cargill, 21 .. K 7
Carloway, 232 .. C 3
Carluke, 8,110 .. E 2
Carnoustie, 5,663 .. L 6
Carnwath, 1,072 .. J 8
Carsphairn, 61 .. H 9
Carstairs Jct., 1,353 .. J 8
Castlebay, 122 .. B 6
Castle Douglas, 3,264 .. H10
Cawdor, 136 .. J 5
Ceres, 609 .. L 7
Chirnside, 821 .. M 8
Clackmannan, 2,476 .. J 7
Closeburn, 218 .. J 9
Clydebank, 49,997 .. C 2
Coatbridge, 52,804 .. D 2
Cockburnspath, 261 .. M 8
Cockenzie and Port Seton, 3,565 .. L 8
Coldingham, 392 .. M 8
Coldstream, 1,267 .. M 8
Colmonell, 231 .. G 9
Corpach, 376 .. F 6
Coupar Angus, 1,978 .. K 6
Cove and Kilcreggan, 1,292 .. B 1
Cowdenbeath, 10,480 .. K 7
Coylton, 233 .. H 9
Craignure, 43 .. E 7
Crail, 968 .. L 7
Crawford, 417 .. J 9
Creetown, 829 .. H10
Crieff, 5,569 .. J 7
Crinan, 34 .. E 7
Cromarty, 587 .. J 4
Cruden Bay, 489 .. N 5
Cullen, 1,253 .. L 4
Cults, 2,448 .. M 5
Cumbernauld, 26,678 .. D 2
Cumnock and Holmhead, 5,920 .. H 9
Cupar, 6,559 .. K 7
Dalbeattie, 3,229 .. J10
Dalkeith, 9,368 .. K 8
Dalmally, 155 .. G 7
Dalmellington, 2,130 .. H 9
Dalry, Ayr, 5,623 .. B 2
Dalry, Kirkcudbright, 448 .. H 9
Dalwhinnie, 132 .. H 6
Darvel, 3,165 .. H 8
Daviot, 38 .. H 5
Denny and Dunipace, 8,587 .. D 1
Dervaig, 82 .. D 6
Dingwall, 3,912 .. H 4
Dores, 143 .. H 5
Dornie, 102 .. F 5
Dornoch, 930 .. H 4
Douglas, 2,075 .. J 8
Doune, 758 .. H 7
Drummore, 390 .. G10
Dufftown, 1,536 .. K 5
Dumbarton, 25,510 .. B 2
Dumfries, 28,149 .. J 9
Dunbar, 2,931 .. M 8
Dunbeath, 159 .. K 3
Dunblane, 3,884 .. D 1
Dundee, 181,950 .. K 7
Dundonald, 1,293 .. H 8
Dunfermline, 50,305 .. J 7
Dunkeld, 279 .. J 6
Dunnet, 72 .. K 2
Dunoon, 9,431 .. A 2
Duns, 1,885 .. M 8
Dunscore, 169 .. J 9
Dunvegan, 157 .. D 5
Durness, 97 .. G 2
Dyce, 1,530 .. M 5
Earlston, 1,367 .. L 8
East Kilbride, 62,243 .. C 2
East Linton, 912 .. L 7
Ecclefechan, 834 .. K 9
Edderton, 52 .. H 4
Eddleston, 181 .. K 8
Edinbain, 149 .. D 5
Edinburgh (cap.), 465,421 .. K 8
Edzell, 644 .. L 6
Elderslie, 4,616 .. C 2
Elgin, 16,416 .. K 4
Elie and Earlsferry, 802 .. L 7
Ellon, 1,877 .. M 5
Elvanfoot, 85 .. J 9
Eriboll, 24 .. G 3
Errol, 744 .. K 7
Ettrick, 38 .. K 9
Evanton, 484 .. H 4
Ewes, 20 .. K 9
Eyemouth, 2,257 .. M 8
Falkirk, 38,625 .. E 1
Fearn, 210 .. J 4
Fetteresso, 20 .. M 6
Findhorn, 629 .. K 4
Findochty, 1,207 .. K 4
Findon, 77 .. M 5
Fochabers, 1,054 .. K 4
Ford, 50 .. F 7
Fordoun, 126 .. M 6
Forfar, 9,870 .. L 6
Forres, 4,711 .. K 4
Fort Augustus, 372 .. G 5
Fort William, 4,006 .. F 6
Fortingall, 33 .. H 6
Fortrose, 1,027 .. H 4
Fraserburgh, 10,898 .. N 4
Gairloch, 104 .. E 4
Galashiels, 12,073 .. L 8
Galston, 4,058 .. H 8
Gardenstown, 906 .. M 4
Garelochhead, 1,042 .. A 1
Gatehouse-of-Fleet, 797 .. H10
Girvan, 6,868 .. G 9
Glamis, 205 .. L 6
Glasgow, 927,948 .. D 2
Glasgow, *1,746,313 .. D 2
Glenbarr, 56 .. E 8
Glenelg, 290 .. E 5
Glenisla, 25 .. K 6
Glenluce, 706 .. G10
Glenrothes, 26,700 .. K 7
Golspie, 1,167 .. H 4
Gourock, 10,618 .. B 2
Grangemouth, 22,701 .. J 8
Grantown-on-Spey, 1,600 .. J 5
Greenlaw, 544 .. M 8
Greenock, 70,267 .. A 2
Gretna Green, 86 .. K 9
Haddington, 4,070 .. L 8
Halkirk, 608 .. K 3
Hamilton, 46,397 .. D 2
Harris (Tarbert), 416 .. C 4
Hawick, 16,685 .. L 9
Helensburgh, 13,594 .. B 1
Helmsdale, 768 .. K 3
Hillswick, 64 .. M 2
Hobkirk, 25 .. L 9
Hopeman, 1,146 .. K 4
Howmore, 38 .. A 5
Huntly, 3,878 .. L 5
Hurlford, 4,152 .. H 8
Hutton, 78 .. K 9
Innerleithen, 2,275 .. K 8
Insch, 917 .. L 5
Insh, 26 .. J 5
Inveraray, 468 .. F 7
Inverbervie, 885 .. M 6
Invergordon, 2,074 .. M 4
Inverie, 36 .. E 5
Inverkeilor, 224 .. M 6
Inverkeithing, 5,367 .. K 7
Inverness, 32,058 .. H 5
Inverurie, 5,351 .. M 5
Irvine, 21,382 .. G 8
Jamestown, 1,193 .. C 1
Jedburgh, 3,714 .. M 9
John O'Groats, 184 .. K 2
Johnshaven, 625 .. M 6
Johnstone, 22,633 .. B 2
Keiss, 364 .. K 2
Keith, 4,091 .. L 4
Kelso, 4,411 .. M 8
Kentallen, 91 .. F 6
Kilbarchan, 2,330 .. B 2
Kilbirnie, 8,158 .. B 2
Kildonan, 22 .. J 3
Kildrummy, 273 .. L 5
Kilfinan, 30 .. F 8
Killin, 583 .. H 7
Kilmacolm, 2,902 .. B 2
Kilmarnock, 47,631 .. G 8
Kilmelford, 69 .. F 7
Kilmore, 78 .. F 7
Kilmory, 81 .. F 9
Kilmuir, 87 .. D 5
Kilrenny and Anstruther, 2,814 .. L 7
Kilsyth, 9,659 .. D 2
Kincardine, 26 .. H 4
Kincardine O'Neil, 166 .. L 5
Kingussie, 1,013 .. H 5
Kinloch Rannoch, 236 .. H 6
Kinlochbervie, 117 .. G 3
Kinlochleven, 1,515 .. G 6
Kinross, 2,361 .. K 7
Kintore, 783 .. M 5
Kirkcaldy, 52,097 .. K 7
Kirkcolm, 318 .. F10
Kirkcowan, 401 .. G10
Kirkcudbright, 2,730 .. H10
Kirkintilloch, 24,601 .. C 2
Kirkoswald, 296 .. G 9
Kirkpatrick Fleming, 231 .. K 9
Kirkwall, 4,688 .. K 2
Kirriemuir, 4,107 .. L 6
Kyle of Lochalsh, 606 .. E 5
Laggan, 43 .. H 5
Lairg, 538 .. H 3
Lamlash, 528 .. F 8
Lanark, 8,407 .. J 8
Langholm, 2,393 .. K 9
Larbert, 4,167 .. D 1
Largs, 8,908 .. B 2
Larkhall, 13,931 .. D 2
Latheron, 51 .. K 3
Lauder, 564 .. L 8
Laurencekirk, 1,365 .. M 6
Leith, 51,378 .. K 8
Lennoxtown, 3,155 .. C 2
Lerwick, 5,919 .. N 3
Leslie, 3,229 .. K 7
Lesmahagow, 3,558 .. H 8
Leuchars, 1,332 .. L 7
Leven, 8,987 .. L 7
Leverburgh, 175 .. C 4
Linlithgow, 5,191 .. K 8
Livingston, 8,100 .. C 1
Lochaline, 200 .. E 6
Lochboisdale, 316 .. B 5
Lochcarron, 210 .. E 5
Lochgelly, 8,021 .. K 7
Lochgilphead, 1,253 .. F 7
Lochinver, 240 .. F 3
Lochmaben, 1,265 .. J 9
Lochmaddy, 303 .. B 4
Lochranza, 95 .. F 8
Lochwinnoch, 2,066 .. B 2
Lockerbie, 2,878 .. K 9
Logierait, 104 .. J 6
Lossiemouth and Branderburgh, 6,419 .. K 4
Lothbeg, 9 .. J 3
Luss, 140 .. B 1
Lybster, 534 .. K 3
Macduff, 3,502 .. M 4
Mallaig, 849 .. E 5
Markinch, 2,349 .. K 7
Marykirk, 126 .. M 6
Mauchline, 3,538 .. H 8
Maybole, 4,548 .. G 9
Meigle, 347 .. K 6
Melrose, 2,242 .. L 8
Melvaig, 36 .. E 4
Melvich, 130 .. H 2
Methlick, 299 .. M 5
Methven, 796 .. J 7
Mid Yell, 166 .. N 2
Millport, 1,159 .. A 2
Milngavie, 9,955 .. C 2
Moffat, 1,866 .. K 9
Moniaive, 409 .. J 9
Monifieth, 5,170 .. L 7
Montrose, 10,269 .. M 6
Motherwell and Wishaw, 75,022 .. D 2
Muirkirk, 3,409 .. H 9
Musselburgh, 17,244 .. L 8
Muthill, 726 .. J 7
Nairn, 4,986 .. J 4
Neilston, 3,795 .. C 2
New Abbey, 352 .. J10
Newarthill, 6,840 .. D 2
Newburgh, Aberdeen, 458 .. N 2
Newburgh, Fife, 2,107 .. K 7
New Cumnock, 5,508 .. H 9
New Deer, 619 .. M 5
New Galloway, 339 .. H 9
Newmilns and Greenholm, 3,506 .. H 8
Newport-on-Tay, 3,427 .. L 7
Newton-Stewart, 1,810 .. G10
Nigg, 33 .. J 4

(continued)

ENGLAND and WALES

CONIC PROJECTION

SCALE OF MILES

SCALE OF KILOMETRES

Capitals of Countries _____ ☆
Other Capitals _____ ◉
Administrative Centers _____ △
County Boundaries _____ — — —
Canals _____ ————

Copyright by C.S. HAMMOND & CO., N.Y.

SCOTLAND (continued)

North Berwick, 4,534 L 7
Oban, 6,743 F 7
Old Meldrum, 1,126 M 5
Oykel Bridge, 45 G 4
Paisley, 95,182 C 2
Peebles, 5,598 K 8
Penicuik, 81,293 K 8
Perth, 41,654 J 7
Peterhead, 13,332 N 4
Pierowall, 108 K 1
Pitlochry, 2,482 J 6
Pittenweem, 1,445 L 7
Plockton, 254 E 5
Poolewe, 81 E 4
Port Appin, 96 F 6
Portaskaig, 30 D 8
Port Ellen, 721 D 8
Port Glasgow, 21,985 B 2
Portknockie, 1,122 L 4
Portlethen, 75 M 5
Portmahomack, 207 J 4
Portobello, 27,141 K 8
Port of Ness, 93 D 3
Portpatrick, 681 F10
Portree, 1,356 D 5
Portsoy, 1,698 L 4
Port William, 528 G10
Prestonpans, 6,816 L 8
Prestwick, 13,741 G 9
Queensferry, 4,256 K 8
Quendale, 11 M 3
Rackwick, 12 K 2
Reay, 187 J 2
Renfrew, 19,114 C 2
Renton, 3,898 B 1
Rhynie, 363 L 5
Rosehearty, 1,144 M 4
Rosneath, 222 A 1
Rothes, 1,099 K 4
Rothesay, 6,329 F 8
Rothiemay, 24 L 4
Rutherglen, 25,213 C 2
Ruthwell, 96 K 9
Saddell, 44 E 8
Saint Andrews, 10,890 L 7
Saint Boswells, 1,007 L 8
Saint Combs, 713 N 4
Saint Cyrus, 347 M 6
Saint Margaret's Hope, 205 L 2
Saint Mary's, 151 L 2
Salen, 171 E 7
Saltcoats, 14,170 G 8
Sandness, 27 M 3
Sandwick, 43 N 3
Sanquhar, 2,066 J 9
Scalasaig, 45 D 7
Scalloway, 878 M 3
Scarinish, 103 C 7
Scone, 3,047 K 7
Scourie, 71 F 3
Scrabster, 129 J 2
Selkirk, 5,527 L 8
Shieldaig, 68 E 5
Shotts, 10,304 E 2
Skipness, 69 F 8
Spean Bridge, 229 G 6
Stevenston, 11,281 G 8
Stewarton, 4,156 H 8
Stirling, 28,786 D 1
Stonehaven, 4,573 M 6
Stonehouse, 3,686 M 8
Stoneykirk, 196 G10
Stornoway, 5,352 C 3
Stow, 453 L 8
Strachur, 36 F 7
Stranraer, 9,401 G10
Strathaven, 4,321 H 8
Strichen, 967 M 4
Stromness, 1,556 K 2
Strontian, 39 E 6
Tain, 1,719 H 4
Tarbert, Argyll, 1,236 F 8
Tarbert, Inverness, 416 C 4
Tarland, 396 L 5
Tayport, 2,916 L 7
Thornhill, 1,482 J 9
Thurso, 9,167 J 2
Tillicoultry, 4,125 J 7
Tobermory, 616 D 6
Tomintoul, 278 K 5
Tongue, 108 H 3
Torridon, 13 F 5
Tranent, 6,988 L 8
Traquair, 55 K 8
Troon, 10,906 G 8
Turriff, 2,784 M 4
Tweedsmuir, 30 J 9
Uig, Inverness, 107 D 4
Uig, Ross and Cromarty, 166 B 3
Ullapool, 676 F 4
Voe, 147 M 3
Walls, 132 M 3
Watten, 251 K 2
West Calder, 1,535 K 8
West Kilbride, 3,042 G 8
West Linton, 667 K 8
Whitburn, 9,596 E 2
Whithorn, 998 H10
Wick, 7,346 K 3
Wigtown, 1,149 H10
Yarrow, 30 K 8
Yetholm, 426 M 8

OTHER FEATURES

Abbey (head) J10
A'Chralaig (mt.) F 5
Affric (lake) G 5
Ailsa Craig (isl.), 10 F 9
Aird (pt.) D 4
Almond (riv.) J 7
Alness (riv.) H 4
Alsh (inlet) E 5
Annan (riv.) K 9
Appin (dist.), 429 F 6
Ardgour (dist.), 299 F 6
Ardivachar (pt.) A 5
Ardle (riv.) K 6
Ardnamurchan (dist.), 772 D 6
Ardnamurchan (pt.) D 6
Argyll (dist.), 4,435 F 7
Arisaig (dist.), 682 E 6
Arkaig (lake) F 6
Arran (isl.), 3,700 F 8
Askival (mt.) D 6
Assynt (dist.), 831 F 3
Assynt (lake) G 3
Athol (dist.), 1,458 H 6
Auskerry (isl.), 3 M 1
Avon (riv.) K 5
Awe (lake) F 7
Ayr (riv.) H 9
Badenoch (dist.), 6,473 H 6
Baleshare (isl.), 59 A 4
Barra (head) A 6
Barra (isl.), 1,369 A 5
Barra (isls.), 1,469 B 6
Barra (passg.) B 6
Battock (mt.) L 6
Beauly (firth) H 5
Beinn Bheigeir (mt.) D 8
Bell Rock (isl.), 3 M 7
Ben Alder (mt.) G 6
Ben Avon (mt.) K 5
Benbecula (isl.), 1,358 A 5
Benbecula (sound) A 5
Ben Dearg (mt.) G 4
Benderloch (dist.) F 7
Beneveian (lake) G 5
Ben Griam More (mt.) H 3
Ben Hee (mt.) G 3
Ben Hope (mt.) G 3
Ben Klibreck (mt.) H 3
Ben Lawers (mt.) H 6
Ben Macdhui (mt.) J 5
Ben Mhor (mt.) B 5
Ben More (mt.), Argyll E 7
Ben More (mt.), Perth G 7
Ben More Assynt (mt.) G 3
Ben Nevis (mt.) F 6
Ben Vorlich (mt.) H 7
Ben Wyvis (mt.) G 4
Bernera (isl.), 317 C 3
Berneray (isl.), 3 A 6
Berneray (isl.), 201 B 4
Black Isle (dist.), 5,673 H 4
Blackwater (res.) G 6
Boisdale (inlet) B 5
Boreray (isl.), 5 B 4
Bracadale (inlet) C 5
Braemar (dist.), 5,091 K 5
Bran (falls) J 6
Breadalbane (dist.), 3,877 H 7
Bressay (isl.), 269 N 3
Brims Ness (prom.) J 2
Broad (bay) D 3
Broad Law (mt.) K 9
Broom (inlet) F 4
Brora (riv.) H 3
Brough (head) K 1
Brough Ness (prom.) L 2
Buchan (dist.), 53,172 M 4
Buchan Ness (prom.) N 5
Buddon Ness (prom.) L 7
Burrow (head) H10
Bute (isl.), 9,793 F 8
Bute (sound) F 8
Butt of Lewis (prom.) D 3
Cairn Gorm (mt.) J 5
Cairngorm (mts.) J 5
Cairn Mor (mt.) K 5
Cairnsmore (mt.) H 9
Cairn Toul (mt.) J 5
Caledonian (canal) G 5
Canna (isl.), 24 C 5
Canna (sound) C 6
Caolisport (inlet) E 8
Carn Eige (mt.) F 5
Carrick (dist.), 21,867 G 9
Carron (inlet) E 5
Carron (river) G 4
Cellar (head) D 3
Cheviot (hills) L 9
Clar Nan (lake) J 3
Clisham (mt.) C 4
Clyde (falls) J 8
Clyde (firth) F 9
Clyde (river) G 8
Cnoc Moy (mt.) E 9
Coire (lake) H 3
Coll (isl.), 147 C 6
Colonsay (isl.), 164 C 6
Conon (river) H 4
Copinsay (isl.), 3 L 2
Corryvreckan (gulf) E 7
Corsewall (pt.) F 9
Cowal (dist.), 16,247 F 7
Creag Meagaidh (mt.) G 6
Cree (river) G 9
Creran (inlet) F 7
Cromarty (firth) H 4
Cuillin (hills) D 5
Cumbraes (isls.), 1,646 A 2
Dee (riv.) H 9
Dee (riv.) M 5
Dennis (head) M 1
Deveron (riv.) L 5
Dhuheartach (isl.), 3 C 6
Don (riv.) L 5
Doon (lake) G 9
Dornoch (firth) J 4
Duich (inlet) F 5
Duirinish (dist.), 1,268 C 5
Dulnain (riv.) J 5
Duncansby (head) L 2
Dunnet (head) J 2
Dunvegan (head) C 4
Durness, Kyle of (inlet) G 2
Earn (lake) H 7
Earn (riv.) J 7
East Loch Tarbert (inlet) C 4
Eck (lake) F 7
Eday (isl.), 198 L 1
Eddrachillis (bay) F 3
Eden (riv.) L 7
Egilsay (isl.), 54 L 1
Eigg (isl.), 74 D 6
Eil (inlet) F 6
Eishort (inlet) D 5
Enard (bay) F 3
Eport (inlet) B 4
Eriboll (inlet) G 2
Ericht (lake) H 6
Eriskay (isl.), 231 B 5
Erisort (inlet) D 3
Esk (riv.) L 9
Etive (inlet) F 7
Ettrick Pen (mt.) K 9
Eye (pen.) D 3
Eynhallow (sound) K 1
Eynort (inlet) B 5
Fair (isl.), 64 L 3
Fannich (lake) F 4
Farrar (riv.) G 5
Fetlar (isl.), 127 N 2
Fife Ness (prom.) L 7
Findhorn (riv.) J 5
Fionn (lake) F 4
Flannan (isls.), 3 A 3
Fleet (inlet) J 4
Foinaven (mt.) G 3
Formartine (dist.), 15,010 M 5
Forth (firth) L 7
Forth (riv.) H 7
Forth and Clyde (canal) H 8
Foula (isl.), 54 L 3
Foyers (falls) H 5
Fyne (inlet) F 8
Gair (inlet) E 4
Gairloch (dist.), 1,788 E 4
Gallan (head) B 3
Galloway (dist.), 57,994 H10
Galloway, Mull of (prom.) G10
Garioch (dist.), 7,950 L 5
Garry (lake) G 5
Garry (riv.) J 6
Gigha (isl.), 163 E 8
Gigha (sound) E 8
Girdle Ness (prom.) N 5
Glas Maol (mt.) K 6
Glass (lake) G 4
Glass (riv.) G 5
Glenelg (dist.), 1,549 E 5
Goat Fell (mt.) F 8
Grampian (mts.) G 6
Greenstone (pt.) E 4
Grimsay (isl.), 239 B 5
Gruinard (bay) E 4
Gruinard (dist.) F 4
Gruinart (inlet) D 8
Gulvain (mt.) F 6
Gunna (sound) C 6
Halladale (riv.) J 3
Harris (dist.), 2,493 C 4
Harris (sound) B 4
Hebrides (isls.), 43,676 A 5
Hebrides, Inner (isls.), 13,964 D 5
Hebrides, Outer (isls.), 29,712 A 5
Hebrides (sea) C 5
Helmsdale (riv.) J 3
Herma Ness (prom.) M 2
Holm (sound) L 2
Holy (isl.), 7 F 9
Holy Loch (inlet) A 2
Hope (lake) G 3
Hourn (inlet) F 5
Hoy (isl.), 511 K 2
Hynish (bay) C 7
Hyskier (isl.), 3 C 6
Inchard (inlet) F 3
Inchcape (Bell) Rock (isl.), 3 M 7
Inchkeith (isl.), 3 K 7
Indaal (inlet) D 8
Inner (sound) E 5
Inner Hebrides (isls.), 13,964 D 5
Inver (inlet) F 3
Iona (isl.), 130 D 7
Isla (riv.) K 6
Islay (isl.), 3,860 D 8
Jura (isl.), 249 E 7
Katrine (lake) G 7
Keal, Na (inlet) D 7
Kebock (head) D 3
Kilbrennan (sound) F 9
Kinnairds (head) N 4
Kintyre (dist.), 9,914 E 9
Kintyre, Mull of (prom.) E 9
Knapdale (dist.), 2,711 E 8
Knoydart (dist.), 1,234 E 5
Kyle (dist.) H 9
Laggan (bay) D 8
Lammermuir (hills) L 8
Langavat (lake) C 3
Laxford (inlet) F 3
Lennox (hills) C 1
Leven (inlet) F 6
Leven (lake) K 7
Lewis (dist.), 21,614 C 3
Lewis, Butt of (prom.) D 3
Liddel Water (riv.) L 9
Linnhe (inlet) F 6
Lismore (isl.), 155 F 7
Little Minch (sound) C 4
Lochaber (dist.), 7,591 F 6
Lochalsh (dist.), 1,651 E 5
Lochnager (mt.) K 6
Lochy (lake) G 6
Lomond (lake) G 7
Long (inlet) B 1
Lorne (dist.), 12,656 F 7
Lorne (firth) E 7
Lothians (dist.) K 8
Loyal (lake) H 3
Lubnaig (lake) H 7
Luce (bay) G10
Lyon (riv.) H 6
Maddy (inlet) B 4
Mainland (isl.), 13,282 N 3
Mainland (isl.), 13,495 K 1
Mam Soul (mt.) F 5
Mar (dist.), 16,918 E 4
Maree (lake) F 4
May (isl.), 7 M 7
Merrick (mt.) H 9
Mhor (lake) H 5
Minginish (dist.), 578 D 5
Moidart (dist.), 247 E 6
Monach (isls.) A 4
Monach (sound) A 4
Monadhliath (mts.) H 5
Monar (lake) F 5
Morar (dist.), 1,106 E 6
Morar (lake) E 6
Moray (firth) J 4
More (lake) G 3
Moriston (riv.) G 5
Morven (dist.), 422 E 6
Morven (mt.) J 3
Muck (isl.), 29 D 6
Muirnag (hill) D 3
Mull (head) L 1
Mull (head) L 2
Mull (isl.), 2,149 E 7
Mull (sound) E 7
Nairn (riv.) J 5
Na Keal (inlet) D 7
Nan Clar (lake) J 3
Naver (lake) H 3
Naver (riv.) H 3
Neist (pt.) C 5
Ness (lake) H 5
Ness (riv.) H 5
Nevis (inlet) E 5
Nith (riv.) J 9
North (chan.) E 9
North (sound) L 1
North Esk (riv.) L 6
North Minch (sound) E 3
North Ronaldsay (firth) M 1
North Ronaldsay (isl.), 161 M 1
North Uist (isl.), 1,620 A 4
Noss (head) L 3
Noup (head) K 1
Oa, Mull of (prom.) D 8
Ochil (hills) J 7
Oich (riv.) G 5
Orchy (riv.) G 7
Orkney (isls.), 17,264 J 1
Oronsay (isl.), 2 D 7
Oronsay (passg.) D 7
Orrin (riv.) G 5
Outer Hebrides (isls.), 29,712 A 5
Oykell (riv.) G 4
Pabbay (isl.), 2 B 4
Papa Stour (isl.), 55 L 3
Papa Westray (isl.), 139 L 1
Paps of Jura (peaks) E 8
Park (dist.), 797 C 3
Peel Fell (mt.) L 9
Pentland (firth) K 2
Pladda (isl.), 6 F 9
Queensberry (mt.) J 9
Quoich (lake) F 5
Raasay (isl.), 211 D 5
Raasay (sound) D 5
Rannoch (dist.), 832 H 6
Rannoch (lake) H 6
Rattray (head) N 4
Renish (pt.) C 4
Resort (inlet) B 3
Rhinns (pt.) C 8
Rhu Coigach (cape) E 3
Roag (inlet) C 3
Rona (isl.), 49 D 4
Ross of Mull (pen.), 471 D 7
Rousay (isl.), 237 K 1
Rudha Hunish (cape) D 4
Rudh Re (cape) E 4
Rum (isl.), 40 D 6
Rum (sound) D 6
Ryan (inlet) F 9
Saint Abb's (head) M 8
Saint Andrews (bay) L 7
Saint Kilda (isl.), 65 B 8
Saint Magnus (bay) M 3
Saint Mary's Loch (lake) K 9
Sanda (isl.), 7 E 9
Sanday (isl.), Inverness D 5
Sanday (isl.), Orkney, 670 M 1
Sanday (sound) L 1
Scalpay (isl.), 470 C 4
Scalpay (isl.), 2 E 5
Scapa Flow (chan.) K 2
Scarba (isl.), 5 E 7
Scarp (isl.), 46 B 3
Scavaig (inlet) D 5
Scradain (inlet) D 7
Scurdie Ness (prom.) M 6
Seaforth (inlet) C 4
Sgurr a Choir Ghlais (mt.) G 5
Sgurr Mhor (mt.) F 4
Sgurr Na Ciche (mt.) F 5
Sgurr Na Lapaich (mt.) F 5
Shapinsay (isl.), 416 L 1
Shee Water (riv.) J 6
Shell (inlet) D 4
Shetland (isls.), 17,089 M 3
Shiel (lake) E 6
Shin (falls) H 4
Shin (lake) G 3
Shona (isl.), 11 E 6
Sidlaw (hills) K 6
Sinclair's (bay) K 2
Skeir Graitich (isl.) D 4
Skerryvore (isl.), 3 B 7
Skye (isl.), 7,478 D 5
Sleat (dist.), 524 E 5
Sleat (pt.) D 5
Sleat (sound) E 5
Small (isls.), 143 C 6
Snizort (inlet) D 4
Soay (isl.), 11 D 5
Solway (firth) J10
South Esk (riv.) K 6
South Ronaldsay (isl.), 980 L 2
South Uist (isl.), 2,376 A 5
Spean (riv.) G 6
Spey (riv.) K 4
Staffin (bay) D 4
Start (pt.) M 1
Stinchar (riv.) G 9
Stoer (pt.) F 3
Stornoway (harb.) D 3
Storr, The (mt.) D 4
Strathbogie (dist.), 9,152 L 5
Strathmore (dist.) J 7
Strathy (pt.) H 2
Stroma (isl.), 12 K 2
Stronsay (firth) L 1
Stronsay (isl.), 497 M 1
Sumburgh (head) M 3
Sunart (inlet) E 6
Swona (isl.), 3 K 2
Taransay (isl.), 5 B 4
Tarbat Ness (prom.) J 4
Tarbert (inlet) D 8
Tay (firth) L 7
Tay (lake) H 7
Tay (riv.) K 7
Teith (riv.) H 7
Teviot (riv.) L 9
Thurso (riv.) J 3
Tilt (riv.) J 6
Tiree (isl.), 993 C 6
Tirry (riv.) H 3
Tiumpan (head) D 3
Toe (head) B 4
Tolsta (head) D 3
Ton Mhor (pt.) C 8
Tongue, Kyle of (inlet) G 2
Tor Ness (prom.) K 2
Torridon (inlet) E 4
Treig (lake) G 6
Trossachs, The (valley) H 7
Trotternish (dist.), 389 D 4
Troup (head) M 4
Tuath (inlet) D 7
Tummel (falls) J 6
Tummel (river) J 6
Turnberry (pt.) G 9
Tweed (riv.) M 8
Tyne (riv.) M 7
Ugie (riv.) N 4
Ulva (isl.), 28 D 7
Unst (isl.), 1,148 N 2
Vaternish (dist.), 198 C 4
Vaternish (pt.) C 4
Vatersay (isl.), 95 A 6
Voil (lake) G 7
Watten (lake) K 3
West Burra (isl.), 561 M 3
West Loch Tarbert (inlet) B 4
Westray (firth) K 1
Westray (isl.), 872 K 1
Whalsay (isl.), 764 N 3
Whiten (head) G 2
Wide (firth) L 1
Wigtown (bay) H10
Wrath (cape) F 2
Yarrow Water (riv.) L 8
Yell (isl.), 1,155 M 2
Yell (sound) M 2
Ythan (riv.) M 5

*City and suburbs.

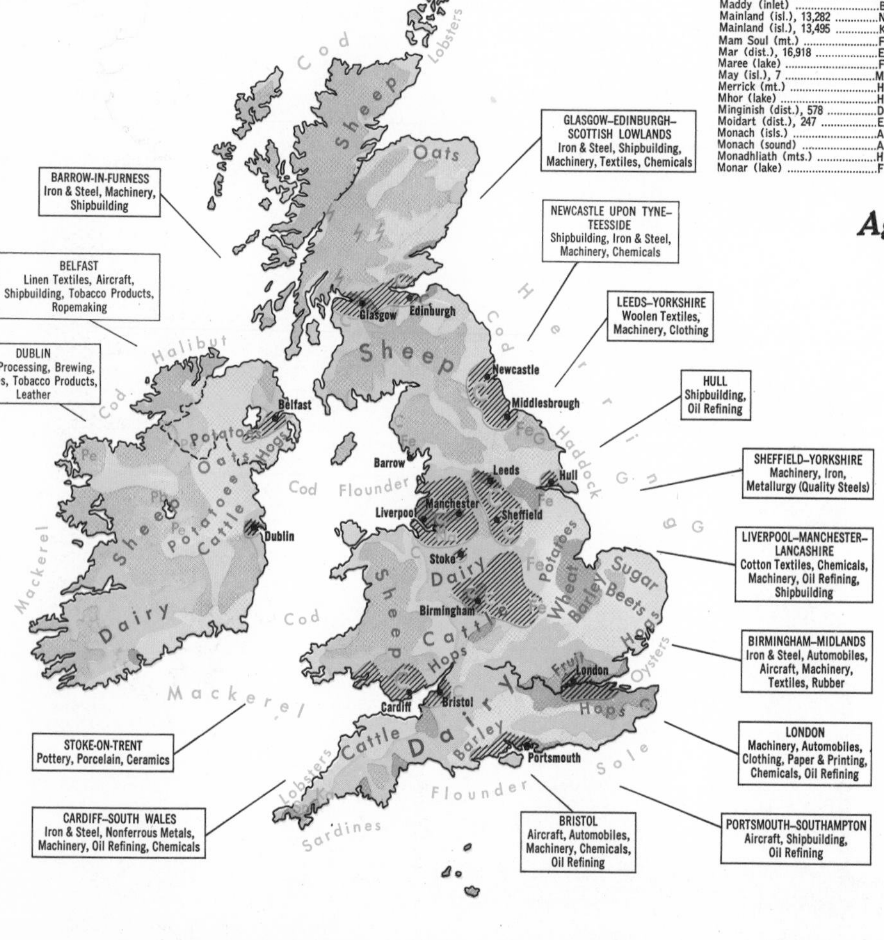

GLASGOW–EDINBURGH–SCOTTISH LOWLANDS
Iron & Steel, Shipbuilding, Machinery, Textiles, Chemicals
BARROW-IN-FURNESS
Iron & Steel, Machinery, Shipbuilding
NEWCASTLE UPON TYNE–TEESSIDE
Shipbuilding, Iron & Steel, Machinery, Chemicals
BELFAST
Linen Textiles, Aircraft, Shipbuilding, Tobacco Products, Ropemaking
LEEDS–YORKSHIRE
Woolen Textiles, Machinery, Clothing
DUBLIN
Food Processing, Brewing, Textiles, Tobacco Products, Leather
HULL
Shipbuilding, Oil Refining
SHEFFIELD–YORKSHIRE
Machinery, Iron, Metallurgy (Quality Steels)
LIVERPOOL–MANCHESTER–LANCASHIRE
Cotton Textiles, Chemicals, Machinery, Oil Refining, Shipbuilding
BIRMINGHAM–MIDLANDS
Iron & Steel, Automobiles, Aircraft, Machinery, Textiles, Rubber
STOKE-ON-TRENT
Pottery, Porcelain, Ceramics
LONDON
Machinery, Automobiles, Clothing, Paper & Printing, Chemicals, Oil Refining
CARDIFF–SOUTH WALES
Iron & Steel, Nonferrous Metals, Machinery, Oil Refining, Chemicals
BRISTOL
Aircraft, Automobiles, Machinery, Chemicals, Oil Refining
PORTSMOUTH–SOUTHAMPTON
Aircraft, Shipbuilding, Oil Refining
Cod
Lobsters
Sheep
Oats
Glasgow
Edinburgh
Halibut
Herring
Haddock
Newcastle
Middlesbrough
Belfast
Potatoes
Oats
Hogs
Barrow
Leeds
Hull
Flounder
Manchester
Liverpool
Sheffield
Dublin
Cattle
Mackerel
Dairy
Stoke
Potatoes
Sugar Beets
Wheat
Barley
Birmingham
Hops
Oysters
Fruit
London
Cardiff
Bristol
Portsmouth
Sole
Sardines

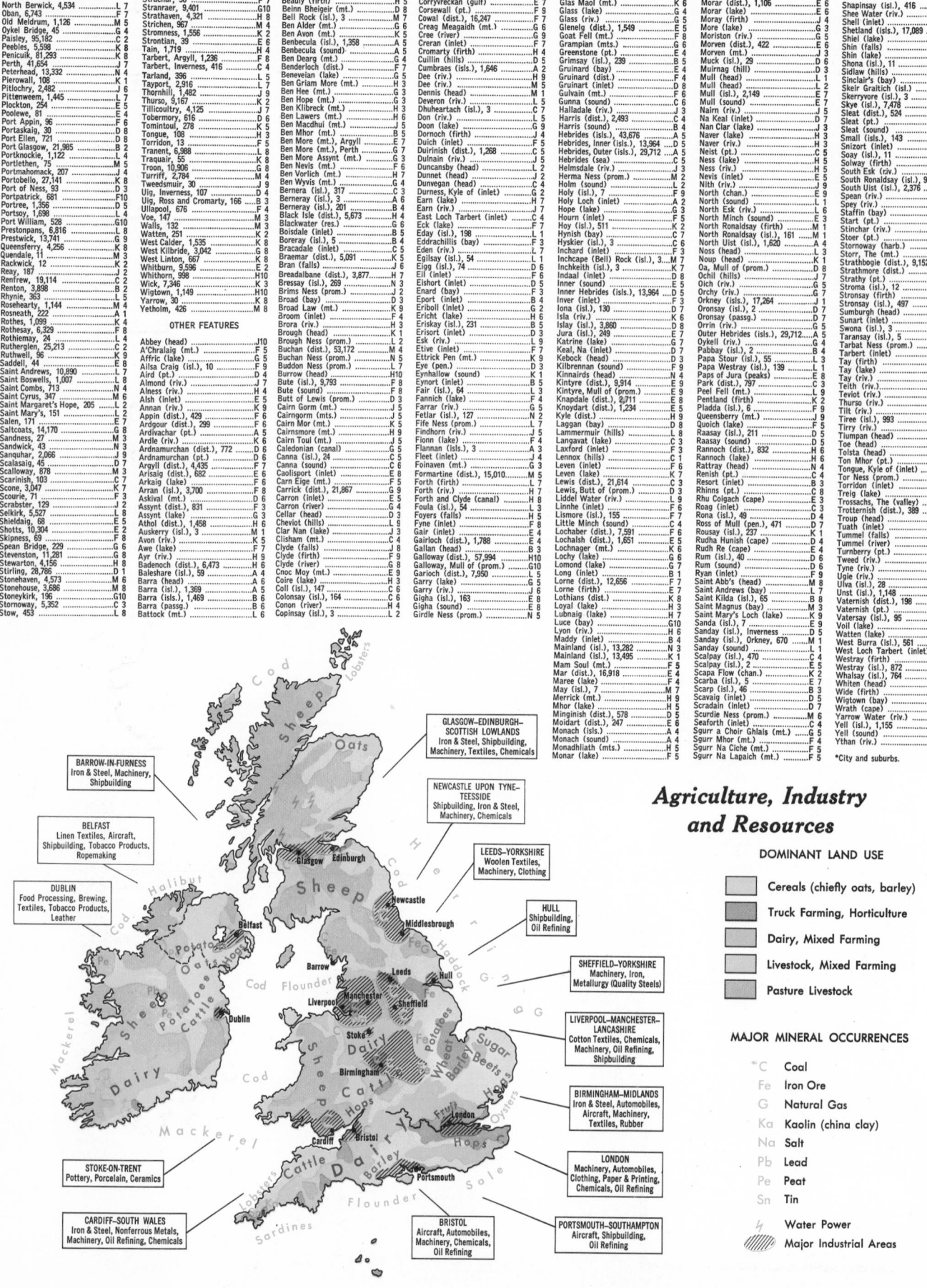

Agriculture, Industry and Resources

DOMINANT LAND USE

- Cereals (chiefly oats, barley)
- Truck Farming, Horticulture
- Dairy, Mixed Farming
- Livestock, Mixed Farming
- Pasture Livestock

MAJOR MINERAL OCCURRENCES

- C Coal
- Fe Iron Ore
- G Natural Gas
- Ka Kaolin (china clay)
- Na Salt
- Pb Lead
- Pe Peat
- Sn Tin
- Water Power
- Major Industrial Areas

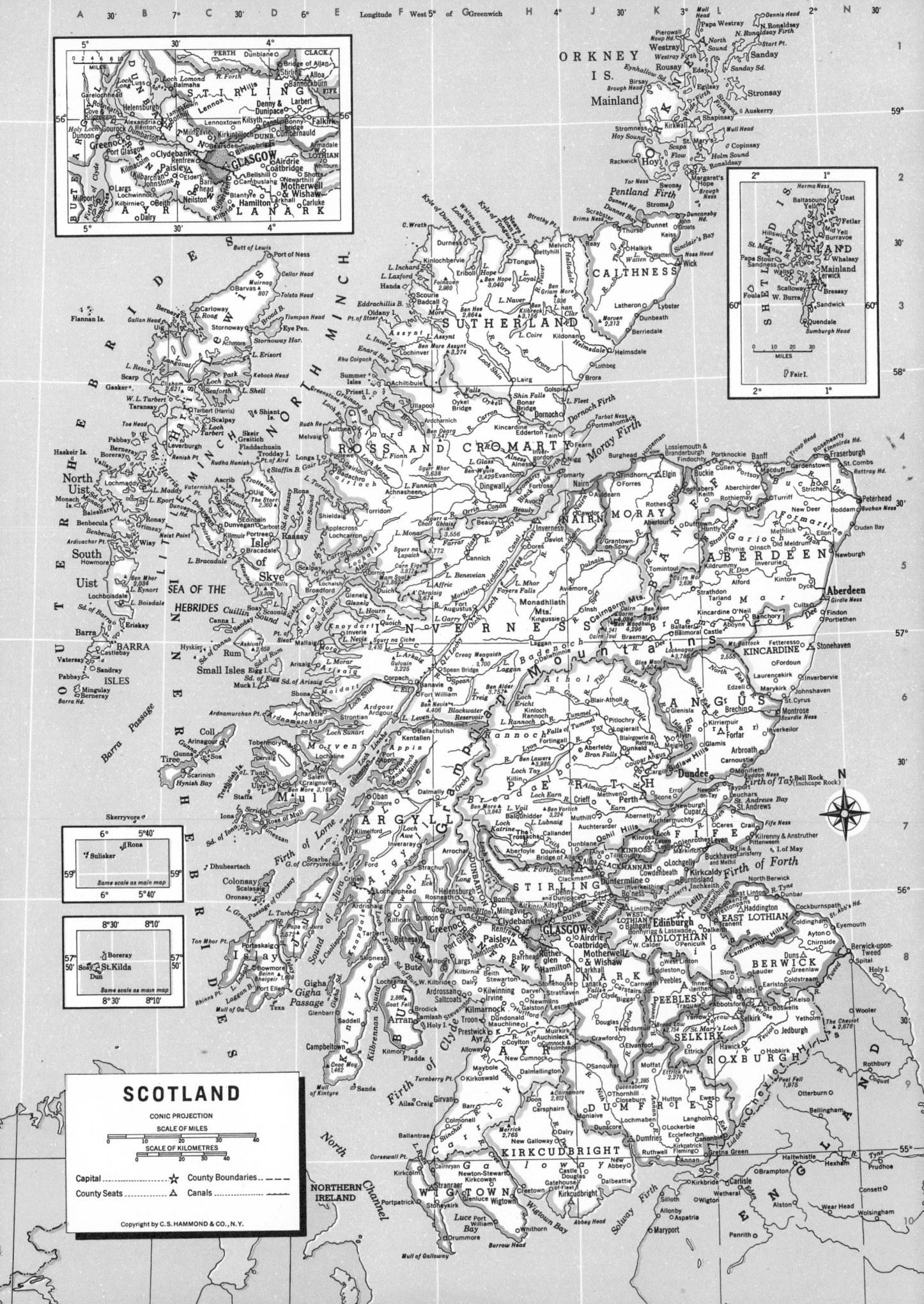

SCOTLAND

CONIC PROJECTION

SCALE OF MILES

SCALE OF KILOMETRES

Capital .... ⋆   County Boundaries ....

County Seats .... △   Canals ....

Copyright by C. S. HAMMOND & CO., N.Y.

14 United Kingdom and Ireland

(continued)

IRELAND

COUNTIES

Carlow, 33,342 ... H 6
Cavan, 56,594 ... G 4
Clare, 73,702 ... D 6
Cork, 330,443 ... D 7
Galway, 149,887 ... D 5
Donegal, 113,842 ... F 2
Dublin, 718,332 ... J 5
Kerry, 116,458 ... B 7
Kildare, 64,402 ... H 5
Kilkenny, 61,668 ... G 6
Laoighis, 45,069 ... G 6
Leitrim, 33,470 ... E 3
Leix (Laoighis), 45,069 ... G 6
Limerick, 133,339 ... D 7
Longford, 30,643 ... F 4
Louth, 67,378 ... J 4
Mayo, 123,330 ... C 4
Meath, 65,122 ... H 4
Monaghan, 47,088 ... H 3
Offaly, 51,533 ... F 5
Roscommon, 59,217 ... E 4
Sligo, 53,561 ... D 3
Tipperary, 123,822 ... F 6
Waterford, 71,439 ... F 7
Westmeath, 52,861 ... G 5
Wexford, 83,308 ... H 7
Wicklow, 58,473 ... J 5

CITIES and TOWNS

Abbeydorney, 164 ... B 7
Abbeyfeale, 1,272 ... C 7
Abbeylara, 113 ... F 4
Abbeyleix, 1,085 ... G 6
Achill Sound, 277 ... B 4
Aclare, 117 ... D 3
Adare, 590 ... D 6
Aghadoe, †371 ... C 7
Aghagower, †558 ... C 4
Ahascragh, 234 ... E 5
Annagassan, 194 ... J 4
Annascaul, 212 ... B 7
An Uaimh, 3,998 ... H 4
Ardagh, Limerick, 122 ... C 7
Ardagh, Longford, 102 ... F 4
Ardara, 547 ... E 2
Ardee, 2,710 ... H 4
Ardfinnan, 428 ... F 7
Ardmore, 290 ... F 8
Arklow, 5,390 ... J 6
Arthurstown, 136 ... H 7
Arva, 512 ... F 4
Ashford, 309 ... J 5
Askeaton, 706 ... D 6
Athboy, 680 ... H 4
Athea, 299 ... C 7
Athenry, 1,266 ... D 5
Athleague, 132 ... E 4
Athlone, 9,624 ... F 5
Athy, 3,842 ... H 6
Aughrim, 528 ... J 6
Avoca, 248 ... J 6
Bagenalstown (Muinebeag), 2,071 ... H 6
Baile Atha Cliath (Dublin) (cap.), 537,448 ... K 5
Bailieborough, 1,136 ... G 4
Balbriggan, 2,943 ... J 4
Balla, 324 ... C 4
Ballaghaderreen, 1,308 ... E 4
Ballina, 6,027 ... C 3
Ballinagh, 389 ... G 4
Ballinakill, 315 ... G 6
Ballinamore, 793 ... F 3
Ballinasloe, 5,711 ... E 5
Ballincollig, 960 ... D 8
Ballindine, 222 ... C 4
Ballingarry, Limerick, 360 ... D 7
Ballingarry, Tipperary, 209 ... F 6
Ballinlough, 252 ... D 4
Ballinrobe, 1,165 ... C 4
Ballintober, †938 ... E 4
Ballintra, 250 ... E 2
Ballisodare, 529 ... E 3
Ballybay, 716 ... G 3
Ballybofey, 1,030 ... F 2
Ballybunion, 1,163 ... B 7
Ballycanew, 168 ... J 6
Ballycastle, 191 ... C 3
Ballyconnell, 592 ... F 3
Ballycotton, 412 ... F 8
Ballydehob, 303 ... C 8
Ballydesmond, 178 ... C 7
Ballyduff, 379 ... B 7
Ballygar, 315 ... E 4
Ballyhaunis, 1,174 ... D 4
Ballyheigue, 417 ... B 7
Ballyjamesduff, 581 ... G 4
Ballylanders, 280 ... E 7
Ballylongford, 594 ... B 6
Ballymahon, 830 ... F 4
Ballymakeery-Ballyvourney, 321 ... C 8
Ballymore, 179 ... F 5
Ballymore Eustace, 348 ... J 5
Ballymote, 965 ... D 3
Ballynacargy, 288 ... G 4
Ballyporeen, 270 ... E 7
Ballyragget, 478 ... G 6
Ballyroan, 122 ... G 6
Ballyshannon, 2,322 ... E 3
Ballytore, 269 ... H 5
Ballyvaughn, 152 ... C 5
Balrothery, 102 ... J 4
Baltimore, 188 ... C 9
Baltinglass, 116 ... H 6
Banagher, 1,050 ... F 5
Bandon, 2,308 ... D 8
Bannow, †820 ... H 7
Bantry, 2,234 ... C 8
Barna, 143 ... C 5
Belmullet, 724 ... B 3
Belturbet, 1,093 ... G 3
Birr, 3,221 ... F 5
Blackwater, 216 ... J 7
Blarney, 995 ... D 8
Blessington, 491 ... J 5
Borris, 413 ... H 6
Borrisokane, 750 ... E 6
Boyle, 1,739 ... E 4
Bray (Brí Chualann), 11,688 ... K 5
Bruff, 545 ... D 7
Bunclody-Carrickduff, 891 ... H 6
Buncrana, 2,960 ... G 1
Bundoran, 1,326 ... E 3
Bunmahon, 265 ... G 7
Burtonport, 224 ... E 2
Buttevant, 981 ... D 7
Cahir, 1,662 ... F 7
Cahirciveen, 1,659 ... A 8
Callan, 1,346 ... G 7
Cappamore, 501 ... E 6
Cappawhite, 318 ... E 6
Cappoquin, 806 ... F 7
Carbury, †926 ... H 5
Carlingford, 471 ... J 3
Carlow, 7,708 ... H 6
Carndonagh, 1,016 ... G 1
Carnew, 551 ... H 6
Carrick, 153 ... D 2
Carrickmacross, 1,940 ... H 4
Carrick-on-Shannon, 1,497 ... F 4
Carrick-on-Suir, 4,672 ... F 7
Carrigaholt, 160 ... B 6
Carrigallen, 202 ... F 4
Carrigart, 196 ... F 1
Carrowkeel, 118 ... G 1
Cashel, 2,679 ... F 7
Castlebar, 5,482 ... C 4
Castlebellingham, 656 ... J 4
Castleblayney, 2,127 ... H 3
Castlebridge, 181 ... J 7
Castlecomer-Donaguile, 1,129 ... G 6
Castledermot, 551 ... H 6
Castlefin, 565 ... F 2
Castlegregory, 235 ... A 7
Castleisland, 1,718 ... B 7
Castlemaine, 171 ... B 7
Castlepollard, 778 ... G 4
Castlerea, 1,568 ... D 4
Castletown, 264 ... F 6
Castletownbere, 721 ... B 8
Castletownroche, 381 ... D 7
Castletownshend, 177 ... C 9
Cavan, 3,208 ... G 3
Ceanannus Mór, 2,193 ... G 4
Celbridge, 1,305 ... H 5
Charlestown-Bellahy, 727 ... D 4
Charleville (Rathluirc), 1,956 ... D 7
Clara, 2,477 ... F 5
Claregalway, 627 ... D 5
Claremorris, 1,519 ... C 4
Clashmore, 175 ... F 8
Clifden, 1,025 ... B 5
Cloghan, 399 ... G 6
Clogh-Chatsworth, 303 ... F 5
Clogheen, 576 ... F 7
Clogherhead, 585 ... J 4
Clonakilty, 2,417 ... D 8
Clonaslee, 275 ... F 5
Clondalkin, 3,434 ... J 5
Clones, 2,107 ... G 3
Clonmacnoise, †411 ... F 5
Clonmany, 238 ... G 1
Clonmel, 10,640 ... F 7
Clonroche, 193 ... H 7
Cloon, 106 ... F 4
Cloughjordan, 479 ... E 6
Cloyne, 612 ... E 8
Coachford, 275 ... D 8
Cóbh, 5,266 ... E 8
Coill Dubh, 645 ... H 5
Collooney, 553 ... E 3
Cong, 178 ... C 4
Convoy, 616 ... F 2
Coolaney, 124 ... D 3
Coole, 344 ... G 4
Coolgreany, 124 ... J 6
Cootehill, 1,296 ... G 3
Cork, 77,980 ... E 8
Corofin, 362 ... C 6
Courtmacsherry, 205 ... D 8
Courtown Harbour-Riverchapel, 396 ... J 6
Crookhaven, 62 ... B 9
Croom, 720 ... D 6
Crosshaven, 858 ... E 8
Crossmolina, 777 ... C 3
Culdaff, 108 ... G 1
Cullen, 113 ... C 7
Daingean, 679 ... G 5
Delvin, 165 ... G 4
Dingle, 1,460 ... A 7
Doaghbeg, †795 ... F 1
Donabate, 318 ... J 5
Donegal, 1,458 ... F 2
Doneraile, 725 ... D 7
Dooagh, 387 ... A 4
Douglas, †3,113 ... D 8
Drishane, †1,511 ... C 7
Drogheda, 17,085 ... J 4
Droichead Nua, 3,668 ... H 5
Dromahair, 229 ... E 3
Dromore West, 99 ... D 3
Drumcar, †1,205 ... J 4
Drumcliffe, 772 ... E 3
Drumconrath, 195 ... H 4
Drumkeerin, 136 ... E 3
Drumlish, 343 ... F 4
Drumshanbo, 565 ... E 3
Dublin (cap.), 537,448 ... K 5
Dublin, *595,288 ... K 5
Duleek, 379 ... J 4
Dunboyne, 521 ... H 5
Duncannon, 226 ... H 7
Dundalk, 19,790 ... H 3
Dunfanaghy, 324 ... F 1
Dungarvan, 5,188 ... F 7
Dungloe, 793 ... E 2
Dunkineely, 261 ... E 2
Dún Laoghaire, 47,792 ... K 5
Dunlavin, 416 ... H 5
Dunleen, 529 ... J 4
Dunmanway, 1,411 ... C 8
Dunmore, 500 ... D 4
Dunmore East, 547 ... G 7
Dunshaughlin, 231 ... H 5
Durrow, Laoighis, 439 ... G 6
Durrow, Westmeath, 435 ... F 5
Easky, 317 ... D 3
Edenderry, 2,691 ... G 5
Elphin, 494 ... E 4
Emyvale, 255 ... G 3
Ennis, 5,699 ... D 6
Enniscorthy, 5,754 ... J 7
Enniskerry, 652 ... J 5
Ennistymon, 1,145 ... C 6
Eyrecourt, 355 ... E 5
Fahan, 322 ... G 1
Feakle, 129 ... D 6
Fenit, 308 ... B 7
Ferbane, 896 ... F 5
Fermoy, 3,241 ... E 7
Ferns, 557 ... J 6
Fethard, Tipperary, 962 ... F 7
Fethard, Wexford, 218 ... H 7
Fiddown, 152 ... G 7
Foxford, 876 ... C 4
Foynes, 686 ... C 6
Frankford (Kilcormac), 1,018 ... F 5
Frenchpark, 155 ... E 4
Freshford, 656 ... G 6
Galbally, 266 ... E 7
Galway, 22,028 ... C 5
Geashill, 170 ... G 5
Glandore, 151 ... C 8
Glencolumbkille, 95 ... D 2
Glencullen, 161 ... J 5
Glengarriff, 392 ... C 8
Glenties, 828 ... E 2
Glenville, 146 ... E 7
Glin, 763 ... C 6
Golden, 153 ... F 7
Gorey, 2,671 ... J 6
Gort, 1,044 ... D 5
Gowran, 365 ... G 6
Granard, 1,044 ... F 4
Greencastle, 233 ... H 1
Greenore, 142 ... J 4
Greystones-Delgany, 3,551 ... K 5
Hacketstown, 509 ... H 6
Holycross, 921 ... F 6
Hospital, 572 ... E 7
Inchigeela, 157 ... C 8
Inniscrone, 533 ... C 3
Johnstown, 326 ... G 6
Kanturk, 1,985 ... D 7
Keel, 459 ... A 4
Kells, 128 ... G 7
Kells (Ceanannus Mór), 2,193 ... G 4
Kenmare, 1,046 ... B 8
Kilbeggan, 799 ... G 5
Kilbehenny, 86 ... E 7
Kilcar, 229 ... D 2
Kilcock, 739 ... H 5
Kilconnell, 113 ... E 5
Kilcoole, 549 ... K 5
Kilcormac, 1,018 ... F 5
Kilcullen, 637 ... H 5
Kildare, 2,551 ... H 5
Kildysart, 295 ... C 6
Kilfenora, 135 ... C 6
Kilfinane, 565 ... D 7
Kilgarvan, 183 ... B 8
Kilkee, 1,392 ... B 6
Kilkelly, 257 ... D 4
Kilkenny, 10,159 ... G 6
Killala, 337 ... C 3
Killaloe, 835 ... D 6
Killarney, 6,825 ... C 7
Killavullen, 167 ... D 7
Killenaule, 531 ... F 6
Killeshandra, 397 ... F 3
Killimor, 195 ... E 5
Killorglin, 1,100 ... B 7
Killucan-Rathwire, 314 ... G 4
Killybegs, 1,065 ... E 2
Kilmacrennan, 251 ... F 1
Kilmacthomas, 446 ... G 7
Kilmallock, 1,159 ... D 7
Kilmeaden, 77 ... G 7
Kilmihill, 264 ... C 6
Kilnaleck, 279 ... G 4
Kilronan, 231 ... B 5
Kilrush, 2,861 ... C 6
Kilsheelan, 172 ... F 7
Kiltimagh, 980 ... C 4
Kilworth, 334 ... E 7
Kingscourt, 793 ... H 4
Kingstown (Dún Laoghaire), 47,792 ... K 5
Kinlough, 203 ... E 3
Kinnegad, 351 ... G 5
Kinnitty, 275 ... F 5
Kinsale, 1,587 ... D 8
Kinvara, 338 ... D 5
Knightstown, 337 ... A 8
Knock, 218 ... D 4
Knocklong, 289 ... D 7
Knocktopher, 127 ... G 7
Labasheeda, 142 ... C 6
Laghey, 184 ... E 2
Lahinch, 389 ... C 6
Lanesborough-Ballyleague, 720 ... E 4
Laracor, 386 ... H 4
Laytown-Bettystown, 766 ... J 4
Leenane, 123 ... B 4
Leighlinbridge, 457 ... H 6
Leitrim, 111 ... F 3
Leixlip, 915 ... H 5
Letterkenny, 4,329 ... F 2
Lifford, 864 ... F 2
Limerick, 50,786 ... D 6
Liscarroll, 228 ... D 7
Lisdoonvarna, 625 ... C 5
Lismore, 810 ... F 7
Listowel, 7,859 ... C 7
Littleton, 274 ... F 6
Longford, 3,558 ... F 4
Lorrha, 84 ... E 5
Loughrea, 2,784 ... E 5
Louisburgh, 346 ... B 4
Louth, 207 ... J 4
Lucan-Doddsborough, 1,657 ... J 5
Luimneach (Limerick), 50,786 ... D 6
Lusk, 495 ... J 4
Macroom, 2,169 ... C 8
Malahide, 2,534 ... J 5
Malin, 164 ... G 1
Mallow, 5,545 ... D 7
Manorhamilton, 920 ... E 3
Manulla, †774 ... C 4
Maryborough (Portlaoighise), 3,133 ... G 5
Maynooth, 1,753 ... H 5
Meathas Truim, 624 ... G 4
Midleton, 2,772 ... E 8
Milford, 611 ... F 1
Millstreet, 1,283 ... D 7
Miltown Malbay, 700 ... C 6
Mitchelstown, 2,655 ... E 7
Moate, 1,261 ... F 5
Mohill, 905 ... F 4
Monaghan, 4,013 ... G 3
Monasterevan, 1,273 ... H 5
Moneygall, 284 ... F 6
Monivea, 222 ... D 5
Mooncoin, 507 ... G 7
Mount Bellew, 306 ... D 5
Mountcharles, 400 ... E 2
Mountmellick, 2,436 ... G 5
Mountrath, 1,051 ... F 5
Moville, 1,097 ... G 1
Moycullen, 127 ... C 5
Moynalty, 128 ... H 4
Muff, 219 ... G 1
Muinebeag, 2,071 ... H 6
Mullagh, 213 ... H 4
Mullaghmore, 137 ... D 3
Mullinahone, 322 ... F 7
Mullinavat, 339 ... G 7
Mullingar, 5,834 ... G 4
Naas, 4,023 ... H 5
Navan (An Uaimh), 3,998 ... H 4
Nenagh, 4,317 ... E 6
Newbliss, 192 ... G 3
Newbridge (Droichead Nua), 3,668 ... H 5
Newcastle, 2,527 ... D 7
New Inn, 164 ... F 7
Newmarket, 791 ... C 7
Newmarket-on-Fergus, 807 ... D 6
New Pallas, 171 ... E 6
Newport, Mayo, 459 ... C 4
Newport, Tipperary, 581 ... E 6
New Ross, 4,494 ... H 7
Newtownforbes, 318 ... F 4
Newtownmountkennedy-Killadreenan, 935 ... J 5
Newtownsandes, 304 ... C 6
O'Briensbridge-Montpelier, 232 ... D 6
Oola, 314 ... E 6
Oranmore, 346 ... D 5
Oughterard, 618 ... C 5
Passage East, 494 ... G 7
Passage West, 2,561 ... E 8
Patrickswell, 305 ... D 6
Pettigo, 313 ... F 2
Portarlington, 2,846 ... G 5
Portlåoighise, 3,133 ... G 5
Portlaw, 1,113 ... G 7
Portmarnock, 669 ... J 5
Portumna, 836 ... E 5
Queenstown (Cóbh), 5,266 ... E 8
Quilty, 190 ... C 6
Rahan, †635 ... F 5
Ramelton, 759 ... F 1
Raphoe, 818 ... F 2
Rathangan, 569 ... G 5
Rathcormac, 267 ... E 7
Rathdowney, 896 ... F 6
Rathdrum, 1,128 ... J 6
Rathkeale, 1,459 ... D 7
Rathluirc, 1,956 ... D 7
Rathmore, 417 ... J 5
Rathmullen, 491 ... F 1
Rathnew-Merrymeeting, 861 ... J 6
Rathowen, 119 ... F 4
Rathvilly, 293 ... H 6
Ratoath, 289 ... J 5
Riverstown, 203 ... E 3
Rockcorry, 190 ... H 3
Rosapenna, †905 ... F 1
Roscommon, 1,600 ... E 4
Roscrea, 3,372 ... F 6
Rosscarbery, 380 ... C 8
Rosslare, 529 ... J 7
Roundstone, 250 ... A 5
Rush, 2,118 ... J 4
Saggart, 426 ... F 2
Saint Johnstown, 458 ... F 2
Sallybrook-Riverstown, 563 ... E 8
Scariff-Tuamgraney, 600 ... E 6
Schull, 419 ... B 8
Scotstown, 199 ... H 3
Shannon Airport, 234 ... D 6
Shercock, 254 ... G 4
Shillelagh, 202 ... J 6
Shinrone, 402 ... F 5
Shrule, 250 ... C 4
Silvermines, 222 ... E 6
Sixmilebridge, 448 ... D 6
Skerries, 2,721 ... J 4
Skibbereen, 2,028 ... C 8
Slane, 421 ... H 4
Sligo, 13,145 ... E 3
Smithborough, 94 ... G 3
Sneem, 282 ... B 8
Spiddal, 134 ... C 5
Stradbally, Laoighis, 792 ... G 5
Stradbally, Waterford, 213 ... F 7
Stranorlar, 848 ... F 2
Strokestown, 707 ... E 4
Swanlinbar, 306 ... F 3
Swinford, 1,115 ... C 4
Swords, 1,816 ... J 5
Taghmon, 347 ... H 7
Tallow, 819 ... F 7
Tarbert, 455 ... C 6
Teltown, †684 ... H 4
Templemore, 1,779 ... F 6
Templetouhy, 156 ... F 6
Termonfeckin, 300 ... J 4
Thomastown, 1,209 ... G 7
Thurles, 6,421 ... F 6
Timoleague, 291 ... D 8
Tinahely, 417 ... H 6
Tipperary, 4,684 ... E 7
Toomevara, 231 ... E 6
Tralee, 10,723 ... B 7
Tramore, 2,882 ... G 7
Trim, 1,371 ... H 4
Tuam, 3,500 ... D 4
Tubbercurry, 878 ... D 3
Tulla, 389 ... D 6
Tullamore, 6,243 ... G 5
Tullaroan, 118 ... G 6
Tullow, 1,725 ... H 6
Tyrellspass, 259 ... G 5
Urlingford, 562 ... F 6
Virginia, 515 ... G 4
Waterford, 28,216 ... G 7
Waterville-Spunkane, 702 ... A 8
Westport, 2,882 ... C 4
Wexford, 11,328 ... H 7
Whitegate, 397 ... E 8
Wicklow, 3,125 ... K 6
Woodford, 264 ... E 5
Youghal, 5,043 ... F 8

OTHER FEATURES

Achill (isl.), 4,220 ... A 4
Aherlow (riv.) ... E 7
Allen (lake) ... E 3
Allen, Bog of (marsh) ... H 5
Allow (riv.) ... D 7
Annalee (riv.) ... G 3
Anner (riv.) ... F 7
Aran (isl.), 948 ... D 2
Aran (isls.), 1,651 ... B 5
Arrow (lake) ... E 3
Awbeg (riv.) ... D 7
Ballinskelligs (bay) ... A 8
Ballyhoura (hills) ... E 7
Ballynakill (harb.) ... A 4
Ballysadare (bay) ... D 3
Ballyteige (bay) ... H 7
Bandon (riv.) ... D 8
Bann (riv.) ... J 6
Bantry (bay) ... B 8
Barrow (riv.) ... H 7
Baurtregaum (mt.) ... A 7
Bear (isl.), 382 ... C 4
Beltra (lake) ... C 4
Ben Dash (hill) ... C 6
Benwee (head) ... B 3
Bertraghboy (bay) ... A 5
Black (head) ... C 5
Blacksod (bay) ... A 3
Blackstairs (mt.) ... H 6
Blackwater (riv.) ... D 7
Blackwater (riv.) ... H 4
Blasket (isls.) ... A 7
Bloody Foreland (prom.) ... E 1
Blue Stack (mts.) ... E 2
Boderg (lake) ... E 4
Boggeragh (mts.) ... D 7
Bolus (head) ... A 8
Bonet (riv.) ... E 3
Boyne (riv.) ... J 4
Brandon (bay) ... A 7
Brandon (mt.) ... A 7
Brannock (isls.) ... A 5
Bray (head) ... A 8
Bride (riv.) ... E 7
Broad Haven (harb.) ... B 3
Brosna (riv.) ... F 5
Bull, The (isl.) ... A 8
Caha (mts.) ... B 8
Cahore (pt.) ... J 6
Cark (mt.) ... F 2
Carlingford (inlet) ... J 3
Carnsore (pt.) ... J 7
Carra (lake) ... C 4
Carrantuohill (mt.) ... B 7
Carrigan (head) ... D 2
Carrowmore (lake) ... B 3
Clare (riv.) ... D 5
Clare with Inishturk (isls.), 313 ... A 4
Clear (cape) ... B 9
Clear (isl.) ... C 9
Clew (bay) ... B 4
Comeragh (mts.) ... F 7
Conn (lake) ... C 3
Connacht (prov.), 419,465 ... C 4
Connemara (dist.), 23,841 ... B 5
Corrib (lake) ... C 5
Courtmacsherry (bay) ... D 8
Croagh Patrick (mt.) ... C 4
Crossfarnoge (pt.) ... J 7
Cuilcagh (mt.) ... F 3
Cullin (lake) ... C 4
Curragh, The ... H 5
Cutra (lake) ... D 5
Dee (riv.) ... H 4
Deel (riv.) ... C 3
Deel (riv.) ... D 7
Deel (riv.) ... F 2
Derg (lake) ... E 6
Derg (lake) ... F 2
Derravaragh (lake) ... G 4
Derryveagh (mts.) ... E 2
Devilsbit (mt.) ... F 6
Dingle (bay) ... A 7
Donegal (bay) ... D 3
Donegal (pt.) ... B 6
Doulus (head) ... A 8
Downpatrick (head) ... C 3
Drum (hills) ... F 7
Dublin (bay) ... J 5
Dunaff (head) ... F 1
Dunany (pt.) ... J 4
Dundalk (bay) ... J 4
Dunkellin (riv.) ... D 5
Dunmanus (bay) ... B 8
Dursey (isl.) ... A 8
Eask (lake) ... E 2
Ennell (lake) ... G 5
Erkina (riv.) ... G 6
Erne (riv.) ... E 3
Erris (head) ... A 3
Errigal (mt.) ... E 1
Fanad (head) ... F 1
Fastnet Rock (isl.) ... B 9
Feale (riv.) ... C 7
Feeagh (lake) ... B 4
Fergus (riv.) ... D 6
Finn (riv.) ... F 2
Finn (riv.) ... G 3
Flesk (riv.) ... C 7
Foul (sound) ... B 5
Foyle (inlet) ... G 1
Foyle (riv.) ... G 2
Galley (head) ... D 9
Galtee (mts.) ... E 7
Galtymore (mt.) ... E 7
Galway (bay) ... C 5
Gara (lake) ... D 4
Garadice (lake) ... F 3
Gartan (lake) ... F 2
Garvan (isls.) ... G 1
Gill (lake) ... E 3
Glen (lake) ... F 1
Glyde (riv.) ... H 4
Gola (isl.) ... E 1
Golden Vale (plain) ... E 7
Gorumna (isl.), †1,730 ... B 5
Gowna (lake) ... G 4
Grand (canal) ... G 5
Great Blasket (isl.) ... A 7
Greenore (pt.) ... J 7
Gregory's (sound) ... B 5
Gweebarra (bay) ... D 2
Gweebarra (riv.) ... E 2
Hags (head) ... B 6
Helvick (head) ... G 7
High (isl.) ... A 4
Hook (head) ... H 7
Horn (head) ... E 1
Iar Connaught (dist.), 4,051 ... C 5
Inishbofin (isl.), 248 ... A 4
Inishbofin (isl.) ... E 1
Inisheer (isl.), 358 ... B 5
Inishmaan (isl.), 357 ... C 5
Inishmore (isl.), 936 ... B 5
Inishmurray (isl.) ... D 3
Inishowen (head) ... H 1
Inishowen (pen.) ... G 1
Inishshark (isl.) ... A 4
Inishtrahull (isl.) ... G 1
Inishturk with Clare (isls.), 313 ... A 4
Inny (riv.) ... A 8
Inny (riv.) ... F 4
Inver (bay) ... E 2
Ireland's Eye (isl.) ... K 5
Irish (sea) ... K 4
Joyce's Country (dist.), 2,425 ... B 4
Keeper (hill) ... E 6
Kenmare (riv.) ... A 8
Kerry (head) ... A 7
Key (lake) ... E 3
Kilkieran (bay) ... B 5
Killary (harb.) ... A 4
Kinsale, Old Head of (head) ... E 8
Kippure (mt.) ... J 5
Knockadoon (head) ... F 8
Knockanefune (mt.) ... C 7
Knockboy (mt.) ... B 8
Knockmealdown (mts.) ... F 7
Lady's Island Lake (inlet) ... J 7
Lambay (isl.) ... K 5
Lamb's (head) ... A 8
Laune (riv.) ... B 7
Leane (lake) ... B 7
Leane (lake) ... G 4
Lee (riv.) ... D 8
Leinster (mt.) ... H 6
Leinster (prov.), 1,332,149 ... G 5
Lettermullen (isl.) ... B 5
Liffey (riv.) ... H 5
Liscannor (bay) ... B 6
Little Brosna (riv.) ... E 5
Long Island (bay) ... B 9
Loop (head) ... A 6
Loughros More (bay) ... D 2
Lugnaquillia (mt.) ... J 5
Lung (riv.) ... D 4
Macgillicuddy's Reeks (mts.) ... B 7
Macnean (lake) ... F 3
Maigue (riv.) ... D 6
Maine (riv.) ... C 7
Malin (head) ... F 1
Mangerton (mt.) ... C 8
Mask (lake) ... C 4
Maumakeogh (mt.) ... C 3
Maumturk (mts.) ... B 5
Melvin (lake) ... E 3
Mine (head) ... F 8
Mizen (head) ... B 9
Mizen (head) ... K 6
Moher (cliffs) ... B 6
Monavullagh (mts.) ... F 7
Moy (riv.) ... C 3
Muckish (mt.) ... E 1
Muckno (lake) ... H 3
Mulkear (riv.) ... E 6
Mullaghareirk (mts.) ... C 7
Mulroy (bay) ... F 1
Munster (prov.), 849,203 ... D 7
Mutton (isl.) ... B 6
Mweelrea (mt.) ... B 4
Mweenish (isl.) ... B 5
Nagles (mts.) ... E 7
Nephin (mt.) ... C 3
Nephin Beg (mt.) ... B 3
Nore (riv.) ... G 7
North (sound) ... B 5
North Inishkea (isl.) ... A 3
Omey (isl.) ... A 5
Oughter (lake) ... G 3
Ovoca (riv.) ... J 6
Owell (lake) ... G 4
Owenmore (riv.) ... B 3
Owenmore (riv.) ... D 3
Owey (isl.) ... D 1
Ox (Slieve Gamph) (mts.) ... D 3
Paps, The (mt.) ... C 7
Partry (mts.) ... C 4
Pollaphuca (res.) ... J 5
Puffin (isl.) ... A 8
Punchestown ... H 5
Ramor (lake) ... G 4
Rathlin O'Birne (isl.) ... C 2
Ree (lake) ... F 5
Rinn (lake) ... F 4
Roaringwater (bay) ... B 9
Rosses (bay) ... D 1
Rosskeeragh (pt.) ... D 3
Rosslare (bay) ... J 7
Royal (canal) ... G 4
Saint Finan's (bay) ... A 8
Saint George's (chan.) ... K 7
Saint John's (pt.) ... D 2
Saltee (isls.) ... H 7
Scarriff (isl.) ... A 8
Seven (heads) ... D 8
Seven Hogs, The (isls.) ... A 7
Shannon (riv.) ... E 6
Shannon, Mouth of the (est.) ... B 6
Sheeffry (hills) ... B 4
Sheep Haven (harb.) ... F 1
Sheeps (head) ... B 8
Shehy (mts.) ... C 8
Sherkin (isl.) ... C 9
Silvermine (mts.) ... E 6
Slaney (riv.) ... H 7
Slieve Anierin (mt.) ... F 3
Slieve Aughty (mts.) ... D 5
Slieve Bernagh (mt.) ... D 6
Slieve Bloom (mts.) ... F 5
Slieve Callan (mt.) ... C 6
Slievecar (mt.) ... B 3
Slieve Elva (mt.) ... C 5
Slievefelim (mts.) ... E 6
Slieve Gamph (mts.) ... D 3
Slieve League (mt.) ... D 2
Slieve Mishkish (mts.) ... B 8
Slievenaman (mt.) ... F 7
Slyne (head) ... A 5
Smerwick (harb.) ... A 7
South (sound) ... C 5
Stacks (mts.) ... B 7
Suck (riv.) ... E 5
Sugarloaf (mt.) ... B 8
Suir (riv.) ... G 7
Swilly (inlet) ... F 1
Tara (hill) ... H 4
Tawin (isl.) ... C 5
Toe (head) ... C 9
Tory (isl.) ... E 1
Tralee (bay) ... B 7
Tramore (bay) ... G 7
Trawbreaga (bay) ... F 1
Truskmore (mt.) ... E 3
Twelve Pins (mt.) ... B 4
Ulster (prov.), 217,524 ... G 2
Valentia (Valencia) (isl.), 926 ... A 8
Veagh (lake) ... F 1
Wexford (bay) ... J 7
Wicklow (mts.) ... J 6
Wicklow (head) ... K 6
Youghal (bay) ... F 8

NORTHERN IRELAND

COUNTIES

Antrim, 333,800 ... J 2
Armagh, 128,200 ... H 3
Belfast (city), 385,900 ... K 2
Down, 300,800 ... J 3
Fermanagh, 49,900 ... F 3
Londonderry, 177,300 ... H 2
Tyrone, 136,600 ... G 2

CITIES and TOWNS

Aghadowey, †679 ... H 1
Ahoghill, 885 ... J 2
Annalong, 553 ... K 3
Antrim, 33,980 ... J 2
Ardglass, 737 ... K 3
Armagh, 11,920 ... H 3
Armoy, 383 ... J 1
Augher, 222 ... G 3
Aughnacloy, 805 ... H 3
Ballycastle, 2,960 ... J 1
Ballyclare, 4,690 ... J 2
Ballygally, 276 ... K 2
Ballygawley, 427 ... G 3
Ballykelly, 367 ... G 1
Ballymena, 16,730 ... J 2
Ballymoney, 3,700 ... J 1
Ballynahinch, 2,042 ... J 3
Ballynure, 291 ... K 2
Ballywalter, 789 ... K 2
Banbridge, 6,620 ... J 3
Bangor, 30,030 ... K 2
Belfast (cap.), 385,900 ... J 2
Belfast, *528,700 ... J 2
Bellaghy, 663 ... H 2
Belleek, 162 ... E 3
Beragh, 349 ... G 2
Bessbrook, 3,199 ... J 3
Brookeborough, 294 ... G 3
Broughshane, 716 ... J 2
Bushmills, 936 ... J 1
Caledon, 350 ... H 3
Carnlough, 586 ... J 2
Carrickfergus, 13,130 ... K 2
Carrowdore, 297 ... K 2
Castledawson, 906 ... H 2
Castlederg, 1,367 ... F 2
Castlewellan, 1,241 ... K 3
Claudy, 286 ... G 2
Clogher, 197 ... G 3
Coalisland, 1,351 ... H 2
Coleraine, 14,090 ... H 1
Comber, 3,987 ... K 2
Cookstown, 6,190 ... H 2
Craigavon, 11,140 ... J 3
Crossgar, 842 ... K 3
Crossmaglen, 932 ... H 3
Crumlin, 394 ... J 2
Cullybackey, 758 ... J 2
Cushendall, 618 ... J 1
Derrygonnelly, 296 ... F 3
Dervock, 558 ... J 1
Doagh, 486 ... J 2
Donaghdee, 3,730 ... K 2
Downpatrick, 5,290 ... K 3
Draperstown, 592 ... H 2
Dromara, 280 ... J 3
Dromore, Down, 1,980 ... J 3
Dromore, Tyrone, 503 ... G 3
Drumquin, 307 ... F 2
Dunbarton, 905 ... J 3
Dundrum, 641 ... K 3
Dungannon, 7.590 ... H 3
Dungiven, 1,102 ... H 2
Dunnamanagh, 352 ... G 2
Ederny, 227 ... F 2
Enniskillen, 7,020 ... F 3
Feeny, 206 ... H 2
Fintona, 990 ... G 3
Fivemiletown, 77 ... G 3
Garvagh, 550 ... H 2
Gilford, 780 ... J 3
Glenarm, 673 ... J 2
Glenavy, 1,306 ... J 2
Glynn, 389 ... K 2
Gortin, 261 ... G 2
Greyabbey, 611 ... K 2
Hillsborough, 806 ... J 3
Hilltown, 309 ... J 3
Holywood, 7,930 ... K 2
Irvinestown, 934 ... F 3
Jonesborough, 274 ... J 3
Keady, 1,960 ... H 3
Kells, 495 ... J 2
Kesh, †689 ... F 3
Kilkeel, 2,570 ... K 3
Killeter, †442 ... F 2
Killough, 504 ... K 3
Killyleagh, 1,876 ... K 3
Kilrea, 952 ... H 2
Kircubbin, 843 ... K 3
Lack, †571 ... F 2
Larne, 17,840 ... K 2
Limavady, 5,230 ... H 1
Lisburn, 24,870 ... J 2
Lisnaskea, 977 ... G 3
Londonderry, 55,000 ... G 2
Loughbrickland, 300 ... J 3
Loughgall, †1,086 ... H 3
Maghera, 1,607 ... H 2
Magherafelt, 2,459 ... H 2
Maguire's Bridge, 339 ... G 3
Markethill, 813 ... H 3
Middletown, 161 ... H 3
Millisle, 386 ... K 2
Moira, 501 ... J 3
Moneymore, 807 ... H 2
Moy, 751 ... H 3
Moygashel, 1,146 ... H 3
Newcastle, 4,450 ... J 3
Newry, 11,960 ... J 3
Newtownabbey, 53,450 ... K 2
Newtownards, 14,180 ... K 2
Newtownbutler, 358 ... G 3
Newtownhamilton, 589 ... H 3
Newtownstewart, 1,125 ... G 2
Omagh, 10,710 ... G 2
Pettigoe, 76 ... F 2
Pomeroy, 349 ... H 2
Portaferry, 1,406 ... K 3
Portavogie, 1,071 ... K 3
Portglenone, 613 ... H 2
Portrush, 4,420 ... H 1
Portstewart, 4,660 ... H 1
Randalstown, 1,579 ... J 2
Rasharkin, 799 ... J 2
Rathfriland, 1,558 ... J 3
Rostrevor, 1,265 ... J 3
Saintfield, 702 ... K 3
Sion Mills, 1,616 ... G 2
Sixmilecross, 245 ... H 2
Stewartstown, 621 ... H 2
Strabane, 9,040 ... G 2
Strangford, 413 ... K 3
Tandragee, 1,570 ... H 3
Templepatrick, †775 ... J 2
Tempo, 269 ... G 3
Trillick, 220 ... G 3
Tynan, †805 ... H 3
Warrenpoint, 3,750 ... J 3
Whitehead, 2,760 ... K 2

OTHER FEATURES

Arney (riv.) ... F 3
Bann (riv.) ... H 2
Beg (lake) ... J 2
Belfast (inlet) ... K 2
Binevenagh (mt.) ... H 1
Blackwater (riv.) ... H 3
Bush (riv.) ... H 1
Copeland (isl.) ... K 2
Derg (riv.) ... F 2
Erne (lake) ... F 3
Fair (head) ... J 1
Foyle (inlet) ... G 1
Foyle (riv.) ... G 2
Garron (pt.) ... K 1
Giant's Causeway ... H 1
Knocklayd (mt.) ... J 1
Lagan (riv.) ... K 2
Larne (inlet) ... K 2
Macnean (lake) ... F 3
Magee, Island (pen.) ... K 2
Magilligan (pt.) ... H 1
Maidens, The (isls.) ... K 2
Main (riv.) ... J 2
Mourne (mts.) ... J 3
Mourne (riv.) ... G 2
Neagh (lake) ... J 2
North (chan.) ... K 1
Owenkillew (riv.) ... G 2
Rathlin (isl.), 159 ... J 1
Red (bay) ... K 1
Roe (riv.) ... H 1
Saint John's (pt.) ... K 3
Slemish (mt.) ... J 2
Slieve Beagh (mt.) ... G 3
Slieve Donard (mt.) ... K 3
Slieve Gullion (mt.) ... J 3
Sperrin (mts.) ... G 2
Strangford (inlet) ... K 3
Torr (head) ... K 1
Trostan (mt.) ... J 1
Ulster (prov.), 1,512,500 ... G 2
Upper Lough Erne (lake) ... F 3

*City and suburbs.
†Population of district.

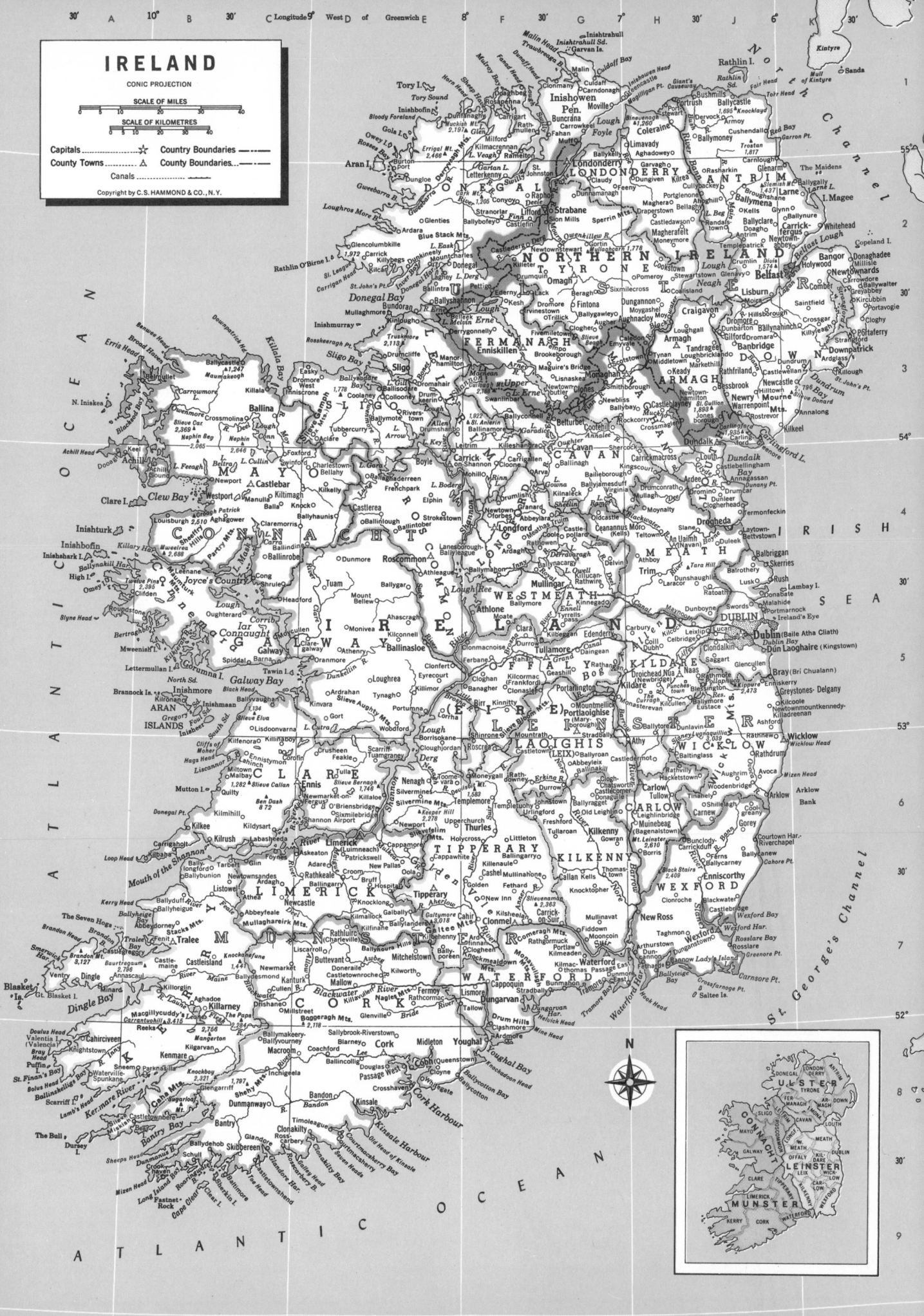

IRELAND

CONIC PROJECTION

SCALE OF MILES

SCALE OF KILOMETRES

Capitals .... ☆   Country Boundaries ——— — ———
County Towns .... △   County Boundaries .....—.....—.....
Canals ——————

Copyright by C.S. HAMMOND & CO., N.Y.

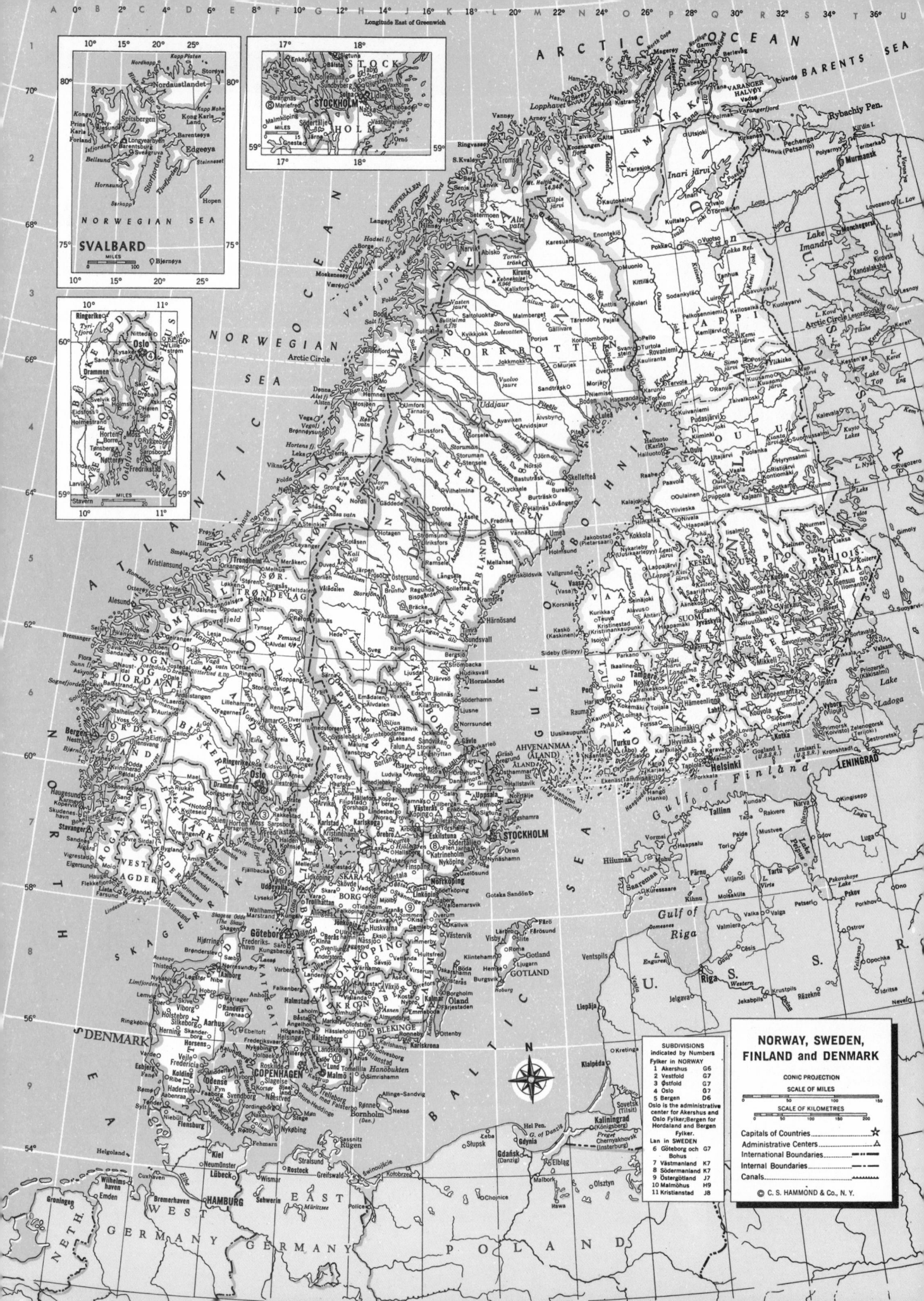

NORWAY, SWEDEN, FINLAND and DENMARK

CONIC PROJECTION

SCALE OF MILES

SCALE OF KILOMETRES

Capitals of Countries .... ★
Administrative Centers .... △
International Boundaries .... ━ ▪ ━ ▪
Internal Boundaries .... ━ ━ ━
Canals .... ⌁⌁⌁⌁

© C. S. HAMMOND & Co., N.Y.

SUBDIVISIONS
indicated by Numbers

Fylker in NORWAY
1 Akershus   G6
2 Vestfold   G7
3 Østfold   G7
4 Oslo   G7
5 Bergen   D6

Oslo is the administrative
center for Akershus and
Oslo Fylker; Bergen for
Hordaland and Bergen
Fylker.

Län in SWEDEN
6 Göteborg och   G7
   Bohus
7 Västmanland   K7
8 Södermanland   K7
9 Östgötland   J7
10 Malmöhus   H9
11 Kristianstad   J8

SVALBARD

STOCKHOLM

Oslo

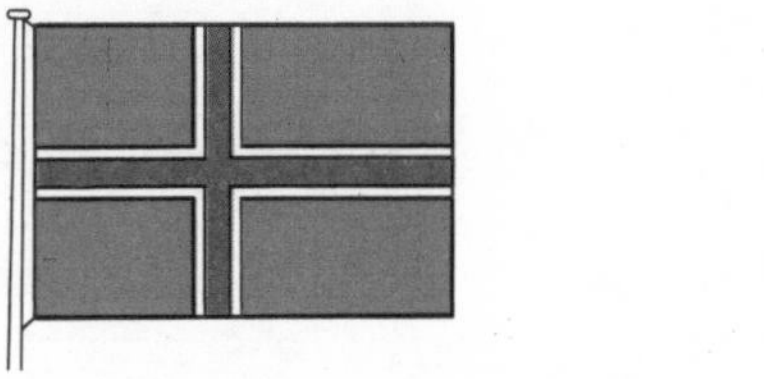

NORWAY

AREA 125,181 sq. mi.
POPULATION 3,893,000
CAPITAL Oslo
LARGEST CITY Oslo
HIGHEST POINT Glittertind 8,110 ft.
MONETARY UNIT krone (crown)
MAJOR LANGUAGE Norwegian
MAJOR RELIGION Protestantism

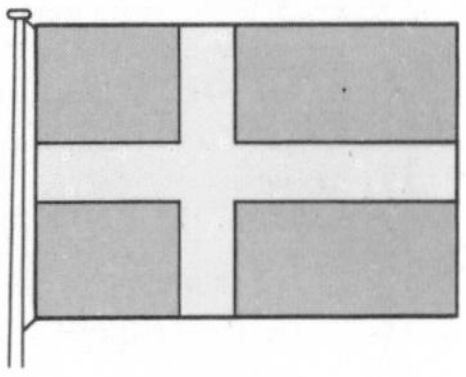

SWEDEN

AREA 173,665 sq. mi.
POPULATION 7,978,000
CAPITAL Stockholm
LARGEST CITY Stockholm
HIGHEST POINT Kebnekaise 6,946 ft.
MONETARY UNIT krona (crown)
MAJOR LANGUAGE Swedish
MAJOR RELIGION Protestantism

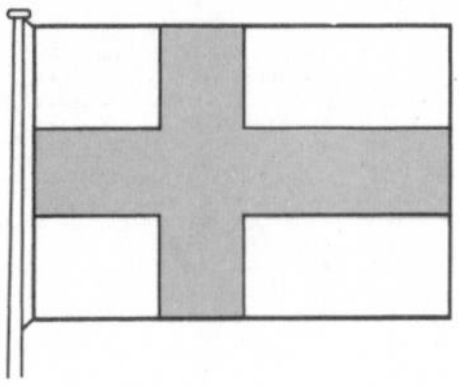

FINLAND

AREA 130,128 sq. mi.
POPULATION 4,706,000
CAPITAL Helsinki
LARGEST CITY Helsinki
HIGHEST POINT Mt. Haltia 4,343 ft.
MONETARY UNIT Markka (Mark)
MAJOR LANGUAGES Finnish, Swedish
MAJOR RELIGION Protestantism

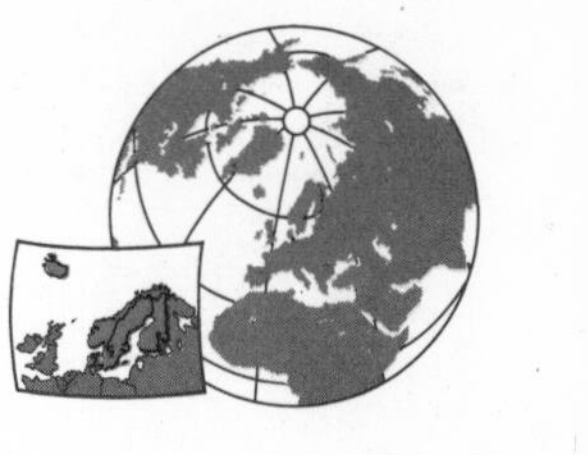

FINLAND

PROVINCES

Ahvenanmaa, 21,584 ....L 6
Häme, 623,756 ....O 6
Keski-Suomi, 248,599 ....O 5
Kuopio, 265,434 ....P 5
Kymi, 348,989 ....Q 6
Lappi, 220,755 ....P 3
Mikkeli, 225,685 ....P 6
Oulu, 422,828 ....P 4
Pohjois-Karjala, 193,199 ....Q 5
Turku-Pori, 680,713 ....N 6
Uusimaa, 999,053 ....O 6
Vaasa, 447,785 ....N 5

CITIES and TOWNS

Äänekoski, 10,977 ....O 5
Åbo (Turku), 155,000 ....N 6
Alavus (Alavo), †11,139 ....N 5
Björneborg (Pori), 71,972 ....M 6
Borgå (Porvoo), 15,738 ....O 6
Brahestad (Raahe), 7,637 ....O 4
Ekenäs (Tammisaari), 6,401 ....N 6
Espoo (Esbo), 88,086 ....O 6
Forssa, 15,260 ....N 6
Fredrikshamn (Hamina), 10,872 ....P 6
Gamlakarleby (Kokkola), 20,715 ....N 5
Haapajärvi, 8,943 ....O 5
Haapamäki, 2,200 ....O 5
Hämeenlinna (Tavastehus), 37,333 ....O 6
Hamina, 10,872 ....P 6
Hangö (Hanko), 9,668 ....N 7
Harjavalta, 8,191 ....N 6
Heinola, 13,696 ....P 6
Helsinki (Helsingfors) (cap.), 531,286 ....O 6
Helsinki, *700,000 ....O 6
Himanka, †3,260 ....N 5
Hyrynsalmi, †5,629 ....Q 4
Hyvinkää (Hyvinge), 33,062 ....O 6
Iisalmi, 7,551 ....P 5
Ilomantsi, †12,050 ....R 5
Imatra, 35,054 ....Q 6
Ivalo ....P 2
Jakobstad (Pietarsaari), 19,114 ....N 5
Joensuu, 35,385 ....R 5
Juuka, †9,925 ....Q 5
Jyväskylä, 56,824 ....O 5
Kajaani, 19,131 ....P 4
Kalajoki, †7,314 ....N 4
Karis (Karjaa), 7,940 ....N 6
Karkkila, 8,504 ....N 6
Kaskö (Kaskinen), 1,436 ....M 5
Kauttua ....M 6
Kemi, 30,199 ....O 4
Kemijärvi, 6,546 ....P 3
Kerava (Kervo), 13,322 ....O 6
Kittilä, †8,347 ....O 3
Kokemäki, †10,922 ....N 6
Kokkola (Gamlakarleby), 20,715 ....N 5
Kotka, 33,953 ....P 6
Kouvola, 25,275 ....P 6
Kristiinankaupunki (Kristinestad), 2,726 ....N 5
Kuhmo, †14,847 ....Q 4
Kuopio, 63,800 ....Q 5
Kurikka, 11,373 ....M 5
Kuusamo, †20,324 ....Q 4
Lahti, 87,237 ....O 6
Lappeenranta, 50,543 ....P 6
Lieksa, 4,703 ....R 5
Loimaa, 6,366 ....N 6
Lovisa (Loviisa), 6,695 ....P 6
Maarianhamina (Mariehamn), 8,512 ....M 7
Mänttä, 7,277 ....O 6
Mariehamn (Maarianhamina), 8,512 ....M 7
Mikkeli (Sankt Michel), 24,962 ....P 6
Muonio, †3,226 ....O 3
Naantali (Nådendal), 6,784 ....M 6
Nivala, †10,784 ....O 5
Nokia, 19,200 ....N 6
Nurmes, 2,329 ....Q 5
Nykarleby (Uusikaarlepyy), 1,289 ....N 5
Nyslott (Savonlinna), 17,618 ....Q 6
Nystad (Uusikaupunki), 6,845 ....M 6
Oulainen, 7,898 ....O 4
Oulu (Uleåborg), 85,094 ....O 4
Outokumpu, 10,862 ....Q 5
Parikkala, †7,052 ....Q 6
Parkano, †8,587 ....N 6
Pello, †7,139 ....O 3
Pieksämäki, 12,821 ....P 5
Pietarsaari (Jakobstad), 19,114 ....N 5
Pori (Björneborg), 71,972 ....M 6
Porvoo (Borgå), 15,738 ....O 6
Posio, †7,454 ....Q 3
Pudasjärvi, †15,622 ....P 4
Raahe (Brahestad), 7,637 ....O 4
Rauma (Raumo), 25,218 ....M 6
Riihimäki, 22,442 ....O 6
Rovaniemi, 28,680 ....O 3
Saarijärvi, †11,586 ....O 5
Salo, 16,715 ....N 6
Sankt Michel (Mikkeli), 24,962 ....P 6
Savonlinna, 17,618 ....Q 6
Savukoski, †2,392 ....Q 3
Seinäjoki, 19,836 ....N 5
Sodankylä, †11,745 ....P 3
Sotkamo, †14,127 ....Q 4
Suolahti, 5,563 ....O 5
Suomussalmi, †15,507 ....Q 4
Suonenjoki, 10,012 ....P 5
Tammerfors (Tampere), 156,100 ....N 6
Tammisaari (Ekenäs), 6,401 ....N 6
Tampere (Tammerfors), 156,000 ....N 6
Tapiola ....O 6
Tavastehus (Hämeenlinna), 37,333 ....O 6
Teuva, †8,280 ....N 5
Toijala, 7,505 ....N 6
Tornio (Torneå), 7,325 ....O 4
Turku (Åbo), 155,000 ....N 6
Uleåborg (Oulu), 85,094 ....O 4
Ulvila (Ulvsby), †7,800 ....N 6
Utsjoki, †1,436 ....P 2
Uusikaarlepyy (Nykarleby), 1,289 ....N 5
Uusikaupunki (Nystad), 6,845 ....M 6
Vaala, †6,675 ....P 4
Vaasa (Vasa), 49,109 ....M 5
Valkeakoski, 15,949 ....N 6
Vammala, 5,605 ....N 6
Varkaus, 24,619 ....Q 5
Vasa (Vaasa), 48,262 ....M 5

OTHER FEATURES

Ahvenanmaa (Åland) (isls.), 21,584 ....L 6
Finland (gulf) ....P 7
Haltia (mt.) ....M 2
Hangöudd (prom.) ....N 7
Hauki (lake) ....Q 5
Ii (river) ....O 4
Inari (lake) ....P 2
Juo (lake) ....Q 5
Kala (river) ....O 4
Kalla (lake) ....P 5
Keitele (lake) ....O 5
Kemi (lake) ....Q 3
Kemi (river) ....O 3
Kiantà (lake) ....Q 4
Kilpis (lake) ....M 2
Kitinen (river) ....P 3
Kivi (lake) ....O 5
Koitere (lake) ....R 5
Kuusamo (lake) ....Q 4
Längelmä (lake) ....O 6
Lapland (reg.) ....O 2
Lapuan (river) ....N 5
Lesti (lake) ....O 5
Lokka (res.) ....P 3
Muo (lake) ....R 4
Muonio (river) ....M 2
Nasi (lake) ....O 6
Onkivesi (lake) ....P 5
Orihvesi (lake) ....Q 5
Oulu (river) ....O 4
Ounas (river) ....O 3
Päijänne (lake) ....O 6
Pasvik (river) ....Q 2
Pielinen (lake) ....Q 5
Puru (lake) ....Q 6
Puula (lake) ....P 5
Pyhä (lake) ....M 6
Pyhä (lake) ....O 5
Saimaa (lake) ....Q 6
Siika (river) ....O 4
Simo (lake) ....P 3
Simo (river) ....O 4
Tana (Teno) (river) ....P 2
Tornio (river) ....O 3
Vallgrund (isl.), 2,063 ....M 5
Ylikitka (lake) ....Q 3

NORWAY

COUNTIES

Akershus, 282,928 ....D 4
Aust-Agder, 78,184 ....E 7
Bergen, 117,465 ....D 6
Buskerud, 191,789 ....F 6
Finnmark, 75,553 ....O 2
Hedmark, 177,300 ....G 6
Hordaland, 243,545 ....E 6
Møre og Romsdal, 219,384 ....E 5
Nord-Trøndelag, 117,376 ....H 4
Nordland, 244,165 ....J 3
Oppland, 168,819 ....F 6
Oslo (city), 485,200 ....D 3
Østfold, 212,450 ....D 4
Rogaland, 256,501 ....E 7
Sogn og Fjordane, 100,711 ....E 6
Sør-Trøndelag, 224,654 ....G 5
Telemark, 155,834 ....F 7
Troms, 132,407 ....L 2
Vest-Agder, 117,226 ....E 7
Vestfold, 167,778 ....D 4

CITIES and TOWNS

Åfjord, †4,105 ....G 5
Ål, †4,377 ....F 6
Ålesund, 18,558 ....D 5
Åndalsnes, 2,202 ....F 5
Arendal, 11,579 ....F 7
Askim, †9,673 ....E 4
Bamble, †8,338 ....F 7
Barentsburg ....C 2
Bergen, 117,465 ....D 6
Bergen, *270,000 ....D 6
Bodø, 14,048 ....J 3
Borre, 6,636 ....D 4
Drammen, 47,261 ....C 4
Drammen, *48,700 ....C 4
Drøbak, 2,683 ....D 4
Eigersund, 9,730 ....D 7
Elverum, †13,604 ....G 6
Farsund, 7,697 ....E 7
Flekkefjord, 8,616 ....E 7
Flora, 7,836 ....D 6
Fredrikstad, 30,006 ....D 4
Gjøvik, 24,256 ....G 6
Grimstad, 2,610 ....F 7
Gulen, †3,212 ....D 6
Halden, 10,006 ....G 7
Hamar, 14,712 ....G 6
Hammerfest, 6,806 ....N 1
Harstad, 18,892 ....K 2
Haugesund, 27,569 ....D 7
Holmestrand, 6,857 ....C 4
Honningsvåg, 2,813 ....O 1
Horten, 13,387 ....D 4
Kirkenes, 4,433 ....Q 2
Kongsberg, 17,578 ....F 7
Kongsvinger, 13,080 ....H 6
Kragerø, †10,067 ....F 7
Kristiansand, 52,542 ....F 8
Kristiansand, *54,900 ....F 8
Kristiansund, 18,466 ....E 5
Kvinnherad, †9,848 ....E 6
Larvik, 10,728 ....C 4
Lenvik, †10,209 ....L 2
Lesja, †2,755 ....F 5
Lillehammer, 19,808 ....F 6
Lillesand, †4,975 ....F 7
Lillestrøm, 10,547 ....E 3
Løkken, †5,054 ....F 5
Longyearbyen ....D 2
Lysaker, 5,393 ....D 3
Mandal, 10,622 ....E 7
Mo, 8,348 ....J 3
Molde, 17,862 ....E 5
Moss, 23,198 ....D 4
Mysen, 2,500 ....G 7
Namsos, 10,998 ....G 4
Narvik, 13,543 ....K 2
Nesttun, 3,827 ....D 6
Notodden, 13,680 ....F 7
Odda, †10,444 ....E 6
Orkanger, 2,874 ....F 5
Oslo (cap.), 483,196 ....D 3
Oslo, *635,700 ....D 3
Porsgrunn, 28,167 ....G 7
Ringerike, 28,577 ....C 3
Risør, 6,110 ....F 7
Rjukan, 6,308 ....F 7
Røros, †5,259 ....G 5
Sandefjord, 6,085 ....C 4
Sandnes, 28,534 ....D 7
Sandvika, 3,751 ....C 3
Sarpsborg, 13,185 ....D 4
Ski, †12,337 ....D 4
Skien, 47,302 ....F 7
Skjåk, †2,692 ....F 6
Stavanger, 79,700 ....D 7
Stavanger, *80,800 ....D 7
Stavern, 2,148 ....D 4
Steinkjer, 19,874 ....G 4
Stor-Elvdal, †4,151 ....G 6
Sulitjelma, 2,129 ....K 3
Sunndalsøra, 2,376 ....F 5
Svolvaer, 3,812 ....J 2
Tana, †3,286 ....Q 1
Telemark ....C 4
Tønsberg, 11,566 ....D 4
Tromsø, 34,600 ....L 2
Trondheim, 118,703 ....F 5
Trondheim, *123,600 ....F 5
Ullensvang, †4,940 ....E 6
Vadsø, 5,320 ....Q 1
Vardø, 4,185 ....R 1
Volda, 2,647 ....E 5
Voss, †13,473 ....E 6

OTHER FEATURES

Alst (fjord) ....G 3
Alsten (isl.), 4,348 ....H 4
Alta (river) ....N 2
Alte (lake) ....L 2
Ands (fjord) ....K 2
Bardu (river) ....L 2
Barentsöya (isl.) ....D 2
Bellsund (bay) ....C 2
Bjørna (fjord) ....D 6
Bjørnøya (isl.) ....D 3
Bokn (fjord) ....D 7
Bremanger (isl.), 2,028 ....D 6
Dønna (isl.), 1,978 ....H 3
Dovrefjeld (mts.) ....F 5
Edgeøya (isl.) ....E 2
Femund (lake) ....G 5
Folda (fjord) ....G 4
Folda (fjord) ....J 3
Frohavet (bay) ....F 5
Frøya (isl.), 4,034 ....F 5
Glittertind (mt.) ....F 6
Glomma (river) ....G 6
Hadsel (fjord) ....J 2
Hardanger (fjord) ....D 7
Hardanger (mts.) ....E 6
Hinlopen (strait) ....C 1
Hinnøy (isl.), 27,599 ....K 2
Hitra (isl.), 3,134 ....F 5
Hopen (isl.) ....E 2
Hornsund (bay) ....C 2
Hortens (fjord) ....G 4
Is (fjord) ....B 2
Jostedals (glacier) ....E 6
Karmøy (isl.), 19,234 ....D 7
Kob (fjord) ....O 1
Kong Karls Land (isls.) ....E 1
Kvaløy (isl.), 6,869 ....O 1
Lagen (river) ....G 6
Lakse (fjord) ....P 1
Langøy (isl.), 16,500 ....J 2
Lapland (reg.) ....K 2
Lindesnes (cape) ....E 8
Lista (pen.), 7,702 ....E 7
Lofoten (isls.), 28,980 ....H 2
Lopphavet (bay) ....M 1
Magerøy (isl.), 5,545 ....P 1
Mohn (cape) ....E 1
Moskenesøy (isl.), 2,318 ....H 3
Namsen (river) ....H 4
Nord (fjord) ....E 6
Nordaustlandet (isl.) ....D 1
Nordkyn (cape) ....Q 1
North (cape) ....P 1
Norwegian (sea) ....F 3
Ofot (fjord) ....K 2
Otter (river) ....E 7
Pasvik (river) ....Q 2
Platen (cape) ....D 1
Porsanger (fjord) ....O 1
Rana (river) ....J 3
Ran (fjord) ....H 3
Rauma (river) ....F 5
Reisa (river) ....M 2
Ringvassøy (isl.), 1,472 ....L 2
Romsdals (fjord) ....E 5
Salt (fjord) ....J 3
Seiland (isl.), 769 ....N 1
Senja (isl.), 10,541 ....K 2
Skagerrak (strait) ....E 8
Smøla (isl.), 2,840 ....E 5
Snåsa (lake) ....H 4
Sogne (fjord) ....D 6
Sørkapp (cape) ....C 2
Sørøy (isl.), 2,350 ....N 1
South Kvaløy (isl.), 3,444 ....K 2
Spitsbergen (isl.) ....C 2
Steinneset (cape) ....E 2
Stor (fjord) ....D 2
Sunn (fjord) ....D 6
Tana (river) ....P 1
Tjuv (fjord) ....D 2
Tunn (lake) ....H 4
Tyri (fjord) ....C 3
Vågå (lake) ....F 6
Vannøy (isl.), 1,112 ....L 1
Varanger (fjord) ....Q 1
Vega (isl.) ....G 4
Vest (fjord) ....H 3

(continued on following page)

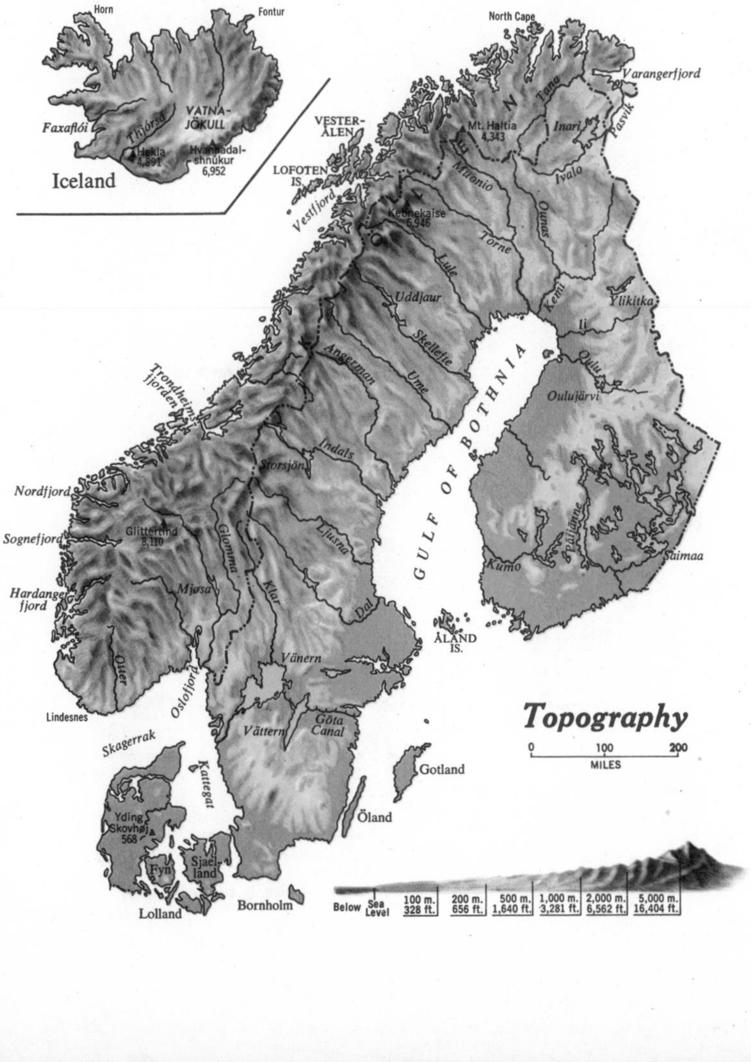

Horn
Fontur
Faxaflói
Thjórsá
VATNA-JÖKULL
Hekla 4,892
Hvannadalshnúkur 6,952
Iceland
North Cape
Varangerfjord
VESTER-ÅLEN
LOFOTEN IS.
Vestfjord
Mt. Haltia 4,343
Inari
Tana
Pasvik
Muonio
Ivalo
Ounas
Kebnekaise 6,946
Torne
Lule
Kemi
Ylikitka
Ii
Uddjaur
Skellefte
Oulu
Ångerman
Ume
GULF OF BOTHNIA
Oulujärvi
Trondheimsfjorden
Indals
Storsjön
Nordfjord
Sognefjord
Glittertind 8,110
Glomma
Ljusna
Päijänne
Saimaa
Kumo
Hardangerfjord
Mjøsa
Klar
Dal
ÅLAND IS.
Vänern
Otter
Oslofjord
Lindesnes
Skagerrak
Göta Canal
Vättern
Kattegat
Gotland
Öland
Yding Skovhøj 568
Fyn
Sjælland
Lolland
Bornholm
Topography
0 100 200
MILES
Below
Sea Level
100 m. 328 ft.
200 m. 656 ft.
500 m. 1,640 ft.
1,000 m. 3,281 ft.
2,000 m. 6,562 ft.
5,000 m. 16,404 ft.

(continued)

NORWAY (continued)

Vesterålen (isls.), 34,385 ....J 2
Vestvågøy (isl.), 11,749 ....H 3
Vikna (isl.), 3,411 ....G 4

SWEDEN

COUNTIES

Älvsborg, 391,851 ....H 7
Blekinge, 150,901 ....J 8
Gävleborg, 294,916 ....K 6
Göteborg och Bohus, 685,449 ....G 7
Gotland, 50,438 ....L 8
Halland, 185,810 ....H 8
Jämtland, 121,552 ....J 5
Jönköping, 292,303 ....H 8
Kalmar, 234,175 ....K 8
Kopparberg, 270,971 ....J 6
Kristianstad, 258,295 ....J 8
Kronoberg, 164,309 ....J 8
Malmöhus, 683,752 ....H 9
Norrbotten, 261,410 ....L 3
örebro, 259,794 ....J 7
östergötland, 369,374 ....J 7
Skaraborg, 248,970 ....H 7
Södermanland, 239,451 ....K 7
Stockholm, 1,406,580 ....L 7
Uppsala, 191,821 ....K 6
Värmland, 273,139 ....H 7
Västerbotten, 235,307 ....K 4
Västernorrland, 277,715 ....K 5
Västmanland, 255,142 ....K 7

CITIES and TOWNS

Åhus, 4,758 ....J 9
Alingsås, 19,810 ....H 7
Älmhult, 6,023 ....H 8
Alvesta, 8,957 ....J 8
Älvsbyn, 4,343 ....M 4
Åmål, 9,397 ....H 7
Anderstorp, 3,960 ....H 8
Ånge, 4,000 ....J 5
Ängelholm, 13,985 ....H 8
Arboga, 12,266 ....J 7
Årjäng, 2,893 ....H 7
Arvidsjaur, 7,767 ....L 4
Arvika, 15,901 ....H 7
Åseda, 3,629 ....J 8
Åsele, 4,727 ....K 4
Åtvidaberg, 9,010 ....K 7
Avesta, 29,232 ....J 6
Båstad, 2,202 ....H 8
Bengtsfors, 3,411 ....H 7
Boden, 24,912 ....M 4
Bollnäs, 17,123 ....K 6
Borås, 70,238 ....H 8
Borlänge, 29,097 ....J 6
Bräcke, 2,658 ....J 5
Brunflo, 2,700 ....J 5
Bureå, 4,583 ....M 4
Burträsk, 6,747 ....M 4
Charlottenberg, 3,112 ....H 6
Danderyd, 15,657 ....H 1
Djursholm, 7,681 ....H 1
Dorotea, 3,964 ....K 4
Edsbyn, 7,132 ....J 6
Eksjö, 9,897 ....J 8
Emmaboda, 3,697 ....J 8
Enköping, 17,684 ....G 1
Eskilstuna, 65,580 ....K 7
Eslöv, 14,737 ....H 9
Fagersta, 16,609 ....J 6
Falkenberg, 12,920 ....H 8
Falköping, 16,032 ....H 7
Falun, 33,840 ....J 6
Filipstad, 7,559 ....H 7
Finspång, 17,616 ....J 7
Flen, 9,112 ....K 7
Forshaga, 4,655 ....H 7
Frösö, 9,520 ....J 5
Frövi, 3,082 ....J 7
Gällivare, 9,718 ....M 3
Gamleby, 3,949 ....K 8
Gävle, 60,868 ....K 6
Gnesta, 3,275 ....G 2
Göteborg, 444,131 ....G 8
Göteborg, *647,122 ....G 8
Gränna, 3,195 ....J 8
Hagfors, 8,964 ....H 6
Hällefors, 12.011 ....J 7
Hallsberg, 12,121 ....J 7
Hallstahammar, 14,099 ....K 7
Halmstad, 46,655 ....H 8
Hälsingborg, 80,801 ....H 8
Haparanda, 9,429 ....N 4
Härnösand, 16,637 ....L 5
Hässleholm, 16,031 ....H 8
Hedemora, 17,744 ....K 6
Hjo, 4,783 ....J 7
Höganäs, 13,846 ....H 8
Holmsund, 5,778 ....M 5
Hudiksvall, 16,057 ....K 6
Hultsfred, 4,979 ....K 8
Huskvarna, 18,198 ....J 8
Järna, 4,591 ....G 2
Järpen, 2,962 ....H 5
Järvsö, 4,850 ....K 6
Jokkmokk, 4,869 ....L 3
Jönköping, 53,774 ....H 8
Jörn, 4,275 ....M 4
Kalmar, 37,938 ....K 8
Karlshamn, 12,351 ....J 8
Karlskoga, 38,284 ....J 7
Karlskrona, 37,358 ....K 8
Karlstad, 54,321 ....H 7
Katrineholm, 21,660 ....K 7
Kinna, 6,386 ....H 8
Kiruna, 29,210 ....L 3
Kisa, 4,353 ....J 8
Köping, 20,807 ....J 7
Kopparberg, 7,985 ....J 7
Kramfors, 11,729 ....K 5
Kristianstad, 27,527 ....J 9
Kristinehamn, 21,925 ....H 7
Kumla, 15,039 ....J 7
Kungälv, 11,213 ....G 8
Kungsbacka, 7,205 ....G 8
Laholm, 3,853 ....H 8
Landskrona, 32,079 ....H 9
Långsele, 4,640 ....K 5
Långshyttan, 3,124 ....K 6
Laxå, 9,498 ....J 7
Leksand, 8,608 ....J 6
Lidingö, 35,400 ....H 1
Lidköping, 19,700 ....H 7
Lindesberg, 6,863 ....J 7
Linköping, 77,881 ....K 7
Ljungby, 11,930 ....J 8
Ljusdal, 10,630 ....J 6
Ljusne, 4,808 ....K 6
Ludvika, 21,989 ....J 6
Luleå, 36,428 ....N 4
Lund, 50,494 ....H 9
Lycksele, 6,333 ....L 4
Lysekil, 8,000 ....G 7
Malmberget, 12,384 ....M 3
Malmköping, 3,450 ....F 1
Malmö, 256,064 ....H 9
Malmö, *428,338 ....H 9
Markaryd, 5,980 ....H 8
Mariefred, 2,502 ....G 1
Mariestad, 15,700 ....H 7
Mellerud, 4,317 ....H 7
Mjölby, 12,790 ....J 7
Mölndal, 31,072 ....H 8
Mönsterås, 6,687 ....K 8
Mora, 13,307 ....J 6
Motala, 27,907 ....J 7
Nacka, 25,798 ....H 1
Nässjö, 20,000 ....J 8
Nora, 9,215 ....J 7
Norberg, 6,160 ....K 6
Norrköping, 94,296 ....K 7
Norrsundet, 4,575 ....K 6
Norrtälje, 11,803 ....L 7
Norsjö, 5,171 ....L 4
Nybro, 10,956 ....J 8
Nyköping, 31,195 ....K 7
Nynäshamn, 10,676 ....L 7
Ockelbo, 5,819 ....K 6
Olofström, 16,218 ....J 8
örbyhus, 2,266 ....K 6
örebro, 86,977 ....J 7
öregrund, 2,026 ....L 6
örnsköldsvik, 16,539 ....L 5
Oskarshamn, 24,873 ....K 8
östersund, 26,600 ....J 5
östhammar, 8,858 ....L 6
övertorneå, 3,589 ....N 3
överum, 2,533 ....K 7
Oxelösund, 14,835 ....K 7
Pajala, 3,871 ....N 3
Piteå, 8,476 ....M 4
Ramnäs, 4,092 ....J 7
Ramsele, 4,547 ....K 5
Rättvik, 7,551 ....J 6
Rimbo, 3,426 ....L 7
Ronneby, 10,125 ....J 8
Ryd, 4,100 ....J 8
Säffle, 12,599 ....H 7
Sala, 11,800 ....K 7
Saltsjöbaden, 6,507 ....J 1
Sandviken, 25,476 ....K 6
Säter, 4,629 ....J 6
Sävsjö, 5,547 ....J 8
Sigtuna, 3,970 ....H 1
Simrishamn, 7,966 ....J 9
Skänninge, 4,482 ....J 7
Skara, 10,376 ....H 7
Skellefteå, 61,880 ....M 4
Skövde, 27,976 ....H 7
Smedjebacken, 10,504 ....J 6
Söderhamn, 13,778 ....K 6
Söderköping, 5,954 ....K 7
Södertälje, 52,601 ....G 1
Sollefteå, 9,715 ....K 5
Sollentuna, 35,038 ....H 1
Solna, 57,707 ....H 1
Sölvesborg, 6,782 ....J 9
Sorsele, 3,550 ....K 4
Stockholm (cap.), 756,697 ....G 1
Stockholm, *1,288,769 ....G 1
Storvik, 2,432 ....K 6
Strängnäs, 9,506 ....F 1
Strömstad, 9,817 ....G 7
Strömsund, 6,058 ....K 5
Sundbyberg, 28,773 ....G 1
Sundsvall, 62,222 ....K 5
Sunne, 11,018 ....H 7
Sveg, 4,975 ....J 5
Svenljunga, 2,925 ....H 8
Täby, 33,694 ....H 1
Tidaholm, 7,250 ....J 7
Tierp, 4,303 ....K 6
Tillberga, 270 ....K 7
Timrå, 12,800 ....K 5
Tomelilla, 6,349 ....J 9
Torsby, 6,796 ....H 6
Torshälla, 7,939 ....K 7
Tranås, 18,845 ....J 7
Trelleborg, 35,249 ....H 9
Trollhättan, 40,945 ....H 7
Uddevalla, 36,510 ....G 7
Ulricehamn, 8,504 ....H 8
Umeå, 51,955 ....M 5
Uppsala, 97,315 ....L 7
Vadstena, 6,893 ....J 7
Vaggeryd, 4,840 ....J 8
Valdemarsvik, 3,590 ....K 7
Vänersborg, 19,975 ....H 7
Vännäs, 4,045 ....L 5
Vansbro, 2,941 ....H 6
Vara, 11,056 ....H 7
Varberg, 18,451 ....G 8
Värnamo, 15,939 ....J 8
Västerås, 110,539 ....J 7
Västerhaninge, 9,814 ....H 1
Västervik, 23,014 ....K 8
Vaxholm, 4,322 ....J 1
Vaxjö, 32,760 ....J 8
Vetlanda, 10,780 ....J 8
Vilhelmina, 9,426 ....K 4
Vimmerby, 7,257 ....J 8
Virserum, 4,650 ....J 8
Visby, 18,338 ....L 8
Vislanda, 2,594 ....H 8
Wallhamn ....G 7
Ystad, 14,002 ....H 9

OTHER FEATURES

Angerman (river) ....K 5
Asnen (lake) ....J 8
Bothnia (gulf) ....M 5
Byske (river) ....L 4
Fårö (isl.), 790 ....L 8
Göta (river) ....H 7
Gotland (isl.), 50,438 ....L 8
Hornslandet (pen.) ....K 6
Kalix (river) ....N 3
Kalmarsund (sound) ....K 8
Kattegat (strait) ....G 8
Kebnekaise (mt.) ....L 3
Lainio (river) ....N 3
Lapland (dist.) ....K 2
Lule (river) ....M 3
Muonio (river) ....M 2
öland (isl.), 20,416 ....K 8
Ornö (isl.), 224 ....J 1
österdal (river) ....H 6
Pite (river) ....M 4
Skellefte (river) ....L 4
Stora Lulevatten (lake) ....L 3
Storuman (lake) ....K 4
Sulitjelma (mt.) ....K 3
Torne (river) ....M 3
Torneträsk (lake) ....L 2
Uddjaur (lake) ....L 4
Ume (river) ....L 4
Vänern (lake) ....H 7
Vättern (lake) ....J 7
Vesterdal (river) ....H 6
Vindel (river) ....L 4
Vojmsjön (lakes) ....J 4

*City and suburbs.
†Population of parish or commune.

DENMARK

INTERNAL DIVISIONS

Aabenraa (dist.), 52,903 ....C 7
Aabenraa-Sønderborg (county), 118,089 ....C 8
Aalborg (county), 252,850 ....D 4
Aarhus (county), 244,099 ....D 5
Assens (dist.), 58,261 ....D 7
Bornholm (county), 48,087 ....F 8
Copenhagen (city-county), 643,262 ....F 6
Copenhagen (county), 828,403 ....F 6
Copenhagen (dist.), 595,781 ....F 6
Faerøe Islands, 38,000 ....B 2
Frederiksborg (county), 244,823..F 6
Haderslev (county), 74,578 ....C 7
Hjørring (county), 184,291 ....C 3
Holbæk (county), 133,920 ....E 6
Maribo (county), 126,628............E 8
Odense (county), 284,368 ....D 7
Odense (dist.), 226,107 ....D 7
Præsto (county), 128,890 ....E 7
Randers (county), 184,859 ....D 5
Ribe (county), 202,005.................B 7
Ringkøbing (county), 227,393 .....B 5
Roskilde (dist.), 129,001 ....E 6
Skanderborg (county), 147,871....D 5
Sønderborg (dist.), 65,186 ....C 8
Sorø (county), 138,810 ....E 7
Svendborg (county), 145,467 .....D 7
Thisted (county), 82,237 ....B 4
Tønder (county), 43,149 ....B 8
Vejle (county), 234,288 ....C 6
Viborg (county), 168,346 ....C 5

CITIES and TOWNS

Aabenraa, 15,101 ....C 7
Aabybro, 2,112 ....C 3
Aakirkeby, 1,524 ....F 9
Aalborg, 82,871 ....D 4
Aalborg, *130,000 ....D 4
Aalestrup, 5,235 ....C 4
Aarhus, 111,266 ....D 5
Aarhus, *192,000 ....D 5
Aars, 3,649 ....C 4
Aarup, 5,008 ....D 7
Ærøskøbing, 1,228 ....D 8
Allingaabro, 1,352 ....D 5
Allinge-Sandvig, 2,086 ....F 8
Ansager, 1,126 ....B 6
Arden, 1,353 ....C 4
Asaa, 1,348 ....D 3
Askov, 725 ....C 7
Asnæs, 1,272 ....E 6
Assens, Odense, 10,868 ....D 7
Assens, Randers, 1,266 ....D 4
Augustenborg, 3,437 ....D 8
Aulum, 1,476 ....B 5
Auning, 1,367 ....D 5
Bælum, 583 ....D 4
Bagenkop, 774 ....D 8
Ballerup, 35,665 ....F 6
Ballum, †821 ....B 7
Bandholm, 668 ....E 8
Bedsted, 890 ....B 4
Birkerød, 18,884 ....F 6
Bjerringbro, 4,276 ....C 5
Bogense, 6,487 ....D 6
Bolderslev, 729 ....C 8
Børkop, 1,126 ....C 6
Borup, 1,072 ....E 7
Brabrand, 7,788 ....C 5
Brædstrup, 3,875 ....C 6
Bramminge, 5,909 ....B 7
Brande, 4,660 ....C 6
Broager, 1,890 ....C 8
Brønderslev, 10,225 ....C 3
Brøns, †877 ....B 7
Brørup, 4,085 ....C 7
Brovst, 8,083 ....C 3
Christiansfeld, 952 ....C 7
Copenhagen (cap.), 643,262 ....F 6
Copenhagen, *1,471,665 ....F 6
Dragør, 4,382 ....F 6
Dronninglund, 1,747 ....D 3
Dybvad, 793 ....D 3
Ebeltoft, 3,039 ....D 5
Egernsund, 1,360 ....C 8
Egtved, 1,169 ....C 6
Ejby, 3,301 ....D 7
Ejstrupholm, 1,054 ....C 6
Elsinore (Helsingør), 29,755 ......F 6
Esbjerg, 62,952 ....B 7
Faaborg, Ribe, †2,232 ....B 6
Faaborg, Svendborg, 5,698 ....D 7
Fakse, 7,314 ....F 7
Fakse Ladeplads, 1,639 ....F 7
Farsø, 1,731 ....C 4
Farum, 6,991 ....F 6
Fjerritslev, 2,014 ....C 3
Fredensborg, 3,977 ....F 6
Fredericia, 34,062 ....C 6
Frederiksberg, 103,621 ....F 6
Frederikshavn, 24,867 ....D 3
Frederikssund, 7,668 ....E 6
Frederiksværk, 4,405 ....E 5
Fuglebjerg, 5,018 ....E 7
Gedser, 1,195 ....F 8
Gedsted, 980 ....C 4
Gelsted, 1,252 ....C 7
Gentofte, 79,947 ....F 6
Gilleleje, 2,558 ....F 5
Give, 8,574 ....C 6
Gjerlev, †1,235 ....D 4
Glamsbjerg, 5,641 ....D 7
Glostrup, 26,898 ....F 6
Glumsø, 819 ....E 7
Gørding, 1,131 ....B 7
Gørlev, 1,468 ....E 7
Graasten, 6,341 ....C 8
Græsted, 1,210 ....F 5
Gram, 3,966 ....C 7
Grenaa, 13,413 ....D 5
Grindsted, †8,629 ....C 6
Gylling, 521 ....D 6
Haarby, 1,366 ....D 7
Haarlev, 980 ....F 7
Haderslev, 20,198 ....C 7
Hadsten, 6,763 ....C 5
Hadsund, 3,707 ....D 4
Hals, 1,596 ....D 3
Hammel, 7,410 ....C 5
Hammerum, 2,415 ....C 5
Hasle, 1,530 ....F 8
Haslev, 9,974 ....E 7
Havdrup, 1,205 ....F 6
Hedensted, 4,807 ....C 6
Hellebæk, 2,240 ....F 5
Helsingør, 29,755 ....F 6
Henne, †1,725 ....B 6
Herning, 32,248 ....B 5
Hillerød, 23,210 ....F 6
Hinnerup, 5,369 ....D 5
Hirtshals, 4,799 ....C 2
Hjallerup, 1,385 ....C 3
Hjerm, 572 ....B 5
Hjørring, 15,658 ....C 3
Hobro, 8,864 ....C 4
Højer, 1,395 ....B 8
Højslev, 1,297 ....C 4
Holbæk, 17,125 ....E 6
Holeby, 4,383 ....E 8
Holstebro, 23,809 ....B 5
Holsted, 1,218 ....B 6
Høng, 7,205 ....E 7
Hornslet, 2,041 ....D 5
Hornum, 827 ....C 4
Horsens, 35,903 ....C 6
Hørsholm, 14,509 ....F 6
Hørve, 1,098 ....E 6
Hov, 607 ....D 6
Humlum, †2,326 ....B 5
Hundested, 4,728 ....E 6
Hurup, 2,172 ....B 4
Hvidbjerg, 946 ....B 4
Hviding, †678 ....B 7
Ikast, 7,559 ....C 5
Jelling, 7,483 ....C 6
Jerslev, 807 ....D 3
Juelsminde, 7,232 ....D 6
Jyderup, 2,477 ....E 6
Kalundborg, 11,726 ....E 6
Karby, †2,465 ....B 4
Karise, 1,010 ....F 7
Karup, 1,471 ....C 5
Kastrup ....F 6
Kerteminde, 10,235 ....D 7
Kjellerup, 3,000 ....C 5
Klaksvík, Færøe Is., 3,894 ....B 2
København (Copenhagen), (cap.), 643,262 ....F 6
Køge, 16,415 ....F 7
Kolding, 39,656 ....C 7
Kolind, 2,586 ....D 5
Kørsør, 15,606 ....E 7
Kværndrup, 855 ....D 7
Langaa, 2,332 ....C 5
Lem, 1,060 ....B 5
Lemvig, 6,788 ....B 4
Løgstør, 3,645 ....C 4
Løgumkloster, 2,051 ....B 7
Lohals, 634 ....E 7
Løjt Kirkeby, 1,013 ....C 7
Løkken, 1,388 ....C 3
Løsning, 1,511 ....C 6
Lundby, 733 ....E 7
Lunderskov, 4,435 ....C 7
Lyngby, 65,015 ....F 6
Malling, 1,287 ....D 5
Mariager, 3,877 ....D 4
Maribo, 5,228 ....E 8
Marstal, 4,160 ....D 8
Middelfart, 9,148 ....C 7
Møgeltønder, 654 ....B 8
Næstved, 24,449 ....E 7
Nakskov, 15,969 ....E 8
Neksø, 3,488 ....F 9
Nibe, 2,757 ....C 4
Nordborg, 2,970 ....C 7
Nordby, 2,085 ....B 7
Nørre-Aaby, 5,237 ....C 7
Nørre-Alslev, 1,145 ....E 8
Nørre-Broby, 858 ....D 7
Nørre-Nebel, 867 ....B 6
Nørresundby, 23,372 ....D 2
Nørre-Vorupør, 632 ....B 4
Nyborg, 11,543 ....D 7
Nykøbing, Holbæk, 4,924 ....E 6
Nykøbing, Maribo, 17,426 ....F 8
Nykøbing, Thisted, 8,780 ....B 4
Nysted, 1,252 ....E 8
Odder, 6,050 ....D 6
Odense, 103,850 ....D 7
Odense, *154,000 ....D 7
Ølgod, 7,139 ....B 6
Ørsted, 1,069 ....D 5
Øster Vraa, 931 ....D 3
Otterup, 10,322 ....D 7

Agriculture, Industry and Resources

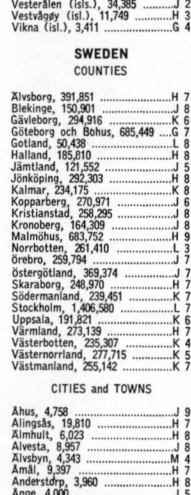

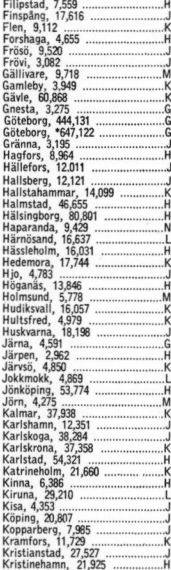

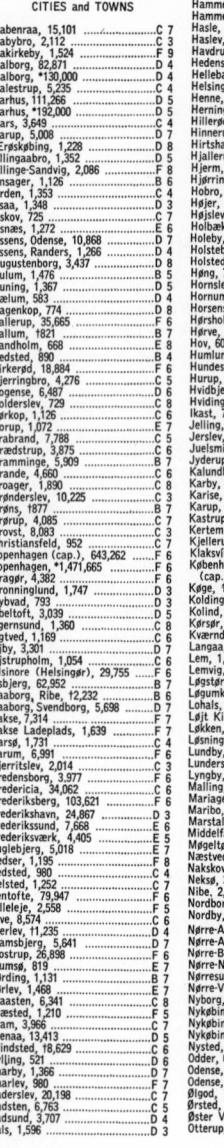

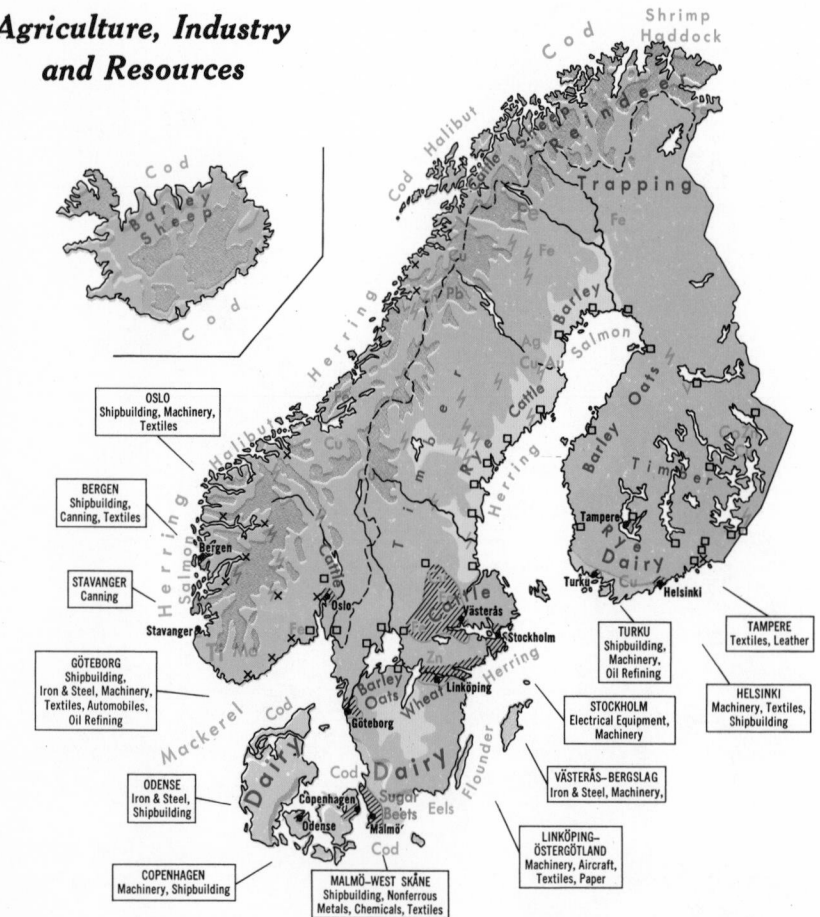

Cod
Barley
Sheep
Shrimp
Haddock
Halibut
Reindeer
Trapping
Herring
Salmon
Timber
Rye
Oats
Cattle
Dairy
Wheat
Mackerel
Sugar Beets
Eels
Flounder
OSLO Shipbuilding, Machinery, Textiles
BERGEN Shipbuilding, Canning, Textiles
STAVANGER Canning
GÖTEBORG Shipbuilding, Iron & Steel, Machinery, Textiles, Automobiles, Oil Refining
ODENSE Iron & Steel, Shipbuilding
COPENHAGEN Machinery, Shipbuilding
MALMÖ–WEST SKÅNE Shipbuilding, Nonferrous Metals, Chemicals, Textiles
LINKÖPING–ÖSTERGÖTLAND Machinery, Aircraft, Textiles, Paper
VÄSTERÅS–BERGSLAG Iron & Steel, Machinery,
STOCKHOLM Electrical Equipment, Machinery
TURKU Shipbuilding, Machinery, Oil Refining
HELSINKI Machinery, Textiles, Shipbuilding
TAMPERE Textiles, Leather
Bergen
Oslo
Stavanger
Göteborg
Linköping
Västerås
Stockholm
Turku
Helsinki
Tampere
Copenhagen
Odense
Malmö

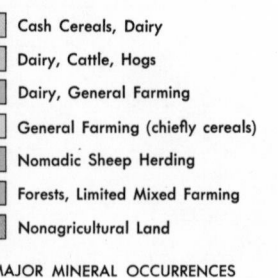

DOMINANT LAND USE

- Cash Cereals, Dairy
- Dairy, Cattle, Hogs
- Dairy, General Farming
- General Farming (chiefly cereals)
- Nomadic Sheep Herding
- Forests, Limited Mixed Farming
- Nonagricultural Land

MAJOR MINERAL OCCURRENCES

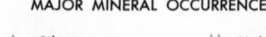

Ag	Silver	Mo	Molybdenum
Au	Gold	Pb	Lead
Co	Cobalt	Ti	Titanium
Cu	Copper	V	Vanadium
Fe	Iron Ore	Zn	Zinc

- Water Power
- Major Industrial Areas
- × Electrochemical & Electrometallurgical Centers
- □ Paper, Pulp & Sawmilling Centers

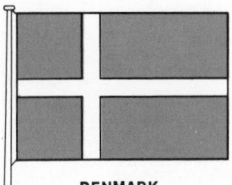

DENMARK

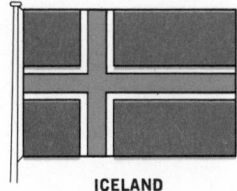

ICELAND

DENMARK

AREA 16,614 sq. mi.
POPULATION 4,910,000
CAPITAL Copenhagen
LARGEST CITY Copenhagen
HIGHEST POINT Yding Skovhøj 568 ft.
MONETARY UNIT krone (crown)
MAJOR LANGUAGE Danish
MAJOR RELIGION Protestantism

ICELAND

AREA 39,768 sq. mi.
POPULATION 203,000
CAPITAL Reykjavík
LARGEST CITY Reykjavík
HIGHEST POINT Hvannadalshnúkur 6,952 ft.
MONETARY UNIT króna (crown)
MAJOR LANGUAGE Icelandic
MAJOR RELIGION Protestantism

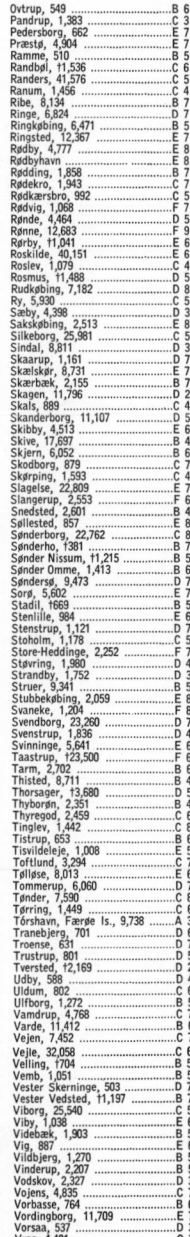

Ovtrup, 549	B 6
Pandrup, 1,383	C 3
Pedersborg, 662	E 7
Præstø, 4,904	E 7
Ramme, 510	B 5
Randbøl, †1,536	C 6
Randers, 41,576	C 5
Ranum, 1,456	C 4
Ribe, 8,134	B 7
Ringe, 6,824	D 7
Ringkøbing, 6,471	B 5
Ringsted, 12,367	E 7
Rødby, 4,777	E 8
Rødbyhavn	E 8
Rødding, 1,858	B 7
Rødekro, 1,943	C 7
Rødkærsbro, 992	C 5
Rødvig, 1,068	F 7
Rønde, 4,464	D 5
Rønne, 12,683	F 9
Rørby, †1,041	E 6
Roskilde, 40,151	E 6
Roslev, 1,079	C 4
Rosmus, †1,488	D 5
Rudkøbing, 7,182	D 8
Ry, 5,930	C 5
Sæby, 4,398	D 3
Sakskøbing, 2,513	E 8
Silkeborg, 25,981	C 5
Sindal, 8,811	D 3
Skaarup, 1,161	D 7
Skælskør, 8,731	E 7
Skærbæk, 2,155	B 7
Skagen, 11,796	D 2
Skals, 889	C 4
Skanderborg, 11,107	D 5
Skibby, 4,513	E 6
Skive, 17,697	B 4
Skjern, 6,052	B 6
Skodborg, 879	C 7
Skørping, 1,593	C 4
Slagelse, 22,809	E 7
Slangerup, 2,553	F 6
Snedsted, 2,601	B 4
Søllested, 857	E 8
Sønderborg, 22,762	C 8
Sønderho, †381	B 7
Sønder Nissum, †1,215	B 5
Sønder Omme, 1,413	B 6
Søndersø, 9,473	D 7
Sorø, 5,602	E 7
Stadil, †669	B 5
Stenlille, 984	E 6
Stenstrup, 1,121	D 7
Stoholm, 1,178	C 5
Store-Heddinge, 2,252	F 7
Støvring, 1,980	D 4
Strandby, 1,752	D 3
Struer, 9,341	B 5
Stubbekøbing, 2,059	E 8
Svaneke, 1,204	F 8
Svendborg, 23,260	D 7
Svenstrup, 1,836	D 4
Svinninge, 5,641	E 6
Taastrup, †23,500	F 6
Tarm, 2,702	B 6
Thisted, 8,711	B 4
Thorsager, †3,680	D 5
Thyborøn, 2,351	B 4
Thyregod, 2,459	C 6
Tinglev, 1,442	C 8
Tistrup, 653	B 6
Tisvildeleje, 1,008	E 5
Toftlund, 3,294	C 7
Tølløse, 8,013	E 6
Tommerup, 6,060	D 7
Tønder, 7,590	C 8
Tørring, 1,449	C 6
Tórshavn, Færøe Is., 9,738	A 3
Tranebjerg, 701	D 6
Troense, 631	D 7
Trustrup, 801	D 5
Tversted, †2,169	D 2
Udby, 588	D 4
Uldum, 802	C 6
Ulfborg, 1,272	B 5
Vamdrup, 4,768	C 7
Varde, 11,412	B 6
Vejen, 7,452	C 7
Vejle, 32,058	C 6
Velling, †704	B 5
Vemb, 1,051	B 5
Vester Skerninge, 503	D 7
Vester Vedsted, †1,197	B 7
Viborg, 25,540	C 5
Viby, 1,038	E 6
Videbæk, 1,903	B 5
Vig, 887	E 6
Vildbjerg, 1,270	B 5
Vinderup, 2,207	B 5
Vodskov, 2,327	D 3
Vojens, 4,835	C 7
Vorbasse, 764	B 6
Vordingborg, 11,709	E 7
Vorsaa, 537	D 3
Vraa, 4,401	C 3

OTHER FEATURES

Aalborg (bay)	D 4
Aarø (isl.), 259	C 7
Ærø (isl.), 9,656	D 8
Als (isl.), 48,676	C 8
Amager (isl.), 177,818	F 6
Anholt (isl.), 237	E 4
Baagø (isl.), 113	C 7
Blaavands Huk (point)	A 6
Bornholm (isl.), 48,087	F 9
Dovns Klint (prom.)	D 8
Endelave (isl.), 317	D 6
Eysturoy (isl.), Færøe Is., 7,714	B 3
Færøe (isls.), 38,000	B 2
Fakse (bay)	F 7
Falster (isl.), 45,906	E 8
Fanø (isl.), 2,750	B 7
Fehmarn (strait)	E 8
Frisian, North (isls.), 3,562	B 7
Fyn (isl.), 389,404	D 7
Fyns Hoved (prom.)	D 6
Gedser Odde (point)	E 8
Gelsaa (river)	C 7
Gilbjerg Hoved (prom.)	F 5
Gjerrild Klint (prom.)	D 5
Gudenaa (river)	C 5
Horsens (fjord)	D 6
Isefjord (fjord)	E 6
Jammerbugt (bay)	C 3
Jutland (Jylland) (pen.), 2,109,370	C 5
Jyske Aas (hills)	D 3
Kattegat (strait)	E 4
Knøsen (mt.)	D 3
Knudshoved (prom.)	D 7
Køge (bay)	F 7
Laaland (Lolland) (isl.), 81,760	E 8
Læsø (isl.), 2,851	D 3
Langeland (isl.), 17,745	D 8
Langelands Bælt (channel)	D 8
Lille Bælt (channel)	C 7
Lilleaa (river)	B 5
Limfjorden (fjord)	A, D 4
Løgstør Bredning (fjord)	C 4
Lolland (Laaland) (isl.), 81,760	E 8
Mariager (fjord)	D 4
Mollebjerg (mt.)	C 6
Møn (isl.), 12,610	F 8
Møns Klint (prom.)	F 8
Mors (isl.), 25,739	B 4
Nissum (fjord)	A 5
North Frisian (isls.), 3,562	B 7
Odense (fjord)	D 7
Omme (river)	B 6
Øresund (sound)	F 6
Ringkøbing (fjord)	B 6
Rømø (isl.), 812	B 7
Røsnaes (prom.)	D 6
Samsø (isl.), 5,361	D 6
Samsø Bælt (channel)	D 6
Sandoy (isl.), Færøe Is., 1,684	B 3
Sejerø (isl.), 576	E 6
Sjælland (Zealand) (isl.), 1,855,500	E 6
Sjællands (point)	E 5
Skagens Odde (The Skaw) (point)	D 2
Skagerrak (strait)	D 2
Skive (river)	C 5
Sound, The (Øresund) (sound)	F 6
Stevns Klint (prom.)	F 7
Storaa (river)	B 5
Store Bælt (channel)	D 6
Streymoy (isl.), Færøe Is. 14,078	A 2
Sudhuroy (isl.), Færøe Is. 5,734	B 3
Susaa (river)	E 7
Tannis (bay)	D 2
Tranebjerg (mt.)	C 6
Varde (river)	B 6
Vejle (fjord)	C 6
Vigsø (bay)	B 3
Vorgod (river)	B 6
Yding Skovhøj (mt.)	C 6
Zealand (Sjælland) (isl.), 1,855,500	E 6

ICELAND

CITIES and TOWNS

Akranes, 4,245	B 1
Akureyri, 10,567	C 1
Hafnarfjördhur, 9,538	B 1
Húsavík, 1,988	C 1
Ísafjördhur, 2,678	B 1
Keflavík, 5,533	B 1
Neskaupstadhur (Nes), 1,527	D 1
Reykjavík (capital), 81,476	B 1
Reykjavík, *96,547	B 1
Saudhárkrókur, 1,507	B 1
Seydhisfjördhur, 905	D 1
Siglufjördhur, 2,248	C 1
Vestmannæyjar, 5,074	B 2

OTHER FEATURES

Bjargtangur (point)	A 1
Breidhafjördhur (fjord)	B 1
Faxaflói (bay)	B 1
Fontur (prom.)	D 1
Gerpir (cape)	D 1
Grímsey (isl.), 89	C 1
Hekla (volcano)	B 1
Horn (cape)	B 1
Hornafjördhur (fjord)	D 1
Húnaflói (bay)	B 1
Hvannadalshnúkur (mt.)	C 1
Hvítá (river)	B 1
Ísafjördhur (fjord)	B 1
Jökulsá (river)	C 1
Lagarfljót (stream)	C 1
Lang (glacier)	B 1
North (Horn) (cape)	B 1
Öndverdharnes (mt.)	A 1
Reykjanestá (cape)	A 2
Rifstangi (cape)	C 1
Skagata (cape)	B 1
Skjálfandafljót (river)	C 1
Surtsey (isl.)	B 2
Thjórsá (river)	C 1
Vatna (glacier)	C 1
Vopnafjörd (fjord)	D 1

*City and suburbs.
†Population of rural municipality.

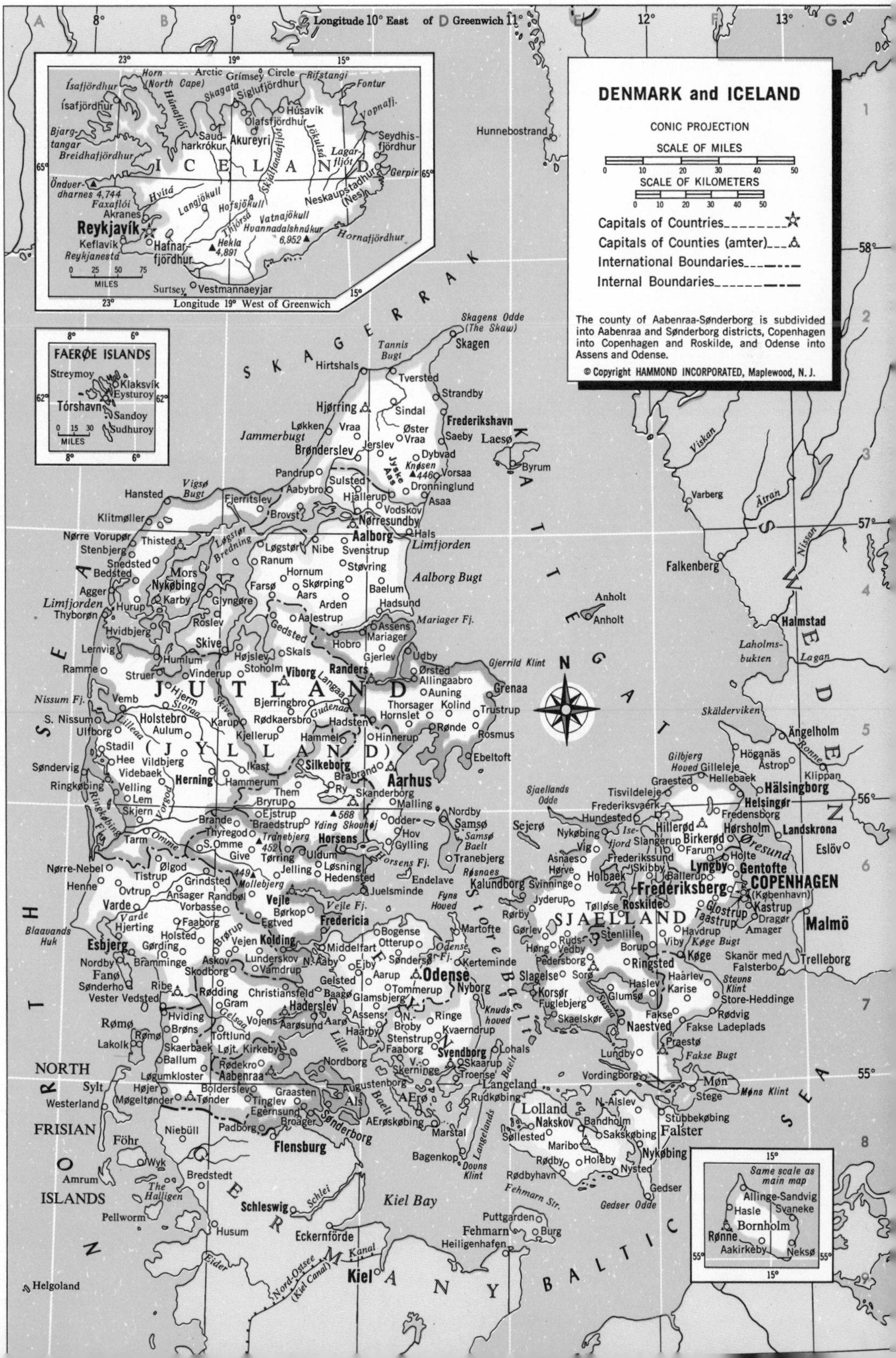

DENMARK and ICELAND
CONIC PROJECTION
SCALE OF MILES
SCALE OF KILOMETERS
Capitals of Countries
Capitals of Counties (amter)
International Boundaries
Internal Boundaries
The county of Aabenraa-Sønderborg is subdivided into Aabenraa and Sønderborg districts, Copenhagen into Copenhagen and Roskilde, and Odense into Assens and Odense.
© Copyright HAMMOND INCORPORATED, Maplewood, N. J.
Longitude 10° East of Greenwich
Longitude 19° West of Greenwich
FAERØE ISLANDS
Same scale as main map
SKAGERRAK
KATTEGAT
JUTLAND (JYLLAND)
SJAELLAND
NORTH FRISIAN ISLANDS
NORTH SEA
BALTIC SEA
SWEDEN
GERMANY
COPENHAGEN (København)

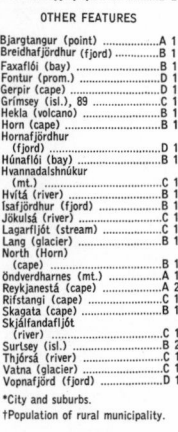

WEST GERMANY

AREA 95,959 sq. mi.
POPULATION 61,194,600
CAPITAL Bonn
LARGEST CITY Berlin (West)
HIGHEST POINT Zugspitze 9,718 ft.
MONETARY UNIT West German Deutsch mark
MAJOR LANGUAGE German
MAJOR RELIGIONS Protestantism, Roman Catholicism

EAST GERMANY

AREA 41,814 sq. mi.
POPULATION 17,117,000
CAPITAL Berlin (East)
LARGEST CITY Berlin (East)
HIGHEST POINT Fichtelberg 3,983 ft.
MONETARY UNIT East German Deutsch mark
MAJOR LANGUAGE German
MAJOR RELIGIONS Protestantism, Roman Catholicism

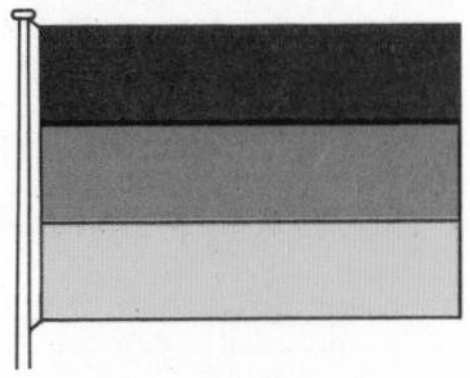

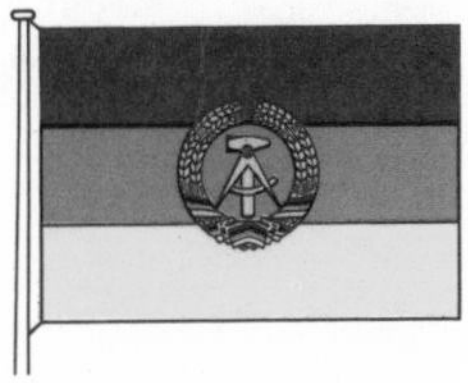

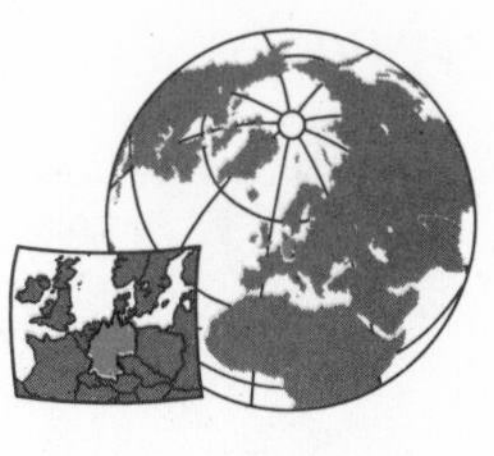

Topography

0 50 100
MILES

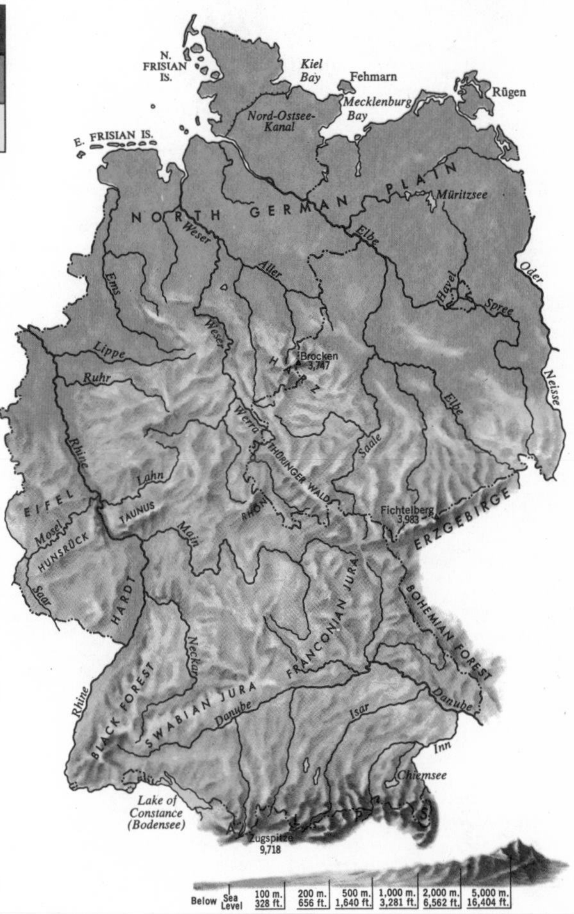
N. FRISIAN IS.
Kiel Bay
Fehmarn
Rügen
Mecklenburg Bay
Nord-Ostsee-Kanal
E. FRISIAN IS.
NORTH GERMAN PLAIN
Müritzsee
Weser
Elbe
Oder
Ems
Aller
Havel
Spree
Lippe
Ruhr
Brocken 3,747
HARZ
Neisse
Werra
THÜRINGER WALD
Saale
Rhine
Lahn
EIFEL
TAUNUS
RHÖN
Fichtelberg 3,983
ERZGEBIRGE
Mosel
HUNSRÜCK
Main
Saar
HARDT
FRANCONIAN JURA
BOHEMIAN FOREST
Neckar
BLACK FOREST
SWABIAN JURA
Danube
Isar
Inn
Chiemsee
Lake of Constance (Bodensee)
Zugspitze 9,718
Below Sea Level
100 m. 328 ft.
200 m. 656 ft.
500 m. 1,640 ft.
1,000 m. 3,281 ft.
2,000 m. 6,562 ft.
5,000 m. 16,404 ft.

EAST GERMANY

DISTRICTS

Berlin (East), 1,084,000 .... F 4
Cottbus, 839,133 .... F 3
Dresden, 1,887,739 .... E 3
Erfurt, 1,249,540 .... D 3
Frankfurt, 660,666 .... F 2
Gera, 735,175 .... D 3
Halle, 1,932,733 .... E 3
Karl-Marx-Stadt, 2,082,927 .... E 3
Leipzig, 1,510,773 .... E 3
Magdeburg, 1,323,644 .... D 2
Neubrandenburg, 633,209 .... E 2
Potsdam, 1,127,498 .... E 2
Rostock, 842,743 .... D 1
Schwerin, 594,786 .... D 2
Suhl, 549,398 .... D 3

CITIES and TOWNS

Aken, 12,126 .... D 3
Altenburg, 47,462 .... E 3
Angermünde, 12,200 .... E 2
Anklam, 19,436 .... E 2
Annaberg-Buchholz, 28,663 .... E 3
Apolda, 29,735 .... D 3
Arnstadt, 27,674 .... D 3
Aschersleben, 36,777 .... D 3
Aue, 31,723 .... E 3
Auerbach, 19,673 .... E 3
Bad Doberan, 13,197 .... D 1
Bad Dürrenberg, 16,500 .... D 3
Bad Freienwalde, 11,845 .... F 2
Bad Langensalza, 16,952 .... D 3
Bad Salzungen, 12,722 .... C 3
Barth, 12,688 .... E 1
Bautzen, 44,041 .... F 3
Bergen, 10,979 .... E 1
Berlin (East) (capital), 1,084,000 .... F 4
Bernau, 14,078 .... E 2
Bernburg, 45,885 .... D 3
Bischofswerda, 11,345 .... F 3
Bitterfeld, 30,916 .... E 3
Blankenburg, 19,595 .... D 3
Boizenburg, 11,370 .... D 2
Borna, 20,669 .... E 3
Brandenburg, 90,753 .... E 2
Burg, 29,906 .... D 2
Calbe, 16,464 .... D 3
Chemnitz (Karl-Marx-Stadt), 295,443 .... D 3
Coswig, 18,600 .... E 3
Cottbus, 75,541 .... F 3
Crimmitschau, 30,752 .... E 3
Delitzsch, 23,480 .... E 3
Demmin, 16,755 .... E 2
Dessau, 95,682 .... E 3
Döbeln, 28,430 .... E 3
Dresden, 499,848 .... E 3
Ebersbach, 11,293 .... F 3
Eberswalde, 33,680 .... E 2
Eilenburg, 21,366 .... E 3
Eisenach, 50,234 .... D 3
Eisenberg, 13,858 .... D 3
Eisenhüttenstadt, 38,138 .... F 2
Eisleben, 32,402 .... D 3
Erfurt, 193,745 .... D 3
Falkensee, 29,884 .... E 3
Falkenstein, 15,269 .... E 3
Finsterwalde, 22,441 .... E 3
Forst, 29,823 .... F 3
Frankfurt-an-der-Oder, 58,866 .... F 2
Freiberg, 49,122 .... E 3
Freital, 42,675 .... E 3
Fürstenwalde, 30,527 .... F 2
Gardelegen, 13,218 .... D 2
Genthin, 15,619 .... E 2
Gera, 109,989 .... E 3
Glauchau, 33,103 .... E 3
Görlitz, 88,632 .... F 3
Gotha, 57,692 .... D 3
Greifswald, 47,402 .... E 1
Greiz, 39,313 .... E 3
Grevesmühlen, 10,914 .... D 2
Grimma, 16,509 .... E 3
Grimmen, 12,943 .... E 1
Grossenhain, 19,848 .... E 3
Grossräschen, 12,737 .... E 3
Guben (Wilhelm-Pieck-Stadt), 26,586 .... F 3
Güstrow, 38,185 .... E 2
Hagenow, 10,434 .... D 2
Halberstadt, 46,071 .... D 3
Haldensleben, 20,547 .... D 2
Halle, 263,928 .... D 3
Heidenau, 20,161 .... E 3
Heiligenstadt, 12,627 .... D 3
Hennigsdorf, 21,398 .... E 3
Hettstedt, 19,218 .... D 3
Hoyerswerda, 43,922 .... F 3
Ilmenau, 19,852 .... D 3
Jena, 85,032 .... D 3
Johanngeorgenstadt, 10,801 .... E 3
Jüterbog, 14,416 .... E 3
Kamenz, 16,236 .... F 3
Karl-Marx-Stadt, 295,443 .... E 3
Kleinmachnow, 13,919 .... E 4
Klingenthal, 14,748 .... E 3
Köpenick, 52,294 .... F 4
Köthen, 38,154 .... E 3
Kottbus (Cottbus), 75,541 .... F 3
Lauchhammer, 28,680 .... E 3
Leipzig, 590,291 .... E 3
Lichtenberg, 62,841 .... F 4
Limbach-Oberfrohna, 26,053 .... E 3
Löbau, 17,068 .... F 3
Lübben, 12,742 .... E 3
Lübbenau, 16,976 .... F 3
Luckenwalde, 29,282 .... E 2
Ludwigslust, 11,512 .... D 2
Magdeburg, 268,269 .... D 2
Markkleeberg, 21,854 .... E 3
Meerane, 24,262 .... E 3
Meiningen, 25,025 .... D 3
Meissen, 47,166 .... E 3
Merseburg, 55,562 .... D 3
Meuselwitz, 10,582 .... E 3
Mittweida, 20,440 .... E 3
Mücheln, 10,842 .... D 3
Mühlhausen, 46,155 .... D 3
Nauen, 12,017 .... E 2
Naumburg, 37,990 .... D 3
Neubrandenburg, 38,740 .... E 2
Neuenhagen, 13,116 .... F 4
Neugersdorf, 11,889 .... F 3
Neuruppin, 22,424 .... E 2
Neustadt, 10,085 .... D 3
Neustrelitz, 27,624 .... E 2
Nordhausen, 42,279 .... D 3
Oelsnitz, 15,954 .... E 3
Oelsnitz im Erzgebirge, 18,377 .... E 3
Olbernhau, 14.240 .... E 3
Oranienburg, 20,401 .... E 2
Oschatz, 15,582 .... E 3
Oschersleben, 18,078 .... D 2
Pankow, 68,785 .... F 3
Parchim, 19,226 .... D 2
Pasewalk, 14,086 .... F 2
Perleberg, 13,707 .... D 2
Pirna, 42,562 .... E 3
Plauen, 81,739 .... E 3
Pössneck, 19,468 .... D 3
Potsdam, 110,671 .... E 2
Prenzlau, 20,276 .... F 2
Quedlinburg, 30,840 .... D 3
Radeberg, 17,410 .... E 3
Radebeul, 41,437 .... E 3
Rathenow, 28,979 .... E 2
Reichenbach, 29,372 .... E 3
Ribnitz-Damgarten, 15,301 .... E 1
Riesa, 43,322 .... E 3
Rosslau, 16,256 .... E 3
Rosswein, 10,649 .... E 3
Rostock, 190,275 .... E 1
Rüdersdorf, 11,837 .... E 2
Rudolstadt, 30,433 .... D 3
Saalfeld, 32,145 .... D 3
Salzwedel, 19,534 .... D 2
Sangerhausen, 29,373 .... D 3
Sassnitz, 13,253 .... E 1
Schkeuditz, 17,131 .... E 3
Schmalkalden, 14,569 .... D 3
Schmölln, 13,992 .... E 3
Schneeberg, 21,225 .... E 3
Schönebeck, 44,551 .... D 2
Schöneiche, 10,101 .... E 2
Schwedt, 23,359 .... F 2
Schwerin, 92,356 .... D 2
Sebnitz, 14,655 .... F 3
Senftenberg, 24,532 .... F 3
Sömmerda, 16,061 .... D 3
Sondershausen, 22,456 .... D 3
Sonneberg, 29,804 .... D 3
Spremberg, 23,367 .... F 3
Stassfurt, 25,622 .... D 3
Stendal, 36,193 .... D 2
Stralsund, 68,925 .... E 1
Strausberg, 17,985 .... F 2
Suhl, 28,698 .... D 3
Tangermünde, 12,992 .... D 2
Teltow, 13,735 .... E 4
Templin, 11,203 .... E 2
Teterow, 11,039 .... E 2
Thale, 17,273 .... D 3
Torgau, 20,941 .... E 3
Torgelow, 13,584 .... F 2
Treptow, 22,302 .... F 4
Ueckermünde, 11,614 .... F 2
Zwickau, 127,688 .... E 3
Waltershausen, 14,250 .... D 3
Waren, 20,008 .... E 2
Weida, 11,950 .... D 3
Weimar, 64,300 .... D 3
Weissenfels, 47,704 .... D 3
Weissensee, 50,691 .... F 3
Weisswasser, 16,016 .... F 3
Werdau, 23,783 .... E 3
Wernigerode, 32,579 .... D 3
Wilhelm-Pieck-Stadt, 26,586 .... F 3
Wismar, 55,235 .... D 2
Wittenberg, 46,816 .... E 3
Wittenberge, 32,621 .... D 2
Wittstock, 10,358 .... E 2
Wolgast, 14,955 .... E 1
Wurzen, 24,349 .... E 3
Zehdenick, 12,306 .... E 2
Zeitz, 46,393 .... E 3
Zella-Mehlis, 17,121 .... D 3
Zerbst, 19,527 .... E 3
Zeulenroda, 18,534 .... D 3
Zittau, 43,259 .... F 3
Zwickau, 127,688 .... E 3

OTHER FEATURES

Altmark (reg.), 288,928 .... D 2
Arkona (cape) .... E 1
Baltic (sea) .... F 1
Black Elster (riv.) .... E 3
Brandenburg (region), 3,726,413 .... E 2
Brocken (mt.) .... D 3
Darsser Ort (point) .... E 1
Elbe (riv.) .... D 2
Elster (riv.) .... E 3
Erzgebirge (Ore) (mts.) .... E 3
Fichtelberg (mt.) .... E 3
Havel (riv.) .... E 2
Kummerowersee (lake) .... E 2
Lusatia (reg.) .... F 3
Malchinersee (lake) .... E 2
Mecklenburg (region), 1,226,685 .... E 2
Mecklenburg (bay) .... D 1
Mulde (riv.) .... E 3
Müritzee (lake) .... E 2
Neisse (riv.) .... F 3
Oder (riv.) .... F 2
Ore (Erzgebirge) (mts.) .... E 3
Penne (riv.) .... E 2
Plauersee (lake) .... E 2
Pomerania (region), 711,075 .... E 2
Pomeranian (bay) .... F 1
Rhön (mts.) .... D 3
Rügen (isl.), 92,348 .... E 1
Saale (riv.) .... D 3
Saxony (region), 5,318,661 .... E 3
Schaalsee (lake) .... D 2
Schwerinersee (lake) .... D 2
Spree (riv.) .... F 3
Spreewald (forest) .... F 3
Stettin (bay) .... F 2
Stubbenkammer (point) .... E 1
Thüringer Wald (forest) .... D 3
Thuringia (Thüringen) (reg.), 2,017,924 .... D 3
Tollensee (lake) .... E 2
Ücker (riv.) .... E 2
Unstrut (riv.) .... D 3
Usedom (isl.) .... F 1
Warnow (riv.) .... D 2
Werra (riv.) .... D 3
White Elster (riv.) .... E 3

WEST GERMANY

STATES

Baden-Württemberg, 8,909,700 .... C 4
Bavaria, 10,568,900 .... D 4
Berlin (West) (free city), 2,134,256 .... E 4
Bremen, 755,977 .... C 2
Hamburg, 1,817,122 .... D 2
Hesse, 5,422,600 .... C 3
Lower Saxony, 7,100,400 .... C 2
North Rhine-Westphalia, 17,129,800 .... B 3
Rhineland-Palatinate, 3,671,300 .... B 4
Saarland, 1,127,400 .... B 4
Schleswig-Holstein, 2,557,200 .... C 1

CITIES and TOWNS

Aachen, 177,642 .... B 3
Aalen, 35,102 .... D 4
Ahlen, 50,411 .... B 3
Ahrensburg, 25,829 .... D 2
Alfeld, 13,726 .... C 2
Alsdorf, 31,726 .... B 3
Altena, 31,164 .... B 3
Altona .... C 2
Alzey, 12,749 .... C 4
Amberg, 42,141 .... E 4
Andernach, 22,367 .... B 3
Ansbach, 30,083 .... D 4
Arnsberg, 22,577 .... C 3
Aschaffenburg, 56,236 .... C 4
Augsburg, 214,376 .... D 4
Aurich, 12,299 .... B 2
Backnang, 28,086 .... C 4
Bad Dürkheim, 15,792 .... C 4
Baden-Baden, 38,852 .... C 4
Bad Harzburg, 11,356 .... D 3
Bad Hersfeld, 23,494 .... C 3
Bad Homburg vor der Höhe, 41,236 .... C 3
Bad Honnef am Rhein, 20,649 .... B 3
Bad Kissingen, 12,672 .... D 3
Bad Kreuznach, 42,707 .... B 4
Bad Mergentheim, 12,552 .... D 4
Bad Nauheim, 15,222 .... C 3
Bad Oeynhausen, 14,127 .... C 2
Bad Oldesloe, 18,915 .... D 2
Bad Pyrmont, 16,527 .... C 2
Bad Reichenhall, 14,894 .... E 5
Bad Salzuflen, 49,030 .... C 2
Bad Schwartau, 16,909 .... D 2
Bad Segeberg, 12,494 .... D 2
Bad Tölz, 12,468 .... D 5
Bad Vilbel, 18,315 .... C 3
Bad Wildungen, 12,189 .... C 3
Balingen, 13,693 .... C 4
Bamberg, 68,713 .... D 4
Bayreuth, 63,387 .... D 4
Bendorf, 14,361 .... B 3
Bensheim, 27,495 .... C 4
Berchtesgaden, 4,074 .... E 5
Bergisch Gladbach, 50,095 .... B 3
Berlin (West), 2,134,256 .... E 4
Betzdorf, 10,388 .... B 3
Biberach an der Riss, 25,597 .... C 4
Bielefeld, 169,347 .... C 2
Bietigheim, 22,488 .... C 4
Bingen, 24,452 .... B 4
Böblingen, 36,644 .... C 4
Bocholt, 48,134 .... B 3
Bochum, 346,886 .... B 3
Bonn (cap.), 299,376 .... B 3
Borghorst, 17,072 .... B 2
Borken, 30,614 .... B 3
Bottrop, 108,161 .... B 3
Brackwede, 40,254 .... C 3
Brake, 19,388 .... C 2
Bramsche, 10,733 .... B 2
Braunschweig (Brunswick), 225,168 .... D 2
Bremen, 607,184 .... C 2
Bremerhaven, 148,793 .... C 2
Brilon, 15,301 .... C 3
Bruchsal, 27,103 .... C 4
Brühl, 41,782 .... B 3
Brunswick, 225,168 .... D 2
Bückeburg, 13,396 .... C 2
Burghausen, 16,630 .... E 4
Burgsteinfurt, 12,554 .... B 2
Buxtehude, 23,140 .... C 2
Celle, 56,335 .... D 2
Charlottenburg .... F 4
Clausthal-Zellerfeld, 15,744 .... D 3
Cloppenburg, 18,162 .... B 2
Coburg, 41,369 .... D 3
Coesfeld, 26,565 .... B 3
Cologne, 866,308 .... B 3
Crailsheim, 16,687 .... D 4
Cuxhaven, 45,218 .... C 2
Dachau, 33,093 .... D 4
Darmstadt, 141,075 .... C 4
Deggendorf, 18,601 .... E 4
Delmenhorst, 63,685 .... C 2
Detmold, 64,473 .... C 3
Diepholz, 11,639 .... C 2
Dillenburg, 10,236 .... C 3
Dillingen an der Donau, 11,606 .... D 4
Dingolfing, 10,747 .... E 4
Donaueschingen, 11,643 .... C 5
Donauwörth, 11,266 .... D 4
Dorsten, 39,393 .... B 3
Dortmund, 648,883 .... B 3
Duderstadt, 10,421 .... D 3
Dudweiler, 30,078 .... B 4
Duisburg, 457,891 .... B 3
Dülmen, 21,094 .... B 3
Düren, 54,867 .... B 3
Düsseldorf, 680,806 .... B 3
Eberbach, 14,369 .... C 4
Ebingen, 22,004 .... C 4
Eckernförde, 21,971 .... D 1
Ehingen, 12,957 .... C 4
Eichstätt, 10,040 .... D 4
Einbeck, 18,618 .... C 3
Eiserfeld, 22,490 .... B 1
Ellwangen, 13,128 .... D 4
Elmshorn, 41,353 .... C 2
Emden, 48,313 .... B 2
Emmendingen, 15,986 .... B 4
Emmerich, 24,512 .... B 3
Erkelenz, 12,275 .... B 3
Erlangen, 85,727 .... D 4
Eschwege, 22,219 .... D 3
Eschweiler, 39,622 .... B 3
Espelkamp, 12,309 .... C 2
Essen, 704,769 .... B 3
Esslingen am Neckar, 86,497 .... C 4
Ettlingen, 21,342 .... C 4
Euskirchen, 41,965 .... B 3
Eutin, 18,177 .... D 1
Fellbach, 29,343 .... C 4
Flensburg, 96,778 .... C 1
Forchheim, 21,582 .... D 4
Frankenthal, 40,505 .... C 4
Frankfurt am Main, 660,410 .... C 3
Frechen, 30,786 .... B 3
Freiburg im Breisgau, 165,960 .... B 5
Freising, 30,264 .... D 4
Freudenstadt, 14,356 .... C 4
Friedberg, 17,401 .... C 3
Friedrichshafen, 42,483 .... C 5
Fulda, 44,262 .... C 3
Fürstenfeldbruck, 22,495 .... D 4
Fürth, 94,310 .... D 4
Füssen, 10,891 .... D 5
Gaggenau, 14,773 .... C 4
Garmisch-Partenkirchen, 27,313 .... D 5
Geesthacht, 23,594 .... D 2
Geislingen an der Steige, 27,209 .... C 4
Geldern, 22,602 .... B 3
Gelsenkirchen, 348,620 .... B 3
Giessen, 74,731 .... C 3
Gifhorn, 23,001 .... D 2
Glückstadt, 16,199 .... C 2
Goch, 27,721 .... B 3
Göggingen, 15,840 .... D 4
Göppingen, 46,899 .... C 4
Goslar, 41,653 .... D 3
Göttingen, 115,227 .... D 3
Grevenbroich, 28,197 .... B 3
Griesheim, 16,392 .... C 4
Gronau, 26,596 .... B 2
Gummersbach, 45,026 .... B 3
Günzburg, 13,449 .... D 4
Gütersloh, 76,343 .... C 3
Haar, 12,388 .... D 4
Hagen, 203,048 .... B 3
Haltern, 15,264 .... B 3
Hamburg, 1,817,122 .... D 2
Hameln, 47,114 .... C 2
Hamm, 84,302 .... B 3
Hanau, 55,674 .... C 3
Hannover, 517,783 .... C 2
Harburg-Wilhelmsburg .... C 2
Hassloch, 17,852 .... C 4
Haunstetten, 22,205 .... D 4
Heide, 23,419 .... C 1
Heidelberg, 121,929 .... C 4
Heidenheim an der Brenz, 50,170 .... D 4
Heilbronn, 99,440 .... C 4
Helmstedt, 27,161 .... D 2
Hennef, 26,589 .... B 3
Herborn, 10,395 .... C 3
Herford, 67,267 .... C 2
Herne, 100,798 .... B 3
Hildesheim, 95,926 .... D 2
Hockenheim, 15,615 .... C 4
Hof, 54,805 .... D 3
Holzminden, 22,273 .... C 3
Homburg, 32,258 .... B 4
Höxter, 32,823 .... C 3
Hürth, 52,011 .... B 3
Husum, 25,037 .... C 1
Hüttental, 40,287 .... C 3
Ibbenbüren, 17,780 .... B 2
Idar-Oberstein, 32,590 .... B 4
Immenstadt, 10,775 .... D 5
Ingolstadt, 71,954 .... D 4
Iserlohn, 57,792 .... B 3
Itzehoe, 35,678 .... C 2
Jülich, 20,152 .... B 3
Kaiserslautern, 99,859 .... B 4
Karlsruhe, 257,144 .... C 4
Kassel, 213,494 .... C 3
Kaufbeuren, 39,940 .... D 5
Kehl, 15,958 .... B 4
Kelheim, 11,701 .... D 4
Kempten, 44,617 .... D 5
Kevelaer, 20,257 .... B 3
Kiel, 276,600 .... C 1
Kirchheim unter Teck, 28,878 .... C 4
Kitzingen, 18,308 .... D 4
Kleve, 44,150 .... B 3
Koblenz, 106,189 .... B 3
Köln (Cologne), 866,308 .... B 3
Konstanz, 61,617 .... C 5
Korbach, 17,324 .... C 3
Kornwestheim, 28,574 .... C 4
Krefeld, 228,726 .... B 3
Kulmbach, 22,768 .... D 3
Lage, 30,949 .... C 3
Lahr, 25,028 .... B 4
Lampertheim, 24,053 .... C 4
Landau in der Pfalz, 32,318 .... C 4
Landsberg am Lech, 14,378 .... D 4
Landshut, 51,393 .... E 4
Langen, 30,230 .... C 4
Langenhagen, 37,077 .... C 2
Lauenburg, 11,445 .... D 2
Lauf an der Pegnitz, 15,771 .... D 4
Leer, 29,919 .... B 2
Lehrte, 21,792 .... D 2
Lemgo, 38,526 .... C 2
Lengerich, 21,451 .... B 2
Leverkusen, 111,588 .... B 3
Lichtenfels, 11,218 .... D 3
Limburg an der Lahn, 14,889 .... C 3
Lindau, 26,260 .... C 5
Lingen, 25,810 .... B 2
Lippstadt, 42,299 .... C 3
Lohr am Main, 11,291 .... C 4
Lörrach, 32,939 .... B 5
Lübbecke, 11,433 .... C 2
Lübeck, 242,191 .... D 2
Lüdenscheid, 80,096 .... B 3
Ludwigsburg, 79,538 .... C 4
Ludwigshafen am Rhein, 174,698 .... C 4
Lüneburg, 59,944 .... D 2
Lünen, 72,195 .... B 3

(continued on following page)

22 Germany
(continued)

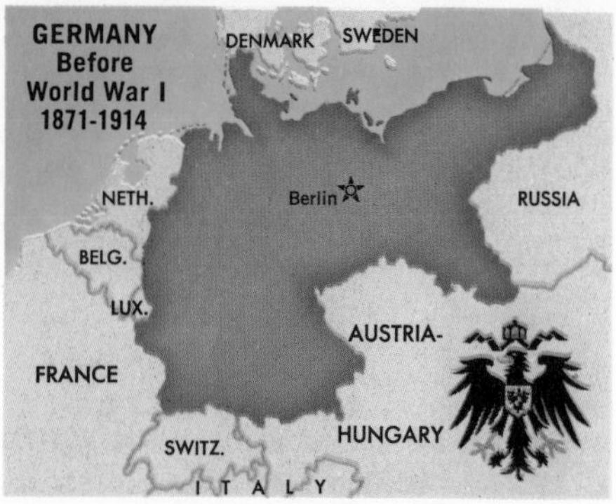
GERMANY
Before
World War I
1871-1914
DENMARK
SWEDEN
NETH.
Berlin
RUSSIA
BELG.
LUX.
AUSTRIA-
FRANCE
HUNGARY
SWITZ.
ITALY

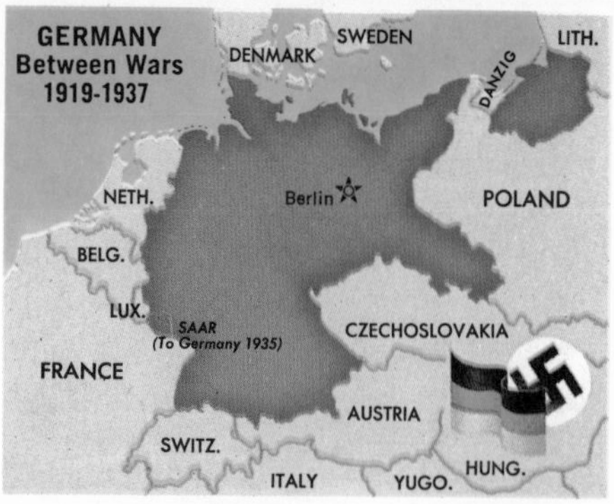
GERMANY
Between Wars
1919-1937
DENMARK
SWEDEN
LITH.
DANZIG
NETH.
Berlin
POLAND
BELG.
LUX.
SAAR
(To Germany 1935)
CZECHOSLOVAKIA
FRANCE
AUSTRIA
SWITZ.
ITALY
YUGO.
HUNG.

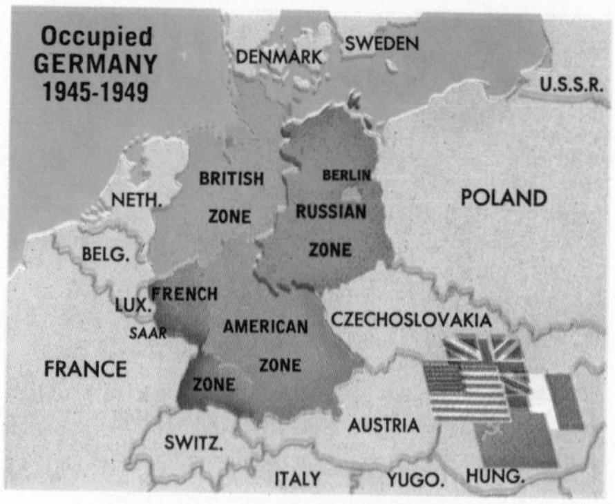
Occupied
GERMANY
1945-1949
DENMARK
SWEDEN
U.S.S.R.
BRITISH
ZONE
BERLIN
RUSSIAN
ZONE
NETH.
POLAND
BELG.
LUX.
FRENCH
SAAR
AMERICAN
ZONE
CZECHOSLOVAKIA
FRANCE
ZONE
AUSTRIA
SWITZ.
ITALY
YUGO.
HUNG.

WEST GERMANY (continued)

Mainz, 176,720 ....C 4
Mannheim, 330,920 ....C 4
Marburg an der Lahn, 51,382 ....C 3
Marktredwitz, 15,605 ....E 3
Marl, 75,779 ....B 3
Mayen, 18,485 ....B 3
Memmingen, 35,454 ....D 5
Meppen, 17,892 ....B 2
Merzig, 12,443 ....B 4
Meschede, 16,222 ....C 3
Metzingen, 14,093 ....C 4
Minden, 51,527 ....C 2
Mittenwald, 10,026 ....D 5
Mölln, 15,307 ....D 2
Mönchengladbach, 152,172 ....B 3
Moosburg an der Isar, 11,730 ....D 4
Mosbach, 13,876 ....C 4
Mühldorf am Inn, 10,998 ....E 4
Mülheim an der Ruhr, 191,080 ....B 3
Münden, 19,111 ....C 3
Munich (München), 1,326,331 ....D 4
Münster, 204,571 ....B 3
Neckarsulm, 18,523 ....C 4
Neheim-Hüsten, 36,864 ....C 3
Neuburg an der Donau, 18,530 ....D 4
Neu-Isenburg, 36,014 ....C 3
Neumarkt in der Oberpfalz, 18,930 ....D 4
Neumünster, 84,636 ....C 1
Neunkirchen, 44,326 ....B 4
Neuss, 117,599 ....B 3
Neustadt an der Weinstrasse, 51,058 ....B 4
Neustadt bei Coburg, 12,496 ....D 3
Neustadt in Holstein, 16,222 ....D 1
Neu-Ulm, 27,710 ....D 4
Neuwied, 31,359 ....B 3
Nienburg, 22,467 ....C 2
Norden, 16,355 ....B 2
Nordenham, 27,368 ....C 2
Nordhorn, 42,895 ....B 2
Nördlingen, 14,238 ....D 4
Northeim, 19,150 ....C 3
Nuremberg (Nürnberg), 477,108 ....D 4
Nürtingen, 21,284 ....C 4
Oberammergau, 4,641 ....D 5
Oberhausen, 249,045 ....B 3
Oberlahnstein, 20,131 ....B 3
Oberursel, 24,933 ....C 3
Ochtrup, 15,823 ....B 2
Offenbach am Main, 118,754 ....C 3
Offenburg, 32,628 ....B 4
Oldenburg, 131,434 ....C 2
Opladen, 43,531 ....B 3
Osnabrück, 141,000 ....C 2
Osterholz-Scharmbeck, 15,211 ....C 2
Osterode am Harz, 16,757 ....D 3
Paderborn, 68,735 ....C 3
Papenburg, 16,714 ....B 2
Passau, 31,574 ....E 4
Peine, 30,882 ....D 2
Penzberg, 10,784 ....D 5
Pforzheim, 90,780 ....C 4
Pfullingen, 15,967 ....C 4
Pinneberg, 36,439 ....C 2
Pirmasens, 56,172 ....B 4
Plettenberg, 30,233 ....C 3
Plön, 11,142 ....D 1
Porz am Rhein, 78,076 ....B 3
Preetz, 14,653 ....D 1
Radolfzell, 15,512 ....C 5
Rastatt, 29,102 ....C 4
Rastede, 16,851 ....C 2
Ratingen, 43,420 ....B 3
Ratzeburg, 12,335 ....D 2
Ravensburg, 31,819 ....C 5
Recklinghausen, 125,535 ....B 3
Regensburg, 128,083 ....E 4
Rehau, 10,565 ....D 3
Remscheid, 137,374 ....B 3
Rendsburg, 35,453 ....C 1
Reutlingen, 77,853 ....C 4
Rheine, 51,167 ....B 2
Rheinfelden, 16,547 ....B 5
Rheinhausen, 71,698 ....B 3
Rheydt, 100,633 ....B 3
Rosenheim, 36,376 ....D 5
Rotenburg, 16,664 ....C 2
Roth bei Nürnberg, 11,550 ....D 4
Rothenburg ob der Tauber, 12,002 ....D 4
Rottenburg am Neckar, 13,495 ....C 4
Rottweil, 19,881 ....C 4
Rüsselsheim, 57,308 ....C 4
Saarbrücken, 130,765 ....B 4
Saarlouis (Saarlautern), 36,251 ....B 4
Säckingen, 12,614 ....C 5
Salzgitter, 118,020 ....D 2
Sankt Ingbert, 28,774 ....B 4
Sankt Wendel, 10,138 ....B 4
Schleswig, 33,317 ....C 1
Schöneberg ....E 4
Schöningen, 14,551 ....D 2
Schramberg, 19,050 ....C 4
Schwabach, 25,774 ....D 4
Schwäbisch Gmünd, 44,628 ....C 4
Schwäbisch Hall, 23,765 ....C 4
Schwandorf in Bayern, 15,995 ....E 4
Schweinfurt, 59,293 ....D 3
Schwelm, 34,199 ....B 3
Schwenningen am Neckar, 35,487 ....C 4
Schwetzingen, 16,613 ....C 4
Seesen, 13,027 ....D 3
Selb, 18,498 ....E 3
Sennestadt, 20,518 ....C 3
Siegburg, 34,586 ....B 3
Siegen, 57,996 ....C 3
Sindelfingen, 41,029 ....C 4
Singen, 39,719 ....C 5
Soest, 40,580 ....C 3
Solingen, 175,895 ....B 3
Soltau, 14,981 ....C 2
Sonthofen, 16,504 ....D 5
Spandau ....E 3
Speyer, 42,323 ....C 4
Springe, 12,698 ....C 2
Stade, 31,637 ....C 2
Stadthagen, 16,876 ....C 2
Starnberg, 10,622 ....D 4
Stolberg, 39,589 ....B 3
Straubing, 36,943 ....E 4
Stuttgart, 628,412 ....C 4
Sulzbach-Rosenberg, 18,691 ....D 4
Tailfingen, 16,787 ....C 4
Tempelhof ....F 4
Traunstein, 14,117 ....E 5
Trier, 103,412 ....B 4
Tübingen, 56,008 ....C 4
Tuttlingen, 26,587 ....C 5
Überlingen, 12,837 ....C 5
Uelzen, 23,775 ....D 2
Uetersen, 16,734 ....C 2
Ulm, 92,486 ....C 4
Varel, 12,759 ....C 2
Vechta, 16,326 ....C 2
Verden, 16,741 ....C 2
Viersen, 83,988 ....B 3
Villingen im Schwarzwald, 37,652 ....C 4
Völklingen, 39,763 ....B 4
Waldshut, 10,621 ....C 5
Walsrode, 13,904 ....C 2
Wangen im Allgäu, 14,159 ....C 5
Wanne-Eickel, 99,923 ....B 3
Warendorf, 18,969 ....B 3
Wedel, 31,134 ....C 2
Weiden in der Oberpfalz, 43,097 ....D 4
Weilheim in Oberbayern, 14,433 ....D 5
Weingarten, 18,420 ....C 5
Weinheim, 29,544 ....C 4
Weissenburg in Bayern, 13,718 ....D 4
Wertheim, 12,035 ....C 4
Wesel, 44,710 ....B 3
Westerstede, 16,387 ....B 2
Wetzlar, 37,230 ....C 3
Wiesbaden, 260,614 ....B 3
Wilhelmshaven, 103,150 ....B 2
Witten, 97,807 ....B 3
Wolfenbüttel, 41,225 ....D 2
Wolfsburg, 89,442 ....D 2
Worms, 78,004 ....C 4
Wunstorf, 17,589 ....C 2
Wuppertal, 414,722 ....B 3
Würzburg, 120,317 ....C 4
Zirndorf, 15,363 ....D 4
Zweibrücken, 32,883 ....B 4
Zwischenahn, 19,906 ....B 2

OTHER FEATURES

Aller (riv.) ....C 2
Allgäu (reg.), 249,600 ....D 5
Alz (riv.) ....E 4
Ammersee (lake) ....D 4
Amrum (isl.), 2,155 ....C 1
Baltrum (isl.), 924 ....B 2
Bavarian (forest) ....E 4
Bavarian Alps (mts.) ....D 5
Black (forest) ....C 4
Bodensee (Constance) (lake) ....C 5
Bohemian (forest) ....E 4
Borkum (isl.), 5,348 ....B 2
Breisgau (reg.), 675,500 ....B 5
Chiemsee (lake) ....E 5
Constance (lake) ....C 5
Danube (Donau) (riv.) ....C 4
Dümmer (lake) ....C 2
East Friesland (region), 599,700 ....B 2
East Frisian (isls.), 20,962 ....B 2
Eder (res.) ....C 3
Eider (riv.) ....C 1
Eifel (mts.) ....B 3
Elbe (riv.) ....C 2
Ems (riv.) ....B 2
Fehmarn (isl.), 12,586 ....D 1
Feldberg (mt.) ....B 5
Fichtelgebirge (mts.) ....D 3
Föhr (isl.), 8,585 ....C 1
Franconian Jura (mts.) ....D 4
Frankenwald (forest) ....D 3
Fulda (riv.) ....C 3
Grosser Arber (mt.) ....E 4
Halligen, The (isls.), 5,112 ....C 1
Hardt (mts.) ....C 4
Harz (mts.) ....D 3
Hegau (reg.), 189,900 ....C 5
Helgoland (isl.), 3,184 ....B 1
Hunsrück (mts.) ....B 4
Iller (riv.) ....D 4
Inn (riv.) ....E 4
Isar (riv.) ....E 4
Jade (bay) ....C 2
Juist (isl.), 2,147 ....B 2
Kaiserstuhl (mt.) ....B 4
Kiel (canal) ....C 1
Königssee (lake) ....E 5
Lahn (riv.) ....C 3
Langeoog (isl.), 2,611 ....B 2
Lech (riv.) ....D 4
Leine (riv.) ....C 2
Lippe (riv.) ....C 3
Lüneburger Heide (dist.) ....C 2
Main (riv.) ....C 4
Mecklenburg (bay) ....D 1
Mosel (riv.) ....B 3
Neckar (riv.) ....C 4
Nord-Ostsee (Kiel) (canal) ....C 1
Norderney (isl.), 8,983 ....B 2
Nordstrand (isl.), 3,079 ....C 1
North (sea) ....A 1
North Friesland (reg.), 163,800 ....C 1
North Frisian (islands), 36,259 ....B 1
Oberpfälzer Wald (forest) ....E 4
Odenwald (forest) ....C 4
Pellworm (isl.), 2,033 ....C 1
Regen (riv.) ....E 4
Regnitz (riv.) ....D 4
Rhine (Rhein) (riv.) ....B 3
Rhön (mts.) ....D 3
Ruhr (riv.) ....B 3
Saar (riv.) ....B 4
Salzach (riv.) ....E 5
Sauer (riv.) ....B 4
Sauerland (reg.) ....B 3
Schwarzwald (Black) (forest) ....C 4
Spessart (range) ....C 4
Spiekeroog (isl.), 823 ....B 2
Starnbergersee (lake) ....D 5
Steigerwald (forest) ....D 4
Steinhuder (lake) ....C 2
Swabian Jura (mts.) ....C 4
Sylt (isl.), 20,407 ....C 1
Tauber (riv.) ....C 4
Taunus (range) ....C 3
Tegernsee (lake) ....D 5
Teutoburger Wald (forest) ....C 2
Vechte (riv.) ....B 2
Vogelsberg (mt.) ....C 3
Walchensee (lake) ....D 5
Wangerooge (isl.), 2,126 ....B 2
Wasserkuppe (mt.) ....C 3
Watzmann (mt.) ....E 5
Werra (riv.) ....D 3
Weser (riv.) ....C 2
Westerwald (forest) ....C 3
Wurmsee (Starnbergersee) (lake) ....D 5
Zugspitze (mt.) ....D 5

Agriculture, Industry and Resources

DOMINANT LAND USE

- Wheat, Sugar Beets
- Cereals (chiefly rye, oats, barley)
- Potatoes, Rye
- Dairy, Livestock
- Mixed Cereals, Dairy
- Truck Farming
- Grapes, Fruit
- Forests

MAJOR MINERAL OCCURRENCES

- Ag Silver
- Ba Barite
- C Coal
- Cu Copper
- Fe Iron Ore
- G Natural Gas
- Gr Graphite
- K Potash
- Lg Lignite
- Mg Magnesium
- Na Salt
- O Petroleum
- Pb Lead
- U Uranium
- Zn Zinc

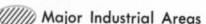

Water Power

Major Industrial Areas

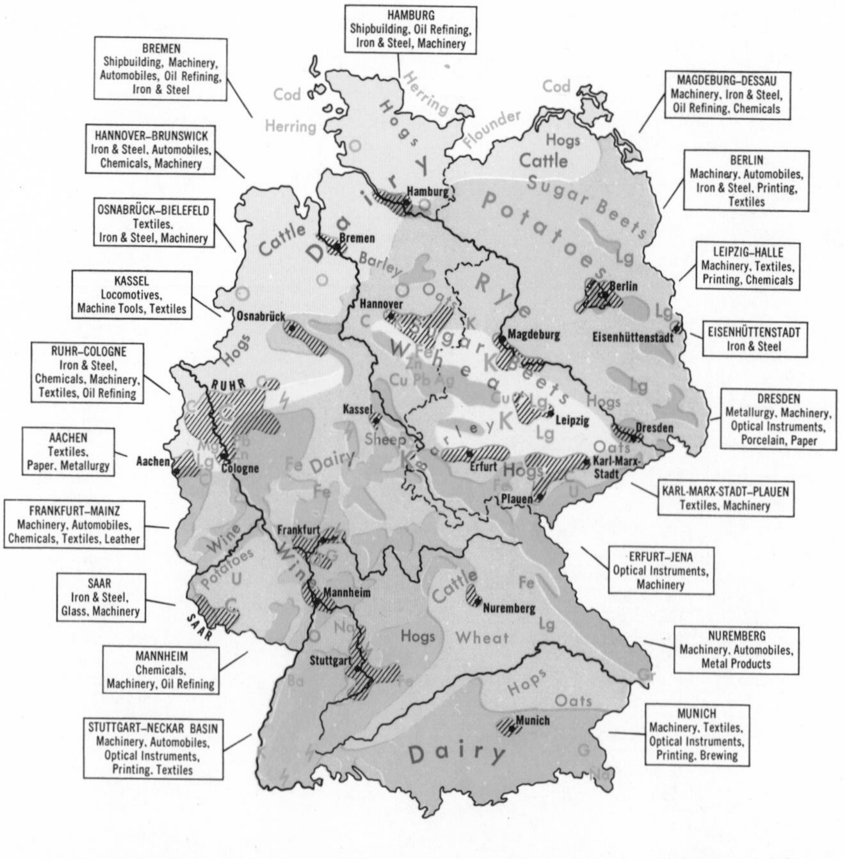
HAMBURG
Shipbuilding, Oil Refining, Iron & Steel, Machinery
BREMEN
Shipbuilding, Machinery, Automobiles, Oil Refining, Iron & Steel
MAGDEBURG-DESSAU
Machinery, Iron & Steel, Oil Refining, Chemicals
HANNOVER-BRUNSWICK
Iron & Steel, Automobiles, Chemicals, Machinery
BERLIN
Machinery, Automobiles, Iron & Steel, Printing, Textiles
OSNABRÜCK-BIELEFELD
Textiles, Iron & Steel, Machinery
LEIPZIG-HALLE
Machinery, Textiles, Printing, Chemicals
KASSEL
Locomotives, Machine Tools, Textiles
EISENHÜTTENSTADT
Iron & Steel
RUHR-COLOGNE
Iron & Steel, Chemicals, Machinery, Textiles, Oil Refining
DRESDEN
Metallurgy, Machinery, Optical Instruments, Porcelain, Paper
AACHEN
Textiles, Paper, Metallurgy
KARL-MARX-STADT-PLAUEN
Textiles, Machinery
FRANKFURT-MAINZ
Machinery, Automobiles, Chemicals, Textiles, Leather
ERFURT-JENA
Optical Instruments, Machinery
SAAR
Iron & Steel, Glass, Machinery
NUREMBERG
Machinery, Automobiles, Metal Products
MANNHEIM
Chemicals, Machinery, Oil Refining
MUNICH
Machinery, Textiles, Optical Instruments, Printing, Brewing
STUTTGART-NECKAR BASIN
Machinery, Automobiles, Optical Instruments, Printing, Textiles
Cod
Herring
Flounder
Hogs
Cattle
Sugar Beets
Potatoes
Dairy
Rye
Barley
Oats
Wheat
Sheep
Wine
Hops
Hamburg
Bremen
Hannover
Osnabrück
Magdeburg
Berlin
Eisenhüttenstadt
Kassel
Leipzig
Dresden
Erfurt
Karl-Marx-Stadt
Plauen
RUHR
Aachen
Cologne
Frankfurt
Mannheim
SAAR
Nuremberg
Stuttgart
Munich

NETHERLANDS
AREA 13,958 sq. mi.
POPULATION 13,077,000
CAPITALS The Hague, Amsterdam
LARGEST CITY Amsterdam
HIGHEST POINT Vaalserberg, 1,056 ft.
MONETARY UNIT guilder
MAJOR LANGUAGE Dutch
MAJOR RELIGIONS Protestantism, Roman Catholicism

BELGIUM
AREA 11,779 sq. mi.
POPULATION 9,660,154
CAPITAL Brussels
LARGEST CITY Brussels (greater)
HIGHEST POINT Botrange 2,277 ft.
MONETARY UNIT Belgian franc
MAJOR LANGUAGES French (Walloon), Flemish
MAJOR RELIGION Roman Catholicism

LUXEMBOURG
AREA 999 sq. mi.
POPULATION 339,000
CAPITAL Luxembourg
LARGEST CITY Luxembourg
HIGHEST POINT Ardennes Plateau, 1,825 ft.
MONETARY UNIT Luxembourg franc
MAJOR LANGUAGES Luxembourgeois (German dialect), French, German
MAJOR RELIGION Roman Catholicism

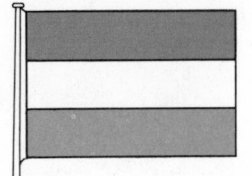
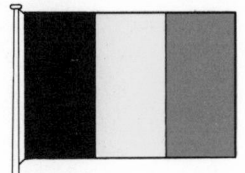
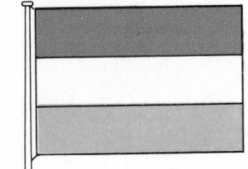

BELGIUM

PROVINCES

Antwerp, 1,529,826 .....F 6
Brabant, 2,166,372 .....F 7
East Flanders, 1,310,638 .....D 7
Hainaut, 1,311,810 .....D 7
Liège, 1,016,131 .....H 7
Limburg, 650,338 .....G 7
Luxembourg, 219,369 .....G 9
Namur, 383,618 .....F 8
West Flanders, 1,052,052 .....B 7

CITIES and TOWNS†

Aalst, 45,900 .....D 7
Aalter, 8,569 .....C 6
Aarlen (Arlon), 14,191 .....H 9
Aarschot, 12,329 .....F 7
Aat (Ath), 11,094 .....D 7
Adinkerke, 2,713 .....A 6
Aiken, 8,054 .....G 7
Alost (Aalst), 45,900 .....D 7
Amay, 7,561 .....G 8
Andenne, 8,068 .....G 8
Anderlecht, 103,832 .....B 9
Anderlues, 12,930 .....E 8
Antoing, 3,435 .....C 7
Antwerp (Antwerpen), 234,099 .....E 6

Antwerp, *673,259 .....E 6
Ardooie, 7,163 .....C 7
Arendonk, 9,516 .....G 6
Arlon, 14,191 .....H 9
As, 4,087 .....H 6
Asse, 12,631 .....E 7
Assebroek, 15,195 .....C 6
Assesse, 1,138 .....G 8
Ath, 11,094 .....D 7
Athus, 7,185 .....H 9
Audenaarde (Oudenaarde), 21,980 .....D 7
Auderghem, 32,782 .....C 9
Autelbas, 1,606 .....H 9
Auvelais, 8,412 .....F 8
Aywaille, 3,813 .....H 8
Baerle-Duc, 2,171 .....F 6
Balen, 14,719 .....G 6
Barvaux, 1,727 .....H 8
Basècles, 4,245 .....D 7
Bastogne (Bastenaken), 6,476 .....H 9
Beaumont, 1,762 .....E 8
Beauraing, 2,703 .....F 8
Berchem, 49,880 .....F 6
Berchem-Sainte-Agathe, 17,689 .....B 9
Bergen (Mons), 27,042 .....E 8
Bertrix, 4,481 .....G 9
Beveren, 15,350 .....E 6

Bilzen, 7,000 .....G 7
Binche, 10,340 .....E 8
Blankenberge, 10,400 .....C 6
Bocholt, 5,582 .....H 6
Boom, 17,280 .....E 6
Borgerhout, 50,226 .....E 6
Borgloon, 3,543 .....G 7
Borgworm (Waremme), 7,623 .....G 7
Bouillon, 3,089 .....G 9
Bourg-Leopold (Leopoldsburg), 9,621 .....G 6
Boussu, 11,626 .....D 8
Bovigny, 1,015 .....H 8
Braine-l'Alleud, 16,028 .....E 7
Braine-le-Comte, 11,343 .....D 7
Bredene, 9,381 .....B 6
Bree, 10,462 .....H 7
Bruges (Brugge), 52,249 .....C 6
Bruges, *112,611 .....C 6
Brussels (Bruxelles) (cap.), 1,073,111 .....C 9
Charleroi, 24,895 .....E 8
Charleroi, *218,089 .....E 8
Châtelet, 15,314 .....E 8
Châtelineau, 20,293 .....E 8
Chièvres, 3,154 .....D 7
Chimay, 3,309 .....E 8
Ciney, 7,431 .....G 8
Comblain-au-Pont, 3,538 .....G 8

Comines, 8,219 .....B 7
Couillet, 15,055 .....E 8
Courcelles, 17,157 .....E 8
Courtrai, 45,310 .....C 7
Couvin, 4,192 .....F 8
Cul-des-Sarts, 993 .....E 9
Deinze, 6,214 .....D 7
Denderleeuw, 9,699 .....D 7
Dendermonde, 9,663 .....E 6
De Panne, 6,792 .....A 6
Dessel, 7,170 .....G 6
Deurne, 75,819 .....F 6
Diegem, 4,760 .....C 9
Diest, 9,587 .....F 7
Diksmuide, 6,557 .....B 6
Dilbeek, 13,620 .....B 9
Dinant, 9,700 .....G 8
Dison, 8,809 .....H 7
Dixmude (Diksmuide), 6,557 .....B 6
Doel, 1,395 .....E 6
Doornik (Tournai), 33,309 .....C 7
Dour, 10,407 .....D 8
Drogenbos, 4,648 .....B 9
Drongen, 8,312 .....C 6
Dudzele, 2,112 .....C 6
Duffel, 13,560 .....F 6
Ecaussines d'Enghien, 6,696 .....E 7
Edingen (Enghien), 4,279 .....D 7

Eeklo, 19,007 .....D 6
Eernegem, 5,865 .....B 6
Eigenbrakel (Braine-l'Alleud), 16,028 .....E 7
Ekeren, 24,535 .....E 6
Ellezelles, 3,676 .....D 7
Enghien, 4,279 .....D 7
Ensival, 5,515 .....H 7
Erquelinnes, 4,812 .....E 8
Esneux, 5,923 .....H 7
Essen, 10,515 .....F 6
Étalle, 1,179 .....H 9
Etterbeek, 52,299 .....C 9
Eupen, 14,856 .....J 7
Evere, 24,289 .....C 9
Evergem, 13,620 .....D 6
Flémalle-Haute, 7,800 .....G 7
Fleurus, 8,475 .....F 8
Florennes, 4,070 .....F 8
Florenville, 2,526 .....G 9
Forest, 55,799 .....B 9
Fosses-la-Ville, 3,887 .....F 8
Frameries, 11,624 .....D 8
Frasnes-lez-Buissenal, 2,672 .....D 7
Furnes (Veurne), 7,475 .....B 6
Ganshoren, 19,164 .....B 9
Gaurain-Ramecroix, 3,599 .....D 7
Gedinne, 1,021 .....F 9
Geel, 28,484 .....F 6
Geldenaken (Jodoigne), 4,194 .....F 7

Gembloux, 11,030 .....F 7
Gemmenich, 2,608 .....H 7
Genk, 55,596 .....H 7
Gent (Ghent), 153,301 .....D 6
Gentbrugge, 22,986 .....D 7
Geraardsbergen, 9,201 .....D 7
Ghent, 153,301 .....D 6
Ghent, *229,687 .....D 6
Gilly, 24,155 .....E 8
Gosselies, 10,970 .....E 8
Grammont (Geraardsbergen), 9,201 .....D 7
Hal (Halle), 20,071 .....E 7
Halen, 5,321 .....G 7
Halle, 20,071 .....E 7
Hamme, 17,083 .....E 6
Hamont, 6,526 .....H 6
Hannut (Hannuit), 3,069 .....G 7
Harelbeke, 17,981 .....C 7
Hasselt, 38,773 .....G 7
Havelange, 1,495 .....G 8
Heer, 578 .....F 8
Heist, 9,289 .....C 6
Heist-op-den-Berg, 13,206 .....F 6
Herbeumont, 590 .....G 9
Herentals, 18,377 .....F 6
Herselt, 7,318 .....F 6
Herstal, 29,602 .....H 7
Herve, 4,357 .....H 7
Hoboken, 31,815 .....E 6
Hoei (Huy), 13,398 .....G 8
Hoeselt, 5,570 .....H 7
Hoogstraten, 4,376 .....F 6
Hornu, 10,905 .....D 8
Houffalize, 1,297 .....H 8
Huy, 13,398 .....G 8
Ieper, 18,461 .....B 7
Ingelmunster, 9,973 .....C 7
Ixelles, 92,532 .....C 9
Izegem, 22,729 .....C 7
Jambes, 14,924 .....G 8
Jemappes, 12,906 .....D 8
Jemeppe, 12,232 .....G 7
Jette, 37,354 .....B 9
Jodoigne, 4,194 .....F 7
Jumet, 28,811 .....E 8
Kain, 4,900 .....C 7
Kalmthout, 12,122 .....F 6
Kapellen, 12,297 .....F 6
Kessel-Lo, 21,351 .....F 7
Knokke, 14,268 .....C 6
Koekelare, 6,423 .....B 6
Koekelberg, 17,348 .....B 9
Koersel, 10,756 .....G 6
Kontich, 13,193 .....E 6
Kortemark, 5,839 .....C 6
Kortrijk (Courtrai), 45,310 .....C 7
Kraainem, 10,560 .....C 9
La Louvière, 23,447 .....E 8
La Louvière, *113,795 .....E 8
La Roche-en-Ardenne, 1,894 .....G 8
Lanaken, 8,216 .....H 7
Landen, 5,247 .....G 7
Langemark, 4,787 .....B 7
Lede, 10,258 .....D 7
Ledeberg, 11,056 .....D 7
Lens, 1,790 .....D 8
Leopoldsburg, 9,621 .....G 6
Lessines (Lessen), 9,047 .....D 7
Leuven (Louvain), 32,125 .....F 7
Leuze, 7,128 .....D 7
Libramont, 2,774 .....G 9
Lichtervelde, 7,372 .....C 6
Liedekerke, 10,273 .....D 7
Liège, 150,127 .....H 7
Liège, *446,990 .....H 7
Lier (Lierre), 28,557 .....F 6
Lierneux, 2,847 .....H 8
Limbourg (Limburg), 3,973 .....J 7
Linkebeek, 4,096 .....C 10
Lokeren, 26,654 .....E 6
Lommel, 20,567 .....G 6
Looz (Borgloon), 3,543 .....G 7
Louvain, 32,125 .....F 7
Luik (Liège), 150,127 .....H 7
Maaseik, 8,363 .....H 6
Machelen, 7,331 .....C 9
Maldegem, 14,182 .....C 6
Malines (Mechelen), 65,728 .....F 6
Malmédy, 6,482 .....J 8
Marche-en-Famenne, 4,423 .....G 8
Marchin, 4,381 .....G 8
Marcinelle, 25,992 .....E 8
Mariembourg, 1,776 .....F 8
Martelange, 1,594 .....H 9
Mechelen, 65,728 .....F 6
Meerhout, 8,359 .....G 6
Meerle, 2,809 .....F 6
Meisbroek, 2,034 .....C 9
Menen (Menin), 22,458 .....C 7
Menin (Menin), 22,458 .....C 7
Merchtem, 8,772 .....D 7
Merelbeke, 13,755 .....D 7

Merksem, 39,011 .....E 6
Merksplas, 4,950 .....F 6
Messancy, 3,064 .....H 9
Mettet, 3,366 .....F 8
Meulebeke, 10,619 .....C 7
Moeskron (Mouscron), 37,624 .....C 7
Mol, 27,320 .....G 6
Molenbeek-Saint-Jean, 67,271 .....B 9
Mons, 27,042 .....E 8
Montegnée, 11,882 .....G 7
Montignies-sur-Sambre, 24,048 .....F 8
Mortsel, 27,999 .....E 6
Mouscron, 37,624 .....C 7
Namur (Namen), 32,621 .....F 8
Neerlinter, 1,431 .....G 7
Neerpelt, 8,273 .....G 6
Neufchâteau, 2,739 .....G 9
Nieuwpoort (Nieuport), 7,165 .....B 6
Ninove, 12,087 .....D 7
Nivelles (Nijvel), 15,384 .....E 7
Oostende (Ostend), 57,749 .....B 6
Oostkamp, 8,560 .....C 6
Ophoven, 2,487 .....H 6
Opwijk, 9,622 .....E 7
Ostend, 57,749 .....B 6
Oud-Turnhout, 8,219 .....F 6
Oudenaarde, 21,980 .....D 7
Ougrée, 21,152 .....H 7
Overijse, 14,119 .....F 7
Overpelt, 10,002 .....G 6
Peer, 5,882 .....G 6
Péruwelz, 7,814 .....D 7
Perwez (Perwijs), 2,858 .....F 7
Philippeville, 1,822 .....F 8
Poperinge, 12,619 .....B 7
Poppel, 2,246 .....G 6
Putte, 6,856 .....F 6
Quaregnon, 18,289 .....D 8
Quiévrain, 5,685 .....D 8
Raeren, 3,490 .....J 7
Rance, 1,443 .....E 8
Rebecq-Rognon, 3,831 .....E 7
Renaix (Ronse), 25,371 .....D 7
Retie, 6,339 .....G 6
Rièzes, 307 .....E 9
Rochefort, 4,242 .....G 8
Roeselare, 40,077 .....C 7
Roeulx, 2,605 .....E 8
Ronse, 25,371 .....D 7
Rouïers (Roeselare), 40,077 .....C 7
Ruisbroek, 5,685 .....C 9
's Gravenbrakel (Braine-le-Comte), 11,343 .....D 7
Saint-Georges, 6,085 .....G 7
Saint-Gérard, 1,626 .....F 8
Saint-Gilles, 57,238 .....B 9
Saint-Hubert, 3,104 .....G 9
Saint-Josse-ten-Noode, 24,335 .....C 9
Saint-Léger, 1,600 .....H 9
Saint-Vith (Sankt-Vith), 2,935 .....J 8
Schaerbeek, 120,650 .....C 9
Schoten, 28,543 .....F 6
Seraing, 40,937 .....H 7
Sint-Amandsberg, 24,778 .....D 6
Sint-Andries, 15,062 .....C 6
Sint-Lenaarts, 4,464 .....F 6
Sint-Niklaas, 48,851 .....E 6
Sint-Pieters-Leeuw, 15,978 .....B 9
Sint-Truiden (Saint-Trond), 21,131 .....G 7
Sivry, 1,384 .....E 8
Soignies, 11,320 .....E 7
Spa, 9,683 .....H 7
Staden, 5,581 .....B 7
Stavelot, 4,461 .....H 8
Steenokkerzeel, 3,877 .....C 9
Stene, 9,304 .....B 6
Stokkem, 3,380 .....H 6
Strombeek-Bever, 10,027 .....C 9
Tamines, 8,139 .....F 8
Tamise (Temse), 14,559 .....E 6
Templeuve, 3,737 .....C 7
Temse, 14,559 .....E 6
Termonde (Dendermonde), 9,663 .....E 6
Tessenderlo, 10,665 .....G 7
Theux, 5,491 .....H 8
Thuin, 5,877 .....E 8
Tielt, Brabant, 3,813 .....F 7
Tielt, West Flanders, 13,887 .....C 7
Tienen (Tirlemont), 22,660 .....G 7
Tongeren (Tongres), 16,880 .....G 7
Torhout, 14,301 .....C 6
Tournai, 33,309 .....C 7
Tronchiennes (Drongen), 8,312 .....D 6
Tubize (Tubeke), 10,269 .....E 7
Turnhout, 37,828 .....F 6
Uccle (Ukkel), 76,579 .....B 9
Verviers, 35,730 .....H 7

(continued on following page)

Agriculture, Industry and Resources

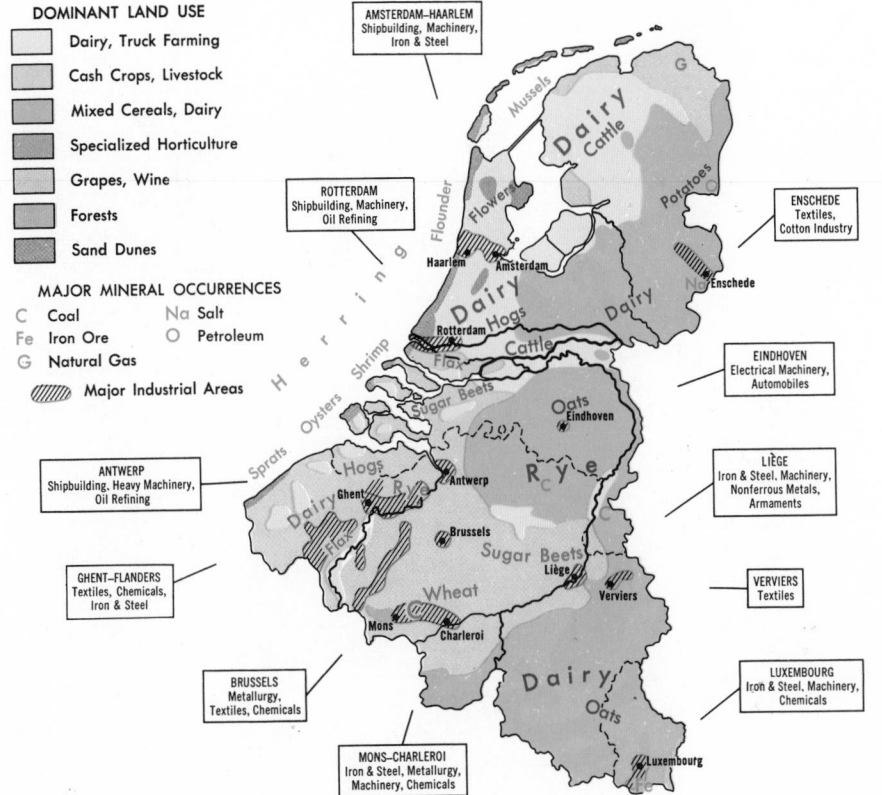

DOMINANT LAND USE

- Dairy, Truck Farming
- Cash Crops, Livestock
- Mixed Cereals, Dairy
- Specialized Horticulture
- Grapes, Wine
- Forests
- Sand Dunes

MAJOR MINERAL OCCURRENCES

C Coal
Fe Iron Ore
G Natural Gas
Na Salt
O Petroleum

///// Major Industrial Areas

AMSTERDAM–HAARLEM
Shipbuilding, Machinery, Iron & Steel

ROTTERDAM
Shipbuilding, Machinery, Oil Refining

ENSCHEDE
Textiles, Cotton Industry

EINDHOVEN
Electrical Machinery, Automobiles

LIÈGE
Iron & Steel, Machinery, Nonferrous Metals, Armaments

VERVIERS
Textiles

LUXEMBOURG
Iron & Steel, Machinery, Chemicals

ANTWERP
Shipbuilding, Heavy Machinery, Oil Refining

GHENT–FLANDERS
Textiles, Chemicals, Iron & Steel

BRUSSELS
Metallurgy, Textiles, Chemicals

MONS–CHARLEROI
Iron & Steel, Metallurgy, Machinery, Chemicals

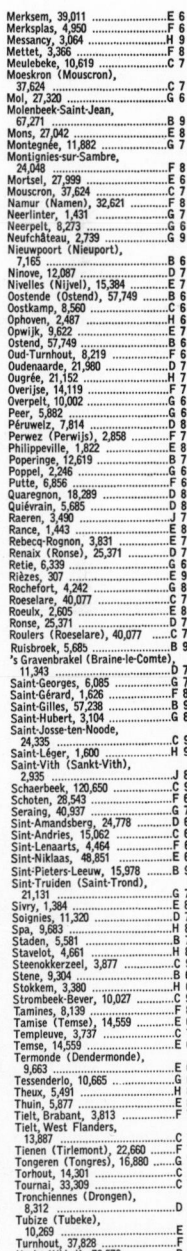

BELGIUM (continued)

Veurne, 7,475 .... B 6
Vielsalm, 3,702 .... J 8
Villers-devant-Orval, 777 .. G 9
Vilvoorde (Vilvorde), 34,040 .. F 7
Virton, 3,956 .... H 9
Visé, 6,595 .... H 7
Vorst (Forest), 55,799 .... B 9
Waarschoot, 7,852 .... D 6
Waasten (Warneton), 3,215 .. B 7
Waha, 2,664 .... G 8
Waimes, 2,787 .... J 8
Walcourt, 2,077 .... F 8
Wandre, 6,833 .... J 7
Waregem, 16,928 .... C 7
Waremme, 7,623 .... G 7
Warneton, 3,215 .... B 7
Wasmes, 13,933 .... D 7
Waterloo, 14,615 .... E 7
Watermael-Boitsfort, 24,730 .. C 9
Watervliet, 1,812 .... D 6
Wavre (Waver), 11,007 .. F 7
Weismes (Waimes), 2,787 .. J 8
Wemmel, 11,404 .... B 9
Wenduine, 1,756 .... C 6
Wervik, 12,728 .... B 7
Westende, 2,746 .... B 6
Westerlo, 7,630 .... F 6
Wetteren, 20,775 .... D 7
Wezembeek-Oppem, 10,536 .. D 9
Wezet (Visé), 6,595 .... H 7
Willebroek, 15,650 ..... E 6
Wilrijk, 42,109 .... E 6
Wingene, 7,178 .... C 7
Woluwe-Saint-Lambert, 44,102 .. C 9
Woluwe-Saint-Pierre, 37,314 .. C 9
Wolvertem, 5,326 .... E 7
Ypres (Ieper), 18,461 .. B 7
Yvoir, 2,837 .... G 8
Zaventem, 9,941 .... C 9
Zeebrugge .... C 6
Zele, 18,386 .... E 6
Zelik, 5,165 .... B 9
Zelzate, 11,751 .... D 6
Zinnik (Soignies), 11,320 .. D 7
Zonhoven, 12,910 ...... G 6
Zottegem, 6,905 .... D 7

OTHER FEATURES

Albert (canal) .... F 6
Ardennes (plateau) .... J 8
Botrange (mt.) .... J 8
Demer (river) .... D 7
Dyle (river) .... D 7
Hohe Venn (plateau) .. H 8
Lesse (river) .... F 8
Mark (river) .... E 6
Meuse (river) .... F 7
Nethe (river) .... F 6
Ourthe (river) .... H 8
Rupel (river) .... E 6
Scheldt (Schelde) (river) .. C 7
Schnee Eifel (plateau) .. J 9
Semois (river) .... G 9
Senne (river) .... E 7
Vesdre (river) .... H 8
Weisserstein (mt.) .... J 8
Yser (river) .... B 7
Zitterwald (plateau) .. J 8

LUXEMBOURG

CITIES and TOWNS

Clervaux, 933 .... J 8

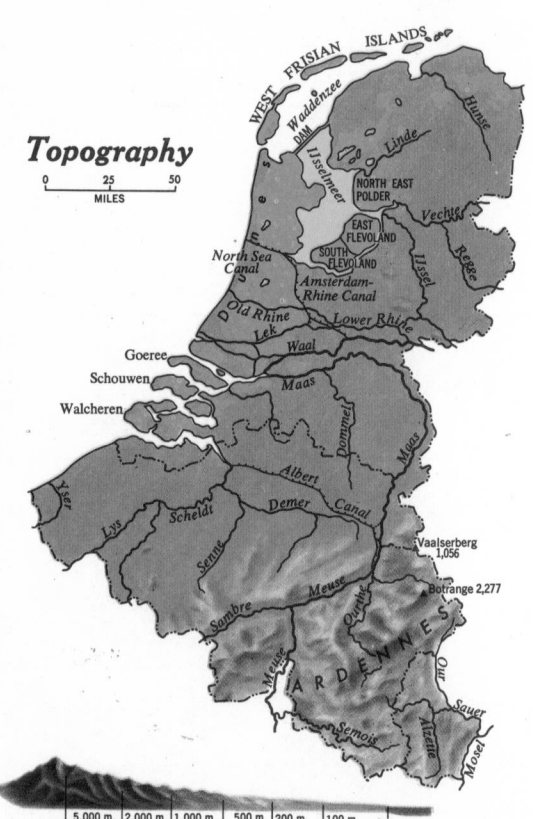

Topography

0 25 50
MILES

5,000 m. | 2,000 m. | 1,000 m. | 500 m. | 200 m. | 100 m. | Sea
16,404 ft. | 6,562 ft. | 3,281 ft. | 1,640 ft. | 656 ft. | 328 ft. | Level Below

Diekirch, 4,899 .... J 9
Differdange, 9,808 ..... H 9
Dudelange, 14,849 ..... H 10
Echternach, 3,472 ..... J 9
Esch-sur-Alzette, 27,921 .. J 9
Esch-sur-Sauer, 265 ... J 9
Ettelbrück, 5,557 ..... J 9
Grevenmacher, 2,850 .. J 9
Luxembourg (cap.), 77,458 .. J 9
Mersch, 1,682 .... J 9
Pétange, 6,251 .... H 9
Redange, 990 .... H 9
Remich, 1,958 .... J 9
Troisvierges, 928 .... J 8
Vianden, 1,381 .... J 9
Wasserbillig, 2,047 .. J 9
Wiltz, 1,538 .... J 9

OTHER FEATURES

Alzette (river) .... J 9
Clerf (river) .... J 8
Eisling (river) .... H 9
Mosel (river) .... J 9
Our (river) .... J 9
Sauer (river) .... J 9

NETHERLANDS

PROVINCES

Drenthe, 366,590 .... K 3
Friesland, 521,751 ..... H 2
Gelderland, 1,505,760 .. G 4
Groningen, 517,305 ..... K 2
North Brabant,
  1,787,783 .... F 5
Limburg, 998,570 ...... H 6
North Holland,
  2,244,456 .... F 3
Overijssel, 920,882 .... J 4
South Holland,
  2,968,670 .... E 5
Utrecht, 801,285 ...... G 4
Zeeland, 305,754 ...... D 6

CITIES and TOWNS

Aalsmeer, ‡18,166 ...... F 4
Aalst, 4,423 .... G 6
Aalten, ‡16,295 .... K 5
Aardenburg, 13,853 .... C 6
Akkrum, 2,495 .... H 3
Alkmaar, †52,091 ..... F 3
Almelo, †58,941 ...... K 4
Amersfoort, †78,189 .. G 4
Amstelveen, †69,167 .. B 5
Amsterdam (cap.)
  831,463 .... F 4
Amsterdam, *918,676 .. B 4
Andijk, 3,482 .... G 3
Anjum, 939 .... J 2
Apeldoorn, 123,628 ... H 4
Apeldoorn, *214,974 .. H 4
Appelscha, 1,622 .... J 3
Appingedam, †10,987 .. K 2
Arnhem, 132,531 ..... H 4
Arnhem, *232,860 .... H 4
Assen, †38,956 ...... K 3
Asten, †11,209 ...... H 6
Axel, 18,904 .... D 6
Baarle-Nassau,
  †4,948 .... F 6
Baarn, 124,106 ...... G 4
Badhoevedorp, 8,699 .. B 5
Balkbrug, 2,468 ..... J 3

Barneveld, 130,046 ..... H 4
Bath, 128 .... D 6
Beilen, †12,289 .... K 3
Bergeijk (Hof), †7,816 .. G 6
Bergen, †13,060 .... F 3
Bergen op Zoom,
  †39,051 .... E 5
Bergum, 14,252 .... H 2
Berkel, 15,936 .... F 4
Berkhout, 13,941 ..... F 3
Beverwijk, †41,357 ... F 4
Blerick, 14,593 ...... H 6
Bloemendaal, †19,253 .. E 4
Blokzijl, †1,105 ..... H 3
Bodegraven, †14,083 .. F 4
Bolsward, †9,247 ..... H 2
Borculo, †8,510 ...... K 4
Borger, †10,972 ...... K 3
Borne, †15,423 .... K 4
Boskoop, †11,600 ..... F 4
Boxmeer, †10,850 ..... H 5
Boxtel, †19,080 ...... G 5
Breda, 121,209 .... F 5
Breda, *233,704 ...... F 5
Breezand, 1,962 ...... F 3
Breskens, †3,851 ..... C 6
Brielle, †8,314 ...... E 5
Broek, 12,260 .... F 4
Brouwershaven, †3,256 .. D 5
Brummen, †18,077 ..... J 4
Buiksloot, 23,738 .... B 4
Bussum, †41,787 ...... G 4
Callantsoog, †1,698 .. *F 3
Coevorden, †12,481 ... K 3
Colijnsplaat, 1,477 .. D 5
Culemborg, †11,083 ... G 5
Cuyk, †12,144 .... H 5
Dalen, 14,630 .... K 3
De Bilt, †29,153 ..... G 4
Dedemsvaart, 8,364 ... J 3
De Koog, 701 .... F 2
Delft, 83,698 .... E 4
Delfzijl, †21,990 .... K 2
Den Burg, 3,579 ..... F 2
Den Helder, †60,612 .. F 2
Denekamp, †10,919 ... L 4
Deurne, †23,949 ..... H 6
Deventer, †65,319 ... J 4
De Wijk, †4,120 ..... J 3
Diemen, †9,558 ...... C 5
Dieren, 8,612 .... J 4
Diever, †3,180 ...... J 3
Dinxperlo, †6,248 ... K 5
Dirksland, †6,092 ... E 5
Doesburg, †9,451 .... J 4
Doetinchem, †31,097 .. J 5
Dokkum, 19,886 ...... J 2
Domburg, †3,154 ..... C 5
Dongen, †16,231 ..... F 5
Doorn, †10,084 ...... G 4
Doornspijk, †10,463 .. H 4
Dordrecht, †88,699 .. F 5
Dordrecht, *99,284 .. F 5
Drachten, 16,529 .... J 2
Driebergen, †15,828 .. G 4
Druten, 19,761 ...... H 5
Duivendrecht, 2,656 .. C 5
Durgerdam, 640 ..... C 4
Echt, 15,795 .... H 6
Edam, 118,184 ...... G 4
Ede, †71,952 .... G 4
Eefde, 2,936 .... J 4
Egmond aan Zee,
  15,554 .... E 3
Eindhoven, 188,631 .. G 6
Eindhoven, *301,049 .. G 6
Elburg, †5,135 ..... H 4
Elst, †15,182 ...... H 5

Emmeloord, 7,251 .... H 3
Emmen, †79,707 .... K 3
Enkhuizen, †11,502 .... G 3
Enschede, 139,245 .... K 4
Epe, †27,515 .... H 4
Erica, 3,026 .... K 3
Ermelo, †37,198 ...... H 4
Etten, †19,698 .... F 5
Flushing, †40,197 .... C 6
Franeker, 19,575 ..... H 2
Geertruidenberg, 15,575 .. F 5
Geldermalsen, †7,946 .. G 5
Geldrop, †26,909 ..... H 6
Geleen, 136,121 ...... H 7
Gemert, †14,329 ...... H 6
Gendringen, 13,688 ... K 5
Gennemuiden, 15,524 .. H 3
Gennep, 16,922 .... H 5
Giessendam, †13,588 .. F 5
Giethoorn, 12,486 .... H 3
Goes, †25,822 .... D 6
Goirle, †11,428 ...... F 6
Goor, 19,702 .... K 4
Gorinchem, 126,380 ... F 5
Gorredijk, 3,006 ..... J 2
Gouda, 145,990 .... F 4
Gouda, *84,695 .... F 4
Graauw, 11,277 .... D 6
Gramsbergen, 15,431 .. K 3
Grave, †7,405 .... H 5
Groenlo, †7,888 ...... K 4
Groesbeek, †17,308 ... H 5
Groningen, 168,843 ... K 2
Groningen, *185,757 .. K 2
Grouw, 3,191 .... J 2
Haamstede, 1,179 ..... D 5
Haarlem, 172,235 ..... F 4
Haarlemmermeer (Hoofddorp),
  4,949 .... F 4
Hague, The (cap.), 550,613 .. E 4
Hague, The, *702,296 . E 4
Halfweg, 2,171 .... A 4
Hallum, 1,424 .... H 2
Hardenberg, 126,011 .. J 3
Harderwijk, 14,054 ... H 4
Hardinxveld, †13,588 .. G 5
Harlingen, †12,552 ... G 2
Hasselt, †5,006 ...... H 3
Hattem, 19,034 .... H 4
Heemstede, 126,507 ... F 4
Heer, †12,217 .... H 7
Heerde, †15,341 ...... H 4
Heerenveen, 131,434 . H 3
Heerlen, †75,147 ..... H 7
Heiloo, †17,736 ...... F 3
Hellendoorn, †29,410 .. J 4
Hellevoetsluis, †19,653 .. E 5
Helmond, †57,889 ..... H 6
Helmond, *†79,164 .... H 6
Hengelo, Gelderland,
  †7,360 .... J 4
Hengelo, Overijssel,
  †69,618 .... K 4
Heusden, 14,587 ...... G 5
Hillegom, †16,963 .... E 4
Hilvarenbeek, †17,358 .. G 6
Hilversum, 99,792 .... G 4
Hindeloopen, †881 .... G 3
Hippolytushoef, 3,035 .. G 3
Hoek, 12,817 .... D 6
Hoek van Holland (Hook of
  Holland), 5,114 ... D 5
Hoensbroek, †22,703 .. H 7
Hof, †7,816 .... K 2
Holijsloot, 344 ..... C 4
Hollum, 890 .... H 2
Holwerd, 1,691 ...... H 2
Hoofddorp, 4,949 .... F 4
Hoogeveen, †37,485 .. J 3
Hoogezand, †30,189 .. K 2
Hoogkarspel, †3,681 .. G 3
Hook of Holland,
  5,114 .... D 5
Hoorn, †18,574 ...... G 3
Horst, †15,310 ...... H 6
Huissen, †9,101 ..... H 5
Huizen, †20,554 ..... G 4
Hulst, †6,699 .... E 6
IJlst, †1,932 .... H 2
IJmuiden, 3,587 ..... E 4
IJsselstein, †9,633 . F 4
IJzendijke, †2,492 .. D 6
Ilpendam, †2,955 ... C 4
Joure, 5,509 .... H 3
Kampen, 128,902 .... H 3
Katwijk aan Zee,
  †36,236 .... E 4
Kerkbuurt en Thij,
  †8,244 .... J 3
Kerkdriel, 3,122 ... G 5
Kerkrade, 148,150 .. J 7
Kesteren, †7,290 ... G 5
Kloosterveen, †17,296 .. K 3
Kollum, 2,543 ...... J 2
Koog aan de Zaan,
  16,114 .... A 4
Krimpen aan den IJssel,
  †17,801 .... F 4
Landsmeer, †6,511 .. C 4
Laren, 16,452 ...... G 4
Leek, †11,628 ...... J 2
Leerdam, 113,282 ... F 5
Leeuwarden, 100,006 . H 2
Leiden, 101,221 .... E 4
Lelystad, 716 ...... H 4
Lemmer, 4,399 ...... H 3
Lent, 2,692 .... H 5
Lisse, †17,049 ..... E 4
Lith, †4,698 .... G 5
Lochem, 19,452 ..... J 4
Lonneker, 1,599 .... K 4
Loon op Zand, †16,437 .. G 5
Losser, 18,713 ..... L 4
Maarssen, 114,734 .. F 4
Maasbree, 17,676 ... H 6
Maassluis, 125,878 . E 5
Maastricht, †93,927 . H 7
Makkum, 2,416 ...... G 2
Margraten, 12,844 .. H 7
Medemblik, 15,192 .. G 3
Meersen, 18,800 .... H 7
Meppel, †19,364 .... H 3
Middelburg, 130,211 . D 6
Middelharnis, †12,488 .. E 5
Middenmeer, 1,775 .. F 3
Millingen aan den Rijn,
  14,764 .... J 5
Moerdijk, 601 ...... F 5
Monnikendam, 16,014 . C 4
Montfoort, 12,392 .. G 4
Muiden, 15,724 ..... G 4
Muntendam, 13,695 .. K 2
Naaldwijk, 122,306 . E 4
Naarden, 117,447 ... G 4
Nagele, 766 .... H 3
Neede, 19,739 ..... K 4
Nes, 894 .... H 2
Nieuw-Buinen, 3,966 . K 3
Nieuw-Schoonebeek,
  1,602 .... L 3

Nieuwe Pekela, †5,163 .. L 2
Nieuwendam, 15,679 ... C 4
Nieuweschans, 11,846 .. L 2
Nieuwkoop, †7,835 .... F 4
Nijkerk, †17,718 ..... H 4
Nijmegen, 148,790 .... H 5
Nijmegen, *210,865 ... H 5
Nijverdal, 11,986 .... J 4
Noordwijk, 120,925 ... E 4
Norg, 15,386 .... J 2
Numansdorp, 15,169 .. E 5
Nunspeet, 7,103 ..... H 4
Odoorn, †11,730 ..... K 3
Oisterwijk, †13,797 .. G 5
Oldenzaal, †22,604 .. K 4
Oost, †8,325 .... J 4
Otterlo, 984 ...... H 4
Ommen, 114,712 .... J 3
Omstwedde, 1,867 .. K 2
Oostburg, 14,064 .. C 6
Oosterend, 118 ... G 2
Oosterhout, †31,826 . F 5
Oostmahorn, 331 .. J 2
Oost-Vlieland, 695 . F 2
Oostzaan, 14,869 .. A 4
Oosterum, 13,339 .. K 4
Oss, †40,085 ...... H 5
Oud-Beijerland, 110,114 .. E 5
Oude-Pekela, †6,385 . K 2
Oude-Tonge, 2,459 . E 5
Oudenbosch, 19,346 . E 5
Oudeschild, 939 ... F 2
Oudewater, 14,846 . F 4
Overloon, 1,007 ... H 5
Purmerend, 123,288 . F 4
Putten, †15,726 ... H 4
Raalte, †19,885 ... J 4
Renkum, 133,619 .. H 5
Reusel, 16,144 ... G 6
Rheden, †48,713 .. J 4
Rhenen, †14,480 .. G 5
Ridderkerk, †41,899 . F 5
Rijnsburg, 18,600 . E 4
Rijssen, †17,360 . J 4
Rijswijk, 150,172 . E 4
Roden, †12,444 ... J 2
Roermond, 135,850 . H 6
Roosendaal, 145,935 . E 5
Rotterdam, 686,586 . E 5
Rotterdam, *1,052,871 . E 5
Rutten, 491 .... H 3
Ruurlo, 16,823 .... J 4
's Gravendeel, 15,830 . E 5
's Gravenhage (The Hague)
  (cap.), 550,613 .. E 4
's Gravenhage, *702,296 . E 4
's Gravenzande, †12,907 . E 4
's Heerenberg, 5,196 . J 5
's Hertogenbosch, 181,574 . G 5
's Hertogenbosch,
  *193,356 .... G 5
Sappemeer, 130,189 . K 2
Schagen, 16,772 ... F 3
Scheveningen, 90,015 . E 4
Schiedam, 183,049 . E 5
Schiermonnikoog, 1814 . J 1
Schijndel, 116,362 . H 5
Schiphol, 3,368 ... A 5
Schoonebeek, †7,426 . L 3
Schoonhoven, †7,565 . F 5
Sint Annaland, †2,826 . D 5
Sint Jacobiparochie, 1,246 . H 2
Sittard, 133,887 ... H 6
Sliedrecht, †19,868 . F 5
Slochteren, †12,901 . K 2
Sloten, Friesland, †751 . H 3
Sloten, North Holland,
  1,332 .... B 5
Sloterdijk, 1,215 .. B 5
Sluis, †2,810 ..... C 6
Smilde (Kloosterveen),
  †7,296 .... K 3
Soest, †35,713 .... G 4
Soesterberg, 4,627 . G 4
Stadskanaal, †32,829 . L 3
Staphorst, †10,498 . J 3
Staveren, 1934 ... G 3
Steenbergen, †12,512 . E 5
Steenwijk, †12,226 . H 3
Steenwijkerwold (Kerkbuurt
  en Thij), †8,244 . J 3
Stiens, 2,008 ..... H 2

Tegelen, †18,168 .... J 6
Ter Apel, 2,508 .... L 3
Termunten, 14,721 .... K 2
Terneuzen, †22,014 ... D 6
Tholen, 19,318 .... E 5
Tiel, †21,789 .... G 5
Tilburg, 152,589 ..... G 6
Tilburg, *268,395 .... G 6
Twello, 5,929 .... J 4
Uden, †23,711 .... H 5
Uitgeest, †7,151 ..... F 3
Uithoorn, †17,492 .... F 4
Uithuizen, 14,939 .... K 2
Ulrum, 13,631 .... J 2
Urk, 8,027 .... H 3
Utrecht, 278,966 ..... G 4
Utrecht, *401,981 .... G 4
Vaals, †10,338 ...... H 7
Valkenswaard, 123,238 . H 6
Van Ewijcksluis, 231 . F 3
Veendam, †23,709 ..... K 2
Veenendaal, 129,637 .. G 4
Veenhuizen, 14,097 .. J 2
Veghel, †18,374 ..... H 5
Velp, 19,488 .... J 5
Velsen, †67,580 ..... F 4
Venlo, †62,694 ...... J 6
Venlo, *95,516 ...... J 6
Venraij, †26,056 .... H 6
Vianen, 18,173 ...... G 5
Vlaardingen, †79,085 . E 5
Vlagtwedde, †16,622 . L 3
Vlijmen, †12,314 .... G 5
Vlissingen (Flushing),
  †40,197 .... C 6
Volendam, 10,123 ... G 4
Voorburg, 145,011 ... E 4
Voorst, 121,379 ..... J 4
Vorden, 16,893 ...... J 4
Vreeswijk, 15,393 .. G 4
Vriesveen, †14,658 . K 4
Vught, 122,633 ..... G 5
Waalwijk, 123,304 .. G 5
Wageningen, 126,572 . H 5
Wamel, 18,217 ...... H 5
Weesp, †17,261 .... G 4
West-Terschelling, 14,294 . G 2
Westkapelle, 12,478 . C 5
Westzaan, 14,502 .. A 4
Wierden, †17,653 .. K 4
Wierum, 628 .... H 2
Wijhe, 16,225 ..... J 4
Wijk aan Zee, 2,414 . E 4
Wijk bij Duurstede, 15,342 . G 5
Wijk en Aalburg, 13,583 . G 5
Willemstad, 4,280 . E 5
Willemstad, 12,306 . F 5
Winkel, 12,450 .... F 3
Winschoten, 118,043 . L 2
Winsum, 13,631 ... K 2
Winterswijk, 126,230 . K 5
Woensdrecht, 17,892 . E 6
Woerden, 118,448 .. F 4
Wolvega, 6,620 ... H 3
Workum, 14,019 .. G 3
Wormerveer, 14,804 . F 4
Yerseke, 4,799 ... E 6
Zaandam, 163,535 . B 4
Zaandijk, 15,696 . B 4
Zaltbommel, †17,092 . G 5
Zandvoort, †15,451 . E 4
Zeist, †55,619 ... G 4
Zevenbergen, †10,270 . E 5
Zierikzee, 17,842 . D 5
Zoutkamp, 1,083 . J 2
Zundert, †12,124 . F 6
Zutphen, †27,810 . J 4
Zwanenburg, 6,999 . B 4
Zwartsluis, 14,091 . H 3
Zwijndrecht, †31,761 . F 5
Zwolle, †76,167 .. J 3

OTHER FEATURES

Alkmaardermeer (lake) .. F 3
Ameland (isl.), †2,899 .. H 2
Bergumer (lake) ...... J 2
Beulaker Wijde (lake) .. H 3
Borndiep (channel) ... H 2
De Fluessen (lake) ... G 3
De Peel (region), 69,356 .. H 6

De Twente (reg.), 491,403 .. K 4
De Zaan (river) .... B 4
Dollart (bay) .... L 2
Dommel (river) .... H 6
Duiveland (isl.), 13,317 . D 5
East Flevoland Polder,
  863 .... H 4
Eastern Scheldt
  (estuary) .... D 5
Eijerlandsche Gat
  (strait) .... F 2
Friesche Gat (channel) . J 2
Galgenberg (hill) ... H 6
Goeree (isl.) .... D 5
Grevelingen (strait) . D 5
Griend (isl.) .... G 2
Groninger Wad (sound) . J 2
Groote IJ Polder, 20 . B 4
Haarlemmermeer Polder,
  59,966 .... B 5
Haringvliet (strait) . D 5
Het IJ (estuary) .... C 4
Hoek van Holland (cape) . D 5
Hondsrug (hills) .... K 3
Houtrak Polder, 339 . A 4
Hunse (river) .... K 3
IJmeer (bay) .... C 4
IJssel (river) ...... J 4
IJsselmeer (lake) ... G 3
Lauwers (channel) .. J 1
Lauwers Zee (bay) .. J 2
Lek (river) .... F 5
Lemelerberg (hill) . J 4
Linde (river) ..... H 3
Lower Rhine (river) . J 5
Maas (river) ...... G 5
Mark (river) ...... F 5
Marken (isl.), 1,865 . G 4
Markerwaard Polder .. G 3
Marsdiep (channel) . F 3
Noordergat (channel) . F 2
North Sea .... E 3
North Beveland (isl.),
  6,777 .... D 5
North East Polder,
  31,929 .... H 3
North Holland (canal) . C 4
North Sea (canal) ... E 4
Old Rhine (river) .. F 4
Ooster Eems (channel) . K 1
Oostzaan Polder, 4,869 . B 4
Orange (canal) ... K 3
Overflakkee (isl.), 27,814 . E 5
Pinkegat (channel) . H 2
Regge (river) .... J 4
Roer (river) ..... H 6
Rottumeroog (isl.), 3 . J 1
Schiermonnikoog (isl.),
  814 .... J 1
Schouwen (isl.), 9,731 . D 5
Simonszand (isl.) . J 1
Slotermeer (lake) . H 3
Sneekermeer (lake) . H 3
South Beveland (isl.),
  61,966 .... D 6
South Flevoland Polder,
  14,925 .... G 4
Terschelling (isl.), 4,294 . G 2
Texel (isl.), 11,394 . F 2
Tjeukemeer (lake) . H 3
Vaalserberg (mt.) . H 7
Vecht (river) ..... J 4
Vechte (river) .... J 3
Veeregat (channel) . D 5
Veluwe (region), 457,834 . H 4
Vlie Stroom (strait) . G 2
Vlieland (isl.), †933 . F 2
Voorne (isl.), 22,742 . D 5
Waal (river) ...... H 5
Waddenzee (sound) . G 2
Walcheren (isl.), 89,793 . C 5
West Frisian (isls.),
  18,336 .... F 2
Wester Eems (channel) . K 1
Western Scheldt (De Honte)
  (estuary) .... D 6
Westgat (channel) . F 3
Wieringermeer Polder,
  16,562 .... G 3
Wilhelmina (canal) . G 5
Willems (canal) ... H 6

*City and suburbs.
†Populations of communes.

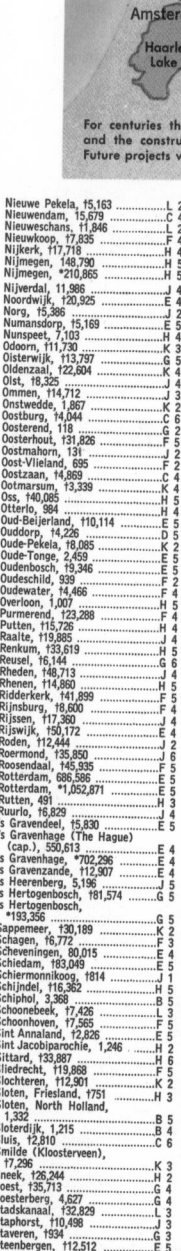

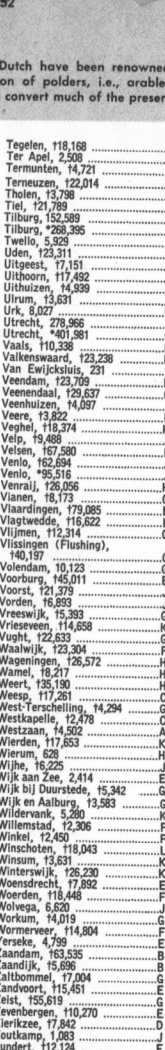

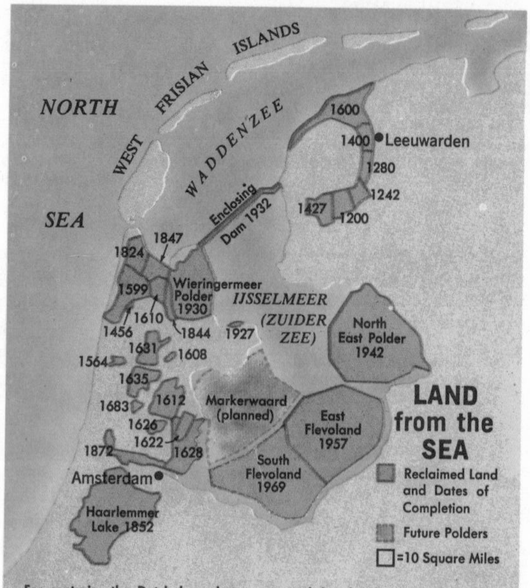

LAND from the SEA

■ Reclaimed Land
  and Dates of
  Completion

■ Future Polders

□ = 10 Square Miles

For centuries the Dutch have been renowned for the drainage of marshes and the construction of polders, i.e., arable land reclaimed from the sea. Future projects will convert much of the present IJsselmeer to agricultural land.

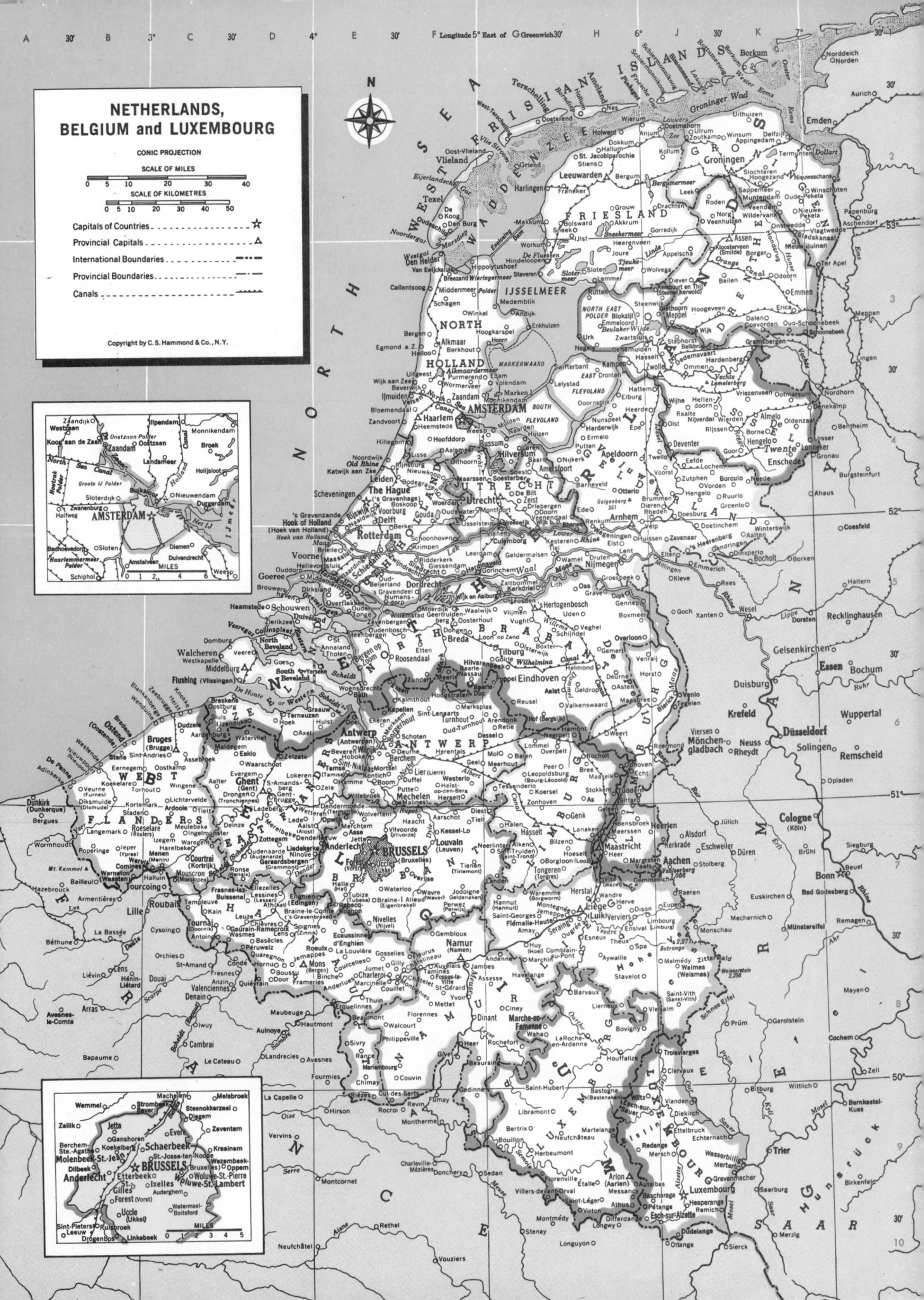

NETHERLANDS, BELGIUM and LUXEMBOURG

CONIC PROJECTION

SCALE OF MILES

SCALE OF KILOMETRES

Capitals of Countries . . . . ☆
Provincial Capitals . . . . △
International Boundaries . . . .
Provincial Boundaries . . . .
Canals . . . .

Copyright by C.S. Hammond & Co., N.Y.

FRANCE

CONIC PROJECTION

SCALE OF MILES

SCALE OF KILOMETRES

Capitals of Countries.................☆
Capitals of Departments.............△
International Boundaries...........
Department Boundaries...........
Canals

© C.S. HAMMOND & Co., N.Y.

PARIS and ENVIRONS

CORSICA
Same Scale as Main Map

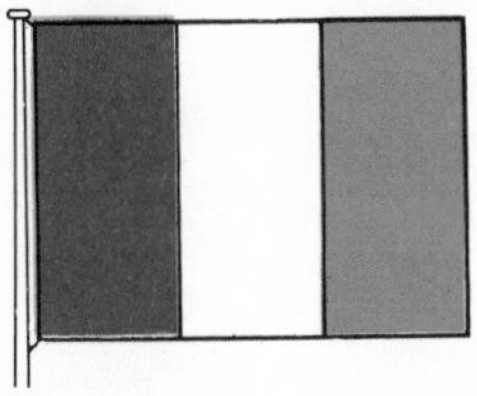

AREA 212,841 sq. mi.
POPULATION 50,770,000
CAPITAL Paris
LARGEST CITY Paris
HIGHEST POINT Mont Blanc 15,771 ft.
MONETARY UNIT franc
MAJOR LANGUAGE French
MAJOR RELIGION Roman Catholicism

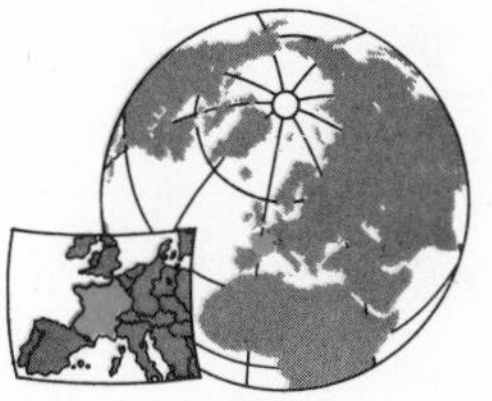

Topography

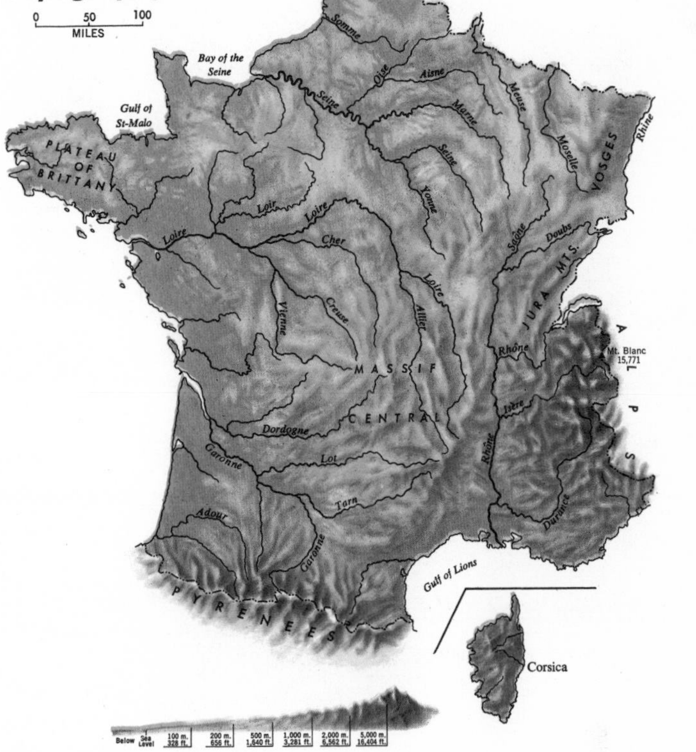

DEPARTMENTS

Ain, 339,262 F 4
Aisne, 526,346 E 3
Allier, 386,533 E 4
Alpes-Maritimes, 722,070 G 6
Ardèche, 256,927 F 5
Ardennes, 309,380 F 3
Ariège, 138,478 D 6
Aube, 270,325 E 3
Aude, 278,323 E 6
Aveyron, 281,568 E 5
Bas-Rhin, 827,367 G 3
Basses-Alpes, 104,813 G 5
Belfort (terr.), 118,450 G 4
Bouches-du-Rhône, 1,470,271 F 6
Calvados, 519,695 C 3
Cantal, 169,330 E 5
Charente, 331,016 D 5
Charente-Maritime, 483,622 C 5
Cher, 304,601 E 4
Corrèze, 237,858 D 5
Corsica (Corse), 269,831 G 6
Côte-d'Or, 421,192 F 4
Côtes-du-Nord, 506,102 B 3
Creuse, 156,876 D 4
Deux-Sèvres, 326,462 C 4
Dordogne, 374,073 D 5
Doubs, 426,363 G 4
Drôme, 342,891 F 5
Essonne, 674,157 E 3
Eure, 383,385 D 3
Eure-et-Loir, 302,207 D 3
Finistère, 768,929 A 3
Gard, 478,544 F 6
Gers, 181,577 D 6
Gironde, 1,009,390 C 5
Haut-Rhin, 585,018 G 4
Haute-Garonne, 690,712 D 6
Haute-Loire, 208,337 E 5
Haute-Marne, 214,336 F 3
Haute-Saône, 214,176 G 4
Haute-Savoie, 378,550 G 5
Haute-Vienne, 341,589 D 5
Hautes-Alpes, 91,790 G 5
Hautes-Pyrénées, 225,730 D 6
Hauts-de-Seine 1.461.619 A 2
Hérault, 591,397 E 6
Ille-et-Vilaine, 652,722 C 3
Indre, 247,178 D 4
Indre-et-Loire, 437,870 D 4
Isère, 768,450 F 5
Jura, 233,547 F 4
Landes, 277,381 C 5
Loir-et-Cher, 267,896 D 4
Loire, 722,383 F 5
Loire-Atlantique, 861,452 C 4
Loiret, 430,629 E 4
Lot, 151,198 D 5
Lot-et-Garonne, 290,592 D 5
Lozère, 77,258 E 5
Maine-et-Loire, 584,709 C 4
Manche, 451,939 C 3
Marne, 485,388 F 3
Mayenne, 252,762 C 3
Meurthe-et-Moselle, 705,413 G 3
Meuse, 209,513 F 3
Morbihan, 540,474 B 4
Moselle, 971,314 G 3
Nièvre, 247,702 E 4
Nord, 2,417,899 E 2
Oise, 540,988 E 3
Orne, 288,524 C 3
Paris, 2,590,771 B 2
Pas-de-Calais, 1,397,159 E 2
Puy-de-Dôme, 547,743 E 5
Pyrénées-Atlantiques, 508,734 C 6
Pyrénées-Orientales, 281,976 E 6
Rhône, 1,325,611 F 5
Saône-et-Loire, 550,362 F 4
Sarthe, 461,839 D 3
Savoie, 288,921 G 5
Seine-et-Marne, 604,340 E 3
Seine-Maritime, 1,113,977 D 3
Seine-Saint-Denis, 1,251,792 B 1
Somme, 512,113 E 3
Tarn, 332,011 E 6
Tarn-et-Garonne, 183,572 D 5
Val-de-Marne, 1,121,340 B 2
Val-d'Oise, 693,269 E 3
Var, 555,926 G 6
Vaucluse, 353,966 F 6
Vendée, 421,250 C 4
Vienne, 340,256 D 4
Vosges, 388,201 G 3
Yonne, 283,376 E 4
Yvelines, 853,386 D 3

CITIES and TOWNS

Abbeville, 23,770 D 2
Agde, 8,812 E 6
Agen, 34,592 D 5
Aix-en-Provence, 74,948 F 6
Aix-les-Bains, 20,594 G 5
Ajaccio, 38,776 F 7
Albert, 10,937 E 2
Albertville, 15,422 G 5
Albi, 38,867 E 6
Alençon, 30,368 D 3
Aléria, 1,000 G 7
Alès, 31,948 E 5
Ambérieu-en-Bugey, 8,570 F 5
Amboise, 8,408 D 4
Amiens, 116,107 D 3
Angers, 127,415 C 4
Angoulême, 46,584 D 5
Annecy, 53,361 G 5
Annonay, 19,591 F 5
Antibes, 47,393 G 6
Antony, 56,556 B 2
Apt, 8,502 F 6
Arcachon, 14,852 C 5
Argentan, 14,418 D 3
Argenteuil, 87,106 A 1
Arles, 33,575 F 6
Armentières, 24,460 E 2
Arras, 48,494 E 2
Asnières, 79,942 A 1
Aubagne, 17,055 F 6
Aubenas, 10,480 F 5
Aubervilliers, 73,559 B 1
Aubusson, 5,641 E 4
Auch, 18,072 D 6
Audincourt, 13,487 G 4
Aulnay-sous-Bois, 61,384 B 1
Auray, 8,180 B 4
Aurignac, 783 D 6
Aurillac, 26,776 E 5
Autun, 17,194 F 4
Auxerre, 33,700 E 4
Avallon, 6,615 E 4
Avesnes-sur-Helpe, 6,253 F 2
Avignon, 78,871 F 6
Avion, 22,390 E 2
Avranches, 9,751 C 3
Bagnères-de-Bigorre, 9,139 D 6
Bagnères-de-Luchon, 4,079 D 6
Bagnolet, 33,607 B 2
Bagnols-sur-Cèze, 15,336 F 5
Bar-le-Duc, 18,874 F 3
Bar-sur-Seine, 2,642 F 3
Barfleur, 825 C 3
Bastia, 48,800 G 6
Bayeux, 11,190 C 3
Bayonne, 39,761 C 6
Beaucaire, 8,820 F 6
Beaune, 16,441 F 4
Beauvais, 46,284 E 3
Bédarieux, 6,929 E 6
Belfort, 53,001 G 4
Belley, 5,958 F 5
Berck, 13,658 D 2
Bergerac, 24,184 D 5
Berney, 9,298 D 3
Besançon, 107,939 G 4
Bessèges, 5,421 F 5
Béthune, 26,144 E 2
Béziers, 74,517 E 6
Biarritz, 26,628 C 6
Blois, 39,279 D 4
Bobigny, 39,321 B 1
Bolbec, 12,517 D 3
Bondy, 51,555 B 1
Bordeaux, 263,808 C 5
Bordeaux, †648,000 C 5
Boulogne-Billancourt, 108,846 A 2
Boulogne-sur-Mer, 49,064 D 2
Bourg-en-Bresse, 35,064 F 4
Bourges, 67,137 E 4
Bressuire, 8,010 C 4
Brest, 150,696 A 3
Briançon, 7,551 G 5
Briare, 4,725 E 4
Brignoles, 8,010 G 6
Brive-la-Gaillarde, 45,314 D 5
Bruay-en-Artois, 38,608 E 2
Caen, 106,790 C 3
Cahors, 17,775 D 5
Calais, 70,153 D 2
Caluire-et-Cuire, 37,541 F 5
Calvi, 2,523 F 6
Cambrai, 37,290 E 2
Cannes, 66,590 G 6
Carcassonne, 40,580 D 6
Carentan, 5,207 C 3
Carmaux, 13,423 E 5
Carpentras, 18,092 F 5
Castelnaudary, 8,550 E 6
Castelsarrasin, 7,912 D 6
Castres, 35,975 E 6
Cavaillon, 14,815 F 6
Cayeux-sur-Mer, 2,489 D 2
Chalon-sur-Saône, 47,004 F 4
Châlons-sur-Marne, 48,558 F 3
Chambéry, 49,858 F 5
Chambord, 200 D 4
Chamonix-Mont Blanc, 5,907 G 5
Champigny-sur-Marne, 70,353 C 2
Chantilly, 10,156 E 3
Charenton-le-Pont, 22,220 B 2
Charleville-Mézières, 55,230 F 3
Chartres, 34,128 D 3
Château-du-Loir, 5,239 D 4
Château-Gontier, 7,881 C 4
Château-Renault, 5,082 D 4
Château-Thierry, 10,858 E 3
Châteaubriant, 11,196 C 4
Châteaudun, 13,715 D 3
Châteauneuf-sur-Loire, 4,603 E 4
Châteauroux, 48,867 D 4
Châtellerault, 33,491 D 4
Châtillon, 24,468 B 2
Châtillon-sur-Seine, 6,128 F 4
Chatou, 22,495 A 1
Chaumont, 25,602 F 3
Chauny, 13,714 E 3
Chelles, 22,111 C 1
Cherbourg, 37,933 C 3
Chinon, 5,435 D 4
Choisy-le-Roi, 41,080 B 2
Cholet, 40,224 C 4
Clamart, 54,866 A 2
Clermont, 7,119 E 3
Clermont-Ferrand, 145,856 E 5
Clichy, 52,398 B 1
Cluny, 3,552 F 4
Cluses, 12,391 G 4
Cognac, 21,137 C 5
Colmar, 58,623 G 3
Colombes, 80,224 A 1
Commentry, 8,129 E 4
Commercy, 7,043 F 3
Compiègne, 28,881 E 3
Concarneau, 16,458 A 4
Cosne-sur-Loire, 8,931 E 4
Coudekerque-Branche, 22,972 E 2
Coulommiers. 11.182 E 3

HISTORIC PROVINCES

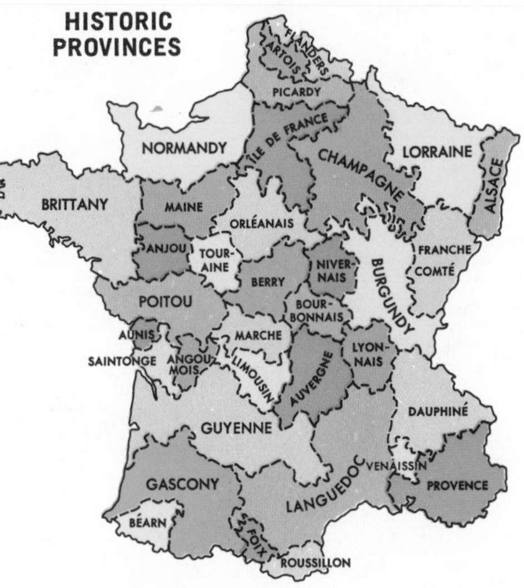

A resident of the city of Caen thinks of himself as a Norman rather than as a citizen of the modern department of Calvados. In spite of the passing of nearly two centuries, the historic provinces which existed before 1790 command the local patriotism of most Frenchmen.

Courbevoie, 57,998 A 1
Coutances, 8,599 C 3
Coutras, 4,251 C 5
Creil, 31,792 E 3
Crépy-en-Valois, 8,506 E 3
Créteil, 48,757 B 2
Cusset, 12,286 E 4
Dax, 18,185 C 6
Deauville, 5,103 C 3
Decazeville, 9,581 E 5
Denain, 27,840 E 2
Dieppe, 29,829 D 3
Digne, 11,973 G 5
Digoin, 9,585 F 4
Dijon, 143,120 F 4
Dinan, 12,999 B 3
Dinard, 9,042 B 3
Dôle, 25,620 F 4
Domrémy-la-Pucelle, 184 F 3
Douai, 47,347 E 2
Douarnenez, 18,442 A 3
Draguignan, 16,139 G 6
Drancy, 69,226 B 1
Dreux, 28,156 D 3
Dunkirk (Dunkerque), 26,038 E 2
Elbeuf, 19,110 D 3
Embrun, 3,986 G 5
Épernay, 26,094 E 3
Épinal, 36,219 G 3
Épinay-sur-Seine, 41,538 B 1
Étampes, 15,542 E 3
Étaples, 9,092 D 2
Eu, 7,866 D 3
Évreux, 41,004 D 3
Évry, 7,047 E 3
Falaise, 6,977 C 3
Fécamp, 21,098 D 3
Figeac, 8,462 D 5
Firminy, 24,545 F 5
Flers, 16,677 C 3
Foix, 9,061 D 6
Fontainebleau, 17,565 E 3
Fontenay-le-Comte, 10,884 C 4
Fontenay-sous-Bois, 38,737 C 2
Forbach, 23,062 G 3
Fougères, 25,745 C 3
Fourmies, 14,895 F 2
Fréjus, 22,567 G 6
Gagny, 35,745 C 1
Gap, 22,027 G 5
Gardanne, 12,601 F 6
Gennevillers, 45,925 B 1
Gentilly, 18,638 B 2
Gex, 3,078 G 4
Gien, 11,655 E 4
Gisors, 7,024 D 3
Givet, 7,697 F 2
Givors, 17,545 F 5
Granville, 12,315 C 3
Grasse, 24,398 G 6
Graulhet, 10,318 E 6
Gray, 7,782 F 4
Grenoble, 161,230 F 5
Guebwiller, 10,684 G 4
Guéret. 12,441 D 4
Guingamp, 9,091 B 3
Guise, 6,732 E 3
Haguenau, 22,335 G 3
Ham, 5,565 E 3
Harfleur, 15,503 D 3
Hautmont, 17,818 F 2
Hayange, 10,218 F 3
Hazebrouck, 16,768 E 2
Hendaye, 7,536 C 6
Hénin-Liétard, 25,067 E 2
Hennebont, 7,605 B 4
Héricourt, 7,376 G 4
Hirson, 11,764 F 3
Honfleur, 9,017 D 3
Hyères, 27,600 G 6
Issoire, 11,745 E 5
Issoudun, 14,559 D 4
Issy-les-Moulineaux, 50,260 A 2
Istres, 8,713 F 6
Ivry-sur-Seine, 60,342 B 2
Joigny, 9,609 E 3
La Baule-Escoublac, 11,962 B 4
La Ciotat, 19,485 F 6
La Courneuve, 42,812 B 1
La Flèche, 9,536 C 4
La Grand-Combe, 8,608 E 5
La Roche-sur-Yon, 32,279 C 4
La Rochelle, 72,075 C 4
La Seyne-sur-Mer, 42,958 F 6
La Tour-du-Pin, 5,649 F 5
L'Aigle, 7,478 D 3
Landerneau, 12,356 B 3
Langeac, 4,584 E 5
Langres, 8,945 F 4
Lannion, 10,066 B 3
Laon, 25,623 E 3
Laval, 45,051 C 3
Lavelanet, 8,512 E 6
Le Blanc-Mesnil, 48,212 B 1
Le Bourget, 9,625 B 1
Le Cateau, 8,922 E 2
Le Chesnay, 13,586 A 2
Le Creusot, 33,581 F 4
Le Croisic, 4,092 B 4
Le Havre, 198,021 C 3
Le Mans, 140,520 C 3
Le Puy, 24,816 F 5
Le Teil, 7,872 F 5
Le Tourquet-Paris-Plage, 4,403 D 2
Le Tréport, 6,194 D 2
Lens, 41,800 E 2
Les Andelys, 6,292 D 3
Les Sables-d'Olonne, 17,856 B 4
Levallois-Perret, 58,890 B 1
Lézignan-Corbières, 7,101 E 6
Libourne, 19,981 C 5
Liévin, 35,733 E 2
Lille, 189,697 E 2
Lille, †1,042,000 E 2
Limoges, 127,605 D 5
Limoux, 9,150 E 6
Lisieux, 23,337 D 3
Livry-Gargan, 32,015 C 1
Lodève, 6,899 E 6
Longwy, 21,052 F 3
Lons-le-Saunier, 18,649 F 4
Lorient, 66,023 B 4
Loudun, 6,118 D 4
Lourdes, 17,627 C 6
Louviers, 15,159 D 3
Lunel, 10,178 E 6
Lunéville, 22,961 G 3
Luxeuil-les-Bains, 9,203 G 4
Lyon, 524,500 F 5
Lyon, †1,305,000 F 5
Mâcon, 33,266 F 4
Maisons-Alfort, 53,118 B 2
Maisons-Laffitte, 24,041 A 1
Malakoff, 36,198 B 2
Manosque, 13,352 G 6
Mantes-la-Jolie, 25,842 D 3
Marmande, 12,145 C 5
Marseille, 880,527 F 6
Marseille, †1,015,000 F 6
Martigues, 17,771 F 6
Maubeuge, 31,992 F 2
Mayenne, 10,010 C 3
Mazamet, 14,650 E 6
Meaux, 29,966 E 3
Melun, 33,345 E 3
Mende, 9,424 E 5
Menton, 23,401 G 6
Metz, 105,533 G 3
Meudon, 30,735 A 2
Millau, 21,420 E 5
Moissac, 7,694 D 5
Mont-de-Marsan, 22,771 C 6
Mont-Dore, 2,045 E 5
Mont-Saint-Michel, 72 C 3
Montargis, 18,087 E 3
Montauban, 33,945 D 5
Montbéliard, 23,402 G 4
Montbrison, 8,733 E 5
Montceau-les-Mines, 18,621 F 4
Montdidier, 5,785 E 3
Montélimar, 23,831 F 5
Montfort, 2,563 C 3
Montigny-les-Metz, 24,417 G 3
Montluçon, 57,638 E 4
Montpellier, 152,105 E 6
Montreuil, 95,420 B 2
Montrouge, 44,788 B 2
Morlaix, 16,750 B 3
Moulins, 25,778 E 4
Moûtiers, 4,066 G 5
Moyeuvre-Grande, 14,559 G 3
Mulhouse, 115,632 G 4
Muret, 10,515 D 6
Nancy, 121,910 G 3
Nanterre, 90,124 A 1
Nantes, 253,105 C 4
Narbonne, 35,236 E 6
Nemours, 8,081 E 3
Neufchâteau, 7,656 F 3
Neufchâtel-en-Bray, 5,734 D 3
Neuilly-sur-Seine, 70,787 B 1
Nevers, 42,092 E 4
Nice, 301,400 G 6
Nîmes, 115,561 F 6
Niort, 46,749 C 4
Nogent-le-Rotrou, 11,040 D 3
Nogent-sur-Seine, 4,271 E 3
Noisy-le-Sec, 34,058 B 1
Noyon, 11,567 E 3
Nyons, 4,311 F 5
Oloron-Sainte-Marie, 12,597 C 6
Orange, 17,582 F 5
Orléans, 94,382 D 3
Orly, 30,151 B 2
Orthez, 8,778 C 6
Oullins, 26,520 F 5
Oyonnax, 19,571 F 4
Pamiers, 13,183 D 6
Pantin, 47,580 B 1
Paray-le-Monial, 10,324 F 4
Paris (cap.), 2,580,010 B 2
Paris, *7,953,065 B 2
Paris, †9,283,000 B 2
Parthenay, 11,177 C 4
Pau, 71,865 C 6
Périgueux, 36,991 D 5
Perpignan, 100,086 E 6
Pessac, 35,343 C 5
Ploërmel, 3,720 B 4
Poitiers, 68,082 D 4
Pont-à-Mousson, 13,283 G 3
Pont-l'Abbé, 6,227 A 4
Pont-l'Évêque, 2,823 D 3
Pontarlier, 16,250 G 4
Pontivy, 9,674 B 3
Pontoise, 16,633 E 3
Port-de-Bouc, 13,447 F 6
Port-Louis, 3,921 B 4

(continued on following page)

(continued)

OTHER FEATURES

*City and suburbs.
†Population of metropolitan area.

MONACO

CITIES and TOWNS

MONACO
AREA 368 acres
POPULATION 23,035

WINE
REGIONS
Caen
CALVADOS
(distilled from cider)
Reims
CHAMPAGNE
ALSACE
Colmar
Chablis
BURGUNDY
Côte d'Or
Anjou
Touraine
Angers
Tours
POUILLY
SANCERRE
LOIRE VALLEY
QUINCY
REUILLY
Beaune
Mâconnais
JURA
Mâcon
COGNAC
Cognac
BORDEAUX
Bordeaux
Bergerac
CÔTES DE DURAS
Valence
CÔTES
DU
RHÔNE
GAILLAC
ARMAGNAC
Auch
LANGUEDOC
Avignon
PROVENCE
Pau
JURANÇON
LIMOUX
ROUSSILLON
Béziers
Toulon

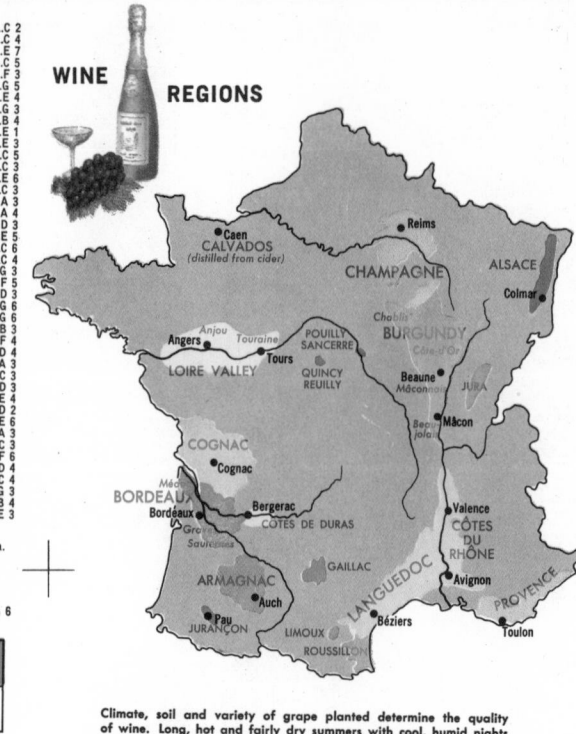

Climate, soil and variety of grape planted determine the quality of wine. Long, hot and fairly dry summers with cool, humid nights constitute an ideal climate. The nature of the soil is such a determining influence that identical grapes planted in Bordeaux, Burgundy and Champagne, will yield wines of widely different types.

Agriculture, Industry and Resources

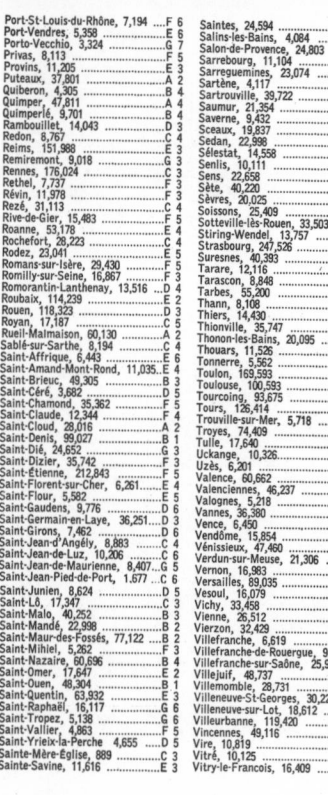

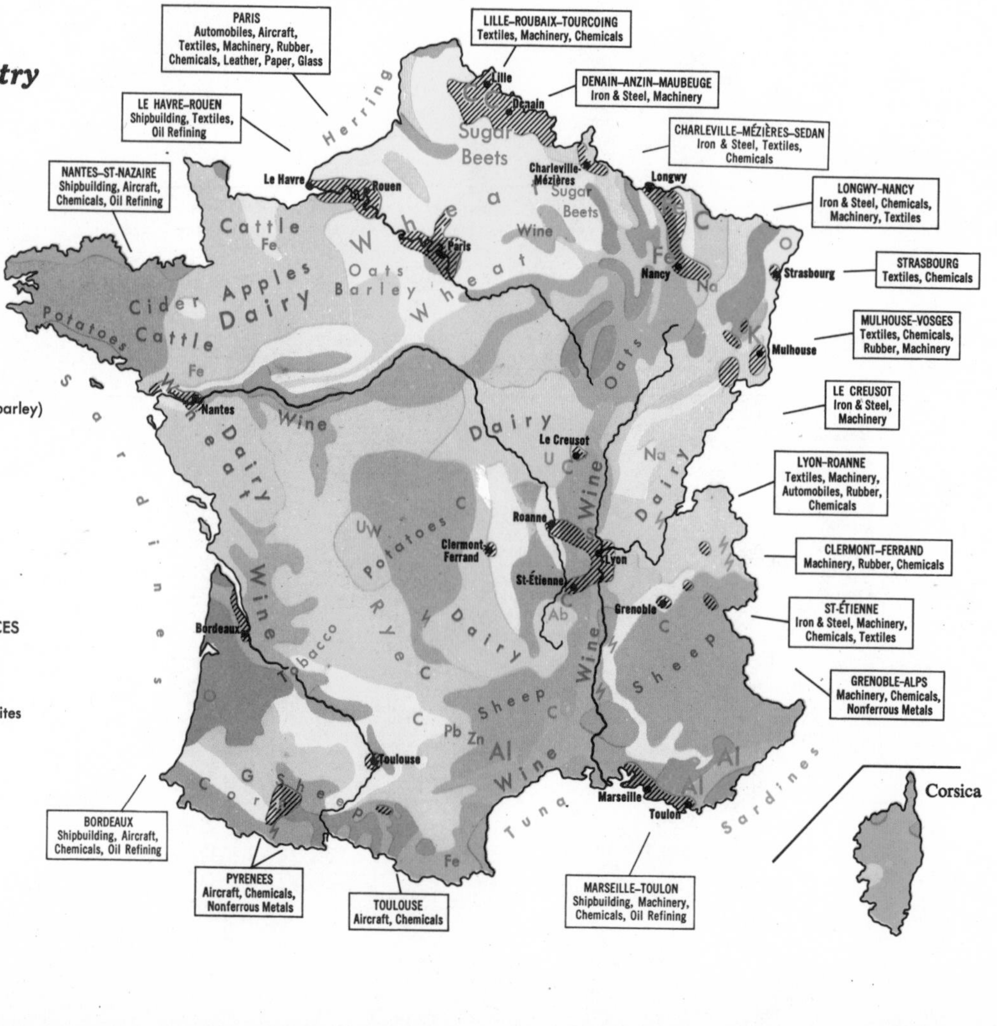

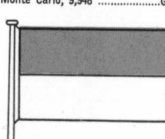

PARIS
Automobiles, Aircraft, Textiles, Machinery, Rubber, Chemicals, Leather, Paper, Glass
LILLE-ROUBAIX-TOURCOING
Textiles, Machinery, Chemicals
DENAIN-ANZIN-MAUBEUGE
Iron & Steel, Machinery
LE HAVRE-ROUEN
Shipbuilding, Textiles, Oil Refining
CHARLEVILLE-MÉZIÈRES-SEDAN
Iron & Steel, Textiles, Chemicals
NANTES-ST-NAZAIRE
Shipbuilding, Aircraft, Chemicals, Oil Refining
LONGWY-NANCY
Iron & Steel, Chemicals, Machinery, Textiles
STRASBOURG
Textiles, Chemicals
MULHOUSE-VOSGES
Textiles, Chemicals, Rubber, Machinery
LE CREUSOT
Iron & Steel, Machinery
LYON-ROANNE
Textiles, Machinery, Automobiles, Rubber, Chemicals
CLERMONT-FERRAND
Machinery, Rubber, Chemicals
ST-ÉTIENNE
Iron & Steel, Machinery, Chemicals, Textiles
GRENOBLE-ALPS
Machinery, Chemicals, Nonferrous Metals
BORDEAUX
Shipbuilding, Aircraft, Chemicals, Oil Refining
PYRENEES
Aircraft, Chemicals, Nonferrous Metals
TOULOUSE
Aircraft, Chemicals
MARSEILLE-TOULON
Shipbuilding, Machinery, Chemicals, Oil Refining
Herring
Sardines
Tuna
Lille
Denain
Le Havre
Rouen
Paris
Charleville-Mézières
Longwy
Nancy
Strasbourg
Mulhouse
Nantes
Le Creusot
Roanne
Clermont-Ferrand
Lyon
St-Étienne
Grenoble
Bordeaux
Toulouse
Marseille
Toulon
Corsica
Sugar Beets
Cattle
Cider Apples
Dairy
Potatoes
Wheat
Oats
Barley
Wine
Potatoes
Rye
Tobacco
Sheep
Corn

DOMINANT LAND USE

- Cereals (chiefly wheat)
- Cereals (chiefly rye, oats, barley)
- Dairy
- Pasture Livestock
- Truck Farming, Horticulture
- Grapes, Wine
- Forests

MAJOR MINERAL OCCURRENCES

Ab	Asbestos	O	Petroleum
Al	Bauxite	Pb	Lead
C	Coal	S	Sulfur, Pyrites
Fe	Iron Ore	U	Uranium
G	Natural Gas	W	Tungsten
K	Potash	Zn	Zinc
Na	Salt		

Water Power
Major Industrial Areas

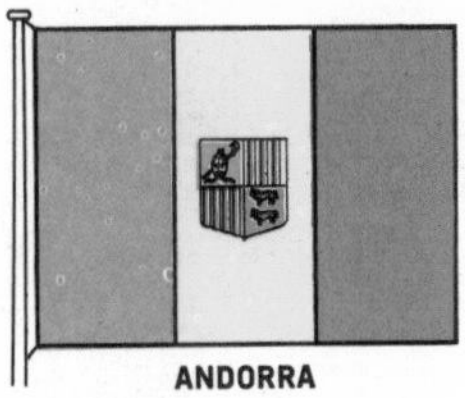

ANDORRA

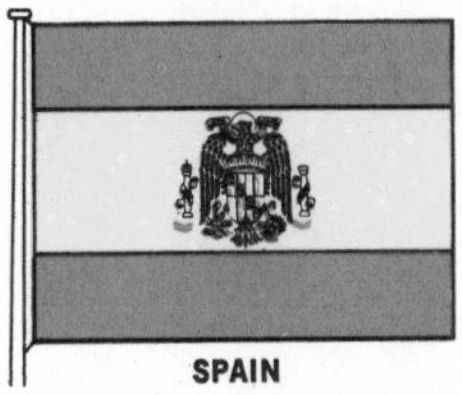

SPAIN

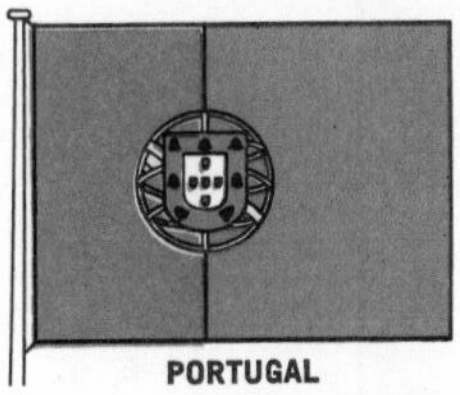

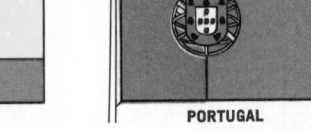

PORTUGAL

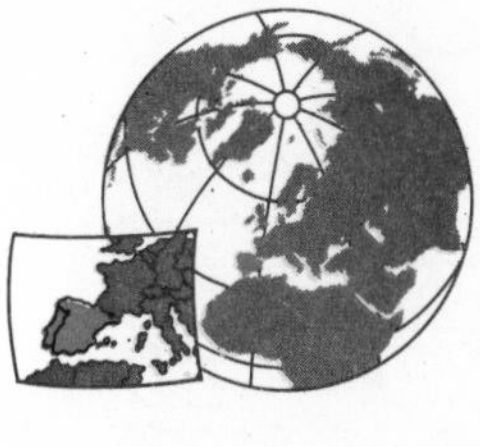

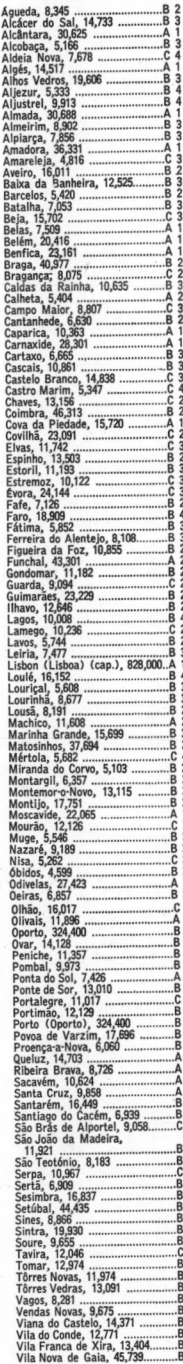

ANDORRA

CITIES and TOWNS

Andorra la Vella (cap.), 2,250....G 1

GIBRALTAR

PHYSICAL FEATURES

Europa (point) ....D 4

PORTUGAL

PROVINCES

Algarve, 315,300 ....B 4
Alto Alentejo, 410,200 ....C 3
Baixo Alentejo, 275,000 ....B 3
Beira Alta, 761,500 ....C 2
Beira Baixa, 321,100 ....C 3
Beira Litoral, 1,448,800 ....B 2
Douro Litoral, 1,352,600 ....B 2
Estremadura, 1,998,600 ....B 3
Madeira, 268,700 ....A 2
Minho, 944,800 ....B 2
Ribatejo, 479,400 ....B 3
Trás-os-Montes e Alto Douro, 586,500 ....C 2

CITIES and TOWNS

Águeda, 8,345 ....B 2
Alcácer do Sal, 14,733 ....B 3
Alcântara, 30,625 ....A 1
Alcobaça, 5,166 ....B 3
Aldeia Nova, 7,678 ....C 4
Algés, 14,517 ....A 1
Alhos Vedros, 19,606 ....B 3
Aljezur, 5,333 ....B 4
Aljustrel, 9,913 ....B 4
Almada, 30,688 ....A 1
Almeirim, 8,902 ....B 3
Alpiarça, 7,856 ....B 3
Amadora, 36,331 ....A 1
Amareleja, 4,816 ....C 3
Aveiro, 16,011 ....B 2
Baixa da Banheira, 12,525..........B 3
Barcelos, 5,420 ....B 2
Batalha, 7,053 ....B 3
Beja, 15,702 ....C 3
Belas, 7,509 ....A 1
Belém, 20,416 ....A 1
Benfica, 23,161 ....A 1
Braga, 40,977 ....B 2
Bragança, 8,075 ....C 2
Caldas da Rainha, 10,635 ....B 3
Calheta, 5,404 ....A 2
Campo Maior, 8,807 ....C 3
Cantanhede, 6,630 ....B 2
Caparica, 10,363 ....A 1
Carnaxide, 28,301 ....A 1
Cartaxo, 6,665 ....B 3
Cascais, 10,861 ....B 3
Castelo Branco, 14,838 ....C 3
Castro Marim, 5,347 ....C 4
Chaves, 13,156 ....C 2
Coimbra, 46,313 ....B 2
Cova da Piedade, 15,720 ....A 1
Covilhã, 23,091 ....C 2
Elvas, 11,742 ....C 3
Espinho, 13,503 ....B 2
Estoril, 11,193 ....B 3
Estremoz, 10,122 ....C 3
Évora, 24,144 ....C 3
Fafe, 7,126 ....B 2
Faro, 18,909 ....B 4
Fátima, 5,852 ....B 3
Ferreira do Alentejo, 8,108..........B 3
Figueira da Foz, 10,855 ....B 2
Funchal, 43,301 ....A 2
Gondomar, 11,182 ....B 2
Guarda, 9,094 ....C 2
Guimarães, 23,229 ....B 2
Ilhavo, 12,646 ....B 2
Lagos, 10,008 ....B 4
Lamego, 10,236 ....C 2
Lavos, 5,744 ....B 2
Leiria, 7,477 ....B 3
Lisbon (Lisboa) (cap.), 828,000..A 1
Loulé, 16,152 ....B 4
Louriçal, 5,608 ....B 3
Lourinhã, 8,677 ....B 3
Lousã, 8,191 ....B 2
Machico, 11,608 ....A 2
Marinha Grande, 15,699 ....B 3
Matosinhos, 37,694 ....B 2
Mértola, 5,682 ....C 4
Miranda do Corvo, 5,103 ....B 2
Montargil, 6,357 ....B 3
Montemor-o-Novo, 13,115 ....B 3
Montijo, 17,751 ....B 3
Moscavide, 22,065 ....A 1
Mourão, 12,126 ....C 3
Muge, 5,546 ....B 3
Nazaré, 9,189 ....B 3
Nisa, 5,262 ....C 3
Óbidos, 4,599 ....B 3
Odivelas, 27,423 ....A 1
Oeiras, 6,857 ....B 3
Olhão, 16,017 ....C 4
Olivais, 11,896 ....A 1
Oporto, 324,400 ....B 2
Ovar, 14,128 ....B 2
Peniche, 11,357 ....B 3
Pombal, 9,973 ....B 3
Ponta do Sol, 7,426 ....A 2
Ponte de Sor, 13,010 ....B 3
Portalegre, 11,017 ....C 3
Portimão, 12,129 ....B 4
Porto (Oporto), 324,400 ....B 2
Povoa de Varzim, 17,696 ....B 2
Proença-a-Nova, 6,060 ....B 3
Queluz, 14,703 ....A 1
Ribeira Brava, 8,726 ....A 2
Sacavém, 10,624 ....A 1
Santa Cruz, 9,858 ....A 2
Santarém, 16,449 ....B 3
Santiago do Cacém, 6,939 ....B 3
São Brás de Alportel, 9,058..............C 4
São João da Madeira, 11,921 ....B 2
São Teotónio, 8,183 ....B 4
Serpa, 10,967 ....C 4
Sertã, 6,909 ....B 3
Sesimbra, 16,837 ....B 3
Setúbal, 44,435 ....B 3
Sines, 8,866 ....B 4
Sintra, 19,930 ....B 3
Soure, 9,655 ....B 2
Tavira, 12,046 ....C 4
Tomar, 12,974 ....B 3
Tôrres Novas, 11,974 ....B 3
Tôrres Vedras, 13,091 ....B 3
Vagos, 8,281 ....B 2
Vendas Novas, 9,675 ....B 3
Viana do Castelo, 14,371 ....B 2
Vila do Conde, 12,771 ....B 2
Vila Franca de Xira, 13,404......................B 3
Vila Nova de Gaia, 45,739........................B 2
Vila Real, 10,263 ....C 2
Vila Real de Sto. António, 11,096 ....C 4
Viseu, 16,961 ....C 2

OTHER FEATURES

Carvoeiro (cape) ....B 3
Desertas (isls.) ....A 2
Douro (river) ....C 2
Estrela, Serra da (mts.) ....C 2
Foia (mt.) ....B 4
Guadiana (river) ....C 4
Lima (river) ....B 2
Madeira (isl.), 265,432 ....A 2
Minho (river) ....B 2
Mira (river) ....B 4
Monchique (mts.) ....B 4
Mondego (cape) ....B 3
Mondego (river) ....C 2
Monsanto (hill) ....A 1
Ossa (mts.) ....C 3
Palha, Mar da (bay) ....A 1
Roca (cape) ....B 3
Sado (river) ....B 3
Saint Vincent (cape) ....B 4
Santa María (cape) ....C 4
Setúbal (bay) ....B 3
Tagus (river) ....B 3
Tâmega (river) ....C 2
Tejo (Tagus) (river) ....B 3
Xarrama (river) ....B 3

SPAIN

AREA 194,896 sq. mi.
POPULATION 33,290,000
CAPITAL Madrid
LARGEST CITY Madrid
HIGHEST POINT Pico de Teide 12,172 ft. (Canary Is.); Mulhacén 11,411 ft. (mainland)
MONETARY UNIT peseta
MAJOR LANGUAGES Spanish, Catalan, Basque
MAJOR RELIGION Roman Catholicism

ANDORRA

AREA 175 sq. mi.
POPULATION 19,000
CAPITAL Andorra la Vella
MONETARY UNIT French franc, Spanish peseta
MAJOR LANGUAGE Catalan
MAJOR RELIGION Roman Catholicism

PORTUGAL

AREA 35,510 sq. mi.
POPULATION 9,560,000
CAPITAL Lisbon
LARGEST CITY Lisbon
HIGHEST POINT Malhão da Estrêla 6,532 ft.
MONETARY UNIT escudo
MAJOR LANGUAGE Portuguese
MAJOR RELIGION Roman Catholicism

GIBRALTAR

AREA 2 sq. mi.
POPULATION 27,000
CAPITAL Gibraltar
MONETARY UNIT pound sterling
MAJOR LANGUAGES English, Spanish
MAJOR RELIGION Roman Catholicism

SPAIN

PROVINCES

Álava, 148,899 ....E 1
Albacete, 358,290 ....E 3
Alicante, 746,917 ....F 3
Almería, 360,798 ....E 4
Ávila, 231,916 ....D 2
Badajoz, 839,363 ....C 3
Baleares (Balearic Is.), 451,343..H 3
Barcelona, 3,213,212 ....G 2
Burgos, 372,138 ....E 1
Cáceres, 540,060 ....C 3
Cádiz, 874,837 ....D 4
Castellón, 344,350 ....G 2
Ciudad Real, 589,262 ....D 3
Córdoba, 802,633 ....D 3
Cuenca, 305,432 ....E 2
Gerona, 361,250 ....H 1
Granada, 760,210 ....E 4
Guadalajara, 174,572 ....E 2
Guipúzcoa, 532,095 ....E 1
Huelva, 413,459 ....C 4
Huesca, 231,376 ....F 1
Jaén, 720,559 ....E 4
La Coruña, 1,004,149 ....B 1
Las Palmas, 492,466 ....C 4
León, 600,935 ....C 1
Lérida, 336,818 ....G 2
Logroño, 228,922 ....E 1
Lugo, 464,922 ....C 1
Madrid, 2,973,619 ....E 2
Málaga, 783,436 ....D 4
Murcia, 817,545 ....F 4
Navarra, 409,239 ....F 1
Orense, 442,420 ....C 1
Oviedo, 1,034,244 ....C 1
Palencia, 230,426 ....D 1
Pontevedra, 681,295 ....B 1
Salamanca, 401,276 ....C 2
Santa Cruz de Tenerife, 525,095 ....B 5
Santander, 443,113 ....D 1
Saragossa, 670,357 ....F 2
Segovia, 192,229 ....D 2
Seville, 1,295,094 ....D 4
Soria, 140,517 ....E 2
Tarragona, 363,830 ....G 2
Teruel, 205,565 ....F 2
Toledo, 516,870 ....D 3
Valencia, 1,462,005 ....F 3
Valladolid, 368,685 ....D 2
Vizcaya, 852,768 ....E 1
Zamora, 293,489 ....D 2

CITIES and TOWNS

Adra, 10,211 ....E 4
Aguilar, 13,760 ....D 4
Aguilas, 11,970 ....F 4
Alagón, 5,270 ....F 2
Alayor, 4,988 ....J 3
Albacete, 61,635 ....F 3
Albox, 4,036 ....E 4
Alburqerque, 9,540 ....C 3
Alcalá de Chivert, 4,049 ....G 2
Alcalá de Guadaira. 27,378 ....D 4
Alcalá de Henares, 20,572 ....G 4
Alcalá de los Gazules, 7,015 ....D 4
Alcalá la Real, 8,351 ....E 4
Alcanar, 6,332 ....G 2
Alcañiz, 9,489 ....F 2
Alcántara, 3,564 ....C 3
Alcantarilla, 15,748 ....F 4
Alcaudete, 9,280 ....E 4
Alcázar de San Juan, 23,788........E 3
Alcira, 22,417 ....F 3
Alcoy, 48,712 ....F 3
Alfaro, 8,570 ....F 1
Algeciras, 51,096 ....D 4
Algemesí, 16,683 ....F 3
Alhama de Granada, 6,989 ....E 4
Alhama de Murcia, 7,175 ....F 4
Alicante, 103,289 ....F 3
Almadén, 13,206 ....D 3
Almagro, 9,232 ....E 3
Almansa, 15,391 ....F 3
Almendralejo, 20,867 ....C 3
Almería, 76,643 ....E 4
Almodóvar del Campo, 8,115............D 3
Almonte, 9,444 ....C 4
Almuñécar, 5,644 ....E 4
Álora, 6,459 ....D 4
Amposta, 11,026 ....G 2
Andújar, 23,897 ....D 3
Antequera, 28,400 ....D 4
Aracena, 5,605 ....C 4
Aranda de Duero, 12,623 ....E 2
Aranjuez, 25,988 ....E 2
Archena, 5,802 ....F 3
Archidona. 7.262 ....D 4
Arcos de la Frontera, 13,536 ......D 4
Arenas de San Pedro, 5,585........D 2
Arenys de Mar, 6,665 ....H 2
Argamasilla de Alba, 6,411 ....E 3
Arganda, 5,253 ....G 4
Arnedo, 7,958 ....E 1
Aroche, 5,319 ....C 4
Arrecife, 12,748 ....C 4
Arroyo de la Luz, 9,781 ....C 3
Arta, 5,173 ....H 3
Arucas, 10,917 ....B 5
Aspe, 9,742 ....F 3
Astorga, 10,101 ....C 1
Ávila de los Caballeros, 26,738 ....D 2
Avilés, 19,992 ....C 1
Ayamonte, 9,608 ....C 4
Ayora, 5,635 ....F 3
Azpeitia, 8,219 ....E 1
Azuaga, 15,477 ....D 3
Badajoz, 23,715 ....C 3
Badalona, 90,655 ....H 2
Baena, 17,612 ....D 4
Baeza, 13,329 ....E 4
Bailén, 11,144 ....E 3
Balaguer, 8,342 ....G 2
Bañolas, 7,531 ....H 1
Barajas, 9,058 ....F 4
Barbastro, 9,730 ....F 1
Barcarrota, 7,443 ....C 3
Barcelona, 1,555,564 ....H 2
Barruelo de Santullán, 3,761......D 1
Baza, 13,323 ....E 4
Beas de Segura, 8,194 ....E 3
Béjar, 14,225 ....D 2
Bélmez, 6,907 ....D 3
Benavente, 11,061 ....D 1
Benicarló, 10,627 ....G 2
Berga, 8,923 ....G 1
Berja, 7,989 ....E 4
Bermeo, 12,398 ....E 1
Betanzos, 6,999 ....B 1
Bilbao, 293,939 ....E 1
Blanes, 9,256 ....H 2
Borja, 4,335 ....F 2
Borjas Blancas, 5,086 ....G 2
Brozas, 5,634 ....C 3
Bujalance, 10,465 ....D 4
Bullas, 7,326 ....F 4
Burgos, 79,810 ....E 1
Burriana, 15,670 ....G 3
Cabeza del Buey, 10,734 ....D 3
Cabra, 15,688 ....D 4
Cáceres, 42,903 ....C 3
Cádiz, 117,871 ....C 4
Calahorra, 14,400 ....E 1
Calasparra, 7,543 ....F 3
Calatayud, 15,777 ....F 2
Calella, 7,947 ....H 2
Callosa de Ensarria, 4,617 ....G 3
Calzada de Calatrava, 7,536..................E 3
Campanario, 8,910 ....D 3
Campillos, 8,791 ....D 4
Campo de Criptana, 13,616......................E 3
Candeleda, 6,507 ....D 2
Cangas, 4,059 ....B 1
Caniles, 5,026 ....E 4
Caravaca, 10,016 ....E 3
Carcagente, 15,791 ....F 3
Carmona, 26,368 ....D 4
Cartagena, 42,424 ....F 4
Casar de Cáceres, 4,560 ....C 3
Caspe, 8,251 ....G 2
Castellón de la Plana, 52,868......G 3
Castro del Río, 11,200 ....D 4
Castro-Urdiales, 7,128 ....E 1
Castuera, 9,905 ....D 3
Caudete, 7,481 ....F 3
Cazalla de la Sierra, 9,414..........D 4
Cazorla, 7,932 ....E 4
Cebreros, 3,898 ....D 2
Ceclavín, 4,778 ....C 3
Cehegín, 10,467 ....F 3
Cervera, 5,215 ....G 2
Cervera del Río Alhama, 3,648....E 1
Ceuta, 88,000 ....D 5
Chiclana de la Frontera, 19,155..C 4
Chinchón, 4,432 ....G 5
Chiva, 3,978 ....F 3
Ciempozuelos, 9,042 ....F 5
Cieza, 20,620 ....F 3
Ciudadela, 10,872 ....H 2
Ciudad Real, 35,015 ....D 3
Cocentaina, 7,405 ....F 3
Coín, 11,441 ....D 4
Colmenar de Oreja, 5,119 ....G 5
Colmenar Viejo, 8,133 ....F 4
Constantina, 12,015 ....D 4
Consuegra, 10,572 ....E 3
Córdoba, 167,808 ....D 4
Corella, 5,591 ....F 1
Coria del Río, 13,781 ....C 4
Corral de Almaguer, 8,621 ....E 3
Crevillente, 12,025 ....F 3
Cuéllar, 5,703 ....D 2
Cuenca, 26,663 ....E 2
Cúllar de Baza, 3,769 ....E 4
Cullera, 13,040 ....F 3
Daimiel, 19,485 ....E 3
Denia, 8,281 ....G 3
Don Benito, 22,642 ....C 3
Dos Hermanas, 21,517 ....D 4
Durango, 11,882 ....E 1
Écija, 29,262 ....D 4
Eibar, 31,371 ....E 1
Ejea de los Caballeros, 9,000..................F 1
El Arahal, 15,107 ....D 4
El Bonillo, 5,215 ....E 3
Elche, 50,989 ....F 3
Elda, 24,182 ....F 3
El Ferrol del Caudillo, 62,010..................B 1
El Puerto de Santa María, 31,848 ....C 4
Énguera, 4,606 ....F 3
Espejo, 8,006 ....D 4
Estella, 8,142 ....E 1
Estepa, 8,628 ....D 4
Estepona, 11,309 ....D 4
Felanitx, 7,860 ....H 3
Fermoselle, 3,885 ....C 2
Figueras, 16,460 ....H 1
Fraga, 8,264 ....G 2

Agriculture, Industry and Resources

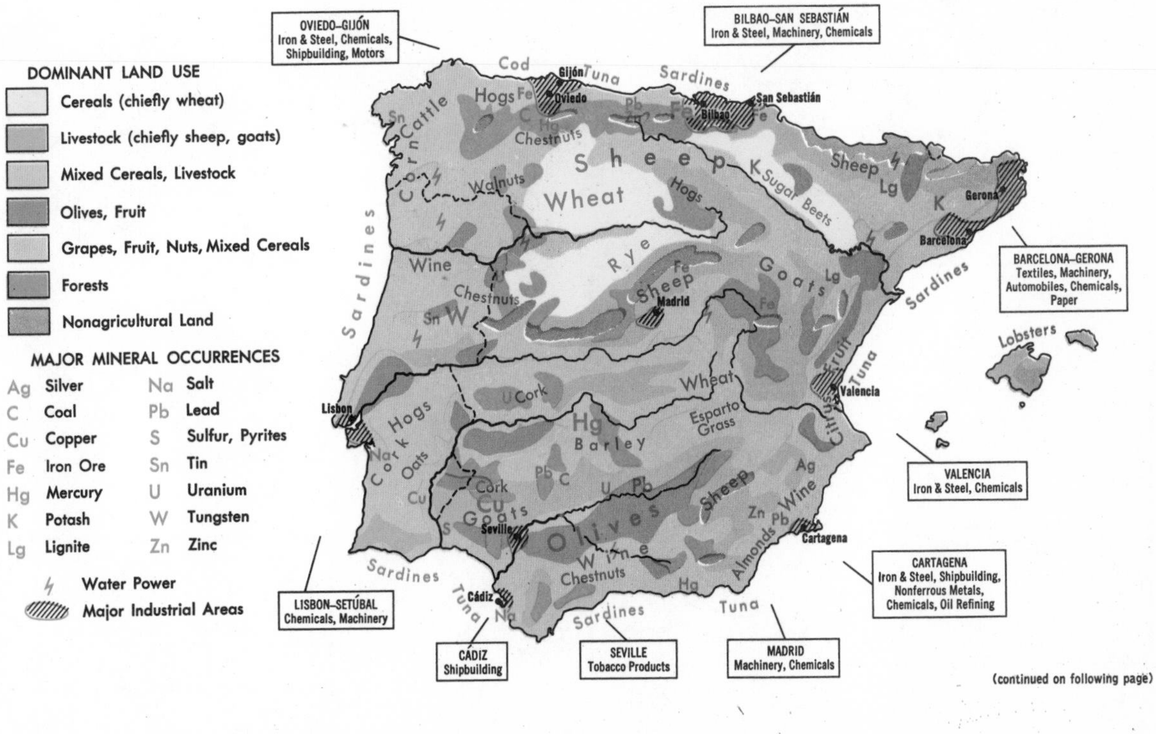

DOMINANT LAND USE
Cereals (chiefly wheat)
Livestock (chiefly sheep, goats)
Mixed Cereals, Livestock
Olives, Fruit
Grapes, Fruit, Nuts, Mixed Cereals
Forests
Nonagricultural Land
MAJOR MINERAL OCCURRENCES
Ag Silver
C Coal
Cu Copper
Fe Iron Ore
Hg Mercury
K Potash
Lg Lignite
Na Salt
Pb Lead
S Sulfur, Pyrites
Sn Tin
U Uranium
W Tungsten
Zn Zinc
Water Power
Major Industrial Areas
OVIEDO–GIJÓN
Iron & Steel, Chemicals, Shipbuilding, Motors
BILBAO–SAN SEBASTIÁN
Iron & Steel, Machinery, Chemicals
BARCELONA–GERONA
Textiles, Machinery, Automobiles, Chemicals, Paper
VALENCIA
Iron & Steel, Chemicals
CARTAGENA
Iron & Steel, Shipbuilding, Nonferrous Metals, Chemicals, Oil Refining
LISBON–SETÚBAL
Chemicals, Machinery
CÁDIZ
Shipbuilding
SEVILLE
Tobacco Products
MADRID
Machinery, Chemicals
Cod
Tuna
Sardines
Gijón
Oviedo
Bilbao
San Sebastián
Gerona
Barcelona
Madrid
Valencia
Lisbon
Seville
Cádiz
Cartagena
Hogs
Cattle
Corn
Chestnuts
Walnuts
Sheep
Wheat
Sugar Beets
Rye
Goats
Wine
Lobsters
Cork
Oats
Esparto Grass
Barley
Olives
Almonds
Citrus Fruit

(continued on following page)

30 Spain and Portugal
(continued)

Topography

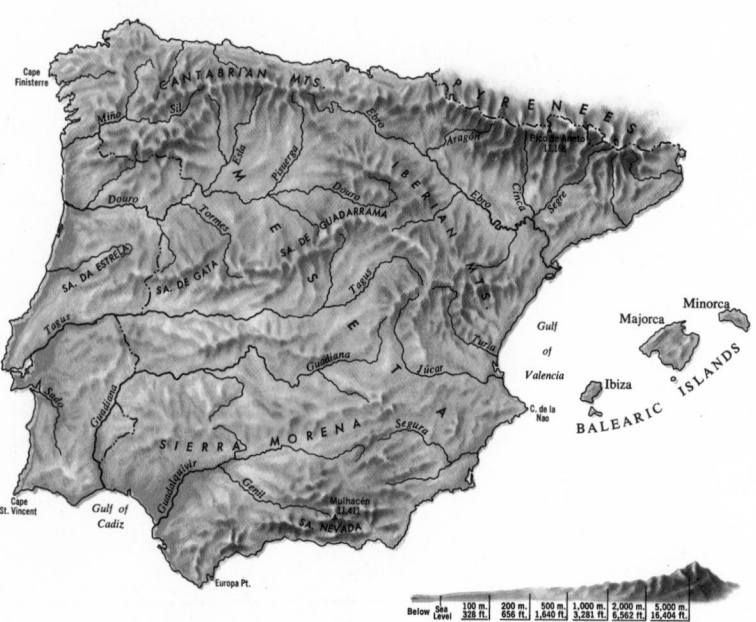

Azores

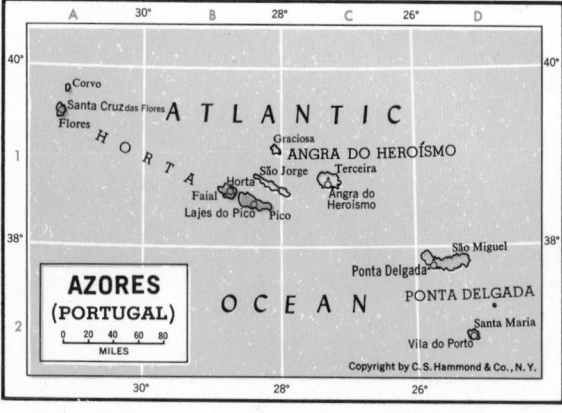

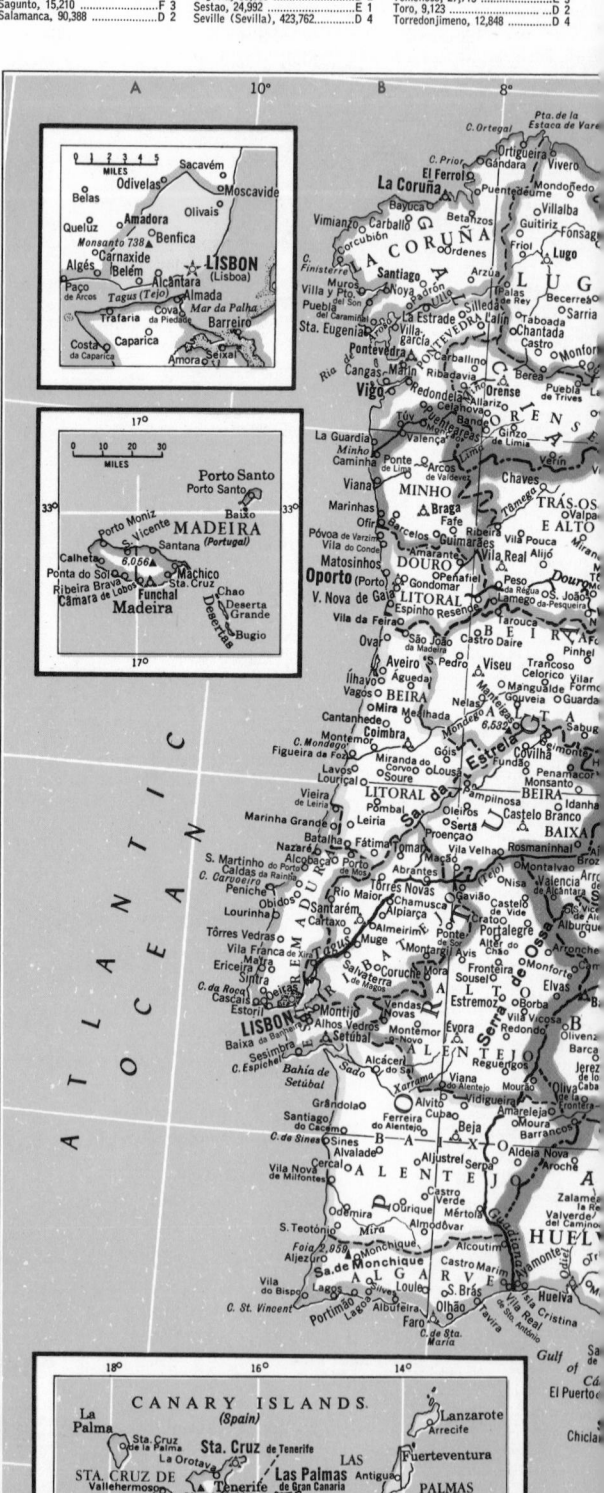

Torrejoncillo, 5,499 .... C 3
Torrelavega, 13,612 .... D 1
Torremolinos, 7,980 .... D 4
Torrente, 23,432 .... F 3
Torrevieja, 8,961 .... F 4
Tortox, 9,211 .... E 3
Tortosa, 18,674 .... G 2
Totana, 10,156 .... F 4
Trigueros, 6,151 .... C 4
Trujillo, 13,326 .... D 3
Tudela, 16,422 .... E 1
Úbeda, 26,930 .... E 3
Ubrique, 8,915 .... D 4
Urda, 5,479 .... E 3
Utiel, 9,720 .... E 3
Utrera, 25,935 .... D 4
Valdepeñas, 24,462 .... E 3
Valdeverdeja, 3,607 .... D 3
Valencia, 466,577 .... F 3
Valencia de Alcántara, 13,159 .... C 3
Valladolid, 133,486 .... D 2
Vall de Uxó, 16,577 .... F 3
Vallehermoso, 887 .... A 5
Valls, 10,890 .... G 2
Valverde del Camino, 10,843 .... C 4

Vejer de la Frontera, 11,853 .... C 4
Vélez-Málaga, 14,348 .... D 4
Vélez Rubio, 4,113 .... E 4
Vich, 18,184 .... H 2
Vigo, 69,429 .... B 2
Vilacañas, 10,113 .... E 3
Villacarrillo, 10,970 .... E 3
Villafranca de los Barros, 14,591 ...... C 3
Villafranca del Panadés, 11,306 .... G 2
Villagarcía, 4,391 .... B 2
Villahermosa, 5,496 .... E 3
Villajoyosa, 7,508 .... F 3
Villanueva de Córdoba, 15,719 .... D 3
Villanueva del Arzobispo, 9,307 .... E 3
Villanueva de la Serena, 17,847 .... D 3
Villanueva de los Infantes, 9,909 ...... E 3
Villanueva y Geltrú, 25,669 .... G 2
Villar del Arzobispo, 3,876 .... F 3
Villarreal de los Infantes,
  20,025 .... G 3
Villarrobledo, 19,585 .... E 3
Villarrubia de los Ojos, 9,043 .... E 3
Villena, 18,333 .... F 3
Vinaroz, 10,968 .... G 2
Vitoria, 65,946 .... E 1

OTHER FEATURES

Alagón (river) .... C 2
Albarán (isl.) .... E 5
Alcudia (bay) .... H 3
Almanzor (mt.) .... D 3
Almanzora (river) .... E 4
Andalusia (reg.), 6,011,026 .... D 4
Aneto (mt.) .... G 1
Aragón (reg.), 1,107,298 .... F 2
Asturias (reg.), 1,034,244 .... D 1
Autza (mt.) .... F 1
Balearic (isls.), 451,343 .... H 3
Bañuelo (river) .... D 3
Barbate (river) .... C 4
Biscay (bay) .... E 1

Cádiz (gulf) .... C 4
Canary (isls.), 1,017,361 .... B 4
Cantabrian (mts.) .... D 1
Castile, New (reg.), 4,559,755 .... E 3
Castile, Old (reg.), 2,207,946 .... D 2
Catalonia (reg.), 4,275,110 .... G 2
Cinca (river) .... G 1
Columbretes (isls.) .... G 3
Costa Brava (reg.) .... H 2
Costa del Sol (reg.) .... D 4
Creus (cape) .... H 1
Cuenca (mts.) .... E 3
Demanda, Sierra de la (mts.) .... E 2
Douro (Duero) (river) .... C 2
Duratón (river) .... D 2
Ebro (river) .... G 2
Eresma (river) .... D 2
Esla (river) .... D 2
Estremadura (region), 1,379,423 .... C 3
Finisterre (cape) .... B 1
Formentor (cape) .... H 3
Fuerteventura (isl.), 18,138 .... C 4
Gata (cape) .... C 4
Gata (mts.) .... C 2

Genil (river) .... D 4
Gibraltar (strait) .... D 5
Gomera (isl.), 27,790 .... A 5
Gran Canaria (isl.), 400,837 .... B 5
Gredos (mts.) .... D 3
Guadalimar (river) .... E 3
Guadalquivir (river) .... C 4
Guadarrama (mts.) .... D 2
Guadarrama (river) .... F 4
Guadiana (river) .... C 3
Gúdar, Sierra da (mts.) .... F 2
Henares (river) .... E 2
Hierro (isl.), 7,957 .... A 5
Huelva (river) .... C 4
Ibiza (Iviza) (isl.), 34,495 .... G 3
Jalón (river) .... E 2
Jarama (river) .... E 2
Júcar (river) .... F 3
Lanzarote (isl.), 34,805 .... C 4
León (reg.), 1,295,700 .... D 2
Lima (river) .... B 2
Llobregat (river) .... G 2
Majorca (isl.), 363,199 .... H 3
Mallorca (Majorca) (isl.),
  363,199 .... H 3

Mancha, La (dist.) .... E 3
Manzanares (river) .... F 4
Marismas, Las (marsh) .... C 4
Menor, Mar (lagoon) .... F 4
Menorca (Minorca) (isl.),
  42,954 .... J 2
Miño (river) .... B 1
Minorca (isl.), 42,954 .... J 2
Moncayo (mt.) .... E 2
Montserrat (mt.) .... G 2
Morena, Sierra (range) .... E 3
Mulhacén (mt.) .... E 4
Murcia (reg.), 1,175,835 .... F 4
Nao (cape) .... G 3
Navia (river) .... C 1
Nevada, Sierra (range) .... E 4
Orbigo (river) .... D 2
Ortegal (cape) .... B 1
Palma, La (isl.), 67,141 .... A 4
Peñalara (mt.) .... D 2
Penibética (mts.) .... E 4
Peñarroya (mt.) .... F 2
Perales (river) .... G 3
Perdido (mt.) .... F 1
Puigmal (mt.) .... H 1

Pyrenees (mts.) .... G 1
Rosas (gulf) .... H 1
Rouge (mt.) .... G 1
San Jorge (gulf) .... G 2
San Pedro (mts.) .... D 3
Sebollera (mt.) .... E 2
Segre (river) .... G 2
Segura (river) .... F 4
Sil (river) .... C 1
Tagus (Tajo) (river) .... D 3
Teide (peak) .... B 5
Tenerife (isl.), 387,767 .... B 5
Ter (river) .... H 1
Tinto (river) .... C 4
Toledo (mts.) .... D 3
Torote (river) .... E 3
Trafalgar (cape) .... C 4
Turia (river) .... F 3
Ulla (river) .... B 1
Urgel (plain) .... G 2
Valencia (gulf) .... G 3
Valencia (lagoon) .... F 3
Valencia (reg.), 2,553,272 .... G 3
Vascongadas (reg.), 1,533,762 .... E 1

*City and suburbs.

SPAIN and PORTUGAL

CONIC PROJECTION

SCALE OF MILES

SCALE OF KILOMETRES

Capitals of Countries .... ☆
Provincial Capitals .... △
International Boundaries _____
Provincial Boundaries -------

© Copyright by C.S. HAMMOND & Co., Maplewood, N.J.

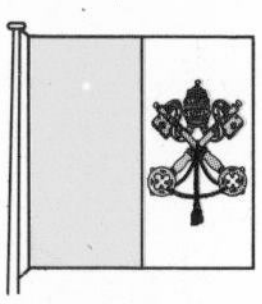

VATICAN CITY
AREA 109 acres
POPULATION 1,000

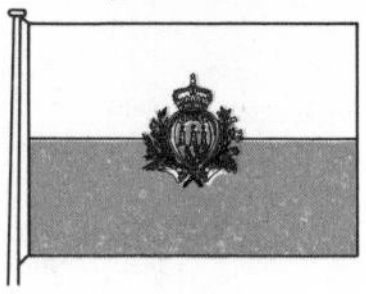

SAN MARINO
AREA 23.4 sq. mi.
POPULATION 19,000

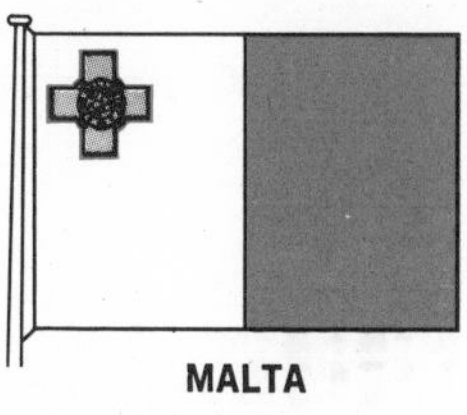

MALTA

AREA 122 sq. mi.
POPULATION 321,000
CAPITAL Valletta
LARGEST CITY Sliema
HIGHEST POINT 787 ft.
MONETARY UNIT Maltese pound
MAJOR LANGUAGES Maltese, English
MAJOR RELIGION Roman Catholicism

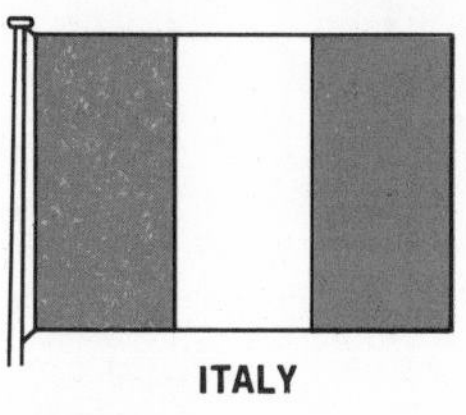

ITALY

AREA 116,303 sq. mi.
POPULATION 54,504,000
CAPITAL Rome
LARGEST CITY Rome
HIGHEST POINT Dufourspitze (Mte. Rosa) 15,203 ft.
MONETARY UNIT lira
MAJOR LANGUAGE Italian
MAJOR RELIGION Roman Catholicism

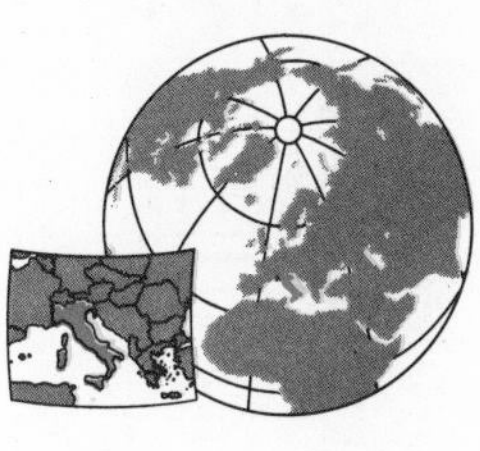

ITALY

REGIONS

Abruzzi, 1,206,266 ....D 3
Apulia, 3,421,217 ....F 4
Basilicata, 644,297 ....F 4
Calabria, 2,045,047 ....F 5
Campania, 4,760,759 ....E 4
Emilia-Romagna, 3,666,680 ....C 2
Friuli-Venezia Giulia, 1,204,298...D 1
Latium, 3,958,957 ....D 4
Liguria, 1,735,349 ....B 2
Lombardy, 7,406,152 ....B 2
Marche, 1,347,489 ....D 3
Molise, 358,052 ....E 4
Piedmont, 3,914,250 ....A 2
Puglia (Apulia), 3,421,217 ....F 4
Sardinia, 1,419,362 ....B 4
Sicily, 4,721,001 ....E 6
Trentino-Alto Adige, 785,967 ......C 1
Tuscany, 3,286,160 ....C 3
Umbria, 794,745 ....D 3
Valle d'Aosta, 100,959 ....A 2
Venetia, 3,846,562 ....C 2

PROVINCES

Agrigento, 472,945 ....D 6
Alessandria, 478,613 ....B 2
Ancona, 405,709 ....D 3
Arezzo, 308,964 ....C 3
Ascoli Piceno, 335,627 ....D 3
Asti, 214,604 ....B 2
Avellino, 464,904 ....E 4
Bari, 1,263,245 ....F 4
Belluno, 234,921 ....D 1
Benevento, 313,020 ....E 4
Bergamo, 744,670 ....B 2
Bologna, 841,474 ....C 2
Bolzano, 373,863 ....C 1
Brescia, 882,949 ....C 2
Brindisi, 345,635 ....G 4
Cagliari, 754,965 ....B 5
Caltanissetta, 302,513 ....D 6
Campobasso, 358,052 ....E 4
Caserta, 649,327 ....E 4
Catania, 893,542 ....E 6
Catanzaro, 741,509 ....F 5
Chieti, 373,632 ....E 3
Como, 622,132 ....B 2
Cosenza, 694,398 ....F 5
Cremona, 351,160 ....B 2
Cuneo, 536,356 ....A 2
Enna, 229,126 ....E 6
Ferrara, 403,218 ....C 2
Florence, 1,012,703 ....C 3
Foggia, 665,286 ....E 4
Forlì, 521,128 ....D 2
Frosinone, 438,254 ....D 4
Genoa, 1,031,091 ....B 2
Gorizia, 137,745 ....D 2
Grosseto, 220,305 ....C 3
Imperia, 202,160 ....B 3
L'Aquila, 328,989 ....D 3
La Spezia, 239,256 ....B 2
Latina, 319,056 ....D 4
Lecce, 678,338 ....G 4
Leghorn, 310,210 ....C 3
Lucca, 365,540 ....C 3
Macerata, 291,412 ....D 3
Mantua, 387,255 ....C 2
Massa-Carrara, 202,981 ....C 2
Matera, 200,131 ....F 4
Messina, 685,260 ....E 5
Milan, 3,156,815 ....B 2
Modena, 511,355 ....C 2
Naples, 2,421,243 ....E 4
Novara, 460,190 ....B 2
Nuoro, 283,206 ....B 4
Padua, 694,017 ....C 2
Palermo, 1,111,397 ....D 5
Parma, 389,199 ....C 2
Pavia, 518,193 ....B 2
Perugia, 570,149 ....D 3
Pesaro e Urbino, 314,741 ....D 3
Pescara, 242,958 ....E 3
Piacenza, 291,059 ....B 2
Pisa, 362,396 ....C 3
Pistoia, 232,999 ....C 2
Pordenone, 241,724 ....D 2
Potenza, 444,166 ....E 4
Ragusa, 252,769 ....E 6
Ravenna, 329,559 ....D 2
Reggio di Calabria, 609,140..........E 5
Reggio nell'Emilia, 379,688 ....C 2
Rieti, 162,405 ....D 3
Rome, 2,775,380 ....F 6
Rovigo, 277,811 ....C 2
Salerno, 912,265 ....E 4
Sassari, 381,191 ....B 4
Savona, 262,842 ....B 2
Siena, 270,062 ....C 3
Sondrio, 161,450 ....B 1
Syracuse, 345,777 ....E 6
Taranto, 468,713 ....F 4
Teramo, 260,687 ....D 3
Terni, 224,596 ....D 3
Trapani, 427,672 ....D 5
Trento, 412,104 ....C 1
Treviso, 607,616 ....D 2
Trieste, 298,645 ....E 2
Turin, 1,824,254 ....A 2
Udine, 526,184 ....D 1
Valle d'Aosta, 100,959 ....A 2
Varese, 581,528 ....B 2
Venice, 749,173 ....D 2
Vercelli, 400,233 ....B 2
Verona, 667,517 ....C 2
Vicenza, 615,507 ....C 2
Viterbo, 263,862 ....C 3

CITIES and TOWNS

Acireale, 26,744 ....E 6
Acqui Terme, 14,070 ....B 2
Acri, 7,660 ....F 5
Adrano, 31,411 ....E 6
Adria, 11,456 ....D 2
Agira, 13,157 ....E 6
Agrigento, 46,947 ....D 6
Agropoli, 7,200 ....E 4
Alassio, 10,492 ....A 2
Alatri, 5,311 ....D 4
Alba, 16,396 ....B 2
Albano Laziale, 13,007 ....F 7
Albenga, 9,429 ....B 3
Albino, 6,875 ....B 2
Alcamo, 42,974 ....D 6
Alessandria, 65,908 ....B 2
Alghero, 22,139 ....B 4
Altamura, 41,528 ....F 4
Amalfi, 5,183 ....E 4
Amantea, 5,910 ....E 5
Ancona, 77,748 ....D 3
Andria, 69,499 ....F 4
Anzio, 12,102 ....D 4
Aosta, 28,637 ....A 2
Aprilia, 8,784 ....D 4
Aragona, 12,119 ....D 6
Arezzo, 43,868 ....C 3
Ariano Irpino, 11,302 ....E 4
Ascoli Piceno, 33,825 ....D 3
Assisi, 5,302 ....D 3
Asti, 44,455 ....B 2
Augusta, 25,774 ....E 6
Avellino, 31,744 ....E 4
Aversa, 40,245 ....E 4
Avezzano, 24,120 ....D 3
Avigliano, 5,119 ....E 4
Avola, 27,197 ....E 6
Bagheria, 31,435 ....D 5
Barcellona Pozzo di Gotto, 32,147 ....D 5
Bari, 293,963 ....F 4
Barletta, 67,419 ....F 4
Bassano del Grappa, 24,077.........C 2
Belluno, 15,400 ....D 1
Benevento, 41,467 ....E 4
Bergamo, 110,666 ....B 2
Biancavilla, 19,858 ....E 6
Biella, 42,994 ....B 2
Bisceglie, 40,520 ....F 4
Bitonto, 34,160 ....F 4
Bitti, 5,623 ....B 4
Bologna, 443,178 ....C 2
Bolzano, 84,685 ....C 1
Bondeno, 6,413 ....C 2
Bonorva, 6,192 ....B 4
Bordighera, 9,045 ....A 3
Borgomanero, 11,843 ....B 2
Borgo San Lorenzo, 6,135 ....C 2
Bosa, 7,890 ....B 4
Bra, 14,472 ....A 2
Bracciano, 6,460 ....C 3
Brescia, 140,518 ....C 2
Bressanone, 10,095 ....C 1
Brindisi, 63,480 ....G 4
Bronte, 19,418 ....E 6
Busto Arsizio, 58,483 ....B 2
Cagliari, 172,925 ....B 5
Caltagirone, 37,634 ....E 6
Caltanissetta, 51,699 ....D 6
Camaiore, 7,130 ....C 3
Campobasso, 27,568 ....E 4
Campo Tures, 1,162 ....C 1
Canicatti, 29,613 ....E 6
Canosa di Puglia, 32,908 ....E 4
Cantù, 17,298 ....B 2
Capua, 13,334 ....E 4
Caravaggio, 9,938 ....B 2
Carbonia, 26,227 ....B 5
Carini, 15,486 ....D 5
Carloforte, 7,153 ....B 5
Carmagnola, 6,583 ....A 2
Carpi, 27,647 ....C 2
Carrara, 37,386 ....C 2
Casale Monferrato, 31,226 ....B 2
Casalmaggiore, 5,995 ....C 2
Cascina-Navacchio, 23,739 ....C 3
Caserta, 36,337 ....E 4
Cassano allo Ionio, 9,250 ....F 5
Cassino, 11,369 ....E 4
Castelfranco Veneto, 9,978 ....D 2
Castel Gandolfo, 2,861 ....F 7
Castellammare del Golfo, 16,581 ....D 5
Castellammare di Stabia, 49,064 ....E 4
Castel San Pietro Terme, 4,824..C 2
Castelvetrano, 30,009 ....D 6
Castrovillari, 13,063 ....F 5
Catania, 358,700 ....E 6
Catanzaro, 44,198 ....F 5
Cava de'Tirreni, 19,883 ....E 4
Cavarzere, 6,109 ....D 2
Cecina, 13,749 ....C 3
Cefalù, 10,360 ....E 5
Ceglie Messapico, 17,891 ....F 4
Celano, 9,743 ....D 3
Cerignola, 43,345 ....E 4
Cernobbio, 6,857 ....B 2
Cesena, 31,153 ....D 2
Cesenatico, 7,684 ....D 2
Chiari, 9,552 ....C 2
Chiavari, 22,835 ....B 2
Chieri, 15,358 ....A 2
Chieti, 31,374 ....E 3
Chioggia, 25,058 ....D 2
Chivasso, 11,806 ....A 2
Ciampino, 10,012 ....F 7
Cittadella, 5,698 ....C 2
Città di Castello, 15,564 ....D 3
Cittanova, 11,567 ....F 5
Cividale del Friuli, 7,698 ....D 1
Civitavecchia, 84,996 ....C 3
Clusone, 5,729 ....C 2
Codriopo, 5,064 ....D 2
Colle di Val d'Elsa, 7,329 ....C 3
Comacchio, 9,743 ....D 2
Comiso, 24,016 ....E 6
Como, 64,301 ....B 2
Conegliano, 16,910 ....D 2
Conversano, 15,543 ....F 4
Corato, 38,774 ....F 4
Cori, 6,930 ....F 7
Corigliano Calabro, 13,526 ....F 5
Corleone, 14,185 ....D 6
Correggio, 8,146 ....C 2
Cortina d'Ampezzo, 4,291 ....D 1
Cosenza, 70,201 ....F 5
Courmayeur, 1,013 ....A 2
Crema, 20,679 ....B 2
Cremona, 64,775 ....B 2
Crotone, 36,516 ....F 5
Cuneo, 32,978 ....A 2
Desenzano del Garda, 8,017 ....C 2
Domodossola, 15,097 ....B 1
Dorgali, 6,976 ....B 4
Eboli, 19,550 ....E 4
Empoli, 22,484 ....C 3
Enna, 26,206 ....E 6
Este, 11,007 ....C 2
Fabriano, 15,127 ....D 3
Faenza, 40,425 ....D 2
Fano, 24,591 ....D 3
Fasano, 17,990 ....F 4
Favara, 27,523 ....D 6
Feltre, 9,446 ....C 1
Fermo, 14,453 ....D 3
Ferrandina, 8,381 ....F 4
Ferrara, 90,419 ....C 2
Fidenza, 13,567 ....B 2
Finale Emilia, 6,711 ....C 2
Finale Ligure, 9,789 ....B 2
Firenze (Florence), 413,455....................C 3
Fiumicino, 9,489 ....F 7
Florence, 413,455 ....C 3
Floridia, 16,104 ....E 6
Foggia, 108,682 ....E 4
Foligno, 23,094 ....D 3
Fondi, 14,991 ....D 4
Forlì, 65,376 ....D 2
Formia, 15,048 ....D 4
Fossano, 12,563 ....A 2
Francavilla Fontana, 27,629...................F 4
Frascati, 12,602 ....F 6
Frosinone, 20,998 ....D 4
Gaeta, 20,436 ....D 4
Galatina, 19,654 ....G 4
Galatone, 13,487 ....F 4
Gallarate, 34,870 ....B 2
Gallipoli, 15,958 ....F 4
Gela, 54,526 ....E 6
Gemona, 7,698 ....D 1
Genoa (Genova), 747,794.........................B 2
Genzano di Roma, 11,666 ....F 7
Giarre, 11,859 ....E 6
Gioia del Colle, 23,734 ....F 4
Giovinazzo, 14,189 ....F 4
Giulianova, 11,220 ....E 3
Gorizia, 35,307 ....D 2
Gravina in Puglia, 30,615 ....F 4
Grosseto, 36,558 ....C 3
Grottaferrata, 5,356 ....F 7
Grottaglie, 22,218 ....F 4
Guastalla, 7,511 ....C 2
Gubbio, 9,730 ....D 3
Iesi, 26,018 ....D 3
Iglesias, 20,518 ....B 5
Imola, 32,148 ....C 2
Imperia, 30,522 ....B 3
Isernia, 9,689 ....E 4
Ivrea, 19,344 ....B 2
La Maddalena, 10,414 ....B 4
Lanciano, 15,182 ....E 3
Lanusei, 5,208 ....B 5
L'Aquila, 29,462 ....D 3
La Spezia, 111,768 ....B 2
Latina, 26,171 ....D 4
Lavello, 12,857 ....E 4
Lecce, 68,385 ....G 4
Lecco, 47,468 ....B 2
Leghorn, 152,517 ....C 3
Legnago, 10,126 ....C 2
Lendinara, 6,475 ....C 2
Lentini, 31,788 ....E 6
Leonforte, 17,690 ....E 6
Licata, 38,222 ....D 6
Lido di Ostia, 25,662 ....F 7
Lido di Venezia, 16,581 ....D 2
Lipari, 3,852 ....E 5
Livorno (Leghorn), 152,517........................C 3
Lodi, 34,281 ....B 2
Lonigo, 5,774 ....C 2
Lucca, 45,398 ....C 3
Lucera, 24,399 ....E 4
Lugo, 16,550 ....D 2
Macerata, 27,054 ....D 3
Macomer, 7,782 ....B 4
Maglie, 12,205 ....G 4
Manduria, 23,971 ....F 4
Manfredonia, 34,583 ....F 4
Mantua, 55,806 ....C 2
Marino, 9,798 ....F 7
Marsala, 34,294 ....D 6
Martina Franca, 27,588 ....F 4
Massa, 46,992 ....C 2
Massafra, 18.884 ....F 4
Massa Marittima, 6,804 ....C 3
Matera, 36,727 ....F 4
Mazara del Vallo, 35,356 ....D 6
Mazzarino, 17,195 ....E 6
Melfi, 15,122 ....E 4
Menfi, 12,335 ....D 6
Merano, 29,196 ....C 1
Mesagne, 25,042 ....G 4
Messina, 202,095 ....E 5
Mestre, 138,822 ....D 2
Milan, 1,573,009 ....B 2
Milazzo, 14,034 ....E 5
Mirandola, 9,272 ....C 2
Mira Taglio, 8,380 ....D 2
Mistretta, 9,979 ....E 6
Modena, 107,814 ....C 2
Modica, 28,998 ....E 6
Mola di Bari, 22,397 ....F 4
Molfetta, 61,226 ....F 4
Moncalieri, 14,339 ....A 2
Mondovì Breo, 9,893 ....A 2
Monfalcone, 26,708 ....D 2
Monopoli, 25,161 ....F 4
Monreale, 18,881 ....D 5
Monselice, 7,766 ....C 2
Montebelluna, 6,088 ....D 2
Montefiascone, 6,428 ....D 3
Monterotondo, 9,616 ....F 6
Monte Sant'Angelo, 20,512 ....F 4
Montevarchi, 12,413 ....C 3
Monza, 79,715 ....B 2
Mortara, 12,243 ....B 2
Naples, 1,119,392 ....E 4
Nardo, 23,006 ....F 4
Narni, 5,551 ....D 3
Naro, 14,295 ....D 6
Nettuno, 16,187 ....D 4
Nicastro, 21,240 ....F 5
Nicosia, 16,624 ....E 6
Niscemi, 24,468 ....E 6
Nizza Monferrato, 6,229 ....B 2
Nocera Inferiore, 38,690 ....E 4
Noto, 21,586 ....E 6
Novara, 79,188 ....B 2
Novi Ligure, 23,349 ....B 2
Nuoro, 22,559 ....B 4
Olbia, 13,795 ....B 4
Oliera, 6,974 ....B 4
Orbetello, 6,800 ....C 3
Oristano, 16,305 ....B 5
Ortona, 11,315 ....E 3
Orvieto, 9,617 ....D 3
Osimo, 9,406 ....D 3
Ostuni, 25,190 ....F 4
Otranto, 3,510 ....G 4
Ozieri, 10,194 ....B 4
Pachino, 20,645 ....E 6
Padua, 169,298 ....C 2
Palazzolo Acreide, 10,802 ....E 6
Palermo, 531,306 ....D 5
Palestrina, 7,897 ....F 7
Palma di Montechiaro, 20,425....D 6
Palmi, 14,576 ....E 5
Pantelleria, 3,100 ....C 6
Paola, 9,701 ....E 5
Parma, 118,602 ....C 2
Partanna, 12,931 ....D 6
Partinico, 25,924 ....D 6
Paterno, 39,912 ....E 6
Patti, 6,748 ....E 5
Pavia, 69,581 ....B 2
Penne, 5,709 ....D 3
Pergine Valsugana, 4,877 ....C 1
Perugia, 52,534 ....D 3
Pesaro, 47,185 ....D 3
Pescara, 81,697 ....E 3
Pescia, 8,737 ....C 3
Piacenza, 78,925 ....B 2
Piazza Armerina, 23,915 ....E 6
Pietrasanta, 6,785 ....B 3
Pinerolo, 25,262 ....A 2
Piombino, 30,843 ....C 3
Piove di Sacco, 6,230 ....C 2
Pisa, 76,846 ....C 3
Pisticci, 11,469 ....F 4
Pistoia, 41,058 ....C 2
Poggibonsi, 12,932 ....C 3
Pont-Canavese, 4,071 ....A 2
Pontecorvo, 5,845 ....D 4
Pontremoli, 4,839 ....C 2
Popoli, 6,749 ....E 3
Pordenone, 29,461 ....D 2
Porto Civitanova, 18,288 ....D 3
Porto Empedocle, 16,110 ....D 6
Portoferraio, 6,318 ....C 3
Portofino, 735 ....B 2
Portogruaro, 8,913 ....D 2
Portomaggiore, 5,532 ....C 2
Porto Recanati, 4,986 ....D 3
Porto Torres, 10,108 ....B 4
Potenza, 34,216 ....F 4
Pozzallo, 11,862 ....E 6
Pozzuoli, 44,038 ....D 4
Prato, 75,402 ....C 3
Prima Porta, 9,978 ....F 6
Priverno, 9,154 ....D 4
Putignano, 15,976 ....F 4
Quartu Sant'Elena, 22,271 ....B 5
Ragusa, 50,718 ....E 6
Rapallo, 16,628 ....B 2
Ravenna, 56,815 ....D 2
Recanati, 7,242 ....D 3
Reggio di Calabria, 93,964.......................................E 5
Reggio nell'Emilia, 83,073 ....C 2
Rho, 27,586 ....B 2
Riesi, 17,899 ....E 6
Rieti, 21,278 ....D 3
Rimini, 72,720 ....D 2
Rionero in Vulture, 13,567 ....E 4
Riva, 7,626 ....C 2
Rome (cap.), 2,043,055 ....F 6
Rome, *2,656,104 ....F 6
Ronciglione, 5,772 ....C 3
Rossano, 13,323 ....F 5
Rovereto, 20,505 ....C 2
Rovigo, 22,804 ....C 2
Ruvo di Puglia, 23,216 ....F 4
Sala Consilina, 6,742 ....E 4
Salemi, 12,237 ....D 6
Salerno, 103,778 ....E 4
Salsomaggiore Terme, 10,376 ....B 2
Saluzzo, 11,991 ....A 2
Sambiase, 11,551 ....F 5
San Bartolomeo in Galdo, 8,745..E 4
San Benedetto del Tronto, 28,053 ....E 3
San Cataldo, 21,778 ....D 6
San Giovanni in Fiore, 16,528 ....F 5
San Giovanni in Persiceto, 8,692 ....C 2
San Marco in Lamis, 17,933 ......E 4
Sannicandro Garganico, 17,238 ....E 4
San Remo, 40,068 ....A 3
Sansepolcro, 10,063 ....D 3
San Severino Marche, 5,582 ......D 3
San Severo, 47,897 ....E 4
Santa Maria Capua Vetere, 29,925 ....E 4
Santeramo in Colle, 19,587..........F 4
San Vito al Tagliamento, 5,278 D 2

(continued on following page)

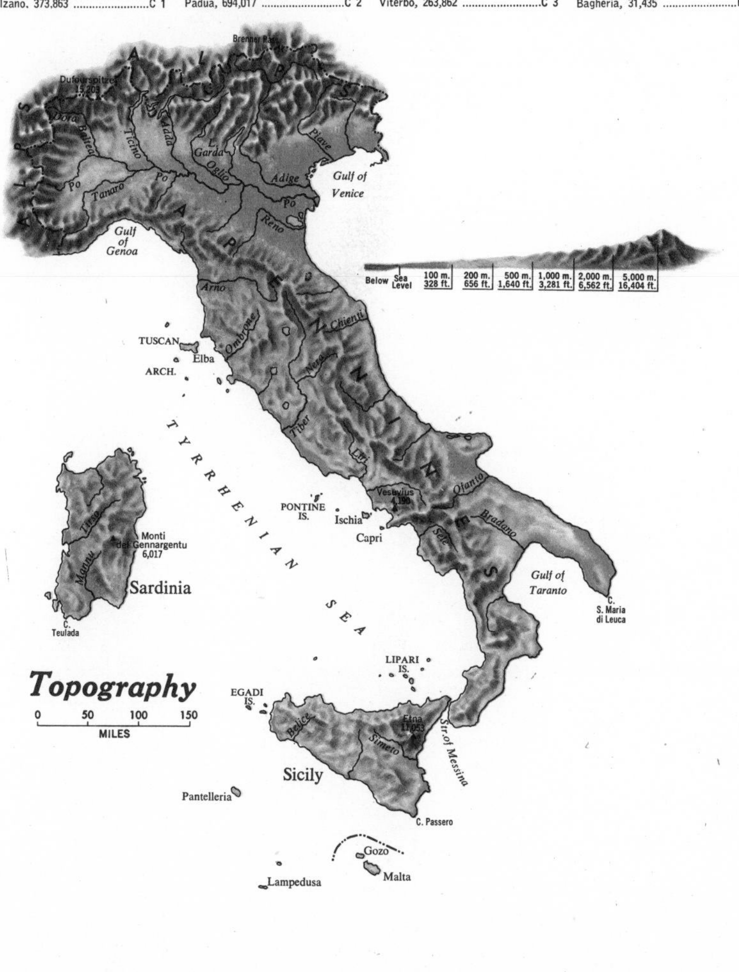

Brenner Pass
Dufourspitze 15,203
Ticino
Adda
Garda
Oglio
Adige
Piave
Po
Tanaro
Gulf of Venice
Reno
Gulf of Genoa
Arno
Ombrone
Tiber
Chienti
Below Sea Level
100 m. 328 ft.
200 m. 656 ft.
500 m. 1,640 ft.
1,000 m. 3,281 ft.
2,000 m. 6,562 ft.
5,000 m. 16,404 ft.
TUSCAN ARCH.
Elba
TYRRHENIAN SEA
PONTINE IS.
Ischia
Capri
Vesuvius 4,190
Ofanto
Bradano
Sele
Gulf of Taranto
C. S. Maria di Leuca
Monti del Gennargentu 6,017
Sardinia
C. Teulada
LIPARI IS.
EGADI IS.
Etna 10,958
Simeto
Str. of Messina
Sicily
Pantelleria
C. Passero
Gozo
Malta
Lampedusa
0 50 100 150
MILES

Topography

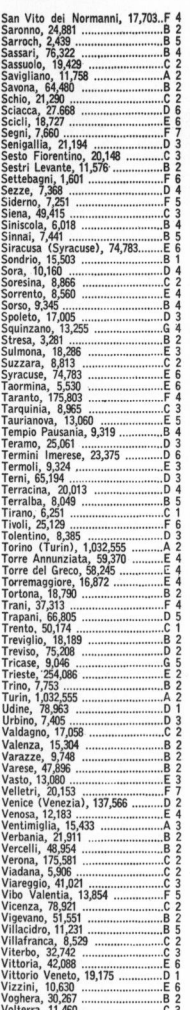

San Vito dei Normanni, 17,703..F 4
Saronno, 24,881 ....B 2
Sarroch, 2,439 ....B 5
Sassari, 76,322 ....B 4
Sassuolo, 19,429 ....C 2
Savigliano, 11,758 ....A 2
Savona, 64,480 ....B 2
Schio, 21,290 ....C 2
Sciacca, 27,668 ....D 6
Scicli, 18,727 ....E 7
Segni, 7,660 ....F 7
Senigallia, 21,194 ....D 3
Sesto Fiorentino, 20,148 ....C 3
Sestri Levante, 11,576 ....B 2
Settebagni, 1,601 ....F 6
Sezze, 7,368 ....E 4
Siderno, 7,251 ....F 5
Siena, 49,415 ....C 3
Sinnicola, 6,018 ....C 3
Sinnai, 7,441 ....B 5
Siracusa (Syracuse), 74,783...E 6
Sondrio, 15,503 ....B 1
Sora, 10,160 ....D 4
Soresina, 8,866 ....C 2
Sorrento, 8,560 ....E 4
Sorso, 9,345 ....B 4
Spoleto, 17,005 ....D 3
Squinzano, 13,255 ....G 4
Stresa, 3,281 ....B 2
Sulmona, 18,286 ....E 3
Suzzara, 8,813 ....C 2
Syracuse, 74,783 ....E 6
Taormina, 5,530 ....E 6
Taranto, 175,803 ....F 4
Tarquinia, 8,965 ....C 3
Taurianova, 13,060 ....E 5
Tempio Pausania, 9,319 ....B 4
Teramo, 25,061 ....D 3
Termini Imerese, 23,375 ....D 6
Termoli, 9,324 ....E 3
Terni, 65,194 ....D 3
Terracina, 20,013 ....D 4
Terralba, 8,049 ....B 5
Tirano, 6,251 ....C 1
Tivoli, 25,129 ....F 6
Tolentino, 8,385 ....D 3
Torino (Turin), 1,032,555 ....A 2
Torre Annunziata, 59,370 ....E 4
Torre del Greco, 58,245 ....E 4
Torremaggiore, 16,872 ....E 4
Tortona, 18,790 ....B 2
Trani, 37,313 ....F 4
Trapani, 66,805 ....D 5
Trento, 50,174 ....C 1
Treviglio, 18,189 ....B 2
Treviso, 75,208 ....D 2
Tricase, 9,046 ....G 5
Trieste, 254,086 ....E 2
Trino, 7,753 ....B 2
Turin, 1,032,555 ....A 2
Udine, 78,963 ....D 2
Urbino, 7,405 ....D 3
Valdagno, 17,058 ....C 2
Valenza, 15,304 ....B 2
Varazze, 9,748 ....B 2
Varese, 47,696 ....B 2
Vasto, 13,080 ....E 3
Velletri, 20,153 ....F 7
Venice (Venezia), 137,566 ......D 2
Venosa, 12,183 ....E 4
Ventimiglia, 15,433 ....A 3
Verbania, 21,911 ....B 2
Vercelli, 48,954 ....B 2
Verona, 175,581 ....C 2
Viadana, 5,906 ....C 2
Viareggio, 41,021 ....C 3
Vibo Valentia, 13,854 ....F 5
Vicenza, 78,921 ....C 2
Vigevano, 51,551 ....B 2
Villacidro, 11,231 ....B 5
Villafranca, 8,529 ....C 2
Viterbo, 32,742 ....C 3
Vittoria, 42,088 ....E 6
Vittorio Veneto, 19,175 ....D 1
Vizzini, 10,630 ....E 6
Voghera, 30,267 ....B 2
Volterra, 11,460 ....C 3

OTHER FEATURES

Adda (river) ....B 2
Adige (river) ....C 2
Adriatic (sea) ....E 7
Albano (lake) ....F 7
Alicudi (isl.), 230 ....E 5
Aniene (river) ....F 6
Apennines (range) ....D 3
Apennines, Central (range) ...D 3
Apennines, Northern (range)..D 2
Apennines, Southern (range)..E 4
Arno (river) ....C 3
Asinara (isl.), 709 ....B 4
Bernina (mt.) ....B 1
Bernina (pass) ....C 1
Blanc (mt.) ....A 2
Bolsena (lake) ....C 3
Bonifacio (strait) ....B 4
Bracciano (lake) ....D 3
Brenner (pass) ....C 1
Cagliari (gulf) ....B 5
Caprala (isl.), 467 ....B 3
Capri (isl.), 10,845 ....E 4
Carbonara (cape) ....B 5
Carnic Alps (range) ....D 1
Castellammare (gulf) ....D 5
Chienti (river) ....D 3
Cimone (mt.) ....C 2
Circeo (cape) ....D 4
Coghinas (river) ....B 4
Como (lake) ....B 1
Cottian Alps (range) ....A 2
Crati (river) ....F 5
Dolomite Alps (range) ....C 1
Dora Baltea (river) ....A 2
Dora Riparia (river) ....A 2
Egadi (isls.), 6,133 ....C 6
Elba (isl.), 27,577 ....C 3
Etna (volcano) ....E 6
Favignana (isl.), 4,726 ....C 6
Filicudi (isl.), 447 ....E 5
Gaeta (gulf) ....D 4
Garda (lake) ....C 2
Gennargentu (mts.) ....B 5
Genoa (gulf) ....B 3
Giannutri (isl.), 3 ....C 3
Giglio (isl.), 2,256 ....C 3
Gorgona (isl.), 292 ....B 3
Graian Alps (range) ....A 2
Gran Paradiso (mt.) ....A 2
Great Saint Bernard (pass)..A 2
Ionian (sea) ....F 6
Ischia (isl.), 34,213 ....D 4
Iseo (lake) ....C 2
Julian Alps (range) ....D 1
Lampedusa (isl.), 4,387 ......D 7
Lepontine Alps (range) ....B 1
Levanzo (isl.), 307 ....D 5
Ligurian (sea) ....B 3
Linosa (isl.), 424 ....D 7
Lipari (isl.), 8,844 ....E 5
Lipari (isls.), 13,741 ....E 5
Liri (river) ....D 4

Maggiore (lake) ....B 1
Malta (channel) ....E 6
Manfredonia (gulf) ....F 4
Mannu (river) ....B 5
Marettimo (isl.), 1,100 ....C 6
Maritime Alps (range) ....A 2
Marmolada (mt.) ....C 1
Mediterranean (sea) ....E 6
Messina (strait) ....E 6
Metauro (river) ....D 3
Mincio (river) ....C 2
Mont Cenis (tunnel) ....A 2
Montecristo (isl.), 8 ....C 3
Nera (river) ....D 3
Ofanto (river) ....E 4
Ombrone (river) ....C 3
Oristano (gulf) ....B 5
Orosei (gulf) ....C 4
Ortles (range) ....C 1
Otranto (strait) ....G 5
Ötztal Alps (range) ....C 1
Palmarola (isl.) ....D 4
Panarea (isl.), 272 ....E 5
Panaro (river) ....C 2
Pantelleria (isl.), 9,601 ....C 6
Parma (river) ....C 2
Pelagie (isls.), 4,811 ....D 7
Pennine Alps (range) ....A 2
Pescara (river) ....D 3
Pianosa (isl.), 878 ....C 3
Piave (river) ....C 2
Po (river) ....C 2
Policastro (gulf) ....E 5
Pompeii (ruins) ....E 4
Pontine (isls.), 5,732 ....D 4
Ponza (isl.), 4,660 ....D 4
Rosa (mt.) ....A 1
Salerno (gulf) ....E 4
Salina (isl.), 2,737 ....E 5
Salso (river) ....D 6
Sangro (river) ....E 4
San Pietro (isl.), 7,275 ....A 5
Santa Maria di Leuca (cape)..G 5
Sant'Antioco (isl.), 10,993 ..A 5
Sant'Eufemia (gulf) ....F 5
San Vito (cape) ....D 5
Sardinia (island), 1,400,103..A 4
Sele (river) ....E 4
Sicily (island), 4,683,076 ....E 6
Sicily (strait) ....D 6
Simeto (river) ....E 6
Spartivento (cape) ....B 5
Spartivento (cape) ....F 6
Squillace (gulf) ....F 5
Stromboli (isl.), 469 ....E 5
Stura (river) ....A 2
Tagliamento (river) ....D 1
Tanaro (river) ....B 2
Taranto (gulf) ....F 4
Testa del Gargano (cape) ....F 4
Teulada (cape) ....B 5
Tiber (river) ....D 3
Trasimeno (lake) ....D 3
Trebbia (river) ....B 2
Tremiti (isls.), 349 ....E 3
Trieste (gulf) ....D 2
Tuscan (arch.), 31,481 ....B 3
Tyrrhenian (sea) ....B 3
Ustica (isl.), 1,262 ....D 5
Varano (lake) ....E 3
Vaticano (cape) ....E 5
Venice (gulf) ....D 2
Ventotene (isl.), 811 ....D 4
Vesuvius (volcano) ....E 4
Volturno (river) ....E 4
Vulcano (isl.), 356 ....E 5

MALTA

CITIES and TOWNS

Sliema, 21,000 ....E 7
Valletta (cap.), 15,432 ....E 7
Victoria, 5,456 ....E 6

OTHER FEATURES

Gozo and Comino (isls.), 29,975..E 6
Malta (isl.), 288,200 ....E 7

SAN MARINO

CITIES and TOWNS

San Marino (cap.), 2,621 .....D 3
San Marino, *3,817 ....D 3

VATICAN CITY

Vatican City, 1,000 ....B 6

*City and suburbs.

Agriculture, Industry and Resources

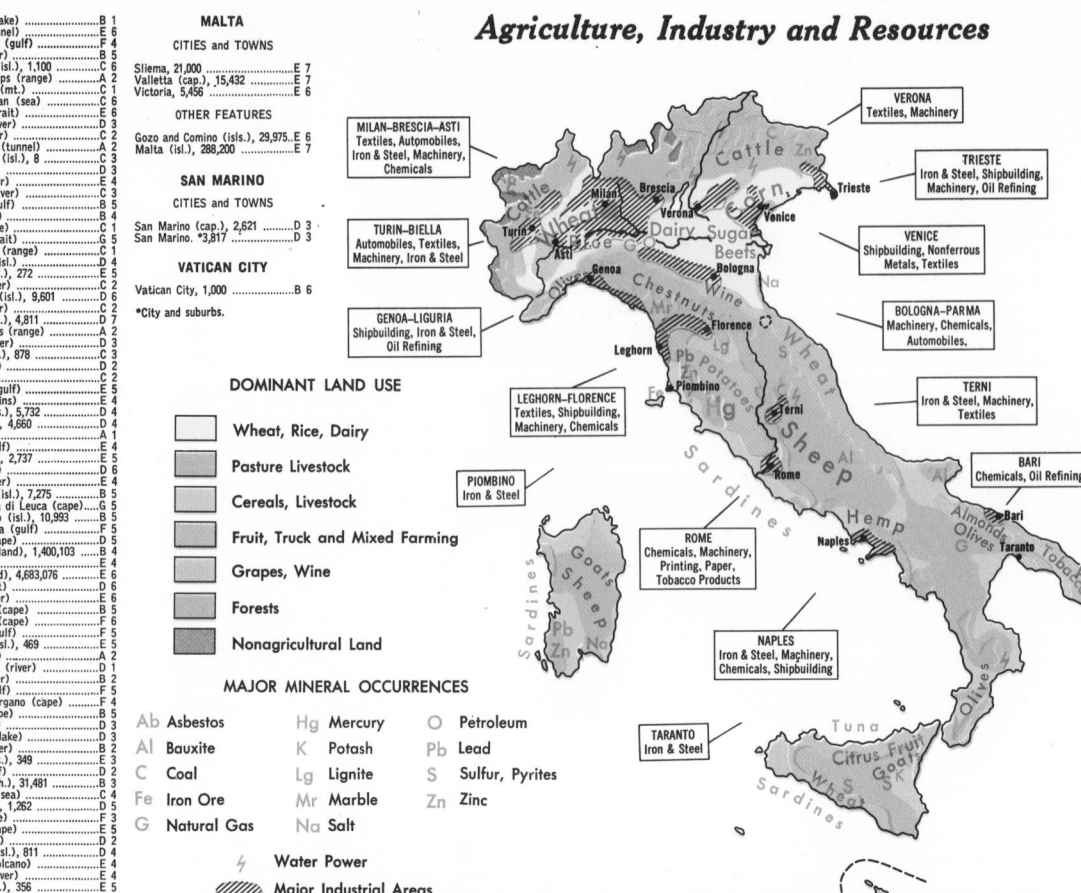

VERONA
Textiles, Machinery

TRIESTE
Iron & Steel, Shipbuilding, Machinery, Oil Refining

MILAN–BRESCIA–ASTI
Textiles, Automobiles, Iron & Steel, Machinery, Chemicals

VENICE
Shipbuilding, Nonferrous Metals, Textiles

TURIN–BIELLA
Automobiles, Textiles, Machinery, Iron & Steel

BOLOGNA–PARMA
Machinery, Chemicals, Automobiles,

GENOA–LIGURIA
Shipbuilding, Iron & Steel, Oil Refining

TERNI
Iron & Steel, Machinery, Textiles

LEGHORN–FLORENCE
Textiles, Shipbuilding, Machinery, Chemicals

BARI
Chemicals, Oil Refining

PIOMBINO
Iron & Steel

ROME
Chemicals, Machinery, Printing, Paper, Tobacco Products

NAPLES
Iron & Steel, Machinery, Chemicals, Shipbuilding

TARANTO
Iron & Steel

DOMINANT LAND USE

Wheat, Rice, Dairy

Pasture Livestock

Cereals, Livestock

Fruit, Truck and Mixed Farming

Grapes, Wine

Forests

Nonagricultural Land

MAJOR MINERAL OCCURRENCES

Ab Asbestos
Al Bauxite
C Coal
Fe Iron Ore
G Natural Gas

Hg Mercury
K Potash
Lg Lignite
Mr Marble
Na Salt

O Petroleum
Pb Lead
S Sulfur, Pyrites
Zn Zinc

Water Power

Major Industrial Areas

THE MEDITERRANEAN

SCALE OF MILES
0 50 100 200 300 400

SCALE OF KILOMETRES
0 50 100 200 300 400

Capitals of Countries .... ☆
Canals ....

SWITZERLAND
AREA 15,941 sq. mi.
POPULATION 6,230,000
CAPITAL Bern
LARGEST CITY Zürich
HIGHEST POINT Dufourspitze (Mte. Rosa) 15,203 ft.
MONETARY UNIT Swiss franc
MAJOR LANGUAGES German, French, Italian, Romansch
MAJOR RELIGIONS Protestantism, Roman Catholicism

LIECHTENSTEIN
AREA 61 sq. mi.
POPULATION 21,000
CAPITAL Vaduz
LARGEST CITY Vaduz
HIGHEST POINT Naafkopf 8,445 ft.
MONETARY UNIT Swiss franc
MAJOR LANGUAGE German
MAJOR RELIGION Roman Catholicism

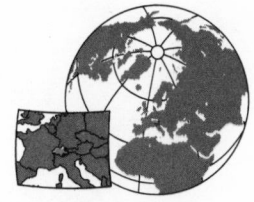

SWITZERLAND

LIECHTENSTEIN

LANGUAGES

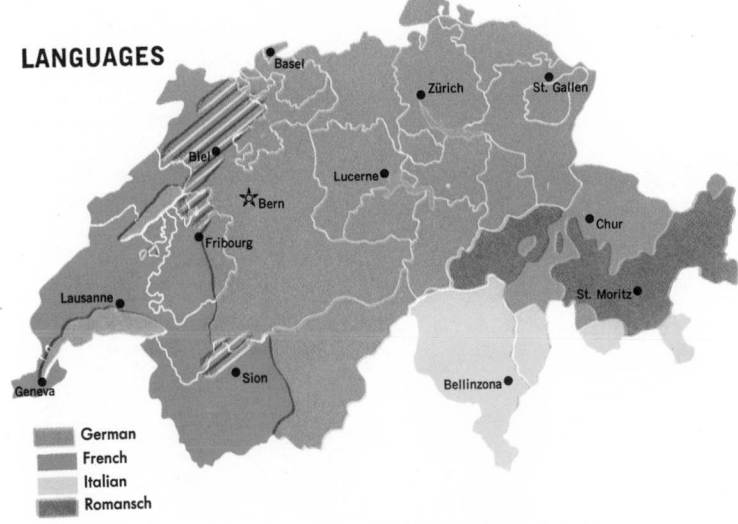

German
French
Italian
Romansch

Switzerland is a multilingual nation with four official languages. 70% of the people speak German, 19% French, 10% Italian and 1% Romansch.

SWITZERLAND

CANTONS

Aargau, 397,000 ....F 2
Appenzell, Ausser Rhoden,
(half-canton), 50,000 .....H 2
Appenzell, Inner Rhoden,
(half-canton), 13,500 .....H 2
Baselland (half-canton),
177,900 ....E 2
Baselstadt (half-canton),
237,300 ....E 1
Bern, 958,000 ....D 2
Fribourg, 163,000 ....D 3
Geneva, 304,400 ....B 4
Glarus, 42,000 ....H 2
Graubünden (Grisons), 155,000..J 3
Luzern (Lucerne), 274,000 ..F 2
Neuchâtel, 161,000 ....C 3
Nidwalden, 25,000 ....F 3
Obwalden, 25,000 ....F 3
Sankt Gallen, 363,000 ......H 2
Schaffhausen, 72,000 ....G 1
Schwyz, 84,800 ....G 2
Solothurn (Soleure), 220,000..E 2
Thurgau, 183,000 ....H 1
Ticino, 220,000 ....G 4
Unterwalden, 50,000 ....F 3
Uri, 33,000 ....G 3
Valais, 191,000 ....E 4
Vaud, 486,000 ....C 3
Zug, 61,000 ....G 2
Zürich, 1,048,000 ....G 2

CITIES AND TOWNS

Aadorf, 2,258 ....G 2
Aarau, 17,400 ....F 2
Aarau, *47,800 ....F 2
Aarberg, 2,355 ....D 2
Aarburg, 5,302 ....E 2
Adelboden, 2,881 ....E 3
Aeschi bei Spiez, 1,319 ....E 3
Affoltern am Albis, 4,904 ..F 2
Affoltern im Emmental, 1,206..E 2
Aigle, 4,381 ....C 4
Airolo, 2,023 ....G 3
Alle, 1,471 ....D 2
Allschwil, 15,500 ....D 1
Alpnach, 3,211 ....F 3
Altdorf, 7,477 ....G 3
Altstätten, 8,751 ....J 2
Amriswil, 6,752 ....H 1
Andermatt, 1,523 ....G 3
Appenzell, 5,082 ....H 2
Arbedo-Castione, 1,467 .....G 4
Arbon, 13,100 ....H 1
Ardon, 1,432 ....D 4
Arlesheim, 5,219 ....E 2
Arosa, 2,600 ....J 3
Arth, 6,321 ....G 2
Ascona, 3,053 ....G 4
Attalens, 1,023 ....C 3
Aubonne, 1,766 ....B 4
Avenches, 1,776 ....D 3
Baar, 9,114 ....F 2
Baden, 14,900 ....F 2
Baden, *54,500 ....F 2
Bad Ragaz, 2,699 ....H 2
Balerna, 3,040 ....G 5
Balsthal, 5,735 ....E 2
Bäretswil, 2,577 ....G 2
Basel, 213,200 ....E 1
Basel, *364,800 ....E 1
Bassecourt, 2,284 ....D 2
Bätterkinden, 1,916 ....E 2
Bauma, 3,214 ....G 2
Beatenberg, 1,303 ....E 3
Beckenried, 2,042 ....G 3

Beinwil am See, 2,346 ......F 2
Bellinzona, 14,900 ....H 4
Bellinzona, *25,700 ....H 4
Belp, 4,922 ....D 3
Bergün-Bravuogn, 551 ....J 3
Bern (cap.), 166,800 ....D 3
Bern, *258,000 ....D 3
Beromünster, 1,443 ....F 2
Bex, 4,667 ....D 4
Biasca, 3,349 ....H 4
Biberist, 7,188 ....D 2
Biel (Bienne), 67,800 ......D 2
Biel, *87,000 ....D 2
Bière, 1,166 ....B 3
Binningen, 13,800 ....D 1
Bischofszell, 3,811 ....H 1
Blumenstein, 1,121 ....E 3
Bodio, 1,276 ....H 4
Bolligen, 19,400 ....E 3
Boltigen, 1,691 ....D 3
Boncourt, 1,493 ....C 2
Bönigen, 1,883 ....E 3
Boswil, 1,663 ....F 2
Boudry, 3,086 ....C 3
Bourg-Saint-Pierre, 524 ....D 5
Breil-Brigels, 1,272 ....H 3
Breitenbach, 1,851 ....E 2
Bremgarten, 4,555 ....F 2
Brienz, 2,864 ....F 3
Brig, 4,647 ....E 4
Brissago, 1,845 ....G 4
Brittnau, 3,070 ....E 2
Brugg, 6,683 ....F 2
Brusio, 1,445 ....K 4
Bubendorf, 1,690 ....E 2
Bubikon, 2,612 ....G 2
Buchs, 6,345 ....H 2
Bülach, 8,188 ....G 1
Bulle, 5,983 ....D 3
Buochs, 2,733 ....F 3
Büren an der Aare, 2,432 ...D 2
Burgdorf, 15,600 ....E 2
Bürglen, 3,175 ....G 3
Bürglen, 1,899 ....H 1
Bussigny-près-Lausanne, 2,381..B 3
Bütschwil, 3,414 ....H 2
Carouge, 15,600 ....B 4
Castagnola, 3,775 ....G 4
Cazis, 1,553 ....H 3
Cernier, 1,545 ....C 2
Chalais, 1,597 ....E 4
Cham, 6,483 ....F 2
Chamoson, 2,088 ....D 4
Charmey, 1,144 ....D 3
Châteaux-d'Oex, 3,378 ......D 4
Châtel-Saint-Denis, 2,666 ..C 3
Chavornay, 1,414 ....C 3
Chexbres, 1,449 ....C 3
Chiasso, 7,377 ....G 5
Chur, 29,100 ....J 3
Churwalden, 877 ....J 3
Coire (Chur), 29,100 ....J 3
Conthey, 3,563 ....D 4
Coppet, 774 ....B 4
Corcelles-près-Payerne, 1,253..C 3
Corgémont, 1,414 ....C 2
Cossonay, 1,264 ....C 3
Courgenay, 1,666 ....D 2
Courroux, 1,667 ....D 2
Court, 1,493 ....D 2
Courtelary, 1,330 ....C 2
Courtételle, 1,618 ....D 2
Couvet, 3,450 ....C 3
Cully, 1,375 ....C 3
Därstetten, 900 ....D 3
Davos (Dorf and Platz), 9,588..J 3
Degersheim, 3,221 ....H 2
Delémont, 9,542 ....D 2
Derendingen, 4,463 ....E 2
Diemtigen, 1,934 ....D 3
Diessenhofen, 2,222 ....G 1
Dietikon, 20,600 ....F 2
Disentis-Mustèr, 2,376 .....G 3
Dombresson, 1,040 ....C 2
Dornach, 4,260 ....E 2
Dübendorf, 17,100 ....G 2
Düdingen, 4,248 ....D 3
Dürnten, 4,271 ....G 2
Dürrenroth, 1,221 ....E 2
Ebnat-Kappel, 4,979 ....H 2
Echallens, 1,428 ....C 3
Egg, 3,018 ....G 2
Eggiwil, 2,591 ....E 3
Eglisau, 1,911 ....G 1
Egnach, 3,483 ....H 1
Einsiedeln, 8,792 ....G 2
Elgg, 2,643 ....G 2
Emmen, 21,400 ....F 2
Engelberg, 2,646 ....F 3
Engi, 1,064 ....H 2
Ennenda, 3,076 ....H 2
Entlebuch, 3,318 ....E 3
Erlenbach im Simmental, 1,471..E 3
Ermatingen, 1,857 ....H 1
Erstfeld, 4,126 ....G 3
Eschenbach, 2,866 ....G 2
Escholzmatt, 3,257 ....E 3
Estavayer-le-Lac, 2,583 ....C 3
Evolène, 1,786 ....D 4
Faido, 1,441 ....G 4

(continued on following page)

Agriculture, Industry and Resources

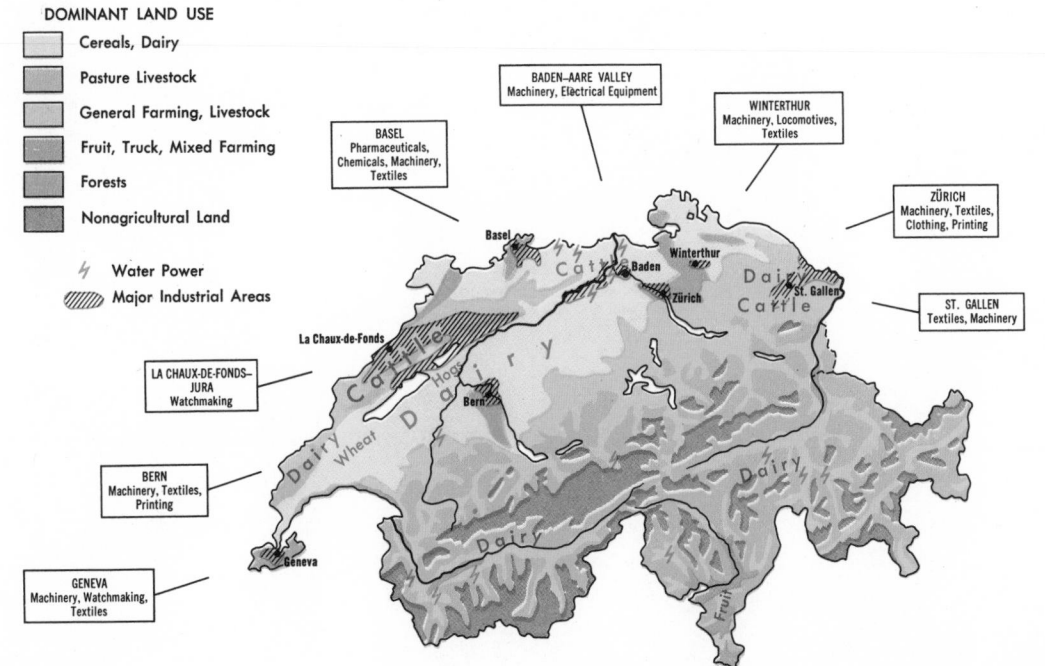

DOMINANT LAND USE
Cereals, Dairy
Pasture Livestock
General Farming, Livestock
Fruit, Truck, Mixed Farming
Forests
Nonagricultural Land

⚡ Water Power
▨ Major Industrial Areas

BASEL
Pharmaceuticals, Chemicals, Machinery, Textiles

BADEN–AARE VALLEY
Machinery, Electrical Equipment

WINTERTHUR
Machinery, Locomotives, Textiles

ZÜRICH
Machinery, Textiles, Clothing, Printing

ST. GALLEN
Textiles, Machinery

LA CHAUX-DE-FONDS–JURA
Watchmaking

BERN
Machinery, Textiles, Printing

GENEVA
Machinery, Watchmaking, Textiles

(continued)

Topography

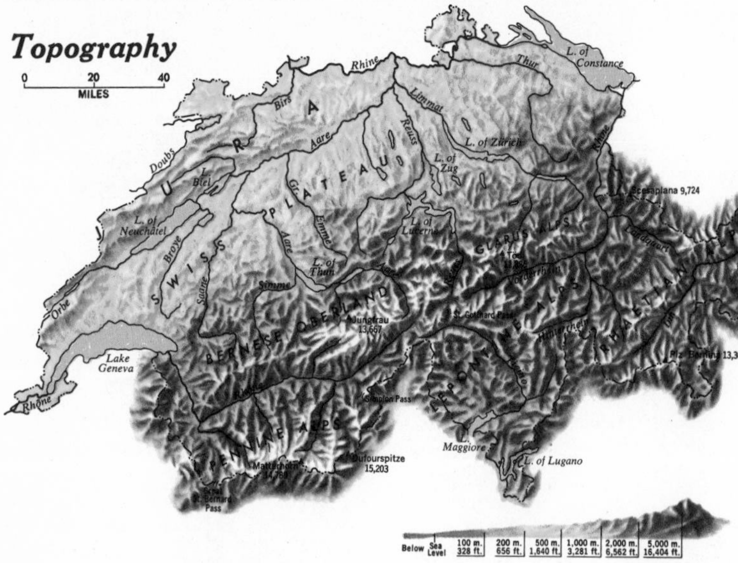

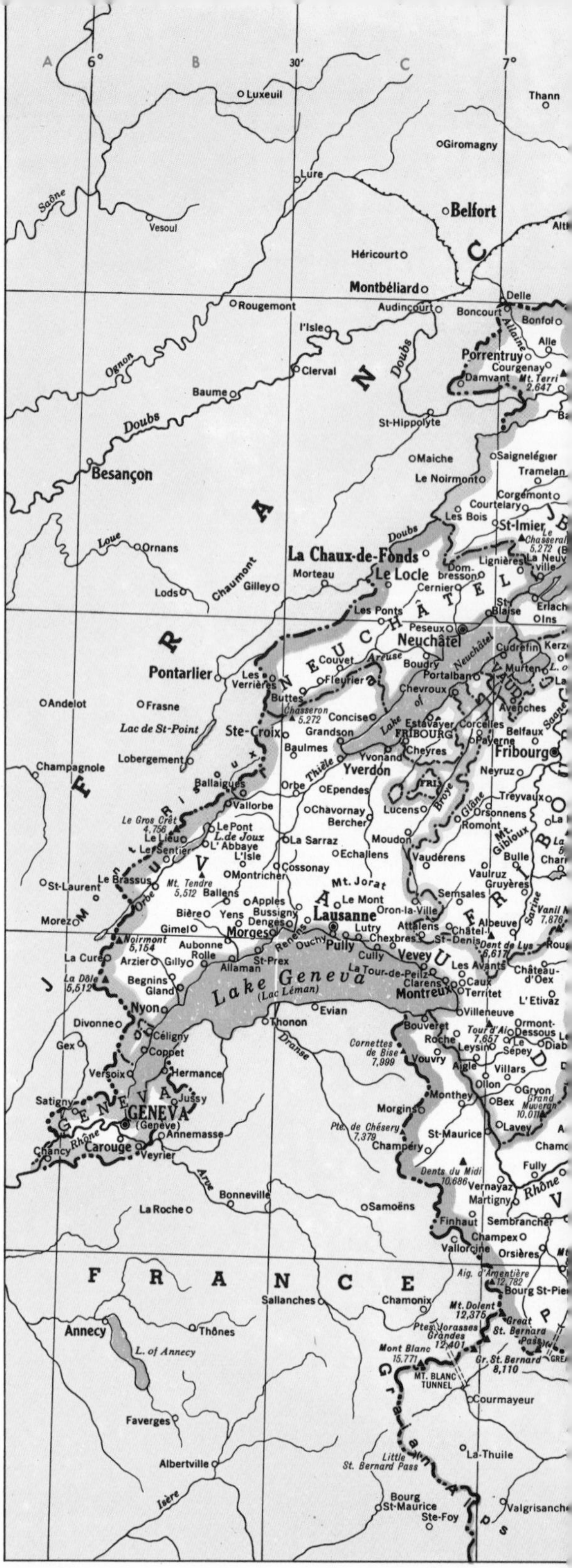

SWITZERLAND (continued)

Flawil, 7,256 H 2
Fleurier, 3,814 C 3
Flims, 1,444 H 3
Flüelen, 1,717 G 3
Flums, 4,462 H 2
Frauenfeld, 16,800 G 1
Fribourg, 38,500 D 3
Fribourg, *47,300 D 3
Frick, 2,123 E 1
Frutigen, 5,565 E 3
Fully, 3,419 D 4
Gais, 2,488 H 2
Gelterkinden, 3,870 E 2
Geneva (Genève), 169,500 B 4
Geneva, *307,500 B 4
Gersau, 1,754 G 2
Gimel, 1,091 B 3
Giornico, 1,063 G 4
Giswil, 2,656 F 3
Giubiasco, 4,281 H 4
Gland, 1,545 B 4
Glarus, 5,852 H 2
Glattfelden, 2,426 F 1
Gordola, 1,794 G 4
Göschenen, 1,284 G 3
Gossau, 9,731 H 2
Grabs, 4,218 H 2
Grandson, 2,091 C 3
Gränichen, 4,411 F 2
Grenchen, 19,800 D 2
Grenchen, *23,400 D 2
Grindelwald, 3,244 E 3
Grossandelfingen, 1,102 G 1
Grosswangen, 2,373 F 2
Gruyères, 1,349 D 3
Gsteig, 937 D 4
Guggisberg, 2,021 D 3
Gurtnellen, 1,048 G 3
Hallau, 1,966 F 1
Heiden, 3,158 H 2
Heimberg, 2,125 E 3
Hemberg, 1,011 H 2
Henau (Uzwil), 7,828 H 2
Hérémence, 1,868 D 4
Herisau, 15,500 H 2
Hermance, 512 B 4
Herzogenbuchsee, 4,641 E 2
Hinwil, 4,811 G 2
Hochdorf, 4,452 F 2
Horgen, 15,300 G 2
Hospental, 289 F 3
Huttwil, 4,664 E 2
Igis, 3,902 J 3
Ilanz, 1,843 H 3
Illnau, 6,160 G 2
Ingenbohl, 5,046 G 2
Innertkirchen, 1,230 F 3
Ins, 2,486 D 2
Interlaken, 4,738 E 3
Jegenstorf, 1,397 D 2
Jenaz, 1,143 J 3
Jona, 5,686 G 2
Jungfraujoch E 3
Kaltbrunn, 2,527 H 2
Kandersteg, 937 E 4
Kerns, 3,553 F 3
Kerzers, 2,228 D 3
Kilchberg, 6,784 F 2
Kirchberg, 3,304 E 2
Kirchberg, 5,554 G 2
Kleinlützel, 1,269 D 2
Klingnau, 2,192 F 1
Klosters, 3,181 J 3
Kloten, 8,446 G 2
Koblenz, 1,114 F 1
Kölliken, 3,007 F 2
Köniz, 30,600 D 3
Kreuzlingen, 14,900 H 1
Kriens, 17,200 F 2
Küsnacht, 12,800 G 2
Küssnacht, 12,400 F 2
Küttigen, 3,457 F 2
L'Abbaye, 1,124 B 3
La Chaux-de-Fonds, 42,800 C 2
Lachen, 3,913 G 2
La Neuveville, 3,216 D 2
Langenthal, 12,400 E 2
Langnau, 9,201 E 3
Langnau am Albis, 2,850 G 2
La Roche, 1,043 D 3
La Sarraz, 1,026 C 3
La Tour-de-Peilz, 6,820 C 4
Läufelfingen, 1,176 E 2
Laufen, 3,955 D 2
Laufenburg, 1,850 F 1
Laupen, 1,607 D 3
Lauperswil, 2,652 E 3
Lausanne, 138,300 C 3
Lausanne, *214,900 C 3
Lauterbrunnen, 3,216 E 3
Le Brassus (Le Chenit), 5,242 B 3
Le Châble, 4,237 D 4
Le Lieu, 970 B 3
Le Locle, 15,100 C 2
Le Mont, 1,719 C 3
Lengnau, 3,524 D 2
Lenk, 1,900 D 4
Le Noirmont, 1,559 C 2
Lens, 1,743 D 4
Lenzburg, 6,378 F 2
Les Bois, 1,098 C 2
Les Ponts-de-Martel, 1,429 C 2
Les Verrières, 1,084 B 3
Leuk, 2,546 E 4
Leukerbad, 619 E 4
Leysin, 2,241 C 4
Liestal, 11,300 E 2
Linthal, 2,645 H 3
Littau, 8,715 F 2
Locarno, 12,200 G 4
Locarno, *21,000 G 4
Lucens, 1,620 C 3
Lucerne, 73,000 F 2
Lucerne, *148,500 F 2
Lugano, 21,100 G 4
Lugano, *50,000 G 4
Lungern, 1,794 F 3
Luthern, 1,801 E 2
Lutry, 3,481 C 3
Lützelflüh, 3,960 E 3
Luzein, 1,013 J 3
Luzern (Lucerne), 73,000 F 2
Lyss, 5,616 D 2
Maienfeld, 1,488 J 2
Malans, 1,358 J 3
Malters, 4,579 F 2
Malvaglia, 1,120 H 4
Männedorf, 6,182 G 2
Marbach, 1,347 E 3
Martigny, 7,593 C 4
Meilen, 8,203 G 2
Meiringen, 3,749 F 3
Melchnau, 1,511 E 2
Melide, 1,046 G 5
Mellingen, 1,941 F 2
Mels, 5,254 H 2
Mendrisio, 5,100 G 5
Menzingen, 3,340 G 2
Menznau, 2,275 E 2
Mesocco, 1,324 H 4
Minusio, 3,663 G 4
Möhlin, 4,681 E 1
Mollis, 2,303 H 2
Montana-Vermala, 1,543 E 4
Monthey, 6,834 C 4
Montreux-Le Châtelard, 20,100 C 4
Morges, 8,420 B 3
Moudon, 2,806 C 3
Moutier, 7,472 D 2
Müllheim, 1,475 G 1
Mümliswil-Ramiswil, 2,714 E 2
Münchenbuchsee, 3,652 E 2
Münsingen, 6,051 E 3
Muotathal, 2,592 G 3
Muri, 3,957 F 2
Muri bei Bern, 7,855 E 3
Murten, 3,330 D 3
Müstair, 717 K 3
Muttenz, 14,000 E 1
Näfels, 3,617 H 2
Naters, 3,797 E 4
Nebikon, 1,206 F 2
Nesslau, 2,002 H 2
Netstal, 2,925 H 2
Neuchâtel, 36,300 C 3
Neuchâtel, *52,600 C 3
Neuenegg, 2,921 D 3
Neuhausen am Rheinfall, 11,800 G 1
Neunkirch, 1,208 F 1
Niederbipp, 3,141 E 2
Niederurnen, 3,347 G 2
Niederweningen, 1,027 F 1
Nunningen, 1,372 E 2
Nyon, 7,643 B 4
Oberägeri, 2,656 G 2
Oberburg, 3,030 E 2
Oberdiessbach, 1,927 E 3
Oberdorf, 1,132 E 2
Oberriet, 5,498 J 2
Obersaxen, 710 H 3
Oberuzwil, 4,394 H 2
Oensingen, 2,907 E 2
Ollon, 4,126 D 4
Olten, 21,900 E 2
Olten, *47,100 E 2
Orbe, 3,824 C 3
Ormont-Dessous, 996 D 4
Orsières, 2,281 D 4
Payerne, 6,024 C 3
Peseux, 4,933 C 3
Pfäffikon, 5,735 G 2
Pfaffnau, 2,575 E 2
Pieterlen, 2,978 D 2
Pontresina, 1,067 J 3
Porrentruy, 7,095 C 2
Poschiavo, 3,743 J 4
Pratteln, 9,492 E 1
Pully, 15,900 C 4
Quinto, 1,365 G 3
Rafz, 1,925 G 1
Ramsen, 1,181 G 1
Rapperswil, 7,585 G 2
Raron, 1,077 E 4
Rechthalten, 1,015 D 3
Regensdorf, 4,997 F 2
Reichenbach, 2,829 E 3
Reiden, 2,795 F 2
Reigoldswil, 1,192 E 2
Reinach, 5,174 F 2
Renens, 15,200 C 3
Rheinau, 2,363 G 1
Rheineck, 3,047 J 2
Rheinfelden, 5,197 E 1
Richterswil, 5,842 G 2
Riehen, 20,100 E 1
Riggisberg, 1,949 E 3
Riva San Vitale, 1,358 G 5
Rivera, 950 G 4
Roggwil, 3,420 E 2
Rohrbach, 1,534 E 2
Rolle, 2,942 B 4
Romanshorn, 7,755 H 1
Romont, 2,982 C 3
Rorschach, 13,400 H 2
Rorschach, *24,500 H 2
Rosenlaui F 3
Rothrist, 5,048 E 2
Rougemont, 860 D 4
Roveredo, 1,878 H 4
Rüeggisberg, 2,035 E 3
Rüschegg, 1,628 D 3
Ruswil, 4,657 F 2
Rüthi, 1,521 J 2
Rüti, Glarus, 738 H 3
Rüti, Zürich, 8,282 G 2
Saanen, 5,649 D 4
Saas-Fee, 739 E 4
Sachseln, 2,721 F 3
Saignelégier, 1,636 D 2
Saint-Blaise, 2,412 D 2
Sainte-Croix, 6,925 B 3
Saint-Imier, 6,704 D 2
Saint-Martin, 1,155 E 4
Saint-Maurice, 3,196 C 4
Saint Moritz, 3,751 J 3
Saint Niklaus, 2,071 E 4
Saint-Prex, 1,897 B 4
Saint-Stephan, 1,227 D 3
Saint-Ursanne, 1,304 D 2
Samedan, 2,106 J 3
Sankt Gallen, 78,900 H 2
Sargans, 2,571 H 2
Sarnen, 6,554 F 3
Satigny, 1,594 A 4
Savièse, 3,203 D 4
Savognin, 632 J 3
Saxon, 2,305 D 4
Schaffhausen, 37,400 G 1
Schaffhausen, *56,900 G 1
Schangnau, 1,031 E 3
Schänis, 2,328 H 2
Schiers, 2,363 J 3
Schinznach-Dorf, 1,081 F 2
Schlarigna-Celerina, 868 J 3
Schleitheim, 1,494 G 1
Schlieren, 11,600 F 2
Schönenwerd, 4,561 E 2
Schüpfheim, 3,771 F 3
Schwanden, 3,020 H 2
Schwyz, 12,200 G 2
Scuol-Schuls, 1,429 K 3
Sedrun, 1,855 G 3
Seewis, 969 J 3
Sembrancher, 710 D 4
Sempach, 1,345 F 2
Semsales, 762 C 3
Seon, 3,006 F 2
Sevelen, 2,370 H 2
Sierre, 8,690 D 4
Siggenthal, 7,376 F 1
Signau, 2,555 E 3
Sigriswil, 3,739 E 3
Silenen, 2,261 G 3
Sils im Domleschg, 737 H 3
Silvaplana, 346 J 4
Sins, 2,195 F 2
Sion, 18,900 D 4
Sirnach, 3,075 G 2
Sissach, 4,574 E 2
Solothurn (Soleure), 18,900 E 2
Solothurn, *36,400 E 2
Sonvico, 1,005 G 4
Spiez, 8,168 E 3
Stäfa, 6,947 G 2
Stalden, 1,007 E 4
Stammheim, 1,460 G 1
Stans, 4,337 F 3
Steckborn, 3,514 G 1
Steffisburg, 12,100 E 3
Stein, 1,060 E 1
Stein am Rhein, 2,588 G 1
Sulgen, 1,252 H 1
Sulz, 1,022 F 1
Sumiswald, 5,525 E 2
Sursee, 5,324 F 2
Tafers, 1,621 D 3
Täuffelen, 1,500 D 2
Tavannes, 3,939 D 2
Thalwil, 13,200 G 2
Thayngen, 3,013 G 1
Therwil, 1,946 E 1
Thun, 33,700 E 3
Thun, *56,700 E 3
Thusis, 1,998 H 3
Trachselwald, 1,269 E 2
Tramelan, 5,567 D 2
Trogen, 2,101 H 2
Trub, 1,981 E 3
Trun, 1,583 G 3
Turbenthal, 2,685 G 2
Turgi, 1,860 F 1
Ueberstorf, 1,536 D 3
Uetendorf, 2,810 E 3
Unterägeri, 3,832 G 2
Unterkulm, 2,149 F 2
Unterseen, 3,783 E 3
Untervaz, 1,142 H 3
Urnäsch, 2,330 H 2
Uster, 20,800 G 2
Utzenstorf, 2,821 E 2
Uznach, 3,173 H 2
Uzwil, 7,828 H 2
Vallorbe, 3,990 B 3
Vals, 968 H 3
Vaz-Obervaz, 1,568 J 3
Vechigen, 3,153 E 3
Vernayaz, 1,188 D 4
Versoix, 3,426 B 4
Vevey, 18,000 C 4
Vevey, *29,600 C 4
Veyrier, 2,705 B 4
Villeneuve, 2,366 C 4
Visp, 3,658 E 4
Vouvry, 1,368 C 4
Wädenswil, 14,300 G 2
Wahlern, 4,723 D 3
Wald, 7,778 G 2
Waldenburg, 1,284 E 2
Waldkirch, 2,487 H 2
Wallenstadt, 3,296 H 2
Walzenhausen, 2,345 J 2
Wangen an der Aare, 1,936 E 2
Wängi, 1,681 H 1
Wartau, 3,284 H 2
Wattwil, 7,480 H 2
Weesen, 1,280 H 2
Weggis, 2,243 F 2
Weinfelden, 6,954 H 1
Wettingen, 19,700 F 2
Wetzikon, 12,600 G 2
Wil, 12,900 H 2
Wilchingen, 1,061 F 1
Wilderswil, 1,701 E 3
Wildhaus, 1,179 H 2
Willisau, 2,508 F 2
Wimmis, 1,756 E 3
Windisch, 5,377 F 1
Winterthur, 92,500 G 1
Winterthur, *104,600 G 1
Wohlen, 8,636 F 2
Wohlen bei Bern, 2,985 D 3
Wolfenschiessen, 1,647 F 3
Wolhusen, 3,446 F 2
Wollerau, 2,415 G 2
Worb, 5,885 E 3
Wynigen, 2,221 E 2
Yverdon, 19,200 C 3
Yvonand, 1,290 C 3
Zäziwil, 1,265 E 3
Zell, Luzern, 1,582 E 2
Zell, Zürich, 3,347 G 2
Zermatt, 2,731 E 4
Zizers, 1,290 J 3
Zofingen, 1,290 F 2
Zollikofen, 6,237 E 3
Zollikon, 12,100 G 2
Zug, 22,300 G 2
Zuoz, 1,001 J 3
Zürich, 432,400 F 2
Zürich, *671,500 F 2
Zurzach, 2,694 F 1
Zweisimmen, 2,676 D 3

OTHER FEATURES

Aa (river) F 3
Aare (river) E 3
Ägerisee (lake) G 2
Albristhorn (mt.) D 4
Aletschhorn (mt.) F 4
Allaine (river) D 2
Areuse (river) C 3
Ault (peak) H 3
Baldeggersee (lake) F 2
Balmhorn (mt.) E 4
Bärenhorn (mt.) H 3
Basodino (mt.) G 4
Bernese Oberland (region) E 3
Bernina, Piz (mt.) J 4
Bernina (pass) K 4
Bernina (river) J 4
Beverin (mt.) H 3
Biel (lake) D 2
Birs (river) D 2
Blindenhorn (mt.) F 4
Blümlisalp (mt.) E 3
Bodensee (Constance) (lake) H 1
Borgne (river) D 4
Breithorn (mt.) E 5
Breithorn (mt.) E 4
Brienz (lake) F 3
Brienzer Rothorn (mt.) F 3
Broye (river) C 3
Brulé (mt.) D 4
Buchegg (mts.) D 2
Bürkelkopf (mt.) K 3
Bütschelegg (mt.) D 3
Calancasca (river) H 4
Campo Tencia (peak) G 4
Ceneri (mt.) G 4
Cheville (pass) D 4
Churfirsten (mt.) H 2
Claridenstock (mt.) G 3
Collon (mt.) D 5
Constance (lake) H 1
Dammastock (mt.) F 3
Davos (valley) J 3
Dent Blanche (mt.) E 4
Dent de Lys (mt.) D 4
Dent de Ruth (mt.) D 3
Dent d'Hérens (mt.) E 5
Dents du Midi (mt.) C 4
Diablerets (mt.) D 4
Doldenhorn (mt.) E 4
Dolent (mt.) C 5
Dom (mt.) E 4
Doubs (river) C 2
Drance (river) D 4
Dufourspitze (mt.) E 5
Emmental (valley) E 3
Engadine (valley) J-K 3-4
Err (mt.) J 3
Finsteraarhorn (mt.) F 3
Finstermünz (pass) K 3
Fletschhorn (mt.) F 4
Flüela (pass) J 3
Fluhberg (mt.) G 2
Fort (mt.) D 4
Furka (pass) F 3
Generoso (mt.) H 5
Geneva (lake) C 4
Giacomo (pass) G 4
Gibloux (mt.) D 3
Glâne (river) C 3
Glärnisch (mt.) H 2

SWITZERLAND and LIECHTENSTEIN

CONIC PROJECTION

SCALE OF MILES

SCALE OF KILOMETRES

Capitals of Countries .... ☆
Capitals of Cantons .... ●
International Boundaries .... – ⋅ – ⋅
Canals ....

Copyright by C.S. HAMMOND & Co., N.Y.

Glarus Alps (mts.)	H 3	Jungfrau (mt.)	E 3
Glatt (river)	G 2	Jura (mts.)	B 2
Goms (valley)	F 4	Kaiseregg (mt.)	D 3
Grand Combin (mt.)	D 5	Kesch (mt.)	H 3
Grande Dixence (dam)	D 4	Kisten (pass)	H 3
Grauhörner (mts.)	F 4	Klausen (pass)	G 3
Great Saint Bernard (mt.)	D 5	Kleine Emme (river)	E 3
Greifensee (lake)	G 2	La Berra (mt.)	D 3
Greina (pass)	G 4	La Dôle (mt.)	B 3
Gridone (mt.)	G 4	Landquart (river)	J 3
Grimsel (pass)	F 3	Le Gros Crêt (mt.)	C 3
Gross Emme (river)	E 3	Léman (Geneva) (lake)	C 4
Gross Litzner (mt.)	K 3	Leone (mt.)	F 4
Hallwilersee (lake)	F 2	Lepontine Alps (range)	F 4
Hausstock (mt.)	H 3	Le Raimeux (mt.)	D 2
Hinterrhein (river)	J 3	Limmat (river)	F 2
Hochwang (mt.)	J 3	Linard (mt.)	K 3
Hohenstollen (mt.)	F 3	Linden (mts.)	K 3
Honegg (mt.)	E 3	Linth (river)	G 3
Hörnli (mt.)	G 2	Lorze (river)*	F 2
Ilfis (river)	E 3	Lötschberg (tunnel)	E 4
Ihn (river)	K 3	Lötschental (valley)*	E 4
Joch (pass)	K 3	Lower Engadine (valley)	K 3
Jorat (mt.)	C 4	Lucerne (Luzern) (lake)	F 3
Joux (lake)	B 3	Lugano (lake)	H 5
Julia (river)	J 4	Madrisahorn (mt.)	K 3
		Maggia (river)	G 4

Maggiore (lake)	G 5	Pennine Alps (range)	E 5
Männliflüh (mt.)	D 3	Pilatus (mt.)	F 3
Marmontana (mt.)	G 4	Plessur (river)	J 3
Matterhorn (mt.)	E 5	Poschiavo (river)	K 4
Mauvoisin (dam)	D 4	Poschiavo (valley)	K 4
Moësa (river)	H 4	Pragel (pass)	G 3
Molare (mt.)	G 3	Quatervals (mt.)	K 3
Montoz (mt.)	C 2	Reuss (river)	F 2
Morat (lake)	D 3	Rhaetian Alps (range)	J 3
Moro (mt.)	E 5	Rhätikon (mts.)	J 2
Moron (mt.)	C 2	Rheinwaldhorn (mt.)	H 4
Muota (river)	G 3	Rhine (river)	E 1, J 2
Muretto (pass)	J 4	Rhône (river)	E 4
Murg (river)	G 2	Rigi (mt.)	F 3
Murtaröl (mt.)	K 3	Rimpfischhorn (mt.)	E 4
Muttler (mt.)	K 3	Ringelspitz (mt.)	H 3
Napf (mt.)	E 3	Risoux (mt.)	B 3
National Park	K 3	Rosa (mt.)	E 5
Neuchâtel (lake)	C 3	Rothorn (mt.)	F 3
Noirmont (mt.)	C 3	Saane (Sarine) (river)	D 3
Oberalp (pass)	G 3	Saint Gotthard (pass)	G 3
Oberalpstock (mt.)	G 3	Saint Gotthard (tunnel)	G 3
Ochsen (mt.)	F 2	San Bernardino (pass)	H 4
Ofen (pass)	K 3	Säntis (mt.)	G 2
Ofenhorn (mt.)	F 4	Sarine (Saane) (river)	D 3
Orbe (river)	B 3		

Sarnen (lake)	F 3	Tamaro (mt.)	G 4
Sasseneire (mt.)	E 4	Tamina (river)	H 3
Scaletta (pass)	J 3	Tendre (peak)	B 3
Schesaplana (mt.)	J 3	Terri (mt.)	H 3
Schreckhorn (mt.)	F 3	Terri (mt.)	H 3
Schwarzhorn (mt.)	F 3	Thiële (river)	E 3
Scopi (mt.)	G 3	Thun (lake)	E 3
Seez (river)	H 3	Thur (river)	G 1
Segnes (pass)	H 3	Ticino (river)	G 4
Sempach (lake)	F 2	Tödi (mt.)	G 3
Sense (river)	D 3	Toggenburg (dist.)	H 2
Septimer (pass)	J 4	Töss (river)*	
Sesvenna (mt.)	K 3	Tour d'Aï (mt.)	C 4
Sihlsee (lake)	G 3	Turnen (mt.)*	D 3
Silvretta (mts.)	K 3	Umbrail (pass)	K 3
Simme (river)	D 3	Untersee (lake)	
Simplon (pass)	F 4	Upper Engadine (valley)	J 3
Simplon (tunnel)	F 4	Uri-Rotstock (mt.)	G 3
Sol (mt.)*	H 3	Vadret (mt.)	
Sonnenhorn (mt.)	G 4	Valserrhein (river)	H 3
Splügen (pass)	H 4	Vélan (mt.)	D 5
Stockhorn (mt.)	D 3	Visp (river)	
Sulzflüh (mt.)	K 3	Vorab (mt.)	H 3
Susten (pass)*	G 3	Vorderrhein (river)	
Sustenhorn (mt.)	G 3	Wallenstadt (lake)	H 2
		Wandfluhhorn (mt.)	

Weissenstein (mts.)	D 2
Weisshorn (mt.)	E 4
Weisshorn (mt.)	J 3
Wetterhorn (mt.)	F 3
Wildhorn (mt.)	E 4
Wildstrubel (mt.)	E 4
Wildersee (lake)*	G 1
Zellersee (lake)*	G 4
Zucchero (mt.)	G 4
Zug (lake)	F 2
Zürich (lake)	G 2
*City and suburbs.	

LIECHTENSTEIN

CITIES and TOWNS

Schaan, 3,022	H 2
Triesen, 1,789	H 2
Vaduz (cap.), 3,514	H 2

OTHER FEATURES

Naafkopf (mt.)	J 2
Ochsenkopf (mt.)	J 2
Rhätikon (mts.)	J 2
Rhine (river)	J 2

AUSTRIA

PROVINCES

Burgenland, 271,001 ... D 3
Carinthia, 495,226 ... B 3
Lower Austria, 1,374,012 ... C 2
Salzburg, 347,292 ... B 3
Styria, 1,137,865 ... C 3
Tirol, 462,899 ... B 3
Upper Austria, 1,131,623 ... C 2
Vienna (city), 1,631,423 ... D 2
Vorarlberg, 226,323 ... A 4

CITIES and TOWNS

Admont, 3,057 ... C 3
Aigen, 1,941 ... C 2
Alt Aussee, 2,026 ... B 3
Altheim, 4,271 ... C 2
Amstetten, 12,086 ... C 2
Andau, 3,011 ... D 3
Arnoldstein, 6,229 ... B 3
Aspang, 2,359 ... D 3
Attnang-Puchheim, 7,525 ... B 2
Bad Aussee, 5,146 ... B 3
Bad Goisern, 6,028 ... B 3
Bad Hofgastein, 4,700 ... B 3
Bad Ischl, 12,703 ... B 3
Bad Sankt Leonhard, 1,939 ... C 3
Baden, 22,484 ... D 2
Badgastein, 5,742 ... B 3
Berndorf, 8,992 ... C 2
Bischofshofen, 8,287 ... B 3
Bludenz, 11,127 ... A 4
Bramberg, 2,620 ... B 3
Braunau, 14,449 ... B 2
Bregenz, 21,428 ... A 4
Bruck an der Leitha, 6,791 ... D 2
Bruck an der Mur, 16,087 ... C 3
Deutsch Feistritz, 3,427 ... C 3
Deutsch Landsberg, 5,227 ... C 3
Deutsch Wagram, 4,207 ... D 2
Deutschkreutz, 3,901 ... D 3
Dornbirn, 28,075 ... A 3
Ebenfurth, 2,342 ... D 2
Ebensee, 9,602 ... B 3
Eferding, 3,151 ... C 2

Hollabrunn, 5,832 ... D 2
Hopfgarten in Nordtirol, 4,163 ... B 3
Horn, 4,705 ... C 2
Hüttenberg, 2,257 ... C 3
Imst, 5,057 ... A 3
Innsbruck, 113,468 ... A 3
Jenbach, 5,479 ... B 3
Judenburg, 9,869 ... C 3
Kapfenberg, 23,859 ... C 3
Kappl, 1,970 ... B 4
Kaprun, 2,164 ... B 3
Kindberg, 5,766 ... C 3
Kirchdorf an der Krems, 2,964 ... C 3
Kitzbühel, 7,744 ... B 3
Klagenfurt, 69,218 ... C 3
Klosterneuburg, 22,787 ... D 2
Knittelfeld, 14,259 ... C 3
Köflach, 12,367 ... C 3
Königswiesen, 2,707 ... C 2
Korneuburg, 8,276 ... D 2
Kössen, 2,361 ... B 3
Kötschach-Mauthen, 2,763 ... B 3
Krems, 21,046 ... C 2
Kufstein, 11,215 ... B 3
Kundl, 2,508 ... A 3
Laa an der Thaya, 4,925 ... D 2
Laakirchen, 6,722 ... B 3
Lambach, 3,019 ... C 2
Landeck, 6,514 ... A 3
Landskron, 9,058 ... B 3
Längenfeld, 2,314 ... B 4
Langenlois, 4,655 ... C 2
Langenwang, 3,734 ... C 3
Lavamünd, 2,506 ... C 3
Leibnitz, 6,356 ... C 3
Lenzing, 5,372 ... B 3
Leoben, 36,257 ... C 3
Leonfelden, 2,546 ... C 2
Lienz, 11,132 ... B 3
Liezen, 5,444 ... C 3
Lilienfeld, 3,307 ... C 2
Linz, 205,762 ... C 2
Lustenau, 12,582 ... A 4
Mannersdorf, 3,909 ... D 2
Marchegg, 2,159 ... D 2
Mariazell, 2,191 ... C 2
Matrei, 3,430 ... B 3
Mattersburg, 4,270 ... D 3
Mattighofen, 3,919 ... B 2
Mauerkirchen, 2,175 ... B 2
Mautern, 2,365 ... C 2
Mauthausen, 3,836 ... C 2

Sankt Veit an der Glan, 10,950 ... C 3
Sankt Wolfgang, 2,234 ... B 3
Schärding, 5,710 ... B 2
Scheibbs, 3,231 ... C 2
Schladming, 3,249 ... B 3
Schrems, 3,080 ... C 2
Schruns, 3,304 ... B 4
Schwarzach, 3,186 ... B 3
Schwaz, 9,455 ... A 3
Schwerberg, 3,369 ... C 2
Sierning, 7,527 ... C 2
Sillian, 1,948 ... B 3
Solbad Hall, 10,750 ... A 3
Spital, 2,421 ... B 3
Spittal, 10,045 ... B 3
Steinach, 2,155 ... A 3
Steyr, 38,306 ... C 2
Stockerau, 11,853 ... D 2
Strassburg, 2,972 ... C 3
Tamsweg, 4,431 ... B 3
Telfs, 5,438 ... A 3
Ternitz, 9,032 ... D 3
Traiskirchen, 7,026 ... D 2
Traun, 16,026 ... C 2
Trieben, 4,023 ... C 3
Trofaiach, 6,909 ... C 3
Tulln, 6,306 ... D 2
Velden, 2,039 ... C 3
Villach, 32,971 ... B 3
Vöcklabruck, 9,353 ... B 2
Voitsberg, 6,353 ... C 3
Völkermarkt, 3,678 ... C 3
Vorderberg, 2,896 ... C 3
Waidhofen an der Thaya, 3,748 ... C 2
Waidhofen an der Ybbs, 5,586 ... C 2
Weitensfeld, 2,998 ... C 3
Weiz, 8,146 ... C 3
Wels, 41,060 ... C 2
Weyer, 2,367 ... C 3
Wiener Neustadt, 33,845 ... D 3
Wildon, 2,020 ... C 3
Wilhelmsburg, 6,196 ... C 2
Wolfsberg, 8,470 ... C 3
Wörgl, 6,828 ... B 3
Ybbs, 5,324 ... C 2
Zams, 2,782 ... A 3
Zell am See, 6,455 ... B 3
Zeltweg, 7,340 ... C 3
Zirl, 3,165 ... A 3
Zistersdorf, 3,011 ... D 2
Zwettl, 3,836 ... C 2

OTHER FEATURES

Allgäu Alps (mts.) ... A 3
Atter (lake) ... A 3
Bavarian Alps (mts.) ... A 3
Bodensee (Constance) (lake) ... A 3
Brenner (pass) ... A 3
Carnic Alps (mts.) ... B 3
Cogliants (Hohe Warte) (peak) ... B 3
Constance (lake) ... A 3
Da..ube (river) ... C 2
Danau (Danube) (river) ... C 2
Drau (river) ... C 3
Enns (river) ... C 2
Fertö tó (Neusiedler) (lake) ... D 3
Greiner (forest) ... C 3
Grossglockner (mt.) ... B 3
Gross Höllkogel (mt.) ... B 3
Gross Peilstein (mt.) ... B 3
Hochgolling (mt.) ... B 3
Hohe Tauern (range) ... B 3
Hohe Warte (peak) ... B 3
Inn (river) ... B 2
Kamp (river) ... C 2
Karawanken (mts.) ... C 3
Lechtaler Alps (mts.) ... A 3
March (river) ... D 2
Mühlviertel (region), 196,037 ... C 2
Mur (river) ... C 3
Mürz (river) ... C 3
Neusiedler (lake) ... D 3
Niedere Tauern (range) ... C 3
Ölsa (river) ... C 3
Ötztal Alps (mts.) ... A 3
Parseierspitze (mt.) ... A 3
Raab (river) ... C 3
Rhine (river) ... A 4
Salzach (river) ... B 3
Salzkammergut (region) ... B 3
Semmering (pass) ... C 3
Thaya (river) ... C 2
Traun (lake) ... B 3
Traun (river) ... C 2
Wildspitze (mt.) ... A 3
Zugspitze (mt.) ... A 3

CZECHOSLOVAKIA

REPUBLICS

Czech, 9,778,000 ... B 1
Slovak, 4,421,000 ... E 2

REGIONS

Jihočeský, 659,000 ... C 2
Jihomoravský, 1,941,000 ... D 2
Prague (city), 1,025,000 ... C 1
Severočeský, 1,122,000 ... C 1
Severomoravský, 1,695,000 ... D 1
Středočeský, 1,271,000 ... C 2
Středoslovenský, 1,379,000 ... E 2
Východočeský, 1,213,000 ... C 1
Východoslovenský, 1,199,000 ... F 2
Západočeský, 852,000 ... B 2
Západoslovenský, 1,843,000 ... D 2

CITIES and TOWNS

As, 10,000 ... B 1
Austerlitz (Slavkov), 4,869 ... D 2
Bánovce, 3,563 ... E 2
Banská Bystrica, 29,000 ... E 2
Banská Štiavnica, 10,381 ... E 2
Bardejov, 11,000 ... F 2
Bechyně, 2,398 ... C 2
Benešov, 10,000 ... C 2
Beroun, 17,000 ... C 2
Bílina, 17,000 ... B 1
Blansko, 11,000 ... D 2
Blatná, 3,596 ... C 2
Blovice, 2,629 ... B 2
Bojkovice, 2,902 ... D 2
Bor, 2,257 ... B 2
Boskovice, 6,396 ... D 2

Brandýs nad Labem-Stará
 Boleslav, 13,161 ... C 1
Bratislava, 278,835 ... D 2
Břeclav, 13,000 ... D 2
Březnice, 11,000 ... C 2
Brno, 333,831 ... D 2
Broumov, 6,370 ... D 1
Brtnice, 2,176 ... C 2
Bruntál, 9,000 ... D 2
Bučovice, 3,381 ... D 2
Budišov, 3,677 ... D 2
Bystřice nad Pernštejnem,
 2,653 ... D 2
Bystřice pod Hostýnem, 4,973 ... D 2
Bytča, 4,528 ... E 2
Čadca, 13,000 ... E 2
Čalovo, 4,536 ... D 2
Čáslav, 10,000 ... C 2
Česká Kamenice, 6,084 ... C 1
Česká Lípa, 15,000 ... C 1
Česká Třebová, 14,000 ... D 2
České Budějovice, 70,000 ... C 2
Český Brod, 5,754 ... C 2
Český Krumlov, 10,000 ... C 2
Český Těšín, 16,000 ... E 1
Cheb, 24,000 ... B 1
Chlumec, 4,345 ... C 1
Choceň, 6,789 ... D 1
Chodov, 5,383 ... B 1
Chomutov, 37,000 ... B 1
Chotěboř, 4,846 ... C 2
Chrastava, 3,618 ... C 1
Chrudim, 17,000 ... C 2

Cukmantl, 2,362 ... D 1
Dačice, 2,810 ... D 2
Děčín, 42,000 ... C 1
Detva, 7,765 ... E 2
Dobřany, 4,905 ... B 2
Dobříš, 4,390 ... C 2
Dobruška, 4,093 ... D 1
Dobšiná, 3,957 ... E 2
Doksy, 3,841 ... C 1
Dolný Kubín, 5,000 ... E 2
Domažlice, 8,000 ... B 2
Dubnica nad Váhom, 11,250 ... E 2
Duchcov, 8,229 ... B 1
Dunajská Streda, 9,000 ... D 3
Dvory, 5,475 ... D 3
Dvůr Králové nad Labem, 16,000 ... C 1
Falknov (Sokolov), 20,000 ... B 1
Fil'akovo, 5,950 ... E 2
Františkovy Lázně, 5,212 ... B 1
Frýdek-Místek, 32,000 ... E 2
Frýdlant nad Ostravicí, 4,178 ... E 2
Frýdlant v Čechách, 5,460 ... C 1
Fulnek, 2,765 ... D 2
Galanta, 8,000 ... D 2
Gelnica, 3,240 ... F 2
Golčův Jeníkov, 1,920 ... C 2
Gottwaldov, 63,000 ... D 2
Handlová, 16,000 ... E 2
Havířov, 72,000 ... E 2
Havlíčkův Brod, 16,000 ... C 2
Hlinsko, 5,189 ... C 2
Hlohovec, 14,000 ... D 2
Hlučín, 11,000 ... D 2
Hodonín, 19,000 ... D 2

(continued)

Topography

MILES
0   50   100

5,000 m. / 2,000 m. / 1,000 m. / 500 m. / 200 m. / 100 m. / Sea Level / Below
16,404 ft. / 6,562 ft. / 3,281 ft. / 1,640 ft. / 656 ft. / 328 ft.

Eggenburg, 3,338 ... C 2
Eisenerz, 12,435 ... C 3
Eisenstadt, 7,167 ... D 3
Enns, 8,919 ... C 2
Feldbach, 3,687 ... C 3
Feldkirch, 17,343 ... A 3
Feldkirchen in Kärnten, 3,181 ... C 3
Ferlach, 5,672 ... C 3
Fieberbrunn, 3,010 ... B 3
Fohnsdorf, 11,571 ... C 3
Frankenmarkt, 2,565 ... B 3
Frauenkirchen, 2,812 ... D 3
Friesach, 3,388 ... C 3
Freistadt, 5,798 ... C 2
Frohnleiten, 4,969 ... C 3
Fulpmes, 2,282 ... B 4
Fürstenfeld, 6,415 ... C 3
Gaming, 4,218 ... C 2
Gänserndorf, 3,378 ... D 2
Gleisdorf, 4,385 ... C 3
Gloggnitz, 7,228 ... C 3
Gmünd, Carinthia, 2,195 ... B 3
Gmünd, Lower Austria, 6,522 ... C 2
Grunden, 12,518 ... B 3
Golling an der Salzach,
 2,845 ... B 3
Götzis, 7,034 ... A 3
Gratwein, 2,515 ... C 3
Graz, 253,000 ... C 3
Grein, 2,518 ... C 2
Grieskirchen, 4,137 ... B 2
Gross Siegharts, 2,599 ... C 2
Grünburg, 3,609 ... C 3
Güssing, 2,715 ... D 3
Haag, 4,671 ... C 2
Hainburg, 6,437 ... D 2
Hainfeld, 3,883 ... C 2
Hallein, 13,329 ... B 3
Hallstatt, 1,373 ... B 3
Hartberg, 3,629 ... C 3
Haslach an der Mühl, 2,565 ... C 2
Heidenreichstein, 3,653 ... C 2
Heiligenblut, 1,195 ... B 3
Hermagor, 2,778 ... B 3
Herzogenburg, 5,166 ... C 2
Hieflau, 2,003 ... C 3
Hohenau an der March, 3,907 ... D 2
Hohenberg, 2,093 ... C 2
Hohenems, 9,188 ... A 3

Mauthen-Kötschach, 2,763 ... B 3
Mayrhofen, 2,523 ... A 3
Melk, 3,534 ... C 2
Mistelbach an der Zaya, 5,434 ... D 2
Mittersill, 3,502 ... B 3
Mödling, 17,274 ... D 2
Mondsee, 2,050 ... B 3
Murau, 2,755 ... C 3
Mürzzuschlag, 11,586 ... C 3
Nassereith, 1,744 ... B 3
Neuberg an der Mürz, 2,411 ... C 3
Neumarkt, Styria, 1,880 ... C 3
Neumarkt am Wallersee, 2,877 ... B 3
Neunkirchen, 10,027 ... D 3
Neusiedl am See, 3,826 ... D 3
Neustift im Stubaital, 2,195 ... A 3
Ober Grafendorf, 3,825 ... C 2
Oberndorf bei Salzburg, 3,084 ... B 3
Obervellach, 2,371 ... B 3
Oberwart, 4,702 ... D 3
Paternion, 5,581 ... B 3
Perg, 4,106 ... C 2
Peuerbach, 2,105 ... C 2
Pinkafeld, 3,826 ... C 3
Pöchlarn, 2,827 ... C 2
Pörtschach, 2,449 ... C 3
Poysdorf, 2,738 ... D 2
Pregarten, 2,818 ... C 2
Radenthein, 5,651 ... B 3
Radstadt, 3,311 ... B 3
Rankweil, 6,451 ... A 3
Rechnitz, 3,374 ... D 3
Reichenau an der Rax, 4,441 ... C 3
Retz, 2,941 ... C 2
Reutte, 4,285 ... A 3
Ried im Innkreis, 9,471 ... B 2
Rottenmann, 4,139 ... C 3
Saalfelden, 8,901 ... B 3
Salzburg, 120,204 ... B 3
Sankt Aegyd am Neuwalde,
 3,206 ... C 3
Sankt Anton am Arlberg, 1,741 ... A 3
Sankt Johann, 4,713 ... B 3
Sankt Michael, 3,433 ... C 3
Sankt Michael im Lungau,
 2,422 ... B 3
Sankt Paul, 1,808 ... C 3
Sankt Pölten, 40,112 ... C 2
Sankt Valentin, ... C 2

AUSTRIA
AREA 32,374 sq. mi.
POPULATION 7,419,341
CAPITAL Vienna
LARGEST CITY Vienna
HIGHEST POINT Grossglockner 12,457 ft.
MONETARY UNIT schilling
MAJOR LANGUAGE German
MAJOR RELIGION Roman Catholicism

CZECHOSLOVAKIA
AREA 49,370 sq. mi.
POPULATION 14,497,000
CAPITAL Prague
LARGEST CITY Prague
HIGHEST POINT Gerlachovka 8,707 ft.
MONETARY UNIT koruna (crown)
MAJOR LANGUAGES Czech, Slovak
MAJOR RELIGIONS Roman Catholicism,
Protestantism

HUNGARY
AREA 35,915 sq. mi.
POPULATION 10,315,597
CAPITAL Budapest
LARGEST CITY Budapest
HIGHEST POINT Kékes 3,330 ft.
MONETARY UNIT forint
MAJOR LANGUAGE Hungarian
MAJOR RELIGIONS Roman Catholicism,
Protestantism

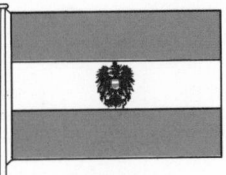

AUSTRIA

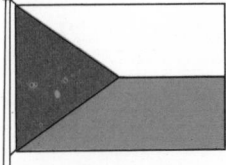

CZECHOSLOVAKIA

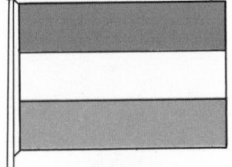

HUNGARY

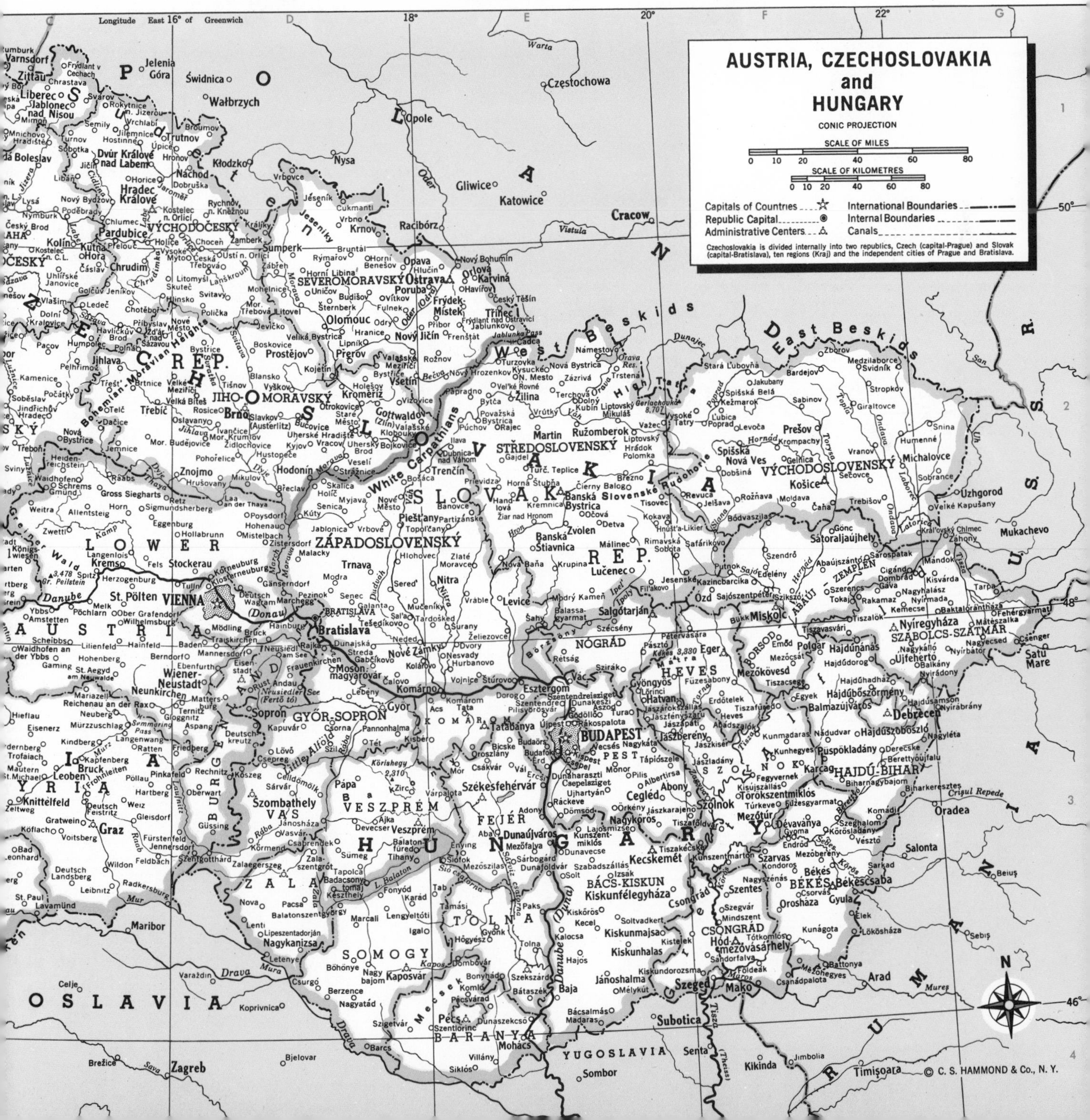

AUSTRIA, CZECHOSLOVAKIA and HUNGARY

CONIC PROJECTION

SCALE OF MILES
0 10 20   40   60   80

SCALE OF KILOMETRES
0 10 20   40   60   80

Capitals of Countries........ ☆   International Boundaries _____
Republic Capital............ ◉   Internal Boundaries _____
Administrative Centers.... △   Canals _____

Czechoslovakia is divided internally into two republics, Czech (capital-Prague) and Slovak
(capital-Bratislava), ten regions (Kraj) and the independent cities of Prague and Bratislava.

© C. S. HAMMOND & Co., N.Y.

CZECHOSLOVAKIA (continued)

Holešov, 6,599	D 2	
Holíč, 5,881	D 2	
Holice, 5,695	D 1	
Horaždovice, 3,098	C 2	
Hořice, 7,133	C 1	
Horní Benešov, 3,181	D 2	
Horní Libina, 4,583	D 2	
Hořovice, 4,697	C 2	
Horšovský Týn, 3,475	B 2	
Hostinné, 4,412	C 1	
Hradec Králové, 62,000	C 1	
Hranice, 12,000	D 2	
Hronov, 11,000	C 1	
Hrušovany, 3,128	C 2	
Humenné, 14,000	G 2	
Humpolec, 5,083	C 2	
Hurbanovo, 3,578	E 3	
Hustopeče, 2,698	D 2	
Ilava, 2,043	D 2	
Ivančice, 4,742	D 2	
Jablonec nad Nisou, 33,000	C 1	
Jablunkov, 4,467	E 2	
Jáchymov, 6,806	B 1	
Jaroměř, 12,000	C 1	
Jelšava, 2,456	F 2	
Jemnice, 3,383	C 2	
Jeseník, 5,873	D 1	
Jesenské, 1,567	F 2	
Jevíčko, 2,881	D 2	
Jičín, 13,000	C 1	
Jihlava, 37,000	C 2	
Jilemnice, 3,562	C 1	
Jindřichův Hradec, 12,000	C 2	
Jirkov, 12,000	B 1	
Kadaň, 5,063	B 1	
Kamenice, 2,692	C 2	
Kaplice, 1,931	C 2	
Karlovy Vary, 45,000	B 1	
Karviná, 70,000	E 2	
Kašperské Hory, 2,814	B 2	
Kdyně, 2,609	B 2	
Kežmarok, 7,372	F 2	
Kladno, 55,000	B 1	
Klatovy, 16,000	B 2	
Kojetín, 5,292	D 2	
Kokava, 5,398	F 2	
Kolárovo, 11,000	D 3	
Kolín, 25,000	C 1	

Mělník, 15,000	C 1	
Michalovce, 18,000	G 2	
Mikulov, 5,220	D 2	
Milevsko, 3,754	C 2	
Mimoň, 5,349	C 1	
Mladá Boleslav, 27,000	C 1	
Mladá Vožice, 1,732	C 2	
Mnichovo Hradiště, 4,647	C 1	
Modra, 6,239	D 2	
Modrý Kameň, 1,836	E 2	
Mohelnice, 4,949	D 2	
Moldava, 2,241	F 2	
Moravská Třebová, 5,844	D 2	
Moravské Budějovice, 4,348	D 2	
Moravský Krumlov, 2,897	D 2	
Most, 56,000	B 1	
Mučeníky, 5,207	D 2	
Myjava, 9,935	D 2	
Náchod, 15,000	D 1	
Neded, 4,553	D 3	
Nejdek, 5,748	B 1	
Nepomuk, 1,860	B 2	
Nesvady, 5,070	E 3	
Netolice, 2,503	C 2	
Nitra, 39,000	D 2	
Nová Baňa, 5,113	E 2	
Nová Bystřice, 2,418	C 2	
Nové Město na Moravě, 3,250	D 2	
Nové Město nad Váhom, 14,000	D 2	
Nové Strašecí, 3,288	B 1	
Nové Zámky, 24,000	D 3	
Nový Bohumín, 12,000	E 2	
Nový Bor, 5,994	C 1	
Nový Bydžov, 6,120	C 1	
Nový Hrozenkov, 5,302	E 2	
Nový Jičín, 17,000	E 2	
Nymburk, 13,000	C 1	
Nýřany, 4,420	B 2	
Nýrsko, 4,124	B 2	
Odry, 5,340	D 2	
Olomouc, 77,000	D 2	
Opava, 46,000	E 2	
Orlová, 22,000	E 2	
Oslavany, 3,606	D 2	
Ostrava, 271,905	E 2	
Ostrov, 19,000	B 1	
Otrokovice-Kvítkovice, 11,000	D 2	
Pacov, 2,775	C 2	
Pardubice, 65,000	C 1	

Rýmařov, 4,328	D 2	
Sabinov, 3,909	F 2	
Šafárikovo, 3,180	F 2	
Šahy, 4,019	E 2	
Šaľa, 4,397	D 2	
Sečovce, 3,354	F 2	
Sedlčany, 3,848	C 2	
Semily, 6,549	C 1	
Senec, 6,194	D 2	
Senica, 8,000	D 2	
Sered', 6,208	D 2	
Skalica, 5,440	D 2	
Skuteč, 3,348	C 1	
Slaný, 12,000	C 1	
Slavkov, 4,869	D 2	
Snina, 5,002	G 2	
Soběslav, 4,643	C 2	
Sobotka, 2,147	C 1	
Sokolov, 20,000	B 1	
Spišská Belá, 3,072	F 2	
Spišská Nová Ves, 20,000	F 2	
Stará Ľubovňa, 1,869	F 2	
Staré Město, 6,350	D 2	
Šternberk, 12,000	D 2	
Stod, 2,502	B 2	
Strakonice, 16,000	B 2	
Strážnice, 5,147	D 2	
Stříbro, 4,659	B 2	
Stropkov, 2,506	F 2	
Štúrovo, 4,082	E 3	
Šumperk, 22,000	D 1	
Šurany, 5,381	D 2	
Sušice, 6,793	B 2	
Svárov, 3,381	C 2	
Svitavy, 14,000	D 2	
Tábor, 21,000	C 2	
Tachov, 8,000	B 2	
Tardošked, 6,689	D 2	
Teč, 4,381	C 2	
Teplá a Toužimě, 2,500	B 2	
Teplice, 32,000	B 1	
Terchová, 4,400	E 2	
Tišnov, 4,885	D 2	
Tisovec, 3,988	F 2	
Topoľčany, 12,000	D 2	
Třebíč, 21,000	D 2	
Třebíšov, 12,000	F 2	
Třeboň, 4,663	C 2	
Trenčín, 26,000	D 2	
Třešť, 4,900	C 2	

Zbiroh, 1,718	B 2	
Zborov, 1,551	F 2	
Žd'ár nad Sázavou, 12,000	C 2	
Železovce, 3,748	E 2	
Žiar nad Hronom, 11,000	E 2	
Žídlochovice, 2,696	D 2	
Žilina, 37,000	E 2	
Zlaté Moravce, 4,003	E 2	
Zlín (Gottwaldov), 63,000	D 2	
Zlutice, 2,114	B 1	
Znojmo, 35,000	D 2	
Zvolen, 23,000	E 2	

OTHER FEATURES

Berounka (river)	B 2	
Beskids, East (mts.)	F 1	
Beskids, West (mts.)	E 2	
Bohemia (region), 6,142,000	C 2	
Bohemian (forest)	B 2	
Bohemian-Moravian Heights	C 2	
Dudváh (river)	D 2	
Dyje (river)	C 2	
Erzgebirge (mts.)	B 1	
Gerlachovka (mt.)	F 2	
Hornád (river)	F 2	
Hron (river)	E 2	
Ipeľ (river)	E 2	
Jablunka (pass)	E 2	
Jeseníky (mts.)	D 1	
Jihlava (river)	C 2	
Kamýcká (res.)	B 2	
Krušné Hory (Erzgebirge) (mts.)	B 1	
Labe (river)	C 1	
Laborec (river)	F 2	
Lipno (res.)	C 2	
Lužnice (river)	C 2	
Moldau (Vltava) (river)	C 2	
Morava (river)	D 2	
Moravia (region), 3,636,000	D 2	
Nitra (river)	D 2	
Oder (Odra) (river)	D 2	
Orava (river)	E 2	
Orava (river)	E 2	
Orlice (river)	C 1	
Orlická (res.)	C 2	
Otava (river)	B 2	

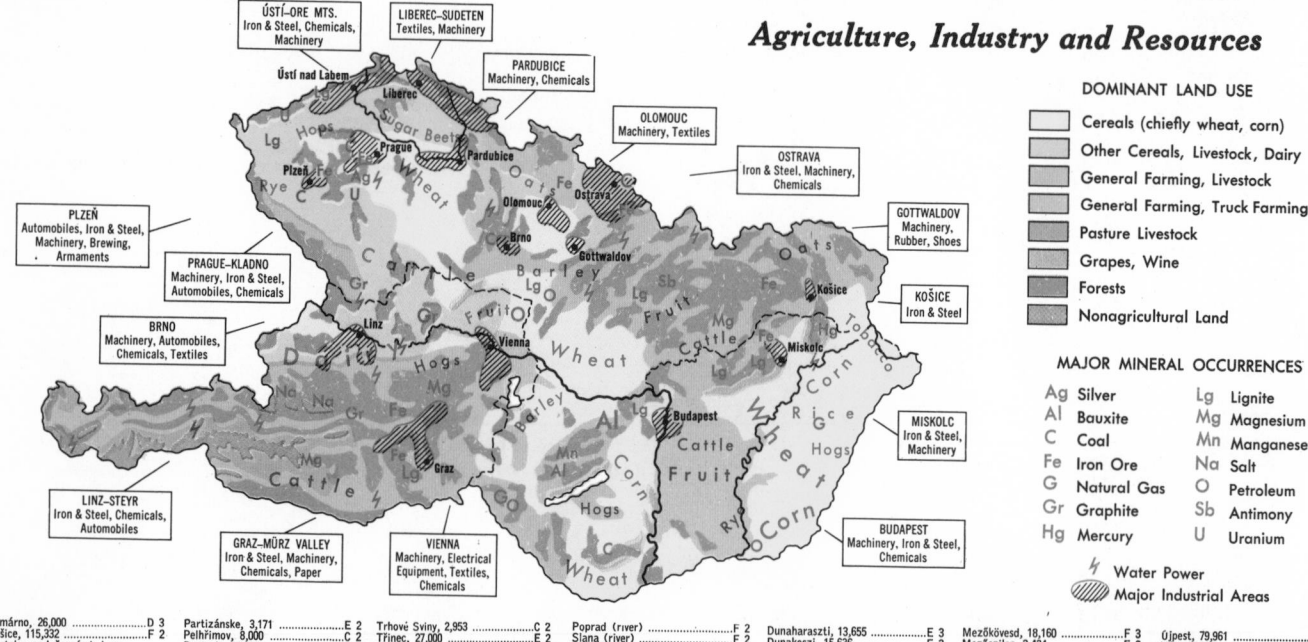

Agriculture, Industry and Resources

ÚSTÍ-ORE MTS.
Iron & Steel, Chemicals, Machinery

LIBEREC–SUDETEN
Textiles, Machinery

PARDUBICE
Machinery, Chemicals

OLOMOUC
Machinery, Textiles

OSTRAVA
Iron & Steel, Machinery, Chemicals

GOTTWALDOV
Machinery, Rubber, Shoes

KOŠICE
Iron & Steel

MISKOLC
Iron & Steel, Machinery

BUDAPEST
Machinery, Iron & Steel, Chemicals

VIENNA
Machinery, Electrical Equipment, Textiles, Chemicals

GRAZ–MÜRZ VALLEY
Iron & Steel, Machinery, Chemicals, Paper

LINZ–STEYR
Iron & Steel, Chemicals, Automobiles

BRNO
Machinery, Automobiles, Chemicals, Textiles

PRAGUE–KLADNO
Machinery, Iron & Steel, Automobiles, Chemicals

PLZEŇ
Automobiles, Iron & Steel, Machinery, Brewing, Armaments

DOMINANT LAND USE

- Cereals (chiefly wheat, corn)
- Other Cereals, Livestock, Dairy
- General Farming, Livestock
- General Farming, Truck Farming
- Pasture Livestock
- Grapes, Wine
- Forests
- Nonagricultural Land

MAJOR MINERAL OCCURRENCES

Ag	Silver	Lg	Lignite
Al	Bauxite	Mg	Magnesium
C	Coal	Mn	Manganese
Fe	Iron Ore	Na	Salt
G	Natural Gas	O	Petroleum
Gr	Graphite	Sb	Antimony
Hg	Mercury	U	Uranium

⚡ Water Power
▨ Major Industrial Areas

Komárno, 26,000	D 3	
Košice, 115,332	F 2	
Kostelec nad Černými, Lesy, 3,616	C 2	
Kostelec nad Orlicí, 5,539	D 1	
Kralíky, 3,895	D 1	
Kralovice, 2,268	B 2	
Kráľovský Chlmec, 3,410	G 2	
Kralupy nad Vltavou, 14,000	C 1	
Kraslice, 6,294	B 1	
Krásna Lípa, 5,041	C 1	
Kremnica, 4,979	E 2	
Kroměříž, 22,000	D 2	
Krompachy, 3,340	F 2	
Krupina, 5,418	E 2	
Krupka, 10,000	B 1	
Kutná Hora, 17,000	C 2	
Kúty, 3,348	D 2	
Kyjov, 5,620	D 2	
Kynšperk, 5,398	B 1	
Kysucké Nové Mesto, 2,318	E 2	
Lanškroun, 6,558	D 2	
Ledeč, 2,625	C 2	
Levice, 15,000	E 2	
Levoča, 7,584	F 2	
Libáň, 2,261	C 1	
Liberec, 76,000	C 1	
Libochovice, 2,879	B 1	
Lidice, 478	B 1	
Lipník, 6,887	D 2	
Liptovský Mikuláš, 14,000	E 2	
Lišov, 2,691	C 2	
Litoměřice, 18,000	C 1	
Litomyšl, 6,384	C 2	
Litovel, 4,496	D 2	
Litvínov, 22,000	B 1	
Lomnice, 2,226	C 1	
Louny, 13,000	B 1	
Lovosice, 4,962	C 1	
Ľubica, 3,335	F 2	
Lúčenec, 18,000	F 2	
Lysá, 6,500	C 1	
Malacky, 11,000	D 2	
Mariánské Lázně, 13,000	B 1	
Martin, 29,000	E 2	

Partizánske, 3,171	E 2	
Pelhřimov, 8,000	C 2	
Pezinok, 12,000	D 2	
Piešťany, 21,000	D 2	
Písek, 22,000	C 2	
Planá, 5,216	B 2	
Plánice, 1,718	B 2	
Plasy, 1,472	B 2	
Plzeň, 143,945	B 2	
Počátky, 2,141	C 2	
Podbořany, 3,893	B 1	
Poděbrady, 13,000	C 1	
Pohořelice, 3,068	D 2	
Polička, 5,600	D 2	
Polná, 4,005	C 2	
Poprad, 18,000	F 2	
Poruba, 21,179	D 2	
Považská Bystrica, 13,000	E 2	
Prachatice, 6,000	B 2	
Prague (Praha) (capital), 1,031,870	C 1	
Přelouč, 4,228	C 1	
Přerov, 35,000	D 2	
Prešov, 39,000	F 2	
Přeštice, 4,616	B 2	
Příbor, 5,491	E 2	
Příbram, 29,000	C 2	
Přibyslav, 2,485	C 2	
Prievidza, 24,000	E 2	
Prostějov, 35,000	D 2	
Protivín, 3,217	C 2	
Rakovník, 4,316	B 2	
Radnice, 2,342	B 2	
Rajec, 2,753	E 2	
Rakovník, 12,000	B 1	
Ričany, 6,376	C 2	
Rimavská Sobota, 12,000	F 2	
Rokycany, 13,000	B 2	
Rokytnice nad Jizerou, 3,893	C 1	
Rosice, 4,900	D 2	
Roudnice nad Labem, 11,000	C 1	
Rožňava, 11,000	F 2	
Rožnov, 3,989	E 2	
Rumburk, 6,759	C 1	
Ružomberok, 20,000	E 2	
Rychnov nad Kněžnou, 5,498	D 1	

Trhové Sviny, 2,953	C 2	
Třinec, 27,000	E 2	
Trnava, 35,000	D 2	
Trstená, 2,468	E 2	
Trutnov, 16,000	D 1	
Turnov, 12,000	C 1	
Turzovka, 9,823	E 2	
Týn, 4,135	C 2	
Uherské Hradiště, 15,000	D 2	
Uherský Brod, 6,457	D 2	
Uhlířské Janovice, 1,979	C 2	
Uničov, 3,325	D 2	
Ústí nad Labem, 72,000	C 1	
Ústí nad Orlicí, 11,000	C 2	
Valašské Klobouky, 2,525	D 2	
Valašské Meziříčí, 15,000	D 2	
Varnsdorf, 14,000	C 1	
Važec, 2,747	E 2	
Vejprty, 5,476	B 1	
Velká Bíteš, 1,714	D 2	
Velká Bystřice, 4,459	D 2	
Veľké Kapušany, 2,371	G 2	
Velké Meziříčí, 6,217	D 2	
Veselí nad Lužnicí, 4,382	C 2	
Veselí nad Moravou, 4,636	D 2	
Vítkov, 2,685	D 2	
Vizovice, 3,583	D 2	
Vlašim, 5,066	C 2	
Vodňany, 5,374	C 2	
Volary, 5,034	B 2	
Volyně, 3,619	B 2	
Vráble, 3,148	E 2	
Vracov, 4,171	D 2	
Vranov, 3,964	F 2	
Vrchlabí, 11,000	C 1	
Vrútky, 5,227	E 2	
Vsetín, 20,000	D 2	
Vyškov, 13,000	D 2	
Vysoké Mýto, 7,983	C 2	
Vysoké Tatry, 1,905	F 2	
Vyšší Brod, 1,905	C 2	
Žamberk, 4,278	D 1	
Žatec, 16,000	B 1	

Poprad (river)	F 2	
Slaná (river)	F 2	
Slapská (res.)	C 2	
Slovakia (region), 4,421,000	E 2	
Slovenske Rudohorie (mts.)	E 2	
Štěchovická (res.)	C 2	
Sudeten (mts.)	C 1	
Tatra, High (mts.)	F 2	
Uh (river)	G 2	
Váh (river)	D 2	
Vltava (river)	C 2	
White Carpathians (mts.)	D 2	

HUNGARY

COUNTIES

Bács-Kiskun, 560,000	E 3	
Baranya, 280,000	E 4	
Békés, 440,000	F 3	
Borsod-Abaúj-Zemplén, 600,000	F 2	
Budapest (city), 1,990,000	E 3	
Csongrád, 320,000	E 3	
Fejér, 390,000	E 3	
Győr-Sopron, 400,000	D 3	
Hajdú-Bihar, 360,000	F 3	
Heves, 340,000	F 3	
Komárom, 300,000	E 3	
Nógrád, 240,000	E 2	
Pest, 870,000	E 3	
Somogy, 360,000	D 3	
Szabolcs-Szatmár, 540,000	G 3	
Szolnok, 440,000	F 3	
Tolna, 260,000	E 3	
Vas, 280,000	D 3	
Veszprém, 420,000	D 3	
Zala, 260,000	D 3	

CITIES and TOWNS

Aba, 4,369	E 3	

Abádszalók, 7,257	F 3	
Abaújszántó, 4,586	F 2	
Abony, 16,048	E 3	
Acs, 8,507	E 3	
Adony, 4,211	E 3	
Ajka, 21,000	D 3	
Albertirsa, 11,490	E 3	
Aszód, 5,361	E 3	
Bácsalmás, 9,514	E 3	
Baja, 34,000	E 3	
Balassagyarmat, 13,000	E 2	
Balatonfüred, 7,561	D 3	
Balkány, 8,224	G 3	
Balmazújváros, 18,645	F 3	
Barcs, 7,245	D 4	
Bátaszék, 7,378	E 3	
Battonya, 11,019	F 3	
Békés, 21,296	F 3	
Békéscsaba, 53,000	F 3	
Berettyóújfalu, 11,577	F 3	
Berzence, 3,651	D 3	
Bicske, 9,106	E 3	
Biharkeresztes, 4,844	F 3	
Biharnagybajom, 4,762	F 3	
Böhönye, 3,809	D 3	
Bonyhád, 9,354	E 3	
Budafok, 39,870	E 3	
Budaörs, 12,882	E 3	
Budapest (capital), 1,990,000	E 3	
Cegléd, 37,000	E 3	
Celldömölk, 9,762	D 3	
Cigánd, 5,220	F 2	
Csákvár, 5,135	E 3	
Csanádpalota, 5,264	F 3	
Csenger, 4,835	G 3	
Csepel, 86,287	E 3	
Cserepreg, 4,348	D 3	
Csongrád, 20,000	E 3	
Csorna, 9,192	D 3	
Csorvás, 7,622	F 3	
Csurgó, 5,400	D 3	
Debrecen, 160,000	F 3	
Derecske, 9,980	F 3	
Dévaványa, 12,137	F 3	
Devecser, 5,271	D 3	
Dombóvár, 15,605	E 3	
Dombrád, 6,868	F 2	
Dömsöd, 6,532	E 3	
Dorog, 9,994	E 3	
Dunaföldvár, 11,039	E 3	

Jászkarajenő, 4,955	E 3	
Jászkisér, 7,280	F 3	
Jászladány, 8,841	F 3	
Kalocsa, 15,000	E 3	
Kaposvár, 50,000	D 3	
Kapuvár, 10,748	D 3	
Karád, 3,438	D 3	
Karcag, 24,000	F 3	
Kazincbarcika, 29,000	F 2	
Kecel, 10,193	E 3	
Kecskemét, 76,000	E 3	
Kemecse, 4,481	G 3	
Keszthely, 17,000	D 3	
Kisbér, 4,967	D 3	
Kiskőrös, 12,954	E 3	
Kiskundorozsma, 8,679	E 3	
Kiskunfélegyháza, 33,000	E 3	
Kiskunhalas, 28,000	E 3	
Kiskunmajsa, 12,311	E 3	
Kispest, 66,547	E 3	
Kistelek, 8,925	E 3	
Kisújszállás, 13,000	F 3	
Kisvárda, 13,050	G 2	
Komádi, 9,850	F 3	
Komárom, 11,000	E 3	
Komló, 28,000	E 3	
Kondoros, 7,462	F 3	
Körmend, 7,548	D 3	
Körösladány, 7,302	F 3	
Kőszeg, 10,000	D 3	
Kunágota, 5,667	F 3	
Kunhegyes, 10,792	F 3	
Kunmadaras, 8,463	F 3	
Kunszentmárton, 13,383	F 3	
Kunszentmiklós, 8,198	E 3	
Lajosmizse, 12,617	E 3	
Lébény, 3,588	D 3	
Lengyeltóti, 3,392	D 3	
Leténye, 4,507	D 3	
Lőkösháza, 2,511	F 3	
Lőrinci, 11,142	E 3	
Madaras, 5,177	E 3	
Makó, 29,000	F 3	
Mándok, 4,828	G 2	
Marcali, 7,877	D 3	
Mátészalka, 11,496	G 3	
Mélykút, 8,168	E 3	
Mezőberény, 12,830	F 3	
Mezőcsát, 6,583	F 3	
Mezőhegyes, 9,137	F 3	

Sándorfalva, 5,815	F 3	
Sárbogárd, 6,853	E 3	
Sarkad, 12,169	F 3	
Sárospatak, 12,799	F 2	
Sárvár, 17,247	D 3	
Sátoraljaújhely, 17,000	F 2	
Siklós, 5,897	E 4	
Siófok, 10,322	E 3	
Solt, 7,199	E 3	
Soltvadkert, 8,244	E 3	
Sopron, 45,000	D 3	
Sümeg, 5,525	D 3	
Szabadszállás, 8,799	E 3	
Szarvas, 19,000	F 3	
Szécsény, 4,410	E 2	
Szeged, 120,000	E 3	
Szeghalom, 10,093	F 3	
Szegvár, 6,970	F 3	
Székesfehérvár, 71,000	E 3	
Szekszárd, 23,000	E 3	
Szendrő, 3,773	F 2	
Szentendre, 13,000	E 3	
Szentes, 32,000	F 3	
Szentgotthárd, 5,421	D 3	
Szerencs, 7,789	F 2	
Szigetvár, 10,000	D 3	
Szikszó, 6,110	F 2	
Szolnok, 81,000	F 3	
Szombathely, 62,000	D 3	
Tab, 4,265	D 3	
Tamási, 7,689	E 3	
Tápiószele, 5,632	E 3	
Tapolca, 10,000	D 3	
Tarpa, 3,966	G 3	
Tata, 19,000	E 3	
Tatabánya, 64,000	E 3	
Tét, 4,861	D 3	
Tiszacsege, 7,002	F 3	
Tiszaföldvár, 12,377	F 3	
Tiszafüred, 11,214	F 3	
Tiszakécske, 12,834	E 3	
Tiszalök, 6,125	F 2	
Tiszavasvári, 12,201	F 3	
Tokaj, 5,031	F 2	
Tolna, 8,741	E 3	
Törökszentmiklós, 24,000	F 3	
Tótkomlós, 9,368	F 3	
Tura, 8,169	E 3	
Túrkeve, 11,000	F 3	
Újfehértó, 14,386	F 3	

Újpest, 79,961	E 3	
Vác, 29,000	E 3	
Várpalota, 27,000	E 3	
Vasvár, 4,293	D 3	
Vecsés, 16,411	E 3	
Veszprém, 33,000	D 3	
Vésztő, 10,463	F 3	
Villány, 2,769	E 4	
Zahony, 2,117	G 2	
Zalaegerszeg, 33,000	D 3	
Zalaszentgrót, 4,470	D 3	
Zirc, 5,427	D 3	

OTHER FEATURES

Bakony (mts.)	D 3	
Balaton (lake)	D 3	
Börzöny (mts.)	E 3	
Bükk (mts.)	F 2	
Csepelsziget (isl.)	E 3	
Danube (river)	E 3	
Dráva (river)	D 3	
Duna (Danube) (river)	E 3	
Fertő tó (Neusiedler) (lake)	D 3	
Great Alföld (plain)	F 3	
Hernád (river)	F 2	
Ipoly (river)	E 2	
Kékes (mt.)	F 2	
Kőrishegy (mt.)	D 3	
Körös (river)	F 3	
Little Alföld (plain)	D 3	
Maros (river)	F 3	
Matra (mts.)	F 2	
Mecsek (mts.)	E 3	
Neusiedler (lake)	D 3	
Rába (river)	D 3	
Sajo (river)	F 2	
Sió (canal)	E 3	
Szentendreisziget (isl.)	E 3	
Tarna (river)	F 2	
Tisza (river)	F 3	
Zala (river)	D 3	

Dunaharaszti, 13,655	E 3	
Dunakeszi, 15,636	E 3	
Dunaújváros, 45,000	E 3	
Dunavecse, 4,908	E 3	
Edelény, 6,851	F 2	
Eger, 45,000	F 2	
Egyek, 8,678	F 3	
Elek, 6,325	F 3	
Emőd, 5,233	F 2	
Endrőd, 9,263	F 3	
Enying, 6,406	E 3	
Ercsi, 7,850	E 3	
Érd, 25,900	E 3	
Erdőtelek, 4,634	F 3	
Esztergom, 30,000	E 3	
Fegyvernek, 7,835	F 3	
Fehérgyarmat, 6,024	G 3	
Földeák, 4,275	F 3	
Füzesabony, 7,125	F 3	
Füzesgyarmat, 7,807	F 3	
Gödöllő, 22,000	E 3	
Gönc, 3,093	F 2	
Gyoma, 10,921	F 3	
Gyöngyös, 32,000	E 3	
Gyönk, 2,984	E 3	
Győr, 81,000	D 3	
Gyula, 25,000	F 3	
Hajdúböszörmény, 30,000	F 3	
Hajdúdorog, 10,559	F 3	
Hajdúhadház, 13,030	F 3	
Hajdúnánás, 17,000	F 3	
Hajdúszoboszló, 22,000	F 3	
Hajós, 5,584	E 3	
Hatvan, 21,000	E 3	
Hercegfalva, 4,951	E 3	
Heves, 11,349	F 3	
Hódmezővásárhely, 53,000	F 3	
Izsák, 8,609	E 3	
Jánoshalma, 12,897	E 3	
Jánosháza, 3,498	D 3	
Jászapáti, 10,495	F 3	
Jászárokszállás, 10,745	F 3	
Jászberény, 30,000	E 3	
Jászfényszaru, 7,542	E 3	

Mezőkövesd, 18,160	F 3	
Mezőszilas, 3,434	E 3	
Mezőtúr, 22,000	F 3	
Mindszent, 9,179	F 3	
Miskolc, 180,000	F 2	
Mohács, 18,000	E 4	
Monor, 15,360	E 3	
Mór, 11,622	E 3	
Mosonmagyaróvár, 25,000	D 3	
Nádudvar, 10,006	F 3	
Nagyatád, 8,791	D 3	
Nagybajom, 4,972	D 3	
Nagyecsed, 8,348	G 3	
Nagyhalász, 6,650	F 2	
Nagykálló, 11,329	F 3	
Nagykanizsa, 38,000	D 3	
Nagykáta, 11,924	E 3	
Nagykőrös, 26,000	E 3	
Nagylété, 6,902	F 3	
Nagyszénás, 7,439	F 3	
Nyírábrány, 4,517	G 3	
Nyírbátor, 7,325	G 3	
Nyírbogdány, 10,167	G 3	
Nyíregyháza, 65,000	G 3	
Nyírmada, 4,826	G 3	
Örkény, 5,001	E 3	
Orosháza, 33,000	F 3	
Oroszlány, 20,000	E 3	
Ózd, 40,000	F 2	
Paks, 11,919	E 3	
Pannonhalma, 3,529	D 3	
Pápa, 27,000	D 3	
Pásztó, 8,091	E 2	
Pécel, 6,640	E 3	
Pécs, 133,000	E 4	
Pécsvárad, 3,199	E 3	
Pétevására, 2,727	F 2	
Pilis, 8,458	E 3	
Pilisvörösvár, 9,627	E 3	
Polgár, 9,053	F 3	
Püspökladány, 15,488	F 3	
Putnok, 6,440	F 2	
Rábacsécsény, 5,381	D 3	
Ráckeve, 7,456	E 3	
Rakamaz, 5,381	F 2	
Rákospalota, 63,344	E 3	
Sajószentpéter, 12,846	F 2	
Salgótarján, 37,000	E 2	

YUGOSLAVIA
AREA 98,766 sq. mi.
POPULATION 20,586,000
CAPITAL Belgrade
LARGEST CITY Belgrade
HIGHEST POINT Triglav 9,393 ft.
MONETARY UNIT Yugoslav dinar
MAJOR LANGUAGES Serbo-Croatian, Slovenian, Macedonian, Albanian
MAJOR RELIGIONS Eastern Orthodoxy, Roman Catholicism, Islam

ALBANIA
AREA 11,100 sq. mi.
POPULATION 2,126,000
CAPITAL Tiranë
LARGEST CITY Tiranë
HIGHEST POINT Korab 9,026 ft.
MONETARY UNIT lek
MAJOR LANGUAGE Albanian
MAJOR RELIGIONS Islam, Eastern Orthodoxy, Roman Catholicism

RUMANIA
AREA 91,699 sq. mi.
POPULATION 20,394,000
CAPITAL Bucharest
LARGEST CITY Bucharest
HIGHEST POINT Moldoveanul 8,343 ft.
MONETARY UNIT leu
MAJOR LANGUAGES Rumanian, Hungarian
MAJOR RELIGION Eastern Orthodoxy

BULGARIA
AREA 42,829 sq. mi.
POPULATION 8,501,000
CAPITAL Sofia
LARGEST CITY Sofia
HIGHEST POINT Musala 9,597 ft.
MONETARY UNIT lev
MAJOR LANGUAGE Bulgarian
MAJOR RELIGION Eastern Orthodoxy

GREECE
AREA 50,548 sq. mi.
POPULATION 8,838,000
CAPITAL Athens
LARGEST CITY Athens
HIGHEST POINT Olympus 9,570 ft.
MONETARY UNIT drachma
MAJOR LANGUAGE Greek
MAJOR RELIGION Eastern (Greek) Orthodoxy

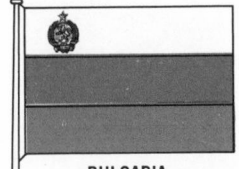
BULGARIA

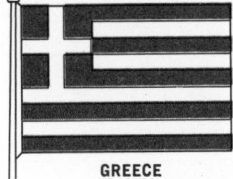
GREECE

YUGOSLAVIA

ALBANIA

RUMANIA

DOMINANT LAND USE
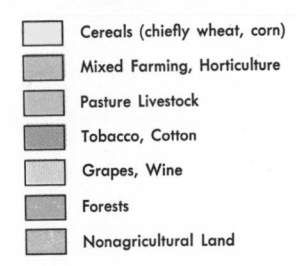

- Cereals (chiefly wheat, corn)
- Mixed Farming, Horticulture
- Pasture Livestock
- Tobacco, Cotton
- Grapes, Wine
- Forests
- Nonagricultural Land

Agriculture, Industry and Resources

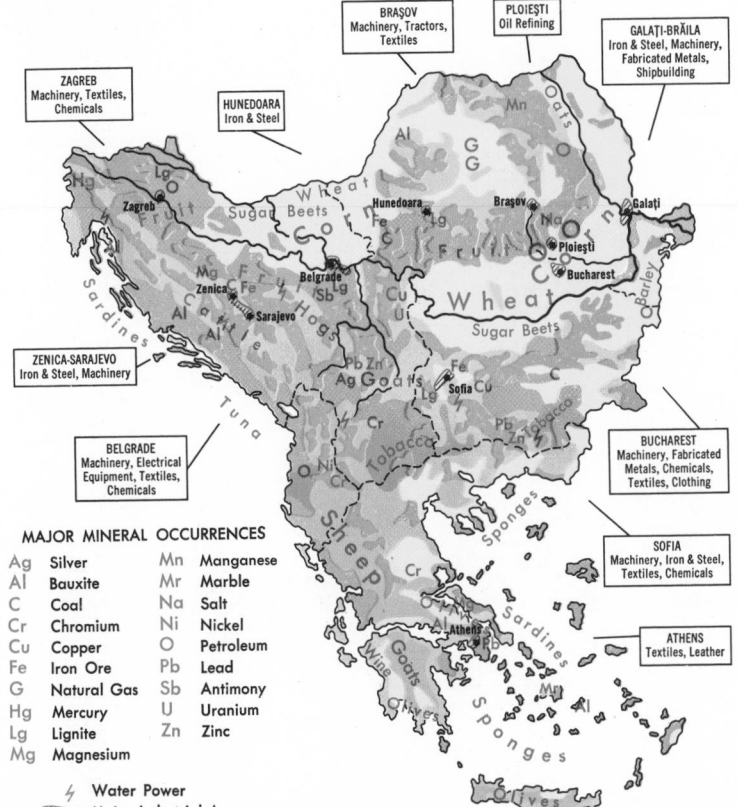

ZAGREB
Machinery, Textiles, Chemicals

HUNEDOARA
Iron & Steel

BRAȘOV
Machinery, Tractors, Textiles

PLOIEȘTI
Oil Refining

GALAȚI-BRĂILA
Iron & Steel, Machinery, Fabricated Metals, Shipbuilding

ZENICA-SARAJEVO
Iron & Steel, Machinery

BELGRADE
Machinery, Electrical Equipment, Textiles, Chemicals

BUCHAREST
Machinery, Fabricated Metals, Chemicals, Textiles, Clothing

SOFIA
Machinery, Iron & Steel, Textiles, Chemicals

ATHENS
Textiles, Leather

MAJOR MINERAL OCCURRENCES

Ag	Silver	Mn	Manganese
Al	Bauxite	Mr	Marble
C	Coal	Na	Salt
Cr	Chromium	Ni	Nickel
Cu	Copper	O	Petroleum
Fe	Iron Ore	Pb	Lead
G	Natural Gas	Sb	Antimony
Hg	Mercury	U	Uranium
Lg	Lignite	Zn	Zinc
Mg	Magnesium		

⚡ Water Power
〰️ Major Industrial Areas

ALBANIA
CITIES and TOWNS

Berat, 22,000	D 5
Bajram Cur, 1,795	D 4
Burrel, 3,150	D 5
Çorovodë, 1,790	E 5
Delvinë, 5,700	D 6
Durrës, 47,900	D 5
Elbasan, 35,300	E 5
Ersekë, 2,150	E 5
Fier, 17,900	D 5
Gjirokastër, 15,000	D 5
Kavajë, 17,700	D 5
Korçë, 43,700	E 5
Kruë, 6,700	D 5
Kuçovë (Stalin), 12,300	D 5
Kukës, 3,900	E 4
Leskovik, 1,625	E 5
Lezh, 3,000	D 5
Lushnje, 16,000	D 5
Peqin, 3,800	D 5
Përmet, 4,000	E 5
Peshkopi, 5,500	E 5
Pogradec, 8,900	E 5
Pukë, 1,700	D 4
Sarandë, 7,700	E 6
Shijak, 5,100	D 5
Shkodër, 47,000	D 5
Stalin, 12,300	D 5
Tepelenë, 2,500	E 5
Tiranë (Tirana) (cap.), 170,000	D 5
Vlorë, 46,900	D 5

OTHER FEATURES

Adriatic (sea)	B 4
Drin (riv.)	E 5
Korab (mt.)	E 5
Ohrid (lake)	E 5
Otranto (str.)	D 5
Prespa (lake)	E 5
Sazan (isl.)	D 5
Scutari (lake)	D 4
Tomor (mt.)	E 5
Vijosë (riv.)	D 5

BULGARIA
CITIES and TOWNS

Alfatar, 3,650	H 4
Akhtopol, 1,058	H 4
Alfatar, 4,042	H 4
Ardino, 2,558	G 5
Asenovgrad, 37,411	G 5
Aytos, 17,769	H 4
Balchik, 8,714	J 4
Bansko, 7,851	F 5
Belogradchik, 5,174	F 4
Berkovitsa, 11,553	F 4
Blagoyevgrad, 32,744	F 5
Botevgrad, 12,051	F 4
Bregovo, 4,725	F 3
Breznik, 4,093	F 4
Burgas, 122,212	H 4
Byala, 9,347	H 4
Byala Slatina, 14,942	H 4
Chirpan, 17,857	G 4
Devin, 4,475	G 5
Dimitrovgrad, 41,787	G 4
Dobrich (Tolbukhin), 55,111	H 4
Dryanovo, 8,187	H 4
Elena, 4,071	G 4
Elin Pelin, 8,074	F 4
Elkhovo, 11,315	H 4
Gabrovo, 57,758	G 4
General Toshevo, 8,251	H 4
Godech, 4,074	F 4
Gorna Dzhumaya (Blagoyevgrad), 32,744	F 5
Gorna Oryakhovitsa, 26,290	G 4
Gotse Delchev, 14,457	F 5
Grudovo, 9,177	H 4
Ikhtiman, 10,325	F 4
Isperikh, 8,445	H 4
Ivaylovgrad, 2,907	H 5
Karapelit, 2,033	H 4
Karlovo (Levskigrad), 20,287	G 4
Karnobat (Polyanovgrad), 18,727	H 4
Kavarna, 8,291	J 4
Kazanlŭk, 44,418	G 4
Kharmanli, 15,478	H 5
Khaskovo, 57,682	G 5
Kolarovgrad (Shumen), 59,362	H 4

Kotel, 7,209	H 4
Krumovgrad, 2,230	G 5
Kubrat, 7,531	H 4
Kula, 6,474	F 4
Kŭrdzhali, 33,319	G 5
Kyustendil, 38,199	F 4
Levskigrad, 20,287	G 4
Lom, 28,189	F 4
Lovech, 30,843	G 4
Lukovit, 9,716	G 4
Malko Tŭrnovo, 3,744	H 4
Maritsa, 8,532	H 4
Michurin, 2,783	H 4
Mikhaylovgrad, 27,240	F 4
Momchilgrad, 6,084	G 5
Nesebŭr, 2,333	H 4
Nikopol, 5,763	G 4
Nova Zagora, 19,257	H 4
Novi Pazar, 12,476	H 4
Omurtag, 8,148	H 4
Oryakhovo, 7,498	F 4
Panagyurishte, 18,298	F 4
Pazardzhik, 55,410	G 4
Pernik, 75,844	F 4
Peshtera, 14,606	G 4
Petrich, 20,653	F 5
Pirdop, 8,252	G 4
Pleven, 79,234	G 4
Plovdiv, 234,547	G 4
Polyanovgrad, 18,727	H 4
Pomorie, 9,567	H 4
Popina, 2,699	H 3
Popovo, 15,609	H 4
Provadiya, 13,837	H 4
Radomir, 8,458	F 4
Razgrad, 26,297	H 4
Razlog, 10,425	F 5
Rositsa, 1,505	H 4
Ruse, 142,894	H 4
Samokov, 21,585	F 4
Sandanski, 14,590	F 5
Sevlievo, 20,396	G 4
Shabla, 3,788	J 4
Shumen, 59,362	H 4
Silistra, 32,996	H 3
Simeonovgrad (Maritsa), 8,532	H 4
Sliven, 68,331	H 4
Smolyan, 17,479	G 5
Smyadovo, 5,349	H 4
Sofia (cap.), 840,113	F 4
Sofia, *923,400	F 4
Sozopol, 3,257	H 4
Stanke Dimitrov, 35,813	F 4
Stara Zagora, 100,565	G 4
Sveti Vrach (Sandanski), 14,590	F 5
Svilengrad, 12,438	G 5
Svishtov, 21,522	G 4
Teteven, 9,807	G 4
Tolbukhin, 55,111	H 4
Topolovgrad, 6,633	H 4
Troyan, 18,382	G 4
Trŭn, 2,922	F 4
Tŭrgovishte, 25,528	H 4
Tutrakan, 9,909	H 4
Varna, 200,827	H 4
Veliko Tŭrnovo, 37,369	G 4
Vidin, 36,820	F 4
Vratsa, 39,052	F 4
Zlatograd, 6,508	G 5

OTHER FEATURES

Balkan (mts.)	G 4
Black (sea)	J 4
Danube (Dunav) (riv.)	H 4
Emine (cape)	J 4
Iskŭr (riv.)	G 4
Kaliakra (cape)	J 4
Lom (riv.)	F 4
Maritsa (riv.)	H 4
Mesta (riv.)	G 5
Musala (mt.)	F 5
Osŭm (riv.)	G 4
Rhodope (mts.)	G 5
Ruen (mt.)	F 5
Struma (riv.)	F 5
Timok (riv.)	G 4
Tundzha (riv.)	H 4
Vit (riv.)	G 4

GREECE
REGIONS

Aegean Islands, 477,476	G 6
Áyion Óros (aut. dist.), 2,687	G 5
Central Greece and Euboea, 2,823,658	G 6
Crete, 483,258	G 8
Epirus, 352,604	E 6
Greater Athens, 1,852,709	F 7
Ionian Islands, 212,573	D 6
Macedonia, 1,890,654	F 5
Pelopónnisos, 1,096,390	F 7
Thessalia, 695,385	F 6
Thrace, 356,555	G 5

CITIES and TOWNS

Agrínion, 24,763	E 6
Aíyina, 4,989	F 7
Aíyion, 17,762	F 6
Alexandroúpolis, 18,712	H 5
Alivérion, 3,523	G 6
Almirós, 6,010	F 6
Amaliás, 15,468	E 7
Amfilokhía, 5,408	E 6
Amfissa, 6,076	F 6
Andíssa, 2,532	H 6
Andravídha, 3,155	E 6
Ándros, 2,032	G 7
Áno Viánnos, 1,820	G 8
Andýia, 2,461	G 8
Ardhéa, 3,523	F 5
Argalastí, 1,864	F 6
Árgos, 16,712	F 7
Argostólion, 7,322	E 6
Arkhángelos, 2,918	J 7
Arnaía, 2,612	G 5
Árta, 16,899	E 6
Astipálaia, 1,205	H 7
Atalándi, 4,552	F 6
Athens (cap.), 627,564	F 7
Athens, *2,347,000	F 7
Áyios Matthaíos, 1,892	D 6
Áyios Nikólaos, 3,709	H 8
Candia (Iráklion), 63,458	G 8
Canea (Khaniá), 38,467	G 8
Chalcis (Khalkís), 24,745	F 6
Corinth, 15,892	F 7
Delvináklon, 1,076	E 6
Dhidhimótikhon, 7,287	H 5
Dhíkaia, 1,181	H 5
Dhimitsána, 1,300	F 7
Dhomokós, 2,017	F 6
Dráma, 32,195	G 5
Edhessa, 15,534	F 5
Elassón, 6,501	F 6
Elevtheroúpolis, 5,448	G 5
Ermoúpolis, 14,402	G 7
Fársala, 6,356	F 6
Filiátes, 3,065	E 6
Filiatrá, 6,753	E 7
Flórina, 11,983	E 5
Gargaliánoi, 6,637	E 7
Grevená, 6,892	E 5
Idhra, 2,546	F 7
Ierápetra, 6,488	G 8
Igoumenítsa, 3,235	E 6
Ioánnina, 34,997	E 6
Iráklion, 63,458	G 8
Istiaía, 3,882	F 6
Itháki, 2,632	E 6
Kalámai, 38,211	F 7
Kalampáka, 4,640	E 6
Kalávrita, 2,039	F 7
Kálimnos, 10,211	H 7
Kardhítsa, 23,708	F 6
Kariá, 1,739	E 6
Karíaí, 429	G 5
Káristos, 3,335	G 6
Karpenísion, 3,523	E 6
Kastéllion, 2,071	F 8
Kastéllion, 1,351	G 8
Kastoría, 10,162	E 5
Kateríni, 28,046	F 5
Kavália, 44,517	G 5
Kéa, 1,788	G 7
Kérkira, 26,991	D 6
Khalkís, 24,745	F 6
Khaniá, 38,467	G 8
Khíos, 24,053	H 6
Kiáton, 6,069	F 6
Kilkís, 10,963	F 5
Kími, 3,285	G 6
Kiparissía, 4,602	E 7
Kíthira, 3,485	F 8
Komotiní, 28,355	H 5
Kónitsa, 3,485	E 5
Koropí, 7,862	G 8
Kos, 8,138	H 7

(continued on following page)

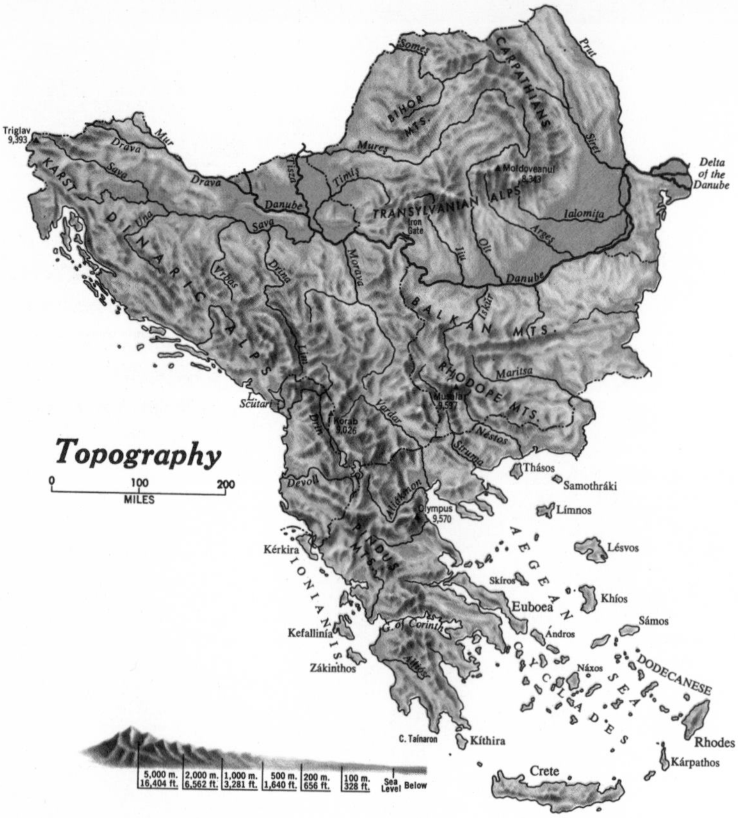

GREECE (continued)

Kozáni, 21,537 ......F 5
Kranídhion, 3,942 ......F 7
Lamía, 21,509 ......F 6
Langadhás, 6,739 ......F 5
Lárisa, 55,391 ......F 6
Lávrion, 6,553 ......G 7
Leonídhion, 3,297 ......F 7
Levádhia, 12,609 ......F 6
Levkás, 6,552 ......E 6
Limenária, 1,999 ......G 5
Limín Vathéos, 5,469 ......H 7
Límni, 2,394 ......F 6
Litókhoron, 5,032 ......F 5
Lixoúrion, 3,977 ......E 6
Loutrá Aidhipsoú, 1,859 ......F 6
Marathón, 2,167 ......G 6
Megalópolis, 2,235 ......E 7
Mégara, 15,450 ......F 6
Meligalá, 1,960 ......F 7
Mesolóngion, 11,266 ......E 6
Messíni, 8,249 ......E 7
Métsovon, 2,976 ......E 6
Mikínai, 361 ......F 7
Mílos, 944 ......G 7
Mírina, 3,460 ......G 6
Missolonghi (Mesolóngion), 11,266 ......E 6
Míthimna, 1,828 ......G 6
Mitilíni, 25,758 ......H 6
Moláoi, 2,526 ......F 7
Monólithos, 496 ......H 7
Moúdhros, 1,236 ......G 6
Náousa, 15,492 ......F 6
Návpaktos, 7,080 ......F 6
Návplion, 8,918 ......F 7
Náxos, 2,458 ......G 7
Néa Filippiás, 3,001 ......E 6
Neápolis, 2,464 ......F 7
Neméa, 4,720 ......F 7
Néon Karlóvasi, 5,308 ......H 7
Nigríta, 9,979 ......F 5
Olimbía, 771 ......E 7
Orestiás, 10,281 ......H 5
Paramithiá, 2,827 ......E 6
Pátrai, 95,364 ......E 6
Péta, 2,522 ......E 6
Pigádhia, 1,281 ......H 8
Pílos, 2,434 ......E 7
Piraiévs (Piraeus), 183,877 ......F 7
Pírgos, 20,558 ......E 7
Piryí, 1,914 ......G 6
Píthion, 1,535 ......H 5
Plomárion, 5,172 ......H 6
Políkastron, 3,821 ......F 5
Políkhnitos, 5,131 ......G 6
Políyiros, 3,541 ......F 5
Póros, 4,392 ......F 7
Préveza, 11,172 ......E 6
Psakhná, 4,433 ......F 6
Ptolemaïs, 12,747 ......E 5
Réthimnon, 14,999 ......G 8
Ródhos (Rhodes), 27,393 ......J 7
Salamís, 11,161 ......F 6
Salonika (Thessaloníki), 448,000 ......F 5
Sámi, 1,065 ......E 6
Samothráki, 1,555 ......G 5
Sápai, 2,589 ......G 5
Sérrai, 40,063 ......F 5
Sérvia, 4,132 ......F 5
Siátista, 4,737 ......E 5
Sidhirókastron, 8,177 ......F 5
Sími, 2,982 ......H 7
Sitía, 5,327 ......H 8
Skíros, 2,411 ......G 6
Skópelos, 2,955 ......F 6
Souflíon, 6,693 ......H 5
Sparta, 10,412 ......F 7
Spétsai, 3,314 ......F 7
Stilís, 4,673 ......F 6
Thebes (Thívai), 15,779 ......F 6
Thessaloníki, 448,000 ......F 5
Thásos, 1,875 ......G 5
Thíra, 1,481 ......G 7
Thívai, 15,779 ......F 6
Timbákion, 2,816 ......G 8
Tínos, 2,888 ......G 7
Tírnavos, 10,805 ......F 6
Tríkkala, 27,876 ......E 6
Trípolis, 18,500 ......F 7
Vartholomión, 3,244 ......E 7
Vathí, 3,161 ......H 7
Velvendós, 4,158 ......F 5
Vérroia, 25,765 ......F 5
Vólos, 49,221 ......F 6
Vólos, *67,424 ......F 6
Vónitsa, 2,996 ......E 6
Vrondádhes, 4,685 ......G 6
Xánthi, 26,377 ......G 5
Yiannitsá, 19,693 ......F 5
Yíthion, 4,992 ......F 7
Zákinthos, 9,506 ......E 7
Zante (Zákinthos), 9,506 ......E 7

OTHER FEATURES

Aegean (sea) ......G 6
Akrítas (cape) ......E 7
Aktí (pen.) ......G 5
Amorgós (isl.), 2,396 ......G 7
Anáfi (isl.), 471 ......G 7
Andikíthira (isl.), 178 ......F 8
Ándros (isl.), 12,928 ......G 7
Arda (riv.) ......G 5
Argolís (gulf) ......F 7
Astipálaia (isl.), 1,539 ......H 7
Áthos (mt.) ......G 5
Áyios Evstrátios (isl.), 1,061 ......G 6
Áyios Yeóryios (cape) ......G 5
Cephalonia (Kefallinía) (isl.), 39,793 ......E 6
Chios (Khíos) (isl.), 60,061 ......G 6
Corfu (Kérkira) (isl.), 99,092 ......D 6
Corinth (gulf) ......F 6
Crete (isl.), 483,075 ......G 8
Crete (sea) ......G 7
Cyclades (isls.), 99,959 ......G 7
Dhrépanon (cape) ......G 6
Dodecanese (isls.), 123,021 ......H 8
Euboea (isl.), 163,215 ......G 6
Évros (riv.) ......H 5
Gávdhos (isl.), 172 ......F 8
Ikaría (isl.), 9,577 ......G 7
Ionian (sea) ......D 7
Íos (isl.), 1,343 ......G 7
Itháki (Ithaca) (isl.), 5,210 ......E 6
Kálimnos (isl.), 10,211 ......H 7
Kafirévs (cape) ......G 6
6,689 ......H 8
Kárpathos (isl.), 6,689 ......H 8
Kásos (isl.), 1,422 ......H 8
Kassándra (pen.) ......F 6
Kéa (isl.), 2,361 ......G 7
Kefallinía (isl.), 39,793 ......E 6
Kérkira (isl.), 99,092 ......D 6
Khálki (isl.), 501 ......H 7
Khani, (gulf) ......G 8
Khíos (isl.), 60,061 ......G 6
Kiparissía (gulf) ......E 7
Kíthira (isl.), 5,340 ......F 7
Kíthnos (isl.), 2,064 ......G 7
Kos (isl.), 18,187 ......H 7
Kriós (cape) ......F 8
Lakonía (gulf) ......F 7
Léros (isl.), 6,611 ......H 7
Lésvos (isl.), 117,371 ......G 6
Levítha (isl.), 7 ......H 7
Levkás (isl.), 2,697 ......E 6
Límnos (isl.), 21,808 ......G 6
Maléa (cape) ......F 7
Matapan (Taínaron) (cape) ......F 7
Merabéllou (gulf) ......H 8
Mesará (gulf) ......G 8
Messíni (gulf) ......E 7
Míkonos (isl.), 3,633 ......G 7
Mílos (isl.), 4,910 ......G 7
Mirtóön (sea) ......F 7
Náxos (isl.), 16,703 ......G 7
Néstos (riv.) ......G 5
Nísiros (isl.), 1,788 ......H 7
Northern Sporades (isls.), 9,810 ......F 6
Olympus (mt.) ......F 5
Óssa (mt.) ......F 6
Parnassus (mt.) ......F 6
Páros (isl.), 7,830 ......G 7
Pátmos (isl.), 2,564 ......H 7
Paxoí (isl.), 2,678 ......D 6
Pindus (mts.) ......E 6
Piniós (riv.) ......E 6
Prespa (lake) ......E 5
Psará (isl.), 576 ......G 6
Rhodes (isl.), 63,951 ......H 7
Rhodope (mts.) ......G 5
Salonika (Thermaic) (gulf) ......F 6
Sámos (isl.), 41,124 ......H 7
Samothráki (isl.), 3,830 ......G 5
Saría (isl.), 18 ......H 8
Saronic (gulf) ......F 7
Sérifos (isl.), 1,878 ......G 7
Sídheros (cape) ......H 8
Sífnos (isl.), 2,258 ......G 7
Sími (isl.), 3,123 ......H 7
Síros (isl.), 19,570 ......G 7
Sithoniá (pen.) ......F 5
Skíros (isl.), 2,882 ......G 6
Spátha (cape) ......F 8
Strimón (gulf) ......G 5
Strofádhes (isls.), 10 ......E 7
Taínaron (cape) ......F 7
Thásos (isl.), 15,916 ......G 5
Thermaic (gulf) ......F 6
Thíra (isl.), 7,751 ......G 7
Tílos (isl.), 789 ......H 7
Tínos (isl.), 9,273 ......G 7
Toronaic (gulf) ......F 5
Vardar (riv.) ......E 5
Voïviïs (lake) ......F 6
Vólvi (lake) ......F 5
Voúxa (cape) ......F 8
Zákinthos (Zante) (isl.), 35,499 ......E 7

RUMANIA

CITIES and TOWNS

Aiud, 11,886 ......F 2
Alba Iulia, 22,225 ......F 2
Alexandria, 21,907 ......G 3
Anina, 11,837 ......E 3
Arad, 132,757 ......E 2
Arad, *137,444 ......E 2
Babadag, 5,549 ......J 3
Bacău, 73,481 ......H 2
Bacău, *87,465 ......H 2
Baia Mare, 62,769 ......F 2
Baia Mare, *108,709 ......F 2
Băileşti, 15,932 ......F 3
Balş, 6,956 ......G 3
Beiuş, 6,467 ......F 2
Bîrlad, 41,061 ......H 2
Bîrlad, *52,497 ......H 2
Bistrița, 25,534 ......G 2
Blaj, 8,731 ......F 2
Botoşani, 35,185 ......H 2
Botoşani, *50,204 ......H 2
Brad, 9,963 ......F 2
Brăila, 147,495 ......H 3
Braşov, 175,264 ......G 3
Braşov, *264,537 ......G 3
Bucharest (Bucureşti) (cap.), 1,431,993 ......G 3
Bucharest, *1,518,725 ......G 3
Buhuş, 12,382 ......H 2
Buzău, 56,380 ......H 3
Buzău, *82,454 ......H 3
Buziaş, 5,140 ......E 3
Călafat, 8,069 ......F 3
Călăraşi, 35,698 ......H 3
Caracal, 22,715 ......G 3
Caransebeş, 15,195 ......F 3
Carei, 16,780 ......F 2
Cernavodă, 8,802 ......J 3
Cîmpio Turzii, 11,514 ......F 2
Cîmpina, 22,862 ......H 3
Cîmpulung, 24,891 ......G 3
Cîmpulung Moldovenesc, 13,627 ......G 2
Cisnădie, 12,246 ......F 3
Cluj, 193,375 ......F 2
Cluj, *223,519 ......F 2
Comaneşti, 12,392 ......H 2
Constanța, 165,245 ......J 3
Constanța, *202,024 ......J 3
Corabia, 11,502 ......G 4
Craiova, 166,249 ......F 3
Craiova, *174,669 ......F 3
Curtea de Argeş, 10,764 ......G 3
Dej, 26,968 ......F 2
Deva, 26,952 ......F 3
Deva, *45,836 ......F 3
Dorohoi, 14,771 ......H 2
Drăgăşani, 9,963 ......F 3
Făgăraş, 22,941 ......G 3
Fălticeni, 13,305 ......H 2
Feteşti, 21,425 ......H 3
Focşani, 35,075 ......H 3
Focşani, *40,701 ......H 3
Găeşti, 7,179 ......G 3
Galați, 160,097 ......H 3
Gheorgheni, 11,969 ......G 2
Gherla, 7,617 ......G 2
Giurgiu, 39,225 ......G 3
Giurgiu, *55,471 ......G 3
Hațeg, 3,853 ......F 3
Hîrşova, 4,761 ......J 3
Hunedoara, 68,303 ......F 3
Hunedoara, *100,953 ......F 3
Huşi, 20,703 ......J 2
Iaşi, 173,569 ......H 2
Iaşi, *196,167 ......H 2
Isaccea, 5,203 ......J 3
Jimbolia, 11,281 ......E 3
Lipova, 10,064 ......E 2
Lugoj, 35,388 ......F 3
Lupeni, 29,377 ......F 3
Mangalia, 4,792 ......J 4
Medgidia, 27,989 ......J 3
Mediaş, 46,396 ......G 2
Miercurea Ciuc, 11,996 ......G 2
Mizil, 7,460 ......H 3
Moineşti, 12,934 ......H 2
Moldova Nouă, 3,582 ......E 3
Moreni, 11,687 ......G 3
Năsăud, 5,725 ......G 2
Ocna Mureş, 10,701 ......G 2
Odobeşti, 4,977 ......H 3
Odorhei, 14,162 ......G 2
Oltenița, 14,111 ......H 3
Oradea, 132,266 ......E 2
Oradea, *136,375 ......E 2
Orăstie, 10,488 ......F 3
Oraşul Gheorghe Georghiu-Dej, 35,689 ......H 2
Oravița, 8,175 ......E 3
Orşova, 6,527 ......F 3
Panciu, 7,679 ......H 3
Paşcani, 15,008 ......H 2
Petrila, 24,804 ......F 3
Petroşeni, 35,237 ......F 3
Petroşeni, *130,111 ......F 3
Piatra Neamț, 45,925 ......G 2
Piatra Neamț, *58,397 ......G 2
Piteşti, 60,094 ......G 3
Piteşti, *78,784 ......G 3
Ploieşti, 156,382 ......H 3
Ploieşti, *191,663 ......H 3
Pucioasa, 9,259 ......G 3
Rădăuti, 15,949 ......G 2
Reghin, 23,317 ......G 2
Reşița, 58,683 ......E 3
Reşița, *121,458 ......E 3
Rîmnicu Sărat, 22,325 ......H 3
Rîmnicu Vîlcea, 23,880 ......F 3
Roman, 38,990 ......H 2
Roman, *49,496 ......H 2
Roşiori de Vede, 21,707 ......G 3
Săcele, 22,822 ......G 3
Salonta, 16,276 ......E 3
Satu Mare, 68,257 ......F 2
Sebeş, 11,628 ......F 3
Sfîntu Gheorge, 20,759 ......G 3
Sibiu, 117,020 ......G 3
Sighetul-Marmației, 29,768 ......F 2
Sighişoara, 25,100 ......G 2
Şimleu Silvaniei, 8,560 ......F 2
Sinaia, 9,006 ......G 3
Sînnicolau Mare, 9,956 ......E 2
Siret, 5,664 ......G 1
Slănic, 6,842 ......G 3
Slatina, 13,381 ......G 3
Slobozia, 9,632 ......H 3
Solca, 2,384 ......G 2
Strehaia, 8,545 ......F 3
Suceava, 37,715 ......G 2
Suceava, *76,327 ......G 2
Sulina, 3,622 ......J 3
Techirghiol, 2,705 ......J 3
Tecuci, 28,458 ......H 3
Timişoara, 184,797 ......E 3
Timişoara, *194,159 ......E 3
Tîrgovişte, 29,754 ......G 3
Tîrgovişte, *48,005 ......G 3
Tîrgu Jiu, 30,837 ......F 3
Tîrgu Jiu, *33,019 ......F 3
Tîrgu Mureş, 86,458 ......G 2
Tîrgu Mureş, *104,922 ......G 2
Tîrgu Neamț, 10,373 ......G 2
Tîrgu Ocna, 11,227 ......H 2
Tîrgu Secuiesc, 7,500 ......H 2
Tîrnăveni, 20,354 ......F 2
Toplița, 8,944 ......G 2
Tulcea, 35,552 ......J 3
Turda, 42,318 ......G 2
Turda, *69,768 ......G 2
Turnu Măgurele, 26,409 ......G 4
Turnu Severin, 45,394 ......F 3
Turnu Severin, *52,497 ......F 3
Urlați, 8,658 ......H 3
Urziceni, 6,061 ......H 3
Vasile Roaită, 3,286 ......J 3
Vaslui, 14,850 ......H 2
Vatra Dornei, 10,822 ......G 2
Vişeu de Sus, 13,956 ......F 2
Zalău, 13,378 ......F 2
Zărneşti, 6,673 ......G 3
Zimnicea, 12,445 ......G 4

OTHER FEATURES

Argeş (riv.) ......G 3
Buzău (riv.) ......H 3
Carpathian (mts.) ......G 2
Crişul Alb (riv.) ......F 2
Crişul Repede (riv.) ......F 2
Danube (river) ......H 4
Ialomița (marshes) ......J 3
Jiu (riv.) ......F 3
Moldoveanul (mt.) ......G 3
Mureş (riv.) ......E 2
Negoiul (mt.) ......G 3
Olt (riv.) ......G 3
Pietrosul (mt.) ......G 2
Prut (riv.) ......J 2
Siret (riv.) ......H 2
Someş (riv.) ......F 2
Timiş (riv.) ......E 3
Transylvanian Alps (mts.) ......G 3

YUGOSLAVIA

INTERNAL DIVISIONS

Bosnia and Hercegovina (rep.), 3,594,000 ......C 3
Croatia (rep.), 4,281,000 ......C 3
Kosovo-Mitohiyan (aut. prov.), 1,089,000 ......E 4
Macedonia (rep.), 1,506,000 ......E 5
Montenegro (rep.), 471,894 ......D 4
Serbia (rep.), 7,637,800 ......E 3
Slovenia (rep.), 1,624,900 ......B 2
Voyvodina (aut. prov.), 1,880,000 ......D 3

CITIES and TOWNS

Aleksinac, 8,828 ......E 4
Apatin, 17,000 ......D 3
Bačka Topola, 14,000 ......D 3
Bakar ......B 3
Banja Luka, 55,000 ......C 3
Bar, 2,184 ......D 4
Bečej, 22,000 ......E 3
Bela Crkva, 11,000 ......E 3
Belgrade (Beograd) (cap.), 745,000 ......E 3
Belgrade, *1,050,000 ......E 3
Bihać, 17,000 ......B 3
Bijeljina, 19,000 ......D 3
Bijelo Polje, 5,856 ......D 4
Bileća, 2,491 ......D 4
Biograd, 2,418 ......B 4
Bitola (Bitolj), 52,000 ......E 5
Bjelovar, 16,000 ......C 3
Bled, 4,156 ......A 2
Bor, 19,000 ......E 3
Bosanska Dubica, 6,259 ......C 3
Bosanska Gradiška, 6,363 ......C 3
Bosaska Kostajnica, 2,034 ......B 3
Bosanska Krupa, 6,191 ......C 3
Bosanski Brod, 7,350 ......D 3
Bosanski Novi, 7,023 ......C 3
Bosanski Petrovac, 3,473 ......C 3
Bosanski Šamac, 3,654 ......D 3
Brčko, 20,000 ......D 3
Brežice, 2,641 ......B 3
Brod, 30,000 ......D 3
Bugojno, 5,453 ......C 3
Buje, 1,955 ......A 3
Čačak, 30,000 ......F 4
Čapljina, 3,275 ......C 4
Caribrod (Dimitrovgrad), 3,665 ......F 4
Celje, 28,000 ......B 2
Cetinje, 9,359 ......D 4
Ćuprija, 12,000 ......E 4
Debar, 6,323 ......E 5
Derventa, 9,843 ......C 3
Dimitrovgrad, 3,665 ......F 4
Djakovica, 22,000 ......E 4
Djakovo, 13,000 ......D 3
Donji Vakuf, 3,764 ......C 3
Drvar, 3,646 ......C 3
Dubrovnik, 24,000 ......C 4
Fiume (Rijeka), 108,000 ......B 3
Foča, 6,763 ......D 4
Fojnica, 1,549 ......C 4
Gacko, 1,368 ......D 4
Gevgelija, 7,332 ......F 5
Glamoč, 1,626 ......C 3
Gnjilane, 14,000 ......E 4
Gornji Vafuf, 1,860 ......C 4
Gospić, 6,767 ......B 3
Gostivar, 14,000 ......E 5
Gračac, 2,183 ......B 3
Gračanica, 7,656 ......D 3
Gradačac, 5,878 ......D 3
Grubišno Polje, 2,655 ......C 3
Gusinje, 2,756 ......D 4
Hercegnovi, 3,797 ......D 4
Ivangrad, 6,969 ......E 4
Jajce, 6,853 ......C 3
Jesenice, 16,000 ......A 2
Kamnik, 5,062 ......B 2
Kanjiža, 10,000 ......D 2
Kardeljevo, 3,267 ......C 4
Karlovac, 35,000 ......B 3
Kavadarci, 13,000 ......E 5
Kičevo, 11,000 ......E 5
Kikinda, 32,000 ......E 3
Kladanj, 2,825 ......D 3
Ključ, 2,320 ......C 3
Knin, 5,116 ......C 3
Knjaževac, 7,448 ......F 4
Kočevje, 5,819 ......B 3
Konjic, 5,927 ......D 4
Koper, 12,000 ......A 3
Koprivnica, 12,000 ......C 2
Korčula, 2,458 ......C 4
Kosovska Mitrovica, 29,000 ......E 4
Kostajnica, 2,080 ......C 3
Kotor, 4,764 ......D 4
Kragujevac, 56,000 ......E 3
Kraljevo (Rankovićevo), 26,000 ......E 4
Kranj, 23,000 ......B 2
Križevci, 6,642 ......C 2
Krk, 1,280 ......B 3
Krško, 3,518 ......B 3
Kruševac, 31,000 ......E 4
Kumanovo, 33,000 ......E 4
Leskovac, 37,000 ......E 4
Livno, 5,181 ......C 4
Ljubljana, 183,000 ......B 3
Ljubuški, 2,168 ......C 4
Loznica, 12,000 ......D 3
Maglaj, 4,556 ......D 3
Makarska, 3,634 ......C 4
Maribor, 89,000 ......B 2
Mladenovac, 12,000 ......E 4
Modriča, 5,053 ......D 3
Mostar, 53,000 ......D 4
Našice, 4,187 ......C 3
Negotin, 8,635 ......F 3
Nevesinje, 2,349 ......D 4
Nikšić, 25,000 ......D 4
Niš, 92,000 ......F 4
Nova Gradiška, 9,229 ......C 3
Novi, 2,075 ......B 3
Novi Pazar, 23,000 ......E 4
Novi Sad, 119,000 ......D 3
Novo Mesto, 6,885 ......B 3
Novska, 3,844 ......C 3
Ogulin, 3,522 ......B 3
Ohrid, 18,000 ......E 5
Omiš, 2,171 ......C 4
Opatija, 7,974 ......A 3
Osijek, 78,000 ......D 3
Pag, 2,431 ......B 3
Pančevo, 49,000 ......E 3
Paraćin, 17,000 ......E 4
Peć, 30,000 ......E 4
Petrinja, 7,366 ......B 3
Piran, 5,474 ......A 3
Pirot, 20,000 ......F 4
Plav, 2,535 ......D 4
Pljevlja, 12,000 ......D 4
Podgorica (Titograd), 37,000 ......D 4
Pola (Pula), 40,000 ......A 3
Poreč, 3,006 ......A 3
Postojna, 4,857 ......B 3
Požarevac, 23,000 ......E 3
Požega, 14,000 ......C 3
Preševo, 5,680 ......E 4
Priboj, 5,490 ......D 4
Prijedor, 13,000 ......C 3
Prijepolje, 4,566 ......D 4
Prilep, 40,000 ......E 5
Priština, 43,000 ......E 4
Prizren, 29,000 ......E 4
Prokuplje, 15,000 ......E 4
Prozor, 1,052 ......C 4
Ptuj, 7,392 ......C 2
Pula, 40,000 ......A 3
Rab, 1,548 ......B 3
Rača, 1,351 ......E 3
Radeče, 1,500 ......B 2
Radoviš, 6,246 ......F 5
Ragusa (Dubrovnik), 24,000 ......C 4
Rankovićevo, 26,000 ......E 4
Raška, 2,278 ......E 4
Rijeka, 108,000 ......B 3
Rogatica, 3,040 ......D 4
Rovinj, 7,155 ......A 3
Ruma, 21,000 ......D 3
Šabac, 30,000 ......D 3
Sanski Most, 5,096 ......C 3
Sarajevo, 223,000 ......D 4
Senj, 3,903 ......B 3
Senta, 22,000 ......D 3
Šibenik, 27,000 ......C 4
Sinj, 4,134 ......C 4
Sisak, 29,000 ......C 3
Škofja Loka, 3,429 ......A 2
Skopje, 230,000 ......E 5
Skradin, 1,118 ......C 4
Smederevo, 29,000 ......E 3
Sombor, 31,000 ......D 3
Split, 106,000 ......C 4
Srebrenica, 1,859 ......D 3
Sremska Mitrovica, 22,000 ......D 3
Sremski Karlovci, 6,390 ......D 3
Stari Majdan, 1,445 ......C 3
Štip, 22,000 ......F 5
Stolac, 2,970 ......D 4
Struga, 6,857 ......E 5
Strumica, 17,000 ......F 5
Subotica, 76,000 ......D 2
Surdulica, 5,007 ......F 4
Svetozarevo, 22,000 ......E 4
Svilajnac, 5,895 ......E 3
Tešanj, 3,148 ......C 3
Tetovo, 27,000 ......E 5
Titograd, 37,000 ......D 4
Titovo Užice, 26,000 ......D 4
Titov Veles, 29,000 ......E 5
Travnik, 12,000 ......C 3
Trbovlje, 16,000 ......B 2
Trebinje, 4,073 ......D 4
Trogir, 5,003 ......C 4
Tržič, 4,881 ......B 2
Tuzla, 55,000 ......D 3
Ulcinj, 5,705 ......D 5
Valjevo, 27,000 ......D 3
Varaždin, 28,000 ......B 2
Vareš, 7,647 ......D 3
Veliki Bečkerek (Zrenjanin), 56,000 ......E 3
Vinkovci, 24,000 ......D 3
Virovitica, 10,000 ......C 3
Višegrad, 3,309 ......D 4
Vranje, 18,000 ......F 4
Vrbas, 19,000 ......D 3
Vršac, 32,000 ......E 3
Vukovar, 25,000 ......D 3
Žabari, 1,984 ......E 3
Zadar, 28,000 ......B 3
Zagreb, 503,000 ......C 3
Zaječar, 18,000 ......E 4
Zara (Zadar), 28,000 ......B 3
Zenica, 50,000 ......C 3
Žepče, 2,709 ......D 3
Zrenjanin, 56,000 ......E 3
Zvornik, 5,444 ......D 3

OTHER FEATURES

Adriatic (sea) ......B 4
Bobotov Kuk (mt.) ......D 4
Bosna (riv.) ......D 3
Brač (isl.), 14,227 ......C 4
Čazma (riv.) ......C 3
Cres (isl.), 4,949 ......B 3
Danube (riv.) ......E 3
Dinaric Alps (mts.) ......B 3
Drava (riv.) ......C 3
Drina (riv.) ......D 3
Dugi Otok (isl.), 4,873 ......B 3
Hvar (isl.), 12,147 ......C 4
Ibar (riv.) ......E 4
Kamenjak (cape) ......A 3
Korab (mt.) ......E 5
Korčula (isl.), 10,245 ......C 4
Kornat (isl.), 6 ......B 4
Krk (isl.), 14,548 ......B 3
Kvarner (gulf) ......B 3
Lastovo (Lagosta) (isl.), 1,449 ......C 4
Lim (riv.) ......D 4
Lošinj (isl.), 5,068 ......B 3
Mljet (isl.), 1,963 ......C 4
Morava (riv.) ......E 3
Mur (riv.) ......B 2
Neretva (riv.) ......D 4
Ohrid (lake) ......E 5
Pag (isl.), 8,017 ......B 3
Pelagruž (Pelagosa) (isl.) ......C 4
Prespa (lake) ......E 5
Rab (isl.), 8,400 ......B 3
Ruen (mt.) ......F 4
Sava (riv.) ......D 3
Scutari (lake) ......D 4
Solta (isl.), 2,735 ......C 4
Tara (riv.) ......D 4
Timok (riv.) ......F 3
Tisza (riv.) ......E 4
Triglav (mt.) ......A 2
Una (riv.) ......C 3
Vardar (riv.) ......E 5
Vis (isl.), 7,004 ......C 4
Vrbas (riv.) ......C 3
Žirje (isl.), 506 ......B 4

*City and suburbs.

THE BALKAN STATES

CONIC PROJECTION

Topography

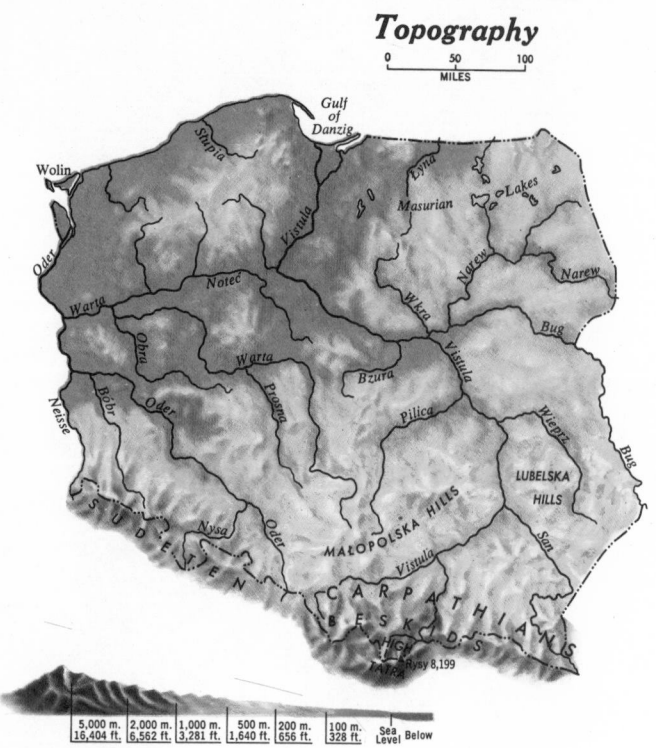

5,000 m. | 2,000 m. | 1,000 m. | 500 m. | 200 m. | 100 m. | Sea Level | Below
16,404 ft. | 6,562 ft. | 3,281 ft. | 1,640 ft. | 656 ft. | 328 ft.

POLAND 1938

Agriculture, Industry and Resources

SZCZECIN
Machinery, Shipbuilding, Chemicals

BYDGOSZCZ
Machinery, Chemicals, Textiles

GDAŃSK
Shipbuilding, Machinery

WROCŁAW—
LOWER SILESIA
Textiles, Machinery, Chemicals

ŁÓDŹ
Textiles, Chemicals

KATOWICE—CRACOW—
UPPER SILESIA
Iron & Steel, Chemicals, Machinery, Nonferrous Metals, Transportation Equipment

WARSAW
Machinery, Textiles, Chemicals

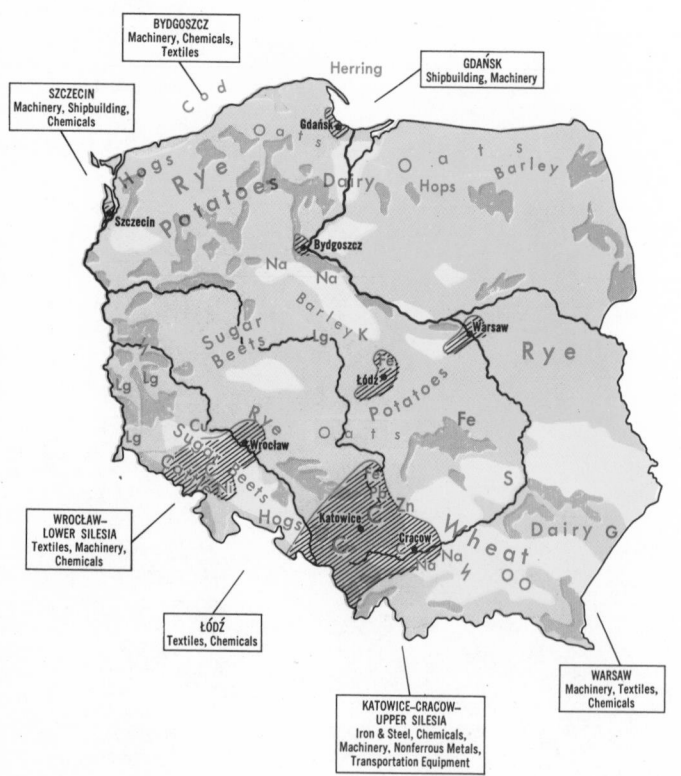

POLAND 1945

DOMINANT LAND USE

Cereals (chiefly wheat)

Rye, Oats, Barley, Potatoes

General Farming, Livestock

Forests

MAJOR MINERAL OCCURRENCES

C Coal
Cu Copper
Fe Iron Ore
G Natural Gas
K Potash
Lg Lignite

Na Salt
Ni Nickel
O Petroleum
Pb Lead
S Sulfur
Zn Zinc

⚡ Water Power
▨ Major Industrial Areas

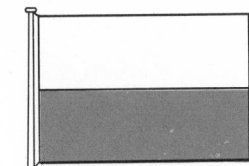

AREA 120,664 sq. mi.
POPULATION 32,889,000
CAPITAL Warsaw
LARGEST CITY Warsaw
HIGHEST POINT Rysy 8,199 ft.
MONETARY UNIT zloty
MAJOR LANGUAGE Polish
MAJOR RELIGION Roman Catholicism

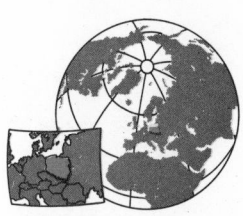

Czechowice-Dziedzice, 24,600	D 4
Czeladź, 31,400	B 4
Częstochowa, 179,400	D 3
Dąbrowa Górnicza, 60,100	C 4
Danzig (Gdańsk), 333,500	D 1
Dębica, 20,900	E 3
Dęblin, 11,700	E 3
Dębno, 10,200	B 2
Dirschau (Tczew), 38,000	D 1
Dzierżoniów, 31,900	C 3
Elbląg (Elbing), 86,700	D 1
Ełk, 25,300	F 2
Frankenstein (Ząbkowice Śląskie), 13,000	C 3
Gdańsk, 333,500	D 1
Gdynia, 171,900	E 1
Giżycko, 16,600	E 1
Glatz (Kłodzko), 25,600	C 3
Gliwice (Gleiwitz), 164,900	A 4
Głowno, 12,700	D 3
Głuchołazy, 14,000	C 3
Gniezno (Gnesen), 48,000	C 2
Gorlice, 14,000	E 4
Görlitz (Zgorzelec), 26,400	B 3
Gorzów Wielkopolski, 69,700	B 2
Gostyń, 12,200	C 3
Gostynin, 10,900	D 2
Graudenz (Grudziądz), 73,700	D 2
Grodziec, 10,500	B 4
Grodzisk Mazowiecki, 19,200	E 2
Grodzisk Wielkopolski, 8,300	C 2
Grudziądz, 73,700	D 2
Grünberg (Zielona Góra), 66,200	B 2
Gryfice, 12,500	B 2
Hajnówka, 14,400	F 2
Haynau (Chojnów), 10,900	B 3
Hindenburg (Zabrze), 197,600	A 4
Hirschberg (Jelenia Góra), 54,900	B 3
Hohensalza (Inowrocław), 52,000	C 2
Hrubieszów, 13,400	G 3
Inowrocław, 52,000	C 2
Jarocin, 17,700	C 2
Jarosław, 27,300	F 3
Jawor (Jauer), 15,300	B 3
Jaworzno, 63,000	D 3
Jędrzejów, 13,700	D 3
Jelenia Góra, 54,900	B 3

Kalisz, 77,500	D 3
Kamienna Góra, 21,100	C 3
Katowice, 291,600	B 4
Kędzierzyn, 27,900	C 3
Kętrzyn, 17,400	E 1
Kielce, 113,200	D 3
Kłobuck, 11,500	D 3
Kłodzko, 25,600	C 3
Kluczbork, 16,300	A 3
Knurów, 23,500	A 4
Koło, 12,100	D 2
Kołobrzeg, 23,000	B 1
Königshütte (Chorzów), 153,100	
Konin, 29,300	D 2
Końskie, 11,700	E 3
Konstantynów, 12,500	D 3
Kościan, 17,300	C 2
Kościerzyna, 13,500	C 1
Koszalin, 56,800	C 1
Kraków (Cracow), 540,200	E 3
Kraśnik, 11,800	F 3
Krasnystaw, 11,800	F 3
Krosno, 24,600	E 4
Krotoszyn, 20,900	C 3
Krynica, 9,300	E 4
Kutno, 28,100	D 2
Kwidzyń, 22,800	D 1
Łańcut, 11,300	F 3
Landeshut (Kamienna Góra), 21,100	C 3
Landsberg (Gorzów Wielkopolski), 69,700	
Langenbielau (Bielawa), 31,500	
Lauban (Lubań), 16,800	B 3
Lębork (Lauenburg), 19,200	
Łęczyca, 13,700	D 2
Lędziny, 13,600	
Legionowo, 13,400	E 2
Legnica, 73,400	C 3
Leszno, 32,500	C 2
Lidzbark Warmiński, 12,200	E 1
Liegnitz (Legnica), 73,400	C 3
Lipno, 11,200	D 2
Łódź, 750,400	D 3
Łomża, 23,700	F 2
Łowicz, 18,800	E 2
Lubań, 16,800	B 3
Lublin, 211,500	F 3
Lubliniec, 18,500	D 3
Luboń, 16,100	C 2
Łuków, 13,400	F 3
Lyck (Ełk), 25,300	F 2
Malbork, 29,500	D 2
Marienburg (Malbork), 29,500	

Marienwerder (Kwidzyń), 22,800	D 2
Międzyrzec Podlaski, 12,900	F 3
Międzyrzecz, 12,200	B 2
Mielec, 26,000	
Mikołów, 20,000	B 4
Mińsk Mazowiecki, 21,700	
Mława, 17,900	E 2
Mrągowo, 12,600	E 2
Mysłowice (Mysłowitz), 44,200	B 4
Nakło nad Notecią, 16,000	C 2
Neisse (Nysa), 29,000	C 3
Neusalz (Nowa Sól), 30,700	B 3
Neustadt (Prudnik), 19,200	
Neustettin (Szczecinek), 27,000	C 1
Nowa Ruda, 18,900	C 3
Nowa Sól, 30,700	B 3
Nowy Dwór, 14,900	E 2
Nowy Sącz, 38,600	E 4
Nowy Targ, 20,600	E 4
Nysa, 29,000	C 3
Oels (Oleśnica), 24,700	C 3
Oława (Ohlau), 15,300	C 3
Oleśnica, 24,700	C 3
Olkusz, 14,500	D 3
Olsztyn, 80,700	E 2
Opoczno, 11,600	E 3
Opole (Oppeln), 78,800	C 3
Ostróda (Osterode), 20,000	D 2
Ostrołęka, 18,600	
Ostrów Mazowiecka, 14,300	
Ostrów Wielkopolski, 47,100	C 3
Ostrowiec Świętokrzyski, 45,600	

Oświęcim, 37,300	D 3
Otwock, 38,200	E 2
Ozorków, 17,400	D 2
Pabianice, 60,100	D 3
Piekary Śląskie, 36,000	B 4
Piła, 40,700	C 2
Pionki, 13,600	E 3
Piotrków Trybunalski, 58,200	D 3
Pleszew, 12,200	
Płock, 60,300	E 2
Płońsk, 10,900	E 2
Poznań, 446,700	C 2
Prudnik, 19,200	C 3
Pruszków, 38,400	E 2
Przemyśl, 51,000	F 4
Pszczyna, 17,400	B 4
Puławy, 26,100	F 3
Pułtusk, 11,900	E 2
Pyskowice, 22,900	A 4
Racibórz, 37,800	C 3
Radom, 148,400	E 3
Radomsko, 29,900	D 3
Ratibor (Racibórz), 37,800	C 3
Rawicz, 13,600	C 3
Ruda Śląska, 142,800	B 4
Rumia, 21,500	D 1
Rybnik, 39,500	B 4
Rzeszów, 74,200	F 3
Sandomierz, 15,600	E 3
Sanok, 19,300	F 4
Schneidemühl (Piła), 40,700	C 2
Schweidnitz (Świdnica), 46,700	C 3
Siedlce, 36,500	F 2
Siemianowice Śląskie, 67,500	B 4
Sieradz, 16,300	D 3
Sierpc, 12,200	D 2
Skarżysko-Kamienna, 38,200	E 3

Skierniewice, 24,900	D 2
Słupsk, 61,800	C 1
Sochaczew, 18,300	D 2
Sopot, 44,300	D 1
Sorau, (Żary), 28,400	
Sosnowiec, 143,300	B 4
Śrem, 12,400	C 2
Środa Wielkopolska, 13,900	C 2
Stalowa Wola, 27,300	E 3
Starachowice, 40,600	E 3
Stargard Szczeciński, 40,600	
Starogard Gdański, 30,600	D 2
Stettin (Szczecin), 322,000	
Stolp (Słupsk), 61,800	C 1
Strzegom, 14,000	C 3
Strzelce Opolskie, 14,000	
Suwałki, 22,900	F 1
Świdnica, 46,700	C 3
Świdnik, 19,300	F 3
Świdwin, 11,500	C 2
Świebodzin, 14,000	B 2
Świecie, 15,700	D 2
Świętochłowice, 58,300	B 4
Świnoujście (Swinemünde), 24,100	
Szamotuły, 12,700	C 2
Szczecin, 322,000	B 2
Szczecinek, 27,000	C 1
Szczytno, 11,600	E 2
Tarnów, 81,000	E 3
Tarnowskie Góry, 32,600	D 3
Tczew, 38,000	D 1
Teschen (Cieszyn), 24,700	D 4
Thorn (Toruń), 117,800	D 2
Tomaszów Mazowiecki, 53,200	E 3

Toruń (Thorn), 117,800	D 2
Turek, 17,500	D 2
Tychy, 66,200	B 4
Wąbrzeźno, 12,100	D 2
Wągrowiec, 14,400	C 2
Wałbrzych, 126,600	C 3
Wałcz, 18,000	C 2
Waldenburg (Wałbrzych), 126,600	C 3
Warsaw (capital), 1,282,600	E 2
Warszawa (Warsaw) (cap.), 1,282,600	E 2
Wejherowo, 30,600	D 1
Wieliczka, 12,800	E 3
Wieluń, 12,900	D 3
Włocławek, 70,200	D 2
Wołomin, 22,800	E 2
Wrocław, 487,000	C 3
Września, 16,100	C 2
Ząbkowice Śląskie, 13,000	C 3
Zabrze, 197,600	A 4
Zagań, 21,100	B 3
Zakopane, 26,100	D 4
Zambrów, 13,200	F 2
Zamość, 31,500	F 3
Żary, 28,400	B 3
Zawiercie, 37,700	D 3
Zduńska Wola, 28,000	D 3
Zgierz, 40,900	D 3
Zgorzelec, 26,400	B 3
Zielona Góra, 66,200	B 2
Złotoryja, 13,700	B 3
Złocieniec, 10,100	C 2
Zoppot (Sopot), 44,300	D 1
Żyrardów, 31,500	E 2
Żywiec, 22,700	D 4

OTHER FEATURES

Alle (Łyna) (river)	E 1
Baltic (sea)	B 1
Beskids (mts.)	E 4

Brda (river)	C 2
Bug (river)	G 2
Bzura (river)	D 2
Danzig (Gdańsk) (gulf)	D 1
Drawa (river)	C 2
Drwęca (river)	D 2
Dukla (pass)	E 4
Dunajec (river)	E 4
Gdańsk (Danzig) (gulf)	D 1
Gwda (river)	C 2
Hel (pen.)	D 1
High Tatra (mts.)	D 4
Kłodnica (river)	A 4
Łyna (river)	E 1
Mamry (Mauer) (lake)	E 1
Mauer (Mamry) (lake)	E 1
Narew (river)	E 2
Neisse (Nysa Łużycka) (river)	B 3
Nitze (Noteć) (river)	B 2
Noteć (Nitze) (river)	C 2
Nysa Kłodzka (river)	C 3
Nysa Łużycka (Neisse) (river)	B 3
Oder (Odra) (river)	B 3
Odra (Oder) (river)	D 4
Orava (river)	D 4
Pilica (river)	E 3
Pomeranian (bay)	B 1
Prosna (river)	C 2
Rysy (mt.)	E 4
San (river)	F 3
Śniardwy (Spirding) (lake)	E 2
Sołokija (river)	G 3
Spirding (Śniardwy) (lake)	E 2
Sudeten (range)	B 3
Uznam (Usedom) (isl.)	B 1
Vistula (Wisła) (river)	D 2
Warta (Warthe) (river)	C 2
Wieprz (river)	F 3
Wisła (Vistula) (river)	D 2
Wkra (river)	E 2
Wolin (Wollin) (isl.), 38,400	B 2

POLAND
CONIC PROJECTION
SCALE OF MILES
0 20 40 60 80 100
SCALE OF KILOMETRES
0 20 40 60 80 100 120 140 160

International Boundaries ....
Internal Boundaries ....
Capitals of Countries .... ☆
Administrative Centers .... ◉
Canals ....

© C. S. HAMMOND & Co., N. Y.

GLOSSARY

PRESENT POLISH	FORMER GERMAN	KEY
Brzeg	Brieg	C-3
Bytom	Beuthen	B-4
Elbląg	Elbing	D-1
Gdańsk	Danzig	D-1
Gliwice	Gleiwitz	A-4
Głogów	Glogau	C-3
Gorzów Wlkp.	Landsberg	B-2
Gubin	Guben	B-3
Jelenia Góra	Hirschberg	B-3
Kołobrzeg	Kolberg	B-1
Kostrzyn	Küstrin	B-2
Koszalin	Köslin	C-1
Legnica	Liegnitz	C-3
Malbork	Marienburg	D-2
Nysa	Neisse	C-3
Olsztyn	Allenstein	E-2
Opole	Oppeln	C-3
Piła	Schneidemühl	C-2
Racibórz	Ratibor	C-3
Słupsk	Stolp	C-1
Świdnica	Schweidnitz	C-3
Świnoujście	Swinemünde	B-2
Szczecin	Stettin	B-2
Wałbrzych	Waldenburg	C-3
Wrocław	Breslau	C-3
Zabrze	Hindenburg	D-3
Zielona Góra	Grünberg	B-3

Post-war territorial changes shown on this map do not necessarily represent the final status of such boundaries. Only after the signing of the Peace Treaties can changes be considered official and definite.

46 Union of Soviet Socialist Republics

UNION REPUBLICS

Armenian S.S.R., 2,493,000 .... E 6
Azerbaidzhan S.S.R., 5,111,000 .... E 5
Estonian S.S.R., 1,357,000 .... C 4
Georgian S.S.R., 4,688,000 .... D 5
Kazakh S.S.R., 12,850,000 .... G 5
Kirghiz S.S.R., 2,933,000 .... H 5
Latvian S.S.R., 2,365,000 .... C 4
Lithuanian S.S.R., 3,129,000 .... C 4
Moldavian S.S.R., 3,572,000 .... C 5
Russian S.F.S.R., 130,090,000
Tadzhik S.S.R., 2,900,000 .... H 6
Turkmen S.S.R., 2,158,000 .... F 6
Ukrainian S.S.R., 47,136,000 .... C 5
Uzbek S.S.R., 11,963,000 .... G 5
White Russian S.S.R., 9,003,000 .... C 4

INTERNAL DIVISIONS

Abkhaz A.S.S.R., 487,000 .... E 5
Adygey Aut. Oblast, 386,000 .... D 5
Adzhar A.S.S.R., 310,000 .... E 5
Aginsk Nat'l Okrug, 66,000 .... M 4
Bashkir A.S.S.R., 3,819,000 .... M 4
Buryat A.S.S.R., 812,000 .... M 4
Chechen-Ingush A.S.S.R., 1,065,000 .... E 5

Chukchi Nat'l Okrug, 101,000 .... R 3
Chuvash A.S.S.R., 1,224,000 .... E 4
Dagestan A.S.S.R., 1,429,000 .... E 5
Evenki Nat'l Okrug, 13,000 .... K 3
Gorno-Altay Aut. Oblast, 168,000 .... J 4
Gorno-Badakhshan Aut. Oblast, 98,000 .... H 6
Jewish Aut. Oblast, 173,000 .... O 5
Kabardin-Balkar A.S.S.R., 589,000 .... E 5
Kalmuck A.S.S.R., 268,000 .... E 5
Kara-Kalpak A.S.S.R., 702,000 .... G 5
Karachay-Cherkess Aut. Oblast, 345,000 .... D 5
Karelian A.S.S.R., 714,000 .... D 3
Khakass Aut. Oblast, 446,000 .... J 4
Khanty-Mansi Nat'l Okrug, 272,000 .... H 3
Komi A.S.S.R., 965,000 .... F 3
Komi-Permyak Nat'l Okrug, 212,000 .... F 4
Koryak Nat'l Okrug, 31,000 .... R 4
Mari A.S.S.R., 685,000 .... E 4
Mordvinian A.S.S.R., 1,030,000 .... E 4
Nagorno-Karabakh Aut. Oblast, 149,000 .... E 5

Nakhichevan' A.S.S.R., 202,000 .... E 6
Nenets Nat'l Okrug, 39,000 .... F 3
North Ossetian A.S.S.R., 553,000 .... E 5
South Ossetian Aut. Oblast, 100,000 .... E 5
Tatar A.S.S.R., 3,131,000 .... E 4
Taymyr Nat'l Okrug, 38,000 .... K 2
Tuvinian A.S.S.R., 231,000 .... K 4
Udmurt A.S.S.R., 1,417,000 .... F 4
Ust'-Ordynskiy Nat'l Okrug, 146,000 .... L 4
Yakut A.S.S.R., 664,000 .... N 3
Yamal-Nenets Nat'l Okrug, 80,000 .... H 3

CITIES and TOWNS

Abakan, 90,000 .... J 4
Adimi .... O 5
Aginskoye, 16,000 .... M 4
Akmolinsk (Tselinograd), 180,000 .... H 4
Aksha .... M 4
Aktyubinsk, 150,000 .... F 4
Aldan .... N 4
Aleksandrovsk-Sakhalinskiy, 22,206 .... P 5
Aleysk, 28,982 .... J 4
Alga, 11,748 .... F 5

Allakh-Yun' .... O 3
Alma-Ata, 730,000 .... H 5
Ambarchik .... R 3
Amderma .... F 3
Amga .... N 4
Anadyr', 6,000 .... T 3
Andizhan, 188,000 .... H 5
Angarsk, 204,000 .... L 4
Anzhero-Sudzhensk, 106,000 .... J 4
Aral'sk, 19,615 .... G 5
Archangel, 343,000 .... E 3
Arkalyk .... G 4
Armavir, 146,000 .... E 5
Artem, 55,531 .... O 5
Artemovskiy .... M 4
Arzamas, 41,518 .... E 4
Ashkhabad, 253,000 .... F 6
Asino, 24,682 .... J 4
Astrakhan', 411,000 .... E 5
Atbasar, 34,316 .... H 4
Atka .... Q 3
Ayaguz, 31,061 .... J 5
Aykhal .... M 3
Bagdarin .... M 4
Bakanas .... H 5
Baku, 1,261,000 .... F 5
Baku, *1,261,000 .... F 5
Balashov, 64,349 .... E 4
Balkhash, 53,031 .... H 5
Balturino, 10,000 .... K 4
Barabinsk, 40,878 .... H 4
Baranovichi, 102,000 .... C 4
Barnaul, 439,000 .... J 4
Batumi, 101,000 .... E 5

Baunt .... M 4
Baykit .... K 3
Baykonur .... G 4
Bayram-Ali, 24,156 .... G 6
Belgorod, 151,000 .... D 4
Belogorsk, 48,831 .... N 4
Belomorsk .... D 3
Beloretsk, 59,315 .... F 4
Berdichev, 53,226 .... C 5
Berezniki, 145,000 .... F 4
Berezovo, 5,700 .... G 3
Beringovskiy .... T 3
Bilibino .... S 3
Birobidzhan, 56,000 .... O 5
Biysk, 186,000 .... J 4
Blagoveshchensk, 128,000 .... N 4
Bobruysk, 138,000 .... C 4
Bodaybo, 18,226 .... M 4
Borisoglebsk, 54,415 .... E 4
Borzya, 23,680 .... M 4
Boshchakul' .... H 4
Bratsk, 155,000 .... L 4
Brest, 122,000 .... C 4
Bryansk, 318,000 .... D 4
Bugul'ma, 60,980 .... F 4
Bukhara, 112,000 .... G 5
Bulun .... N 2
Buzuluk, 54,851 .... F 4
Chagda .... O 4
Chapayevsk, 83,263 .... E 4
Chara .... M 4
Chardzhou, 66,112 .... G 6
Cheboksary, 216,000 .... E 4
Chelkar, 17,236 .... F 5
Chelyabinsk, 874,000 .... G 4

Cheremkhovo .... L 4
Cherepovets, 189,000 .... D 4
Cherkessk, 67,000 .... E 5
Chernigov, 159,000 .... D 4
Chernovtsy, 187,000 .... C 5
Chernyshevsk .... M 4
Chernyshevskiy .... L 3
Chimbay, 15,954 .... F 5
Chimkent, 247,000 .... G 5
Chita, 242,000 .... M 4
Chokurdakh .... O 3
Chu'man .... N 4
Chumikan .... O 4
Daugavpils, 101,000 .... C 4
Dikson .... J 2
Dnepropetrovsk, 863,000 .... D 5
Dolinsk .... P 5
Donetsk, 879,000 .... D 5
Drogobych, 42,145 .... C 5
Druzhina .... O 3
Dudinka, 16,332 .... J 3
Dushanbe, 374,000 .... G 6
Dzerzhinsk, 221,000 .... E 4
Dzhalal-Abad, 31,234 .... H 5
Dzhalinda .... N 4
Dzhambul, 188,000 .... H 5
Dzhelinda .... M 2
Dzhezkazgan, 12,442 .... G 5
Dzhetygara, 14,672 .... G 4
Dzhezkazgan, 32,442 .... G 5
Ege-Khaya .... O 3
Ekibastuz, 25,705 .... H 4
Ekimchan .... O 4
El'dikan .... O 3
Elista, 50,000 .... E 5
Engel's, 130,000 .... E 4

Erivan, 767,000 .... E 6
Evensk .... R 3
Fergana, 111,000 .... H 5
Fort-Shevchenko, 11,393 .... F 5
Frolovo, 26,438 .... E 4
Frunze, 431,000 .... H 5
Gasan-Kuli .... F 6
Gizhiga .... R 3
Gol'chikha .... J 2
Gomel', 272,000 .... D 4
Gor'kiy, 1,170,000 .... E 4
Gorno-Altaysk, 34,000 .... J 4
Grodno, 132,000 .... C 4
Groznyy, 341,000 .... E 5
Gubakha .... F 4
Gulistan, 31,000 .... G 5
Gur'yev, 113,000 .... F 5
Gusinoozersk .... L 4
Gydy .... H 2
Igarka, 14,500 .... J 3
Ilanskiy, 26,911 .... K 4
Iliysk .... H 5
Iman, 25,411 .... O 5
Indiga .... E 3
Inta, 36,154 .... G 3
Iolotan', 9,640 .... G 6
Irkutsk, 451,000 .... L 4
Ishim, 47,793 .... G 4
Ishimbay, 46,568 .... F 4
Isil'-Kul', 23,120 .... H 4
Ivano-Frankovsk, 105,000 .... C 5
Ivanovo, 419,000 .... E 4
Izhevsk, 422,000 .... F 4
Izmail, 48,103 .... C 5

UNION OF SOVIET SOCIALIST REPUBLICS

CONIC PROJECTION

SCALE OF MILES
0 100 200 300 400 500 600

SCALE OF KILOMETRES
0 100 200 300 400 500 600

Capitals   **Boundaries**
⍟ National .... — · —
☆ Union Republic .... — · · —
◉ A.S.S.R. .... — — —
◎ Autonomous Oblast .... — — —
◦ National Okrug .... — — —

ADMINISTRATIVE DIVISIONS NOT NAMED ON MAP

Division	Ref.	Division	Ref.
1. Abkhaz A.S.S.R.	E5	13. Khakass Aut. Oblast	J4
2. Adygey Aut. Oblast	D5	14. Komi-Permyak Nat'l Okrug	F4
3. Adzhar A.S.S.R.	E5	15. Mari A.S.S.R.	E4
4. Aginsk Nat'l Okrug	M4	16. Mordvinian A.S.S.R.	E4
5. Chechen-Ingush A.S.S.R.	E5	17. Nagorno-Karabakh Aut. Oblast	E5
6. Chuvash A.S.S.R.	E4	18. Nakhichevan' A.S.S.R.	E5
7. Gorno-Altay Aut. Oblast	J4	19. North Ossetian A.S.S.R.	E5
8. Gorno-Badakhshan Aut. Oblast	H6	20. South Ossetian Aut. Oblast	E5
9. Jewish Aut. Oblast	O5	21. Tatar A.S.S.R.	E4
10. Kabardin-Balkar A.S.S.R.	E5	22. Tuvinian A.S.S.R.	K4
11. Karachay-Cherkess Aut. Oblast	D5	23. Udmurt A.S.S.R.	F4
12. Kara-Kalpak A.S.S.R.	G5	24. Ust'-Ordynskiy Nat'l Okrug	L4

AREA 8,649,498 sq. mi.
POPULATION 241,748,000
CAPITAL Moscow
LARGEST CITY Moscow
HIGHEST POINT Mt. Communism 24,590 ft.
MONETARY UNIT ruble
MAJOR LANGUAGES Russian, Ukrainian, White Russian, Uzbek, Azerbaidzhani, Tatar, Georgian, Lithuanian, Armenian, Yiddish, Latvian, Mordvinian, Kirghiz, Tadzhik, Estonian, Kazakh, Moldavian, German, Chuvash, Turkmenian, Bashkir
MAJOR RELIGIONS Eastern (Russian) Orthodoxy, Islam, Judaism, Protestantism (Baltic States)

UNION REPUBLICS

	AREA (sq. mi.)	POPULATION	CAPITAL and LARGEST CITY
RUSSIAN S.F.S.R.	6,592,819	130,090,000	Moscow 6,942,000
KAZAKH S.S.R.	1,048,301	12,850,000	Alma-Ata 730,000
UKRAINIAN S.S.R.	232,046	47,136,000	Kiev 1,632,000
TURKMEN S.S.R.	188,456	2,158,000	Ashkhabad 253,000
UZBEK S.S.R.	173,591	11,963,000	Tashkent 1,385,000
WHITE RUSSIAN S.S.R.	80,154	9,003,000	Minsk 907,000
KIRGHIZ S.S.R.	76,641	2,933,000	Frunze 431,000
TADZHIK S.S.R.	55,251	2,900,000	Dushanbe 374,000
AZERBAIDZHAN S.S.R.	33,436	5,111,000	Baku 847,000
GEORGIAN S.S.R.	26,911	4,688,000	Tbilisi 889,000
LITHUANIAN S.S.R.	25,174	3,129,000	Vilna 372,000
LATVIAN S.S.R.	24,595	2,365,000	Riga 733,000
ESTONIAN S.S.R.	17,413	1,357,000	Tallinn 363,000
MOLDAVIAN S.S.R.	13,012	3,572,000	Kishinev 357,000
ARMENIAN S.S.R.	11,500	2,493,000	Erivan 767,000

...achug .... L 4
...agan, 21,103 .... G 6
...alachinsk, 18,987 ...... H 4
...alakan .... M 4
...alevala .... D 3
...alinin, 345,000 .... D 4
...aliningrad, 297,000 .... B 4
...almykovo .... F 5
...aluga, 211,000 .... D 4
...amensk-Ural'skiy, 169,000 G 4
...amenskoye .... R 3
...amyshin, 56,511 .... E 4
...amyshlov, 30,137 ....
...andalaksha, 37,045 ..... C 3
...ansk, 73,814 .... K 4
...arabekaul ....
...aragandа, 522,000 ...... H 5
...arasuk, 19,961 .... H 4

Karkaralinsk, 6,874 .... H 5
Karshi, 71,000 .... G 6
Kaunas, 306,000 .... C 4
Kazach'ye .... O 2
Kazalinsk, 7,697 .... G 5
Kazan', 869,000 .... F 4
Kazandzhik, 7,807 .... F 6
Kem', 18,127 .... D 3
Kemerovo, 385,000 .... J 4
Kerki, 11,838 .... G 6
Kezhma .... K 4
Khabarovsk, 437,000 ...... O 5
Khandyga .... N 3
Khanty-Mansiysk, 20,677 .. H 3
Khar'kov, 1,223,000 ...... D 4
Kharovsk .... D 3
Khatanga .... L 2
Kherson, 261,000 .... D 5

Khilok, 15,855 .... M 4
Khiva, 17,460 .... G 5
Khodzheyli, 20,525 .... F 5
Kholmsk, 31,541 .... P 5
Khorog, 12,000 .... H 6
Kiev, 1,632,000 .... D 4
Kirensk .... L 4
Kirov, 332,000 .... E 4
Kirovabad, 190,000 .... G 5
Kirovograd, 189,000 ...... D 5
Kiselevsk, 126,000 .... J 4
Kishinev, 357,000 .... D 5
Kizel', 60,687 .... F 4
Kizyl-Arvat, 16,199 ...... F 6
Klaipeda, 140,000 .... C 4
Kokchetav, 81,000 .... H 4
Kolomna, 136,000 .... D 4
Kolpashevo, 22,595 .... J 4
Komsomol'sk, 218,000 ..... O 4
Kondopoga, 16,060 .... D 3
Kopeysk, 156,000 .... G 4
Korf .... R 3
Korkino, 84,962 .... G 4
Korsakov, 32,914 .... P 5
Koslan .... E 3
Kostroma, 223,000 .... E 4
Kotlas, 39,162 .... E 3
Kovel', 24,666 .... C 4
Kovrov, 123,000 .... E 4

Kozhevnikovo .... L 2
Krasino .... F 2
Krasnodar, 465,000 .... E 5
Krasnokamsk, 54,715 ...... F 4
Krasnotur'insk, 61,990 ... G 3
Krasnoural'sk, 39,245 .... G 4
Krasnovishersk, 15,207 ... F 3
Krasnovodsk, 39,272 ...... F 5
Krasnoyarsk, 648,000 ..... K 4
Kremenchug, 148,000 ...... D 5
Krivoy Rog, 573,000 ...... D 5
Kudymkar, 21,801 .... F 4
Kul'sary .... F 5
Kungur, 64,796 .... F 4
Kupino, 23,185 .... H 4
Kurgan, 244,000 .... G 4
Kurgan-Tyube, 23,560 ..... G 6
Kuril'sk .... P 5
Kursk, 284,000 .... D 4
Kushka .... G 6
Kustanay, 123,000 .... G 4
Kutaisi, 161,000 .... E 5
Kuybyshev, 1,047,000 ..... F 4
Kyakhta, 10,000 .... L 4
Kyusyur .... N 2
Kyzyl, 52,000 .... K 4
Kyzyl-Orda, 123,000 ...... G 5
Labytnangi .... G 3
Leninabad, 103,000 .... G 5

Leninakan, 164,000 .... E 5
Leningrad, 3,513,000 ..... D 4
Leningrad, *3,950,000 .... D 4
Leninogorsk, 66,812 ...... J 5
Leninsk-Kuznetskiy, 128,000 J 4
Leninskoye .... O 5
Lenkoran', 25,209 .... E 6
Lensk .... M 3
Lesozavodsk, 32,124 ...... O 5
Liepāja, 71,464 .... B 4
Lipetsk, 290,000 .... E 4
Luga, 25,540 .... D 4
Lutsk, 94,000 .... C 4
Luza .... E 3
L'vov, 553,000 .... C 4
Lys'va, 72,989 .... F 4
Magadan, 92,000 .... N 4
Magdagachi .... N 4
Magnitogorsk, 364,000 .... G 4
Makhachkala, 186,000 ..... E 5
Makinsk .... G 4
Maklakovo .... K 4
Makov .... M 4
Markovo .... S 3
Mary, 48,125 .... G 6
Maykop, 111,000 .... D 5
Mednogorsk, 36,303 .... F 4
Medvezhiy Yar .... K 2

Medvezh'yegorsk, 15,824 .. D 3
Megion .... H 3
Melekess, 50,696 .... F 4
Menza .... L 5
Mezen' .... E 3
Michurinsk, 80,653 .... E 4
Millerovo, 30,005 .... E 5
Minsk, 907,000 .... C 4
Minsk, *916,000 .... C 4
Minusinsk, 38,318 .... K 4
Mirnyy, 15,000 .... M 3
Mogilev, 202,000 .... D 4
Mogocha .... N 4
Molodechno, 26,275 .... C 4
Monchegorsk, 45,523 ...... C 3
Mongolia .... M 2
Moscow (cap.), 6,942,000 . D 4
Moscow, *7,061,000 .... D 4
Motygino .... K 4
Mozyr', 25,710 .... D 4
Murgab .... H 6
Murmansk, 309,000 .... D 3
Muya .... M 4
Muynak, 10,428 .... F 5
Nagornyy .... N 4
Nakama .... L 3
Nakhichevan', 33,000 ..... E 6
Nakhodka, 105,000 .... O 5
Nal'chik, 146,000 .... E 5
Namangan, 175,000 .... G 5

Naminga, 3,000 .... M 4
Napas .... J 4
Nar'yan-Mar, 13,200 ...... F 3
Naryn, 14,857 .... H 5
Nebit-Dag, 32,903 .... F 6
Nepa .... L 4
Nel'kan .... O 4
Nepa .... L 4
Nerchinsk, 11,600 .... N 4
Nikolayev, 331,000 .... D 5
Nikolayevsk, 30,923 ...... P 4
Nikol'skoye .... R 4
Nimnyrskiy .... N 4
Nizhne-Angarsk .... M 4
Nizhneudinsk, 38,761 ..... K 4
Nizhniy Tagil, 378,000 ... G 4
Nordvik .... M 2
Noril'sk, 136,000 .... J 3
Novaya Kazanka .... F 4
Novgorod, 128,000 .... D 4
Novokuznetsk, 499,000 .... J 4
Novomoskovsk, 134,000 .... E 4
Novorossiysk, 133,000 .... D 5
Novosibirsk, 1,161,000 ... J 4
Novouzensk .... E 4
Novozybkov, 25,852 .... D 4
Novyy Port .... G 3
Nukus, 74,000 .... F 5
Nyandoma, 21,668 .... E 3
Nyda .... H 3

Topography

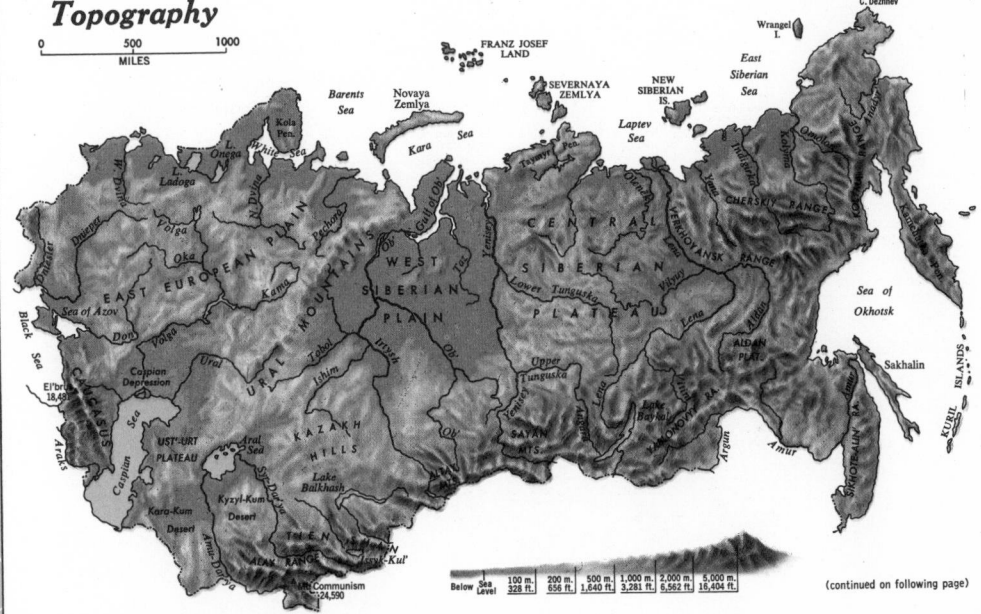

0 ——— 500 ——— 1000
MILES

| Below Sea Level | 100 m. 328 ft. | 200 m. 656 ft. | 500 m. 1,640 ft. | 1,000 m. 3,281 ft. | 2,000 m. 6,562 ft. | 5,000 m. 16,404 ft. |

(continued on following page)

Agriculture, Industry and Resources

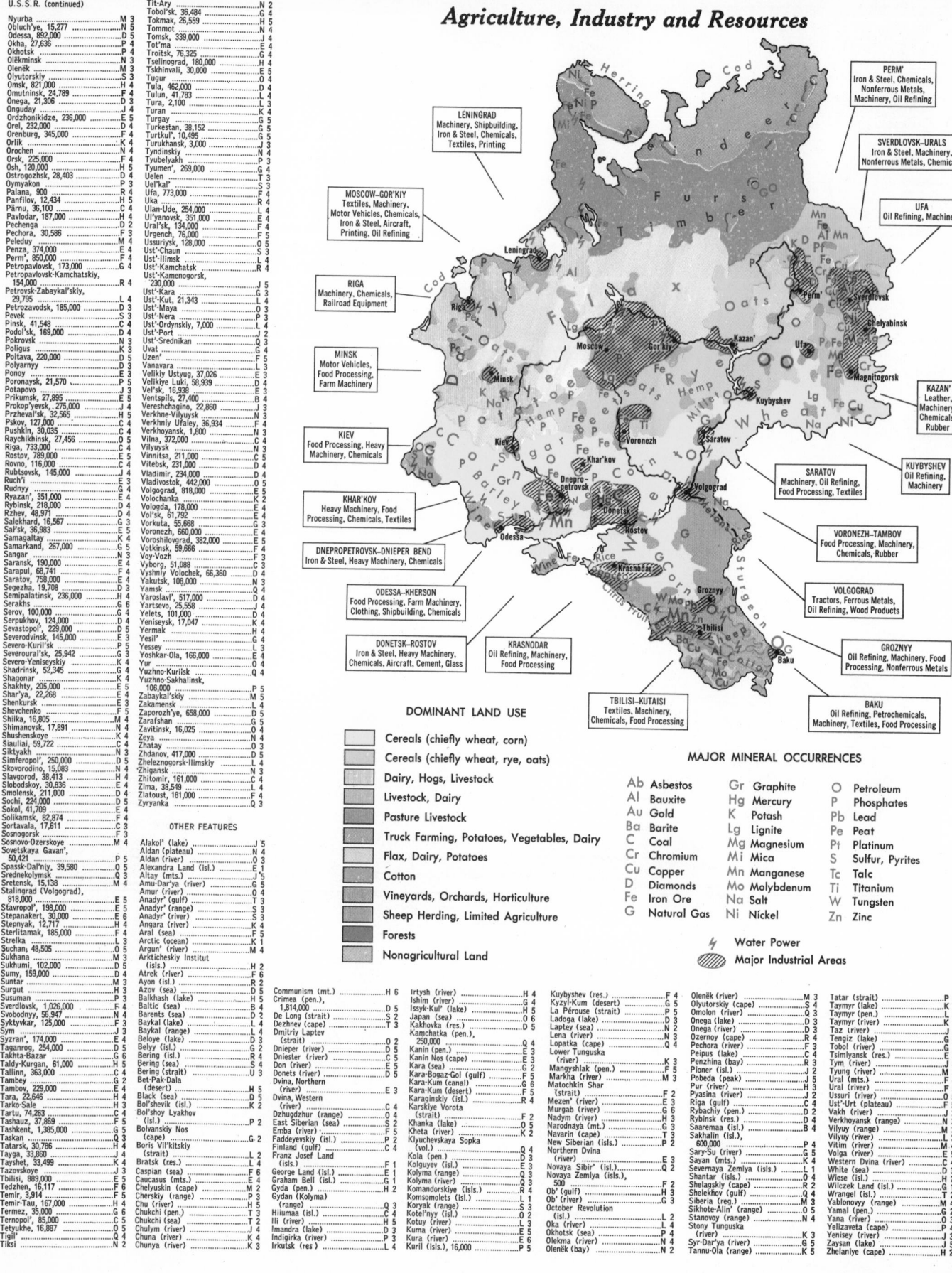

PERM'
Iron & Steel, Chemicals,
Nonferrous Metals,
Machinery, Oil Refining

SVERDLOVSK–URALS
Iron & Steel, Machinery,
Nonferrous Metals, Chemicals

UFA
Oil Refining, Machinery

LENINGRAD
Machinery, Shipbuilding,
Iron & Steel, Chemicals,
Textiles, Printing

MOSCOW–GOR'KIY
Textiles, Machinery,
Motor Vehicles, Chemicals,
Iron & Steel, Aircraft,
Printing, Oil Refining

RIGA
Machinery, Chemicals,
Railroad Equipment

MINSK
Motor Vehicles,
Food Processing,
Farm Machinery

KAZAN'
Leather,
Machinery,
Chemicals,
Rubber

KIEV
Food Processing, Heavy
Machinery, Chemicals

KHAR'KOV
Heavy Machinery, Food
Processing, Chemicals, Textiles

SARATOV
Machinery, Oil Refining,
Food Processing, Textiles

KUYBYSHEV
Oil Refining,
Machinery

VORONEZH–TAMBOV
Food Processing, Machinery,
Chemicals, Rubber

VOLGOGRAD
Tractors, Ferrous Metals,
Oil Refining, Wood Products

GROZNYY
Oil Refining, Machinery, Food
Processing, Nonferrous Metals

DNEPROPETROVSK–DNIEPER BEND
Iron & Steel, Heavy Machinery, Chemicals

ODESSA–KHERSON
Food Processing, Farm Machinery,
Clothing, Shipbuilding, Chemicals

DONETSK–ROSTOV
Iron & Steel, Heavy Machinery,
Chemicals, Aircraft, Cement, Glass

KRASNODAR
Oil Refining, Machinery,
Food Processing

TBILISI–KUTAISI
Textiles, Machinery,
Chemicals, Food Processing

BAKU
Oil Refining, Petrochemicals,
Machinery, Textiles, Food Processing

DOMINANT LAND USE

- Cereals (chiefly wheat, corn)
- Cereals (chiefly wheat, rye, oats)
- Dairy, Hogs, Livestock
- Livestock, Dairy
- Pasture Livestock
- Truck Farming, Potatoes, Vegetables, Dairy
- Flax, Dairy, Potatoes
- Cotton
- Vineyards, Orchards, Horticulture
- Sheep Herding, Limited Agriculture
- Forests
- Nonagricultural Land

MAJOR MINERAL OCCURRENCES

Ab	Asbestos	Gr	Graphite	O	Petroleum
Al	Bauxite	Hg	Mercury	P	Phosphates
Au	Gold	K	Potash	Pb	Lead
Ba	Barite	Lg	Lignite	Pe	Peat
C	Coal	Mg	Magnesium	Pt	Platinum
Cr	Chromium	Mi	Mica	S	Sulfur, Pyrites
Cu	Copper	Mn	Manganese	Tc	Talc
D	Diamonds	Mo	Molybdenum	Ti	Titanium
Fe	Iron Ore	Na	Salt	W	Tungsten
G	Natural Gas	Ni	Nickel	Zn	Zinc

⚡ Water Power

Major Industrial Areas

Agriculture, Industry and Resources

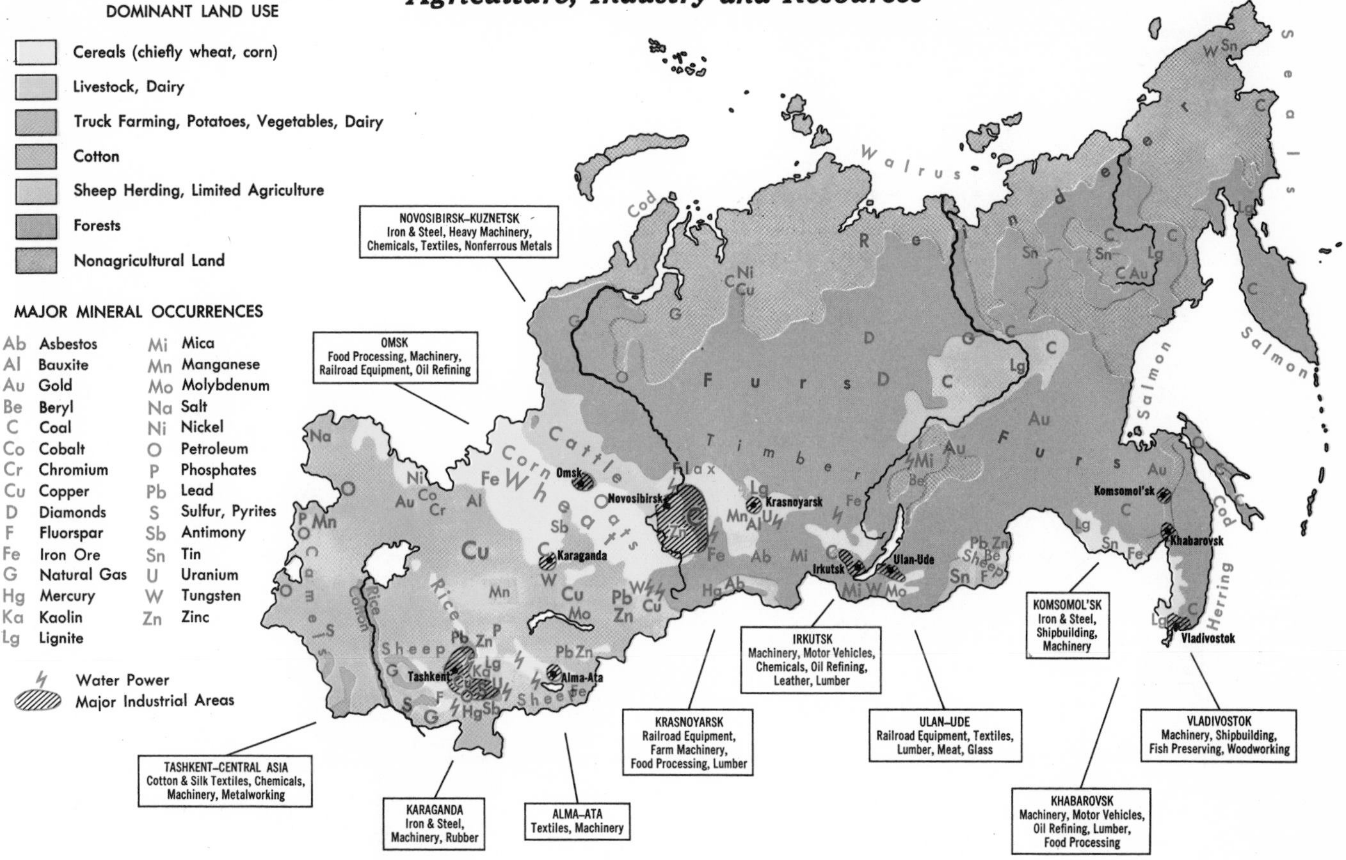
DOMINANT LAND USE
Cereals (chiefly wheat, corn)
Livestock, Dairy
Truck Farming, Potatoes, Vegetables, Dairy
Cotton
Sheep Herding, Limited Agriculture
Forests
Nonagricultural Land
MAJOR MINERAL OCCURRENCES
Ab Asbestos
Al Bauxite
Au Gold
Be Beryl
C Coal
Co Cobalt
Cr Chromium
Cu Copper
D Diamonds
F Fluorspar
Fe Iron Ore
G Natural Gas
Hg Mercury
Ka Kaolin
Lg Lignite
Mi Mica
Mn Manganese
Mo Molybdenum
Na Salt
Ni Nickel
O Petroleum
P Phosphates
Pb Lead
S Sulfur, Pyrites
Sb Antimony
Sn Tin
U Uranium
W Tungsten
Zn Zinc
Water Power
Major Industrial Areas
NOVOSIBIRSK–KUZNETSK
Iron & Steel, Heavy Machinery, Chemicals, Textiles, Nonferrous Metals
OMSK
Food Processing, Machinery, Railroad Equipment, Oil Refining
TASHKENT–CENTRAL ASIA
Cotton & Silk Textiles, Chemicals, Machinery, Metalworking
KARAGANDA
Iron & Steel, Machinery, Rubber
ALMA–ATA
Textiles, Machinery
KRASNOYARSK
Railroad Equipment, Farm Machinery, Food Processing, Lumber
IRKUTSK
Machinery, Motor Vehicles, Chemicals, Oil Refining, Leather, Lumber
ULAN–UDE
Railroad Equipment, Textiles, Lumber, Meat, Glass
KOMSOMOL'SK
Iron & Steel, Shipbuilding, Machinery
KHABAROVSK
Machinery, Motor Vehicles, Oil Refining, Lumber, Food Processing
VLADIVOSTOK
Machinery, Shipbuilding, Fish Preserving, Woodworking
Walrus
Seals
Reindeer
Furs
Timber
Cattle
Corn
Wheat
Oats
Flax
Rice
Cotton
Camels
Sheep
Cod
Salmon
Herring
Omsk
Novosibirsk
Karaganda
Tashkent
Alma-Ata
Krasnoyarsk
Irkutsk
Ulan-Ude
Komsomol'sk
Khabarovsk
Vladivostok

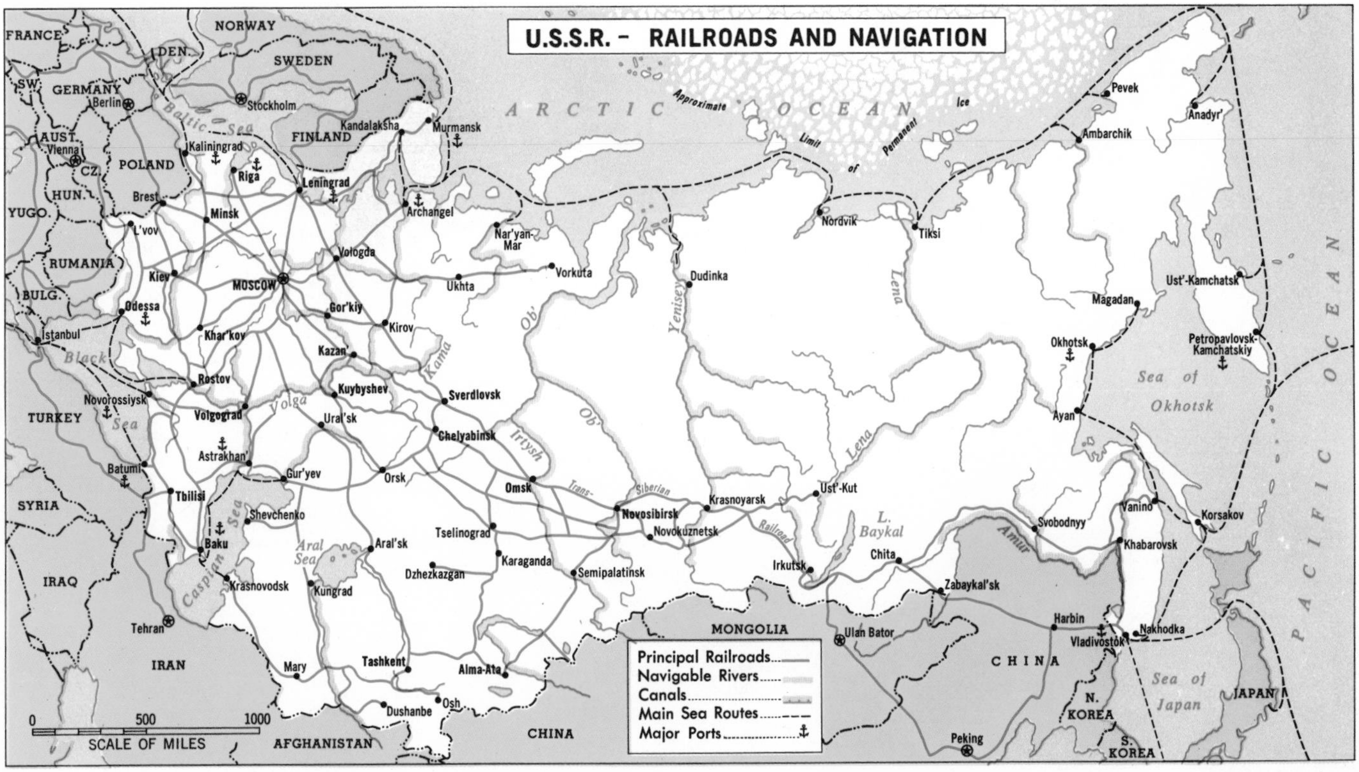
U.S.S.R. - RAILROADS AND NAVIGATION
ARCTIC OCEAN
Approximate Limit of Permanent Ice
PACIFIC OCEAN
Sea of Okhotsk
Sea of Japan
Black Sea
Caspian Sea
Aral Sea
Baltic Sea
L. Baykal
NORWAY
SWEDEN
FINLAND
FRANCE
DEN.
SW.
GERMANY
AUST.
CZ.
POLAND
HUN.
YUGO.
RUMANIA
BULG.
TURKEY
SYRIA
IRAQ
IRAN
AFGHANISTAN
CHINA
MONGOLIA
N. KOREA
S. KOREA
JAPAN
Stockholm
Berlin
Vienna
Kaliningrad
Riga
Leningrad
Kandalaksha
Murmansk
Archangel
Brest
Minsk
L'vov
Kiev
Odessa
Istanbul
MOSCOW
Vologda
Gor'kiy
Kirov
Khar'kov
Kazan'
Rostov
Novorossiysk
Volgograd
Kuybyshev
Astrakhan'
Batumi
Tbilisi
Baku
Shevchenko
Krasnovodsk
Tehran
Gur'yev
Ural'sk
Orsk
Sverdlovsk
Chelyabinsk
Kungrad
Aral'sk
Mary
Tashkent
Dushanbe
Osh
Alma-Ata
Dzhezkazgan
Tselinograd
Karaganda
Semipalatinsk
Omsk
Novosibirsk
Novokuznetsk
Krasnoyarsk
Irkutsk
Ust'-Kut
Chita
Zabaykal'sk
Ulan Bator
Peking
Harbin
Vladivostok
Nakhodka
Khabarovsk
Vanino
Korsakov
Svobodnyy
Ayan
Okhotsk
Magadan
Petropavlovsk-Kamchatskiy
Ust'-Kamchatsk
Anadyr'
Pevek
Ambarchik
Tiksi
Nordvik
Dudinka
Vorkuta
Ukhta
Nar'yan-Mar
Volga
Kama
Ob'
Irtysh
Yenisey
Lena
Amur
Trans-Siberian Railroad
Principal Railroads
Navigable Rivers
Canals
Main Sea Routes
Major Ports
0 500 1000
SCALE OF MILES

(continued on following page)

UNION OF SOVIET SOCIALIST REPUBLICS
European Part

CONIC PROJECTION

SCALE OF MILES

0   50   100   200   300

SCALE OF KILOMETRES

0 50 100   200   300

National Capitals	☆
Capitals of Union Republics	⬡
Administrative Centers	△
International boundaries	▬▬▬
Union Republic boundaries	▬·▬·▬
A.S.S.R., Oblast, Kray boundaries	▬▬▬
Autonomous Oblast boundaries	·········
National Okrug boundaries	·········
Canals	

The government of the United States has not recognized the incorporation of Estonia, Latvia and Lithuania into the Soviet Union, nor does it recognize as final the de facto western limit of Polish administration in Germany (the Oder-Neisse line).

Copyright by C. S. HAMMOND & CO., N.Y.

Administrative Divisions bear same names as their respective Capitals or Centers, except:

Abkhaz A.S.S.R.	Sukhumi	F6
Adygey Aut. Oblast	Maykop	F6
Adzhar A.S.S.R.	Batumi	F6
Bashkir A.S.S.R.	Ufa	J4
Chechen-Ingush A.S.S.R.	Groznyy	G6
Chuvash A.S.S.R.	Cheboksary	G3
Crimean Oblast	Simferopol'	D6
Dagestan A.S.S.R.	Makhachkala	G6
Kabardin-Balkar A.S.S.R.	Nal'chik	F6
Kalmuck A.S.S.R.	Elista	F5
Karachay-Cherkess Aut. Obl.	Cherkessk	F6
Karelian A.S.S.R.	Petrozavodsk	D2
Komi A.S.S.R.	Syktyvkar	H2
Komi-Permyak Nat'l Okrug	Kudymkar	H3
Mari A.S.S.R.	Yoshkar-Ola	G3
Mordvinian A.S.S.R.	Saransk	G4
Nagorno-Karabakh Aut. Obl.	Stepanakert	G7
Nenets Nat'l Okrug	Nar'yan-Mar	H1
North Ossetian A.S.S.R.	Ordzhonikidze	F6
South Ossetian Aut. Obl.	Tskhinvali	F6
Tatar A.S.S.R.	Kazan'	G3
Trans-Carpathian Oblast	Uzhgorod	B5
Udmurt A.S.S.R.	Izhevsk	H3
Volyn Oblast	Lutsk	C4

(continued)

U.S.S.R. - EUROPEAN

UNION REPUBLICS

Place	Key
Armenian S.S.R., 2,493,000	F 6
Azerbaidzhan S.S.R., 5,111,000	G 6
Estonian S.S.R., 1,357,000	C 3
Georgian S.S.R., 4,688,000	F 6
Latvian S.S.R., 2,365,000	B 3
Lithuanian S.S.R., 3,129,000	B 3
Moldavian S.S.R., 3,572,000	C 5
Russian S.F.S.R., 130,090,000	F 3
Ukrainian S.S.R., 47,136,000	D 5
White Russian S.S.R., 9,003,000	C 4

INTERNAL DIVISIONS

Place	Key
Abkhaz A.S.S.R., 487,000	F 6
Adygey Aut. Oblast, 386,000	F 6
Adzhar A.S.S.R., 310,000	F 6
Bashkir A.S.S.R., 3,819,000	J 4
Chechen-Ingush A.S.S.R., 1,065,000	G 6
Chuvash A.S.S.R., 1,224,000	G 3
Crimean Oblast, 1,814,000	D 6
Dagestan A.S.S.R., 1,429,000	G 6
Kabardin-Balkar A.S.S.R., 589,000	F 6
Kalmuck A.S.S.R., 268,000	F 5
Karachay-Cherkess Aut. Oblast, 345,000	F 6
Karelian A.S.S.R., 714,000	D 2
Komi A.S.S.R., 965,000	H 2
Komi-Permyak Nat'l Okrug, 212,000	H 3
Mari A.S.S.R., 685,000	G 3
Mordvinian A.S.S.R., 1,030,000	G 4
Nagorno-Karabakh Aut. Oblast, 149,000	G 7
Nakhichevan' A.S.S.R., 202,000	F 7
Nenets Nat'l Okrug, 39,000	H 1
North Ossetian A.S.S.R., 553,000	F 6
South Ossetian Aut. Oblast, 100,000	F 6
Tatar A.S.S.R., 3,131,000	G 3
Trans-Carpathian Oblast, 1,057,000	B 5
Udmurt A.S.S.R., 1,417,000	H 3
Volyn Oblast, 975,000	C 4

CITIES and TOWNS

Place	Key
Abdulino, 29,976	H 4
Agdam, 16,061	G 6
Agryz, 20,270	H 3
Akhaltsikhe, 16,868	F 6
Akhtubinsk, 15,221	G 5
Akhtyrka, 31,563	E 4
Akkerman (Belgorod-Dnestrovskiy), 21,832	D 5
Alagir, 15,163	F 6
Alatyr', 36,933	G 4
Aleksandriya, 35,190	D 5
Aleksandrov, 36,738	E 3
Alekseyevka, 20,148	E 4
Aleksin, 46,313	E 4
Ali-Bayramly, 13,427	G 7
Al'met'yevsk, 48,611	H 3
Alushta, 12,337	D 6
Anapa, 18,512	E 6
Apatity, 19,938	D 1
Apsheronsk, 29,837	F 6
Archangel (Arkhangel'sk), 343,000	F 2
Armavir, 146,000	F 5
Artemovsk, 60,626	E 5
Arzamas, 41,518	F 3
Astara, 5,381	G 7
Astrakhan', 411,000	G 5
Atkarsk, 27,771	G 4
Azov, 39,931	E 5
Bakhchisaray, 10,852	D 6
Bakhmach, 13,066	D 4
Baku, 847,000	H 6
Baku, *1,261,000	H 6
Balakhna, 29,846	F 3
Balaklava	D 6
Balakovo, 103,000	G 4
Balashov, 64,349	F 4
Baltiysk, 17,378	A 4
Baranovichi, 102,000	C 4
Barysh, 17,909	G 4
Bataysk, 52,242	E 5
Batumi, 101,000	F 6
Belaya Tserkov', 109,000	C 5
Belebey, 26,172	H 4
Belev, 17,153	E 4
Belgorod, 151,000	E 4
Belgorod-Dnestrovskiy, 21,832	D 5
Beloretsk, 59,315	J 4
Bel'tsy, 102,000	C 5
Bendery, 43,109	C 5
Berdichev, 53,206	C 5
Berdyansk, 100,000	E 5
Beregovo, 25,730	B 5
Berezniki, 145,000	J 3
Berislav, 10,507	D 5
Beslan, 19,385	F 6
Bezhetsk, 26,921	E 3
Birsk, 24,837	J 3
Bobrinets, 11,453	D 5
Bobruysk, 138,000	C 4
Bologoye, 30,301	D 3
Borisoglebsk, 54,415	F 4
Borislav, 28,603	B 5
Borisov, 59,280	C 4
Borovichi, 44,123	D 3
Borzhomi, 15,332	F 6
Brest, 122,000	B 4
Bryansk, 318,000	D 4
Bugul'ma, 60,980	H 4
Buguruslan, 42,476	H 4
Buy, 27,221	F 3
Buynaksk, 32,956	G 6
Buzuluk, 54,851	H 4
Bykhov, 13,227	C 4
Cēsis, 13,800	C 3
Chadyr-Lunga, 13,193	B 5
Chapayevsk, 83,263	G 4
Chaykovskiy	H 3
Cheboksary, 216,000	G 3
Cherepovets, 189,000	E 3
Cherkassy, 159,000	D 5
Cherkessk, 67,000	F 6
Chernigov, 159,000	D 4
Chernovtsy, 187,000	C 5
Chervonograd, 12,241	B 4
Chiatura, 21,521	F 6
Chistopol', 51,864	H 3
Chkalov (Orenburg), 345,000	J 4
Chortkov, 15,294	B 5
Chusovoy, 60,658	J 3
Danilov, 16,902	E 3
Daugavpils, 101,000	C 3
Davlekanovo, 17,072	H 4
Derbent, 47,318	G 6
Dmitrov, 34,415	E 3
Dneprodzerzhinsk, 227,000	D 5
Dnepropetrovsk, 863,000	D 5
Dobrush, 14,270	D 4
Donetsk, 879,000	E 5
Drogobych, 42,145	B 5
Dubna, 32,626	E 3
Dubna	E 4
Dvinsk (Daugavpils), 101,000	C 3
Dzerzhinsk, 221,000	F 3
Dzhankoy, 28,457	D 5
Dzhul'fa, 4,017	G 7
Elista, 50,000	F 5
Engel's, 130,000	G 4
Erivan, 767,000	F 6
Fastov, 30,240	C 4
Feodosiya, 46,327	D 5
Frolovo, 26,438	F 5
Furmanov, 38,225	F 3
Gadyach, 11,725	D 4
Gagra, 14,023	E 6
Galich, 16,119	F 3
Gandzha (Kirovabad), 190,000	G 6
Gaysin, 17,680	C 5
Genichesk, 14,420	E 5
Georgiu-Dezh, 37,638	E 4
Glazov, 59,012	H 3
Glukhov, 22,962	D 4
Gomel', 272,000	D 4
Gori, 35,061	F 6
Gorki, 15,099	D 4
Gor'kiy, 1,170,000	F 3
Gorlovka, 335,000	E 5
Gornyatskiy, 28,457	K 1
Gorodets, 27,019	F 3
Gremyachinsk, 38,014	J 3
Grodno, 132.000	B 4
Groznyy, 341,000	G 6
Gryazi, 34,425	F 4
Gubakha, 47,094	J 3
Gubkin, 21,333	E 4
Gudauta, 13,019	F 6
Gukovo, 52,969	F 5
Gus-Khrustal'nyy, 54,158	F 3
Ichnya, 13,131	D 4
Inta, 36,154	K 1
Inza, 18,612	G 4
Ishimbay, 46,568	J 4
Ivano-Frankovsk, 105,000	B 5
Ivanovo, 419,000	E 3
Izhevsk, 422,000	H 3
Izmail, 48,103	C 5
Izyaslav, 11,587	C 4
Izyum, 37,595	E 5
Jelgava, 36,300	B 3
Kadiyevka, 137,000	E 5
Kagul, 16,223	C 5
Kakhovka, 19,107	D 5
Kalach, 16,906	F 5
Kalinin, 345,000	E 3
Kaliningrad, 297,000	B 4
Kalinkovichi, 14,942	F 4
Kaluga, 211,000	E 4
Kamenets-Podol'skiy, 40,299	C 5
Kamenka, 27,634	F 4
Kamensk-Shakhtinskiy, 57,525	E 5
Kamyshin, 56,511	F 4
Kanash, 32,897	G 3
Kandalaksha, 37,045	D 1
Kapsukas, 19,600	B 4
Kashin, 16,162	E 3
Kasimov, 27,855	F 4
Kaspiysk, 25,178	G 6
Kaunas, 306,000	B 4
Kazan', 869,000	G 3
Kazatin, 22,784	C 5
Kem', 18,127	D 2
Kerch', 128,000	E 5
Khachmas, 17,123	G 6
Khar'kov, 1,223,000	E 5
Khasavyurt, 34,194	G 6
Kherson, 261,000	D 5
Khmel'nitskiy, 113,000	C 5
Khorol, 12,357	D 5
Khotin, 10,319	C 5
Khvalynsk, 17,036	G 4
Kiev, 1,632,000	D 4
Kiliya, 20,304	C 5
Kimovsk, 39,490	E 4
Kimry, 41,243	E 3
Kinel', 32,447	H 4
Kineshma, 85,418	F 3
Kirov, 16,647	D 4
Kirov, 332,000	G 3
Kirovabad, 190,000	G 6
Kirovakan, 107,000	G 6
Kirovo-Chepetsk, 28,726	H 3
Kirovograd, 189,000	D 5
Kirovsk, 39,047	D 1
Kirsanov, 15,654	F 4
Kishinev, 357,000	C 5
Kislovodsk, 79,097	F 6
Kizel', 60,687	J 3
Kizlyar, 25,573	G 6
Klaipėda, 140,000	B 3
Klimovichi, 11,586	D 4
Klintsy, 42,033	D 4
Kobrin, 13,686	B 4
Kobuleti, 12,598	F 6
Kohtla-Järve, 29,200	C 3
Kolomna, 136,000	E 4
Kommunarsk, 123,000	E 5
Komrat, 14,361	C 5
Kondopoga, 16,060	D 2
Königsberg (Kaliningrad), 297,000	B 4
Konotop, 54,097	D 4
Korosten', 38,041	C 4
Kostroma, 223,000	F 3
Kotel'nich, 27,640	G 3
Kotel'nikovo, 17,605	F 5
Kotlas, 39,162	G 2
Kotovsk, 25,511	F 4
Kotovsk, 27,383	C 5
Kovel', 24,666	C 4
Kovrov, 123,000	F 3
Kramatorsk, 151,000	E 5
Krasnodar, 465,000	E 6
Krasnograd, 14,941	E 5
Krasnokamsk, 54,715	H 3
Krasnoslobodsk, 18,993	F 4
Krasnovishersk, 15,207	J 2
Krasnyy Liman, 28,911	E 5
Kremenchug, 148,000	D 5
Krichev, 19,028	D 4
Krivoy Rog, 573,000	D 5
Krolevets, 13,996	D 4
Kronshtadt	C 3
Kropotkin, 53,997	F 5
Krymsk, 32,803	E 6
Kuba, 15,947	G 6
Kudymkar, 21,801	H 3
Kulebaki, 44,720	F 3
Kumertau, 30,937	J 4
Kungur, 64,796	J 3
Kupyansk, 25,644	E 5
Kursk, 284,000	E 4
Kutaisi, 161,000	F 6
Kuvandyk, 21,383	J 4
Kuybyshev, 1,047,000	H 4
Kuznetsk, 56,880	G 4
Labinsk, 41,944	F 6
Lebedin, 24,741	D 4
Leninakan, 164,000	F 6
Leningrad, 3,513,000	C 3
Leningrad, *3,950,000	C 3
Leninogorsk, 38,565	H 4
Lenkoran', 25,209	G 7
L'gov, 21,328	E 4
Lida, 28,541	C 4
Liepāja, 71,464	B 3
Lipetsk, 290,000	E 4
Lisichansk, 117,000	E 5
Livny, 23,900	E 4
Lodeynoye Pole, 17,485	D 2
Lozovaya, 27,144	E 5
Lubny, 29,442	D 4
Luga, 25,540	C 3
Luninets, 10,328	C 4
Lutsk, 94,000	B 4
L'vov (Lwów), 553,000	B 5
Lyubotin, 31,540	E 4
Lyskovo, 16,167	F 3
Lys'va, 72,989	J 3
Lyudinovo, 26,433	D 4
Makeyevka, 393,000	E 5
Makhachkala, 186,000	G 6
Makharadze, 19,131	F 6
Malaya Vishera, 16,109	D 3
Manturovo, 16,345	F 3
Marganets, 34,422	E 5
Mariupol' (Zhdanov), 417,000	E 5
Maykop, 111,000	F 6
Mednogorsk, 36,303	J 4
Medvezh'yegorsk, 15,824	D 2
Melekess, 50,696	G 4
Melenki, 17,462	F 3
Meieuz, 17,772	J 4
Melitopol', 137,000	D 5
Memel (Klaipėda), 140,000	B 3
Merefa, 26,307	E 5
Michurinsk, 80,653	F 4
Mikhaylovka, 34,645	F 4
Millerovo, 30,005	F 5
Mineralnye Vody, 40,131	F 6
Mingechaur, 19,904	G 6
Minsk, 907,000	C 4
Minsk, *916,000	C 4
Mirgorod, 25,069	D 5
Mogilev, 202,000	C 4
Mogilev-Podol'skiy, 21,208	C 5
Molodechno, 26,275	C 4
Molotov (Perm'), 850,000	J 3
Molotovsk (Severodvinsk), 145,000	E 2
Monchegorsk, 45,523	D 1
Morozovsk, 26,952	F 5
Morshansk, 40,924	F 4
Moscow (Moskva) (cap.), 6,942,000	E 3
Moscow, *7,061,000	E 3
Mozhaysk, 15,697	E 3
Mozhga, 29,987	H 3
Mozyr', 25,710	C 4
Mukachevo, 46,423	B 5
Murmansk, 309,000	D 1
Murom, 71,567	F 3
Naberezhnye Chelny, 16,214	H 3
Nakhichevan', 33,000	F 7
Nal'chik, 146,000	F 6
Naro-Fominsk, 35,419	E 3
Narva, 27,600	C 3
Nar'yan-Mar, 13,200	H 1
Nelidovo, 26,465	D 3
Nerekhta, 22,310	F 3
Nevinnomyssk, 39,806	F 6
Nezhin, 46,211	D 4
Nikel', 16,305	C 1
Nikolayev, 331,000	D 5
Nikol'sk, 16,818	G 3
Nikopol', 125,000	D 5
Noginsk, 104,000	E 3
Novaya Kakhovka, 19,885	D 5
Novgorod, 128,000	D 3
Novgorod-Severskiy, 11,249	D 4
Novoanninskiy, 18,664	F 4
Novocherkassk, 162,000	F 5
Novograd-Volynskiy, 27,580	C 4
Novogrudok, 12,624	C 4
Novokuybyshevsk, 104,000	G 4
Novomoskovsk, 134,000	E 4
Novopolotsk, 20,000	C 3
Novorossiysk, 133,000	E 6
Novoshakhtinsk, 102,000	E 5
Novotroitsk, 54,484	J 4
Novoukrainka, 16,098	D 5
Novovolynsk, 23,895	B 4
Novyy Bug, 15,354	D 5
Nyandoma, 21,668	F 2
Obruch, 11,536	C 4
Ochamchire, 16,500	F 6
Odessa, 892,000	D 5
Oktyabr'sk, 33,771	G 4
Oktyabr'skiy, 64,717	H 4
Omutninsk, 24,789	H 3
Onega, 21,306	E 2
Oni, 4,385	F 6
Ordzhonikidze, 236,000	F 6
Orekhovo-Zuyevo, 120,000	E 3
Orel, 232,000	E 4
Orenburg, 345,000	J 4
Orgeyev, 14,391	C 5
Orsha, 101,000	C 4
Orsk, 225,000	J 4
Osipenko (Berdyansk), 100,000	E 5
Osipovichi, 15,777	C 4
Ostashkov, 19,542	D 3
Ostrogozhsk, 28,403	E 4
Ostrov, 17,646	C 3
Otradnyy, 27,889	H 4
Panevėžys, 41,100	B 3
Pärnu, 36,100	C 3
Pavlovo, 47,890	F 3
Pechora, 30,586	J 1
Penza, 374,000	F 4
Perm', 850,000	J 3
Pervomaysk, 44,330	D 5
Pervomayskiy, 16,341	F 2
Petrovsk, 24,987	G 4
Petrozavodsk, 185,000	D 2
Pinsk, 41,548	C 4
Piryatin, 15,203	D 4
Pochep, 15,700	D 4
Podol'sk, 169,000	E 3
Polonnoye, 19,775	C 4
Polotsk, 41,308	C 3
Poltava, 220,000	D 5
Polyarnyy	D 1
Postavy, 10,566	C 3
Poti, 42,068	F 6
Povorino, 19,274	F 4
Prikumsk, 27,895	F 6
Priluki, 43,719	D 4
Primorsko-Akhtarsk, 22,006	E 5
Priyutovo, 18,941	H 4
Promyshlennyy, 20,405	K 1
Pskov, 127,000	C 3
Pugachev, 32,725	G 4
Pushkin, 30,035	D 3
Pyatigorsk, 69,617	F 6
Pyatikhatki, 21,359	D 5
Radomyshl', 11,427	C 4
Rakhov, 10,849	B 5
Rakvere, 14,300	C 3
Rasskazovo, 33,785	F 4
Rechitsa, 30,602	C 4
Revel (Tallinn), 363,000	B 3
Rēzekne, 21,400	C 3
Riga, 733,000	B 3
Rogachev, 10,156	D 4
Romny, 35,792	D 4
Roslavl', 37,433	D 4
Rossosh', 30,184	E 4
Rostov, 29,230	E 3
Rostov, 789,000	F 5
Rovno, 116,000	C 4
Rtishchevo, 32,739	F 4
Rubezhnoye, 35,122	E 5
Rustavi, 62,395	G 6
Ruzayevka, 24,909	F 4
Ryazan', 351,000	E 4
Rybinsk, 218,000	E 3
Rybnitsa, 18,649	C 5
Rzhev, 48,971	D 3
Sabirabad, 8,872	G 6
Safonovo, 31,709	D 3
Saki, 18,122	D 5
Salavat, 114,000	H 4
Sal'sk, 36,983	F 5
Sal'yany, 17,197	G 7
Samara (Kuybyshev), 1,047,000	H 4
Saransk, 190,000	G 4
Sarapul, 68,741	H 3
Saratov, 758,000	G 4
Sarny, 10,174	C 4
Sasovo, 20,735	F 4
Segezha, 19,708	D 2
Semenov, 19,837	F 3
Serdobel (Sortavala), 17,611	D 2
Serdobsk, 26,119	F 4
Serpukhov, 124,000	E 4
Sevastopol', 229,000	D 6
Severodvinsk, 145,000	E 2
Severomorsk, 32,234	D 1
Shakhty, 205,000	F 5
Shakhun'ya, 21,305	G 3
Shar'ya, 22,268	G 3
Shatura, 19,629	E 3
Shcherbakov (Rybinsk), 218,000	E 3
Sheki, 34,348	G 6
Shemakha, 13,066	G 6
Shepetovka, 31,898	C 4
Shostka, 38,884	D 4
Shumerlya, 30,213	G 3
Shuya, 64,562	F 3
Šiauliai, 59,722	B 3
Sibay, 28,822	J 4
Simferopol', 250,000	D 6
Skopin, 17,957	F 4
Slantsy, 35,303	C 3
Slavgorod, 38,413	D 4
Slavuta, 20,216	C 4
Slavyansk, 124,000	E 5
Slavyansk-na-Kubani, 38,954	E 5
Slobodskoy, 30,836	H 3
Slutsk, 22,740	C 4
Smela, 44,534	D 5
Smolensk, 211,000	D 4
Sochi, 224,000	E 6
Sokol, 41,709	F 3
Sol'-Iletsk, 21,614	J 4
Solikamsk, 82,874	J 3
Sorochinsk, 19,359	H 4
Soroki, 15,195	C 5
Sortavala, 17,611	D 2
Sosnogorsk, 15,799	H 2
Sovetsk, 31,941	B 4
Stalingrad (Volgograd), 818,000	F 5
Stalino (Donetsk), 879,000	E 5
Staraya Russa, 25,409	D 3
Starobel'sk, 19,519	E 5
Staryy Oskol, 27,474	E 4
Stavropol', 198,000	F 5
Stepanakert, 30,000	G 7
Stepnoy (Elista), 50,000	G 5
Sterlitamak, 185,000	J 4
Stupino, 40,343	E 4
Sukhumi, 102,000	F 6
Sumgait, 124,000	G 6
Sumy, 159,000	E 4
Syktyvkar, 125,000	H 2
Syzran', 174,000	G 4
Taganrog, 254.000	E 5
Tallinn, 363,000	B 3
Tambov, 229,000	F 4
Tartu, 74,263	C 3
Tauragė, 12,000	B 3
Tbilisi, 889,000	F 6
Telavi, 15,328	G 6
Telšiai, 13,500	B 3
Temryuk, 22,182	E 5
Ternopol', 85,000	C 5
Teykovo, 28,298	E 3
Tiflis (Tbilisi), 889,000	F 6
Tighina (Bendery), 43,109	C 5
Tikhoretsk, 49,658	F 5
Tikhvin, 18,412	D 3
Tiraspol', 106,000	D 5
Togliatti, 251,000	G 4
Tokmak, 28,575	E 5
Toropets, 15,154	D 3
Torzhok, 34,921	D 3
Tskhinvali, 30,000	F 6
Tuapse, 36,650	E 6
Tukums, 10,800	B 3
Tula, 462,000	E 4
Tul'chin, 12,492	C 5
Tutayev, 17,210	E 3
Tuymazy, 23,408	H 4
Uchaly	J 4
Ufa, 773,000	J 4
Uglich, 28,890	E 3
Ukmergė, 14,900	C 3
Ul'yanovsk, 351,000	G 4
Uman', 44,546	D 5
Uryupinsk, 31,546	F 4
Uzhgorod, 65,000	B 5
Uzlovaya, 53,912	E 4
Valga, 13,400	C 3
Valmiera, 11,600	C 3
Valuyki, 18,068	E 4
Varnek	J 1
Vasil'kov, 20,450	D 4
Velikiy Ustyug, 37,026	F 2
Velikiye Luki, 58,939	D 3
Vel'sk, 16,938	F 2
Ventspils, 27,400	B 3
Vichuga, 51,676	F 3
Viipuri (Vyborg), 51,088	C 2
Vilna (Vilnius), 372,000	C 4
Vinnitsa, 211,000	C 5
Vitebsk, 231,000	C 3
Vladimir, 234,000	F 3
Volgodonsk, 15,710	F 5
Volgograd, 818,000	F 5
Volkhov, 36,630	D 3
Volkovysk, 18,283	B 4
Vologda, 178,000	F 3
Vol'sk, 61,792	G 4
Volzhsk, 33,412	G 3
Volzhskiy, 142,000	G 5
Vorkuta, 55,668	K 1
Voronezh, 660,000	E 4
Voroshilovgrad, 382,000	F 5
Votkinsk, 59,666	H 3
Voznesensk, 31,043	D 5
Vyatskiye Polyany, 25,717	H 3
Vyaz'ma, 31,883	D 3
Vyborg, 51,088	C 2
Vyksa, 40,275	F 3
Vyshniy Volochek, 66,360	D 3
Yalta, 43,994	D 6
Yanaul, 15,843	J 3
Yaroslavl', 517,000	E 3
Yartsevo, 25,558	D 3
Yasnyy	J 4
Yefremov, 28,672	E 4
Yegor'yevsk, 59,341	E 3
Yelabuga, 21,992	H 3
Yelets, 101,000	E 4
Yenakiyevo, 92,306	E 5
Yershov, 19,977	G 4
Yessentuki, 48,101	F 6
Yevpatoria, 56,992	D 5
Yeysk, 55,324	E 5
Yoshkar-Ola, 166,000	G 3
Yur'yevets, 19,746	F 3
Zagorsk, 73,578	E 3
Zaporozh'ye, 658,000	E 5
Zelenodol'sk. 60.472	G 3
Zhdanov, 417,000	E 5
Zherdevka, 15,267	F 4
Zhigulevsk. 46.117	G 4
Zhitomir, 161,000	C 4
Zhlobin, 19,216	D 4
Zhmerinka, 29,368	C 5
Zhodino, 13,000	C 4
Znamenka, 22,297	D 5
Zolotonosha, 24,603	D 5
Zugdidi, 31,081	F 6
Zvenigorodka, 17,154	D 5

OTHER FEATURES

Place	Key
Apsheron (pen.)	H 6
Araks (river)	G 7
Azov (sea)	E 5
Baltic (sea)	B 3
Belaya (river)	H 3
Beloye (lake)	E 2
Berezina (river)	C 4
Black (sea)	D 6
Bug (river)	B 4
Bug (river)	D 5
Caspian (sea)	G 6
Caucasus (mts.)	F 6
Central Ural (mts.)	J 2
Cheshskaya (bay)	G 1
Chir (river)	F 5
Crimea (pen.), 1,814,000	D 5
Dagö (Hiiumaa) (isl.)	B 3
Denezhkin Kamen' (mt.)	J 2
Desna (river)	D 4
Dnieper (river)	D 5
Dniester (river)	C 5
Dolgiy (isl.)	J 1
Don (river)	F 5
Donets (river)	E 5
Dvina (bay)	E 2
Dvina, Northern (river)	F 2
Dvina, Western (river)	C 3
Dykh-Tau (mt.)	F 6
El'brus (mt.)	F 6
Finland (gulf)	C 3
Goryn' (river)	C 4
Hiiumaa (isl.)	B 3
Ilek (river)	J 4
Il'men (lake)	D 3
Izhma (river)	H 2
Kakhovka (res.)	D 5
Kama (river)	H 3
Kandalaksha (gulf)	D 1
Kanin (pen.)	G 1
Kapydzhik (mt.)	G 7
Kara (sea)	K 1
Kazbek (mt.)	F 6
Khoper (river)	F 4
Kil'din (isl.)	D 1
Kinel' (river)	H 4
Kola (pen.)	E 1
Kolguyev (isl.)	G 1
Kolva (river)	J 1
Kuban' (river)	E 5
Kubeno (lake)	E 3
Kura (river)	G 6
Kuyto (lake)	D 2
Lacha (lake)	E 2
Ladoga (lake)	D 2
Lapland (reg.)	C 1
Lovat' (river)	D 3
Mansel'ka (mts.)	C 1
Manych-Gudilo (lake)	F 5
Matveyev (isl.)	J 1
Medveditsa (river)	F 4
Mezen' (bay)	F 1
Mezen' (river)	G 1
Mezhdusharskiy (isl.)	G 1
Moksha (river)	F 4
Moskva (river)	E 3
Msta (river)	D 3
Niemen (river)	B 4
North Ural (mts.)	K 1
Northern Dvina (river)	F 2
Novaya Zemlya (isls.), 500	H 1
Oka (river)	F 4
Onega (bay)	E 2
Onega (lake)	E 2
Ösel (Saaremaa) (isl.)	B 3
Pay-Yer (mt.)	K 1
Pechora (river)	H 1
Pechora (sea)	H 1
Peipus (lake)	C 3
Pinega (river)	G 2
Ponoy (river)	E 1
Pripet (marsh)	C 4
Pripyat' (river)	C 4
Prut (river)	C 5
Psel (river)	D 4
Riga (gulf)	B 3
Russkiy Zavorot (cape)	H 1
Rybachiy (pen.)	D 1
Saaremaa (isl.)	B 3
Samara (river)	H 4
Seg (lake)	D 2
Sevan (lake)	G 6
Seym (river)	D 4
Solovetskiye (isls.)	E 1
South Ural (mts.)	J 4
Suda (river)	E 3
Sukhona (river)	F 2
Sura (river)	G 4
Svir' (river)	D 2
Sysola (river)	H 2
Tel'pos-Iz (mt.)	K 2
Timan Ridge (mts.)	H 1
Top (lake)	D 1
Tuloma (river)	D 1
Ufa (river)	J 3
Undzha (river)	F 3
Ural (mts.)	J 2
Ural (river)	J 4
Usa (river)	K 1
Vaga (river)	F 2
Valday (hills)	D 3
Vaygach (isl.)	K 1
Velikaya (river)	C 3
Vetluga (river)	G 3
Vodl (lake)	E 2
Volga (river)	G 5
Volga-Don (canal)	F 5
Volkhov (river)	D 3
Vorona (river)	F 4
Vorskla (river)	E 4
Vozhe (lake)	F 2
Vyatka (river)	H 3
Vychegda (river)	G 2
Vyg (lake)	E 2
Vym' (river)	H 2
Western Dvina (river)	C 3
White (sea)	E 1
Yamantau (mt.)	J 4
Yug (river)	G 2
Yugorskiy (pen.)	K 1

*City and suburbs.

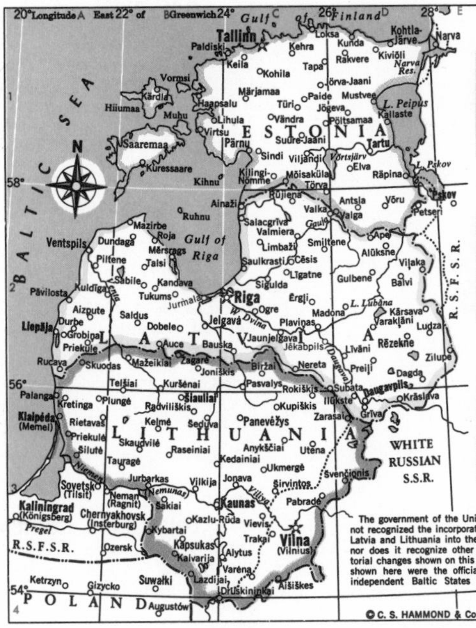

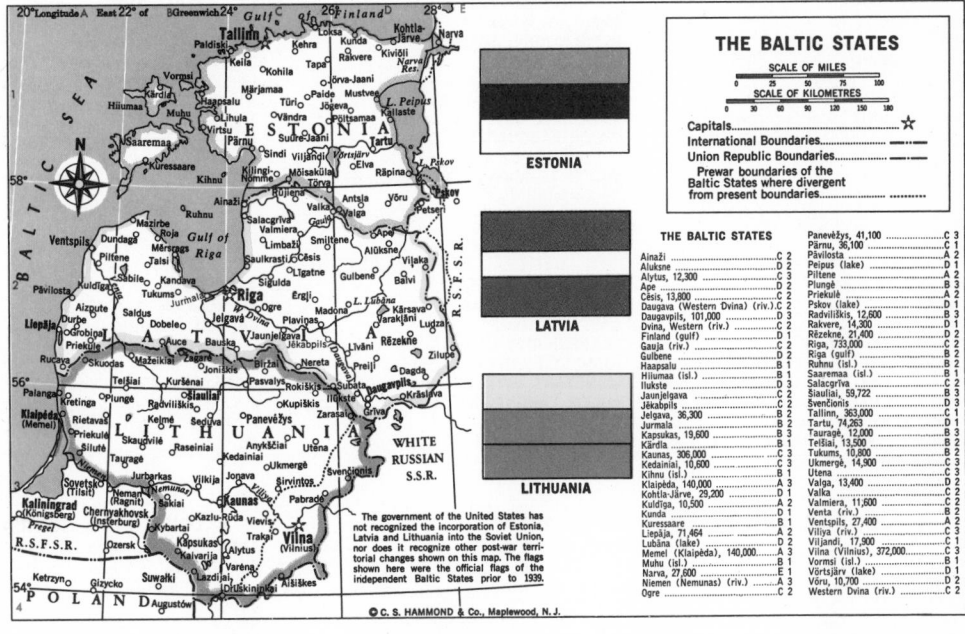

ESTONIA

LATVIA

LITHUANIA

The government of the United States has not recognized the incorporation of Estonia, Latvia and Lithuania into the Soviet Union, nor does it recognize other post-war territorial changes shown on this map. The flags shown here were the official flags of the independent Baltic States prior to 1939.

© C. S. HAMMOND & Co., Maplewood, N. J.

THE BALTIC STATES

SCALE OF MILES: 0 25 50 75 100

SCALE OF KILOMETRES: 0 30 60 90 120 150 180

Capitals ☆
International Boundaries
Union Republic Boundaries
Prewar boundaries of the Baltic States where divergent from present boundaries

THE BALTIC STATES

Place	Key
Ainaži	C 2
Aluksne	D 2
Alytus, 12,300	C 3
Ape	D 2
Cēsis, 13,800	C 2
Daugava (Western Dvina) (riv.)	C 2
Daugavpils, 101,000	D 3
Dvina, Western (riv.)	C 2
Finland (gulf)	D 1
Gauja (riv.)	C 2
Gulbene	D 2
Haapsalu	B 1
Hiiumaa (isl.)	B 1
Ilukste	D 3
Jaunjelgava	C 2
Jēkabpils	C 2
Jelgava, 36,300	B 2
Jurmala	B 2
Kapsukas, 19,600	B 3
Kärdla	B 1
Kaunas, 306,000	C 3
Kedainiai, 10,600	C 3
Kihnu (isl.)	B 1
Klaipėda, 140,000	A 3
Kohtla-Järve, 29,200	D 1
Kuldīga, 10,500	A 2
Kunda	D 1
Kuressaare	B 1
Liepāja, 71,464	A 2
Lubāna (lake)	D 2
Memel (Klaipėda), 140,000	A 3
Muhu (isl.)	B 1
Narva, 27,600	E 1
Niemen (Nemunas) (riv.)	A 3
Ogre	C 2
Panevėžys, 41,100	C 3
Pärnu, 36,100	C 1
Pāvilosta	A 2
Peipus (lake)	D 1
Piltene	A 2
Plungė	B 3
Priekulė	A 2
Pskov (lake)	D 1
Radviliškis, 12,600	B 3
Rakvere, 14,300	D 1
Rēzekne, 21,400	D 2
Riga, 733,000	C 2
Riga (gulf)	B 2
Ruhnu (isl.)	B 2
Saaremaa (isl.)	B 1
Salacgrīva	C 2
Šiauliai, 59,722	B 3
Švenčionis	D 3
Tallinn, 363,000	C 1
Tartu, 74,263	D 1
Tauragė, 12,000	B 3
Telšiai, 13,500	B 2
Tukums, 10,800	B 2
Ukmergė, 14,900	C 3
Utena	C 3
Valga, 13,400	D 2
Valka	C 2
Valmiera, 11,600	C 2
Venta (riv.)	B 2
Ventspils, 27,400	A 2
Viliya (riv.)	C 3
Viljandi, 17,900	C 1
Vilna (Vilnius), 372,000	C 3
Vormsi (isl.)	B 1
Võrtsjärv (lake)	D 1
Võru, 10,700	D 2
Western Dvina (riv.)	C 2

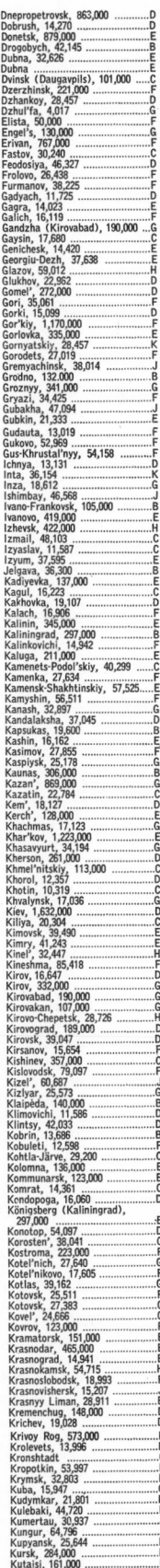

ALGERIA
AREA 919,595 sq. mi.
POPULATION 13,547,000
CAPITAL Algiers
LARGEST CITY Algiers
HIGHEST POINT Tahat 9,850 ft.
MONETARY UNIT Algerian franc
MAJOR LANGUAGES Arabic, Berber, French
MAJOR RELIGION Islam

ANGOLA
AREA 481,351 sq. mi.
POPULATION 5,430,000
CAPITAL Luanda
LARGEST CITY Luanda
HIGHEST POINT Mt. Moco 8,597 ft.
MONETARY UNIT Portuguese escudo
MAJOR LANGUAGES Mbundu, Kongo, Lunda, Portuguese
MAJOR RELIGIONS Tribal religions, Roman Catholicism

BOTSWANA
AREA 219,815 sq. mi.
POPULATION 629,000
CAPITAL Gaborone
LARGEST CITIES Serowe and Kanye
HIGHEST POINT Tsodilo Hill 5,922 ft.
MONETARY UNIT pound sterling
MAJOR LANGUAGES Setswana, Shona, Bushman, English
MAJOR RELIGIONS Tribal religions, Protestantism

BURUNDI
AREA 10,747 sq. mi.
POPULATION 3,475,000
CAPITAL Bujumbura
LARGEST CITY Bujumbura
HIGHEST POINT 8,858 ft.
MONETARY UNIT Rwanda-Burundi fra
MAJOR LANGUAGES Kirundi, French
MAJOR RELIGIONS Tribal religions, R Catholicism

CAMEROON
AREA 183,568 sq. mi.
POPULATION 5,836,000
CAPITAL Yaoundé
LARGEST CITY Douala
HIGHEST POINT Cameroon 13,350 ft.
MONETARY UNIT CFA franc
MAJOR LANGUAGES Fang, Bamileke, Fulani, Duala, French, English
MAJOR RELIGIONS Tribal religions, Christianity, Islam

CENTRAL AFRICAN REPUBLIC
AREA 240,534 sq. mi.
POPULATION 1,518,000
CAPITAL Bangui
LARGEST CITY Bangui
HIGHEST POINT Gao 4,659 ft.
MONETARY UNIT CFA franc
MAJOR LANGUAGES Banda, Gbaya, Sango, French
MAJOR RELIGIONS Tribal religions, Christianity, Islam

CHAD
AREA 495,753 sq. mi.
POPULATION 3,510,000
CAPITAL Fort-Lamy
LARGEST CITY Fort-Lamy
HIGHEST POINT Emi Koussi 11,204 ft.
MONETARY UNIT CFA franc
MAJOR LANGUAGES Arabic, Bagirmi, French
MAJOR RELIGIONS Islam, Tribal religions

DEMOCRATIC REPUBLIC OF THE CONGO
AREA 905,563 sq. mi.
POPULATION 21,637,876
CAPITAL Kinshasa
LARGEST CITY Kinshasa
HIGHEST POINT Margherita 16,795 ft.
MONETARY UNIT Congo franc
MAJOR LANGUAGES Luba, Mongo, Ko Kinyarwanda, Zande, Lingala, Swahili
MAJOR RELIGIONS Tribal religions, Christianity

REPUBLIC OF CONGO
AREA 175,676 sq. mi.
POPULATION 915,000
CAPITAL Brazzaville
LARGEST CITY Brazzaville
HIGHEST POINT Leketi Mts. 3,412 ft.
MONETARY UNIT CFA franc
MAJOR LANGUAGES Kongo, Bateke, Lingala, French
MAJOR RELIGIONS Christianity, Tribal religions

DAHOMEY
AREA 44,290 sq. mi.
POPULATION 2,640,000
CAPITAL Porto-Novo
LARGEST CITY Cotonou
HIGHEST POINT Atakora Mts. 2,083 ft.
MONETARY UNIT CFA franc
MAJOR LANGUAGES Fon, Somba, Yoruba, Bariba, French
MAJOR RELIGIONS Tribal religions, Islam, Roman Catholicism

EQUATORIAL GUINEA
AREA 10,832 sq. mi.
POPULATION 286,000
CAPITAL Santa Isabel
LARGEST CITY Santa Isabel
HIGHEST POINT 9,868 ft.
MONETARY UNIT peseta
MAJOR LANGUAGES Fang, Bubi, Spanish
MAJOR RELIGIONS Tribal religions, Christianity

ETHIOPIA
AREA 471,776 sq. mi.
POPULATION 24,764,000
CAPITAL Addis Ababa
LARGEST CITY Addis Ababa
HIGHEST POINT Ras Dashan 15,157 ft.
MONETARY UNIT Ethiopian dollar
MAJOR LANGUAGES Amharic, Galla, Tigrinya, Somali, Sidamo
MAJOR RELIGIONS Coptic Christianity

GABON
AREA 103,346 sq. mi.
POPULATION 500,000
CAPITAL Libreville
LARGEST CITY Libreville
HIGHEST POINT Ibounzi 5,165 ft.
MONETARY UNIT CFA franc
MAJOR LANGUAGES Fang and other Bantu languages, French
MAJOR RELIGIONS Tribal religions, Christianity

GAMBIA
AREA 4,003 sq. mi.
POPULATION 357,000
CAPITAL Bathurst
LARGEST CITY Bathurst
HIGHEST POINT 100 ft.
MONETARY UNIT West African pound
MAJOR LANGUAGES Mandingo, Fulani, Wolof, English
MAJOR RELIGIONS Islam, Tribal religions, Christianity

GHANA
AREA 91,843 sq. mi.
POPULATION 8,545,561
CAPITAL Accra
LARGEST CITY Accra
HIGHEST POINT Togo Hills 2,900 ft.
MONETARY UNIT cedi
MAJOR LANGUAGES Twi, Fante, Dagomba, Ewe, Ga, English
MAJOR RELIGIONS Tribal religions, Christianity

GUINEA
AREA 94,925 sq. mi.
POPULATION 3,890,000
CAPITAL Conakry
LARGEST CITY Conakry
HIGHEST POINT Nimba Mts. 6,070 ft.
MONETARY UNIT Guinean franc
MAJOR LANGUAGES Fulani, Mandingo, Susu, French
MAJOR RELIGIONS Islam, Tribal religions

IVORY COAST
AREA 124,503 sq. mi.
POPULATION 4,800,000
CAPITAL Abidjan
LARGEST CITY Abidjan
HIGHEST POINT Nimba Mts. 5,745 ft.
MONETARY UNIT CFA franc
MAJOR LANGUAGES Bale, Bete, Senufu, French
MAJOR RELIGIONS Tribal religions, Islam

KENYA
AREA 224,960 sq. mi.
POPULATION 10,880,200
CAPITAL Nairobi
LARGEST CITY Nairobi
HIGHEST POINT Kenya 17,058 ft.
MONETARY UNIT East African shilling
MAJOR LANGUAGES Kikuyu, Luo, Kavirondo, Kamba, Swahili, English
MAJOR RELIGIONS Tribal religions, Christianity

LESOTHO
AREA 11,716 sq. mi.
POPULATION 930,000
CAPITAL Maseru
LARGEST CITY Maseru
HIGHEST POINT 11,425 ft.
MONETARY UNIT rand
MAJOR LANGUAGES Sesotho, English
MAJOR RELIGIONS Tribal religions, Christianity

LIBERIA
AREA 43,000 sq. mi.
POPULATION 1,200,000
CAPITAL Monrovia
LARGEST CITY Monrovia
HIGHEST POINT Wutivi 5,584 ft.
MONETARY UNIT Liberian dollar
MAJOR LANGUAGES Kru, Kpelle, Bass Vai, English
MAJOR RELIGIONS Christianity, Tribal religions

LIBYA
AREA 679,359 sq. mi.
POPULATION 1,900,000
CAPITALS Tripoli, Benghazi
LARGEST CITY Tripoli
HIGHEST POINT Bette Pk. 7,500 ft.
MONETARY UNIT Libyan pound
MAJOR LANGUAGES Arabic, Berber
MAJOR RELIGION Islam

MALAGASY REPUBLIC
AREA 226,657 sq. mi.
POPULATION 7,011,563
CAPITAL Tananarive
LARGEST CITY Tananarive
HIGHEST POINT Maromokotro 9,436 ft.
MONETARY UNIT CFA franc
MAJOR LANGUAGES Malagasy, French
MAJOR RELIGIONS Tribal religions, Roman Catholicism, Protestantism

MALAWI
AREA 45,483 sq. mi.
POPULATION 4,530,000
CAPITAL Zomba
LARGEST CITY Blantyre
HIGHEST POINT Mlanje 9,843 ft.
MONETARY UNIT Malawi pound
MAJOR LANGUAGES Chichewa, Yao, English
MAJOR RELIGIONS Tribal religions, Islam

MALI
AREA 463,948 sq. mi.
POPULATION 4,929,000
CAPITAL Bamako
LARGEST CITY Bamako
HIGHEST POINT Hombori Mts. 3,789 ft.
MONETARY UNIT Malian franc
MAJOR LANGUAGES Bambara, Senufu, Fulani, Soninke, French
MAJOR RELIGIONS Islam, Tribal religio

MAURITANIA
AREA 397,954 sq. mi.
POPULATION 1,140,000
CAPITAL Nouakchott
LARGEST CITY Nouakchott
HIGHEST POINT 2,972 ft.
MONETARY UNIT CFA franc
MAJOR LANGUAGES Arabic, French, Wolof
MAJOR RELIGION Islam

MAURITIUS
AREA 709 sq. mi.
POPULATION 823,000
CAPITAL Port Louis
LARGEST CITY Port Louis
HIGHEST POINT 2,711 ft.
MONETARY UNIT Mauritius rupee
MAJOR LANGUAGES English, French, French Creole, Hindi
MAJOR RELIGIONS Hinduism, Christianity

MOROCCO
AREA 172,413 sq. mi.
POPULATION 15,577,000
CAPITAL Rabat
LARGEST CITY Casablanca
HIGHEST POINT Jeb. Toubkal 13,665 ft.
MONETARY UNIT dirham
MAJOR LANGUAGES Arabic, Berber, French
MAJOR RELIGIONS Islam, Judaism

MOZAMBIQUE
AREA 302,328 sq. mi.
POPULATION 7,376,000
CAPITAL Lourenço Marques
LARGEST CITY Lourenço Marques
HIGHEST POINT Mt. Binga 7,992 ft.
MONETARY UNIT Portuguese escudo
MAJOR LANGUAGES Makua, Thonga, Shona, Portuguese
MAJOR RELIGIONS Tribal religions, Roman Catholicism

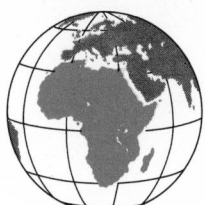

NIGER
489,189 sq. mi.
ILATION 4,016,000
TAL Niamey
EST CITY Niamey
EST POINT Banguezane 6,234 ft.
ETARY UNIT CFA franc
OR LANGUAGES Hausa, Songhai, Fulani, French
OR RELIGIONS Islam, Tribal religions

NIGERIA
AREA 356,669 sq. mi.
POPULATION 66,174,000
CAPITAL Lagos
LARGEST CITY Lagos
HIGHEST POINT Vogel 6,700 ft.
MONETARY UNIT Nigerian pound
MAJOR LANGUAGES Hausa, Yoruba, Ibo, Fulani, Tiv, Kanuri, Ibibio, English
MAJOR RELIGIONS Islam, Christianity

AFRICA
AREA 11,682,000 sq. mi.
POPULATION 345,000,000
LARGEST CITY Cairo
HIGHEST POINT Kilimanjaro 19,304 ft.
LOWEST POINT Qattara Depression -436 ft.

PORTUGUESE GUINEA
13,948 sq. mi.
ILATION 530,000
TAL Bissau
EST CITY Bissau
EST POINT 689 ft.
ETARY UNIT Portuguese escudo
OR LANGUAGES Balante, Fulani, Mandjako, Mandingo, Portuguese
OR RELIGIONS Islam, Tribal religions, Roman Catholicism

RHODESIA
AREA 150,332 sq. mi.
POPULATION 5,310,000
CAPITAL Salisbury
LARGEST CITY Salisbury
HIGHEST POINT Mt. Inyangani 8,517 ft.
MONETARY UNIT Rhodesian pound
MAJOR LANGUAGES English, Shona, Ndabele
MAJOR RELIGIONS Tribal religions, Protestantism

RWANDA
AREA 10,169 sq. mi.
POPULATION 3,500,000
CAPITAL Kigali
LARGEST CITY Kigali
HIGHEST POINT Karisimbi 14,780 ft.
MONETARY UNIT Rwanda-Burundi franc
MAJOR LANGUAGES Kinyarwanda, French
MAJOR RELIGIONS Tribal religions, Roman Catholicism

SENEGAL
AREA 75,750 sq. mi.
POPULATION 3,780,000
CAPITAL Dakar
LARGEST CITY Dakar
HIGHEST POINT Futa Jallon 1,640 ft.
MONETARY UNIT CFA franc
MAJOR LANGUAGES Wolof, Fulani, Serer, French
MAJOR RELIGIONS Islam, Tribal religions, Roman Catholicism

SIERRA LEONE
A 27,925 sq. mi.
ILATION 2,512,000
TAL Freetown
EST CITY Freetown
EST POINT Loma Mts. 6,390 ft.
ETARY UNIT leone
OR LANGUAGES Mende, Temne, Vai, English
OR RELIGIONS Tribal religions, Islam, Christianity

SOMALIA
AREA 246,200 sq. mi.
POPULATION 2,730,000
CAPITAL Mogadishu
LARGEST CITY Mogadishu
HIGHEST POINT Surud Ad 7,900 ft.
MONETARY UNIT somalo
MAJOR LANGUAGES Somali, Arabic, Italian, English
MAJOR RELIGIONS Islam, Roman Catholicism

SOUTH AFRICA
AREA 471,663 sq. mi.
POPULATION 21,282,000
CAPITALS Cape Town, Pretoria
LARGEST CITY Johannesburg
HIGHEST POINT Injasuti 11,182 ft.
MONETARY UNIT rand
MAJOR LANGUAGES Afrikaans, English, Xhosa, Zulu, Sesotho, Pedi
MAJOR RELIGIONS Protestantism, Roman Catholicism, Islam, Hinduism

SOUTH-WEST AFRICA
AREA 317,838 sq. mi.
POPULATION 615,000
CAPITAL Windhoek
LARGEST CITY Windhoek
HIGHEST POINT Brandberg 8,550 ft.
MONETARY UNIT rand
MAJOR LANGUAGES Ovambo, Hottentot, Herero, Afrikaans, English
MAJOR RELIGIONS Tribal religions, Protestantism

SPANISH SAHARA
A 102,702 sq. mi.
ULATION 63,000
TAL El Aaiún
GEST CITY El Aaiún
HEST POINT 2,700 ft.
ETARY UNIT Spanish peseta
OR LANGUAGES Arabic, Spanish
OR RELIGION Islam

SUDAN
AREA 967,495 sq. mi.
POPULATION 15,312,000
CAPITAL Khartoum
LARGEST CITY Omdurman
HIGHEST POINT Jeb. Marra 10,073 ft.
MONETARY UNIT Sudanese pound
MAJOR LANGUAGES Arabic, Dinka, Nubian, Beja, Nuer
MAJOR RELIGIONS Islam, Tribal religions

SWAZILAND
AREA 6,704 sq. mi.
POPULATION 411,879
CAPITAL Mbabane
LARGEST CITY Mbabane
HIGHEST POINT Emlembe 6,109 ft.
MONETARY UNIT rand
MAJOR LANGUAGES Swazi, English
MAJOR RELIGIONS Tribal religions, Christianity

TANZANIA
AREA 362,819 sq. mi.
POPULATION 12,896,000
CAPITAL Dar es Salaam
LARGEST CITY Dar es Salaam
HIGHEST POINT Kilimanjaro 19,340 ft.
MONETARY UNIT East African shilling
MAJOR LANGUAGES Nyamwezi-Sukuma, Swahili, English
MAJOR RELIGIONS Tribal religions, Christianity, Islam

TOGO
A 21,853 sq. mi.
ULATION 2,004,711
ITAL Lomé
GEST CITY Lomé
HEST POINT Agou 3,445 ft.
ETARY UNIT CFA franc
OR LANGUAGES Ewe, Kabre, Gurma, French
OR RELIGIONS Tribal religions, Roman Catholicism, Islam

TUNISIA
AREA 63,378 sq. mi.
POPULATION 5,027,000
CAPITAL Tunis
LARGEST CITY Tunis
HIGHEST POINT Jeb. Chambi 5,066 ft.
MONETARY UNIT Tunisian dinar
MAJOR LANGUAGES Arabic, French
MAJOR RELIGION Islam

UGANDA
AREA 92,674 sq. mi.
POPULATION 9,764,000
CAPITAL Kampala
LARGEST CITY Kampala
HIGHEST POINT Margherita 16,795 ft.
MONETARY UNIT East African shilling
MAJOR LANGUAGES Ganda, Acholi, Teso, Nyoro, Soga, Nkole, English
MAJOR RELIGIONS Tribal religions, Christianity

UNITED ARAB REPUBLIC
AREA 386,100 sq. mi.
POPULATION 33,329,000
CAPITAL Cairo
LARGEST CITY Cairo
HIGHEST POINT Jeb. Katherina 8,651 ft.
MONETARY UNIT Egyptian pound
MAJOR LANGUAGE Arabic
MAJOR RELIGIONS Islam, Christianity

UPPER VOLTA
A 105,841 sq. mi.
ULATION 5,330,000
ITAL Ouagadougou
RGEST CITY Ouagadougou
HEST POINT 2,352 ft.
ETARY UNIT CFA franc
OR LANGUAGES Mossi, Lobi, Fulani, Bobo, French
OR RELIGIONS Islam, Tribal religions, Roman Catholicism

ZAMBIA
AREA 290,586 sq. mi.
POPULATION 4,056,995
CAPITAL Lusaka
LARGEST CITY Lusaka
HIGHEST POINT Sunzu 6,782 ft.
MONETARY UNIT kwacha
MAJOR LANGUAGES Bemba, Tonga, Lozi, Luvale, Nyanje, English
MAJOR RELIGIONS Tribal religions

TERRITORY OF THE AFARS AND ISSAS
EA 8,498 sq. mi.
ULATION 125,050
ITAL Djibouti

COMORO ISLANDS
AREA 838 sq. mi.
POPULATION 270,000
CAPITAL Moroni

SÃO TOMÉ E PRÍNCIPE
AREA 372 sq. mi.
POPULATION 66,000
CAPITAL São Tomé

CAPE VERDE ISLANDS
EA 1,557 sq. mi.
ULATION 250,000
PITAL Praia

RÉUNION
AREA 969 sq. mi.
POPULATION 436,000
CAPITAL St-Denis

SEYCHELLES
AREA 109 sq. mi.
POPULATION 51,396
CAPITAL Victoria

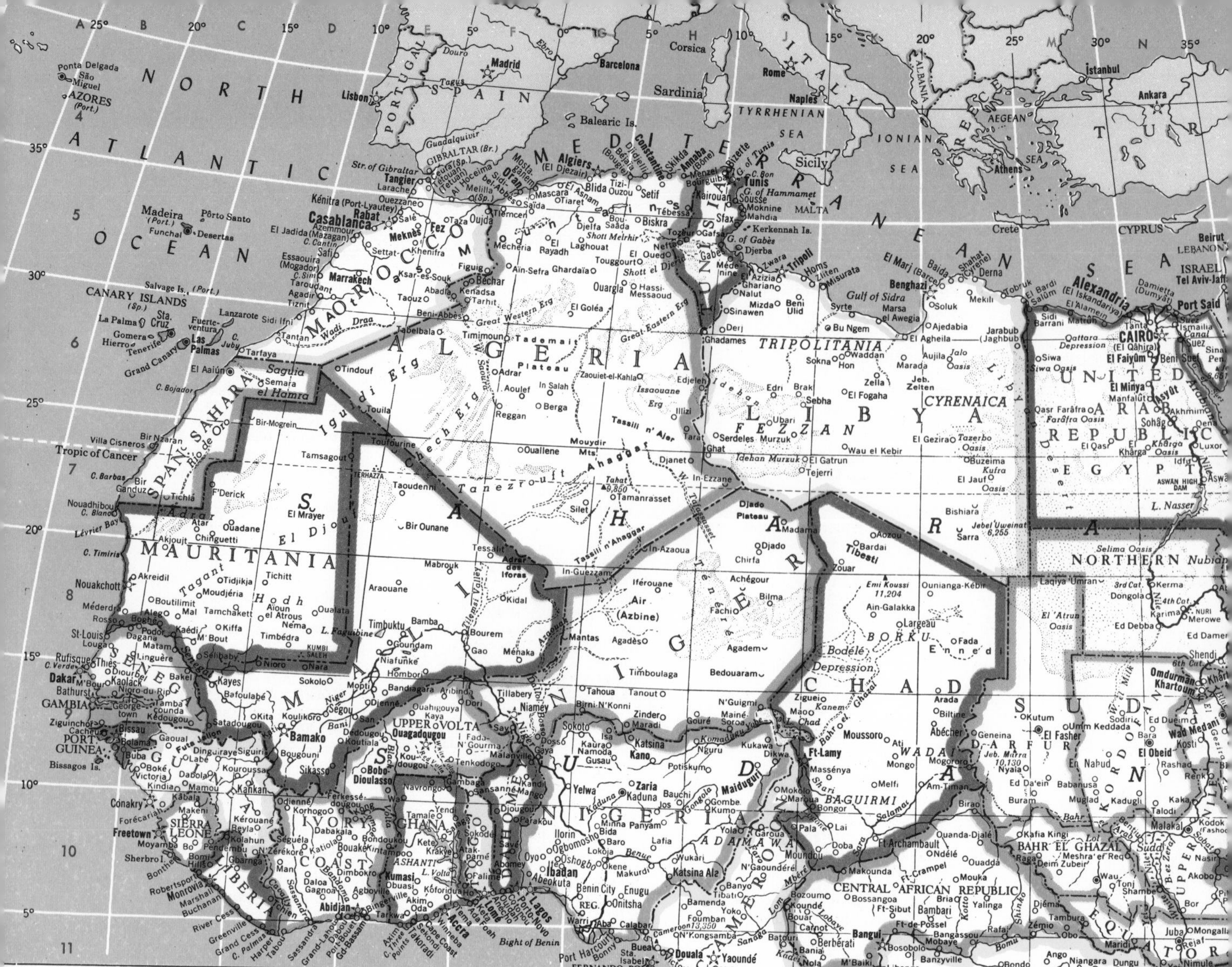

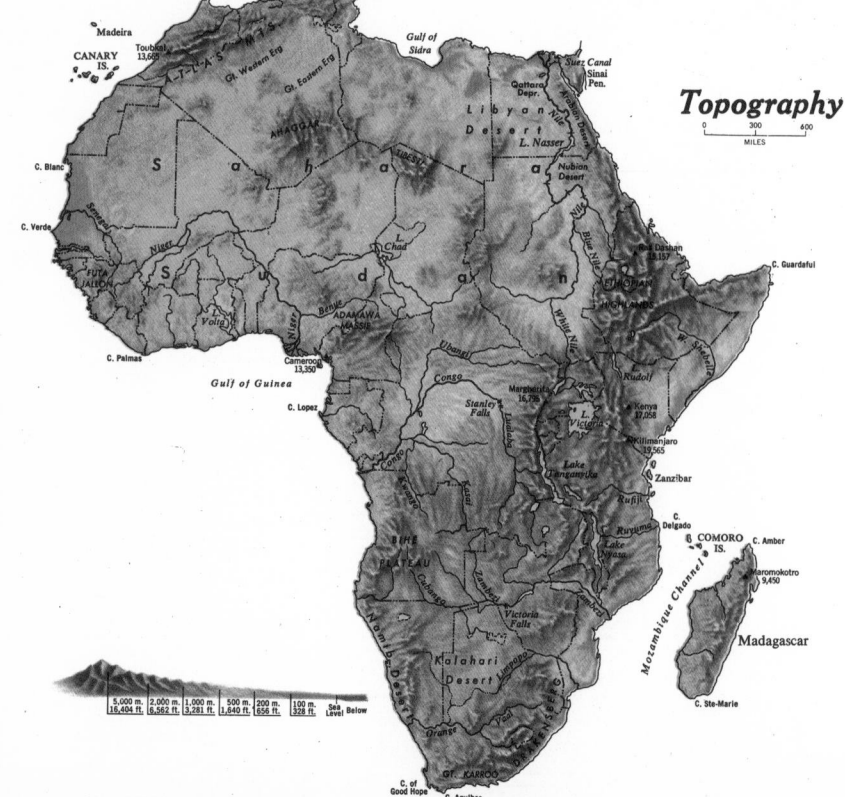

Main map — Northern Africa

NORTH ATLANTIC OCEAN

PORTUGAL · SPAIN · Madrid · Lisbon · Barcelona · Corsica · Sardinia · ITALY · Rome · Naples · TYRRHENIAN SEA · IONIAN SEA · GREECE · Athens · Crete · İstanbul · Ankara · TURKEY · CYPRUS · LEBANON · Beirut · ISRAEL · Tel Aviv-Jaffa

AZORES (Port.) · Ponta Delgada · São Miguel

MEDITERRANEAN SEA · MALTA · Sicily · Tunis · Algiers · Tangier · GIBRALTAR (Br.) · Str. of Gibraltar · Tripoli · Benghazi

Madeira (Port.) · Funchal · CANARY ISLANDS (Sp.) · Las Palmas · Santa Cruz · Tenerife · Grand Canary

MOROCCO · Casablanca · Rabat · Marrakech · Fez · Meknès

ALGERIA · Great Western Erg · Great Eastern Erg · Ahaggar · Tassili n' Ajjer

SPANISH SAHARA · Villa Cisneros · Tropic of Cancer

MAURITANIA · Nouakchott · Atar · El Djouf · Hodh

SENEGAL · Dakar · GAMBIA · PORTUGUESE GUINEA · Bissau

MALI · Bamako · Timbuktu · Gao

UPPER VOLTA · Ouagadougou · Bobo-Dioulasso

NIGER · Niamey · Agadès · Air (Azbine)

LIBYA · TRIPOLITANIA · FEZZAN · CYRENAICA · Sebha · Murzuk

UNITED ARAB REPUBLIC · EGYPT · CAIRO (El Qâhira) · Alexandria · Port Said · Suez · Aswân · L. Nasser · ASWAN HIGH DAM

SUDAN · Khartoum · Omdurman · El Obeid · DARFUR · KORDOFAN · NORTHERN · Nubian Desert

CHAD · Fort-Lamy · BORKU · ENNEDI · Tibesti · Emi Koussi 11,204 · Bodélé Depression · WADAI · BAGUIRMI

NIGERIA · Lagos · Ibadan · Kano · Kaduna · Maiduguri · Zaria · ADAMAWA · Benin City · Enugu · Port Harcourt · Calabar · Bight of Benin · FERNANDO PO

CAMEROON · Yaoundé · Douala

CENTRAL AFRICAN REPUBLIC · Bangui · Bambari

GUINEA · Conakry · SIERRA LEONE · Freetown · LIBERIA · Monrovia · IVORY COAST · Abidjan · GHANA · Accra · Kumasi · TOGO · DAHOMEY · Cotonou · ASHANTI · Gulf of Guinea · Bight of Benin · EQUATOR

Topography (inset map)

Topography

0 300 600 MILES

CANARY IS. · Madeira · C. Bon · Gulf of Sidra · Suez Canal · Sinai Pen. · Qattoro Depr.

ATLAS MTS. · Gt. Western Erg · Gt. Eastern Erg · Libyan Desert · L. Nasser · Nubian Desert

Sahara · C. Blanc · C. Verde · FUTA JALLON · Niger · AHAGGAR · TIBESTI · Chad

Sudan · ADAMAWA MASSIF · Cameroon 13,350 · C. Palmas · Gulf of Guinea · C. Lopez · Congo · Ubangi

Toubkal 13,665 · Kilimanjaro 19,565 · Kenya 17,058 · L. Victoria · L. Tanganyika · L. Nyasa · Stanley Falls · Ruwenzori 16,795 · Rudolf

C. Guardaful · Ras Dashan 15,157 · ETHIOPIAN HIGHLANDS · Blue Nile · White Nile · L. Albert · Victoria Falls

Zanzibar · COMORO IS. · C. Delgado · C. Amber · Madagascar · Maromokotro 9,450 · Mozambique Channel · C. Ste-Marie

Kalahari Desert · KARROO · Orange · C. of Good Hope · C. Agulhas

5,000 m. 16,404 ft. / 2,000 m. 6,562 ft. / 1,000 m. 3,281 ft. / 500 m. 1,640 ft. / 200 m. 656 ft. / 100 m. 328 ft. / Sea Level / Below

Gazetteer Index

BOTSWANA
CITIES and TOWNS
Francistown, 3,225 ...M16
Gaborone (cap.), 18,000 ...M16
Kanye, 35,000 ...L16
Lobatse, 3,949 ...M16
Mahalapye, 13,199 ...M16
Maun, 4,591 ...L15
Mochudi, 17,712 ...M16
Molepolole, 29,625 ...M16
Palapye, 5,137 ...M16
Serowe, 35,000 ...M16

OTHER FEATURES
Kalahari (desert) ...L16
Makgadikgadi (salt pan) ...L16
Ngami (lake) ...L16
Ngamiland (region), 42,395 ...L16
Okovango (basin) ...L15

BRITISH INDIAN OCEAN TERR.
PHYSICAL FEATURES
Aldabra (isls.), 100 ...P13
Farquhar (isls.), 172 ...S14

BURUNDI
CITIES and TOWNS
Bujumbura (cap.), 90,000 ...N12
Gitega, 3,579 ...N12

OTHER FEATURES
Tanganyika (lake) ...N13

CAMEROON
CITIES and TOWNS
Buea, 3,000 ...H11
Douala, 230,000 ...J11
Ebolowa, 16,000 ...J11
Foumban, 20,000 ...J10
Garoua, 30,000 ...J10
Kribi, 7,000 ...J11
Maroua, 24,979 ...J 9
M'Balmayo, 5,500 ...J11
Moloundou, 8,575 ...K11
N'Gaoundéré, 15,000 ...J10
N'Kongsamba, 39,800 ...J11
Victoria, 15,000 ...H11
Yaoundé (cap.), 130,000 ...J11

OTHER FEATURES
Biafra (bight) ...H11
Cameroon (mt.) ...H11
Kadéi (river) ...J11
Lom (river) ...J10
Mbéré (river) ...J10
Sanaga (river) ...J11

CANARY ISLANDS
CITIES and TOWNS
Las Palmas (cap.), 166,236 ...D 6
Santa Cruz (cap.), 82,520 ...C 6

OTHER FEATURES
Fuerteventura (isl.), 18,138 ...D 6
Gomera (isl.), 27,790 ...C 6
Grand Canary (isl.), 400,837 ...C 6
Hierro (isl.), 7,957 ...C 6
La Palma (isl.), 67,141 ...C 6
Lanzarote (isl.), 34,805 ...D 6
Tenerife (isl.), 387,767 ...C 6

CENTRAL AFRICAN REPUBLIC
CITIES and TOWNS
Bambari, 32,000 ...L10
Bangassou, 28,000 ...L10
Bangui (cap.), 111,266 ...K10
Bangui, *240,000 ...K10
Berbérati, 40,000 ...K11
Bossangoa, 36,000 ...D10
Bouar, 29,000 ...K10
Bozoum, 4,700 ...K10
Bria, 25,000 ...L10
Carnot, 4,000 ...K10
Fort-Crampel, 5,000 ...L10
M'Baiki, 18,000 ...K11
Ndélé, 4,013 ...L10
Obo, 3,000 ...M10
Rafai, 9,891 ...L10
Yalinga, 1,500 ...L10
Zémio, 1,500 ...M10

OTHER FEATURES
Lobaye (river) ...K10
Shinko (river) ...L10

CHAD
CITIES and TOWNS
Abécher, 19,650 ...L 9
Ati, 6,000 ...K 9
Biltine, 4,000 ...L 9
Bongor, 11,000 ...
Doba, 7,375 ...
Fort-Archambault, 35,00...
Fort-Lamy (cap.), 132,5...
Lai, 8,000 ...
Largeau, 5,200 ...
Melfi, 3,000 ...
Mongo, 7,000 ...
Moundou, 34,100 ...
Pala, 4,200 ...

OTHER FEATU...
Baguirmi (reg.), 81,666
Borku (region), 21,962 ...
Chad (lake) ...
Emi Koussi (mt.) ...
Ennedi (plateau) ...
Kanem (region), 261,108
Logone (river) ...
Sahara (desert) ...
Salamat (river) ...
Shari (river) ...
Sudan (region) ...
Tibesti (mts.) ...
Wadai (region), 314,775

COMORO ISLA...
CITIES and TOW...
Dzaoudzi, 196 ...
Moroni (cap.), 11,515 ...

OTHER FEATU...
Anjouan (island), 83,486
Grand Comoro (island), 118,443 ...
Mayotte (island), 32,494
Mohéli (isl.), 9,525 ...

DEMOCRATIC RE... OF THE CON...
CITIES and TOW...
Aketi, 15,339 ...
Banana ...
Bandundu, 74,467 ...
Banzyville, 6,608 ...
Basankusu, 5,613 ...
Bikoro, 6,491 ...
Boma, 33,143 ...
Bukavu, 134,861 ...
Bumba, 5,182 ...
Bunia, 12,410 ...
Buta, 10,845 ...
Butembo, 9,980 ...
Elisabethville (Lubumba... 318,000 ...

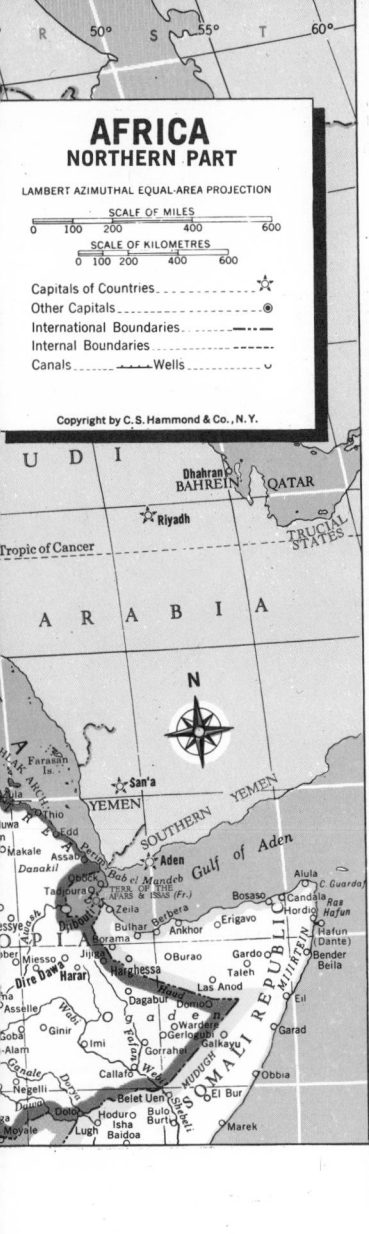

AFRICA
NORTHERN PART
LAMBERT AZIMUTHAL EQUAL-AREA PROJECTION

SCALE OF MILES
0 100 200 400 600

SCALE OF KILOMETRES
0 100 200 400 600

Capitals of Countries .... ☆
Other Capitals .... ◉
International Boundaries .... ———
Internal Boundaries .... — — —
Canals .... Wells .... ᵕ

Copyright by C.S. Hammond & Co., N.Y.

FLAGS OF AFRICA

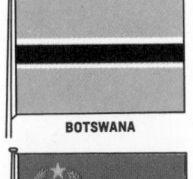
ALGERIA

BOTSWANA

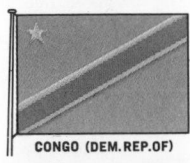
BURUNDI

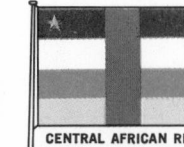
CAMEROON

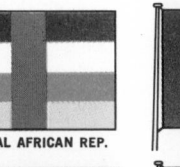
CENTRAL AFRICAN REP.

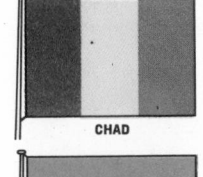
CHAD

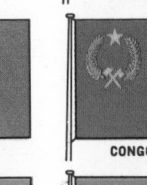
CONGO (REP. OF)

CONGO (DEM. REP. OF)

DAHOMEY

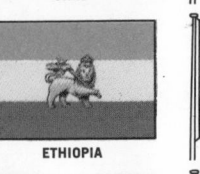
EQUATORIAL GUINEA

ETHIOPIA

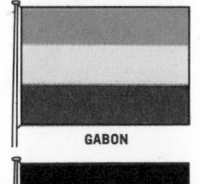
GABON

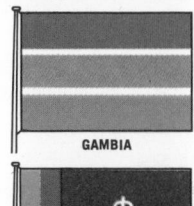
GAMBIA

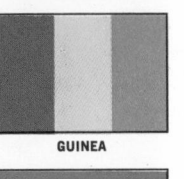
GHANA

GUINEA

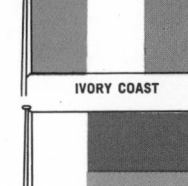
IVORY COAST

KENYA

LESOTHO

LIBERIA

LIBYA

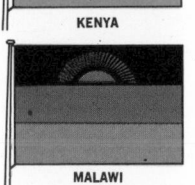
MALAGASY REP

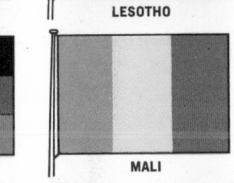
MALAWI

MALI

MAURITANIA

MAURITIUS

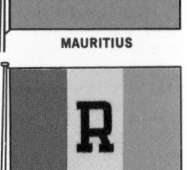
MOROCCO

NIGER

NIGERIA

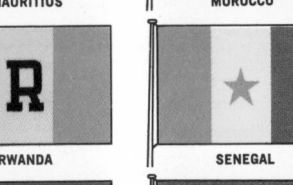
RHODESIA

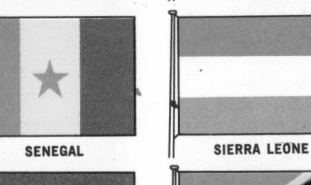
RWANDA

SENEGAL

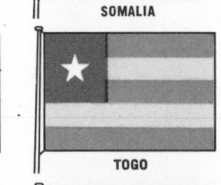
SIERRA LEONE

SOMALIA

SOUTH AFRICA

SUDAN

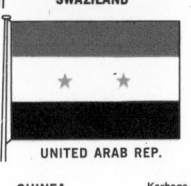
SWAZILAND

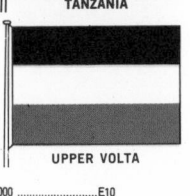
TANZANIA

TOGO

TUNISIA

UGANDA

UNITED ARAB REP.

UPPER VOLTA

ZAMBIA

(continued on following page)

Agriculture, Industry and Resources

DOMINANT LAND USE

- Cereals, Horticulture, Livestock
- Cash Crops, Mixed Cereals
- Cotton, Cereals
- Diversified Tropical Crops
- Plantation Agriculture
- Oases
- Pasture Livestock
- Nomadic Livestock Herding
- Forests
- Nonagricultural Land

MAJOR MINERAL OCCURRENCES

Ab	Asbestos	Mi	Mica
Ag	Silver	Mn	Manganese
Al	Bauxite	Na	Salt
Au	Gold	O	Petroleum
Be	Beryl	P	Phosphates
C	Coal	Pb	Lead
Co	Cobalt	Pt	Platinum
Cr	Chromium	Sb	Antimony
Cu	Copper	Sn	Tin
D	Diamonds	So	Soda Ash
Fe	Iron Ore	Ti	Titanium
G	Natural Gas	U	Uranium
Gp	Gypsum	V	Vanadium
Gr	Graphite	W	Tungsten
K	Potash	Zn	Zinc

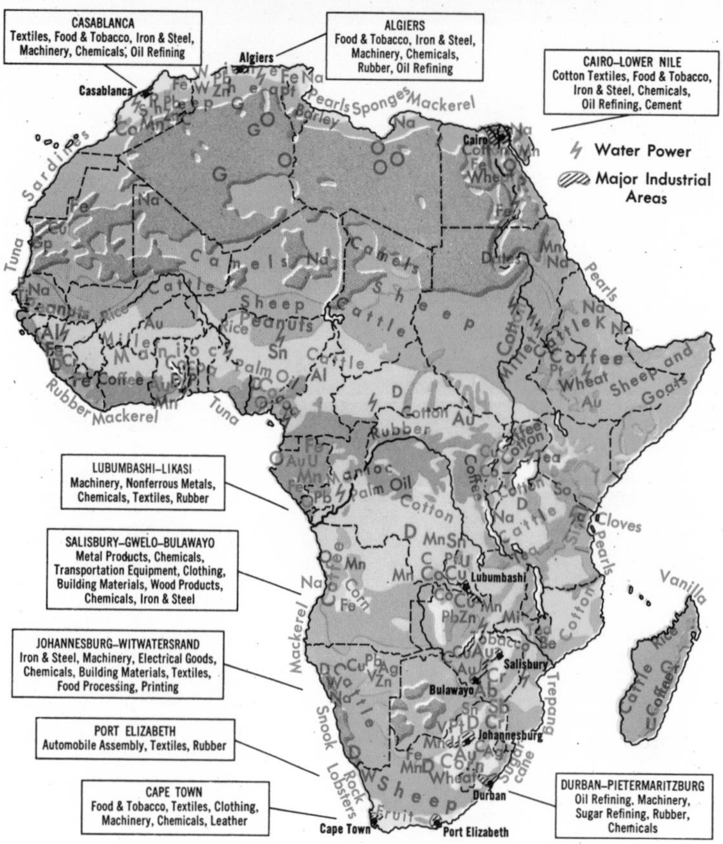
CASABLANCA
Textiles, Food & Tobacco, Iron & Steel, Machinery, Chemicals, Oil Refining
ALGIERS
Food & Tobacco, Iron & Steel, Machinery, Chemicals, Rubber, Oil Refining
CAIRO–LOWER NILE
Cotton Textiles, Food & Tobacco, Iron & Steel, Chemicals, Oil Refining, Cement
Water Power
Major Industrial Areas
LUBUMBASHI–LIKASI
Machinery, Nonferrous Metals, Chemicals, Textiles, Rubber
SALISBURY–GWELO–BULAWAYO
Metal Products, Chemicals, Transportation Equipment, Clothing, Building Materials, Wood Products, Chemicals, Iron & Steel
JOHANNESBURG–WITWATERSRAND
Iron & Steel, Machinery, Electrical Goods, Chemicals, Building Materials, Textiles, Food Processing, Printing
PORT ELIZABETH
Automobile Assembly, Textiles, Rubber
CAPE TOWN
Food & Tobacco, Textiles, Clothing, Machinery, Chemicals, Leather
DURBAN–PIETERMARITZBURG
Oil Refining, Machinery, Sugar Refining, Rubber, Chemicals
Algiers
Casablanca
Cairo
Lubumbashi
Salisbury
Bulawayo
Johannesburg
Durban
Cape Town
Port Elizabeth
Sardines
Tuna
Mackerel
Sponges
Pearls
Camels
Cattle
Sheep
Peanuts
Millet
Rice
Palm Oil
Coffee
Rubber
Cotton
Wheat
Goats
Cloves
Vanilla
Snoek
Rock Lobsters
Fruit
Trepang
Sugar cane

Syrte, 7,093 ....K 5
Tobruk, 15,867 ....L 5
Tripoli (cap.), 247,365 ....J 5
Waddan, ‡3,519 ....K 6
Zliten, ‡17,950 ....K 5
Zwara, ‡14,578 ....J 5

OTHER FEATURES

Cyrenaica (reg.), 450,954 ....L 6
Fezzan (reg.), 79,326 ....J 6
Libyan (desert) ....M 6
Jalo (oasis), 3,910 ....L 6
Kufra (oasis), 5,509 ....L 7
Sahara (desert) ....L 7
Sidra (gulf) ....K 5
Tazerbo (oasis), ‡1,307 ....L 6
Tripolitania (reg.), 1,034,089........J 5

MADEIRA

CITIES and TOWNS

Funchal (cap.), 43,301 ....C 5

OTHER FEATURES

Madeira (isl.), 265,432 ....C 5
Pôrto Santo (isl.), 3,505 ....C 5

MALAGASY REPUBLIC

CITIES and TOWNS

Ambalavao, 6,045 ....R16
Ambanja, 5,198 ....R14
Ambatondrazaka, 14,297 ....R15
Ambilobe, 7,877 ....R14
Ambositra, 15,131 ....R16
Antalaha, 18,083 ....S14
Antsirabe, 29,914 ....R16
Arivonimamo, 7,011 ....R15
Belo-sur-Tsiribihina, 4,391 ....P15
Betroka, 4,071 ....R16
Diégo-Suarez, 40,237 ....R14
Farafangana, 10,753 ....R16
Fénérive, 7,080 ....S15
Fianarantsoa, 45,790 ....R16
Fort-Dauphin, 12,677 ....R16
Hell-Ville, 9,481 ....R14
Ihosy, 6,578 ....R16
Maevatanana, 5,147 ....R15
Maintirano, 4,594 ....P15
Majunga, 47,654 ....R15
Manakara, 17,567 ....R16
Mananjary, 13,019 ....R16
Manja, 4,671 ....P16
Maroantsetra, 7,184 ....S15
Marovoay, 18,074 ....R15
Moramanga, 10,706 ....R15
Morombe, 6,684 ....P16
Morondava, 15,032 ....P16
Sambava, 6,198 ....S14
Tamatave, 53,173 ....S15
Tananarive (cap.), 332,885 ....R15
Tuléar, 33,842 ....P16
Vangaindrano, 2,665 ....R16
Vohémar, 3,622 ....S14

OTHER FEATURES

Amber (cape) S14
Madagascar (island) R16
Mangoky (river) P16

Mozambique (channel) O16
Nossi-Bé (isl.), 26,462 ....R14
Sainte-Marie (isl.), 9,090 ....S15
Tsiafajavona (mt.) R15
Tsiribihina (river) R15

MALAWI

CITIES and TOWNS

Blantyre, 109,461 ....N15
Fort Johnston, 1,467 ....N14
Karonga, 1,128 ....N13
Lilongwe, 19,425 ....N14
Mzimba, 4,156 ....N14
Nsanje, 1,373 ....O15
Zomba (cap.), 19,666 ....N15

OTHER FEATURES

Mlanje (mt.) O15
Nyasa (lake) N14
Shire (river) N15

MALI

CITIES and TOWNS

Bamako (cap.), 88,500 ....E 9
Bamako, *182,000 ....E 9
Bandiagara, 6,700 ....F 9
Bougouni, 5,500 ....E 9
Djenné, 8,200 ....F 9
Gao, 15,400 ....G 8
Goundam, 10,000 ....F 8
Hombori, 3,600 ....F 8
Kati, 5,900 ....E 9
Kayes, 23,600 ....D 9
Kita, 8,600 ....E 9
Koulikoro, 10,000 ....E 9
Koutiala, 11,300 ....F 9
Mopti, 32,000 ....F 9
Niafunké, 5,100 ....F 8
Nioro, 11,000 ....E 8
San, 14,900 ....F 9
Ségou, 27,200 ....E 9
Sikasso, 21,800 ....E 9
Sokolo, 3,457 ....E 9
Timbuktu, 14,900 ....F 8

OTHER FEATURES

Niger (river) ....E 9
Sahara (desert) ....F 7
Terhazza (ruins) ....F 7

MAURITANIA

CITIES and TOWNS

Aïoun el Atrous, 3,054 ....E 8
Akjoujt, 2,500 ....D 7
Atar, 7,120 ....D 7
Boghé, 2,316 ....D 8
Boutilimit, 3,000 ....D 8
Kaédi, 11,000 ....D 8
Kiffa; 2,600 ....D 8
M'Bout, 1,400 ....D 8
Méderdra, 1,473 ....C 8
Néma, 2,946 ....E 8
Nouadhibou, 11,250 ....C 7
Nouakchott (cap.), 14,500 ....C 8
Rosso, 3,923 ....C 8
Sélibaby, 2,600 ....D 8
Tidjikja, 5,900 ....D 8

OTHER FEATURES

Adrar (region), 50,920 ....D 7
Blanc (cape) ....C 7
Hodh (region), 183,945 ....E 8
Kumbi Saleh (ruins) ....E 8
Lévrier (bay) ....C 7
Sahara (desert) ....E 7
Senegal (river) ....D 8
Tagant (region), 52,703 ....D 8

MAURITIUS

CITIES and TOWNS

Curepipe, 49,000 ....S19
Mahébourg, 13,005 ....T19
Port Louis (cap.), 131,000 ....S19
Quatre Bornes, 28,389 ....S19

OTHER FEATURES

Black River (mt.) S19
Mascarene (isls.), 1,259,000........R20

MOROCCO

CITIES and TOWNS

Agadir, 16,695 ....D 5
Al Hoceima, 11,262 ....F 4
Azemmour, 12,449 ....E 5
Casablanca, 1,320,000 ....E 5
El Jadida, 40,302 ....E 5
Essaouira, 26,392 ....D 5
Fez, 280,000 ....F 5
Figuig, 12,108 ....F 5
Kénitra, 125,000 ....E 5
Khenifra, 18,503 ....F 5
Larache, 30,763 ....E 4
Marrakech, 295,000 ....E 5
Meknès, 235,000 ....E 5
Ouezzane, 26,203 ....E 5
Oujda, 150,000 ....F 5
Port-Lyautey (Kénitra), 125,000..E 5
Rabat (cap.), 227,445 ....E 5
Rabat, *435,000 ....E 5
Safi, 125,000 ....E 5
Salé, 75,799 ....E 5
Settat, 29,617 ....E 5
Sidi Ifni, 12,751 ....D 6
Tangier, 160,000 ....E 4
Taroudant, 17,141 ....E 5
Taza, 31,667 ....F 5
Tétouan, 120,000 ....F 4

OTHER FEATURES

Atlas (mts.) ....E 5
Draa, Wadi (dry river) ....E 6
Juby (cape) ....D 6

MOZAMBIQUE

DISTRICTS

Cabo Delgado, 542,165 ....O14
Gaza, 675,150 ....N16
Inhambane, 583,772 ....N16
Lourenço Marques, 436,897 ....N17
Manica e Sofala, 781,070 ....N15
Moçambique, 1,444,555 ....O14
Niassa, 276,810 ....O14
Tete, 470,100 ....N15
Zambézia, 1,363,619 ....O15

CITIES and TOWNS

António Enes, ‡33,245 ....P15
Beira, ‡58,235 ....O15
Caniçado, ‡30,647 ....N16
Chemba, ‡28,317 ....N15
Chibuto, ‡122,989 ....N16
Chicoa, ‡11,852 ....N15
Homoíne, ‡57,959 ....O16
Ibo, ‡4,394 ....P14
Inhambane, ‡22,016 ....O16
Inharrime, ‡40,721 ....O16
João Belo, ‡48,959 ....O17
Lourenço Marques (cap.), 65,716 ....N17
Lourenço Marques, *177,929 ....N17
Magude, ‡44,183 ....N16
Maniamba, ‡11,708 ....O14
Marromeu, ‡33,096 ....O15
Massinga, ‡80,526 ....O16
Meconta, ‡28,187 ....O14
Memba, ‡51,703 ....P14
Moçambique, ‡12,166 ....P15
Mocímboa da Praia, ‡28,335 ....P14
Mocuba, ‡43,484 ....O15
Moma, ‡64,685 ....O15
Nacala, ‡43,439 ....P14
Nampula, ‡104,648 ....P15
Nova Sofala, ‡16,468 ....O16
Pebane, ‡18,826 ....O15
Porto Amélia, ‡21,005 ....P14
Quelimane, ‡62,717 ....O15
Tete, ‡38,196 ....N15
Vila Cabral, ‡28,701 ....O14
Vila de Manica, ‡14,151 ....N15
Vila de Sena, ‡46,616 ....N15
Vila do Chinde, ‡25,617 ....O15
Vila Fontes, ‡29,434 ....N15
Vila Pery, ‡36,406 ....N15
Zumbo, ‡9,978 ....N15

OTHER FEATURES

Delagoa (bay) N17
Delgado (cape) P14
Mozambique (channel) O16
Namuli (mt.) O15
Nyasa (lake) N14
Ruvuma (river) O14
Save (river) N16
Zambezi (river) N15

NIGER

CITIES and TOWNS

Agadès, 7,100 ....H 8
Birni-N'Konni, 7,900 ....H 9
Dosso, 3,500 ....G 9
Gaya, 4,200 ....G 9
Gouré, 2,100 ....J 9
Maradi, 22,400 ....H 9
N'Guigmi, 4,000 ....J 9
Niamey (cap.), 42,000 ....G 9
Niamey, *122,672 ....G 9
Say, 2,700 ....G 9
Tahoua, 18,100 ....H 9
Zinder, 24,000 ....H 9

OTHER FEATURES

Air (mt.) ....H 8
Djado (plateau) ....J 7
Niger (river) ....G 9
Sahara (desert) ....J 7
Ténéré (desert) ....J 8

NIGERIA

CITIES and TOWNS

Aba, 151,923 ....H10
Abeokuta, 217,201 ....G10
Bauchi ....H 9
Benin City, 116,774 ....H10
Calabar, 46,705 ....H10
Enugu, 160,567 ....H10
Gusau, 40,202 ....H 9
Ibadan, 727,565 ....G10
Ife, 150,818 ....G10
Ilorin, 241,849 ....G10
Jos, 38,527 ....H 9
Kaduna, 173,849 ....H 9
Kano, 342,610 ....H 9
Katsina, 52,672 ....H 9
Lagos (cap.), 841,749 ....G10
Lokoja, 13,103 ....H10
Maiduguri, 162,316 ....J 9
Nguru, 23,084 ....J 9
Ogbomosho, 370,963 ....H10
Okene, 32,602 ....H10
Onitsha, 189,067 ....H10
Oshogbo, 242,336 ....H10
Oyo, 130,290 ....G10
Port Harcourt, 208,237 ....H11
Sokoto, 47,643 ....H 9
Warri, 19,526 ....H10
Zaria, 192,706 ....H 9

OTHER FEATURES

Adamawa (region) J10
Benin (bight) G11
Benue (river) H10
Gongola (river) ....J 9
Guinea (gulf) F11
Kaduna (river) ....H 9
Niger (river) ....G 9
Sudan (region) ....H 9

PORTUGUESE GUINEA

CITIES and TOWNS

Bissau (cap.), 20,000 ....D 9
Bolama, ‡4,642 ....D 9

OTHER FEATURES

Bijagós (isls.), 9,332 ....C 9

RÉUNION

CITIES and TOWNS

Le Port, 13,281 ....P20
Saint-Benoït, 4,095 ....R20
Saint-Denis (cap.), 37,047 ....P19
Saint-Denis, *65,614 ....P19
Saint-Joseph, 5,969 ....P20
Saint-Louis, 7,753 ....P20
Saint-Paul, 5,624 ....P20
Saint-Pierre, 8,752 ....P20

OTHER FEATURES

Bassas da India (isls.) O16
Europa (isl.) P16
Glorioso (isls.) R14
Juan de Nova (isl.) P15
Mascarene (isls.), 1,259,000 ....R20
Piton des Neiges (mt.) P20

RHODESIA

CITIES and TOWNS

Bulawayo, †270,000 ....M16
Dett, 2,180 ....M15
Fort Victoria, †12,000 ....N15
Gatooma, †23,000 ....M15
Gwaai, ‡2,160 ....M15
Gwanda, 5,880 ....M16
Gwelo, †50,000 ....M15
Hartley, 7,170 ....M15
Kariba, 5,950 ....M15
Matopos, ‡9,390 ....M16
Rusape, 3,960 ....N15
Salisbury (cap.), 385,530 ....N15
Salisbury, ‡423,000 ....N15
Selukwe, 3,030 ....M15
Sinoia, ‡14,000 ....M15
Umtali, ‡50,000 ....N15
Wankie, ‡21,000 ....M15
West Nicholson, 2,640 ....N16

OTHER FEATURES

Kariba (lake) M15
Limpopo (river) N16
Lundi (river) N16
Sabi (river) N16
Victoria (falls) M15
Zimbabwe (ruins) N16

RWANDA

CITIES and TOWNS

Kigali (cap.), 24,000 ....N12

SÃO TOMÉ E PRÍNCIPE

CITIES and TOWNS

Santo António, ‡4,605 ....H11
São Tomé (cap.), 7,364 ....H11

OTHER FEATURES

Príncipe (isl.), 4,605 ....H11
São Tomé (island), 58,880 ....H11

SENEGAL

CITIES and TOWNS

Bakel, 2,500 ....D 9
Dagana, 4,000 ....D 8
Dakar (cap.), 550,000 ....C 9
Dakar, *661,000 ....C 9
Diourbel, 30,000 ....C 9
Kaolack, 70,000 ....C 9
Kédougou, 1,938 ....D 9
Louga, 15,000 ....C 8
Matam, 5,000 ....D 8
M'Bour, 15,000 ....C 9
Nioro-du-Rip, 2,788 ....D 9
Podor, 5,000 ....D 8
Rufisque, 50,000 ....C 9
Saint-Louis, 50,000 ....C 8
Tambacounda, 10,027 ....D 9
Thiès, 70,000 ....C 9
Ziguinchor, 30,000 ....C 9

OTHER FEATURES

Senegal (river) ....D 8
Verde (cape) ....C 9

SEYCHELLES

PHYSICAL FEATURES

Assumption (island), 31 ....R14
Astove (isl.), 50 ....R14
Cerf (isl.), 34 ....S13
Cosmoledo (islands), 57 ....R13
Providence (isl.), 70 ....S13
Saint Pierre (island), 45 ....S13

SIERRA LEONE

CITIES and TOWNS

Bo, 26,613 ....D10
Bonthe, 6,230 ....D10
Freetown (cap.), 170,600 ....D10
Kabala, 4,610 ....D10
Makeni, 12,304 ....D10
Moyamba, 4,564 ....D10
Pendembu, 2,696 ....D10

OTHER FEATURES

Sherbro (isl.), 6,894 ....D10

SOMALIA

CITIES and TOWNS

Afmadu, ◉2,580 ....P11
Alula, ◉6,063 ....S 9
Baidoa, ◉14,962 ....P11
Barawa (Brava), ◉6,168 ....P11
Bardera, ◉7,874 ....P11
Belet Uen, ◉11,426 ....P11
Bender Beila, ◉6,084 ....S10
Berbera, ◉12,219 ....R 9
Borama, ◉3,244 ....P 9
Bosaso, ◉7,560 ....R 9
Brava, ◉6,168 ....P11
Bulo Burti, ◉5,247 ....P11
Bur Acaba, ◉10,924 ....P11
Burao, ◉12,617 ....R10
Candala, ◉3,213 ....S 9
Dante (Hafun) ....S 9
Eil, ◉2,234 ....S10
El Bur, ◉3,224 ....R11
Erigavo, ◉4,279 ....R 9
Galkayu, ◉9,477 ....R10
Gardo, ◉4,076 ....R10
Hafun ....S 9
Harghessa, ◉40,254 ....P10
Hodur, ◉3,137 ....P11
Hordio ....S 9
Jamama, ◉22,030 ....P12
Jelib, ◉3,232 ....P11
Johar, ◉13,156 ....R11
Kismayu, ◉17,872 ....P12
Las Anod, ◉2,441 ....R10
Lugh, ◉3,768 ....P11
Marek R11
Merka, ◉56,385 ....R11
Mogadishu (cap.), 172,677 ....R11
Obbia, ◉2,106 ....R10
Zeila, ◉1,226 ....P 9

OTHER FEATURES

Benadir (region), 392,189 ....P11
Chiamboni (cape) P12
Guardafui (cape) ....S 9
Hafun (cape) ....S 9
Juba (river) P11
Mijirtein (region), 82,710 ....R10
Mudugh (region), 141,197 ....R10
Webi Shebeli (river) R11

SOUTH AFRICA

PROVINCES

Cape of Good Hope, 3,936,226 ....
Natal, 2,979,920 ....
Orange Free State, 1,386,547 ....
Transkei, 1,439,195 ....
Transvaal, 6,273,477 ....

CITIES and TOWNS

Alexander Bay, 2,073 ....
Aliwal North, 10,700 ....
Barkly East, 3,650 ....
Beaufort West, 16,300 ....
Bellville, 42,500 ....
Benoni, 126,700 ....
Bethlehem, 31,400 ....
Bloemfontein, †147,000 ....
Brandvlei, 1,419 ....
Britstown, 2,834 ....
Caledon, 4,300 ....
Calvinia, 6,700 ....
Cape Town (cap.), 625,000 ....
Cape Town, †817,000 ....
Carnarvon, 4,800 ....
Ceres, 6,200 ....
Clanwilliam, 2,216 ....
Cradock, 21,300 ....
De Aar, 16,600 ....
Durban, †690,000 ....
Durbanville, 3,057 ....
East London, 134,100 ....
Franschhoek, 1,534 ....
George, 19,600 ....
Germiston, †222,000 ....
Goodwood, 82,600 ....
Graaff-Reinet, 17,700 ....
Grabouw, 5,200 ....
Grahamstown, 37,600 ....
Griquatown, 2,526 ....
Hawston, 1,211 ....
Hermanus, 5,200 ....
Hopetown, 2,631 ....
Johannesburg, †1,305,000 ....
Kimberley, 95,200 ....
King William's Town, 15,000 ....
Knysna, 13,900 ....
Kraaifontein, 4,800 ....
Kroonstad, 50,700 ....
Ladysmith, 27,900 ....
Louis Trichardt, 14,800 ....
Lydenburg, 8,000 ....
Maclear, 3,550 ....
Mafeking, 6,200 ....
Malmesbury, 8,800 ....
Messina, 12,500 ....
Middelburg, Cape of Good Hope, 11,700 ....
Middelburg, Transvaal, 25,100........
Moorreesburg, 4,000 ....
Mossel Bay, 15,600 ....
Muizenberg, 10,000 ....
Newcastle, 16,900 ....
Nylstroom, 6,700 ....
Okiep, 2,973 ....
Oudtshoorn, 25,800 ....
Paarl, 48,800 ....
Parow, 48,100 ....
Pietermaritzburg, †128,598 ....
Pietersburg, 35,700 ....
Pinelands, 14,100 ....
Port Elizabeth, †448,000 ....
Port Nolloth, 2,624 ....
Port Shepstone, 4,200 ....
Potchefstroom, 51,800 ....M
Potgietersrus, 12,700 ....M
Pretoria (cap.), 479,700 ....M
Prieska, 7,600 ....
Prince Albert, 4,500 ....
Queenstown, 42,200 ....M
Riversdale, 5,100 L
Saldanha, 2,243 ....
Simonstown, 8,900 ....
Somerset West, 9,500 ....
Springbok, 4,100 ....
Stellenbosch, 29,000 ....
Strand, 21,200 ....
Swellendam, 4,900 ....
Uitenhage, 63,400 ....M
Umtata, 17,200 ....M
Upington, 28,000 L
Vanrhynsdorp, 2,133 ....
Victoria West, 4,100 L
Villiersdorp, 1,590 ....H
Vishoek, 7,500 ....
Vryburg, 17,100 ....
Walvis Bay, 12,234 ....
Warrenton, 8,600 ....M
Wellington, 13,200 ....H
Willowmore, 4,200 L
Worcester, 37,000 ....

OTHER FEATURES

Agulhas (cape) ....K
Algoa (bay) ....M
Bot (river) ....H
Breede (river) ....H
British Bechuanaland (reg.), 271,517 L
Cape (peninsula) ....F
Cape (point) ....F
Diep (river) ....G
False (bay) ....G
Good Hope (cape) ....F
Great Berg (river) ....H
Hangklip (cape) ....G
Hex River (mts.) ....J
Hoeks (river) ....H
Kasteel (mts.) ....G
Limpopo (river) ....N
Maclear (cape) ....F
Orange (river) ....K
Robben (isl.) ....F
Saint Helena (bay) ....K
Sandown (bay) ....G
Seal (isl.) ....G
Slangkop (point) ....F
Sneeuwkop (mt.) ....H
Table (bay) ....F
Table (mt.) ....F
Vaal (river) ....M
Walker (bay) ....H
Zonderend (mts.) ....J
Zonderend (river) ....H
Zululand (district), 570,160 ....N

SOUTH-WEST AFRICA

CITIES and TOWNS

Bethanie, 1,142 ....K1
Gobabis, 4,326 ....K1
Grootfontein, 1,919 ....K1
Karasburg, 2,234 ....K1
Karibib, 1,398 ....K1

anshoop, 8,064 ....K17
z, 3,633 ....J17
öhe, 1,048 ....K16
tal, 3,498 ....K16
dja, 2,977 ....K16
u, 2,698 ....K16
nund, 3,125 ....K17
1,303 ....K15
ongo, 6,368 ....K16
2,963 ....K15
th, 2,973 ....K16
omund, 4,701 ....J16
, 7,823 ....K15
, 4,278 ....K16
oek (cap.), 36,050 ....K16

OTHER FEATURES

Strip (reg.), 15,871 ....L15
(river) J15
aland (reg.) K16
(salt pan) J15
river) K17
cape) J15
Namaland (reg.) K17
veld (mts.) J15
(desert) J15
ngo (river) K15
(river) K17
oland (reg.), 203,862 ....K15

SPANISH SAHARA

CITIES and TOWNS

iún, 10,000 ....D 6
a, 1,000 ....D 6
Cisneros, 4,000 ....C 7

OTHER FEATURES

s (cape) ....C 7
or (cape) ....C 6
Oro (region) ....D 7
a el Hamra (region) ....D 6
(well) ....D 7

SUDAN

PROVINCES

el Ghazal, 1,238,779 ....M10
Nile, 2,724,968 ....N 9
r, 1,467,688 ....L 9
toria, 1,129,388 ....N11
ala, 1,413,069 ....O 8
toum, 749,932 ....N 8
ofan, 2,022,201 ....M 9
hern, 982,046 ....M 7
r Nile, 1,110,769 ....N10

CITIES and TOWNS

Hamed ....N 8
ra, 36,000 ....N 8
, 4,885 ....N 9
er, 10,977 ....N 8
Zubeir M10
ola, 3,350 ....M 8
Damer, 5,458 ....N 8
Dueim, 12,319 ....N 9
asher, 26,161 ....M 9
beid, 53,000 ....N 9
Nahud, 16,499 ....M 9
Roseires, 3,927 ....O 9
aka ....N 9
oda (Kodok), 9,100 ....N10
aref, 17,537 ....O 9
eina, 11,817 ....L 9
, 10,660 ....N10
ugli, 4,716 ....M 9
ma, 5,989 ....N 8
sala, 40,000 ....O 8
rtoum (cap.), 194,000 ....N 8
rtoum North, 40,000 ....N 8
ok, 9,100 ....N10
i, 22,688 ....N 9
akal, 9,680 ....N10
idi, 839 ....M11
owe, 1,620 ....N 8
hra' er Req M10
galla N10
lad, 3,735 ....M 9
ammad Qol ....O 7
ule N11
la, 12,278 ....L 9
urman, 206,000 ....N 8
Sudan, 110,000 ....O 8
had, 1,683 ....N 9
f N11
k ....N 9
nar, 8,093 ....N 9
ndi, 11,031 ....N 8
ga, 9,436 ....N 9
kat, 5,175 ....O 8
iri, 1,804 ....M 9
kin, 4,228 ....O 8
odi, 2,736 ....N 9
kar, 16,802 ....O 8
j, 2,071 ....M10
kitat ....O 8
m Keddada, 2,410 ....M 9
d Medani, 48,000 ....N 9
u, 8,009 ....M10
, 739 ....N11

OTHER FEATURES

Shagara, Ras (cape) ....O 7
oara (river) ....O 8
r el 'Arab (river) M10
e Nile (river) ....N 9

Cataract, 3rd (rapids) ....M 8
Cataract, 4th (rapids) ....N 8
Cataract, 5th (rapids) ....N 8
Cataract, 6th (rapids) ....N 8
Gezira, El (region) ....N 9
Lol (dry river) M10
Marra, Jebel (mt.) ....L 9
Meroe (ruins) ....N 8
Naqa (ruins) ....N 8
Nasser (lake) ....N 7
Nile (river) ....N 8
Nubian (desert) ....N 7
Nuri (ruins) ....N 8
Sahara (desert) ....M 7
Sobat (river) N10
Sudan (region) ....M 9
Sudd (swamp) N10
White Nile (river) N10
Yei (river) N10

SWAZILAND

CITIES and TOWNS

Mbabane (cap.), 13,803 ....N17

TANZANIA

CITIES and TOWNS

Arusha, 32,452 ....O12
Bagamoyo, 5,112 ....O13
Biharamulo, 1,011 ....N12
Bukoba, 8,141 ....N12
Chake Chake, 4,862 ....P13
Chunya, 2,398 ....N13
Dar es Salaam (cap.), 272,821....P13
Dodoma, 23,559 ....O13
Geita, 3,066 ....N12
Iringa, 21,746 ....O13
Kasanga, ‡10,462 ....N13
Kigoma-Ujiji, 21,369 ....N12
Kilosa, 4,458 ....O13
Kilwa Kivinje, 2,790 ....P13
Kondoa, 4,514 ....O12
Kongwa, ‡27,411 ....O13
Lindi, 13,352 ....O14
Liwale, ‡22,205 ....O13
Lushoto, 1,803 ....O12
Mahenge, ‡32,047 ....O13
Manyoni, 14,362 ....N13
Mbeya, 12,479 ....N13
Mombo, ‡29,782 ....O13
Morogoro, 25,262 ....O13
Moshi, 26,864 ....O12
Mtwara-Mikindani, 20,413....P14
Musoma, 15,412 ....N12
Mwadui, 7,383 ....N12
Mwanza, 34,861 ....N12
Mwaya, ‡15,940 ....N13
Nachingwea, 3,751 ....O14
Pangani, 2,955 ....O13
Shinyanga, 5,135 ....N12
Singida, 9,478 ....N12
Songea, 5,430 ....O14
Tabora, 21,012 ....N12
Tanga, 61,058 ....O12
Zanzibar, 68,490 ....P13
Zanzibar, *95,047 ....P13

OTHER FEATURES

Eyasi (lake) O12
Great Ruaha (river) O13
Juani (island), 696 ....P13
Kilimanjaro (mt.) O12
Mafia (island), 15,459 ....P13
Natron (lake) O12
Nyasa (lake) N14
Pangani (river) O12
Bukoba, 8,141 ....N12
Chake Chake, 4,862 ....P13
Chunya, 2,398 ....N13
Dar es Salaam (cap.), 272,821....P13
Dodoma, 23,559 ....O13
Geita, 3,066 ....N12
Iringa, 21,746 ....O13
Kasanga, ‡10,462 ....N13
Kigoma-Ujiji, 21,369 ....N12
Kilosa, 4,458 ....O13
Kilwa Kivinje, 2,790 ....P13
Kondoa, 4,514 ....O12
Kongwa, ‡27,411 ....O13
Lindi, 13,352 ....O14
Liwale, ‡22,205 ....O13
Pemba (island), 164,321 ....P13
Rufiji (river) O13
Rukwa (lake) N13
Ruvuma (river) O14
Tanganyika (lake) N13
Victoria (lake) N12
Zanzibar (island), 190,494 ....P13

TOGO

CITIES and TOWNS

Anécho, †11,040 ....G10
Atakpamé, †18,008 ....G10
Lomé (cap.), 90,600 ....G10
Lomé, *149,879 ....G10
Palimé, †20,331 ....G10
Sansanné-Mango ....G 9
Sokodé, †30,271 ....G10

TUNISIA

CITIES and TOWNS

Bizerte, 51,700 ....J 4
Gabès, 32,300 ....H 5
Gafsa, 32,400 ....H 5
Kairouan, 46,200 ....H 4
Mahdia, 10,000 ....J 4
Médenine, 8,000 ....J 5
Menzel Bourguiba, 36,700 ....H 4
Moknine, 18,500 ....J 4
Nefta, 15,000 ....H 5
Sfax, 65,000 ....J 5
Sousse, 48,200 ....J 4
Tozeur, 11,820 ....H 5
Tunis (cap.), 662,000 ....J 4
Tunis, *800,000 ....J 4

OTHER FEATURES

Bon (cape) ....J 4
Djerba (isl.), 62,445 ....J 5
Gabès (gulf) ....J 5
Hammamet (gulf) ....J 4
Kerkennah (islands), 13,704 ....J 5
Tunis (gulf) ....J 4

UGANDA

CITIES and TOWNS

Arua, 4,645 ....N11
Butiaba, 1,216 ....N11
Entebbe, 10,941 ....N12
Fort Portal, 8,317 ....N11
Jinja, 29,741 ....N11
Kabale, 10,919 ....N12
Kampala (cap.), 330,000 ....N11
Masindi, 1,571 ....N11
Mbarara, 3,844 ....N12
Soroti, 6,645 ....N11

OTHER FEATURES

Kioga (lake) N11
Ruwenzori (mt.) N11
Victoria (lake) N12

UNITED ARAB REPUBLIC (EGYPT)

CITIES and TOWNS

Akhmim, 41,580 ....N 6
Alexandria, 1,803,900 ....M 5
Aswân, 127,700 ....N 7
Asyût, 154,100 ....N 6
Beni Suef, 78,829 ....N 6
Cairo (cap.), 4,219,853 ....N 5
Damietta, 71,780 ....N 5
Dumyât (Damietta), 71,780 ....N 5
El 'Alamein, 593 ....M 5
El Faiyûm, 133,800 ....M 6
El Iskandariya (Alexandria), 1,803,900 ....M 5
El Khârga, 9,277 ....N 6
El Minya, 112,800 ....M 6
El Qâhira (Cairo) (cap.), 4,219,853 ....N 5
El Qasr, 1,789 ....M 6
El Quseir, 4,336 ....O 6
Idfu, 25,105 ....N 7
Ismailia, 156,500 ....N 5
Luxor, 35,074 ....N 6
Manfalût, 28,540 ....M 6
Matruh, 9,254 ....M 5
Port Said, 283,400 ....N 5
Qena, 57,417 ....N 6
Salûm, 1,348 ....M 5
Sidi Barrani, 1,583 ....M 5
Sohâg, 61,944 ....N 6
Suez, 264,500 ....N 6
Tanta, 230,400 ....N 5

OTHER FEATURES

'Aqaba (gulf) ....O 6
Arabian (desert) ....N 6
Aswân High (dam) ....N 7
Bânâs, Ras (cape) ....O 7
Farâfra (oasis), 747 ....M 6
Katherina, Jebel (mt.) ....O 6
Khârga (oasis), 12,346 ....N 6
Libyan (desert) ....M 6
Nasser (lake) ....N 7
Nile (river) ....N 7
Qattâra (depression) ....M 5
Sahara (desert) ....M 7
Sinai (peninsula), 49,769 ....N 6
Siwa (oasis), 3,839 ....M 6
Suez (canal) ....N 5
Suez (gulf) ....N 6

UPPER VOLTA

CITIES and TOWNS

Bobo-Dioulasso, 56,100 ....F 9
Dédougou, 3,680 ....F 9
Dori, 3,500 ....G 9
Fada-N'Gourma, 4,867 ....G 9
Gaoua, 5,907 ....F 9
Kaya, 10,304 ....F 9
Koudougou, 7,940 ....F 9
Ouagadougou (cap.), 77,500 ....F 9
Ouagadougou, *100,000 ....F 9
Ouanigouya, 12,960 ....F 9
Tenkodogo, 6,561 ....G 9

OTHER FEATURES

Black Volta (river) ....F 9
Red Volta (river) ....F 9
Sudan (region) ....F 9
White Volta (river) ....F 9

ZAMBIA

CITIES and TOWNS

Balovale, 2,260 ....L14
Chipata, †13,300 ....N14
Choma, †11,300 ....M15
Kabwe, †67,200 ....M14
Kalomo, 2,560 ....M15
Kasama, †8,900 ....N13
Lealui L15
Livingstone, †43,000 ....L15
Lusaka (cap.), †238,200 ....M15
Mankoya, 1,600 ....L14
Mansa, †5,700 ....M14
Mazabuka, †9,400 ....M15
Mbala, †5,200 ....N13
Mongu, †10,700 ....L15
Monze, †4,300 ....M15
Ndola, †150,800 ....M14
Nkana, 54,500 ....M14
Senanga, 1,500 ....L15
Serenje, 1,650 ....N14
Solwezi, 1,930 ....M14

OTHER FEATURES

Bangweulu (lake) N14
Barotseland (region), 417,000....L15
Kafue (river) M15
Kariba (lake) M15
Luangwa (river) N14
Mweru (lake) M13
Tanganyika (lake) N13
Victoria (falls) M15
Zambezi (river) M15

*City and suburbs.
†Population of urban area.
‡Population of sub-division.
◉Population of municipality.

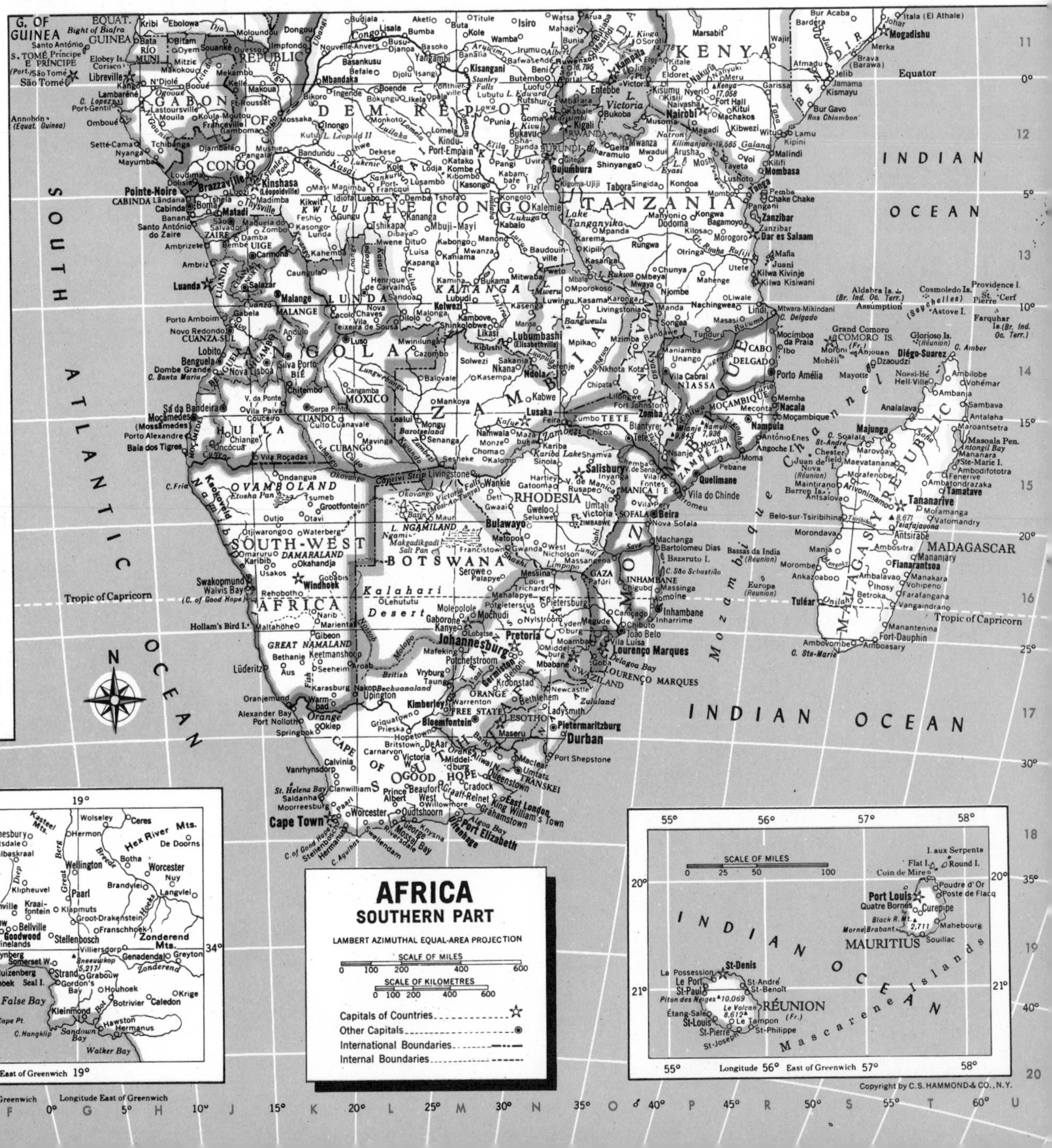

AFRICA
SOUTHERN PART
LAMBERT AZIMUTHAL EQUAL-AREA PROJECTION
SCALE OF MILES
0 100 200 400 600
SCALE OF KILOMETRES
0 100 200 400 600
Capitals of Countries
Other Capitals
International Boundaries
Internal Boundaries
SOUTH ATLANTIC OCEAN
INDIAN OCEAN
Tropic of Capricorn
Equator
Mozambique Channel
DEM. REP. OF THE CONGO
CONGO
GABON
ANGOLA
ZAMBIA
TANZANIA
KENYA
UGANDA
RWANDA
BURUNDI
MALAWI
MOZAMBIQUE
RHODESIA
BOTSWANA
SOUTH-WEST AFRICA
MALAGASY REPUBLIC
MADAGASCAR
LESOTHO
SWAZILAND
TRANSKEI
MAURITIUS
RÉUNION
Copyright by C.S. HAMMOND & CO., N.Y.
Longitude West of Greenwich
Longitude East of Greenwich
SCALE OF MILES
0 5 10 20 30
SOUTH ATLANTIC OCEAN
Cape Town
Table Mtn. 3,549
Robben I.
False Bay
Cape Peninsula
Cape of Good Hope
Stellenbosch
Paarl
Wellington
Worcester
Hex River Mts.
Longitude East of Greenwich 19°

ASIA

LAMBERT AZIMUTHAL EQUAL-AREA PROJECTION

SCALE OF MILES

0 150 300   600   900   1200

SCALE OF KILOMETRES

0   300   600   900   1200

Capitals of Countries....☆   Canals ------

International Boundaries -------

Copyright by C.S. HAMMOND & CO., N.Y.

POPULATION DISTRIBUTION

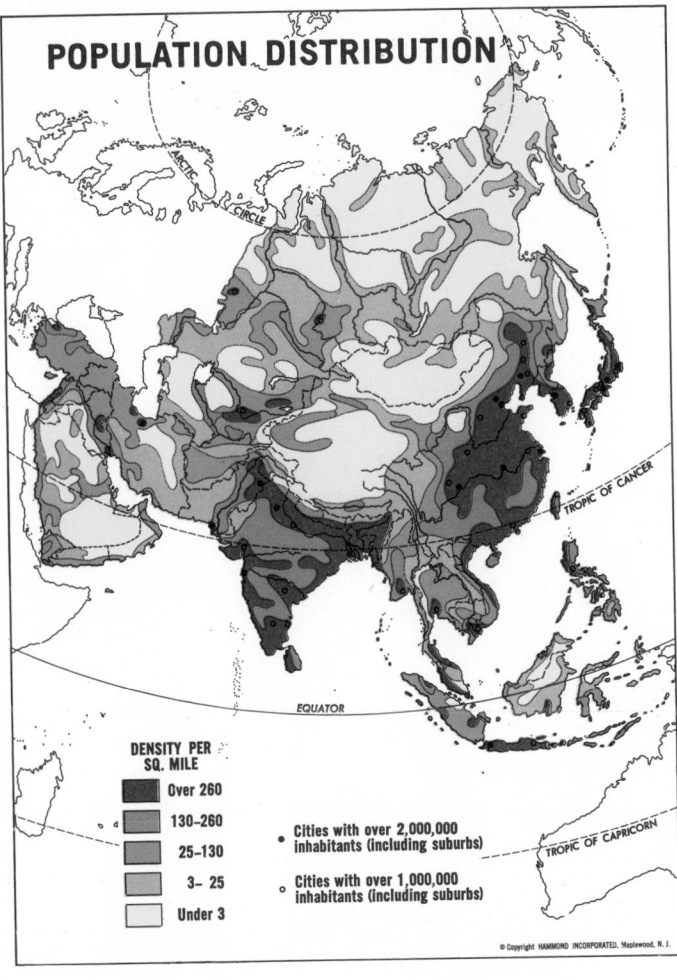

AREA 17,032,000 sq. mi.
POPULATION 2,043,997,000
LARGEST CITY Tokyo
HIGHEST POINT Mt. Everest 29,028 ft.
LOWEST POINT Dead Sea -1,290 ft.

VEGETATION

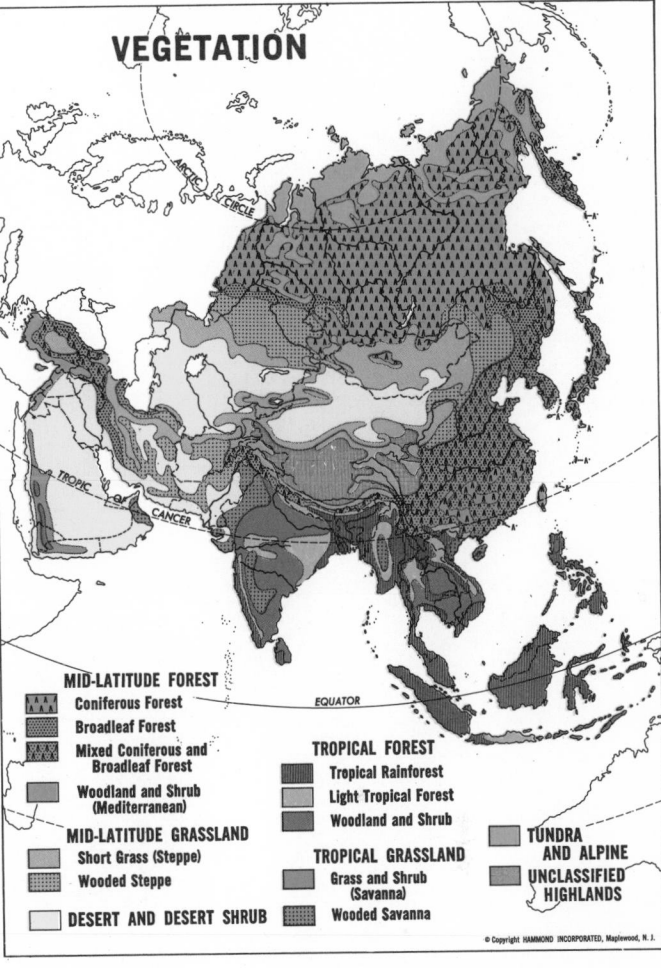

DENSITY PER SQ. MILE
- Over 260
- 130–260
- 25–130
- 3–25
- Under 3

• Cities with over 2,000,000 inhabitants (including suburbs)
○ Cities with over 1,000,000 inhabitants (including suburbs)

© Copyright HAMMOND INCORPORATED, Maplewood, N. J.

MID-LATITUDE FOREST
- Coniferous Forest
- Broadleaf Forest
- Mixed Coniferous and Broadleaf Forest
- Woodland and Shrub (Mediterranean)

MID-LATITUDE GRASSLAND
- Short Grass (Steppe)
- Wooded Steppe

DESERT AND DESERT SHRUB

TROPICAL FOREST
- Tropical Rainforest
- Light Tropical Forest
- Woodland and Shrub

TROPICAL GRASSLAND
- Grass and Shrub (Savanna)
- Wooded Savanna

TUNDRA AND ALPINE

UNCLASSIFIED HIGHLANDS

© Copyright HAMMOND INCORPORATED, Maplewood, N. J.

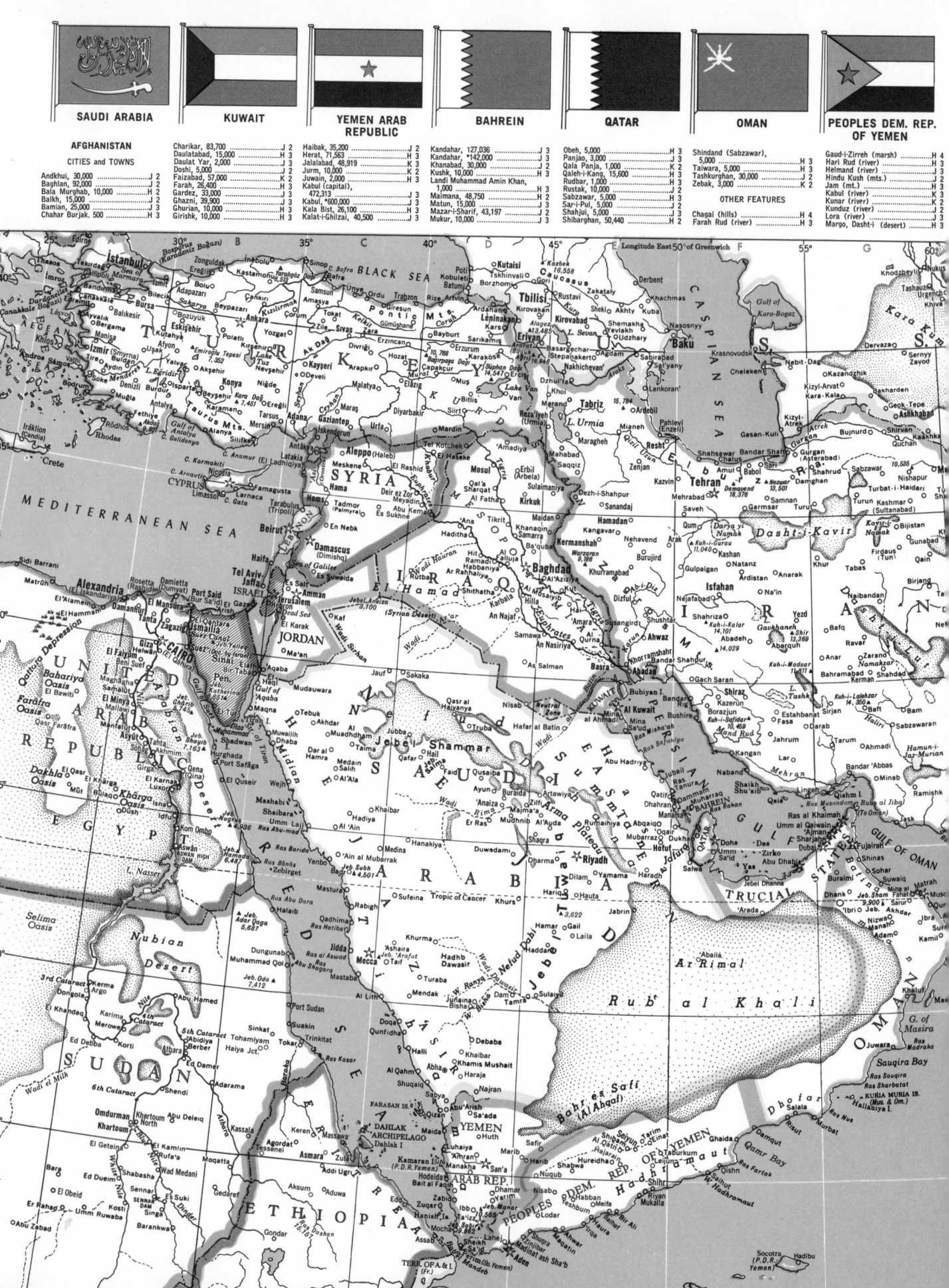

| SAUDI ARABIA | KUWAIT | YEMEN ARAB REPUBLIC | BAHREIN | QATAR | OMAN | PEOPLES DEM. REP. OF YEMEN |

AFGHANISTAN

CITIES and TOWNS

Andkhui, 30,000 .... J 2
Baghlan, 92,000 .... J 2
Bala Murghab, 10,000 .... H 2
Balkh, 15,000 .... J 2
Bamian, 25,000 .... J 3
Chahar Burjak, 500 .... H 3

Charikar, 83,700 .... J 2
Daulatabad, 15,000 .... H 3
Daulat Yar, 2,000 .... J 3
Doshi, 5,000 .... J 2
Faizabad, 57,000 .... K 2
Farah, 26,400 .... H 3
Gardez, 33,000 .... J 3
Ghazni, 39,900 .... J 3
Ghurian, 10,000 .... H 3
Girishk, 10,000 .... H 3

Haibak, 35,200 .... J 2
Herat, 71,563 .... H 3
Jalalabad, 48,919 .... K 3
Jurm, 10,000 .... K 2
Juwain, 2,000 .... H 3
Kabul (capital),
 472,313 .... J 3
Kabul, *600,000 .... J 3
Kala Bist, 26,100 .... H 3
Kalat-i-Ghilzai, 40,500 ...... J 3

Kandahar, 127,036 .... H 3
Kandahar, *142,000 .... J 3
Khanabad, 30,000 .... J 2
Kushk, 10,000 .... H 3
Landi Muhammad Amin Khan,
 1,000 .... H 3
Maimana, 48,750 .... H 2
Matun, 15,000 .... J 3
Mazar-i-Sharif, 43,197 ...... J 2
Mukur, 10,000 .... J 3

Obeh, 5,000 .... H 3
Panjao, 3,000 .... H 3
Qala Panja, 1,000 .... K 2
Qaleh-i-Kang, 15,600 .... H 3
Rudbar, 1,000 .... H 3
Rustak, 10,000 .... J 2
Sabzawar, 5,000 .... H 3
Sar-i-Pul, 5,000 .... J 2
Shahjui, 5,000 .... J 3
Shibarghan, 50,440 .... J 2

Shindand (Sabzawar),
 5,000 .... H 3
Taiwara, 5,000 .... H 3
Tashkurghan, 30,000 .... J 2
Zebak, 3,000 .... K 2

OTHER FEATURES

Chagai (hills) .... H 4
Farah Rud (river) .... H 3

Gaud-i-Zirreh (marsh) .... H 3
Hari Rud (river) .... H 3
Helmand (river) .... H 3
Hindu Kush (mts.) .... J 2
Jam (mt.) .... H 3
Kabul (river) .... K 3
Kunar (river) .... K 2
Kunduz (river) .... J 2
Lora (river) .... H 3
Margo, Dasht-i (desert) ..... H 3

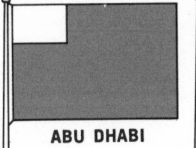

ABU DHABI

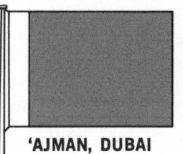

'AJMAN, DUBAI

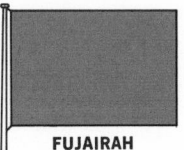

FUJAIRAH

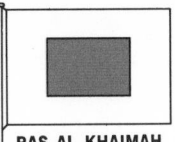

RAS AL KHAIMAH SHARJAH

UMM AL QAIWAIN

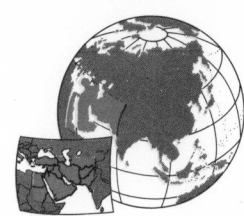

Murghab (river) ....H 2
Namaksar (salt lake) ......H 3
Paropamisus (mts.) ....H 3
Pyandzh (river) ....K 2
Registan (desert) ....H 3

BAHREIN
CITIES and TOWNS

Manama (capital),
  79,098 ....F 4
Muharraq, 34,430 ....F 4

IRAN
CITIES and TOWNS

Abadan, 272,962 ....E 3
Abadeh, 16,000 ....F 3

Abarquh, 8,000 ....F 3
Ahwaz, 206,375 ....E 3
Amul, 40,076 ....F 3
Anarak, 2,038 ....F 3
Arak, 71,925 ....E 3
Ardebil, 83,596 ....E 2
Ardistan, 6,645 ....F 3
Asterabad (Gurgan),
  51,181 ....F 2
Babol, 49,973 ....F 2

Bafq, 5,000 ....G 3
Baft, 6,000 ....G 4
Bahramabad, 21,000 ......G 3
Bam, 22,000 ....G 4
Bandar 'Abbas, 34,627 ...G 4
Bandar Shah, 13,000 .....F 2
Bandar Shahpur, 6,000 ...E 3
Barfrush (Babol),
  49,973 ....F 2
Birjand, 25,854 ....G 3

Borazjun, 20,000 ....F 4
Bujnurd, 31,248 ....G 2
Burujird, 71,476 ....E 3
Bushire, 26,032 ....F 4
Chalus, 15,000 ....F 2
Damghan, 13,000 ....F 2
Darab, 13,000 ....G 4
Dizful, 84,499 ....E 3
Duzdab (Zahidan),
  40,000 ....H 4

(continued on following page)

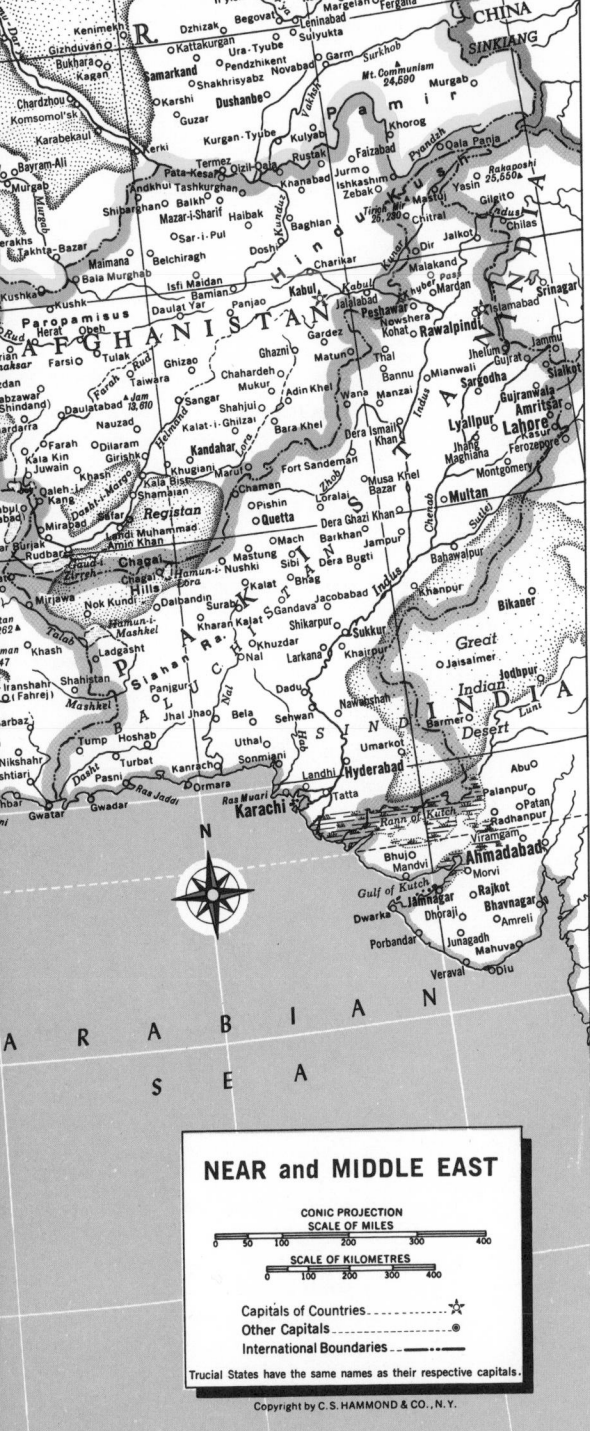

SAUDI ARABIA
AREA 920,000 sq. mi.
POPULATION 7,200,000
CAPITALS Riyadh, Mecca
MONETARY UNIT riyal
MAJOR LANGUAGE Arabic
MAJOR RELIGION Islam

YEMEN ARAB REPUBLIC
AREA 75,000 sq. mi.
POPULATION 5,000,000
CAPITALS San'a, Ta'izz
MONETARY UNIT bakcha
MAJOR LANGUAGE Arabic
MAJOR RELIGION Islam

BAHREIN
AREA 231 sq. mi.
POPULATION 207,000
CAPITAL Manama
MONETARY UNIT Indian rupee
MAJOR LANGUAGE Arabic
MAJOR RELIGION Islam

TRUCIAL STATES
AREA 32,278 sq. mi.
POPULATION 179,126
CAPITALS (several)
MONETARY UNIT Indian rupee
MAJOR LANGUAGE Arabic
MAJOR RELIGION Islam

KUWAIT
AREA 8,000 sq. mi.
POPULATION 733,196
CAPITAL Al Kuwait
MONETARY UNIT Kuwaiti dinar
MAJOR LANGUAGE Arabic
MAJOR RELIGION Islam

PEOPLES DEMOCRATIC REPUBLIC OF YEMEN
AREA 111,075 sq. mi.
POPULATION 1,220,000
CAPITALS Aden, Madinat ash Sha'b
MONETARY UNIT East African shilling
MAJOR LANGUAGE Arabic
MAJOR RELIGION Islam

QATAR
AREA 8,500 sq. mi.
POPULATION 100,000
CAPITAL Doha
MONETARY UNIT Indian rupee
MAJOR LANGUAGE Arabic
MAJOR RELIGION Islam

OMAN
AREA 82,000 sq. mi.
POPULATION 565,000
CAPITAL Muscat
MONETARY UNIT rupee, Maria Theresa dollar
MAJOR LANGUAGE Arabic
MAJOR RELIGION Islam

NEAR and MIDDLE EAST
CONIC PROJECTION
SCALE OF MILES
50   100   200   300   400
SCALE OF KILOMETRES
100   200   300   400

Capitals of Countries ....☆
Other Capitals ....◉
International Boundaries ....

Trucial States have the same names as their respective capitals.

Copyright by C.S. HAMMOND & CO., N.Y.

Topography

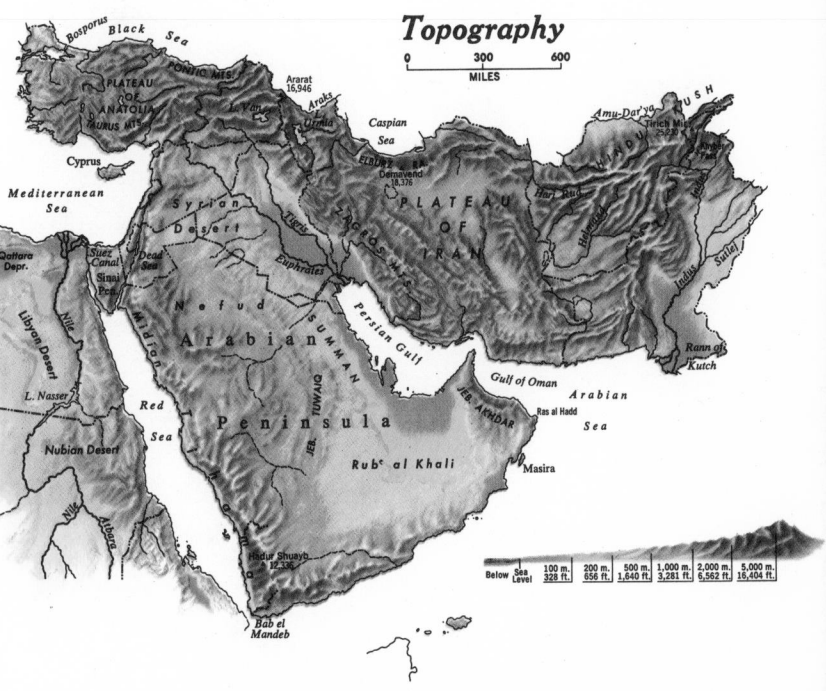

IRAN (continued)

Enzeli (Pahlevi), 41,785 .....E 2
Estahbanat, 18,187 .....F 4
Fahrej (Iranshahr),
  5,000 .....H 4
Fasa, 19,000 .....G 3
Firdaus, 11,000 .....G 3
Gach Saran .....F 4
Garmsar, 4,723 .....F 2
Gulpaigan, 20,515 .....F 3
Gunabad, 8,000 .....G 3
Gurgan, 51,181 .....F 2
Hamadan, 124,167 .....E 3
Iranshahr, 5,000 .....H 4
Isfahan, 424,045 .....F 3
Jahrum, 38,236 .....F 4
Juimand (Gunabad),
  8,000 .....G 3
Kangavar, 9,414 .....E 3
Kashan, 58,468 .....F 3
Kashmar, 17,000 .....G 2
Kazerun, 39,758 .....F 4
Kazvin, 88,106 .....E 2
Kerman, 85,404 .....G 3
Kermanshah, 187,930 .....E 3
Khaf, 5,000 .....H 3
Khoi, 47,648 .....E 2
Khorramshahr, 88,536 .....E 3
Khur, 2,912 .....G 3
Khurramabad, 59,578 .....E 3
Lar, 22,000 .....F 4
Mahabad, 28,610 .....E 2
Maragheh, 54,106 .....E 2
Marand, 24,000 .....E 2
Meshed, 409,616 .....H 2
Mianeh, 28,447 .....E 2
Mirjawa, 11,000 .....H 4
Na'in, 5,925 .....F 3
Naishapur (Nishapur),
  33,482 .....G 2
Nasratabad (Zabul), 20,000 .....H 3
Natanz, 4,370 .....F 3
Nehavend, 24,000 .....E 3
Nejafabad, 43,384 .....F 3
Nishapur, 33,482 .....G 2
Pahlevi, 41,785 .....E 2
Qain, 6,000 .....G 3
Quchan, 29,133 .....G 2
Qum, 134,292 .....F 3
Ravar, 7,000 .....G 3
Resht, 143,557 .....E 2
Reza'iyeh, 110,749 .....D 2
Sabzavar, 42,415 .....G 2
Sabzawaran, 7,000 .....G 4
Samnan, 31,058 .....F 2
Saqqiz, 17,000 .....E 2
Sari, 44,547 .....F 2
Saveh, 17,565 .....F 3
Shahr-i-Tajan (Sari),
  44,547 .....F 2
Shahriza, 34,220 .....F 3
Shahrud, 30,767 .....G 2
Shahsawar, 12,000 .....F 2
Shiraz, 269,865 .....F 4
Shirvan, 11,000 .....G 2
Shushtar, 24,000 .....E 3
Sirjan, 12,160 .....G 4
Sultanabad (Arak), 71,925 .....E 3
Sultanabad (Kashmar),
  17,000 .....G 2
Susangird, 21,000 .....E 3
Tabas (Tabas-Masina),
  10,000 .....G 3
Tabriz, 403,413 .....E 2
Tehran (capital), 2,719,730 .....F 2
Tun (Firdaus), 11,000 .....G 3
Turbat-i-Haidari,
  30,106 .....G 2

Turbat-i-Shaikh Jam,
  13,000 .....H 2
Turshiz (Kashmar),
  17,000 .....G 2
Turun .....G 2
Urmia (Reza'iyeh),
  110,749 .....D 2
Yezd, 93,241 .....F 3
Zabul, 20,000 .....H 3
Zahidan, 39,732 .....H 3
Zarand, 5,000 .....G 3
Zenjan, 58,714 .....E 2

OTHER FEATURES

Araks (river) .....E 2
Atrek (river) .....G 2
Bazman, Kuh-i (mt.) .....H 4
Demavend (mt.) .....F 2
Diz, Ab-i (river) .....E 3
Elburz (mts.) .....F 2
Galvkhaneh (lake) .....F 3
Gurgan (river) .....G 2
Haliri (river) .....G 4
Jaz Murian, Hamun-i-
  (marsh) .....G 4
Karun (river) .....E 3
Kavir, Dasht-i-
  (salt desert) .....G 3
Kavir-i-Namak
  (salt desert) .....G 3
Kurdistan (reg.) .....D 2
Lut, Dasht-i-
  (desert) .....G 3
Maidani, Ras (cape) .....G 4
Mand Rud (river) .....H 4
Mashkel (river) .....H 4
Mehran (river) .....G 4
Namak, Darya-i-
  (salt lake) .....F 3
Namaksar (salt lake) .....H 3
Namakzar (marsh) .....H 3
Nezwar (river) .....F 2
Oman (gulf) .....G 5
Persian (gulf) .....F 4
Qais (isl.) .....F 4
Qishm (isl.) .....G 4
Qizil Uzun (river) .....E 2
Safidar, Kuh-i (mt.) .....F 4
Shaikh Shu'aib (isl.) .....F 4
Shir (mt.) .....F 4
Taftan (mt.) .....H 4
Talab (river) .....H 4
Tashk (lake) .....F 4
Urmia (lake) .....E 2
Zagros (mts.) .....E 3

IRAQ

CITIES and TOWNS

Al 'Aziziya, 7,450 .....E 3
Al Falluja, 38,072 .....D 3
Al Musaiyib, 15,955 .....D 3
Al Qurna, 5,638 .....E 4
'Amadiya, 2,578 .....D 2
'Amara, 64,847 .....E 3
An Najaf, 128,096 .....D 3
An Nasiriya, 60,405 .....E 3
'Ana, 6,884 .....D 3
Ar Rahhaliya .....D 3
Arbela (Erbil), 90,320 .....D 2
As Salman, 1,789 .....E 3
Baghdad (capital),
  502,503 .....E 3
Baghdad, 1,745,328 .....E 3
Ba'quba, 34,575 .....D 3
Basra, 313,327 .....E 3
Erbil, 90,320 .....D 2

OTHER FEATURES

Akhdar, Jebel (range) .....G 5

Habbaniya, 14,405 .....D 3
Haditha, 6,870 .....D 3
Hai, 16,988 .....E 3
Hilla, 84,717 .....D 3
Hit, 9,131 .....D 3
Karbala', 83,301 .....D 3
Khanaqin, 23,522 .....D 3
Kirkuk, 167,413 .....D 2
Kut, 42,116 .....E 3
Maidan, 354 .....D 3
Mosul, 315,157 .....D 2
Qal'a Sharqat, 2,434 .....D 2
Ramadi, 28,723 .....D 3
Rutba, 5,091 .....D 3
Samarra, 24,746 .....D 3
Samawa, 33,473 .....D 3
Shithatha, 2,326 .....D 3
Sulaimaniya, 86,822 .....E 2
Tikrit, 9,921 .....D 3

OTHER FEATURES

Al Batin, Wadi (river) .....E 4
'Aneiza, Jebel (mt.) .....D 3
'Ar'ar, Wadi (dry river) .....D 3
El Hamad (desert) .....D 3
Euphrates (river) .....D 3
Hauran, Wadi (dry river) .....D 3
Kurdistan (reg.) .....E 2
Mesopotamia (reg.) .....D 3
Tigris (river) .....E 3

QATAR

CITIES and TOWNS

Doha (capital), 45,000 .....F 4
Dukhan, 2,500 .....F 4
Umm Sa'id, 3,500 .....F 5

OTHER FEATURES

Persian (gulf) .....F 4
Rakan, Ras (cape) .....F 4

KUWAIT

CITIES and TOWNS

Al Kuwait (capital),
  80,008 .....E 4
Al Kuwait, *217,364 .....E 4
Mina al-Ahmadi .....E 4

OTHER FEATURES

Bubiyan (isl.) .....E 4
Persian (gulf) .....E 4

OMAN

CITIES and TOWNS

Adam .....G 5
Buraimi .....G 5
Dhank .....G 5
Ibra .....G 5
'Ibri .....G 5
Juwara .....G 6
Kamil .....G 5
Khaluf .....G 6
Khasab .....G 4
Manah .....G 5
Matrah, 15,000 .....G 5
Mina al Fahal .....G 5
Murbat .....G 6
Muscat (capital),
  7,500 .....G 5
Nizwa .....G 5
Quryat .....G 5
Risut .....F 6
Salala, 6,000 .....F 6
Sarur .....G 5
Shinas .....G 4
Sohar .....G 5
Sur .....G 5
Suwaiq .....G 5

OTHER FEATURES

Akhdar, Jebel (range) .....G 5

SAUDI ARABIA

PROVINCES

'Asir, 900,000 .....D 6
Eastern, 2,250,000 .....E 4
Hejaz, 1,250,000 .....C 4
Nejd, 1,500,000 .....D 4

CITIES and TOWNS

'Abaila .....F 5
Abha .....D 6
Abqaiq .....E 4
Abu 'Arish .....D 6
Abu Hadriya .....E 4
'Ain al Mubarrak .....C 4
Akhdar .....C 4
Al 'Ain .....C 4
Al 'Ala .....C 4
Al 'Auda .....E 4
Al Lith .....C 5
Al Muaddham .....C 4
Al Qalm .....D 6
'Anaiza .....D 4
Artawiya .....D 4
Ashaira .....C 5
Ayun .....D 4
Badr .....C 5
Bisha .....D 5
Buraida .....D 4
Buraimi .....C 4
Dam .....C 4
Dammam, 9,200 .....F 4
Dar al Hamra .....C 4
Debaba .....D 4
Dhaba .....C 4
Dhahran, 12,500 .....E 4
Dharma .....D 4
Dilam .....E 5
Doqa .....D 6
Duwadami .....D 4
Er Ras .....D 4
Faid .....D 4
Gail .....E 5
Haddar .....E 5

Hadiya .....C 4
Hafar al Batin .....E 4
Hail, 20,000 .....D 4
Halil .....D 6
Hamar .....E 5
Hanakiya .....D 5
Haql .....C 4
Haradh .....E 5
Haraja .....D 6
Hauta .....E 5
Hofuf, 83,000 .....E 4
Jabrin .....E 5
Jauf, 5,000 .....C 4
Jidda, 194,000 .....C 5
Jubail .....E 4
Jubba .....D 4
Junaina .....C 3
Kaf .....C 3
Khaibar .....D 6
Khamis Mushait .....D 6
Khurma .....D 5
Khurs .....D 5
Laila .....E 5
Majma'a .....D 4
Maqna .....C 4
Mastaba .....C 5
Mastura .....C 5
Mecca (capital), 185,000 .....C 5
Medain Salih .....C 4
Medina, 72,000 .....C 5
Mendak .....D 5
Mina Sa'ud .....E 4
Mubarraz .....E 4
Mudhnib .....D 4
Muwailih .....C 4
Najran .....D 6
Nisab .....E 4
Oqair .....E 4
Qadhima .....C 5
Qafar .....D 4
Qasr al Haiyana .....E 4
Qatif .....E 4
Qizan .....D 6
Qunfidha .....C 5
Qusaiba .....D 4
Rabigh .....C 5
Ras Tanura .....E 4
Riyadh (capital),
  225,000 .....E 5
Rumaihiya .....E 4
Sabya .....D 6
Sakaka .....D 4
Salwa .....F 5
Shaqra .....D 5
Shuqaiq .....D 6
Sufeina .....D 5
Sulaiyil .....D 5
Taif, 54,000 .....D 5
Taima .....C 4
Tamra .....D 5
Tebuk .....C 4
Truba .....D 5
Turaba .....D 5
Umm Lajj .....C 5
Wejh .....C 4
Yamama .....E 5
Yenbo .....C 5
Zilfi .....E 4

OTHER FEATURES

Abu-mad (cape) .....C 5
'Ar'ar, Wadi (dry river) .....D 3
Al Ahqaf (Bahr es Safi)
  (desert) .....E 6
'Aneiza, Jebel (mt.) .....D 3
'Aqaba (gulf) .....C 4
Arafat, Jebel (mt.) .....D 5

Ar'ar, Wadi (dry river) .....D 3
Arma (plateau) .....E 4
Aswad, Ras (cape) .....C 5
Bahr es Safi (desert) .....E 6
Barida, Ras (cape) .....C 4
Bisha, Wadi
  (dry river) .....D 5
Dahana (desert) .....E 4
Dawasir, Wadi
  (dry river) .....E 5
Dawasir, Hadb (range) .....D 5
Farasan (isls.) .....D 6
Hasa (reg.) .....E 4
Hatiba, Ras (cape) .....C 5
Jafura (desert) .....F 5
Mashabi (isl.) .....C 4
Midian (district) .....C 4
Misha'ab, Ras (cape) .....E 4
Nefud (desert) .....D 4
Nefud Dahi (desert) .....D 5
Persian (gulf) .....E 4
Ranya, Wadi
  (dry river) .....D 5
Red (sea) .....C 5
Red (Nefud) (desert) .....D 4
Rima, Wadi (river) .....D 4
Rimal, Ar (desert) .....F 5
Rub' al Khali (desert) .....E 5
Safaniya, Ras (cape) .....E 4
Salma, Jebel (mts.) .....D 4
Shaibara (isl.) .....C 5
Shammar, Jebel
  (plateau) .....D 4
Sirhan, Wadi .....C 3
Subh, Jebel (mt.) .....C 5
Summan (plateau) .....E 4
Tihama (reg.) .....C 5
Tiran (isl.) .....B 4
Tiran (str.) .....B 4
Tuwaiq, Jebel (range) .....D 5

TRUCIAL STATES

CITIES and TOWNS

Abu Dhabi (capital), 22,000 .....F 5
Abu Dhabi, *35,000 .....F 5
'Ajman (capital), 3,725 .....G 4
'Arada .....F 5
Buraimi .....G 5
Dubai (capital), *57,400 .....F 4
Fujairah (capital), 761 .....G 4
Jebel Dhauna .....F 5
Ras al Khaimah (capital),
  5,244 .....F 4
Ras al Khaimah, *8,764 .....F 4
Sharjah (capital), 19,198 .....F 4
Sharjah, *20,621 .....F 4
Umm al Qaiwain (capital),
  2,928 .....F 4

OTHER FEATURES

Das (isl.) .....F 4
Persian (gulf) .....F 4
Yas (isl.) .....F 5
Zirko (isl.) .....F 4

YEMEN ARAB REP.

CITIES and TOWNS

'Amran .....D 6
Bait al Faqih .....D 7
Dhamar .....D 7
Harib .....E 6
Hodeida, 40,000 .....D 7
Huth .....D 6
Ibb .....D 7

Luhaiya (Loheia) .....D 6
Maida, 2,500 .....D 6
Manakha .....D 6
Marib .....D 6
Mocha .....D 7
Sa'ada .....D 6
Safir .....E 6
San'a (capital),
  100,000 .....D 6
Sheikh Sa'id .....D 7
Ta'izz (capital),
  80,000 .....D 7
Yarim, 5,000 .....D 7
Zabid, 8,000 .....D 7

OTHER FEATURES

Hanish (isls.) .....D 7
Manar, Jebel (mt.) .....D 7
Red (sea) .....C 5
Sabir, Jebel (mt.) .....D 7
Tihama (reg.) .....D 7
Zuqar (isl.) .....D 7

YEMEN, PEOPLES DEM.
REPUBLIC OF

CITIES and TOWNS

Aden (capital), 150,000 .....E 7
Aden, *225,000 .....E 7
Ahwar .....E 6
Al Qatn .....E 6
Balhaf .....F 6
Bir 'Ali .....F 6
'Einat .....F 6
Ghaida .....G 6
Hadibu .....G 7
Hajarain .....E 6
Haura .....F 6
Hureidha .....E 6
Irqa .....E 6
Lahej .....E 7
Leijun .....F 6
Lodar .....E 7
Madinat ash Sha'b (capital),
  29,897 .....E 7
Magatin .....F 6
Meifa .....F 6
Mukalla, 30,000 .....F 6
Nisab .....E 6
Nuqub .....E 6
Qishn .....G 6
Riyan .....F 6
Saihut, 10,000 .....G 6
Seiyun .....F 6
Shabwa .....E 6
Shibam, 6,000 .....F 6
Shihr .....F 6
Shugra .....E 7
Taburkum .....F 6
Tarim .....F 6
Yeshbum .....E 6
Zinjibar .....E 7

OTHER FEATURES

Fartak, Ras (cape) .....F 6
Hadhramaut (dist.),
  350,000 .....E 7
Hadhramaut, Wadi
  (river) .....F 7
Kamaran (island),
  2,200 .....D 6
Mandeb, Bab el (str.) .....D 7
Perim (isl.), 381 .....D 7
Socotra (island),
  14,000 .....F 7

*City and suburbs.

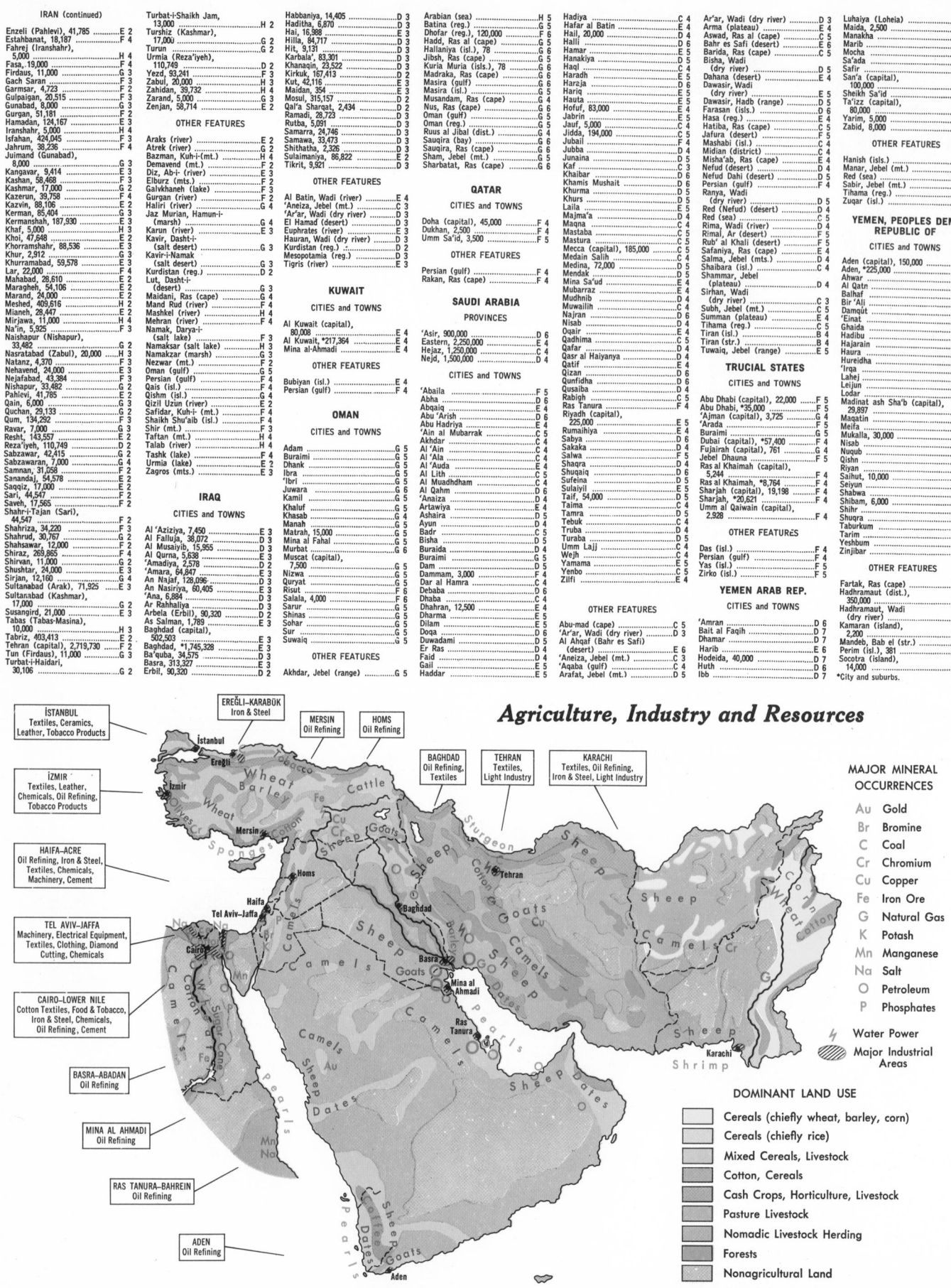

Agriculture, Industry and Resources

İSTANBUL Textiles, Ceramics, Leather, Tobacco Products

EREĞLİ–KARABÜK Iron & Steel

MERSIN Oil Refining

HOMS Oil Refining

BAGHDAD Oil Refining, Textiles

TEHRAN Textiles, Light Industry

KARACHI Textiles, Oil Refining, Iron & Steel, Light Industry

İZMIR Textiles, Leather, Chemicals, Oil Refining, Tobacco Products

HAIFA–ACRE Oil Refining, Iron & Steel, Textiles, Chemicals, Machinery, Cement

TEL AVIV–JAFFA Machinery, Electrical Equipment, Textiles, Clothing, Diamond Cutting, Chemicals

CAIRO–LOWER NILE Cotton Textiles, Food & Tobacco, Iron & Steel, Chemicals, Oil Refining, Cement

BASRA–ABADAN Oil Refining

MINA AL AHMADI Oil Refining

RAS TANURA–BAHREIN Oil Refining

ADEN Oil Refining

MAJOR MINERAL OCCURRENCES

Au — Gold
Br — Bromine
C — Coal
Cr — Chromium
Cu — Copper
Fe — Iron Ore
G — Natural Gas
K — Potash
Mn — Manganese
Na — Salt
O — Petroleum
P — Phosphates

⚡ Water Power
▨ Major Industrial Areas

DOMINANT LAND USE

Cereals (chiefly wheat, barley, corn)
Cereals (chiefly rice)
Mixed Cereals, Livestock
Cotton, Cereals
Cash Crops, Horticulture, Livestock
Pasture Livestock
Nomadic Livestock Herding
Forests
Nonagricultural Land

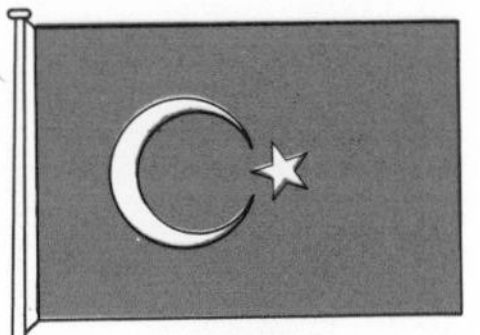

TURKEY

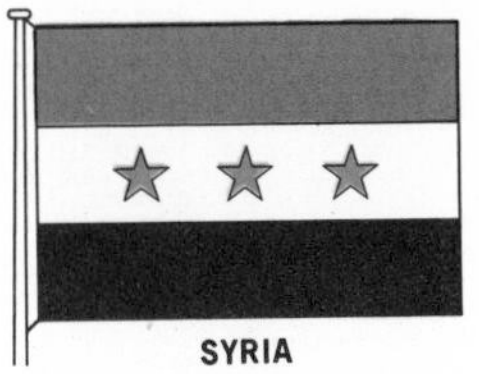

SYRIA

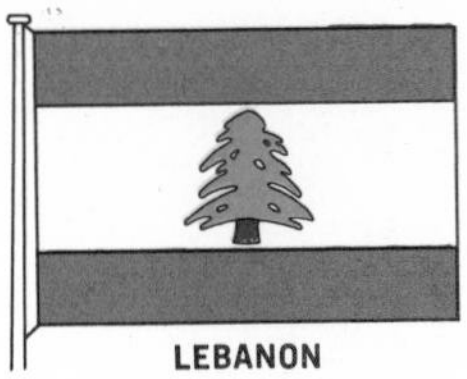

LEBANON

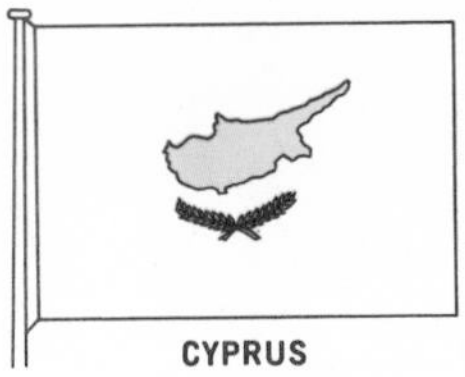

CYPRUS

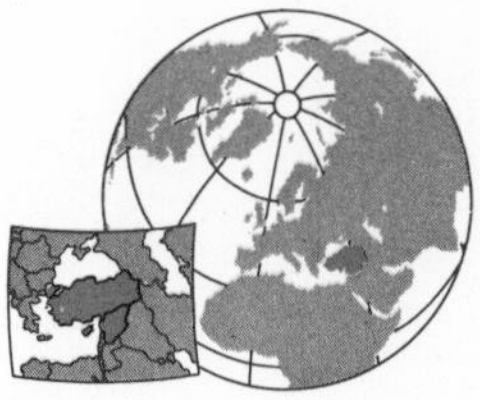

TURKEY

AREA 301,381 sq. mi.
POPULATION 34,375,000
CAPITAL Ankara
LARGEST CITY Istanbul (greater)
HIGHEST POINT Ararat 16,916 ft.
MONETARY UNIT Turkish pound (lira)
MAJOR LANGUAGES Turkish, Kurdish
MAJOR RELIGION Islam

SYRIA

AREA 71,498 sq. mi.
POPULATION 5,866,000
CAPITAL Damascus
LARGEST CITY Damascus
HIGHEST POINT Hermon 9,232 ft.
MONETARY UNIT Syrian pound
MAJOR LANGUAGES Arabic, Kurdish, Armenian
MAJOR RELIGIONS Islam, Christianity

LEBANON

AREA 4,015 sq. mi.
POPULATION 2,800,000
CAPITAL Beirut
LARGEST CITY Beirut
HIGHEST POINT Qurnet es Sauda 10,131 ft.
MONETARY UNIT Lebanese pound
MAJOR LANGUAGE Arabic
MAJOR RELIGIONS Christianity, Islam

CYPRUS

AREA 3,473 sq. mi.
POPULATION 649,000
CAPITAL Nicosia
LARGEST CITY Nicosia
HIGHEST POINT Troodos 6,406 ft.
MONETARY UNIT Cypriot pound
MAJOR LANGUAGES Greek, Turkish
MAJOR RELIGIONS Eastern (Greek) Orthodoxy, Islam

CYPRUS

CITIES and TOWNS

Famagusta, 38,000	F 5
Famagusta, *41,000	F 5
Kyrenia, 3,500	E 5
Kyrenia, *4,500	E 5
Larnaca, 20,000	E 5
Larnaca, *21,000	E 5
Lefka, 3,673	E 5
Lefkara, 2,075	E 5
Limassol, 46,500	E 5
Limassol, *50,000	E 5
Morphou, 6,642	E 5
Nicosia (capital), 47,000	E 5
Nicosia, *112,000	E 5
Paphos, 10,000	E 5
Paphos, *11,500	E 5
Yialousa, 2,541	F 5

OTHER FEATURES

Andreas (cape)	F 5
Arnauti (cape)	E 5
Famagusta (bay)	F 5
Gata (cape)	E 5
Greco (cape)	F 5
Klides (isls.)	F 5
Kormakiti (cape)	E 5
Larnaca (bay)	E 5
Morphou (bay)	E 5
Sovereign Base Area, 3,602	E 5
Troodos (mt.)	E 5

LEBANON

CITIES and TOWNS

'Aleih, 18,630	F 6
Amyun, 7,926	F 5
Ba'albek, 15,560	G 5
Batrun, 5,976	F 5
Beirut (capital), 700,000	F 6
Beirut, *840,000	F 6
En Naqura, 967	F 6
Hermil, 2,652	G 5
Merj 'Uyun, 9,318	F 6
Rasheiya, 6,731	F 6
Rayak, 1,480	G 6
Saida, 32,200	F 6
Sidon (Saida), 32,200	F 6
Sur, 16,483	F 6
Tarabulus (Tripoli), 127,611	F 5
Tyre (Sur), 16,483	F 6
Zahle, 53,121	F 6
Zegharta, 18,210	G 5

OTHER FEATURES

Hermon (mt.)	F 6
Lebanon (range)	F 6
Litani (Leontes) (river)	F 6
Sauda, Qurnet es (mt.)	G 5

SYRIA

GOVERNORATES

Aleppo, 1,131,854	G 4
Damascus, 1,060,484	G 6
Damascus (municipality), 630,063	G 6
Deir es Zor, 286,010	H 5
Der'a, 221,275	G 6
El Quneitra, 6,396	F 6
Es Suweida, 151,500	G 6
Hama, 390,084	G 5
Haseke, 309,279	J 4
Homs, 504,098	G 5
Idlib, 374,751	G 5
Latakia, 625,473	G 5
Rashid, 124,876	H 5

CITIES and TOWNS

Abu Kemal, 6,907	J 5
Aleppo, 566,770	G 4
A'zaz, 13,923	G 4
Baniyas, 8,537	F 5
Damascus (cap.), 789,840	G 6
Deir ez Zor, 60,335	H 5
Der'a, 20,465	G 6
Dimishq (Damascus) (capital), 789,840	G 6
Duma, 30,050	G 6
El Bab, 27,366	G 4
El Haseke, 23,074	J 4
El Ladhiqiya (Latakia), 72,378	F 5
El Quneitra, 206	F 6
El Rashid, 11,998	H 5
En Nebk, 16,334	G 5
Es Suweida, 17,592	G 6
Haleb (Aleppo), 566,770	G 4
Hama, 196,224	G 5
Harim, 6,837	G 4
Homs, 231,877	G 5
Idlib, 37,501	G 5
Jeble, 15,715	F 5
Jerablus, 8,610	G 4
Jisr esh Shughur, 13,131	G 5
Latakia, 72,378	F 5
Masyaf, 7,058	G 5
Membij, 13,796	G 4
Meyadin, 12,515	J 5
Palmyra (Tadmor), 10,670	H 5
Qamishliye, 31,448	J 4
Quteife, 4,993	G 6
Raqqa (El Rashid), 11,998	H 5
Safita, 9,650	G 5
Selemiya, 25,728	G 5
Tadmor, 10,670	H 5
Tartus, 19,137	F 5
Zebdani, 10,010	G 6

OTHER FEATURES

'Abdul 'Aziz, Jebel (mts.)	J 4
Abu Rujmein, Jebel (mts.)	H 5
'Asi (river)	G 5
Druz, Jebel ed (mts.)	G 6
Euphrates (El Furat) (river)	J 5
Furat, El (river)	H 4
Hermon (mt.)	F 6
Khabur (river)	J 5
Orontes ('Asi) (river)	G 5
Ruad (island)	F 5
Sharqi, Jebel esh (range)	G 5
Tigris (river)	K 4

TURKEY

PROVINCES

Adana, 902,712	F 4
Adıyaman, 267,288	H 4
Afyon-Karahisar, 502,248	D 3
Ağrı, 246,961	K 3
Amasya, 285,729	G 2
Ankara, 1,644,302	E 3
Antalya, 486,910	D 4
Artvin, 210,065	J 2
Aydın, 524,918	B 4
Balıkesir, 708,342	B 3
Bilecik, 139,041	D 2
Bingöl, 150,521	J 3
Bitlis, 154,069	J 3
Bolu, 383,939	D 2
Burdur, 194,950	D 4
Bursa, 755,504	C 2
Çanakkale, 350,317	B 2
Çankırı, 250,706	E 2
Çorum, 485,567	F 2
Denizli, 463,369	C 4
Diyarbakır, 475,916	H 4
Edirne, 303,234	B 2
Elâzığ, 322,727	H 3
Erzincan, 258,586	H 3
Erzurum, 628,001	J 3
Eskişehir, 415,101	D 3
Gaziantep, 511,026	G 4
Giresun, 428,015	H 2
Gümüşhane, 262,731	H 2
Hakkâri, 83,937	K 4
Hatay, 506,154	G 4
Içel, 511,273	F 4
Isparta, 266,240	D 4
Istanbul, 2,293,823	C 2
Izmir, 1,234,667	B 3
Kars, 606,313	K 2
Kastamonu, 441,638	E 2
Kayseri, 536,206	F 3
Kırklareli, 258,386	B 2
Kırsehir, 196,836	F 3
Kocaeli, 335,518	D 2
Konya, 1,122,622	E 4
Kütahya, 398,081	C 3
Malatya, 452,624	H 3
Manisa, 748,545	B 3
Maraş, 438,423	G 4
Mardin, 397,880	J 4
Muğla, 334,973	C 4
Muş, 198,716	J 3
Nevşehir, 203,316	F 3
Niğde, 362,044	F 4
Ordu, 543,863	G 2
Rize, 281,099	J 2
Sakarya, 404,078	D 2
Samsun, 755,946	F 2
Siirt, 264,832	J 4
Sinop, 266,069	F 2
Sivas, 705,186	G 3
Tekirdağ, 287,381	B 2
Tokat, 495,352	G 2
Trabzon, 595,782	H 2
Tunceli, 154,175	H 3
Urfa, 450,798	H 4
Uşak, 190,536	C 3
Van, 266,840	K 3
Yozgat, 437,883	F 3
Zonguldak, 650,191	D 2

CITIES and TOWNS

Abana, 2,455	F 1
Acıgol, 3,265	F 3
Acıpayam, 4,118	C 4
Adalia (Antalya), 71,833	D 4
Adana, 289,919	F 4
Adapazarı, 86,124	D 2
Adilcevaz, 6,148	K 3
Adıyaman, 22,153	H 4
Afşin, 8,069	G 3
Afyon, 44,026	D 3
Ağlasun, 3,730	D 4
Ağlı, 3,425	E 2
Ağrı (Karaköse), 24,168	K 3
Ahlat, 5,879	K 3
Akçaabat, 7,600	H 2
Akçadağ, 5,995	G 3
Akçakale, 4,526	H 4
Akçakoca, 7,179	D 2
Akdağmadeni, 4,321	F 3
Akhisar, 46,167	B 3
Aksaray, 24,414	F 3
Akşehir, 25,269	D 3
Akseki, 2,505	D 4
Akviran, 3,786	E 4
Akyazi, 9,090	D 2
Alaca, 8,288	F 2
Alaçam, 7,833	F 2
Alanya, 12,436	D 4
Alaşehir, 16,012	C 3
Alexandretta (Iskenderun), 69,382	G 4
Aliağa, 3,087	B 3
Alibeyköyü, 15,199	D 6
Almus, 4,110	G 2
Alpu, 2,709	D 3
Altindağ, 89,838	E 2
Altınova, 6,368	B 3
Altıntaş, 2,361	C 3
Amasya, 34,168	G 2
Anadoluhisari, 13,959	D 6
Anamur, 11,246	E 4
Andırın, 3,695	G 4
Ankara (capital), 905,660	E 3
Antâkya, 57,855	G 4
Antalya, 71,833	D 4
Araç, 2,820	E 2
Aralık, 2,879	L 3
Arapkir, 7,056	H 3
Ardahan, 9,117	K 2
Ardeşen, 5,488	J 2
Arhavi, 4,510	J 2
Arnavutköy, 22,468	D 6
Arsin, 4,028	H 2
Artova, 2,863	G 2
Artvin, 9,847	J 2
Aşkale, 6,943	J 3
Aslanköy, 3,656	F 4
Avanos, 5,675	F 3
Ayancik, 5,320	F 2
Ayas, 3,873	E 2
Aybastı, 7,450	G 2
Aydın, 43,483	B 4
Ayvacık, 2,277	B 3
Ayvalık, 16,283	B 3
Babadağ, 5,511	C 4
Babaeski, 13,879	B 2
Bafra, 26,239	F 2
Bahçe, 2,264	G 4
Bakırköy, 65,285	D 6
Baklan, 2,680	C 4
Balâ, 3,646	E 3
Balıkesir, 69,341	B 3
Banaz, 3,495	C 3
Bandırma, 33,116	B 2
Barak, 3,117	G 4
Bartın, 14,259	E 2
Başkale, 4,007	K 3
Başmakçı, 5,093	D 4
Batman, 24,990	J 4
Bayburt, 15,184	H 2
Bayındır, 11,273	B 3
Bayramiç, 4,607	B 3
Bergama, 24,121	B 3
Beşiktaş, 58,814	D 6
Besni, 11,625	G 4
Beykoz, 37,730	D 5
Beylerbeyi, 21,741	D 6
Beyoğlu, 39,984	D 6
Beypazarı, 9,860	D 2
Beyşehir, 7,456	D 4
Biga, 12,063	B 2
Bigadiç, 4,820	C 3
Bilecik, 9,722	D 2
Bingöl (Çapakçur), 11,727	J 3
Birecik, 15,317	H 4
Bismil, 4,444	J 4
Bitlis, 18,725	J 3
Bodrum, 5,136	B 4
Boğazlıyan, 7,925	F 3
Bolu, 21,700	D 2
Bolvadin, 20,139	D 3
Bor, 14,309	F 4
Borçka, 3,763	J 2
Bornova, 30,445	B 3
Boyabat, 9,418	F 2
Bozdoğan, 6,739	C 4
Bozkır, 3,112	E 4
Bozkurt, 2,954	F 2
Bozova, 3,425	H 4
Bozüyük, 10,842	D 3
Bucak, 10,094	D 4
Bulancak, 9,343	G 2
Bulanık, 6,186	K 3
Buldan, 9,813	C 3
Bünyan, 8,467	G 3
Burdur, 29,268	D 4
Burhaniye, 12,597	B 3

(continued on following page)

Agriculture, Industry and Resources

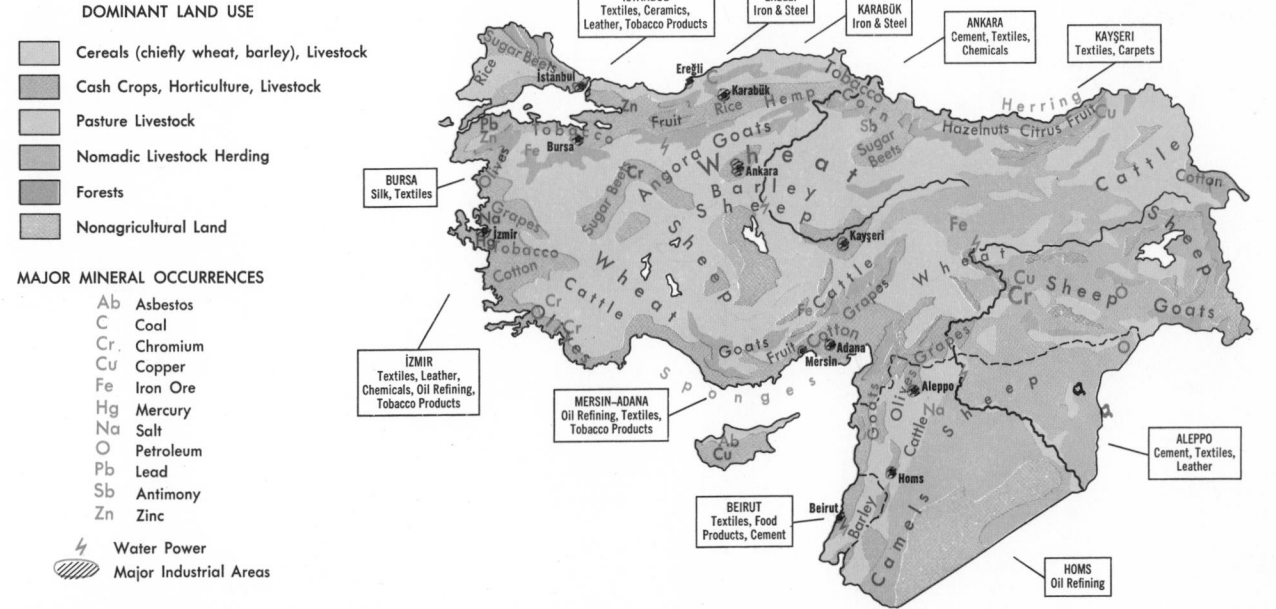

DOMINANT LAND USE

- Cereals (chiefly wheat, barley), Livestock
- Cash Crops, Horticulture, Livestock
- Pasture Livestock
- Nomadic Livestock Herding
- Forests
- Nonagricultural Land

MAJOR MINERAL OCCURRENCES

- Ab Asbestos
- C Coal
- Cr Chromium
- Cu Copper
- Fe Iron Ore
- Hg Mercury
- Na Salt
- O Petroleum
- Pb Lead
- Sb Antimony
- Zn Zinc

- Water Power
- Major Industrial Areas

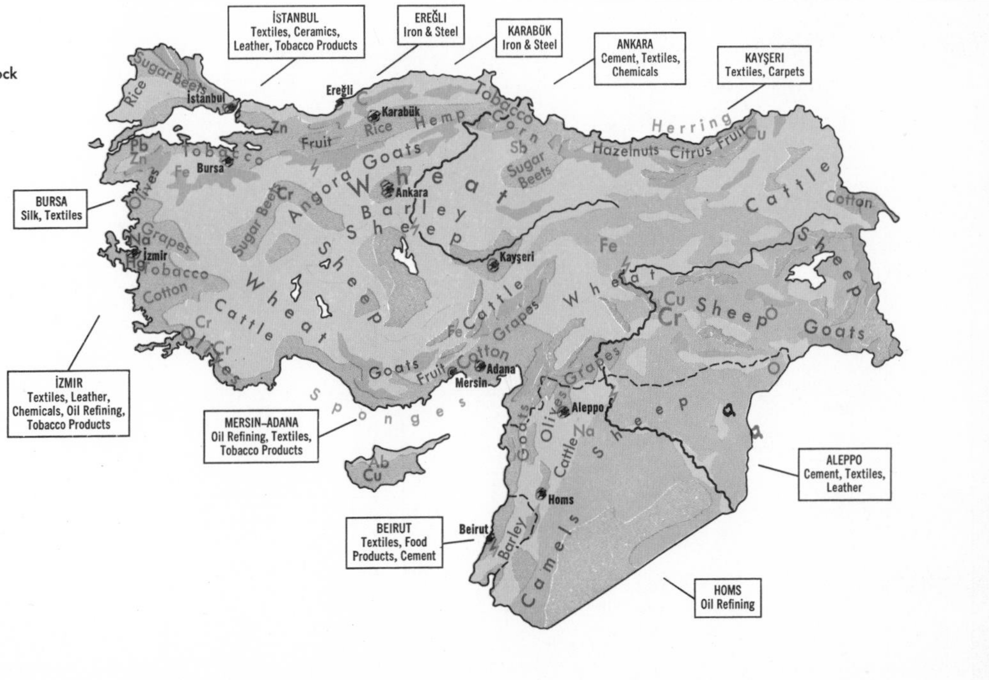

İSTANBUL
Textiles, Ceramics, Leather, Tobacco Products
EREĞLI
Iron & Steel
KARABÜK
Iron & Steel
ANKARA
Cement, Textiles, Chemicals
KAYŞERI
Textiles, Carpets
BURSA
Silk, Textiles
İZMIR
Textiles, Leather, Chemicals, Oil Refining, Tobacco Products
MERSIN-ADANA
Oil Refining, Textiles, Tobacco Products
ALEPPO
Cement, Textiles, Leather
BEIRUT
Textiles, Food Products, Cement
HOMS
Oil Refining
Sugar Beets
Rice
Tobacco
Zn
Fruit
Hemp
Corn
Herring
Hazelnuts
Citrus Fruit
Sb
Goats
Wheat
Barley
Sheep
Angora Goats
Cattle
Cotton
Olives
Grapes
Fe
Cr
Cu
Sponges
Ab
Na
Camels
Kayşeri
Mersin
Adana
Aleppo
Homs
Beirut
Bursa
Ankara
Karabük
Ereğli

Turkey is divided into provinces bearing the same names as their capital towns, except:

Province	Capital	
AFYON-KARAHISAR	Afyon	D 3
AĞRI	Karaköse	K 3
BİNGÖL	Çapakçur	J 3
HAKKÂRİ	Çölemerik	K 4
HATAY	Antakya	G 4
İÇEL	Mersin	F 4
KOCAELİ	İzmit	C 2
SAKARYA	Adapazarı	D 2
TUNCELİ	Kalan	H 3

Ilica, 7,612 .... J 3	Kalan, 5,825 .... H 3
İmranlı, 3,176 .... H 3	Kale, 3,166 .... C 4
İmroz, 2,721 .... A 3	Kalecik, 4,022 .... E 2
İncesu, 5,775 .... F 3	Kaman, 10,067 .... E 3
İnebolu, 5,935 .... E 1	Kandıra, 5,992 .... D 2
İnegöl, 27,777 .... C 3	Kangal, 4,412 .... G 3
İnönü, 4,246 .... D 3	Karabük, 46,169 .... E 2
İpsala, 6,544 .... B 2	Karacabey, 18,368 .... C 3
İpsile, 2,246 .... G 2	Karahallı, 4,367 .... C 3
İskenderun, 69,382 .... G 4	Karaçoban, 2,965 .... J 3
İskilip, 12,400 .... F 2	Karaköse, 24,168 .... K 3
İslâhiye, 13,775 .... G 4	Karaman, 26,051 .... E 4
Isparta, 42,901 .... D 4	Karamanlı, 4,694 .... C 4
İspir, 2,294 .... J 2	Karapınar, 12,989 .... E 4
İstanbul, 1,742,978 .... D 6	Karasu, 7,060 .... D 2
İstanbul, *2,043,447 .... D 6	Karataş, 2,493 .... F 4
İzmir, 263,521 .... B 3	Karayaka, 3,631 .... G 2
İzmir, *411,626 .... B 3	Kargı, 3,954 .... F 2
İzmit, 89,547 .... D 2	Kars, 41,376 .... K 2
İznik, 8,213 .... D 3	Karşıyaka, 82,574 .... B 3
Kadıköy, 81,945 .... D 6	Kartal, 20,139 .... D 6
Kadınhanı, 8,398 .... E 3	Kastamonu, 23,485 .... E 2
Kadirli, 15,926 .... F 4	Kavak, 2,135 .... C 5
Kâğıthane, 56,157 .... D 6	Kavak, 2,473 .... F 2
Kağızman, 9,417 .... K 2	Kayseri, 126,653 .... F 3
Kâhta, 6,885 .... H 3	Kazanlı, 3,360 .... F 4

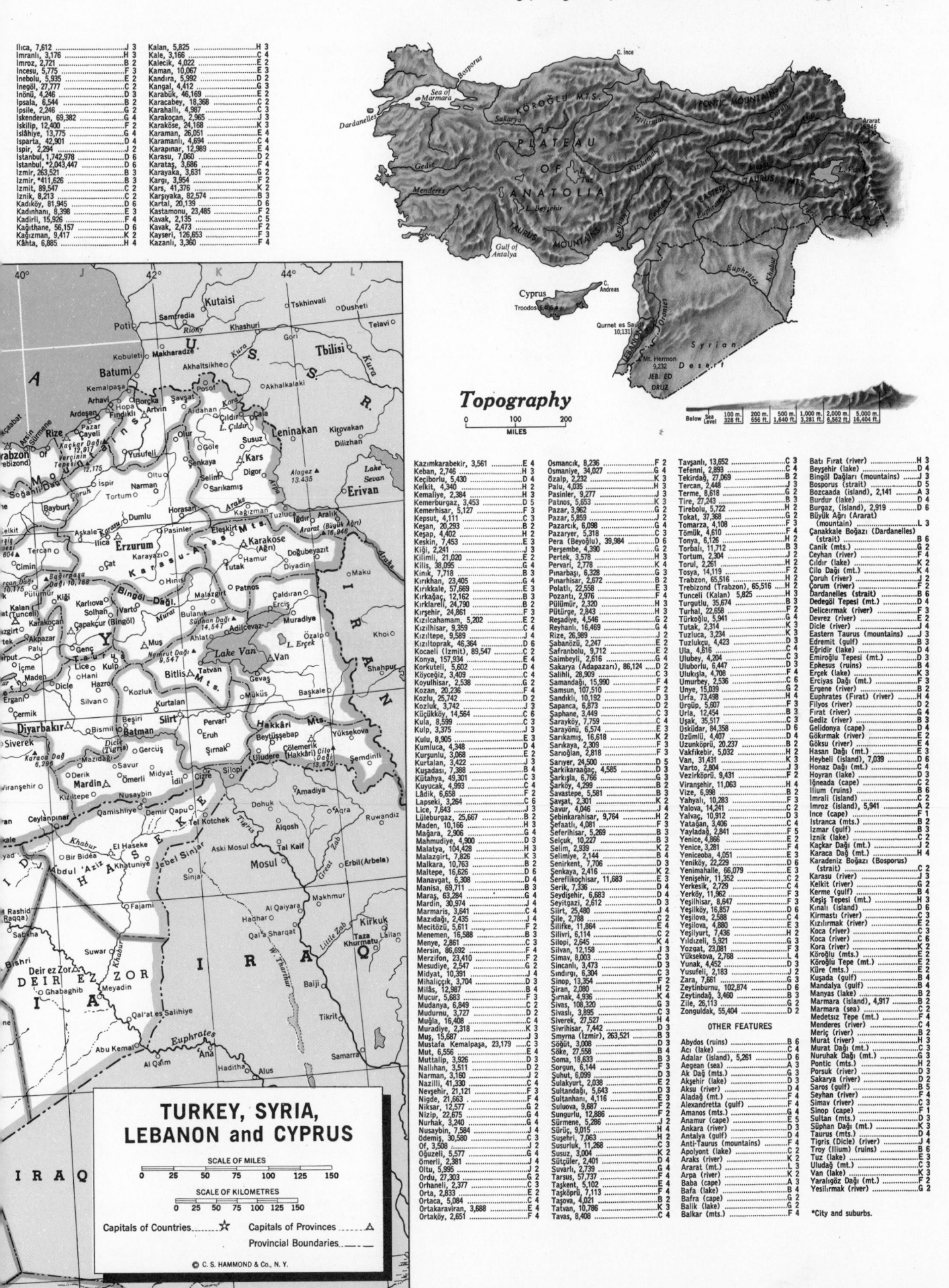

Topography

0   100   200
MILES

Below Sea Level | 100 m. 328 ft. | 200 m. 656 ft. | 500 m. 1,640 ft. | 1,000 m. 3,281 ft. | 2,000 m. 6,562 ft. | 5,000 m. 16,404 ft.

Kazımkarabekir, 3,561 ... E 4	Osmancık, 8,236 ... F 2	Tavşanlı, 13,652 ... C 3
Keban, 2,746 ... H 3	Osmaniye, 34,027 ... F 4	Tefenni, 2,893 ... C 4
Keçiborlu, 5,430 ... D 4	Özalp, 2,232 ... K 3	Tekirdağ, 27,069 ... B 2
Kelkit, 4,340 ... H 2	Palu, 4,035 ... H 3	Tercan, 2,449 ... H 3
Kemaliye, 2,384 ... H 3	Pasinler, 9,277 ... J 3	Terme, 8,618 ... G 2
Kemerburgaz, 3,453 ... D 5	Patnos, 5,653 ... K 3	Tire, 27,243 ... B 3
Kemerhisar, 5,127 ... F 3	Pazar, 3,962 ... G 2	Tirebolu, 5,722 ... H 2
Kepsut, 4,111 ... C 3	Pazar, 5,859 ... J 2	Tokat, 37,368 ... G 2
Keşan, 20,293 ... B 2	Pazarcık, 6,098 ... G 4	Tomarza, 4,108 ... F 3
Keşap, 4,402 ... H 2	Pazaryer, 5,318 ... D 3	Tömük, 4,610 ... F 4
Keskin, 7,453 ... E 3	Pera (Beyoğlu), 39,984 ... D 6	Tonya, 6,126 ... H 2
Kiği, 2,241 ... H 3	Perşembe, 4,390 ... G 2	Torbalı, 11,712 ... B 3
Kilimli, 21,020 ... D 2	Pertek, 3,578 ... H 3	Tortum, 2,304 ... J 2
Kilis, 38,095 ... G 4	Pervari, 2,778 ... K 4	Torul, 2,261 ... H 2
Kınık, 7,718 ... B 3	Pınarbaşı, 6,328 ... G 3	Tosya, 14,119 ... F 2
Kırıkhan, 23,405 ... G 4	Pınarhisar, 2,672 ... B 2	Trabzon, 65,516 ... H 2
Kırıkkale, 37,669 ... E 3	Polatlı, 22,558 ... E 3	Trebizond (Trabzon), 65,516 ... H 2
Kırkağaç, 12,162 ... B 3	Pozantı, 2,976 ... F 4	Tunceli (Kalan), 5,825 ... H 3
Kırklareli, 24,790 ... B 2	Pülümür, 2,320 ... H 3	Turgutlu, 35,674 ... B 3
Kırşehir, 24,861 ... F 3	Pütürge, 2,843 ... H 3	Turhal, 22,658 ... G 2
Kızılcahamam, 5,202 ... E 2	Reşadiye, 4,546 ... G 2	Türkoğlu, 5,941 ... G 4
Kızılhisar, 9,359 ... C 4	Reyhanlı, 16,469 ... G 4	Tutak, 2,314 ... K 3
Kızıltepe, 9,589 ... H 4	Rize, 26,989 ... J 2	Tuzla, 2,306 ... D 6
Kızıltoprak, 46,364 ... D 6	Sabanözü, 2,247 ... E 2	Tuzlukçu, 4,423 ... E 3
Kocaeli (İzmit), 89,547 ... E 4	Safranbolu, 9,712 ... E 2	Ula, 4,616 ... C 4
Konya, 157,934 ... E 4	Saimbeyli, 2,616 ... G 4	Ulubey, 5,607 ... C 3
Korkuteli, 5,602 ... D 4	Sakarya (Adapazarı), 86,124 ... D 2	Uluborlu, 6,447 ... D 3
Köyceğiz, 3,409 ... C 4	Salihli, 28,909 ... C 3	Uluköyla, 4,706 ... F 2
Koyulhisar, 2,538 ... G 2	Samandağ, 15,990 ... F 4	Umurbey, 2,536 ... C 6
Kozan, 20,236 ... F 4	Samsun, 107,510 ... G 2	Ürgüp, 5,607 ... F 3
Kozlu, 25,742 ... D 2	Sandıklı, 10,192 ... D 3	Urfa, 73,498 ... H 4
Kozluk, 3,742 ... J 3	Sapanca, 6,873 ... D 2	Urla, 12,654 ... B 3
Küçükköy, 14,564 ... F 2	Saraçhane, 3,449 ... C 3	Uşak, 35,517 ... C 3
Kula, 8,599 ... C 3	Sarayköy, 7,759 ... C 4	Üsküdar, 84,358 ... D 6
Kulp, 3,375 ... J 3	Sarayönü, 6,574 ... E 3	Üzümlü, 4,407 ... C 4
Kulu, 8,905 ... E 3	Sarıkamış, 16,618 ... K 2	Uzunköprü, 20,237 ... B 2
Kumluca, 4,348 ... D 4	Sarıkaya, 2,309 ... F 3	Vakfıkebir, 5,602 ... H 2
Kurşunlu, 3,068 ... E 2	Sarıoğlan, 2,818 ... F 3	Van, 23,417 ... K 3
Kurtalan, 3,422 ... J 3	Sarıyer, 24,500 ... D 6	Varto, 2,894 ... J 3
Kuşadası, 7,388 ... B 4	Sarızkağanağac, 4,585 ... D 3	Vezirköprü, 9,431 ... F 2
Kütahya, 46,301 ... C 3	Sarkışla, 8,766 ... G 3	Viranşehir, 11,063 ... H 4
Kuyucak, 4,593 ... C 4	Şarköy, 4,299 ... B 2	Vize, 6,998 ... B 2
Lâdik, 6,658 ... F 2	Savastepe, 5,581 ... B 3	Yalova, 14,241 ... D 2
Lapseki, 3,264 ... C 6	Savur, 4,046 ... J 4	Yalvaç, 10,912 ... D 3
Lice, 7,643 ... J 3	Şebinkarahisar, 9,764 ... H 2	Yatağan, 3,406 ... C 4
Lüleburgaz, 25,667 ... B 2	Şefaatli, 4,081 ... F 3	Yayladağ, 2,841 ... G 5
Maden, 10,166 ... H 3	Şereflihisar, 5,269 ... B 3	Yenice, 4,866 ... E 2
Mağara, 2,906 ... G 4	Selçuk, 10,227 ... B 3	Yenice, 3,281 ... C 3
Mahmudiye, 4,900 ... D 3	Selim, 2,939 ... K 2	Yenicoba, 4,051 ... D 3
Malatya, 104,428 ... H 3	Selimiye, 2,144 ... B 3	Yeniköy, 22,229 ... D 6
Malazgirt, 7,826 ... J 3	Senkent, 7,706 ... D 3	Yenimahalle, 66,079 ... E 3
Maltepe, 10,763 ... D 6	Senkaya, 2,416 ... J 2	Yenişehir, 11,352 ... C 3
Maltepe, 16,626 ... B 6	Şereflikoçhisar, 11,683 ... E 3	Yerkesik, 2,729 ... C 4
Manavgat, 6,308 ... D 4	Serik, 7,336 ... D 4	Yerköy, 11,962 ... F 3
Manisa, 69,711 ... B 3	Seydişehir, 6,883 ... D 4	Yeşilışar, 8,647 ... F 3
Maraş, 63,284 ... G 4	Seyitgazi, 2,612 ... D 3	Yeşilhisar, 16,857 ... F 3
Mardin, 30,974 ... J 4	Siirt, 25,480 ... J 3	Yeşilova, 2,588 ... C 4
Marmaris, 3,641 ... C 4	Sile, 2,788 ... D 6	Yeşilova, 4,880 ... C 4
Mazıdağı, 2,435 ... J 4	Silifke, 11,864 ... E 4	Yeşilyurt, 7,436 ... H 3
Meciözü, 5,611 ... F 2	Silivri, 6,114 ... C 2	Yıldızeli, 5,921 ... G 3
Menemen, 16,588 ... B 3	Silopi, 2,645 ... K 4	Yozgat, 25,081 ... F 3
Menye, 2,861 ... C 3	Silvan, 12,158 ... J 3	Yüksekova, 2,768 ... K 4
Mersin, 86,692 ... F 4	Simav, 8,003 ... C 3	Yunak, 4,452 ... D 3
Merzifon, 23,410 ... F 2	Sincanlı, 3,473 ... D 3	Yusufeli, 2,183 ... J 2
Mesudiye, 2,547 ... G 2	Sındırgı, 6,304 ... C 3	Zara, 7,661 ... G 3
Midyat, 10,391 ... J 4	Sinop, 13,354 ... F 2	Zeytinburnu, 102,874 ... D 6
Mihaliçcik, 3,704 ... D 3	Şiran, 2,080 ... H 2	Zeytindağ, 3,460 ... B 3
Milâs, 12,987 ... B 4	Şırnak, 4,936 ... K 4	Zile, 26,113 ... G 2
Mucur, 5,683 ... F 3	Sivas, 108,320 ... G 3	Zonguldak, 55,404 ... D 2
Mudanya, 6,849 ... C 3	Sivaslı, 3,895 ... C 3	
Muduran, 3,722 ... D 2	Siverek, 27,527 ... H 3	
Muğla, 16,408 ... C 4	Sivrihisar, 7,442 ... D 3	**OTHER FEATURES**
Muradiye, 2,318 ... K 3	Smyrna (İzmir), 263,521 ... B 3	
Muş, 15,687 ... J 3	Söğüt, 3,008 ... D 3	Abydos (ruins) ... B 6
Mustafa Kemalpaşa, 23,179 ... C 3	Söke, 27,558 ... B 3	Acı (lake) ... D 6
Mut, 6,556 ... E 4	Soma, 18,633 ... B 3	Adalar (island), 5,261 ... C 6
Muttalip, 3,926 ... D 3	Sorgun, 6,144 ... F 3	Aegean (sea) ... A 3
Nallıhan, 3,511 ... D 2	Susuz, 3,004 ... K 2	Ak Dağ (mts.) ... D 3
Narman, 3,160 ... J 2	Suhut, 6,099 ... D 3	Akşehir (lake) ... D 3
Nazilli, 41,330 ... C 4	Sulakyurt, 2,038 ... E 2	Aksu (river) ... D 4
Nevşehir, 21,121 ... F 3	Sultandağı, 5,643 ... D 3	Aladağ (mt.) ... F 4
Niğde, 21,663 ... F 3	Sultanhanı, 4,116 ... E 3	Alexandretta (gulf) ... G 4
Niksar, 12,577 ... G 2	Sulova, 9,687 ... F 2	Amanos (mts.) ... G 4
Nizip, 22,675 ... G 4	Sungurlu, 12,067 ... F 2	Amara (river) ... J 4
Nurhak, 3,240 ... G 4	Sürmene, 5,286 ... H 2	Ankara (river) ... E 2
Nusaybin, 7,584 ... J 4	Sürüç, 9,015 ... H 4	Antalya (gulf) ... D 4
Ödemiş, 30,580 ... C 3	Suşehri, 7,063 ... G 2	Anti-Taurus (mountains) ... F 4
Of, 3,508 ... J 2	Susurluk, 11,268 ... C 3	Apolyont (lake) ... C 3
Öğürelli, 5,577 ... D 4	Süzce, 3,004 ... K 2	Ararat (lake) ... K 3
Ömerli, 2,381 ... J 4	Sütçüler, 2,401 ... D 4	Ararat (mt.) ... K 3
Oltu, 5,995 ... J 2	Suvarlı, 2,739 ... G 4	
Ordu, 27,303 ... G 2	Tarsus, 57,737 ... F 4	Baba (cape) ... A 3
Orhaneli, 2,377 ... C 3	Taşkent, 5,102 ... E 4	Bafa (lake) ... B 4
Orta, 2,833 ... E 2	Taşköprü, 7,113 ... F 2	Bafra (river) ... F 2
Ortaca, 5,084 ... C 4	Taşova, 4,021 ... G 2	Balık (lake) ... E 2
Ortakaravıran, 3,888 ... E 4	Tatvan, 10,786 ... J 3	Balkar (mts.) ... F 4
Ortaköy, 2,651 ... F 4	Tavas, 8,408 ... C 4	

Batı Fırat (river) ... H 3	
Beyşehir (lake) ... D 4	
Bingöl Dağları (mountains) ... J 3	
Bosporus (strait) ... D 5	
Bozcaada (island), 2,141 ... A 3	
Burdur (lake) ... D 4	
Burgaz, (island), 2,919 ... D 6	
Büyük Ağrı (Ararat) (mountain) ... K 3	
Çanakkale Boğazı (Dardanelles) (strait) ... B 6	
Canik (mts.) ... G 2	
Ceyhan (river) ... F 4	
Çıldır (lake) ... K 2	
Cilo Dağı (mt.) ... K 4	
Çoruh (river) ... J 2	
Çorum (river) ... F 2	
Dardanelles (strait) ... B 6	
Dedegöl Tepesi (mt.) ... D 4	
Delicırmak (river) ... F 2	
Devrez (river) ... E 2	
Dicle (river) ... J 4	
Eastern Taurus (mountains) ... J 3	
Edremit (gulf) ... B 3	
Eğridir (lake) ... D 4	
Emiroğlu Tepesi (mt.) ... E 4	
Ephesus (ruins) ... B 3	
Erçek (lake) ... K 3	
Erciyas Dağı (mt.) ... F 3	
Ergene (river) ... B 2	
Euphrates (Fırat) (river) ... H 4	
Filyos (river) ... D 2	
Fırat (river) ... H 4	
Gediz (river) ... B 3	
Gelidonya (cape) ... D 4	
Gökırmak (river) ... E 2	
Göksu (river) ... E 4	
Hasan Dağı (mt.) ... E 3	
Heybeli (island), 7,039 ... D 6	
Honaz Dağı (mt.) ... C 4	
Hoyran (lake) ... D 3	
İğneada (cape) ... B 2	
Ilium (ruins) ... B 6	
İmralı (island) ... C 3	
İmroz (island), 5,941 ... A 3	
İnce (cape) ... F 1	
İstranca (mts.) ... B 2	
İzmar (gulf) ... B 3	
İznik (lake) ... D 3	
Kaçkar Dağı (mt.) ... J 2	
Karaca Dağı (mt.) ... H 4	
Karadeniz Boğazı (Bosporus) (strait) ... D 5	
Karasu (river) ... J 2	
Kelkit (river) ... H 2	
Kerme (gulf) ... B 4	
Keşiş Tepesi (mt.) ... D 3	
Kınalı (island) ... D 6	
Kırmastı (river) ... C 3	
Kızılırmak (river) ... E 2	
Koca (river) ... K 3	
Koca (river) ... C 2	
Kora (river) ... K 2	
Köroğlu (mts.) ... D 2	
Köroğlu Tepe (mt.) ... D 2	
Küre (mt.) ... E 2	
Kuşada (gulf) ... B 3	
Mandalya (gulf) ... B 4	
Manyas (lake) ... C 3	
Marmara (island), 4,917 ... C 3	
Marmara (sea) ... C 3	
Medetsiz Tepe (mt.) ... F 4	
Meriç (river) ... B 2	
Menderes (river) ... C 4	
Murat (river) ... J 3	
Murat Dağı (mt.) ... C 3	
Nuruhak Dağı (mt.) ... G 4	
Pontic (mts.) ... H 2	
Porsuk (river) ... D 3	
Sakarya (river) ... D 2	
Saros (gulf) ... B 2	
Seyhan (river) ... F 4	
Simav (river) ... C 3	
Sinop (cape) ... F 1	
Sultan (mts.) ... D 3	
Süphan Dağı (mt.) ... J 3	
Taurus (mts.) ... D 4	
Tigris (Dicle) (river) ... J 4	
Troy (Ilium) (ruins) ... B 6	
Tuz (lake) ... E 3	
Uludağ (mt.) ... C 3	
Van (lake) ... K 3	
Yaralıgöz Dağı (mt.) ... E 2	
Yeşilırmak (river) ... G 2	
*City and suburbs.	

TURKEY, SYRIA, LEBANON and CYPRUS

SCALE OF MILES
0   25   50   75   100   125   150

SCALE OF KILOMETRES
0   25   50   75   100   125   150

Capitals of Countries .... ★
Capitals of Provinces .... △
Provincial Boundaries .... — — —

© C. S. HAMMOND & Co., N.Y.

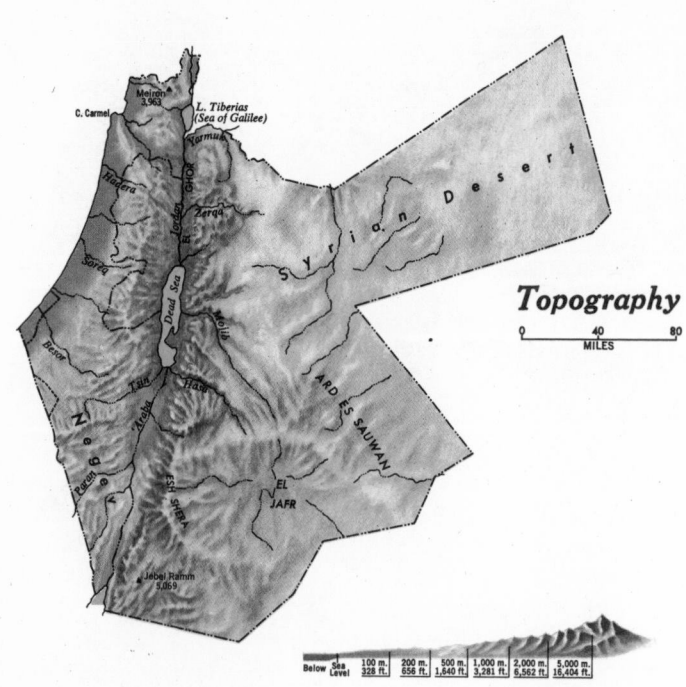

Topography

0   40   80
MILES

| Below Sea Level | 100 m. 328 ft. | 200 m. 656 ft. | 500 m. 1,640 ft. | 1,000 m. 3,281 ft. | 2,000 m. 6,562 ft. | 5,000 m. 16,404 ft. |

ISRAEL

DISTRICTS

Central, 426,454 ....B 3
Haifa, 391,380 ....C 2
Jerusalem, 201,749 ....B 4
Northern, 363,159 ....C 2
Southern, 213,283 ....B, D 5
Tel Aviv, 735,776 ....B 3

CITIES and TOWNS

Acre, 28,100 ....C 2
Afiqim, 1,243 ....D 2
Afula, 15,000 ....C 2
Ahuzzam, 407 ....B 4
Akko (Acre), 28,100 ....C 2
Arad ....C 5
'Arrabe, 3,636 ....C 2
Ashdod, 11,700 ....B 4
Ashdot Ya'aqov,
  1,197 ....D 2
Ashqelon, 28,400 ....A 4
Atlit, 1,516 ....B 2
Avihayil, 579 ....B 3
Azor, 3,687 ....B 3
Bat Shelomo, 218 ....B 2
Bat Yam, 39,100 ....B 3
Beer Ora ....D 5
Be'er Tuveya, 602 ....B 4
Be'eri, 390 ....A 5
Beersheba, 51,600 ....C 4
Bene Beraq, 51,700 ....B 3
Bet Dagan, 2,932 ....B 4
Bet Hagaddi, 566 ....B 5
Bet Qama, 228 ....B 5
Bet She'an, 10,900 ....D 3
Bet Shemesh, 8,200 ....B 4
Binyamina, 2,950 ....B 2
Carmel ....C 2
Dafna, 577 ....D 1
Daliyat al-Karmel,
  4,124 ....B 2
Dan, 498 ....D 1
Dimona, 12,100 ....D 4
Dor, 195 ....B 2
'Ein Harod, 1,372 ....C 2
El 'Auja ....D 5
Elath (Elat), 7,000 ....D 5
Elyakim, 568 ....C 2
Elyashiv, 435 ....B 3
Even Yehuda, 3,464 ....B 3
Gal'on, 356 ....B 4
Gan Yavne, 2,668 ....B 4
Gat, 430 ....B 4
Gedera, 4,561 ....B 4
Gesher, 360 ....D 2
Gesher Haziv, 238 ....C 1
Gevar'am, 283 ....B 4
Gilat, 561 ....B 5
Gimosar, 473 ....C 2
Giv'atayim, 30,932 ....B 3
Giv'at Brenner, 1,505 ....B 4
Giv'at Hayyim, 1,360 ....B 3
Gosh Halav (Jish), 1,498 .....C 1
Habonim, 189 ....B 2
Hadera, 27,200 ....B 2
Haifa, 212,200 ....B 2
Haifa, *447,800 ....B 2
Hazerim, 127 ....B 5
Helez, 466 ....B 4
Herzeliyya, 30,000 ....B 3

Hod Hasharon ....B 3
Hodiyya, 400 ....B 4
Holon, 55,200 ....B 3
Iksal, 2,156 ....C 2
Jerusalem (capital),
  275,000 ....C 4
Jish, 1,498 ....C 1
Kafar Kanna, 3,549 ....C 2
Kafar Yasif, 2,975 ....C 2
Karkur, 2,856 ....C 3
Kefar Atta, 16,300 ....C 2
Kefar Blum, 565 ....D 1
Kefar Gil'adi, 701 ....D 1
Kefar Ruppin, 306 ....D 2
Kefar Sava, 19,000 ....B 3
Kefar Vitkin, 808 ....B 3
Kefar Yona, 2,372 ....B 3
Kefar Zekhariya, 420 ....B 4
Kinneret, 909 ....D 2
Kurnub ....C 5
Lod (Lydda), 21,000 ....B 4
Lydda, 21,000 ....B 4
Magen, 149 ....A 5
Malkiya ....D 1
Mash' Abbe Sade, 238 ....B 6
Mavqi'im, 177 ....B 4
Megiddo ....C 2
Me'ona, 317 ....C 1
Metula, 317 ....D 1
Migdal, 688 ....C 2
Mikhmoret, 608 ....B 3
Mishmar Hanegev, 336 ....B 5
Mishmar Hayarden ....D 1
Mivtahim, 398 ....A 5
Mizpe Ramon, 331 ....D 5
Moza Illit, 219 ....C 2
Mughar, 4,010 ....C 2
Muqeible, 459 ....C 2
Nahariyya, 15,900 ....C 1
Nazareth, 26,400 ....C 2
Neqba, 453 ....A 4
Nes Ziyyona, 11,200 ....B 4
Nesher, 8,450 ....C 2
Netanya, 46,200 ....B 3
Nevatim, 436 ....B 5
Newe Yam, 211 ....B 2
Nir Am, 331 ....A 5
Nir Yitzhaq, 209 ....A 5
Nizzanim, 479 ....B 4
'Omer ....C 6
Oron ....C 6
Pardes Hanna, 8,200 ....B 2
Peduyim, 361 ....B 5
Petah Tiqwa, 58,700 ....B 3
Qadima, 2,937 ....B 3
Qedma, 157 ....B 4
Qiryat Bialik, 10,400 ....C 2
Qiryat Gat, 10,111 ....B 4
Qiryat Haayin, 9,256 ....B 2
Qiryat Motzkin, 10,300 ....C 2
Qiryat Shemona, 13,900 .....C 1
Qiryat Tiv'on, 9,650 ....C 2
Qiryat Yam, 11,600 ....C 2
Ra'anana, 10,000 ....B 3
Ramat Gan, 109,400 ....B 3
Ramat Hasharon, 11,100 .....B 3
Rame, 2,986 ....C 1
Ramla, 23,900 ....B 4
Rehovot, 30,400 ....B 4
Re'im, 155 ....A 5
Revadim, 175 ....B 4
Revivim, 258 ....B 5
Rishon Le Ziyyon, 30,000 ....B 4

Rosh Pinna, 700 ....D 2
Ruhama, 497 ....B 5
Sa'ad, 418 ....B 5
Safad (Zefat), 11,500 ....C 2
Sakhnin, 5,500 ....C 2
Sede Boqer ....D 5
Sedom ....D 5
Sedot Yam, 511 ....B 2
Shave Ziyyon, 269 ....C 2
Shefar'am, 7,650 ....C 2
Shefayim, 614 ....B 3
Shoval, 393 ....B 5
Tayibe, 8,100 ....C 3
Tel Aviv-Jaffa, 384,700 ....B 3
Tel Aviv-Jaffa, *838,000 ......B 3
Tiberias, 22,300 ....D 2
Tirat Hakarmel, 11,300 ....B 2
Tirat Zevi, 353 ....D 2
Tur'an, 2,304 ....C 2
Umm el Fahm, 8,100 ....C 2
Urim, 203 ....B 5
Uzza, 487 ....B 5
Yad Mordekhai, 416 ....A 1
Yagur, 1,266 ....C 2
Yavne, 6,200 ....B 4
Yavne'el, 1,580 ....C 2
Yehud, 7,000 ....B 3
Yeroham, 1,574 ....B 4
Yesodot, 293 ....B 4
Yesud Hama'ala, 428 ....D 1
Yiftah ....D 1
Yirka, 2,715 ....C 2
Yoqne'am, 2,884 ....C 2
Yotvata ....D 5
Zavdi'el, 396 ....B 4
Ze'elim, 148 ....A 5
Zefat, 11,500 ....C 2
Zikhron Ya'aqov, 4,393 ....B 2
Zippori, 241 ....C 2

OTHER FEATURES

'Araba, Wadi
  (dry river) ....D 5
Beer Efe' (well) ....C 5
Beer Sheva', Wadi
  (dry river) ....B 4
Besor (river) ....B 5
Borot Kidod (well) ....C 5
Carmel (cape) ....B 2
Carmel (mt.) ....C 2
Dead (sea) ....C 4
Dimona (mt.) ....C 5
'Ein Gedi (well) ....C 5
'Ein Netafim (well) ....D 5
Galilee (region) ....C 2
Galilee, Sea of (sea) ....C 2
Gerar, Wadi (dry river) ....B 5
Hadera (river) ....B 2
Haifa (bay) ....C 2
Hatira (mt.) ....B 6
Hemar, Wadi
  (dry river) ....C 5
Judaea (region) ....C 5
Lakhish, Wadi
  (dry river) ....B 4
Meiron (mt.) ....C 1
Negev (region) ....D 5
Paran, Wadi
  (dry river) ....D 5
Qarn (river) ....C 1
Qishon (river) ....C 2
Ramon (mt.) ....D 5

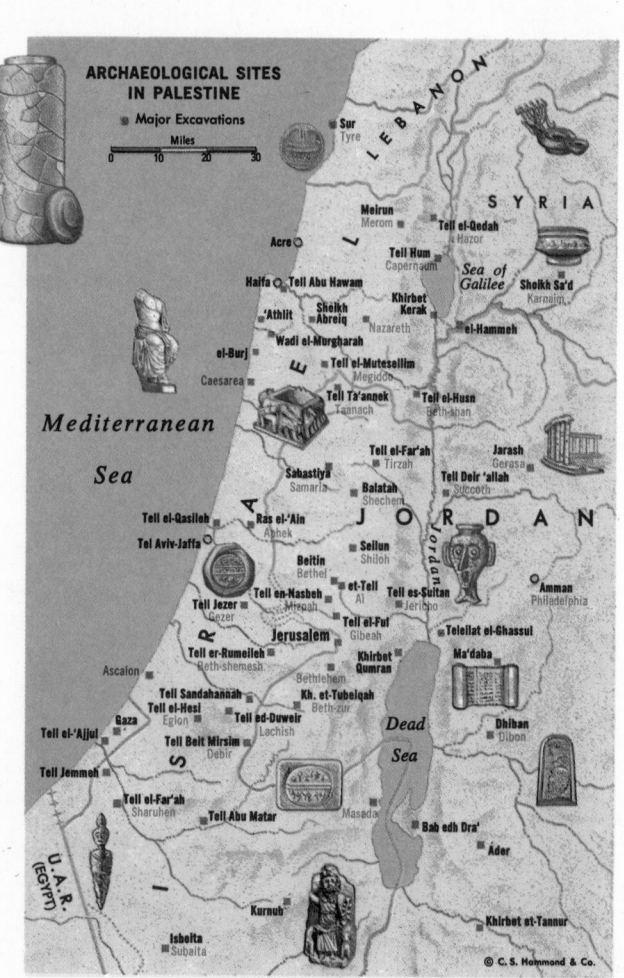

ARCHAEOLOGICAL SITES IN PALESTINE

■ Major Excavations

Miles
0   10   20   30

LEBANON

SYRIA

Sur / Tyre

Meirun / Merom
Tell el-Qedah / Hazor
Acre
Tell Hum / Capernaum
Haifa / Tell Abu Hawam
Khirbet Kerak
Sea of Galilee
Sheikh Sa'd / Karnaim
'Athlit
Sheikh Abreiq / Nazareth
el-Hammeh
el-Burj
Wadi el-Murgharah
Tell el-Mutesellim / Megiddo
Caesarea
Tell Ta'annek / Taanach
Tell el-Husn / Beth-shan
Jarash / Gerasa
Mediterranean Sea
Tell el-Far'ah / Tirzah
Sabastiya / Samaria
Tell Deir 'alla / Succoth
Balatah / Shechem
JORDAN
Tell el-Qasileh
Ras el-'Ain / Aphek
Tel Aviv-Jaffa
Seilun / Shiloh
Beitin / Bethel
et-Tell / Ai
Tell en-Nasbeh / Mizpah
Tell es-Sultan / Jericho
Amman / Philadelphia
Tell Jezer / Gezer
Tell el-Ful / Gibeah
Jerusalem
Khirbet Qumran
Tell er-Rumeileh / Beth-shemesh
Bethlehem
Ma'daba
Ascalon
Tell Sandahannah
Tell el-Hesi / Eglon
Kh. et-Tubeiqah / Beth-zur
Gaza
Tell ed-Duweir / Lachish
Dhiban / Dibon
Tell el-'Ajjul
Tell Beit Mirsim / Debir
Dead Sea
Tell Jemmeh
Tell el-Far'ah / Sharuhen
Tell Abu Matar
Masada
Bab edh Dra'
Åder
U.A.R. (EGYPT)
Kurnub
Khirbet et-Tannur
Isbeita / Subaita

© C. S. Hammond & Co.

Agriculture, Industry and Resources

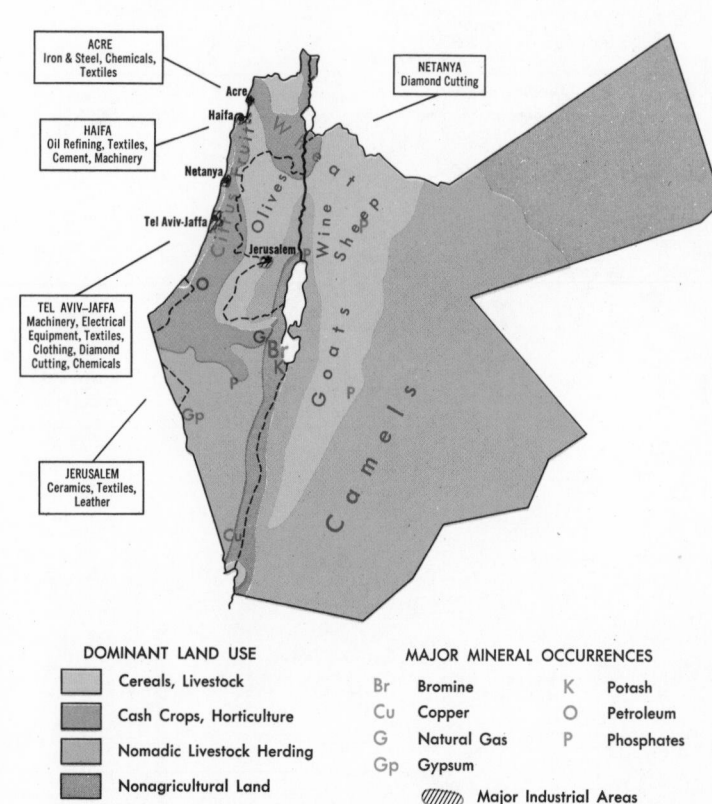

ACRE
Iron & Steel, Chemicals, Textiles

NETANYA
Diamond Cutting

HAIFA
Oil Refining, Textiles, Cement, Machinery

TEL AVIV-JAFFA
Machinery, Electrical Equipment, Textiles, Clothing, Diamond Cutting, Chemicals

JERUSALEM
Ceramics, Textiles, Leather

DOMINANT LAND USE

Cereals, Livestock

Cash Crops, Horticulture

Nomadic Livestock Herding

Nonagricultural Land

MAJOR MINERAL OCCURRENCES

Br Bromine
Cu Copper
G   Natural Gas
Gp Gypsum

K   Potash
O   Petroleum
P   Phosphates

/// Major Industrial Areas

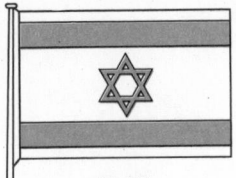

ISRAEL

JORDAN

ISRAEL
AREA 7,993 sq. mi.
POPULATION 2,911,000
CAPITAL Jerusalem
LARGEST CITY Tel Aviv-Jaffa
HIGHEST POINT Meiron 3,963 ft.
MONETARY UNIT Israeli pound
MAJOR LANGUAGES Hebrew, Arabic
MAJOR RELIGIONS Judaism, Islam, Christianity

JORDAN
AREA 37,297 sq. mi.
POPULATION 2,300,000
CAPITAL Amman
LARGEST CITY Amman
HIGHEST POINT Jeb. Ramm 5,069 ft.
MONETARY UNIT Jordanian dinar
MAJOR LANGUAGE Arabic
MAJOR RELIGION Islam

ISRAEL and JORDAN
CYLINDRICAL PROJECTION
SCALE OF MILES
0 5 10 15 20 25 30
SCALE OF KILOMETRES
0 5 10 15 20 25 30

Capitals of Countries .... ★
District Capitals ------------------ ◉
International Boundaries _____
District Boundaries —·—·—·—
Demilitarized Zone Boundaries ....
Neutral Zone Boundaries _____

Copyright by C. S. Hammond & Co., N.Y.

(Index — Jordan / Other Features)

Rubin, Wadi (dry river) ...... B 4
Shiqma (river) ...... B 4
Tabor (mt.) ...... C 2
Tiberias (Galilee) (sea) ...... D 2
Tseelim, Wadi (dry river) ...... C 5
Tsin, Wadi (dry river) ...... D 5
Yarmuk (river) ...... D 2
Yarqon (river) ...... B 3

JORDAN

DISTRICTS

'Ajlun, 334,000 ...... D 3
Amman, 526,000 ...... D 4
El Balqa, 95,000 ...... D 3
El Karak, 81,000 ...... E 5
Hebron, 145,000 ...... C 4
Jerusalem, 418,000 ...... C 4
Ma'an, 58,000 ...... D 5
Nablus, 414,000 ...... C 3

CITIES and TOWNS

'Ajja, 1,322 ...... C 3
'Ajlun, 5,390 ...... D 3
Amman (capital), 330,220 ...... D 4
'Anabta, 4,018 ...... C 3
Anin, 914 ...... C 2
'Anjara, 3,163 ...... D 3
'Anza, 807 ...... C 3
'Aqaba, 8,908 ...... D 6
'Aqraba, 2,501 ...... C 3
Ariha (Jericho), 5,312 ...... C 4
'Arraba, 4,231 ...... C 3
Arura, 849 ...... C 4
'Attil, 3,808 ...... C 3
Bal'ama, 769 ...... C 3
Baqura, 3,042 ...... D 2
Beit Fajjar, 2,474 ...... C 4
Beit Hanina, 3,067 ...... C 4
Beit Jala, 6,041 ...... C 4
Beit Lahm (Bethlehem), 14,439 ...... C 4
Beit Nuba, 1,350 ...... B 4
Beit Sahur, 5,380 ...... C 4
Bethlehem, 14,439 ...... C 4
Biddu, 1,259 ...... C 4
Bir Zeit, 2,311 ...... C 4
Birqin, 2,036 ...... C 3
Burqa, 2,477 ...... C 3
Damiya, 483 ...... D 3
Dana, 844 ...... E 5
Deir Abu Sa'id, 1,927 ...... D 3
Deir Ballut, 1,058 ...... C 3
Deir Sharaf, 973 ...... C 3
Dhahiriya, 4,875 ...... B 5
Dhira', 214 ...... C 3
Duma, 524 ...... C 3
Dura, 4,954 ...... C 4
El 'Al, 492 ...... D 4
El Bira, 9,674 ...... C 4
El Husn, 9,272 ...... D 3
El Karak, 7,422 ...... E 4
El Khalil (Hebron), 38,309 ...... C 4
El Kitta, 987 ...... D 3
El Madwar, 164 ...... E 3
El Mafraq, 9,499 ...... E 3
El Majdal, 259 ...... D 4
El Quweira, 268 ...... D 5
El Yaduda, 251 ...... D 4
Er Rafid, 782 ...... D 2
Er Ramtha, 10,791 ...... E 3
Er Rihiya, 555 ...... C 5
Er Rumman, 293 ...... D 3
Er Ruseifa, 6,200 ...... E 3
Es Salt, 16,176 ...... D 3
Es Sukhna, 649 ...... E 3
Esh Shaubak ...... D 5
Et Tafila, 4,506 ...... D 5
Et Taiyiba, 2,606 ...... D 2
Ez Zababida, 1,474 ...... C 3
Ez Zarqa, 121,303 ...... E 3
Falama, 162 ...... C 3
Halhul, 6,041 ...... C 4
Harima, 635 ...... D 2
Haris, 641 ...... C 3
Hawara, 2,342 ...... C 3
Hebron, 38,309 ...... C 4
Hisban, 718 ...... D 4
Idhna, 3,713 ...... B 4
'Ibbin, 1,364 ...... D 3
'Imwas, 1,955 ...... C 4
Irbid, 44,685 ...... D 2
Jaba', 2,817 ...... C 3
Jabir, 135 ...... E 2
Jalama, 784 ...... C 2
Jalud, 221 ...... D 3
Jarash, 3,796 ...... D 3
Jenin, 8,346 ...... C 3
Jericho, 5,312 ...... C 4
Jerusalem (old city), 60,488 ...... C 4
Jifna, 655 ...... C 4

Kharas, 1,364 ...... C 4
Kitim, 1,026 ...... D 3
Kuraiyima ...... D 3
Ma'ad, 125 ...... D 3
Ma'an, 6,643 ...... E 5
Ma'daba, 11,224 ...... D 4
Ma'in, 1,271 ...... D 4
Manja, 353 ...... D 4
Mazra', 1,194 ...... C 5
Nablus, 41,709 ...... C 3
Nablus (Nablus), 41,709 ...... C 3
Nahhalin, 1,109 ...... C 4
Na'ur, 2,382 ...... D 4
Ni'lin, 1,227 ...... C 4
Nitil, 348 ...... D 4
Qabalan, 1,891 ...... C 3
Qabatiya, 6,005 ...... C 3
Qaffin, 2,480 ...... C 3
Qalqiliya, 8,926 ...... C 3
Qibya, 926 ...... C 4
Qumeim, 955 ...... D 2
Rafidiya, 1,123 ...... C 3
Ramallah, 12,134 ...... C 4
Rammun, 1,198 ...... C 4
Rantis, 897 ...... C 3
Ra's en Naqb, 225 ...... E 5
Safi, 3,468 ...... C 5
Safut, 421 ...... D 3
Salfit, 3,201 ...... C 3
Samar, 716 ...... D 2
Sarih, 3,784 ...... D 3
Sarih, 3,390 ...... D 3
Shu'fat, 2,732 ...... C 4
Shunat Nimrin, 109 ...... D 4
Shuweika, 2,332 ...... C 3
Silat Dhahr, 3,566 ...... C 3
Sinjil, 1,823 ...... C 3
Siris, 1,285 ...... C 3
Subeihi, 514 ...... D 3
Suf, 3,259 ...... D 3
Suweilih, 3,457 ...... D 4
Suweima, 315 ...... D 4
Tammun, 2,952 ...... C 3
Tarqumiya, 2,412 ...... C 4
Tubas, 5,262 ...... C 3
Tulkarm, 10,255 ...... C 3
Tur, 4,289 ...... C 4
Um Jauza, 582 ...... D 3
Wadi es Sir, 4,455 ...... D 4
Wadi Musa, 654 ...... D 5
Waqqas, 2,321 ...... D 2
Ya'bad, 4,857 ...... C 3
Yabrud, 277 ...... C 4
Yamun, 4,173 ...... C 3
Yatta, 7,281 ...... C 5
Zububa, 633 ...... C 2
Zuweiza, 126 ...... D 4

OTHER FEATURES

'Ajlun (range) ...... D 3
Anabta (mt.) ...... C 3
'Aqaba (gulf) ...... D 6
'Araba, Wadi (dry river) ...... D 5
Dead (sea) ...... C 4
Ebal (mt.) ...... C 3
El Ghor (reg.) ...... C 5
El Lisan (pen.) ...... C 5
Hasa, Wadi (dry river) ...... E 5
Hebron (mt.) ...... C 4
Jordan (river) ...... D 3
Judaea (region) ...... C 4
Khirbet Qumran (site) ...... D 4
Kufrinja (mt.) ...... D 3
Kufrinja, Wadi (dry river) ...... D 3
Mashash, Wadi ...... C 4
Nebo (mt.) ...... D 4
Petra (ruins) ...... D 5
Samaria (region) ...... C 3
Shallala, Wadi ...... D 2
Shu'eib, Wadi ...... D 4
Tell 'Asur (mt.) ...... C 4
Tur (mt.) ...... C 4
Yabis, Wadi (dry river) ...... D 3
Zarqa' (river) ...... D 3

GAZA STRIP

Total Population, 480,000

CITIES and TOWNS

'Abasan, 1,481 ...... A 5
Bani Suheila, 7,561 ...... A 4
Beit Hanun, 4,756 ...... A 4
Deir el Balah, 10,854 ...... A 5
Gaza, 87,793 ...... A 4
Gaza, 118,272 ...... A 4
Jabaliya, 10,508 ...... A 4
Khan Yunis, 29,522 ...... A 5
Rafah, 10,812 ...... A 5

City and suburbs.

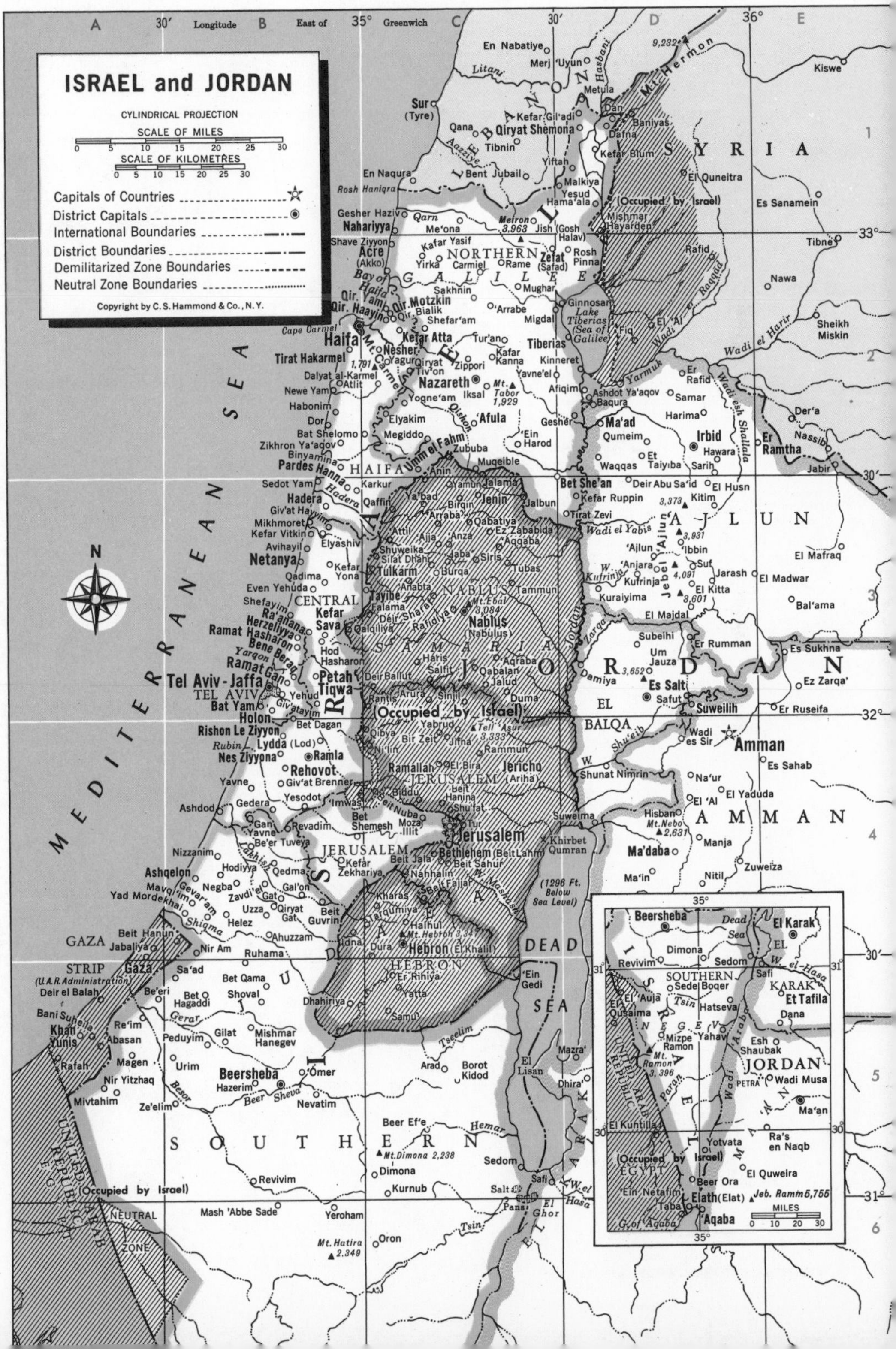

IRAN

INTERNAL DIVISIONS

Bakhtiari (governorate), 298,448	F 4
Boyer Ahmedi and Kahkiluye (governorate),	G 5
East Azerbaijan (province), 2,596,439	E 1
Fars (province), 1,429,804	H 6
Gilan (province), 1,752,504	F 2
Hamadan (governorate), 889,888	F 3
Ilam (governorate)	E 4
Isfahan (province), 1,703,701	H 4
Kerman (province), 761,851	K 6
Kermanshah (province), 924,717	E 3
Khurasan (province), 2,497,381	K 3
Khuzistan (province), 1,578,079	F 5
Kurdistan (province), 619,573	E 2
Luristan (governorate), 686,307	F 4
Mazanderan (province), 1,841,637	H 2
Samnan (governorate), 207,786	J 3
Sea of Oman-Persian Gulf (province), 598,331	H 7
Seistan and Baluchistan (prov.), 454,996	M 6
Tehran (province), 4,979,081	H 3
West Azerbaijan (province), 1,087,182	D 1

CITIES and TOWNS

Abadan, 272,962	F 5
Abadeh, 16,000	H 5
Abarquh, 8,000	H 5
Abhar, 11,000	F 2
Ahar, 24,000	E 1
Ahwaz, 206,375	F 5
Amul, 40,076	H 2
Anarak, 2,038	H 4
Andimeshk, 16,000	F 4
Aradan, 18,978	F 3
Arak, 71,925	F 3
Ardebil, 83,596	F 1
Ardistan, 6,645	H 4
Asadabad, 7,000	F 3
Asterabad (Gurgan), 51,181	J 2
Azarshahr, 6,000	D 2
Azna, 5,000	F 3
Babol, 49,973	H 2
Babulsar, 12,000	H 2
Bafq, 6,000	J 5
Baft, 6,000	K 6
Bahramabad, 21,000	K 5
Bam, 22,000	L 6
Bandar Abbas, 34,627	J 7
Bandar Ma'shur, 17,000	F 5
Bandar Shah, 13,000	H 2
Bandar Shahpur, 5,000	F 5
Behbehan, 39,874	G 5
Behshahr, 26,032	J 2
Bijar, 12,000	E 2
Birjand, 25,854	L 4
Borazjun, 20,000	G 6
Bujnurd, 31,248	L 2
Bukan, 9,000	D 2
Burujird, 71,476	F 4
Bushire, 26,032	G 6
Chalus, 15,000	G 2
Dalijan, 6,000	G 4
Damghan, 13,000	J 2
Darab, 13,000	J 6
Daran, 4,509	G 4
Darreh Gaz, 11,000	L 2
Daulatabad (Malayer), 28,434	F 3
Deh Haqq, 4,115	H 3
Demavend, 5,391	H 3
Dizful, 84,499	F 4
Duzdab (Zahidan), 40,000	M 6
Enzeli (Pahlevi), 41,785	F 2
Estahbanat, 18,187	H 6
Fahrej (Iranshahr), 5,000	M 7
Fariman, 8,000	L 3
Farrashband, 3,532	G 6
Fasa, 19,000	H 6
Firdaus, 11,000	K 3
Firuzabad, 8,718	H 6
Firuzkuh, 4,684	H 3
Fumen, 9,000	F 2
Gach Saran, 9,000	G 5
Ganaveh, 9,000	G 5
Garmsar, 4,723	H 3
Golshan (Tabas), 10,000	K 4
Gulpaigan, 20,515	G 4
Gumishan, 6,000	J 2
Gunabad, 8,000	L 3
Gunbad-i-Qabus, 40,667	K 3
Gurgan, 51,181	J 2
Haft Kel, 10,000	F 5
Hamadan, 124,167	F 3
Hashtpar, 5,000	F 2
Homayunshahr, 46,836	G 4
Ilam, 15,000	E 4
Iranshahr, 5,000	M 7
Isfahan, 424,045	H 4
Jahrum, 38,236	H 6
Kangavar, 9,414	F 3
Karaj, 44,243	G 3
Kashan, 58,468	G 3
Kashmar, 17,000	L 3
Kazerun, 39,758	G 6
Kazvin, 88,106	G 3
Qasr-i-Shirin, 15,904	E 3
Kerman, 85,404	K 5
Kermanshah, 187,930	E 3
Khaf, 25,000	M 3
Khorramshahr, 88,536	F 5
Khunsar, 10,947	G 4
Khur, 2,912	J 4
Khurramabad, 59,578	F 4
Khoi, 47,648	D 1
Lahijan, 25,725	F 2
Lar, 12,000	J 6
Mahabad, 28,610	D 2
Mahallat, 12,000	G 4
Mahan, 8,000	K 5
Maibud, 15,000	J 4
Maku, 15,000	D 1
Malayer, 28,434	F 3
Maragheh, 54,106	E 2
Marand, 24,000	E 1
Mardasht, 25,498	H 6
Masjid-i-Sulaiman, 64,488	F 5
Meshed, 409,616	L 2
Meshed-i-Sar (Babulsar), 12,000	H 2
Meshkinshahr, 9,000	F 1
Mianeh, 28,447	E 2
Mirjawa, 11,000	M 6
Miyanduab, 19,000	D 2
Naft-i-Shah, 3,043	E 4
Na'in, 6,925	H 4
Nasratabad (Zabul), 20,000	M 5
Natanz, 4,370	H 4
Naushahr, 8,000	H 2
Nehavend, 24,000	F 3
Nejafabad, 43,384	G 4
Niriz, 16,114	J 6
Nishapur, 33,482	L 2
Pahlevi (Enzeli), 41,785	F 2
Qain, 6,000	L 4
Qasr-i-Shirin, 15,904	E 3
Quchan, 29,133	L 2
Qum, 134,292	G 3
Rafsenjan (Bahramabad), 21,000	K 5
Rai, 102,825	G 3
Ram Hormuz, 9,000	F 5
Ramsar, 12,000	G 2
Ravar, 7,000	K 5
Resht, 143,557	F 2
Reza'iyeh, 110,749	D 1
Sabzawar, 42,415	K 2
Sabzawar, 7,000	G 5
Saidabad (Sirjan), 20,000	J 6
Samnan, 31,058	H 3
Sanandaj, 54,578	E 2
Sang-i-Sar, 9,000	H 3
Saqiz, 17,000	D 2
Sarab, 16,000	E 2
Sardasht, 6,000	D 2
Savanat (Estahbanat), 18,187	H 6
Shushtar, 24,000	F 4
Sinneh (Sanandaj), 54,578	E 2
Sirjan, 20,000	J 6
Sultanabad (Kashmar), 17,000	L 3
Sunqur, 10,433	E 3
Susangird, 21,000	F 5
Tabas, 10,000	K 4
Tabriz, 403,413	E 1
Taft, 7,000	J 5
Tajrish, 157,486	G 3
Takistan, 13,485	F 2
Tehran (capital), 2,719,730	H 3
Tuiserkan, 12,000	F 3
Tun (Firdaus), 11,000	K 3
Turbat-i-Haidari, 30,106	L 3
Turbat-i-Shaikh Jam, 13,000	M 3
Urmia (Reza'iyeh), 110,749	D 1
Ushnuiyeh, 5,000	D 2
Veramin, 11,183	H 3
Yezd, 93,241	J 5
Zabul, 20,000	M 5
Zahidan, 39,732	M 6
Zarand, 5,000	K 5
Zarghan, 7,000	H 6
Zenjan, 58,714	F 2

OTHER FEATURES

Ab-i-Diz (river)	F 4
Aji Chai (river)	E 1
Arabi (isl.)	G 7
Aras (Araks) (river)	D 1
Atrek (river)	K 2
Bakhtegan (lake)	H 6
Baluchistan (region)	M 7
Bampur (river)	M 7
Behistun (ruins)	E 3
Caspian (sea)	H 1
Darya-yi-Namak (salt lake)	G 3
Dasht-i-Kavir (salt desert)	J 3
Dasht-i-Lut (desert)	L 5
Demavend (mt.)	H 3
Dez (Ab-i-Diz) (river)	F 4
Elburz (range)	H 2
Farsi (isl.)	G 7
Gurgan (river)	J 2
Hamun-i-Helmand (marsh)	M 6
Hamun-i-Jaz-Murian (marsh)	L 7
Hamun-i-Sabari (lake)	M 5
Hanjam (isl.)	J 7
Hari Rud (river)	M 3
Hashtadan (reg.)	M 3
Hormuz (strait)	K 7
Kalar, Kuh-i- (mt.)	E 4
Karkheh (river)	E 4
Kashaf Rud (river)	L 2
Kharg (isl.), 647	F 6
Kuh, Ras el (cape)	K 8
Kuh-i-Aladagh (mts.)	K 2
Kuh-i-Bagraband (mts.)	M 8
Kuh-i-Bazqush (mts.)	E 2
Kuh-i-Dinar (mts.)	G 5
Kuh-i-Gugird (mts.)	K 5
Kuh-i-Jagatai (mts.)	K 2
Kuh-i-Shah Jehan (mts.)	L 2
Kuhistan (region)	L 4
Kur Rud (river)	H 6
Kurang (river)	G 4
Laristan (region)	J 7
Maidani (cape)	M 8
Makran (region)	M 8
Mand Rud (river)	G 6
Mashkel (river)	M 7
Mehran (river)	M 4
Mura, Qal'eh-i- (river)	M 4
Namaksar (lake)	M 3

IRAN and IRAQ

CONIC PROJECTION

SCALE OF MILES
0 25 50 100 150 200

SCALE OF KILOMETRES
0 25 50 100 150 200

Capitals of Countries	★
Capitals of Provinces	△
Capitals of Governorates	◉
International Boundaries	
Provincial Boundaries	
Governorate Boundaries	

Iran consists of fourteen provinces called ostans. Attached to six of these provinces are six governorates.

Namakzar (dry lake) ....L 4
Nezwar (mt.) ....H 3
Nihing (river) ....N 7
Oman (gulf) ....M 8
Pasargadae (ruins) ....H 5
Persepolis (ruins) ....H 6
Persian (gulf) ....F 4
Pusht-i-Kuh (mts.) ....E 4
Qais (isl.) ....J 7
Qarajeh Dagh (mts.) ....E 1
Qara Su (river) ....E 1
Qara Su (river) ....G 3
Qaranqu (river) ....E 2
Qishm (isl.) ....J 7
Qizil Uzun (river) ....F 2
Sefid Rud (river) ....F 2
Shaikh Shu'aib (island) ....H 7
Shelagh (river) ....M 5
Shirvan (river) ....E 3
Shur (river) ....J 7
Siahkuh (mt.) ....J 5
Silop (river) ....M 8
Susa (ruins) ....F 4
Talab (river) ....N 6
Tashk (lake) ....J 6
Urmia (lake) ....D 2
Yezd (region) ....J 5
Zagros (mts.) ....G 4
Zaindeh Rud (river) ....H 4
Zarineh (river) ....E 2
Zilbir Chai (river) ....D 1
Zuhreh Rud (river) ....F 5

IRAQ
PROVINCES

'Amara, 346,663 ....E 5
Baghdad, 2,124,323 ....C 3

Ash Shabicha, 249 ....C 5
Az Zubair, 41,408 ....E 5
Badra, 3,564 ....D 4
Baghdad (capital),
  502,503 ....D 3
Baghdad*, 1,745,328 ....D 3
Baiji, 6,785 ....C 2
Ba'quba, 34,575 ....D 4
Basra, 313,327 ....E 5
Dohuk, 16,998 ....C 2
Erbil, 90,320 ....D 2
Fao, 15,399 ....F 6
Habbaniya, 14,405 ....C 3
Hadhar, 1,019 ....C 3
Haditha, 6,870 ....C 3
Hai, 16,988 ....D 4
Halabja, 11,206 ....D 3
Hilla, 84,717 ....D 4
Hindiya, 16,436 ....D 4
Hit, 9,131 ....C 3
Karbala*, 83,301 ....C 4
Khanaqin, 23,522 ....D 3
Kifri, 8,500 ....D 3
Kirkuk, 167,413 ....D 3
Kut, 42,116 ....D 4
Lailan, 1,526 ....D 3
Maidan, 354 ....D 3
Makhmur, 2,556 ....C 3
Mandali, 11,262 ....D 4
Mosul, 315,157 ....C 2
Muqdadiyah, 12,181 ....D 4
Na'maniya, 11,943 ....D 4
An Najaf, 128,096 ....D 5
An Nasiriya, 60,405 ....D 5
'Ana, 6,884 ....B 3
'Aqra, 8,659 ....D 2
Ar Rahhaliya ....D 4
Arbela (Erbil), 90,320 ....D 2
As Busaiya, 295 ....E 5
As Salman, 1,789 ....D 5

Basra, 673,623 ....E 5
Diwaniya, 548,830 ....D 5
Diyala, 400,049 ....D 4
Hilla, 448,023 ....D 4
Karbala*, 339,692 ....C 4
Kirkuk, 462,027 ....D 3
Kut, 335,495 ....D 4
Mosul, 954,157 ....C 2
Nasiriya, 500,033 ....E 5
Ramadi, 319,289 ....C 4
Sulaimaniya, 408,220 ....D 3

CITIES and TOWNS

Ad Diwaniya, 60,553 ....D 5
'Afaq, 5,390 ....D 4
Al 'Azair, 2,255 ....E 5
Al 'Aziziya, 7,450 ....D 4
Al Faluja, 38,072 ....C 4
Al Kufa, 30,862 ....D 4
Al Kumait, 2,225 ....E 4
Al Musaiyib, 15,955 ....D 4
Al Qa'im, 3,372 ....B 3
Al Qaiyara, 3,060 ....C 2
Al Qosh, 3,863 ....C 2
Al Qurna, 5,638 ....E 5
'Ali Gharbi, 5,735 ....E 4
'Ali Sharqi, 1,980 ....E 4
'Amadiya, 2,578 ....D 2

IRAN
AREA 636,293 sq. mi.
POPULATION 28,448,000
CAPITAL Tehran
LARGEST CITY Tehran
HIGHEST POINT Demavend 18,376 ft.
MONETARY UNIT rial
MAJOR LANGUAGES Persian, Azerbaijani, Kurdish
MAJOR RELIGIONS Islam, Parsiism

IRAQ
AREA 167,924 sq. mi..
POPULATION 9,431,000
CAPITAL Baghdad
LARGEST CITY Baghdad
HIGHEST POINT Haji Ibrahim 11,811 ft.
MONETARY UNIT Iraqi dinar
MAJOR LANGUAGES Arabic, Kurdish
MAJOR RELIGION Islam

IRAN

IRAQ

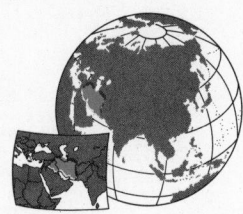

Ramadi, 28,723 ....C 4
Refa'i, 7,881 ....E 5
Rumaitha, 10,222 ....D 5
Rutba, 5,091 ....B 4
Ruwandiz, 5,807 ....D 2
Sa'diya, 5,285 ....D 3
Samarra, 24,746 ....C 3
Samawa, 33,473 ....D 5
Shaikh Sa'ad, 2,958 ....E 4
Shaqlawa, 6,814 ....D 2
Shatra, 18,822 ....E 5
Shithatha, 2,326 ....C 4
Sinjar, 7,942 ....B 2
Sulaimaniya, 86,822 ....D 3
Tal Kaif, 7,482 ....C 2
Tauq, 845 ....D 3
Taza Khurmatu, 2,681 ....D 3
Tikrit, 9,921 ....C 3
Tuz Khurmatu, 13,860 ....D 3
Zakho, 14,790 ....C 2
Zorbatiya, 1,602 ....D 4

OTHER FEATURES

Adhaim (river) ....D 3
Al Hajara (plain) ....C 5
'Aneiza, Jebel (mt.) ....A 4
'Arab, Shatt-al- (river) ....F 5
'Ar'ar, Wadi (dry river) ....B 5
Babylon (ruins) ....D 4
Bahr al Milh (lake) ....C 4
Batin, Wadi al (dry river) ....E 6
Ctesiphon (ruins) ....D 4
Darbandikhan (dam) ....D 3
Euphrates (river) ....C 2
Great Zab (river) ....C 2
Hajara, Al (plain) ....D 5
Haji Ibrahim (mt.) ....D 2
Hammar, Hor al
  (lake) ....E 5
Hauran, Wadi (dry river) ....B 4
Ibrahim, Haji (mt.) ....D 2
Kurdistan (region) ....C 2
Little Zab (river) ....C 2
Mesopotamia (region) ....C 3
Nineveh (ruins) ....C 2
Sa'diya, Hor (lake) ....E 4
Saniya, Hor (lake) ....D 4
Sha'ib Hisb, Wadi
  (dry river) ....C 5
Shatt-al-'Arab (river) ....F 5
Sinjar, Jebel (mts.) ....B 2
Siyah Kuh (mt.) ....B 2
Syrian (desert) ....B 4
Tigris (river) ....C 2
Ubaiyidh, Wadi (dry river) ....B 5
Ur (ruins) ....D 5

*City and suburbs.
†Population of sub-district.

Topography

0   200   400
MILES

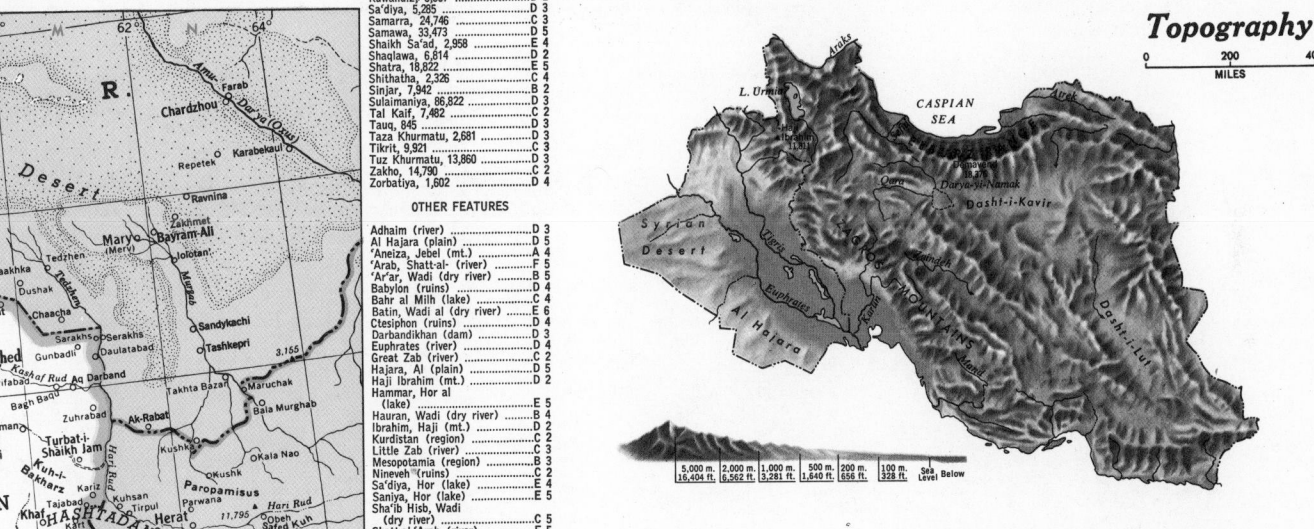

5,000 m. 2,000 m. 1,000 m. 500 m. 200 m. 100 m. Sea
16,404 ft. 6,562 ft. 3,281 ft. 1,640 ft. 656 ft. 328 ft. Level   Below

Agriculture, Industry and Resources

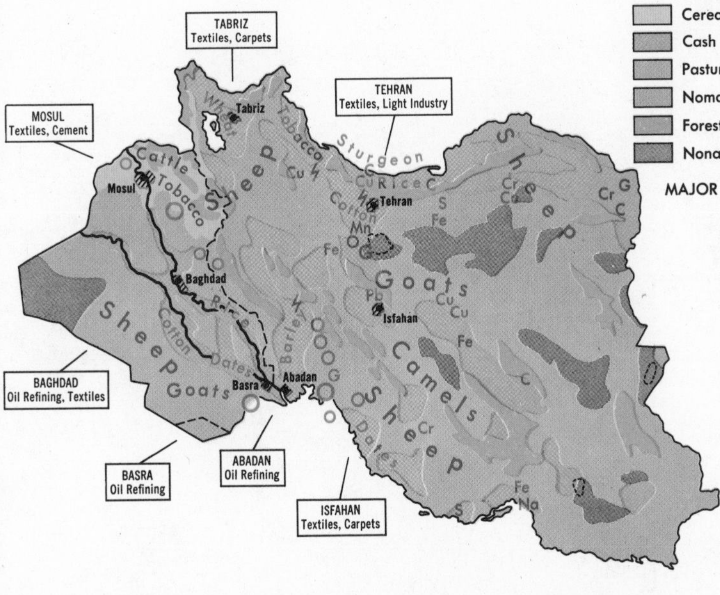

DOMINANT LAND USE

Cereals, Livestock
Cash Crops, Horticulture, Livestock
Pasture Livestock
Nomadic Livestock Herding
Forests
Nonagricultural Land

MAJOR MINERAL OCCURRENCES

C   Coal
Cr Chromium
Cu Copper
Fe Iron Ore
G   Natural Gas
Mn Manganese
Na Salt
O   Petroleum
Pb Lead
S   Sulfur, Pyrites

⚡ Water Power
▨ Major Industrial Areas

TABRIZ
Textiles, Carpets

TEHRAN
Textiles, Light Industry

MOSUL
Textiles, Cement

BAGHDAD
Oil Refining, Textiles

BASRA
Oil Refining

ABADAN
Oil Refining

ISFAHAN
Textiles, Carpets

INDIAN SUBCONTINENT and AFGHANISTAN

CONIC PROJECTION

SCALE OF MILES

0 50 100   200   300

SCALE OF KILOMETRES

0 50 100   200   300

Capitals of Countries.................☆
Provincial and State Capitals.............◉
International Boundaries...........————
Provincial and State Boundaries...—·—·—
Canals....................................

Copyright by C. S. HAMMOND & CO., N. Y.

INDIA

PAKISTAN

CEYLON

AFGHANISTAN

NEPAL

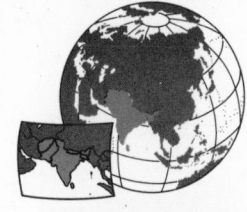

MALDIVES

INDIA
AREA 1,261,483 sq. mi.
POPULATION 546,955,945
CAPITAL New Delhi
LARGEST CITY Calcutta (greater)
HIGHEST POINT K2 (Godwin Austen) 28,250 ft.
MONETARY UNIT Indian rupee
MAJOR LANGUAGES Hindi, English, Bihari, Telugu, Marathi, Bengali, Tamil, Gujarati, Rajasthani, Kanarese, Malayalam, Oriya, Punjabi, Assamese, Kashmiri
MAJOR RELIGIONS Hinduism, Islam, Christianity, Sikhism, Buddhism, Jainism, Parsiism, Animism

NEPAL
AREA 54,362 sq. mi.
POPULATION 10,845,000
CAPITAL Katmandu
LARGEST CITY Katmandu
HIGHEST POINT Mt. Everest 29,028 ft.
MONETARY UNIT Nepalese rupee
MAJOR LANGUAGES Nepali, Maithili, Tamang, Newari, Tharu
MAJOR RELIGIONS Hinduism, Buddhism

MALDIVES
AREA 115 sq. mi.
POPULATION 110,770
CAPITAL Malé
LARGEST CITY Malé
HIGHEST POINT 20 ft.
MONETARY UNIT Indian & Ceylonese rupees
MAJOR LANGUAGE Maldivian
MAJOR RELIGION Islam

AFGHANISTAN
AREA 250,000 sq. mi.
POPULATION 17,078,263
CAPITAL Kabul
LARGEST CITY Kabul
HIGHEST POINT Hindu Kush 24,556 ft.
MONETARY UNIT afghani
MAJOR LANGUAGES Pushtu, Dari, Uzbek
MAJOR RELIGION Islam

PAKISTAN
AREA 365,527 sq. mi.
POPULATION 112,600,000
CAPITALS Islamabad, Ayubnagar
LARGEST CITY Karachi (greater)
HIGHEST POINT Tirich Mir 25,230 ft.
MONETARY UNIT Pakistani rupee
MAJOR LANGUAGES Urdu, Bengali, English, Punjabi, Pushtu, Sindhi, Baluchi
MAJOR RELIGIONS Islam, Hinduism, Sikhism, Christianity

CEYLON
AREA 25,332 sq. mi.
POPULATION 12,300,000
CAPITAL Colombo
LARGEST CITY Colombo
HIGHEST POINT Pidurutalagala 8,281 ft.
MONETARY UNIT Ceylonese rupee
MAJOR LANGUAGES Singhalese, Tamil, English
MAJOR RELIGIONS Buddhism, Hinduism, Christianity

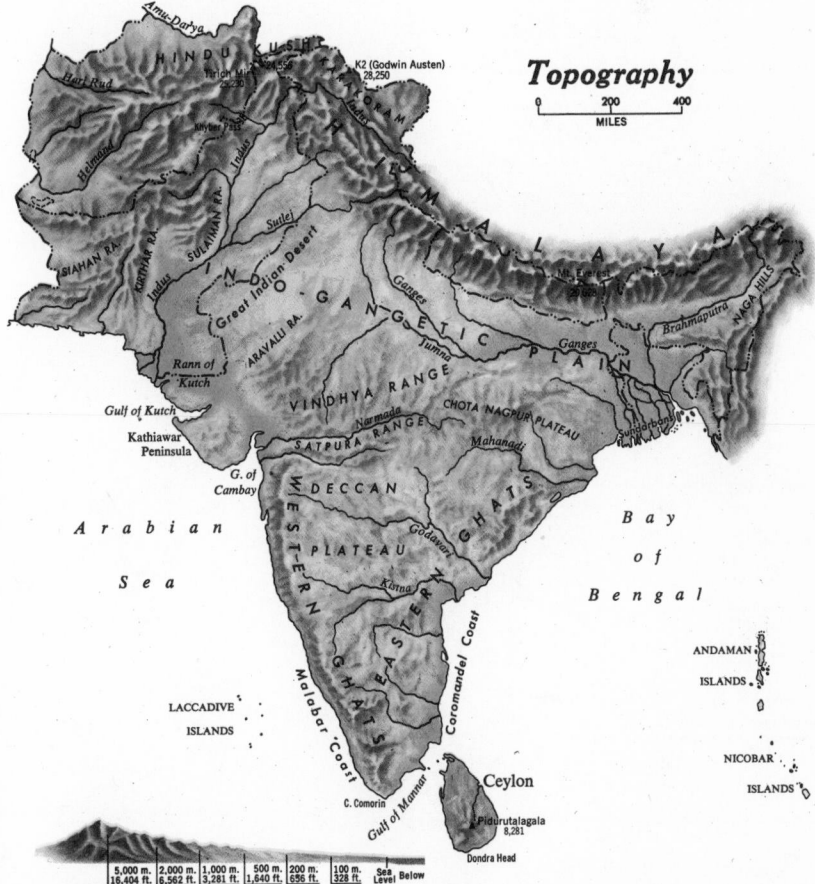

Topography

0 200 400
MILES

AFGHANISTAN
CITIES and TOWNS

Andkhui, 30,000 ....B 1
Baghlan, 92,000 ....B 1
Balkh, 15,000 ....B 1
Bamian, 25,000 ....B 2
Charikar, 83,700 ....B 2
Faizabad, 57,000 ....C 1
Farah, 26,400 ....A 2
Gardez, 33,000 ....B 2
Ghazni, 39,900 ....B 2
Haibak, 35,200 ....B 1
Herat, 71,563 ....A 2
Jalalabad, 48,919 ....C 2
Kabul (cap.), 472,313 ....B 2
Kabul, *600,000 ....B 2
Kala Bist, 26,100 ....A 2
Kalat-i-Ghilzai, 40,500 ....B 2
Kandahar, 127,036 ....B 2
Kandahar, *142,000 ....B 2
Khanabad, 30,000 ....B 1
Maimana, 48,750 ....A 1
Mazar-i-Sharif, 43,197 ....B 1
Shibarghan, 50,440 ....B 1
Tashkurghan, 30,000 ....B 1

OTHER FEATURES

Hari Rud (river) ....A 1
Helmand (river) ....B 2
Hindu Kush (range) ....C 2
Kabul (river) ....C 2
Kunar (river) ....C 1
Kunduz (river) ....B 1
Paropamisus (range) ....A 2
Registan (desert) ....B 2

CEYLON
CITIES and TOWNS

Anuradhapura, 29,397 ....E 7
Badulla, 27,088 ....E 7
Batticaloa, 22,957 ....E 7
Colombo (cap.), 551,200 ......D 7
Galle, 64,942 ....D 7
Jaffna, 94,248 ....E 7
Kalutara, 25,286 ....D 7
Kandy, 67,768 ....E 7
Kurunegala, 21,293 ....E 7
Matara, 32,284 ....E 7
Moratuwa, 77,632 ....D 7
Negombo, 47,028 ....D 7
Nuwara Eliya, 19,988 ....E 7
Ratnapura, 21,582 ....D 7
Trincomalee, 34,872 ....E 7

OTHER FEATURES

Adam's Bridge (shoals) ....D 7
Dondra (head) ....D 7
Mannar (gulf) ....D 7
Palk (strait) ....D 7
Pidurutalagala (mt.) ....E 7

INDIA
INTERNAL DIVISIONS

Andaman and Nicobar Islands (terr.), 115,092 ....G 6
Andhra Pradesh (state), 43,394,951 ....D 5
Assam (state), 15,851,338 .....G 3
Bhutan (protectorate), 770,000 ....G 3
Bihar (state), 56,387,296 ......F 4
Chandigarh (terr.), 150,000 ..D 2
Dadra and Nagar-Haveli (terr.), 69,000 ....C 4
Delhi (terr.), 4,044,281 ....D 2
Goa, Daman and Diu (terr.), 675,000 ....C 4
Gujarat (state), 25,189,000 ...C 4
Haryana (state), 9,914,145 ....D 2
Himachal Pradesh (state), 3,432,000 ....D 2

Jammu and Kashmir (state), 4,615,025 ....D 2
Kerala (state), 20,296,000 ....D 6
Laccadive, Minicoy and Amindivi Islands (terr.), 27,000 ....C 6
Madhya Pradesh (state), 41,449,729 ....D 4
Maharashtra (state), 50,295,081 .C 5
Manipur (terr.), 1,035,000 .....G 4
Mysore (state), 27,985,000 ...D 6
Nagaland (state), 515,551 .....G 3
North East Frontier Agency, 381,000 ....G 3
Orissa (state), 20,674,000 .....E 5
Pondicherry (terr.), 430,000 ..E 6
Punjab (state), 13,935,000 ....D 2
Rajasthan (state), 25,724,595 ..C 3
Sikkim (state), 191,000 ....F 3
Tamil Nadu (state), 33,686,953 .D 6
Tripura (terr.), 1,424,000 ......G 4
Uttar Pradesh (state), 88,299,453 ....D 3
West Bengal (state), 44,440,095 ....F 4

CITIES and TOWNS

Achalpur, 36,538 ....D 4
Achalpur, *54,028 ....D 4
Adoni, 69,951 ....D 5
Agartala, 54,878 ....G 4
Agra, 610,328 ....D 3
Agra, *658,781 ....D 3
Ahmadabad, 1,507,921 ....C 4
Ahmadabad, *1,746,111 ......C 4
Ahmadnagar, 131,973 ....C 5
Ajmer, 265,156 ....C 3
Akola, 143,919 ....D 4
Aligarh, 232,278 ....D 3
Allahabad, 521,568 ....E 3
Allahabad, *537,047 ....E 3
Alleppey, 161,279 ....D 7
Alwar, 72,707 ....D 3
Amalner, 46,963 ....C 4
Ambala, 87,750 ....D 2
Ambala, *200,576 ....D 2
Amravati, 177,066 ....D 4
Amreli, 34,869 ....C 4
Amritsar, 424,961 ....C 2
Amritsar, *459,179 ....C 2
Anakapalle, 46,402 ....E 5
Anantapur, 52,280 ....D 6
Andheri, 122,401 ....B 7
Arcot, 25,029 ....D 6
Arrah, 76,766 ....E 3
Aruppukkottai, 50,200 ....D 7
Aruppukkottai, *55,977 ....D 7
Asansol, 134,056 ....F 4
Asansol, *278,350 ....F 4
Aurangabad, 87,579 ....D 5
Aurangabad, *97,701 ....D 5
Azamgarh, 32,391 ....E 3
Badagara, 43,908 ....D 6
Bagalkot, 39,934 ....D 5
Bahraich, 56,033 ....E 3
Baidyabati, 44,312 ....F 1
Balasore, 33,931 ....F 4
Ballia, 38,216 ....E 3
Bally, 247,844 ....F 1
Balrampur, 31,776 ....E 3
Banda, 37,744 ....D 3
Bandra, 38,099 ....B 7
Bangalore, 1,027,327 ....D 6
Bangalore, *1,648,232 ....D 6
Bankura, 62,833 ....F 4
Bansberia, 45,463 ....F 1
Barasat, 29,281 ....F 1
Barasat, *61,621 ....F 1
Bareilly, 325,560 ....D 3
Bareilly, *343,559 ....D 3
Baripada, 20,301 ....F 4
Barmer, 27,600 ....C 3
Barnagore, 143,621 ....F 1
Baroda, 400,725 ....C 4
Barrackpore, 63,778 ....F 1
Barrackpore, *158,244 ....F 1
Barsi, 50,385 ....D 5
Basirhat, 53,943 ....F 1
Bassein, 22,598 ....C 5

Bassein, *28,238 ....C 5
Batala, 51,300 ....D 2
Beawar, 53,931 ....C 3
Belgaum, 156,105 ....C 5
Belgaum, *176,857 ....C 5
Bellary, 85,673 ....D 5
Benares (Varanasi), 619,822 .E 3
Berhampore, 62,317 ....F 4
Berhampur, 76,931 ....E 5
Bettiah, 39,990 ....E 3
Bhadrak, 25,285 ....F 4
Bhadreswar, 35,489 ....F 1

Bhagalpur, 174,538 ....F 4
Bhandara, 27,710 ....E 4
Bhandup, 30,000 ....B 7
Bharatpur, 49,776 ....D 3
Bhatinda, 52,253 ....C 2
Bhatpara, 159,219 ....F 1
Bhavnagar, 217,533 ....C 4
Bhilai, 86,116 ....E 4
Bhilwara, 43,499 ....C 3
Bhimavaram, 43,281 ....D 5
Bhir (Bir), 33,066 ....D 5
Bhiwandi, 47,630 ....C 5
Bhiwani, 58,194 ....D 3

Bhopal, 310,733 ....D 4
Bhopal, *441,939 ....D 4
Bhubaneswar, 38,211 ....F 4
Bhuj, 38,953 ....B 4
Bhuj, *40,180 ....B 4
Bhusawal, 73,994 ....D 4
Bhusawal, *79,121 ....D 4
Bidar, 32,420 ....D 5
Bihar, 78,581 ....F 3
Bijapur, 78,854 ....D 5
Bijnor, 33,821 ....D 3
Bikaner, 186,560 ....C 3
Bilaspur, 86,706 ....E 4

Bina, 27,476 ....D 4
Bir, 33,066 ....D 5
Bobbili, 25,592 ....E 5
Bodhan, 30,929 ....D 5
Bodinayakkanur, 44,914 ....D 7
Bombay, *5,931,989 ....B 7
Broach, 73,639 ....C 4
Budaun, 58,770 ....D 3
Budge-Budge, 39,824 ....F 1
Bulsar, 35,028 ....C 4
Bulsar, *37,586 ....C 4
Bundi, 26,478 ....D 3
Burdwan, 147,528 ....F 4

(continued on following page)

Burhanpur, 82,090 ....D 4
Calcutta, 7,040,345 ....F 2
Calicut (Kozhikode), 315,786 ....D 6
Cambay, 51,291 ....C 4
Cannanore, 46,101 ....C 6
Cannanore, *48,960 ....B 6
Cawnpore (Kanpur), 1,163,524 ....E 3
Champdani, 42,129 ....F 1
Chanda, 51,484 ....D 5
Chandernagore, 67,105 ....F 1
Chandigarh, 89,321 ....D 2
Chandigarh, *110,614 ....D 2
Chapra, 75,580 ....F 3
Chembur, 85,582 ....B 7
Chhindwara, 37,244 ....D 4
Chidambaram, 40,694 ....E 6
Chikmagalur, 30,253 ....D 6
Chingleput, 25,977 ....E 6
Chirala, 45,410 ....E 5
Chitradurga, 33,336 ....D 6
Chittoor, 47,876 ....D 6
Churu, 41,727 ....D 3
Cocanada (Kakinada), 146,332 ..E 5
Cochin, 35,076 ....D 6
Coimbatore, 393,145 ....D 6
Cooch Behar, 41,922 ....F 3
Cuddalore, 79,168 ....E 6
Cuddapah, 49,027 ....D 6
Cuttack, 198,405 ....F 4
Dabhoi, 30,841 ....C 4
Daltonganj, 25,270 ....E 4
Damoh, 46,656 ....D 4
Darbhanga, 121,438 ....F 3
Darjeeling, 40,651 ....F 3
Datia, 29,430 ....D 3
Davangere, 78,124 ....D 6
Dehra Dun, 136,469 ....D 2
Dehra Dun, *167,297 ....D 2
Delhi, *3,629,842 ....D 3
Deoghar, 35,105 ....F 4
Deolali, 37,264 ....C 5
Deoria, 28,407 ....E 3
Dewas, 34,577 ....D 4
Dhamtari, 31,552 ....E 4
Dhanbad, 57,400 ....F 4
Dhar, 28,325 ....C 4
Dharwar, 77,163 ....C 5
Dholpur, 27,412 ....D 3
Dhoraji, 48,951 ....C 4
Dhubri, 28,355 ....G 3
Dhulia, 98,893 ....C 4
Dibrugarh, 58,480 ....G 3
Dindigul, 92,947 ....D 6
Dohad, 35,483 ....C 4
Dohad, *50,434 ....C 4
Domjor, *30,843 ....F 1
Dum Dum, 20,041 ....F 1
Dum Dum, *174,177 ....F 1
Durg, 64,132 ....E 4
Durg, *204,784 ....E 4
Durgapur, *41,696 ....F 4
Eluru, 130,166 ....E 5

Ernakulam, 203,493 ....D 6
Ernakulam, *474,187 ....D 6
Erode, 73,762 ....D 6
Erode, *96,528 ....D 6
Etawah, 69,681 ....D 3
Faizabad, 83,717 ....E 3
Faizabad, *88,296 ....E 3
Fatehgarh, 87,793 ....D 3
Fatehgarh, *94,591 ....D 3
Fatehpur, 27,039 ....C 3
Fatehpur, 28,323 ....E 3
Ferozepore, 47,060 ....C 2
Ferozepore, *97,932 ....C 2
Firozabad, 98,611 ....D 3
Gadag, 76,614 ....D 5
Ganganagar, 63,854 ....C 3
Gangtok, 6,848 ....F 3
Garden Reach, 152,347 ....F 2
Garulia, 29,041 ....F 1
Gauhati, 210,561 ....G 3
Gaya, 167,500 ....F 4
Ghat Kopar, 34,256 ....B 7
Ghaziabad, 63,190 ....D 3
Ghaziabad, *70,438 ....D 3
Ghazipur, 37,147 ....E 3
Godhra, 52,167 ....C 4
Gonda, 43,496 ....E 3
Gondal, 45,069 ....C 4
Gorakhpur, 234,497 ....E 3
Gudur, 25,618 ....D 6
Gulbarga, 97,069 ....D 5
Guna, 31,031 ....D 4
Guntakal, 48,083 ....D 5
Guntur, 264,138 ....D 5
Gwalior, 361,780 ....D 3
Harda, 22,279 ....D 4
Hardoi, 36,725 ....E 3
Hardwar, 58,513 ....D 2
Hardwar, *59,960 ....D 2
Hassan, 32,172 ....D 6
Hathras, 64,045 ....D 3
Hazaribagh, 40,958 ....F 4
Hindupur, 32,445 ....D 6
Hinganghat, 36,890 ....D 4
Hingoli, 23,407 ....D 5
Hissar, 60,222 ....D 3
Hooghly-Chinsura, 83,104 ....F 1
Hospet, 53,242 ....D 5
Howrah, 590,385 ....F 2
Hubli, 217,284 ....C 5
Hubli, *303,696 ....C 5
Hyderabad, 1,294,800 ....D 5
Hyderabad, *1,798,910 ....D 5
Imphal, 67,717 ....G 4
Indore, 483,969 ....D 4
Itarsi, 33,611 ....D 4
Jabalpur, 406,214 ....D 4
Jabalpur, *497,946 ....D 4
Jaipur, 533,151 ....D 3
Jalgaon, 80,351 ....D 4
Jalna, 67,158 ....D 4
Jalpaiguri, 48,738 ....F 3
Jamalpur, 57,039 ....F 3

Jammu, 102,738 ....D 2
Jammu, *108,257 ....D 2
Jamnagar, 200,918 ....B 4
Jamshedpur, 402,462 ....F 4
Jamshedpur, *465,740 ....F 4
Jaora, 31,140 ....D 4
Jaunpur, 61,851 ....E 3
Jeypore, 25,291 ....E 5
Jhansi, 177,456 ....D 3
Jhansi, *216,736 ....D 3
Jhunjhunu, 24,962 ....D 3
Jind, 24,216 ....D 3
Jodhpur, 270,404 ....C 3
Jorhat, 24,953 ....G 3
Jubbulpore (Jabalpur), 406,214 ....D 4
Jullundur, 281,623 ....D 2
Jullundur, *333,938 ....D 2
Junagadh, 74,298 ....B 4
Kadayanallur, 41,249 ....D 7
Kadiri, 24,307 ....D 6
Kakinada, 146,332 ....E 5
Kalyan, 73,482 ....C 5
Kalyan, *194,334 ....C 5
Kamarhati, 190,695 ....F 1
Kamptee, 40,859 ....D 4
Kamptee, *46,643 ....D 4
Kanchipuram, 92,714 ....E 6
Kannauj, 24,646 ....D 3
Kanpur, 1,163,524 ....E 3
Kanpur, *1,273,042 ....E 3
Karad, 33,772 ....C 5
Karaikudi, 43,698 ....D 7
Karanja, 26,440 ....D 4
Karikal, 22,252 ....E 6
Karnal, 72,109 ....D 3
Karur, 50,564 ....D 6
Karwar, 23,906 ....C 6
Kasaragod, 27,635 ....C 6
Kasganj, 37,559 ....D 3
Katihar, 46,837 ....F 3
Katihar, *59,344 ....F 3
Katni (Murwara), 46,169 ....E 4
Kavaratti, 2,828 ....C 6
Khamgaon, 44,432 ....D 4
Khamman, 35,888 ....D 5
Khandwa, 63,505 ....D 4
Kharagpur, 163,929 ....F 4
Khardah, 28,362 ....F 1
Kirkee, 58,496 ....C 5
Kishangarh, 25,244 ....D 3
Kolar, 32,587 ....D 6
Kolar Gold Fields, 167,610 ....D 6
Kolhapur, 245,206 ....C 5
Kolhapur, *259,482 ....C 5
Konnagar, 29,443 ....F 1
Kota, 205,429 ....D 3
Kotrung, 31,031 ....F 1
Kottayam, 52,685 ....D 7
Kozhikode, 315,786 ....D 6
Kozhikode, *381,096 ....D 6
Krishnanagar, 70,440 ....F 4
*Kumbakonam, 92,581 ....D 6

Kumbakonam, *96,746 ....D 6
Kurla, 98,018 ....B 7
Kurnool, 157,448 ....D 5
Latur, 40,913 ....D 5
Lucknow, 763,604 ....E 3
Lucknow, *830,298 ....E 3
Ludhiana, 363,403 ....D 2
Machilipatnam, 126,855 ....E 5
Madhubani, 28,229 ....F 3
Madras, 2,047,735 ....E 6
Madras, *2,470,288 ....E 6
Madurai, 486,480 ....D 7
Mahbubnagar, 35,588 ....D 5
Mahuva, 31,668 ....C 4
Mahuva, *32,732 ....C 4
Malad, 88,287 ....B 6
Malegaon, 243,474 ....C 4
Maler-Kotla, 39,543 ....D 2
Malkapur, 29,687 ....D 4
Mandsaur, 41,876 ....C 4
Mandvi, 26,609 ....B 4
Mangalore, 168,646 ....C 6
Mangalore, *234,680 ....C 6
Mangrol, 21,089 ....B 4
Manmad, 23,570 ....C 4
Manmad, *31,551 ....C 4
Mannargudi, 33,558 ....E 6
Mathura, 135,166 ....D 3
Mathura, *144,485 ....D 3
Mattancheri, 83,896 ....D 7
Mau, 48,785 ....E 3
Mayuram, 51,393 ....D 6
Meerut, 244,824 ....D 3
Meerut, *335,565 ....D 3
Mehsana, 32,577 ....C 4
Mhow, 48,032 ....D 4
Midnapore, 59,532 ....F 4
Miraj, 53,345 ....D 5
Mirzapur, 113,177 ....E 4
Monghyr, 89,768 ....F 3
Moradabad, 205,509 ....D 3
Moradabad, *221,433 ....D 3
Morvi, 50,192 ....C 4
Mulund, 56,430 ....B 6
Murwara, 46,169 ....E 4
Murwara, *60,472 ....E 4
Muzaffarnagar, 87,622 ....D 3
Muzaffarpur, 152,831 ....E 3
Mysore, 262,136 ....D 6
Nadiad, 78,952 ....C 4
Nagapattinam, 59,063 ....E 6
Nagapattinam, *61,305 ....E 6
Nagaur, 24,296 ....C 3
Nagercoil, 136,264 ....D 7
Nagina, 30,247 ....D 3
Nagpur, 876,020 ....D 4
Nagpur, *933,344 ....D 4
Naihati, 58,457 ....F 1
Nander, 81,087 ....D 5
Nandurbar, 41,055 ....C 4
Nandyal, 42,927 ....D 5
Nasik, 169,451 ....C 4
Nasik, *282,782 ....C 4

Navsari, 51,300 ....C 4
Navsari, *53,600 ....C 4
Nellore, 134,404 ....E 6
New Delhi (cap.), 324,283 ....D 3
Nimach, 36,287 ....D 4
Nizamabad, 79,093 ....D 5
Ongole, 35,804 ....E 5
Ootacamund, 50,140 ....D 6
Orai, 29,587 ....D 3
Palanpur, 29,139 ....C 4
Palayankottai, 51,002 ....D 7
Palghat, 77,620 ....D 6
Pali, 33,303 ....C 3
Palni, 39,832 ....D 6
Palni, *56,909 ....D 6
Panchur, 25,131 ....F 2
Pandharpur, 45,421 ....D 5
Panihati, 93,749 ....F 1
Panipat, 67,026 ....D 3
Panjim, †79,437 ....C 5
Parbhani, 36,795 ....D 5
Parlakhemundi, 22,708 ....E 5
Parvatipuram, 25,281 ....E 5
Patan, 50,264 ....C 4
Patiala, 154,414 ....D 2
Patna, 449,471 ....F 3
Patna, *451,520 ....F 3
Pilibhit, 57,527 ....D 3
Pondicherry, 40,421 ....E 6
Poona, 718,220 ....C 5
Poona, *1,123,399 ....C 5
Porbandar, 74,476 ....B 4
Porbandar, *75,081 ....B 4
Port Blair, 14,075 ....G 6
Proddatur, 50,616 ....D 6
Pudukkottai, 50,488 ....D 6
Puri, 60,815 ....F 5
Purnea, 40,602 ....F 3
Purulia, 48,134 ....F 4
Quilon, 91,018 ....D 7
Raichur, 63,329 ....D 5
Raigarh, 36,933 ....E 4
Raipur, 204,632 ....E 4
Rajahmundry, 155,450 ....E 5
Rajapalaiyam, 71,203 ....D 7
Rajkot, 270,186 ....C 4
Rajnandgaon, 44,678 ....E 4
Rajpipla, 21,426 ....C 4
Rajpur, 24,812 ....F 2
Rampur, 136,349 ....D 3
Ranchi, 137,280 ....F 4
Ranchi, *176,789 ....F 4
Ratangarh, 26,631 ....C 3
Ratlam, 87,472 ....C 4
Ratnagiri, 31,091 ....C 5
Raurkela, 90,287 ....F 4
Rewa, 43,065 ....E 4
Rewari, 36,994 ....D 3
Rishra, 38,535 ....F 1
Sagar, 97,556 ....D 4
Sagar, *120,262 ....D 4
Saharanpur, 223,459 ....D 3
Salem, 297,168 ....D 6

Samalkot, 31,924 ....E 5
Sambalpur, 38,915 ....E 4
Sambhal, 68,940 ....D 3
Sangli, 88,753 ....C 5
Sangli, *150,407 ....C 5
Santa Cruz, 101,232 ....B 7
Santipur, 51,190 ....F 4
Sardarshahr, 32,072 ....C 3
Sasaram, 37,782 ....E 4
Satara, 44,353 ....C 5
Satara, *48,709 ....C 5
Satna, 38,046 ....E 4
Savanur, 16,930 ....D 6
Secunderabad, 187,471 ....D 5
Sehore, 28,489 ....D 4
Seoni, 30,274 ....D 4
Serampore, 91,521 ....F 1
Shahjahanpur, 121,107 ....E 3
Shahjahanpur, *129,737 ....E 3
Sheo, †56,033 ....C 3
Shillong, 84,269 ....G 3
Shillong, *130,195 ....G 3
Shimoga, 63,764 ....D 6
Shivpuri, 28,681 ....D 3
Sholapur, 398,996 ....D 5
Sidhpur, 33,850 ....C 4
Sikar, 50,636 ....D 3
Silchar, 41,062 ....G 4
Siliguri, 65,471 ....F 3
Simla, 42,597 ....D 2
Sirsa, 33,363 ....D 3
Sitapur, 53,884 ....E 3
South Suburban, 307,471 ....F 2
South Suburban, *513,337 ....F 2
Srikakulam, 35,071 ....E 5
Srinagar, 285,257 ....D 2
Surat, 368,917 ....C 4
Surendranagar, 48,602 ....C 4
Tanda, 32,687 ....E 3
Tellicherry, 44,763 ....C 6
Tenali, 78,525 ....E 5
Tezpur, 24,159 ....G 3
Thana, 154,770 ....B 6
Thana, *164,896 ....B 6
Thanjavur, 120,681 ....D 6
Thimphu ....G 3
Tinsukia, 28,468 ....H 3
Tiruchchirappalli, 279,283 ....D 6
Tirunelveli, 87,988 ....D 7
Tirupati, 35,845 ....D 6
Tiruppattur, 30,799 ....D 6
Tiruvannamalai, 46,441 ....D 6
Titagarh, 76,429 ....F 1
Tonk, 43,413 ....D 3
Trichur, 73,038 ....D 6
Trivandrum, 336,757 ....D 7
Trivandrum, *435,566 ....D 7
Trombay, 17,258 ....B 7
Tumkur, 47,277 ....D 6
Tuni, 22,452 ....E 5
Tuticorin, 150,784 ....D 7
Tuticorin, *157,943 ....D 7
Udaipur, 133,368 ....C 4
Udipi, 24,610 ....C 6
Ujjain, 157,435 ....D 4
Ulhasnagar, 137,636 ....C 5
Umrer, 22,682 ....D 4
Unnao, 29,780 ....E 3
Uttarpara, 21,132 ....F 1
Vaniyambadi, 42,048 ....D 6
Vaniyambadi, *47,918 ....D 6
Varanasi, 619,822 ....E 3
Varanasi, *643,720 ....E 3
Vellore, 120,643 ....D 6
Vellore, *138,914 ....D 6
Veraval, 46,637 ....C 4
Veraval, *60,857 ....C 4
Vidisha, 27,718 ....D 4
Vijayawada, 312,822 ....D 5
Villupuram, 43,496 ....D 6
Viramgam, 38,955 ....C 4
Visakhapatnam, 285,837 ....E 5
Visnagar, 25,982 ....C 4
Vizagapatam (Visakhapatnam), 285,837 ....E 5
Vizianagaram, 76,808 ....E 5
Warangal, 178,559 ....D 5
Wardha, 49,113 ....D 4
Wun, 18,176 ....D 5
Yeola, 21,039 ....C 4
Yeotmal, 45,587 ....D 4

OTHER FEATURES

Agatti (isl.), 2,411 ....C 6
Amindivi (isls.), 7,854 ....C 6
Amini (isl.), 3,530 ....C 6
Andaman (isls.) ....G 6
Andaman (sea) ....G 6
Androth (isl.), 4,183 ....C 6
Arabian (sea) ....B 5
Baltistan (region) ....D 1
Bengal (bay) ....F 5
Berar (region), 4,580,302 ....D 4
Brahmaputra (river) ....G 3
Cambay (gulf) ....C 4
Chenab (river) ....D 2
Chetlat (isl.), 953 ....C 6
Chomo Lhari (mt.) ....F 3
Comorin (cape) ....D 7
Coromandel Coast (reg.)........E 6
Daman (dist.), 22,390 ....C 4
Damodar (river) ....F 4
Deccan (plateau) ....D 6
Diu (dist.), 14,280 ....C 4
Eastern Ghats (mts.) ....D 6
Elephanta (isl.) ....B 7
Ganges (Ganga) (river) ....F 3
Goa (dist.), 589,997 ....C 5
Godavari (river) ....D 5
Godwin Austen (K2) (mt.)........D 1
Golconda (ruins) ....D 5
Great Indian (des.) ....C 3
Himalaya (mts.) ....D 2
Hooghly (river) ....F 2
Indravati (river) ....E 5
Indus (river) ....D 2
Jhelum (river) ....C 2
Jumna (river) ....E 3
K2 (mt.) ....D 1
Kadmat (isl.), 1,851 ....C 6
Kalpeni (isl.), 2,613 ....C 7
Kamet (mt.) ....D 2
Kanchenjunga (mt.) ....F 3
Karakoram (mts.) ....D 1
Kiltan (isl.), 1,520 ....C 6
Kistna (Krishna) (river) ....D 5
Kula Kangri (mt.) ....G 3
Kunlun (range) ....D 1
Kutch (gulf) ....B 4
Kutch, Rann of (salt marsh) ....B 4
Laccadive (isls.), 12,115 ....C 6
Ladakh (region), 88,651 ....D 2
Mahanadi (river) ....E 4
Malabar (hill) ....B 7
Malabar Coast (reg.) ....C 6
Mannar (gulf) ....D 7
Minicoy (isl.), 4,139 ....C 7
Nanda Devi (mt.) ....D 2
Nanga Parbat (mt.) ....D 1

Narmada (river) ....
Nicobar (isls.) ....
Palk (strait) ....
Penganga (river) ....
Pitti (isl.), 80 ....
Rakaposhi (mt.) ....
Salsette (isl.), 1,566,572 ....
Saraswati (river) ....
Satpura (range) ....
Shipki (pass) ....
Sundarbans (swamp) ....F
Sutlej (river) C
Towers of Silence ....B
Travancore (region) ....D
Tungabhadra (river) ....D
Vindhya (range) ....D
Western Ghats (mts.) C
Yamuna (Jumna) (river) ....E

NEPAL

CITIES and TOWNS

Bhaktapur, 33,877 ....F
Biratnagar, 35,355 ....F
Birganj, 10,769 ....F
Janakpur, 8,928 ....F
Katmandu (cap.), 121,019 ....E
Lalitpur, 47,713 ....E
Nepalganj, 15,817 ....E
Pokhara, 5,413 ....E

OTHER FEATURES

Annapurna (mt.) ....E
Dhaulagiri (mt.) ....E
Everest (mt.) ....F
Himalaya (mts.) ....F
Kanchenjunga (mt.) ....F

PAKISTAN

PROVINCES

Baluchistan, 1,400,000 ....B
Capital Territory, 50,000 C
East Pakistan, 53,460,000 ....G
North-West Frontier, 9,500,000....C
Punjab, 36,290,000 C
Sind, 11,900,000 ....B

CITIES and TOWNS

Abbottabad, 31,036 C
Ahmadpur East, 20,423 C
Ayubnagar (cap.) ....F
Bahawalnagar, 36,290 C
Bahawalpur, 84,377 C
Bahawalpur, *147,000 C
Bannu, 31,623 C
Barisal, 69,936 ....G
Bogra, 33,784 ....F
Chittagong, 364,205 ....G
Chittagong, *437,000 ....G
Comilla, 54,504 ....G
Dacca, 556,712 ....G
Dacca, *829,000 ....G
Dera Ghazi Khan, 47,105 C
Dera Ismail Khan, 46,140 C
Dinajpur, 37,711 ....F
Faridpur, 28,333 ....F
Gujranwala, 196,154 C
Gujranwala, *289,000 C
Gujrat, 59,608 C
Hyderabad, 434,537 ....B
Hyderabad, *698,000 ....B
Islamabad (cap.), 50,000 C
Jacobabad, 35,278 ....B
Jessore, 46,366 ....F
Jhang-Maghiana, 94,971 C
Jhang-Maghiana, *118,000 C
Jhelum, 52,585 C
Karachi, 1,912,598 ....B
Karachi, *3,060,000 ....B
Khairpur, 34,144 ....B
Khulna, 127,970 ....F
Khulna, *320,000 ....F
Kohat, 49,854 C
Lahore, 1,296,477 C
Lahore, *1,823,000 C
Larkana, 48,008 ....B
Lyallpur, 425,248 C
Lyallpur, *854,000 C
Mardan, 77,932 C
Mardan, *113,000 C
Mianwali, 31,398 C
Mirpur Khas, 60,861 ....B
Multan, 358,201 C
Multan, *597,000 C
Mymensingh, 53,256 ....G
Narayanganj, 162,054 ....G
Narayanganj, *327,000 ....G
Nawabshah, 45,651 ....B
Pabna, 40,792 ....F
Parachinar, 22,953 ....B
Peshawar, 218,691 C
Peshawar, *296,000 C
Quetta, 106,633 ....B
Quetta, *130,000 ....B
Rahimyar Khan, 43,548 C
Rahimyar Khan, *130,000........C
Rajshahi, 56,885 ....F
Rangpur, 40,634 ....F
Rawalpindi, 340,175 C
Rawalpindi, *445,000 C
Sargodha, 129,291 C
Sargodha, *194,000 C
Sialkot, 164,346 C
Sialkot, *167,000 C
Sukkur, 103,216 ....B
Sukkur, *131,000 ....B
Sylhet, 37,740 ....G

OTHER FEATURES

Arabian (sea) ....B
Bengal (bay) ....F
Brahmaputra (river) ....G
Chagai (hills) ....A
Chenab (river) C
Ganges (river) ....F
Hindu Kush (range) C
Indus (river) ....B
Jhelum (river) C
Kabul (river) C
Khyber (pass) C
Kutch, Rann of (salt marsh) ....B
Mohenjo Daro (ruins) ....B
Ravi (river) C
Sulaiman (range) C
Sundarbans (swamp) ....F
Sutlej (river) C
Taxila (ruins) C
Tirich Mir (mt.) C

*City and suburbs.
†Population of sub-division.
‡Population of district.

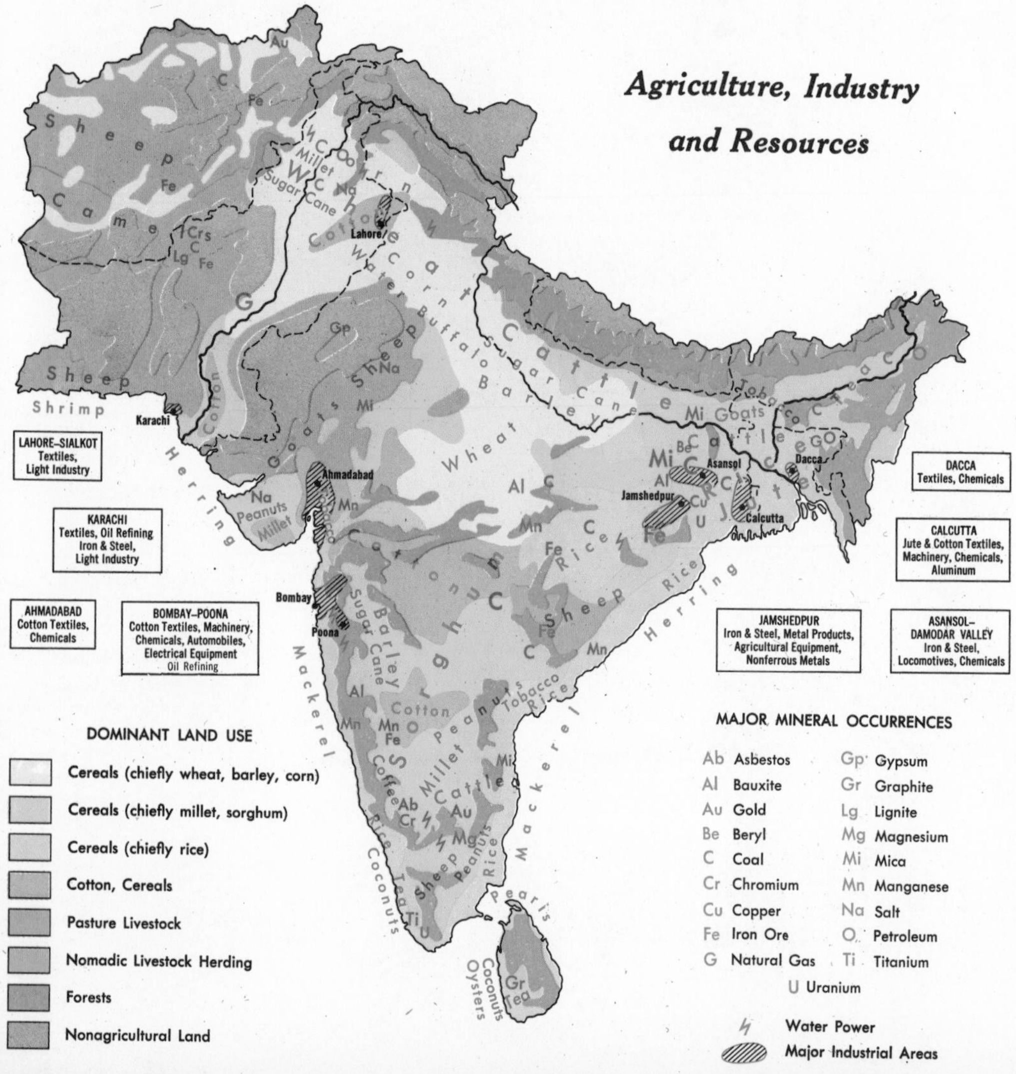

Agriculture, Industry and Resources
LAHORE–SIALKOT Textiles, Light Industry
KARACHI Textiles, Oil Refining Iron & Steel, Light Industry
AHMADABAD Cotton Textiles, Chemicals
BOMBAY–POONA Cotton Textiles, Machinery, Chemicals, Automobiles, Electrical Equipment Oil Refining
DACCA Textiles, Chemicals
CALCUTTA Jute & Cotton Textiles, Machinery, Chemicals, Aluminum
JAMSHEDPUR Iron & Steel, Metal Products, Agricultural Equipment, Nonferrous Metals
ASANSOL–DAMODAR VALLEY Iron & Steel, Locomotives, Chemicals
Karachi
Lahore
Ahmadabad
Bombay
Poona
Jamshedpur
Asansol
Calcutta
Dacca
Sheep
Camel
Shrimp
Herring
Mackerel
Pearls
Coconuts
Oysters
Cotton
Wheat
Millet
Sugar Cane
Rice
Peanuts
Barley
Corn
Buffalo
Goats
Cattle
Tobacco
Tea
Jute
Coffee
DOMINANT LAND USE
Cereals (chiefly wheat, barley, corn)
Cereals (chiefly millet, sorghum)
Cereals (chiefly rice)
Cotton, Cereals
Pasture Livestock
Nomadic Livestock Herding
Forests
Nonagricultural Land
MAJOR MINERAL OCCURRENCES
Ab Asbestos
Al Bauxite
Au Gold
Be Beryl
C Coal
Cr Chromium
Cu Copper
Fe Iron Ore
G Natural Gas
Gp Gypsum
Gr Graphite
Lg Lignite
Mg Magnesium
Mi Mica
Mn Manganese
Na Salt
O Petroleum
Ti Titanium
U Uranium
Water Power
Major Industrial Areas

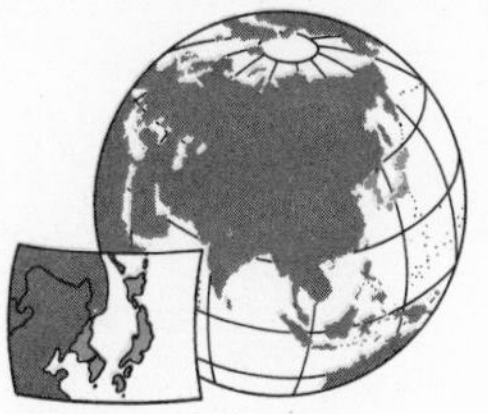

JAPAN

AREA 142,774 sq. mi.
POPULATION 103,540,000
CAPITAL Tokyo
LARGEST CITY Tokyo
HIGHEST POINT Fuji 12,389 ft.
MONETARY UNIT yen
MAJOR LANGUAGE Japanese
MAJOR RELIGIONS Buddhism, Shintoism

NORTH KOREA

AREA 46,540 sq. mi.
POPULATION 13,300,000
CAPITAL P'yŏngyang
LARGEST CITY P'yŏngyang
HIGHEST POINT Paektu 9,003 ft.
MONETARY UNIT won
MAJOR LANGUAGE Korean
MAJOR RELIGIONS Confucianism, Buddhism, Christianity

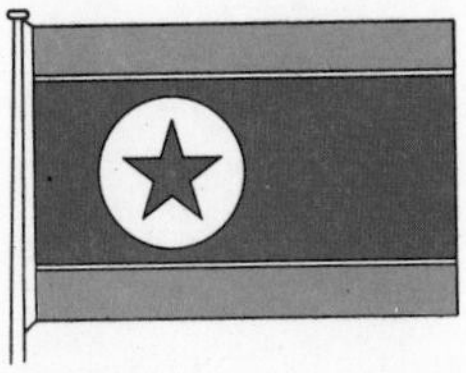

SOUTH KOREA

AREA 38,452 sq. mi.
POPULATION 31,683,000
CAPITAL Seoul
LARGEST CITY Seoul
HIGHEST POINT Halla 6,398 ft.
MONETARY UNIT hwan
MAJOR LANGUAGE Korean
MAJOR RELIGIONS Confucianism, Buddhism, Chondogyo, Christianity

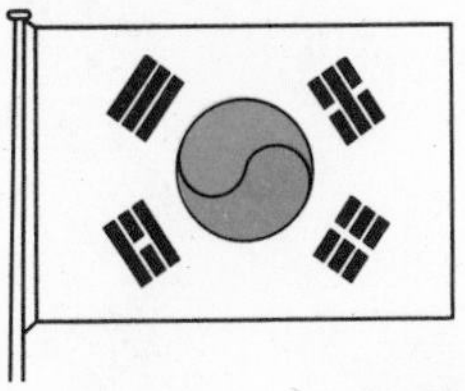

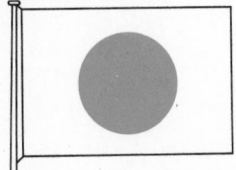

JAPAN

PREFECTURES

Aichi, 4,798,653 ....H 6
Akita, 1,279,835 ....J 4
Aomori, 1,416,591 ....K 3
Chiba, 2,701,770 ....P 2
Ehime, 1,446,384 ....F 7
Fukui, 750,557 ....G 5
Fukuoka, 3,964,611 ....D 7
Fukushima, 1,983,754 ....K 5
Gifu, 1,700,365 ....H 6
Gumma, 1,605,584 ....J 5
Hiroshima, 2,281,146 ....E 6
Hokkaido, 5,171,800 ....K 2
Hyogo, 4,309,944 ....H 7
Ibaraki, 2,056,154 ....K 5
Ishikawa, 980,499 ....H 5
Iwate, 1,411,118 ....K 4
Kagawa, 900,845 ....G 6
Kagoshima, 1,853,541 ....E 8
Kanagawa, 4,430,743 ....O 2
Kochi, 812,714 ....F 7
Kumamoto, 1,770,736 ....E 7
Kyoto, 2,102,808 ....J 7
Mie, 1,514,467 ....H 6
Miyagi, 1,753,126 ....F 4
Miyazaki, 1,080,692 ....E 8
Nagano, 1,958,007 ....J 5
Nagasaki, 1,641,245 ....D 7
Nara, 825,965 ....J 8
Niigata, 2,398,931 ....J 5
Oita, 1,187,480 ....E 7
Okayama, 1,645,135 ....F 6
Osaka, 6,657,189 ....J 8
Saga, 871,885 ....E 7
Saitama, 3,014,983 ....O 2
Shiga, 853,385 ....J 7
Shimane, 821.620 ....F 6
Shizuoka, 2,912,521 ....H 6
Tochigi, 1,521,656 ....K 5
Tokushima, 815,115 ....G 7
Tokyo, 10,869,244 ....O 2
Tottori, 579,853 ....G 6
Toyama, 1,025,465 ....H 5
Wakayama, 1,026,975 ....G 6
Yamagata, 1,263,103 ....K 4
Yamaguchi, 1,543,573 ....E 6
Yamanashi, 763,194 ....J 6

CITIES and TOWNS

Abashiri, 44,195 ....M 1
Ageo, 54,776 ....O 2
Aikawa, 16,454 ....H 4
Aizuwakamatsu, 104,000 ....J 5
Ajigasawa, 20,504 ....J 3
Akabira, 46,646 ....K 2
Akashi, 187,000 ....H 8
Aki, 26,605 ....F 7
Akita, 233,000 ....J 4
Akkeshi, 19,039 ....M 2
Akune, 36,026 ....E 7
Amagasaki, 532,000 ....H 8
Amagi, 44,060 ....E 7
Amaha, 18,062 ....O 3
Anan, 59,105 ....G 7
Aomori, 252,000 ....K 3
Asahi, 31,063 ....K 6
Asahikawa, 293,000 ....L 2
Ashibetsu, 52,123 ....L 2
Ashikaga, 153,000 ....J 5
Ashiya, 63,195 ....H 8
Atami, 54,540 ....J 6
Atsugi, 61,383 ....O 2
Awaji, 9,972 ....H 8
Ayabe, 48,339 ....G 6
Beppu, 144,000 ....E 7
Bibai, 63,051 ....L 2
Ьiratori, 12,930 ....L 2
Chiba, 407,000 ....P 2
Chichibu, 60,330 ....J 6
Chigasaki, 119,000 ....O 3
Chitose, 51,243 ....K 2
Chofu, 145,000 ....O 2
Choshi, 91,492 ....K 6
Daito, 57,107 ....J 8
Ebetsu, 44,510 ....K 2
Esashi, Hokkaido, 15,380 ....J 3
Esashi, Hokkaido, 11,401 ....L 1
Esashi, Iwate, 42,666 ....K 4
Fuchu, Hiroshima, 45,341 ....F 6
Fuchu, Tokyo, 148,000 ....O 2
Fuji, 173,000 ....J 6
Fujieda, 70,789 ....J 6
Fujisawa, 211,000 ....O 3
Fukuchiyama, 58,223 ....G 6
Fukue, 36,876 ....D 7
Fukui, 193,000 ....G 5
Fukuoka, 812,000 ....D 7
Fukushima, 225,000 ....K 5
Fukuyama, 233,000 ....F 6
Funabashi, 281,000 ....P 2
Furukawa, 52,853 ....K 4
Futtsu, 16,445 ....O 3
Gifu, 398,000 ....H 6
Gobo, 30,040 ....G 7
Gose, 35,788 ....J 8
Gosen, 38,113 ....J 5
Goshogawara, 47,433 ....K 3
Gotsu, 30,209 ....F 6
Habikino, 50,333 ....J 8
Haboro, 30,266 ....K 1
Hachinohe, 209,000 ....K 3
Hachioji, 229,000 ....O 2
Hagi, 53,905 ....E 6
Hakodate, 249,000 ....K 3
Hakui, 29,090 ....H 5
Hamada, 44,439 ....E 6
Hamamatsu, 420,000 ....H 6
Hanamaki, 62,710 ....K 4
Hanawa, 20,507 ....K 3
Hanno, 47,825 ....O 2
Haramachi, 40,643 ....K 5
Hayama, 17,617 ....O 3
Higashiosaka, 454,000 ....J 8
Hikone, 62,740 ....H 6
Himeji, 403,000 ....G 6
Himi, 62,452 ....H 5
Hirakata, 164,000 ....J 7
Hirata, 33,128 ....F 6
Hiratsuka, 151,000 ....O 3
Hiroo, 13,598 ....L 2
Hirosaki, 162,000 ....K 3
Hiroshima, 542,000 ....E 6
Hitachi, 184,000 ....K 5
Hitachiota, 36,974 ....K 5
Hitoyoshi, 44,831 ....E 7
Hofu, 94,342 ....E 6
Hondo, 39,790 ....E 7
Honjo, 38,361 ....J 4
Hyuga, 43,678 ....E 7
Ibaraki, 143,000 ....J 7
Ibusuki, 32,386 ....E 8
Ichihara, 134,000 ....P 2
Ichikawa, 236,000 ....P 2
Ichinohe, 25,165 ....K 3
Ichinomiya, 210,000 ....H 6
Ichinoseki, 57,238 ....K 4
Ide, 8,199 ....J 7
Iida, 79,145 ....H 6
Iizuka, 82,033 ....E 7
Ikeda, Hokkaido, 15,529 ....L 2
Ikeda, Osaka, 82,478 ....H 7
Ikuno, 9,466 ....G 6
Imabari, 109,000 ....F 6
Imari, 67,316 ....D 7
Imazu, 11,245 ....G 6
Ina, 51,944 ....H 6
Isahaya, 63,886 ....D 7
Ise, 104,000 ....H 6
Ishige, 18,481 ....P 2
Ishinomaki, 106,000 ....K 4
Ishioka, 36,789 ....K 5
Itami, 141,000 ....H 7
Ito, 59,404 ....J 6
Itoigawa, 39,332 ....H 5
Iwaizumi, 24,846 ....K 4
Iwaki, 337,000 ....K 5
Iwakuni, 106,000 ....E 6
Iwami, 18,004 ....G 6
Iwamisawa, 65,508 ....L 2
Iwanai, 25,405 ....K 2
Iwasaki, 5,432 ....J 3
Iwata, 58,940 ....H 6
Iwatsuki, 41,946 ....O 2
Iyo, 28,611 ....F 7
Izuhara, 21,989 ....D 6
Izumi, 84,771 ....J 8
Izumiotsu, 53,312 ....J 8
Izumisano, 66,521 ....G 6
Izumo, 68,765 ....F 6
Joyo, 20,038 ....J 7
Kadoma, 121,000 ....J 7
Kaga, 54,860 ....H 5
Kagoshima, 406,000 ....E 8
Kaizuka, 69,365 ....H 8
Kakogawa, 115,000 ....G 6
Kamaishi, 82,104 ....L 4
Kamakura, 136,000 ....O 3
Kameoka, 43,335 ....J 7
Kaminoyama, 38,679 ....J 4
Kamiyaku, 12,458 ....E 8
Kamo, 9,034 ....J 7
Kanazawa, 344,000 ....H 5
Kanonji, 44,200 ....F 6
Kanoya, 70,519 ....E 8
Kanuma, 77,240 ....J 5
Karatsu, 73,999 ....D 7
Kaseda, 28,565 ....D 8
Kashihara, 57,065 ....J 8
Kashiwa, 133,000 ....P 2
Kashiwazaki, 71,465 ....J 5
Kasugai, 141,000 ....H 6
Kasukabe, 42,460 ....O 2
Katsuta, 52,625 ....K 5
Katsuura, 29,133 ....K 6
Kawachi, 91,853 ....J 8
Kawachinagano, 40,109 ....J 8
Kawagoe, 148,000 ....O 2
Kawaguchi, 284.000 ....O 2
Kawanishi, 61,282 ....H 7
Kawasaki, 910.000 ....J 6
Kazusa, 12,787 ....P 3
Kembuchi, 8,013 ....L 1
Kesennuma, 59,884 ....K 4
Kikonai, 11,353 ....K 3
Kiryu, 132,000 ....J 5
Kisarazu, 54,928 ....P 3
Kishiwada, 156,000 ....J 8
Kitaibaraki, 55,334 ....K 5
Kitakata, 40,424 ....J 5
Kitakyushu, 1,042,319 ....E 6
Kitami, 74,841 ....L 2
Kizu, 10,814 ....J 7
Kobayashi, 41,922 ....E 8
Kobe, 1,288,754 ....H 7
Kochi, 242,000 ....F 7
Kodaira, 125,000 ....O 2
Kofu, 185,000 ....J 6
Kokubu, 31,249 ....E 8
Komagane, 28,327 ....H 6
Komatsu, 91,163 ....H 5
Koriyama, 240,000 ....K 5
Koshigaya, 112,000 ....P 2
Kuji, 38,374 ....K 3
Kuki, 26,773 ....O 2
Kumagaya, 119,000 ....J 5
Kumamoto, 432,000 ....E 7
Kumano, 30,041 ....H 7
Kumiyama, 7,231 ....J 7
Kurashiki, 332,000 ....F 6
Kurayoshi, 50,114 ....F 6
Kure, 237,000 ....F 6
Kurume, 188,000 ....E 7
Kushikino, 31,781 ....E 8
Kushima, 36,425 ....E 8
Kushimoto, 20.252 ....G 7
Kushiro, 195,000 ....M 2
Kutchan, 19,738 ....K 2
Kyonan, 13,980 ....O 3
Kyoto, 1,418,933 ....J 7
Machida, 154,000 ....O 2
Maebashi, 225,000 ....J 5
Maibara, 13,415 ....G 6
Maizuru, 96,641 ....G 6
Mashike, 13,063 ....K 2
Masuda, 52,729 ....E 6
Matsubara, 71,406 ....H 8
Matsudo, 206,000 ....P 2
Matsue, 115,000 ....F 6
Matsumae, 19,111 ....J 3
Matsumoto, 159,000 ....H 5
Matsunaga, 34,610 ....F 6
Matsusaka, 104,000 ....H 6
Matsuto, 29,649 ....H 5
Matsuyama, 310,000 ....F 7
Mihara, 82,175 ....F 6
Miki, 38,542 ....H 7
Mikuni, 22,135 ....G 5
Minamata, 45,577 ....E 7
Minobu, 12,250 ....J 6
Minoo, 43,851 ....J 7
Misawa, 36,326 ....K 3
Mishima, 43,479 ....J 7
Mitaka, 146,000 ....O 2
Mito, 167,000 ....K 5
Mitsukaido, 36,584 ....P 2
Miura, 42,601 ....O 3
Miyako, 56,575 ....L 4
Miyakonojo, 121,000 ....E 8
Miyazaki, 212,000 ....E 8
Miyazu, 33,285 ....G 6
Miyoshi, 37,871 ....F 6
Mizusawa, 45,985 ....K 4
Mobara, 42,486 ....K 6
Mombetsu, 40,389 ....L 1
Mooka, 38,117 ....K 5
Mori, 18,330 ....K 2
Moriguchi, 164,000 ....J 7
Morioka, 191,000 ....K 4
Muko, 20,730 ....J 7
Murakami, 32,651 ....J 4
Muroran, 181,000 ....K 2
Muroto, 28,746 ....G 7
Musashino, 135,000 ....O 2
Mutsu, 39,282 ....K 3
Nachikatsuura, 24,889 ....H 7
Nagahama, Ehime, 16,193 ....F 7
Nagahama, Shiga, 49,871 ....H 6
Nagano, 280,000 ....J 5
Nagaoka, 27,522 ....J 7
Nagaoka, 159,000 ....J 5
Nagasaki, 422,000 ....D 7
Nagato, 29,246 ....E 6
Nagoya, 2,036,022 ....H 6
Nakaminato, 33,620 ....K 5
Nakamura, 35,717 ....F 7
Nakasato, 15,898 ....K 3
Nakatsu, 58,371 ....E 7
Nakoso, 46,731 ....K 5
Nanao, 48,715 ....H 5
Nankoku, 41,237 ....F 7
Naoetsu, 45,650 ....H 5
Nara, 191,000 ....J 8
Narashino, 64,897 ....P 2
Nayoro, 36,106 ....L 1
Naze, 44,111 ....O 5
Nemuro, 45,149 ....M 2
Neyagawa, 174,000 ....J 7
Nichinan, 57,612 ....E 8
Niigata, 379,000 ....J 5
Niihama, 130,000 ....F 6
Niimi, 34,063 ....F 6
Niitsu, 56,594 ....J 5
Nikko, 32,031 ....J 5
Nishinomiya, 357,000 ....H 8
Nishinoomote, 30,490 ....E 8
Nobeoka, 134,000 ....E 7
Noboribetsu, 39,101 ....K 2
Noda, 59,799 ....P 2
Nogata, 57,839 ....E 7
Nose, 9,906 ....J 7
Noshiro, 61,921 ....J 3
Noto, 17,719 ....H 5
Numata, 44,347 ....J 5
Numazu, 186.000 ....J 6
Obama, 35,160 ....G 6
Obihiro, 129,000 ....L 2
Oda, 42,322 ....F 6
Odate, 59,662 ....K 3
Odawara, 151.000 ....J 6
Ofunato, 38,347 ....K 4
Oga, 43,333 ....J 4
Ogaki, 134,000 ....H 6
Ogi, 5,500 ....J 5
Ohata, 13,015 ....K 3

(continued on following page)

Agriculture, Industry and Resources

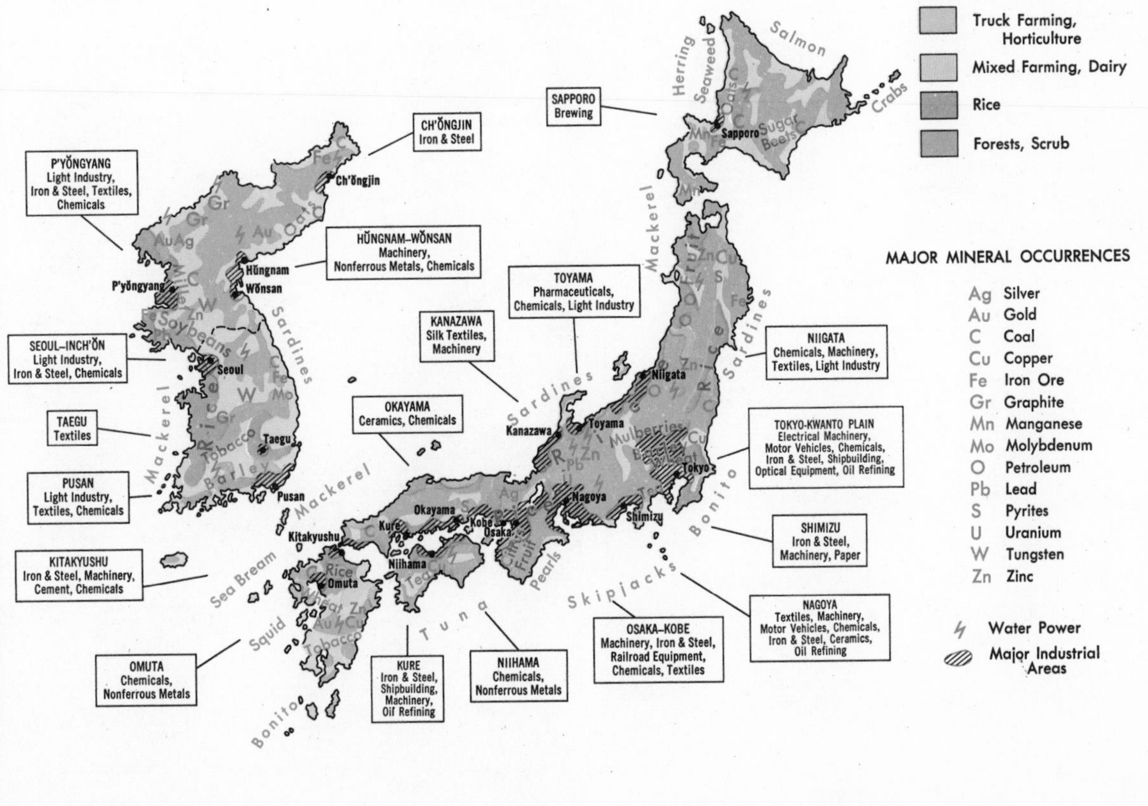

P'YŎNGYANG Light Industry, Iron & Steel, Textiles, Chemicals
CH'ŎNGJIN Iron & Steel
HŬNGNAM–WŎNSAN Machinery, Nonferrous Metals, Chemicals
SEOUL–INCH'ŎN Light Industry, Iron & Steel, Chemicals
TAEGU Textiles
PUSAN Light Industry, Textiles, Chemicals
KITAKYUSHU Iron & Steel, Machinery, Cement, Chemicals
OMUTA Chemicals, Nonferrous Metals
KURE Iron & Steel, Shipbuilding, Machinery, Oil Refining
NIIHAMA Chemicals, Nonferrous Metals
OSAKA–KOBE Machinery, Iron & Steel, Railroad Equipment, Chemicals, Textiles
NAGOYA Textiles, Machinery, Motor Vehicles, Chemicals, Iron & Steel, Ceramics, Oil Refining
SHIMIZU Iron & Steel, Machinery, Paper
TOKYO-KWANTO PLAIN Electrical Machinery, Motor Vehicles, Chemicals, Iron & Steel, Shipbuilding, Optical Equipment, Oil Refining
NIIGATA Chemicals, Machinery, Textiles, Light Industry
OKAYAMA Ceramics, Chemicals
KANAZAWA Silk Textiles, Machinery
TOYAMA Pharmaceuticals, Chemicals, Light Industry
SAPPORO Brewing
Salmon
Herring
Seaweed
Crabs
Sugar Beets
Mackerel
Sardines
Sea Bream
Squid
Bonito
Tuna
Skipjacks
Pearls
Soybeans
Rice
Tobacco
Barley
Mulberries
Fruit
Tea
DOMINANT LAND USE
Cereals, Cash Crops
Truck Farming, Horticulture
Mixed Farming, Dairy
Rice
Forests, Scrub
MAJOR MINERAL OCCURRENCES
Ag Silver
Au Gold
C Coal
Cu Copper
Fe Iron Ore
Gr Graphite
Mn Manganese
Mo Molybdenum
O Petroleum
Pb Lead
S Pyrites
U Uranium
W Tungsten
Zn Zinc
Water Power
Major Industrial Areas

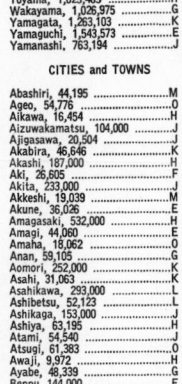

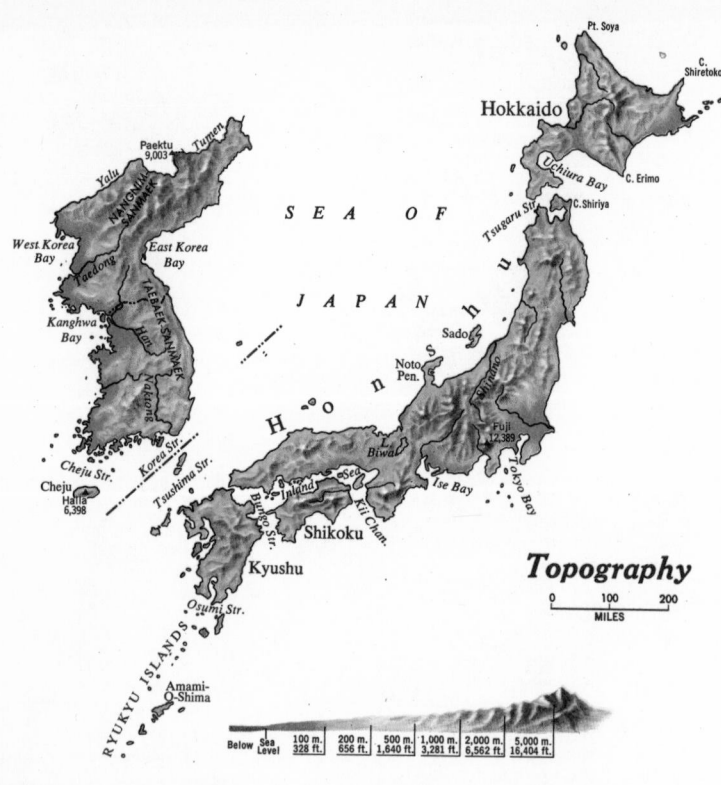

SEA OF JAPAN

Hokkaido

Honshu

Shikoku

Kyushu

Topography

0   100   200
MILES

Below Sea Level | 100 m. 328 ft. | 200 m. 656 ft. | 500 m. 1,640 ft. | 1,000 m. 3,281 ft. | 2,000 m. 6,562 ft. | 5,000 m. 16,404 ft.

Osumi (isls.), 82,372	E 8
Osumi (pen.)	E 8
Osumi (str.)	E 8
Otakine (mt.)	O 5
Rebun (isl.), 8,374	K 1
Rikuchu-Kaigan Nat'l Park	L 4
Rishiri (isl.), 17,663	K 1
Sado (isl.), 102,925	J 4
Sagami (bay)	O 3
Sagami (river)	O 2
Sagami (sea)	O 6
Saikai Nat'l Park	D 7
San'in Kaigan Nat'l Park	G 6
Sata (cape)	E 8
Setonaikai Nat'l Park	F 6
Shikoku (isl.), 3,975,058	F 7
Shikotan (isl.)	N 2
Shikotsu (lake)	K 2
Shikotsu-Toya Nat'l Park	K 2
Shimane (pen.)	F 6
Shimokita (pen.)	K 3
Shinano (river)	J 5
Shiono (cape)	H 7
Shiragami (cape)	J 3
Shirane (mt.)	J 6

Shirane (mt.)	H 6
Shiretoko (cape)	M 1
Shiriya (cape)	L 3
Soya (point)	L 1
Soya (sea)	E 7
Suruga (bay)	J 6
Suwanose (isl.)	D 8
Suzu (point)	H 5
Takeshima (isls.)	F 5
Tama (river)	O 2
Tanega (isl.), 60,130	E 8
Tappi (cape)	J 3
Tazawa (lake)	K 4
Teshio (mt.)	L 1
Teshio (river)	L 1
Tobi (isl.)	L 1
Tokachi (mt.)	L 2
Tokachi (river)	L 2
Tokara (arch.), 2,722	O 5
Tokuno (isl.)	
18,920	O 5
Tokyo (bay)	O 2
Tone (river)	J 6
Tosa (bay)	F 7
Towada (lake)	K 3

Towada-Hachimantai Nat'l Park	K 3
Toya (lake)	K 2
Toyama (bay)	H 5
Tsu (isls.), 65,304	D 6
Tsugaru (strait)	K 3
Tsurugi (mt.)	H 5
Tsushima (isls.), 65,304	D 6
Tsushima (strait)	D 7
Uchiura (bay)	K 2
Unzen (mt.)	D 7
Unzen-Amakusa Nat'l Park	D 7
Volcano (isls.)	M 4
Wakasa (bay)	G 6
Yaku (isl.), 22,242	E 8
Yoron (isl.)	O 6
Yoshino (river)	F 7
Yoshino-Kumano Nat'l Park	H 7
Zao (mt.)	K 5

KOREA (NORTH)
CITIES and TOWNS
Aniu	B 4

JAPAN (continued)
Oita, 243,000	E 7
Ojiya, 47,376	J 5
Okawa, 51,197	E 7
Okaya, 56,986	J 5
Okayama, 322,000	F 6
Okazaki, 200,000	H 6
Omagari, 39,900	K 4
Omiya, 248,000	O 2
Omu, 9,494	L 1
Omura, Bonin Islands, 203	M 3
Omura, Nagasaki, 56,425	D 7
Omuta, 206,000	E 7
Onagawa, 18,080	K 4
Ono, 43,747	H 6
Onoda, 43,584	E 6
Onomichi, 90,740	F 6
Osaka, 2,980,409	J 7
Ota, 87,898	J 5
Otaru, 205,000	K 2
Otawara, 41,026	K 5
Otsu, 164,000	J 6
Owase, 34,019	H 6
Oyabe, 35,646	H 5
Oyama, 90,632	J 5
Ozu, 40,165	F 7
Rausu, 8,931	M 1
Rikuzentakata, 31,040	K 4
Rumoi, 40,231	K 2
Ryotsu, 26,494	J 4
Ryugasaki, 34,917	P 2
Sabae, 50,114	H 5
Saga, 153,000	E 7
Sagamihara, 224,000	O 2
Saigo, 16,569	F 5
Saiki, 51,145	E 7
Saito, 42,543	E 7
Sakado, 24,854	O 2
Sakai, Ibaraki, 21,689	P 1
Sakai, Osaka, 544,000	J 7
Sakaide, 61,284	F 6
Sakaiminato, 32,846	F 6
Sakata, 95,982	J 4
Saku, 55,149	J 5
Sakurai, 49,939	J 7
Sanda, 32,265	H 7
Sanjo, 74,080	J 5
Sapporo, 1,010,122	K 2
Sarufutsu, 7,450	L 1
Sasebo, 268,000	D 7
Satte, 25,169	O 1
Sawara, 47,561	P 2
Sayama, 40,183	O 2
Sendai, Kagoshima, 67,142	E 8
Sendai, Miyagi, 515,000	K 4
Seta, 20,327	J 7
Shari, 18,015	M 2
Shibata, 73,992	J 5
Shibetsu, 36,502	M 2
Shimabara, 44,175	D 7
Shimizu, 230,000	J 6
Shimoda, 28,645	J 6
Shimonoseki, 276,000	E 6
Shingu, 40,051	H 7
Shinjo, 43,057	K 4
Shiogama, 58,363	K 4
Shiroishi, 41,928	K 4
Shizunai, 26,533	L 2
Shizuoka, 392,000	J 6
Shobara, 26,515	F 6
Soka, 102,000	O 2
Soma, 38,430	K 4
Sonobe, 15,241	J 7
Suita, 239,000	J 7
Sukagawa, 46,999	K 5
Sukumo, 26,992	E 7
Sumoto, 46,313	G 6
Sunagawa, 30,325	K 2
Susaki, 37,020	F 7

Suttsu, 8,043	J 2
Suwa, 46,276	J 6
Suzu, 32,122	H 5
Suzuka, 115,000	H 6
Tachikawa, 115,000	O 2
Tajimi, 60,175	H 6
Takada, 73,668	J 5
Takaishi, 45,679	H 7
Takamatsu, 271,000	G 6
Takaoka, 158,000	H 5
Takarazuka, 109,000	H 7
Takasaki, 184,000	J 5
Takatsuki, 178,000	J 7
Takawa, 74,063	E 7
Takayama, 53,399	H 5
Takefu, 62,588	G 6
Tanabe, Kyoto, 17,333	J 7
Tanabe, Wakayama, 62,276	H 7
Tateyama, 55,866	K 6
Tendo, 43,903	J 4
Tenri, 54,169	J 7
Teshio, 9,493	K 1
Toba, 30,098	H 6
Tobetsu, 19,406	K 2
Togane, 31,922	K 2
Tojo, 16,866	F 6
Tokushima, 225,000	G 7
Tokuyama, 100,000	E 6
Tokyo (capital), 8,832,647	O 2
Tokyo, *11,350,000	O 2
Tomakomai, 81,812	K 2
Tomiyama, 7,863	O 3
Tondabayashi, 47,985	J 7
Tosa, 30,772	F 7
Tosashimizu, 26,725	F 7
Yosu, 44,449	F 7
Tottori, 117,000	G 6
Towada, 46,713	K 3
Toyama, 264,000	H 5
Toyohashi, 253,000	H 6
Toyonaka, 334,000	J 7
Toyooka, 43,259	G 6
Toyota, 161,000	H 6
Tsubame, 40,134	J 5
Tsuchiura, 78,971	K 5
Tsuruga, 54,508	G 6
Tsuruoka, 95,615	J 4
Tsuyama, 76,007	F 6
Ube, 149,000	E 6
Uchinoura, 10,036	E 8
Ueda, 73,940	J 5
Ugo, 25,661	K 4
Uji, 68,934	J 7
Uozu, 46,854	H 5
Urakawa, 21,552	L 2
Urawa, 250,000	O 2
Ushibuka, 30,995	D 7
Usuki, 42,731	E 7
Utsunomiya, 283,000	K 5
Uwajima, 66,484	E 7
Wajima, 35,798	H 5
Wakasa, 8,455	J 6
Wakayama, 353,000	G 6
Wakkanai, 51,539	K 1
Warabi, 69,715	O 2
Yaizu, 77,008	J 6
Yakumo, 22,487	K 2
Yamaguchi, 103,000	E 6
Yamato, 64,991	O 2
Yamatokoriyama, 45,765	J 7
Yamatotakada, 47,371	J 7
Yao, 197,000	J 7
Yatabe, 20,093	P 2
Yatsushiro, 105,000	E 7
Yawata, 19,204	J 7
Yawatahama, 50,005	E 7
Yoichi, 26,154	K 2

Yokawa, 8,146	H 7
Yokkaichi, 230,000	H 6
Yokohama, 2,237,513	O 3
Yokosuka, 340,000	O 3
Yokote, 44,331	K 4
Yonago, 108,000	F 6
Yonezawa, 94,435	K 5
Yono, 51,746	O 2
Yotsukura, 20,226	L 5
Yubari, 85,141	L 2
Yubetsu, 9,720	L 1
Yukuhashi, 47,495	E 7
Yuzawa, 39,879	K 4
Zushi, 43,211	O 3

OTHER FEATURES
Abashiri (river)	M 1
Abukuma (river)	K 4
Agano (river)	J 4
Akan Nat'l Park	M 2
Amakusa (isls.), 233,465	D 7
Amami (isls.), 186,193	N 5
Amami-O-Shima (isl.), 94,348	N 5
Ara (river)	O 2
Asahi (mt.)	J 4
Asama (mt.)	J 5
Ashizuri (cape)	E 7
Aso Nat'l Park	E 7
Atsumi (bay)	H 6
Awa (isl.), 771	J 4
Awaji (isl.), 185,473	G 6
Bandai (mt.)	K 5
Bandai-Asahi Nat'l Park	K 4
Biwa (lake)	H 6
Bonin (isls.), 203	M 3
Boso (pen.)	K 6
Bungo (strait)	E 7
Chichi (isl.), 203	M 3
Chichibu-Tama Nat'l Park	J 6
Chokai (mt.)	J 4
Chubu Sangaku Nat'l Park	H 5
Dai (mt.)	F 6
Daimanji (mt.)	J 6
Daio (cape)	H 6
Daisen-Oki National Park	F 6
Daisetsu (mt.)	L 2
Daisetsu-Zan Nat'l Park	L 2
Dogo (isl.), 23,669	F 5
Dozen (isl.), 12,516	F 5
East China (sea)	C 8
Edo (river)	O 2
Erabu (isl.), 22,049	N 5
Erimo (cape)	L 2
Esan (point)	K 3
Fuji (mt.)	J 6
Fuji (river)	J 6
Fuji-Hakone-Izu Nat'l Park	J 6
Gassan (mt.)	J 4
Goto (isls.), 159,190	D 7
Habomai (isls.)	N 2
Hachijo (lagoon)	K 6
Haha (isl.)	M 3
Hakken (isl.)	H 7
Haku (mt.)	H 5
Haku san Nat'l Park	H 5

Harima (sea)	G 6
Hida (river)	H 6
Hodaka (mt.)	H 5
Hokkaido (isl.), 5,171,800	L 2
Honshu (isl.), 76,757,913	J 5
Iki (isl.), 45,654	D 7
Ina (river)	H 6
Inawashiro (lake)	K 5
Inubo (cape)	K 6
Iro (cape)	J 6
Ise (bay)	H 6
Ise-Shima Nat'l Park	H 6
Ishikari (bay)	K 2
Ishikari (river)	K 2
Ishizuchi (mt.)	F 7
Iwaki (mt.)	K 3
Iwate (mt.)	K 4
Iwo (isl.)	M 4
Iyo (sea)	E 7
Izu (isls.)	J 6
Izu (pen.), 35,592	J 6
Izu (isl.)	J 6
Japan (sea)	G 4
Joshinetsu-Kogen Nat'l Park	J 5
Kagoshima (bay)	E 8
Kamui (cape)	K 2
Kariba (mt.)	K 2
Kasumiga (lagoon)	K 5
Kazan-Retto (Volcano) (isls.)	M 4
Kii (channel)	G 7
Kikai (isl.), 14,231	O 5
Kino (river)	G 6
Kirishima-Yaku Nat'l Park	E 8
Kitakami (river)	K 4
Koma (mt.)	K 2
Koshiki (isls.), 16,301	D 8
Kuchino (isl.)	O 5
Kuju (mt.)	E 7
Kutcharo (lake)	M 2
Kyushu (isl.), 12,370,190	E 7
Meakan (mt.)	M 2
Miura (pen.)	O 3
Mogami (river)	J 4
Motsuta (cape)	K 2
Muko (sea)	G 7
Muroto (point)	G 7
Mutsu (bay)	K 3
Naka (river)	K 5
Nampo-Shoto (isls.), 203	M 3
Nantai (mt.)	J 5
Nasu (mt.)	K 5
Nemuro (strait)	M 1
Nii (isl.), 3,913	J 6
Nikko Nat'l Park	J 5
Nojima (cape)	K 6
Noshappu (point)	N 2
Noto (cape)	J 4
Nyudo (cape)	K 3
Oani (river)	K 3
Obitsu (river)	K 6
Oga (pen.)	J 4
Ogasawara-Gunto (Bonin) (isls.), 203	M 3
Oki (isls.)	F 5
Okinoshima (isl.), 7,142	J 2
Oma (cape)	K 3
Omono (river)	K 4
Ono (river)	E 7
Ontake (mt.)	H 6
Osaka (bay)	H 6
Oshima (isl.), 11,840	J 6

JAPAN is divided into prefectures bearing the same names as their capitals except:

Prefecture	Capital	Ref.
AICHI	NAGOYA	H 6
EHIME	MATSUYAMA	F 7
GUMMA	MAEBASHI	J 5
HOKKAIDO	SAPPORO	K 2
HYOGO	KOBE	H 7
IBARAKI	MITO	K 5
ISHIKAWA	KANAZAWA	H 5
IWATE	MORIOKA	K 4
KAGAWA	TAKAMATSU	G 6
KANAGAWA	YOKOHAMA	O 3
MIE	TSU	H 6
MIYAGI	SENDAI	K 4
SAITAMA	URAWA	O 2
SHIGA	OTSU	J 7
SHIMANE	MATSUE	F 6
TOCHIGI	UTSUNOMIYA	K 5
YAMANASHI	KOFU	J 6

Changjon ....D 4	Pak'chŏn ....B 4	Kŏmdŏk (mt.) ....D 3
Chasŏng ....C 3	Pukch'ŏng ....C 3	Kumgang (mt.) ....D 4
Chŏngjin, 1250,000 ....E 3	P'yŏngyang ....C 4	Myohyang (mt.) ....C 3
Chungsŏng ....C 4	P'yŏngyang (cap.), 1,800,000 ....C 4	Nangnim-sanmaek (range) ....C 3
Haeju, 1140,000 ....B 4	P'yŏngyang, *1,221,300 ....C 4	Paektu (Baktu) (mt.) ....D 2
Hamhŭng-Hŭngnam, 1,200,000 ....D 3	Sariwŏn ....C 4	Puksubaek (mt.) ....C 3
Hoeryŏng ....D 2	Sinp'o ....D 3	Supong (res.) ....C 2
Hongwŏn ....D 3	Sinŭiju, 1300,000 ....B 3	Taedong (river) ....C 4
Hŭngnam-Hamhŭng, 1,200,000 ....C 4	Sŏnch'ŏn ....B 4	Tumen (river) ....D 2
Hyesan ....D 3	Sŏngrim ....C 4	Tuun (mt.) ....C 3
Iwŏn ....D 3	Sunch'ŏn ....C 4	West Korea (bay) ....B 4
Kaesŏng, 1175,000 ....C 4	Tanch'ŏn ....D 3	Yalu (river) ....B 3
Kanggye ....C 3	Uiju ....B 3	
Kapsan ....D 3	Unggi ....E 2	
Kilchu ....D 3	Unsan ....C 3	**KOREA (SOUTH)**
Kimchaek, 1,100,000 ....D 3	Wŏnsan, 1275,000 ....C 4	**CITIES and TOWNS**
Kosŏng ....D 4	Yangdŏk ....C 4	
Kusŏng ....C 3	Yongamp'o ....B 4	Andong, 63,816 ....D 5
Manp'o ....C 3		Ansŏng, 23,698 ....C 6
Musan ....D 2	**OTHER FEATURES**	Changhŭng, 30,166 ....C 6
Najin ....E 2		Changsŏng, 26,816 ....C 6
Namp'o, 1140,000 ....C 4	Baktu (mt.) ....C 3	Chech'ŏn, 49,883 ....C 5
Nanam ....D 3	Chang Pai Shan (range) ....C 3	Cheju, 87,569 ....C 7
Ongjin ....B 5	Changjin (res.) ....C 3	Chinhae, 80,804 ....D 6
	East Korea (bay) ....D 4	Chinju, 107,126 ....D 6

Choch'iwŏn, 25,423 ....C 5	Posŏng, 22,247 ....C 6	Cheju (isl.), 336,694 ....C 7
Ch'ŏnan, 71,315 ....C 5	Pusan, 1,425,703 ....D 6	Cheju (strait) ....C 7
Ch'ŏngju, 123,736 ....C 5	Samch'ŏk, 35,117 ....D 5	Dagelet (Ullŭng) (isl.), 27,032 ....E 5
Chŏngŭp, 47,036 ....C 6	Samangjin, 21,936 ....D 6	Halla (mt.) ....C 7
Chŏnju, 220,654 ....C 6	Sangju, 47,558 ....D 5	Han (river) ....C 5
Ch'ungju, 100,043 ....C 5	Seoul (cap.), 4,100,000 ....C 5	Kōje (isl.), 117,906 ....D 6
Ch'ungju, 80,212 ....C 5	Sŏsan, 30,416 ....C 5	Korea (strait) ....D 6
Hongch'ŏn, 23,473 ....D 5	Sunch'ŏn, 79,313 ....C 6	Kŭm (river) ....C 5
Hongsŏng, 21,912 ....C 5	Suwŏn, 127,752 ....C 5	Naktong (river) ....D 6
Inch'ŏn, 525,072 ....C 5	Taegu, 845,073 ....D 6	Port Hamilton (isl.) ....C 7
Iri, 78,448 ....C 6	Taejŏn, 315,094 ....C 5	Quelpart (Cheju) (isl.), 336,694 ....C 7
Kanggyŏng, 26,430 ....C 5	Tamyang, 14,856 ....C 6	So (isl.) ....C 5
Kangnŭng, 65,422 ....D 5	Uisŏng, 21,306 ....D 6	Taebaek (mt.) ....D 5
Kimch'ŏn, 56,981 ....D 5	Ulchin, 27,579 ....D 5	Ullŭng (isl.), 22,032 ....E 5
Koch'ang, 34,707 ....C 6	Ulsan, 112,858 ....D 6	
Konju, 30,320 ....C 5	Wŏnju, 103,852 ....C 5	**RYUKYU ISLANDS**
Kunsan, 102,343 ....C 6	Yangyang, 10,832 ....D 5	**CITIES and TOWNS**
Kwangju, 403,737 ....C 6	Yŏngch'ŏn, 44,305 ....D 6	
Kyŏngju, 85,895 ....D 6	Yŏngdŏk, 19,220 ....D 5	Hirara, 32,591 ....L 7
Masan, 154,873 ....D 6	Yŏnju, 46,338 ....C 6	Ishigaki, 41,315 ....L 7
Miryang, 40,288 ....D 6	Yŏsu, 102,011 ....C 6	Itoman, 34,065 ....N 6
Mokp'o, 162,322 ....C 6		Koza, 55,923 ....N 6
Muju, 18,174 ....C 6	**OTHER FEATURES**	Motobu, 15,068 ....N 6
Namwŏn, 44,193 ....C 6		
P'ohang, 66,190 ....D 5		

Nago, 19,601 ....N 6	
Naha (cap.), 284,000 ....N 6	
Shuri, 28,282 ....N 6	

OTHER FEATURES

Ie (isl.), 7,059 ....N 6	
Iheya (isl.), 3,083 ....N 6	
Iriomote (isl.), 7,026 ....K 7	
Ishigaki (isl.), 41,315 ....L 7	
Kerama (isls.), 2,467 ....M 6	
Kume (isl.), 5,922 ....M 6	
Miyako (isl.), 47,150 ....L 7	
Miyako (isls.), 69,825 ....L 7	
Okinawa (isl.), 782,267 ....N 6	
Okinawa (isls.), 812,339 ....N 6	
Sakishima (isls.), 121,837 ....L 7	
So (isl.) ....K 7	
Tarama (isl.), 2,603 ....L 7	
Yaeyama (isls.), 52,012 ....K 7	
Yonaguni (isl.), 3,671 ....K 7	

*City and suburbs.

†Populations courtesy of Kingsley Davis, Office of Int'l Pop. & Urban Research, Inst. of Int'l Studies, Univ. of California.

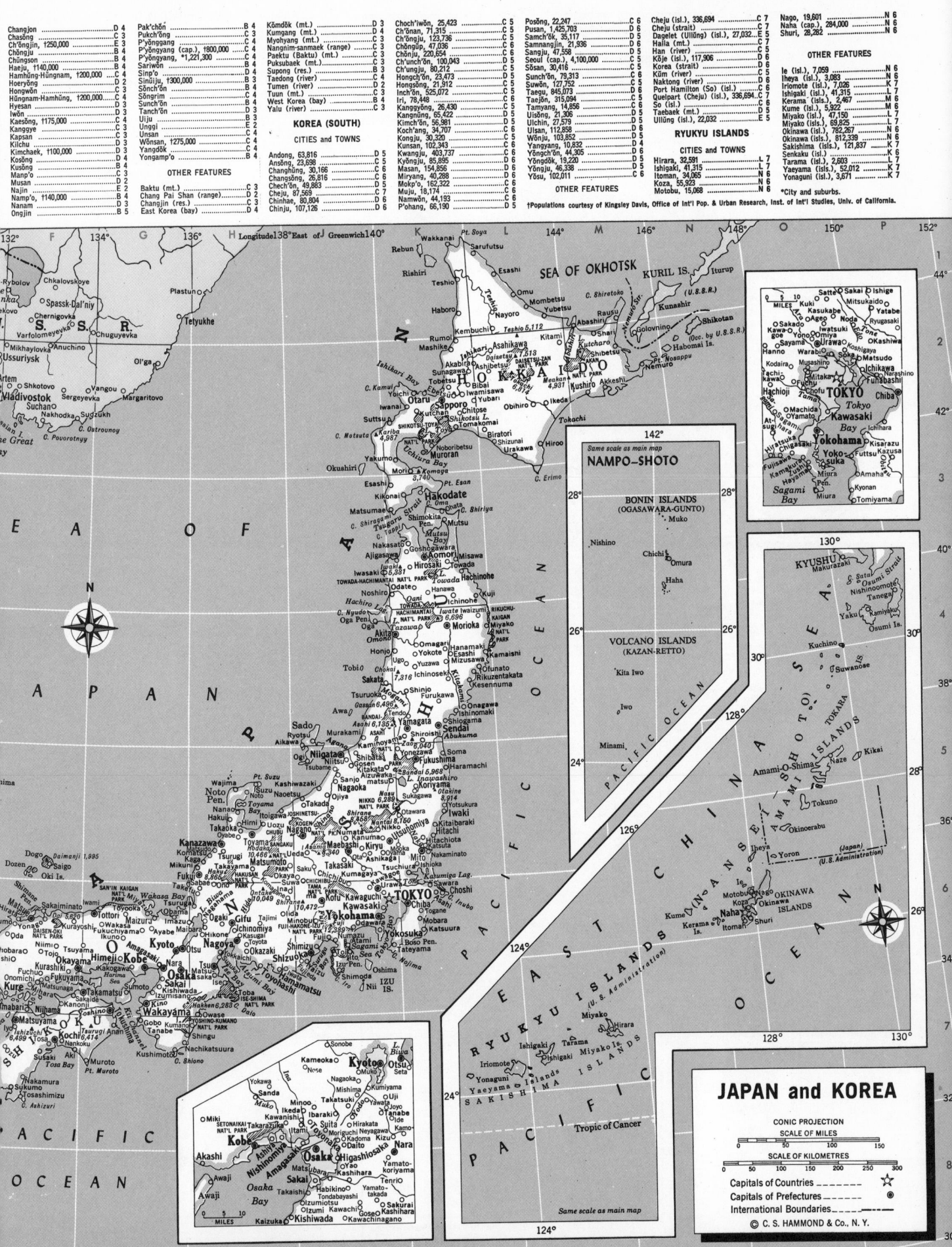

JAPAN and KOREA

CONIC PROJECTION

SCALE OF MILES

SCALE OF KILOMETRES

Capitals of Countries ⭐
Capitals of Prefectures ◉
International Boundaries

© C. S. HAMMOND & Co., N.Y.

76 China and Mongolia

CHINA (MAINLAND)

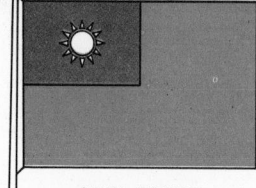

CHINA (TAIWAN)

MONGOLIA

CHINA (MAINLAND)
AREA 3,691,506 sq. mi.
POPULATION 740,000,000
CAPITAL Peking
LARGEST CITY Shanghai
HIGHEST POINT Mt. Everest 29,028 ft.
MONETARY UNIT yüan
MAJOR LANGUAGES Chinese, Chuang, Uigur, Yi,
Tibetan, Miao, Mongol
MAJOR RELIGIONS Confucianism, Buddhism,
Taoism, Islam

Topography

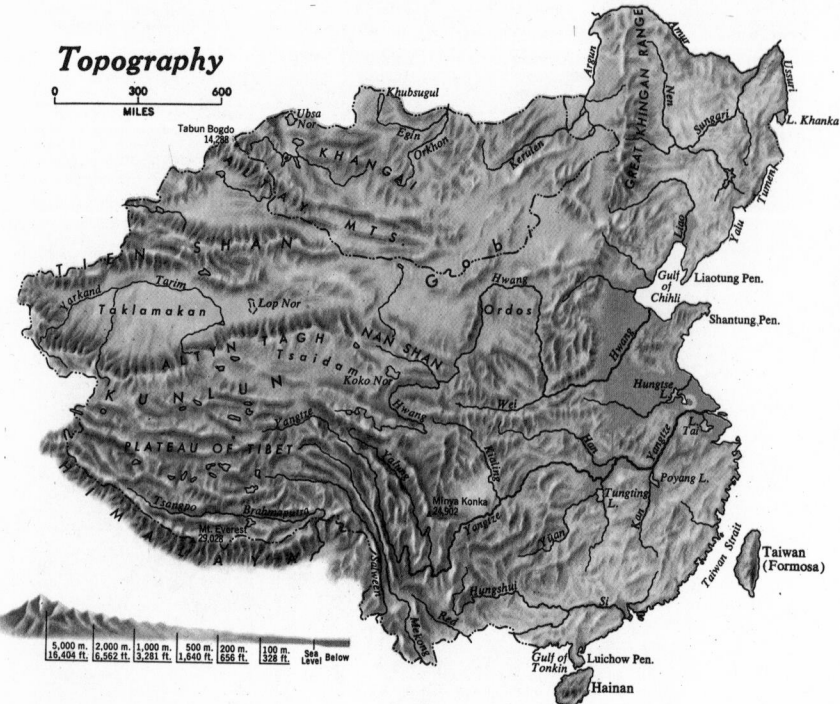

0   300   600
MILES

5,000 m. 2,000 m. 1,000 m. 500 m. 200 m. 100 m. Sea
16,404 ft. 6,562 ft. 3,281 ft. 1,640 ft. 656 ft. 328 ft. Level Below

CHINA

PROVINCES

Anhwei, 33,560,000 .... J 5
Chekiang, 25,280,000 .... J 6
Fukien, 14,650,000 .... J 6
Heilungkiang, 14,860,000 .... L 2
Honan, 48,670,000 .... H 5
Hopei, 44,720,000 .... H 4
Hunan, 36,220,000 .... H 6
Hupei, 30,790,000 .... H 5
Inner Mongolian Autonomous
Region, 9,200,000 .... G 3
Kansu, 12,800,000 .... F 4
Kiangsi, 18,610,000 .... J 6
Kiangsu, 45,230,000 .... K 5
Kirin, 12,550,000 .... L 3
Kwangsi Chuang Autonomous
Region, 19,390,000 .... G 7
Kwangtung, 37,960,000 .... H 7
Kweichow, 16,890,000 .... G 6
Liaoning, 24,090,000 .... K 3
Ningsia Hui Autonomous Region,
1,810,000 .... G 4
Shansi, 15,960,000 .... G 4
Shantung, 54,030,000 .... J 4
Shensi, 18,130,000 .... G 5
Sinkiang-Uigur Autonomous
Region, 5,640,000 .... B 3
Szechwan, 72,160,000 .... F 5
Taiwan, 14,577,000 .... K 7
Tibet Autonomous Region,
1,270,000 .... C 5
Tsinghai, 2,050,000 .... E 4
Yünnan, 19,100,000 .... F 7

CITIES and TOWNS†

Ahpa .... F 5
Aicheng .... G 8
Aigun .... L 1
Aihui (Aigun) .... L 1
Aliho .... L 2
Altai .... C 2
Amoy, 400,000 .... J 7
Ankang .... G 5
Anking, 160,000 .... J 5
Anshan, 1,500,000 .... K 3
Anshun, 40,000 .... G 6
Ansi .... E 3
Antung (Tantung),
450,000 .... K 3
Anyang, 225,000 .... H 4
Aqsu .... A 4
Atushi, 5,000 .... A 4
Awati .... B 3
Baba Hatim .... B 3
Bai .... B 3
Barkha .... B 5
Barkhatu .... B 4
Barkol .... D 3
Bayinhot .... F 4
Bayinkt .... B 3
Canton, 2,300,000 .... H 7

Chalainor .... J 2
Chamdo .... E 5
Changchih, 300,000 .... H 4
Changchow, 400,000 .... J 6
Changchow, 81,200 .... J 7
Changchun, 1,500,000 .... K 3
Changsha, 850,000 .... H 6
Changteh, 225,000 .... H 5
Changyeh, 45,000 .... F 4
Chankiang, 220,000 .... H 7
Chaoan, 101,000 .... J 7
Chaotung, 50,000 .... F 6
Chaoyang, 30,000 .... K 3
Charkhliq .... C 4
Chefoo, 180,000 .... K 4
Chendo .... D 5
Chengchow, 1,500,000 .... H 5
Chengteh, 200,000 .... J 3
Chengtu, 2,000,000 .... F 5
Chenpa .... G 5
Cherchen .... C 4
Chiai, 221,817 .... K 7
Chiehmo (Cherchen) .... C 4
Chihfeng, 49,000 .... J 3
Chinchow, 750,000 .... J 3
Chinkiang, 250,000 .... K 5
Chinsi, 45,000 .... K 3
Chinwangtao, 400,000 .... J 4
Chomo Dzong .... D 6
Chüanchow, 130,000 .... J 7
Chuchow, 350,000 .... H 6
Chuguchak .... B 2
Chumatien, 45,000 .... H 5
Chungking, 3,500,000 .... G 6
Chungning .... G 4
Chungshan, 135,000 .... H 7
Chushul .... D 6
Dairen (in Lüta) .... K 4
Denchin .... E 5
Depung .... D 6
Durbuljin .... B 2
Ed Dzong .... D 5
Fatshan, 120,000 .... H 7
Fengfeng, 45,000 .... H 4
Fengyang, 25,000 .... J 5
Foochow, 900,000 .... J 6
Fowyang, 75,000 .... J 5
Fuchin .... M 2
Fuhai .... C 2
Fushun, 1,700,000 .... K 3
Fusin, 350,000 .... K 3
Fusingchen, 20,000 .... F 7
Fuyü, 62,969 .... K 3
Gartok .... B 4
Giamda Dzong (Taichao) .... D 5
Guma .... A 4
Gyangtse .... C 6
Gyatsa Dzong .... D 5
Haikow (Hoihow),
500,000 .... H 7
Hailar, 60,000 .... J 2
Hailun .... L 2
Hailung, 20,000 .... K 3
Hami .... D 3
Hanchung, 120,000 .... G 5
Hangchow, 1,100,000 .... J 5
Hankow (in Wuhan) .... H 5
Hantan, 500,000 .... H 4

Hanyang (in Wuhan) .... H 5
Harbin, 2,750,000 .... L 2
Hengshui .... J 4
Hengyang, 310,000 .... H 6
Hochwan, 75,000 .... G 5
Hofei, 400,000 .... J 5
Hofeng .... G 2
Hoihow, 500,000 .... H 7
Hokang, 350,000 .... M 2
Hopo, 80,000 .... A 4
Hotien (Khotan) .... A 4
Hsüchang, 58,000 .... H 5
Huhehot, 700,000 .... H 3
Huma .... L 1
Hunchun, 13,246 .... M 3
Hwainan, 350,000 .... J 5
Hwaiteh, 60,000 .... K 3
Hwangchung .... F 4
Hwangling .... G 4
Hwangshih, 200,000 .... J 5
Hwangyüan .... F 4
Hwohsien .... G 4
Ichang, 150,000 .... H 5
Ichun, 200,000 .... L 2
Ierhsieh .... J 2
Ining (Kuldja),
160,000 .... B 3
Ipin, 275,000 .... F 6
Ishan .... G 7
Jechiang (Charkhliq) .... C 4
Jyekundo .... E 5
Kaifeng, 330,000 .... H 5
Kalgan, 1,000,000 .... H 3
Kanchow, 135,000 .... H 6
Kangting .... F 6
Kaohsiung, 719,899 .... K 7
Karamai, 43,000 .... B 2
Kashgar, 175,000 .... A 4
Kashing, 132,000 .... K 5
Keelung, 304,740 .... K 6
Kelpin (Koping) .... A 3
Keriya .... B 4
Khabakhe .... C 2
Khetinsiring .... D 5
Khobuk-Saur (Hofeng) .... C 2
Khotan .... A 4
Kiamusze, 275,000 .... L 2
Kian, 100,000 .... H 6
Kiayükwan .... E 4
Kienow .... J 6
Kienyang .... J 6
Kinghung .... F 7
Kingku .... F 7
Kingtehchen, 300,000 .... J 6
Kinhwa, 46,200 .... J 6
Kirin, 1,200,000 .... L 3
Kisi, 350,000 .... M 2
Kital .... C 3
Kiuchüan, 50,000 .... E 4
Kiukiang, 120,000 .... H 6
Kokiu, 150,000 .... F 7
Kongmoon, 150,000 .... H 7
Koping .... A 3
Kucha .... B 3
Kulang .... F 4
Kuldja, 160,000 .... B 3
Kungju .... B 3
Kunming, 1,700,000 .... F 7

Kwanghwa .... H 5
Kweilin, 225,000 .... G 6
Kweisui (Huhehot),
700,000 .... H 3
Kweiyang, 1,500,000 .... G 6
Lanchow, 1,500,000 .... F 4
Lantsang .... F 7
Lhakang Dzong .... D 6
Lhasa, 175,000 .... D 6
Lhatse Dzong .... C 6
Lhuntse Dzong .... D 6
Liaoyang, 250,000 .... K 3
Liaoyüan, 300,000 .... L 3
Lienyünkang, 300,000 .... K 5
Likiang .... F 6
Linchwan, 45,000 .... J 6
Linsia, 75,000 .... F 4
Lintsing, 45,000 .... J 4
Liuchow, 250,000 .... G 6
Loho, 55,000 .... H 5
Loshan, 250,000 .... F 6
Loyang, 750,000 .... H 5
Luchow, 225,000 .... F 6
Lungchen, 14,000 .... L 2
Lüshun (Port Arthur)
(in Lüta) .... K 4
Lüta, 14,000,000 .... K 4
Mahai .... D 4
Manass .... C 3
Manchouli, 30,000 .... J 2
Mani .... B 4
Manning (Wanning) .... H 8
Maralbashi .... A 4
Markham Dzong .... E 6
Mato .... E 4
Mendong Gomba .... C 5
Merket .... A 4
Minhsien .... F 5
Mowming, 15,000 .... H 7
Moyü (Qara Qash) .... B 4
Mukden, 3,750,000 .... K 3
Muli .... F 6
Mutankiang, 400,000 .... M 3
Nachii .... D 5
Nanchang, 900,000 .... H 6
Nancheng, 50,000 .... J 6
Nanchung, 275,000 .... G 5
Nanking, 2,000,000 .... J 5
Nanning, 375,000 .... G 7
Nanping, 53,445 .... J 6
Nanyang, 150,000 .... H 5
Neikiang, 240,000 .... F 6
Ningpo, 350,000 .... K 6
Ningsia (Yinchwan),
175,000 .... F 4
Omin (Durbuljin) .... B 2
Pachen .... D 5
Pachu (Maralbashi) .... A 4
Paicheng, 75,000 .... K 2
Paiyin, 50,000 .... F 4
Paiyü .... E 5
Pakhoi, 175,000 .... G 7
Paoki, 275,000 .... G 5
Paoting, 350,000 .... H 4
Paotow, 800,000 .... G 3
Pehan, 130,000 .... L 2
Peihai (Pakhoi),
175,000 .... G 7

(continued on following page)

China and Mongolia 77

CHINA (TAIWAN)
AREA 13,948 sq. mi.
POPULATION 14,577,000
CAPITAL Taipei
LARGEST CITY Taipei
HIGHEST POINT Hsinkao Shan 12,959 ft.
MONETARY UNIT new Taiwan dollar
MAJOR LANGUAGES Chinese, Formosan
MAJOR RELIGIONS Confucianism, Buddhism, Taoism, Christianity, Tribal religions

MONGOLIA
AREA 604,247 sq. mi.
POPULATION 1,300,000
CAPITAL Ulan Bator
LARGEST CITY Ulan Bator
HIGHEST POINT Tabun Bogdo 15,266 ft.
MONETARY UNIT tugrik
MAJOR LANGUAGES Mongolian, Kazakh
MAJOR RELIGION Buddhism

HONG KONG
AREA 398 sq. mi.
POPULATION 4,089,000
CAPITAL Victoria
MONETARY UNIT Hong Kong dollar
MAJOR LANGUAGES Chinese, English
MAJOR RELIGIONS Confucianism, Buddhism, Christianity

MACAO
AREA 6.2 sq. mi.
POPULATION 292,000
CAPITAL Macao
MONETARY UNIT pataca
MAJOR LANGUAGES Chinese, Portuguese
MAJOR RELIGIONS Confucianism, Buddhism, Taoism, Christianity

CHINA and MONGOLIA
CONIC PROJECTION
SCALE OF MILES
0 100 200 300 400 500
SCALE OF KILOMETRES
0 100 200 300 400 500

Capitals of Countries....☆   International Boundaries
Provincial Capitals......◉   Provincial Boundaries
Canals   Walls

© Copyright by C.S. HAMMOND & CO., N.Y.

*Wuhan municipality consists of Hankow, Hanyang and Wuchang

78 China and Mongolia

(continued)

Peiping (Peking) (capital), ‡8,000,000 J 3
Peking (capital), ‡8,000,000 J 3
Pengpu, 400,000 J 5
Penki, 750,000 K 3
Pingliang, 60,000 G 4
Pingsiang, 7,000 G 7
Pingtung, 153,953 K 7
Pishan (Guma) A 4
Pohsien, 75,000 J 5
Port Arthur (in Lüta) K 4
Poseh G 7
Puèrh F 7
Qara Qash B 4
Qara Shahr C 3
Qarghaliq A 4
Rima E 6
Rudok B 5
Rungmar Thok B 5
Saka C 6
Sanga Cho Dzong E 6
Sanho K 1
Shahyar B 3
Shanghai, ‡8,500,000 K 5
Shanghsien H 5
Shangjao, 100,000 J 6
Shangkiu, 250,000 J 5
Shangshui, 100,000 J 5
Shaohing, 225,000 K 6
Shaoyang, 275,000 H 6
Sharasume (Altai) C 2
Shasi, 125,000 H 5
Shenyang (Mukden), 3,750,000 K 3
Shigatse, 26,000 C 6
Shihhotzu, 70,000 C 3
Shihkiachwang, 1,500,000 J 4
Shiukwan, 125,000 H 7
Shobando E 5
Shwangyashan, 150,000 M 2
Siakwan, 26,200 F 6
Sian, 1,900,000 G 5
Siangfan, 150,000 H 5
Siangtan, 300,000 H 6
Sienyang, 120,000 G 5
Silinhot, 20,000 J 3
Sinchu, 188,062 K 7
Singi Obo C 5
Singsingsia D 3
Singtai, 75,000 H 4
Sinhailien (Lienyünkang), 300,000 J 5
Sining, 250,000 F 4
Sinsiang, 300,000 H 4
Sinyang, 125,000 H 5
Soche (Yarkand), 80,000 A 4
Solun K 2
Soochow, 1,300,000 K 5
Süchow, 1,500,000 J 5
Suihwa, 36,000 L 2
Suining, 75,000 F 5
Sutsien J 5
Süyung F 6
Swatow, 400,000 J 7
Szeping, 180,000 K 3
Tahcheng (Chuguchak) B 2
Taian, 20,000 J 4
Taichung, 407,054 J 7
Tainan, 441,556 J 7
Taipei (capital), 1,604,543 K 7
Taitung, 69,984 K 7
Taiyüan, 2,725,000 H 4
Taklakhar B 5
Talai, 20,000 K 2
Tali E 6
Tangshan, 1,200,000 J 4
Tantung, 450,000 K 3
Taoan, 75,000 K 2
Tapanshang J 3
Tash Qurghan A 4
Tashigong A 5
Tatung, 300,000 H 3
Tehchow, 45,000 J 4
Tengchung E 7
Tengkow G 4
Thok Daurakpa C 5
Thok Jalung B 5
Tiehling, 52,945 K 3
Tienshui, 100,000 F 5
Tientsin, ‡4,500,000 J 4
Tingri Dzong C 6
Tokoto H 3
Tolun J 3
Tradom B 6
Tsoachwang J 4
Tsangchow, 75,000 J 4
Tsiaotso, 300,000 H 4
Tsinan, 1,500,000 J 4
Tsingkiang, 110,000 J 5
Tsingshih, 100,000 H 6
Tsingtao, 1,900,000 K 4
Tsining, 160,000 H 3
Tsining, 86,200 J 4
Tsitsihar, 1,500,000 K 2
Tsunyi, 275,000 G 6
Tungchwan, 45,000 G 4
Tungfang G 8
Tunghwa, 275,000 L 3
Tungjen G 6
Tungkiang, 96,652 M 2
Tungliao, 40,000 K 3
Tunhwa, 80,000 L 3
Tunki, 75,000 J 6
Tushantze B 3
Turfan C 3
Tuyün, 60,000 G 6
Tzekung, 350,000 G 6
Tzepo, 1,750 J 4
Uch Turfan A 3
Ulanhot, 100,000 K 2
Ulughchat A 4
Uniket J 2
Urumchi, 500,000 C 3
Wanhsien, 175,000 G 5
Wanning H 8
Weifang, 260,000 J 4
Weihai, 50,000 K 4
Wenchow, 250,000 J 6
Wuchang (in Wuhan) H 5
Wuchow, 150,000 H 7
Wuchung, 45,000 G 4
Wuhan, ‡4,250,000 H 5
Wuhing, 160,000 J 5
Wuhu, 300,000 J 5
Wusih, 900,000 K 5
Wusu B 3
Wuta G 3
Wuwei F 4
Yaan, 100,000 F 6
Yangchow, 210,000 K 5
Yangchüan, 350,000 H 4
Yangi Hissar A 4
Yarkand, 80,000 A 4
Yatung C 6
Yenan G 4
Yenki (Qara Shahr) C 3
Yenki, 130,000 L 3
Yinchwan, 175,000 F 4
Yingkow, 215,000 K 3
Yingtak H 7
Yiyang, 75,000 H 6
Yüehsi F 6
Yühsien H 4
Yülin G 8
Yümen, 325,000 E 4
Yungkia (Wenchow), 250,000 J 6
Yüshu (Jyekundo) E 5
Yütien (Keriya) B 4
Yütze, 100,000 H 4

OTHER FEATURES

Achchik Kol (lake) C 4
Alashan (desert) F 4
Altay (mts.) C 2
Altyn Tagh (range) C 4
Amne Machin (mts.) F 5
Amur (river) L 2
Argun (river) J 1
Bagrach Kol (lake) C 3
Bam Tso (lake) D 5
Bashi (channel) K 7
Bayan Kara Shan (range) E 5
Black (river) F 7
Bogdo Ula (mts.) C 3
Bor Nor (lake) J 2
Chang Tang (plat.) B 5
Cherchen (river) C 4
Chihli (gulf) K 4
Chushan (arch.) K 5
Dre Chu (river) E 5
Dza Chu (river) E 5
Dzungaria (region) C 3
East China (sea) L 6
Ebi Nor (lake) B 2
Erh Hai (lake) F 6
Everest (mt.) C 6
Fen Ho (river) H 4
Formosa (Taiwan) (isl.), 12,888,478 K 7
Formosa (Taiwan) (str.) J 7
Gashun Nor (lake) E 3
Genghis Khan Wall (ruins) H 2
Gobi (desert) G 3
Grand (canal) J 4
Great Khingan (range) K 2
Great Wall (ruins) G 4
Gurla Mandhata (mt.) B 5
Hainan (isl.) G 8
Hangchow (bay) K 5
Han Kiang (river) H 5
Himalaya (mts.) B-D 6
Hulun Nor (lake) J 2
Hungtow (isl.), 2,465 K 7
Hwang Ho (river) H 5
Indus (river) A 5
Inner Mongolia (reg.) H 3
Jiggitai Tso (lake) C 4
Kailas (mt.) B 5
Kaopao (lake) J 5
Karakhoto (ruins) F 3
Karakoram (mts.) A 4
Kara Nor (lake) E 4
Kashum Tso (lake) C 5
Kerulen (river) H 2
Khanka (lake) M 3
Khotan (river) B 4
Kialing Kiang (river) G 5
Kiungchow (str.) G 7
Koko Nor (lake) E 4
Kumara (river) K 1
Kunlun (mts.) C 4
Kyaring Tso (lake) C 5
Kyaring Tso (lake) E 4
Liao Ho (river) J 3
Liaotung (pen.) K 4
Lighten Tso (lake) B 5
Lop Nor (dry lake) D 3
Luichow (pen.) G 7
Manasarowar (lake) B 5
Manass (river) C 3
Manchuria (reg.), 51,500,000 K 2
Matsu (isl.) K 6
Mekong (river) F 7
Min Kiang (river) F 5
Min Kiang (river) J 6
Min Shan (range) F 5
Minya Konka (mt.) F 6
Montcalm (lake) C 5
Muztagh (mt.) B 4
Muztagh Ata (mt.) A 4
Nam Tso (lake) D 5
Namcha Barwa (mt.) E 6
Nan Shan (range) E 4
Nen (river) K 2
Nganglaring Tso (lake) B 5
Ngangtse Tso (lake) C 5
Ngoring Tso (lake) E 5
Nyenchen Tanglha (range) C 6
Olwanpi (cape) K 7
Ordos (desert) G 4
Pangong Tso (lake) A 5
Penghu (isls.), 113,503 J 7
Pescadores (Penghu) (isls.), 113,503 J 7
Pobeda (peak) B 3
Po Hai (Chihli) (gulf) K 4
Poyang (lake) J 6
Pratas (isl.) J 7
Quemoy (isl.) J 7
Red (river) F 7
Salween (river) E 6
Shamo (Gobi) (des.) G 3
Siang Kiang (river) H 7
Si Kiang (river) H 7
Sinkao Shan (mt.) K 7
South China (sea) H 7
Sungari (river) M 2
Sutlej (river) A 5
Tachen (isls.) K 6
Tahsüeh Shan (range) F 6
Tai (lake) J 5
Taiwan (isl.), 12,888,478 K 7
Taiwan (str.) J 7
Taklamakan (desert) B 4
Tanglha (range) C 5
Tangra Tso (lake) C 5
Tapa Shan (range) G 5
Tarbagatay (range) B 2
Tarim (river) C 3
Tarok Tso (lake) B 5
Tien Chih (lake) F 7
Tien Shan (range) B 3
Tonkin (gulf) G 8
Trans-Himalayas (range) C 5
Tsaidam (swamp) E 4
Tsangpo (river) C 6
Tsing Hai (Koko Nor) (lake) E 4
Tsinling Shan (range) G 5
Tungsha (Pratas) (isl.) J 7
Tungting (lake) H 6
Turfan (depr.) C 3
Ulan Muren (river) D 5
Ulugh Muztagh (mt.) C 4
Ulyungur Nor (lake) C 2
Urungu (river) C 2
Ussuri (river) M 2
Wei Ho (river) G 5
West Korea (bay) K 4
Wu Kiang (river) G 6
Wuyi Shan (range) J 6
Yalu (river) L 3
Yalung Kiang (river) E 5
Yamdrok Tso (lake) D 6
Yangtze Kiang (river) K 5
Yarkand (river) A 4
Yellow (Hwang Ho) (river) J 4
Yellow (sea) J 4
Yüan Kiang (river) G 6
Yü Kiang (river) G 7
Zilling Tso (lake) C 5

HONG KONG

CITIES and TOWNS

Kowloon, 692,800 H 7
Victoria (capital), 694,500 H 7
Victoria, *1,034,000 H 7

MACAO

CITIES and TOWNS

Macao (capital), 262,000 H 7

MONGOLIA

PROVINCES

Bayan Khongor, 43,600 E 2
Bayan Ulegei, 45,100 C 2
Bulagan, 31,200 F 2
Central, 50,400 G 2
Dzabkhan, 56,800 E 2
Eastern, 34,300 H 2
East Gobi, 26,300 G 3
Gobi-Altay, 40,500 D 2
Khentei, 35,400 G 2
Khubsugul, 61,100 E 1
Kobdo, 44,800 D 2
Middle Gobi, 27,500 G 2
North Khangai, 60,300 F 2
Selenga, 43,300 G 2
South Gobi, 21,900 F 3
South Khangai, 53,800 F 2
Sukh-Batar, 30,400 H 2
Ubsa Nor, 49,000 D 2

CITIES and TOWNS

Arbai Khere, 6,000 F 2
Altay, 7,000 E 2
Baishintu H 2
Baruun Urta, 6,000 H 2
Bayan Khongor, 4,400 F 2
Bayan Tumen (Choibalsan), 14,000 H 2
Bayan Ulegei, 8,000 D 2
Bulagan, 8,000 F 2
Chindamani Suma E 2
Choibalsan, 14,000 H 2
Dalan Dzadagad, 4,000 G 3
Darkhan, 30,000 G 2
Delger Khangai F 2
Delger Tsogtu G 2
Dzamyn Ude G 3
Dzun Modo, 6,000 G 2
Erdeni Dzuu F 2
Jibhalanta (Uliassutai), 7,000
Jirgalanta (Kobdo), 11,000
Khan Bogda
Khongor Obo
Khonichi
Kobdo, 11,000
Mandal Gobi, 5,000
Munku Khan
Muren, 9,000
Nalaikha, 14,000
Nomogon
Noyan
Onon
Sain Shanda, 7,000
Sair Usa
Sukhe Bator, 9,000
Suok
Tamtsak
Tsagan Ula
Tsetserlig, 14,000
Tszaq
Ulan Bator (capital), 268,800
Ulangom, 10,000
Uliassutai, 7,000
Undur Khan, 7,000
Yugodzyr
Yusun Bulak (Altay), 7,000

OTHER FEATURES

Altay (mts.)
Bor Nor (lake)
Durga Nor (lake)
Dzabkhan (river)
Egin (river)
Genghis Khan Wall (ruins)
Gobi (desert)
Höbsögöl (Khubsugul) (lake)
Ider (river)
Karakorum (ruins)
Kerulen (river)
Khangai (mts.)
Khara Usu (lake)
Khentei (mts.)
Khubsugul (lake)
Kirgis Nor (lake)
Kobdo (river)
Munku-Sardyk (mt.)
Onon (river)
Orkhon (river)
Selenga (river)
Shamo (Gobi) (des.)
Tabun Bogdo (mt.)
Tannu-Ola (range)
Tesin (river)
Ubsa Nor (lake)

*City and suburbs.
‡Population of municipality.

Agriculture, Industry and Resources

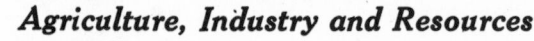

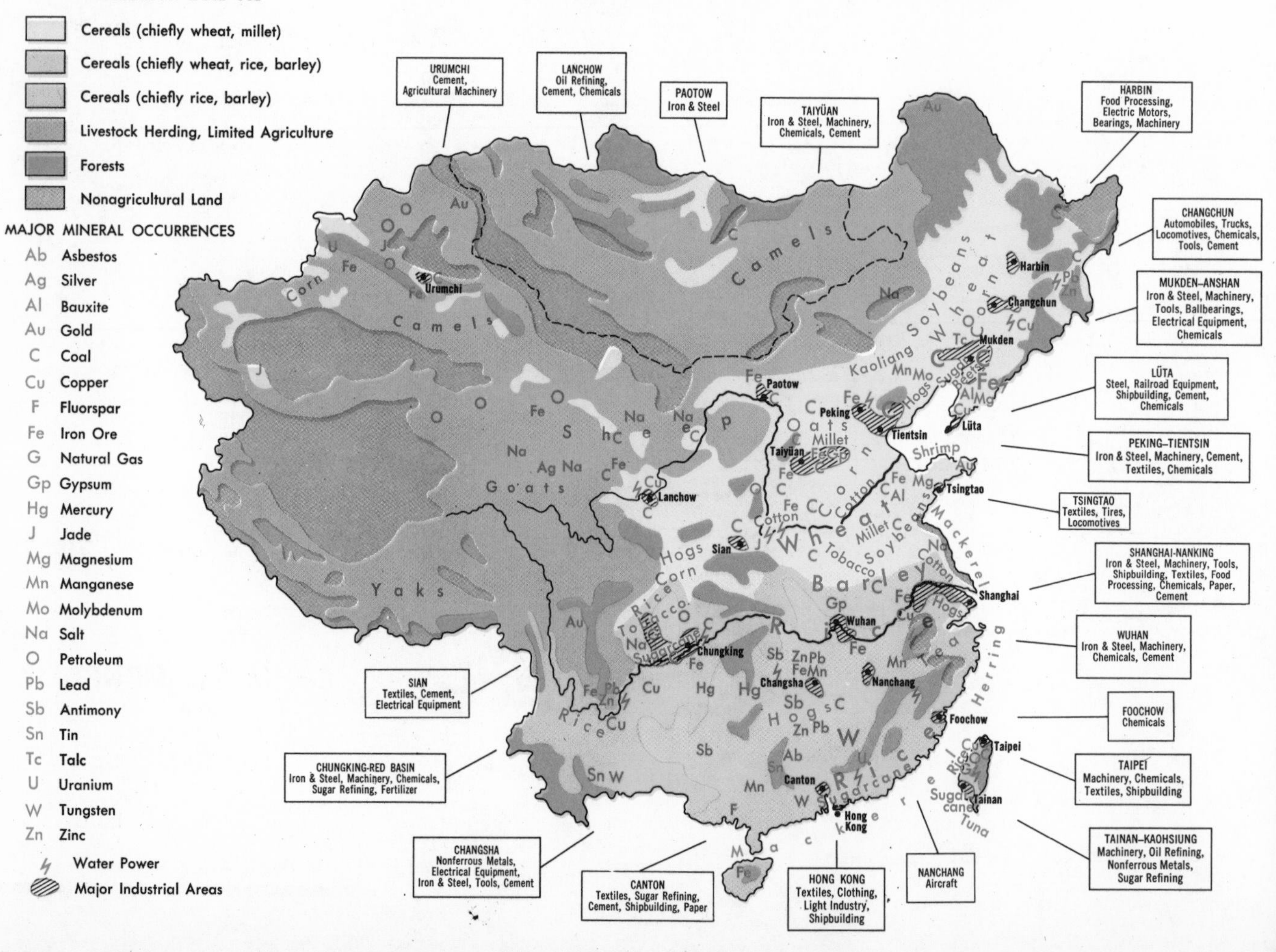

DOMINANT LAND USE
Cereals (chiefly wheat, millet)
Cereals (chiefly wheat, rice, barley)
Cereals (chiefly rice, barley)
Livestock Herding, Limited Agriculture
Forests
Nonagricultural Land
MAJOR MINERAL OCCURRENCES
Ab Asbestos
Ag Silver
Al Bauxite
Au Gold
C Coal
Cu Copper
F Fluorspar
Fe Iron Ore
G Natural Gas
Gp Gypsum
Hg Mercury
J Jade
Mg Magnesium
Mn Manganese
Mo Molybdenum
Na Salt
O Petroleum
Pb Lead
Sb Antimony
Sn Tin
Tc Talc
U Uranium
W Tungsten
Zn Zinc
Water Power
Major Industrial Areas
URUMCHI Cement, Agricultural Machinery
LANCHOW Oil Refining, Cement, Chemicals
PAOTOW Iron & Steel
TAIYÜAN Iron & Steel, Machinery, Chemicals, Cement
HARBIN Food Processing, Electric Motors, Bearings, Machinery
CHANGCHUN Automobiles, Trucks, Locomotives, Chemicals, Tools, Cement
MUKDEN–ANSHAN Iron & Steel, Machinery, Tools, Ballbearings, Electrical Equipment, Chemicals
LÜTA Steel, Railroad Equipment, Shipbuilding, Cement, Chemicals
PEKING–TIENTSIN Iron & Steel, Machinery, Cement, Textiles, Chemicals
TSINGTAO Textiles, Tires, Locomotives
SHANGHAI-NANKING Iron & Steel, Machinery, Tools, Shipbuilding, Textiles, Food Processing, Chemicals, Paper, Cement
WUHAN Iron & Steel, Machinery, Chemicals, Cement
FOOCHOW Chemicals
TAIPEI Machinery, Chemicals, Textiles, Shipbuilding
TAINAN–KAOHSIUNG Machinery, Oil Refining, Nonferrous Metals, Sugar Refining
SIAN Textiles, Cement, Electrical Equipment
CHUNGKING-RED BASIN Iron & Steel, Machinery, Chemicals, Sugar Refining, Fertilizer
CHANGSHA Nonferrous Metals, Electrical Equipment, Iron & Steel, Tools, Cement
CANTON Textiles, Sugar Refining, Cement, Shipbuilding, Paper
HONG KONG Textiles, Clothing, Light Industry, Shipbuilding
NANCHANG Aircraft
Urumchi
Lanchow
Paotow
Peking
Tientsin
Taiyüan
Harbin
Changchun
Mukden
Lüta
Tsingtao
Sian
Shanghai
Wuhan
Chungking
Changsha
Nanchang
Foochow
Taipei
Tainan
Canton
Hong Kong
Camels
Corn
Goats
Yaks
Soybeans
Wheat
Kaoliang
Hogs
Oats
Millet
Cotton
Tobacco
Barley
Rice
Sugarcane
Shrimp
Mackerel
Herring
Tuna

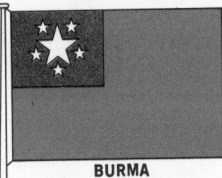

BURMA

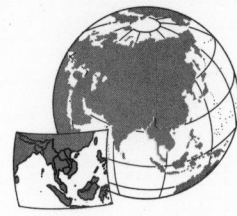

BURMA
AREA 261,789 sq. mi.
POPULATION 27,000,000
CAPITAL Rangoon
LARGEST CITY Rangoon
HIGHEST POINT Hkakabo Razi 19,296 ft.
MONETARY UNIT kyat
MAJOR LANGUAGES Burmese, Karen, Shan
MAJOR RELIGIONS Buddhism, Tribal religions

THAILAND
AREA 198,456 sq. mi.
POPULATION 35,448,000
CAPITAL Bangkok
LARGEST CITY Bangkok
HIGHEST POINT Doi Inthanon 8,452 ft.
MONETARY UNIT baht
MAJOR LANGUAGES Thai, Lao, Chinese
MAJOR RELIGIONS Buddhism, Tribal religions

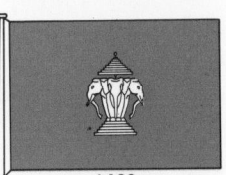

THAILAND

LAOS
AREA 91,459 sq. mi.
POPULATION 2,900,000
CAPITAL Vientiane
LARGEST CITY Vientiane
HIGHEST POINT Phu Bia 9,252 ft.
MONETARY UNIT kip
MAJOR LANGUAGES Lao, French
MAJOR RELIGION Buddhism

CAMBODIA
AREA 69,898 sq. mi.
POPULATION 6,701,000
CAPITAL Phnom Penh
LARGEST CITY Phnom Penh
HIGHEST POINT 5,948 ft.
MONETARY UNIT riel
MAJOR LANGUAGES Khmer (Cambodian), French
MAJOR RELIGION Buddhism

NORTH VIETNAM
AREA 61,293 sq. mi.
POPULATION 21,340,000
CAPITAL Hanoi
LARGEST CITY Hanoi
HIGHEST POINT Fan Si Pan 10,308 ft.
MONETARY UNIT dong
MAJOR LANGUAGES Vietnamese, Thai, Muong, Meo, Yao
MAJOR RELIGIONS Buddhism, Taoism, Confucianism

LAOS

SOUTH VIETNAM
AREA 66,263 sq. mi.
POPULATION 16,543,434
CAPITAL Saigon
LARGEST CITY Saigon
HIGHEST POINT Ngoc Linh 8,524 ft.
MONETARY UNIT piaster
MAJOR LANGUAGES Vietnamese, Chinese, Khmer, Jarai, French
MAJOR RELIGIONS Buddhism, Taoism, Confucianism, Roman Catholicism, Cao-Dai

MALAYSIA
AREA 128,308 sq. mi.
POPULATION 10,583,000
CAPITAL Kuala Lumpur
LARGEST CITY Kuala Lumpur
HIGHEST POINT Mt. Kinabalu 13,455 ft.
MONETARY UNIT Malayan dollar
MAJOR LANGUAGES Malay, Chinese, English, Tamil, Dayak, Kadazan
MAJOR RELIGIONS Islam, Confucianism, Buddhism, Tribal religions, Hinduism, Taoism

SINGAPORE
AREA 226 sq. mi.
POPULATION 2,034,000
CAPITAL Singapore
LARGEST CITY Singapore
HIGHEST POINT Bukit Timah 581 ft.
MONETARY UNIT Malayan dollar
MAJOR LANGUAGES Chinese, Malay, Tamil, English
MAJOR RELIGIONS Confucianism, Buddhism, Taoism, Hinduism, Islam, Christianity

CAMBODIA

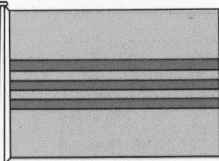

NORTH VIETNAM

SOUTH VIETNAM

MALAYSIA

SINGAPORE

Topography

0   200   400
MILES

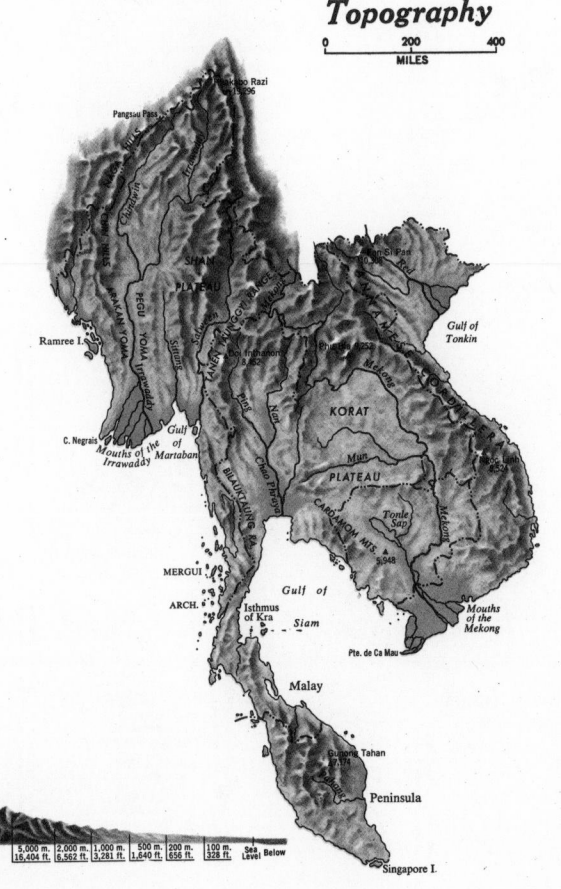

5,000 m.   2,000 m.   1,000 m.   500 m.   200 m.   100 m.   Sea   Below
16,404 ft.   6,562 ft.   3,281 ft.   1,640 ft.   656 ft.   328 ft.   Level

(continued on following page)

(continued)

CAMBODIA

CITIES and TOWNS

Banam, †87,048 E 5
Battambang, 38,846 D 4
Cheom Ksan E 4
Chhlong, †46,108 E 4
Chong Kal, †16,918 D 4
Kampot, 12,558 E 5
Kep, 7,565 E 5
Khemarak Phouinville D 5
Kohnieh E 4
Kompong Cham, 28,534 E 4
Kompong Chhnang, 12,847 D 4
Kompong Kleang E 4
Kompong Som, 6,578 D 5
Kompong Speu, 7,453 E 5
Kompong Thom, 9,682 E 4
Kompong Trabek, †108,227 E 5
Koulen E 4
Kratie, 11,908 E 4
Krauchmar, †63,262 E 4
Moung, †88,321 D 4
Pailin, †15,536 D 4
Phnom Penh (capital), *500,000 E 5
Phsar Babau D 4
Phsar Oudong, †50,456 E 5
Phum Rovieng, †21,151 E 4
Phum Troun E 4
Poipet D 4
Prek Po E 5
Prey Veng, 8,792 E 5
Pursat, 14,329 D 4
Ream D 5
Sambor, †11,213 E 4
Siem Pang, †8,959 E 4
Siem Reap, 10,230 D 4
Sisophon, †29,581 D 4
Sre Khtum E 4
Stung Treng, 3,369 E 4
Suong E 5
Svay Rieng, 11,184 E 5
Takeo, 11,312 E 5
Virachei, †16,912 E 4

OTHER FEATURES

Angkor Wat (ruins) E 4
Dang Raek, Phanom (mts.) D 4
Joncs (plain) E 5
Kas Kong (isl.) D 5
Kas Tang (isl.) D 5
Kong, Kas (isl.) D 5
Mekong (river) E 4
Phanom Dang Raek (mts.) D 4
Preapatang (rapids) E 4
Rong, Koh (isl.) D 5
Samit (point) D 5
Se Khong (river) E 4
Se San (river) E 4
Siam (gulf) D 5
Srepok (river) E 4
Stung Sen (river) E 4
Tang, Kas (isl.) D 5
Tonle Sap (lake) D 4

LAOS

CITIES and TOWNS

Attopeu, 2,750 E 4
Ban Bung Sai E 4
Borikhane D 3
Botene D 3
Boun Neua, 2,500 D 2
Boun Tai, †1,681 D 2
Champassak, 3,500 E 4
Houei Sai, 1,500 D 2
Hua Muong D 2
Keng Kok, 2,000 E 3
Kham Keut, †31,206 E 3
Khone E 4
Khong, 1,750 E 4
Khong Sédone, 2,000 E 4
Luang Prabang, 7,596 D 3
Mahaxay, 2,000 E 3
Muong Beng, †2,305 D 2
Muong Bo D 3
Muong Hai, †476 D 2
Muong Hôm D 3
Muong Lan, †836 D 3
Muong May E 4
Muong Phalane E 3
Muong Phine E 3
Muong Phong D 3
Muong Sai, 2,000 D 2
Muong Sing, 1,091 D 2
Muong Son D 2
Muong Song Khone, 2,000 E 3
Muong Wapi E 4
Muong Yo D 2
Nam Tha, 1,459 D 2
Napé E 3
Nong Het D 3
Ou Neua, †4,300 D 2
Pak Beng, †2,964 D 3
Pak Hin Boun, 1,750 E 3
Pak Sane, 2,500 D 3
Paklay, 2,000 D 3
Pakse, 8,000 E 4
Phiafay, †17,216 E 4
Phon Tiou E 3
Phong Saly, 2,500 D 2
Sam Neua, 3,000 E 2
Saravane, 2,350 E 4
Savannakhet, 8,500 E 3
Sayaboury, 2,500 D 3
Tchepone, 1,250 E 3
Tha-deua D 3
Thakhek, 5,500 E 3
Tourakom D 3
Vang Vieng, 1,250 D 3
Vien Phou Kha D 2
Vientiane (capital), 132,253 D 3
Vientiane, *162,297 D 3
Xieng Khouang, 3,500 D 3

OTHER FEATURES

Bolovens (plateau) E 4
Hou, Nam (river) D 2
Jars (plain) D 3
Mekong (river) D 3
Nam Hou (river) D 2
Nam Tha (river) D 2
Phu Bia (mt.) D 3
Phu Co Pi (mt.) E 3
Phu Loi (mt.) D 2
Rao Co (mt.) E 3
Se Khong (river) E 4
Tha, Nam (river) D 2
Tran Ninh (plateau) D 3

MALAYSIA

STATES

Johor, 1,236,412 D 7
Kedah, 885,775 D 6
Kelantan, 645,200 D 6
Melaka, 391,003 D 7
Negeri Sembilan, 488,318 D 7
Pahang, 405,156 D 7
Perak, 1,568,024 D 6
Perlis, 113,350 D 6
Pinang, 724,169 D 6
Selangor, 1,339,142 D 7
Terengganu, 360,388 D 6

CITIES and TOWNS

Alor Gajah, 2,135 D 7
Alor Setar, 52,915 D 6
Baling, 4,121 D 6
Bandar Maharani, 39,046 D 7
Bandar Penggaram, 39,294 D 7
Batu Gajah, 10,143 D 6
Bentong, 18,845 D 7
Butterworth, 42,504 D 6
Cameron Highlands D 6
Chukai, 10,803 D 6
Gemas, 4,873 D 7
George Town (Pinang), 234,903 C 6
Ipoh, 125,770 D 6
Johor Baharu, 74,909 F 5
Kajang, 9,630 D 7
Kampar, 24,602 D 6
Kangar, 6,064 D 6
Kelang, 75,649 D 7
Keluang, 31,181 D 7
Kota Baharu, 38,103 D 6
Kota Tinggi, 7,475 F 5
Kuala Dungun, 12,515 D 6
Kuala Lipis, 8,753 D 6
Kuala Lumpur (cap.), 325,000 D 7
Kuala Pilah, 12,024 D 7
Kuala Selangor, 2,285 D 7
Kuala Terengganu, 29,446 D 6
Kuantan, 23,034 D 7
Kulai, 7,759 F 5
Lumut, 2,947 D 6
Melaka (Malacca), 69,848 D 7
Mersing, 7,228 E 7
Pekan, 2,070 D 7
Pekan Nanas, 7,129 E 5
Pinang, 234,903 C 6
Pontian Kechil, 8,459 E 5
Port Dickson, 4,416 D 7
Port Swettenham, 16,925 D 7
Port Weld, 2,260 D 6
Raub, 15,363 D 7
Segamat, 18,445 D 7
Sematan D 6
Seremban, 52,091 D 7
Sungei Petani, 22,916 C 6
Taiping, 48,206 D 6
Tanah Merah, 775 D 6
Telok Anson, 37,042 D 6
Tumpat, 8,946 D 6

OTHER FEATURES

Aur, Pulau (isl.), 415 E 7
Belumut, Gunong (mt.) D 7
Gelang, Tanjong (point) D 6
Johor (river) F 5
Johore (str.) E 6
Kelantan (river) D 6
Langkawi, Palau (isl.), 16,535 C 6
Ledang, Gunong (mt.) D 7
Lima, Pulau (isl.) F 6
Malacca (str.) D 7
Malaya (region), 9,000,000 E 6
Pahang (river) D 7
Pangkor, Pulau (isl.), 2,580 D 6
Perak, Gunong (mt.) D 6
Perhentian (isls.), 447 D 6
Pulai (river) E 5
Pinang, Pulau (isl.), 338,898 C 6
Ramunia, Tanjong (point) F 6
Redang, Pulau (isl.), 470 D 6
Sedili Kechil, Tanjong (point) F 5
Tahan, Gunong (mt.) D 6
Temiang, Bukit (mt.) D 6
Tenggol, Pulau (isl.), 2,386 D 6
Tinggi, Pulau (isl.), 440 E 7

SINGAPORE

CITIES and TOWNS

Jurong E 6
Nee Soon, 6,043 F 6
Paya Lebar, 45,440 F 6
Serangoon, 3,798 F 6
Singapore (cap.), *1,987,900 F 6
Woodlands, 737 F 6

OTHER FEATURES

Johore (str.) E 6
Keppel (harb.) F 6
Main (str.) F 6
Singapore (str.) F 6
Tekong Besar, Pulau (isl.), 4,074 F 6

THAILAND (SIAM)

CITIES and TOWNS

Amnat, 11,335 E 4
Ang Thong, 6,458 C 4
Ayutthaya, 24,597 D 4
Ban Aranyaprathet, 11,112 D 4
Ban Kantang, 5,076 C 6
Ban Khlong Yai, 3,815 D 5
Ban Pak Phanang, 11,963 D 5
Ban Pua, 12,317 D 3
Ban Sattahip, 22,942 D 4
Ban Tha Uthen, 7,297 D 3
Bang Lamung, 9,087 D 4
Bang Saphan, 6,959 C 5
Bangkok (capital), 1,299,528 D 4
Bangkok, *2,000,000 D 4
Banphot Phisai, 6,036 C 3
Buriram, 12,579 D 4
Chachoengsao, 19,809 G 4
Chai Badan, 6,158 D 4
Chai Buri, †31,135 D 3
Chainat, 4,652 D 4
Chaiya, 3,607 C 5
Chaiyaphum, 9,633 D 4
Chang Khoeng, 6,037 C 3
Chanthaburi, 10,780 D 4
Chiang Dao, 8,017 C 3
Chiang Khan, 5,810 D 3
Chiang Rai, 11,663 C 3
Chiang Saen, 5,443 C 2
Chiengmai, 65,600 C 3
Chon Buri, 32,496 D 4
Chumphon, 9,342 C 5
Dan Sai, 6,710 D 3
Den Chai, 12,732 C 3
Hat Yai, 35,504 C 6
Hua Hin, 17,078 D 4
Kabin Buri, 3,703 D 4
Kalasin, 11,043 D 3
Kamphaeng Phet, 7,171 C 3
Kanchanaburi, 12,957 C 4
Khemmarat, 5,426 E 4
Khon Kaen, 19,591 D 3
Khorat (Nakhon Ratchasima), 41,037 D 4
Khu Khan, †122,206 E 4
Kra Buri, 3,717 C 5
Krung Thep (Bangkok) (cap.), 1,299,528 D 4
Kumphawapi, 20,759 D 3
Lae, 5,743 D 3
Lampang, 36,488 C 3
Lamphun, 10,602 C 3
Lang Suan, 4,108 C 5
Loei, 7,301 D 3
Lom Sak, 8,386 D 3
Lop Buri, 21,244 D 4
Maha Sarakham, 15,680 D 3
Mukdahan, 17,738 E 3
Nakhon Nayok, 8,048 D 4
Nakhon Pathom, 28,426 C 4
Nakhon Phanom, 14,799 D 3
Nakhon Ratchasima, 41,037 D 4
Nakhon Sawan, 34,947 D 4
Nakhon Si Thammarat, 25,919 D 5
Nan, 13,843 D 3
Nang Rong, 15,623 D 4
Narathiwat, 17,508 D 6
Ngao, †32,643 D 3
Nong Khai, 21,120 D 3
Pattani, 16,804 D 6
Phanat Nikhom, 9,307 D 4
Phangnga, 4,782 C 5
Phatthalung, 10,420 D 6
Phayao, 17,959 C 3
Phet Buri, 24,654 C 4
Phetchabun, 5,947 D 3
Phichai, 5,258 D 3
Phichit, 9,258 D 3
Phitsanulok, 30,364 D 3
Phon Phisai, 6,745 D 3
Phrae, 16,005 D 3
Phuket, 28,163 C 6
Phutthaisong, 9,315 D 4
Prachin Buri, 13,420 D 4
Prachuap Khiri Khan, 6,303 D 5
Pran Buri, 7,795 D 4
Rahaeng (Tak), 13,274 C 3
Ranong, 5,993 C 5
Rat Buri, 20,383 C 4
Rayong, 9,680 D 4
Roi Et, 12,930 D 4
Rong Kwang, †39,375 D 3
Sakon Nakhon, 16,457 E 3
Samut Prakan, 21,769 D 4
Samut Sakhon, 27,802 D 4
Samut Songkhram, 12,801 C 4
Sara Buri, 17,572 D 4
Satun, 4,369 C 6
Sawankhalok, 7,880 C 3
Selaphum, 10,395 E 3
Sing Buri, 8,384 D 4
Singora (Songkhla), 31,014 D 6
Sisaket, 9,519 E 4
Songkhla, 31,014 D 6
Sukhothai, 8,627 D 3
Suphan Buri, 13,859 C 4
Surat Thani, 19,738 C 5
Surin, 13,860 D 4
Suwannaphum, 15,731 D 4
Tak, 13,274 C 3
Takua Pa, 6,308 C 5
Thoen, 17,283 C 3
Thonburi, 403,818 D 4
Thonburi, *460,000 D 4
Trang, 17,158 C 6
Trat, 3,813 D 4
Ubon, 27,092 E 4
Udon Thani, 29,965 D 3
Uthai Thani, 10,729 C 4
Uttaradit, 9,120 D 3
Warin Chamrap, 7,067 E 4
Yala, 18,083 D 6
Yasothon, 9,717 D 4

OTHER FEATURES

Amya (pass) C 4
Bilauktaung (range) C 4
Chao Phraya, Mae Nam (river) D 4
Chi, Mae Nam (river) D 3
Chong Pak Phra (cape) C 5
Dang Raek, Phanom (mts.) D 4
Doi Inthanon (mt.) C 3
Doi Pha Hom Pok (mt.) C 2
Doi Pia Fai (mt.) D 4
Kao Prawa (mt.) C 3
Khao Luang (mt.) C 5
Khwae Noi, Mae Nam (river) C 4
Ko Chang (isl.) D 4
Ko Kut (isl.) D 5
Ko Lanta (isl.), 9,486 C 6
Ko Phangan (isl.) D 5
Ko Phuket (isl.), 75,652 C 5
Ko Samui (isl.), 30,818 D 5
Ko Tao (isl.) C 5
Ko Terutao (isl.) C 6
Ko Thalu (isls.) C 5
Kra (isthmus) C 5
Laem Pho (cape) D 6
Laem Talumphuk (cape) D 5
Luang (mt.) C 5
Mae Klong, Mae Nam (river) C 4
Mekong (river) E 3
Mulayit Taung (mt.) C 3
Mun, Mae Nam (river) D 4
Nan, Mae Nam (river) D 3
Nong Lahan (lake) D 3
Pa Sak, Mae Nam (river) D 4
Pakchan (river) C 5
Phanom Dang Raek (mts.) D 4
Ping, Mae Nam (river) C 3
Samui (str.) D 5
Siam (gulf) D 5
Tapi, Mae Nam (river) C 5
Tha Chin, Mae Nam (river) C 4
Thale Luang (lagoon) D 6
Three Pagodas (pass) C 4
Wang, Mae Nam (river) C 3

VIETNAM (NORTH)

CITIES and TOWNS

Ba Don E 3
Bac Can E 2
Bac Ninh, 22,560 E 2
Bai Thuong E 3
Bao Ha D 2
Bao Lac E 2
Cao Bang E 2
Co Lieu E 3
Con Cuong E 3
Cua Rao E 3
Dien Bien Phu D 2
Dong Hoi E 3
Ha Giang E 2
Ha Tinh E 3
Haiphong, 182,496 E 2
Haiphong, ‡*600,000 E 2
Hanoi (capital), 414,620 E 2
Hanoi, ‡*1,400,000 E 2
Hoa Binh E 2
Hoi Xuan E 2
Hon Gay, ‡100,000 E 2
Huong Khe E 3
Ke Bao E 2
Lai Chau D 2
Lang Mo E 3
Lang Son, 15,071 E 2
Lao Cai E 2
Loc Chou E 3
Luc An Chau E 2
Mon Cay E 2
Muong Khuong E 2
Nam Dinh, ‡125,000 E 2
Nghia Lo D 2
Ninh Binh E 2
Phuc Loi E 3
Phu Dien E 3
Phu Lang Thuong E 2
Phuly E 2
Phu Qui E 3
Phu Tho, 10,888 E 2
Quang Khe E 3
Quang Yen E 2
Ron E 3
Son La D 2
Son Tay, 19,213 E 2
Thai Binh, 14,739 E 2
Thai Nguyen, ‡110,000 E 2
Thanh Hoa, 31,211 E 3
That Khe E 2
Tien Yen E 2
Trung Khanh Phu E 2
Tuyen Quang E 2
Van Hoa E 2
Van Yen E 2
Vinh, 43,954 E 3
Vinh Yen E 2
Vu Liet E 3
Yen Bai E 2
Yen Minh E 2

OTHER FEATURES

Bach Long Vi, Dao (isl.) F 2
Black (river) D 2
Cat Ba, Dao (isl.) E 2
Dao Bach Long Vi (isl.) F 2
Demilitarized Zone E 3
Fan Si Pan (mt.) D 2
Lay (cape) E 3
Mui Duong (cape) E 3
Nightingale (Bach Long Vi) (isl.) F 2
Rao Co (mt.) E 3
Red (river) E 2
Sip Song Chau Thai (mts.) D 2
Song Bo (Black) (river) D 2
Song Ca (river) E 3
Song Coi (Red) (river) E 2
Tigre (isl.) E 3
Tonkin (gulf) E 3

VIETNAM (SOUTH)

CITIES and TOWNS

An Khe F 4
An Loc, 15,276 E 5
Bac Lieu (Vinh Loi), 53,841 E 5
Ban Me Thuot, 68,771 F 4
Bien Hoa, 87,135 E 5
Binh Dinh F 4
Binh Son F 4
Bong Son F 4
Bu Dop E 4
Cam Ranh, 84,281 F 5
Can Tho, 92,132 E 5
Cao Lanh, 16,482 E 5
Cap Saint-Jacques (Vung Tau), 79,270 E 5
Chau Phu, 37,175 E 5
Cheo Reo E 4
Chu Lai F 4
Da Lat, 83,992 F 5
Da Nang, 363,343 E 3
Dak Bla E 4
Dam Doi E 5
Di Linh F 5
Duong Dong D 5
Go Cong, 33,191 E 5
Go Quao E 5
Ha Tien E 5
Ham Tan, 19,323 E 5
Hoa Da F 5
Hoi An, 45,059 F 4
Hon Chong E 5
Hue, 170,884 E 3
Khanh Hoa F 4
Khanh Hung, 59,015 E 5
Kontum, 33,554 E 4
Loc Ninh E 5
Long Xuyen, 72,658 E 5
Mo Duc F 4
Moc Hoa, 3,191 E 5
My Tho, 109,967 E 5
Nha Trang, 103,184 F 4
Phan Rang, 33,377 F 5
Phan Ri F 5
Phan Thiet, 80,122 F 5
Phoc Tuy, 16,419 E 5
Phu Cuong, 28,267 E 5
Phu Loc E 5
Phu My F 4
Phu Rieng E 5
Phu Vinh (Tra Vinh), 48,485 E 5
Pleiku, 23,720 E 4
Pleime E 4
Quan Long, 59,331 E 5
Quang Nam E 4
Quang Ngai, 14,119 F 4
Quang Tri, 15,874 E 3
Qui Nhon, 116,821 F 4
Rach Gia, 66,745 E 5
Sa Dec, 51,867 E 5
Saigon (capital), 1,706,869 E 5
Song Cau F 4
Son Ha F 4
Tam Ky, 38,532 F 4
Tam Quan F 4
Tan An, 38,082 E 5
Tay Ninh, 22,957 E 5
Tra Vinh, 48,485 E 5
Truc Giang, 68,629 E 5
Tuy Hoa, 63,552 F 4
Van Gia F 4
Vinh Loi, 53,841 E 5
Vinh Long, 30,667 E 5
Vo Dat E 5
Vung Tau, 79,270 E 5

OTHER FEATURES

Batangan (cape) F 4
Bên Gôi (bay) F 4
Ca Mau (Mui Bai Bung) (pt.) E 5
Cam Ranh (bay) F 5
Chon May (bay) F 3
Chu Yang Sin (mt.) F 4
Con Son (isls.), 3,147 E 5
Cù Lao Hon (isls.) F 5
Dama, Poulo (isls.) D 5
Dao Phu Quoc (isl.) D 5
Darlac (plateau) F 4
Demilitarized Zone E 3
Dent du Tigre (mt.) E 3
Deux Frères, Les (isls.) E 5
Hon Khoai (isl.) E 5
Hon Panjang (isl.) D 5
Ia Drang (riv.) E 4
Joncs (plain) E 5
Ke Ga (point) F 5
Kontum (plateau) E 4
Lang Bian (mts.) E 4
Mekong, Mouths of the (delta) E 5
Mui Bai Bung (pt.) E 5
Mui Dinh (cape) F 5
Nam Tram (cape) F 4
Nui Ba Den (mt.) E 5
Phu Quoc, Dao (isl.) D 5
Poulo Dàma (isls.) D 5
Poulo Way (isls.) D 5
Se San (river) E 4
Siam (gulf) D 5
Song Ba (river) F 4
Song Cai (river) E 4
South China (sea) F 4
Varella (cape) F 4
Way, Poulo (isls.) D 5

*City and suburbs.
†Population of district.

‡City populations courtesy of Kingsley Davis, Office of Int'l Pop. & Urban Research, Inst. of Int'l Studies, Univ. of California.

Agriculture, Industry and Resources

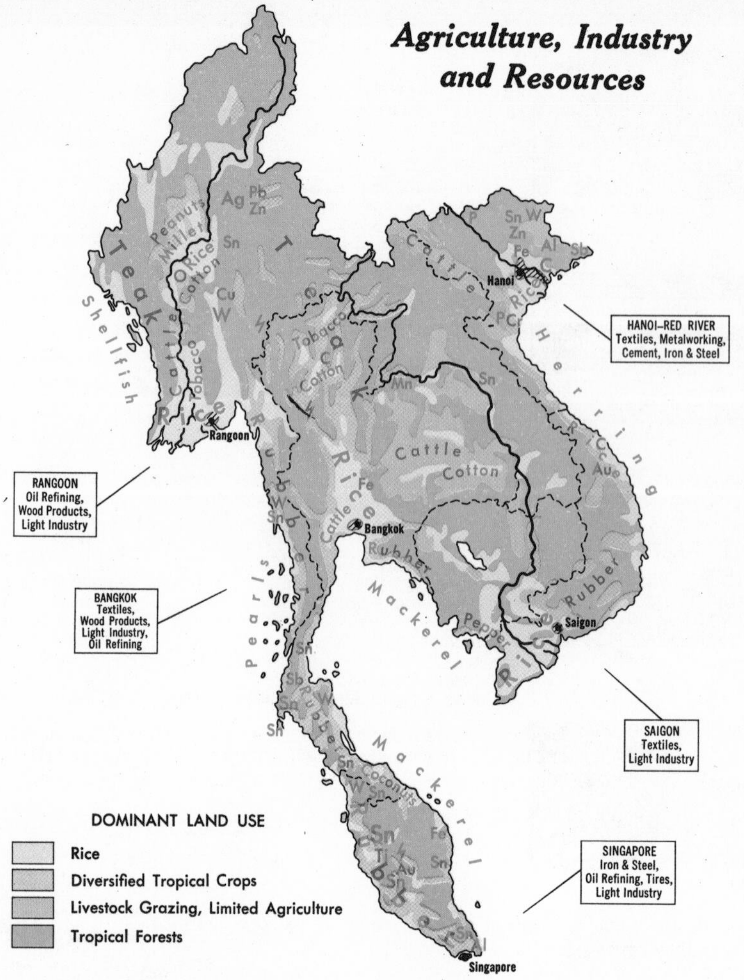
Hanoi
HANOI-RED RIVER
Textiles, Metalworking, Cement, Iron & Steel
Rangoon
RANGOON
Oil Refining, Wood Products, Light Industry
Bangkok
BANGKOK
Textiles, Wood Products, Light Industry, Oil Refining
Saigon
SAIGON
Textiles, Light Industry
Singapore
SINGAPORE
Iron & Steel, Oil Refining, Tires, Light Industry
Cattle
Cotton
Rice
Rubber
Mackerel
Herring
Pearls
Shellfish

DOMINANT LAND USE

- Rice
- Diversified Tropical Crops
- Livestock Grazing, Limited Agriculture
- Tropical Forests

MAJOR MINERAL OCCURRENCES

Ag	Silver	Cr	Chromium	O	Petroleum	Sn	Tin
Al	Bauxite	Cu	Copper	P	Phosphates	Ti	Titanium
Au	Gold	Fe	Iron Ore	Pb	Lead	W	Tungsten
C	Coal	Mn	Manganese	Sb	Antimony	Zn	Zinc

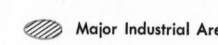

Water Power

Major Industrial Areas

BURMA, THAILAND,
INDOCHINA
and MALAYA

CONIC PROJECTION

SCALE OF MILES

SCALE OF KILOMETRES

International Boundaries ----------
Provincial and State Boundaries ----------
Capitals of Countries ----------☆
Provincial and State Capitals ----------◉

Copyright by C.S. HAMMOND & Co., N.Y.

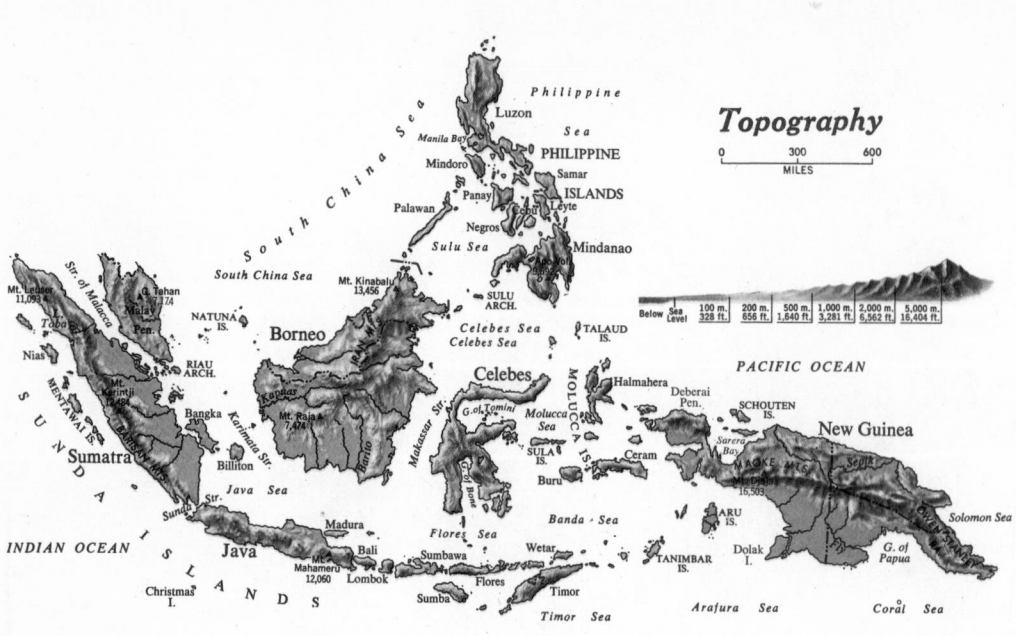

Topography

0   300   600
MILES

Below Sea Level | 100 m. 328 ft. | 200 m. 656 ft. | 500 m. 1,640 ft. | 1,000 m. 3,281 ft. | 2,000 m. 6,562 ft. | 5,000 m. 16,404 ft.

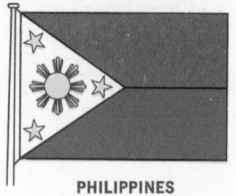

PHILIPPINES

BRUNEI
CITIES and TOWNS
Bandar Seri Begawan (cap.), 37,000 .... E 4

INDONESIA
CITIES and TOWNS

Agats, 300 .... K 7
Amahai, 18,017 .... H 6
Amboina, 70,000 .... H 6
Ambon (Amboina), 70,000 .... H 6
Balikpapan, 113,000 .... E 6
Banda Atjeh, 49,000 .... A 4
Bandanaira, 13,686 .... H 6
Bandjarmasin, 264,000 .... E 6
Bandung, 1,006,000 .... H 2
Bangil, 34,112 .... K 2
Bangkalan, 129,536 .... K 2
Banjuwangi, 53,576 .... L 2
Bantul, 30,572 .... J 2
Barabai, 9,366 .... F 6
Barus, 135,716 .... B 5
Batang, 57,561 .... J 2
Batavia (Djakarta), 3,429,000 .... H 1
Baturadja, 126,706 .... C 6
Batusangkar, 10,437 .... C 6
Bekasi, 32,012 .... H 2
Bengkajang, 117,029 .... E 5
Bengkalis, 136,433 .... C 5
Bengkulu, 31,000 .... C 6
Benteng, 7,035 .... G 7
Bindjai, 56,000 .... B 5
Bitung, 15,249 .... H 5
Blitar, 78,000 .... K 2

Blora, 49,296 .... K 2
Bodjonegoro, 161,749 .... J 2
Bogor, 172,000 .... H 2
Bondowoso, 144,215 .... L 2
Bonthain, 140,289 .... F 7
Brebes, †72,971 .... H 2
Bukittinggi, 62,000 .... B 6
Bula, 3,116 .... J 6
Bulukumba, 14,137 .... G 7
Bumiaju, 52,790 .... H 2
Buntok, 3,884 .... F 6
Demak, †42,915 .... J 2
Denpasar, †52,000 .... E 7
Djailolo, 110,170 .... H 5
Djajapura, 14,462 .... K 6
Djakarta, (cap.), 3,429,000 .... H 1
Djakarta, *5,692,000 .... H 1
Djambi (Telanaipura) 139,000 .... C 6
Djeneponto, 10,350 .... F 7
Djepara, 154,025 .... J 2
Djokdjakarta, 385,000 .... J 2
Djombang, 157,370 .... K 2
Dompu, 8,886 .... F 7
Fakfak, 2,430 .... J 6
Galela, †7,384 .... H 5
Garut, 167,542 .... H 2
Gorontalo, 88,000 .... G 5
Gresik, 36,790 .... K 2
Gunungsitoli, †44,712 .... B 5
Hollandia (Djajapura), 14,462 .... K 6
Indramaju, 156,117 .... H 2
Isimu, 4,304 .... G 5
Kaimana, 1,128 .... J 6
Kajuagung, 15,000 .... D 6
Kalianda, †31,073 .... D 7
Kampung Baru (Tolitoli), 8,333 .... G 5
Karangasem, 16,022 .... F 7
Kau, 17,497 .... H 5
Kebumen, 164,874 .... J 2

Kediri, 196,000 .... K 2
Kendal, 23,129 .... J 2
Kendari, 191,065 .... G 6
Kendawangan, 6,845 .... D 6
Kepi, 617 .... K 7
Klaten, 33,400 .... J 2
Kolaka, †18,671 .... G 6
Kotaagung, 125,314 .... C 7
Kragan, 23,786 .... J 2
Krawang, 49,867 .... H 2
Kualakurun, 111,489 .... E 6
Kudus, 62,130 .... J 2
Kumai, 8,835 .... E 6
Kuningan, †77,181 .... H 2
Kupang, 17,171 .... G 8
Kutaradja (Banda Atjeh), 49,000 .... A 4
Kutoardjo, 44,962 .... J 2
Labuan, †22,259 .... G 2
Lahat, 125,781 .... C 6
Lamongan, 134,825 .... K 2
Langsa, †47,044 .... A 4
Lawang, 140,239 .... K 2
Longiram, 7,776 .... F 5
Longnawan, 116,234 .... F 5
Lubuklinggau, 14,890 .... C 6
Lubuksikaping, 11,778 .... B 5
Lumadjang, 55,700 .... K 2
Madiun, 152,000 .... J 2
Madjalengka, †47,055 .... H 2
Madjene, †37,727 .... F 6
Magelang, 119,000 .... J 2
Magetan, 154,159 .... J 2
Makassar, 473,000 .... F 7
Malang, 419,000 .... K 2
Malili, 5,735 .... G 6
Malinau, 9,677 .... F 5
Mamudju, †47,309 .... F 6
Manado, 160,000 .... G 5
Manokwari, 10,461 .... J 6

Marabahan, 8,893 .... E 6
Martapura, †53,216 .... F 6
Masamba, 115,152 .... G 6
Medan, 590,000 .... B 5
Menggala, 20,343 .... D 6
Meulaboh, 6,544 .... B 5
Merak, †36,293 .... G 1
Merauke, 5,989 .... K 7
Mindiptana, 1,577 .... L 7
Modjokerto, 64,000 .... K 2
Muarabungo, 10,706 .... C 6
Muarateweh, 6,135 .... F 6
Muntok, 125,883 .... D 6
Namlea, 16,018 .... H 6
Nangapinoh, 124,836 .... E 6
Nangatajap, 18,285 .... E 6
Negara, 10,161 .... E 7
Ngabang, 124,516 .... D 5
Ngawi, 29,220 .... K 2
Padang, 178,000 .... B 6
Padangpandjang, 32,000 .... B 6
Padangsidimpuan, 171,704 .... B 5
Painan, 12,060 .... C 6
Pajakumbuh, 174,393 .... C 6
Pakanbaru, 87,000 .... C 5
Palangkaraja, 9,000 .... E 6
Paleleh, 5,466 .... G 5
Palembang, 585,000 .... D 6
Pamangkat, 151,871 .... D 5
Pamekasan, 142,650 .... L 2
Pameungpeuk, 124,662 .... H 2
Panarukan, 6,846 .... K 2
Pandeglang, 124,823 .... G 1
Pangkalanberandan, 123,806 .... B 5
Pangkalpinang, 74,000 .... D 6
Pare, 185,528 .... K 2
Parepare, 84,000 .... F 6
Pariaman, 145,812 .... B 6
Pasuruan, 78,000 .... K 2
Pati, 156,749 .... J 2

Patjitan, 44,383 .... J 2
Pekalongan, 125,000 .... J 2
Pemalang, 193,608 .... J 2
Pematangsiantar, 142,000 .... B 5
Perahbumulih, 41,951 .... C 6
Pinrang, 23,818 .... F 6
Piru, 123,633 .... H 6
Ponorogo, 49,993 .... J 2
Pontianak, 185,000 .... D 6
Poso, †41,292 .... G 6
Prapat, 5,552 .... B 5
Probolinggo, 85,000 .... B 5
Purbolinggo, 31,719 .... J 2
Purwakarta, 188,680 .... H 2
Purwodadi, 154,648 .... J 2
Purwokerto, 22,623 .... H 2
Purworedjo, 23,209 .... J 2
Putussibau, 18,357 .... E 5
Rangkasbitung, 151,176 .... G 2
Rantauprapat, 25,707 .... C 5
Rembang, 39,939 .... K 2
Rengat, †22,982 .... C 6
Ruteng, 15,814 .... G 7
Sabang, 6,747 .... B 4
Salatiga, 72,000 .... J 2
Samarinda, 87,000 .... F 6
Sambas, †53,290 .... D 5
Sampang, 47,596 .... K 2
Sanana, 23,388 .... H 6
Sanggau, †26,039 .... E 5
Sangkulirang, 6,108 .... F 5
Saparua, 53,390 .... H 6
Saumlaki, †22,732 .... J 7
Sawahlunto, 15,000 .... C 6
Semarang, 619,000 .... J 2
Semitau, 19,255 .... E 5
Sengkang, †17,948 .... F 6
Serang, †43,661 .... G 1
Serui, 2,743 .... K 6

(continued on following page)

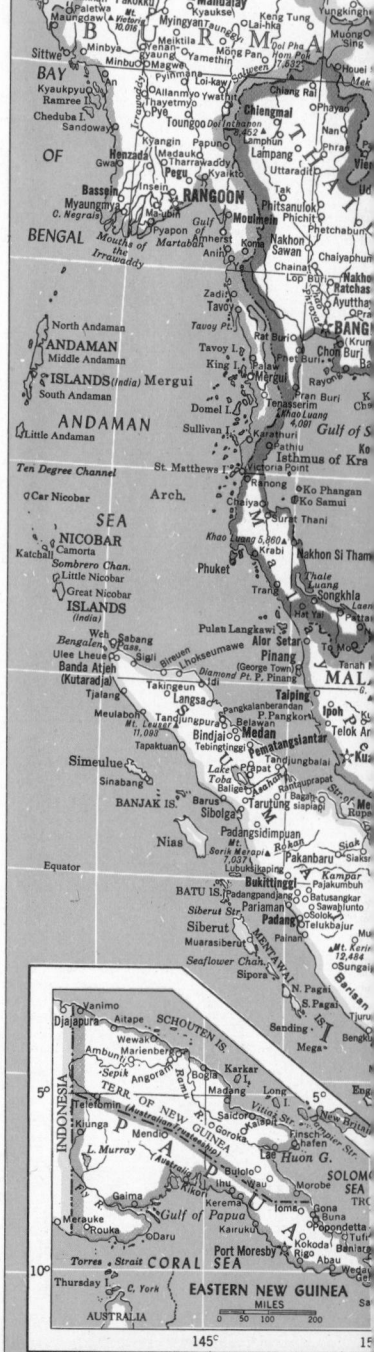

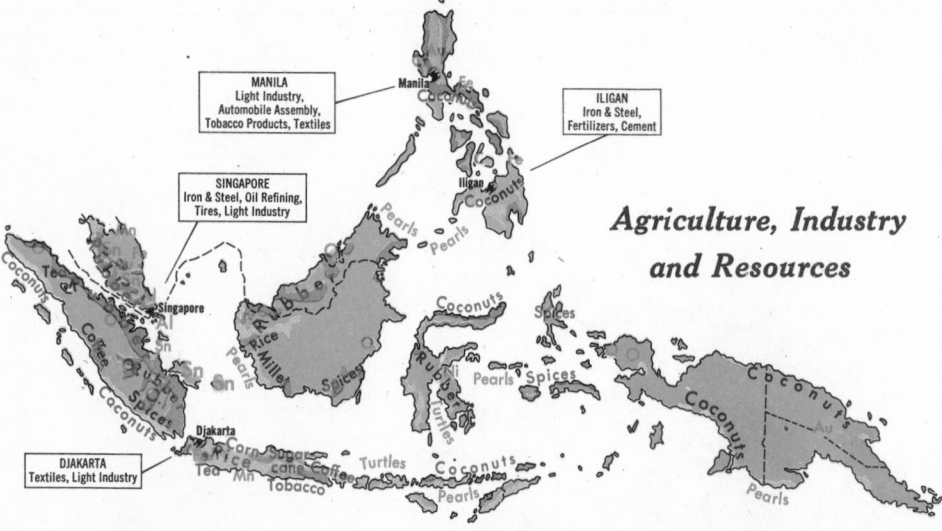

MANILA
Light Industry, Automobile Assembly, Tobacco Products, Textiles

ILIGAN
Iron & Steel, Fertilizers, Cement

SINGAPORE
Iron & Steel, Oil Refining, Tires, Light Industry

Agriculture, Industry and Resources

DJAKARTA
Textiles, Light Industry

DOMINANT LAND USE

Cereals (chiefly rice, corn)
Diversified Tropical Crops
Forests

MAJOR MINERAL OCCURRENCES

Al Bauxite
Au Gold
C   Coal

Cr Chromium
Fe Iron Ore

Mn Manganese
Ni Nickel

O   Petroleum
Sn Tin

Major Industrial Areas

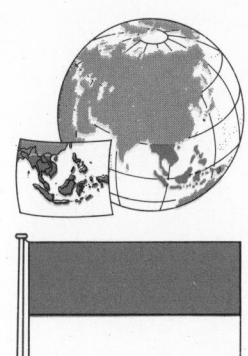

INDONESIA

INDONESIA
AREA 735,264 sq. mi.
POPULATION 119,572,000
CAPITAL Djakarta
LARGEST CITY Djakarta
HIGHEST POINT Mt. Djaja 16,400 ft.
MONETARY UNIT rupiah
MAJOR LANGUAGES Bahasa Indonesian, local
  Indonesian languages, Papuan languages
MAJOR RELIGIONS Islam, Tribal religions,
  Christianity, Hinduism

PORTUGUESE TIMOR
AREA 5,762 sq. mi.
POPULATION 590,000
CAPITAL Dili

BRUNEI
AREA 2,226 sq. mi.
POPULATION 130,000
CAPITAL Bandar Seri Begawan

PHILIPPINES
AREA 115,707 sq. mi.
POPULATION 39,079,000
CAPITAL Quezon City
LARGEST CITY Manila
HIGHEST POINT Apo 9,692 ft.
MONETARY UNIT Philippine peso
MAJOR LANGUAGES Pilipino (Tagalog), English,
  Spanish, Bisayan, Ilocano, Bikol
MAJOR RELIGIONS Roman Catholicism, Islam,
  Tribal religions

SOUTHEAST ASIA

LAMBERT AZIMUTHAL EQUAL-AREA PROJECTION

SCALE OF MILES
0   100   200   300   400   500   600

SCALE OF KILOMETRES
0   100   200   300   400   500   600

Capitals of Countries........☆
Administrative Center........◉
International Boundaries........
Other Boundaries........

Copyright by C.S. HAMMOND & CO., N.Y.

JAVA
MILES
0   25   50

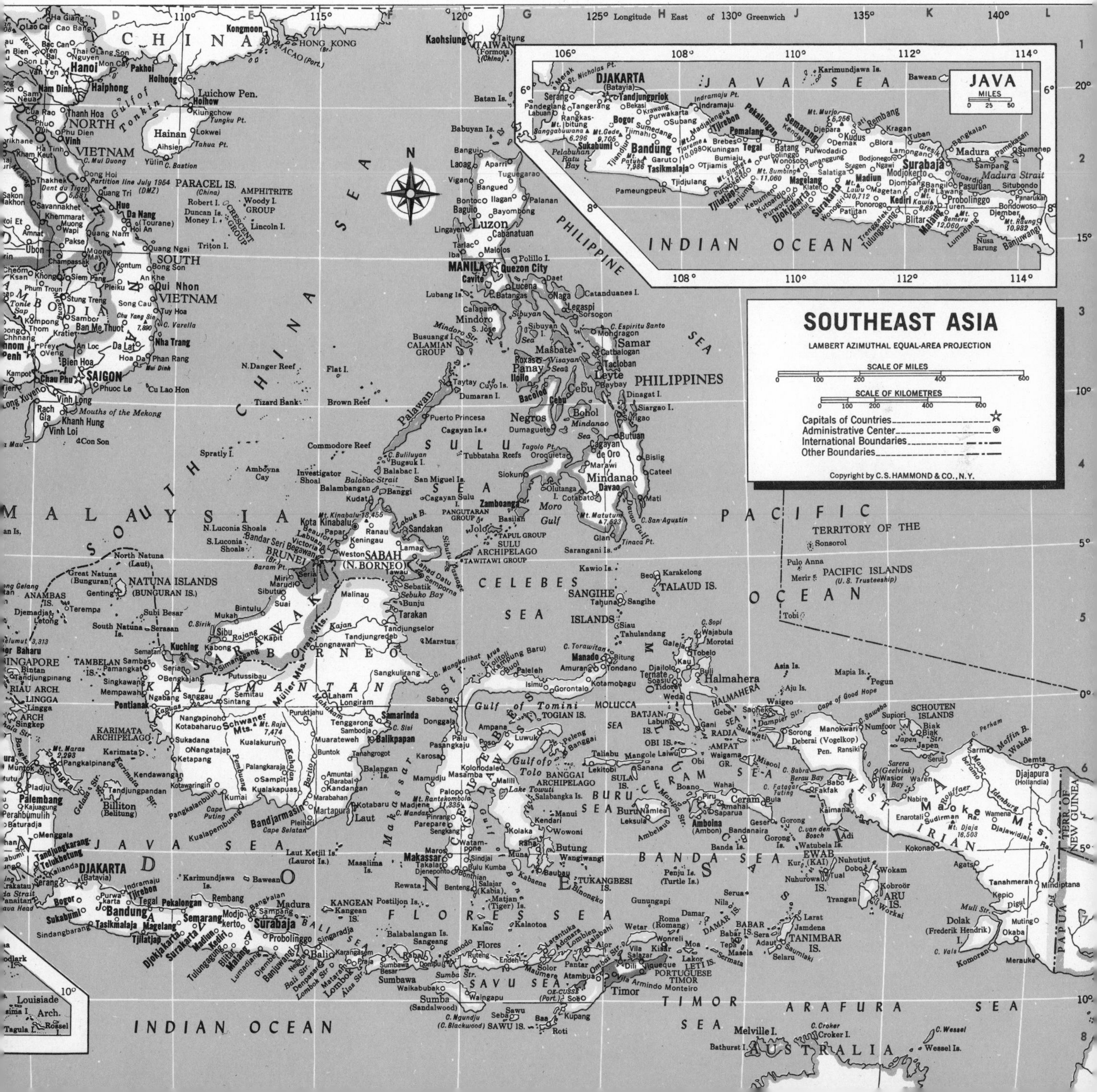

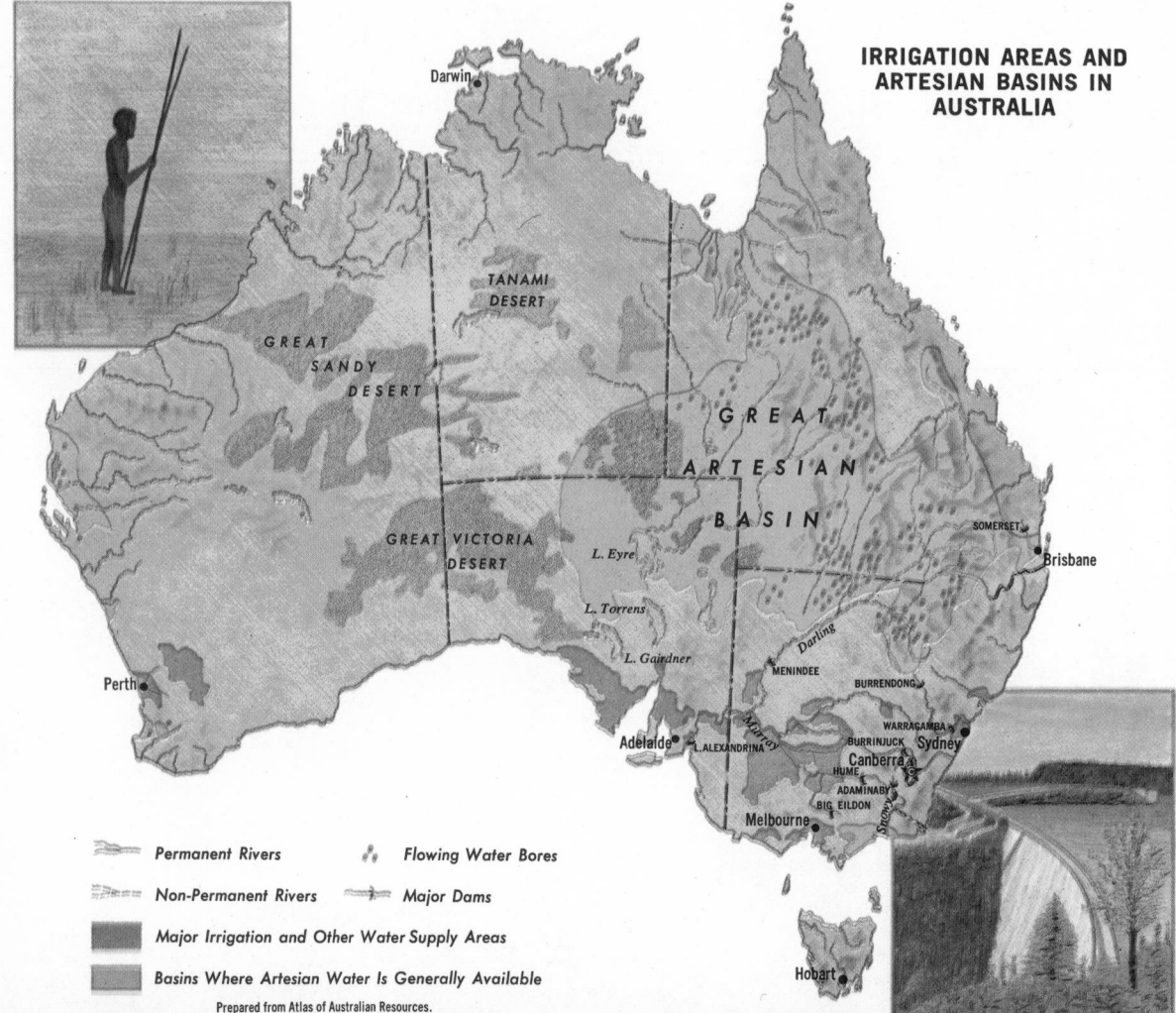

IRRIGATION AREAS AND ARTESIAN BASINS IN AUSTRALIA

Darwin · TANAMI DESERT · GREAT SANDY DESERT · GREAT VICTORIA DESERT · GREAT ARTESIAN BASIN · SOMERSET · Brisbane · L. Eyre · L. Torrens · L. Gairdner · Perth · MENINDEE · BURRENDONG · Darling · WARRAGAMBA · BURRINJUCK · Sydney · Adelaide · L. ALEXANDRINA · Murray · Canberra · HUME · ADAMINABY · BIG EILDON · Melbourne · Snowy · Hobart

Permanent Rivers
Non-Permanent Rivers
Flowing Water Bores
Major Dams
Major Irrigation and Other Water Supply Areas
Basins Where Artesian Water Is Generally Available

Prepared from Atlas of Australian Resources.

AUSTRALIA
2,967,741 sq. mi.
LATION 12,630,000
'AL Canberra
EST CITY Sydney (greater)
EST POINT Mt. Kosciusko 7,316 ft.
ST POINT Lake Eyre -39 ft.
'TARY UNIT Australian dollar
R LANGUAGE English
R RELIGIONS Protestantism, Roman Cath.

NEW ZEALAND
AREA 103,736 sq. mi.
POPULATION 2,815,000
CAPITAL Wellington
LARGEST CITY Auckland
HIGHEST POINT Mt. Cook 12,349 ft.
MONETARY UNIT New Zealand dollar
MAJOR LANGUAGES English, Maori
MAJOR RELIGION Protestantism

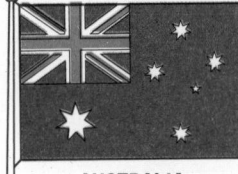

AUSTRALIA

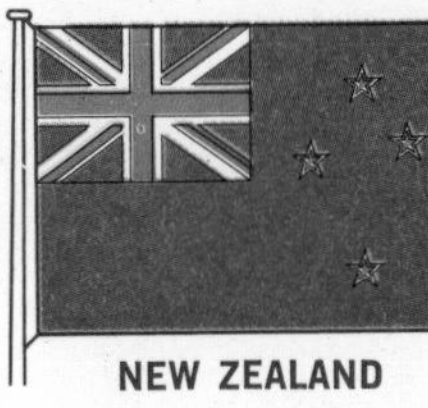
NEW ZEALAND

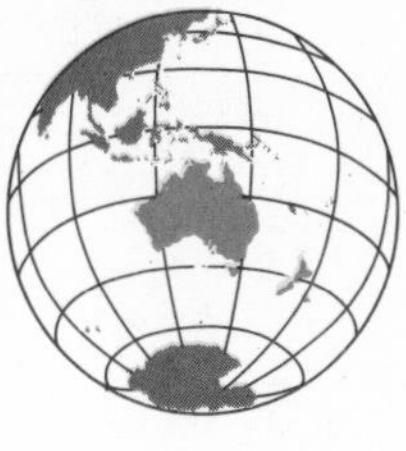

AUSTRALIA

STATES and TERRITORIES

Australian Capital Terr., 136,300 .... J 7
Coral Sea Islands Terr., 3 .... J 3
New South Wales, 4,595,400 .... H 6
Northern Territory, 73,000 .... E 3
Queensland, 1,810,000 .... G 4
South Australia, 1,169,600 .... F 6
Tasmania, 393,700 .... H 8
Victoria, 3,461,400 .... G 7
Western Australia, 991,300 .... C 5

CITIES and TOWNS

Adelaide (capital), S.A., †727,916 .... D 7
Adelaide River, N.T., ‡300 .... E 2
Albany, W.A., 11,419 .... B 6
Albury, N.S.W., 25,112 .... H 7
Alice Springs, N.T., 6,037 .... E 4
Aramac, Q. .... H 4
Ararat, V., 8,233 .... G 7
Armadale, W.A., 3,463 .... B 2
Armidale, N.S.W., 14,984 .... J 6
Augathella, Q. .... H 5
Ayr, Q., 8,674 .... H 3
Bacchus Marsh, V., 3,707 .... K 1
Bairnsdale, V., 7,785 .... H 7
Balhannah, S.A. .... E 8
Ballarat, V., *56,290 .... G 7
Ballina, N.S.W., 4,931 .... J 5
Balranald, N.S.W., 1,490 .... G 6
Bankstown, N.S.W., 159,981 .... L 3
Barcaldine, Q., 1,779 .... G 4
Bargo, N.S.W. .... K 4
Barraba, N.S.W., 1,425 .... J 6
Bathurst, N.S.W., 17,222 .... H 6
Beachport, S.A., ‡1,903 .... F 7
Bega, N.S.W., 3,925 .... J 7
Bendigo, V., *42,208 .... G 7
Beverley, W.A., ‡1,773 .... B 2
Bingara, N.S.W., 1,504 .... H 5
Blackall, Q., 2,004 .... G 4
Blacktown, N.S.W., 111,488 .... K 3
Blair Athol, Q. .... H 4
Blue Mts., N.S.W., 30,731 .... H 6
Bombala, N.S.W., 1,495 .... H 7
Bordertown, S.A., 1,758 .... G 7
Botany, N.S.W., 31,871 .... L 3
Boulder, W.A., 5,234 .... C 6
Bourke, N.S.W., 3,262 .... H 6
Bowen, Q., 5,144 .... H 3
Brewarrina, N.S.W., 1,255 .... H 5
Bridgetown, W.A., 1,569 .... B 6
Bright, V., 747 .... H 7
Brighton, V., 40,617 .... L 2
Brisbane (capital), Q., †718,822 .... J 5
Broken Hill, N.S.W., 30,014 .... G 6
Brookton, W.A., ‡1,341 .... B 2
Broome, W.A., 1,570 .... C 3
Bullfinch, W.A. .... B 6
Bulli, N.S.W. .... L 4
Bunbury, W.A., 15,459 .... A 6
Bundaberg, Q., 25,402 .... J 5
Burnie, T., 15,806 .... H 8
Busselton, W.A., 4,278 .... A 6
Cairns, Q., 29,326 .... H 3
Camberwell, V., 99,908 .... L 2
Camden, N.S.W., 3,427 .... K 4
Camooweal, Q. .... F 4
Campbelltown, N.S.W., 25,695 .... L 3
Canberra, A.C.T. (cap.), Australia, *136,300 .... H 7
Cardwell, Q. .... H 3
Carnarvon, W.A., 2,956 .... A 4
Casino, N.S.W., 8,502 .... J 5
Casterton, V., 2,492 .... G 7
Caulfield, V., 76,119 .... L 2
Ceduna, S.A., 1,406 .... E 6
Cessnock, N.S.W., *34,515 .... J 6
Charleville, Q., 4,871 .... H 5
Charters Towers, Q., 7,602 .... G 4
Chelsea, V., 24,789 .... L 2
Clermont, Q., 1,649 .... H 4
Cloncurry, Q., 2,149 .... G 4
Cobar, N.S.W., 2,348 .... H 6
Coburg, V., 68,568 .... L 1
Coffs Harbour, N.S.W., 7,667 .... J 6
Coleraine, V., 1,518 .... G 7
Collie, W.A., 7,628 .... B 6
Collinsville, Q., 1,887 .... H 4
Condobolin, N.S.W., 3,571 .... H 6
Coober Pedy, S.A. .... E 5
Cooktown, Q. .... H 3
Coolgardie, W.A., ‡762 .... C 6
Cooma, N.S.W., 9,103 .... H 7
Coonamble, N.S.W., 3,396 .... H 6
Cootamundra, N.S.W., 6,219 .... H 6
Corio, V. .... K 2
Corrigin, W.A., ‡2,099 .... B 5
Corrimal, N.S.W. .... L 4
Cowra, N.S.W., 7,076 .... H 6
Cudgewa, V. .... H 7
Cue, W.A., ‡430 .... B 5
Culcairn, N.S.W., 1,019 .... H 7
Cunnamulla, Q., 1,980 .... H 5
Cygnet, T. .... H 8
Dalby, Q., 8,860 .... J 5
Daly Waters, N.T., ‡265 .... E 3
Dandenong, V., 31,698 .... L 2
Darwin (capital), N.T., 18,042 .... E 2
Daylesford, V., 2,664 .... G 7
Deloraine, T., 1,793 .... H 8
Deniliquin, N.S.W., 6,239 .... H 7
Derby, W.A., 1,424 .... C 3
Devonport, T., 14,874 .... H 8
Dirranbandi, Q. .... H 5
Dubbo, N.S.W., 15,561 .... H 6
Echuca, V., 7,043 .... G 7
Echunga, S.A. .... E 7
Eidsvold, Q. .... J 5
Elizabeth, S.A., 32,949 .... D 7
Emerald, Q., 2,193 .... H 4
Esperance, W.A., 2,677 .... C 6
Essendon, V., 58,258 .... K 2
Footscray, V., 58,823 .... K 2
Forbes, N.S.W., 7,369 .... H 6
Frankston, V., 38,718 .... L 2
Fremantle, W.A., 25,284 .... B 2
Gawler, S.A., 5,703 .... D 7
Geelong, V., *105,059 .... K 2
Geraldton, W.A., 12,125 .... A 5
Gingin, W.A., ‡1,021 .... B 1
Gladstone, Q., 12,426 .... J 4
Glen Innes, N.S.W., 5,737 .... J 5
Glenmorgan, Q. .... H 5
Gold Coast, Q., 49,481 .... J 5
Goomalling, W.A., ‡1,567 .... B 1
Goondiwindi, Q., 3,529 .... H 5
Goulburn, N.S.W., 20,871 .... J 7
Grafton, N.S.W., 15,951 .... J 5
Griffith, N.S.W., 9,537 .... H 6
Gunnedah, N.S.W., 7,507 .... H 6
Gympie, Q., 11,279 .... J 5
Halls Creek, W.A., ‡577 .... D 3
Hamilton, V., 10,054 .... G 7
Hay, N.S.W., 2,952 .... H 6
Heidelberg, V. 63,929 .... L 1
Helensburgh, N.S.W., 2,334 .... L 4
Henley and Grange, S.A., 14,146 .... D 7
Hillston, N.S.W., 1,034 .... G 6
Hindmarsh, S.A., 11,352 .... D 7
Hobart (capital), T., †119,469 .... H 8
Home Hill, Q., 3,507 .... H 3
Horsham, V., 10,562 .... G 7
Hughenden, Q., 2,033 .... G 4
Hurstbridge, V. .... L 1
Hurstville, N.S.W., 64,851 .... L 3
Ingham, Q., 5,354 .... H 3
Injune, Q. .... H 5
Innisfail, Q., 7,432 .... H 3
Inverell, N.S.W., 8,413 .... J 5
Ipswich, Q., 54,531 .... J 5
Iron Knob, S.A. .... F 6
Ivanhoe, N.S.W. .... G 6
Jamestown, S.A. 1,282 .... F 6
Jandowae, Q. .... J 5
Jericho, Q. .... H 4
Junee, N.S.W., 3,904 .... H 6
Kadina, S.A., 1,865 .... F 6
Kalgoorlie, W.A., *19,908 .... C 6
Katanning, W.A., 3,506 .... B 6
Katherine, N.T., 1,302 .... E 2
Kelmscott, W.A., 914 .... B 2
Kempsey, N.S.W., 8,181 .... J 6
Kensington and Norwood, S.A., 11,928 .... D 8
Kerang, V., 4,164 .... G 7
Kew, V., 32,816 .... L 1
Kingaroy, Q., 5,080 .... J 5
Kingscote, S.A., 1,071 .... F 7
Kingston, S.A., 1,065 .... F 7
Kogarah, N.S.W., 47,654 .... L 3
Kwinana, W.A., 1,272 .... B 2
Lake Cargelligo, N.S.W., 1,128 .... H 6
Larrimah, N.T., ‡88 .... E 3
Launceston, T., 37,217 .... H 8
Laverton, W.A., ‡206 .... C 5
Leigh Creek, S.A., 1,014 .... F 6
Leonora, W.A., 623 .... C 5
Lismore, N.S.W., 19,734 .... J 5
Lithgow, N.S.W., 13,165 .... J 6
Liverpool, N.S.W., 68,959 .... K 3
Longford, T., 1,688 .... H 8
Longreach, Q., 3,871 .... G 4
Loxton, S.A., 2,418 .... G 6
Mackay, Q., 24,578 .... H 4
Maitland, N.S.W., 28,428 .... J 6
Mandurah, W.A., 2,730 .... B 2
Manilla, N.S.W., 1,761 .... J 6
Manly, N.S.W., 38,141 .... L 3
Maralinga and Woomera, S.A., 4,745 .... E 5
Marble Bar, W.A., ‡567 .... C 4
Mareeba, Q., 4,799 .... H 3
Marion, S.A., 66,950 .... D 8
Maryborough, Q., 20,393 .... J 5
Maryborough, V., 7,707 .... G 7
Mataranka, N.T., ‡114 .... E 2
Meekatharra, W.A., ‡1,011 .... B 5
Melbourne (cap.), V., †2,110,168 .... L 1
Merredin, W.A., 3,599 .... B 6
Midland, W.A., 9,335 .... B 2
Mildura, V., 12,931 .... G 6
Miles, Q., 1,485 .... H 5
Mingenew, W.A., ‡978 .... B 5
Mitchell, Q., 1,704 .... H 5
Moonta, S.A., 1,122 .... F 6
Moora, W.A., 1,185 .... B 6
Morawa, W.A., ‡1,718 .... B 5
Mordialloc, V., 28,076 .... L 2
Moree, N.S.W., 8,031 .... H 5
Mornington, V., 7,349 .... L 2
Mossman, Q., 1,614 .... G 3
Mount Barker, S.A., 1,934 .... E 8
Mount Gambier, S.A., 17,251 .... F 7
Mount Garnet, Q. .... G 3
Mount Isa, Q., 16,877 .... F 4
Mount Lofty, S.A. .... D 8
Mount Magnet, W.A. .... B 5
Mount Morgan, Q., 4,055 .... H 4
Mount Pleasant, S.A., ‡1,433 .... E 7
Mount Torrens, S.A. .... E 7
Mudgee, N.S.W., 5,372 .... J 6
Mullewa, W.A., ‡1,825 .... B 5
Murray Bridge, S.A., 5,957 .... F 7
Murwillumbah, N.S.W., 7,311 .... J 5
Muswellbrook, N.S.W., 6,312 .... J 6
Nanango, Q., 1,300 .... J 5
Nannup, W.A., ‡1,272 .... B 6
Naracoorte, S.A., 4,378 .... F 7
Narembeen, W.A., ‡1,590 .... B 6
Narrabri, N.S.W., 5,953 .... H 6
Narrandera, N.S.W., 4,905 .... H 6
Narrogin, W.A., 4,861 .... B 6
Narromine, N.S.W., 2,465 .... H 6
Nedlands, W.A., 23,320 .... B 2
New Norfolk, T., 5,770 .... H 8
Newcastle, N.S.W., *233,936 .... J 6
Normanton, Q. .... G 3
Norseman, W.A., 1,863 .... C 6
Northam, W.A., 7,400 .... B 2
Northampton, W.A., ‡2,021 .... A 5
Nowra, N.S.W., 9,633 .... J 6
Nyngan, N.S.W., 2,584 .... H 6
Orange, N.S.W., 22,196 .... H 6
Orbost, V., 2,797 .... H 7
Parkes, N.S.W., 8,438 .... H 6
Parramatta, N.S.W., 106,996 .... K 3
Penrith, N.S.W., 46,357 .... K 3
Perth (capital), W.A., †499,969 .... B 2
Peterborough, S.A., 3,117 .... F 6
Picton, N.S.W., 1,327 .... K 4
Pine Creek, N.T., ‡577 .... E 2
Pingelly, W.A., ‡1,453 .... B 2
Pinnaroo, S.A., ‡1,717 .... G 7
Port Adelaide, S.A., 39,823 .... D 7
Port Albert, V. .... H 7
Portarlington, V., 1,224 .... K 2
Port Augusta, S.A., 10,103 .... F 6
Port Fairy, V., 2,579 .... G 7
Port Hedland, W.A., 1,778 .... B 3
Port Kembla, N.S.W. .... J 6
Portland, V., 6,690 .... G 7
Port Lincoln, S.A., 8,888 .... E 6
Port Macquarie, N.S.W., 7,063 .... J 6
Port Melbourne, V., 12,591 .... K 2
Port Pirie, S.A., 15,566 .... F 6
Port Wakefield, S.A., ‡1,020 .... F 6
Proserpine, Q., 2,951 .... H 4
Queenstown, T., 4,295 .... G 8
Quirindi, N.S.W., 2,730 .... H 6
Quorn, S.A., 588 .... F 6
Radium Hill, S.A. .... G 6
Randwick, N.S.W., 113,634 .... L 3
Ravensthorpe, W.A., ‡782 .... C 6
Renmark, S.A., 6,275 .... G 6
Reynella-Port Noarlunga, 11,818 .... D 8
Richmond, V., 32,530 .... L 2
Ringwood, V., 29,141 .... L 1
Rockdale, N.S.W., 81,463 .... L 3
Rockhampton, Q., 46,083 .... J 4
Rockingham, W.A., 3,767 .... B 2
Roebourne, W.A., ‡1,782 .... B 4
Roma, Q., 5,996 .... H 5
Ryde, N.S.W., 81,291 .... L 3
Saint Arnaud, V., 3,004 .... G 7
Saint George, Q., 2,233 .... H 5
Saint Kilda, V., 58,129 .... L 2
Sale, V., 8,640 .... H 7
Salisbury, S.A., 35,762 .... D 7
Sandgate, Q., 22,621 .... J 5
Sandringham, V., 36,671 .... L 2
Sarina, Q., 2,422 .... H 4
Scone, N.S.W., 2,915 .... J 6
Singleton, N.S.W., 6,188 .... J 6
Spalding, S.A., ‡705 .... F 6
Stanthorpe, Q., 3,641 .... J 5
Stawell, V., 5,909 .... G 7
Strathalbyn, S.A., 1,449 .... D 8
Strathfield, N.S.W., 26,704 .... L 3
Streaky Bay, S.A., ‡2,134 .... E 6
Subiaco, W.A., 16,621 .... B 2
Sunbury, V., 3,526 .... K 1
Swan Hill, V., 7,381 .... G 7
Sydney (cap.), N.S.W., †2,446,345 .... L 3
Tamworth, N.S.W., 21,680 .... J 6
Taree, N.S.W., 10,560 .... J 6
Temora, N.S.W., 4,536 .... H 6
Tennant Creek, N.T., 1,001 .... E 3
Tenterfield, N.S.W., 3,270 .... J 5
Theodore, Q. .... H 4
Thursday Island, Q., 2,551 .... G 2
Toowoomba, Q., 55,799 .... J 5
Townsville, Q., 58,847 .... H 3
Truro, S.A., ‡588 .... F 6
Tully, Q., 2,860 .... H 3
Tumbarumba, N.S.W., 1,443 .... H 7
Tumut, N.S.W., 4,277 .... H 7
Ulverstone, T., 6,842 .... H 8
Unley, S.A., 39,727 .... D 8
Victor Harbor, S.A., 2,160 .... F 7
Wagga Wagga, N.S.W., 25,819 .... H 7
Wagin, W.A., 1,750 .... B 6
Walcha, N.S.W., 1,544 .... J 6
Walgett, N.S.W., 1,985 .... H 6
Wallaroo, S.A., 2,094 .... F 6
Wandoan, Q. .... H 5
Wangaratta, V., 15,175 .... H 7
Waroona, W.A., 1,013 .... B 2

(continued on following page)

Agriculture, Industry and Resources

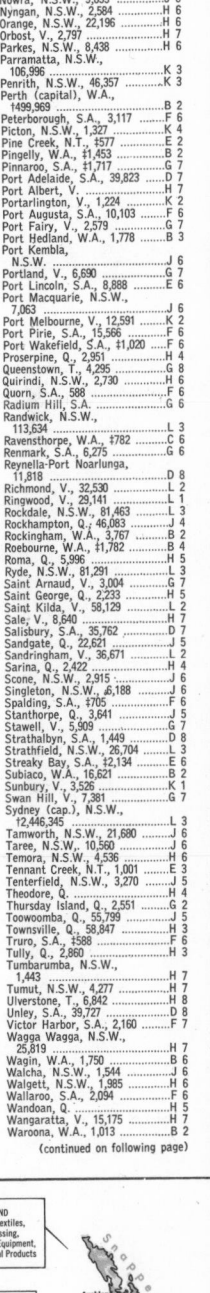

DOMINANT LAND USE

- Cereals (chiefly wheat), Livestock
- Dairy, Truck Farming
- Cash Crops, Horticulture, Fruit
- Pasture Livestock
- Range Livestock
- Forests
- Nonagricultural Land

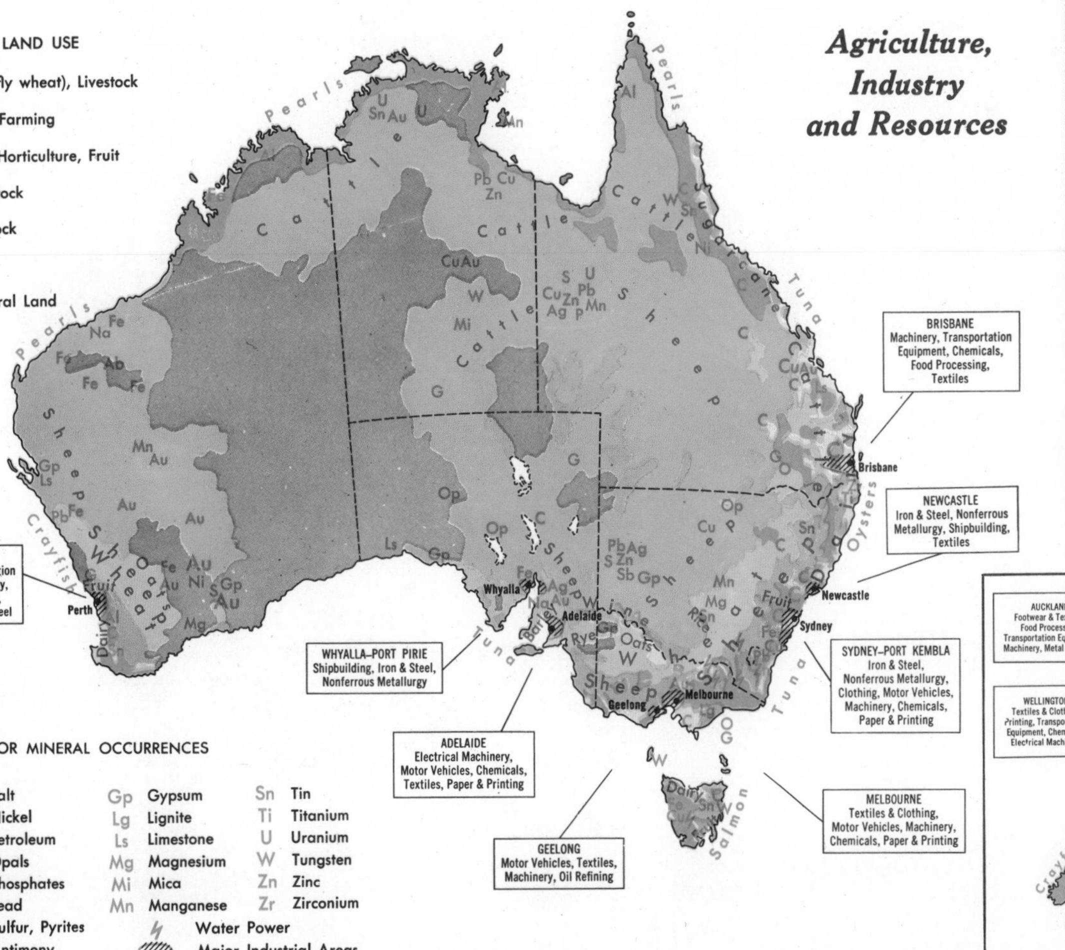
Pearls
Cattle
Sheep
Sugarcane
Tuna
Oysters
Crayfish
Salmon
Wheat
Fruit
Dairy
BRISBANE
Machinery, Transportation Equipment, Chemicals, Food Processing, Textiles
NEWCASTLE
Iron & Steel, Nonferrous Metallurgy, Shipbuilding, Textiles
PERTH
Machinery, Transportation Equipment, Metallurgy, Chemicals, Textiles, Oil Refining, Iron & Steel
WHYALLA–PORT PIRIE
Shipbuilding, Iron & Steel, Nonferrous Metallurgy
ADELAIDE
Electrical Machinery, Motor Vehicles, Chemicals, Textiles, Paper & Printing
GEELONG
Motor Vehicles, Textiles, Machinery, Oil Refining
MELBOURNE
Textiles & Clothing, Motor Vehicles, Machinery, Chemicals, Paper & Printing
SYDNEY–PORT KEMBLA
Iron & Steel, Nonferrous Metallurgy, Clothing, Motor Vehicles, Machinery, Chemicals, Paper & Printing
Perth
Whyalla
Adelaide
Geelong
Melbourne
Sydney
Newcastle
Brisbane

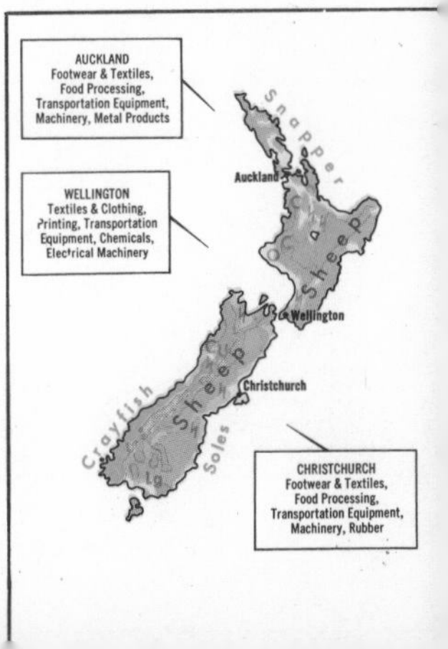
AUCKLAND
Footwear & Textiles, Food Processing, Transportation Equipment, Machinery, Metal Products
WELLINGTON
Textiles & Clothing, Printing, Transportation Equipment, Chemicals, Electrical Machinery
CHRISTCHURCH
Footwear & Textiles, Food Processing, Transportation Equipment, Machinery, Rubber
Auckland
Wellington
Christchurch
Snapper
Sheep
Crayfish
Soles

MAJOR MINERAL OCCURRENCES

Asbestos	Na Salt	Gp Gypsum	Sn Tin
Silver	Ni Nickel	Lg Lignite	Ti Titanium
Bauxite	O Petroleum	Ls Limestone	U Uranium
Gold	Op Opals	Mg Magnesium	W Tungsten
Coal	P Phosphates	Mi Mica	Zn Zinc
Copper	Pb Lead	Mn Manganese	Zr Zirconium
Iron Ore	S Sulfur, Pyrites	Water Power	
Natural Gas	Sb Antimony	Major Industrial Areas	

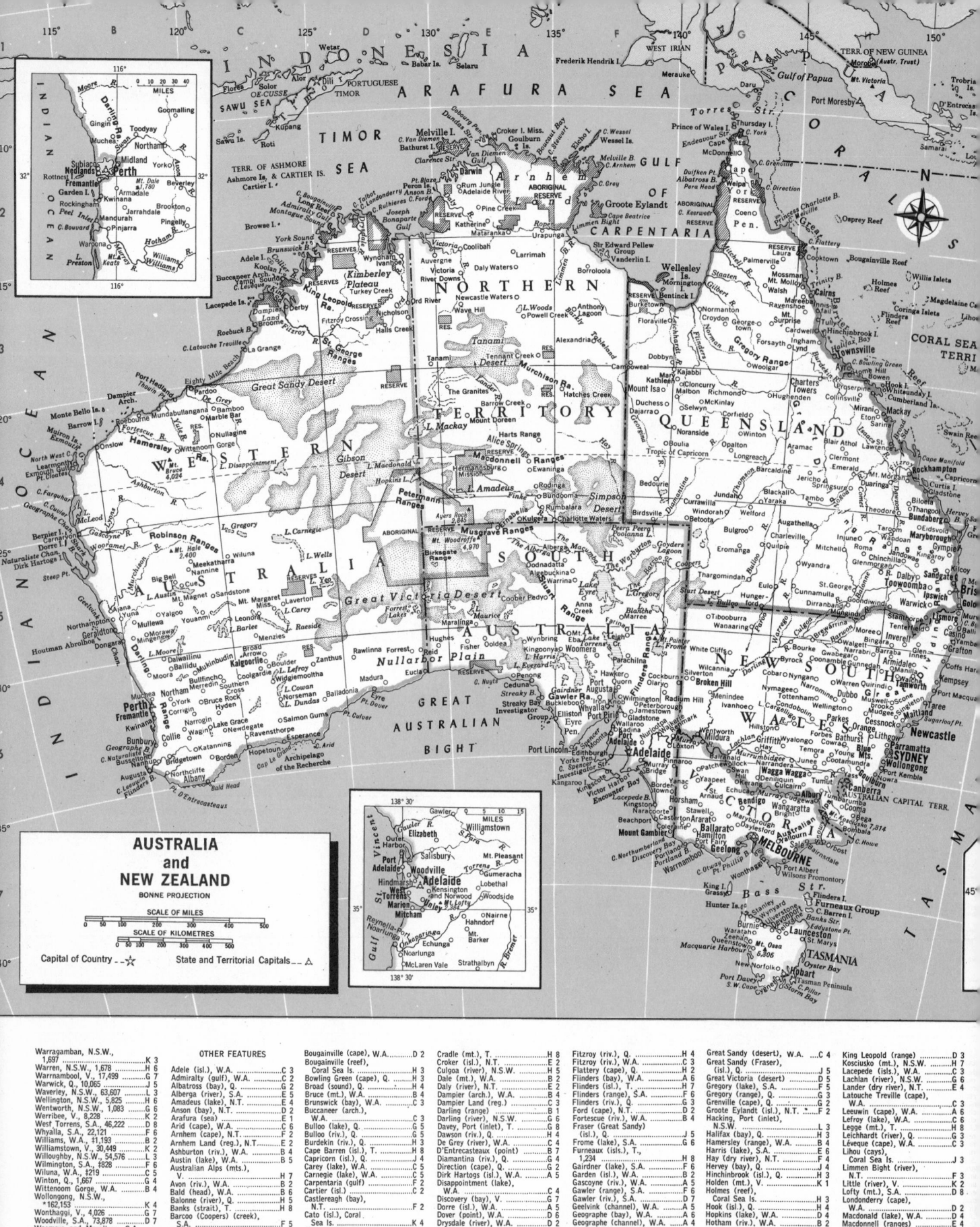

AUSTRALIA and NEW ZEALAND

BONNE PROJECTION

SCALE OF MILES

SCALE OF KILOMETRES

Capital of Country ⋯ ☆   State and Territorial Capitals ⋯ △

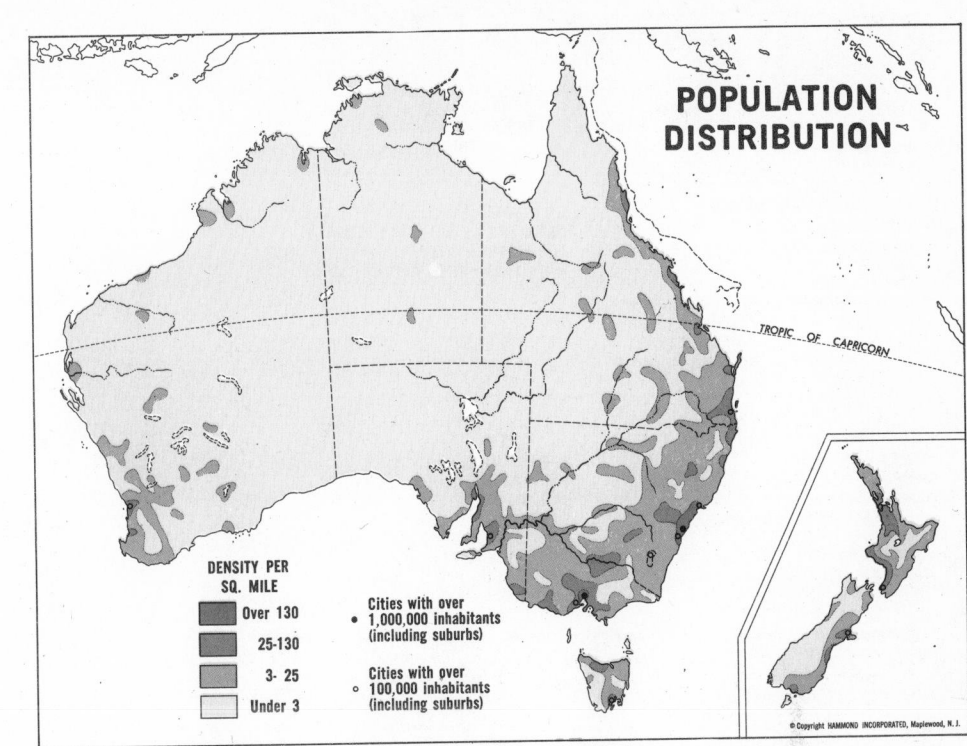

POPULATION DISTRIBUTION

DENSITY PER SQ. MILE

- Over 130
- 25-130
- 3- 25
- Under 3

- ● Cities with over 1,000,000 inhabitants (including suburbs)
- ○ Cities with over 100,000 inhabitants (including suburbs)

© Copyright HAMMOND INCORPORATED, Maplewood, N. J.

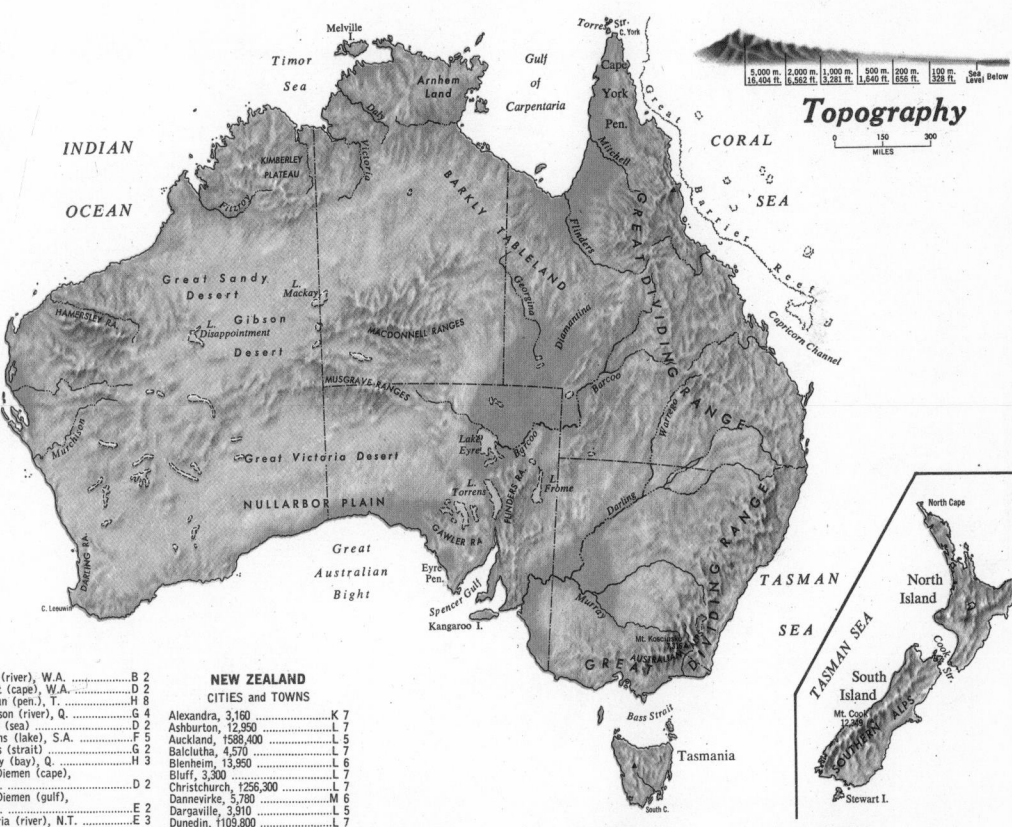

Topography

5,000 m. 16,404 ft. | 2,000 m. 6,562 ft. | 1,000 m. 3,281 ft. | 500 m. 1,640 ft. | 200 m. 656 ft. | 100 m. 328 ft. | Sea Level | Below

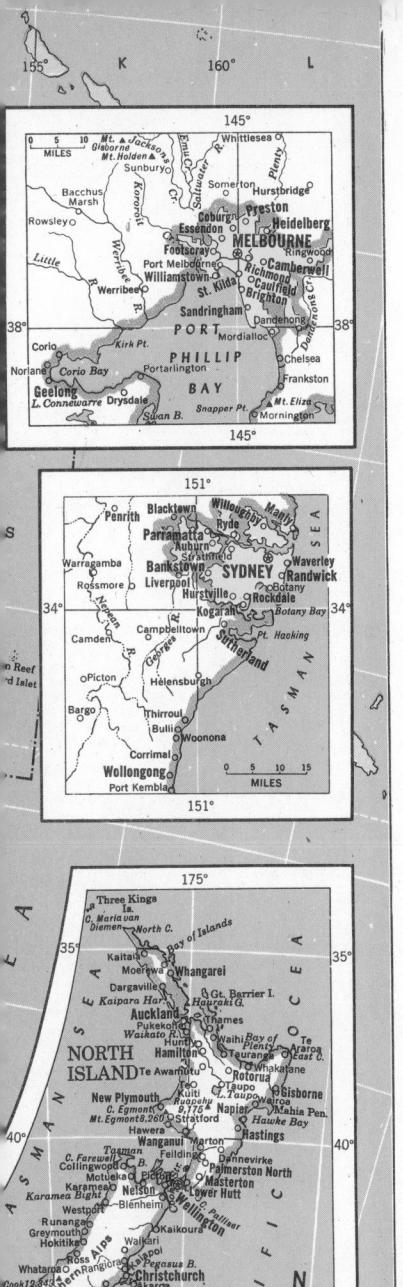

NEW ZEALAND
CITIES and TOWNS

Name	Pop.	Grid
Alexandra, 3,160		K 7
Ashburton, 12,950		L 7
Auckland, 588,400		L 5
Balclutha, 4,570		L 7
Blenheim, 13,950		L 6
Bluff, 3,300		L 7
Christchurch, 256,300		L 7
Dannevirke, 5,780		M 6
Dargaville, 3,910		L 5
Dunedin, 109,800		L 7
Feilding, 9,360		L 6
Gisborne, 128,500		M 6
Gore, 8,380		L 7
Greymouth, 8,590		L 6
Hamilton, 168,000		L 6
Hastings, ‡39,200		M 6
Hawera, 8,210		L 6
Hokitika, 3,310		L 7
Invercargill, 147,800		K 7
Kaiapoi, 3,610		L 7
Kaitaia, 3,110		L 5
Lower Hutt, 58,700		L 6
Marton, 4,780		L 6
Masterton, 17,950		M 6
Motueka, 3,840		L 6
Napier, ‡39,900		M 6
Nelson, 128,400		L 6
New Plymouth, ‡35,800		L 6
Oamaru, 13,350		L 7
Palmerston North, ‡50,900		M 6
Picton, 2,610		L 6
Pukekohe, 6,800		L 5
Rangiora, 4,270		L 7
Rotorua, 135,300		M 6
Runanga, 1,683		L 6
Stratford, 5,470		L 6
Tauranga, ‡33,500		M 5
Te Awamutu, 6,780		L 6
Te Kuiti, 4,830		L 6
Temuka, 3,190		L 7
Thames, 5,680		L 6
Timaru, ‡28,400		L 7
Tuatapere, 954		K 7
Waihi, 3,170		L 6
Wairoa, 5,190		M 6
Wanganui, ‡38,500		L 6
Wellington (capital) ‡175,500		L 6
Westport, 5,230		L 6
Whakatane, 9,080		M 5
Whangarei, 131,600		L 5

OTHER FEATURES

Name		Grid
Aspiring (mt.)		K 7
Canterbury (bight)		L 7
Cook (mt.)		L 7
Cook (strait)		L 6
East (cape)		M 5
Egmont (cape)		L 6
Egmont (mt.)		L 6
Farewell (cape)		L 6
Foveaux (strait)		K 7
Great Barrier (isl.), 272		L 5
Hauraki (gulf)		L 5
Hawke (bay)		M 6
Islands (bay)		L 5
Karamea (bight)		K 6
Maria van Diemen (cape)		L 5
North (isl.), 1,956,411		L 6
Otago (pen.)		L 7
Pegasus (bay)		L 7
Plenty (bay)		M 5
Ruapehu (vol.)		L 6
South (cape)		L 8
South (isl.), 798,681		L 7
Southern Alps (mts.)		L 7
Stewart (isl.), 332		K 8
Tasman (bay)		L 6
Tasman (sea)		K 6
Taupo (lake)		L 6
Te Anau (lake)		K 7
Waikato (river)		L 6

*City and suburbs.
†Population of metropolitan area.
‡Population of district or sub-division.

Australia index (left columns)

Name		Grid
...ntague (sound), W.A.		C 2
...nte Bello (isls.), W.A.		A 4
...ore (lake), W.A.		B 5
...ore (river), W.A.		B 1
...reston (isl.), Q.		J 5
...rnington (range), Q.		G 3
...rchison (river),		E 4
...W.A.		
...rray (river), V.		B 5
...rray (river), V.		G 6
...rray (river), W.A.		B 2
...rumbidgee (river),		
...N.S.W.		E 5
...sgrave (range)		E 5
...turaliste (cape), W.A.		A 6
...turaliste (channel), W.A.		A 5
...bean (river), N.S.W.		A 1
...rman (river), Q.		G 3
...rth West (cape),		
...A.		A 4
...thumberland (cape),		
...T.		F 3
...larbor (plain)		D 6
...kaparinga (river), S.A.		D 8
...d (river), W.A.		A 2
...ter (bay), T.		H 8
...too (river), N.S.W.		G 5
...r (inlet), W.A.		B 2
...era Peera Poolanna (lake),		
...A.		F 5
...head), Q.		G 2
...on (islands), N.T.		D 2
...et (cape), T.		H 8

Plenty (river), V.		L 1
Port Philip (bay), V.		K 2
Portland (cape), V.		G 7
Preston (lake), W.A.		B 2
Prince of Wales (isl.), Q.		G 2
Princess Charlotte (bay), Q.		G 2
Recherche (arch.), W.A.		C 6
Roebuck (bay), W.A.		C 3
Roper (river), N.T.		E 2
Rottnest (isl.), W.A.		A 2
Rulhieres (cape), W.A.		D 2
Saint George (ranges), W.A.		D 3
Saint Vincent (gulf), S.A.		D 7
Saltwater (river), V.		K 1
Sandy (cape), Q.		J 4
Shark (bay), W.A.		A 4
Simpson (desert), N.T.		F 5
Sir Edward Pellew (isls.), N.T.		F 2
South Para (river), S.A.		E 7
South West (cape), T.		G 8
Spencer (cape), S.A.		F 7
Spencer (gulf), S.A.		F 7
Steep (point), W.A.		A 4
Stewart (cape), N.T.		F 2
Storm (bay), T.		H 8
Stuart (range), S.A.		E 5
Sturt (desert), S.A.		G 5
Swain (reefs), Q.		J 4
Swan (bay), V.		K 2

Swan (river), W.A.		B 2
Talbot (cape), W.A.		D 2
Tasman (pen.), T.		H 8
Thomson (river), Q.		G 4
Timor (sea)		D 2
Torrens (lake), S.A.		F 5
Torres (strait)		G 2
Trinity (bay), Q.		H 3
Van Diemen (cape), N.T.		D 2
Van Diemen (gulf), N.T.		E 2
Victoria (river), N.T.		E 3
Warrego (river), N.S.W.		H 5
Wellesley (isls.), Q.		F 3
Wells (lake), W.A.		C 5
Werribee (river), V.		K 2
Wessel (cape), N.T.		F 2
Wessel (isls.), N.T.		F 2
Whitsunday (isl.), Q.		H 4
Wilberforce (river), N.T.		F 2
Williams (river), W.A.		B 3
Willis (islets)		
Coral Sea Is., 3		J 3
Wilsons (promontory), V.		
Wooramel (river), W.A.		A 5
York (cape), Q.		G 2
York (sound), W.A.		C 2
Yorke (pen.), S.A.		F 7
Yule (river), W.A.		B 4

Copyright by C. S. Hammond & Co., N. Y.

NORTH ISLAND

SOUTH ISLAND

NEW ZEALAND
Same scale as main map

Longitude 170° East of 175° Greenwich 180°

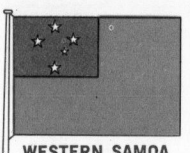
WESTERN SAMOA

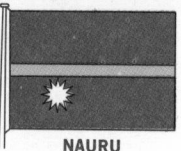
NAURU

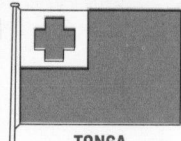
TONGA

FIJI

WESTERN SAMOA

AREA 1,097 sq. mi.
POPULATION 139,810
CAPITAL Apia
LARGEST CITY Apia
HIGHEST POINT Mt. Silisili 6,094 ft.
MONETARY UNIT West Samoan pound
MAJOR LANGUAGES Samoan, English
MAJOR RELIGIONS Protestantism,
Roman Catholicism

NAURU

AREA 8.2 sq. mi.
POPULATION 7,000
MONETARY UNIT Australian dollar

TONGA

AREA 270 sq. mi.
POPULATION 83,000
CAPITAL Nuku'alofa
LARGEST CITY Nuku'alofa
HIGHEST POINT 3,389 ft.
MONETARY UNIT Tongan pound
MAJOR LANGUAGES Tongan, English
MAJOR RELIGION Protestantism

FIJI

AREA 7,015 sq. mi.
POPULATION 519,000
CAPITAL Suva
LARGEST CITY Suva
HIGHEST POINT Tomaniivi (Mt. Victoria) 4,341 ft.
MONETARY UNIT Fijian pound
MAJOR LANGUAGES Fijian, Hindi, English
MAJOR RELIGIONS Protestantism, Hinduism

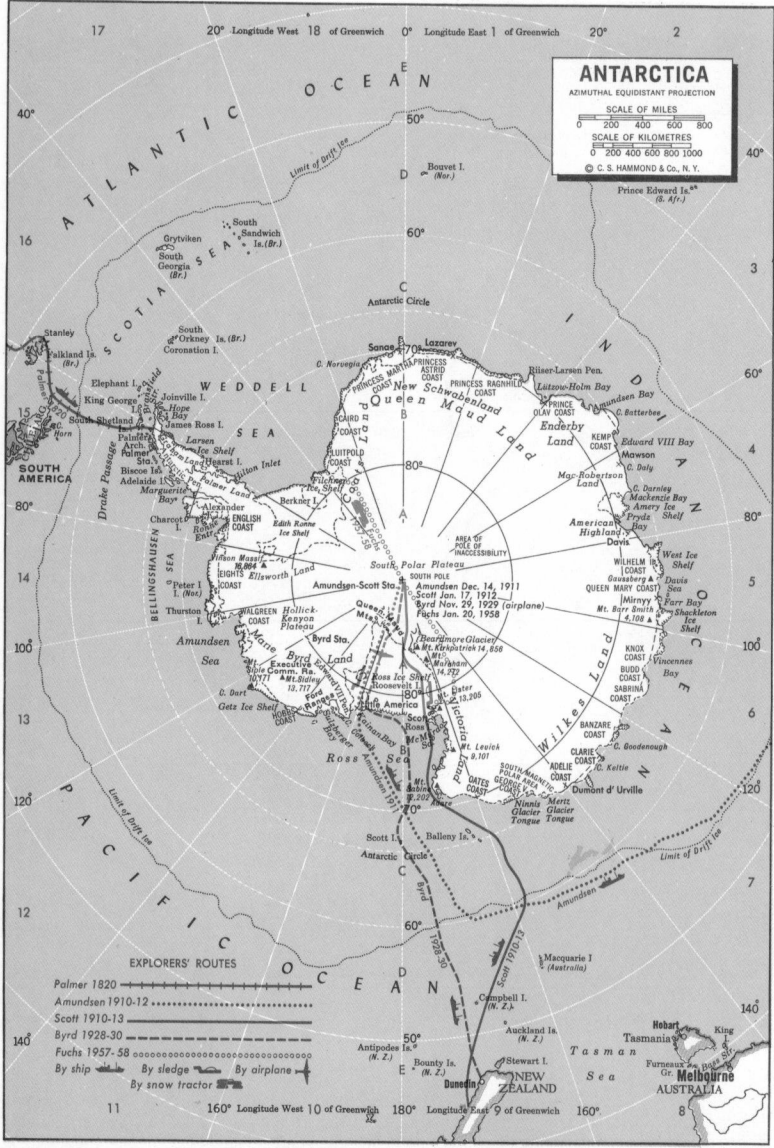

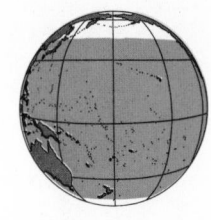

Mitiaro (isl.), 293 .... L 7
Moen (isl.), 4,966 .... F 5
Moerai, 684 .... L 8
Mokil (atoll), 393 .... G 5
Molokai (isl.), 5,089 .... L 3
Moorea (isl.), 4,370 .... L 7
Morobe, 12,132 .... E 6
Mount Gambier, 17,251 .... D 9
Mururoa (isl.) .... M 8
Namatanai, ‡2,221 .... F 5
Namonuito (atoll) .... F 5
Namorik (atoll), 490 .... G 5
Nandi, 2,542 .... H 7
Nanumea (atoll), 1,076 .... H 6
Napier, 36,700 .... H 9
Nassau (isl.), 167 .... K 7
Nauru, 7,000 .... G 6
Ndeni (isl.) .... G 6
Ndeu, 3,593 .... F 4
Nelson, 27,900 .... H10
New Britain (isl.), 138,689 .... F 6
New Caledonia, 100,579 .... G 8
New Caledonia, 86,802 .... G 8
Newcastle, 233,936 .... F 9
New Georgia (isl.) .... F 6
New Guinea (isl.) .... E 6
New Guinea, Terr. of, 1,722,572 .... E 6
New Hebrides (isls.), 80,000 .... G 7
New Ireland (isl.), 48,774 .... F 5
New South Wales (state),
  4,595,400 .... E 9
New Zealand, 2,815,000 .... G 9
Ngatik (atoll), 442 .... F 5
Ngulu (isl.), 43 .... D 5
Niihau (isl.), 237 .... K 3
Nikumaroro (Gardner) (isl.),
  230 .... J 6
Ninigo Group (isls.), 1,051 .... E 6

Niuafo'ou (isl.), 599 .... J 7
Niuatoputapu (isl.), 1,294 .... J 7
Niue (isl.), 5,323 .... K 7
Niutao (atoll), 796 .... H 6
Niutao (atoll), 796 .... H 6
Norfolk (isl.), 1,147 .... G 8
North (isl.), 1,956,411 .... H 9
North East New Guinea (reg.),
  1,420,568 .... E 6
Northern Territory (terr.),
  73,000 .... D 7
Nouméa, 41,853 .... G 8
Nouméa, *47,966 .... G 8
Nui (atoll), 569 .... H 6
Nuku'alofa, 15,685 .... J 8
Nukuhiva (isl.), 1,351 .... M 6
Nukulaelae (atoll), 354 .... H 6
Nukumanu (atoll), 675 .... F 6
Nukuono (atoll), 528 .... F 5
Nukuoro (atoll), 408 .... F 5
Oahu (isl.), 629,176 .... L 3
Ocean (isl.), 2,192 .... G 6
Oeno (isl.) .... O 8
Onotoa (atoll), 1,960 .... H 6
Ontong Java (isl.), 900 .... G 6
Orange, 22,196 .... E 9
Orona (Hull) (isl.), 583 .... J 6
Pacific Islands, Terr. of, 98,009 .... F 5
Pagan (isl.), 62 .... E 4
Pago Pago, 2,481 .... J 7
Palau (isls.), 12,291 .... D 5
Palmerston (atoll), 86 .... K 7
Palmerston North, 49,200 .... H10
Palmyra (isl.) .... K 5
Pangai, 1,670 .... J 8
Papeete, 22,278 .... M 7
Papeete, *37,485 .... M 7
Papua, 648,000 .... E 6

Peleliu (isl.), 810 .... D 5
Penrhyn (Tongareva) (atoll),
  545 .... L 6
Perth, 1,499,969 .... B 9
Phoenix (isls.), 1,018 .... H 6
Pines, Isle of (isl.), 978 .... G 8
Pingelap (atoll), 815 .... G 5
Pitcairn (isl.), 74 .... O 8
Polynesia (reg.) .... K 7
Ponape (isl.), 13,976 .... F 5
Port Augusta, 10,103 .... D 9
Port Hedland, 1,778 .... B 8
Port Lincoln, 8,888 .... D 9
Port Moresby, 56,206 .... E 6
Port Pirie, 15,566 .... D 9
Puka-Puka (atoll), 98 .... L 7
Pukapuka (atoll), 684 .... K 7
Pulap (atoll), 302 .... E 5
Pulo Anna (isl.), 13 .... D 5
Pulusuk (atoll), 305 .... E 5
Puluwat (atoll), 412 .... E 5
Queensland (state), 1,810,000 .... E 8
Rabaul, 8,737 .... F 6
Raiatea (isl.), 6,187 .... L 7
Raivavae (isl.), 999 .... M 8
Rakahanga (atoll), 323 .... K 6
Ralik Chain (isls.), 9,268 .... G 5
Rangiroa (atoll), 868 .... M 7
Rapa (isl.), 363 .... M 8
Rapa Nui (Easter) (isl.), 1,598 .... Q 8
Raroia (atoll) 52 .... M 7
Rarotonga (isl.), 9,971 .... K 8
Ratak Chain (isls.), 10,060 .... G 5
Reao (atoll), 255 .... N 7
Rennell (isl.), 1,169 .... G 7
Rimatara (isl.), 747 .... L 8
Rockhampton, 45,376 .... F 8
Roma, 5,996 .... E 8

Rongelap (atoll), 107 .... G 4
Rota (isl.), 1,344 .... E 4
Rotuma (isl.), 3,365 .... H 7
Rururu (isl.), 1,546 .... L 8
Saipan (isl.), 9,590 .... E 4
Sala y Gómez (isl.) .... P 8
Samarai, 2,201 .... F 6
Samoa (isls.), 167,579 .... J 7
San Cristobal (isl.), 8,500 .... G 7
Santa Isabel (isl.) .... G 6
Santa Cruz (isls.), 2,800 .... G 6
Satawal (isl.), 345 .... E 5
Savai'i (isl.), 36,159 .... J 7
Senyavin (isls.) .... F 5
Society (isls.), 81,487 .... L 7
Sohano, 877 .... F 6
Solomon (isls.), 234,186 .... F 6
Solomon (sea) .... F 6
Solomon Islands Prot., 161,525 .... F 6
Sonsorol (isl.), 92 .... D 5
Sorol (atoll), 15 .... D 5
South (isl.), 798,681 .... G10
South Australia (state),
  1,169,600 .... D 8
Starbuck (isl.) .... L 6
Stewart (isl.), 332 .... G10
Suva, 54,157 .... H 7
Suva, *80,248 .... H 7
Swains (isl.), 74 .... J 7
Sydney, 12,446,345 .... F 9
Sydney (isl.) .... J 6
Tabiteuea (atoll), 4,419 .... H 6
Tahaa (isl.), 3,567 .... L 7
Tahiti (isl.), 61,519 .... L 7
Takaroa (atoll), 161 .... M 7
Tamworth, 21,680 .... E 9
Tanna (isl.), 10,500 .... H 7

Taongi (atoll) .... G 4
Tarawa (atoll), 13,700 .... H 6
Tasman (sea) .... G 9
Tasmania (state), 393,700 .... E10
Taveuni (isl.), 6,351 .... H 7
Tennant Creek, 1,001 .... D 7
Tikopia (isl.), 1,400 .... G 7
Timaru, 27,800 .... H10
Tinian (isl.), 696 .... E 4
Tobi (isl.), 80 .... D 5
Tokelau (isls.), 2,000 .... J 6
Tonga, 83,000 .... J 8
Tongareva (atoll), 545 .... L 6
Tongatapu (isl.), 47,606 .... J 8
Toowoomba, 52,139 .... F 8
Torres (isls.), 200 .... G 7
Townsville, 56,768 .... E 7
Trobriand (isls.), 10,199 .... F 6
Truk (isls.), 18,792 .... F 5
Tuamotu (archipelago), 6,148 .... M 7
Tubuai (isl.), 1,398 .... L 8
Tubuai (Austral) (isls.), 5,053 .... L 8
Tureia (atoll), 40 .... N 8
Tutuila (isl.), 25,557 .... J 7
Uahuka (isl.), 359 .... N 6
Uapou (isl.), 1,414 .... N 6
Ujelang (atoll), 281 .... F 5
Ulithi (atoll), 523 .... D 5
Upolu (isl.), 94,691 .... J 7
Uturoa, 2,394 .... L 7
Uvéa (isl.), 2,001 .... H 7
Vahitahi (atoll), 109 .... N 7
Vaitupu (atoll), 876 .... H 6
Vanua Levu (isl.), 71,933 .... H 7
Vava'u Group (isl.), 13,533 .... J 7
Victoria (state), 3,461,400 .... E 9
Vila, 7,000 .... G 7
Viti Levu (isl.), 341,784 .... H 7

Wagga Wagga, 25,819 .... E 9
Wake (isl.), 1,097 .... G 4
Wallis (isls.), 6,000 .... J 7
Wallis and Futuna, 8,546 .... J 7
Wanganui, 36,400 .... H 9
Warrnambool, 17,499 .... D 9
Washington (isl.), 437 .... L 5
Wau, 1,072 .... E 6
Wellington, 134,400 .... H10
Western Australia (state),
  991,300 .... C 8
Western Samoa, 139,810 .... J 7
Wewak, 5,090 .... E 6
Whangarei, 29,600 .... H 9

Whyalla, 22,121 .... D 9
Willis (islets), 3 .... F 7
Wiluna, 1,219 .... C 8
Woleai (atoll), 586 .... E 5
Wollongong, *162,153 .... F 9
Wonthaggi, 4,026 .... E 9
Woomera, 4,571 .... D 8
Wotje (atoll), 376 .... H 5
Wyndham, 1,156 .... C 7
Yap (isls.), 4,380 .... D 5

*City and suburbs.
†Population of metropolitan area.
‡Population of sub-district.

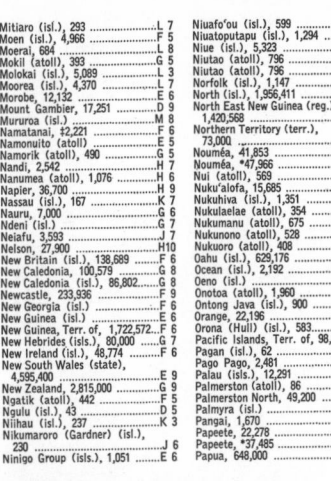

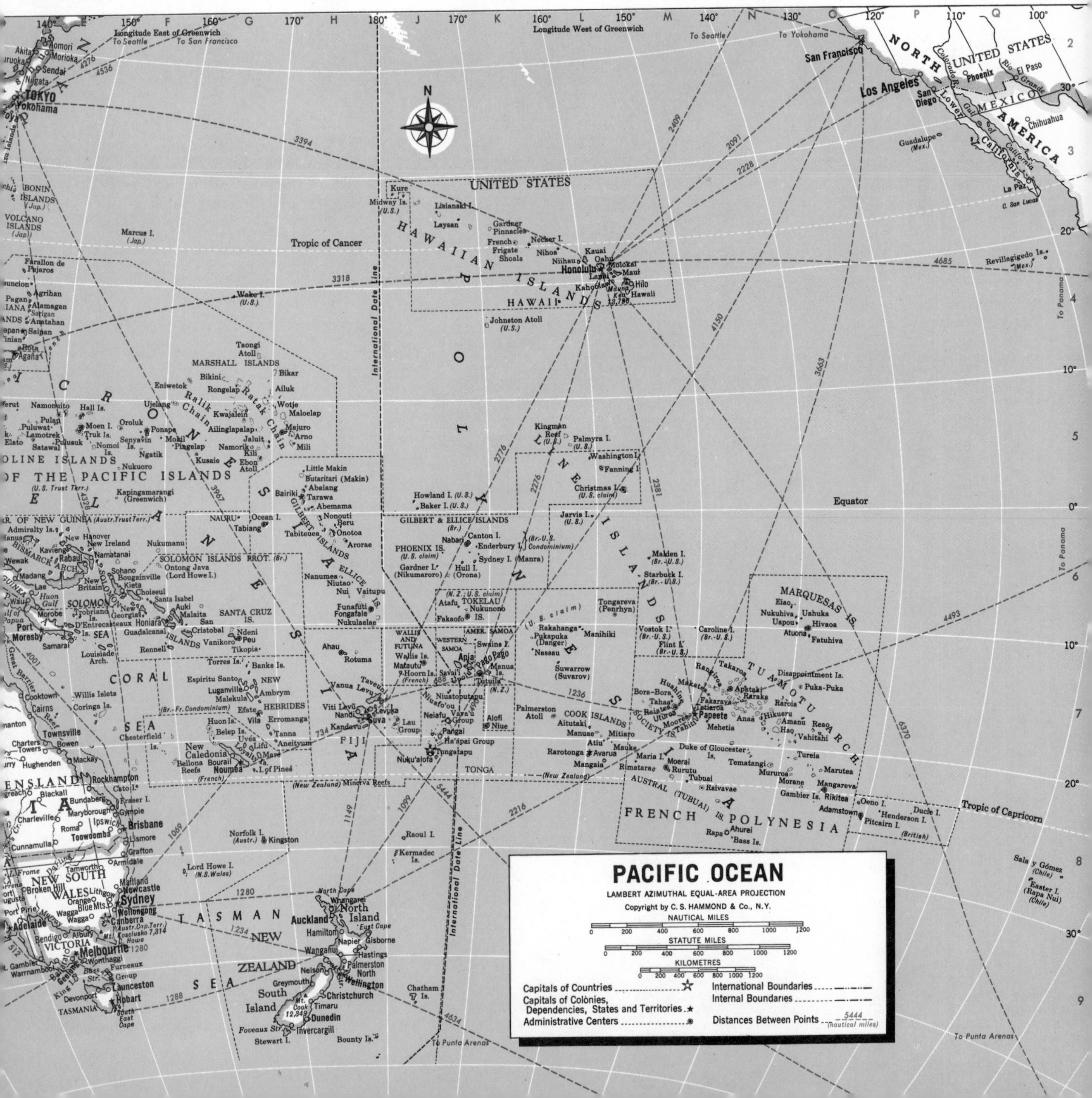

PACIFIC OCEAN
LAMBERT AZIMUTHAL EQUAL-AREA PROJECTION
Copyright by C. S. Hammond & Co., N.Y.

NAUTICAL MILES
0   200   400   600   800   1000   1200

STATUTE MILES
0   200   400   600   800   1000   1200

KILOMETRES
0   200   400   600   800   1000   1200

Capitals of Countries .... ★ International Boundaries .... ——
Capitals of Colònies,
  Dependencies, States and Territories .... ★ Internal Boundaries .... ——
Administrative Centers .... ◉ Distances Between Points 5444
                                              (nautical miles)

POPULATION DISTRIBUTION

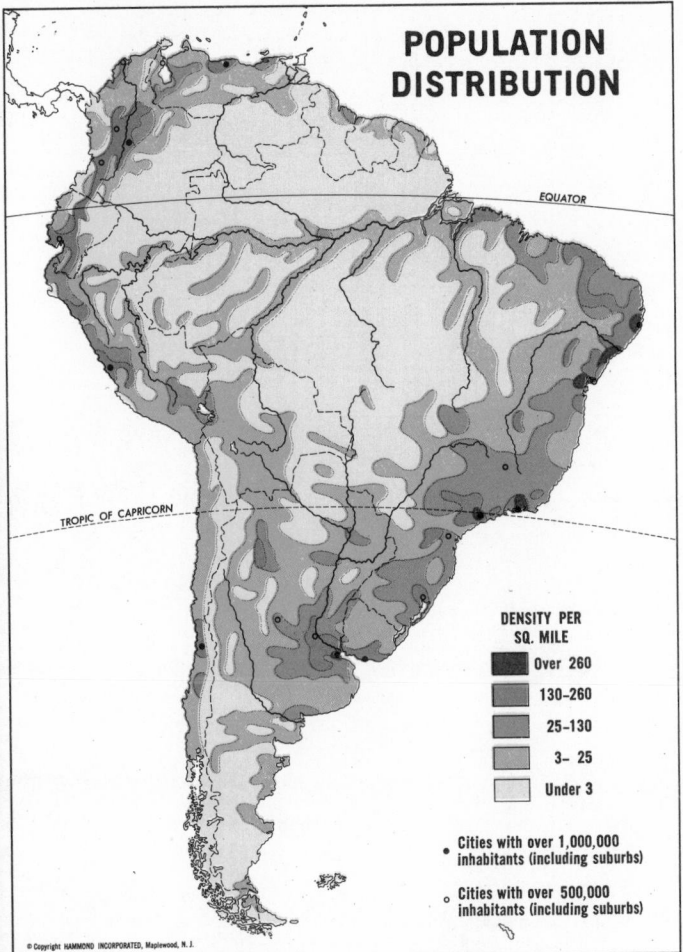

AREA 6,875,000 sq. mi.
POPULATION 186,000,000
LARGEST CITY Buenos Aires (greater)
HIGHEST POINT Cerro Aconcagua 22,831 ft.
LOWEST POINT Salina Grande -131 ft.

EQUATOR

TROPIC OF CAPRICORN

DENSITY PER SQ. MILE

- Over 260
- 130–260
- 25–130
- 3– 25
- Under 3

● Cities with over 1,000,000 inhabitants (including suburbs)

○ Cities with over 500,000 inhabitants (including suburbs)

© Copyright HAMMOND INCORPORATED, Maplewood, N. J.

VEGETATION

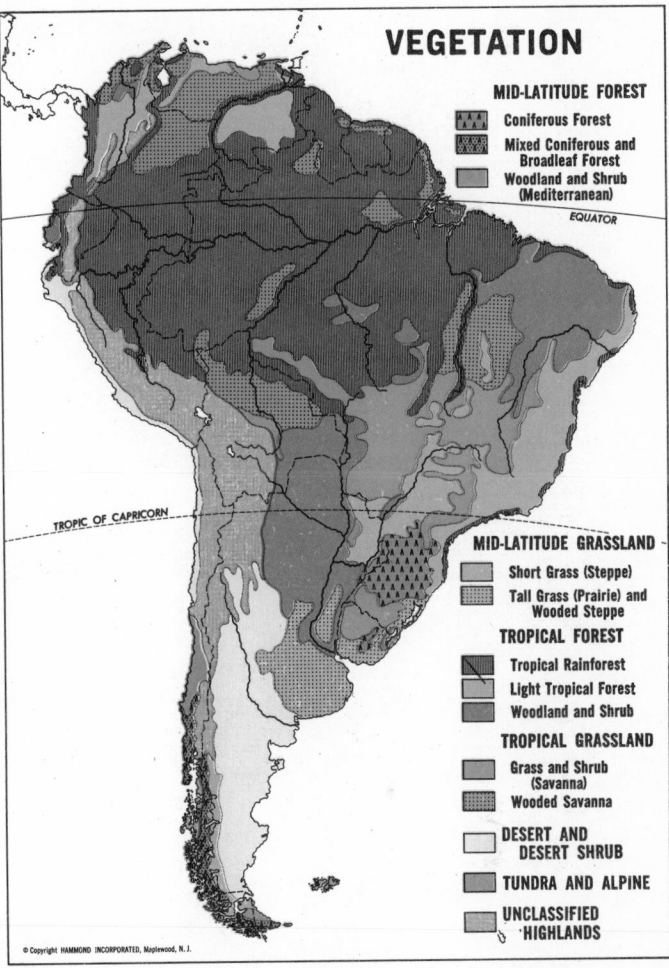

MID-LATITUDE FOREST

- Coniferous Forest
- Mixed Coniferous and Broadleaf Forest
- Woodland and Shrub (Mediterranean)

EQUATOR

TROPIC OF CAPRICORN

MID-LATITUDE GRASSLAND

- Short Grass (Steppe)
- Tall Grass (Prairie) and Wooded Steppe

TROPICAL FOREST

- Tropical Rainforest
- Light Tropical Forest
- Woodland and Shrub

TROPICAL GRASSLAND

- Grass and Shrub (Savanna)
- Wooded Savanna

DESERT AND DESERT SHRUB

TUNDRA AND ALPINE

UNCLASSIFIED HIGHLANDS

© Copyright HAMMOND INCORPORATED, Maplewood, N. J.

92 Venezuela

INTERNAL DIVISIONS

Amazonas (terr.), 12,831 .... E 5
Anzoátegui (state),
  501,384 .... F 3
Apure (state), 158,487 ...... D 4
Aragua (state), 429,344 ..... E 3
Barinas (state), 193,914 .... D 3
Bolívar (state), 383,315 .... F 4
Carabobo (state), 512,173 ... D 2
Cojedes (state), 95,177 ..... D 3
Delta Amacuro (terr.), 34,278 .. H 3
Dependencias Federales (terr.),
  1,000 .... F 2
Distrito Federal, 2,009,561 .. D 2
Falcón (state), 406,051 ..... D 2
Guárico (state), 330,147 .... E 3
Lara (state), 611,192 .... C 2
Mérida (state), 335,428 ..... C 3
Miranda (state), 702,603 .... E 2
Monagas (state), 316,732 .... G 3
Nueva Esparta (state),
  112,611 .... G 2
Portuguesa (state),
  284,523 .... D 3
Sucre (state), 493,840 ...... G 2
Táchira (state), 525,840 .... B 3
Trujillo (state), 382,441 ... C 3
Yaracuy (state), 222,041 .... D 2
Zulia (state), 1,342,994 .... B 2

CITIES and TOWNS

Acarigua, 30,683 .... D 3

Achaguas, 1,934 .... D 4
Adícora, 563 .... D 2
Aguada Grande, 1,601 .... D 2
Agua Fría, 539 .... D 2
Agua Linda, 25 .... E 5
Aguasay, 1,458 .... G 3
Altagracia, 7,362 .... C 2
Altagracia de Orituco, 13,013 .. E 3
Amuay, 986 .... D 2
Anaco, 23,105 .... F 3
Aparurén .... G 5
Apurito, 739 .... D 4
Arabopó .... H 5
Aragua de Barcelona,
  8,241 .... F 3
Aragua de Maturín,
  2,643 .... G 3
Araure, 12,316 .... D 3
Aricagua, 230 .... C 3
Arichuna, 983 .... D 4
Aripao, 400 .... F 4
Arismendi, 1,243 .... D 3
Aroa, 6,356 .... D 2
Atapirire, 203 .... F 3
Bachaquero, 14,490 .... C 2
Baraguá, 831 .... D 2
Barbacoas, 1,579 .... E 2
Barcelona, 42,379 .... F 3
Barinas, 25,748 .... C 3
Barinitas, 7,008 .... C 3
Barquisimeto, 280,086 .... C 2
Barrancas, Barinas, 3,154 ... C 3
Barrancas, Monagas,
  4,189 .... G 3

Betijoque, 3,915 .... C 3
Biruaca, 631 .... E 4
Biscucuy, 3,900 .... D 3
Bobare, 970 .... D 2
Bobures, 2,159 .... C 3
Boca de Aroa, 1,674 .... D 2
Boca del Mangle, 1,075 ...... C 2
Boca del Pao, 283 .... E 4
Bocono, 10,430 .... C 3
Borbón, 373 .... E 4
Borojó, 367 .... C 2
Bruzual, 556 .... D 4
Buena Vista, Anzoátegui, 2,335 .. F 3
Buena Vista, Apure, 64 ...... D 4
Buena Vista, Falcón, 786 .... D 2
Cabimas, 141,314 .... C 2
Cabruta, 813 .... E 4
Cabudare, 4,480 .... D 2
Cabure, 1,440 .... D 2
Cachipo, 1,091 .... G 3
Cacuri, 45 .... F 5
Cagua, 16,233 .... E 2
Caicara, 4,776 .... D 2
Caicara de Orinoco, 3,281 ... E 4
Calabozo, 15,739 .... E 3
Calderas, 631 .... C 3
Camaguán, 1,917 .... E 3
Camatagua, 1,419 .... E 3
Campo Claro, 1,620 .... C 2
Candelaria, 158 .... E 4
Cantaura, 14,068 .... F 3
Capatárida, 1,278 .... C 2
Capure, 459 .... G 2
Carabobo, Bolívar .... H 4

Carabobo, Carabobo,
  2,319 .... D 2
Caracas (cap.), 786,710 ..... E 2
Caracas, *2,064,033 .... E 2
Carache, 2,635 .... C 3
Carapa, 115 .... E 4
Cariaco, 4,281 .... G 2
Caribén, 25 .... E 4
Caripe, 3,583 .... G 2
Caripito, 21,598 .... G 2
Carirubana, 3,421 .... D 2
Carmelo, 1,944 .... C 2
Carora, 23,227 .... C 2
Carrasquero, 1,353 .... B 2
Carúpano, 38,197 .... G 2
Casanay, 3,561 .... G 2
Casigua, Falcón, 406 .... C 2
Casigua, Zulia, 5,320 .... B 3
Cazorla, 657 .... E 3
Chaguaramas, 1,363 .... E 3
Chichiriviche, 2,512 .... D 2
Chivacoa, 12,871 .... D 2
Choroní, 352 .... E 2
Churuguara, 4,458 .... D 2
Ciudad Bolívar, 63,266 ...... G 3
Ciudad Bolivia, 2,080 .... C 3
Ciudad de Nutrias, 541 ...... D 3
Ciudad Guayana, 127,681 ..... G 3
Ciudad Ojeda, 53,745 .... C 2
Ciudad Piar, 4,598 .... G 4
Clarines, 2,018 .... F 3
Cojoro, 156 .... B 2
Colón, 169 .... E 6

Comunidad, 44 .... E 6
Coporito, 659 .... H 3
Coro, 45,506 .... D 2
Corozo Pando, 286 .... E 3
Cúa, 5,567 .... E 2
Cubiro, 1,742 .... D 2
Cuchívero, 122 .... F 4
Cumaná, 69,937 .... F 2
Cumanacoa, 7,354 .... G 2
Curiapo, 375 .... H 3
Dabajuro, 3,927 .... C 2
Delicias, 1,398 .... B 4
Democracia, 12 .... G 4
Dolores, 1,122 .... D 3
Duaca, 5,771 .... D 2
Ejido, 5,457 .... C 3
El Almacén, 31 .... E 4
El Amparo de Apure, 1,087 ... C 4
El Baúl, 1,550 .... D 3
El Callao, 5,039 .... G 4
El Calvario, 567 .... E 3
El Carmen .... E 7
El Chaparro, 1,703 .... F 3
El Cristo, 328 .... C 4
El Dorado, 2,094 .... H 4
El Empedrado, 1,739 .... C 2
El Guapo, 842 .... E 2
El Manteco, 999 .... G 4
El Miamo, 269 .... G 4
Elorza, 2,121 .... C 4
El Palmar, 1,986 .... G 4
El Pao, Anzoátegui, 586 ..... F 3
El Pao, Bolívar, 2,115 ...... G 4

El Pao, Cojedes, 1,081 ...... D 3
El Perú, 1,487 .... H 4
El Pilar, 3,326 .... G 2
El Rastro, 748 .... E 3
El Roque, 348 .... G 4
El Samán de Apure, 1,099 .... C 3
El Socorro, 3,153 .... F 3
El Sombrero, 5,712 .... E 3
El Tigre, 41,961 .... F 3
El Tocuyo, 14,560 .... C 3
El Toro, 199 .... H 3
El Vigía, 8,874 .... C 3
El Vínculo, 1,224 .... D 1
El Yagual, 435 .... D 4
Encontrados, 2,991 .... B 3
Esperanza, 15 .... C 2
Espino, 470 .... F 3
Garcitas, 1,224 .... C 3
Guacara, 11,353 .... D 2
Guáchara, 462 .... D 3
Guadarrama, 461 .... D 3
Guaína, 87 .... E 4
Guanare, 18,452 .... D 3
Guanarito, 1,048 .... D 3
Guanoco, 437 .... G 2
Guanta, 8,048 .... F 2
Guardatinajas, 704 .... E 3
Guárero, 646 .... B 2
Guárico, 3,653 .... D 3
Guariquén, 633 .... G 2
Guasdualito, 4,586 .... C 4
Guasimal, 303 .... D 3
Guasipati, 3,446 .... G 4

Guayabal, 40 .... E 6
Guayabal, 841 .... E 3
Güiria, 11,061 .... G 2
Gurí, 158 .... G 4
Guzmán Blanco, 151 .... E 6
Higüerote, 3,852 .... E 2
Icabarú, 475 .... G 5
Independencia, 3,658 .... B 4
Irapa, 4,532 .... G 2
Juangriego, 4,505 .... G 2
Judibana, 4,375 .... D 2
Juasepín, 2,471 .... G 3
Kavanayén, 401 .... H 5
La Aduana, 106 .... D 3
La Asunción, 5,517 .... G 2
La Canoa, 256 .... F 3
La Ceiba, Apure, 13 .... D 4
La Ceiba, Trujillo, 199 .... C 3
La Concepción, 18,015 ...... B 2
La Concepción, 9,488 .... C 2
La Esmeralda, 30 .... F 5
La Esperanza .... G 2
La Fría, 4,771 .... B 3
La Grita, 7,866 .... C 3
La Guaira, 20,497 .... E 2
Lagunetas, 522 .... C 2
La Horqueta, 330 .... G 2
La Inglesa, 522 .... G 3
La Leona, 327 .... F 3
La Luz, 414 .... D 3
La Margarita .... C 2
La Paragua, 833 .... G 4
Las Bonitas, 306 .... F 4
Las Lajitas .... F 4

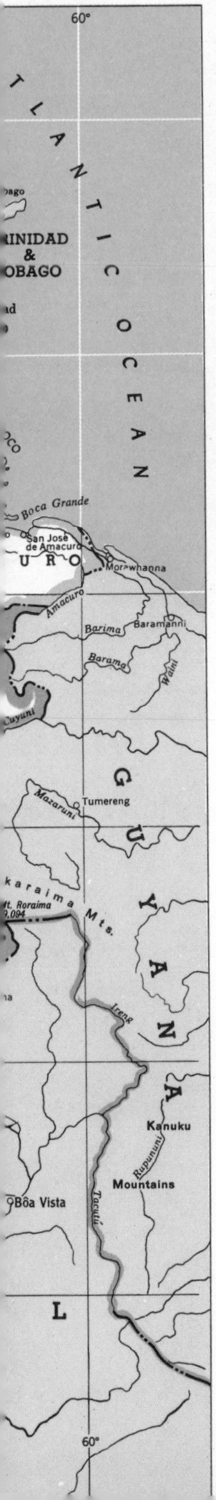

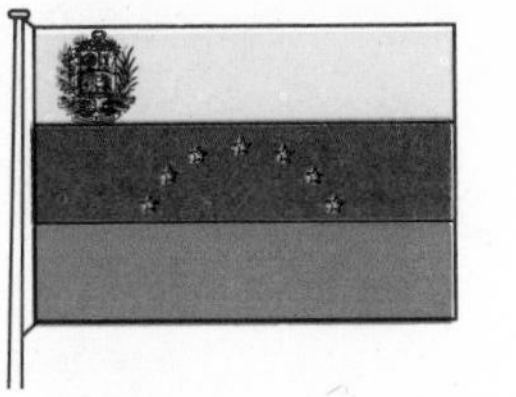

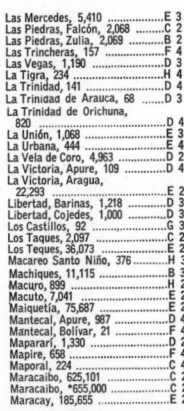

AREA 352,143 sq. mi.
POPULATION 10,398,907
CAPITAL Caracas
LARGEST CITY Caracas
HIGHEST POINT Pico Bolívar 16,427 ft.
MONETARY UNIT bolívar
MAJOR LANGUAGE Spanish
MAJOR RELIGION Roman Catholicism

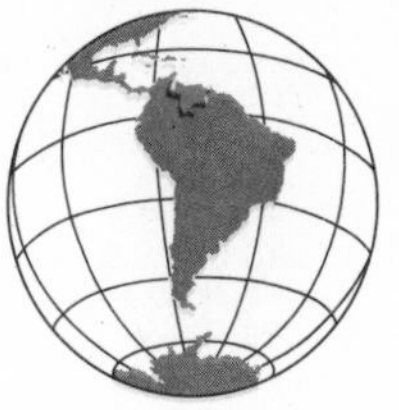

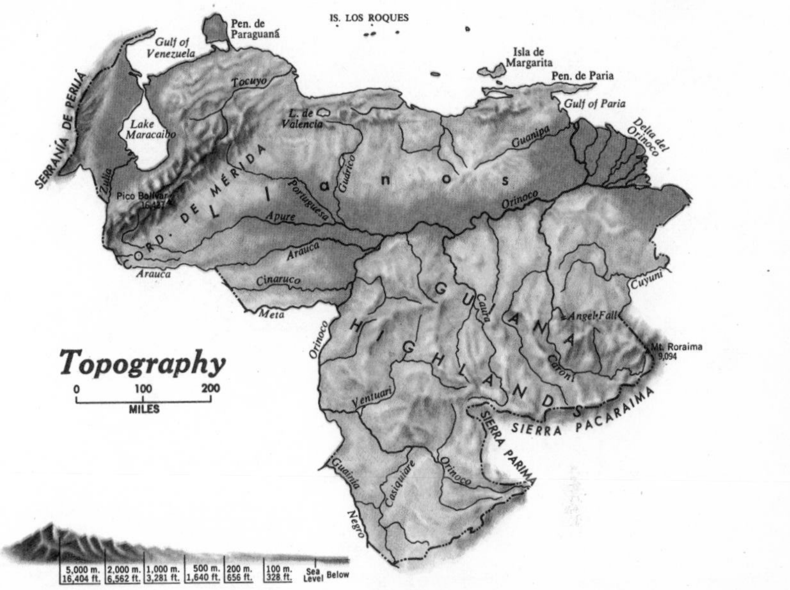

Topography
0 100 200
MILES
IS. LOS ROQUES
Pen. de Paraguaná
Gulf of Venezuela
Isla de Margarita
Pen. de Paria
Gulf of Paria
Delta del Orinoco
Tocuyo
L. de Valencia
Lake Maracaibo
SERRANÍA DE PERIJÁ
Zulia
Pico Bolívar 16,427
CORD. DE MÉRIDA
L l a n o s
Guanipa
Guárico
Portuguesa
Apure
Orinoco
Arauca
Cinaruco
Meta
Caura
Caroní
Cuyuni
Angel Fall
Mt. Roraima 9,094
G U I A N A H I G H L A N D S
Ventuari
SIERRA PACARAIMA
SIERRA PARIMA
Casiquiare
Guainía
Negro
5,000 m. 16,404 ft.
2,000 m. 6,562 ft.
1,000 m. 3,281 ft.
500 m. 1,640 ft.
200 m. 656 ft.
100 m. 328 ft.
Sea Level
Below

Las Mercedes, 5,410	E 3
Las Piedras, Falcón, 2,068	C 2
Las Piedras, Zulia, 2,069	B 2
Las Trincheras, 157	F 4
Las Vegas, 1,190	D 3
La Tigra, 234	H 4
La Trinidad, 141	D 4
La Trinidad de Arauca, 68	D 3
La Trinidad de Orichuna, 820	D 4
La Unión, 1,068	E 3
La Urbana, 444	E 4
La Vela de Coro, 4,963	D 2
La Victoria, Apure, 109	D 4
La Victoria, Aragua, 22,293	E 2
Libertad, Barinas, 1,218	D 3
Libertad, Cojedes, 1,000	D 3
Los Castillos, 92	G 3
Los Taques, 2,097	C 2
Los Teques, 36,073	E 2
Macareo Santo Niño, 376	H 3
Machiques, 11,115	B 3
Macuro, 899	H 2
Macuto, 7,041	E 2
Maiquetía, 75,687	E 2
Mantecal, Apure, 987	D 4
Mantecal, Bolívar, 21	F 4
Mapararí, 1,330	D 2
Mapire, 658	F 4
Maporal, 224	C 4
Maracaibo, 625,101	C 2
Maracaibo, *655,000	C 2
Maracay, 185,655	E 2
Marigüitar, 3,075	G 2
Maripa, 802	F 4
Maroa, 417	E 6
Matu, 87	F 4
Maturín, 54,362	G 3
Mene de Mauroa, 3,597	C 2
Mene Grande, 11,673	C 3
Mérida, 46,339	C 3
Mesa Bolívar, 1,227	C 3
Mirimire, 1,473	D 2
Moitaco, 364	F 4
Morganito, 103	E 5
Morón, 7,079	D 2
Mucuchachí, 391	C 3
Mucuchíes, 1,034	C 3
Naricual, 656	F 2
Nirgua, 7,371	D 2
Nuevo Mamo, 284	G 3
Obispos, 651	D 3
Ocumare de la Costa, 1,332	E 2
Ocumare del Tuy, 15,006	E 2
Onoto, 1,090	F 3
Ortiz, 1,309	E 3
Ospino, 1,590	D 3
Palmarejo, 943	C 2
Palmarito, Apure, 1,176	D 4
Palmarito, Guárico, 74	F 3
Palmarito, Mérida, 903	C 3
Papelón, 414	D 3
Paraguaipoa, 1,443	C 2
Paraíso de Chabasquén, 2,324	D 3
Pariaguán, 6,236	F 3
Parmana, 322	F 4
Pedernales, 788	G 3
Pedregal, 1,483	C 2
Peraitepuí, 81	H 5
Piacoa, 377	H 3
Pimichín, 19	E 6
Píritu, Anzoátegui, 1,438	F 2
Píritu, Falcón, 1,859	D 2
Píritu, Portuguesa, 4,879	D 3
Platanal, 8	F 6
Porlamar, 21,787	G 2
Pozuelos, 6,488	F 2
Pregonero, 2,894	C 3
Pueblo Nuevo, 2,680	D 1
Puerto Ayacucho, 5,465	E 5
Puerto Cabello, 52,493	E 2
Puerto Cumarebo, 8,029	D 2
Puerto de Nutrias, 565	D 3
Puerto Hierro, 1,096	H 2
Puerto La Cruz, 59,033	F 2
Puerto Miranda, 374	E 4
Puerto Páez, 767	E 4
Puerto Píritu, 2,407	F 2
Punta Cardón, 7,461	C 2
Punta de Mata, 6,525	G 3
Punta de Piedras, 2,342	F 2
Punto Fijo, 34,457	D 2
Puruey, 343	F 4
Puruname, 8	E 6
Quibor, 7,046	D 3
Quiriquire, 7,393	G 3
Quisiro, 816	C 2
Río Caribe, 7,774	G 2
Río Chico, 2,612	F 2
Río Claro, 1,374	D 3
Río Tocuyo, 1,650	C 2
Rosario, 10,442	B 2
Rubio, 11,774	B 4
Sabaneta, Barinas, 1,997	D 3
Sabaneta, Falcón, 414	D 2
Samariapo, 19	E 5
San Antonio, Monagas, 3,337	G 2
San Antonio, Zulia, 510	C 3
San Antonio de Caparo, 1,412	C 4
San Antonio del Táchira, 14,247	B 4
San Antonio de Orinoco, 48	E 6
San Antonio de Tabasca, 434	G 3
Sanare, 3,599	D 3
San Carlos, Cojedes, 11,934	D 3
San Carlos, Zulia, 686	C 2
San Carlos del Zulia, 14,480	C 3
San Carlos de Río Negro, 474	E 7
San Casimiro, 3,485	E 3
San Cristóbal, 149,063	B 4
San Diego de Cabrutica, 455	F 3
San Felipe, Yaracuy, 28,744	D 2
San Felipe, Zulia, 570	B 3
San Félix, 424	C 2
San Fernando, 24,470	E 4
San Fernando de Atabapo, 898	E 5
San Francisco, 967	C 2
San Ignacio, 697	B 2
San José, Amazonas	E 5
San José, Zulia, 2,991	B 3
San José de Amacuro, 22	H 3
San José de Areocuar, 1,000	G 2
San José de Guanipa, 20,746	G 3
San José de la Costa, 505	D 2
San José de Río Chico, 3,368	F 2
San José de Tiznados, 504	E 3
San Juan de Colón, 8,944	B 3
San Juan de las Galdonas, 1,104	G 2
San Juan de los Cayos, 1,191	D 2
San Juan de los Morros, 28,556	E 3
San Juan de Manapiare, 46	E 5
San Juan de Payara, 945	E 4
San Lorenzo, Falcón, 527	D 2
San Lorenzo, Zulia, 1,552	C 3
San Luis, 1,266	D 2
San Mateo, 1,849	F 3
San Mauricio, 43	E 3
San Pedro de las Bocas, 288	G 4
San Rafael, 6,390	C 2
San Rafael de Atamaica, 597	E 4
San Rafael de Orituco, 991	E 3
San Sebastián, 4,090	E 2
Santa Ana, Anzoátegui, 3,609	F 3
Santa Ana, Táchira, 3,677	B 4
Santa Bárbara, Amazonas	E 6
Santa Bárbara, Barinas, 2,029	C 4
Santa Bárbara, Monagas, 1,720	G 3
Santa Bárbara, Zulia, 105	C 3
Santa Catalina, Barinas, 425	D 4
Santa Catalina, Delta Amacuro, 440	H 3
Santa Cruz, 3,224	C 3
Santa Cruz de Bucaral, 1,829	D 2
Santa Cruz del Zulia, 2,041	B 3
Santa Cruz de Mara, 1,919	C 2
Santa Cruz de Orinoco, 419	F 3
Santa Elena, 752	H 5
Santa Inés, Anzoátegui, 917	F 3
Santa Inés, Barinas, 257	C 3
Santa Isabel	F 7
Santa Lucía, 563	D 3
Santa María, Bolívar, 468	G 3
Santa Mariá de Erebató, 468	F 5
Santa María de Ipire, 3,167	F 3
Santa María del Orinoco, 57	E 4
Santa Rita, Guárico, 306	E 3
Santa Rita, Zulia, 5,342	C 2
Santa Rosa, Anzoátegui, 1,036	F 3
Santa Rosa, Apure, 27	D 4
Santa Rosa, Barinas, 957	D 3
Santa Rosa de Amanadona, 163	E 7
Santa Rosalía, 239	F 4
Santa Teresa del Tuy, 6,958	E 2
San Timoteo, 2,823	C 3
San Tomé, 5,625	F 3
San Vicente, Amazonas, 14	E 5
San Vicente, Apure, 252	D 4
Sarare, 2,664	D 3
Seboruco, 2,440	B 3
Simaraña	G 5
Sinamaica, 1,345	B 2
Siquisique, 2,579	D 2
Solano	E 6
Soledad, 5,653	G 3
Sucre, 65	D 3
Suripa, 128	D 4
Tamatama, 35	F 6
Táriba, 9,835	B 4
Temblador, 2,041	G 3
Tia Juana, 5,846	C 2
Timotes, 2,548	C 3
Tinaco, 4,485	D 3
Tinaquillo, 8,142	D 3
Tocópero, 721	D 2
Tocuyo de la Costa, 3,351	D 2
Torunos, 676	C 3
Tovar, 9,614	C 3
Trujillo, 18,957	C 3
Tucacas, 3,853	D 2
Tucupido, 7,016	F 3
Tucupita, 9,922	H 3
Tumeremo, 3,926	H 4
Tupí, 91	D 2
Turén, 341	D 3
Turiamo, 31	E 2
Turmero, 7,639	E 2
Upata, 12,717	G 3
Urachiche, 3,630	D 2
Uracoa, 858	G 3
Urica, 1,577	F 3
Urimán, 237	G 5
Urumaco, 941	C 2
Uruyén	G 5
Uverito, 336	F 3
Valencia, 177,199	E 2
Valencia, *224,552	E 2
Valera, 46,643	C 3
Valle de Guanape, 3,254	F 3
Valle de la Pascua, 24,308	F 3
Villa Bruzual, 10,278	D 3
Villa de Cura, 19,945	E 2
Villa Frontado, 1,597	G 2
Yaguaraparo, 2,673	G 2
Yaritagua, 14,740	D 2
Yavita, 49	E 6
Yerichaña	F 5
Yoco, 2,181	G 2
Zanja de Lira, 58	E 3
Zaraza, 10,084	F 3
Zuata, 783	F 3

OTHER FEATURES

Amacuro (river)	H 4
Angel (Salto Angel) (fall)	G 5
Apongua (river)	H 5
Apure (river)	E 4
Arauca (river)	E 4
Arichuna (river)	D 4
Aro (river)	F 4
Atabapo (river)	E 6
Auyantepui (mt.)	G 5
Baria (river)	E 7
Blanquilla, La (isl.), 46	F 2
Bolívar (mt.)	C 3
Bolívar (mt.)	G 4
Canagua (river)	C 3
Caño Capure (river)	H 3
Caño Macareo (river)	H 3
Caño Mánamo (river)	G 3
Capanaparo (river)	E 4
Caparo (river)	C 4
Caroní (river)	G 4
Carrao (river)	G 5
Caruai (river)	H 5
Casiquiare, Brazo (river)	E 6
Catatumbo (river)	B 3
Caura (river)	F 5
Cerbatana, La (mts.)	E 4
Chicanán (river)	H 4
Chimantá–tepuí (mt.)	G 5
Chivapure (river)	E 4
Cinaruco (river)	D 4
Coche (isl.)	F 2
Codera (cape)	F 2
Cojedes (river)	D 3
Cuao (river)	E 5
Cubagua (isl.)	F 2
Cuchivero (river)	F 4
Cuquenán (river)	H 5
Curutú (river)	G 5
Cuyuni (river)	H 4
Delgado Chalbaud (mt.)	G 6
Dragons Mouth (strait)	H 2
Duida (mt.)	F 6
Erebato (river)	F 5
Gran Sabana, La (plain)	G 5
Guainía (river)	E 6
Guampí (mts.)	F 4
Guanare (river)	D 3
Guanare Viejo (river)	D 3
Guanipa (river)	G 3
Guárico (res.)	E 3
Guárico (river)	E 3
Guayapo (mts.)	E 5
Güere (river)	F 3
Guri (dam)	G 4
Guri (res.)	G 4
Hermanos, Los (isls.)	F 2
Icabaru (river)	G 5
Imataca (mts.)	H 4
Imeri (mts.)	F 7
La Blanquilla (isl.), 46	F 2
La Grand Sabana (plain)	G 5
La Orchila (isl.), 35	F 2
Las Aves (isl.), 6	E 2
La Tortuga (isl.), 25	F 2
Los Hermanos (isls.)	F 2
Los Monjes (isls.)	C 1
Los Roques (isls.), 537	E 2
Los Testigos (isls.), 59	G 2
Macanao (pen.)	F 2
Maigualida (mts.)	F 4
Manapire (river)	E 3
Maracaibo (lake)	C 3
Margarita (isl.), 85,296	F 2
Mavaca (river)	F 6
Médanos (isthmus)	D 2
Merevari (river)	E 4
Mérida (mts.)	C 3
Meta (river)	E 4
Monjes, Los (isls.)	C 1
Morichal Largo (river)	G 3
Neblina (Phelps) (pk.)	E 7
Negro (river)	E 7
Nuria (mts.)	H 4
Ocamo (river)	F 6
Orchila, La (isl.), 35	F 2
Orinoco (delta)	H 3
Orinoco (river)	G 3
Orituco (river)	E 3
Pacaraima (mts.)	G 5
Pao (river)	D 3
Pao (river)	F 3
Paragua (river)	G 4
Paraguaná (peninsula), 104,535	C 1
Paria (gulf)	H 2
Paria (pen.)	G 2
Parida, La (Bolívar) (mt.)	G 4
Parima (mts.)	F 6
Perijá (mts.)	B 2
Phelps (pk.)	E 7
Portuguesa (river)	D 3
Roques, Los (isls.), 537	E 2
Roraima (mt.)	H 5
Salto Angel (fall)	G 5
Sarare (river)	C 4
Serpents Mouth (strait)	H 3
Siapa (river)	E 7
Sipapo (river)	E 5
Suapure (river)	E 4
Suripá (river)	C 4
Tapirapecó (mts.)	F 7
Testigos, Los (isls.), 59	G 2
Tigre (river)	G 3
Tocuco (river)	B 3
Tocuyo (river)	D 2
Tortuga, La (isl.), 25	F 2
Tramán–tepuí (mt.)	G 5
Triste (gulf)	D 2
Turagua (mts.)	F 4
Tuy (river)	E 2
Unare (river)	F 3
Valencia (lake)	E 2
Venamo (mt.)	H 4
Venamo (river)	H 4
Venezuela (gulf)	C 2
Ventuari (river)	E 5
Votamo (river)	F 6
Yatua (river)	E 7
Yuruari (river)	H 4
Zuata (river)	F 3
Zulia (river)	B 3

*City and suburbs.

Agriculture, Industry and Resources

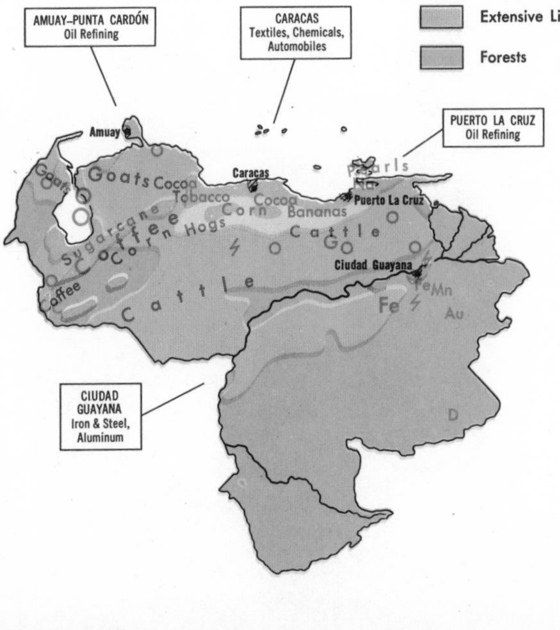

AMUAY–PUNTA CARDÓN Oil Refining
CARACAS Textiles, Chemicals, Automobiles
PUERTO LA CRUZ Oil Refining
CIUDAD GUAYANA Iron & Steel, Aluminum
Amuay
Caracas
Puerto La Cruz
Ciudad Guayana
Pearls
Goats
Cocoa
Tobacco
Cocoa
Corn
Bananas
Sugarcane
Coffee
Corn
Hogs
Cattle
Coffee
Cattle
Fe
Mn
Au
D

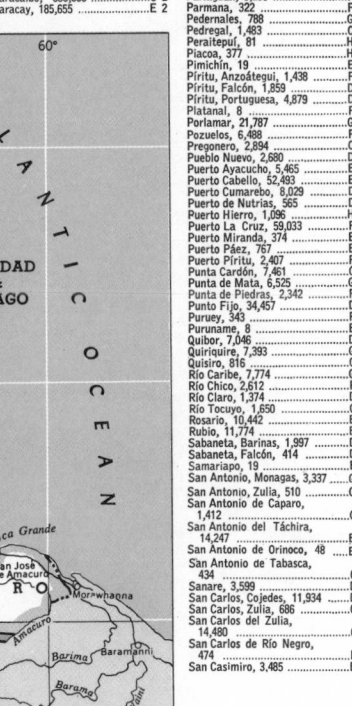

DOMINANT LAND USE

- Diversified Tropical Crops (chiefly plantation agriculture)
- Upland Cultivated Areas
- Upland Livestock Grazing, Limited Agriculture
- Extensive Livestock Ranching
- Forests

MAJOR MINERAL OCCURRENCES

- Au Gold
- C Coal
- D Diamonds
- Fe Iron Ore
- G Natural Gas
- Mn Manganese
- Na Salt
- O Petroleum

- Water Power
- Major Industrial Areas

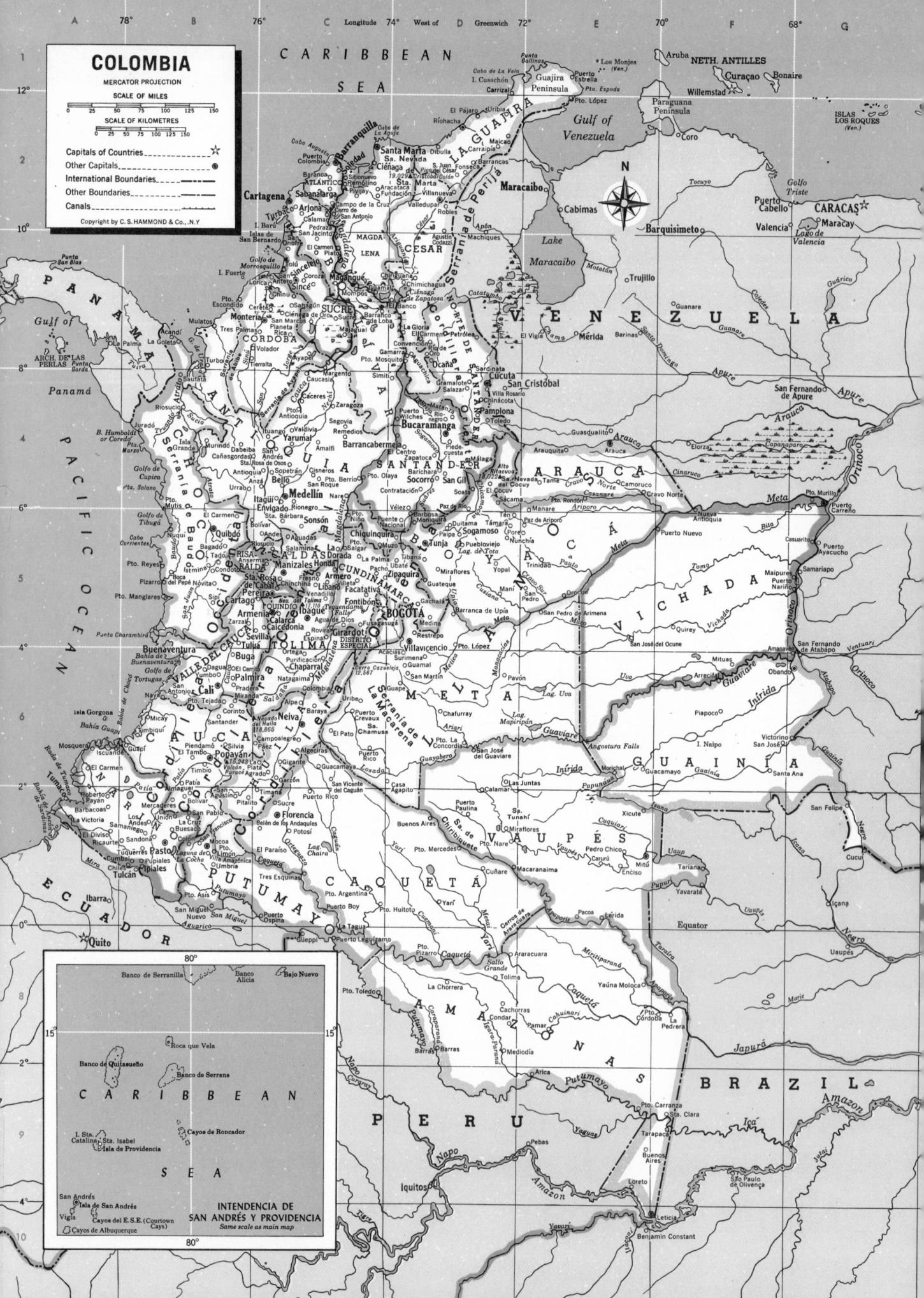

COLOMBIA

MERCATOR PROJECTION

SCALE OF MILES

0 25 50 75 100 125 150

SCALE OF KILOMETRES

0 25 50 75 100 125 150

Capitals of Countries _____ ☆
Other Capitals _____ ●
International Boundaries _____
Other Boundaries _____
Canals _____

Copyright by C. S. HAMMOND & Co., .,N.Y

Longitude West of Greenwich

CARIBBEAN SEA

NETH. ANTILLES

PANAMA

PACIFIC OCEAN

VENEZUELA

CARACAS ☆

BOGOTA

ECUADOR

PERU

BRAZIL

INTENDENCIA DE
SAN ANDRÉS Y PROVIDENCIA
Same scale as main map

CARIBBEAN SEA

Colombia 95

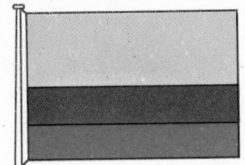

AREA 439,513 sq. mi.
POPULATION 21,117,000
CAPITAL Bogotá
LARGEST CITY Bogotá
HIGHEST POINT Pico Cristóbal Colón 19,029 ft.
MONETARY UNIT Colombian peso
MAJOR LANGUAGE Spanish
MAJOR RELIGION Roman Catholicism

INTERNAL DIVISIONS

Amazonas (intendency), 16,000....D 8
Antioquia (dept.), 3,031,000....C 4
Arauca (commissary), 32,000....C 4
Atlántico (dept.), 903,000....C 2
Bolívar (dept.), 849,000....C 3
Boyacá (dept.), 1,194,000....D 5
Caldas (dept.), 810,000....C 4
Caquetá (intendency), 157,000....C 7
Cauca (dept.), 696,000....B 6
Cesar (dept.), 357,000....C 2
Chocó (dept.), 210,000....B 4
Córdoba (dept.), 760,000....C 3
Cundinamarca (dept.), 1,187,000....C 5
Distrito Especial, 2,416,000....C 5
Guainía (comm.), 5,000....F 6
Guajira, La (dept.), 173,000....D 2
Huila (dept.), 485,000....C 6
La Guajira (dept.), 173,000....D 2
Magdalena (dept.), 683,000....D 3
Meta (dept.), 248,000....D 6
Nariño (dept.), 767,000....B 7
Norte de Santander (dept.), 615,000....D 4
Putumayo (comm.), 77,000....C 7
Quindío (dept.), 346,000....C 5
Risaralda (dept.), 512,000....C 5
San Andrés y Providencia (intendency), 27,000....B10
Santander (dept.), 1,137,000....D 4
Sucre (dept.), 361,000....C 2
Tolima (dept.), 902,000....C 5
Valle del Cauca (dept.), 2,114,000....B 6
Vaupés (commissary), 18,000....E 7
Vichada (commissary), 9,000....F 5

CITIES and TOWNS

Acacías, 6,508....D 6
Acandí, 1,886....B 3
Agrado, 2,751....C 6
Agua de Dios, 7,401....C 5
Aguachica, 8,556....D 3
Aguadas, 10,822....C 4
Agustín Codazzi, 11,673....D 3
Aipe, 3,404....C 6
Algeciras, 3,778....C 6
Almaguer, 1,251....B 7
Amalfi, 4,667....C 4
Amanavén, 11,164....F 6
Andes, 11,135....B 5
Anserma, 14,129....B 5
Antioquia, 6,002....B 4
Anza, 680....B 4
Aracataca, 5,304....D 2
Aracatuara....E 8
Arauca, 4,280....E 4
Arauquita, 413....E 4
Arjona, 16,510....C 2
Armenia, 162,837....B 5
Armero, 17,495....C 5
Ayapel, 5,610....C 3
Bagadó, 865....B 5
Baranoa, 14,064....C 2
Baraya, 2,696....C 6
Barbacoas, 4,011....A 7
Barbosa, 6,018....C 4
Barichara, 2,798....D 4
Barrancabermeja, 59,625....D 4
Barrancas, 2,010....D 2
Barranco de Loba, 1,648....C 3
Barranquilla, 816,706....C 2
Belén de los Andaquíes, 1,420....C 7
Bello, 127,377....B 4
Boca del Pepé, 566....B 4
Bogotá (cap.), 2,037,904....D 5
Bogotá, *2,416,000....D 5
Bolívar, Antioquia, 9,532....C 5
Bolívar, Cauca, 3,641....B 7
Bucaramanga, 279,703....D 4
Buenaventura, 113,301....B 6
Buesaco, 2,278....B 7
Buga, 65,535....B 6
Caicedonia, 16,327....C 5
Calamar, Bolívar, 6,055....C 3
Calamar, Vaupés....D 7
Calarcá, 30,342....C 5
Cali, 820,809....B 6
Camoruco....E 4
Campo de la Cruz, 10,044....C 2
Campoalegre, 9,768....C 6
Cañasgordas, 4,464....B 4
Cartagena, 229,040....C 2
Cartago, 55,682....B 5
Carurú, 277....E 7
Casuarito, 175....G 4
Caucasia, 5,616....C 3
Cereté, 11,849....C 3
Cerro de San Antonio, 3,397....C 2
Chaparral, 13,261....C 5
Chimichagua, 5,093....D 3
Chinácota, 4,081....D 4
Chinchiná, 15,944....C 5
Chinú, 7,552....C 3
Chiquinquirá, 16,926....D 4
Chiriguaná, 6,516....D 3
Ciénaga, 142,893....C 2
Ciénaga de Oro, 8,047....C 3
Cisneros, 7,554....C 4
Colombia, 1,599....C 6
Colón, 1,133....C 7
Condoto, 4,094....B 5
Contratación, 3,117....D 4
Convención, 7,371....D 3
Corinto, 5,008....B 6
Corozal, 14,000....C 3
Cravo Norte, 566....F 4
Cúcuta, 207,091....D 4
Cumbal, 2,549....B 7
Cuñare....D 7
Dabeiba, 4,218....B 4
Dagua, 4,635....B 6
Dibulla....D 2
Duitama, 31,865....D 4
El Banco, 14,889....D 3
El Carmen, Chocó, 1,689....B 5
El Carmen, Norte de Santander, 2,737....D 3
El Carmen de Bolívar, 19,196....C 3
El Cerrito, 12,200....B 6
El Cocuy, 2,869....D 4
El Tambo, 4,003....B 6
Envigado, 40,686....C 4
Espinal, 22,591....C 5
Facatativá, 20,742....C 5
Florencia, 17,709....C 7
Fonseca, 5,190....D 2
Fontibón....C 5
Fresno, 7,058....C 5
Fundación, 14,128....D 2
Fusagasugá, 18,755....C 5
Gachalá, 1,253....D 5
Gamarra, 4,664....D 3
Garzón, 11,999....C 6
Gigante, 4,594....C 6
Girardot, 66,584....C 5
Gramalote, 5,098....D 4
Guacamaya....C 6
Guamal, Magdalena, 4,695....C 3
Guamal, Meta, 2,113....D 6
Guape....C 6
Guapi, 3,066....B 6
Guateque, 4,646....D 5
Honda, 19,945....C 5
Ibagué, 178,821....C 5
Ipiales, 23,320....B 7
Iscuandé, 1,777....A 6
Istmina, 3,996....B 5
Itagüí, 101,066....C 4
Ituango, 3,466....C 4
Juradó, 708....B 4
La Cruz, 4,014....B 7
La Dorada, 26,168....C 5
La Gloria, 2,915....D 3
La Palma, 4,594....C 5
La Plata, 5,863....C 6
La Unión, 3,875....B 7
Leticia, 4,013....F10
Líbano, 18,640....C 5
Lorica, 12,880....C 3
Los Andes, 1,392....B 7
Macaranaima....E 7
Magangué, 27,354....C 3
Maicao, 9,347....D 2
Maipures....F 5
Majagual, 2,197....C 3
Málaga, 9,674....D 4
Manare....D 5
Maní, 586....D 5
Manizales, 267,543....C 5
Matanza, 1,264....D 4
Medellín, 967,825....C 4
Medina, 899....D 5
Mercaderes, 2,376....B 7
Micay....B 6
Miraflores, Boyacá, 3,257....D 5
Miraflores, Vaupés, 245....E 7
Miranda, 5,527....B 6
Mitú, 1,623....F 6
Mituas....F 6
Mocoa, 2,571....B 7
Mompós, 10,965....C 3
Moniquirá, 4,882....D 4
Montería, 167,446....C 3
Morichal, 572....E 7
Mosquera, 766....A 6
Murindó, 319....B 4
Muzo, 792....C 5
Natagaima, 8,372....C 6
Naya....B 6
Neiva, 111,727....C 6
Nóvita, 883....B 5
Nueva Antioquia, 1,236....F 5
Nunchía, 461....D 5
Nuquí, 1,500....B 5
Obando....G 6
Ocaña, 28,028....D 3
Orocué, 1,600....D 5
Ortega, 4,450....C 6
Pacho, 7,192....C 5
Pacoa, 1960....D 7
Páez, 1,570....C 6
Pailitas, 3,105....D 3
Palmira, 164,394....B 6
Pamplona, 25,502....D 4
Pasto, 123,153....B 7
Patía, 3,045....B 6
Paz de Ariporo, 2,126....E 5
Paz del Río, 2,748....D 4
Pedraza, 1,757....C 2
Pereira, 224,421....C 5
Piedecuesta, 12,278....D 4
Pitalito, 10,818....B 7
Pivijay, 8,200....C 2
Planeta Rica, 5,959....C 3
Plato, 13,364....C 3
Popayán, 58,500....B 6
Pore, 193....D 5
Potosí, 1,149....B 7
Pradera, 11,223....B 6
Puente Nacional, 2,913....D 4
Puerto Asís, 2,902....B 7
Puerto Berrío, 15,812....C 4
Puerto Carreño, 1,115....G 4
Puerto Colombia, 7,143....C 2
Puerto Escondido, 1,543....B 3
Puerto Leguízamo, 3,014....C 8
Puerto López, La Guajira....E 2
Puerto López, Meta, 3,586....D 5
Puerto Murillo, 11,014....C 4
Puerto Nariño, 1926....F 5
Puerto Rico, Caquetá, 110,328....C 7
Puerto Rico, Meta....C 6
Puerto Rondón, 951....E 4
Puerto Salgar, 6,398....C 5
Puerto Tejada, 14,863....B 6
Puerto Wilches, 4,635....D 4
Pupiales, 2,432....B 7
Purificación, 7,044....C 6
Quibdó, 19,989....B 5
Remedios, 2,090....C 4
Remolino, 3,373....C 2
Restrepo, 2,803....D 5
Ricaurte, 866....A 7
Río de Oro, 2,482....D 3
Riohacha, 11,708....D 2
Rionegro, Antioquia, 2,708....C 4
Rionegro, Santander, 12,541....C 4
Riosucio, Caldas, 11,274....C 5
Riosucio, Chocó, 1,817....B 4
Roberto Payán, 402....A 7
Robles, 4,278....D 2
Rovira, 4,582....C 5
Sabanalarga, 20,254....C 2
Sácama, 54....D 4
Sahagún, 11,560....C 3
Salamina, 14,263....C 4
Salazar, 3,020....D 4
Samaniego, 3,373....B 7
San Agustín, 3,250....B 7
San Andrés, Antioquia, 1,773....C 4
San Andrés, San Andrés y Providencia, 9,040....A10
San Antero, 6,596....C 3
San Felipe, 187....G 7
San Francisco, 1,248....D 4
San Gil, 18,518....D 4
San Jacinto, 10,210....C 3
San José del Guaviare, 215....D 6
San José del Ocune, 105....E 5
San Juan del César, 9,347....D 2
San Marcos, 7,083....C 3
San Martín, 6,739....D 6
San Onofre, 10,737....C 2
San Pablo, 4,103....B 7
San Roque, 3,272....C 4
San Vicente del Caguán, 1,764....C 6
Sandoná, 6,776....B 7
Santa Bárbara, 7,779....C 5
Santa Isabel, 468....B 9
Santa Marta, 137,474....C 2
Santa Rosa de Cabal, 31,646....C 5
Santa Rosa de Osos, 6,860....C 4
Santander, 11,426....B 6
Santiago, 929....B 7
Sardinata, 2,964....D 4
Segovia, 9,234....C 4
Sevilla, 26,757....C 5
Sibundoy-Las Casas, 1,999....B 7
Silvia, 3,180....B 6
Simití, 2,825....C 4
Sincé, 10,631....C 3
Sincelejo, 44,001....C 3
Sipí, 155....B 5
Sitionuevo, 5,969....C 2
Soatá, 4,361....D 4
Socorro, 13,716....D 4
Sogamoso, 32,274....D 5
Soledad, 37,617....C 2
Sonsón, 16,955....C 4
Sucre, Bolívar, 3,035....C 3
Sucre, Caquetá....C 7
Támara, 1,034....D 5
Tame, 3,063....E 4
Cazuelá (mt.)....D 5
Tierralta, 4,415....C 3
Timaná, 2,999....C 7
Timbío, 4,145....B 6
Timbiquí, 1,406....B 6
Toledo, 2,314....D 4
Tolú, 7,954....C 3
Trinidad, 572....E 5
Tuluá, 56,539....B 6
Tumaco, 25,145....A 7
Tunja, 40,451....D 5
Túquerres, 10,698....B 7
Turbaco, 14,259....C 2
Turbo, 7,375....B 3
Ubaté, 6,261....D 5
Uribia, 1,763....D 2
Urrao, 7,712....B 4
Valdivia, 2,264....C 4
Valledupar, 120,009....C 2
Vélez, 7,033....D 4
Venadillo, 6,931....C 5
Villanueva, 8,288....D 2
Villa Amazónica, 1,344....D 7
Villa Rosario, 5,184....D 4
Villavicencio, 45,277....D 5
Villeta, 5,290....C 5
Yarumal, 16,823....C 4
Yavaraté, 11,963....F 7
Yopal, 2,878....D 5
Yumbo, 15,270....B 6
Zapatoca, 7,305....D 4
Zaragoza, 2,134....C 4
Zarzal, 17,768....C 5
Zipaquirá, 22,648....C 5

OTHER FEATURES

Abibe (mts.)....B 4
Aguja (cape)....C 2
Albuquerque (cays)....A10
Alicia (bank)....B 8
Alto Ritacuva (mt.)....D 4
Amazon (Amazonas) (river)....E 9
Ancón de Sardinas (bay)....A 7
Angostura (falls)....F 8
Araracuara (mts.)....E 8
Arauca (river)....E 4
Ariari (river)....D 6
Ariguaní (river)....D 2
Ariporo (river)....E 5
Atabapo (river)....G 6
Atrato (river)....B 3
Augusta (lake)....C 2
Ayapel (mts.)....C 4
Bajo Nuevo (shoal)....C 8
Baudó (mts.)....B 5
Baudó (river)....B 4
Bita (river)....F 5
Caguán (river)....C 7
Cahuinarí (river)....E 8
Caquetá (river)....D 8
Caraparaná (river)....D 8
Casanare (river)....E 5
Cauca (river)....C 3
Central (mts.)....C 5
Chaira (lagoon)....C 7
Chamusa (mts.)....C 4
Charambirá (point)....B 5
Chiribiquete (mts.)....D 7
Chocó (bay)....B 4
Cocha (lake)....B 7
Cocuy (mts.)....D 4
Coredó (Humboldt) (bay)....B 4
Corrientes (cape)....B 4
Courtown (Este Sudeste) (cays)....A10
Cravo Norte (river)....E 4
Cravo Sur (river)....D 5
Cristóbal Colón (mt.)....D 2
Cuemaní (river)....C 8
Cupica (gulf)....B 4
Cuquiarí (river)....F 6
Cusiana (river)....D 5
Este Sudeste (cays)....A10
Gallinas (point)....E 1
Grande (isl.)....C 2
Guainía (river)....E 6
Guajira (pen.)....D 2
Guapi (bay)....A 6
Guaviare (river)....E 6
Guayabero (river)....D 6
Huila (mt.)....C 6
Humboldt (Coredó) (bay)....B 4
Igara-Paraná (river)....D 8
Inírida (river)....E 6
Isana (river)....F 7
Lebrija (river)....D 4
Llanos (plains)....D 5
Losada (river)....C 6
Macarena (mts.)....D 6
Magdalena (river)....C 6
Manacacías (river)....D 6
Mapiripán (lake)....D 6
Marzo (cape)....B 4
Mesai (river)....D 7
Meta (river)....E 5
Metica (river)....D 6
Mirritiparaná (river)....E 8
Morrosquillo (gulf)....C 3
Muco (river)....E 5
Naipo (isl.)....C 6
Nechí (river)....C 3
Occidental, Cordillera (mts.)....B 5
Oriental, Cordillera (mts.)....C 5
Ortequaza (river)....C 7
Papunáua (river)....E 6
Patía (river)....B 6
Pauto (river)....E 5
Perijá (mts.)....D 2
Providencia (isl.), 2,318....B 9
Pupurí (river)....F 7
Puracé (volcano)....B 6
Putumayo (river)....C 8
Quitasueño (bank)....A 9
Riosucio (river)....B 3
Roncador (bank)....B 9
Saldaña (river)....C 5
Salto Grande (falls)....A 7
San Andrés (isl.), 14,413....A10
San Jorge (river)....C 3
San Juan (river)....B 5
Santa Marta, Nev. de (range)....D 2
Serrana (bank)....B 9
Serranilla (bank)....C 8
Sinú (river)....C 3
Sogamoso (river)....D 4
Solano (point)....B 4
Suárez (river)....D 4
Taraira (river)....F 7
Tequendama (falls)....C 5
Tibugá (gulf)....B 4
Tolima (mt.)....C 5
Tomo (river)....F 5
Tortugas (gulf)....B 6
Truandó (river)....B 4
Tumaco (inlet)....A 6
Tunahí (mts.)....E 7
Upía (river)....D 5
Urabá (gulf)....B 3
Uva (lake)....E 6
Uva (river)....E 6
Vaupés (river)....E 7
Vela (cape)....D 1
Vela, Roca que (cay)....D 1
Vichada (river)....E 5
Yarí (river)....D 7
Zapatosa (swamp)....D 3

*City and suburbs.

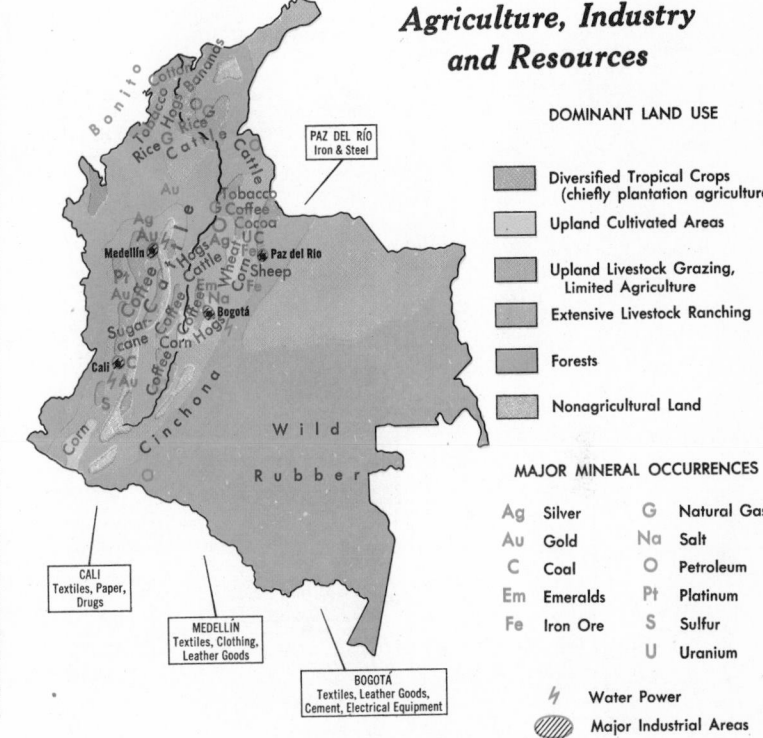

Agriculture, Industry and Resources

DOMINANT LAND USE

Diversified Tropical Crops (chiefly plantation agriculture)
Upland Cultivated Areas
Upland Livestock Grazing, Limited Agriculture
Extensive Livestock Ranching
Forests
Nonagricultural Land

MAJOR MINERAL OCCURRENCES

Ag Silver
Au Gold
C Coal
Em Emeralds
Fe Iron Ore
G Natural Gas
Na Salt
O Petroleum
Pt Platinum
S Sulfur
U Uranium

⚡ Water Power
▨ Major Industrial Areas

PAZ DEL RÍO — Iron & Steel
CALI — Textiles, Paper, Drugs
MEDELLÍN — Textiles, Clothing, Leather Goods
BOGOTÁ — Textiles, Leather Goods, Cement, Electrical Equipment

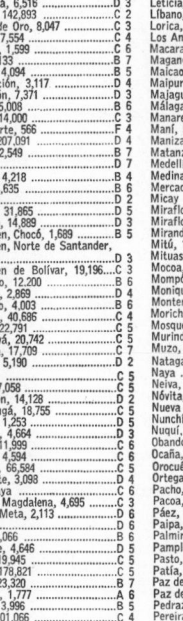

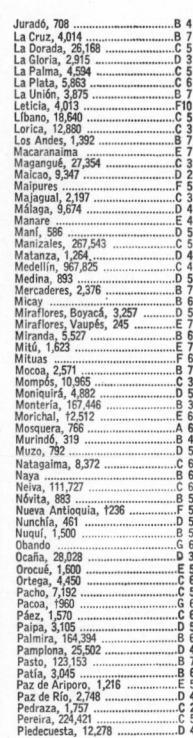

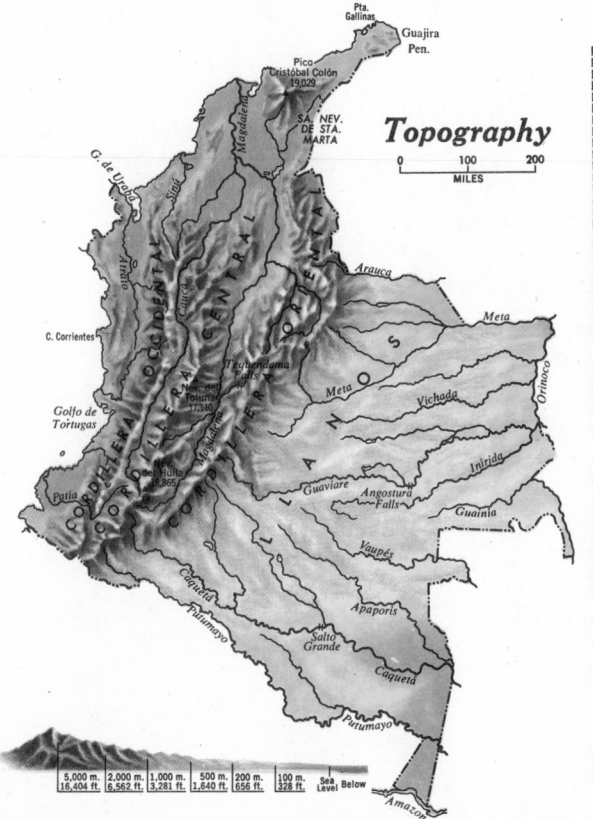

Topography

0   100   200
MILES

5,000 m. 16,404 ft. | 2,000 m. 6,562 ft. | 1,000 m. 3,281 ft. | 500 m. 1,640 ft. | 200 m. 656 ft. | 100 m. 328 ft. | Sea Level | Below

96 Guianas

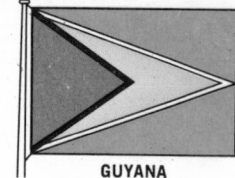

GUYANA

FRENCH GUIANA
AREA 35,135 sq. mi.
POPULATION 48,000
CAPITAL Cayenne
LARGEST CITY Cayenne
HIGHEST POINT 2,723 ft.
MONETARY UNIT French franc
MAJOR LANGUAGE French
MAJOR RELIGIONS Roman Cath.
Protestantism

GUYANA
AREA 83,000 sq. mi.
POPULATION 763,000
CAPITAL Georgetown
LARGEST CITY Georgetown
HIGHEST POINT Mt. Roraima 9,094 ft.
MONETARY UNIT British West Indian dollar
MAJOR LANGUAGES English, Hindi
MAJOR RELIGIONS Christianity, Hinduism, Islam

SURINAM
AREA 55,144 sq. mi.
POPULATION 389,000
CAPITAL Paramaribo
LARGEST CITY Paramaribo
HIGHEST POINT Julianatop 4,200 ft.
MONETARY UNIT Surinam guilder
MAJOR LANGUAGES Dutch, Hindi, Indonesian
MAJOR RELIGIONS Christianity, Islam, Hinduism

FRENCH GUIANA

DISTRICTS

Cayenne, 41,724	E 3
Inini, 2,668	E 4

CITIES and TOWNS

Bélizon	E 3
Bienvenue	E 4
Camopi, 1276	E 4
Cayenne, *24,581	E 4
Cayenne, (cap.), 19,668	E 3
Clément	E 4
Counamama	E 3
Délices	E 3
Edmond	E 3
Grand-Santi, 60	D 3
Guisambourg	E 3
Inini	E 4
Iracoubo, 504	E 3
Kaw, 258	E 3
Kourou, 868	E 3
Macouria (Tonate), 301	E 3
Malmanoury	E 3
Mana, 568	E 3
Maripa	E 4
Maripasoula, 166	D 4
Montsinéry, 107	E 3
Organobo	E 3
Oscar	E 4
Ouanary, 79	F 3
Ouaqui	D 4
P. I. (Paul Isnard), 147	D 3
Paul Isnard, 147	E 3
Régina	E 3
Rémire, 650	E 3
Roura, 84	E 3
Saint-Élie, 78	E 3
Saint-Georges-de-l'Oyapoc, 502	F 4
Saint-Jean	E 3
Saint-Laurent-du-Maroni, 3,486	E 3
Saül, 81	D 3
Saut-Tigre	E 3
Sinnamary, 1,355	E 3
Tonate, 301	E 3

OTHER FEATURES

Approuague (river)	E 4
Araous (mts.)	D 4
Béhague (point)	F 3
Camopi (river)	E 4
Chaîne Granitique (range)	E 4
Comté (river)	E 3
Connétable (isl.)	F 3
Devil's (isl.)	E 3
Granitique, Chaîne (range)	E 4
Inini (river)	E 4
Itany (river)	D 4
Mana (river)	D 3
Maroni (river)	D 3
Marouini (river)	D 4
Oyapock (river)	E 3
Rémire (isl.)	F 3
Saint-Marcel (mt.)	E 3
Salut (isls.)	F 3
Sinnamary (river)	E 3
Tampoc (river)	E 4

GUYANA

DISTRICTS

East Berbice, 115,511	C 3
East Demerara, 256,908	B 2
Essequibo, 29,729	B 2
Essequibo Islands, 15,728	B 2
Mazaruni-Potaro, 12,029	A 2
North West, 12,809	A 2
Rupununi, 30,588	B 4
West Berbice, 26,524	C 2
West Demerara, 81,061	B 3

CITIES and TOWNS

Adventure, 507	B 2
Anna Regina, 848	B 4
Annai	B 4
Apoteri	B 2
Arakaka	B 2
Atkinson Field	B 2
Aurora	B 2
Baramanni	B 2
Baramita	A 2
Bartica, 2,352	B 2
Biloku	B 5
Charity, 838	B 2
Christianburg-Wismar-Mackenzie, 5,843	B 2
Dadanawa	B 4
Danielstown, 478	B 2
Enmore	C 2
Enterprise	B 2
Epira	A 2
Five Stars	A 2
Fort Wellington	B 2
Georgetown (cap.), 97,190	B 2
Georgetown, *102,688	B 2
Imbaimadai	A 3
Issano	A 3
Isseru	A 2

Kamarang, 510	A 3
Karasabai	B 4
Kwakwani	C 3
Lethem	B 4
Lumid Pau	B 4
Mabaruma, 343	B 1
Mahaica, 8,646	C 2
Mahaicony, 8,272	B 2
Mahdia	B 3
Mara	B 2
Morawhanna, 305	B 1
Mount Everard	B 2
New Amsterdam, 14,300	C 2
Orealla	C 3
Paradise	C 2
Parika, 577	B 2
Pickersgill, 334	B 2
Port Kaituma	B 2
Queenstown, 1,067	B 2
Rockstone	B 2
Rosignol, 1,204	C 2
Skeldon, 4,367	C 2
Springlands, 181	C 2
Suddie, 512	B 2
Tumereng	B 2
Vreed-en-Hoop, 3,156	B 2
Wichabai	B 4
Yupukari	B 4

OTHER FEATURES

Akarai (mts.)	B 5
Amakara (river)	A 2
Amuku (river)	A 2
Barama (river)	A 2
Barima (river)	A 2
Berbice (river)	B 3
Burro-Burro (river)	B 3
Cabural (mt.)	A 3
Canje (river)	C 3
Courantyne (river)	C 3
Cuyuni (river)	B 2
Demerara (river)	B 2
Enwarak (mt.)	B 3
Essequibo (river)	B 3
Great (fall)	B 3
Ireng (river)	B 3
Kaieteur (fall)	B 3
Kamaria (falls)	B 2
Kamoa (river)	B 5
Kanuku (mts.)	B 4
Kurungku (mts.)	A 3
Kuyuwini (river)	B 4
Kwitaro (river)	B 4
Leguan (isl.), 6,567	B 2
Marudi (mts.)	B 5
Mazaruni (river)	A 2
Moruka (river)	B 2
New (river)	C 4
Pakaraima (mts.)	A 3
Playa (point)	B 1
Pomeroon (river)	B 2
Potaro (river)	B 3
Puruni (river)	B 2
Roraima (mt.)	A 3
Rupununi (river)	B 4
Venamo (mt.)	A 3
Waini (river)	A 3
Wenamu (river)	A 2

SURINAM

DISTRICTS

Brokopondo, 1,376	D 4
Commewijne, 18,796	D 3
Coronie, 4,069	C 3
Marowijne, 10,074	D 4
Nickerie, 24,730	C 3
Para	D 3
Paramaribo, 122,634	D 3
Saramacca, 10,979	D 3
Suriname, 80,870	D 3

CITIES and TOWNS

Albina, 1,000	D 3
Berg-en-Dal	D 3
Brokopondo	D 3

Calcutta, 1,100	D 3
Cottica	D 4
Domburg, 1,200	D 3
Groningen, 600	D 3
Lelydorp, 300	D 3
Marienburg, 3,500	D 3
Moengo, 2,100	D 3
Nieuw-Amsterdam, 1,400	D 3
Nieuw-Nickerie, 7,400	C 3
Paramaribo (cap.), 110,867	D 3
Paramaribo, *182,100	D 3
Paranam	D 3
Saramaccapolder	D 3
Totness, 1,300	C 3
Wageningen, 800	C 3

OTHER FEATURES

Bakhuys (mts.)	C 3
Blanche Marie (fall)	C 4
Coeroeni (river)	C 4
Commewijne (river)	D 3
Coppename (river)	C 3
Corantijn (river)	C 3
Cottica (river)	D 3
Frederik Willem IV (falls)	C 4
Julianatop (mt.)	C 4
Kayser (mts.)	D 3
Lely (mts.)	D 3
Litani (river)	D 4
Lucie (river)	C 4
Marowijne (river)	D 4
Nickerie (river)	C 3
Oelemari (river)	D 4
Orange (mts.)	D 4
Saramacca (river)	C 3
Sipaliwini (river)	C 4
Suriname (river)	D 3
Tapanahoni (river)	D 3
Toekomstig (res.)	D 3
Van Blommestein (lake)	D 3
Wilhelmina (mts.)	C 4

*City and suburbs.
†Population of municipality.

Topography

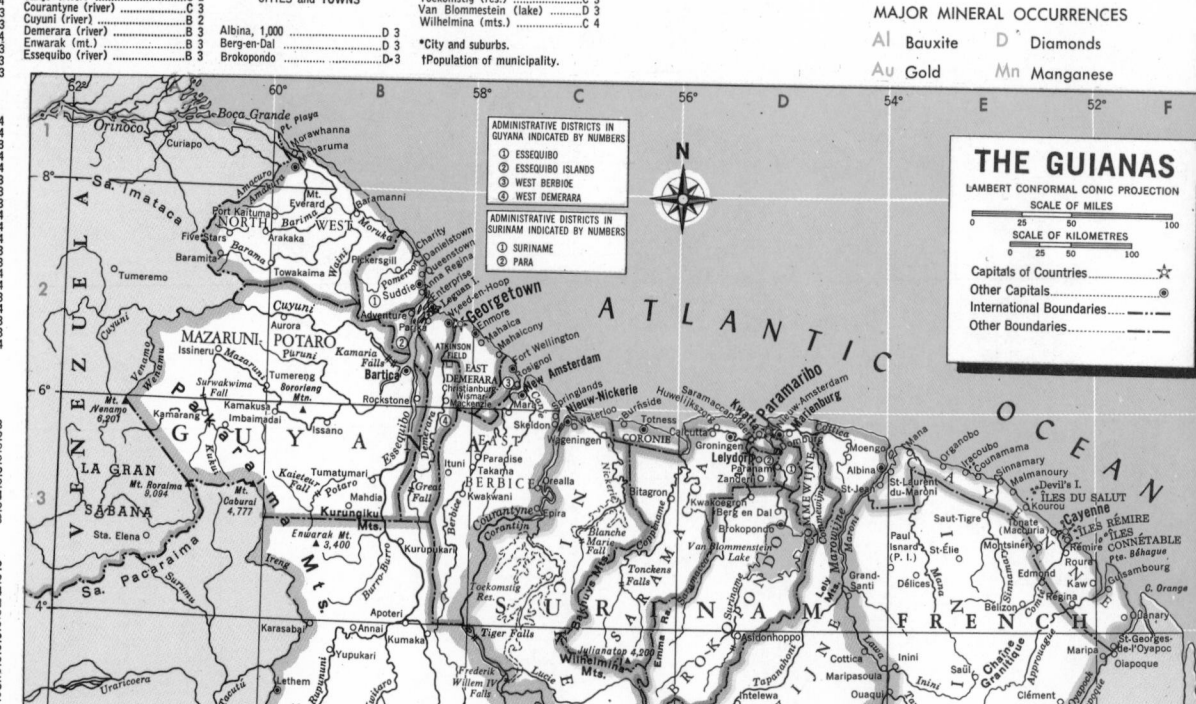

DOMINANT LAND USE

Agriculture, Industry and Resources

- Diversified Tropical Crops (chiefly plantation agriculture)
- Extensive Livestock Ranching
- Forests
- Water Power

MAJOR MINERAL OCCURRENCES

Al	Bauxite	D	Diamonds
Au	Gold	Mn	Manganese

THE GUIANAS
LAMBERT CONFORMAL CONIC PROJECTION
SCALE OF MILES
SCALE OF KILOMETRES

Capitals of Countries ☆
Other Capitals ◉
International Boundaries
Other Boundaries

ADMINISTRATIVE DISTRICTS IN GUYANA INDICATED BY NUMBERS
① ESSEQUIBO
② ESSEQUIBO ISLANDS
③ WEST BERBICE
④ WEST DEMERARA

ADMINISTRATIVE DISTRICTS IN SURINAM INDICATED BY NUMBERS
① SURINAME
② PARA

Copyright by C. S. HAMMOND & Co., Maplewood, N. J.

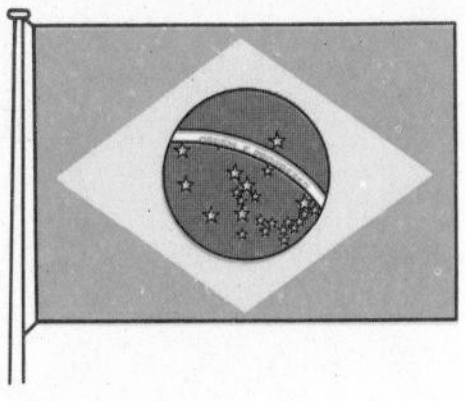

AREA 3,284,426 sq. mi.
POPULATION 90,840,000
CAPITAL Brasília
LARGEST CITY São Paulo (greater)
HIGHEST POINT Pico da Neblina 9,889 ft.
MONETARY UNIT cruzeiro
MAJOR LANGUAGE Portuguese
MAJOR RELIGION Roman Catholicism

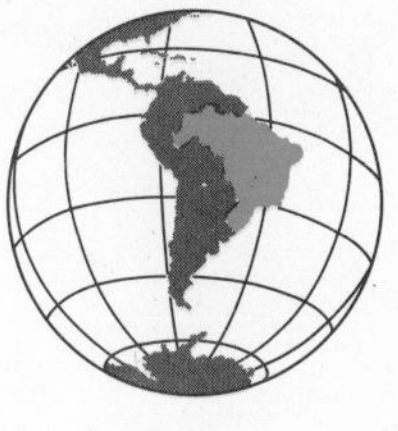

STATES and TERRITORIES

Acre, 196,000 ....G10
Alagoas, 1,381,000 ....G 5
Amapá (terr.), 100,000 ....D 2
Amazonas, 875,000 ....G 9
Bahia, 6,778,000 ....F 6
Ceará, 3,764,000 ....G 4
Espírito Santo, 1,446,000 ....F 7
Federal District, 348,000 ....E 6
Goiás, 2,950,000 ....D 6
Guanabara, 4,007,000 ....F 8, †E 3
Guaporé (Rondônia) (terr.), 97,000 ....H10
Maranhão, 3,314,000 ....E 4
Mato Grosso, 1,293,000 ....B 6
Minas Gerais, 11,230,000 ....E 7, †D 2
Pará, 1,872,000 ....C 4
Paraíba, 2,219,000 ....G 4
Paraná, 6,743,000 ....D 9, †B 4
Pernambuco, 4,645,000 ....G 5
Piauí, 1,391,000 ....F 4
Rio de Janeiro, 4,340,000 ....F 8, †E 3
Rio Grande do Norte, 1,271,000 ....G 4
Rio Grande do Sul, 6,397,000 ....C10
Rondônia (terr.), 107,000 ....H10
Roraima (terr.), 40,000 ....H 8
Santa Catarina, 2,624,000 ....D 9
São Paulo, 16,081,000 ....D 8, †B 2
Sergipe, 838,000 ....G 5

CITIES and TOWNS

Abaeté, 7,988 ....E 7
Abaetetuba, 11,196 ....D 3
Acaraú, 3,042 ....F 3
Acopiara, 3,953 ....G 4
Acorizal, 892 ....C 6
Açu, 8,158 ....G 4
Afuá, 600 ....D 3
Agudos, 6,564 ....†B 3
Alagoa Grande, 12,115 ....H 4
Alagoinhas, 38,246 ....G 6
Alcobaça, 1,812 ....G 7
Alegre, 7,487 ....†F 2
Alegrete, 33,735 ....B10
Além Paraíba, 18,399 ....†E 2
Alenquer, 7,027 ....C 3
Alfenas, 16,051 ....†C 2
Alfredo Chaves, 1,209 ....F 8
Altamira, 2,939 ....C 3
Alto Araguaia, 2,077 ....C 7
Alto Longa, 784 ....F 4
Alto Parnaiba, 1,300 ....E 5
Altos, 5,056 ....F 4
Amambaí, 2,601 ....C 8
Amarante, 3,199 ....F 4
Amargosa, 6,059 ....F 6
Americana, 32,000 ....†C 3
Amparo, 14,348 ....†C 3
Anápolis, 48,847 ....D 7
Andaraí, 2,510 ....F 6
Angra dos Reis, 10,634 ....†D 3
Anicuns, 3,642 ....D 7
Andrelândia, 4,617 ....†D 2
Antonina, 8,520 ....†B 4
Aparecida, 15,290 ....†D 3
Apiaí, 2,728 ....†B 4
Aquidauana, 11,997 ....C 8
Aracaju, *156,243 ....G 5
Aracati, 11,016 ....G 4
Araçatuba, 53,563 ....†A 2
Araçuaí, 6,763 ....F 7
Araguacema, 1,745 ....D 5
Araguaiana, 568 ....C 6
Araguari, 35,520 ....D 7
Araioses, 1,487 ....F 3
Araranguá, 7,775 ....D10
Araraquara, 58,076 ....†B 2
Araras, 23,898 ....†C 3
Arari, 4,004 ....E 3
Araxá, 24,041 ....E 7
Arcoverde, 18,008 ....G 5
Areia Branca, 8.904 ....G 4
Aripuanã, 178 ....B 5
Arraias, 1,446 ....E 6
Assis, 30,207 ....†A 3
Aurora, 3,622 ....G 4
Avaré, 20,334 ....†B 3
Bacabal, *19,753 ....E 4
Bagé, 47,930 ....C10
Bahia (Salvador), *892,392 ....G 6
Baião, 2,265 ....D 3
Baixo Guandu, 6,975 ....F 7
Balsas, 1,946 ....E 4
Bambuí, 8,148 ....†C 2
Barão de Cocais, 7,223 ....†E 1
Barbacena, 41,931 ....†E 2
Barcelos, 1,904 ....H 9
Bariri, 8,403 ....†B 3
Barra, 7,237 ....F 5
Barra-do-Bugres, 658 ....B 6
Barra-do-Corda, 3,723 ....E 4
Barra do Piraí, 29,398 ....†E 3
Barra Mansa, 47,398 ....†D 3
Barras, 3,388 ....F 4
Barreiras, 7,175 ....E 6
Barreirinha, 701 ....B 3
Barreirinhas, 2,184 ....F 3
Barreiros, 10,402 ....H 5
Barretos, 39,950 ....†B 2
Batalha, 15,559 ....F 3
Batatais, 15,266 ....†C 2
Baturité, 7,198 ....G 4
Bauru, *110,961 ....†B 3
Bebedouro, 18,249 ....†B 2
Bela Vista, 8,878 ....C 8
Bela Vista de Goiás, 2,687 ....D 7
Belém, *563,996 ....E 3
Belmonte, 7,897 ....G 6
Belo Horizonte, *1,167,026 ....†D 1
Belo Horizonte, ‡1,300,000 ....†D 1
Beneditinos, 828 ....F 4
Benjamin Constant, 3,224 ....G 9
Bento Gonçalves, 13,662 ....C10
Bertolínia, 714 ....F 4
Betim, 8,963 ....†D 2
Bicas, 7,469 ....†E 2
Birigui, 18,721 ....†A 2
Blumenau, 46,591 ....D 9
Boa Esperança, 9,263 ....†D 2
Boa Vista, 10,180 ....H 8
Bôca do Acre, 2,994 ....G10
Bocaiúva, 5,952 ....E 7
Boiaçu, 180 ....H 8
Bom Conselho, 6,840 ....G 5
Bom Despacho, 13,568 ....†D 1
Bom Jesus, 1,431 ....E 5
Bom Jesus da Lapa, 6,107 ....F 6
Bom Retiro, 1,601 ....D10
Bom Sucesso, 6,173 ....†D 2
Borba, 1,304 ....H 9
Botucatu, 33,878 ....†B 3
Bragança, 12,848 ....E 3
Bragança Paulista, 27,328 ....†C 3
Brasiléia, 1,902 ....G10
Brasília (capital), 130,968 ....D 6
Brasília, ‡379,699 ....D 6
Brasília, 3,182 ....F 7
Brumado, 7,054 ....F 6
Brusque, 16,127 ....D 9
Buri, 2,666 ....†B 3
Buriti, 1,951 ....F 3
Buriti Alegre, 5,042 ....D 7
Buriti dos Lopes, 1,812 ....F 3
Cabedelo, 10,738 ....H 4
Cabo Frio, 13,117 ....†F 3
Caçador, 10,480 ....D 9
Caçapava, 7,987 ....†D 3
Caçapava do Sul, 6,712 ....C10
Cáceres, 8,246 ....B 7
Cachoeira, 11,415 ....G 6
Cachoeira do Arari, 2,532 ....D 3
Cachoeira do Sul, 38,661 ....C10
Cachoeiro de Itapemirim, *110,301 ....G 8
Caeté, 10,840 ....†E 1
Caetité, 4,823 ....F 6
Cafelândia, 6,573 ....†B 2
Caiapônia, 2,476 ....C 7
Caicó, 15,826 ....G 4
Cajàzeiras, 15,884 ....G 4
Cajuru, 4,971 ....†C 2
Camaquã, 9,732 ....C10
Cambará, 6,028 ....†A 3
Cametá, 5,695 ....D 3
Camocim, 10,788 ....F 3
Campanha, 6,178 ....†D 2
Campina Grande, *157,149 ....G 4
Campinas, *252,145 ....†C 3
Campina Verde, 4,464 ....D 7
Campo Belo, 15,742 ....†D 2
Campo Florido, 1,307 ....†B 1
Campo Formoso, 3,925 ....F 5
Campo Grande, *111,205 ....C 8
Campo Largo, 7,915 ....†B 4
Campo Maior, 13,939 ....F 4
Campos, *389,045 ....†F 2
Campos Altos, 5,243 ....†C 1
Cananéia, 1,948 ....†C 4
Canavieiras, 10,264 ....G 6
Cândido Mendes, 819 ....E 3
Canguaretama, 4,261 ....H 4
Canindé, 5,854 ....G 4
Canoas, *122,040 ....D10
Canoinhas, 9,252 ....D 9
Cantagalo, 3,479 ....†E 3
Canto do Buriti, 1,636 ....F 5
Canutama, 977 ....G 9
Capanema, 9,678 ....E 3
Capão Bonito, 6,829 ....†B 4
Capela, 5,172 ....G 5
Caraguatatuba, 4,655 ....†D 3
Carandaí, 2,792 ....†E 2
Carangola, 11,896 ....†E 2
Caratinga, *123,344 ....†E 1
Caraúbas, 3,066 ....G 4
Caravelas, 3,096 ....G 7
Carinhanha, 2,163 ....E 6
Carolina, 8,137 ....E 4
Caruaru, *115,414 ....G 5
Carutapera, 2,477 ....E 3
Casa Branca, 8,980 ....†C 2
Casa Nova, 1,525 ....F 5
Cascatinha, 19,497 ....†E 3
Cascavel, 3,336 ....G 4
Cássia, 7,034 ....†C 2
Castanhal, 9,528 ....E 3
Castelo, 5,729 ....F 8
Castelo do Piauí, 1,185 ....F 4
Castro, 9,249 ....†B 4
Castro Alves, 7,388 ....G 6
Cataguases, 21,476 ....†E 2
Catalão, 11,471 ....D 7
Catanduva, 37,307 ....†B 2
Catolé do Rocha, 5,217 ....G 4
Cavalcante, 660 ....D 6
Caxambu, 10,491 ....†D 2
Caxias, *124,403 ....F 4
Caxias do Sul, *110,241 ....D10
Ceará (Fortaleza), *846,069 ....G 3
Ceará-Mirim, 8,290 ....H 4
Ceres, 6,895 ....D 7
Cêrro Azul, 1,460 ....†B 4
Chaves, 428 ....D 3
Cicero Dantas, 2,972 ....G 5
Coari, 5,908 ....H 9
Codajás, 1,505 ....H 9
Codó, *100,933 ....E 4
Colatina, *140,729 ....F 7
Colinas, 2,972 ....F 4
Conceição da Barra, 2,229 ....G 7
Conceição do Araguaia, 2,332 ....D 5
Concórdia, 5,864 ....D 9
Conde, 4,190 ....G 5
Conselheiro Lafaiete, 29,208 ....†E 2
Corinto, 12,247 ....E 7
Cornélio Procópio, 17,524 ....D 8
Coroatá, 7,720 ....F 3
Coromandel, 5,148 ....E 7
Corrente, 2,214 ....E 5
Correntina, 2,636 ....E 6
Corumbá, 36,744 ....B 7
Coxim, 1,371 ....C 7
Crateús, 14,572 ....F 4
Crato, 27,649 ....G 4
Criciúma, 25,331 ....D10
Cristalina, 3,810 ....E 7
Cruz Alta, 33,190 ....C10
Cruzeiro, 27,005 ....†D 3
Cruzeiro do Sul, 2,826 ....G10
Cubatão, 18,885 ....†C 3
Cuiabá, 43,112 ....C 6
Curaça, 1,264 ....G 5
Curitiba, *616,548 ....†B 4
Currais Novos, 7,782 ....G 4
Curuçá, 3,871 ....E 3
Cururupu, 4,822 ....E 3
Curvelo, 21,772 ....E 7
Diamantina, 14,252 ....F 7
Diamantino, 645 ....B 6
Dianópolis, 2,145 ....E 5
Divinópolis, 41,544 ....†D 2
Dois Córregos, 7,272 ....†B 3
Dom Pedrito, 15,429 ....C10
Dores do Indaiá, 10,354 ....E 7
Dourados, 10,757 ....C 8
Duque de Caxias, *324,261 ....†E 3
Eirunepé, 3,023 ....G10
Eldorado, 1,524 ....†B 4
Erechim, 24,941 ....C 9
Erval, 1,404 ....C11
Escada, 13,761 ....H 5
Esperança, 9,105 ....G 4
Esplanada, 3,792 ....G 5
Estância, 16,106 ....G 5
Exu, 2,549 ....G 4
Faro, 1,434 ....B 3
Feira de Santana, *136,000 ....G 5
Fernandópolis, 14,375 ....†A 2
Ferreira Gomes, 439 ....D 2
Ferros, 2,456 ....F 7
Flores, 2,102 ....G 4
Floriano, 16,063 ....F 4
Florianópolis, *130,012 ....E 9
Formiga, 18,763 ....†D 2
Formosa, 9,449 ....E 6
Fortaleza, *846,069 ....G 3
Foz do Iguaçu, 7,407 ....C 9
Franca, 47,244 ....†C 2
Fronteiras, 1,320 ....F 4
Frutal, 8,252 ....†B 2
Garanhuns, 34,050 ....G 5
Garça, 18,155 ....†B 3
Gilbués, 588 ....E 5
Goiana, 19,026 ....H 4
Goiandira, 3,169 ....E 7
Goiânia, *345,085 ....D 7
Goiás, 7,121 ....D 6
Governador Valadares, *124,606 ....F 7
Grajaú, 2,539 ....E 4
Granja, 5,074 ....F 3
Guacuí, 7,724 ....†F 2
Guajará-Mirim, 7,115 ....H10
Guamá, 2,470 ....E 3
Guarabira, 15,848 ....H 4
Guarapuava, *126,080 ....C 9
Guaratinguetá, 38,293 ....†D 3
Guarujá, 6,506 ....†C 4
Guarulhos, *119,572 ....†C 3
Guarus, 21,492 ....†F 2
Guaxupé, 14,168 ....†C 2
Guimarães, 1,512 ....E 3
Guiratinga, 4,203 ....C 7
Gurupá, 912 ....D 3
Gurupi, 4,148 ....D 5
Humaitá, 1,192 ....H10
Ibaiti, 3,628 ....†A 3
Ibiá, 6,999 ....E 7
Ibipetuba, 2,298 ....F 5
Ibitinga, 8,881 ....†B 2
Icó, 5,586 ....G 4
Icoraci, 11,512 ....D 3
Igarapava, 9,083 ....†C 2
Igarapé-Miri, 2,591 ....D 3
Iguape, 5,465 ....†C 4
Iguatu, 16,540 ....G 4
Ijuí, 19,671 ....C10
Ilhéus, *100,687 ....G 6
Imbituba, 6,638 ....D10
Imbituva, 3,290 ....†A 4
Imperatriz, 9,004 ....E 4
Inhumas, 8,298 ....D 7
Ipameri, 8,987 ....E 7
Ipiaú, 13,164 ....G 6
Ipu, 7,724 ....F 4
Irati, 12,764 ....†A 4
Itabaiana, Paraíba, 11,847 ....H 4
Itabaiana, Sergipe, 11,050 ....G 5
Itaberaba, 8,555 ....F 6
Itabira, 15,539 ....F 7
Itabirito, 10,511 ....†E 2
Itabuna, 54,268 ....G 6
Itacoatiara, 8,818 ....B 3
Itaguatins, 1,596 ....D 4
Itaí, 1,601 ....†B 3
Itajaí, 38,889 ....D 9
Itajubá, 31,262 ....†D 3
Itamarandiba, 2,404 ....F 7
Itanhaém, 5,376 ....†C 4
Itapecerica, 7,696 ....†D 2
Itapecuru-Mirim, 3,385 ....F 3
Itapemirim, 4,095 ....F 8
Itaperuna, 18,095 ....†F 2
Itapetininga, 29,468 ....†B 3
Itapeva, 13,510 ....†B 3
Itapicuru, 900 ....G 5
Itapipoca, 7,186 ....G 3
Itapira, 16,859 ....†C 3
Itapiranga, 477 ....B 3
Itápolis, 7,430 ....†B 2
Itaporanga, 5,328 ....G 4
Itaqui, 13,223 ....B10
Itararé, 12,812 ....†B 4
Itariri, 1,318 ....†C 4
Itatiba, 12,336 ....†C 3
Itaúna, 22,319 ....†D 2
Itu, 23,435 ....†C 3
Ituaçu, 1,431 ....F 6
Ituberá, 4,097 ....G 6
Ituiutaba, 29,724 ....D 7
Itumbiara, 12,575 ....D 7
Iturama, 1,518 ....†A 1
Ituverava, 11,890 ....†C 2
Jaboticabal, 20,231 ....†B 2
Jacareí, 28,131 ....†D 3
Jacarèzinho, 14,813 ....†A 3
Jacobina, 12,373 ....F 5
Jacupiranga, 2,144 ....†B 4
Jaguaquara, 5,363 ....F 6
Jaguarão, 12,336 ....C11
Jaguariaíva, 6,465 ....†B 4
Jaicós, 1,308 ....F 4
Januária, 9,741 ....E 6
Jaraguá, 3,813 ....D 6
Jardim, 3,104 ....G 4
Jataí, 14,022 ....D 7
Jaú, 31,229 ....†B 3
Jequié, 40,158 ....F 6
Jequitinhonha, 5,410 ....F 7
Jeremoabo, 3,177 ....G 5
Joaçaba, 7,921 ....D 9
João Pessoa, *189,096 ....H 4
João Pinheiro, 3,433 ....E 7
Joaquim Tavora, 3,574 ....†B 3
Joinville, 44,255 ....D 9
Juàzeiro, 21,196 ....G 5
Juàzeiro do Norte, 53,421 ....F 4
Juiz de Fora, *194,135 ....†E 2
Jundiaí, *124,368 ....†C 3
Lábrea, 2,080 ....G10
Laguna, 17,451 ....D10
Lajes, 35,112 ....D 9
Lambari, 6,825 ....†D 2
Lapa, 7,167 ....D 9
Laranjeiras, 4,296 ....G 5
Laranjeiras do Sul, 3,802 ....C 9
Lavras, 23,793 ....†D 2
Leme, 11,785 ....†C 3
Lençóis, 2,483 ....F 6
Leopoldina, 17,726 ....†E 2
Lima Duarte, 3,554 ....†E 2
Limeira, 45,256 ....†C 3
Limoeiro, 21,252 ....H 4
Limoeiro do Norte, 5,705 ....G 4
Linhares, 5,751 ....F 7
Lins, 32,204 ....†B 2
Londrina, *226,332 ....D 8
Lorena, 26,068 ....†D 3
Luís Correia, 1,523 ....F 3
Luz, 5,633 ....†D 1
Luziânia, 4,849 ....E 7
Luzilândia, 3,434 ....F 3
Macaé, 19.830 ....†F 3
Macapá, 27,585 ....D 2
Macau 11.876 ....G 4
Macaúbas, 2,504 ....F 6
Maceió, *221,250 ....H 5
Machado, 8,373 ....†C 2
Mafra, 12,981 ....D 9
Magé, 10,712 ....†E 3
Mallet, 1,816 ....D 9
Manacapuru, 2,584 ....H 9
Manaus, *249,797 ....H 9
Manga, 2,000 ....E 6
Manhuaçu, 10,546 ....†E 2
Manhumirim, 9,477 ....†E 2
Manicoré, 2,268 ....H 9
Marabá, 8,533 ....D 4
Maragogipe, 12,575 ....G 6
Maranguape, 8,715 ....G 3
Marapanim, 3,542 ....E 3
Marechal-Deodoro, 5,269 ....H 5
Mariana, 6,378 ....†E 2
Marília, *107,305 ....†A 3
Marques de Valença, 18,935 ....†D 3
Massapê, 4,760 ....G 3
Mata de São João, 8,117 ....G 6
Mato Grosso, 520 ....B 6
Maués, 4,161 ....B 3
Mazagão, 919 ....B 3
Miguel Alves, 4,537 ....F 4
Mimoso do Sul, 5,278 ....†F 2
Minas Novas, 1,708 ....F 7
Mineiros, 5,105 ....C 7
Miracema, 9,810 ....†E 2
Mirador, 818 ....B 4
Miranda, 2,075 ....C 8
Mirassol, 13,674 ....†B 2
Mocajuba, 1,352 ....D 3
Mococa, 14,306 ....†C 2
Mogi das Cruzes, *111,554 ....†C 3
Mogi-Mirim, 18,345 ....†C 3
Monte Alegre, 3,911 ....C 3
Monte Alegre de Minas, 4,464 ....D 7
Monte Aprazível, 7,235 ....†A 2
Monte Azul, 4,860 ....F 6
Monteiro, 6,028 ....G 4
Montenegro, 14,491 ....D10
Monte Santo, 1,607 ....G 5
Montes Claros, *121,428 ....E 7
Morrinhos, 9,879 ....D 7
Morro do Chapéu, 2,039 ....F 5
Mossoró, 38,833 ....G 4
Mucugê, 723 ....F 6
Mucuri, 603 ....G 7
Mundo Novo, 3,237 ....F 5
Muqui, 4,262 ....F 8
Muriaé, 22,571 ....†E 2
Muzambinho, 18,073 ....†C 2
Natal, *239,590 ....H 4

(continued on following page)

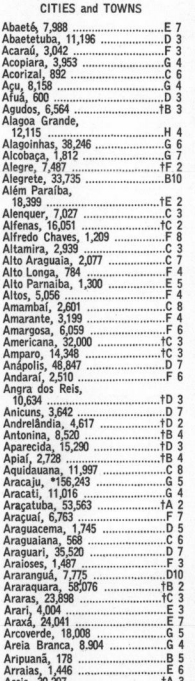

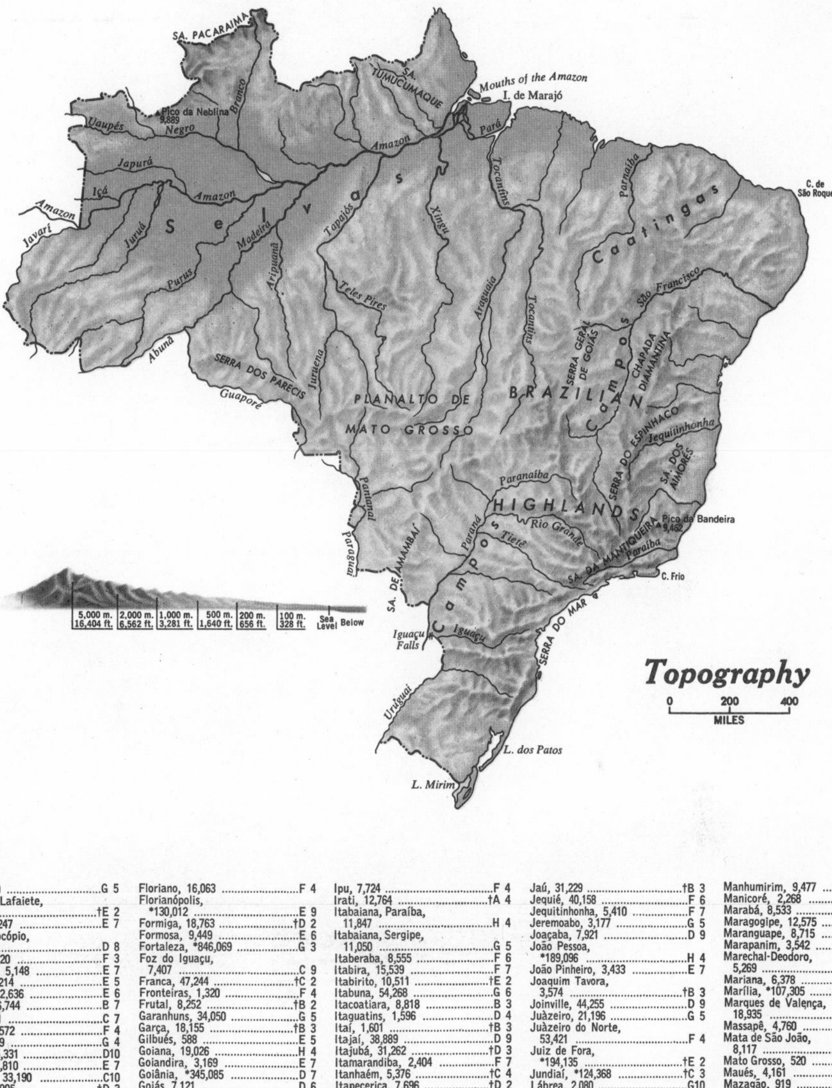
SA. PACARAIMA
SA. TUMUCUMAQUE
Mouths of the Amazon
I. de Marajó
Pico da Neblina 9,889
Uaupés
Negro
Branco
Amazon
Pará
Japurá
Içá
Amazon
Javari
Juruá
Purus
Madeira
Selvas
Tapajós
Xingu
Tocantins
Parnaíba
C. de São Roque
Caatingas
São Francisco
Teles Pires
Araguaia
Aripuanã
Juruena
Abunã
Guaporé
SERRA DOS PARECIS
PLANALTO DE MATO GROSSO
BRAZILIAN HIGHLANDS
SERRA GERAL DE GOIÁS
CHAPADA DIAMANTINA
Campos
SERRA DO ESPINHAÇO
Jequitinhonha
SA. DOS AIMORÉS
Paranaíba
Rio Grande
Pico da Bandeira 9,462
Tietê
Paraíba
SA. DA MANTIQUEIRA
C. Frio
Pantanal
Paraguai
Paraná
SA. DE AMAMBAÍ
SERRA DO MAR
Iguaçu
Iguaçu Falls
Uruguai
L. dos Patos
L. Mirim
5,000 m. 16,404 ft.
2,000 m. 6,562 ft.
1,000 m. 3,281 ft.
500 m. 1,640 ft.
200 m. 656 ft.
100 m. 328 ft.
Sea Level
Below
Topography
0 200 400
MILES

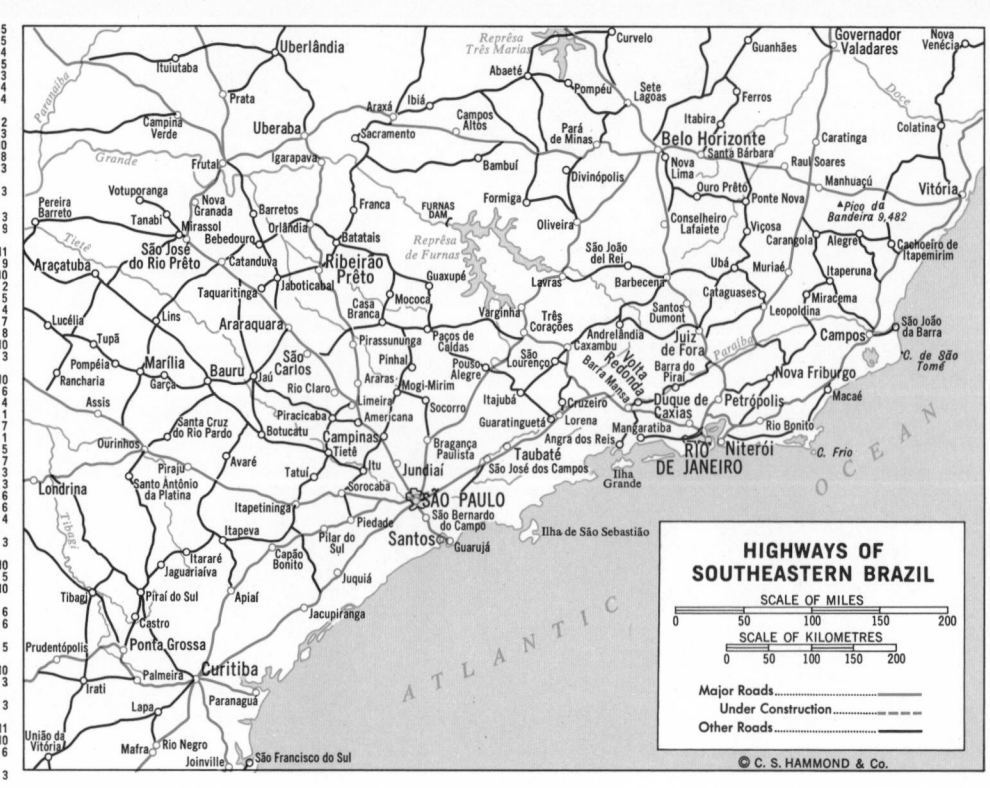

HIGHWAYS OF
SOUTHEASTERN BRAZIL

SCALE OF MILES
0   50   100   150   200

SCALE OF KILOMETRES
0   50   100   150   200

Major Roads ....
Under Construction ....
Other Roads ....

© C. S. HAMMOND & Co.

Agriculture, Industry and Resources

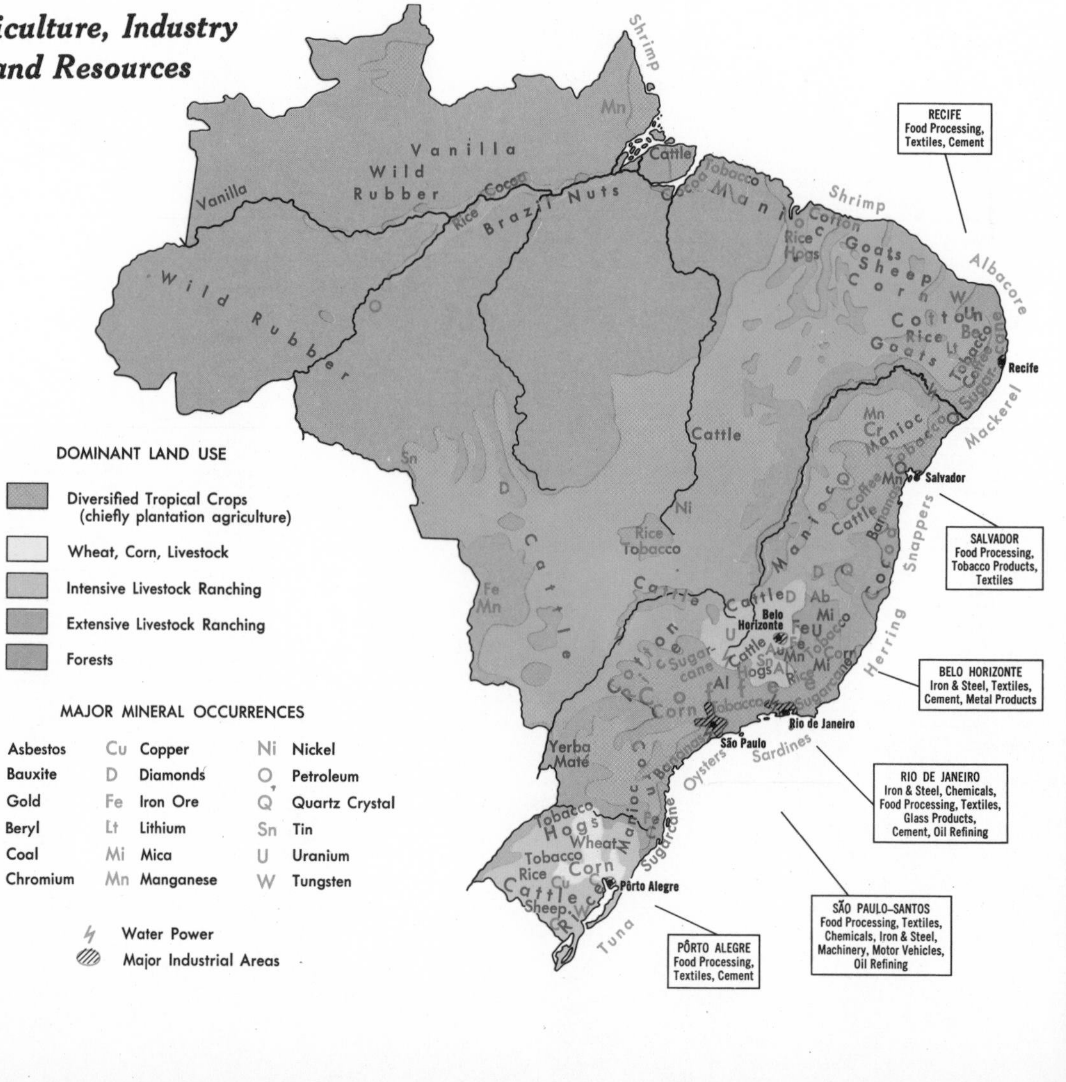

RECIFE
Food Processing,
Textiles, Cement

SALVADOR
Food Processing,
Tobacco Products,
Textiles

BELO HORIZONTE
Iron & Steel, Textiles,
Cement, Metal Products

RIO DE JANEIRO
Iron & Steel, Chemicals,
Food Processing, Textiles,
Glass Products,
Cement, Oil Refining

SÃO PAULO–SANTOS
Food Processing, Textiles,
Chemicals, Iron & Steel,
Machinery, Motor Vehicles,
Oil Refining

PÔRTO ALEGRE
Food Processing,
Textiles, Cement

DOMINANT LAND USE

Diversified Tropical Crops
(chiefly plantation agriculture)

Wheat, Corn, Livestock

Intensive Livestock Ranching

Extensive Livestock Ranching

Forests

MAJOR MINERAL OCCURRENCES

Ab	Asbestos	Cu	Copper	Ni	Nickel
Al	Bauxite	D	Diamonds	O	Petroleum
Au	Gold	Fe	Iron Ore	Q	Quartz Crystal
Be	Beryl	Lt	Lithium	Sn	Tin
C	Coal	Mi	Mica	U	Uranium
Cr	Chromium	Mn	Manganese	W	Tungsten

Water Power

Major Industrial Areas

PERU and ECUADOR

BIPOLAR OBLIQUE CONIC CONFORMAL PROJECTION

SCALE OF MILES
0   50   100   150   200

SCALE OF KILOMETRES
0 50   100   150   200

Capitals of Countries .... ☆
Other Capitals .... ◉
International Boundaries _ _ _ _ _
Other Boundaries ....

Copyright by C.S. Hammond & Co., N.Y.

GALÁPAGOS ISLANDS
(ARCHIPIÉLAGO DE COLÓN)
(Ecuador)
Same scale as main map

PACIFIC OCEAN

ECUADOR

PERU

PROVINCES OF ECUADOR
INDICATED BY NUMBERS

1 Imbabura	C-2	5 Bolívar	C-3
2 Cotopaxi	C-3	6 Chimborazo	C-3
3 Tungurahua	C-3	7 Cañar	C-4
4 Los Ríos	C-3	8 El Oro	C-4

PERU
DEPARTMENTS

Amazonas, 171,100	C 5
Ancash, 744,700	D 7
Apurímac, 330,400	F 9
Arequipa, 518,300	F10
Ayacucho, 474,100	E 9
Cajamarca, 1,007,600	C 6
Callao (province), 335,400	D 9
Cuzco, 756,100	F 9
Huancavelica, 367,100	E 9
Huánuco, 430,100	D 7
Ica, 362,700	E10
Junín, 699,100	E 8
La Libertad, 784,900	C 6
Lambayeque, 485,500	B 6
Lima, 3,155,800	D 8
Loreto, 504,600	E 5
Madre de Dios, 24,200	G 8
Moquegua, 68,800	G11
Pasco, 188,000	D 8
Piura, 922,300	B 5
Puno, 848,200	G10
San Martín, 229,400	D 6
Tacna, 93,900	G11
Tumbes, 84,000	B 4

CITIES and TOWNS

Abancay, 9,053	
Acarí, 1,428	
Acobamba, 2,167	
Acolla, 4,415	
Acomayo, Cuzco, 1,874	
Acomayo, Huánuco, 1,198	
Acora, 941	
Acuracay, 96	
Aija, 1,710	
Alca, 539	
Ambo, 1,606	
Ancón, 3,760	
Andahuaylas, 4,674	
Andamarca, 339	
Anta, 2,574	
Antabamba, 2,294	
Aplao, 1,316	
Aquia, 897	
Arequipa, 194,700	
Ascope, 3,845	
Astillero	
Atalaya, 307	
Atico, 297	
Ayabaca, 3,415	
Ayacucho, 28,500	
Ayaviri, 7,553	
Azángaro, 4,771	
Bagua, 2,343	
Balsapuerto, 203	
Bambamarca, 4,281	
Barranca, Lima, 11,320	
Barranca, Loreto, 184	
Bartra Antiguo	
Bartra Nuevo	
Bayóvar	
Bellavista, 2,129	
Bolívar, 1,057	
Bolognesi	
Bolognesi, 516	
Borja, 300	
Bretaña, 766	
Buldibuyo, 616	
Caballococha, 1,197	
Cabana, 1,910	
Cabo Blanco	
Cahuapanas, 125	
Cailloma, 607	
Cajabamba, 5,253	
Cajacay, 809	
Cajamarca, 28,200	
Cajatambo, 2,257	
Calca, 3,489	
Callalli, 133	
Callao, 335,400	
Camaná, 5,120	
Candarave, 859	
Cangallo, 1,578	
Canta, 2,491	
Capachica, 193	
Caraś, 6,033	
Caravelí, 1,954	
Carhuás, 2,175	
Carumás, 727	
Cascas, 2,403	
Casma, 4,975	
Castilla, 29,541	
Castrovirreyna, 784	
Catacaos, 12,135	
Celendín, 5,646	
Cerro Azul, 1,571	
Cerro de Pasco, 23,400	
Chachapoyas, 6,860	
Chala, 1,054	
Chalhuanca, 2,840	
Chancay, 6,145	
Chao	
Chepén, 16,119	
Chicama, 1,362	
Chiclayo, 140,800	
Chilca (Pucusana), 1,331	
Chilete, 1,105	
Chimbote, 102,800	
Chincha Alta, 26,500	
Chiquián, 3,354	
Chirinos, 490	
Chivay, 2,320	
Chorrillos, 31,703	
Chosica	
Chota, 4,961	
Chulucanas, 19,714	
Chupaca, 2,180	
Chuquibamba, 2,983	
Chuquibambilla, 1,423	
Churín, 610	
Cocachacra, 2,869	

ıa ... G 8
ı, 763 ... H10
ay, 466 ... C 5
mar, 1,370 ... D 6
ca, 1,408 ... E 9
oción, 4,184 ... E 8
rdia, 66 ... E 5
mana, 4,708 ... E 6
mazá, 2,532 ... C 6
ora, 4,116 ... F10
va, 620 ... E10
go, 2,241 ... D 7
uasi, 1,618 ... F10
ras ... C 7
ría ... F 7
wo, 4,702 ... C 6
uyo, 708 ... H10
, 108,900 ... F 9
guadero, 948 ... H11
ua, 416 ... G10
de Mayo, 970 ... E 6
rate, 374 ... F 9
ortugués ... C 7
ranza, 261 ... G 7
ñafe, 12,112 ... C 6
arrald ... G 8
isco de Orellana, 306 ... F 4
alupe, 2,896 ... E 9
oi ... E 3
ho, 29,400 ... D 8
rachuco, 757 ... D 7
ayoc, 1,223 ... C 6
a, 2,586 ... F 9
anca, Ancash, 491 ... D 7
anca, Huánuco, 1,202 ... D 7
nachuco, 5,730 ... D 6
acabamba, 3,215 ... C 5
cané, 4,053 ... H10
capi, 2,415 ... E 9
cavelica, 11,039 ... E 9
acayo, 95,000 ... E 9
chaco, 1,006 ... C 7
ata, 5,728 ... E 9
uco, 34,500 ... E 7
al, 11,481 ... D 8
áz, 20,345 ... D 7
i, 2,467 ... D 7
iaca, 1,534 ... E 8
mey, 5,232 ... C 8
ochirí, 2,125 ... D 9
rocondo, 2,921 ... F 9
ara, 1,442 ... D 8
las, 1,258 ... C 7
a, 526 ... F 5
72,300 ... E10
ña, 183 ... G11
, 4,278 ... H11
9,986 ... G11
erial, 6,345 ... D 9
ibari, 9 ... H 9
ari, 159 ... H 8
tu, 344 ... E 4
ia, 171 ... E 7
tos, 76,100 ... F 4
, 4,420 ... C 5
a, 12,751 ... E 8
anca, 4,240 ... B 6
eros, 1,842 ... D 5
ajuí, 5,105 ... D 6
3,874 ... H11
aca, 35,000 ... G10
billa, 876 ... C 5
n, 5,004 ... E 8
unas, 3,637 ... E 5
luaca, 1,863 ... B 5
alca, 1,401 ... D 6
loya, 1,305 ... G11
eas, 7,139 ... D 6
bayeque, 10,629 ... B 6
pa, 3,123 ... G10
nud, 2,609 ... C 6
lacuni Bajo, 229 ... G 9
Oroya, 32,600 ... D 8
Piedras, 13 ... H 9
Yaras, 367 ... G11
ina ... B 5
Jnión, 2,013 ... D 7
nebamba, 1,026 ... D 6
a (capital), *2,541,300 ... D 8
abani, 903 ... H10
cay, 2,077 ... E 9

Llata, 2,255 ... D 7
Lobitos, 3,071 ... B 5
Locumba, 349 ... G11
Lomas, 111 ... E10
Lucerna ... H 9
Lurín, 2,741 ... D 9
Machupicchu, 1,026 ... F 9
Macusani, 1,601 ... G10
Madre de Dios, †802 ... G 9
Máncora, 7,943 ... B 5
Manú, †686 ... G 9
Marcapata, 334 ... G 9
Marcona, 6,744 ... E10
Margos, 1,195 ... D 8
Masisea, 1,520 ... E 7
Matarani ... F11
Matucana, 2,883 ... D 8
Mavila ... H 8
Mazán, 411 ... F 4
Mazocruz, 156 ... H11
Mendoza, 1,002 ... D 6
Miraflores, 52,142 ... G11
Mishagua ... F 8
Moho, 1,377 ... H10
Mollendo, 12,483 ... F11
Monsefú, 11,141 ... C 6
Moquegua, 7,795 ... G11
Morales, 2,430 ... D 6
Morococha, 6,519 ... D 8
Morropón, 4,730 ... C 5
Motupe, 1,286 ... C 6
Moyobamba, 8,373 ... D 6
Nauta, 1,905 ... F 5
Nazca, 13,587 ... E10
Negritos, 14,810 ... B 5
Nueva Alejandría, †264 ... F 5
Nuñoa, 2,137 ... G10
Ocoña, 1,207 ... F11
Ocros, 1,204 ... D 8
Ollachea, 903 ... G 9
Ollantaytambo, 1,632 ... F 9
Olmos, 3,628 ... C 5
Omaguas ... F 4
Omas, 217 ... D 9
Omate, 856 ... G11
Orcotuna, 2,716 ... E 8
Orellana, 1,596 ... E 6
Otuzco, 4,311 ... C 6
Oxapampa, 2,535 ... E 8
Oyón, 2,171 ... D 8
Pacasmayo, 11,956 ... C 6
Pachiza, 1,307 ... D 6
Paijan, 5,815 ... C 6
Paita, 9,615 ... B 5
Palpa, 2,615 ... E10
Pampachiri, 448 ... F10
Pampacolca, 1,876 ... F10
Pampas, 2,495 ... E 9
Panao, 1,262 ... E 7
Pantoja, 528 ... E 3
Parinari, 126 ... E 5
Paruro, 1,905 ... F 9
Pataz, 324 ... D 6
Pativilca, 15,325 ... D 8
Paucarbamba, 715 ... E 9
Paucartambo, Cuzco, 1,928 ... E 8
Paucartambo, Pasco, 1,717 ... G 9
Pevas, 696 ... G 4
Picota, 2,014 ... D 6
Pimentel, 6,252 ... B 6
Pinquén ... G 9
Pisac, 1,230 ... G 9
Pisco, 27,300 ... D 9
Piura, 111,400 ... B 5
Pizacoma, 86 ... H11
Pomabamba, 2,522 ... D 7
Porvenir ... E 5
Poto, 161 ... H10
Pozuzo, 121 ... E 8
Puca Barranca ... F 4
Pucallpa, 45,600 ... E 7
Pucará, 1,119 ... G10
Pucauro, 12 ... G 4
Pucusana, 1,331 ... D 9
Puerto Alianza ... D 5
Puerto América, 150 ... D 5
Puerto Arturo ... F 3
Puerto Bermúdez, 230 ... E 8
Puerto Caballas ... E10
Puerto Chicama, 3,002 ... C 6
Puerto Eten, 2,192 ... B 6

PERU

AREA 496,222 sq. mi.
POPULATION 13,586,300
CAPITAL Lima
LARGEST CITY Lima
HIGHEST POINT Huascarán 22,205 ft.
MONETARY UNIT sol
MAJOR LANGUAGES Spanish, Quechua, Aymara
MAJOR RELIGION Roman Catholicism

ECUADOR

AREA 109,483 sq. mi.
POPULATION 6,144,000
CAPITAL Quito
LARGEST CITY Guayaquil
HIGHEST POINT Chimborazo 20,561 ft.
MONETARY UNIT sucre
MAJOR LANGUAGES Spanish, Quechua
MAJOR RELIGION Roman Catholicism

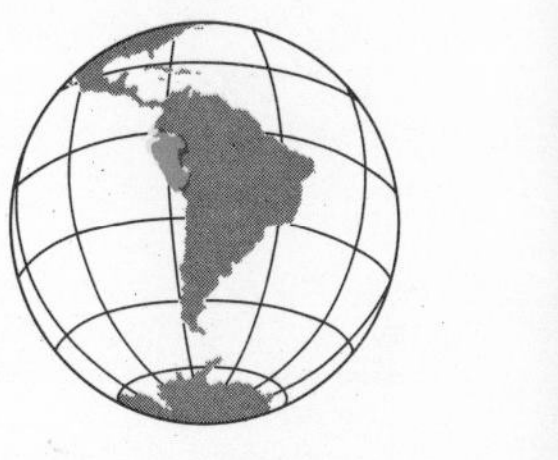

Puerto José Pardo ... D 4
Puerto Leguía, Loreto ... D 4
Puerto Leguía, Puno ... G 9
Puerto Maldonado, 3,518 ... H 9
Puerto Morín ... C 7
Puerto Ocopa, 1,304 ... E 8
Puerto Pardo ... F 7
Puerto Pizarro ... B 4
Puerto Portillo, 49 ... F 7
Puerto Prado, 419 ... E 8
Puerto Samanco, 1,733 ... C 7
Puerto Tahuantinsuyo ... G 9
Puerto Victoria ... E 7
Puno, 32,100 ... G10
Punta de Bombón, 3,943 ... F11
Punta Moreno ... C 6
Puquina, 1,030 ... G11
Puquio, 8,144 ... E10
Putina, 3,512 ... H10
Querecotillo, 6,205 ... B 5
Quicacha, 299 ... F10
Quilca, 171 ... F11
Quillabamba, 8,644 ... F 9
Quince Mil ... G 9
Ramón Castilla, †8,106 ... G 5
Recuay, 1,755 ... D 7
Requena, 3,931 ... F 5
Reventazón ... B 6
Rioja, 4,361 ... D 6
Salaverry, 4,605 ... C 7
San José, 2,612 ... B 6
San José de Sisa, 4,190 ... D 6
San Juan, 717 ... E10
San Lorenzo, 84 ... H 8
San Martín ... E 3
San Miguel, Ayacucho, 1,271 ... F 9
San Miguel, Cajamarca, 1,871 ... C 6
San Pedro de Lloc, 7,497 ... C 6
San Ramón, 3,016 ... E 8
San Vicente de Cañete, 7,184 ... D 9
Saña, 18,421 ... C 6
Sandia, 3,026 ... H10
Santa, 2,966 ... C 7
Santa Clotilde, 824 ... E 4
Santa Cruz, Cajamarca, 1,729 ... C 6
Santa Cruz, Loreto, 739 ... E 5
Santa Elena, 271 ... F 5
Santa Isabel de Sihuas, 118 ... F11
Santa María de Nanay, 123 ... F 4
Santiago, 1,613 ... E10
Santiago de Cao, 1,033 ... C 6
Santiago de Chocorvos, 344 ... E 9
Santiago de Chuco, 4,649 ... C 7
Santo Tomás, Amazonas, 1,097 ... C 6
Santo Tomás, Cuzco, 1,659 ... G10
Santo Tomás de Andoas, 65 ... D 4
Saposoa, 4,456 ... D 6
Saquena, 688 ... F 5
Satipo, 2,499 ... E 8
Sauce, 1,761 ... D 6
Sayán, 1,764 ... D 8
Sechura, 5,157 ... B 5
Sicuani, 10,664 ... G10
Sihuas, 1,404 ... D 7
Sullana, 43,500 ... B 5
Sumbay ... G10
Sumbilca, 1,365 ... D 8
Supe, 2,499 ... D 8

Tacna, 41,200 ... G11
Tahuamanu, †4,011 ... H 8
Talara, 39,600 ... B 5
Tambo de Mora, 1,128 ... D 9
Tambo Grande, 4,404 ... B 5
Tamshiyacu, 1,623 ... F 5
Tarapoto, 13,907 ... D 6
Tarata, 2,673 ... H11
Tarma, 15,452 ... E 8
Tarqui ... E 3
Tayabamba, 1,519 ... D 7
Ticaco, 1,206 ... H11
Tingo María, 5,208 ... D 7
Tiruntán, 847 ... E 6
Tocache, 1,607 ... D 7
Tonegrama ... D 4
Topara, 1,437 ... D 9
Toquepala ... G11
Torata, 669 ... G11
Tournavista ... E 7
Trujillo, 156,200 ... C 7
Tumbes, 30,000 ... B 4
Ubinas, 348 ... G11
Uchiza, 1,006 ... D 7
Unini ... F 8
Urcos, 2,733 ... G 9
Urubamba, 3,325 ... F 9
Vinchos, 473 ... E 9
Virú, 2,647 ... C 7
Vitor, 117 ... G11
Yambrasbamba, 306 ... D 5
Yanahuanca, 962 ... D 8
Yanaoca, 1,146 ... G10
Yauca, 2,364 ... E10
Yauli, 1,696 ... D 8
Yauri, 2,834 ... G10
Yauyos, 1,456 ... E 9
Yunguyo, 2,506 ... H11
Yurimaguas, 11,655 ... E 5
Zarumilla, 3,499 ... B 4
Zorritos, 2,862 ... B 4

OTHER FEATURES

Aguaytía (river) ... E 7
Aguja (point) ... B 5
Amazon (river) ... F 4
Andes, Cordillera de los (mts.) ... F10
Apurímac (river) ... F 9
Azángaro (river) ... G10
Azul, Cordillera (mts.) ... E 7
Blanca, Cordillera (mts.) ... D 7
Blanco (cape) ... B 5
Cañete (river) ... D 9
Chincha (isls.) ... D 9
Chira (river) ... B 5
Coles (point) ... G11
Cóndor, Cordillera del (mts.) ... C 5
Coropuna, Nudo (mt.) ... F10
Corrientes (river) ... E 4
El Boquerón (pass) ... E 7
El Misti (mt.) ... G11
Ene (river) ... E 8
Guañape (isls.) ... C 7
Heath (river) ... H 9
Huallaga (river) ... D 5
Huascarán (mt.) ... D 7
Huayabamba (river) ... D 6
Ica (river) ... E10
Inambari (river) ... H 9
Independencia (bay) ... D10
La Montaña (reg.) ... F 8
Lachay (Salinas) (point) ... D 8
Las Piedras (river) ... G 8
Lobos de Tierra (isl.) ... B 6
Locumba (river) ... G11
Madre de Dios (river) ... G 9
Majes (river) ... F11
Marañón (river) ... E 5
Montaña, La (reg.) ... F 8
Morona (river) ... D 5
Napo (river) ... F 4
Negra, Cordillera (mts.) ... D 7
Negra (point) ... B 6
Occidental, Cordillera (mts.) ... F10
Ocoña (river) ... F11
Oriental, Cordillera (mts.) ... H10
Pachitea (river) ... E 7
Pampas (river) ... E 9
Paracas (pen.), †727 ... D 9
Pariñas (point) ... B 5
Pastaza (river) ... D 5
Pativilca (river) ... D 8
Perené (river) ... E 8
Piedras, Las (river) ... G 8
Pirua (river) ... B 5
Puinagua, Canal de (river) ... E 5
Purus (river) ... G 8
Putumayo (river) ... G 4
Rímac (river) ... D 9
Salinas (Lachay) (point) ... D 8
San Lorenzo (isl.) ... D 9
Santa (river) ... C 7
Santiago (river) ... D 4
Tambo (river) ... G11
Tigre (river) ... E 4
Titicaca (lake) ... H10
Tumbes (river) ... B 4
Ucayali (river) ... F 5
Urubamba (river) ... F 8
Vilcabamba, Cordillera (mts.) ... F 9
Vilcanota (mt.) ... G10
Vitor (river) ... F11
Yaguas (river) ... G 4
Yavarí (river) ... G 5

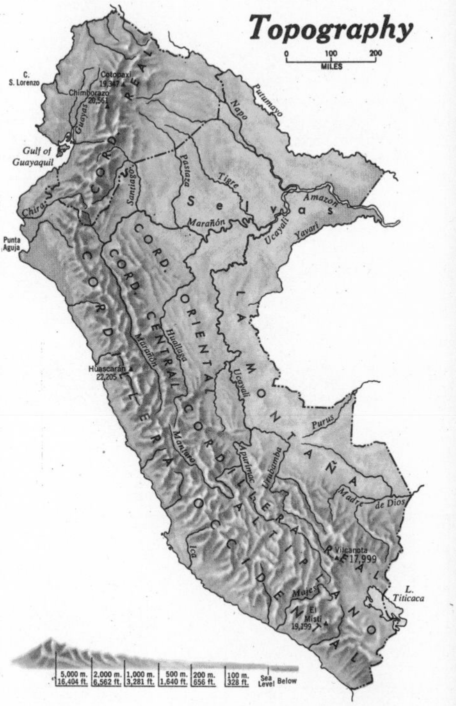

Topography
MILES
C. S. Lorenzo
Gulf of Guayaquil
Punta Aguja
Cotopaxi
Chimborazo
Huascarán 22,205
Vilcanota 17,999
El Misti 19,199
L. Titicaca
Amazon
Napo
Putumayo
Marañón
Ucayali
Purus
Madre de Dios
Yavari
Tigre
Pastaza
Huallaga
LA MONTAÑA
5,000 m. 16,404 ft.
2,000 m. 6,562 ft.
1,000 m. 3,281 ft.
500 m. 1,640 ft.
200 m. 656 ft.
100 m. 328 ft.
Sea Level
Below

ECUADOR

PROVINCES

Azuay, 274,642 ... C 4
Bolívar, 131,651 ... C 3
Cañar, 112,733 ... C 4
Carchi, 94,649 ... C 2
Chimborazo, 276,668 ... C 3
Colón, Archipiélago de (terr.), 2,391 ... C 8
Cotopaxi, 154,971 ... C 3
El Oro, 160,650 ... C 4
Esmeraldas, 124,881 ... C 2
Guayas, 979,223 ... B 4
Imbabura, 174,039 ... C 2
Loja, 285,448 ... C 4
Los Ríos, 250,062 ... C 3
Manabí, 612,542 ... B 3
Morona-Santiago, 25,503 ... C 4
Napo, 24,253 ... D 3
Pastaza, 13,693 ... D 3
Pichincha, 587,835 ... C 3
Tungurahua, 178,709 ... C 3
Zamora-Chinchipe, 11,464 ... C 5

CITIES and TOWNS

Alausí, 6,676 ... C 4
Ambato, 53,372 ... C 3
Andoas Nuevo ... D 4
Arapicos ... D 3
Archidona ... D 3
Arenillas, 3,925 ... B 4
Atuntaqui, 8,759 ... C 2
Azogues, 8,075 ... C 4
Baba, 693 ... C 3
Babahoyo, 16,444 ... C 3
Baeza, 213 ... D 3
Bahía de Caráquez, 8,845 ... C 3
Balao, 1,415 ... C 4
Balzar, 6,588 ... C 3
Bolívar, 410 ... C 2
Cajabamba, 2,094 ... C 3
Calceta, 4,946 ... C 3
Cañar, 4,935 ... C 4
Canelos ... D 3
Cariamanga, 5,381 ... C 5
Carondelet, 318 ... C 2
Catacocha, 3,796 ... C 5
Catamayo, 4,097 ... C 4
Catarama, 2,424 ... C 3
Cayambe, 8,101 ... D 3
Celica, 3,467 ... B 4
Chone, 12,832 ... B 3
Chunchi, 2,388 ... C 4
Coca ... D 3
Cojimíes, 1,538 ... B 2
Cononaco ... E 3
Cuenca, 60,402 ... C 4
Cuyabeno ... E 3
Daule, 7,428 ... B 3
Edén ... E 3
El Ángel, 4,009 ... C 2
El Corazón, 1,118 ... C 3
El Progreso ... C 9
El Pun, 612 ... D 2
Esmeraldas, 33,403 ... B 2
Farfán ... D 2
Floreana ... B10
Girón, 1,914 ... C 4
Gualaceo, 3,065 ... C 4
Gualaquiza, 635 ... C 4
Guale ... B 3
Guamote, 2,640 ... C 3
Guano, 4,455 ... C 3
Guaranda, 9,900 ... C 3
Guayaquil, 738,591 ... B 4
Ibarra, 25,835 ... D 2
Jama, 1,743 ... B 3
Jipijapa, 13,367 ... B 3
La Libertad, 13,565 ... B 4
La Tola, 650 ... C 2
Latacunga, 14,856 ... C 3
Loja, 26,785 ... C 4
Loreto ... D 3
Macará, 5,027 ... C 5
Macas, 1,355 ... D 4
Machachi, 3,951 ... C 3
Machala, 29,036 ... B 4
Machalilla, 615 ... B 3
Manglaralto, 799 ... B 3
Manta, 33,622 ... B 3
Méndez, 527 ... C 4
Mera ... C 3
Miazal ... D 4
Milagro, 28,148 ... C 4
Montecristi, 4,540 ... B 3
Morona ... D 4
Mulaló, 427 ... C 3
Napo ... D 3
Nuevo Rocafuerte, 435 ... E 3
Otavalo, 8,630 ... C 2
Pajan, 1,818 ... B 3
Palanda ... C 5
Papallacta ... D 3
Pasaje, 13,215 ... C 4
Paute, 1,511 ... C 4
Pedernales, 610 ... B 2
Pelileo, 2,545 ... C 3
Píllaro, 2,714 ... C 3
Piñas, 3,344 ... C 4
Playas, 5,067 ... B 4
Portoviejo, 32,228 ... B 3
Posorja, 2,086 ... B 4
Puerto Baquerizo Moreno ... C 9
Puerto de Cayo, 713 ... B 3
Pujilí, 2,534 ... C 3
Putumayo ... E 2
Puyo, 2,290 ... D 3
Quevedo, 20,602 ... C 3
Quito (capital), 496,410 ... C 3
Río Tigre ... E 3
Riobamba, 41,625 ... C 3
Rocafuerte, 4,349 ... B 3
Rosa Zárate, 1,662 ... C 2
Salinas, 5,460 ... B 4
San Gabriel, 6,803 ... D 2
San Lorenzo, 575 ... C 2
San Miguel, 2,410 ... C 3
San Miguel de Salcedo, 3,442 ... C 3
Sangolquí, 5,501 ... C 3
Santa Ana, 3,940 ... B 3
Santa Cruz ... B 9
Santa Elena, 4,241 ... B 4
Santa Isabel, 1,602 ... C 4
Santa Rosa, 8,935 ... C 4
Santa Rosa de Sucumbíos, 132 ... D 2
Santo Domingo de los Colorados, 6,951 ... C 3
Saraguro, 1,562 ... C 4
Sarayacu ... D 3
Sigsig, 1,228 ... C 4
Sigüe ... D 2
Sucre, 2,578 ... B 3
Sucúa, 1,153 ... C 4
Tabacundo, 2,009 ... C 2
Tachina ... C 2
Tena, 1,029 ... D 3
Tulcán, 16,448 ... D 2
Valdez, 3,358 ... C 2
Viche, 230 ... C 2
Villamil ... B 9
Vinces, 5,901 ... C 3
Yacuambí, 405 ... C 4
Yaguachi, 2,996 ... C 4
Yaupi ... D 4
Zamora, 1,030 ... C 5
Zapotillo, 460 ... B 5
Zaruma, 9,000 ... C 4
Zumba, 450 ... C 5

OTHER FEATURES

Aguarico (river) ... D 3
Ancón de Sardinas (bay) ... C 2
Antisana (mt.) ... D 3
Baltra (isl.) ... B 9
Banks (bay) ... B 9
Bobonaza (river) ... D 3
Cayambe (mt.) ... D 2
Chaves (Santa Cruz) (isl.), 626 ... C 9
Chimborazo (mt.) ... C 3
Cotopaxi (mt.) ... C 3
Cristóbal (point) ... B 9
Curaray (river) ... D 3
Esmeraldas (river) ... C 2
Española (isl.) ... C10
Fernandina (isl.) ... B 9
Floreana (Santa María) (isl.), 46 ... B10
Galápagos (isls.), 2,391 ... C 8
Galera (point) ... B 2
Guayaquil (gulf) ... B 4
Guayas (river) ... C 4
Isabel (bay) ... B 9
Isabela (isl.), 336 ... B 9
La Puntilla (cape) ... B 4
Mira (river) ... C 2
Napo (river) ... D 3
Naranjal (river) ... C 4
Pastaza (river) ... D 4
Puná (isl.), 5,459 ... B 4
Puntilla, La (cape) ... B 4
Putumayo (river) ... E 2
Rosa (cape) ... B10
San Cristóbal (isl.), 1,404 ... C 9
San Francisco (cape) ... B 2
Sangay (mt.) ... C 4
San Lorenzo (cape) ... B 3
San Salvador (isl.) ... B 9
Santa Cruz (isl.), 626 ... C 9
Santa María (isl.), 46 ... B10
Santiago (San Salvador) (isl.) ... C 9
Tumbes (river) ... B 4
Zamora (river) ... C 4

*City and suburbs.
†Population of district.

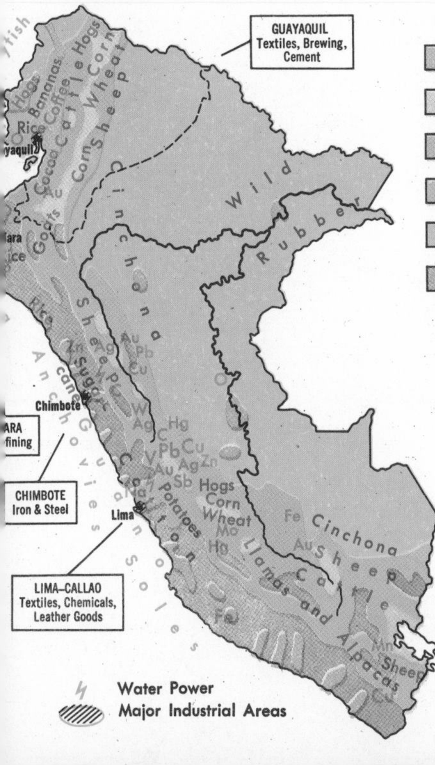

GUAYAQUIL
Textiles, Brewing, Cement
Chimbote
CHIMBOTE
Iron & Steel
Lima
LIMA-CALLAO
Textiles, Chemicals, Leather Goods
Water Power
Major Industrial Areas

Agriculture, Industry and Resources

DOMINANT LAND USE

Diversified Tropical Crops (chiefly plantation agriculture)
Upland Cultivated Areas
Upland Livestock Grazing, Limited Agriculture
Extensive Livestock Ranching
Forests
Nonagricultural Land

MAJOR MINERAL OCCURRENCES

Ag Silver
Au Gold
C Coal
Cu Copper
Fe Iron Ore
Hg Mercury
Mn Manganese
Mo Molybdenum
Na Salt
O Petroleum
P Phosphates
Pb Lead
Sb Antimony
V Vanadium
W Tungsten
Zn Zinc

DEPARTMENTS

Beni, 181,000 .... C 3
Chuquisaca, 427,400 .... C 6
Cochabamba, 741,100 .... C 5
La Paz, 1,433,000 .... A 4
Oruro, 317,700 .... A 5
Pando, 29,900 .... B 2
Potosí, 807,400 .... B 6
Santa Cruz, 432,300 .... E 5
Tarija, 191,600 .... C 7

CITIES and TOWNS

Abapó, 466 .... D 6
Acchilla, 208 .... C 7
Achacachi, 3,621 .... A 5

Aiquile, 3,465 .... C 6	Aroma, 1,254 .... B 6	Betanzos, 1,097 .... C 6	Camargo, 1,609 .... C 7	Cataricahua, 3,240 .... B 6	Chocaya, 444 .... B 7
Alcalá, 236 .... C 6	Arque, 1,254 .... B 5	Bolívar .... B 3	Camatindi .... D 7	Cavari, 249 .... B 5	Choquecota .... A 5
Alejandría .... C 3	Arroyo Grande .... A 2	Bolpebra .... A 2	Camiri, 4,969 .... D 7	Cavinas .... A 3	Chorrillos .... C 2
Alto Seco .... D 6	Ascención, 2,097 .... D 4	Boyuibe, 537 .... D 7	Cañas .... C 7	Chachacomani, 159 .... A 6	Chulumani, 2,362 .... C 5
Amarete, 992 .... A 4	Asunción .... E 4	Buena Hora .... E 4	Candelaria .... F 5	Chaguaya, 643 .... C 7	Chuma, 931 .... A 5
Amboró .... D 5	Asunta, 45 .... A 4	Buena Vista .... D 4	Canquela, 148 .... A 7	Challacollo, 284 .... A 5	Chuquichambi .... A 5
Ananea, 302 .... A 4	Atén, 199 .... A 4	Buena Vista, 435 .... D 5	Capinota, 1,734 .... B 5	Challacota .... B 6	Chuquichuqui .... C 6
Ancoraimes, 769 .... A 4	Atocha .... B 7	Cabezas, 298 .... D 7	Capirenda .... D 7	Challana .... A 5	Cliza, 3,121 .... C 5
Andamarca .... B 6	Ayacucho, 729 .... D 5	Cachuela Esperanza, 1,073 .... C 2	Caquiavirí, 760 .... A 5	Challapata, 2,529 .... B 6	Cobija, 2,537 .... B 2
Añimbo, 443 .... C 7	Ayata, 479 .... A 5	Caíza, 838 .... C 6	Carabuco, 626 .... A 4	Chapacura .... A 1	Cocani .... C 5
Anzaldo, 1,056 .... C 5	Azurduy, 1,234 .... C 6	Cajuata, 447 .... B 5	Caracollo, 909 .... B 5	Chaquí, 291 .... C 6	Cocapata .... B 5
Apolo, 1,043 .... A 4	Barrera .... B 3	Calacoto, 415 .... A 5	Caranavi .... A 5	Charagua, 1,185 .... D 6	Cochabamba, 157,000 .... C 5
Aquío .... A 6	Baures, 592 .... B 2	Calamarca, 802 .... A 5	Carandaití, 1,403 .... D 7	Charaña, 794 .... A 5	Cohoni, 890 .... C 5
Araca .... B 5	Bella Flor .... B 2	Calcha .... B 7	Carangas .... A 5	Chayanta, 1,272 .... B 6	Coipasa .... A 6
Arampampa, 829 .... B 5	Bella Vista .... E 3	Calcha .... C 6	Caraparí, 351 .... D 7	Chiguana, 154 .... A 7	Collpa, 481 .... B 5
Arani, 2,200 .... C 5	Berenguela .... A 5	Callapa, 636 .... A 5	Carmen .... B 2	Chiñijo, 27 .... A 4	Colquechaca, 1,070 .... B 6
Arcopongo .... B 5	Bermejo .... C 8	Camacho .... C 7	Carrizal .... C 7	Chivé .... A 3	Colquiri, 806 .... B 5

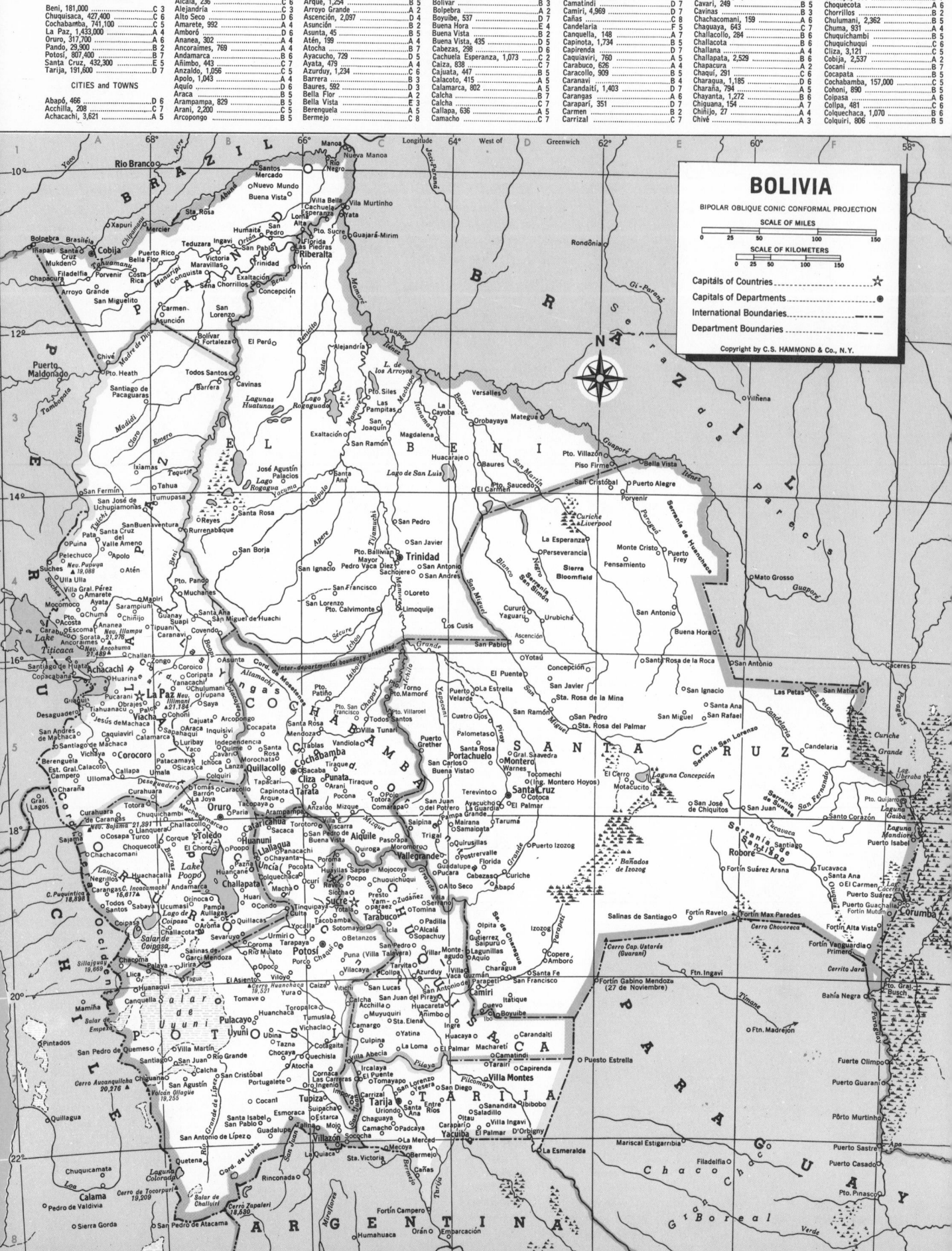

Comarapa, 1,096 ..... C 5
Concepción ..... B 2
Concepción, 1,056 ..... D 5
Condo ..... B 6
Conquista ..... B 2
Copacabana, 1,981 ..... A 5
Copere ..... D 6
Coripata, 1,647 ..... B 5
Cornaca, 264 ..... C 7
Corocoro, 4,431 ..... A 5
Coroico, 2,235 ..... B 5
Coroma ..... B 6
Corque, 423 ..... B 6
Cosapa, 297 ..... A 6
Costa Rica ..... A 2
Cotagaita, 1,353 ..... C 7
Cotoca, 915 ..... D 5
Covendo, 71 ..... B 4
Cuatro Ojos ..... D 5
Cuevo, 902 ..... D 7
Culpina, 981 ..... C 7
Culta ..... B 6
Curahuara, 510 ..... A 5
Curahuara de Carangas, 235 ..... A 5
Curiche, 257 ..... D 6
Cururú ..... D 4
Desaguadero, 201 ..... A 5
D'Orbigny ..... D 7
El Asiento ..... B 6
El Carmen, 232 ..... D 3
El Carmen ..... F 6
El Cerro, 117 ..... E 5
El Choro, 224 ..... B 6
El Palmer ..... D 7
El Palmar, 437 ..... D 5
El Palmar, 832 ..... D 7
El Perú ..... B 3
El Puente ..... C 7
El Puente ..... D 5
Entre Ríos, 1,011 ..... C 7
Escoma, 220 ..... A 4
Esmoraca ..... B 7
Estación General Campero ..... A 5
Estarca ..... C 7
Exaltación ..... B 2
Exaltación, 405 ..... C 3
Filadelfia ..... A 2
Florida ..... C 2
Florida, 128 ..... D 6
Fortaleza ..... B 3
Fortín Alta Vista ..... F 6
Fortín Campero ..... C 8
Fortín Max Paredes ..... F 6
Fortín Mutum ..... F 6
Fortín Ravelo ..... E 6
Fortín Suárez Arana ..... F 6
Fortín Vanguardia Primero ..... F 6
General Saavedra, 1,006 ..... D 5
Guadalupe, 71 ..... B 7
Guadalupe, 2,355 ..... C 6
Guanay, 574 ..... B 4
Guaqui, 2,266 ..... A 5
Gutiérrez, 770 ..... D 6
Huacaraje, 673 ..... D 3
Huacareta, 239 ..... C 7
Huacaya, 229 ..... D 7
Huachacalla, 801 ..... A 6
Huanaqui, 359 ..... A 7
Huancané, 148 ..... B 6
Huanchaca ..... B 7
Huanuni, 5,696 ..... B 6
Huari, 1,070 ..... B 6
Huarina, 1,151 ..... A 5
Huayllas, 206 ..... C 6
Humaitá ..... B 2
Ibibobo ..... D 7
Ibo, 425 ..... D 7
Ichoca, 591 ..... B 5
Icla, 196 ..... C 6
Impora, 274 ..... C 7
Independencia, 1,742 ..... B 5
Ingavi ..... B 2
Ingeniero Montero Hoyos (Tocomechi), 575 ..... D 5
Ingre, 162 ..... D 7
Inquisivi, 520 ..... B 5
Ipitá, 441 ..... D 6
Ircalaya ..... C 7
Irupana, 1,937 ..... B 5
Itatique ..... D 7
Itaú, 102 ..... D 7
Ivón ..... C 2
Ixiamas, 292 ..... A 3
Izozog ..... D 6
Jesús de Machaca, 529 ..... A 5
Jirira ..... B 6
José Agustín Palacios ..... B 3
La Cayoba ..... C 3
La Esmeralda ..... D 8
La Esperanza ..... D 4
La Estrella ..... D 5
La Guardia, 470 ..... D 5
La Joya, 401 ..... B 5
La Loma ..... C 7
La Merced ..... C 8
La Paz (cap.), 525,000 ..... B 5
Lagunillas, 840 ..... D 6
Lanza, 526 ..... B 5
Las Carreras, 155 ..... C 7
Las Pampitas ..... C 3
Las Petas ..... F 5
Las Piedras ..... C 2
Limoquije ..... C 4
Llallagua, 6,719 ..... B 6
Llanquera, 613 ..... A 6
Llica, 560 ..... A 6
Loma Alta ..... B 2
Loreto, 589 ..... C 4
Los Cusis ..... D 4
Luribay, 392 ..... B 5
Macha, 1,050 ..... B 6
Machacamarca, 1,746 ..... B 5
Machareti ..... D 7
Magdalena, 1,724 ..... C 3
Mairana, 508 ..... D 6
Manoa ..... C 1
Mapiri, 289 ..... B 4
Maravillas ..... B 2
Mategua, 38 ..... D 3
Mayor Pedro Vaca Diez, 358 ..... C 4
Mecoya ..... C 8
Mendoza ..... C 5
Mercier ..... B 2
Mizque, 870 ..... C 5
Mocomoco, 977 ..... A 4
Mojo, 469 ..... C 7
Mojocoya, 498 ..... C 6
Monte Cristo ..... E 4
Monteagudo, 971 ..... D 6
Montero, 2,713 ..... D 5
Morochata, 461 ..... B 5
Moromoro, 556 ..... C 6
Motacucito ..... E 5
Muchanes ..... B 4
Mukden ..... A 2
Muyuquiri ..... C 7
Negrillos, 85 ..... A 6
Nueva Manoa ..... C 1
Nuevo Mundo ..... B 2
Obrajes ..... A 5
Ocurí, 1,531 ..... C 6
Opoco ..... B 6
Orinoca ..... B 6
Oro Ingenio ..... C 7
Orobayaya ..... D 3
Oruro, 86,985 ..... B 5
Padcaya, 324 ..... C 7
Padilla, 2,462 ..... C 6
Palaya, 300 ..... A 6
Palca, 887 ..... A 5
Palometas ..... D 5
Pampa Aullagas ..... B 6
Pampa Grande, 727 ..... D 5
Panacachi, 952 ..... B 6
Paria, 335 ..... B 5
Pasorapa, 1,016 ..... C 6
Pata, 122 ..... A 4
Patacamaya, 1,278 ..... B 5
Pazña, 671 ..... B 6
Pelechuco, 873 ..... A 4
Pensamiento ..... E 4
Perseverancia ..... D 4
Piso Firme ..... D 3
Pocoata, 859 ..... B 6
Pocona, 518 ..... C 5
Pocpo ..... C 6
Pojo, 1,047 ..... C 5
Poopó, 736 ..... B 6
Porco, 817 ..... B 6
Poroma, 171 ..... C 6
Portachuelo, 2,456 ..... D 5
Portugalete ..... B 7
Porvenir ..... A 2
Porvenir ..... E 4
Postrervalle, 750 ..... D 6
Potosí, 55,233 ..... C 6
Presto, 725 ..... C 6
Pucara, 762 ..... C 6
Pucarani, 1,041 ..... A 5
Puerto Acosta, 1,302 ..... A 4
Puerto Alegre ..... E 3
Puerto Ballivián ..... C 4
Puerto Calvimonte ..... C 4
Puerto Frey ..... E 4
Puerto General Busch ..... G 7
Puerto Grether ..... C 5
Puerto Guachalla ..... F 6
Puerto Heath ..... A 3
Puerto Isabel ..... G 6
Puerto Izozog ..... D 6
Puerto Mamoré ..... C 5
Puerto Pando ..... B 4
Puerto Patiño ..... C 5
Puerto Quijarro, 1,006 ..... G 5

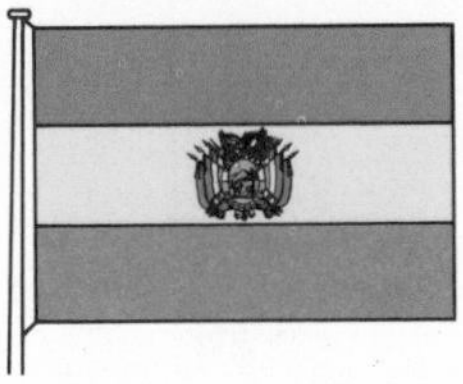

AREA 424, 163 sq. mi.
POPULATION 4,804,000
CAPITALS La Paz, Sucre
LARGEST CITY La Paz
HIGHEST POINT Nevada Ancohuma 21,489 ft.
MONETARY UNIT Bolivian peso
MAJOR LANGUAGES Spanish, Quechua, Aymara
MAJOR RELIGION Roman Catholicism

Puerto Rico ..... B 2
Puerto San Francisco ..... C 5
Puerto Saucedo ..... D 3
Puerto Siles, 357 ..... C 3
Puerto Suárez, 1,159 ..... F 6
Puerto Sucre, 1,470 ..... C 2
Puerto Torno ..... C 5
Puerto Velarde ..... D 5
Puerto Villaroel ..... C 5
Puerto Villazón ..... D 3
Puina ..... A 4
Pulacayo, 7,984 ..... B 7
Puna, 852 ..... C 6
Punata, 5,014 ..... C 5
Quechisla, 171 ..... C 7
Quetena, 183 ..... B 8
Quillacas, 1,170 ..... B 6
Quillacollo, 9,123 ..... B 5
Quime, 1,256 ..... B 5
Quiroga ..... C 6
Quirusillas, 433 ..... D 6
Ravelo, 907 ..... C 6
Reyes, 1,404 ..... B 4
Riberalta, 6,549 ..... C 2
Río Grande, 281 ..... B 7
Río Mulato, 381 ..... B 6
Río Negro ..... C 1
Roboré, 3,715 ..... F 6
Rurrenabaque, 1,225 ..... B 4
Sabaya, 649 ..... A 6
Sacaba, 2,752 ..... C 5
Sacaca, 1,778 ..... B 6
Sachojere, 401 ..... C 4
Saipina, 573 ..... C 6
Saipurú ..... D 6
Sajama, 231 ..... A 6
Saladillo ..... D 7
Salinas de Garci Mendoza, 335 ..... B 6
Salinas de Santiago ..... E 6
Samaipata, 1,656 ..... D 6
San Agustín ..... B 7
San Andrés, 399 ..... C 4
San Andrés de Machaca, 101 ..... A 5
San Antonio, 436 ..... C 4
San Antonio ..... E 4
San Antonio de Lípez ..... B 7
San Antonio del Parapetí, 497 ..... D 7
San Borja, 708 ..... B 4
San Buenaventura, 307 ..... A 4
San Carlos, 570 ..... D 5
San Cristóbal ..... B 7
San Cristóbal ..... E 3
San Diego ..... D 7
San Fermín ..... A 3
San Francisco, 185 ..... C 4
San Francisco ..... D 7
San Ignacio, 1,757 ..... C 4
San Ignacio, 1,819 ..... E 5
San Javier, 233 ..... C 4
San Javier, 564 ..... D 5
San Joaquín, 1,959 ..... C 3
San José de Chiquitos, 1,933 ..... E 5
San José de Uchupiamonas, 277 ..... A 4
San Juan, 131 ..... B 7
San Juan ..... F 5
San Juan del Piray, 541 ..... C 7
San Juan del Potrero, 263 ..... C 5
San Lorenzo ..... B 2
San Lorenzo, 496 ..... C 4
San Lorenzo, 785 ..... C 7
San Lucas, 925 ..... C 7
San Matías, 887 ..... F 5
San Miguel, 502 ..... E 5
San Miguel de Huachi, 25 ..... B 4
San Miguelito ..... A 2
San Pablo ..... B 2
San Pablo, 11 ..... B 7
San Pablo ..... D 4
San Pedro ..... B 2
San Pedro, 262 ..... C 4
San Pedro, 182 ..... C 6
San Pedro, 80 ..... D 5
San Pedro de Buena Vista, 1,094 ..... C 6
San Pedro de Quemes ..... A 7
San Rafael ..... E 5
San Ramón, 1,161 ..... C 3
San Ramón, 379 ..... D 5
Sanandita, 379 ..... D 7
Santa Ana, 171 ..... B 4
Santa Ana, 2,225 ..... C 3
Santa Ana ..... C 7
Santa Ana, 275 ..... E 5
Santa Ana, 663 ..... F 6
Santa Cruz ..... A 2
Santa Cruz, 108,720 ..... D 5
Santa Cruz del Valle Ameno, 442 ..... A 4
Santa Elena ..... C 7
Santa Fe ..... D 6
Santa Isabel ..... B 7
Santa Rosa ..... B 2
Santa Rosa, 765 ..... B 4
Santa Rosa, 491 ..... B 5
Santa Rosa ..... C 5
Santa Rosa, 995 ..... D 5
Santa Rosa de la Mina, 99 ..... D 5
Santa Rosa de la Roca, 101 ..... E 5
Santa Roso del Palmar, 441 ..... E 5
Santiago, 172 ..... A 7
Santiago, 765 ..... F 6
Santiago de Huata, 948 ..... A 5
Santiago de Machaca, 218 ..... A 5
Santiago de Pacaguaras ..... A 3
Santo Corazón ..... F 5
Santos Mercado ..... B 2
Sapahaqui, 55 ..... B 5
Sapse ..... C 6
Sarampiuni, 138 ..... A 4
Saya, 339 ..... B 5
Sena ..... B 2
Sevaruyo, 475 ..... B 6
Sicasica, 1,486 ..... B 5
Siccha ..... C 6
Sococha ..... C 7
Sopachuy, 713 ..... C 6
Sorata, 2,087 ..... A 4
Sotomayor, 510 ..... C 6
Suapi ..... B 4
Suches ..... A 4
Sucre (capital), 58,359 ..... C 6
Suipacha ..... C 7
Tablas ..... C 5
Tacobamba ..... C 6
Tacopaya, 795 ..... B 5
Tagua ..... B 6
Tahua, 114 ..... B 3
Talina, 122 ..... B 7
Tapacarí, 980 ..... B 5
Tarabuco, 2,833 ..... C 6
Tarairí ..... D 7
Tarapaya, 357 ..... B 6
Tarata, 3,016 ..... C 5
Tarija, 20,851 ..... C 7
Tarumá ..... D 6
Tarvita, 404 ..... C 6
Tazna ..... B 7
Teduzara ..... B 2
Terevinto ..... D 5
Tiahuanacu, 1,227 ..... A 5
Tinquipaya, 766 ..... C 6
Tipuani ..... B 4
Tiraque, 1,390 ..... C 5
Tiraque, 234 ..... C 5
Tocomechi (Ingeniero Montero Hoyos), 575 ..... D 5
Todos Santos, 68 ..... A 6
Todos Santos ..... B 3
Todos Santos, 408 ..... C 5
Toledo, 3,273 ..... B 6
Tomás Barrón, 1,852 ..... B 5
Tomave, 201 ..... B 7
Tomayapo ..... C 7

Topography

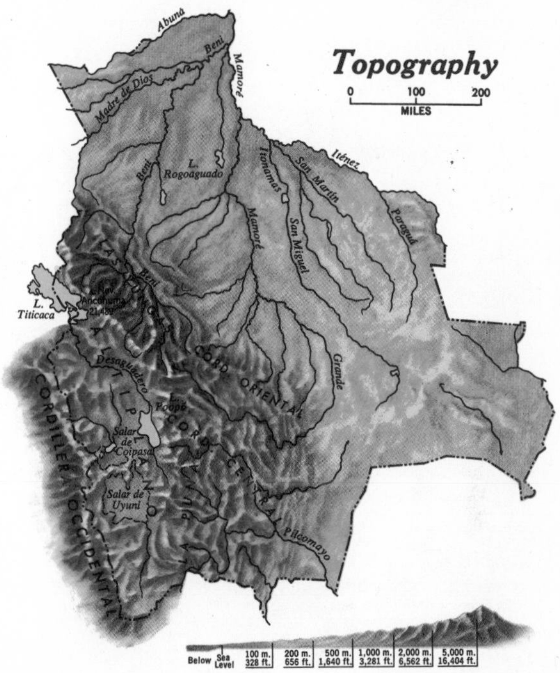
0 100 200
MILES
Abuná
Beni
Madre de Dios
Mamoré
L. Rogoaguado
Itonamas
San Martín
Iténez
Paraguá
Mamoré
San Miguel
Beni
L. Titicaca
Desaguadero
Poopó
Salar de Coipasa
Salar de Uyuni
CORD. ORIENTAL
CORDILLERA OCCIDENTAL
Grande
Pilcomayo
Below Sea Level
100 m. 328 ft.
200 m. 656 ft.
500 m. 1,640 ft.
1,000 m. 3,281 ft.
2,000 m. 6,562 ft.
5,000 m. 16,404 ft.

Tomina, 708 ..... C 6
Toropalca ..... B 7
Torotoro, 1,233 ..... C 6
Totora, 210 ..... A 5
Totora, 2,290 ..... C 5
Trigal, 749 ..... C 6
Trinidad ..... B 2
Trinidad, 14,505 ..... C 4
Tucavaca ..... F 6
Tumupasa, 349 ..... B 4
Tumusla ..... C 7
Tupiza, 8,248 ..... C 7
Turco, 131 ..... A 6
Ubina ..... B 7
Ucumasi ..... B 6
Ulla Ulla, 52 ..... A 4
Ulloma, 116 ..... A 5
Umala, 481 ..... B 5
Uncía, 4,507 ..... B 6
Uriondo, 860 ..... C 7
Urmiri ..... B 6
Urubichá, 1,369 ..... D 4
Uyuni, 6,968 ..... B 7
Vallegrande, 5,094 ..... C 6
Vandiola ..... C 5
Versalles, 83 ..... D 3
Viacha, 6,607 ..... A 5
Vichacla, 317 ..... C 7
Vichaya, 422 ..... A 5
Victoria ..... B 2
Vilacaya, 200 ..... C 6
Villa Abecia, 539 ..... C 7
Villa Bella, 88 ..... C 2
Villa E. Viscarra, 658 ..... C 6
Villa General Pérez, 802 ..... A 4
Villa Ingavi, 122 ..... D 7
Villa Martín, 543 ..... B 7
Villa Montes, 3,105 ..... D 7
Villa Serrano, 1,570 ..... C 6
Villa Talavera (Puna), 852 ..... C 6
Villa Tunari, 510 ..... C 5
Villa Vaca Guzmán, 699 ..... D 6
Villar, 322 ..... C 6
Villazón, 6,261 ..... C 7
Viloyo ..... B 6
Vitichi, 1,515 ..... C 7
Warnes, 1,571 ..... D 5
Yaco, 835 ..... B 5
Yacuiba, 5,027 ..... D 7
Yaguarú ..... D 4
Yamparáez, 725 ..... C 6
Yanacachi ..... B 5
Yata ..... C 2
Yatina ..... C 7
Yesera ..... C 7
Yocalla ..... B 6
Yotala, 1,554 ..... C 6
Yotaú ..... D 5
Yura, 136 ..... B 7
Zongo, 141 ..... B 5
Zudáñez, 1,868 ..... C 6

OTHER FEATURES

Altamachi (river) ..... B 5
Ancohuma, Nevada (mt.) ..... A 4
Andes (mts.) ..... A 3
Apere (river) ..... C 4
Arroyas, Los (lake) ..... C 3
Barras (river) ..... B 6
Baures (river) ..... D 3
Beni (river) ..... B 2
Bermejo (river) ..... C 8
Blanco (river) ..... D 4
Bloomfield, Sierra (mts.) ..... D 4
Boopi (river) ..... B 4
Cáceres (lagoon) ..... F 6
Candelaria (river) ..... F 5
Capitán Ustarés, Cerro (mt.) ..... E 6
Central, Cordillera (mts.) ..... C 6
Challviri (salt depr.) ..... B 8
Chaparé (river) ..... C 5
Charagua (mts.) ..... D 6
Chipamanu (river) ..... A 2
Coipasa (lake) ..... B 6
Coipasa (salt depr.) ..... A 6
Colorada (lagoon) ..... A 8
Concepción (lagoon) ..... E 5
Cotacajes (river) ..... B 5
Desaguadero (river) ..... B 5
Empexa (salt depr.) ..... A 7
Gaiba (lagoon) ..... G 5
Grande (marsh) ..... F 5
Grande (river) ..... C 4
Grande (river) ..... C 6
Grande de Lípez (river) ..... B 7
Guaporé (river) ..... C 3
Guaraní (Capitán Ustarés) (mt.) ..... E 6
Heath (river) ..... A 3
Huanchaca, Cerro (mt.) ..... B 7
Huanchaca, Serranía de (mts.) ..... E 4
Ichilo (river) ..... C 5
Illampu, Nevada (mt.) ..... A 4
Illimani, Nevada (mt.) ..... B 5
Incacamachi, Cerro (mt.) ..... A 6
Isiboro (river) ..... C 5
Iténez (Guaporé) (river) ..... C 3
Itonamas (river) ..... C 3
Izozog (swamp) ..... E 6
Las Petas (river) ..... F 5
Las Yungas (region) ..... B 5
Lauca (river) ..... A 6
Lípez, Cordillera de (mts.) ..... B 8
Liverpool (swamp) ..... D 4
Machupo (river) ..... C 3
Madidi (river) ..... A 3
Madre de Dios (river) ..... A 3
Mamoré (river) ..... C 2
Mandioré (lagoon) ..... G 6
Manuripi (river) ..... B 2
Mizque (river) ..... C 6
Mosetenes, Cordillera de (mts.) ..... B 5
Negro (river) ..... D 4
Occidental, Cordillera (mts.) ..... A 6
Ollagüe (volcano) ..... A 7
Oriental, Cordillera (mts.) ..... C 5
Ortón (river) ..... B 2
Otuquis (river) ..... F 6
Paraguá (river) ..... E 4
Paraguay (river) ..... F 7
Parapetí (river) ..... D 6
Petas, Las (river) ..... F 5
Pilaya (river) ..... C 7
Pilcomayo (river) ..... D 7
Piray (river) ..... D 5
Poopó (lake) ..... B 6
Pupuya, Nevada (mt.) ..... A 4
Puquintica, Cerro (mt.) ..... A 6
Rápulo (river) ..... C 4
Real, Cordillera (mts.) ..... A 5
Rogagua (lake) ..... B 3
Rogaguado (lake) ..... C 3
Sajama, Nevada (mt.) ..... A 6
San Fernando (river) ..... F 5
San Juan (river) ..... C 7
San Luis (lake) ..... C 3
San Martín (river) ..... D 3
San Miguel (river) ..... D 4
San Simón, Serranía (mts.) ..... D 4
Santiago, Serranía de (mts.) ..... F 6
Sillajguay (mt.) ..... A 6
Suches (river) ..... A 4
Tahuamanu (river) ..... A 2
Tarija (river) ..... C 8
Titicaca (lake) ..... A 4
Tocorpuri, Cerros de (mt.) ..... A 8
Tucavaca (river) ..... F 6
Tuichi (river) ..... A 4
Uberaba (lagoon) ..... F 5
Uyuni (salt depr.) ..... B 7
Yacuma (river) ..... B 3
Yapacani (river) ..... C 5
Yata (river) ..... C 3
Yungas, Las (region) ..... B 5
Zapaleri, Cerro (mt.) ..... B 8

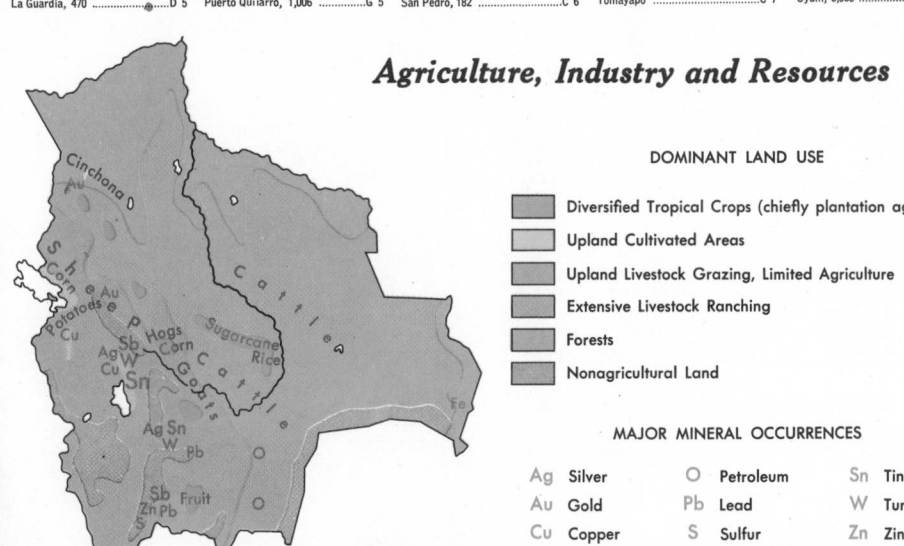

Agriculture, Industry and Resources

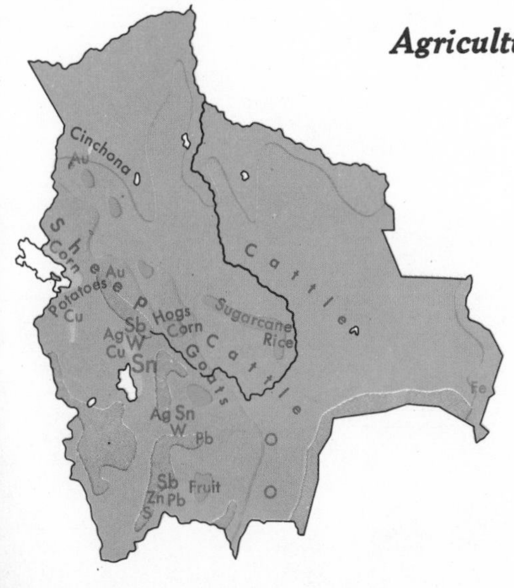
Cinchona
Au
Sheep
Corn
Au
Potatoes
Cu
Sb
Hogs
Corn
Sugarcane
Rice
Ag
W
Cu
Sn
Cattle
Goats
Ag Sn
W
Pb
Sb
Zn Pb
Fruit
Fe

DOMINANT LAND USE

- Diversified Tropical Crops (chiefly plantation agriculture)
- Upland Cultivated Areas
- Upland Livestock Grazing, Limited Agriculture
- Extensive Livestock Ranching
- Forests
- Nonagricultural Land

MAJOR MINERAL OCCURRENCES

Ag	Silver	O	Petroleum	Sn	Tin
Au	Gold	Pb	Lead	W	Tungsten
Cu	Copper	S	Sulfur	Zn	Zinc
Fe	Iron Ore	Sb	Antimony		

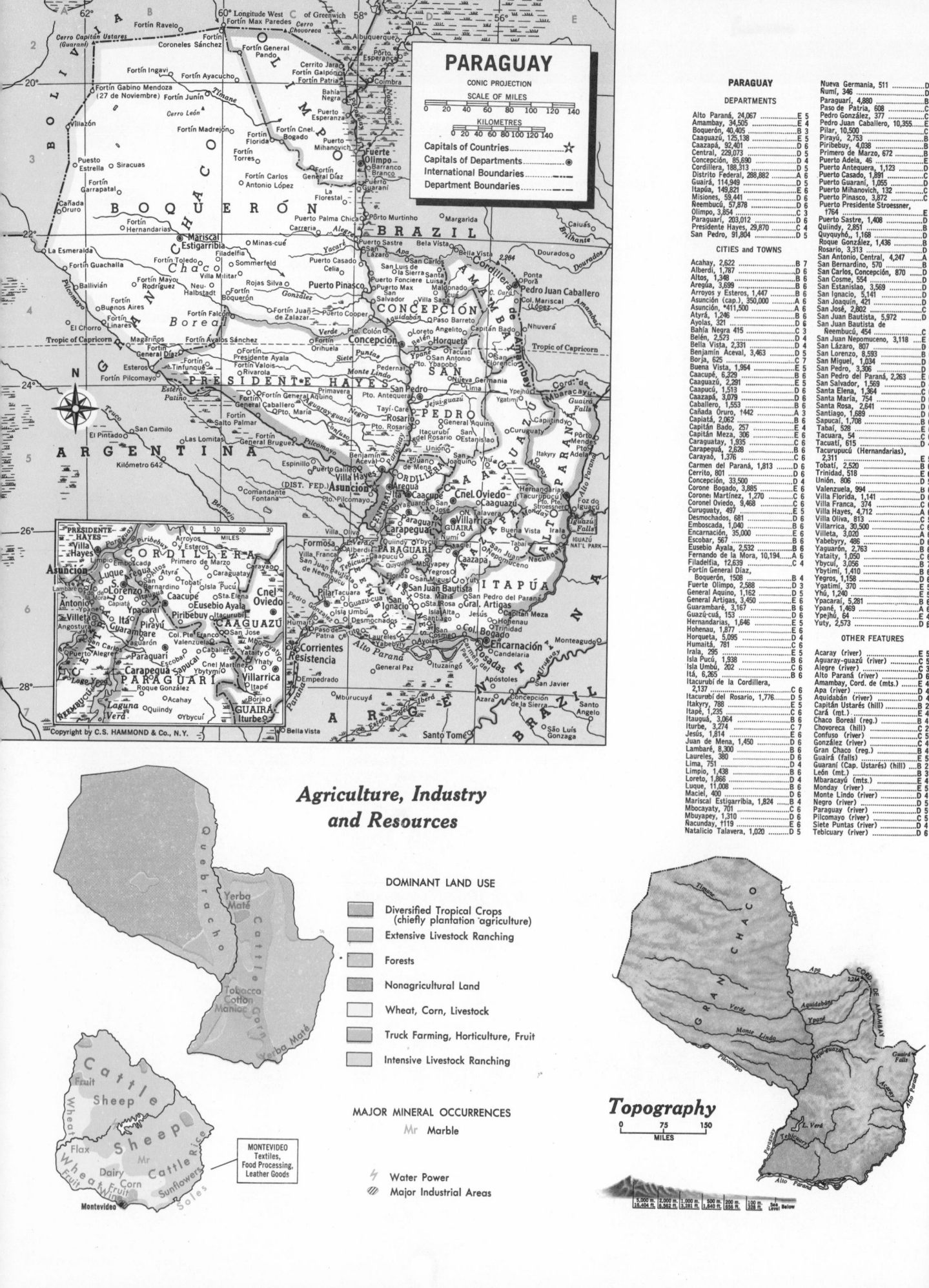

PARAGUAY

CONIC PROJECTION

SCALE OF MILES
0 20 40 60 80 100 120 140

KILOMETRES
0 20 40 60 80 100 120 140

Capitals of Countries .... ☆
Capitals of Departments .... ◉
International Boundaries ....
Department Boundaries ....

PARAGUAY

DEPARTMENTS

Alto Paraná, 24,067	E 5
Amambay, 34,505	E 4
Boquerón, 40,405	B 3
Caaguazú, 125,138	E 5
Caazapá, 92,401	D 6
Central, 229,073	D 5
Concepción, 85,690	D 4
Cordillera, 188,313	D 5
Distrito Federal, 288,882	A 6
Guairá, 114,949	D 5
Itapúa, 149,821	E 6
Misiones, 59,441	D 6
Ñeembucú, 57,878	D 6
Olimpo, 3,854	C 2
Paraguarí, 203,012	D 6
Presidente Hayes, 29,870	C 4
San Pedro, 91,804	D 5

CITIES and TOWNS

Acahay, 2,622	B 7
Alberdi, 1,787	B 6
Altos, 1,348	B 6
Aregúa, 3,699	B 6
Arroyos y Esteros, 1,447	B 6
Asunción (cap.), 350,000	A 6
Asunción, *411,500	A 6
Atyrá, 1,246	B 6
Ayolas, 321	D 6
Bahía Negra 415	C 3
Belén, 2,523	D 4
Bella Vista, 2,331	D 4
Benjamín Aceval, 3,463	C 5
Borja, 625	C 7
Buena Vista, 1,954	E 5
Caacupé, 6,329	B 6
Caaguazú, 2,291	E 5
Caapucú, 1,513	C 7
Caazapá, 3,079	D 6
Caballero, 1,553	B 6
Cañada Oruro, 1442	A 3
Capiatá, 2,062	B 6
Capitán Bado, 257	E 4
Capitán Meza, 306	C 7
Caraguatay, 1,935	C 6
Carapeguá, 2,628	B 6
Carayá, 1,376	D 6
Carmen del Paraná, 1,813	D 6
Cerrito, 801	C 6
Concepción, 33,500	D 4
Corone Bogado, 3,885	D 6
Coronel Martínez, 1,270	C 6
Coronel Oviedo, 9,468	C 6
Curuguaty, 497	E 5
Desmochados, 681	C 6
Emboscada, 1,040	B 6
Encarnación, 25,000	E 6
Escobar, 567	C 6
Eusebio Ayala, 2,532	B 6
Fernando de la Mora, 10,194	A 6
Filadelfia, 12,639	C 4
Fortín General Díaz, Boquerón, 1508	B 4
Fuerte Olimpo, 2,588	D 3
General Aquino, 1,162	D 5
General Artigas, 3,450	E 6
Guarambaré, 3,167	B 6
Guazú-cuá, 153	D 6
Hernandarias, 1,646	E 5
Hohenau, 1,877	E 6
Horqueta, 5,095	D 4
Humaitá, 781	C 6
Irala, 295	E 5
Isla Pucú, 1,938	B 6
Isla Umbú, 202	B 6
Itá, 6,265	B 6
Itacurubí de la Cordillera, 2,137	C 6
Itacurubí del Rosario, 1,776	D 5
Itakyry, 788	E 5
Itapé, 1,235	C 6
Itauguá, 3,064	B 6
Iturbe, 3,274	C 7
Jesús, 1,814	E 6
Juan de Mena, 1,450	C 6
Lambaré, 8,300	A 6
Laureles, 380	D 6
Lima, 751	D 4
Limpio, 1,438	D 4
Loreto, 1,866	D 4
Luque, 11,008	D 5
Maciel, 400	C 6
Mariscal Estigarribia, 1,824	B 4
Mbocayaty, 701	D 6
Mbuyapey, 1,310	D 6
Ñacunday, 1119	E 6
Natalicio Talavera, 1,020	D 5

Nueva Germania, 511	D 5
Numi, 346	B 6
Paraguarí, 4,880	D 6
Paso de Patria, 608	C 6
Pedro González, 377	C 6
Pedro Juan Caballero, 10,355	E 4
Pilar, 10,500	C 6
Pirayú, 2,753	B 6
Piribebuy, 4,038	B 6
Primero de Marzo, 672	C 6
Puerto Adela, 46	E 5
Puerto Antequera, 1,123	C 5
Puerto Casado, 1,891	C 4
Puerto Guaraní, 1,055	C 3
Puerto Mihanovich, 132	C 3
Puerto Pinasco, 3,872	C 4
Puerto Presidente Stroessner, 1764	E 5
Puerto Sastre, 1,408	C 4
Quiindy, 2,851	B 7
Quyquyhó, 1,168	B 7
Rosario, 3,313	A 5
San Antonio, Central, 4,247	A 6
San Bernardino, 570	B 6
San Carlos, Concepción, 870	C 3
San Cosme, 554	D 6
San Estanislao, 3,569	D 5
San Ignacio, 5,141	D 6
San Joaquín, 427	D 5
San José, 2,802	C 6
San Juan Bautista, 5,972	D 6
San Juan Bautista de Ñeembucú, 454	C 6
San Juan Nepomuceno, 3,118	C 7
San Lázaro, 807	D 4
San Lorenzo, 8,593	A 6
San Miguel, 1,034	D 6
San Pedro, 3,306	D 5
San Pedro del Paraná, 2,263	C 6
San Salvador, 1,569	D 5
Santa Elena, 1,364	C 6
Santa María, 754	D 6
Santa Rosa, 2,641	D 7
Santiago, 1,689	D 6
Sapucaí, 1,708	B 6
Tabaí, 528	C 6
Tacuara, 54	D 4
Tacuatí, 615	D 4
Tacurupucú (Hernandarias), 2,311	E 5
Tobatí, 2,520	B 6
Trinidad, 518	E 6
Unión, 806	D 5
Valenzuela, 994	D 6
Villa Florida, 1,141	D 6
Villa Franca, 374	C 6
Villa Hayes, 4,712	A 6
Villa Oliva, 813	C 6
Villarrica, 30,500	C 6
Villeta, 2,763	A 6
Yabebyry, 486	D 6
Yataity, 1,050	C 6
Ybycuí, 3,056	B 7
Ybytimí, 1,410	B 7
Ygatimí, 370	E 5
Yhú, 1,240	E 5
Ypacaraí, 5,281	B 6
Ypané, 3,493	A 6
Ypejhú, 64	E 4
Yuty, 2,573	D 7

OTHER FEATURES

Acaray (river)	E 5
Aguaray-guazú (river)	C 3
Alegre (river)	C 3
Alto Paraná (river)	E 5
Amambay, Cord. de (mts.)	E 4
Apa (river)	D 4
Aquidabán (river)	C 4
Cará (river)	E 4
Chaco Boreal (reg.)	B 4
Chovoreca (hill)	C 2
Confuso (river)	B 4
González (river)	C 4
Gran Chaco (reg.)	B 4
Guairá (falls)	E 4
Guaraní (Cap. Ustarés) (hill)	B 2
León (mt.)	C 7
Mbaracayú (mts.)	E 4
Monday (river)	E 5
Monte Lindo (river)	D 4
Negro (river)	D 5
Paraguay (river)	D 5
Pilcomayo (river)	B 4
Siete Puntas (river)	D 4
Tebicuary (river)	D 6

Agriculture, Industry and Resources

DOMINANT LAND USE

- Diversified Tropical Crops (chiefly plantation agriculture)
- Extensive Livestock Ranching
- Forests
- Nonagricultural Land
- Wheat, Corn, Livestock
- Truck Farming, Horticulture, Fruit
- Intensive Livestock Ranching

MAJOR MINERAL OCCURRENCES
Mr Marble

⚡ Water Power
▨ Major Industrial Areas

MONTEVIDEO
Textiles,
Food Processing,
Leather Goods

Topography

0   75   150
MILES

Copyright by C.S. HAMMOND & Co., N.Y.

Tímane (river) ....C 3
Verá (lagoon) ....B 7
Verde (river) ....C 4
Yacaré (river) ....C 4
Ypané (river) ....D 4
Ypoá (lake) ....B 6

URUGUAY

DEPARTMENTS

Artigas, 52,261 ....B 1
Canelones, 211,644 ....D 5
Cerro Largo, 118,880 ....E 3
Colonia, 135,185 ....B 5
Durazno, 113,797 ....D 4
Flores, 35,457 ....C 4
Florida, 104,739 ....D 4
Lavalleja, 114,090 ....E 4
Maldonado, 62,344 ....E 5
Montevideo, 1,173,114 ....D 5
Paysandú, 89,906 ....B 3
Río Negro, 49,258 ....B 3
Rivera, 86,430 ....D 2
Rocha, 84,210 ....E 4
Salto, 105,698 ....B 2
San José, 94,541 ....C 5
Soriano, 78,234 ....B 4
Tacuarembó, 119,690 ....D 3
Treinta y Tres, 81,887 ....E 4

CITIES and TOWNS

Achar, 460 ....C 3
Aiguá, 2,715 ....E 4
Algorta, 650 ....C 4
Arroyo Grande, 1,000 ....C 4
Artigas, 23,429 ....B 1
Balneario El Tesoro, 84 ....E 5
Balneario La Barra, 124 ....E 5
Balneario Solís, 225 ....D 5
Baltasar Brum, 1,764 ....B 1
Belén, 2,933 ....B 1
Bella Unión, 4,955 ....B 1
Bernabé Rivera, 683 ....B 1
Bizcocho, 117 ....B 4
Campamento, 187 ....C 1
Cañada Nieto, 407 ....B 4
Canelones, 27,000 ....D 5
Cardona, 4,110 ....C 4
Carlos Reyles, 940 ....C 4
Carmelo, 11,923 ....A 4
Carmen, 1,687 ....D 4
Castillos, 5,345 ....F 5
Casupá, 1,652 ....D 5
Cerro Chato, Treinta y
Tres, 2,045 ....D 4
Clara, 1,000 ....D 3
Colonia, 9,825 ....A 5
Colonia Agraciada, 409 ....A 4
Colonia Arrué ....B 5
Colonia Artigas, 234 ....B 1
Colonia Concordia, 755 ....C 4
Colonia Itacumbú, 738 ....B 1
Colonia Lavalleja ....C 4
Colonia Palma, 94 ....D 4
Colonia Rossel y Rius ....D 4
Colonia Valdense, 1,126 ....B 5
Conchillas, 590 ....C 1
Constancia, 150 ....B 3
Constitución, 1,600 ....A 2
Corrales (J. P. Varela), 2,700 ....E 4
Cuaró ....D 2
Cufré ....C 3
Curtina ....C 3
Diego Lamas, 94 ....B 1
Dolores, 12,480 ....A 4
Durazno, 19,486 ....D 4
Egaña, 675 ....B 4
Estación Atlántida, 1,007 ....C 6
Estación Cuaró, 203 ....C 1
Estación José Ignacio, 131 ....E 5
Estación Rincón ....C 4
Estación Sosa Díaz ....C 6
Estación Villasboas ....C 4
Estanzuela ....A 4
Florida, 17,243 ....D 4
Fortaleza de Santa Teresa ....F 5
Fraile Muerto, 1,876 ....E 3
Fray Bentos, 14,625 ....A 4
Fray Marcos, 1,095 ....D 5
Garzón, 345 ....E 5
Guichón, 4,625 ....C 3
Itapeby ....C 2
Javier de Viana, 317 ....C 1
Joaquín Suárez, Canelones,
1,752 ....B 6
Joaquín Suárez, Colonia ....B 5
José Batlle y Ordóñez, 1,781 ....D 4
José Enrique Rodó, 1,319 ....C 4
José Pedro Varela (Corrales),
2,955 ....E 4
Juan D. Jackson, 163 ....C 4
Juan L. Lacaze, 9,916 ....B 5
La Bolsa, 274 ....C 1
La Cruz, 2,000 ....C 4
La Paz, Canelones, 5,214 ....B 6
La Paz, Colonia ....B 5
La Sierra, 241 ....D 5
Las Flores, 404 ....B 2

Las Piedras, 15,724 ....B 6
Lascano, 4,204 ....E 5
Libertad, 4,622 ....C 5
Mal Abrigo, 630 ....C 5
Maldonado, 15,005 ....E 5
Manga ....C 5
Mariscala, 1,305 ....E 4
Martín Chico ....A 5
Mazangano ....E 3
Melo, 28,673 ....E 3
Mercedes, 31,325 ....B 4
Merinos, 1,200 ....C 3
Migues, 1,017 ....D 5
Minas, 23,127 ....D 5
Minas de Corrales, 2,320 ....D 2
Molles (Carlos Reyles), 940 ....D 4
Montevideo (cap.), 1,154,465 ....B 7
Montevideo, *1,400,000 ....C 5
Nico Pérez ....D 4
Nueva Helvecia ....B 5
Nueva Palmira, 4,611 ....A 4
Nuevo Berlín, 1,531 ....B 3
Olimar, 2,499 ....E 3
Ombúes de Lavalle, 1,067 ....B 4
Palmitas, 1,288 ....B 4
Pan de Azúcar, 4,190 ....D 5
Pando, 11,623 ....C 5
Parada Esperanza, 250 ....B 3
Paso de Andrés Pérez ....B 1
Paso de León, 184 ....D 4
Paso de los Toros, 10,624 ....C 4
Paso de Ramos, 23 ....C 1
Paso del Borracho ....D 2
Paso del Parque ....D 4
Paysandú, 47,875 ....B 3
Piedras Coloradas, 200 ....C 3
Piñera, 1,000 ....B 1
Pintado, 160 ....D 4
Pirarajá, 1,000 ....E 4
Piriápolis, 4,546 ....E 5
Polanco del Yí, 300 ....D 4
Porvenir, 1,000 ....B 3
Progreso ....C 5
Puerto Amaro ....F 2
Puerto Arazatí ....C 5
Punta del Este, 5,272 ....F 5
Quebracho, 1,002 ....C 3
Río Branco, 3,345 ....F 3
Rivera, 42,623 ....D 2
Rocha, 19,895 ....E 5
Rodríguez, 1,097 ....C 5
Rosario, 6,398 ....C 5
Salto, 55,425 ....B 2
San Bautista, 1,500 ....D 5
San Carlos, 13,695 ....E 5
San Gregorio, San José ....C 4
San Gregorio, Tacuarembó,
1,606 ....D 3
San José de Mayo, 21,048 ....D 5
San Ramón, 3,983 ....D 5
Sánchez ....C 5
Santa Catalina, 824 ....B 4
Santa Clara de Olimar ....E 3
Santa Lucía, 9,126 ....B 6
Santa Rosa, 1,596 ....D 5
Sarandí del Yí, 5,900 ....D 4
Sarandí de Navarro, 630 ....C 3
Sarandí Grande, 5,620 ....C 4
Sauce, Canelones, 1,570 ....D 5
Sauce, Rocha ....E 5
Sequeira, 880 ....C 1
Soca, 1,200 ....C 5
Solís, 1,531 ....D 5
Soriano, 1,036 ....A 4
Tacuarembó, 17,854 ....D 3
Tala, 1,957 ....D 5
Tambores, 1,273 ....C 2
Toledo, 1,200 ....B 6
Tomás Gomensoro, 2,144 ....B 1
Topador, 183 ....C 1
Tranqueras, 3,340 ....D 2
Treinta y Tres, 18,856 ....E 4
Tres Árboles, 400 ....C 3
Trinidad, 17,233 ....C 4
Tupambaé, 1,359 ....E 3
Veinticinco de Agosto, 1,139 ....A 6
Velázquez, 1,198 ....F 5
Vergara, 2,480 ....E 3
Villa Darwin, 445 ....B 4
Young, 6,485 ....B 3
Zapicán, 1,500 ....E 4

OTHER FEATURES

Aiguá (river) ....E 4
Alférez (river) ....E 5
Arapey Chico (river) ....B 1
Arapey Grande (river) ....B 2
Arroyo Negro (river) ....B 3
Belén (range) ....C 1
Bonete (dam) ....D 4
Brava (point) ....E 7
Cañas (range) ....C 2
Caraguatá (river) ....D 3
Castillos (lagoon) ....F 5
Cebollatí (river) ....E 4
Cordobés (river) ....D 4
Cuñapirú (river) ....D 2
Daymán (range) ....B 2
Daymán (river) ....B 2

Durazno (range) ....D 4
Espinillo (point) ....D 6
Este (point) ....E 5
Flores (isl.) ....D 6
Garzón (lagoon) ....E 5
Grande (range) ....B 4
Grande (river) ....C 4
Grande Inferior (range) ....B 1
Haedo (range) ....C 3
India Muerta (river) ....E 4
José Ignacio (lagoon) ....E 5
La Plata (river) ....B 5
Lobos (isl.), 11 ....C 6
Maciel (river) ....C 4
Mirador Nacional (mt.) ....D 4
Mirim (lagoon) ....F 4
Negra (lagoon) ....F 5
Negra (range) ....D 3
Negro (river) ....B 4
Olimar Grande (river) ....E 3
Pando (river) ....C 5
Parao (river) ....E 3
Plata, La (river) ....B 5

Polonio (cape) ....F 5
Queguay Chico (river) ....B 3
Queguay Grande (river) ....B 3
Río Negro (res.) ....D 3
Rocha (river) ....E 5
Salto Grande (falls) ....A 2
San José (river) ....C 5
San Miguel (swamp) ....F 4
San Salvador (river) ....B 4
Santa Ana (range) ....D 2
Santa Lucía (river) ....C 5
Santa Lucía Chico (river) ....D 5
Santa María (cape) ....F 5
Sauce (lagoon) ....D 5
Sopas (river) ....C 2
Tacuarembó (river) ....D 3
Tacuarí (river) ....F 3
Tigre (isl.) ....A 7
Uruguay (river) ....B 4
Yaguarón (river) ....F 3
Yí (river) ....B 4

*City and suburbs.
†Population of district.

PARAGUAY

AREA 157,047 sq. mi.
POPULATION 2,314,000
CAPITAL Asunción
LARGEST CITY Asunción
HIGHEST POINT Amambay Range 2,264 ft.
MONETARY UNIT guaraní
MAJOR LANGUAGES Spanish, Guaraní
MAJOR RELIGION Roman Catholicism

URUGUAY

AREA 72,172 sq. mi.
POPULATION 2,900,000
CAPITAL Montevideo
LARGEST CITY Montevideo
HIGHEST POINT Mirador Nacional 1,644 ft.
MONETARY UNIT Uruguayan peso
MAJOR LANGUAGE Spanish
MAJOR RELIGION Roman Catholicism

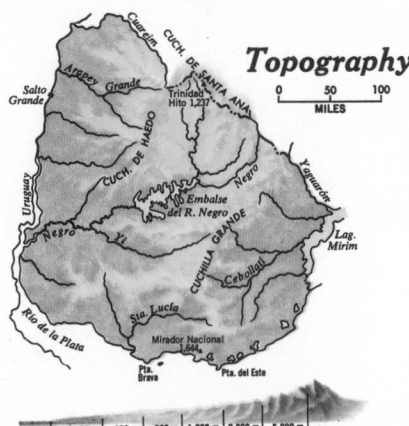

Topography

0   50   100
MILES

Below Sea Level | 100 m. 328 ft. | 200 m. 656 ft. | 500 m. 1,640 ft. | 1,000 m. 3,281 ft. | 2,000 m. 6,562 ft. | 5,000 m. 16,404 ft.

URUGUAY

CONIC PROJECTION

SCALE OF MILES
20   40   60

SCALE OF KILOMETRES
0   20   40   60

Capitals of Countries ············☆
Department Capitals ············●
International Boundaries ············
Department Boundaries ············

Copyright by C.S. Hammond & Co., N.Y.

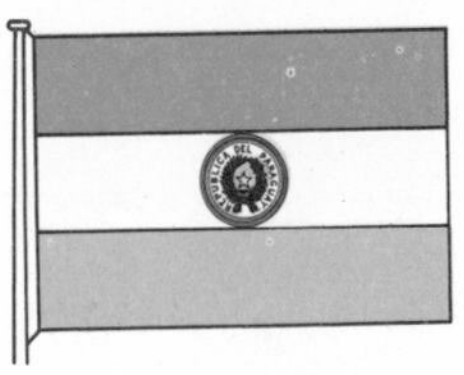

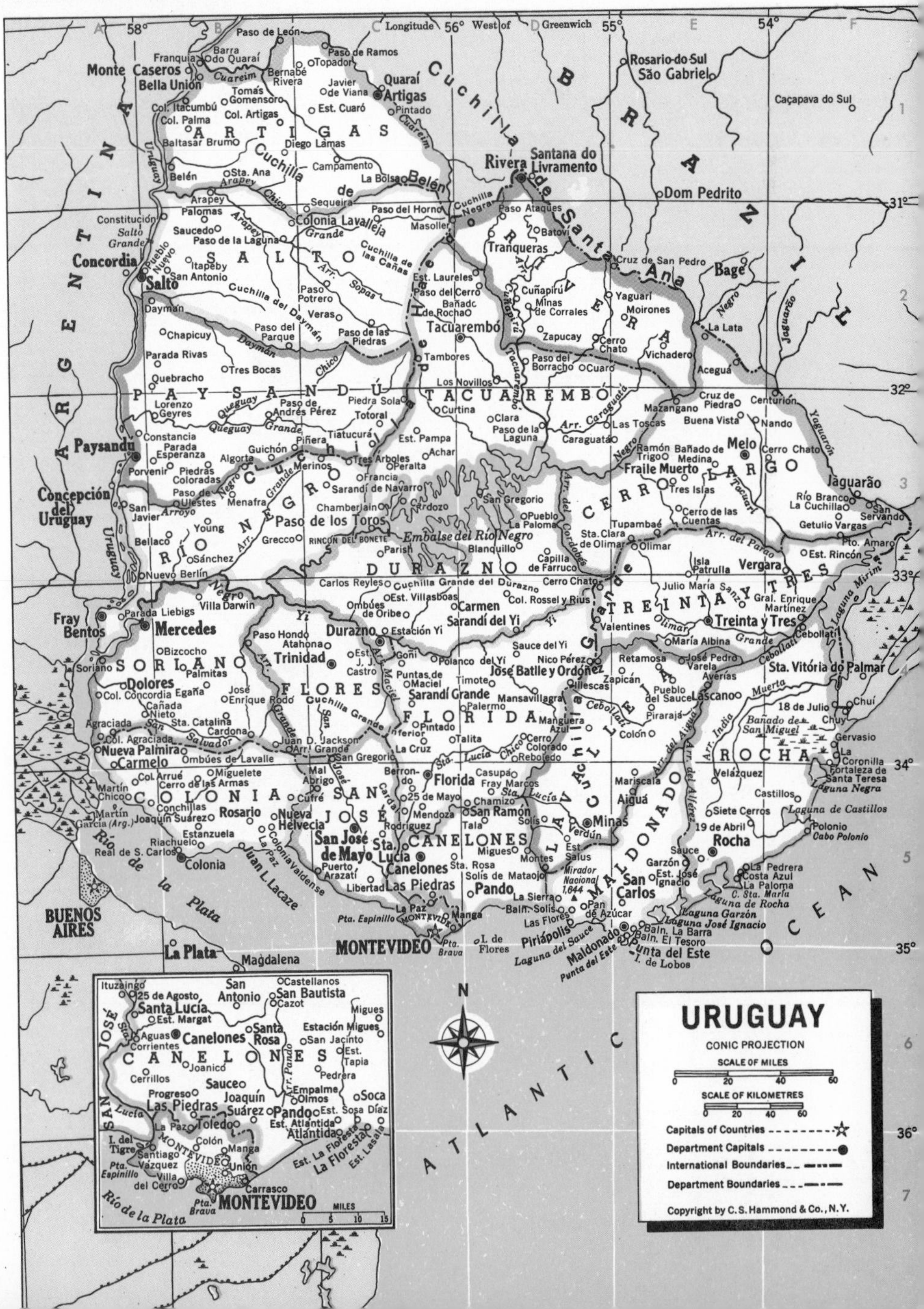

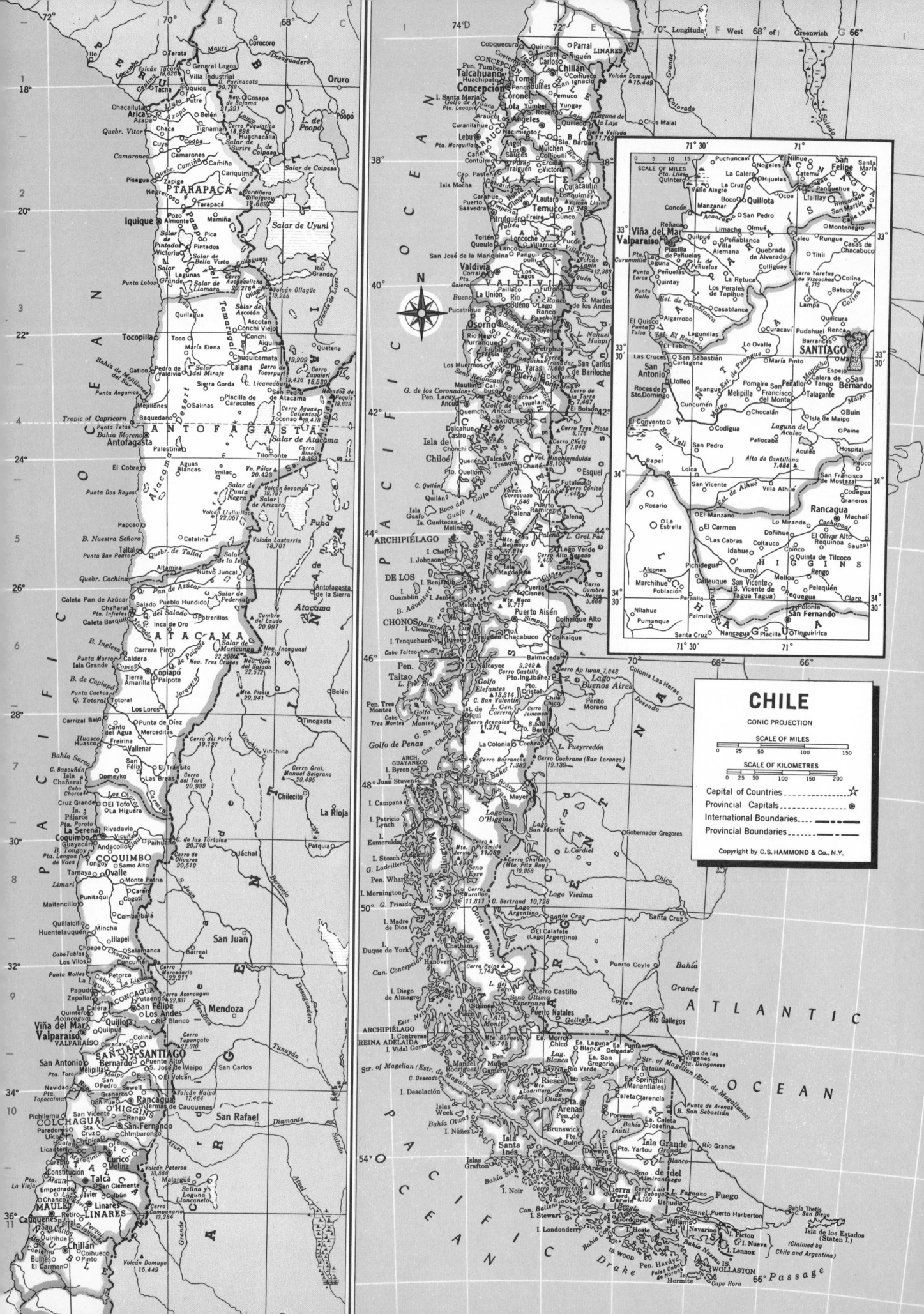

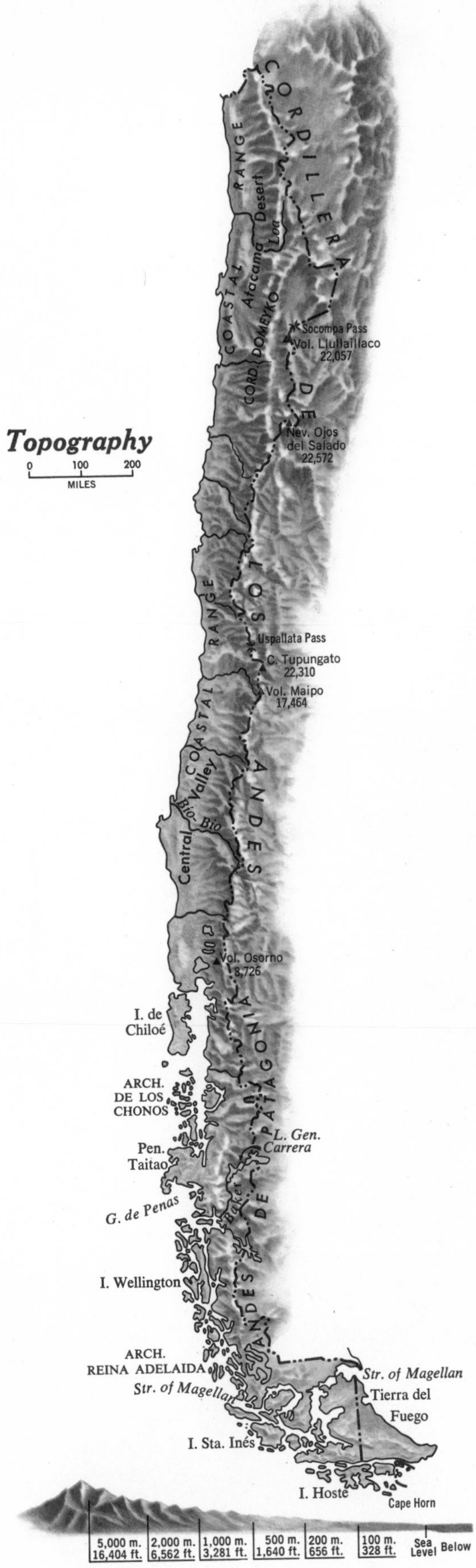
Topography
0 100 200
MILES
CORDILLERA
DE
LOS
ANDES
COASTAL RANGE
COASTAL RANGE
COASTAL
Atacama Desert
Loa
DOMEYKO
CORD.
Socompa Pass
Vol. Llullaillaco
22,057
Nev. Ojos del Salado
22,572
Uspallata Pass
C. Tupungato
22,310
Vol. Maipo
17,464
Central Valley
Bío Bío
Vol. Osorno
8,726
I. de Chiloé
ARCH. DE LOS CHONOS
L. Gen. Carrera
Pen. Taitao
G. de Penas
Baker
ANDES DE PATAGONIA
I. Wellington
ARCH. REINA ADELAIDA
Str. of Magellan
Str. of Magellan
Tierra del Fuego
I. Sta. Inés
I. Hoste
Cape Horn
5,000 m. 16,404 ft.
2,000 m. 6,562 ft.
1,000 m. 3,281 ft.
500 m. 1,640 ft.
200 m. 656 ft.
100 m. 328 ft.
Sea Level
Below

AREA 292,257 sq. mi.
POPULATION 8,834,820
CAPITAL Santiago
LARGEST CITY Santiago
HIGHEST POINT Ojos del Salado 22,572 ft.
MONETARY UNIT Chilean escudo
MAJOR LANGUAGE Spanish
MAJOR RELIGION Roman Catholicism

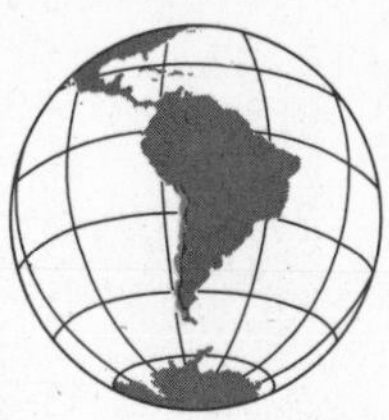

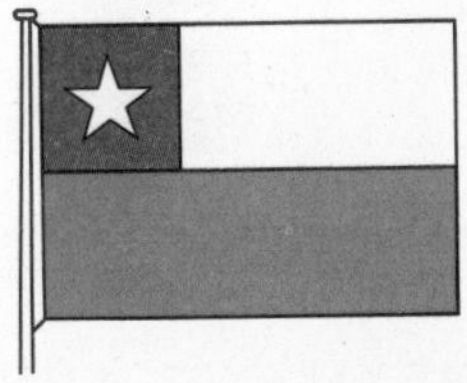

PROVINCES

Aconcagua, 160,821	A 9
Aisén, 51,022	D 6
Antofagasta, 250,665	B 4
Arauco, 98,810	D 1
Atacama, 152,326	B 6
Bío-Bío, 193,002	D 1
Cautín, 420,682	E 2
Chiloé, 110,728	D 4
Colchagua, 167,899	A10
Concepción, 638,118	D 1
Coquimbo, 336,821	A 8
Curicó, 113,710	A10
Linares, 189,010	A11
Llanquihue, 197,986	D 3
Magallanes, 88,706	E10
Malleco, 176,060	E 2
Maule, 82,339	A11
Ñuble, 314,738	E 1
O'Higgins, 306,739	A10
Osorno, 158,673	D 3
Santiago, 3,217,870	A 9
Talca, 231,088	A11
Tarapacá, 174,730	B 2
Valdivia, 275,404	D 3
Valparaíso, 726,953	A 9

CITIES and TOWNS

Achao, †11,501	D 4
Aculeo, 20	G 4
Aguas Blancas, †203	B 4
Aiquina, 105	B 3
Alcones, 682	F 5
Algarrobo, †3,941	F 3
Altamira, 93	B 5
Ancud, †22,127	D 4
Andacollo, †9,987	A 8
Angol, †35,995	D 1
Antofagasta, †126,252	A 4
Arauco, †20,018	D 1
Arica, †92,394	A 1
Ascotán, 23	B 3
Azapa, 225	A 1
Balmaceda, 735	E 6
Baquedano, 1,412	A 4
Barrancas, †184,241	G 3
Batuco, 1,125	G 3
Belén, †925	B 1
Boco, 1,655	F 2
Buin, †31,233	G 4
Bulnes, †16,107	E 1
Cabildo, †13,018	A 9
Calama, †71,983	B 3
Calbuco, †21,673	D 4
Caldera, †3,268	A 6
Calera de Tango, †6,198	G 4
Caleta Barquito, 932	A 6
Caleta Clarencia, 60	E10
Caleta Pan de Azúcar, 8	A 6
Caleu, 187	G 2
Calle Larga, †7,172	G 2
Calleuque	F 5
Camarones, 259	B 2
Camiña, 234	B 2
Cañete, †15,179	D 2
Canto del Agua, 269	A 7
Capitán Pastene, 1,669	D 2
Carahue, †12,733	D 2
Carén, 225	A 8
Cariquima, 20	B 2
Carrera Pinto, 68	B 6
Carrizal Bajo, 207	A 7
Cartagena, †7,124	F 3
Casablanca, †12,292	F 3
Castro, †22,682	D 4
Catalina, †1,637	B 5
Catemu, †8,728	G 2
Cauquenes, †38,476	A11
Cerro Castillo, †537	E 9
Chaca, 37	B 1
Chacalluta, 75	A 1
Chaitén, †4,067	E 4
Chañaral, †36,949	A 6
Chanco, †12,433	A11
Chépica, †11,199	A10
Chile Chico, 1,926	E 6
Chillán, †102,361	A11
Chimbarongo, †17,592	A10
Choapa, 258	A 9
Chocalán, 187	F 4
Chonchi, †8,911	D 4
Chuquicamata, 24,798	B 3
Cobquecura, †6,298	D 1
Cochamó, †5,042	E 3
Codegua, †6,757	G 4
Codigua, 530	F 4
Codpa, †950	B 1
Coelemu, †11,967	D 1
Cogotí, 212	A 8
Coihaique, †24,032	E 6
Coihaique Alto, 24	E 6
Coihueco, †17,276	A11
Coinco, †4,942	G 5
Colbún, †12,924	A11
Colina, †18,058	G 3
Collaguasi, 8	B 3
Colliguay, 102	F 3
Collipulli, †15,058	E 2
Coltauco, †11,857	F 5
Combarbalá, †17,332	A 8
Concepción, †189,929	D 1
Conchi, 9	B 3
Conchi Viejo, 17	B 3
Concón, 5,381	F 2
Constitución, †23,543	A11
Contulmo, †13,987	D 2
Copiapó, †51,809	B 6
Coquimbo, †55,360	A 8
Coronel, †73,568	D 1
Corral, †5,533	D 3
Cruz Grande, 478	A 7
Cunco, †18,836	E 2
Cuncumén, Coquimbo, 1,052	A 9
Cuncumén, Santiago	F 4
Curacautín, †15,862	E 2
Curacaví, †11,481	G 3
Curanilahue, †21,207	D 1
Curepto, †13,020	A10
Curicó, †59,621	A10
Cuya, 86	B 2
Dalcahue, †7,084	D 4
Domeyko, 1,814	A 7
Doñihue, †8,837	G 5
El Carmen, Ñuble, †13,226	A11
El Carmen, O'Higgins, 625	F 5
El Cobre, 7	A 4
El Convento, 733	F 4
El Manzano, 1,073	F 5
El Ñilhue, 341	G 1
El Olivar Alto, †5,414	G 5
El Quisco, †2,152	E 3
El Tabo, †2,180	F 3
El Tofo, 1,175	A 7
El Tránsito, 235	B 7
El Volcán, 250	B10
Empedrado, †7,887	A11
Ercilla, †8,061	E 2
Espejo, 3,481	G 3
Estancia Caleta Josefina, †1,042	F10
Estancia Laguna Blanca, 119	E 9
Estancia Morro Chico, †785	E 9
Estancia Punta Delgada, 233	E 9
Estancia San Gregorio, †1,156	E 9
Estancia Springhill (Manantiales), 291	F10
Freire, †23,313	E 2
Freirina, †5,523	A 7
Fresia, †15,359	D 3
Frutillar, †12,721	D 3
Fuerte Bulnes, 18	E10
Futaleufú, †2,366	E 4
Futrono, †7,109	E 3
Galvarino, †9,495	D 2
Gatico, 16	A 4
General Lagos, †810	B 1
Graneros, †13,523	G 5
Guayacán, 1,514	A 8
Hijuelas, †7,128	F 2
Hospital, 460	G 4
Huachipato, †16,336	D 1
Hualaihué, 391	E 4
Hualañé, †6,912	A10
Huara, †1,934	B 2
Huasco, †4,971	A 7
Huentelauquén, 355	A 8
Idahue, 1,832	F 5
Illapel, †20,660	A 8
Imalac, 27	B 4
Inca de Oro, 1,406	B 6
Iquique, †64,900	A 2
Isla de Maipo, †12,903	G 4
La Calera, †28,728	F 2
La Colonia, 41	D 7
La Cruz, †8,907	F 2
La Estrella, †3,707	F 5
La Higuera, †6,991	A 7
La Laguna, 316	F 2
La Ligua, †15,719	A 9
La Retuca, 173	F 3
La Serena, †71,898	A 8
La Unión, †32,010	D 3
Lago Ranco, †12,767	D 3
Lago Verde, 193	E 5
Lagunas, †5,653	B 3
Lagunillas, 468	F 3
Lampa, †10,220	G 3
Lanco, †14,479	D 2
Las Breas, 14	B 7
Las Cabras †12,119	F 5
Las Cruces, 612	F 3
Lautaro, †26,011	E 2
Lebu, †16,946	D 1
Licantén, †6,354	A10
Limache, †22,472	F 2
Linares, †61,011	A11
Llaillay, †14,074	G 2
Llico, 330	A10
Llolleo, 9,846	F 4
Lo Miranda, 2,270	G 5
Lo Ovalle, 129	F 3
Loica, 446	F 4
Loncoche, †17,539	D 2
Longaví, †15,909	A11
Lonquimay, †9,524	E 2
Los Andes, †30,408	B 9
Los Ángeles, †89,810	D 1
Los Lagos, †14,934	D 3
Los Loros, 269	A 6
Los Muermos, †9,296	D 3
Los Perales de Tapihue, 176	F 3
Los Sauces, †7,613	D 2
Los Vilos, †10,453	A 9
Lota, †51,548	D 1
Machalí, †28,415	G 5
Maipú, †117,872	G 3
Maitencillo, 31	A 8
Malloa, †9,742	G 5
Mamiña, 341	B 2
Manantiales, 291	F10
Manzanar, 248	F 2
Marchihue, †4,451	F 5
María Elena, 9,572	B 3
María Pinto, †5,980	G 3
Maullín, †14,544	D 4
Mayer, 29	E 7
Mejillones, †3,333	A 4
Melinca, 166	D 5
Melipilla, †49,306	F 4
Merceditas, 33	B 7
Mincha, †11,329	A 8
Molina, †30,398	A10
Montenegro, 327	G 2
Monte Patria, †18,927	A 8
Mulchén, †23,379	E 1
Nacimiento, †17,651	D 1
Nancagua, †11,076	F 6
Navidad, †6,618	A10
Negreiros, †1,144	B 2
Nilahue, 428	E 6
Ñiquén, †13,640	E 1
Nogales, †18,529	F 2
Nueva Imperial, †30,286	D 2
Nuevo Juncal, 2	B 5
Ocoa, 871	G 2
Ollagüe, 333	B 3
Olmué, †8,804	F 2
Osorno, †105,793	D 3
Ovalle, †53,433	A 8
Paihuano, †6,048	B 8
Paillaco, †13,612	D 3
Paine, †21,876	G 4
Paipote, 2,278	B 6
Palena, †2,508	E 5
Palestina, 7	B 4
Paliocabe, 77	F 4
Palmilla, †12,429	F 6
Panguipulli, †32,834	E 2
Panquehue, †4,230	G 2
Paposo, 87	A 5
Papudo, †2,594	A 9
Paredones, †7,404	A10
Parral, †30,427	A11
Pedro de Valdivia, 11,028	B 4
Pelequen, 1,068	G 5
Pemuco, †7,577	E 1
Peñablanca, 5,586	F 2
Peñaflor, †37,788	G 4
Penco, †33,962	D 1
Peñuelas, 359	F 3
Peralillo, †7,965	F 5
Petorca, †8,343	A 9
Petrohué, 40	E 3
Peuco, 211	G 4
Peumo, †11,308	F 5
Pica, †1,487	B 2
Pichidegua, †13,550	F 5
Pichilemu, †8,042	A10
Pintados, 144	B 2
Pinto, †8,687	A11
Pisagua, †1,880	A 2
Pitrufquén, †16,797	D 2
Placilla, †6,411	F 6
Placilla de Caracoles, 2	B 4
Placilla de Peñuelas, 1,495	F 2
Población, 1,026	F 5
Polonia	G 6
Pomaire, 1,366	F 4
Porvenir, †3,600	E10
Potrerillos, 6,168	B 6
Pozo Almonte, †1,798	B 2
Puangue	F 4
Pucatrihue, 60	D 3
Puchuncaví, †7,542	F 2
Pucón, †16,872	E 2
Pudahuel, 172	G 3
Pueblo Hundido, 2,123	B 6
Puente Alto, †81,031	B10
Puerto Aisén, †15,000	E 6
Puerto Bertrand, 52	E 7
Puerto Chacabuco, 130	D 6
Puerto Cisnes, †2,800	E 5
Puerto Cristal, 698	E 6
Puerto Ingeniero Ibáñez, †1,900	E 6
Puerto Montt, †86,750	E 4
Puerto Natales, †13,577	E 9
Puerto Palena, 105	D 5
Puerto Quellón, †7,734	D 4
Puerto Ramírez, 82	E 5
Puerto Saavedra, 805	D 2
Puerto Varas, †21,003	E 3
Puerto Williams, †949	F11
Puerto Yartou, 14	E10
Pumanque, †3,137	F 6
Punitaqui, †16,167	A 8
Punta Arenas, †64,958	E10
Punta de Díaz, 11	B 7
Puquios, 105	B 1
Purén, †11,604	D 2
Purranque, †18,201	D 3
Putaendo, †12,806	A 9
Putre, †855	B 1
Puyehue, 39	E 3
Quebrada de Alvarado, 429	F 2
Queilén, †6,055	D 4
Quemchi, †6,707	D 4
Queule, 235	D 2
Quilicura, †22,644	G 3
Quillagua, 288	B 3
Quillaicillo, 195	A 8
Quilleco, †16,043	E 1
Quillota, †49,202	F 2
Quilpué, †56,399	F 2
Quinta de Tilcoco, †6,513	G 5
Quintay, 166	F 3
Quintero, †11,847	F 2
Quirihue, †11,178	E 1
Rancagua, †95,030	G 5
Rapel, 699	F 4
Reñaca, 1,267	F 2
Renca, †67,168	G 3
Rengo, †28,230	G 5
Requegua, 1,699	G 5
Requíhoa, †10,730	G 5
Retiro, †15,146	A11
Rinconada San Martín, †4,118	G 2
Río Blanco, 456	B 9
Río Bueno, †28,469	D 3
Río Cisnes, 244	E 5
Río Negro, †15,582	D 3
Río Verde, †554	E10
Rivadavia, 443	A 7
Rocas de Santo Domingo, †4,114	F 4
Rolecha, 573	D 4
Rosario, †3,383	F 5
Rungue, 312	G 2
Salado, 1,375	A 6
Salamanca, †18,741	A 9
Salinas, 7	B 4
Samo Alto, †5,689	A 8
San Antonio, †53,100	F 3
San Bernardo, †117,766	G 4
San Carlos, †30,651	E 1
San Clemente, †23,273	A11
San Felipe, †34,292	G 2
San Félix, 495	A 7
San Fernando, †44,160	G 6
San Francisco de Mostazal, †11,439	G 4
San Francisco del Monte, †14,897	G 4
San Ignacio, †13,523	E 1
San Javier, †27,592	A11
San José de la Mariquina, 2,878	D 2
San José de Maipo, †9,601	B10
San Pablo, †7,978	D 3
San Pedro, Santiago, †8,255	F 4
San Pedro, Valparaíso, 1,420	F 2
San Pedro de Atacama, 515	C 4
San Rosendo, †14,337	E 1
San Sebastián, 494	F 3
San Vicente, 230	F 4
San Vicente (San Vicente de Tagua Tagua), †28,333	F 5
Santa Bárbara, †14,345	E 1
Santa Cruz, †19,338	F 6
Santa María, †8,162	G 2
Santiago (capital), 2,596,929	G 3
Sewell, 10,866	A10
Sierra Gorda, †8,805	B 4
Talagante, †23,619	G 4
Talca, †102,522	A11
Talcahuano, †150,011	D 1
Taltal, †7,417	A 5
Tamaya, 248	A 8
Tarapacá, 130	B 2
Temuco, †146,039	E 2
Teno, †17,675	A10
Termas de Cauquenes, 210	B10
Tierra Amarilla, †6,842	A 6
Tignamar, 226	B 1
Tilomonte, 3	B 4
Tiltil, †9,198	G 2
Tinguiririca, 1,012	G 6
Toco, †8,734	B 3
Toconao, 452	C 4
Tocopilla, †22,301	A 3
Toltén, †16,265	D 2
Tomé, †44,480	D 1
Tongoy, 935	A 8
Totoral, 109	A 6
Traiguén, †21,084	D 2
Valdivia, †90,942	D 3
Valle Alegre, 241	F 2
Vallenar, †41,907	A 7
Valparaíso, †251,459	E 2
Victoria, Malleco, †28,382	E 2
Victoria, Tarapacá, 4,943	B 3
Vicuña, †13,806	A 8
Villa Alemana, †37,547	F 2
Villa Alhué, †5,078	G 4
Villa Industrial, 28	B 1
Villarrica, †23,924	E 2
Viña del Mar, †184,332	F 2
Yumbel, †21,858	E 1
Yungay, †10,725	E 1
Zapallar, †2,894	A 9

OTHER FEATURES

Aconcagua (river)	F 2
Aculeo (lagoon)	G 4
Adventure (bay)	D 5
Aguas Calientes (mt.)	C 4
Alhué (river)	F 4
Almirantazgo (bay)	F11
Almeida (mts.)	C 4
Almirante Montt (gulf)	D 9
Alto Nevado (mt.)	E 5
Ancho (channel)	D 8
Ancud (gulf)	D 4
Angamos (isl.)	D 8
Angamos (point)	A 4
Ap Iwan (mt.)	E 6
Arauco (gulf)	D 1
Arenales (mt.)	D 7
Ascotán (salt deposit)	B 3
Atacama (desert)	B 4
Atacama (salt deposit)	C 4
Aucanquilcha (mt.)	B 3
Azapa (river)	B 1
Baker (river)	D 7
Ballenero (channel)	E11
Barrancos (mt.)	D 7
Bascuñán (cape)	A 7
Beagle (channel)	E11
Bella Vista (salt deposit)	B 3
Benjamín (isl.), 16	D 5
Bertrand (mt.)	D 8
Bío-Bío (river)	E 2
Blanca (lagoon)	E10
Blanco (lake)	F10
Bravo (river)	D 7
Brunswick (pen.)	E10

(continued on following page)

Agriculture, Industry and Resources

DOMINANT LAND USE

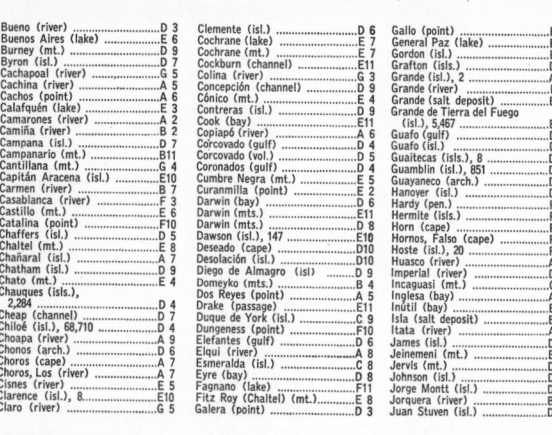

- Cereals, Livestock
- Mediterranean Agriculture (cereals, fruit, livestock)
- Pasture Livestock
- Extensive Livestock Ranching
- Limited Seasonal Grazing
- Forests
- Nonagricultural Land

MAJOR MINERAL OCCURRENCES

Ag	Silver	Hg	Mercury
Au	Gold	Id	Iodine
C	Coal	Mn	Manganese
Cu	Copper	Mo	Molybdenum
Fe	Iron Ore	N	Nitrates
G	Natural Gas	Na	Salt
Gp	Gypsum	O	Petroleum
		S	Sulfur

⚡ Water Power   ▨ Major Industrial Areas

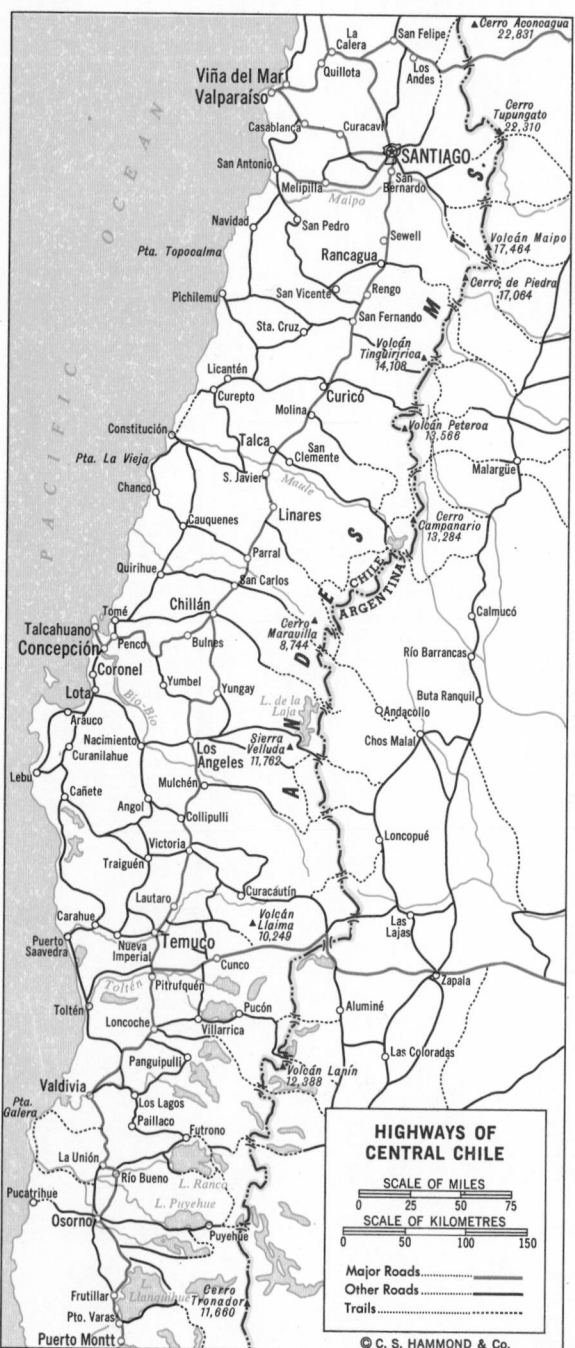

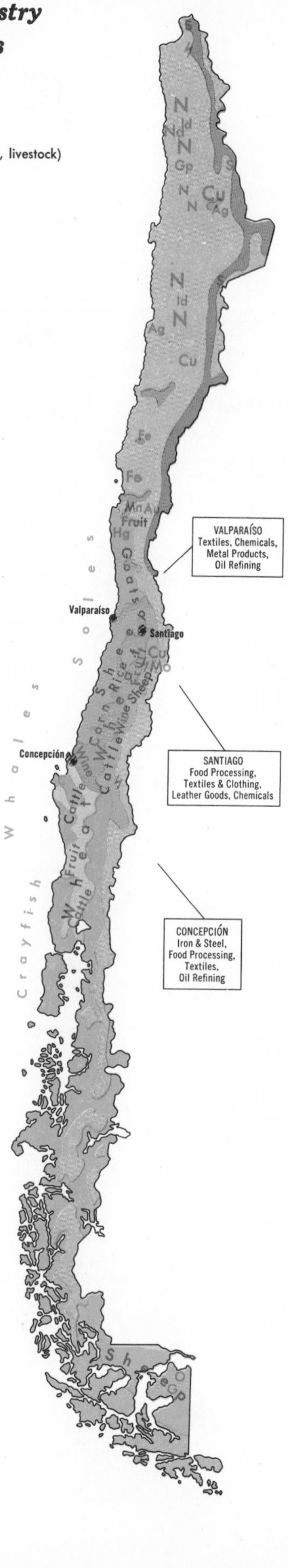

HIGHWAYS OF CENTRAL CHILE

SCALE OF MILES
0 25 50 75

SCALE OF KILOMETRES
0 50 100 150

Major Roads ————
Other Roads ————
Trails --------

© C. S. HAMMOND & Co.

Agriculture, Industry and Resources

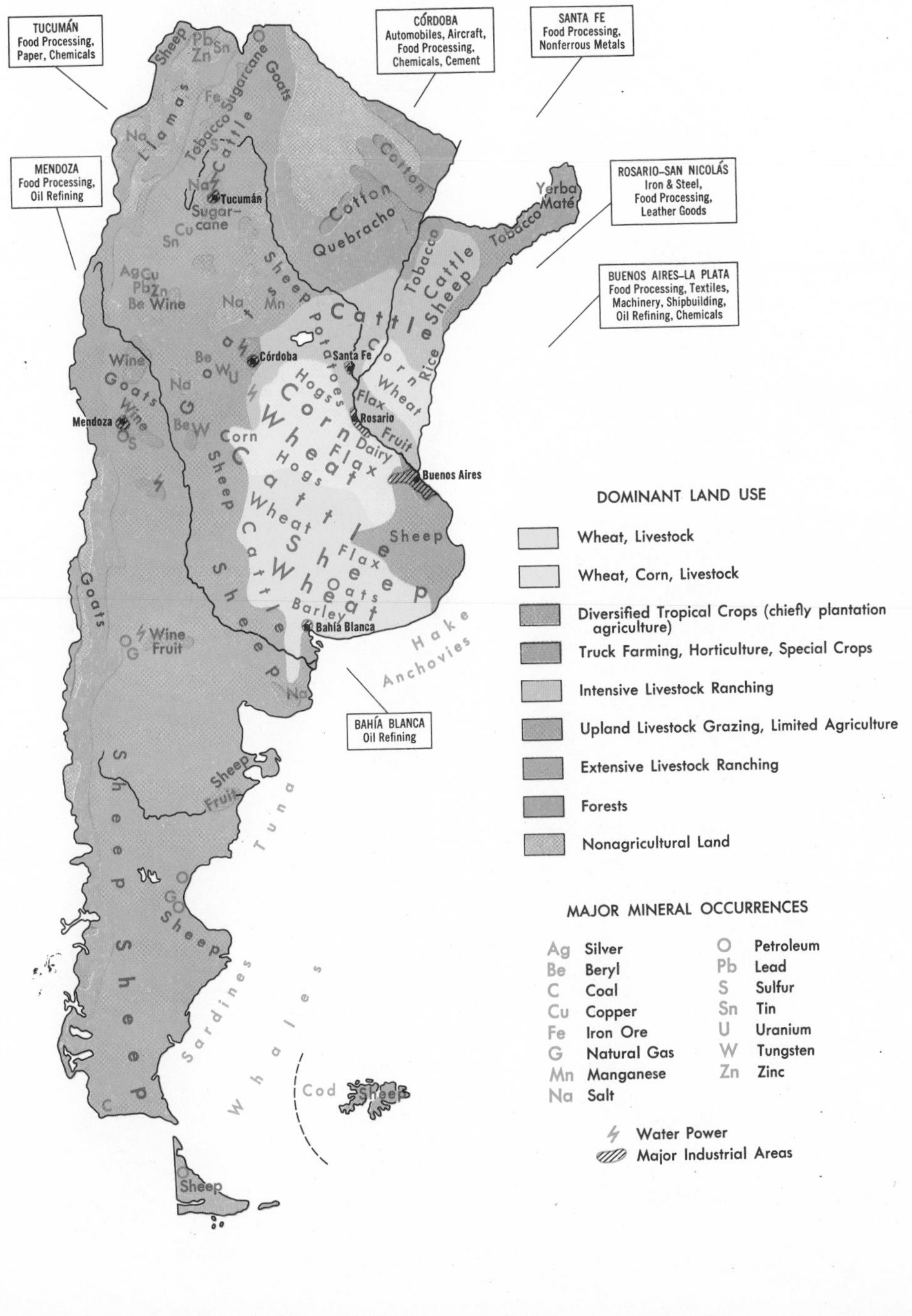

AREA 1,072,070
POPULATION 23,983,000
CAPITAL Buenos Aires
LARGEST CITY Buenos Aires
HIGHEST POINT Cerro Aconcagua 22,831 ft.
MONETARY UNIT Argentine peso
MAJOR LANGUAGE Spanish
MAJOR RELIGION Roman Catholicism

TUCUMÁN
Food Processing,
Paper, Chemicals

CÓRDOBA
Automobiles, Aircraft,
Food Processing,
Chemicals, Cement

SANTA FE
Food Processing,
Nonferrous Metals

MENDOZA
Food Processing,
Oil Refining

ROSARIO–SAN NICOLÁS
Iron & Steel,
Food Processing,
Leather Goods

BUENOS AIRES–LA PLATA
Food Processing, Textiles,
Machinery, Shipbuilding,
Oil Refining, Chemicals

BAHÍA BLANCA
Oil Refining

DOMINANT LAND USE

- Wheat, Livestock
- Wheat, Corn, Livestock
- Diversified Tropical Crops (chiefly plantation agriculture)
- Truck Farming, Horticulture, Special Crops
- Intensive Livestock Ranching
- Upland Livestock Grazing, Limited Agriculture
- Extensive Livestock Ranching
- Forests
- Nonagricultural Land

MAJOR MINERAL OCCURRENCES

Ag	Silver	O	Petroleum
Be	Beryl	Pb	Lead
C	Coal	S	Sulfur
Cu	Copper	Sn	Tin
Fe	Iron Ore	U	Uranium
G	Natural Gas	W	Tungsten
Mn	Manganese	Zn	Zinc
Na	Salt		

⚡ Water Power
▨ Major Industrial Areas

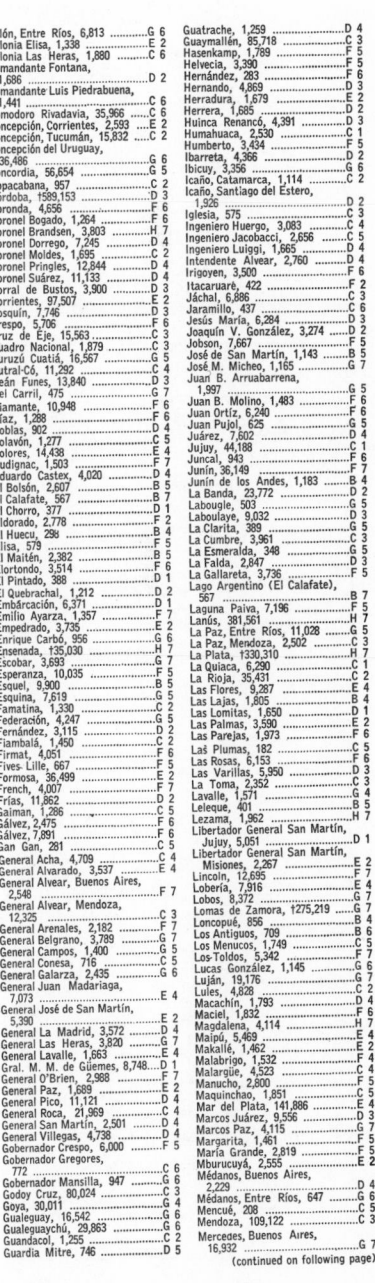

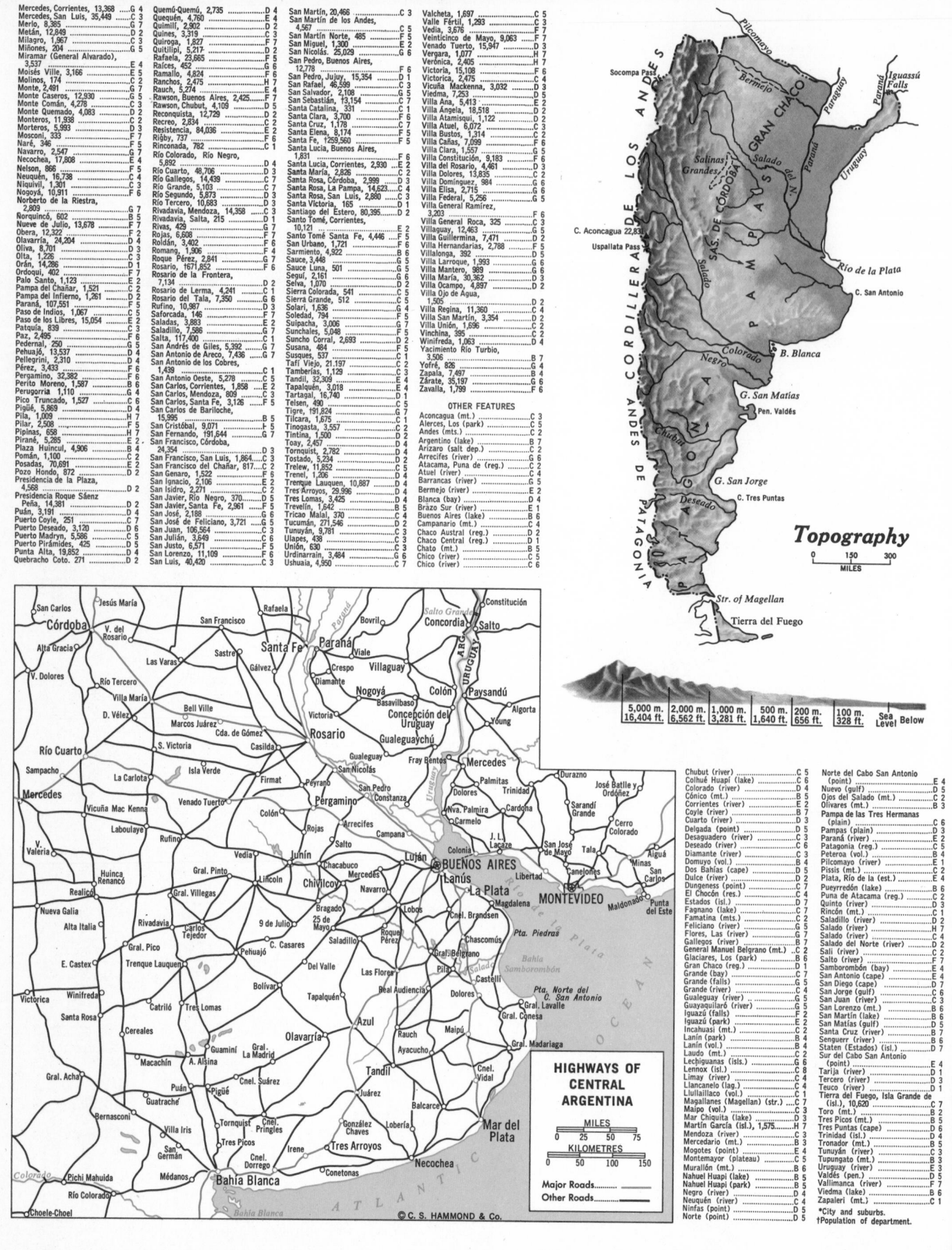

Mercedes, Corrientes, 13,368 .....G 4
Mercedes, San Luis, 35,449 .....C 3
Merlo, 8,385 .....G 7
Metán, 12,849 .....D 2
Milagro, 1,967 .....C 3
Miñones, 204 .....G 5
Miramar (General Alvarado), 3,537 .....E 4
Moisés Ville, 3,166 .....E 5
Molinos, 174 .....C 2
Monte, 2,401 .....G 7
Monte Caseros, 12,930 .....G 5
Monte Comán, 1,938 .....C 3
Monte Quemado, 4,083 .....D 2
Monteros, 11,938 .....C 2
Morteros, 5,593 .....F 7
Mosconi, 333 .....F 7
Naré, 346 .....F 5
Navarro, 2,547 .....G 7
Necochea, 17,808 .....E 4
Nelson, 866 .....F 5
Neuquén, 16,738 .....C 4
Niquivil, 1,301 .....C 2
Nogoyá, 10,911 .....F 6
Norberto de la Riestra, 2,809 .....G 7
Norquincó, 602 .....B 5
Nueve de Julio, 13,678 .....F 2
Obera, 12,322 .....F 2
Olavarría, 24,204 .....D 4
Oliva, 8,701 .....D 3
Olta, 1,226 .....C 3
Orán, 14,286 .....D 1
Ordoquí, 402 .....F 7
Palo Santo, 1,123 .....E 1
Pampa del Chañar, 1,521 .....C 2
Pampa del Infierno, 1,261 .....D 2
Paraná, 107,551 .....F 5
Paso de Indios, 1,067 .....C 5
Paso de los Libres, 15,054 .....C 3
Patquía, 839 .....C 2
Paz, 4,568 .....G 6
Pedernal, 250 .....G 5
Pehuajó, 13,537 .....D 4
Pellegrini, 2,310 .....D 4
Pérez, 3,433 .....F 6
Pergamino, 22,382 .....F 6
Perito Moreno, 1,587 .....B 6
Perugorría, 1,110 .....G 4
Pico Truncado, 1,527 .....C 6
Pigüé, 5,869 .....D 4
Pila, 1,009 .....H 7
Pilar, 2,508 .....G 7
Pipinas, 658 .....H 7
Piran, 5,285 .....E 2
Plaza Huincul, 4,906 .....B 4
Pomán, 1,100 .....C 2
Posadas, 70,691 .....E 2
Pozo Hondo, 872 .....D 2
Presidencia de la Plaza, 4,568 .....D 2
Presidencia Roque Sáenz Peña, 14,381 .....D 2
Puán, 3,511 .....D 4
Puerto Coyle, 251 .....C 7
Puerto Deseado, 3,120 .....D 6
Puerto Madryn, 5,586 .....C 5
Puerto Pirámides, 425 .....D 5
Punta Alta, 19,852 .....D 4
Quebracho Coto. 271 .....D 2

Quemú-Quemú, 2,735 .....D 4
Quequén, 4,760 .....E 4
Quimilí, 2,902 .....D 2
Quines, 3,319 .....C 3
Quiroga, 1,827 .....D 7
Quitilipi, 5,217 .....D 2
Rafaela, 23,665 .....D 5
Raíces, 452 .....G 7
Ramallo, 4,824 .....F 6
Ranchos, 2,475 .....H 7
Rauch, 5,274 .....E 4
Rawson, Buenos Aires, 2,425 .....F 7
Rawson, Chubut, 4,109 .....D 5
Reconquista, 12,729 .....D 5
Recreo, 2,834 .....C 2
Resistencia, 84,036 .....E 2
Rigby, 737 .....F 6
Rinconada, 782 .....C 1
Río Colorado, Río Negro, 5,892 .....D 4
Río Cuarto, 48,706 .....D 3
Río Gallegos, 14,439 .....C 7
Río Grande, 5,103 .....C 7
Río Segundo, 5,873 .....D 3
Río Tercero, 10,683 .....D 3
Rivadavia, Mendoza, 14,358 .....C 3
Rivadavia, Salta, 215 .....D 1
Rivas, 429 .....G 7
Rojas, 6,608 .....F 7
Roldán, 3,402 .....F 6
Romang, 1,906 .....F 4
Roque Pérez, 2,841 .....G 5
Rosario, 1671,852 .....F 6
Rosario de la Frontera, 7,134 .....D 2
Rosario de Lerma, 4,241 .....C 1
Rosario del Tala, 7,350 .....G 6
Rufino, 10,987 .....D 3
Saforcada, 146 .....F 7
Saladillo, 7,586 .....D 7
Salta, 117,400 .....C 1
San Andrés de Giles, 5,392 .....G 7
San Antonio de Areco, 7,436 .....G 7
San Antonio de los Cobres, 1,439 .....C 1
San Antonio Oeste, 5,278 .....C 5
San Carlos, Corrientes, 1,858 .....E 2
San Carlos, Mendoza, 809 .....C 3
San Carlos, Santa Fe, 3,126 .....F 5
San Carlos de Bariloche, 15,995 .....B 5
San Cristóbal, 9,071 .....E 5
San Fernando, 191,644 .....H 7
San Francisco, Córdoba, 24,354 .....E 3
San Francisco, San Luis, 1,864 .....C 3
San Francisco del Chañar, 817 .....C 2
San Genaro, 1,522 .....F 5
San Ignacio, 2,106 .....E 2
San Isidro, 2,271 .....C 2
San Javier, Río Negro, 370 .....D 5
San Javier, Santa Fe, 2,961 .....F 5
San José, 2,188 .....G 5
San José de Feliciano, 3,721 .....G 5
San Juan, 106,564 .....C 3
San Julián, 3,649 .....C 6
San Justo, 6,571 .....F 5
San Lorenzo, 11,109 .....F 6
San Luis, 40,420 .....C 3

San Martín, 20,466 .....C 3
San Martín de los Andes, 4,567 .....C 5
San Martín Norte, 485 .....F 5
San Miguel, 1,300 .....E 2
San Nicolás, 25,029 .....G 6
San Pedro, Buenos Aires, 12,378 .....G 6
San Pedro, Jujuy, 15,354 .....D 1
San Rafael, 46,599 .....C 3
San Salvador, 2,108 .....G 5
Santa Catalina, 331 .....C 1
Santa Clara, 3,700 .....F 6
Santa Cruz, 1,178 .....C 7
Santa Elena, 8,174 .....F 5
Santa Fe, 1259,560 .....F 5
Santa Lucía, Buenos Aires, 1,831 .....F 6
Santa Lucía, Corrientes, 2,930 .....E 2
Santa María, 2,826 .....C 2
Santa Rosa, Córdoba, 2,999 .....D 3
Santa Rosa, La Pampa, 14,523 .....C 4
Santa Rosa, San Luis, 2,880 .....C 3
Santa Victoria, 165 .....D 1
Santiago del Estero, 80,395 .....D 2
Santo Tomé, Corrientes, 10,121 .....E 2
Santo Tomé Santa Fe, 4,446 .....F 5
San Urbano, 1,721 .....F 6
Sarmiento, 4,922 .....C 6
Sauce, 3,448 .....G 5
Sauce Luna, 501 .....G 5
Seguí, 2,161 .....G 6
Selva, 1,070 .....D 2
Sierra Colorada, 541 .....C 5
Sierra Grande, 512 .....C 5
Solari, 1,636 .....G 4
Soledad, 794 .....F 5
Suipacha, 3,006 .....G 7
Sunchales, 5,468 .....E 5
Suncho Corral, 2,693 .....D 2
Susana, 484 .....F 5
Susques, 337 .....C 1
Taff Viejo, 21,197 .....C 2
Tamberías, 1,129 .....C 2
Tandil, 32,309 .....D 4
Tapalqué, 3,018 .....E 4
Tartagal, 16,740 .....D 1
Telsen, 490 .....C 5
Tigre, 191,824 .....G 7
Tilcara, 1,675 .....C 1
Tinogasta, 3,557 .....C 2
Tintina, 1,500 .....D 2
Toay, 2,457 .....D 4
Tornquist, 2,782 .....D 4
Tostado, 5,234 .....D 2
Trelew, 11,852 .....C 5
Trenel, 1,206 .....D 4
Trenque Lauquen, 10,887 .....D 4
Tres Arroyos, 29,996 .....D 4
Tres Lomas, 3,425 .....D 4
Trevelín, 1,642 .....B 5
Tricao Malal, 370 .....C 4
Tucumán, 271,546 .....C 2
Tunuyán, 9,781 .....C 3
Ulapes, 438 .....C 3
Unión, 630 .....D 4
Urdinarrain, 3,484 .....G 6
Ushuaia, 4,950 .....C 7

Valcheta, 1,697 .....C 5
Valle Fértil, 1,293 .....C 3
Vedia, 3,676 .....F 7
Veinticinco de Mayo, 9,063 .....F 7
Venado Tuerto, 15,947 .....D 3
Vergara, 1,077 .....H 7
Verónica, 2,405 .....H 7
Victoria, 15,108 .....F 5
Victorica, 2,475 .....C 4
Vicuña Mackenna, 3,032 .....D 3
Viedma, 7,253 .....D 5
Villa Ana, 5,413 .....E 2
Villa Ángela, 18,518 .....D 2
Villa Atamisqui, 1,122 .....D 2
Villa Atuel, 6,072 .....C 3
Villa Bustos, 1,314 .....C 2
Villa Cañas, 7,099 .....F 6
Villa Clara, 1,557 .....G 5
Villa Constitución, 9,183 .....F 6
Villa del Rosario, 4,461 .....D 3
Villa Dolores, 13,835 .....C 3
Villa Domínguez, 984 .....G 5
Villa Elisa, 2,715 .....G 6
Villa Federal, 5,256 .....G 5
Villa General Ramírez, 3,203 .....F 6
Villa General Roca, 325 .....C 3
Villaguay, 12,463 .....G 5
Villa Guillermina, 7,471 .....E 2
Villa Hernandarias, 2,788 .....F 5
Villalonga, 392 .....D 5
Villa Larroque, 1,993 .....G 6
Villa Mantero, 989 .....G 6
Villa María, 30,362 .....D 3
Villa Ocampo, 4,897 .....E 2
Villa Ojo de Agua, 1,505 .....D 2
Villa Regina, 11,360 .....C 4
Villa San Martín, 3,354 .....C 2
Villa Unión, 1,696 .....C 2
Vinchina, 395 .....C 2
Winifreda, 1,063 .....D 4
Yacimiento Río Turbio, 3,506 .....B 7
Yofré, 826 .....B 4
Zapala, 7,497 .....B 4
Zárate, 35,197 .....G 7
Zavalla, 1,799 .....F 6

OTHER FEATURES

Aconcagua (mt.) .....C 3
Alerces, Los (park) .....B 5
Andes (mts.) .....C 2
Argentino (lake) .....B 7
Arizaro (salt dep.) .....C 2
Arrecifes .....G 6
Atacama, Puna de (reg.) .....C 1
Atuel (river) .....C 4
Barrancas (river) .....G 5
Bermejo (river) .....E 2
Blanca (bay) .....D 4
Brazo Sur (river) .....E 1
Buenos Aires (lake) .....B 6
Campanario (mt.) .....C 4
Chaco Austral (reg.) .....D 2
Chaco Central (reg.) .....D 1
Chato (mt.) .....B 5
Chico (river) .....C 6
Chico (river) .....C 6

Chubut (river) .....C 5
Colhué Huapí (lake) .....C 6
Colorado (river) .....D 4
Cónico (mt.) .....B 4
Corrientes (river) .....E 2
Coyle (river) .....C 7
Cuarto (river) .....D 3
Delgada (point) .....D 5
Desaguadero (river) .....C 3
Deseado (river) .....C 6
Diamante (river) .....C 3
Domuyo (mt.) .....B 4
Dos Bahías (cape) .....C 5
Dulce (river) .....D 2
Dungeness (point) .....C 7
El Chocón (res.) .....C 4
Estados (isl.) .....D 7
Fagnano (lake) .....C 7
Famatina (river) .....C 2
Feliciano (river) .....G 5
Flores, Las (river) .....D 1
Gallegos (river) .....C 7
General Manuel Belgrano (mt.) .....C 2
Glaciares, Los (park) .....B 6
Gran Chaco (reg.) .....C 2
Grande (bay) .....C 7
Grande (falls) .....C 3
Grande (river) .....C 4
Gualeguay (river) .....G 6
Guayaquilaró (river) .....G 5
Iguazú (falls) .....F 2
Iguazú (park) .....F 2
Incahuasi (mt.) .....C 2
Lanín (park) .....B 4
Lanín (vol.) .....B 4
Laudo (mt.) .....C 3
Lechiguanas (isls.) .....G 6
Lennox (isl.) .....C 8
Limay (river) .....C 4
Llancanelo (lake) .....C 4
Llullaillaco (vol.) .....C 2
Maipó (vol.) .....C 3
Mar Chiquita (lake) .....D 3
Martín García (isl.), 1,575 .....H 7
Mendoza (river) .....C 3
Mercedario (mt.) .....C 3
Mogotes (cape) .....E 4
Montemayor (plateau) .....C 5
Murallón (mt.) .....B 6
Nahuel Huapí (lake) .....B 5
Nahuel Huapí (park) .....B 5
Negro (river) .....C 4
Neuquén (river) .....C 4
Ninfas (point) .....D 5
Norte (point) .....D 5

Norte del Cabo San Antonio (point) .....E 4
Nuevo (gulf) .....D 5
Ojos del Salado (mt.) .....C 2
Olivares (mt.) .....B 3
Pampa de las Tres Hermanas (plain) .....C 6
Pampas (plain) .....C 3
Paraná (river) .....E 2
Patagonia (reg.) .....B 4
Pilcomayo (river) .....E 1
Pissis (mt.) .....C 2
Plata, Río de la (est.) .....E 4
Pueyrredón (lake) .....B 6
Puna de Atacama (reg.) .....C 1
Quinto (river) .....D 3
Rincón (river) .....C 3
Saladillo (river) .....D 3
Salado (river) .....H 7
Salado (river) .....C 4
Salado del Norte (river) .....D 2
Salí (river) .....C 2
Salto (river) .....F 7
Samborombón (bay) .....H 7
San Antonio (cape) .....E 4
San Diego (cape) .....D 7
San Jorge (gulf) .....C 6
San Juan (river) .....C 3
San Lorenzo (mt.) .....B 6
San Martín (lake) .....B 6
San Matías (gulf) .....C 5
Santa Cruz (river) .....C 6
Senguerr (river) .....C 6
Staten (Estados) (isl.) .....D 7
Sur del Cabo San Antonio (point) .....E 4
Tarija (river) .....D 1
Tercero (river) .....D 3
Teuco (river) .....D 1
Tierra del Fuego, Isla Grande de (isl.), 10,620 .....C 7
Toro (mt.) .....B 2
Tres Picos (mt.) .....D 4
Tres Puntas (cape) .....D 6
Trinidad (isl.) .....D 4
Tronador (mt.) .....B 5
Tunuyán (river) .....C 3
Tupungato (mt.) .....B 3
Uruguay (river) .....E 3
Valdés (pen.) .....D 5
Vallimanca (river) .....D 4
Viedma (lake) .....B 6
Vilama (lake) .....C 1
Zapaleri (mt.) .....C 1

*City and suburbs.
†Population of department.

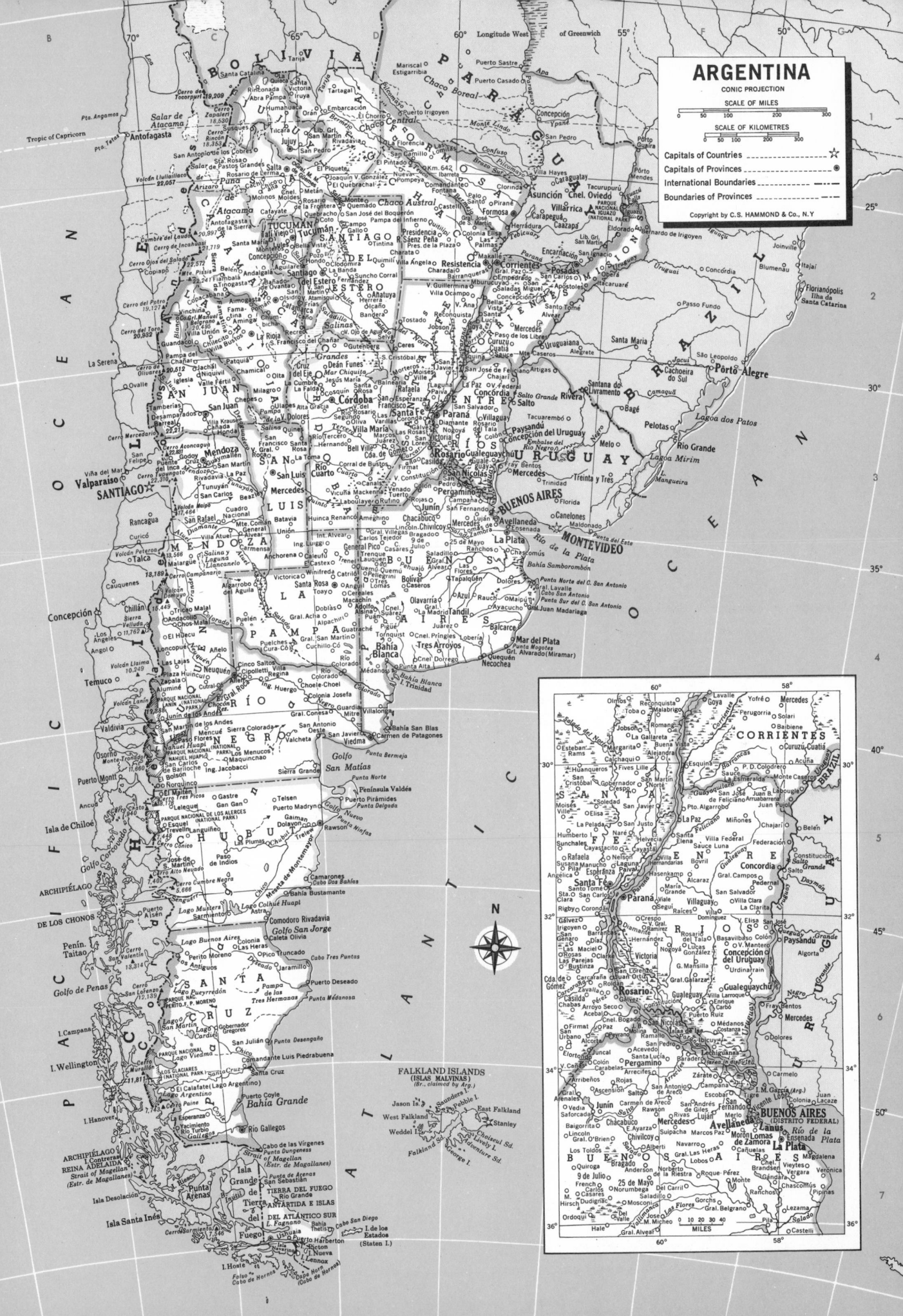

NORTH AMERICA

LAMBERT AZIMUTHAL EQUAL-AREA PROJECTION

SCALE OF MILES

0 100 200   400   600   800

SCALE OF KILOMETRES

0   200   400   600   800

Capitals of Countries .... ☆
International Boundaries .... __ __ __
Other Boundaries .... __ . __ . __
Canals ....

© C.S. HAMMOND & Co., N.Y.

POPULATION DISTRIBUTION

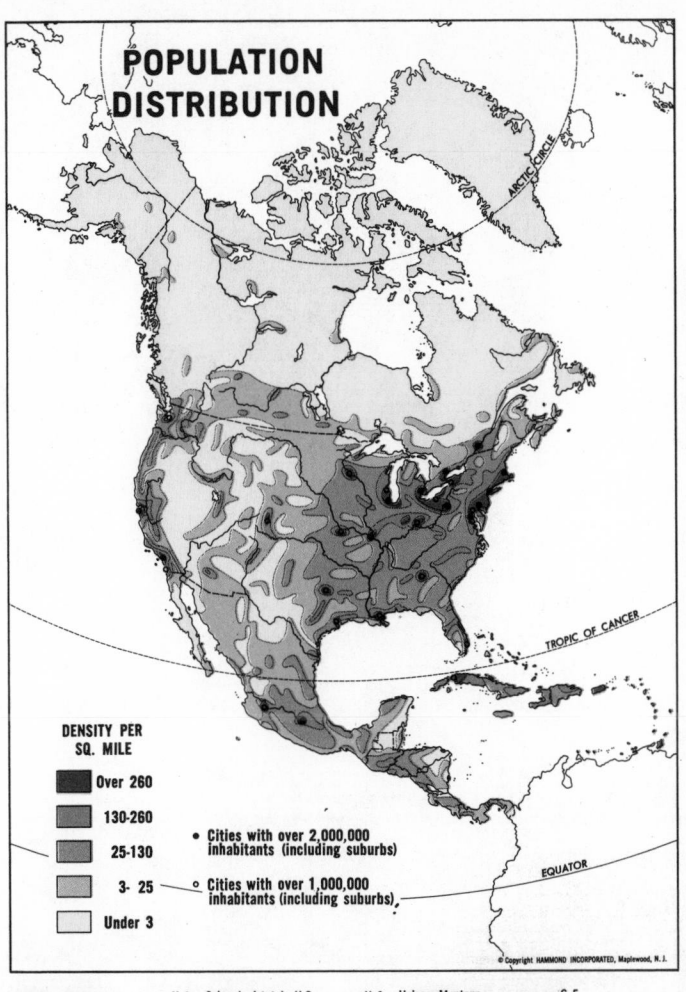

AREA 9,363,000 sq. mi.
POPULATION 314,000,000
LARGEST CITY New York
HIGHEST POINT Mt. McKinley 20,320 ft.
LOWEST POINT Death Valley 282 ft.

DENSITY PER SQ. MILE

- Over 260
- 130-260
- 25-130
- 3- 25
- Under 3

• Cities with over 2,000,000 inhabitants (including suburbs)
○ Cities with over 1,000,000 inhabitants (including suburbs)

© Copyright HAMMOND INCORPORATED, Maplewood, N.J.

VEGETATION

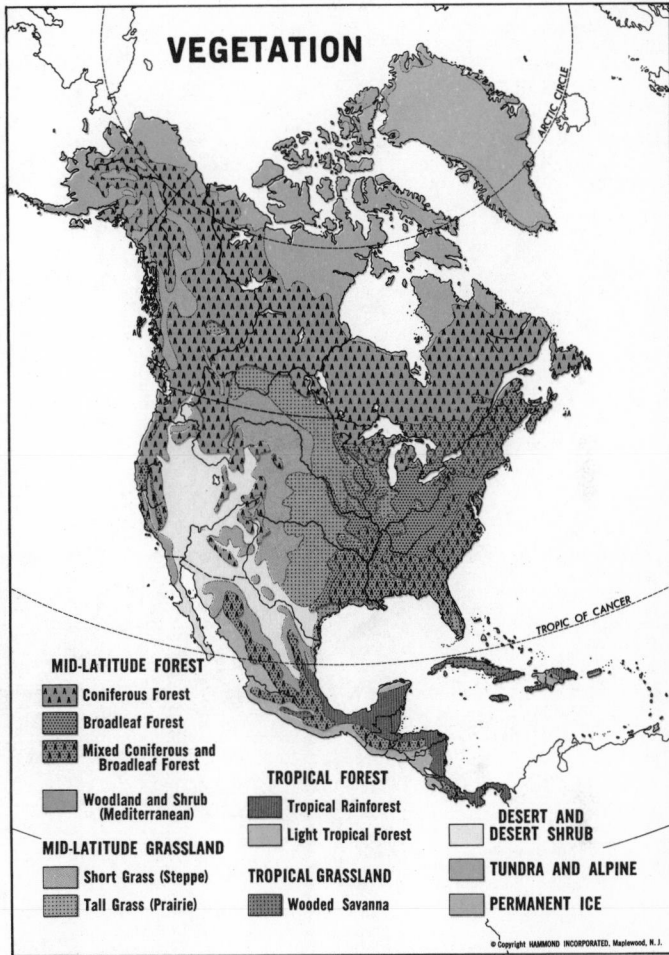

MID-LATITUDE FOREST
- Coniferous Forest
- Broadleaf Forest
- Mixed Coniferous and Broadleaf Forest
- Woodland and Shrub (Mediterranean)

MID-LATITUDE GRASSLAND
- Short Grass (Steppe)
- Tall Grass (Prairie)

TROPICAL FOREST
- Tropical Rainforest
- Light Tropical Forest

TROPICAL GRASSLAND
- Wooded Savanna

DESERT AND DESERT SHRUB

TUNDRA AND ALPINE

PERMANENT ICE

© Copyright HAMMOND INCORPORATED, Maplewood, N.J.

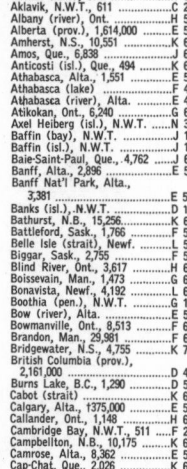

CANADA

CONIC PROJECTION

SCALE
0 50 100   200   300   400   500MI.
0 50 100   200   300   400   500KM.

Capitals of Countries .... ★
Provincial & Territorial Capitals .... △
International Boundaries .... – – –
Provincial Boundaries .... –·–·–
Canals ....

© C.S. HAMMOND & Co., N.Y.

Abitibi (lake), Ont. ....H 6
Aklavik, N.W.T., 611 ....C 2
Albany (river), Ont. ....H 5
Alberta (prov.), 1,614,000 ....E 5
Amherst, N.S., 10,551 ....K 6
Amos, Que., 6,838 ....J 6
Anticosti (isl.), Que., 494 ....K 6
Athabasca, Alta., 1,551 ....E 5
Athabasca (lake) ....E 4
Athabasca (river), Alta. ....E 4
Atikokan, Ont., 6,240 ....H 6
Axel Heiberg (isl.), N.W.T. ....N 3
Baffin (bay) ....J 1
Baffin (isl.), N.W.T. ....J 1
Baie-Saint-Paul, Que., -4,762 ......J 6
Banff, Alta., 2,755 ....E 5
Banff Nat'l Park, Alta.,
  3,381 ....D 1
Banks (isl.), N.W.T. ....D 1
Bathurst, N.B., 15,256 ....K 6
Battleford, Sask., 1,766 ....F 5
Belle Isle (strait), Newf. ....L 6
Biggar, Sask., 2,755 ....F 5
Blind River, Ont., 3,617 ....H 6
Boissevain, Man., 1,473 ....F 6
Bonavista, Newf., 4,192 ....L 6
Boothia (pen.), N.W.T. ....G 1
Bow (river), Alta. ....E 5
Bowmanville, Ont., 8,513 ....J 7
Brandon, Man., 29,981 ....F 6
Bridgewater, N.S., 4,755 ....K 7
British Columbia (prov.),
  2,161,000 ....D 4
Burns Lake, B.C., 1,290 ....D 5
Cabot (strait) ....L 6
Calgary, Alta., 1375,000 ....E 5
Callander, Ont., 1,148 ....H 6
Cambridge Bay, N.W.T., 511 ....F 2
Campbellton, N.B., 10,175 ....K 6
Camrose, Alta., 8,362 ....E 5
Cap-Chat, Que., 2,026 ....K 6

Cape Breton (isl.), N.S.,
  162,359 ....K 6
Cardston, Alta., 2,721 ....E 6
Carman, Man., 1,922 ....G 6
Chandler, Que., 3,608 ....K 6
Channel-Port aux Basques,
  Newf., 5,692 ....L 6
Chapleau, Ont., 3,778 ....H 6
Charlottetown (cap.), P.E.I.,
  18,427 ....K 6
Chatham, N.B., 8,136 ....K 6
Chesterfield Inlet, N.W.T., 199 ....G 3
Chibougamau, Que., 8,902 ....J 2
Chicoutimi, Que., 32,526 ....J 6
Chidley (cape) ....K 3
Chilliwack, B.C., 8,681 ....D 6
Churchill, Man., 1,689 ....G 4
Churchill (falls), Newf. ....C 4
Coast (mts.) ....C 4
Cobalt, Ont., 2,211 ....H 6
Cochrane, Ont., 4,775 ....H 6
Coleman, Alta., 1,507 ....E 6
Columbia (river), B.C. ....D 6
Coppermine, N.W.T., 536 ....E 2
Corner Brook, Newf., 27,116 ....L 6
Cornwall, Ont., 45,766 ....J 7
Courtenay, B.C., 4,913 ....D 6
Cranbrook, B.C., 7,849 ....E 6
Cree (lake), Sask. ....F 4
Dartmouth, N.S., 58,745 ....K 7
Dauphin, Man., 8,655 ....F 5
Davis (strait), N.W.T. ....K 1
Dawson, Yukon, 742 ....C 2
Devon (isl.), N.W.T. ....M 3
Didsbury, Alta., 1,586 ....E 5
Drumheller, Alta., 3,574 ....E 5
Edmonton (cap.), Alta.,
  1437,000 ....E 5
Edmundston, N.B., 12,517 ....K 6
Edson, Alta., 3,788 ....E 5
Elk Island Nat'l Park, Alta., 63 ..E 5

Ellesmere (isl.), N.W.T. ....N 3
Englehart, Ont., 1,790 ....H 6
Eskimo Point, N.W.T., 464 ....G 3
Estevan, Sask., 9,062 ....F 6
Eston, Sask., 1,548 ....F 5
Fernie, B.C., 2,715 ....E 6
Finlay (river), B.C. ....D 4
Flin Flon, Man.-Sask., 10,201 ......F 4
Fogo (isl.), Newf., 4,494 ....L 6
Fond du Lac (river), Sask. ....F 4
Fort Frances, Ont., 9,524 ....G 6
Fort Franklin, N.W.T., 311 ....D 2
Fort George, Que., 1,300 ....J 5
Fort Good Hope, N.W.T., 335 ....D 2
Fort McMurray, Alta., 2,614 ....E 4
Fort McPherson, N.W.T., 654 ....C 2
Fort Nelson, B.C., 954 ....D 4
Fort Providence, N.W.T., 378 ....E 3
Fort Reliance, N.W.T., 698 ....F 3
Fort Resolution, N.W.T., 677 ....E 3
Fort Saskatchewan, Alta., 4,152 ....E 5
Fort Simpson, N.W.T., 712 ....D 3
Fort Smith, N.W.T., 2,120 ....E 3
Foxe (basin), N.W.T. ....J 2
Franklin (dist.), N.W.T., 7,167 ....H 1
Fraser (river), B.C. ....D 5
Fredericton (cap.), N.B., 22,460 ...K 6
Frobisher Bay, N.W.T., 1,631 ....K 3
Fundy (bay) ....K 6
Gagnon, Que., 3,999 ....K 5
Gander, Newf., 7,183 ....L 6
Gaspé, Que., 2,938 ....K 6
Gatineau (river), Que. ....J 6
Georgian (bay), Ont. ....H 6
Geraldton, Ont., 3,658 ....H 6
Glace Bay, N.S., 23,516 ....L 6
Goose Bay, Newf., 2,364 ....K 5
Gouin (res.), Que. ....J 6
Grand Falls, Newf., 7,451 ....L 6
Grande-Prairie, Alta., 11,417 ......E 4

Great Bear (lake), N.W.T. ....D 2
Great Slave (lake), N.W.T. ....E 3
Great Whale (river), Que. ....J 4
Guelph, Ont., 57,377 ....H 7
Halifax (cap.), N.S., 1204,000 .....K 7
Hamilton, Ont., 1479,000 ....J 7
Hanna, Alta., 2,633 ....E 5
Harbour Grace, Newf., 2,811 ....L 6
Havre-Saint-Pierre, Que., 2,687 ....K 5
Hay River, N.W.T., 2,002 ....E 3
Hearst, Ont., 2,882 ....H 6
Hecate (strait), B.C. ....C 5
High River, Alta., 2,239 ....E 5
Hope, B.C., 2,948 ....D 6
Hull, Que., 60,176 ....J 6
Humboldt, Sask., 3,979 ....F 5
Indian Head, Sask., 1,891 ....F 5
Inuvik, N.W.T., 2,040 ....C 2
Inverness, N.S., 2,022 ....K 6
Iroquois Falls, Ont., 1,834 ....H 6
Jasper, Alta., 2,505 ....D 5
Jasper Nat'l Park, Alta., 2,791 ....E 5
Jonquière, Que., 29,663 ....J 6
Juan de Fuca (strait), B.C. ....D 6
Kamloops, B.C., 10,759 ....D 5
Kamsack, Sask., 2,982 ....F 5
Kane (basin), N.W.T. ....M 2
Kapuskasing, Ont., 12,617 ....H 6
Keewatin (dist.), N.W.T., 2,886 ....G 3
Kelowna, B.C., 17,006 ....D 6
Kenora, Ont., 11,295 ....G 6
Killarney, Man., 1,836 ....G 6
Kindersley, Sask., 3,534 ....F 5
Kingston, Ont., 59,004 ....J 7
Kirkland Lake, Ont., 14,008 ....H 6
Kitimat, B.C., 9,782 ....C 5
Kluane (lake), Yukon ....C 3
Kootenay (lake), B.C. ....E 5
La Tuque, Que., 13,554 ....J 6
Labrador (reg.), Newf., 21,157 .....K 4
Labrador (sea) ....L 5

Lac La Biche, Alta., 1,490 ....E 5
Lacombe, Alta., 3,035 ....E 5
Lake Louise, Alta., 121 ....E 5
Lancaster (sound), N.W.T. ....H 1
Leduc, Alta., 2,856 ....E 5
Lesser Slave (lake), Alta. ....E 4
Lethbridge, Alta., 37,186 ....E 6
Lilloet, B.C., 1,379 ....D 5
Lloydminster, Alta.-Sask.,
  7,071 ....E 5
Logan (mt.), Yukon ....B 3
London, Ont., 1224,000 ....H 7
Lunenburg, N.S., 3,154 ....K 7
Mackenzie (river), N.W.T. ....C 2
Magdalen (isls.), Que., 13,213 .....K 6
Manitoba (prov.), 979,000 ....G 5
Manitoba (lake), Man. ....G 5
Maple Creek, Sask., 2,359 ....F 6
Marathon, Ont., 2,532 ....H 6
Mattawa, Ont., 3,143 ....J 6
Mayo, Yukon, 479 ....C 2
M'Clintock (chan.), N.W.T. ....F 1
Medicine Hat, Alta., 25,574 ....E 5
Melfort, Sask., 4,386 ....F 5
Melville, Sask., 5,690 ....F 5
Melville (isl.), N.W.T. ....E 1
Merritt, B.C., 4,500 ....D 5
Minto (lake), Que. ....J 4
Mistassini (river), Que. ....J 5
Mistassini (lake), Que. ....J 5
Moncton, N.B., 45,847 ....K 6
Mont-Joli, Que., 6,366 ....K 6
Mont-Laurier, Que., 6,140 ....J 6
Montréal, Que., 12,553,000 ....J 7
Moose Jaw, Sask., 33,417 ....F 5
Moosomin, Sask., 2,141 ....F 5
Moosonee, Ont., 1,110 ....H 5

Morden, Man., 3,097 ....G 6
Nanaimo, B.C., 15,188 ....D 6
Nares (strait), N.W.T. ....M 2
Nelson, B.C., 9,504 ....E 6
Nelson (river), Man. ....G 4
Newcastle, N.B., 5,911 ....K 6
New Glasgow, N.S., 10,565 ....K 6
New Liskeard, Ont., 5,258 ....H 6
New Westminster, B.C. 38,013 ....D 6
Niagara Falls, Ont., 56,891 ....J 7
Nipigon, Ont., 2,199 ....H 6
Noranda, Que., 11,521 ....J 6
North Battleford, Sask., 12,262 ....F 5
North Bay, Ont., 23,635 ....J 6
North Magnetic Pole ....F 1
North Saskatchewan (river) ....E 5
North Vancouver, B.C., 26,851 ......D 6
Northwest Territories, 34,000 ......E 2
Nottaway (river), Que. ....J 5
Nova Scotia (prov.), 767,000 ....K 7
Okanagan (lake), B.C. ....D 6
Ontario (prov.), 7,707,000 ....H 5
Ottawa (cap.), Canada, 1527,000 ....J 6
Ottawa (river) ....J 6
Owen Sound, Ont., 17,769 ....H 7
Parry Sound, Ont., 5,901 ....J 6
Peace (river) ....D 4
Peace River, Alta., 4,087 ....E 4
Peel (river) ....C 2
Pelly (river), Yukon ....C 3
Pembroke, Ont., 16,262 ....J 6
Penticton, B.C., 18,146 ....D 6
Peterborough, Ont., 56,177 ....J 7
Pincher Creek, Alta., 2,882 ....E 6
Portage-la-Prairie, Man., 13,012 ...G 5
Port Radium, N.W.T., 412 ....E 2
Prince Albert, Sask., 26,269 ....F 5
Prince Albert Nat'l Park, Sask.,
  216 ....F 5

Prince Edward Island (prov.),
  110,000 ....K 6
Prince George, B.C., 24,471 ....D 5
Prince Patrick (isl.), N.W.T. ......D 1
Prince Rupert, B.C., 14,677 ....C 5
Québec (prov.), 6,023,000 ....J 5
Québec (cap.), Que., 1430,000 ......J 6
Queen Charlotte (isls.),
  B.C., 2,763 ....C 5
Queen Elizabeth (isls.), N.W.T. ...N 2
Quesnel, B.C., 5,725 ....D 5
Race (cape), Newf. ....L 6
Radville, Sask., 1,053 ....F 6
Rae, N.W.T., 779 ....E 3
Rainy (lake), Ont. ....G 6
Rainy River, Ont., 1,149 ....G 6
Raymond, Alta., 1,950 ....E 6
Red Deer, Alta., 26,171 ....E 5
Regina (cap.), Sask., 1140,000 .....F 5
Reindeer (lake) ....F 4
Renfrew, Ont., 9,502 ....J 6
Revelstoke, B.C., 4,791 ....D 5
Rimouski, Que., 20,330 ....K 6
Rivière-du-Loup, Que., 11,637 ......K 6
Roberval, Que., 8,552 ....J 6
Robson (mt.), B.C. ....D 5
Rocky (mts.) ....C 3
Rocky Mtn. House, Alta., 2,446 .....E 5
Rosetown, Sask., 2,658 ....F 5
Rossland, B.C., 4,264 ....E 6
Rosthern, Sask., 1,414 ....F 5
Rouyn, Que., 18,581 ....J 6
Sable (cape), N.S. ....K 7
Sable (isl.), N.S., 12 ....L 7
Saint-Boniface, Man., 43,214 ....G 5
Saint Elias (mt.), Yukon ....B 3
Saint John, N.B., 1101,000 ....K 6
Saint John's (cap.), Newf.,
  †110,000 ....

QUEEN ELIZABETH
ISLANDS

0 50 100   200 MI.
0 50 100 200 KM.

AREA 3,851,809 sq. mi.
POPULATION 21,489,000
CAPITAL Ottawa
LARGEST CITY Montréal
HIGHEST POINT Mt. Logan 19,850 ft.
MONETARY UNIT Canadian dollar
MAJOR LANGUAGES English, French
MAJOR RELIGIONS Protestantism, Roman Catholicism

POPULATION DISTRIBUTION

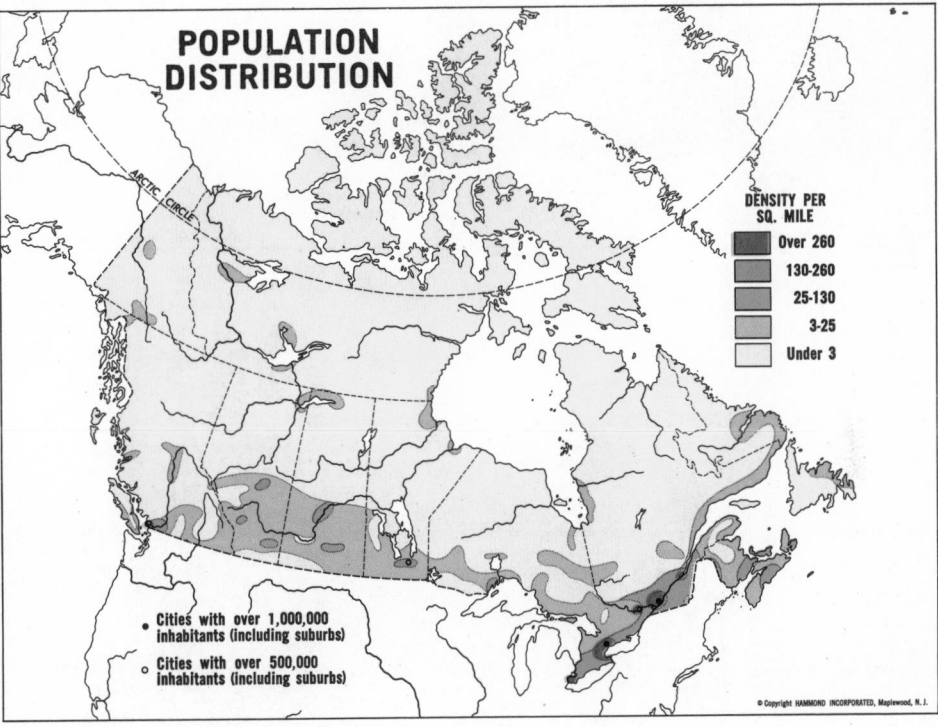

DENSITY PER
SQ. MILE

Over 260
130-260
25-130
3-25
Under 3

• Cities with over 1,000,000
  inhabitants (including suburbs)
○ Cities with over 500,000
  inhabitants (including suburbs)

© Copyright HAMMOND INCORPORATED, Maplewood, N.J.

VEGETATION

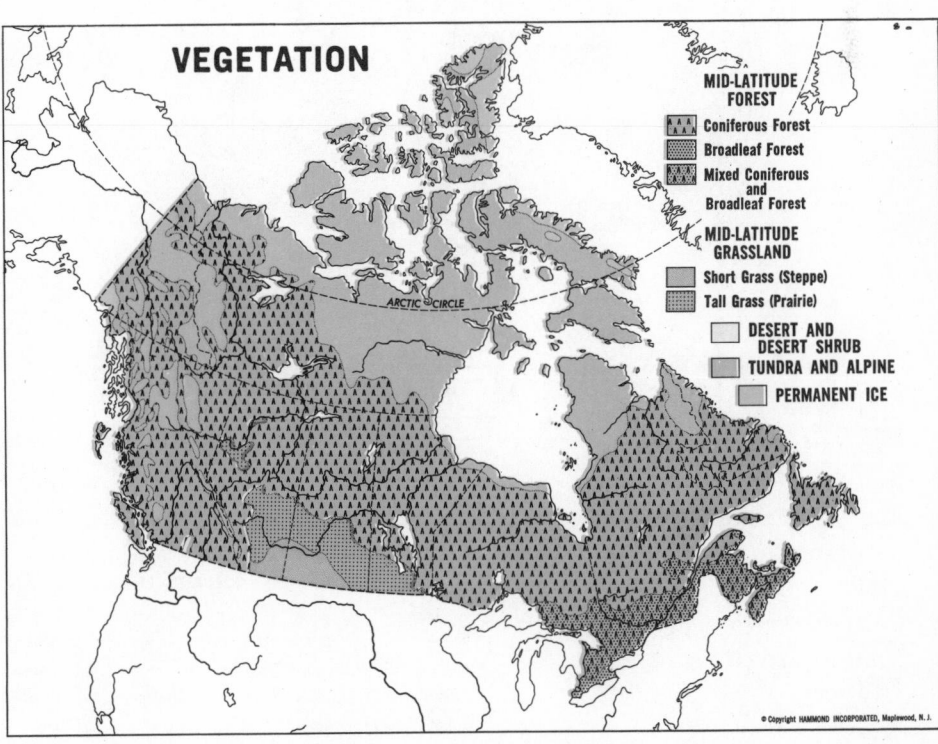

MID-LATITUDE
FOREST

Coniferous Forest
Broadleaf Forest
Mixed Coniferous
  and
Broadleaf Forest

MID-LATITUDE
GRASSLAND

Short Grass (Steppe)
Tall Grass (Prairie)

DESERT AND
DESERT SHRUB
TUNDRA AND ALPINE
PERMANENT ICE

© Copyright HAMMOND INCORPORATED, Maplewood, N.J.

AVERAGE JANUARY TEMPERATURE
ARCTIC CIRCLE
FAHRENHEIT
Over 32°
14° to 32°
-4° to 14°
-22° to -4°
Under -22°
Resolute Bay -26°
Dawson -18°
Baker Lake -27°
Frobisher Bay -16°
Inoucdjouac -13°
Edmonton 5°
Vancouver 39°
Kamloops 21°
Winnipeg -2°
Thunder Bay 7°
Québec 9°
Montréal 16°
Toronto 25°
Gander 21°
Winnipeg -2
Average January temperature at selected stations
© Copyright HAMMOND INCORPORATED, Maplewood, N. J.

AVERAGE JULY TEMPERATURE
ARCTIC CIRCLE
FAHRENHEIT
Over 68°
50° to 68°
Under 50°
Resolute Bay 40°
Dawson 60°
Baker Lake 51°
Frobisher Bay 46°
Inoucdjouac 48°
Edmonton 61°
Vancouver 59°
Kamloops 70°
Winnipeg 66°
Thunder Bay 64°
Québec 66°
Montréal 71°
Toronto 72°
Gander 62°
Winnipeg 66
Average July temperature at selected stations
© Copyright HAMMOND INCORPORATED, Maplewood, N. J.

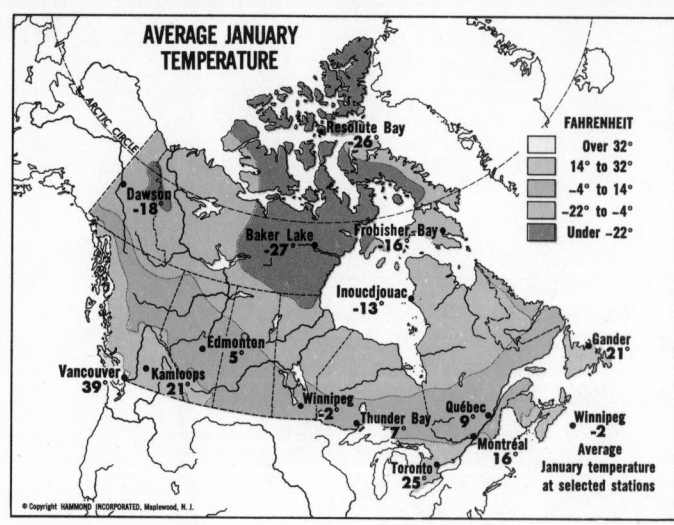

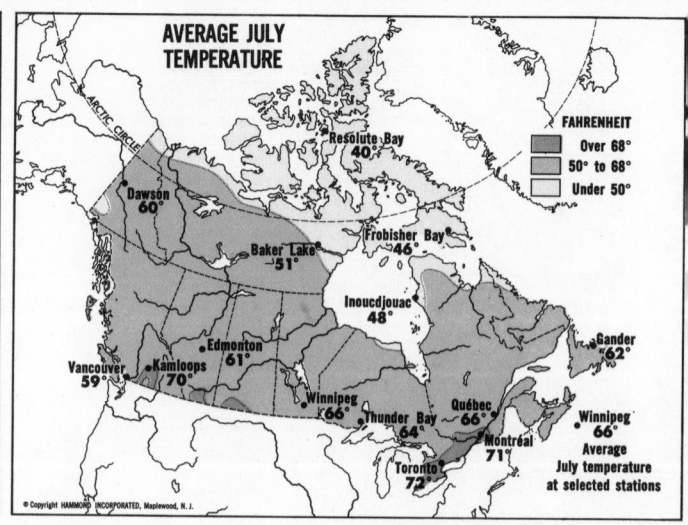

Agriculture, Industry and Resources

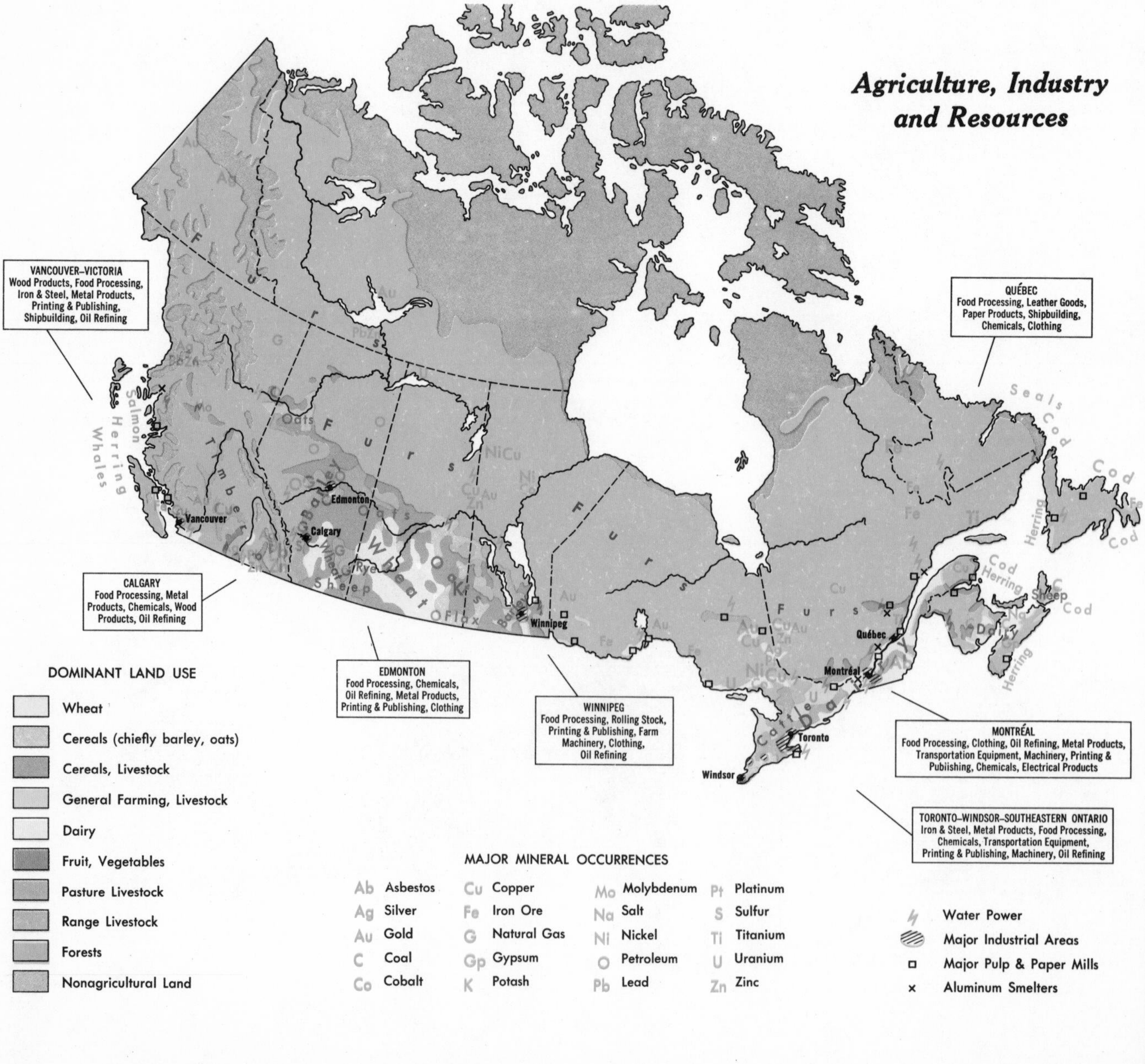

VANCOUVER–VICTORIA
Wood Products, Food Processing, Iron & Steel, Metal Products, Printing & Publishing, Shipbuilding, Oil Refining
QUÉBEC
Food Processing, Leather Goods, Paper Products, Shipbuilding, Chemicals, Clothing
CALGARY
Food Processing, Metal Products, Chemicals, Wood Products, Oil Refining
EDMONTON
Food Processing, Chemicals, Oil Refining, Metal Products, Printing & Publishing, Clothing
WINNIPEG
Food Processing, Rolling Stock, Printing & Publishing, Farm Machinery, Clothing, Oil Refining
MONTRÉAL
Food Processing, Clothing, Oil Refining, Metal Products, Transportation Equipment, Machinery, Printing & Publishing, Chemicals, Electrical Products
TORONTO–WINDSOR–SOUTHEASTERN ONTARIO
Iron & Steel, Metal Products, Food Processing, Chemicals, Transportation Equipment, Printing & Publishing, Machinery, Oil Refining
Vancouver
Calgary
Edmonton
Winnipeg
Québec
Montréal
Toronto
Windsor
Furs
Timber
Wheat
Oats
Sheep
Flax
Barley
Rye
Dairy
Salmon
Herring
Whales
Seals
Cod
DOMINANT LAND USE
Wheat
Cereals (chiefly barley, oats)
Cereals, Livestock
General Farming, Livestock
Dairy
Fruit, Vegetables
Pasture Livestock
Range Livestock
Forests
Nonagricultural Land
MAJOR MINERAL OCCURRENCES
Ab Asbestos
Ag Silver
Au Gold
C Coal
Co Cobalt
Cu Copper
Fe Iron Ore
G Natural Gas
Gp Gypsum
K Potash
Mo Molybdenum
Na Salt
Ni Nickel
O Petroleum
Pb Lead
Pt Platinum
S Sulfur
Ti Titanium
U Uranium
Zn Zinc
Water Power
Major Industrial Areas
Major Pulp & Paper Mills
Aluminum Smelters

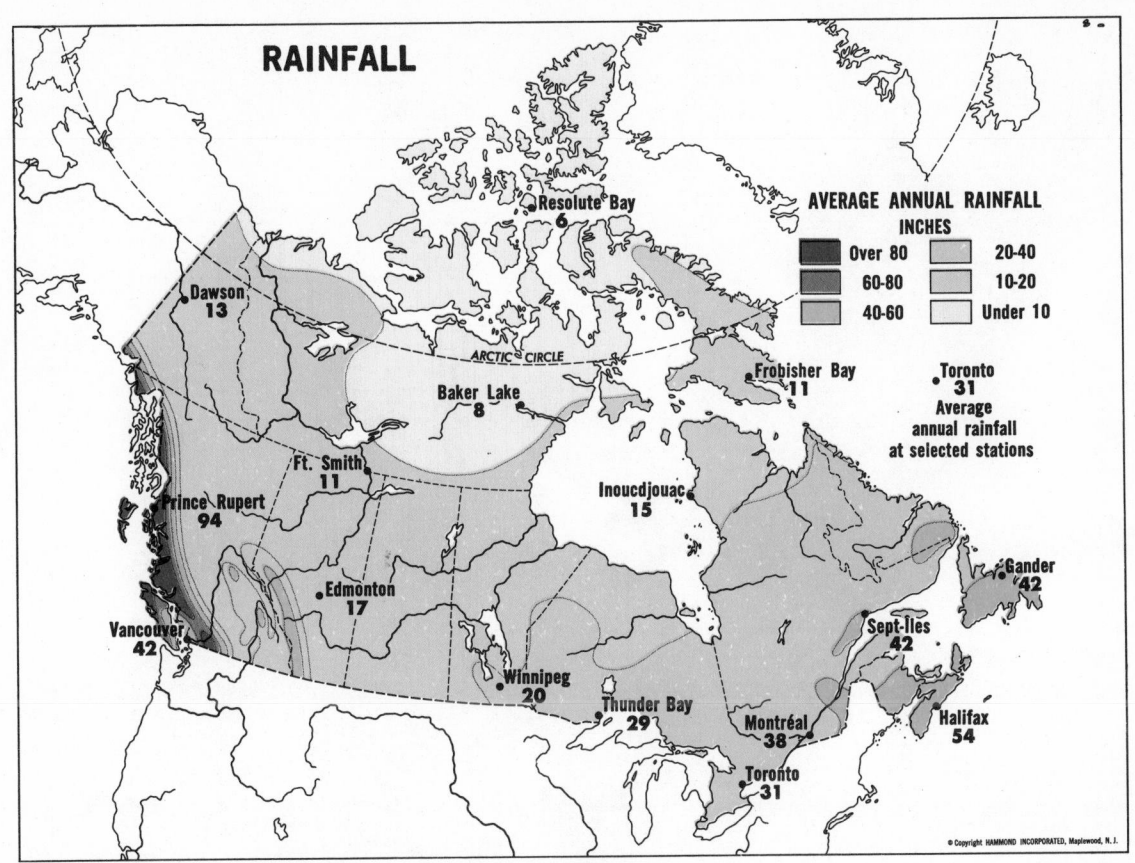

RAINFALL

AVERAGE ANNUAL RAINFALL
INCHES

Over 80 · 60-80 · 40-60 · 20-40 · 10-20 · Under 10

Resolute Bay 6
Dawson 13
ARCTIC CIRCLE
Baker Lake 8
Frobisher Bay 11
Toronto 31 — Average annual rainfall at selected stations
Ft. Smith 11
Prince Rupert 94
Inoucdjouac 15
Edmonton 17
Gander 42
Vancouver 42
Sept-Iles 42
Winnipeg 20
Thunder Bay 29
Montréal 38
Halifax 54
Toronto 31

© Copyright HAMMOND INCORPORATED, Maplewood, N.J.

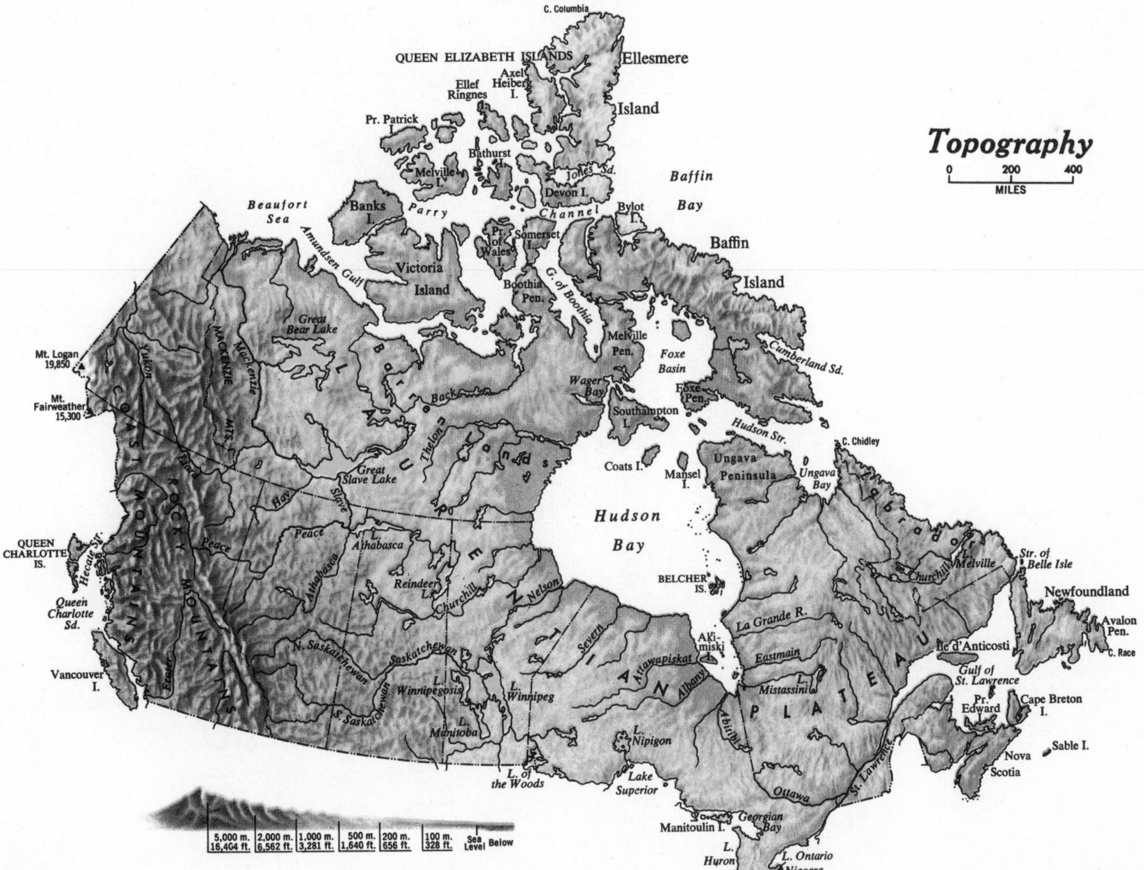

Topography

0 200 400
MILES

(Topographic map of Canada with labeled features: Queen Elizabeth Islands, Ellesmere Island, Baffin Island, Hudson Bay, Rocky Mts., Mackenzie, Great Bear Lake, Great Slave Lake, Newfoundland, Nova Scotia, etc.)

5,000 m. 2,000 m. 1,000 m. 500 m. 200 m. 100 m. Sea Level Below
16,404 ft. 6,562 ft. 3,281 ft. 1,640 ft. 656 ft. 328 ft.

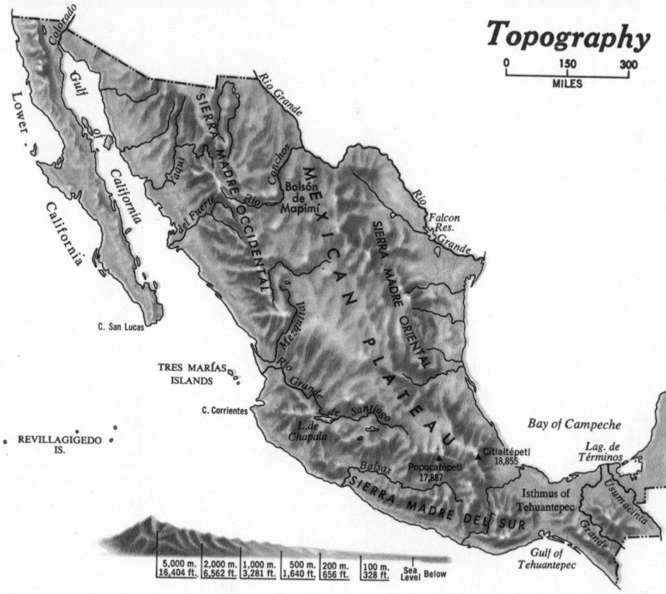

STATES and TERRITORIES

Aguascalientes, 334,936 ... H 6
Baja California, 856,773 ... B 1
Baja California Sur (terr.), 123,786 ... C 3
Campeche, 250,391 ... O 7
Chiapas, 1,578,180 ... N 8
Chihuahua, 1,730,012 ... F 2
Coahuila, 1,140,989 ... H 3
Colima, 240,235 ... G 7
Distrito Federal, 7,005,855 ... L 1
Durango, 919,381 ... G 4
Guanajuato, 2,285,249 ... J 6
Guerrero, 1,573,098 ... J 8
Hidalgo, 1,156,177 ... K 6
Jalisco, 3,322,750 ... H 6
México, 3,797,861 ... K 7
Michoacán, 2,341,556 ... H 7
Morelos, 620,392 ... K 7
Nayarit, 547,992 ... G 6
Nuevo León, 1,653,808 ... K 4
Oaxaca, 2,011,946 ... L 8
Puebla, 2,483,770 ... L 7
Querétaro, 464,226 ... J 6
Quintana Roo (terr.), 91,044 ... P 7
San Luis Potosí, 1,257,028 ... J 5
Sinaloa, 1,273,228 ... F 4
Sonora, 1,092,458 ... D 2
Tabasco, 766,346 ... N 7
Tamaulipas, 1,438,350 ... K 4
Tlaxcala, 418,334 ... N 1
Veracruz, 3,813,613 ... L 7
Yucatán, 774,011 ... P 6
Zacatecas, 949,663 ... H 5

CITIES and TOWNS

Acámbaro, 80,259 ... J 7
Acaponeta, 29,829 ... G 5
Acapulco de Juárez, 234,866 ... J 8
Acatlán, 22,507 ... K 7
Acatzingo, 14,809 ... N 2
Acayucan, 36,352 ... M 8
Aconchi, 2,313 ... D 2
Actopan, 26,608 ... Q 1
Agualeguas, 5,536 ... J 3
Agua Prieta, 21,627 ... E 1
Aguascalientes, 222,105 ... H 6
Aguililla, 20,752 ... H 7
Ahuacatlán, 14,180 ... G 6
Ajalpan, 20,413 ... L 7
Alamos, 24,123 ... E 3
Aldama, Chihuahua, 14,117 ... G 2
Aldama, Tamaulipas, 15,336 ... L 5
Aljojuca, 5,520 ... O 1
Allende, Chihuahua, 11,039 ... G 3
Allende, Coahuila, 12,736 ... J 2
Allende, Nuevo León, 14,263 ... J 4
Almoloya del Río, 3,692 ... K 1
Altamira, 28,667 ... K 5
Altar, 3,811 ... D 1
Altotonga, 31,231 ... P 1
Alvarado, 33,152 ... M 7
Amatlán de los Reyes, 21,011 ... P 2
Amealco, 26,222 ... K 6
Ameca, 42,016 ... H 6
Amecameca de Juárez, 21,753 ... L 1
Amozoc de Mota, 13,381 ... N 2
Angostura, 29,709 ... E 4
Apan, 21,550 ... M 1
Apatzingán de la Constitución, 67,384 ... J 7
Apizaco, 20,998 ... N 1
Aquiles Serdán, 5,159 ... G 2
Aramberri, 16,051 ... J 5
Arandas, 41,958 ... H 6
Arcelia, 25,631 ... J 7
Arizpe, 4,415 ... D 1
Armeria, 16,334 ... G 7
Arriaga, 23,582 ... N 8
Arteaga, 17,455 ... H 7
Ascensión, 8,810 ... E 1
Atlixco, 72,256 ... M 2
Atotonilco, 35,297 ... H 6
Autlán de Navarro, 30,853 ... G 7
Ayutla de los Libres, 23,668 ... K 8
Azcapotzalco, 545,513 ... L 1
Azoyú, 23,554 ... K 8
Bacadéhuachi, 1,470 ... D 2
Bacerac, 2,306 ... E 1
Bácum, 17,598 ... D 3
Badiraguato, 28,995 ... F 4
Balancán, 27,241 ... O 8
Balleza, 15,122 ... F 3
Batopilas, 8,780 ... F 3
Baviácora, 4,202 ... E 2
Bavispe, 2,048 ... E 1
Benjamín Hill, 5,807 ... D 1
Boca del Río, 27,884 ... Q 1
Buenaventura, 14,629 ... F 2
Burgos, 5,529 ... K 4
Cadereyta, 28,093 ... K 6
Cadereyta Jiménez, 30,429 ... K 4
Calera, 13,030 ... H 5
Calkiní, 24,503 ... O 6
Calpulalpan, 14,633 ... M 1
Calvillo, 24,039 ... H 6
Campeche, 81,147 ... O 7
Cananea, 21,824 ... D 1
Canatlán, 63,871 ... G 4
Cancún ... Q 6
Candela, 2,202 ... J 3
Carbo, 3,242 ... D 2
Cárdenas, S. Luis Potosí, 18,091 ... K 6
Cárdenas, Tabasco, 78,477 ... N 8
Carmen, 71,240 ... N 7
Casas Grandes, 11,207 ... F 1
Catemaco, 23,671 ... M 7
Cedral, 12,426 ... J 5
Celaya, 143,703 ... J 6
Celestún, 1,535 ... O 6
Cerralvo, 6,831 ... J 3
Cerritos, 18,868 ... K 5
Chalchihuites, 11,347 ... G 5
Chalco, 41,145 ... M 1
Champotón, 27,581 ... O 7
Chapulco, 2,807 ... O 2
Charcas, 22,388 ... J 5
Chetumal, 34,237 ... Q 7
Chiapa de Corzo, 22,640 ... N 8
Chiautempan, 33,820 ... N 1
Chicoloapan de Juárez, 8,995 ... M 1
Chietla, 26,921 ... M 2
Chignahuapan, 29,556 ... N 1
Chignautla, 8,348 ... N 1
Chihuahua, 363,850 ... G 2
Chilapa, 53,263 ... K 8
Chilpancingo, 56,904 ... K 8
China, 9,018 ... K 4
Chocamán, 7,270 ... P 2
Choix, 27,515 ... E 3
Cholula, 20,913 ... M 1
Cihuatlán, 16,314 ... G 7
Cintalapa, 31,252 ... M 8
Ciudad Acuña, 32,760 ... J 2
Ciudad Camargo, Chihuahua, 29,185 ... G 3
Ciudad Camargo, Tamaulipas, 16,097 ... K 3
Ciudad Delicias, 64,385 ... G 2
Ciudad del Maíz, 35,502 ... K 5
Ciudad de Valles, 71,098 ... K 5
Ciudad Guerrero, 35,631 ... F 2
Ciudad Guzmán, 48,142 ... H 7
Ciudad Juárez, 436,054 ... F 1
Ciudad Lerdo, 53,551 ... H 4
Ciudad Madero, 89,994 ... L 5
Ciudad Mante, 79,130 ... K 5
Ciudad Miguel Alemán, 18,134 ... K 3
Ciudad Obregón, 181,972 ... E 3
Ciudad Río Bravo, 70,814 ... K 4
Ciudad Serdán, 25,288 ... O 2
Ciudad Victoria, 94,304 ... K 5
Coalcomán de Matamoros, 13,480 ... H 7
Coatepec, 34,161 ... P 1
Coatzacoalcos, 108,818 ... M 7
Cocula, 20,273 ... G 6
Colima, 72,074 ... H 7
Colón, 20,392 ... K 6
Colotlán, 14,316 ... H 5
Comala, 13,715 ... G 7
Comalcalco, 71,651 ... N 7
Comitán, 38,137 ... O 8
Comondú, 30,872 ... D 3
Compostela, 59,422 ... G 6
Concepción del Oro, 15,711 ... J 4
Concordia, 21,023 ... G 5
Córdoba, 92,870 ... P 2
Cosalá, 16,202 ... F 4
Cosamaloapan de Carpio, 75,412 ... M 7
Cosautlán de Carvajal, 8,015 ... P 1
Coscomatepec de Bravo, 19,890 ... P 2
Cosío, 7,031 ... H 5
Cosoleacaque, 20,251 ... M 7
Cotija, 17,296 ... H 7
Coyame, 3,798 ... G 2
Coyoacán, 338,850 ... L 1
Coyotepec, 8,658 ... L 1
Coyuca, 25,128 ... J 7
Coyuca de Benítez, 36,032 ... J 8
Coyutla, 12,008 ... L 6
Cozumel, 12,634 ... Q 6
Cuatrociénegas de Carranza, 9,512 ... H 3
Cuauhtémoc, 65,160 ... F 2
Cuautitlán, 40,622 ... L 1
Cuautla Morelos, 67,869 ... L 2
Cuencamé, 31,170 ... H 4
Cuernavaca, 159,909 ... L 2
Cuicatlán, 45,013 ... L 8
Cuitlahuac, 13,078 ... P 2
Culiacán, 358,812 ... F 4
Cumpas, 6,186 ... D 2
Cuna de la Independencia Nacional, 71,212 ... J 6
Cunduacán, 42,872 ... N 7
Doctor Arroyo, 45,889 ... K 5
Durango, 192,934 ... G 4
Ejutla de Crespo, 34,890 ... L 8
El Ebano, 20,571 ... K 5
El Fuerte, 62,001 ... E 3
El Oro, Durango, 18,668 ... G 4
El Oro, México, 17,086 ... K 7
El Salto, 19,604 ... G 5
Empalme, 32,541 ... D 2
Encarnación de Díaz, 29,533 ... H 6
Ensenada, 113,320 ... A 1
Escuinapa de Hidalgo, 30,763 ... G 5
Escuintla, 13,754 ... N 9
Etchojoa, 53,767 ... E 3
Fortín de las Flores, 21,370 ... P 2
Fresnillo, 101,316 ... H 5
Frontera, 43,007 ... N 7
Galeana, Chihuahua, 3,176 ... F 1
Galeana, Nuevo León, 39,143 ... J 4
García de la Cadena, 4,755 ... H 6
General Bravo, 6,063 ... K 4
General Cepeda, 13,332 ... J 4
Gómez Palacio, 135,743 ... G 4
González, 23,748 ... K 5
Guadalajara, 1,196,218 ... H 6
Guadalupe, Nvo. León, 153,454 ... J 4
Guadalupe, Zacatecas, 31,976 ... H 5
Guadalupe-Bravos, 9,649 ... F 1
Guadalupe Victoria, 27,450 ... G 4
Guadalupe y Calvo, 31,131 ... F 2
Guanacevi, 12,035 ... G 4
Guanajuato, 65,258 ... J 6
Guasave, 148,475 ... E 4
Guaymas, 84,730 ... D 3
Gutiérrez Zamora, 20,534 ... L 6
Halachó, 8,547 ... O 6
Hecelchakán, 10,974 ... O 6
Hermosillo, 206,663 ... D 2
Heroica Caborca, 29,486 ... C 1
Heroica Huamantla, 26,191 ... N 1
Heroica Nogales, 52,865 ... D 1
Hidalgo, 21,434 ... K 4
Hopelchén, 23,509 ... P 7
Huajuapan de León, 83,939 ... L 8
Huaquechula, 16,702 ... M 2
Huatabampo, 43,963 ... D 3
Huatusco de Chicuellar, 20,621 ... P 2
Huauchinango, 37,211 ... L 6
Huehuetlán, 6,962 ... M 2
Huejotzingo, 21,728 ... M 1
Huejutla de Reyes, 45,771 ... K 6
Huetamo de Núñez, 35,414 ... J 7
Hueyotlipan, 6,786 ... M 1
Huimanguillo, 70,525 ... N 8
Huitzuco, 28,159 ... K 7
Huixtla, 25,884 ... N 9
Hunucmá, 10,600 ... O 6
Ignacio de la Llave, 16,345 ... Q 2
Iguala, 60,980 ... K 7
Imuris, 5,853 ... D 1
Indé, 11,969 ... G 4
Irapuato, 175,966 ... J 6
Isla de Aguada ... O 7
Isla Mujeres, 10,469 ... Q 6
Ixmiquilpan, 35,851 ... K 6
Ixtacalco, 474,700 ... L 1
Ixtapalapa, 533,569 ... L 1
Ixtlán del Río, 16,228 ... G 6
Izamal, 16,188 ... P 6
Izúcar de Matamoros, 44,074 ... M 2
Jala, 11,174 ... G 6
Jalacingo, 15,436 ... P 1
Jalapa Enríquez, 127,081 ... P 1
Jalpa, Tabasco, 29,904 ... N 7
Jalpa, Zacatecas, 26,050 ... H 6
Jalpan, 15,319 ... K 6
Jáltipan, 19,676 ... M 8
Jaumave, 13,504 ... K 5
Jerez de Garcia Salinas, 49,202 ... H 5
Jico, 14,153 ... P 1
Jilotepec, 34,866 ... K 7
Jiménez, Chihuahua, 27,044 ... G 3
Jiménez, Coahuila, 8,019 ... J 2
Jojutla de Juárez, 31,196 ... L 2
Jonatatepec, 7,478 ... M 2
Jonuta, 14,227 ... N 7
Juan Aldama, 13,661 ... H 4
Juárez, 1,664 ... J 3
Juchipila, 14,517 ... H 6
Juchique de Ferrer, 14,094 ... Q 1
Juchitán de Zaragoza, 178,388 ... M 8
La Barca, 40,331 ... H 6
La Concordia, 15,296 ... N 9
La Cruz, Chihuahua, 3,899 ... G 3
La Cruz, Sinaloa, 19,055 ... F 5
Lagos, 66,273 ... J 6
La Paz, 49,637 ... D 5
La Piedad, 51,484 ... H 6
La Trinitaria, 28,028 ... N 9
La Yesca, 9,010 ... G 6
León, 453,976 ... J 6
Libres, 12,973 ... O 1
Linares, 49,397 ... K 4
Llera de Canales, 21,117 ... K 5
Loreto, 21,544 ... J 5
Los Mochis, 165,612 ... E 4
Los Reyes, 33,879 ... H 7
Macuspana, 75,013 ... N 8
Madera, 32,367 ... F 2
Magdalena, 13,485 ... D 1
Manuel Benavides, 5,135 ... H 2
Manzanillo, 46,170 ... G 7
Mapastepec, 16,911 ... N 9
Mapimí, 19,053 ... G 4
Martínez de la Torre, 62,707 ... L 6
Mascota, 15,260 ... G 6
Matamoros, Coahuila, 44,103 ... H 4
Matamoros, Tamaulipas, 182,887 ... L 4
Matehuala, 48,368 ... J 5
Maxcanú, 10,620 ... O 6
Mazapil, 28,656 ... J 4
Mazatán, 1,561 ... E 2
Mazatlán, 171,835 ... F 5
Melchor Múzquiz, 45,945 ... J 3
Melchor Ocampo, 4,180 ... H 4
Melchor Ocampo del Balsas, 23,248 ... H 8
Meoquí, 27,000 ... G 2
Mérida, 253,856 ... P 6
Mexicali, 390,411 ... B 1
Mexico City (México) (capital), 3,025,564 ... L 1
Mexico City, *7,157,000 ... L 1
Mezquital, 4,663 ... G 5
Miacatlán, 12,579 ... L 2
Mier, 5,916 ... K 3
Miguel Azua, 15,330 ... H 4
Minatitlán, 89,412 ... M 8
Mineral del Monte, 10,943 ... K 6
Miquihuana, 3,099 ... K 5
Misantla, 44,268 ... P 1
Mocorito, 49,957 ... F 4
Moctezuma, S. L. Potosí, 13,628 ... J 5
Moctezuma, Sonora, 3,476 ... E 2
Monclova, 80,252 ... J 3
Montemorelos, 34,067 ... K 4
Monterrey, 830,336 ... J 4
Morelia, 209,507 ... J 7
Morelos, 4,721 ... J 2
Morelos Cañada, 11,463 ... O 2
Moroleón, 33,765 ... J 6
Motozintla de Mendoza, 31,518 ... N 9
Motul, 21,087 ... P 6
Mulegé, 19,282 ... C 3
Muna, 6,147 ... P 6
Naco, 3,639 ... D 1
Nacozari de García, 3,483 ... E 1
Nadadores, 3,869 ... J 3
Nanacamilpa, 8,658 ... M 1
Naolinco de Victoria, 11,077 ... P 1
Naranjos, 21,371 ... L 6
Naucalpan, 373,605 ... L 1
Nautla, 9,425 ... L 6
Nava, 5,669 ... J 2
Navojoa, 69,792 ... E 3
Nazas, 13,189 ... G 4
Nieves, 19,938 ... H 5
Nochistlán, Oaxaca, 58,609 ... L 8
Nochistlán, Zacatecas, 28,463 ... H 6
Nogales, 19,158 ... P 2
Nombre de Dios, 17,742 ... G 5
Nonoava, 4,054 ... F 3
Nopalucan, 8,401 ... O 1
Nueva Casas Grandes, 5,333 ... F 1
Nueva Ciudad Guerrero, 4,065 ... K 3
Nuevo Laredo, 150,922 ... J 3
Nuevo Morelos, 2,245 ... K 5
Oaxaca, 156,587 ... L 8
Ocampo, Chihuahua, 4,947 ... E 2
Ocampo, Coahuila, 10,072 ... H 3
Ocampo, Tamaulipas, 15,998 ... K 5
Ocotlán, 43,394 ... H 6
Ocotlán de Morelos, 45,752 ... L 8
Ojinaga, 23,854 ... G 2
Ojocaliente, 20,280 ... H 5
Ometepec, 23,604 ... K 8
Opódepe, 3,312 ... D 2
Oriental, 7,375 ... O 1
Orizaba, 92,728 ... P 2
Otumba de Gómez Farías, 11,960 ... M 1
Oxkutzcab, 10,295 ... P 7
Ozuluama, 22,382 ... L 6
Ozumba, 11,013 ... M 1
Pachuca, 84,543 ... K 6
Padilla, 13,643 ... K 5
Palenque, 22,684 ... O 8
Palizada, 7,445 ... O 7
Palmar de Bravo, 15,898 ... O 2
Palmillas, 2,420 ... K 5
Pánuco, 49,077 ... K 6
Papantla de Olarte, 94,623 ... L 6
Paraíso, 30,439 ... N 7
Parral, 61,729 ... G 3
Parras, 32,664 ... H 4
Pátzcuaro, 44,591 ... J 7
Pedro Montoya, 10,760 ... K 6
Pénjamo, 89,548 ... J 6
Peñón Blanco, 10,541 ... H 4
Perote, 23,556 ... P 1
Petatlán, 31,088 ... J 8
Peto, 11,986 ... P 6
Piedras Negras, 65,883 ... J 2
Pijijiapan, 20,350 ... N 9
Pitiquito, 6,100 ... D 1
Pochutla, 84,033 ... L 9
Poza Rica de Hidalgo, 121,341 ... L 6
Progreso, 22,100 ... P 6

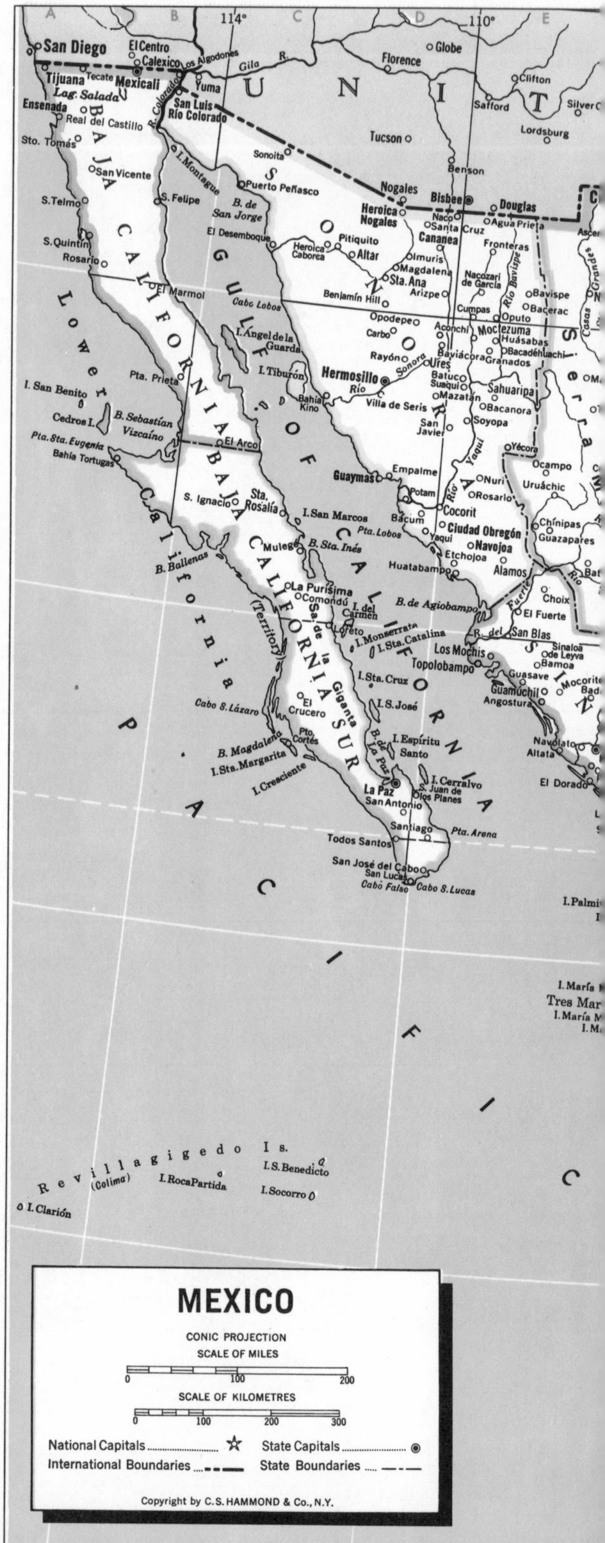

(continued on following page)

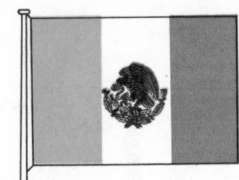

AREA 761,601 sq. mi.
POPULATION 48,313,438
CAPITAL Mexico City
LARGEST CITY Mexico City
HIGHEST POINT Citlaltépetl 18,855 ft.
MONETARY UNIT Mexican peso
MAJOR LANGUAGE Spanish
MAJOR RELIGION Roman Catholicism

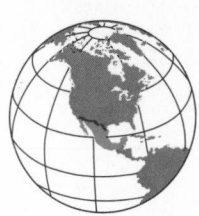

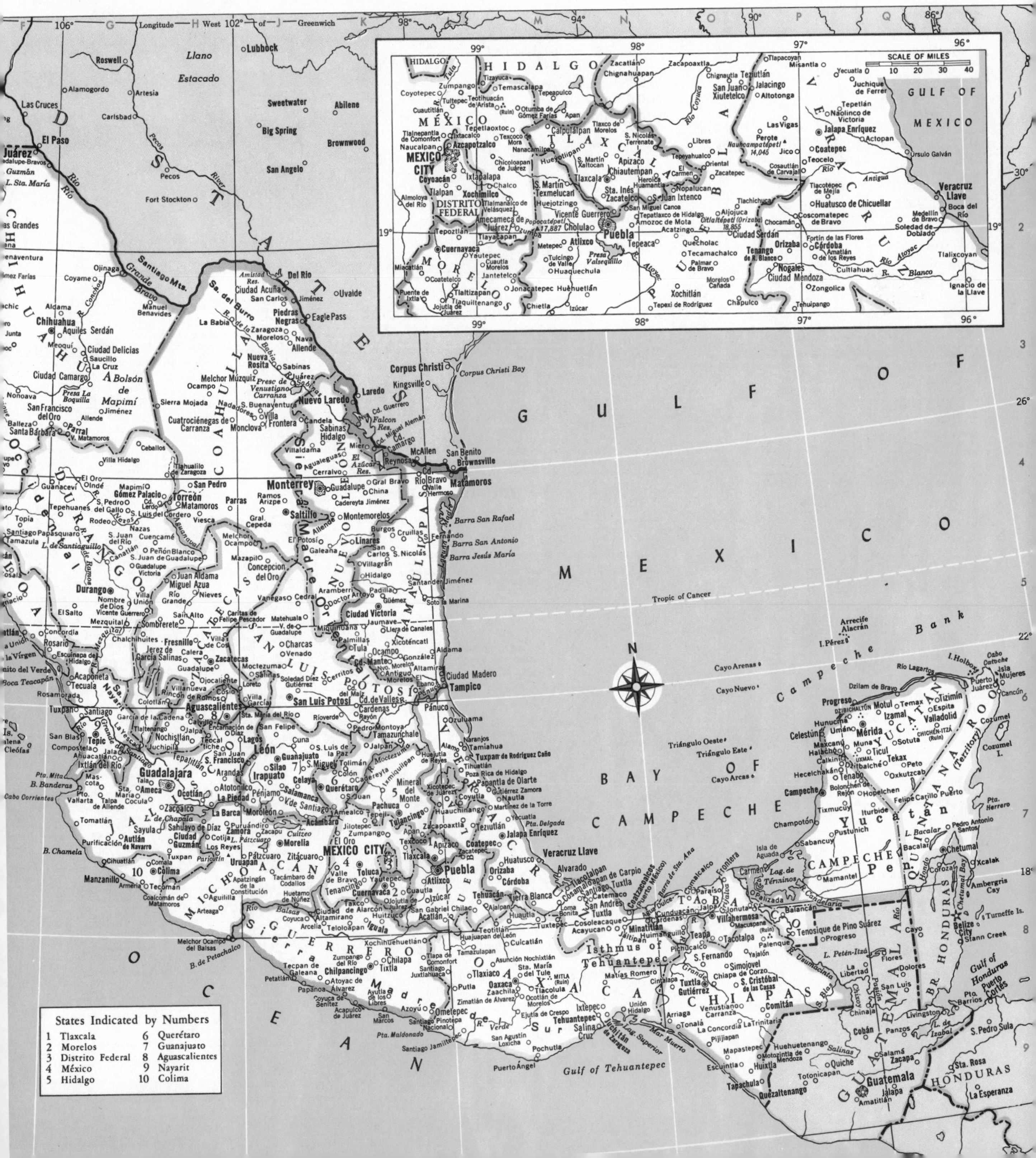

San Gabriel Chilac, 7,303 ....K 7
San Ignacio, 22,116 ....F 5
San Javier, 390 ....D 2
San José del Cabo, 9,382 ....H 6
San Juan, Jalisco, 31,389 ....H 6
San Juan, Querétaro, 53,332 ....K 6
San Juan de Guadalupe, 8,877 ....H 4
San Juan del Río, 14,639 ....G 4
San Juan Ixtenco, 4,894 ....N 1
San Juan Xiutetelco, 11,771 ....O 1
San Luis de la Paz, 26,819 ....J 6
San Luis del Cordero, 3,155 ....H 4
San Luis Potosí, 274,320 ....J 6
San Luis Río Colorado, 63,644 ....B 1
San Marcos, 33,954 ....K 8
San Martín Texmelucan, 50,071 ....M 1
San Martín Xaltocan, 6,142 ....N 1
San Miguel, 63,937 ....J 6
San Nicolás, 1,023 ....K 4
San Nicolás Terrenate, 7,160 ....N 1
San Pedro, 70,407 ....H 4
San Pedro del Gallo, 3,843 ....G 4
Santa Ana, 10,416 ....D 1
Santa Bárbara, 20,117 ....F 3
Santa Cruz, 1,659 ....D 1
Santa Inés Zacatelco, 19,972 ....N 1
Santa María, 6,260 ....G 6
Santa María del Río, 30,072 ....J 6
Santa María del Tule ....K 8
Santander Jiménez, 5,323 ....K 4
Santa Rosalía ....C 3
Santiago, Baja California, 4,978 ....E 5
Santiago, Nayarit, 84,167 ....G 6
Santiago Jamiltepec, 104,275 ....K 8
Santiago Juxtlahuaca, 37,095 ....K 8
Santiago Papasquiaro, 35,828 ....F 4
Santiago Tuxtla, 33,471 ....M 7
Saucillo, 30,781 ....F 2
Sayula, 18,878 ....H 7
Sierra Mojada, 5,517 ....H 3
Silao, 69,866 ....J 6
Simojovel, 14,896 ....N 8
Sinaloa de Leyva, 53,639 ....E 4
Soledad de Doblado, 19,467 ....Q 2
Soledad Díez Gutiérrez, 28,337 ....J 5
Sombrerete, 48,411 ....H 5
Soturta, 5,417 ....E 2
Soyopa, 2,314 ....E 2
Suaqui, 1,061 ....E 2
Tacámbaro de Codallos, 33,690 ....J 7
Tacotalpa, 20,912 ....N 8
Tala, 33,369 ....H 6
Talpa de Allende, 13,027 ....G 6
Tamazunchale, 60,976 ....K 6
Tamiahua, 23,689 ....L 6
Tampico, 196,147 ....L 5
Tapachula, 108,464 ....N 9
Taxco de Alarcón, 64,368 ....K 7
Teapa, 19,787 ....N 8

Tecamachalco, 21,688 ....O 2
Tecate, 17,917 ....A 1
Tecomán, 45,933 ....H 7
Tecpan de Galeana, 44,820 ....J 8
Tecuala, 41,129 ....G 5
Tehuacán, 67,520 ....L 2
Tehuantepec, 100,176 ....M 9
Tehuipango, 7,163 ....P 2
Tekax, 16,370 ....P 6
Teloloapan, 48,458 ....J 7
Temascalapa, 9,428 ....M 1
Temax, 5,821 ....P 6
Temósachic, 8,378 ....F 2
Tenabo, 3,992 ....P 6
Tenancingo, 31,808 ....K 7
Tenango de Río Blanco, 27,266 ....O 2
Tenosique de Pino Suárez, 26,954 ....O 8
Teocaltiche, 29,330 ....H 6
Teocelo, 7,441 ....P 1
Teotihuacán de Arista, 15,704 ....L 1
Teotitlán, 103,209 ....L 8
Tepatitlán, 53,683 ....H 6
Tepatlaxco de Hidalgo, 8,768 ....N 1
Tepeaca, 26,334 ....N 2
Tepeapulco, 26,254 ....L 1
Tepehuanes, 16,361 ....G 4
Tepeji, 24,167 ....K 6
Tepetlaoxtoc, 6,987 ....L 1
Tepexi de Rodríguez, 12,655 ....L 2
Tepeyahualco, 9,504 ....N 1
Tepic, 111,344 ....G 6
Tepoztlán, 12,635 ....L 1
Texcoco de Mora, 67,220 ....L 1
Teziutlán, 41,502 ....O 1
Ticul, 16,537 ....P 6
Tierra Blanca, 48,733 ....L 7
Tihuatlán, 53,447 ....L 6
Tijuana, 333,125 ....A 1
Tixtla, 19,735 ....K 8
Tizayuca, 8,717 ....L 1
Tizimín, 29,895 ....Q 6
Tlachichuca, 15,225 ....O 1
Tlacolula, 78,684 ....L 8
Tlacotalpan, 13,404 ....M 7
Tlacotepec de Mejía, 1,948 ....P 1
Tlahualilo de Zaragoza, 21,646 ....H 3
Tlalixcoyan, 28,625 ....Q 2
Tlaltizapán, 20,716 ....L 1
Tlapacoyan, 23,623 ....P 1
Tlapa de Comonfort, 23,261 ....K 8
Tlaquiltenango, 16,335 ....L 2
Tlaxcala, 21,424 ....M 1
Tlaxco de Morelos, 16,128 ....N 1
Tlaxiaco, 85,929 ....L 8
Tlayacapan, 5,240 ....L 1
Todos Santos, 4,506 ....D 5
Tolimán, 12,017 ....K 6
Toluca, 220,195 ....K 7
Tomatlán, 17,201 ....G 6

Tonalá, 41,562 ....N 8
Topolobampo ....E 4
Torreón, 257,045 ....H 4
Tula, 21,201 ....K 5
Tulancingo, 45,449 ....K 7
Tulcingo de Valle, 6,718 ....M 2
Tultepec, 13,693 ....L 1
Tuxpan, Jalisco, 23,569 ....H 7
Tuxpan, Nayarit, 28,345 ....G 6
Tuxpan de Rodríguez Cano, 65,211 ....L 6
Tuxtepec, 184,757 ....L 7
Tuxtla Gutiérrez, 69,326 ....N 8
Umán, 14,258 ....P 6
Ures, 10,366 ....D 2

Úrsulo Galván, 16,772 ....Q 1
Uruáchic, 7,585 ....E 3
Uruapan, 104,475 ....H 7
Valladolid, 25,367 ....P 6
Valle de Bravo, 23,591 ....J 7
Valle de Santiago, 80,504 ....J 6
Valle Hermoso, 41,546 ....L 4
Vanegas, 6,384 ....J 5
Venado, 12,147 ....J 5
Venustiano Carranza, 32,131 ....N 8
Veracruz Llave, 242,351 ....Q 1
Vicente Guerrero, Durango, 13,529 ....G 5
Vicente Guerrero, Puebla, 10,207 ....M 2

Viesca, 15,046 ....H 4
Villa de Cos, 18,012 ....H 5
Villa de Guadalupe, 12,436 ....J 5
Villa de Seris ....D 2
Villa Frontera, 31,055 ....J 3
Villa García, 9,116 ....J 5
Villagrán, 10,338 ....K 4
Villahermosa, 162,678 ....N 8
Villaldama, 4,639 ....J 3
Villa Matamoros, 5,928 ....G 3
Villanueva, 35,553 ....H 5
Villa Unión, 20,002 ....H 5
Xicoténcatl, 21,144 ....K 5
Xicotepec de Juárez, 27,372 ....K 6

Xochihuehuetlán, 6,046 ....K 8
Xochimilco, 117,083 ....L 1
Xochitlán, 8,166 ....N 2
Yajalón, 8,497 ....N 8
Yautepec, 26,182 ....L 1
Yécora, 4,896 ....E 2
Yecuatla, 10,382 ....P 1
Zaachila, 22,739 ....L 8
Zacapoaxtla, 25,479 ....O 1
Zacapu, 52,649 ....J 7
Zacatecas, 56,829 ....H 5
Zacatlán, 37,261 ....N 1
Zacoalco, 21,929 ....H 6
Zamora, 82,712 ....H 7
Zaragoza, 8,955 ....J 2
Zitlala de Álvarez, 40,302 ....L 8
Zitácuaro, 67,173 ....J 7
Zongolica, 24,372 ....P 2
Zumpango, 35,035 ....L 1
Zumpango del Río, 21,894 ....J 8

OTHER FEATURES

Agiabampo (bay) ....E 3
Aguanaval (river) ....H 4
Amistad (res.) ....J 2
Ángel de la Guarda (island) ....C 2
Antigua (river) ....Q 1
Arena (point) ....D 5
Arenas (cay) ....N 2
Atoyac (river) ....N 2
Atoyac (river) ....K 7
Babía (lake) ....D 7
Bacalar (lake) ....P 7
Ballenas (bay) ....C 3
Balsas (river) ....G 8
Banderas (bay) ....G 6
Bavispe (river) ....E 1
Blanco (river) ....Q 2
Bravo (river) ....G 2
Burro, Sierra del (mts.) ....J 2
California (gulf) ....D 3
Campeche (bank) ....O 5
Campeche (bay) ....N 7
Candelaria (river) ....O 8
Carmen (island) ....D 4
Casas Grandes (river) ....F 1
Catoche (cape) ....Q 6
Cedros (island) ....B 2
Cerralvo (island) ....D 5
Chamela (bay) ....G 7
Chapala (lake) ....H 6
Chetumal (bay) ....P 7
Chichén-Itzá (ruins) ....P 6
Chixoy (river) ....O 8
Citlaltépetl (mt.) ....O 2
Clarión (island) ....B 7
Colorado (river) ....B 1
Conchos (river) ....G 2
Corrientes (cape) ....F 6
Coyuca (river) ....J 8
Cresciente (island) ....D 5
Cuitzeo (lake) ....J 7
Delgada (point) ....L 7
Dzibilchaltún (ruins) ....P 6
El Azúcar (res.) ....K 4
Espíritu Santo (island) ....D 4
Falcón (res.) ....K 3
Falso (cape) ....E 5
Fuerte (river) ....E 3
Giganta, Sierra de la (mts.) ....D 4
Grande (river) ....N 8
Grande (river) ....B 1
Grande de Santiago (river) ....G 6
Grijalva (river) ....N 8
Guzmán (lake) ....E 1
Herrero (point) ....P 7
Holbox (island) ....Q 6
Hondo (river) ....P 7
Jesús María, Barra (inlet) ....L 4
La Boquilla (res.) ....G 3
La Paz (bay) ....D 4
Lobos (cape) ....D 2
Lobos (point) ....D 3

Lower California (pen.), 980,559 ....B 3
Madre (lagoon) ....L 4
Madre del Sur, Sierra (mts.) ....J-L 8
Madre Occidental, Sierra (mts.) ....F 3
Madre Oriental, Sierra (mts.) ....J 4
Magdalena (bay) ....C 4
Maldonado (point) ....K 8
Mapimí, Bolsón de (depression) ....G 3
María Cleófas (island) ....F 6
María Madre (island) ....F 6
María Magdalena (island) ....F 6
Mexico (gulf) ....N 4
Mezquital (river) ....G 5
Mita (point) ....G 5
Mitla (ruins) ....M 8
Moctezuma (river) ....K 6
Monserrate (isl.) ....D 4
Montague (isl.) ....C 1
Muerto, Mar (lagoon) ....N 7
Nauhcampatépetl (mt.) ....O 1
Nayarit, Sierra (mts.) ....G 4
Nazas (river) ....G 4
Nuevo (cay) ....Q 5
Orizaba (Citlaltépetl) (mt.) ....O 2
Palenque (ruins) ....O 8
Palmito de la Virgen (isl.) ....F 5
Palmito del Verde (isl.) ....F 5
Pánuco (river) ....K 5
Parícutin (vol.) ....H 7
Pátzcuaro (lake) ....J 7
Pérez (isl.) ....H 5
Petacalco (bay) ....H 8
Popocatépetl (mt.) ....M 1
Ramos (river) ....G 4
Revillagigedo (isls.) ....C 8
Río Grande (river) ....F 1
Roca Partida (isl.) ....C 8
Sabinas (river) ....H 2
Salada (lagoon) ....A 1
San Antonio, Barra de (inlet) ....L 4
San Benedicto (isl.) ....B 8
San Benito (isl.) ....B 2
San Blas (river) ....F 2
San Jorge (isl.) ....D 4
San José (isl.) ....D 4
San Lázaro (cape) ....C 4
San Lucas (cape) ....E 5
San Marcos (isl.) ....D 3
San Rafael, Barra de (inlet) ....L 4
Santa Ana, Barra de (inlet) ....N 7
Santa Catalina (isl.) ....D 4
Santa Cruz (isl.) ....D 4
Santa Eugenia (point) ....B 3
Santa Inés (isl.) ....D 3
Santa Margarita (isl.) ....C 4
Santa María (lake) ....F 1
Santa María (river) ....G 2
Santiaguillo (lake) ....G 4
Sebastián Vizcaíno (bay) ....C 2
Socorro (isl.) ....B 8
Sonora (river) ....D 2
Superior (lagoon) ....M 9
Teacapán, Boca (inlet) ....G 5
Tehuantepec (gulf) ....M 9
Tehuantepec (isthmus) ....M 8
Teotihuacán (ruins) ....M 1
Términos (lagoon) ....O 7
Tiburón (isl.) ....C 2
Tres Marías (isls.) ....N 6
Triángulo Este (isl.) ....N 6
Triángulo Oeste (isl.) ....N 6
Tula (ruins) ....L 1
Urique (river) ....F 3
Usumacinta (river) ....O 8
Uxmal (ruins) ....P 6
Valsequillo, Presa (res.) ....N 2
Verde (river) ....H 6
Yaqui (river) ....E 2

*City and suburbs.

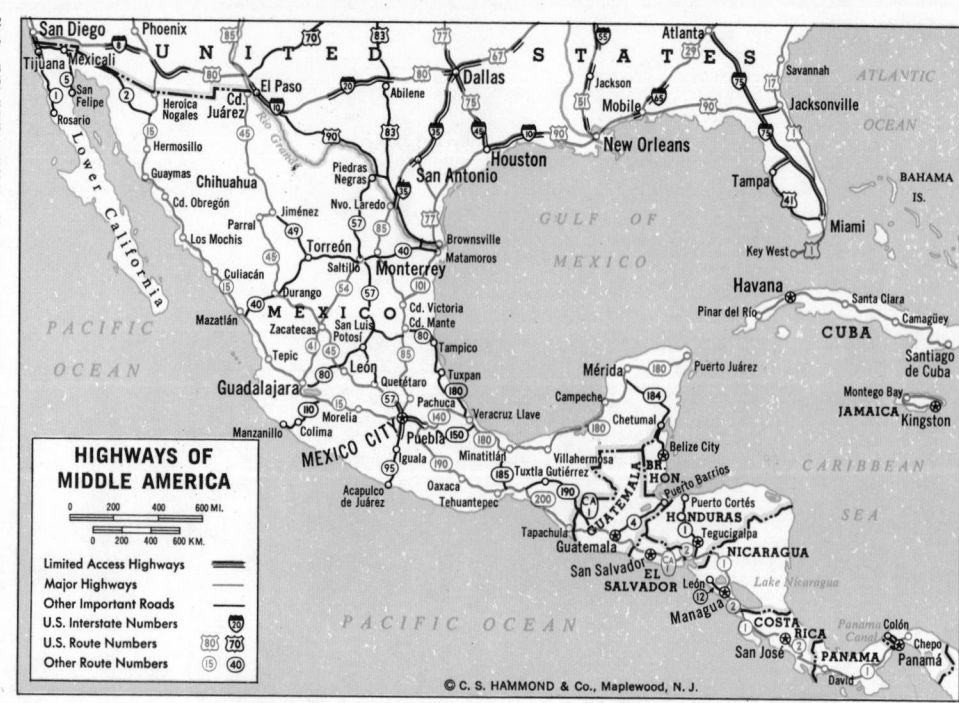

HIGHWAYS OF MIDDLE AMERICA

0 200 400 600 MI.
0 200 400 600 KM.

Limited Access Highways
Major Highways
Other Important Roads
U.S. Interstate Numbers
U.S. Route Numbers
Other Route Numbers

© C. S. HAMMOND & Co., Maplewood, N.J.

Agriculture, Industry and Resources

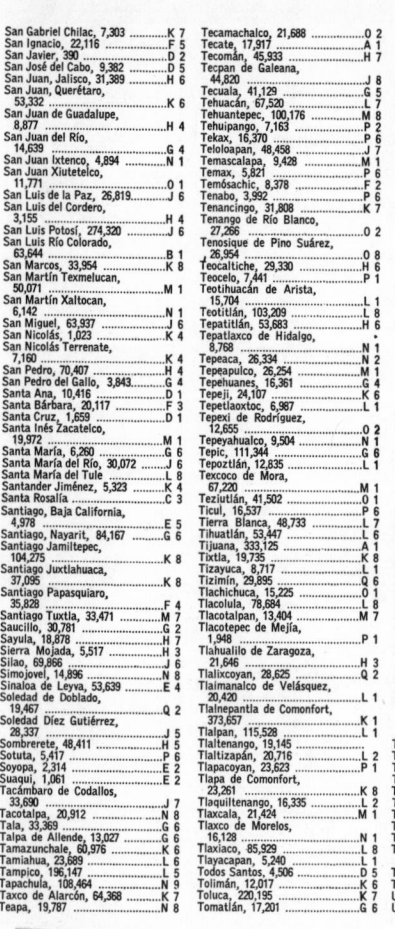

CHIHUAHUA — Nonferrous Metals

PIEDRAS NEGRAS — Iron & Steel

MONCLOVA — Iron & Steel, Chemicals

MONTERREY–SALTILLO — Iron & Steel, Nonferrous Metals, Metalworking, Chemicals, Food Processing

TORREÓN — Nonferrous Metals, Chemicals, Textiles

SAN LUIS POTOSÍ — Nonferrous Metals, Textiles

TAMPICO — Oil Refining, Chemicals, Food Processing

SALAMANCA — Chemicals, Textiles, Food Processing

GUADALAJARA — Metalworking, Textiles, Food Processing, Leather Products

VERACRUZ LLAVE — Iron & Steel, Textiles, Metalworking

ORIZABA — Textiles, Cement

MEXICO CITY–PUEBLA — Metalworking, Textiles, Leather Products, Food Processing, Chemicals, Automobile Assembly

DOMINANT LAND USE

- Wheat, Livestock
- Cereals (chiefly corn), Livestock
- Diversified Tropical Cash Crops
- Cotton, Mixed Cereals
- Livestock, Limited Agriculture
- Range Livestock
- Forests
- Nonagricultural Land

Water Power
Major Industrial Areas

MAJOR MINERAL OCCURRENCES

Ag	Silver	G	Natural Gas	O	Petroleum
Au	Gold	Gr	Graphite	Pb	Lead
C	Coal	Hg	Mercury	S	Sulfur
Cu	Copper	Mn	Manganese	Sb	Antimony
F	Fluorspar	Mo	Molybdenum	Sn	Tin
Fe	Iron Ore	Na	Salt	W	Tungsten
				Zn	Zinc

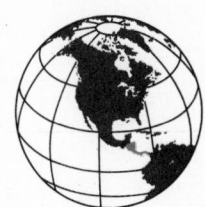

GUATEMALA
AREA 42,042 sq. mi.
POPULATION 5,200,000
CAPITAL Guatemala
LARGEST CITY Guatemala
HIGHEST POINT Tajumulco 13,845 ft.
MONETARY UNIT quetzal
MAJOR LANGUAGES Spanish, Quiché
MAJOR RELIGION Roman Catholicism

BRITISH HONDURAS
AREA 8,867 sq. mi.
POPULATION 122,000
CAPITAL Belize City
LARGEST CITY Belize City
HIGHEST POINT Victoria Peak, 3,681 ft.
MONETARY UNIT British Honduran dollar
MAJOR LANGUAGES English, Spanish, Mayan
MAJOR RELIGIONS Protestantism, Roman Catholicism

EL SALVADOR
AREA 8,260 sq. mi.
POPULATION 3,418,455
CAPITAL San Salvador
LARGEST CITY San Salvador
HIGHEST POINT Santa Ana 7,825 ft.
MONETARY UNIT colón
MAJOR LANGUAGE Spanish
MAJOR RELIGION Roman Catholicism

HONDURAS
AREA 43,277 sq. mi.
POPULATION 2,495,000
CAPITAL Tegucigalpa
LARGEST CITY Tegucigalpa
HIGHEST POINT Las Minas 9,347 ft.
MONETARY UNIT lempira
MAJOR LANGUAGE Spanish
MAJOR RELIGION Roman Catholicism

NICARAGUA
AREA 45,698 sq. mi.
POPULATION 1,984,000
CAPITAL Managua
LARGEST CITY Managua
HIGHEST POINT Cerro Mocotón 6,913 ft.
MONETARY UNIT córdoba
MAJOR LANGUAGE Spanish
MAJOR RELIGION Roman Catholicism

COSTA RICA
AREA 19,575 sq. mi.
POPULATION 1,800,000
CAPITAL San José
LARGEST CITY San José
HIGHEST POINT Chirripó Grande 12,530 ft.
MONETARY UNIT colón
MAJOR LANGUAGE Spanish
MAJOR RELIGION Roman Catholicism

PANAMA
AREA 29,209 sq. mi.
POPULATION 1,425,343
CAPITAL Panamá
LARGEST CITY Panamá
HIGHEST POINT Vol. Chiriquí 11,401 ft.
MONETARY UNIT balboa
MAJOR LANGUAGE Spanish
MAJOR RELIGION Roman Catholicism

CANAL ZONE
AREA 647 sq. mi.
POPULATION 44,650
CAPITAL Balboa Heights

Agriculture, Industry and Resources

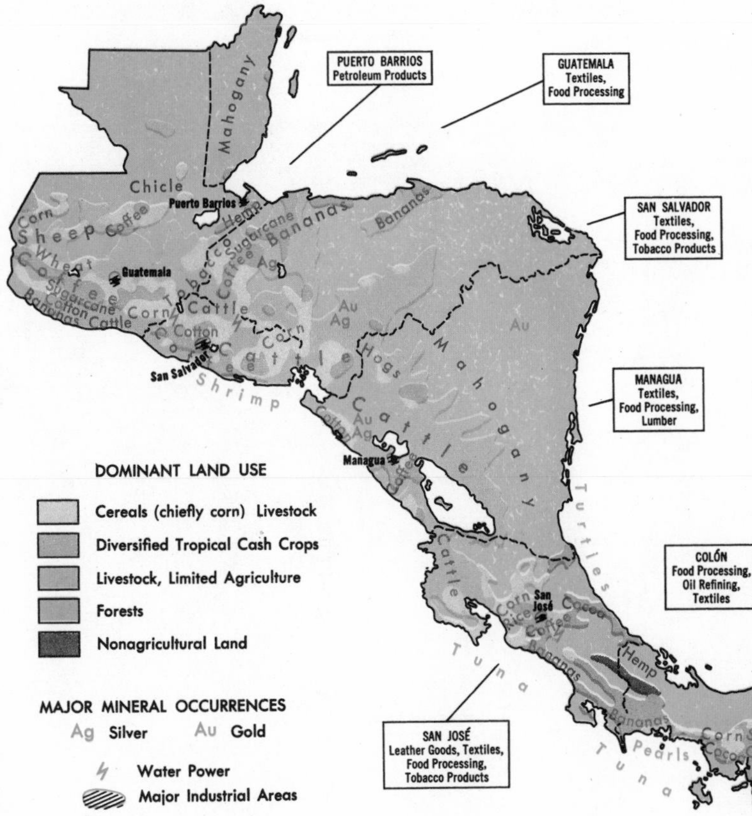

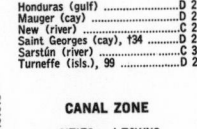

PUERTO BARRIOS
Petroleum Products
GUATEMALA
Textiles,
Food Processing
SAN SALVADOR
Textiles,
Food Processing,
Tobacco Products
MANAGUA
Textiles,
Food Processing,
Lumber
PANAMÁ
Food Processing,
Textiles
COLÓN
Food Processing,
Oil Refining,
Textiles
SAN JOSÉ
Leather Goods, Textiles,
Food Processing,
Tobacco Products
Mahogany
Chicle
Puerto Barrios
Guatemala
San Salvador
Managua
San José
Colón
Panamá
Shrimp
Turtles
Tuna
Pearls
DOMINANT LAND USE
Cereals (chiefly corn) Livestock
Diversified Tropical Cash Crops
Livestock, Limited Agriculture
Forests
Nonagricultural Land
MAJOR MINERAL OCCURRENCES
Ag Silver
Au Gold
Water Power
Major Industrial Areas

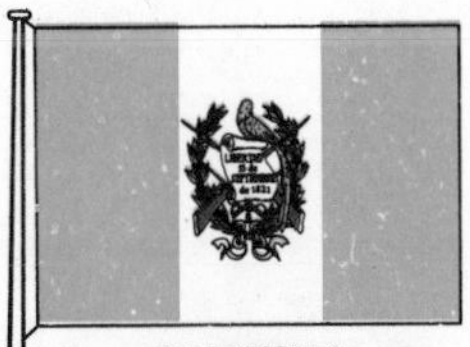

GUATEMALA

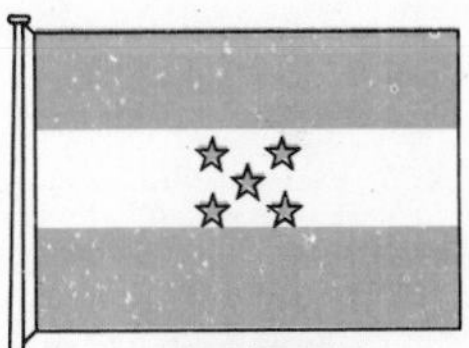

HONDURAS

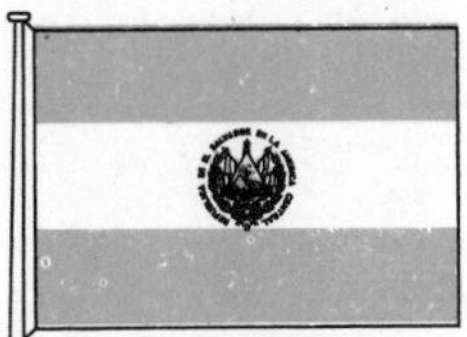

EL SALVADOR

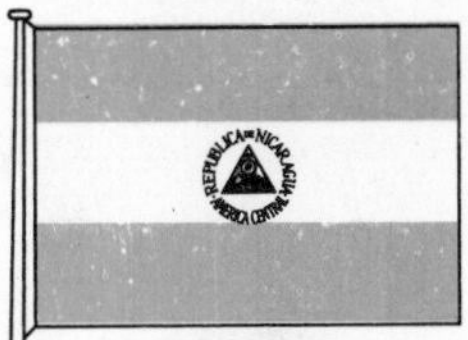

NICARAGUA

COSTA RICA

PANAMA

BRITISH HONDURAS

CITIES and TOWNS

Belize City (cap.), 37,000	C 2
Belize City, *48,421	C 2
Benque Viejo, 1,607	C 2
Cayo, 1,890	C 2
Corozal, 3,171	C 1
Hill Bank, 78	C 2
Monkey River, 417	C 2
Orange Walk, 2,157	C 1
Punta Gorda, 1,789	C 2
San José, 365	C 2
San Pedro, 170	D 2
Stann Creek, 5,287	C 2

OTHER FEATURES

Ambergris (cay), †572	D 1
Belize (river)	C 2
Bokel (cay)	D 2
Cockscomb (mts.)	C 2
Corker (cay), †360	D 2
Glovers (reef)	D 2
Half Moon (cay)	D 2
Hondo (river)	C 1
Honduras (gulf)	D 2
Mauger (cay)	D 2
New (river)	C 2
Saint Georges (cay), †34	D 2
Sarstún (river)	C 3
Turneffe (isls.), 99	D 2

CANAL ZONE

CITIES and TOWNS

Balboa, 2,568	H 6
Cristóbal, 817	G 6

COSTA RICA

CITIES and TOWNS

Alajuela, 25,195	E 6
Atenas, 963	E 6
Atlanta	F 6
Bagaces, 1,175	E 5
Beverly	F 6
Boruca, ‡1,049	F 6
Buenos Aires, ‡4,624	F 6
Cañas, 2,991	E 5
Carmen	F 5
Cartago, 19,038	F 6
Chomes, ‡1,991	E 5
Ciudad Quesada, 3,696	E 5
El Salvador	F 5
Esparta, 2,860	E 5
Filadelfia, 1,574	E 5
Golfito, 6,859	F 6
Grecia, 4,862	E 5
Guácimo, 5,731	F 5
Guápiles, 983	F 5
Heredia, 20,523	E 5
Las Juntas, 827	E 5
Liberia, 11,171	E 5
Limón, 30,676	F 6
Miramar, 1,122	E 5
Nicoya, 3,196	E 5
Orotina, 1,749	E 6
Palmares, 1,529	F 6
Paquera	E 6
Paraíso, 4,427	F 6
Pejivalle	F 6
Platanilla	F 6
Playa Bonita	E 6
Puerto Cortés, 1,757	F 6
Puntarenas, 27,527	E 6
Quepos, 1,858	E 6
San Ignacio, 315	E 6
San José (cap.), 182,961	F 5
San José, *408,000	F 5
San Marcos, 411	E 6
San Ramón, 6,444	E 5
Santa Cruz, 3,849	E 5
Santa Rosa, ‡1,750	E 5
Santo Domingo, 3,333	F 6
Sibube	F 6
Siquirres, 2,157	F 5
Turrialba, 8,629	F 6
Vesta	F 6

OTHER FEATURES

Blanca (point)	F 5
Blanco (cape)	E 6
Blanco (mt.)	F 6
Burica (point)	F 6
Cahuita (point)	F 6
Caño (isl.)	F 6

(continued on following page)

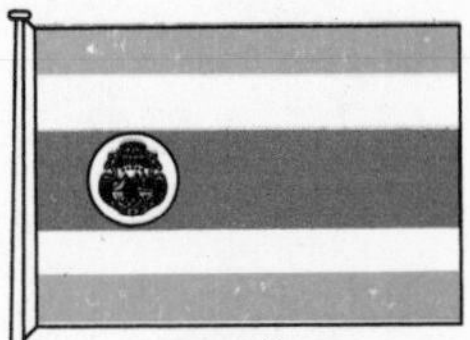

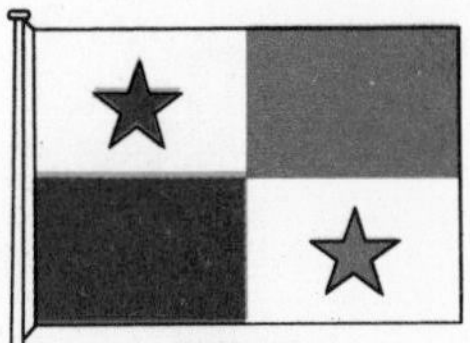

122 Central America
(continued)

CENTRAL AMERICA

CONIC PROJECTION

SCALE OF MILES
0   25   50   100   150

SCALE OF KILOMETRES
0   25   50   100   150

Capitals of Countries .... ☆
International Boundaries .... ▬▬▬
Canals .... ▬ ▪ ▬ ▪

Copyright by C. S. HAMMOND & Co., N.Y.

El Paraíso, Copán, 1,787 .... C 3
El Paraíso, El Paraíso, 5,758 .... D 4
El Porvenir, 529 .... D 3
El Progreso, 8,718 .... D 3
El Triunfo, 2,136 .... D 4
Goascorán, 1,184 .... D 4
Gracias, 2,484 .... C 3
Guaimaca, 2,620 .... D 3
Gualpatanta .... E 3
Guanaja, 1,253 .... E 2
Guarita, 599 .... C 3
Guayape, 610 .... D 3
Iriona, 119 .... E 2
Jacaleapa, 992 .... D 3
Jesús de Otoro, 2,775 .... C 3
Jutiapa, 1,711 .... D 3
Juticalpa, 7,912 .... D 3
La Ceiba, 33,934 .... D 3
La Concepción .... E 3
La Esperanza, 2,000 .... C 3
La Guata, 281 .... D 3
La Paz, 5,542 .... D 3
La Protección .... D 3
Lauterique, 272 .... D 4
Limón. 1,934 .... E 3
Manto, 943 .... D 3
Marcala, 1,968 .... C 3
Melcher .... D 3
Morazán, 3,924 .... D 3
Morocelí, 1,472 .... D 3
Nacaome, 4,376 .... D 4
Namasigüe, 1,024 .... D 4
Naranjito, 3,291 .... C 3
Nueva Armenia, 866 .... D 4
Nueva Ocotepeque, 4,608 .... C 3
Olanchito, 5,008 .... D 3
Omoa, 1,384 .... C 3
Paso Real .... E 3
Patuca .... E 3
Pespire, 1,758 .... D 4
Puerto Castilla .... D 3
Puerto Cortés, 21,600 .... D 2
Roatán, 1,883 .... D 2
Sabanagrande, 1,657 .... D 4
Salado .... D 3
San Esteban, 763 .... D 3
San Francisco, 1,122 .... D 3
San Francisco de la Paz, 1,971 .... D 3
San Juan de Flores, 1,174 .... D 3
San Luis, 2,631 .... C 3
San Marcos, 1,576 .... C 3
San Pedro Sula, 90,538 .... C 3
San Pedro Zacapa, 765 .... D 3
Santa Bárbara, 6,129 .... C 3
Santa Cruz de Yojoa, 1,833 .... D 3

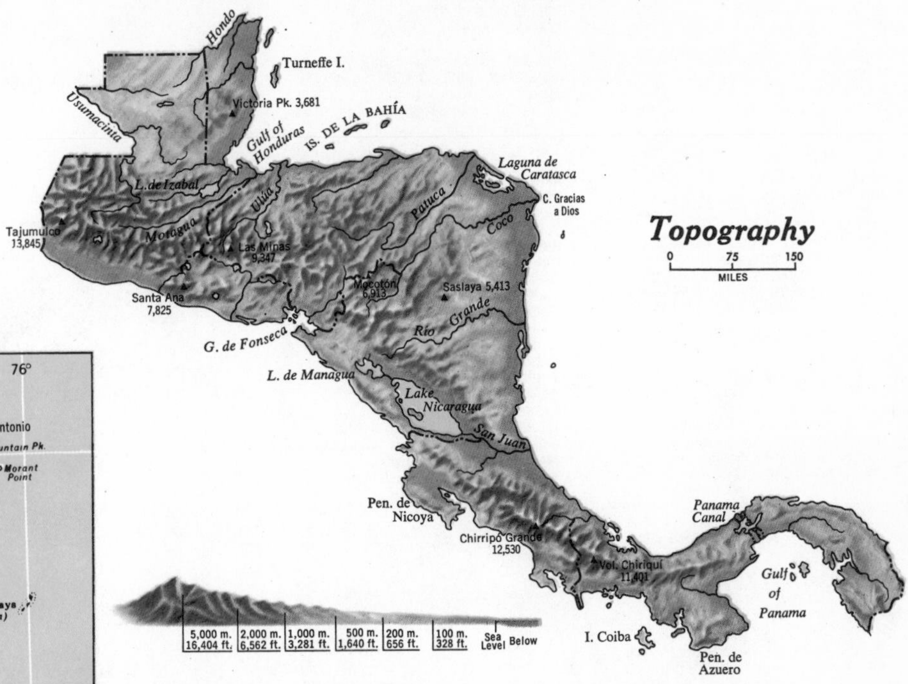

Topography
0 75 150
MILES
Hondo
Turneffe I.
Usumacinta
Victoria Pk. 3,681
IS. DE LA BAHÍA
Gulf of Honduras
L. de Izabal
Laguna de Caratasca
C. Gracias a Dios
Tajumulco 13,845
Motagua
Ulúa
Patuca
Coco
Las Minas 9,347
Mocotón 6,913
Saslaya 5,413
Santa Ana 7,825
Río Grande
G. de Fonseca
L. de Managua
Lake Nicaragua
San Juan
Pen. de Nicoya
Chirripó Grande 12,530
Panama Canal
Vol. Chiriquí 11,401
Gulf of Panama
I. Coiba
Pen. de Azuero
5,000 m. 16,404 ft.
2,000 m. 6,562 ft.
1,000 m. 3,281 ft.
500 m. 1,640 ft.
200 m. 656 ft.
100 m. 328 ft.
Sea Level
Below

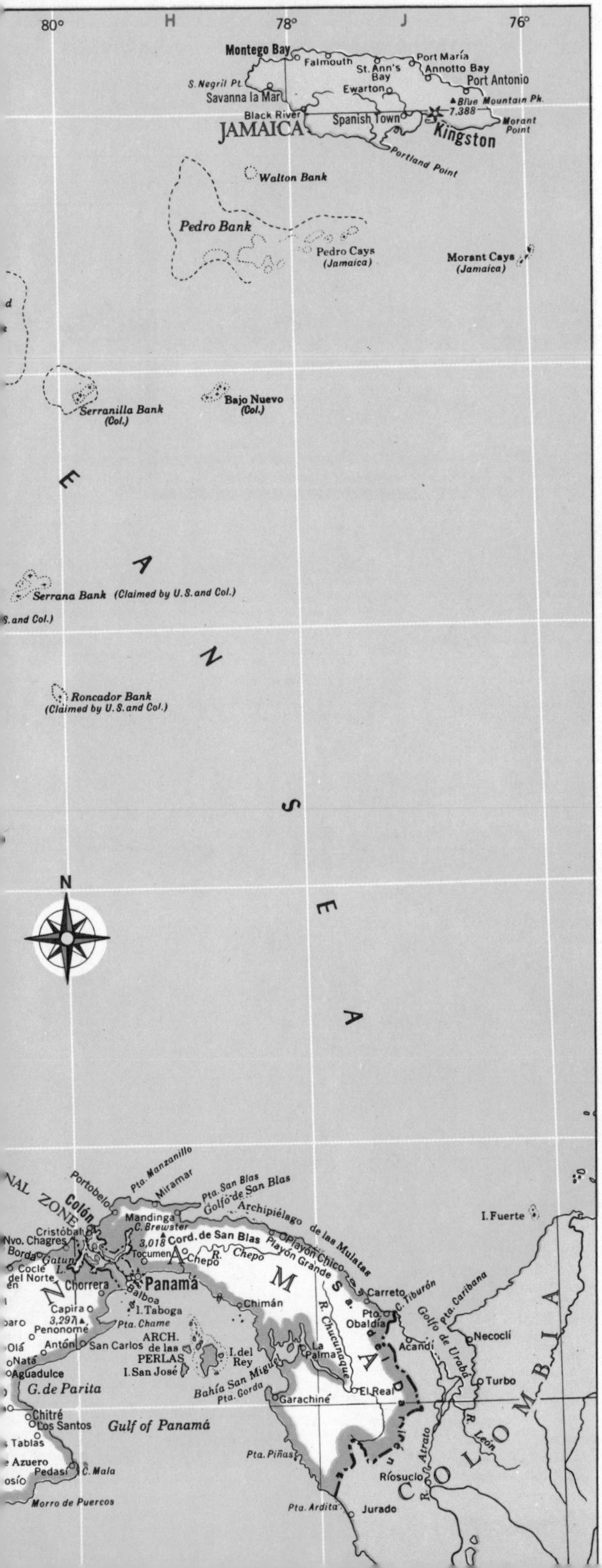

80°
H
78°
J
76°
Montego Bay
Falmouth
St. Ann's Bay
Port María
Annotto Bay
Port Antonio
S. Negril Pt.
Savanna la Mar
Ewarton
Blue Mountain Pk. 7,388
Black River
Spanish Town
Kingston
Morant Point
JAMAICA
Portland Point
Walton Bank
Pedro Bank
Pedro Cays (Jamaica)
Morant Cays (Jamaica)
Serranilla Bank (Col.)
Bajo Nuevo (Col.)
Serrana Bank (Claimed by U.S. and Col.)
Roncador Bank (Claimed by U.S. and Col.)
N
I. Fuerte
Portobelo
Pta. Manzanillo
Miramar
Pta. San Blas
Golfo de San Blas
Archipiélago de las Mulatas
Colón
Mandinga
C. Brewster
Cristóbal
Nvo. Chagres
Gatún
Coclé del Norte
Chorrera
Panamá
Tocumen
Chepo
Cord. de San Blas
Playón Chico
Playón Grande
R. Chepo
Carreto
C. Tiburón
Pto. Obaldía
Golfo de Urabá
Pta. Caribana
Necoclí
Turbo
Capira
Penonomé
Antón
Natá
Aguadulce
I. Taboga
Pta. Chame
San Carlos
ARCH. DE LAS PERLAS
I. San José
I. del Rey
Chimán
Bahía San Miguel
Pta. Gorda
La Palma
Acandí
El Real
Garachiné
G. de Parita
Chitré
Los Santos
Tablas
Gulf of Panamá
Azuero
Pedasí
C. Mala
Morro de Puercos
Pta. Piñas
Riosucio
Pta. Ardita
Jurado
R. León
Atrato
COLOMBIA

Santa Rita, 3,976 .... D 3
Santa Rosa de Aguán, 1,701 .... E 2
Santa Rosa de Copán, 9,109 .... C 3
Siguatepeque, 9,462 .... D 3
Sinuapa, 882 .... C 3
Sonaguera, 1,344 .... D 3
Sulaco, 1,071 .... D 3
Tegucigalpa (cap.), 253,283 .... D 3
Tela, 14,103 .... D 3
Teupasenti, 829 .... D 3
Tocoa, 1,605 .... E 3
Trinidad, 2,817 .... C 3
Trujillo, 4,656 .... E 3
Uji .... F 3
Utila, 967 .... D 2
Villa de San Antonio, 2,287 .... D 3
Yocón, 269 .... D 3
Yorito, 869 .... D 3
Yoro, 4,129 .... D 3
Yuscarán, 1,854 .... D 4

OTHER FEATURES

Aguán (river) .... D 3
Bahía (isls.), 9,702 .... D 2
Bonacca (Guanaja) (isl.), 2,039 .... E 2
Brus (lagoon) .... E 2
Camarón (cape) .... E 2
Caratasca (cays) .... F 2
Caratasca (lagoon) .... F 3
Choluteca (river) .... D 4
Coco (river) .... E 3
Colón (mts.) .... E 3
Esperanza (mts.) .... E 3
Falso (cape) .... F 3
Fonseca (gulf) .... D 4
Gorda (bank) .... F 3
Gorda (cay) .... F 3
Guanaja (isl.), 2,039 .... E 2
Half Moon (reefs) .... F 3
Honduras (cape) .... E 2
Honduras (gulf) .... D 2
Patuca (point) .... E 3
Patuca (river) .... E 3
Paulaya (river) .... E 3
Pigeon (cays) .... F 3
Pija (mts.) .... D 3
Roatán (isl.), 6,552 .... D 2
San Pablo, Sierra de (mts.) .... E 3
Segovia (Coco) (river) .... F 3
Sico (river) .... E 3
Sulaco (river) .... D 3
Swan (isls.), 28 .... F 2
Ulúa (river) .... D 3
Utila (isl.), 1,111 .... D 2
Vivario (cays) .... F 3
Wanks (Coco) (river) .... F 3
Yojoa (lake) .... D 3

NICARAGUA

CITIES and TOWNS

Acoyapa, 1,755 .... E 5
Alamikamba .... E 4
Barra de Río Grande .... F 4
Bilwaskarma .... F 3
Bluefields, 9,292 .... F 4
Boaco, 4,656 .... E 4
Bocay .... E 3
Bonanza, 2,175 .... E 4
Bragman's Bluff (Puerto Cabezas), 5,983 .... F 3
Cabo Gracias a Dios, 511 .... F 3
Camoapa, 2,617 .... E 4
Chichigalpa, 6,657 .... D 4
Chinandega, 22,409 .... D 4
Ciudad Darío, 3,851 .... D 4
Comalapa, 441 .... E 4
Condega, 2,229 .... D 4
Corinto, 9,177 .... D 4
Cuicuina .... E 4
Cuyu Tigni .... F 3
Diriamba, 10,499 .... D 5
El Gallo .... E 4
El Jicaral, 239 .... D 4
El Jícaro, 1,114 .... D 4
El Sauce, 2,944 .... D 4
El Viejo, 7,190 .... D 4
Esquipulas, 1,636 .... E 4
Estelí, 12,742 .... D 4
Granada, 28,507 .... E 5
Greytown (San Juan del Norte), 199 .... F 5
Jalapa, 1,868 .... E 4
Jinotega, 7,693 .... E 4
Jinotepe, 9,113 .... D 5
Juigalpa, 6,146 .... E 4
La Conquista, 364 .... D 5
La Cruz, 155 .... E 4
Laguna de Perlas .... F 4
La Libertad, 1,355 .... E 4
La Paz Central, 4,431 .... D 4
La Paz de Oriente, 828 .... E 5
La Trinidad, 2,340 .... D 4
León, 44,053 .... D 4
Managua (capital), 262,047 .... D 4
Masatepe, 4,831 .... D 5
Masaya, 23,402 .... D 5
Matagalpa, 15,030 .... E 4
Mateare, 1,254 .... D 4
Morrito, 324 .... E 5
Moyogalpa, 1,252 .... E 5
Muleculus .... E 4
Muy Muy, 691 .... E 4
Muy Muy Viejo .... E 4
Nagarote, 5,241 .... D 4
Nandaime, 5,051 .... E 5
Ocotal, 4,339 .... D 4
Ocotal .... E 4
Palsagua .... E 4
Playa Grande .... D 4
Poneloya, 995 .... D 4
Poteca .... E 4
Prinzapolka, 230 .... F 4
Puerto Cabezas, 5,983 .... F 3
Quilalí, 710 .... E 4
Rama (El Rama), 600 .... E 4
Rivas, 7,721 .... E 5
San Carlos, 1,547 .... E 5
Sandy Bay .... F 3
San Francisco .... E 5
San Jorge, 1,657 .... E 5
San Juan del Norte, 199 .... F 5
San Juan del Sur, 2,103 .... D 5
San Miguelito, 885 .... E 5
San Pedro .... E 4
San Rafael del Norte, 1,298 .... E 4
San Rafael del Sur, 2,411 .... D 5
San Ramón, 436 .... E 4
Santa Cruz .... E 4
Santo Domingo, 1,779 .... E 4
Santo Tomás, 1,530 .... E 5
Siuna, 3,743 .... E 4
Somotillo, 1,435 .... D 4
Somoto, 3,967 .... D 4
Telpaneca, 1,019 .... D 4
Terrabona, 690 .... E 4
Teustepe, 764 .... E 4
Tipitapa, 3,600 .... E 4
Tunki .... E 4
Waspán, 973 .... E 3
Yablis .... F 4

OTHER FEATURES

Alargate (reef) .... F 3
Coco (river) .... E 3
Cosegüina (point) .... D 4
Dariense (range) .... E 4
Dipilto (range) .... D 4
Escondido (river) .... F 4
Fonseca (gulf) .... D 4
Gorda (point) .... F 5
Gracias a Dios (cape) .... F 3
Grande (river) .... E 4
Huapí (mts.) .... E 4
Isabelia (range) .... E 4
King (cays) .... F 4
Kukalaya (river) .... F 4
Managua (lake) .... E 4
Miskito (cays) .... F 3
Monkey (point) .... F 5
Nicaragua (lake) .... E 5
Ometepe (isl.), 12,556 .... E 5
Pearl (cays) .... F 4
Perlas (lagoon) .... F 4
Prinzapolca (river) .... F 4
Salinas (bay) .... D 5
San Juan (river) .... E, F 5
San Juan del Norte (bay) .... F 5
Segovia (Coco) (river) .... E 3
Solentiname (isls.) .... E 5
Tuma (river) .... E 4
Tyra (cays) .... F 4
Wanks (Coco) (river) .... F 3
Waspuk (river) .... E 3
Wawa (river) .... F 3
Zapatera (isl.) .... E 5

PANAMA

CITIES and TOWNS

Aguadulce, 8,192 .... G 6
Alanje, †1,544 .... F 6
Almirante, 4,134 .... F 6
Antón, 3,022 .... G 6
Bajo Boquete, 2,625 .... F 6
Belén .... G 6
Bocas del Toro, 2,462 .... F 6
Calobre, †1,933 .... G 6
Cañazas, †5,516 .... G 6
Capira, †2,168 .... G 6
Carreto .... J 6
Chepo, †598 .... H 6
Chimán, †972 .... H 6
Chiriquí Grande, †1,517 .... F 6
Chitré, 12,575 .... G 7
Chorrera, 26,026 .... H 6
Coclé del Norte, †1,329 .... G 6
Colón, 67,641 .... H 6
David, 35,538 .... F 6
Dolega, †3,710 .... F 6
El Real .... J 6
Garachiné, †1,471 .... H 6
Guabito, †3,531 .... F 6
Gualaca, †3,125 .... F 6
Horconcitos .... F 6
La Concepción, 9,179 .... F 6
La Palma, 1,845 .... H 6
Las Palmas, †3,115 .... G 6
Las Tablas, 3,571 .... G 7
Loma Escobar (La Pintada) .... G 6
Los Santos, 3,940 .... G 7
Mandinga .... H 6
Miguel de la Borda .... G 6
Miramar, †132 .... H 6
Montijo, †3,600 .... G 6
Natá, 3,195 .... G 6
Nuevo Chagres .... G 6
Ocú, †5,267 .... G 7
Olá, †987 .... G 6
Panamá (cap.), 418,013 .... H 6
Parita, †2,320 .... G 6
Pedasí, †1,302 .... G 7
Penonomé, 5,067 .... G 6
Playón Chico .... H 6
Playón Grande .... H 6
Portobelo, †626 .... H 6
Potrerillos .... F 6
Puerto Armuelles, 12,022 .... F 6
Puerto Obaldía .... J 6
San Carlos, †1,421 .... H 6
San Cristóbal .... G 6
San Félix, †1,314 .... G 6
San Francisco, †1,576 .... G 6
Santa Fé, †1,768 .... G 6
Santiago, 14,391 .... G 6
Soná, 4,066 .... G 6
Tocumen, †5,905 .... H 6
Tolé, †4,734 .... G 6
Tonosí, †1,301 .... G 7

OTHER FEATURES

Azuero (pen.) .... G 7
Bastimentos (isl.), 574 .... G 6
Brewster (mt.) .... H 6
Burica (point) .... F 6
Cébaco (isl.) .... G 7
Chepo (river) .... H 6
Chiriquí (gulf) .... F 7
Chiriquí (lagoon) .... G 6
Chiriquí (volcano) .... F 6
Chucunaque (river) .... J 6
Coiba (isl.) .... F 7
Colón (isl.) .... G 6
Contreras (isls.) .... F 7
Darién (mts.) .... J 6
Escudo de Veraguas (isl.) .... G 6
Gatun (lake) .... G 6
Gorda (point) .... H 6
Jicarón (isl.) .... F 7
Ladrones (isls.) .... F 7
Manzanillo (point) .... H 6
Montijo (gulf) .... G 7
Mosquito (gulf) .... G 6
Mulatas (arch.) .... J 6
Panamá (gulf) .... H 7
Pando (mt.) .... F 6
Parida (isl.) .... F 6
Parita (gulf) .... G 6
Perlas (arch.) .... H 6
Puercos (prom.) .... H 7
Rey (isl.) .... H 6
Rincón (point) .... G 6
San Blas (gulf) .... H 6
San Blas (range) .... H 6
San José (isl.) .... H 6
San Miguel (bay) .... H 6
Santiago (mt.) .... G 6
Secas (isls.) .... G 7
Tabasará (mts.) .... G 6
Taboga (isl.), 1,747 .... H 6
Tiburón (cape) .... J 6
Urabá (gulf) .... J 6
Valiente (pen.) .... G 6

CENTRAL AMERICA

Great Corn (isl.), 1,896 .... F 4
Guardian (bank) .... D 6
Little Corn (isl.) .... F 4
Mosquito Coast (reg.) .... E 4
Rosalind (bank) .... G 2

City and suburbs.
†Population of sub-district.
‡Population of district.

124 West Indies

CUBA
AREA 44,206 sq. mi.
POPULATION 8,553,395
CAPITAL Havana
LARGEST CITY Havana
HIGHEST POINT Pico Turquino 6,561 ft.
MONETARY UNIT Cuban peso
MAJOR LANGUAGE Spanish
MAJOR RELIGION Roman Catholicism

HAITI
AREA 10,694 sq. mi.
POPULATION 4,867,190
CAPITAL Port-au-Prince
LARGEST CITY Port-au-Prince
HIGHEST POINT Pic La Selle 8,793 ft.
MONETARY UNIT gourde
MAJOR LANGUAGES Creole French, French
MAJOR RELIGION Roman Catholicism

DOMINICAN REPUBLIC
AREA 18,704 sq. mi.
POPULATION 4,011,589
CAPITAL Santo Domingo
LARGEST CITY Santo Domingo
HIGHEST POINT Pico Duarte 10,417 ft.
MONETARY UNIT Dominican peso
MAJOR LANGUAGE Spanish
MAJOR RELIGION Roman Catholicism

JAMAICA
AREA 4,411 sq. mi.
POPULATION 1,972,000
CAPITAL Kingston
LARGEST CITY Kingston
HIGHEST POINT Blue Mountain Peak, 7,402 ft.
MONETARY UNIT Jamaican pound
MAJOR LANGUAGE English
MAJOR RELIGIONS Protestantism, Roman
  Catholicism

TRINIDAD AND TOBAGO
AREA 1,980 sq. mi.
POPULATION 1,040,000
CAPITAL Port of Spain
LARGEST CITY Port of Spain
HIGHEST POINT Mt. Aripo 3,084 ft.
MONETARY UNIT British West Indian dollar
MAJOR LANGUAGES English, Hindi
MAJOR RELIGIONS Roman Catholicism, Prot.
  Hinduism, Islam

BARBADOS
AREA 166 sq. mi.
POPULATION 253,620
CAPITAL Bridgetown
LARGEST CITY Bridgetown
HIGHEST POINT Mt. Hillaby 1,104 ft.
MONETARY UNIT British West Indian dollar
MAJOR LANGUAGE English
MAJOR RELIGION Protestantism

CUBA

HAITI

DOMINICAN REPUBLIC

JAMAICA

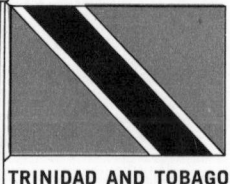
TRINIDAD AND TOBAGO

BARBADOS

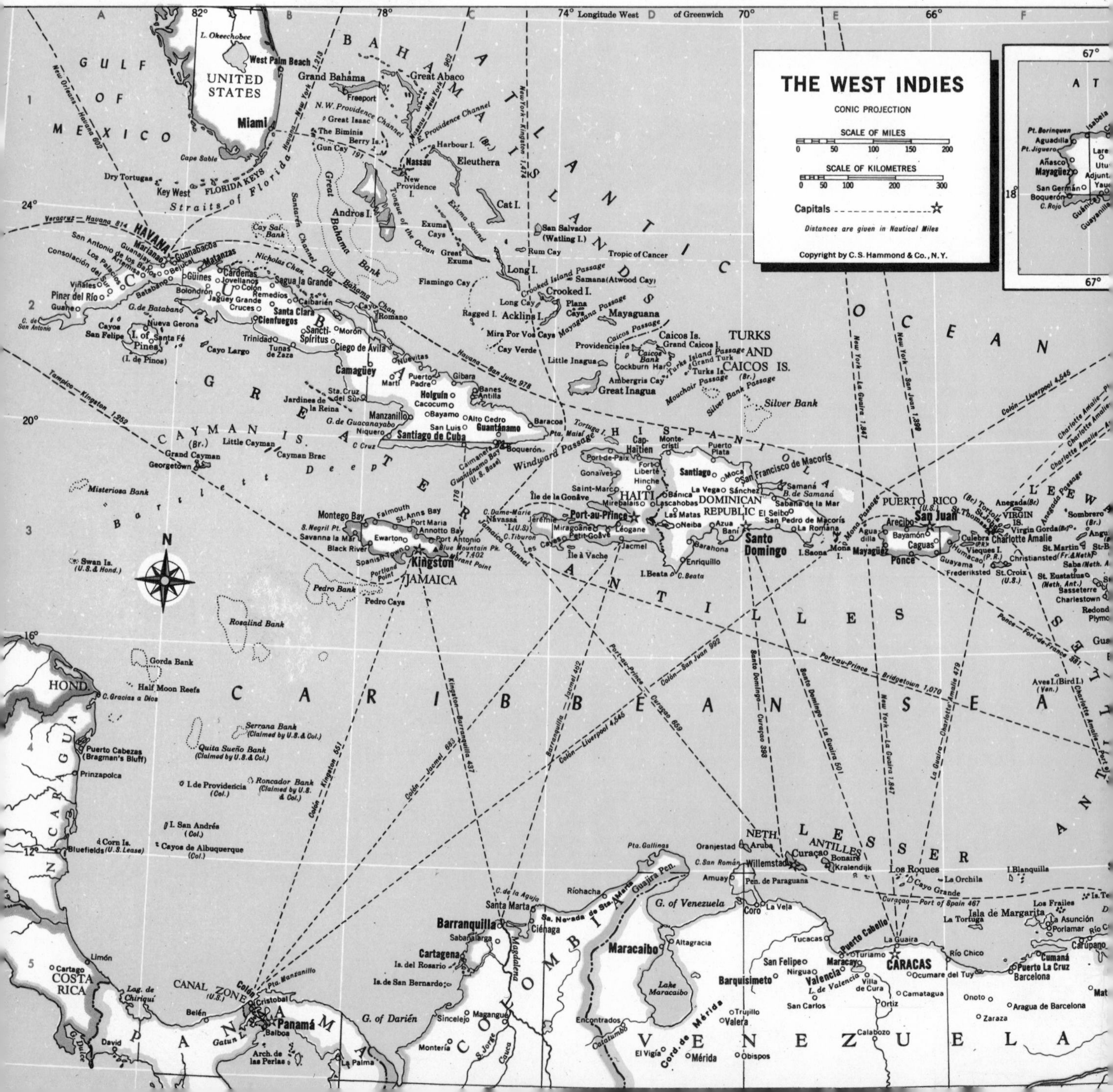

THE WEST INDIES
CONIC PROJECTION

SCALE OF MILES
0   50   100   150   200

SCALE OF KILOMETRES
0   50 100   200   300

Capitals .... ☆

Distances are given in Nautical Miles

Copyright by C.S. Hammond & Co., N.Y.

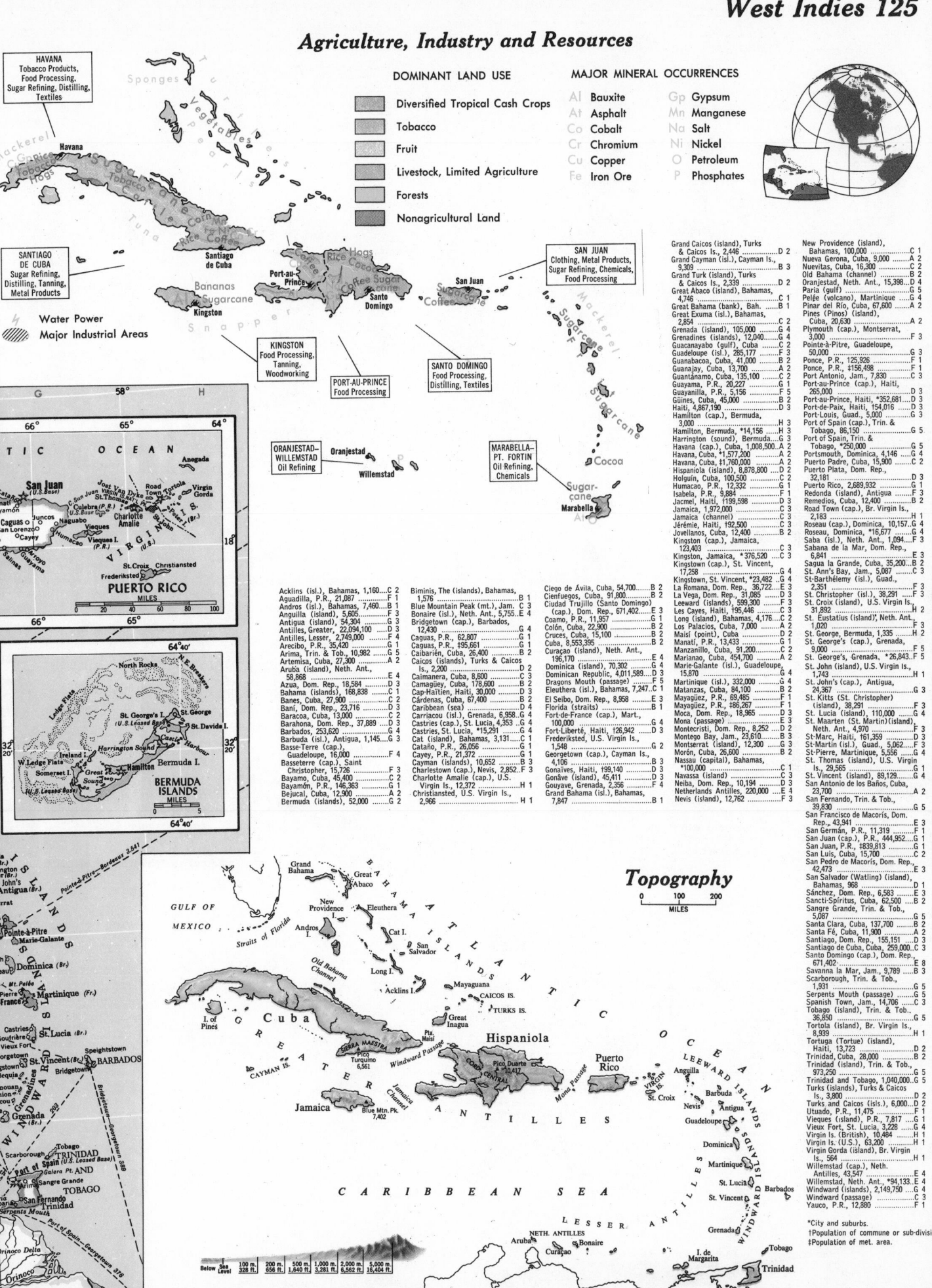

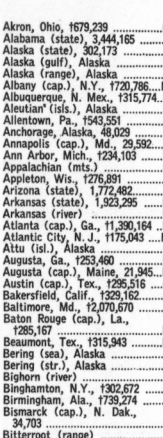

UNITED STATES

POLYCONIC PROJECTION

SCALE

0 50 100 200 300 400MI.

0 50 100 200 300 400KM.

Capitals of Countries............☆
State Capitals..................△
International Boundaries.........– – –
State Boundaries................— — —

© C.S. HAMMOND & Co., N.Y.

Akron, Ohio, †679,239 ....K 2
Alabama (state), 3,444,165 ....J 4
Alaska (state), 302,173 ....C 5
Alaska (range), Alaska ....C 5
Alaska (gulf), Alaska ....D 6
Albany, N.Y., †720,786 ....M 2
Albany, Oreg. ....B 2
Albuquerque, N. Mex, 1315,774 ....E 3
Aleutian° (isls.), Alaska ....D 6
Allentown, Pa., 1543,551 ....L 2
Anchorage, Alaska, 48,029 ....D 6
Annapolis (cap.), Md., 29,592 ....L 3
Ann Arbor, Mich., 1234,103 ....K 2
Appalachian (mts.) ....K 3
Appleton, Wis., 1276,891 ....J 2
Arizona (state), 1,772,482 ....D 4
Arkansas (state), 1,923,295 ....H 4
Arkansas (river) ....G 4
Charleston (cap.), W. Va. ....K 3
†229,515
Atlanta (cap.), Ga., 11,390,164 ....K 4
Atlantic City, N. J., 1175,043 ....M 3
Attu (isl.), Alaska ....D 6
Augusta, Ga., 1253,460 ....K 4
Augusta (cap.), Maine, 21,945 ....N 2
Austin (cap.), Tex., 1295,516 ....G 4
Bakersfield, Calif. 1329,162 ....C 3
Baltimore, Md., 12,070,670 ....L 3
Baton Rouge (cap.), La.,
†285,167 ....H 4
Beaumont, Tex., 1315,943 ....H 4
Bering (sea), Alaska ....C 5
Bering (str.), Alaska ....C 5
Bighorn (river) ....E 2
Binghamton, N.Y., 1302,672 ....L 2
Birmingham, Ala., 1739,274 ....J 4
Bismarck (cap.), N. Dak., ...F 1
34,703
Bitterroot (range) ....D 1
Black Hills (mts.) ....F 2
Boise (cap.), Idaho, 1112,230 ....C 2
Borah (peak), Idaho ....D 2

Boston (cap.), Mass., 12,753,700 ....M 2
Brazos (river), Tex. ....G 4
Bridgeport, Conn., 1388,953 ....M 2
Brooks (range), Alaska ....C 5
Buffalo, N.Y., 11,349,211 ....L 2
California (state), 19,953,134 ....B 3
Canadian (river) ....E 3
Canaveral (Kennedy) (cape), ...L 5
Fla.
Canton, Ohio, 1372,210 ....K 2
Cape Fear (river), N.C. ....L 4
Carson City (cap.), Nev., 15,468 ....C 3
Cascade (range) ....B 2
Cedar Rapids, Iowa, 1163,213 ....H 2
Champlain (lake) ....M 2
Charleston, S.C., 1303,849 ....L 4
Charleston (cap.), W. Va. ....K 3
†229,515
Charlotte, N.C. 1409,370 ....K 3
Chattahoochee (river) ....K 4
Chattanooga, Tenn., 1304,927 ....J 3
Chesapeake (bay) ....L 3
Cheyenne (cap.), Wyo., 40,914 ....F 2
Cheyenne (river) ....F 2
Chicago, Ill., †6,978,947 ....J 2
Cimarron (river) ....G 3
Cincinnati, Ohio, 11,384,911 ....K 3
Cleveland, Ohio, 12,064,194 ....K 2
Coast (range) ....B 2
Cod (cape), Mass. ....N 2
Colorado (state), 2,207,259 ....E 3
Colorado (river) ....D 4
Colorado (river), Tex. ....G 4
Colorado Sprs., Colo., 1235,972 ....F 3
Columbia (cap.), S.C., 1322,880 ....K 4
Columbia (river) ....C 1
Columbus, Ga., 1238,584 ....K 4
Columbus (cap.), Ohio, 1916,228 ....K 3
Concord (cap.), N.H., 30,022 ....M 2

Connecticut (state), 3,032,217 ....M 2
Connecticut (river) ....M 2
Corpus Christi, Tex., 1284,832 ....G 5
Cumberland (river) ....J 3
Dallas, Tex., 11,555,950 ....G 4
Davenport, Iowa, 1362,638 ....H 2
Dayton, Ohio, 1850,266 ....K 3
Death Valley (depr.), Calif. ....C 3
Delaware (state), 548,104 ....L 3
Delaware (bay) ....L 3
Denver (cap.), Colo., 11,227,529 ....F 3
Des Moines (cap.), Iowa, ...H 2
1286,101
Detroit, Mich., 14,199,931 ....K 2
District of Columbia, 756,510 ....L 3
Dover (cap.), Del., 17,488 ....L 3
Duluth, Minn., 1265,350 ....H 1
Durham, N.C., 1190,388 ....L 3
Elbert (mt.), Colo. ....E 3
El Paso, Tex., 1359,291 ....E 4
Erie, Pa., 1263,654 ....L 2
Erie (lake) ....L 2
Eugene, Oreg., 1213,358 ....B 2
Evansville, Ind., 1232,775 ....J 3
Everglades (swamp), Fla. ....K 5
Fayetteville, N.C., 1212,042 ....L 3
Flint, Mich., 1496,658 ....K 2
Florida (state), 6,789,443 ....K 5
Florida (keys), Fla. ....K 6
Ft. Smith, Ark., 1160,421 ....H 3
Ft. Wayne, Ind., 1280,455 ....J 2
Ft. Worth, Tex., 1762,086 ....G 4
Frankfort (cap.), Ky., 21,356 ....K 3
Fresno, Calif., 1413,053 ....C 3
Galveston, Tex., 1169,812 ....H 5
Gary, Ind., 1633,367 ....J 2
Georgia (state), 4,589,575 ....K 4
Gila (river) ....D 4
Glacier Nat'l Park, Mont. ....D 1

Golden Gate (chan.), Calif. ....B 3
Grand Canyon Nat'l Park, Ariz. ....D 3
Grand Rapids, Mich., 1539,225 ....J 2
Great Salt (lake), Utah ....D 2
Greensboro, N.C., 1603,895 ....K 3
Greenville, S.C., 1299,502 ....K 4
Hamilton, Ohio, 1226,207 ....K 3
Harrisburg (cap.), Pa., 1410,626 ....L 2
Hartford (cap.), Conn., ...M 2
1663,891
Hatteras (cape), N.C. ....M 3
Havasu (lake) ....D 3
Hawaii (state), 769,913 ....F 6
Hawaii (isl.), Hawaii ....F 6
Helena (cap.), Mont., 22,730 ....D 1
Honolulu (cap.), Hawaii, ...F 6
1629,176
Houston, Tex., 11,985,031 ....G 5
Huntington, W. Va., 1253,743 ....K 3
Huntsville, Ala., 1228,239 ....J 4
Huron (lake), Mich. ....K 2
Idaho (state), 713,008 ....D 2
Illinois (state), 11,113,976 ....J 3
Indiana (state), 5,193,669 ....J 3
Indianapolis (cap.), Ind., ...J 3
11,109,882
Iowa (state), 2,825,041 ....H 2
Jackson (cap.), Miss., 1258,906 ....H 4
Jacksonville, Fla., 1528,865 ....K 4
Jefferson City (cap.), Mo. ....H 3
32,407
Jersey City, N.J., 1609,266 ....M 2
Johnstown, Pa., 1262,822 ....L 2
Juneau (cap.), Alaska, 13,556 ....E 6
Kalamazoo, Mich., 1201,550 ....J 2
Kansas (state), 2,249,071 ....G 3
Kansas City, Kans.-Mo., ...H 3
11,256,649
Kauai (isl.), Hawaii ....E 5

Kennedy (cape), Fla. ....L 5
Kentucky (state), 3,219,311 ....J 3
Kentucky (lake) ....J 3
Knoxville, Tenn., 1400,337 ....K 3
Lancaster, Pa., 1319,693 ....L 2
Lansing (cap.), Mich., 1378,423 ....K 2
Las Vegas, Nev., 1273,288 ....D 3
Lawrence, Mass., 1232,395 ....M 2
Lexington, Ky., 1174,323 ....K 3
Lima, Ohio, 1171,472 ....K 2
Lincoln (cap.), Nebr., 1167,972 ....G 2
Little Rock (cap.), Ark., ...H 4
†323,296
Long (isl.), N.Y. ....M 2
Long Beach, Calif., 358,633 ....C 4
Los Angeles, Calif., 17,032,075 ....C 4
Louisiana (state), 3,643,180 ....H 4
Louisville, Ky., 1826,553 ....J 3
Lowell, Mass., 1212,860 ....M 2
Lubbock, Tex., 1179,295 ....F 4
Macon, Ga., 1206,342 ....K 4
Madison (cap.), Wis., 1290,272 ....H 2
Maine (state), 993,663 ....N 1
Maryland (state), 3,922,399 ....L 3
Massachusetts (state), ...M 2
5,689,170
Maui (isl.), Hawaii ....F 5
Mauna Kea (mt.), Hawaii ....F 6
Mauna Loa (mt.), Hawaii ....F 6
May (cape), N.J. ....M 3
McKinley (mt.), Alaska ....C 5
Mead (lake) ....D 3
Memphis, Tenn., 1770,120 ....J 3
Mendocino (cape), Calif. ....B 2
Mexico (gulf) ....J 5
Miami, Fla., 11,267,792 ....K 5
Michigan (state), 8,875,083 ....J 2
Michigan (lake) ....J 2
Milwaukee, Wis., 11,403,887 ....J 2

Minneapolis, Minn., 11,813,647 ....H 1
Minnesota (state), 3,805,069 ....H 1
Mississippi (state), 2,216,912 ....J 4
Mississippi (river) ....J 3
Missouri (state), 4,677,399 ....H 3
Missouri (river) ....J 2
Mitchell (mt.), N.C. ....K 3
Mobile, Ala., 1376,690 ....J 4
Montana (state), 694,409 ....E 1
Montgomery (cap.), Ala., ...J 4
1201,325
Montpelier (cap.), Vt., 8,609 ....M 2
Nantucket (isl.), Mass. ....N 2
Nashville (cap.), Tenn., 1540,982 ....J 3
Nebraska (state), 1,483,791 ....F 2
Nevada (state), 488,738 ....C 3
Newark, N. J., 11,856,556 ....M 2
New Hampshire(state), 737,681 ....M 2
New Haven, Conn., 1355,538 ....M 2
New Jersey (state), 7,168,164 ....M 2
New Mexico (state), 1,016,000 ....E 4
New Orleans, La., 11,045,809 ....H 5
Newport News, Va., 1292,159 ....L 3
New York (state), 18,190,740 ....L 2
New York, N.Y., 11,528,649 ....M 2
Norfolk, Va., 1680,600 ....L 3
North Carolina(state), 5,082,059 ....L 3
North Dakota (state), 617,761 ....F 1
Oahu (isl.), Hawaii ....E 5
Oakland, Calif., 361,561 ....B 3
Ohio (state), 10,652,017 ....K 2
Ohio (river) ....J 3
Oklahoma (state), 2,559,253 ....G 3
Oklahoma City (cap.), Okla., ...G 3
1640,889
Olympia (cap.), Wash., 23,111 ....B 1
Olympic Nat'l Park, Wash. ....A 1
Omaha, Nebr., 1541,453 ....G 2
Ontario (lake), N.Y. ....L 2

Oregon (state), 2,091,385 ....B 2
Orlando, Fla., 1428,003 ....K 5
Ozark (mts.) ....H 3
Paterson, N. J., 11,358,794 ....M 2
Pennsylvania (state), 11,793,909 ....L 2
Pensacola, Fla., 1243,075 ....J 4
Peoria, Ill., 1341,979 ....J 2
Philadelphia, Pa., 14,817,914 ....M 2
Phoenix (cap.), Ariz., 1968,487 ....D 4
Pierre (cap.), S. Dak., 9,699 ....F 2
Pikes (peak), Colo. ....F 3
Pittsburgh, Pa., 12,401,245 ....L 2
Platte (river), Nebr. ....G 2
Pontchartrain (lake), La. ....H 4
Portland, Maine, 1141,625 ....N 2
Portland, Oreg., 11,009,129 ....B 1
Potomac (river) ....L 3
Providence (cap.), R.I., 1914,110 ....M 2
Racine, Wis., 1170,838 ....J 2
Rainier (mt.), Wash. ....B 1
Raleigh (cap.), N.C., 1228,453 ....L 3
Reading, Pa., 1296,382 ....L 2
Red (river) ....H 4
Red River of the North (river) ....G 1
Rhode Island (state), 949,723 ....M 2
Richmond (cap.), Va., 1518,319 ....L 3
Rio Grande (river) ....F 5
Roanoke, Va., 1181,436 ....K 3
Rochester, N.Y., 1882,667 ....L 2
Rockford, Ill., 1272,063 ....J 2
Rocky (mts.) ....E 2
Sacramento (cap.), Calif., ...B 3
1800,592
Saginaw, Mich., 1219,743 ....K 2
Saint Clair (lake) ....K 2
Saint Lawrence (river), N.Y. ....N 1
Saint Louis, Mo., 12,363,017 ....H 3
Saint Paul (cap.), Minn., ...H 1
309,980

AREA 3,615,123 sq. mi.
POPULATION 203,184,772
CAPITAL Washington
LARGEST CITY New York
HIGHEST POINT Mt. McKinley 20,320 ft.
MONETARY VALUE U.S. dollar
MAJOR LANGUAGE English
MAJOR RELIGIONS Protestantism, Roman Catholicism, Judaism

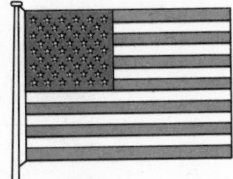

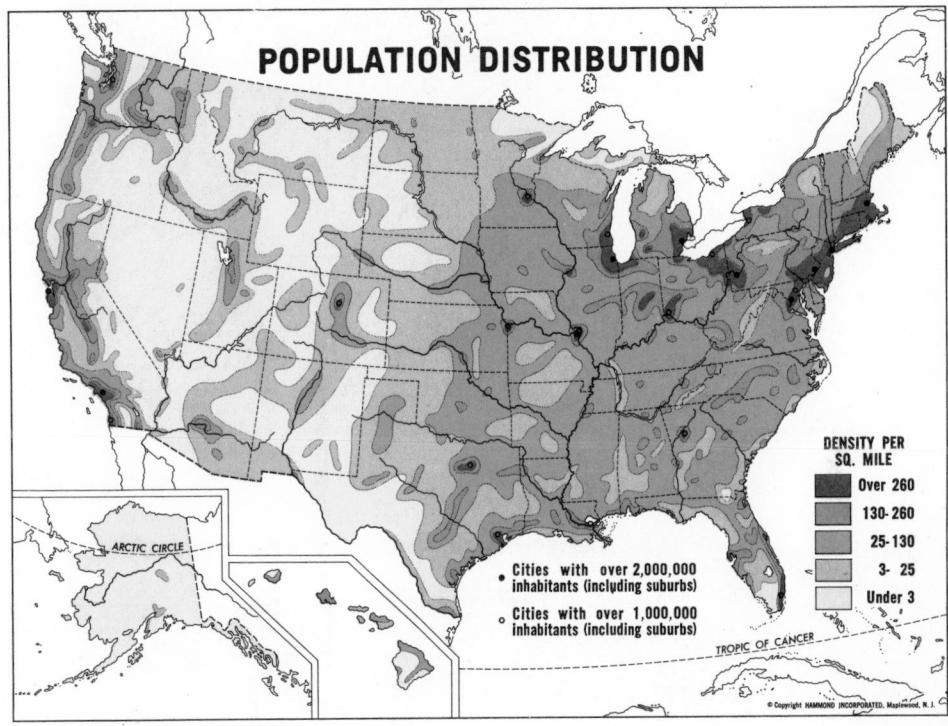

POPULATION DISTRIBUTION

- Cities with over 2,000,000 inhabitants (including suburbs)
- Cities with over 1,000,000 inhabitants (including suburbs)

DENSITY PER SQ. MILE

- Over 260
- 130- 260
- 25-130
- 3- 25
- Under 3

ARCTIC CIRCLE

TROPIC OF CANCER

© Copyright HAMMOND INCORPORATED, Maplewood, N.J.

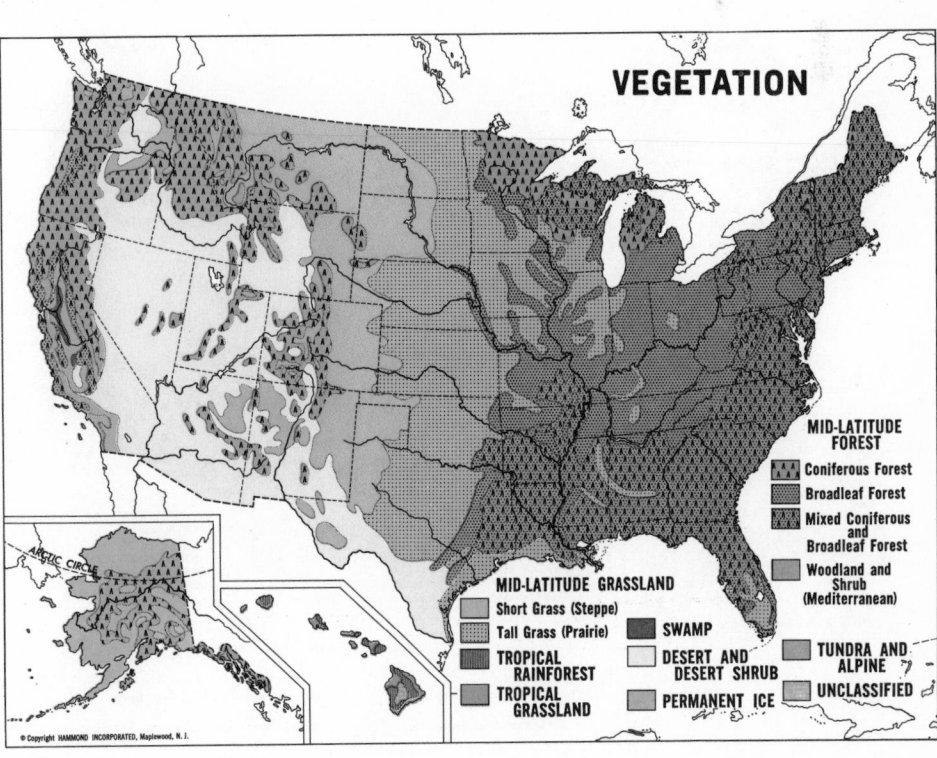

VEGETATION

MID-LATITUDE FOREST
- Coniferous Forest
- Broadleaf Forest
- Mixed Coniferous and Broadleaf Forest
- Woodland and Shrub (Mediterranean)

MID-LATITUDE GRASSLAND
- Short Grass (Steppe)
- Tall Grass (Prairie)
- SWAMP
- TROPICAL RAINFOREST
- DESERT AND DESERT SHRUB
- TROPICAL GRASSLAND
- PERMANENT ICE
- TUNDRA AND ALPINE
- UNCLASSIFIED

ARCTIC CIRCLE

© Copyright HAMMOND INCORPORATED, Maplewood, N.J.

Topography

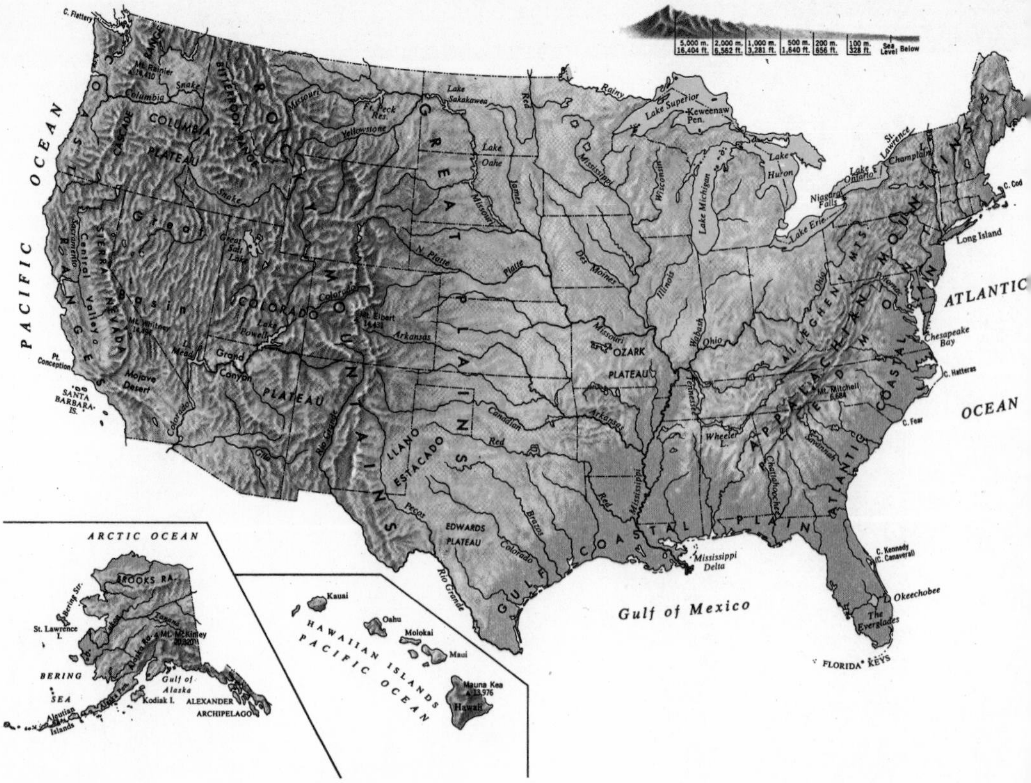
5,000 m. 16,404 ft.
2,000 m. 6,562 ft.
1,000 m. 3,281 ft.
500 m. 1,640 ft.
200 m. 656 ft.
100 m. 328 ft.
Sea Level Below
PACIFIC OCEAN
ATLANTIC OCEAN
Gulf of Mexico
ROCKY MOUNTAINS
GREAT PLAINS
COLUMBIA PLATEAU
COLORADO PLATEAU
Great Basin
OZARK PLATEAU
LLANO ESTACADO
EDWARDS PLATEAU
APPALACHIAN MTS.
GULF COASTAL PLAIN
ARCTIC OCEAN
BROOKS RA.
BERING SEA
Gulf of Alaska
ALEXANDER ARCHIPELAGO
HAWAIIAN ISLANDS
PACIFIC OCEAN
Mauna Kea 13,796
FLORIDA KEYS
0 200 400
MILES

Agriculture, Industry and Resources

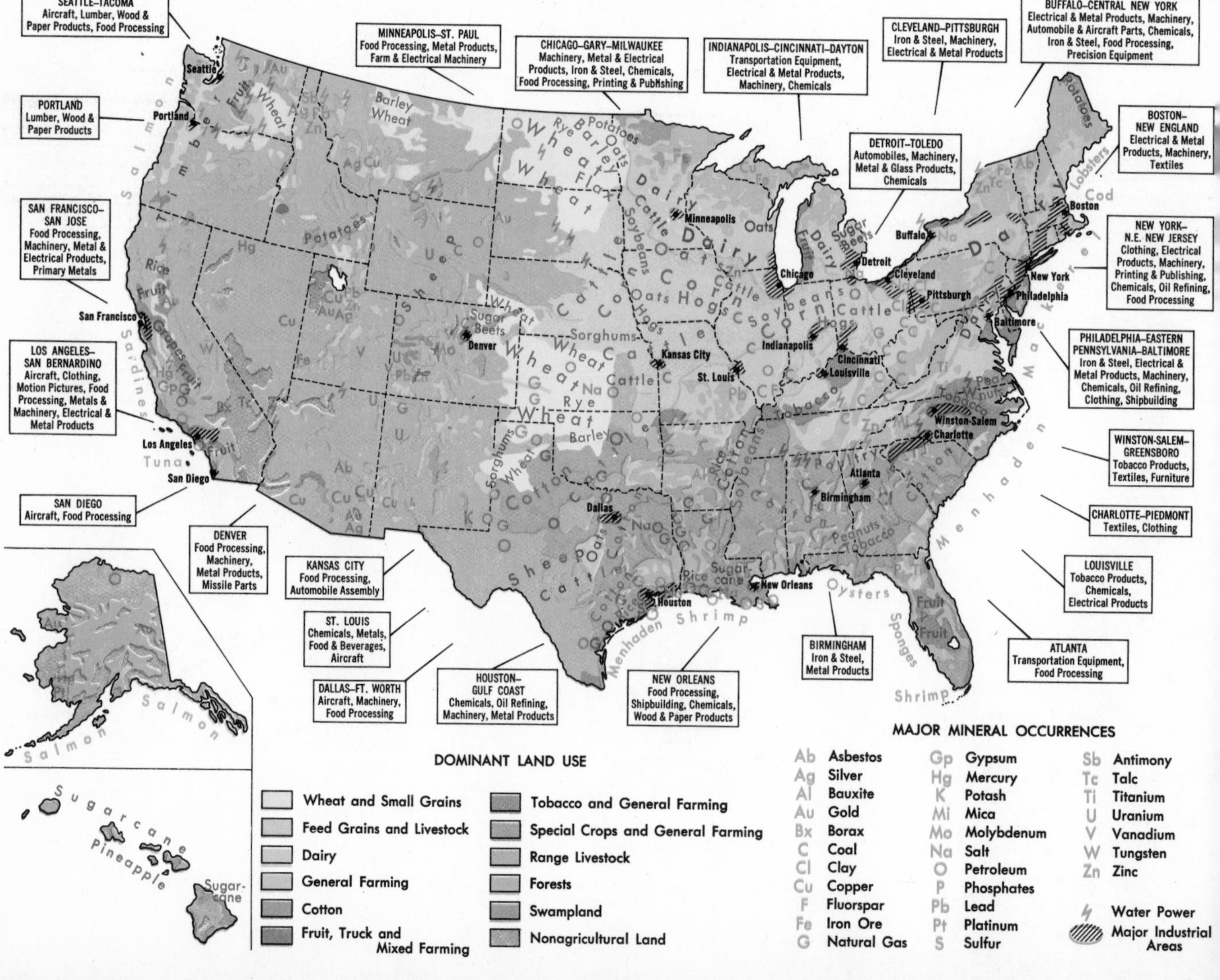
SEATTLE–TACOMA
Aircraft, Lumber, Wood & Paper Products, Food Processing
PORTLAND
Lumber, Wood & Paper Products
SAN FRANCISCO–SAN JOSE
Food Processing, Machinery, Metal & Electrical Products, Primary Metals
LOS ANGELES–SAN BERNARDINO
Aircraft, Clothing, Motion Pictures, Food Processing, Metals & Machinery, Electrical & Metal Products
SAN DIEGO
Aircraft, Food Processing
DENVER
Food Processing, Machinery, Metal Products, Missile Parts
KANSAS CITY
Food Processing, Automobile Assembly
ST. LOUIS
Chemicals, Metals, Food & Beverages, Aircraft
DALLAS–FT. WORTH
Aircraft, Machinery, Food Processing
HOUSTON–GULF COAST
Chemicals, Oil Refining, Machinery, Metal Products
NEW ORLEANS
Food Processing, Shipbuilding, Chemicals, Wood & Paper Products
BIRMINGHAM
Iron & Steel, Metal Products
MINNEAPOLIS–ST. PAUL
Food Processing, Metal Products, Farm & Electrical Machinery
CHICAGO–GARY–MILWAUKEE
Machinery, Metal & Electrical Products, Iron & Steel, Chemicals, Food Processing, Printing & Publishing
INDIANAPOLIS–CINCINNATI–DAYTON
Transportation Equipment, Electrical & Metal Products, Machinery, Chemicals
CLEVELAND–PITTSBURGH
Iron & Steel, Machinery, Electrical & Metal Products
DETROIT–TOLEDO
Automobiles, Machinery, Metal & Glass Products, Chemicals
BUFFALO–CENTRAL NEW YORK
Electrical & Metal Products, Machinery, Automobile & Aircraft Parts, Chemicals, Iron & Steel, Food Processing, Precision Equipment
BOSTON–NEW ENGLAND
Electrical & Metal Products, Machinery, Textiles
NEW YORK–N.E. NEW JERSEY
Clothing, Electrical Products, Machinery, Printing & Publishing, Chemicals, Oil Refining, Food Processing
PHILADELPHIA–EASTERN PENNSYLVANIA–BALTIMORE
Iron & Steel, Electrical & Metal Products, Machinery, Chemicals, Oil Refining, Clothing, Shipbuilding
WINSTON-SALEM–GREENSBORO
Tobacco Products, Textiles, Furniture
CHARLOTTE–PIEDMONT
Textiles, Clothing
LOUISVILLE
Tobacco Products, Chemicals, Electrical Products
ATLANTA
Transportation Equipment, Food Processing
DOMINANT LAND USE
Wheat and Small Grains
Feed Grains and Livestock
Dairy
General Farming
Cotton
Fruit, Truck and Mixed Farming
Tobacco and General Farming
Special Crops and General Farming
Range Livestock
Forests
Swampland
Nonagricultural Land
MAJOR MINERAL OCCURRENCES
Ab Asbestos
Ag Silver
Al Bauxite
Au Gold
Bx Borax
C Coal
Cl Clay
Cu Copper
F Fluorspar
Fe Iron Ore
G Natural Gas
Gp Gypsum
Hg Mercury
K Potash
Mi Mica
Mo Molybdenum
Na Salt
O Petroleum
P Phosphates
Pb Lead
Pt Platinum
S Sulfur
Sb Antimony
Tc Talc
Ti Titanium
U Uranium
V Vanadium
W Tungsten
Zn Zinc
Water Power
Major Industrial Areas

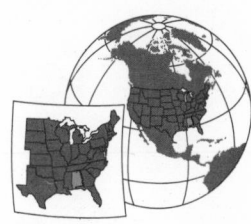

COUNTIES

Autauga, 24,460 ....E 5
Baldwin, 59,382 ....C 9
Barbour, 22,543 ....H 7
Bibb, 13,812 ....D 5
Blount, 26,853 ....E 2
Bullock, 11,824 ....G 6
Butler, 22,007 ....E 7
Calhoun, 103,092 ....G 3
Chambers, 36,356 ....H 5
Cherokee, 15,606 ....G 2
Chilton, 25,180 ....E 5
Choctaw, 16,589 ....B 6
Clarke, 26,724 ....C 7
Clay, 12,636 ....G 4
Cleburne, 10,996 ....G 3
Coffee, 34,872 ....G 8
Colbert, 49,632 ....C 1
Conecuh, 15,645 ....E 8
Coosa, 10,662 ....F 5
Covington, 34,079 ....F 8
Crenshaw, 13,188 ....F 7
Cullman, 52,445 ....E 2
Dale, 52,938 ....G 8
Dallas, 55,296 ....D 6
De Kalb, 41,981 ....F 1
Elmore, 33,535 ....F 5
Escambia, 34,906 ....D 8
Etowah, 94,144 ....F 2
Fayette, 16,252 ....C 3
Franklin, 23,933 ....C 2
Geneva, 21,924 ....G 8
Greene, 10,650 ....C 5
Hale, 15,888 ....C 5
Henry, 13,254 ....H 7
Houston, 56,574 ....H 8
Jackson, 39,202 ....F 1
Jefferson, 644,991 ....E 3
Lamar, 14,335 ....B 3
Lauderdale, 68,111 ....C 1
Lawrence, 27,281 ....D 1
Lee, 61,268 ....H 5
Limestone, 41,699 ....E 1
Lowndes, 12,897 ....E 6
Macon, 24,841 ....G 6
Madison, 186,540 ....E 1
Marengo, 23,819 ....C 6
Marion, 23,788 ....C 2
Marshall, 54,211 ....F 2
Mobile, 317,308 ....B 9
Monroe, 20,883 ....D 7
Montgomery, 167,790 ....F 6
Morgan, 77,306 ....E 2
Perry, 15,388 ....D 5
Pickens, 20,326 ....B 4
Pike, 25,038 ....G 7
Randolph, 18,331 ....H 4
Russell, 45,394 ....H 6
Saint Clair, 27,956 ....F 3
Shelby, 38,037 ....E 4
Sumter, 16,974 ....B 5
Talladega, 65,280 ....F 4
Tallapoosa, 33,840 ....G 5

Tuscaloosa, 116,029 ....C 4
Walker, 56,246 ....D 3
Washington, 16,241 ....B 8
Wilcox, 16,303 ....D 7
Winston, 16,654 ....D 2

CITIES and TOWNS

Zip	Name/Pop.	Key
36310	Abbeville⊙, 2,996	H 7
35440	Abernant, 602	D 4
35005	Adamsville, 2,412	D 3
35540	Addison, 692	D 2
35006	Adger, 1,550	D 4
35441	Akron, 535	C 5
35007	Alabaster, 2,642	E 4
35950	Albertville, 9,963	F 2
† 35115	Aldrich, 476	E 4
35010	Alexander City, 12,358	G 5
36250	Alexandria, 600	G 3
35442	Aliceville, 2,807	B 4
35013	Allgood, 272	F 3
† 35616	Allsboro, 300	B 1
35015	Alton, 500	D 4
35952	Altoona, 781	F 2
36420	Andalusia⊙, 10,092	E 8
35610	Anderson, 400	D 1
36201	Anniston⊙, 31,533	G 3
35016	Arab, 4,399	E 2
35805	Ardmore, 761	E 1
36311	Ariton, 643	G 7
35033	Arkadelphia, 325	E 3
† 35035	Ashby, 500	E 4
36312	Ashford, 1,980	H 8
36251	Ashland⊙, 1,921	G 4
35953	Ashville, 986	F 3
35611	Athens⊙, 14,360	E 1
36502	Atmore, 8,293	C 8
35954	Attalla, 7,510	F 2
36830	Auburn, 22,767	H 5
36003	Autaugaville, 870	E 6
† 36312	Avon, 374	H 8
36605	Axis, 600	B 9
35019	Baileyton, 500	E 2
36004	Baker Hill, 350	H 7
36506	Barlow Bend, 300	C 8
† 36532	Barnwell, 700	C 10
36533	Battles Wharf, 300	C 10
36507	Bay Minette⊙, 6,727	C 9
36509	Bayou La Batre, 2,664	B 10
35543	Bear Creek, 336	C 2
36425	Beatrice, 455	D 7
35544	Beaverton, 265	B 3
† 35653	Belgreen, 500	C 2
36901	Bellamy, 700	B 6
35546	Berry, 679	D 3
35020	Bessemer, 33,428	D 4
* 35201	Birmingham⊙, 300,910	D 3
	Birmingham, ‡739,274	D 3
36902	Bladon Springs, 300	B 7
36874	Bleecker, 250	H 5
35031	Blountsville, 1,254	E 2
36201	Blue Mountain, 446	G 3
35226	Bluff Park, 12,372	E 4

35957	Boaz, 5,621	F 2
36903	Bolinger, 250	B 7
36007	Bolling, 250	E 7
36511	Bon Secour, 850	C 10
36110	Boylston, 2,943	F 6
36009	Brantley, 1,066	F 7
35034	Brent, 2,093	D 5
36426	Brewton⊙, 6,747	D 8
35740	Bridgeport, 2,908	G 1
35035	Brierfield, 950	E 4
35020	Brighton, 2,277	D 4
35548	Brilliant, 726	C 2
36429	Brooklyn, 350	E 8
35036	Brookside, 990	E 3
35444	Brookwood, 450	D 4
35445	Brownville, 300	C 4
36010	Brundidge, 2,709	G 7
35446	Buhl, 500	C 4
36725	Burkville, 250	E 6
36431	Burnt Corn, 250	D 7
36429	Butler⊙, 2,064	B 6
† 36767	Cahaba, 50	D 6
35040	Calera, 1,655	E 4
36012	Calhoun, 950	F 6
36513	Calvert, 500	B 8
36726	Camden⊙, 1,742	D 7
36850	Camp Hill, 1,554	G 5
36514	Canoe, 560	D 8
† 36726	Canton Bend, 250	D 6
35549	Carbon Hill, 1,929	D 3
36515	Carlton, 275	C 8
35447	Carrollton⊙, 923	B 4
† 36023	Carrville, 895	G 5
36548	Carson, 250	C 8
36432	Castleberry, 666	D 8
36013	Cecil, 250	F 6
35559	Cedar Bluff, 956	G 2
36014	Central, 300	F 5
35960	Centre⊙, 2,418	G 2
35042	Centreville⊙, 2,233	D 5
36729	Chance, 350	C 7
36015	Chapman, 400	E 7
36518	Chatom⊙, 1,059	B 8
35043	Chelsea, 615	E 4
35616	Cherokee, 1,484	C 1
36611	Chickasaw, 8,447	B 9
35044	Childersburg, 4,831	F 4
36254	Choccolocco, 300	G 3
36905	Choctaw, 600	B 6
36520	Chrysler, 300	C 8
36521	Chunchula, 400	B 9
36522	Citronelle, 1,935	B 8
35045	Clanton⊙, 5,868	E 5
36015	Clayton⊙, 1,626	G 7
35049	Cleveland, 413	E 3
36017	Clio, 1,065	G 7
35617	Cloverdale, 650	C 1
35449	Coaling, 300	D 4
36523	Coden, 500	B 10
36318	Coffee Springs, 329	G 8
36524	Coffeeville, 441	B 7
35452	Coker, 800	C 4
35961	Collinsville, 1,300	G 2
36319	Columbia, 891	H 8
35051	Columbiana⊙, 2,248	E 4

AREA 51,609 sq. mi.
POPULATION 3,444,165
CAPITAL Montgomery
LARGEST CITY Birmingham
HIGHEST POINT Cheaha Mtn. 2,407 ft.
SETTLED IN 1702
ADMITTED TO UNION December 14, 1819
POPULAR NAME Heart of Dixie; Cotton State
STATE FLOWER Camellia
STATE BIRD Yellowhammer

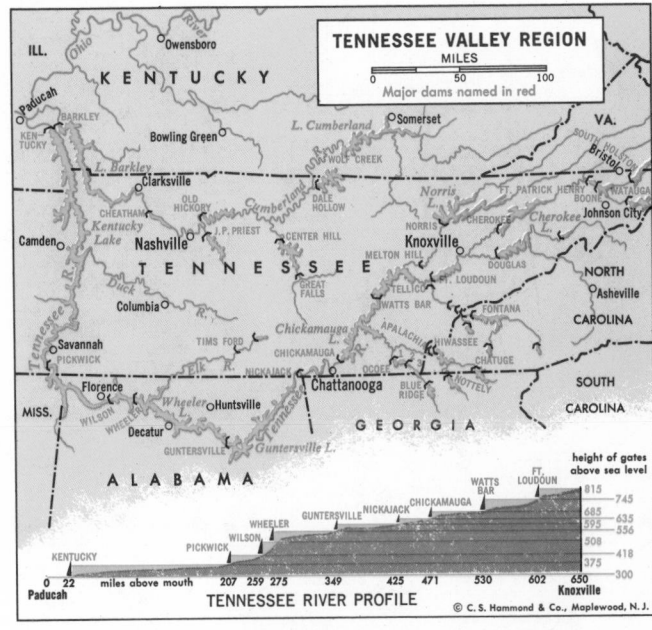

TENNESSEE VALLEY REGION
MILES
0   50   100
Major dams named in red

TENNESSEE RIVER PROFILE

© C. S. Hammond & Co., Maplewood, N. J.

36019	Cooper, 250	E 5
36020	Coosada, 600	F 5
35550	Cordova, 2,750	D 3
† 35546	Corona, 300	C 3
35088	Cottage Grove, 300	F 5
35453	Cottondale, 600	D 4
36851	Cottonton, 415	H 6
36320	Cottonwood, 1,149	H 8
35618	Courtland, 547	D 1
36321	Cowarts, 350	H 8
36435	Coy, 950	D 7
36525	Creola, 950	B 9
36906	Cromwell, 700	B 6
35962	Crossville, 1,035	G 2
36907	Cuba, 386	B 6
35055	Cullman⊙, 12,601	E 2
36920	Cullomburg, 325	B 7
36852	Cusseta, 250	H 5
36853	Dadeville⊙, 2,847	G 5
36322	Daleville, 5,182	G 8
35619	Danville, 400	D 2
36526	Daphne, 2,382	C 9
36528	Dauphin Island, 950	B 10
36256	Daviston, 247	G 4
36257	De Armanville, 500	G 3
36022	Deatsville, 350	F 5
36601	Decatur⊙, 38,044	D 1
36529	Deer Park, 300	B 8
36732	Demopolis, 7,651	C 6
36436	Dickinson, 350	C 7
36736	Dixons Mills, 285	C 6
35061	Dolomite, 1,237	D 4
35062	Dora, 1,862	D 3
36301	Dothan⊙, 36,733	H 8
35553	Double Springs⊙, 957	D 2
35964	Douglas, 527	F 2
36028	Dozier, 304	F 7
36259	Duke, 250	G 3
35744	Dutton, 423	G 1
† 36507	Dyas, 250	C 9
36260	Eastaboga, 500	F 3
36426	East Brewton, 2,336	E 8
35457	Echola, 300	C 4
36024	Eclectic, 1,184	F 5
† 36317	Edwin, 296	H 7
36323	Elba⊙, 4,634	F 8
36530	Elberta, 395	C 10
35554	Eldridge, 350	C 3
35620	Elkmont, 394	E 1
36025	Elmore, 656	F 5
35458	Elrod, 600	C 4
35459	Emelle, 300	B 5
35063	Empire, 400	D 3
36330	Enterprise, 15,591	G 8
35460	Epes, 293	B 5
36027	Eufaula, 9,102	H 7
35462	Eutaw⊙, 2,805	C 5
36401	Evergreen⊙, 3,924	E 8
36439	Excel, 422	D 7
35746	Fackler, 250	G 1

36854	Fairfax, 2,772	H 5
35064	Fairfield, 14,369	E 3
36532	Fairhope, 5,720	C 10
35208	Fairview, 313	E 2
35622	Falkville, 946	E 2
35555	Fayette⊙, 4,568	C 3
36440	Fitzburg, 300	H 7
36855	Five Points, 247	H 4
† 35129	Flat Creek-Wegra, 1,066	D 3
35966	Flat Rock, 750	G 1
36739	Flatwood, 300	C 6
† 35601	Flint City, 404	D 1
36441	Flomaton, 1,584	D 8
36442	Florala, 2,701	F 8
35639	Florence⊙, 34,031	C 1
36535	Foley, 3,368	C 10
35214	Forestdale, 6,091	E 3
36030	Forest Home, 450	E 7
36740	Forkland, 400	C 5
36031	Fort Davis, 500	G 6
36032	Fort Deposit, 1,438	E 7
36856	Fort Mitchell, 2,400	H 6
35967	Fort Payne⊙, 8,435	G 2
35463	Fosters, 400	C 4
36444	Franklin, 500	D 7
36538	Frankville, 550	B 7
† 31833	Fredonia, 300	H 5
36445	Frisco City, 1,286	D 8
36539	Fruitdale, 275	B 8
36446	Fulton, 628	C 7
35068	Fultondale, 5,163	E 3
36741	Furman, 300	E 6
35971	Fyffe, 311	G 2
* 35901	Gadsden⊙, 53,928	G 2
	Gadsden, ‡94,144	G 2
36540	Gainestown, 300	C 8
35464	Gainesville, 255	B 5
35972	Gallant, 475	F 2
36038	Gantt, 380	F 8
35070	Garden City, 745	E 2
35071	Gardendale, 6,502	E 3
36340	Geneva⊙, 4,398	G 8
36033	Georgiana, 2,148	E 7
35974	Geraldine, 610	G 2
35559	Glen Allen, 276	C 3
35905	Glencoe, 2,901	G 3
36034	Glenwood, 378	F 7
† 36024	Good Hope, 840	E 2
35072	Goodwater, 2,172	F 4
35466	Gordo, 1,991	C 4
36343	Gordon, 312	H 8
35561	Gorgas, 500	D 3
36035	Goshen, 279	F 7
36450	Gosport, 400	C 7
36036	Grady, 298	F 7
36541	Grand Bay, 950	B 10
35747	Grant, 382	F 1
35073	Graysville, 3,182	D 3
35074	Green Pond, 500	D 4
35746	Greensboro⊙, 3,371	C 5

(continued on following page)

Agriculture, Industry and Resources

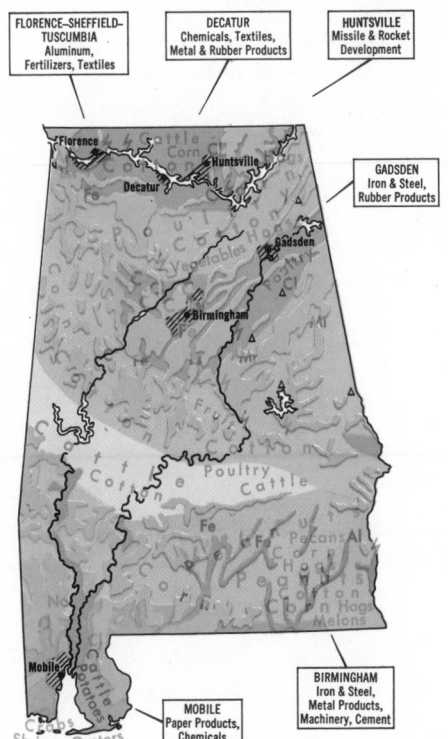

FLORENCE–SHEFFIELD–TUSCUMBIA
Aluminum, Fertilizers, Textiles

DECATUR
Chemicals, Textiles, Metal & Rubber Products

HUNTSVILLE
Missile & Rocket Development

GADSDEN
Iron & Steel, Rubber Products

BIRMINGHAM
Iron & Steel, Metal Products, Machinery, Cement

MOBILE
Paper Products, Chemicals

DOMINANT LAND USE

Specialized Cotton

Cotton, Livestock

Cotton, General Farming

Cotton, Hogs, Peanuts

Cotton, Forest Products

Peanuts, General Farming

Truck and Mixed Farming

Forests

Swampland, Limited Agriculture

MAJOR MINERAL OCCURRENCES

Al Bauxite
At Asphalt
C   Coal
Cl Clay
Fe Iron Ore

Ls Limestone
Mi Mica
Mr Marble
Na Salt
O   Petroleum

⚡ Water Power

▨ Major Industrial Areas

△ Major Textile Manufacturing Centers

ALABAMA

SCALE

0   5   10   20   30   40 MI.

0 5 10   20   30   40 KM.

State Capitals .... ⊛

County Seats .... ⊙

© C.S. HAMMOND & Co., N.Y.

Topography

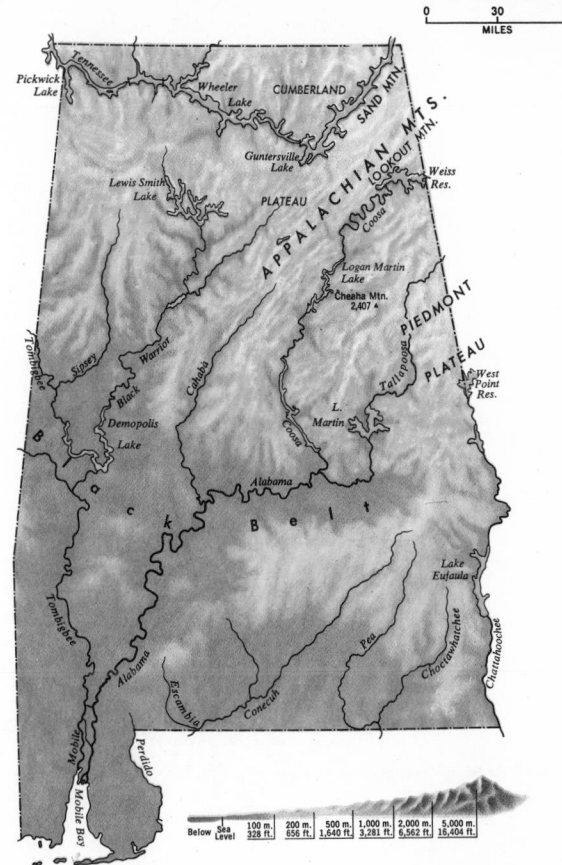

Railroad tracks form tangled spider webs leading to voracious steel furnaces. Native coal, iron ore and limestone are delivered to Ensley (Birmingham), Alabama plant.

Shostal Associates

36037 Greenville◉, 8,033............E 7	35091 Kimberly, 847..............E 3	† 35150 Mignon, 1,726..............F 4
36451 Grove Hill◉, 1,825..........C 7	36746 Kimbrough, 250............C 6	36760 Millbrook, 800..............D 4
35975 Groveoak, 275...............F 2	36453 Kinston, 540...............F 8	36867 Millers Ferry, 300..........D 6
35563 Guin, 2,220.................C 3	35469 Knoxville, 500..............C 4	35576 Millport, 1,070.............B 3
36542 Gulf Shores, 909...........C10	35754 Laceys Spring, 500..........E 1	36558 Millry, 911.................B 7
35976 Guntersville◉, 6,491........F 2	36862 Lafayette◉, 3,530...........H 5	36761 Minter, 450.................D 6
35748 Gurley, 647.................F 1	36747 Lamison, 275................C 6	* 36601 Mobile◉, 190,026...........B 9
35564 Hackleburg, 726.............C 2	36863 Lanett, 6,908...............H 5	Mobile, ‡376,690..............B 9
35565 Haleyville, 4,134...........C 2	36864 Langdale, 2,235.............H 5	36460 Monroeville◉, 4,846.........D 7
36909 Halsell, 250................B 6	35755 Langston, 250..............G 1	† 35804 Monrovia, 500..............E 1
35570 Hamilton◉, 3,088............C 2	36046 Lapine, 300.................F 7	35115 Montevallo, 3,719...........E 4
35077 Hanceville, 2,027...........E 2	† 35768 Larkinsville, 425..........F 1	* 36101 Montgomery (cap.)◉,.......F 6
36039 Hardaway, 300...............G 6	36911 Lavaca, 550.................B 6	133,386......................F 6
35078 Harpersville, 639...........F 4	35094 Leeds, 8,991...............E 3	Montgomery, ‡201,325..........F 6
36344 Hartford, 2,648.............G 8	35646 Leighton, 1,231............D 1	36559 Montrose, 900...............C 9
35640 Hartselle, 7,355............E 2	36548 Leroy, 350..................B 8	35125 Moody, 504..................F 3
35749 Harvest, 500................E 1	36047 Letohatchee, 250............E 6	35116 Morris, 519.................E 3
36858 Hatchechubbee, 250..........H 6	35648 Lexington, 278.............D 1	36762 Morvin, 450.................D 7
† 35672 Hatton, 950................D 1	36549 Lillian, 600...............D10	36772 Putnam, 305.................B 6
36040 Hayneville◉, 473............E 6	35096 Lincoln, 1,127.............F 3	35131 Ragland, 1,239..............F 3
36345 Headland, 2,545.............H 8	36748 Linden◉, 2,697.............C 6	35901 Rainbow City, 3,107.........F 3
36264 Heflin◉, 2,872.............G 3	36266 Lineville, 1,984...........G 4	35986 Rainsville, 2,099...........G 2
35080 Helena, 1,110...............E 4	35020 Lipscomb, 3,225.............E 4	35480 Ralph, 500..................C 4
35978 Henagar, 812................G 1	36912 Lisman, 628.................B 6	36069 Ramer, 750..................F 6
35979 Higdon, 450.................G 1	36550 Little River, 400..........C 8	36273 Ranburne, 371...............H 3
35081 Hissop, 250.................F 5	† 35876 Little Shawmut, 2,682......H 5	36473 Range, 250..................D 8
36201 Hobson City, 1,124..........G 3	35654 Littleville, 858...........D 1	36527 Spanish Fort, 983...........C 9
35903 Hokes Bluff, 2,133..........G 3	35470 Livingston◉, 2,358.........B 5	† 35674 Spring Valley, 600.........C 1
35082 Hollins, 600................F 4	36865 Loachapoka, 400............G 5	35146 Springville, 1,153.........E 3
35083 Holly Pond, 325.............E 2	36455 Lockhart, 698..............F 9	35585 Spruce Pine, 600............C 2
35751 Hollytree, 245..............F 1	† 35045 Lomax, 300................E 5	35987 Steele, 798.................F 3
35752 Hollywood, 301..............G 1	36048 Louisville, 785............G 7	35147 Sterrett, 450...............F 4
35401 Holt, 2,000.................D 4	36751 Lower Peach Tree, 950.......C 7	35203 Republic, 500...............E 3
36859 Holy Trinity, 400...........H 6	36551 Loxley, 859................C 9	35574 Stewartville, 250...........F 4
35209 Homewood, 21,245............E 4	36049 Luverne◉, 2,440............E 7	36579 Stockton, 1,400............C 9
† 35226 Hoover, 1,393.............E 4	35575 Lynn, 286..................C 2	35586 Sulligent, 1,762...........B 3
36043 Hope Hull, 975..............F 6	35758 Madison, 3,086.............E 1	35148 Sumiton, 2,374.............D 3
35980 Horton, 271................F 2	36754 Magnolia, 350..............C 6	36580 Summerdale, 550............C10
35020 Hueytown, 7,095.............D 4	36555 Magnolia Springs, 726......C10	36780 Sunny South, 300...........C 7
* 35801 Huntsville◉, 137,802......E 1	36556 Malcolm, 300...............B 8	36781 Suttle, 256................D 5
Huntsville, ‡228,339..........E 1	36586 Manila, 300................D 3	36782 Sweet Water, 265...........C 6
† 36507 Hurricane, 300............C 9	35579 Oakman, 853................D 3	35149 Sycamore, 800..............F 4
36860 Hurtsboro, 937.............H 6	35120 Odenville, 533.............E 3	35150 Sylacauga, 12,255..........F 4
36452 Hybart, 250................D 7	36271 Ohatchee, 445..............G 3	35988 Sylvania, 476..............G 1
35981 Ider, 500..................G 1	36801 Opelika◉, 19,027...........H 5	35160 Talladega◉, 17,662.........F 4
35210 Irondale, 3,166............E 3	36467 Opp, 6,493................E 8	36078 Tallassee, 4,809...........G 5
36910 Jachin, 250................B 6	36561 Orange Beach, 300..........C10	35160 Talladega◉
36545 Jackson, 5,957.............C 8	35767 Orrville, 362.............D 6	36783 Thomaston, 450............C 7
36861 Jacksons Gap, 450..........G 5	35763 Owens Cross Roads, 767.....E 1	36784 Thomasville, 3,769.........C 7
36265 Jacksonville, 7,715.........G 3	36201 Oxford, 4,361.............G 3	35171 Thorsby, 944..............E 5
35501 Jasper◉, 10,798............D 3	36360 Ozark◉, 13,555.............G 8	36582 Theodore, 1,950...........B 9
36745 Jefferson, 500.............C 6	36456 McKenzie, 491..............E 7	35180 Trafford, 628.............D 3
35085 Jemison, 1,423.............E 5	36753 McWilliams, 525............D 7	35173 Trussville, 2,985.........E 3

SENATORIAL DISTRICTS

Name/Pop.	Key
Central, 70,996	H 2
Northwestern, 16,763	E 2
South Central, 170,058	G 3
Southeastern, 42,565	L 3

CITIES and TOWNS

	Zip	Name/Pop.	Key
	99615	Akhiok, 115	H 3
	99551	Akiachak, 312	F 2
	99552	Akiak, 171	F 2
	99553	Akutan, 101	E 4
	99554	Alakanuk, 265	E 2
	99555	Aleknagik, 128	G 3
	99720	Allakaket, 174	H 1
	99786	Ambler, 169	G 1
	99721	Anaktuvuk Pass, 99	H 1
*	99501	Anchorage⊙, 48,029	B 1
	99556	Anchor Point, 102	B 2
†	99760	Anderson, 362	H 2
†	99658	Andreafski (Saint Marys), 384	F 2
	99820	Angoon, 400	M 1
	99557	Aniak, 205	G 2
	99920	Annette, 195	N 2
	99558	Anvik, 83	F 2
	99722	Arctic Village, 85	K 1
†	99701	Aurora Lodge, 250	J 2
	99723	Barrow, 2,104	G 1
†	99747	Barter Island (Kaktovik), 123	K 1
	99724	Beaver, 101	J 1
†	99612	Belkofski, 59	F 3
	99559	Bethel, 2,416	F 2
†	99726	Bettles, 65	H 1
	99726	Bettles Field, 49	H 1
†	99740	Birch Creek, 45	J 1
†	99567	Birchwood, 1,219	C 1
	99785	Brevig Mission, 123	E 1
	99727	Buckland, 104	F 1
	99729	Cantwell, 62	J 2
†	99901	Cape Pole, 123	M 2
	99730	Central, 26	J 1
	99788	Chalkyitsik, 130	K 1
†	99620	Chaneliak, 100	F 2
	99561	Chefornak, 146	F 2
	99563	Chevak, 387	E 2
	99732	Chicken, 25	K 2
	99564	Chignik, 83	G 3
	99565	Chignik Lagoon, 70	G 3
†	99564	Chignik Lake, 117	G 3
†	99586	Chistochina, 33	K 2
	99566	Chitina, 38	K 2
	99567	Chugiak, 489	C 1
	99733	Circle, 54	K 1
	99568	Clam Gulch, 47	B 1
	99569	Clarks Point, 95	G 3
	99704	Clear, 504	J 2
	99570	Cohoe, 60	B 1
	99571	Cold Bay, 256	F 3
	99701	College, 3,434	J 1
	99572	Cooper Landing, 31	C 1
	99573	Copper Center, 206	J 2
	99574	Cordova, 1,164	D 1
	99921	Craig, 272	M 2
	99575	Crooked Creek, 59	G 2
†	99746	Cutoff (Huslia), 159	G 1
	99736	Deering, 85	F 1
	99737	Delta Junction, 703	J 2
	99576	Dillingham, 914	G 3
†	99762	Diomede, 84	E 1
	99737	Dot Lake, 42	K 2
†	99685	Dutch Harbor, 30	E 4
	99738	Eagle, 36	K 2
	99577	Eagle River, 2,437	C 1
†	99901	Edna Bay, 112	M 2
	99578	Eek, 186	F 2
	99579	Egegik, 148	G 3
†	99569	Ekuk, 51	G 3
	99580	Ekwok, 103	G 3
	99825	Elfin Cove, 49	M 1
	99739	Elim, 174	F 2
	99581	Emmonak, 439	E 2
†	99603	English Bay, 58	B 2
†	99674	Eska, 50	B 1
	99725	Ester, 264	J 2
	99701	Fairbanks⊙, 14,771	J 2
	99583	False Pass, 62	F 4
	99585	Fortuna Ledge, 175	F 2
	99740	Fort Yukon, 448	J 1
	99586	Gakona, 88	K 2
	99741	Galena, 302	G 2
	99742	Gambell, 372	D 2
	99587	Girdwood, 144	C 1
	99588	Glennallen, 363	D 1
	99762	Golovin, 117	F 2
	99589	Goodnews Bay, 218	F 3
†	99586	Gulkana, 53	J 2
	99826	Gustavus, 64	M 1
	99827	Haines, 463	M 1
	99743	Healy, 79	H 2
†	99665	Holikachuk, 100	G 2
	99602	Holy Cross, 199	G 2
	99603	Homer, 1,083	B 2
	99829	Hoonah, 748	M 1
	99604	Hooper Bay, 490	E 2
	99605	Hope, 51	C 1
†	99687	Houston, 69	B 1
	99745	Hughes, 85	H 1
	99746	Huslia, 159	G 1
	99922	Hydaburg, 214	M 2
	99923	Hyder, 49	P 2
†	99625	Igiugig, 36	G 3
	99606	Iliamna, 58	G 3
	99801	Juneau (cap.)⊙, 6,050	N 1
†	99663	Kachemak, 76	B 2
†	99608	Kaguyak, 59	H 3
	99830	Kake, 448	M 1
†	99647	Kakhonak, 88	H 3
	99747	Kaktovik, 123	K 1
	99607	Kalskag, 122	F 2
	99748	Kaltag, 206	G 2
	99608	Karluk, 98	H 3
	99924	Kasaan, 30	N 2
†	99668	Kashegelok, 200	G 2
	99609	Kasigluk, 526	F 2
	99610	Kasilof, 71	B 1
	99611	Kenai, 3,533	B 1
	99901	Ketchikan, 6,994	N 2
	99749	Kiana, 278	F 1
	99612	King Cove, 283	F 4
†	99762	King Island, 100	E 1
	99613	King Salmon, 202	G 3
	99614	Kipnuk, 325	F 2
	99750	Kivalina, 188	E 1
	99925	Klawock, 213	M 2
†	99827	Klukwan, 103	M 1
	99751	Kobuk, 75	G 1
	99615	Kodiak, 3,798	H 3
	99576	Koliganek, 142	G 3
	99620	Kotlik, 228	F 2
	99752	Kotzebue, 1,696	F 1
	99753	Koyuk, 122	F 1
	99754	Koyukuk, 124	G 1
†	99625	Kvichak, 75	G 3
	99621	Kwethluk, 408	F 2
	99622	Kwigillingok, 148	F 3
†	99655	Kwinhagak (Quinhagak), 340	F 3
	99624	Larsen Bay, 109	H 3
	99625	Levelock, 74	G 3
†	99566	Lower Tonsina, 65	J 2
	99756	Manley Hot Springs, 34	H 2
	99628	Manokotak, 214	G 3
†	99585	Marshall (Fortuna Ledge), 175	F 2
	99627	McGrath, 279	H 2
	99630	Mekoryuk, 249	E 2
†	99579	Meshik, 75	G 3
	99926	Metlakatla, 1,050	N 2
	99903	Meyers Chuck, 37	N 2
	99758	Minto, 168	J 2
†	99676	Montana, 33	B 1
	99631	Moose Pass, 53	C 1
†	99901	Mountain Point, 459	N 2
	99632	Mountain Village, 419	E 2
	99835	Mount Edgecumbe, 835	M 1
†	99589	Mumtrak (Goodnews Bay), 218	F 3
†	99764	Nabesna, 40	K 2
	99633	Naknek, 178	G 3
†	99559	Napaiskak, 259	F 2
	99634	Napakiak, 270	F 2
	99760	Nenana, 362	J 2
†	99606	Newhalen, 88	H 3
	99636	New Stuyahok, 216	G
	99559	Newtok, 114	F
†	99603	Nikolaevsk, 70	B
	99691	Nikolai, 112	H
	99638	Nikolski, 57	E
	99639	Ninilchik, 134	B
	99761	Noatak, 293	F
	99762	Nome⊙, 2,488	E
	99640	Nondalton, 184	G
	99763	Noorvik, 462	F
	99705	North Pole, 265	J
	99764	Northway, 40	K
	99765	Nulato, 308	G
	99641	Nunapitchuk, 400	F
	99643	Old Harbor, 290	H
†	99559	Oscarville, 41	F
	99644	Ouzinkie, 160	H
	99645	Palmer, 1,140	C
	99646	Pauloff Harbor, 39	F
	99737	Paxson, 32	J
	99647	Pedro Bay, 65	H
	99832	Pelican, 133	M
	99648	Perryville, 94	G
	99833	Petersburg, 2,042	N
	99649	Pilot Point, 68	G
	99650	Pilot Station, 290	F
†	99658	Pitkas Point, 70	F
	99651	Platinum, 55	F
	99766	Point Hope, 386	E
†	99587	Portage, 80	C
	99834	Port Alexander, 36	M
†	99827	Port Chilkoot, 220	N
†	99603	Port Graham, 107	B
†	99579	Port Heiden, 66	G
	99550	Port Lions, 227	H

Agriculture, Industry and Resources

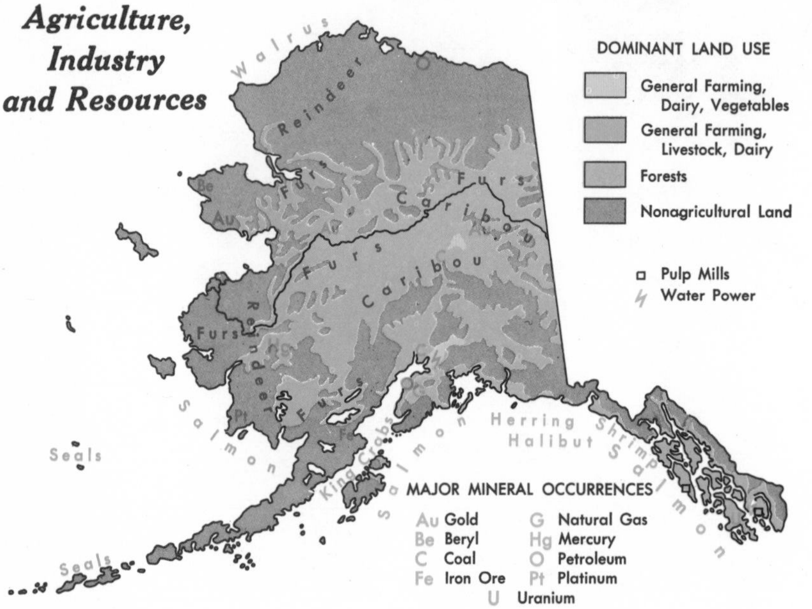

DOMINANT LAND USE
General Farming, Dairy, Vegetables
General Farming, Livestock, Dairy
Forests
Nonagricultural Land
Pulp Mills
Water Power
MAJOR MINERAL OCCURRENCES
Au Gold
Be Beryl
C Coal
Fe Iron Ore
G Natural Gas
Hg Mercury
O Petroleum
Pt Platinum
U Uranium
Walrus
Reindeer
Furs
Caribou
Seals
Salmon
Herring
Halibut
Shrimp
King Crabs

Topography

0 200 400
MILES
Pt. Barrow
Pt. Hope
Chukchi Sea
BROOKS RANGE
Colville
Seward Pen.
Norton Sound
Yukon
Koyukuk
Tanana
ALASKA RANGE
KUSKOKWIM MTS.
Mt. McKinley
WRANGELL MTS.
ST. ELIAS MTS.
COAST MTS.
ALEXANDER ARCH.
St. Lawrence I.
St. Matthew I.
Nunivak I.
Bering Sea
PRIBILOF IS.
Kuskokwim Bay
Bristol Bay
Iliamna L.
Kenai Pen.
Cook Inlet
Montague I.
Gulf of Alaska
Kodiak I.
Alaska Pen.
Unimak I.
Unalaska I.
Umnak I.
Atka I.
Attu I.
NEAR IS.
Kiska I.
RAT IS.
ANDREANOF IS.
FOX IS.
ALEUTIAN ISLANDS
Below Sea Level
100 m. 328 ft.
200 m. 656 ft.
500 m. 1,640 ft.
1,000 m. 3,281 ft.
2,000 m. 6,562 ft.
5,000 m. 16,404 ft.

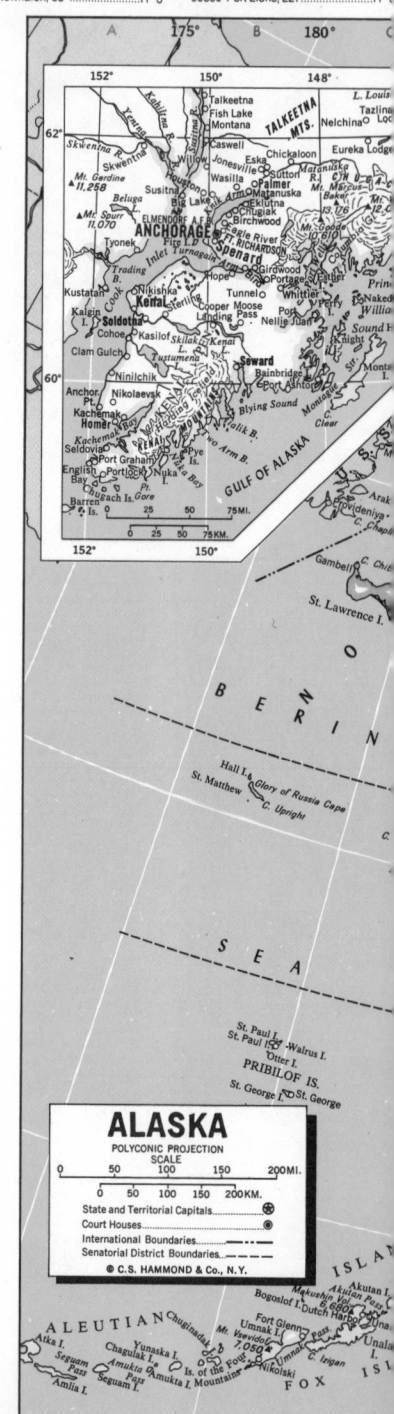

ALASKA
POLYCONIC PROJECTION
SCALE
0 50 100 150 200 MI.
0 50 100 150 200 KM.
State and Territorial Capitals
Court Houses
International Boundaries
Senatorial District Boundaries
© C.S. HAMMOND & Co., N.Y.
ANCHORAGE
Talkeetna
Kenai
Seward
Homer
Soldotna
GULF OF ALASKA
BERING SEA
St. Lawrence I.
St. Matthew
PRIBILOF IS.
ALEUTIAN
FOX IS.

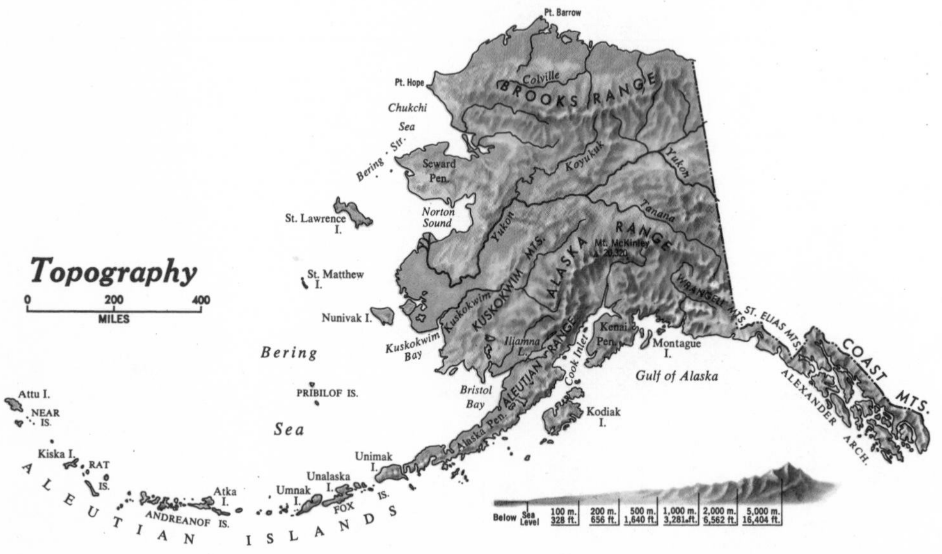

99723	Prudhoe Bay, 49	J	1
99655	Quinhagak, 340	F	3
99767	Rampart, 36	H	1
99656	Red Devil, 81	G	2
99768	Ruby, 145	G	2
99657	Russian Mission, 146	F	2
99660	Saint George, 163	E	3
99658	Saint Marys, 384	F	2
99659	Saint Michael, 207	F	2
99660	Saint Paul Island, 450	D	3
99661	Sand Point, 360	G	3
99769	Savoonga, 364	E	2
99901	Saxman, 135	N	2
99662	Scammon Bay, 166	E	2
99770	Selawik, 429	G	1
99663	Seldovia, 437	B	2
99664	Seward, 1,587	C	1
99665	Shageluk, 167	G	2
99771	Shaktoolik, 151	F	2
99666	Sheldon Point, 125	E	2
99772	Shishmaref, 267	E	1
99773	Shungnak, 165	G	1
99835	Sitka, 3,370	M	1
99840	Skagway, 675	M	1
99668	Sleetmute, 109	G	2
99669	Soldotna, 1,202	B	1
99670	South Naknek, 154	G	3
99503	Spenard, 18,089	C	1
99671	Stebbins, 231	F	2
99672	Sterling, 30	B	1
99774	Stevens Village, 74	J	1
99673	Stony River, 74	G	2
99729	Summit, 34	J	2
99743	Suntrana, 67	J	2
99501	Susitna, 50	B	1
99674	Sutton, 76	C	1
99676	Talkeetna, 182	B	1
99776	Tanacross, 84	K	2
99777	Tanana, 120	H	1
99677	Tatitlek, 111	D	1
99778	Teller, 220	E	1
99841	Tenakee Springs, 86	M	1
99779	Tetlin, 114	K	2
† 99801	Thane, 70	N	1
† 99901	Thorne Bay, 443	M	2
99678	Togiak, 383	F	3
99780	Tok, 214	K	2
99679	Tuluksak, 195	F	2
99680	Tuntutuliak, 158	F	2
99681	Tununak, 274	E	2
99682	Tyonek, 232	B	1
† 99701	Umiat, 45	H	1
99684	Unalakleet, 434	G	2
99685	Unalaska, 178	E	4
99686	Valdez, 1,005	D	1
99781	Venetie, 112	J	1
99782	Wainwright, 315	F	1
99783	Wales, 131	E	1
99928	Ward Cove, 105	N	2
99687	Wasilla, 300	B	1
99784	White Mountain, 87	F	2
99501	Whittier, 130	C	1
99688	Willow, 38	B	1
† 99615	Woody Island, 41	H	3
99929	Wrangell, 2,029	N	2
99689	Yakutat, 190	L	3

⊙ Court House
† Zip of nearest p.o.
* Multiple zips

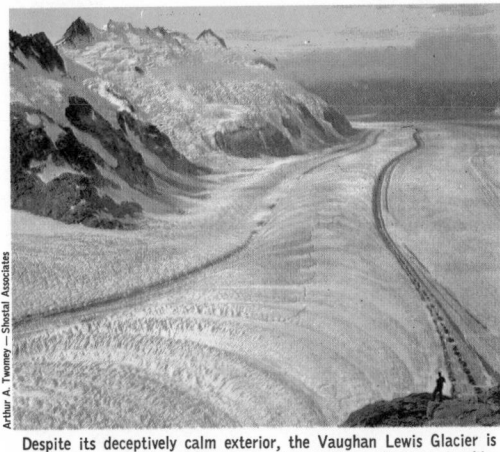

Arthur A. Twomey — Shostal Associates

Despite its deceptively calm exterior, the Vaughan Lewis Glacier is actually a river of ice, hundreds of feet deep, flowing steadily. Ridges (eskers) are formed by streams under the ice.

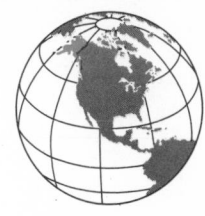

AREA 586,412 sq. mi.
POPULATION 302,173
CAPITAL Juneau
LARGEST CITY Anchorage
HIGHEST POINT Mt. McKinley 20,320 ft.
SETTLED IN 1801
ADMITTED TO UNION January 3, 1959
POPULAR NAME Great Land
STATE FLOWER Forget-me-not
STATE BIRD Willow Ptarmigan

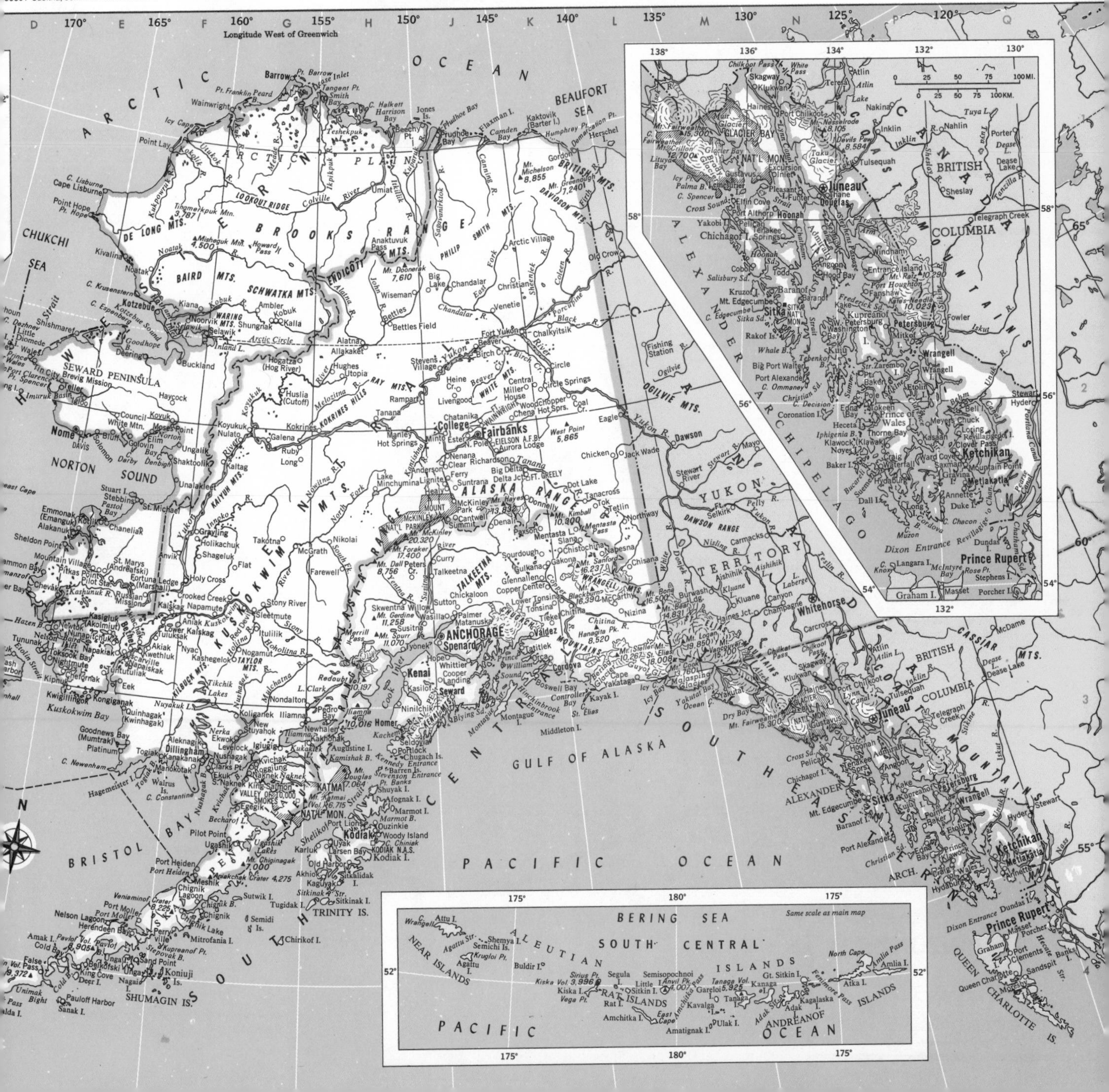

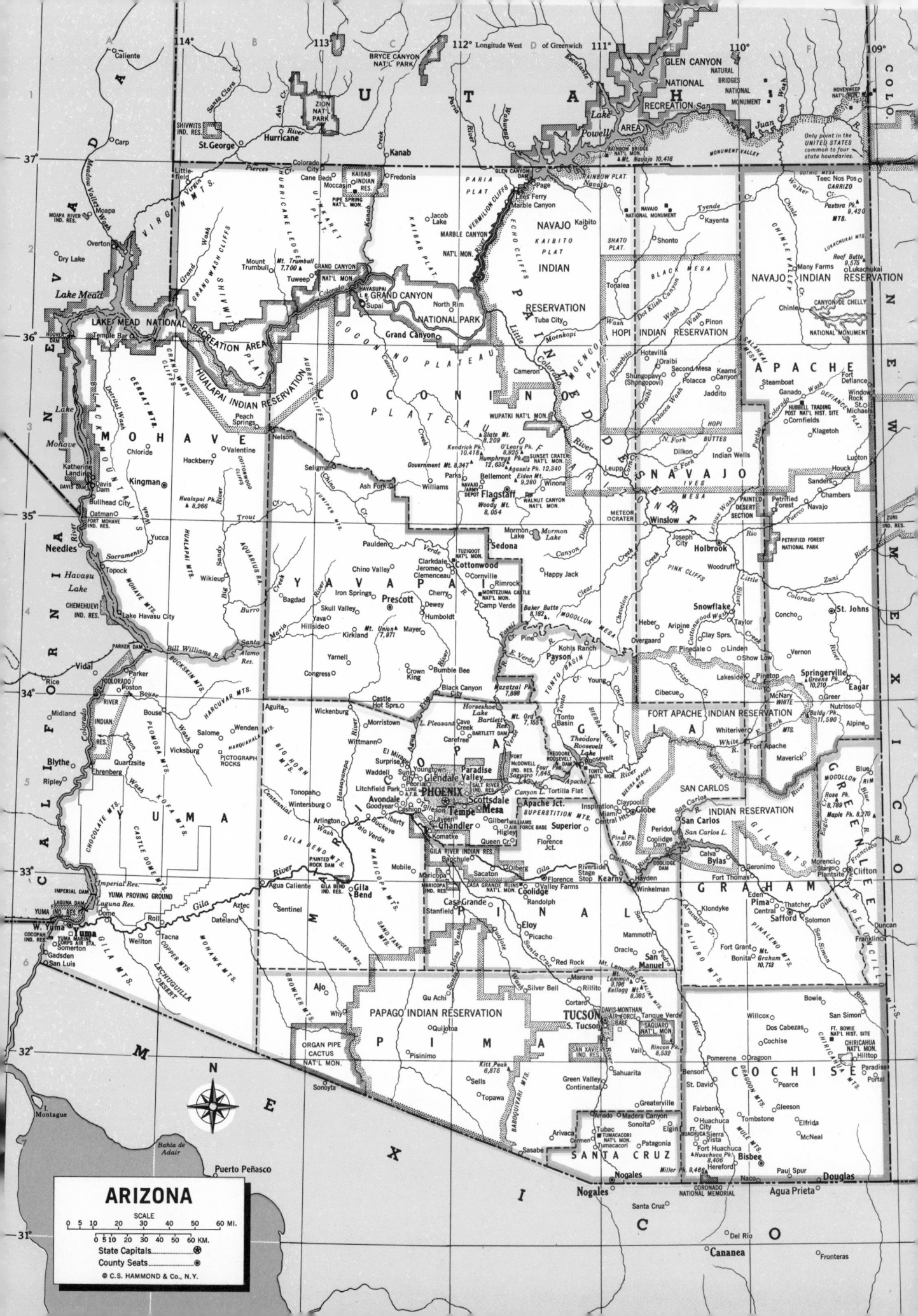

Topography

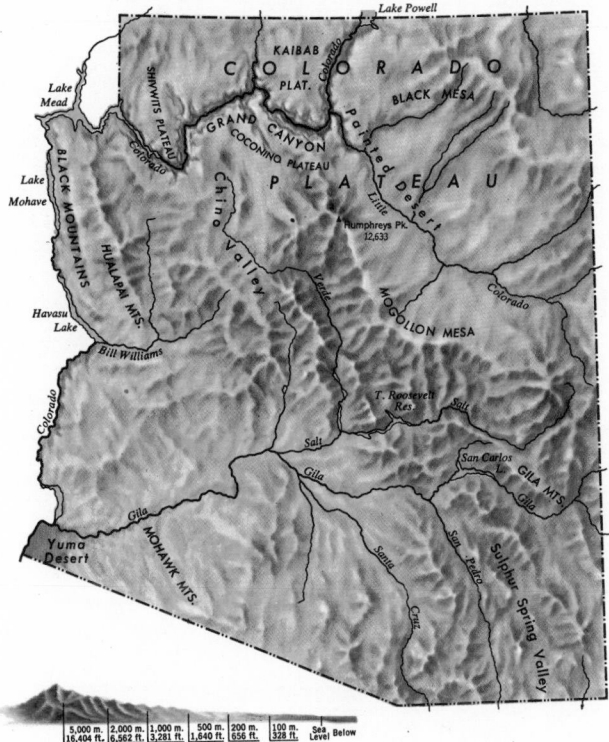

0   50   100
MILES

| 5,000 m. | 2,000 m. | 1,000 m. | 500 m. | 200 m. | 100 m. | Sea | Below |
| 16,404 ft. | 6,562 ft. | 3,281 ft. | 1,640 ft. | 656 ft. | 328 ft. | Level | |

AREA 113,909 sq. mi.
POPULATION 1,772,482
CAPITAL Phoenix
LARGEST CITY Phoenix
HIGHEST POINT Humphreys Pk. 12,633 ft.
SETTLED IN 1580
ADMITTED TO UNION February 14, 1912
POPULAR NAME Grand Canyon State
STATE FLOWER Saguaro Cactus Blossom
STATE BIRD Cactus Wren

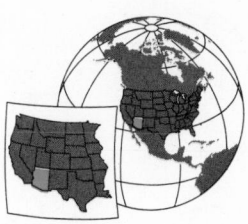

Agriculture, Industry and Resources

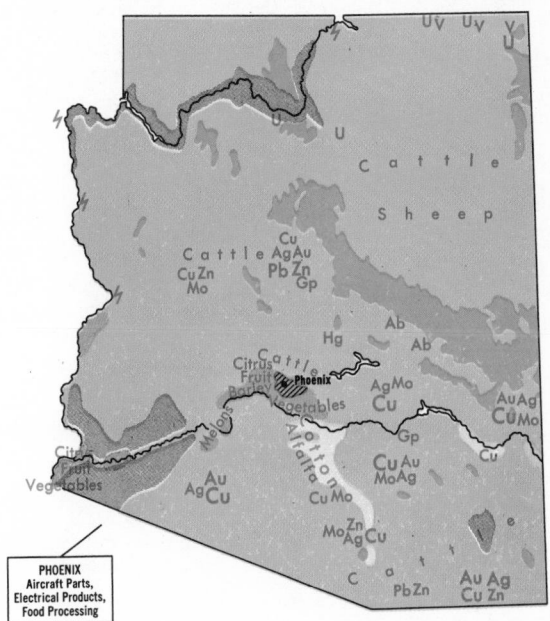

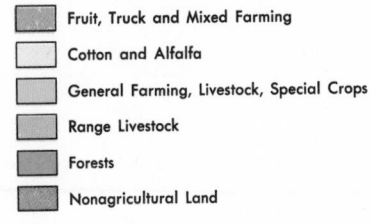

PHOENIX
Aircraft Parts,
Electrical Products,
Food Processing

MAJOR MINERAL OCCURRENCES

Ab	Asbestos	Gp	Gypsum	U	Uranium	
Ag	Silver	Hg	Mercury	V	Vanadium	
Au	Gold	Mo	Molybdenum	Zn	Zinc	
Cu	Copper	Pb	Lead			

DOMINANT LAND USE

- Fruit, Truck and Mixed Farming
- Cotton and Alfalfa
- General Farming, Livestock, Special Crops
- Range Livestock
- Forests
- Nonagricultural Land

⚡ Water Power

▨ Major Industrial Areas

COUNTIES

Apache, 32,298	F	3
Cochise, 61,910	F	7
Coconino, 48,326	C	3
Gila, 29,255	E	5
Graham, 16,578	E	6
Greenlee, 10,330	F	5
Maricopa, 967,522	C	5
Mohave, 25,857	A	3
Navajo, 47,715	E	3
Pima, 351,667	D	6
Pinal, 67,916	D	6
Santa Cruz, 13,966	E	7
Yavapai, 36,733	C	4
Yuma, 60,827	A	5

CITIES and TOWNS

Zip	Name/Pop.	Key
† 85333	Agua Caliente, 30	B 6
85320	Aguila, 450	B 5
85321	Ajo, 5,881	C 6
85920	Alpine, 450	F 5
85640	Amado, 75	D 7
85220	Apache Junction, 2,390	D 5
† 85901	Aripine, 25	E 4
85601	Arivaca, 165	D 7
85322	Arlington, 950	C 5
86320	Ash Fork, 800	C 3
85323	Avondale, 6,304	C 5
‡ 85333	Aztec, 20	B 6
86321	Bagdad, 2,079	B 4
85221	Bapchule, 300	D 5
86001	Bellemont, 6	D 3
85602	Benson, 2,839	E 7
85603	Bisbee⊙, 8,328	F 7
85324	Black Canyon City, 600	C 4
85922	Blue, 50	F 5
† 85643	Bonita, 20	E 6
85325	Bouse, 200	A 5
85605	Bowie, 600	F 6
85326	Buckeye, 2,599	C 5
86430	Bullhead City, 2,900	A 3
85327	Bumble Bee, 15	C 4
85530	Bylas, 1,125	E 5
† 85530	Calva, 10	E 5
86020	Cameron, 600	D 3
86322	Camp Verde, 1,500	D 4
† 86022	Cane Beds, 30	B 2
85331	Carefree, 350	D 5
† 85640	Carmen, 200	D 7
85222	Casa Grande, 10,536	D 6
85329	Cashion, 2,705	C 5
‡ 85342	Castle Hot Springs, 50	C 4
85331	Cave Creek, 300	D 5
85531	Central, 300	F 6
† 85501	Central Heights, 2,289	E 5
86502	Chambers, 500	F 3

85224	Chandler, 13,763	D 5
† 86327	Cherry, 20	C 4
86503	Chinle, 500	F 2
86323	Chino Valley, 970	C 4
86431	Chloride, 225	A 3
† 85292	Christmas, 201	E 5
85901	Cibecue, 100	E 4
86324	Clarkdale, 892	C 4
85532	Claypool, 2,245	E 5
† 85934	Clay Springs, 225	E 4
† 86326	Clemenceau, 300	C 4
85553	Clifton⊙, 5,087	F 5
85606	Cochise, 150	F 7
86021	Colorado City, 350	B 2
85924	Concho, 100	F 4
85332	Congress, 350	C 4
† 85640	Continental, 250	D 7
85228	Coolidge, 4,651	D 6
‡ 85542	Coolidge Dam, 42	E 5
86505	Cornfields, 200	F 3
86325	Cornville, 425	D 4
85230	Cortaro, 75	D 6
86326	Cottonwood, 2,815	C 4
86333	Crown King, 100	C 4
85333	Dateland, 100	B 6
86430	Davis Dam, 125	A 3
86327	Dewey, 100	C 4
† 86047	Dilkon, 90	E 3
† 85364	Dome, 48	A 6
85643	Dos Cabezas, 30	F 6
85607	Douglas, 12,462	F 7
85609	Dragoon, 150	F 6
85534	Duncan, 773	F 6
85925	Eagar, 1,279	F 4
85535	Eden, 89	E 6
85334	Ehrenberg, 93	A 5
85617	Elfrida, 700	F 7
† 85637	Elgin, 247	E 7
85335	El Mirage, 3,258	C 5
85231	Eloy, 5,381	D 6
85612	Fairbank, 100	E 7
86001	Flagstaff⊙, 26,117	D 3
85232	Florence⊙, 2,173	D 5
85233	Florence Junction, 35	D 5
85926	Fort Apache, 500	F 4
86504	Fort Defiance, 900	F 2
85643	Fort Grant, 240	E 6
85613	Fort Huachuca, 159	E 7
85536	Fort Thomas, 450	E 6
85534	Franklin, 300	F 6
86022	Fredonia, 798	C 2
85336	Gadsden, 250	A 6
86505	Ganado, 300	F 3
† 85337	Gila Bend, 1,795	C 6
85234	Gilbert, 1,971	D 5
† 85617	Gleeson, 15	F 7
85301	Glendale, 36,228	C 5
85501	Globe⊙, 7,333	E 5

85338	Goodyear, 2,140	C 5
86023	Grand Canyon, 1,011	C 2
† 85637	Greaterville, 15	E 7
85614	Green Valley, 5,971	D 7
85927	Greer, 60	F 4
† 85634	Gu-Achi, 339	C 6
86401	Hackberry, 250	B 3
86024	Happy Jack, 50	D 4
85235	Hayden, 1,283	E 5
85928	Heber, 750	E 4
85615	Hereford, 10	E 7
85236	Higley, 500	D 5
† 86301	Hillside, 100	B 4
85632	Hilltop, 9	F 6
86025	Holbrook⊙, 4,759	E 4
86030	Hotevilla, 600	E 3
86506	Houck, 325	F 3
86329	Humboldt, 424	C 4
86031	Indian Wells, 150	E 3
85537	Inspiration, 500	E 5
86330	Iron Springs, 175	C 4
86022	Jacob Lake, 16	C 2
† 86025	Jeddito, 20	E 3
86331	Jerome, 290	C 4
86032	Joseph City, 650	E 4
86044	Kaibito, 275	D 2
† 86401	Katherine Landing, 102	A 3
86033	Kayenta, 500	E 2
86034	Keams Canyon, 400	E 3
85237	Kearny, 2,829	E 5
86332	Kirkland, 100	C 4
† 86505	Klagetoh, 200	F 3
85643	Klondyke, 86	E 6
85538	Kohls Ranch, 100	D 4
85239	Komatke, 300	C 5
86403	Lake Havasu City, 5,700	A 4
85929	Lakeside, 700	E 4
85339	Laveen, 800	C 5
86036	Lees Ferry, 10	D 2
† 85326	Liberty, 150	C 5
† 85901	Linden, 50	E 4
85340	Litchfield Park, 1,664	C 5
86432	Littlefield, 40	B 2
86507	Lukachukai, 350	F 2
85341	Lukeville, 50	C 7
86508	Lupton, 250	F 3
† 85637	Madera Canyon, 75	E 7
85618	Mammoth, 1,953	E 6
86503	Many Farms, 250	F 2
85238	Marana, 2,900	D 6
86036	Marble Canyon, 6	D 2
85239	Maricopa, 750	C 5
† 85920	Maverick, 50	F 5
86333	Mayer, 810	C 4
85930	McNary, 950	F 4
85617	McNeal, 100	F 7

(continued on following page)

Indigo-blue Lake Mead is surrounded by color-streaked cliffs and ranges, set off by the bright concrete of Arizona's Hoover Dam. One of the world's largest man-made lakes, Lake Mead provides water storage, dependable water supply and water sports.

Ray Manley — Shostal Associates

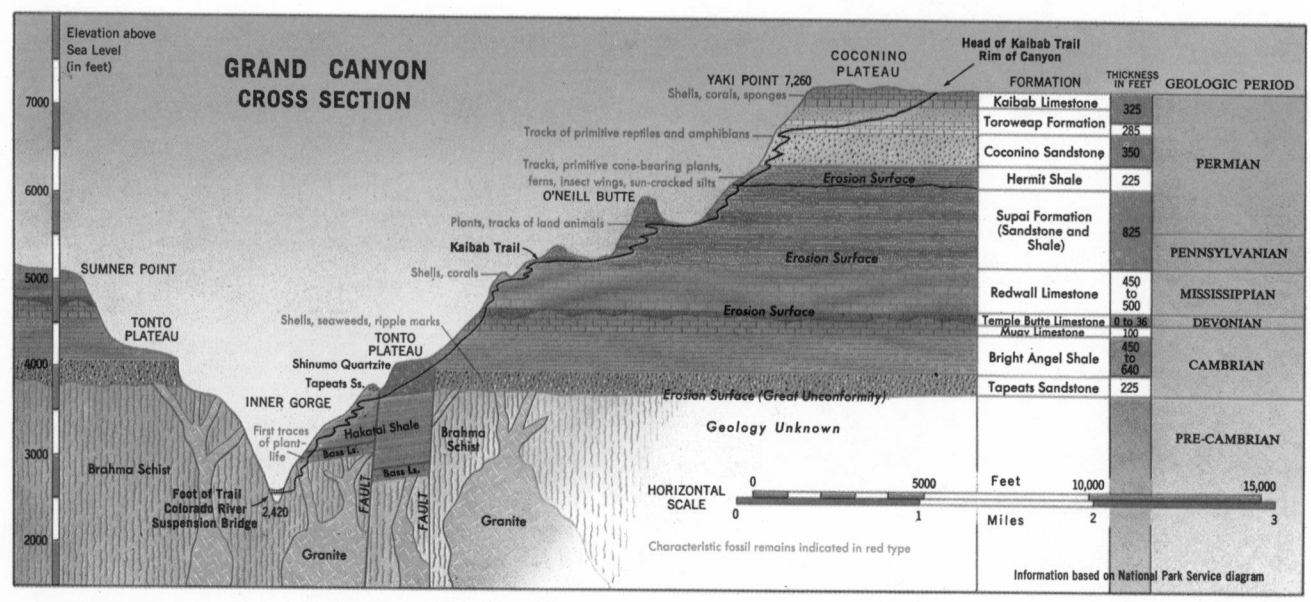

COUNTIES

Arkansas, 23,347	H 5
Ashley, 24,976	G 7
Baxter, 15,319	F 1
Benton, 50,476	B 1
Boone, 19,073	D 1
Bradley, 12,778	F 7
Calhoun, 5,573	E 6
Carroll, 12,301	C 1
Chicot, 18,164	H 7
Clark, 21,537	D 5
Clay, 18,771	K 1
Cleburne, 10,349	F 2
Cleveland, 6,605	F 6
Columbia, 25,952	D 7
Conway, 16,805	E 3
Craighead, 52,068	J 2
Crawford, 25,677	B 2
Crittenden, 48,106	K 3
Cross, 19,783	J 3
Dallas, 10,022	E 6
Desha, 18,761	H 6
Drew, 15,157	G 6
Faulkner, 31,572	F 3

Franklin, 11,301	C 2
Fulton, 7,699	G 1
Garland, 54,131	D 4
Grant, 9,711	F 5
Greene, 24,765	J 1
Hempstead, 19,308	C 6
Hot Spring, 21,963	E 5
Howard, 11,412	C 5
Independence, 22,723	G 2
Izard, 7,381	G 1
Jackson, 20,452	H 2
Jefferson, 85,329	G 5
Johnson, 13,630	C 2
Lafayette, 10,018	C 7
Lawrence, 16,320	H 1
Lee, 18,884	J 4
Lincoln, 12,913	G 6
Little River, 11,194	B 6
Logan, 16,789	C 3
Lonoke, 34,518	G 4
Madison, 9,453	C 1
Marion, 7,000	E 1
Miller, 33,385	C 7
Mississippi, 62,060	K 2
Monroe, 15,657	H 4
Montgomery, 5,821	C 4

Nevada, 10,111	D 6
Newton, 5,844	D 2
Ouachita, 30,896	E 6
Perry, 5,634	E 4
Phillips, 40,046	J 5
Pike, 8,711	C 5
Poinsett, 26,822	J 2
Polk, 13,297	B 5
Pope, 28,607	D 3
Prairie, 10,249	G 4
Pulaski, 287,189	F 4
Randolph, 12,645	H 1
Saint Francis, 30,799	J 3
Saline, 36,107	E 4
Scott, 8,207	B 3
Searcy, 7,731	E 2
Sebastian, 79,237	B 3
Sevier, 11,272	B 6
Sharp, 8,233	G 1
Stone, 6,838	F 2
Union, 45,428	E 7
Van Buren, 8,275	E 2
Washington, 77,370	B 2
White, 39,253	G 3
Woodruff, 11,566	H 3
Yell, 14,208	D 3

AREA 53,104 sq. mi.
POPULATION 1,923,295
CAPITAL Little Rock
LARGEST CITY Little Rock
HIGHEST POINT Magazine Mtn. 2,753 ft.
SETTLED IN 1685
ADMITTED TO UNION June 15, 1836
POPULAR NAME Land of Opportunity; Wonder State
STATE FLOWER Apple Blossom
STATE BIRD Mockingbird

Agriculture, Industry and Resources

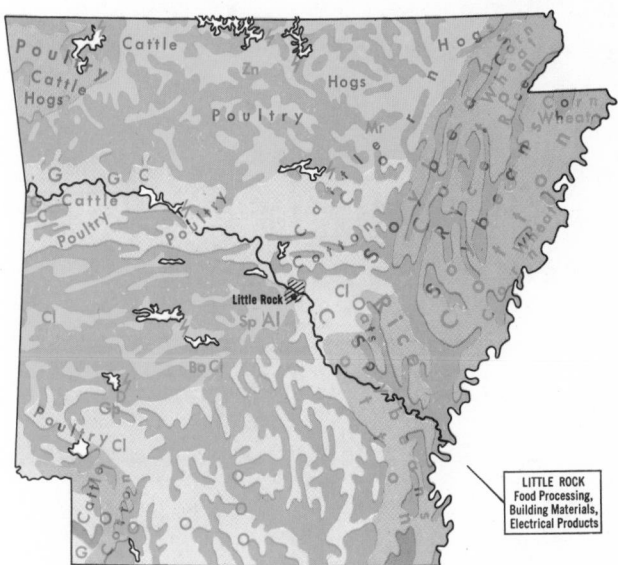

LITTLE ROCK
Food Processing,
Building Materials,
Electrical Products

DOMINANT LAND USE

- Fruit and Mixed Farming
- Specialized Cotton
- Cotton, General Farming
- Rice, General Farming
- General Farming, Livestock, Truck Farming, Cotton
- Forests
- Swampland, Limited Agriculture

MAJOR MINERAL OCCURRENCES

Al	Bauxite	G	Natural Gas
Ba	Barite	Gp	Gypsum
C	Coal	Mr	Marble
Cl	Clay	O	Petroleum
D	Diamonds	Sp	Soapstone
		Zn	Zinc

⚡ Water Power   ▨ Major Industrial Areas

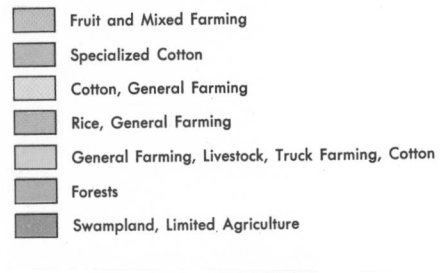

Soybeans, Arkansas' leading cash crop, valued primarily as high protein food and feed, also has a wide range of uses, including plastics and agricultural sprays.

Eric Carle — Shostal Associates

CITIES and TOWNS

Zip	Name/Pop.	Key
72920	Abbott, 210	B 3
72001	Adona, 204	E 3
72510	Agnos, 130	G 1
72002	Alexander, 297	F 4
72410	Alicia, 246	H 2
72820	Alix, 250	C 3
† 72046	Allport, 307	G 4
72921	Alma, 1,613	B 3
72003	Almyra, 220	H 5
72611	Alpena, 309	D 1
72004	Altheimer, 1,037	G 5
72821	Altus, 418	C 3
72005	Amagon, 136	H 2
71921	Amity, 614	D 5
71922	Antoine, 182	D 5
72822	Appleton, 150	E 3
71923	Arkadelphia⊙, 9,841	D 5
71630	Arkansas City⊙, 615	H 6
† 72055	Arkansas Post, 15	H 5
72310	Armorel, 300	L 2
71822	Ashdown⊙, 3,522	B 6
72513	Ash Flat⊙, 211	G 1
72823	Atkins, 2,015	E 3
72311	Aubrey, 351	J 4
72006	Augusta⊙, 2,777	H 3
72007	Austin, 236	G 4
72008	Auvergne, 150	H 2
72711	Avoca, 173	B 1
72010	Bald Knob, 2,094	G 3
71631	Banks, 189	F 6
72923	Barling, 1,739	B 3
72312	Barton, 400	J 4
72313	Bassett, 265	K 2
72501	Batesville⊙, 7,209	G 2
72411	Bay, 751	J 2
71720	Bearden, 1,272	E 6
72012	Beebe, 2,805	G 3
72014	Beedeville, 144	H 3
71721	Beirne, 140	D 6
72712	Bella Vista, 500	B 1
72601	Bellefonte, 300	D 1
72824	Belleville, 379	D 3
71823	Ben Lomond, 155	B 6
72015	Benton⊙, 16,499	E 4
72712	Bentonville⊙, 5,508	B 1
72615	Bergman, 249	E 1
72616	Berryville⊙, 2,271	C 1
72764	Bethel Heights, 284	B 1
72501	Bethesda, 285	G 2
72016	Bigelow, 258	E 3
72617	Bigflat, 189	F 1
72413	Biggers, 372	J 1
† 72386	Birdsong, 150	K 3
72017	Biscoe, 340	H 4
71929	Bismarck, 200	D 5

Zip	Name/Pop.	Key
72414	Black Oak, 272	K 2
72415	Black Rock, 498	H 1
† 72069	Blackton, 175	H 4
71825	Blevins, 265	C 6
72933	Bloomer, 150	B 3
71722	Bluff City, 244	D 6
72827	Bluffton, 198	C 4
72315	Blytheville⊙, 24,752	L 2
† 71858	Bodcaw, 158	D 6
72926	Boles, 163	B 4
72901	Bonanza, 342	B 3
72416	Bono, 428	J 2
72927	Booneville⊙, 3,239	C 3
72020	Bradford, 826	G 3
71826	Bradley, 706	C 7
72928	Branch, 325	C 3
72017	Brasfield, 200	H 4
72828	Briggsville, 200	C 4
72021	Brinkley, 5,275	H 4
72417	Brookland, 465	J 2
72618	Bruno, 130	E 1
72022	Bryant, 1,199	F 4
71827	Buckner, 392	D 7
72619	Bull Shoals, 430	E 1
72321	Burdette, 173	L 2
72023	Cabot, 2,903	F 4
71935	Caddo Gap, 125	C 5
72322	Caldwell, 292	J 3
72519	Calico Rock, 723	F 1
71724	Calion, 535	E 7
71701	Camden⊙, 15,147	E 6
† 72201	Cammack Village, 1,165	E 4
72473	Campbell Station, 218	H 2
71829	Canfield, 365	C 7
72419	Caraway, 952	K 2
72024	Carlisle, 2,048	G 4
71725	Carthage, 566	E 5
72025	Casa, 208	D 3
72421	Cash, 265	J 2
72026	Casscoe, 200	H 4
† 72951	Caulksville, 208	C 3
72521	Cave City, 807	G 2
72718	Cave Springs, 469	B 1
72930	Cecil, 234	C 3
72450	Center Hill, 1,201	J 1
71830	Center Point, 144	C 6
72027	Center Ridge, 220	E 3
72719	Centerton, 312	B 1
71901	Central City, 150	B 3
† 71832	Chapel Hill, 154	B 5
72933	Charleston⊙, 1,497	B 3
72522	Charlotte, 158	H 2
72323	Chatfield, 150	K 3
72542	Cherokee Village, 1,300	G 1
† 71953	Cherry Hill, 250	B 4
72324	Cherry Valley, 556	J 3
71726	Chidester, 232	D 6
72029	Clarendon⊙, 2,563	H 4

Zip	Name/Pop.	Key
72325	Clarkedale, 250	K 3
72830	Clarksville⊙, 4,616	D 3
72031	Clinton⊙, 1,029	F 2
72832	Coal Hill, 733	C 3
72476	College City, 645	J 1
71655	College Heights, 2,050	G 6
72326	Colt, 301	J 3
71831	Columbus, 258	C 6
72523	Concord, 163	G 2
72032	Conway⊙, 15,510	F 3
72422	Corning⊙, 2,705	J 1
72626	Cotter, 858	E 1
72036	Cotton Plant, 1,657	H 3
71937	Cove, 334	B 5
72037	Coy, 240	G 4
72327	Crawfordsville, 831	K 3
71635	Crossett, 6,191	G 7
71728	Curtis, 500	D 6
72526	Cushman, 427	G 2
† 71923	Dalark, 132	E 5
72039	Damascus, 255	F 3
72833	Danville⊙, 1,362	D 3
72834	Dardanelle⊙, 3,297	D 3
72424	Datto, 142	J 1
72722	Decatur, 847	A 1
72723	Delaney, 150	C 2
72425	Delaplaine, 145	J 1
72835	Delaware, 200	D 3
71940	Delight, 439	C 5
72426	Dell, 358	K 2
72836	Denning, 203	C 3
71832	De Queen⊙, 3,863	B 5
71638	Dermott, 4,250	H 7
72040	Des Arc⊙, 1,714	G 4
72041	De Valls Bluff⊙, 622	H 4
72042	De Witt⊙, 3,728	H 5
72644	Diamond City, 282	E 1
72043	Diaz, 283	H 2
71833	Dierks, 1,101	C 5
71834	Doddridge, 125	C 7
71941	Donaldson, 500	D 5
72837	Dover, 662	D 3
72530	Drasco, 300	G 2
† 72943	Driggs, 125	C 3
71639	Dumas, 4,600	H 6
72935	Dyer, 486	B 3
71729	Eagle Mills, 149	E 6
72331	Earle, 3,146	K 3
71701	East Camden, 589	E 6
72044	Edgemont, 125	F 2
72332	Edmondson, 412	K 3
72333	Elaine, 1,210	J 5
71730	El Dorado⊙, 25,283	E 7
72727	Elkins, 418	C 1
72728	Elm Springs, 260	B 1
72045	El Paso, 131	F 3
71740	Emerson, 393	D 7
71835	Emmet, 433	D 6

(continued on following page)

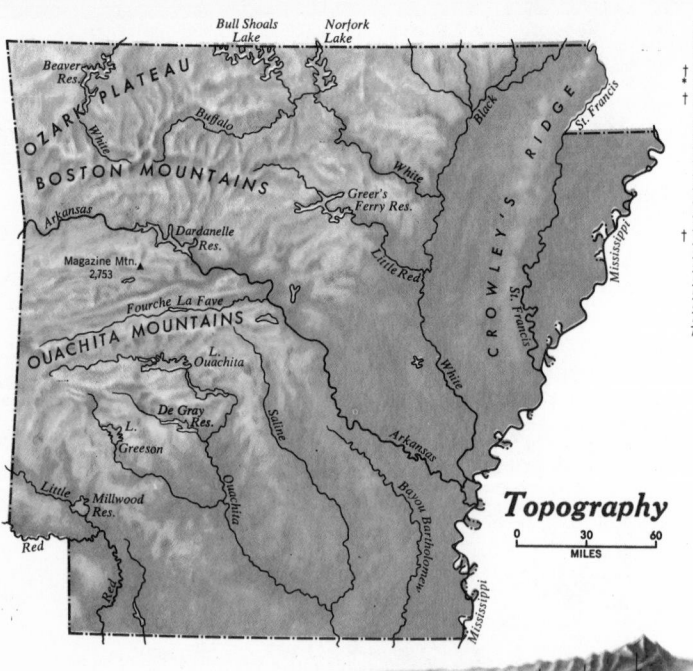

Topography

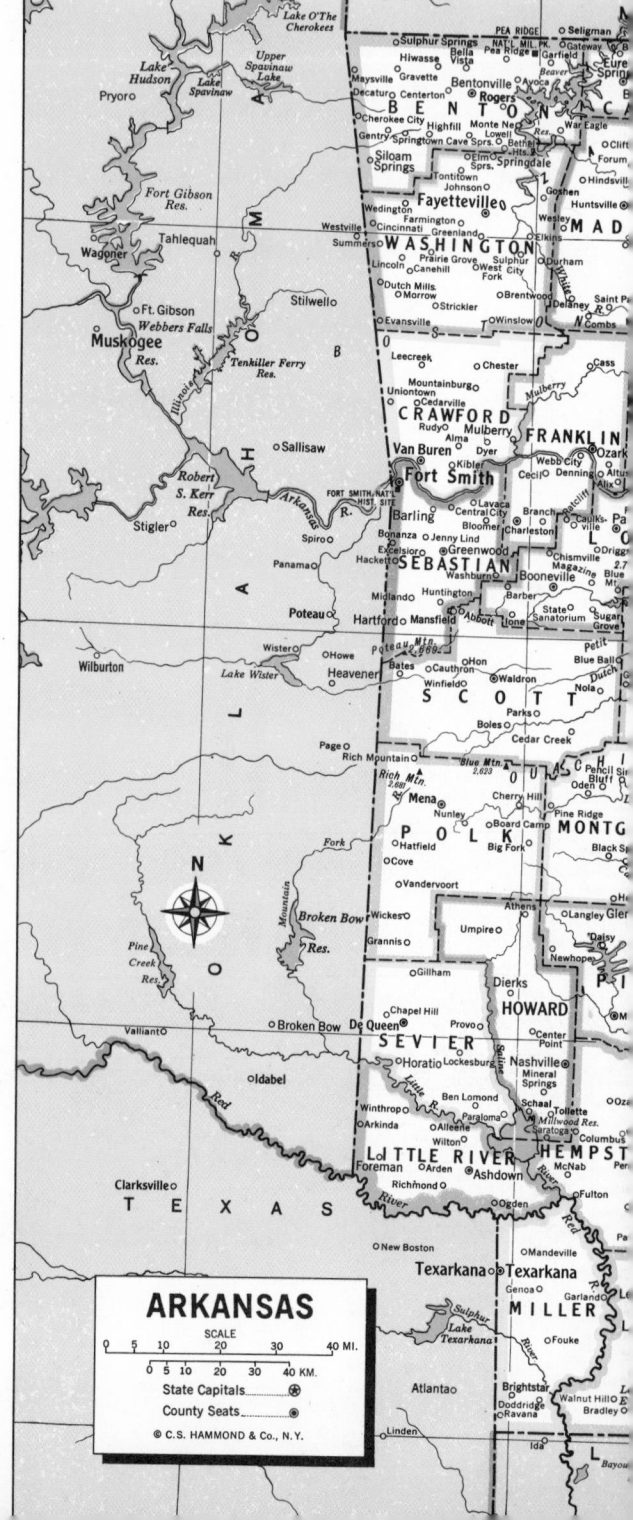

ARKANSAS

SCALE
0   5 10   20   30   40 MI.
0 5 10   20   30   40 KM.
State Capitals.....⊛
County Seats.....◉
© C.S. HAMMOND & Co., N.Y.

⊚ County seat.
‡ Population of metropolitan area.
† Zip of nearest p.o.
* Multiple zips.

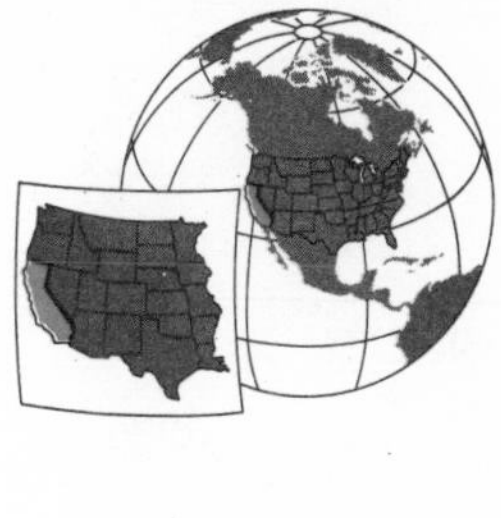

AREA 158,693 sq. mi.
POPULATION 19,953,134
CAPITAL Sacramento
LARGEST CITY Los Angeles
HIGHEST POINT Mt. Whitney 14,494 ft.
SETTLED IN 1769
ADMITTED TO UNION September 9, 1850
POPULAR NAME Golden State
STATE FLOWER Golden Poppy
STATE BIRD California Valley Quail

COUNTIES

County, Pop.	Key
Alameda, 1,073,184	D 6
Alpine, 484	F 5
Amador, 11,821	E 5
Butte, 101,969	D 4
Calaveras, 13,585	E 5
Colusa, 12,430	C 4
Contra Costa, 558,389	D 6
Del Norte, 14,580	B 2
El Dorado, 43,833	E 5
Fresno, 413,053	E 7
Glenn, 17,521	C 4
Humboldt, 99,692	B 3
Imperial, 74,492	K 10
Inyo, 15,571	H 7
Kern, 329,162	G 8
Kings, 64,610	F 8
Lake, 19,548	C 4
Lassen, 14,960	E 3
Los Angeles, 7,032,075	G 9
Madera, 41,519	F 6
Marin, 206,038	C 5
Mariposa, 6,015	E 6
Mendocino, 51,101	B 4
Merced, 104,629	E 6
Modoc, 7,469	E 2
Mono, 4,016	F 5
Monterey, 250,071	D 7
Napa, 79,140	C 5
Nevada, 26,346	E 4
Orange, 1,420,386	H 10
Placer, 77,306	E 4
Plumas, 11,707	E 4
Riverside, 459,074	J 10
Sacramento, 631,498	D 5
San Benito, 18,226	D 7
San Bernardino, 684,072	J 9
San Diego, 1,357,854	J 10
San Francisco (city county), 715,674	J 2
San Joaquin, 290,208	D 6
San Luis Obispo, 105,690	E 8
San Mateo, 556,234	C 6
Santa Barbara, 264,324	E 9
Santa Clara, 1,064,714	D 6
Santa Cruz, 123,790	C 6
Shasta, 77,640	C 3
Sierra, 2,365	E 4
Siskiyou, 33,225	C 2
Solano, 169,941	D 5
Sonoma, 204,885	C 5
Stanislaus, 194,506	D 6
Sutter, 41,935	D 4
Tehama, 29,517	C 3
Trinity, 7,615	B 3
Tulare, 188,322	G 7
Tuolumne, 22,169	F 5
Ventura, 376,430	F 9
Yolo, 91,788	D 5
Yuba, 34,736	D 4

CITIES and TOWNS

Zip	Name/Pop.	Key
92301	Adelanto, 2,115	H 9
96006	Adin, 550	E 2
93601	Ahwahnee, 503	E 6
94501	Alameda, 70,968	J 2
94507	Alamo-Danville, 14,059	K 2
94706	Albany, 14,674	J 2
* 91801	Alhambra, 62,125	C 10
93201	Alpaugh, 800	F 8
92001	Alpine, 1,570	J 11
91001	Altadena, 42,380	C 10
91701	Alta Loma, 6,100	E 10
96101	Alturas⊙, 2,799	E 2
† 95101	Alum Rock, 18,355	L 3
* 92801	Anaheim, 166,701	D 11
	Anaheim-Santa Ana-Garden Grove, ‡1,420,386	D 11
96007	Anderson, 5,492	C 3
95222	Angels Camp, 1,710	E 5
94508	Angwin, 2,690	C 5
94509	Antioch, 28,060	L 1
92307	Apple Valley, 6,702	H 9
95003	Aptos, 8,704	K 4
95912	Arbuckle, 1,037	C 4
95825	Arcade-Arden, 82,498	B 8
91006	Arcadia, 42,868	C 10
95521	Arcata, 8,985	A 3
93202	Armona, 1,392	F 7
93420	Arroyo Grande, 7,454	E 8
90701	Artesia, 14,757	C 11
93203	Arvin, 5,090	G 8
† 94578	Ashland, 14,810	K 2
95413	Asti, 50	C 5
93422	Atascadero, 10,290	E 8
94025	Atherton, 8,085	K 3
95301	Atwater, 11,640	E 6
93602	Auberry, 515	F 6
95603	Auburn⊙, 6,570	C 8
90704	Avalon, 1,520	G 10
93204	Avenal, 3,035	E 8
91702	Azusa, 25,217	D 10
92309	Baker, 600	J 8
* 93301	Bakersfield, 69,515	F 8
	Bakersfield, ‡329,162	F 8
91706	Baldwin Park, 47,285	D 10
92220	Banning, 12,034	J 10
92311	Barstow, 17,442	H 9
† 95501	Bayview, 2,340	A 3
† 93401	Baywood Park-Los Osos, 3,487	E 8
92223	Beaumont, 5,484	J 10
90201	Bell, 21,836	C 11
90706	Bellflower, 51,454	C 11
94002	Belmont, 23,667	J 3
94920	Belvedere, 2,599	H 2
94510	Benicia, 8,783	K 1
95005	Ben Lomond, 2,793	K 4
* 94701	Berkeley, 116,716	J 2
94511	Bethel Island, 1,398	L 1
* 90210	Beverly Hills, 33,416	B 10
92314	Big Bear City, 850	J 9
92315	Big Bear Lake, 5,268	J 9
95917	Biggs, 1,115	D 4
93513	Big Pine, 839	G 6
93920	Big Sur, 500	D 7
93606	Biola, 950	E 7
93514	Bishop, 3,498	G 6
† 94947	Black Point, 500	J 1
92316	Bloomington, 11,957	E 10
95525	Blue Lake, 1,112	A 3
92225	Blythe, 7,047	L 10
94923	Bodega Bay, 700	B 5
94924	Bolinas, 700	H 1
95415	Boonville, 715	B 5
93516	Boron, 1,999	H 8
92004	Borrego Springs, 860	J 10
95006	Boulder Creek, 1,806	J 4
95707	Bowman, 2,089	C 8
91010	Bradbury, 1,098	D 10
92227	Brawley, 13,746	K 11
92621	Brea, 18,447	D 11
94513	Brentwood, 2,649	L 2
93517	Bridgeport⊙, 525	F 5
94005	Brisbane, 3,003	J 2
95605	Broderick-Bryte, 12,782	B 8
95007	Brookdale, 630	J 4
95605	Bryte-Broderick, 12,782	B 8
93427	Buellton, 1,402	E 9
90620	Buena Park, 63,646	D 11
* 91501	Burbank, 88,871	C 10
94010	Burlingame, 27,320	J 2
96013	Burney, 2,190	D 3
93206	Buttonwillow, 1,193	F 8
94514	Byron, 800	L 2
92230	Cabazon, 598	J 10
92231	Calexico, 10,625	K 11
93501	California City, 1,309	H 8
92233	Calipatria, 1,824	K 10
94515	Calistoga, 1,882	C 5
95418	Calpella, 900	B 4
93745	Calwa, 5,191	F 7
93010	Camarillo, 19,219	F 9
93428	Cambria, 1,716	D 8
95709	Camino, 800	E 5
95008	Campbell, 24,770	K 3
92006	Campo, 850	J 11
95226	Campo Seco, 700	D 9
* 91303	Canoga Park, 109,127	B 10
92672	Capistrano Beach, 4,149	H 10
95010	Capitola, 5,080	K 4
92007	Cardiff-by-the-Sea, 5,724	H 10
92008	Carlsbad, 14,944	H 10
93921	Carmel, 4,525	D 7
93924	Carmel Valley, 3,026	D 7
95608	Carmichael, 37,625	C 8
93013	Carpinteria, 6,982	F 9
90744	Carson, 71,150	C 11
93609	Caruthers, 950	E 7
† 93001	Casitas Springs, 1,113	F 9
95420	Caspar, 578	B 4
91310	Castaic, 800	G 9
94546	Castro Valley, 44,760	K 2
95012	Castroville, 3,235	D 7
92234	Cathedral City, 3,640	J 10
93430	Cayucos, 1,772	E 8
96104	Cedarville, 825	E 2
96019	Central Valley, 2,361	C 3
95307	Ceres, 6,029	D 6
90701	Cerritos, 15,856	C 11
91311	Chatsworth, 24,000	B 10
95044	Chemeketa Park-Redwood Estates, 1,452	K
† 94521	Cherryland, 9,969	K 2
96020	Chester, 1,531	D 3
95926	Chico, 19,580	D 4
93555	China Lake, 11,105	H 8
95309	Chinese Camp, 150	E 6
91710	Chino, 20,411	D 10
93610	Chowchilla, 4,349	E 6
* 92010	Chula Vista, 67,901	J 11
95610	Citrus Heights, 21,760	C 8
91711	Claremont, 23,464	D 10
95612	Clarksburg, 554	B 9
94517	Clayton, 1,385	K 2
95422	Clearlake Highlands, 2,836	C 5
95423	Clearlake Oaks, 975	C 4
95425	Cloverdale, 3,251	B 5
93612	Clovis, 13,856	F 7
92236	Coachella, 8,353	J 10
93210	Coalinga, 6,161	E 7
95713	Colfax, 796	E 4
94014	Colma, 537	J 2
92324	Colton, 19,974	E 10
95932	Colusa⊙, 3,842	C 4
† 90001	Commerce, 10,536	C 10
90220	Compton, 78,611	C 11
* 94520	Concord, 85,164	K 1
93212	Corcoran, 5,249	F 7
96021	Corning, 3,573	C 4
91720	Corona, 27,519	E 11
92118	Coronado, 20,910	H 11
95076	Corralitos, 600	L 4
94925	Corte Madera, 8,464	J 2
* 92626	Costa Mesa, 72,660	D 11
96022	Cottonwood, 1,288	C 3
95428	Covelo, 900	B 4
91722	Covina, 30,380	D 10
95531	Crescent City⊙, 2,586	A 2
92325	Crestline, 3,509	H 9
94525	Crockett, 2,900	J 1
91730	Cucamonga, 5,796	E 10
90230	Culver City, 31,035	B 10
95014	Cupertino, 18,216	K 3
93615	Cutler, 2,503	F 7
95534	Cutten, 2,228	A 3
90630	Cypress, 31,026	D 11
92327	Daggett, 950	H 9
* 94014	Daly City, 66,922	H 2
92629	Dana Point, 4,745	H 10
94526	Danville-Alamo, 14,059	K 2
95616	Davis, 23,488	B 8
94576	Deer Park, 975	C 5
93215	Delano, 14,559	F 8
95315	Delhi, 2,063	E 6
92014	Del Mar, 3,956	H 11
93940	Del Rey Oaks, 1,823	D 7
92404	Del Rosa, 8,000	E 10
92240	Desert Hot Springs, 2,738	J 9
† 93550	Desert View Highlands, 2,172	G 9
94528	Diablo, 950	K 2
95619	Diamond Springs, 900	D 8
93618	Dinuba, 7,917	F 7
95620	Dixon, 4,432	B 9
96023	Dorris, 840	D 2
93620	Dos Palos, 2,496	E 6
* 90240	Downey, 88,445	C 11
95936	Downieville⊙, 375	E 4
91010	Duarte, 14,981	D 10
94566	Dublin, 13,641	K 2
95937	Dunnigan, 550	C 5
96025	Dunsmuir, 2,214	C 2
95938	Durham, 700	D 4
92241	Eagle Mountain, 2,453	K 10
93219	Earlimart, 3,080	F 8
† 92225	East Blythe, 1,252	L 10
90804	East Los Angeles, 105,033	C 10
93706	Easton, 1,065	F 7
93523	Edwards, 900	G 9
* 92020	El Cajon, 52,273	J 11
92243	El Centro⊙, 19,272	K 11
94530	El Cerrito, 25,190	J 2
95623	El Dorado, 900	C 8
95630	El Dorado Hills, 2,000	C 8
94018	El Granada, 1,473	H 3
95624	Elk Grove, 3,721	B 9
* 91731	El Monte, 69,837	D 10
95318	El Portal, 675	F 6
93030	El Rio, 6,173	F 9
90245	El Segundo, 15,620	B 11
92330	Elsinore, 3,530	F 11
92630	El Toro, 8,654	E 11
94608	Emeryville, 2,681	J 2
95319	Empire, 2,016	D 6
92024	Encinitas, 5,375	H 10
91316	Encino, 40,000	B 10
96001	Enterprise, 11,486	C 3
95320	Escalon, 2,366	E 6
92025	Escondido, 36,792	J 10
95627	Esparto, 1,088	C 5
91739	Etiwanda, 900	E 10
96027	Etna, 667	C 2
95501	Eureka⊙, 24,337	A 3
93221	Exeter, 4,475	F 7
94930	Fairfax, 7,661	H 1
94533	Fairfield⊙, 44,146	K 1
95628	Fair Oaks, 11,256	C 8
92028	Fallbrook, 6,945	H 10
96028	Fall River Mills, 600	D 3
93223	Farmersville, 3,456	F 7
93224	Fellows, 530	F 8
95018	Felton, 2,062	K 4
95536	Ferndale, 1,352	A 3
93015	Fillmore, 6,285	G 9
93622	Firebaugh, 2,517	E 7
95628	Florin, 9,646	B 8
95630	Folsom, 5,810	C 8
92335	Fontana, 20,673	E 10
† 93268	Ford City, 3,503	F 8
† 95703	Foresthill, 900	E 4
94933	Forest Knolls, 900	H 1
95437	Fort Bragg, 4,455	B 4
95538	Fort Dick, 850	A 2
96032	Fort Jones, 515	C 2
95540	Fortuna, 4,203	A 3
94404	Foster City, 9,327	J 2
92708	Fountain Valley, 31,826	D 11
93625	Fowler, 2,239	F 7
93225	Frazier Park, 1,167	F 9
95019	Freedom, 5,563	L 4
* 94536	Fremont, 100,869	K 3
† 93701	Fresno⊙, 165,972	F 7
	Fresno, ‡413,053	F 7
* 92631	Fullerton, 3,200	D 11
95632	Galt, 3,200	C 9
* 90247	Gardena, 41,021	C 11
* 92640	Garden Grove, 122,524	D 11
95634	Georgetown, 700	E 5
96035	Gerber, 800	C 3
95441	Geyserville, 887	B 5
95020	Gilroy, 12,665	D 6
† 92501	Glen Avon Heights, 5,759	E 10
* 91201	Glendale, 132,752	C 10
91740	Glendora, 31,349	D 10
93017	Goleta, 3,500	F 9
93926	Gonzales, 2,575	D 7
93227	Goshen, 1,324	F 7
91344	Granada Hills, 50,000	B 10
92324	Grand Terrace, 5,901	E 10
95945	Grass Valley, 5,149	D 4
95444	Graton, 975	C 5
93308	Greenacres, 2,116	F 8
93927	Greenfield, 2,608	D 7
95947	Greenville, 1,073	E 3
95948	Gridley, 3,534	D 4
93433	Grover City, 5,939	E 8
93434	Guadalupe, 3,145	E 9
95445	Gualala, 585	B 5
95446	Guerneville, 900	B 5
95322	Gustine, 2,793	D 6
94019	Half Moon Bay, 4,023	H 3
95951	Hamilton City, 961	C 4
93230	Hanford⊙, 15,179	F 7
96039	Happy Camp, 925	B 2
90710	Harbor City, 17,500	C 11
90250	Hawthorne, 53,304	C 11
96041	Hayfork, 900	B 3
* 94541	Hayward, 93,058	K 2
95448	Healdsburg, 5,438	B 5
92249	Heber, 875	K 11
92343	Hemet, 12,252	H 10
96113	Herlong, 900	E 3
90254	Hermosa Beach, 17,412	B 11
92345	Hesperia, 4,592	H 9
† 91302	Hidden Hills, 1,529	B 10
92507	Highgrove, 2,158	E 10
92346	Highland, 13,290	H 9
95324	Hilmar, 813	E 6
92347	Hinkley, 900	H 9
95023	Hollister⊙, 7,663	D 7
90028	Hollywood, 85,047	C 10
92250	Holtville, 3,496	K 11
† 91720	Home Gardens, 5,116	E 11
92348	Homeland, 1,187	H 10
95546	Hoopa, 850	B 2
95449	Hopland, 817	B 5
95326	Hughson, 2,144	E 6
* 92646	Huntington Beach, 115,960	C 11
90255	Huntington Park, 33,744	C 11
93234	Huron, 1,525	E 7
92349	Idyllwild, 950	J 10
94947	Ignacio, 4,500	H 1
92251	Imperial, 3,094	K 11
92032	Imperial Beach, 20,244	H 11
93526	Independence⊙, 748	G 7
92201	Indio, 14,459	J 10
* 90301	Inglewood, 89,985	B 11
94937	Inverness, 800	B 5
95640	Ione, 2,369	C 9
93017	Isla Vista, 13,441	E 9
95641	Isleton, 909	L 1
93235	Ivanhoe, 1,595	F 7
95642	Jackson⊙, 1,924	C 9
92034	Jacumba, 700	J 11
95327	Jamestown, 950	E 6
92252	Joshua Tree, 1,211	J 9
95451	Kelseyville, 950	C 5
† 94701	Kensington, 5,823	J 2
93600	Kerman, 2,667	E 7
93238	Kernville, 900	G 8
93239	Kettleman City, 600	E 7
95328	Keyes, 1,875	E 6
93930	King City, 3,717	D 7
95719	Kings Beach, 600	F 4
93631	Kingsburg, 3,843	F 7
95645	Knights Landing, 846	B 8
91011	La Canada, 20,652	C 10
91214	La Crescenta-Montrose, 19,594	C 10
94549	Lafayette, 20,484	K 2
* 92651	Laguna Beach, 14,550	G 10
92653	Laguna Hills, 13,676	D 11
92677	Laguna Niguel, 4,644	H 10
90631	La Habra, 41,350	D 11
94020	La Honda, 650	J 3
92037	La Jolla, 30,000	H 11
92352	Lake Arrowhead, 2,682	H 9
93532	Lake Hughes, 750	G 9
93240	Lake Isabella, 850	G 8
* 92330	Lakeland Village, 1,724	E 11
95453	Lakeport⊙, 3,005	C 4
* 90712	Lakewood, 82,973	C 11
92041	La Mesa, 39,178	H 11
90638	La Mirada, 30,808	D 11
93241	Lamont, 7,007	G 8
93534	Lancaster, 30,948	G 9
* 91744	La Puente, 31,092	D 10
94939	Larkspur, 10,487	H 1
95076	La Selva Beach, 1,171	K 4
95330	Lathrop, 2,137	D 6
93242	Laton, 1,071	F 7
91750	La Verne, 12,965	D 10

(continued on following page)

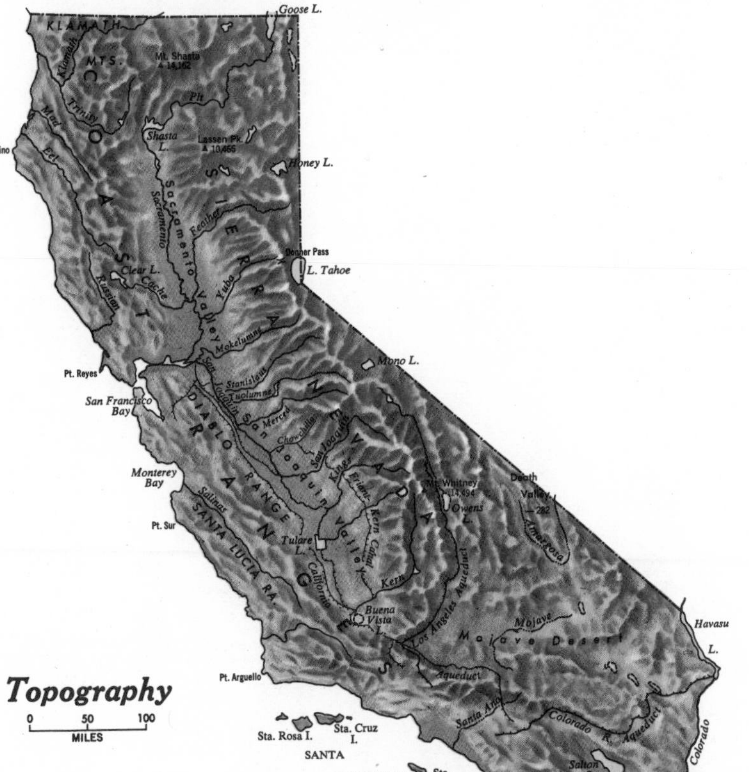
KLAMATH
MTS.
Mt. Shasta 14,162
Goose L.
Klamath
Trinity
Pit
Shasta L.
Lassen Pk. 10,466
Honey L.
Cape Mendocino
Mad
Eel
COAST
Sacramento
Feather
SIERRA
Clear L.
Cache
Yuba
Donner Pass
L. Tahoe
Russian
Valley
Mokelumne
Pt. Reyes
San Francisco Bay
San Joaquin
Stanislaus
Tuolumne
Merced
Mono L.
DIABLO
RANGE
Chowchilla
San Joaquin
Kings
Monterey Bay
Salinas
Mt. Whitney 14,494
Owens L.
Death Valley -282
Amargosa
Pt. Sur
SANTA LUCIA RA.
Tulare L.
Kern Canal
Kern
Buena Vista L.
Los Angeles Aqueduct
Mojave
Mojave Desert
Havasu L.
Pt. Arguello
Aqueduct
Santa Ana
Colorado R. Aqueduct
Colorado
Salton Sea
Imperial Valley
Sta. Rosa I.
Sta. Cruz I.
SANTA BARBARA IS.
Sta. Catalina I.
San Clemente I.

Topography

0 50 100
MILES

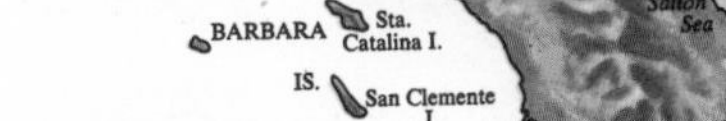
5,000 m. 16,404 ft.
2,000 m. 6,562 ft.
1,000 m. 3,281 ft.
500 m. 1,640 ft.
200 m. 656 ft.
100 m. 328 ft.
Sea Level
Below

(continued)

90260 Lawndale, 24,825 ... B 11
95454 Laytonville, 917 ... B 4
95333 Le Grand, 995 ... E 6
92045 Lemon Grove, 19,690 ... J 11
93245 Lemoore, 4,219 ... F 7
90304 Lennox, 16,121 ... B 11
92311 Lenwood, 3,834 ... H 9
92024 Leucadia, 5,900 ... H 10
95648 Lincoln, 3,176 ... B 8
† 95901 Linda, 7,731 ... D 4
93247 Lindsay, 5,206 ... F 7
95953 Live Oak, 2,645 ... D 4
95953 Live Oak, 6,443 ... K 4
94550 Livermore, 37,703 ... L 2
95334 Livingston, 2,588 ... E 6
95237 Lockeford, 890 ... C 9
95240 Lodi, 28,691 ... C 9
95551 Loleta, 800 ... A 3
92354 Loma Linda, 9,797 ... F 10
90717 Lomita, 19,784 ... C 11
93436 Lompoc, 25,284 ... E 9
93545 Lone Pine, 1,241 ... H 7
* 90801 Long Beach, 358,633 ... C 11
95650 Loomis, 1,108 ... C 8
90720 Los Alamitos, 11,346 ... D 11
93440 Los Alamos, 750 ... E 9
94022 Los Altos, 24,956 ... K 3
94022 Los Altos Hills, 6,865 ... J 3
* 90001 Los Angeles⊙, 2,816,061 ... C 10
Los Angeles-Long Beach, ‡7,032,075 ... C 10
93635 Los Banos, 9,188 ... E 6
95030 Los Gatos, 23,735 ... K 4
96055 Los Molinos, 900 ... D 3
† 93401 Los Osos-Baywood Park, 3,487 ... E 8
95457 Lower Lake, 850 ... C 5
96118 Loyalton, 945 ... E 4
95458 Lucerne, 1,300 ... C 4
92356 Lucerne Valley, 850 ... J 9
90262 Lynwood, 43,353 ... C 11
93637 Madera⊙, 16,044 ... E 7
90265 Malibu, 15,000 ... B 10
90266 Manhattan Beach, 35,352 ... B 11
95336 Manteca, 13,845 ... D 6
93252 Maricopa, 740 ... F 8
† 94901 Marinwood, 6,000 ... H 1
95338 Mariposa⊙, 900 ... F 6
96120 Markleeville⊙, 150 ... F 5
94553 Martinez⊙, 16,506 ... K 1
95901 Marysville⊙, 9,353 ... D 4
95955 Maxwell, 850 ... C 4
90270 Maywood, 16,996 ... C 10
96057 McCloud, 1,643 ... C 2
93250 McFarland, 4,177 ... F 8
92254 Mecca, 900 ... K 10
93023 Meiners Oaks, 7,025 ... F 9
95460 Mendocino, 975 ... B 4
93640 Mendota, 2,705 ... E 7
94025 Menlo Park, 26,734 ... J 3
92359 Mentone, 2,900 ... H 9
95340 Merced⊙, 22,670 ... E 6
95461 Middletown, 800 ... C 5
92655 Midway City, 5,900 ... D 11
94030 Millbrae, 20,781 ... J 2
94941 Mill Valley, 12,942 ... H 2
95035 Milpitas, 27,149 ... L 3
91752 Mira Loma, 8,482 ... E 10
92675 Mission Viejo, 11,933 ... D 11
* 95350 Modesto⊙, 61,712 ... D 6
93501 Mojave, 2,573 ... G 8
95245 Mokelumne Hill, 560 ... E 5
91016 Monrovia, 30,015 ... D 10
96064 Montague, 890 ... C 2
93003 Montalvo, 2,400 ... F 9
94037 Montara, 1,459 ... H 3
91763 Montclair, 22,546 ... D 10
90640 Montebello, 42,807 ... C 10
93103 Montecito, 4,900 ... F 9
93940 Monterey, 26,302 ... D 7
91754 Monterey Park, 49,166 ... C 10
95462 Monte Rio, 900 ... B 5
95030 Monte Sereno, 3,089 ... K 4
91020 Montrose-La Crescenta, 19,594 ... C 10
93021 Moorpark, 3,380 ... G 9
94556 Moraga, 14,205 ... K 2
95037 Morgan Hill, 6,485 ... L 4
93442 Morro Bay, 7,109 ... D 8
94038 Moss Beach, 700 ... H 3
95039 Moss Landing, 600 ... C 7
94040 Mountain View, 51,092 ... K 3
96067 Mount Shasta, 2,163 ... C 2
† 95926 Mulberry, 1,795 ... D 4
95247 Murphys, 780 ... E 5
92362 Murrieta, 850 ... H 10
92405 Muscoy, 7,091 ... E 10
94558 Napa⊙, 35,978 ... C 5
92050 National City, 43,184 ... J 11
92363 Needles, 4,051 ... L 9
95959 Nevada City⊙, 2,314 ... D 4
94560 Newark, 27,153 ... K 3
92365 Newberry Springs, 710 ... J 9
95658 Newcastle, 900 ... C 8
91321 Newhall, 9,651 ... G 9
95360 Newman, 2,505 ... D 6
* 92660 Newport Beach, 49,422 ... D 11
92257 Niland, 900 ... K 10
93444 Nipomo, 3,642 ... E 8
91760 Norco, 14,511 ... E 11
93643 North Fork, 575 ... F 6
95660 North Highlands, 31,854 ... B 8
* 91601 North Hollywood, 190,000 ... B 10
90650 Norwalk, 91,827 ... C 11
94947 Novato, 31,006 ... H 1
95361 Oakdale, 6,594 ... E 6
93644 Oakhurst, 800 ... F 6
* 94601 Oakland⊙, 361,561 ... J 2
94561 Oakley, 1,306 ... L 1
93022 Oak View, 4,872 ... F 9
93445 Oceano, 2,564 ... E 8
92054 Oceanside, 40,494 ... H 10
93308 Oildale, 20,879 ... F 8
93023 Ojai, 5,591 ... F 9
* 91761 Ontario, 64,118 ... D 10
95060 Opal Cliffs, 5,425 ... K 4
* 92666 Orange, 77,374 ... D 11

93646 Orange Cove, 3,392 ... F 7
93454 Orcutt, 8,500 ... E 9
95555 Orick, 950 ... A 2
94563 Orinda, 6,790 ... J 2
95963 Orland, 2,884 ... C 4
95556 Orleans, 850 ... B 2
92368 Oro Grande, 700 ... H 9
93647 Orosi, 2,757 ... F 7
95965 Oroville⊙, 7,536 ... D 4
93030 Oxnard, 71,225 ... F 9
Oxnard-Ventura, ‡376,430 ... F 9
94044 Pacifica, 36,020 ... H 2
92109 Pacific Beach, 59,000 ... H 11
93950 Pacific Grove, 13,505 ... C 7
† 95076 Pajaro, 1,407 ... D 7
95968 Palermo, 1,966 ... D 4
93550 Palmdale, 8,511 ... G 9
92260 Palm Desert, 6,171 ... J 10
92262 Palm Springs, 20,936 ... J 10
* 94301 Palo Alto, 55,966 ... K 3
90274 Palos Verdes Estates, 13,641 ... B 11
95969 Paradise, 14,539 ... D 4
90723 Paramount, 34,734 ... C 11
93648 Parlier, 1,993 ... F 7
* 91101 Pasadena, 113,327 ... C 10
† 95060 Pastiempo, 1,115 ... K 4
93446 Paso Robles, 7,168 ... E 8
95363 Patterson, 3,147 ... D 6
93553 Pearblossom, 900 ... H 9
93953 Pebble Beach, 5,000 ... C 7
92370 Perris, 4,228 ... F 11
94060 Pescadero, 625 ... J 4
94952 Petaluma, 24,870 ... H 1
95466 Philo, 700 ... B 4
90660 Pico Rivera, 54,170 ... C 10
94611 Piedmont, 10,917 ... J 2
93650 Pinedale, 1,900 ... F 7
94564 Pinole, 15,850 ... J 1
93040 Piru, 975 ... G 9
93449 Pismo Beach, 4,043 ... E 8
94565 Pittsburg, 20,651 ... L 1
93256 Pixley, 1,584 ... F 8
92670 Placentia, 21,948 ... D 11
95667 Placerville⊙, 5,416 ... C 8
95365 Planada, 2,056 ... E 6
94523 Pleasant Hill, 24,610 ... K 2
94566 Pleasanton, 18,328 ... L 2
95669 Plymouth, 501 ... C 8
95726 Pollock Pines, 850 ... E 5
* 91766 Pomona, 87,384 ... D 10
93257 Poplar, 1,239 ... F 7
93257 Porterville, 12,602 ... G 7
93041 Port Hueneme, 14,295 ... F 9
96122 Portola, 1,625 ... E 4
94025 Portola Valley, 4,999 ... J 3
95469 Potter Valley, 975 ... B 4
92064 Poway, 9,422 ... J 11
96079 Project City, 1,431 ... C 3
93534 Quartz Hill, 4,935 ... G 9
95971 Quincy⊙, 3,343 ... E 4
92065 Ramona, 3,554 ... J 10
95670 Rancho Cordova, 30,451 ... C 8
† 91321 Rancho Santa Clarita, 4,860 ... G 9
92067 Rancho Santa Fe, 975 ... H 10
96080 Red Bluff⊙, 7,676 ... C 3
96001 Redding⊙, 16,659 ... C 3
92373 Redlands, 36,355 ... H 9
* 90277 Redondo Beach, 56,075 ... B 11
* 94061 Redwood City⊙, 55,686 ... J 3
95044 Redwood Estates-Chemeketa Park, 1,452 ... K 4
93654 Reedley, 8,131 ... F 7
91335 Reseda, 60,862 ... B 10
92376 Rialto, 28,370 ... E 10
93261 Richgrove, 1,023 ... F 8
* 94801 Richmond, 79,043 ... J 1
93555 Ridgecrest, 7,629 ... H 8
95562 Rio Dell, 2,817 ... A 3
95673 Rio Linda, 7,524 ... B 8
94571 Rio Vista, 3,135 ... L 1
95366 Ripon, 2,679 ... D 6
95367 Riverbank, 3,949 ... E 6
93656 Riverdale, 1,722 ... E 7
* 92501 Riverside⊙, 140,089 ... E 11
95677 Rocklin, 3,039 ... B 8
94572 Rodeo, 5,356 ... J 1
94928 Rohnert Park, 6,133 ... C 5
95540 Rohnerville, 2,781 ... B 3
90274 Rolling Hills, 2,050 ... B 11
90274 Rolling Hills Estates, 6,027 ... B 11
93560 Rosamond, 2,281 ... G 9
91770 Rosemead, 40,972 ... C 10
95678 Roseville, 17,895 ... B 8
94957 Ross, 2,742 ... H 1
92509 Rubidoux, 13,969 ... E 10
* 95801 Sacramento (cap.)⊙, 254,413 ... B 8
Sacramento, ‡800,592 ... B 8
94574 Saint Helena, 3,173 ... C 5
93901 Salinas⊙, 58,896 ... D 7
Salinas-Monterey, ‡250,071 ... D 7
95563 Salyer, 700 ... B 3
95564 Samoa, 585 ... A 3
95249 San Andreas⊙, 1,564 ... E 5
94960 San Anselmo, 13,031 ... H 1
93450 San Ardo, 750 ... E 7
* 92401 San Bernardino⊙, 104,251 ... E 10
San Bernardino-Riverside-Ontario, ‡1,143,146 ... E 10
94066 San Bruno, 36,254 ... J 2
94070 San Carlos, 25,924 ... J 3
92672 San Clemente, 17,063 ... H 10
* 92101 San Diego⊙, 696,769 ... H 11
San Diego, ‡1,357,854 ... H 11
91773 San Dimas, 15,692 ... D 10
* 91340 San Fernando, 16,571 ... C 10
* 94101 San Francisco⊙, 715,674 ... H 2
San Francisco-Oakland, ‡3,109,519 ... H 2
* 91775 San Gabriel, 29,176 ... C 10
93657 Sanger, 10,088 ... F 7
92383 San Jacinto, 4,385 ... H 10
93660 San Joaquin, 1,506 ... E 7
* 95101 San Jose⊙, 445,779 ... L 3
San Jose, ‡1,064,714 ... L 3

Agriculture, Industry and Resources

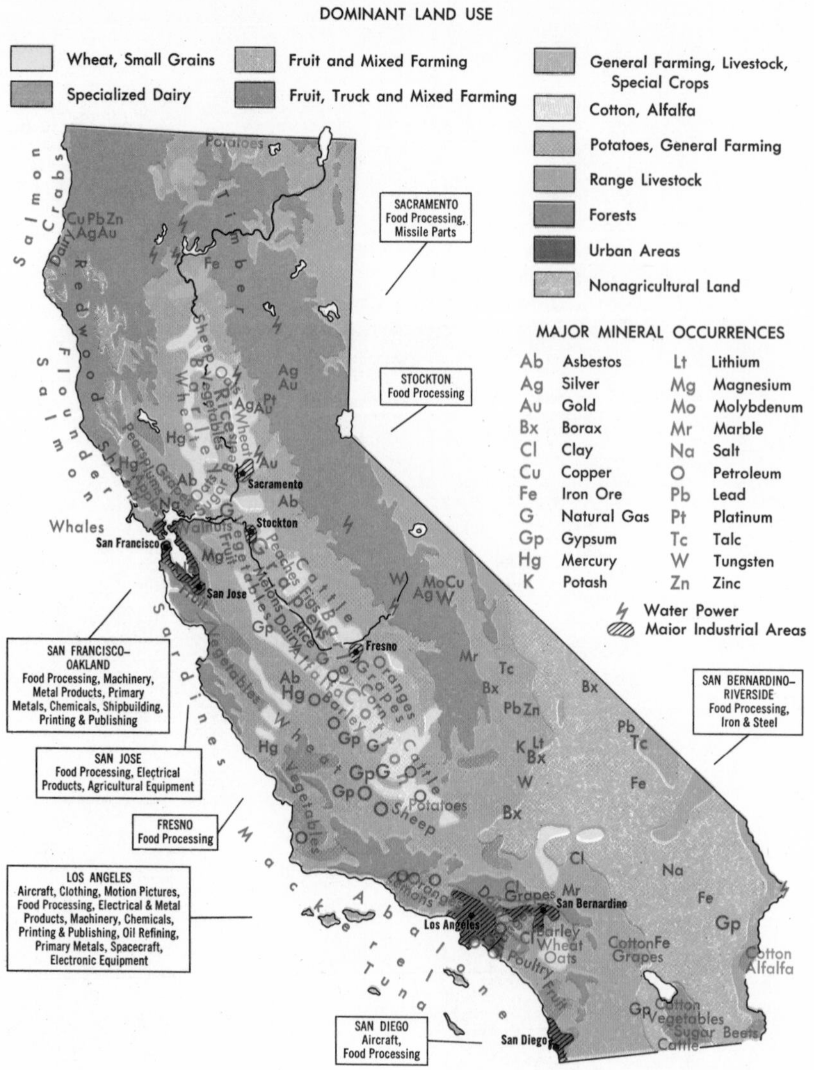
DOMINANT LAND USE
Wheat, Small Grains
Specialized Dairy
Fruit and Mixed Farming
Fruit, Truck and Mixed Farming
General Farming, Livestock, Special Crops
Cotton, Alfalfa
Potatoes, General Farming
Range Livestock
Forests
Urban Areas
Nonagricultural Land
MAJOR MINERAL OCCURRENCES
Ab Asbestos
Ag Silver
Au Gold
Bx Borax
Cl Clay
Cu Copper
Fe Iron Ore
G Natural Gas
Gp Gypsum
Hg Mercury
K Potash
Lt Lithium
Mg Magnesium
Mo Molybdenum
Mr Marble
Na Salt
O Petroleum
Pb Lead
Pt Platinum
Tc Talc
W Tungsten
Zn Zinc
Water Power
Major Industrial Areas
SACRAMENTO
Food Processing, Missile Parts
STOCKTON
Food Processing
SAN FRANCISCO-OAKLAND
Food Processing, Machinery, Metal Products, Primary Metals, Chemicals, Shipbuilding, Printing & Publishing
SAN JOSE
Food Processing, Electrical Products, Agricultural Equipment
FRESNO
Food Processing
LOS ANGELES
Aircraft, Clothing, Motion Pictures, Food Processing, Electrical & Metal Products, Machinery, Chemicals, Printing & Publishing, Oil Refining, Primary Metals, Spacecraft, Electronic Equipment
SAN DIEGO
Aircraft, Food Processing
SAN BERNARDINO-RIVERSIDE
Food Processing, Iron & Steel
Sacramento
Stockton
San Francisco
San Jose
Fresno
Los Angeles
San Bernardino
San Diego
Whales
Salmon
Crabs
Flounder
Sardines
Mackerel
Tuna
Potatoes
Timber
Cattle
Sheep
Rice
Oranges
Grapes
Cotton
Vegetables
Poultry
Barley
Wheat
Oats
Alfalfa
Sugar Beets

95045 San Juan Bautista, 1,164 ... D 7
92675 San Juan Capistrano, 3,781 ... H 10
* 94577 San Leandro, 68,698 ... J 2
94580 San Lorenzo, 24,633 ... K 2
93401 San Luis Obispo⊙, 28,036 ... E 8
92069 San Marcos, 3,896 ... H 10
91108 San Marino, 14,177 ... D 10
95046 San Martin, 1,392 ... L 4
* 94401 San Mateo, 78,911 ... J 3
93451 San Miguel, 600 ... E 8
94806 San Pablo, 21,461 ... J 1
* 90731 San Pedro, 91,000 ... C 11
* 94901 San Rafael⊙, 38,977 ... J 1
94583 San Ramon, 4,084 ... K 2
* 92701 Santa Ana⊙, 156,601 ... D 11
* 93101 Santa Barbara⊙, 70,215 ... F 9
Santa Barbara, ‡264,324 ... F 9
* 95050 Santa Clara, 87,717 ... K 3
95060 Santa Cruz⊙, 32,076 ... K 4
90670 Santa Fe Springs, 14,750 ... C 11
93453 Santa Margarita, 750 ... E 8
93454 Santa Maria, 32,749 ... E 9
* 90401 Santa Monica, 88,289 ... B 10
93060 Santa Paula, 18,001 ... F 9
* 95401 Santa Rosa⊙, 50,006 ... C 5
93063 Santa Susana, 2,900 ... B 10
† 94901 Santa Venetia, 2,500 ... J 1
92071 Santee, 21,107 ... J 11
95070 Saratoga, 27,110 ... K 4
93003 Saticoy, 2,400 ... F 9
94965 Sausalito, 6,158 ... H 2
95565 Scotia, 950 ... A 3
95060 Scotts Valley, 3,621 ... K 4
90740 Seal Beach, 24 441 ... C 11
93955 Seaside, 35,935 ... D 7
95472 Sebastopol, 3,993 ... C 5
92273 Seeley, 952 ... K 11
93662 Selma, 7,459 ... F 7
91343 Sepulveda, 40,000 ... B 10
93263 Shafter, 5,327 ... F 8
96087 Shasta, 750 ... C 3
93449 Shell Beach, 1,900 ... E 8
91024 Sierra Madre, 12,140 ... D 10
90806 Signal Hill, 5,582 ... C 11

92676 Silverado, 950 ... E 11
93065 Simi Valley, 56,464 ... G 9
92075 Solana Beach, 5,023 ... H 11
93960 Soledad, 6,843 ... D 7
93463 Solvang, 2,004 ... E 9
95476 Sonoma, 4,112 ... C 5
95370 Sonora⊙, 3,100 ... E 6
95073 Soquel, 5,795 ... K 4
93665 South Dos Palos, 850 ... E 7
91733 South El Monte, 13,443 ... C 10
90280 South Gate, 56,909 ... C 11
95705 South Lake Tahoe, 12,921 ... F 5
† 95965 South Oroville, 4,111 ... D 4
91030 South Pasadena, 22,979 ... C 10
† 95801 South Sacramento, 28,574 ... B 8
94080 South San Francisco, 46,646 ... J 2
† 93268 South Taft, 2,214 ... F 8
93265 Springville, 720 ... G 7
94305 Stanford, 8,691 ... J 3
90680 Stanton, 17,947 ... D 11
94970 Stinson Beach, 800 ... H 2
* 95201 Stockton⊙, 107,644 ... D 6
Stockton, ‡290,208 ... D 6
93266 Stratford, 750 ... F 7
93267 Strathmore, 1,221 ... F 7
94585 Suisun City, 2,917 ... K 1
93067 Summerland, 781 ... F 9
92381 Sun City, 5,519 ... F 11
96089 Summit City, 900 ... C 3
91040 Sunland, 22,200 ... C 10
92388 Sunnymead, 6,708 ... F 11
* 94086 Sunnyvale, 95,408 ... K 3
94586 Sunol, 750 ... L 2
90742 Sunset Beach, 1,900 ... C 11
96130 Susanville⊙, 6,608 ... E 3
95982 Sutter, 1,488 ... D 4
95685 Sutter Creek, 1,508 ... C 9
93268 Taft, 4,285 ... F 8
95730 Tahoe City, 1,394 ... E 4
91356 Tarzana, 24,165 ... B 10
93561 Tehachapi, 4,211 ... G 8
91780 Temple City, 29,673 ... D 10
93465 Templeton, 900 ... E 8

93270 Terra Bella, 1,037 ... G 8
92274 Thermal, 975 ... J 10
† 95965 Thermalito, 4,217 ... D 4
95686 Thornton, 850 ... B 9
91360 Thousand Oaks. 36,334 ... G 9
92276 Thousand Palms, 600 ... J 10
94920 Tiburon, 6,209 ... J 2
93272 Tipton, 969 ... F 7
90290 Topanga, 4,800 ... B 10
† 90290 Topanga Beach, 4,500 ... B 10
* 90501 Torrance, 134,584 ... C 11
95376 Tracy, 14,724 ... D 6
93668 Tranquillity, 800 ... E 7
93562 Trona, 975 ... H 8
95734 Truckee, 1,392 ... E 4
91042 Tujunga, 22,000 ... C 10
93274 Tulare, 16,235 ... F 7
96134 Tulelake, 857 ... D 2
95379 Tuolumne, 1,365 ... E 6
95380 Turlock, 13,992 ... E 6
92680 Tustin, 21,178 ... D 11
95383 Twain Harte, 1,484 ... E 6
92277 Twentynine Palms, 5,667 ... K 9
† 95060 Twin Lakes, 3,012 ... K 4
95482 Ukiah⊙, 10,095 ... B 4
94587 Union City, 14,724 ... K 2
90007 University Park, 3,100 ... D 11
91786 Upland, 32,551 ... E 10
95485 Upper Lake, 975 ... C 4
95688 Vacaville, 21,690 ... D 5
91355 Valencia, 4,243 ... G 9
94590 Vallejo, 66,733 ... J 1
Vallejo-Napa, ‡249,081 ... J 1
95252 Valley Springs, 800 ... C 9
* 91401 Van Nuys, 231,600 ... B 10
90291 Venice, 80,500 ... B 11
* 93001 Ventura⊙, 55,797 ... F 9
92392 Victorville, 10,845 ... H 9
92667 Villa Park, 2,723 ... D 11
93277 Visalia⊙, 27,268 ... F 7
92083 Vista, 24,688 ... H 10
91789 Walnut, 5,992 ... D 10
* 94595 Walnut Creek, 39,844 ... K 2
95690 Walnut Grove, 800 ... B 9

93280 Wasco, 8,269 ... F 8
95386 Waterford, 2,243 ... E 6
95076 Watsonville, 14,569 ... D 7
96093 Weaverville⊙, 1,489 ... B 3
96094 Weed, 2,983 ... C 2
* 91790 West Covina, 68,034 ... D 10
† 90025 West Hollywood, 29,448 ... B 10
90025 West Los Angeles, 38,805 ... B 10
92683 Westminster, 59,865 ... D 11
92281 Westmorland, 1,175 ... K 10
94565 West Pittsburg, 5,969 ... K 1
95255 West Point, 950 ... E 5
95691 West Sacramento, 12,002 ... B 8
96137 Westwood, 1,862 ... D 3
96137 Westwood, 45,000 ... B 10
95692 Wheatland, 1,280 ... D 4
* 90601 Whittier, 72,863 ... D 11
95987 Williams, 1,571 ... C 4
95490 Willits, 3,091 ... B 4
95988 Willows⊙, 4,085 ... C 4
90744 Wilmington, 38,000 ... C 11
95492 Windsor, 2,359 ... C 5
92283 Winterhaven, 850 ... L 11
95694 Winters, 2,419 ... D 5
95388 Winton, 3,393 ... E 6
95258 Woodbridge, 1,397 ... B 9
93286 Woodlake, 3,371 ... G 7
95695 Woodland⊙, 20,677 ... B 8
91364 Woodland Hills, 56,420 ... B 10
94062 Woodside, 4,731 ... J 3
92398 Yermo, 1,304 ... J 9
92686 Yorba Linda, 11,856 ... D 11
95389 Yosemite National Park, 857 ... F 6
94599 Yountville, 2,332 ... C 5
96097 Yreka⊙, 5,394 ... C 2
95991 Yuba City⊙, 13,986 ... D 4
92399 Yucaipa, 19,284 ... J 9
92284 Yucca Valley, 3,893 ... J 9

⊙ County seat.
‡ Population of metropolitan area.
† Zip of nearest p.o.
* Multiple zips

AREA 104,247 sq. mi
POPULATION 2,207,259
CAPITAL Denver
LARGEST CITY Denver
HIGHEST POINT Mt. Elbert 14,433 ft.
SETTLED IN 1858
ADMITTED TO UNION August 1, 1876
POPULAR NAME Centennial State
STATE FLOWER Mountain Columbine
STATE BIRD Lark Bunting

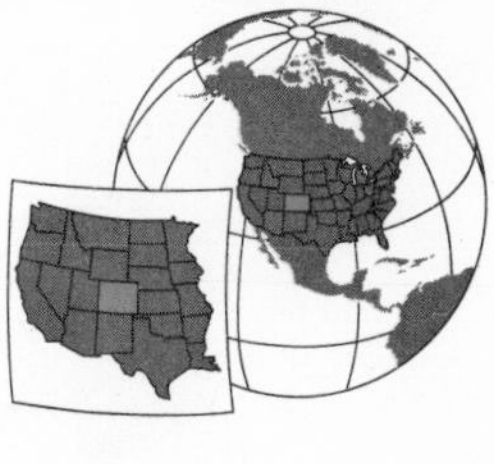

COUNTIES

County	Key
Adams, 185,789	L 3
Alamosa, 11,422	H 7
Arapahoe, 162,142	L 3
Archuleta, 2,733	E 8
Baca, 5,674	O 8
Bent, 6,493	N 7
Boulder, 131,889	J 2
Chaffee, 10,162	G 5
Cheyenne, 2,396	O 5
Clear Creek, 4,819	H 3
Conejos, 7,846	G 8
Costilla, 3,091	J 8
Crowley, 3,086	M 6
Custer, 1,120	J 6
Delta, 15,286	D 5
Denver, 514,678	K 3
Dolores, 1,641	C 7
Douglas, 8,407	K 4
Eagle, 7,498	F 3
Elbert, 3,903	L 4
El Paso, 235,972	K 5
Fremont, 21,942	J 5
Garfield, 14,821	C 3
Gilpin, 1,272	H 3
Grand, 4,107	G 2
Gunnison, 7,578	E 5
Hinsdale, 202	E 7
Huerfano, 6,590	K 7
Jackson, 1,811	G 1
Jefferson, 233,031	J 3
Kiowa, 2,029	O 6
Kit Carson, 7,530	O 4
Lake, 8,282	G 4
La Plata, 19,199	D 8
Larimer, 89,900	H 1
Las Animas, 15,744	L 8
Lincoln, 4,836	M 5
Logan, 18,852	N 1
Mesa, 54,374	B 5
Mineral, 786	F 7
Moffat, 6,525	C 1
Montezuma, 12,952	B 8
Montrose, 18,366	C 6
Morgan, 20,105	M 2
Otero, 23,523	M 7
Ouray, 1,546	D 6
Park, 2,185	H 4
Phillips, 4,131	P 1
Pitkin, 6,185	F 4
Prowers, 13,258	P 7
Pueblo, 118,238	K 6
Rio Blanco, 4,842	C 3
Rio Grande, 10,494	G 7
Routt, 6,592	E 1
Saguache, 3,827	G 6
San Juan, 831	D 7
San Miguel, 1,949	C 6
Sedgwick, 3,405	P 1
Summit, 2,665	G 3
Teller, 3,316	J 5
Washington, 5,550	N 3
Weld, 89,297	L 1
Yuma, 8,544	P 2

CITIES and TOWNS

Zip	Name/Pop.	Key
80101	Agate, 120	M 4
81020	Aguilar, 699	K 8
80720	Akron⊙, 1,775	N 2
81101	Alamosa⊙, 6,985	H 8
80510	Allenspark, 100	J 2
80420	Alma, 73	G 4
81210	Almont, 15	F 5
80721	Amherst, 105	P 1
80801	Anton, 65	N 3
81120	Antonito, 1,113	H 8
80802	Arapahoe, 100	P 5
81021	Arlington, 10	N 6
80804	Arriba, 254	N 4
† 81323	Arriola, 50	B 8
80002	Arvada, 46,814	J 3
81611	Aspen⊙, 2,404	F 4
80722	Atwood, 75	N 1
80610	Ault, 841	K 1
80010	Aurora, 74,974	K 3
81410	Austin, 1,163	D 5
81620	Avon, 50	F 3
81022	Avondale, 750	L 6
80421	Bailey, 200	H 4
† 80624	Barnesville, 20	L 2
81621	Basalt, 419	E 4
81122	Bayfield, 320	D 8
81411	Bedrock, 20	B 6
† 80758	Beecher Island, 5	P 3
80512	Bellvue, 335	J 1
80102	Bennett, 613	L 3
80513	Berthoud, 1,446	J 2
† 80438	Berthoud Pass, 200	H 3
80805	Bethune, 99	P 4
81023	Beulah, 425	K 6
80908	Black Forest, 700	K 4
80422	Black Hawk, 217	J 3
81123	Blanca, 212	H 8
† 81001	Blende, 950	K 6
† 80424	Blue River, 8	G 4
† 81155	Bonanza, 10	G 6
81024	Boncarbo, 50	K 8
80423	Bond, 63	F 3
81025	Boone, 448	L 6
* 80301	Boulder⊙, 66,870	J 2
† 81428	Bowie, 18	D 5
80806	Boyero, 25	N 5
81026	Brandon, 10	P 6
81027	Branson, 70	M 8
80424	Breckenridge⊙, 548	G 4
80611	Briggsdale, 440	L 1
80601	Brighton⊙, 8,309	K 3
81028	Bristol, 250	P 6
† 80901	Broadmoor, 3,871	K 5
† 81212	Brookside, 173	J 6
80020	Broomfield, 7,261	J 3
80723	Brush, 3,377	M 2
† 80742	Buckingham, 6	L 1
81211	Buena Vista, 1,962	G 5
80425	Buffalo Creek, 150	J 4
80807	Burlington⊙, 2,828	P 4
80426	Burns, 100	F 3
80103	Byers, 490	L 3
81320	Cahone, 125	B 7
80808	Calhan, 465	L 4
81029	Campo, 206	O 8
81212	Canon City⊙, 9,206	J 6
81124	Capulin, 600	G 8
81623	Carbondale, 726	E 4
80612	Carr, 47	K 1
80809	Cascade, 950	K 5
80104	Castle Rock⊙, 1,531	K 4
81413	Cedaredge, 581	D 5
81125	Center, 1,470	G 7
80427	Central City⊙, 228	J 3
81126	Chama, 400	J 8
81030	Cheraw, 129	N 6
80810	Cheyenne Wells⊙, 982	P 5
81127	Chimney Rock, 51	E 8
81031	Chivington, 15	O 6
81128	Chromo, 150	F 8
81220	Cimarron, 25	D 6
80428	Clark, 55	F 1
† 80731	Clarkville, 4	P 2
81520	Clifton, 950	C 4
80429	Climax, 975	G 4
81221	Coal Creek, 225	J 6
81222	Coaldale, 104	H 6
80430	Coalmont, 12	F 1
81032	Cokedale, 101	K 8
81624	Collbran, 225	C 4
† 81401	Colona, 54	D 6
81004	Colorado City, 411	K 6
* 80901	Colorado Springs⊙, 135,060	K 5
	Colorado Springs, ‡235,972	K 5
† 80428	Columbine, 12	E 1
80022	Commerce City, 17,407	K 3
80432	Como, 35	H 4
81129	Conejos⊙, 100	G 8
80812	Cope, 125	O 3
80611	Cornish, 2	L 2
81321	Cortez⊙, 6,032	B 8
81223	Cotopaxi, 150	H 6
80434	Cowdrey, 10	G 1
81625	Craig⊙, 4,205	D 2
81415	Crawford, 171	D 5
81130	Creede⊙, 653	E 7
81224	Crested Butte, 372	E 5
81131	Crestone, 34	H 7
80813	Cripple Creek⊙, 425	J 5
80726	Crook, 199	O 1
81033	Crowley, 216	M 6
81055	Cuchara, 43	J 8
80514	Dacono, 360	K 2
† 80728	Dailey, 20	O 1
81630	De Beque, 155	C 4
† 80135	Deckers, 4	J 4
80105	Deer Trail, 374	M 3
81034	Delhi, 10	M 7
81132	Del Norte⊙, 1,569	G 7
81416	Delta⊙, 3,694	D 5
* 80201	Denver (cap.)⊙, 514,678	K 3
	Denver, ‡1,227,529	K 3
81035	Deora, 2	O 7
80435	Dillon, 182	H 3
81610	Dinosaur, 247	B 2
80814	Divide, 50	J 5
81323	Dolores, 820	C 8
81324	Dove Creek⊙, 619	A 7
† 81239	Doyleville, 75	F 6
80515	Drake, 75	J 2
81301	Durango⊙, 10,333	D 8
81036	Eads⊙, 795	O 6
81631	Eagle⊙, 790	F 3
† 81212	East Canon, 1,805	J 6
80615	Eaton, 1,389	K 1
81418	Eckert, 850	C 5
80727	Eckley, 193	P 2
80214	Edgewater, 4,866	J 3
81632	Edwards, 100	F 3
81325	Egnar, 84	B 7
80106	Elbert, 150	L 4
80437	Eldora, 100	H 3
80107	Elizabeth, 493	K 4
81633	Elk Springs, 56	C 2
80438	Empire, 249	H 3
80110	Englewood, 33,695	K 3
80516	Erie, 1,090	K 2
80517	Estes Park, 1,616	J 2
† 81433	Eureka, 25	D 7
80620	Evans, 2,570	K 2
80439	Evergreen, 2,321	J 3
80440	Fairplay⊙, 419	H 4
81037	Farisita, 45	J 7
† 80030	Federal Heights, 1,502	J 3
80520	Firestone, 570	K 2
† 80810	Firstview, 6	O 5
80815	Flagler, 615	N 4
80728	Fleming, 349	O 1
81226	Florence, 2,846	J 6
80816	Florissant, 75	J 5
80521	Fort Collins⊙, 43,337	J 1
81133	Fort Garland, 400	J 8
80621	Fort Lupton, 2,489	K 2
81038	Fort Lyon, 135	N 6
80701	Fort Morgan⊙, 7,594	M 2
80817	Fountain, 3,515	K 5
81039	Fowler, 1,241	L 6
80441	Foxton, 75	J 4
80116	Franktown, 157	K 4
80442	Fraser, 221	H 3
80530	Frederick, 696	K 2
80820	Freshwater (Guffey), 24	H 5
80443	Frisco, 471	G 3
81521	Fruita, 1,822	B 4
† 81501	Fruitvale, 950	C 4
80622	Galeton, 200	K 1
81134	Garcia, 90	J 8
81040	Gardner, 75	J 7
81227	Garfield, 11	G 5
81522	Gateway, 250	B 5
80818	Genoa, 161	N 4
80444	Georgetown⊙, 542	H 3
80623	Gilcrest, 382	K 2
80624	Gill, 250	L 2
81634	Gilman, 400	G 3
81523	Glade Park, 69	B 5
80485	Glendevey, 50	H 1
80532	Glen Haven, 50	H 2
81601	Glenwood Springs⊙, 4,106	E 4
80401	Golden⊙, 9,817	J 3
80625	Goodrich, 85	M 2
80445	Gould, 12	G 2
81041	Granada, 551	P 6
80446	Granby, 554	H 2
81501	Grand Junction⊙, 20,170	B 4
80447	Grand Lake, 189	H 2
81635	Grand Valley, 270	D 4
81228	Granite, 23	G 4
80448	Grant, 50	H 4
80631	Greeley⊙, 38,902	K 2
† 80118	Greenland, 47	K 4
80819	Green Mountain Falls, 359	K 5
81636	Greystone, 2	B 1
80729	Grover, 121	L 1
80820	Guffey, 24	H 5
81042	Gulnare, 100	K 8
81230	Gunnison⊙, 4,613	E 5
81637	Gypsum, 420	F 3
80730	Hale, 12	P 3
81638	Hamilton, 30	D 2
81043	Hartman, 129	P 6
80449	Hartsel, 75	H 4
81044	Hasty, 150	O 6
81045	Haswell, 135	N 6
80731	Haxtun, 899	O 1
81639	Hayden, 763	E 2
80732	Hereford, 50	L 1
81326	Hesperus, 78	C 8
80733	Hillrose, 121	N 2
81232	Hillside, 79	H 6
81046	Hoehne, 400	L 8
81047	Holly, 993	P 6
80734	Holyoke⊙, 1,640	P 1
81136	Hooper, 80	H 7
81419	Hotchkiss, 507	D 5
80451	Hot Sulphur Springs⊙, 220	H 2
81233	Howard, 175	H 6
80641	Hoyt, 175	L 2
80642	Hudson, 518	K 2
80821	Hugo⊙, 759	N 4
80533	Hygiene, 400	J 2
80452	Idaho Springs, 2,003	H 3
80735	Idalia, 100	P 3
81137	Ignacio, 613	D 8
80736	Iliff, 193	N 1
81427	Ironton, 1	D 7
† 80901	Ivywild, 12,000	K 5
80455	Jamestown, 185	J 2
81048	Jansen, 267	K 8
81138	Jaroso, 56	H 8
80456	Jefferson, 45	H 4
80822	Joes, 100	O 3
80534	Johnstown, 1,191	K 2
80737	Julesburg⊙, 1,578	P 1
80823	Karval, 70	N 5
80643	Keenesburg, 427	L 2
80738	Keota, 6	L 1
80644	Kersey, 474	L 2
81049	Kim, 200	N 8
80117	Kiowa⊙, 235	L 4
80824	Kirk, 100	P 3
80825	Kit Carson, 220	O 5
† 80435	Kokomo, 75	G 4
80459	Kremmling, 764	G 2
80826	Kutch, 2	M 5
80026	Lafayette, 3,498	K 3
81139	La Garita, 50	G 7
80739	Laird, 105	P 2
81140	La Jara, 768	H 8
81050	La Junta⊙, 7,938	M 7
81235	Lake City⊙, 91	E 6
80827	Lake George, 29	J 5
80215	Lakewood, 92,787	J 3
81052	Lamar⊙, 7,797	O 6
80535	Laporte, 950	J 1
80118	Larkspur, 350	K 4
80645	La Salle, 1,227	K 2
81054	Las Animas⊙, 3,148	N 6
† 81151	Lasauces, 120	H 8
† 81153	Lavalley, 237	J 8
81055	La Veta, 589	J 8
† 80452	Lawson, 108	H 3
81625	Lay, 8	D 2
81420	Lazear, 60	D 5
80461	Leadville⊙, 4,314	G 4
† 81323	Lebanon, 50	B 8
81327	Lewis, 350	B 8
80828	Limon, 1,814	M 4
† 81212	Lincoln Park, 2,984	J 6
80740	Lindon, 50	N 3
80120	Littleton⊙, 26,466	K 3
80536	Livermore, 20	J 1
† 80701	Log Lane Village, 329	M 2
81524	Loma, 100	B 4
80501	Longmont, 23,209	J 2
† 80135	Longview, 10	J 4
80027	Louisville, 2,409	J 3
80131	Louviers, 306	K 4
80537	Loveland, 16,220	J 2
80646	Lucerne, 150	K 2
81056	Lycan, 4	P 7
80540	Lyons, 958	J 2
81525	Mack, 175	B 4
81421	Maher, 80	D 5
† 80461	Malta, 200	G 4
81141	Manassa, 814	H 8
81328	Mancos, 709	C 8
80829	Manitou Springs, 4,278	J 5
81058	Manzanola, 451	M 6
† 81623	Marble, 1	E 4
81329	Marvel, 100	C 8
80541	Masonville, 200	J 2
† 80649	Masters, 50	L 2
80830	Matheson, 100	M 4
81640	Maybell, 82	C 2
81057	McClave, 165	O 6
80463	McCoy, 14	F 3
80542	Mead, 195	K 2
81641	Meeker⊙, 1,597	D 2
81642	Meredith, 48	F 4
80741	Merino, 260	N 2
81005	Mesa, 295	C 4
81330	Mesa Verde National Park, 70	C 8
81142	Mesita, 50	H 8
80543	Milliken, 702	K 2
80477	Milner, 75	F 2
81645	Minturn, 706	G 3
81059	Model, 19	L 8
81143	Moffat, 98	H 6
81646	Molina, 120	D 4
81144	Monte Vista, 3,909	G 7
80464	Montezuma, 6	H 3

(continued on following page)

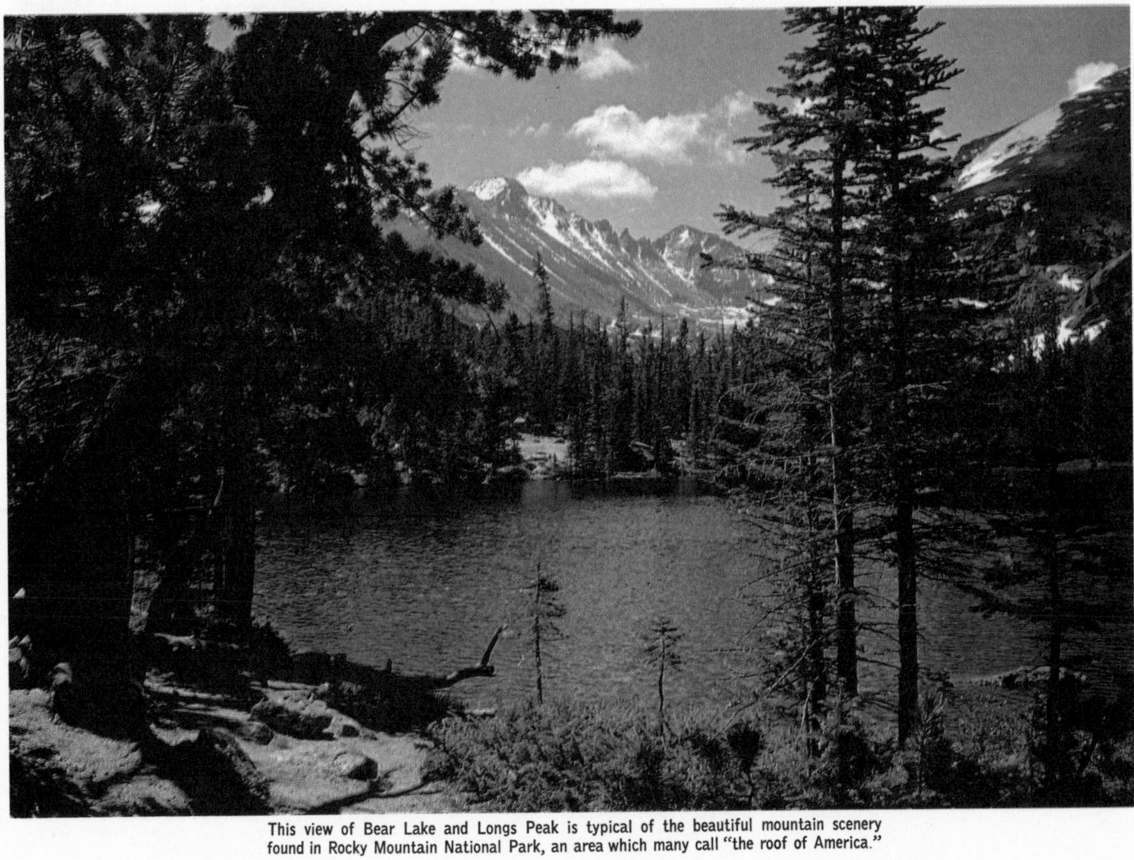
This view of Bear Lake and Longs Peak is typical of the beautiful mountain scenery found in Rocky Mountain National Park, an area which many call "the roof of America."

Colorado Department of Public Relations

Topography

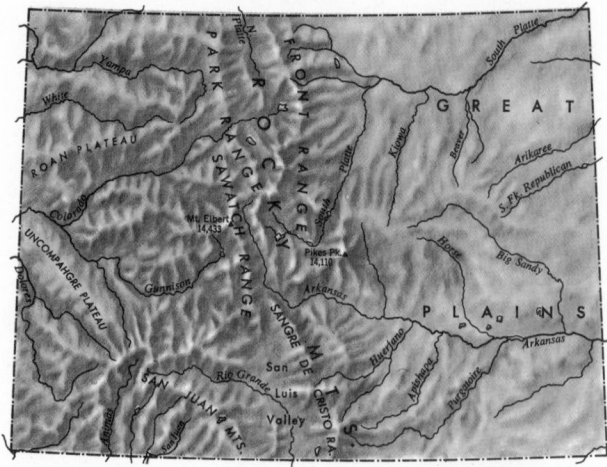

Agriculture, Industry and Resources

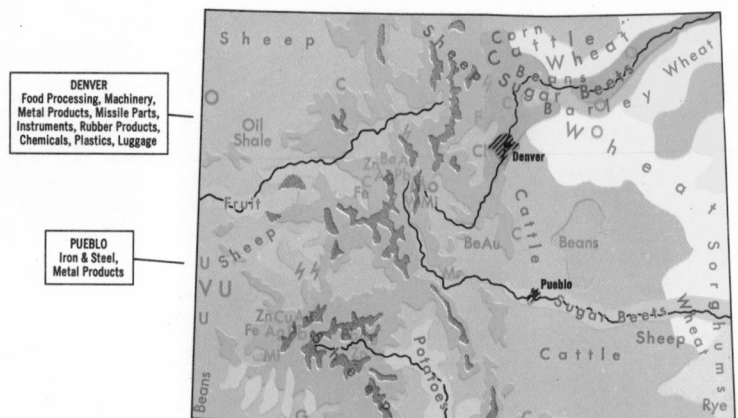

DENVER
Food Processing, Machinery, Metal Products, Missile Parts, Instruments, Rubber Products, Chemicals, Plastics, Luggage

PUEBLO
Iron & Steel, Metal Products

DOMINANT LAND USE

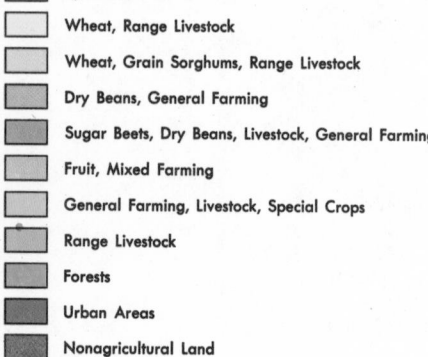

- Specialized Wheat
- Wheat, Range Livestock
- Wheat, Grain Sorghums, Range Livestock
- Dry Beans, General Farming
- Sugar Beets, Dry Beans, Livestock, General Farming
- Fruit, Mixed Farming
- General Farming, Livestock, Special Crops
- Range Livestock
- Forests
- Urban Areas
- Nonagricultural Land

MAJOR MINERAL OCCURRENCES

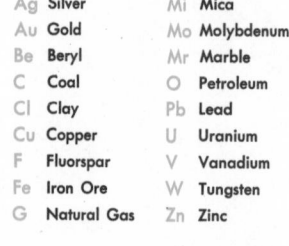

Ag	Silver	Mi	Mica
Au	Gold	Mo	Molybdenum
Be	Beryl	Mr	Marble
C	Coal	O	Petroleum
Cl	Clay	Pb	Lead
Cu	Copper	U	Uranium
F	Fluorspar	V	Vanadium
Fe	Iron Ore	W	Tungsten
G	Natural Gas	Zn	Zinc

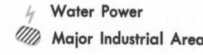

Water Power

Major Industrial Areas

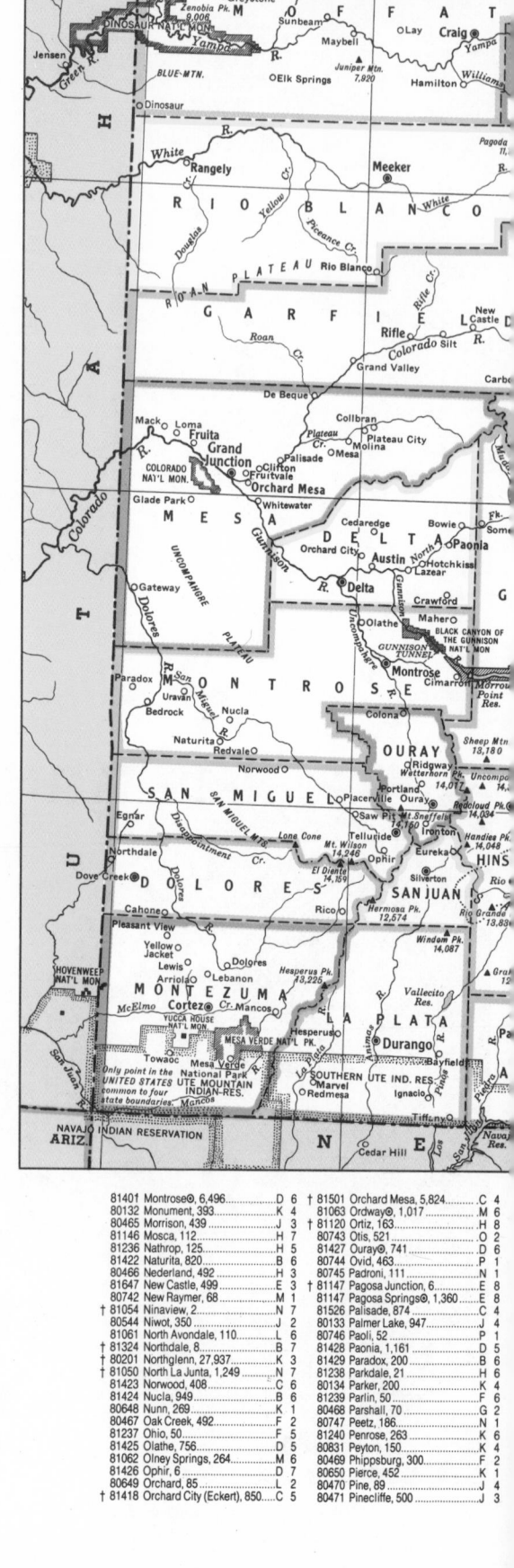

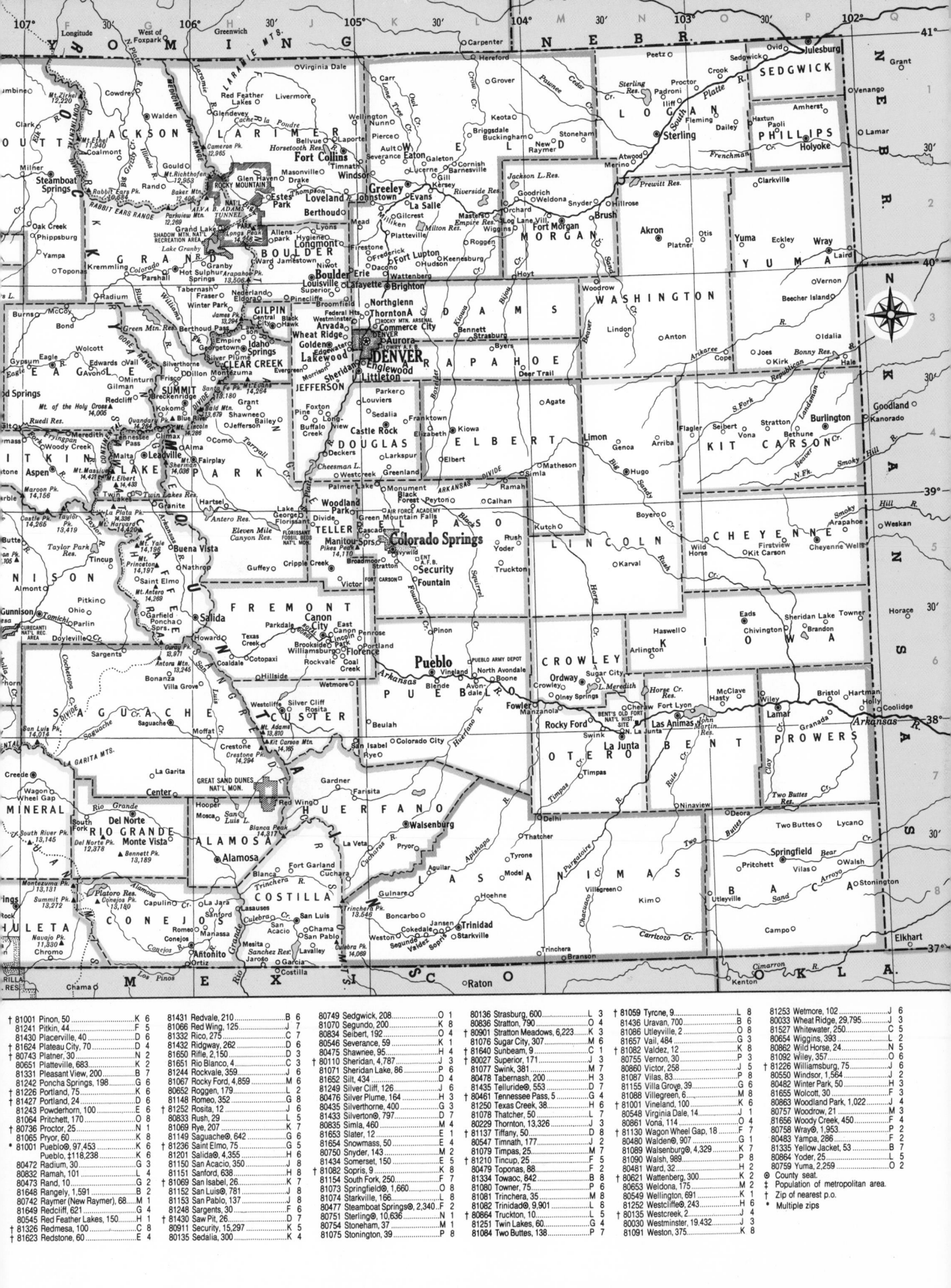

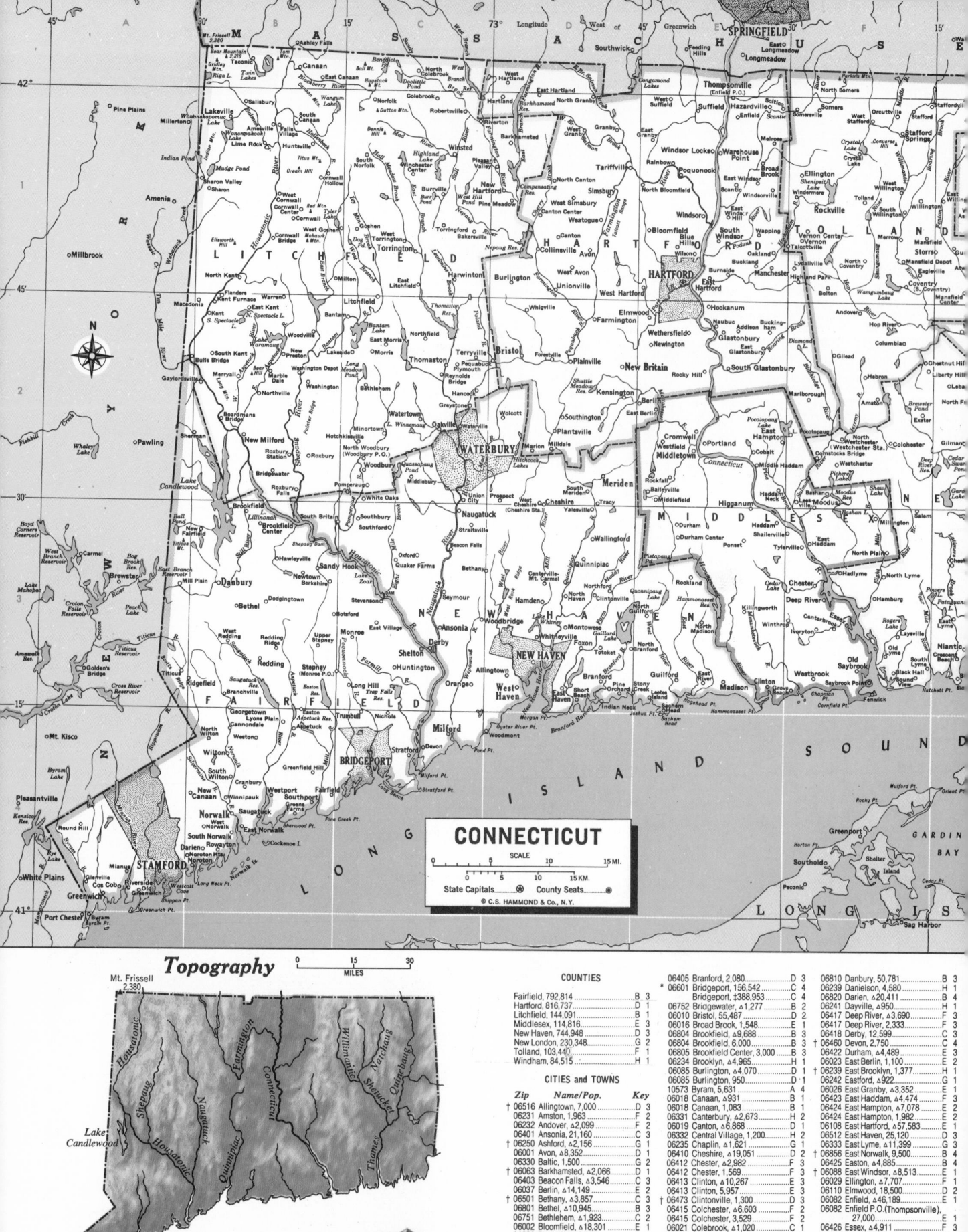

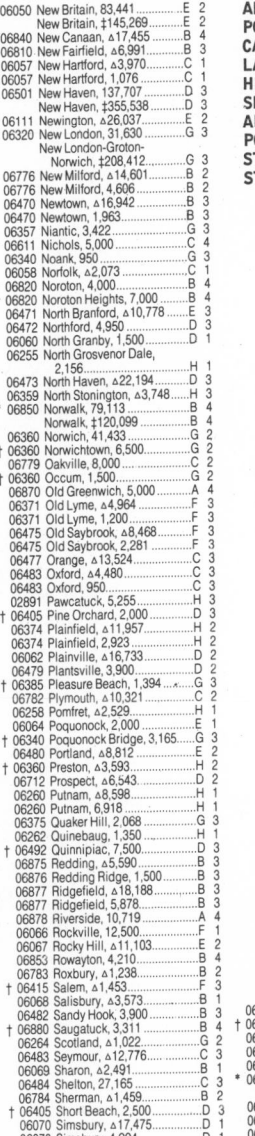

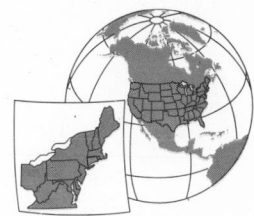

* 06050 New Britain, 83,441	E	2
New Britain, ‡145,269	E	2
06840 New Canaan, △17,455	B	4
06810 New Fairfield, ∆6,991	B	3
06057 New Hartford, ∆3,970	C	1
06057 New Hartford, 1,076	C	1
* 06501 New Haven, 137,707	D	3
New Haven, ‡355,538	D	3
06111 Newington, ∆26,037	E	2
06320 New London, 31,630	G	3
New London-Groton-		
Norwich, ‡208,412	G	3
06776 New Milford, ∆14,601	B	2
06776 New Milford, 4,606	B	2
06470 Newtown, ∆16,942	B	3
06470 Newtown, 1,963	B	3
06357 Niantic, 3,422	G	3
† 06611 Nichols, 5,000	C	4
06340 Noank, 950	G	3
06058 Norfolk, ∆2,073	C	1
06820 Noroton, 4,000	B	4
† 06820 Noroton Heights, 7,000	B	4
06471 North Branford, ∆10,778	E	3
06472 Northford, 4,950	D	3
06060 North Granby, 1,500	D	1
06255 North Grosvenor Dale,		
2,156	H	1
06473 North Haven, ∆22,194	D	3
06359 North Stonington, △3,748	H	3
* 06850 Norwalk, 79,113	B	4
Norwalk, ‡120,099	B	4
06360 Norwich, 41,433	G	2
06360 Norwichtown, 6,500	G	2
06779 Oakville, 8,000	C	2
06360 Occum, 1,500	G	2
06870 Old Greenwich, 5,000	A	4
06371 Old Lyme, ∆4,964	F	3
06371 Old Lyme, 1,200	F	3
06475 Old Saybrook, ∆8,468	F	3
06475 Old Saybrook, 2,281	F	3
06477 Orange, ∆13,524	C	3
06483 Oxford, ∆4,480	C	3
06483 Oxford, 950	C	3
02891 Pawcatuck, 5,255	H	3
† 06405 Pine Orchard, 2,000	D	3
06374 Plainfield, ∆11,957	H	2
06374 Plainfield, 2,923	H	2
06062 Plainville, ∆16,733	D	2
06479 Plantsville, 3,900	D	2
† 06385 Pleasant Beach, 1,394	G	3
06782 Plymouth, ∆10,321	C	2
06258 Pomfret, ∆2,529	H	1
06064 Poquonock, 2,000	E	1
† 06340 Poquonock Bridge, 3,165	G	3
06480 Portland, ∆8,812	E	2
† 06360 Preston, ∆3,593	H	2
06712 Prospect, ∆6,543	D	2
06260 Putnam, ∆8,598	H	1
06260 Putnam, 6,918	H	1
06375 Quaker Hill, 2,068	G	3
06262 Quinebaug, 1,350	H	1
† 06492 Quinnipiac, 7,500	D	3
06875 Redding, ∆5,590	B	3
06876 Redding Ridge, 1,500	B	3
06877 Ridgefield, ∆18,188	B	3
06877 Ridgefield, 5,878	B	3
06878 Riverside, 10,719	A	4
06066 Rockville, 12,500	F	1
06067 Rocky Hill, ∆11,103	E	2
06853 Rowayton, 4,210	B	4
06783 Roxbury, ∆1,238	B	2
† 06415 Salem, ∆1,453	F	3
06068 Salisbury, ∆3,573	B	1
06482 Sandy Hook, 3,900	B	3
† 06880 Saugatuck, 3,311	B	4
06264 Scotland, ∆1,022	G	2
06483 Seymour, ∆12,776	C	3
06484 Shelton, 27,165	C	3
06784 Sherman, ∆1,459	B	2
* 06405 Short Beach, 2,500	D	3
06070 Simsbury, ∆17,475	D	1
06070 Simsbury, 4,994	D	1
06071 Somers, ∆6,893	F	1
06071 Somers, 1,274	F	1
06488 Southbury, ∆7,852	C	3
† 06238 South Coventry (Coventry),		
3,735	F	1
06073 South Glastonbury, 3,000	E	2
06489 Southington, ∆30,946	D	2
06850 South Norwalk, 21,000	B	4
06490 Southport, 3,500	C	4
† 06897 South Wilton, 1,400	B	4
06075 Stafford, ∆8,680	F	1
06076 Stafford Springs, 3,339	F	1
06077 Staffordville, 1,200	G	1
† 06901 Stamford, 108,798	A	4
Stamford, ‡206,419	A	4
† 06468 Stepney, 2,300	B	3
06377 Sterling, ∆1,853	H	2
06491 Stevenson, 1,500	C	3
06378 Stonington, ∆15,940	H	3
06378 Stonington, 1,413	H	3
* 06405 Stony Creek, 2,800	E	3
06268 Storrs, 10,691	F	1
06497 Stratford, ∆49,775	C	4
06078 Suffield, ∆8,634	E	1
06380 Taftville, 2,000	G	2
06081 Tariffville, 1,337	D	1
06786 Terryville, 6,900	C	2
† 06360 Thamesville, 1,500	G	2
06787 Thomaston, ∆6,233	C	2
06277 Thompson, ∆7,580	H	1
06277 Thompson, 1,200	H	1
06082 Thompsonville, 27,000	E	1
06084 Tolland, ∆7,857	F	1
06790 Torrington, 3,500	C	1
06790 Torrington, 31,952	C	1
† 06405 Totoket, 950	D	3

06492 Wallingford, ∆35,714	D	3
† 06074 Wapping, 1,600	E	1
06088 Warehouse Point, 2,400	E	1
06754 Warren, ∆827	B	2
06793 Washington, ∆3,121	B	2
* 06701 Waterbury, 108,033	C	2
Waterbury, ‡208,956	C	2
06385 Waterford, ∆17,227	G	3
06795 Watertown, ∆18,610	C	2
06795 Watertown, 9,000	C	2
06714 Waterville, 4,295	C	2
06387 Wauregan, 1,100	H	2
06089 Weatogue, 2,396	D	1
* 06001 West Avon, 4,500	D	1
06498 Westbrook, ∆3,820	F	3
06498 Westbrook, 1,507	F	3
06410 West Cheshire, 2,000	D	3
06457 Westfield, 9,000	E	2
06107 West Hartford, ∆68,031	D	1
06516 West Haven, 52,851	D	3
06388 West Mystic, 3,694	H	3
* 06856 West Norwalk, 950	B	4
06880 Weston, ∆7,417	B	4
06880 Weston, 3,000	B	4
06880 Westport, ∆27,414	B	4
06896 West Redding, 1,200	B	3
06092 West Simsbury, 1,419	D	1
06093 West Suffield, 2,400	E	1
06109 Wethersfield, 26,662	E	2
06517 Whitneyville, 18,458	D	3
06226 Willimantic, 14,402	G	2
† 06279 Willington, ∆3,755	F	1
06897 Wilton, ∆13,572	B	4
06897 Wilton, 4,200	B	4
06094 Winchester, ∆11,106	C	1
06094 Winchester Center, ∆350	C	1
06280 Windham, ∆19,626	G	2
06095 Windsor, ∆22,502	E	1
06096 Windsor Locks, ∆15,080	E	1
06098 Winsted, 8,954	C	1
06716 Wolcott, ∆12,495	D	2
† 06501 Woodbridge, ∆7,673	D	3
06798 Woodbury, ∆5,869	C	2
06798 Woodbury, 1,800	C	2
06798 Woodbury P.O. (North		
Woodbury), 1,342	C	2
† 06460 Woodmont, 2,400	D	3
06281 Woodstock, ∆4,311	H	1
† 06492 Yalesville, 3,500	D	3
06389 Yantic, 1,200	G	2

AREA 5,009 sq. mi.
POPULATION 3,032,217
CAPITAL Hartford
LARGEST CITY Hartford
HIGHEST POINT Mt. Frissell (S. Slope) 2,380 ft.
SETTLED IN 1635
ADMITTED TO UNION January 9, 1788
POPULAR NAME Constitution State; Nutmeg State
STATE FLOWER Mountain Laurel
STATE BIRD Robin

Agriculture, Industry and Resources

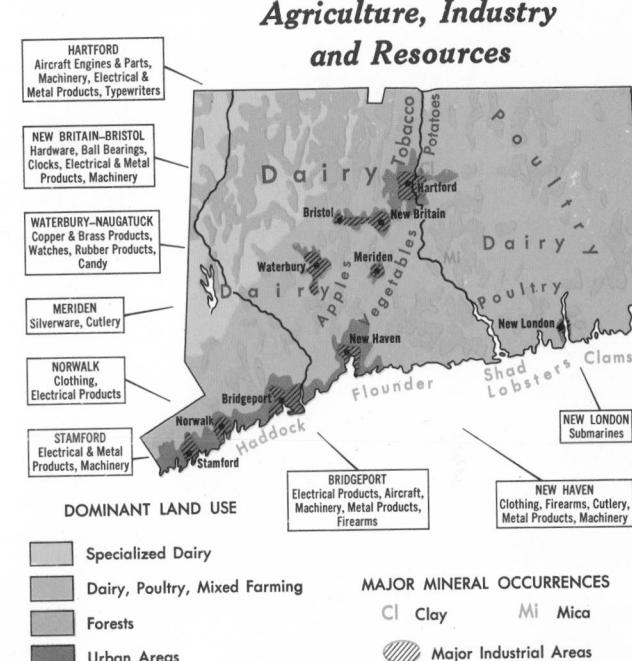

HARTFORD Aircraft Engines & Parts, Machinery, Electrical & Metal Products, Typewriters

NEW BRITAIN–BRISTOL Hardware, Ball Bearings, Clocks, Electrical & Metal Products, Machinery

WATERBURY–NAUGATUCK Copper & Brass Products, Watches, Rubber Products, Candy

MERIDEN Silverware, Cutlery

NORWALK Clothing, Electrical Products

STAMFORD Electrical & Metal Products, Machinery

BRIDGEPORT Electrical Products, Aircraft, Machinery, Metal Products, Firearms

NEW LONDON Submarines

NEW HAVEN Clothing, Firearms, Cutlery, Metal Products, Machinery

DOMINANT LAND USE

- Specialized Dairy
- Dairy, Poultry, Mixed Farming
- Forests
- Urban Areas

MAJOR MINERAL OCCURRENCES
Cl Clay   Mi Mica

Major Industrial Areas

Bark whaler "Charles W. Morgan," on view at Mystic, Connecticut, covered more miles and caught more whales than any other ship of her kind.

Edmund V. Ballman

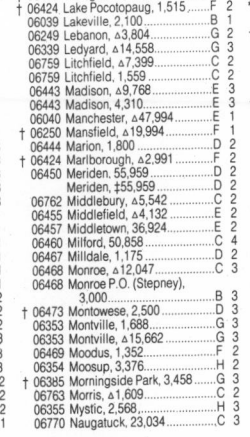

† 06254 Franklin, ∆1,356	G	2
06335 Gales Ferry, 6,200	G	3
06829 Georgetown, 1,101	B	4
06033 Glastonbury, ∆20,651	E	2
06756 Goshen, ∆1,351	C	1
06035 Granby, ∆6,150	D	1
† 06430 Greenfield Hill, 2,500	B	4
06436 Greens Farms, 3,147	B	4
06830 Greenwich, ∆59,755	A	4
06340 Groton, ∆38,523	G	3
06340 Groton, 8,933	G	3
06437 Guilford, ∆12,033	E	3
06437 Guilford, 3,632	E	3
06438 Haddam, ∆4,934	E	3
06438 Haddam, 950	E	3
06514 Hamden, ∆49,357	D	3
06247 Hampton, ∆1,129	G	1
* 06101 Hartford (cap.), 158,017	E	1
Hartford, ‡663,891	E	1
† 06091 Hartland, ∆1,303	C	1
06790 Harwinton, ∆4,318	C	1
06082 Hazardville, 10,000	E	1
06248 Hebron, ∆3,815	F	2
06441 Higganum, 2,600	E	2
† 06108 Hockanum, 6,500	F	1
06484 Huntington, 2,000	C	3
06442 Ivoryton, 1,500	F	3
06351 Jewett City, 3,372	H	2
06037 Kensington, 6,000	E	2
06757 Kent, ∆1,990	B	2
† 06241 Killingly, ∆13,573	H	1

06413 Killingworth, ∆2,435	E	3
† 06424 Lake Pocotopaug, 1,515	F	2
06039 Lakeville, 2,100	B	1
06249 Lebanon, ∆3,804	G	2
06339 Ledyard, ∆14,558	G	3
06759 Litchfield, ∆7,399	C	2
06759 Litchfield, 1,559	C	2
06443 Madison, ∆9,768	E	3
06443 Madison, 4,310	E	3
06040 Manchester, ∆47,994	E	1
† 06250 Mansfield, ∆19,994	F	1
06444 Marion, 1,800	D	2
† 06424 Marlborough, ∆2,991	F	2
06450 Meriden, 55,959	D	2
Meriden, ‡55,999	D	2
06762 Middlebury, ∆5,542	C	2
06455 Middlefield, ∆4,132	E	2
06457 Middletown, 36,924	E	2
06460 Milford, 50,858	C	4
06467 Milldale, 1,175	D	2
06468 Monroe, ∆12,047	C	3
06468 Monroe P.O. (Stepney),		
2,300	B	3
† 06473 Montowese, 2,500	D	3
06353 Montville, 1,688	G	3
06353 Montville, ∆15,662	G	2
06469 Moodus, 1,352	F	2
06354 Moosup, 3,376	H	2
† 06385 Morningside Park, 3,458	G	3
06763 Morris, ∆1,609	C	2
06355 Mystic, 2,568	H	3
06770 Naugatuck, 23,034	C	3

‡ Population of metropolitan area.
∆ Population of town or township.
† Zip of nearest p.o.
* Multiple zips

FLORIDA

SCALE
0 5 10   20   30   40   50 MI.
0 5 10 20 30 40 50 KM.

State Capitals............⊛
County Seats.............⊚
Canals...................

© C.S. HAMMOND & CO., N.Y.

WESTERN PART OF
FLORIDA

Same scale as main map

AREA 58,560 sq. mi.
POPULATION 6,789,443
CAPITAL Tallahassee
LARGEST CITY Jacksonville
HIGHEST POINT 345 ft. (Walton County)
SETTLED IN 1565
ADMITTED TO UNION March 3, 1845
POPULAR NAME Sunshine State; Peninsula State
STATE FLOWER Orange Blossom
STATE BIRD Mockingbird

COUNTIES

Alachua, 104,764 ....D 2
Baker, 9,242 ....D 1
Bay, 75,283 ....C 6
Bradford, 14,625 ....D 2
Brevard, 230,006 ....F 3
Broward, 620,100 ....F 5
Calhoun, 7,624 ....C 6
Charlotte, 27,559 ....E 5
Citrus, 19,196 ....D 3
Clay, 32,059 ....E 2
Collier, 38,040 ....E 5
Columbia, 25,250 ....D 1
Dade, 1,287,792 ....F 6
De Soto, 13,060 ....E 4
Dixie, 5,480 ....C 2
Duval, 528,865 ....E 1
Escambia, 205,334 ....B 6
Flagler, 4,454 ....E 2
Franklin, 7,065 ....B 2
Gadsden, 39,184 ....B 1
Gilchrist, 3,551 ....D 2
Glades, 3,669 ....E 5
Gulf, 10,096 ....D 7
Hamilton, 7,787 ....D 1
Hardee, 14,889 ....E 4
Hendry, 11,859 ....E 5
Hernando, 17,004 ....D 3
Highlands, 29,507 ....E 4
Hillsborough, 490,265 ....D 4
Holmes, 10,720 ....C 5
Indian River, 35,992 ....F 4
Jackson, 34,434 ....D 5
Jefferson, 8,778 ....C 1
Lafayette, 2,892 ....C 2
Lake, 69,305 ....E 3
Lee, 105,216 ....E 5
Leon, 103,047 ....B 1
Levy, 12,756 ....D 2
Liberty, 3,379 ....B 1
Madison, 13,481 ....C 1
Manatee, 97,115 ....D 4
Marion, 69,030 ....D 2
Martin, 28,035 ....F 4
Monroe, 52,586 ....E 7
Nassau, 20,626 ....E 1
Okaloosa, 88,187 ....C 6
Okeechobee, 11,233 ....F 4
Orange, 344,311 ....E 3
Osceola, 25,267 ....E 3
Palm Beach, 348,753 ....F 5
Pasco, 75,955 ....D 3
Pinellas, 522,329 ....D 4
Polk, 227,222 ....E 4
Putnam, 36,290 ....E 2
Saint Johns, 50,727 ....F 4
Saint Lucie, 50,836 ....F 4
Santa Rosa, 37,741 ....B 6
Sarasota, 120,413 ....D 4
Seminole, 83,692 ....E 3
Sumter, 14,839 ....D 3

Suwannee, 15,559 ....C 1
Taylor, 13,641 ....C 1
Union, 8,112 ....D 1
Volusia, 169,487 ....E 2
Wakulla, 6,308 ....B 1
Walton, 16,087 ....C 6
Washington, 11,453 ....C 6

CITIES and TOWNS

Zip	Name/Pop.	Key
32615	Alachua, 2,252	D 2
32420	Alford, 402	D 6
32421	Altha, 423	A 1
32702	Altoona, 800	E 3
33820	Alturas, 468	E 4
33920	Alva, 900	E 4
33501	Anna Maria, 1,137	D 4
32617	Anthony, 500	D 2
32320	Apalachicola⊙, 3,102	A 2
33570	Apollo Beach, 1,042	C 3
32703	Apopka, 4,045	E 3
33821	Arcadia⊙, 6,658	E 4
32618	Archer, 898	D 2
32422	Argyle, 155	C 6
33502	Aripeka, 300	D 3
†32327	Arran, 160	B 1
32705	Astatula, 388	E 3
32002	Astor, 300	E 2
33823	Auburndale, 5,386	E 4
†32344	Aucilla, 150	C 1
33825	Avon Park, 6,712	E 4
33827	Babson Park, 950	E 4
32530	Bagdad, 850	B 6
32531	Baker, 500	C 5
32234	Baldwin, 1,272	E 1
†33101	Bal Harbour, 2,038	C 4
32005	Barberville, 300	E 2
†32533	Barrineau Park, 150	B 6
32532	Barth, 200	B 6
33830	Barterow⊙, 12,891	E 4
32423	Bascom, 200	A 1
33428	Basinger, 300	F 4
†33101	Bay Harbour Islands, 4,619	B 4
33504	Bay Pines, 1,100	D 4
†33902	Bayshore, 150	E 5
36502	Bay Springs, 125	B 6
33429	Bean City, 155	F 5
33578	Bee Ridge, 2,100	D 4
32619	Bell, 227	D 2
33540	Belleair, 2,962	B 2
†33540	Belleair Beach, 952	B 2
33540	Belleair Bluffs, 1,910	B 2
33430	Belle Glade, 15,949	F 5
†33430	Belle Glade Camp, 1,892	F 5
†32801	Belle Isle, 2,705	E 3
32620	Belleview, 916	D 2
33152	Biscayne Park, 2,717	B 4
†32801	Bithlo, 684	E 3
32424	Blountstown⊙, 2,384	A 1
†32535	Bluffsprings, 160	B 6
33921	Boca Grande, 600	D 5

33432	Boca Raton, 28,506	F 5
33922	Bokeelia, 750	D 5
32425	Bonifay⊙, 2,068	C 5
33923	Bonita Springs, 1,932	E 5
32007	Bostwick, 500	E 2
33834	Bowling Green, 1,357	E 4
33435	Boynton Beach, 18,115	F 5
33505	Bradenton⊙, 21,040	D 4
33510	Bradenton Beach, 1,370	D 4
33835	Bradley, 1,276	D 4
33511	Brandon, 12,749	D 4
32008	Branford, 820	D 2
33435	Briny Breezes, 481	G 5
32321	Bristol⊙, 626	B 1
32621	Bronson⊙, 698	D 2
32622	Brooker, 340	D 2
33512	Brooksville⊙, 4,060	D 3
33101	Browns Village, 23,442	B 4

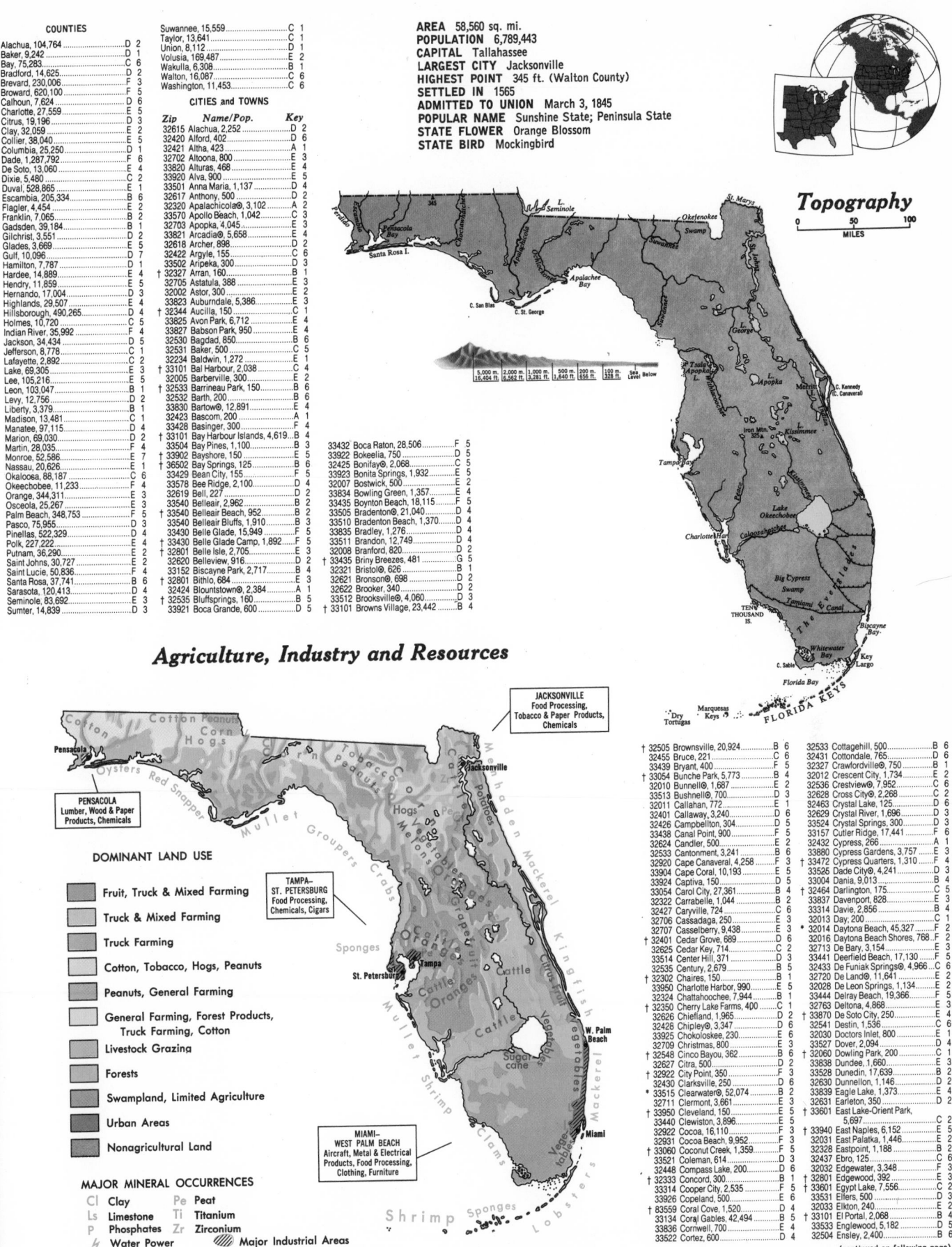

Topography

0   50   100
MILES

5,000 m. / 2,000 m. / 1,000 m. / 500 m. / 200 m. / 100 m. / See
16,404 ft. / 6,562 ft. / 3,281 ft. / 1,640 ft. / 656 ft. / 328 ft. / Level Below

Agriculture, Industry and Resources

JACKSONVILLE
Food Processing,
Tobacco & Paper Products,
Chemicals

PENSACOLA
Lumber, Wood & Paper
Products, Chemicals

TAMPA–
ST. PETERSBURG
Food Processing,
Chemicals, Cigars

MIAMI–
WEST PALM BEACH
Aircraft, Metal & Electrical
Products, Food Processing,
Clothing, Furniture

DOMINANT LAND USE

Fruit, Truck & Mixed Farming

Truck & Mixed Farming

Truck Farming

Cotton, Tobacco, Hogs, Peanuts

Peanuts, General Farming

General Farming, Forest Products,
Truck Farming, Cotton

Livestock Grazing

Forests

Swampland, Limited Agriculture

Urban Areas

Nonagricultural Land

MAJOR MINERAL OCCURRENCES

Cl	Clay	Pe	Peat
Ls	Limestone	Ti	Titanium
P	Phosphates	Zr	Zirconium
⚡	Water Power		

▨ Major Industrial Areas

†32505	Brownsville, 20,924	B 6
32455	Bruce, 221	C 6
33439	Bryant, 400	F 5
†33054	Bunche Park, 5,773	B 4
32010	Bunnell⊙, 1,687	E 2
33513	Bushnell⊙, 700	D 3
32011	Callahan, 772	E 1
32401	Callaway, 3,240	D 6
32426	Campbellton, 304	D 5
33438	Canal Point, 900	F 5
32624	Candler, 500	E 2
32533	Cantonment, 3,241	B 6
32920	Cape Canaveral, 4,258	F 3
33904	Cape Coral, 10,193	E 5
33924	Captiva, 150	D 5
†33054	Carol City, 27,361	B 4
32322	Carrabelle, 1,044	B 2
32427	Caryville, 724	C 6
32706	Cassadaga, 250	E 3
32707	Casselberry, 9,438	E 3
†32401	Cedar Grove, 689	D 6
32625	Cedar Key, 714	C 2
33514	Center Hill, 371	D 3
32535	Century, 2,679	B 5
†32302	Chaires, 150	B 1
33950	Charlotte Harbor, 990	E 5
32324	Chattahoochee, 7,944	B 1
†32350	Cherry Lake Farms, 400	C 1
32626	Chiefland, 1,965	D 2
32428	Chipley⊙, 3,347	D 6
33925	Chokoloskee, 230	E 6
32709	Christmas, 800	E 3
†32548	Cinco Bayou, 362	B 6
32627	Citra, 500	D 2
†32922	City Point, 350	F 3
32430	Clarksville, 250	D 6
*33515	Clearwater⊙, 52,074	B 2
32711	Clermont, 3,661	E 3
†33950	Cleveland, 150	E 5
33440	Clewiston, 3,896	E 5
32922	Cocoa, 16,110	F 3
32931	Cocoa Beach, 9,952	F 3
33060	Coconut Creek, 1,359	F 6
33521	Coleman, 614	D 3
32448	Compass Lake, 200	D 6
†32333	Concord, 300	B 1
33314	Cooper City, 2,535	F 6
33926	Copeland, 500	E 6
†83559	Coral Cove, 1,520	C 4
33134	Coral Gables, 42,494	B 5
33836	Cornwell, 700	D 4
33522	Cortez, 600	D 4

32533	Cottagehill, 500	B 6
32431	Cottondale, 765	D 6
32327	Crawfordville⊙, 750	B 1
32012	Crescent City, 1,734	E 2
32536	Crestview⊙, 7,952	C 6
32628	Cross City⊙, 2,268	C 2
32463	Crystal Lake, 125	D 6
32629	Crystal River, 1,696	D 3
33524	Crystal Springs, 300	D 3
33157	Cutler Ridge, 17,441	F 6
32432	Cypress, 266	A 1
33880	Cypress Gardens, 3,757	E 3
†33472	Cypress Quarters, 1,310	F 4
33525	Dade City⊙, 4,241	D 3
33004	Dania, 9,013	F 6
32464	Darlington, 175	C 5
33837	Davenport, 828	E 3
33314	Davie, 2,856	B 4
32013	Day, 200	C 1
*32014	Daytona Beach, 45,327	F 2
32016	Daytona Beach Shores, 768	F 2
32713	De Bary, 3,154	E 3
33441	Deerfield Beach, 17,130	F 6
32433	De Funiak Springs⊙, 4,966	C 6
32720	De Land⊙, 11,641	E 2
32028	De Leon Springs, 1,134	E 2
33444	Delray Beach, 19,366	F 5
32763	Deltona, 4,868	E 3
†33870	De Soto City, 250	E 4
32541	Destin, 1,536	C 6
32030	Doctors Inlet, 800	E 1
33527	Dover, 2,094	D 4
†32060	Dowling Park, 200	C 1
33838	Dundee, 1,660	E 3
33528	Dunedin, 17,639	D 2
32630	Dunnellon, 1,146	D 2
33839	Eagle Lake, 1,373	E 4
32631	Earleton, 350	D 2
†33601	East Lake-Orient Park, 5,697	C 2
†33940	East Naples, 6,152	E 5
32031	East Palatka, 1,446	E 2
32328	Eastpoint, 1,188	B 2
32437	Ebro, 125	C 6
32032	Edgewater, 3,348	F 3
†32801	Edgewood, 392	E 3
†33601	Egypt Lake, 7,556	C 2
33531	Elfers, 500	D 3
32033	Elkton, 240	E 2
†33101	El Portal, 2,068	B 4
33533	Englewood, 5,182	D 5
32504	Ensley, 2,400	B 6

(continued on following page)

(continued)

Joseph Brocas — Shostal Associates

Over 150 miles of inland waterways provide a Venetian atmosphere in the modern city of Fort Lauderdale, Florida.

† 32010 Espanola, 300 .... E 2
33928 Estero, 950 .... E 5
32425 Esto, 210 .... C 5
32726 Eustis, 6,722 .... E 3
33929 Everglades City, 462 .... E 6
† 32601 Fairbanks, 380 .... D 2
† 32804 Fairvilla, 950 .... E 3
33930 Felda, 125 .... E 5
32948 Fellsmere, 813 .... F 4
32034 Fernandina Beach⊙, 6,955 .... E 1
† 33301 Fern Crest Village, 1,009 .... B 4
32036 Flagler Beach, 1,042 .... E 2
32635 Florahome, 400 .... E 2
32636 Floral City, 975 .... D 3
33030 Florida City, 5,133 .... F 6
† 32570 Floridatown, 297 .... B 6
† 32569 Florosa, 200 .... B 6
† 32347 Foley, 500 .... C 1
† 33935 Fort Denaud, 300 .... E 5
† 33472 Fort Drum, 100 .... F 4
33834 Fort Green, 300 .... E 4
* 33301 Fort Lauderdale⊙, 139,590 .... C 4
Fort Lauderdale-Hollywood, ‡620,100 .... C 4
32637 Fort McCoy, 900 .... E 2
33841 Fort Meade, 4,374 .... E 4
* 33901 Fort Myers⊙, 27,351 .... E 5
33931 Fort Myers Beach, 4,305 .... E 5
33842 Fort Ogden, 700 .... E 4
33450 Fort Pierce⊙, 29,721 .... F 4
32548 Fort Walton Beach, 19,994 .... C 6
32038 Fort White, 365 .... D 2
32438 Fountain, 650 .... D 6
32439 Freeport, 950 .... C 6
† 32430 Frink, 275 .... D 6
33843 Frostproof, 2,814 .... E 4
32731 Fruitland Park, 1,359 .... D 3
33578 Fruitville, 1,531 .... D 4
32601 Gainesville⊙, 64,510 .... D 2
32732 Geneva, 950 .... E 3
32039 Georgetown, 687 .... E 2
33534 Gibsonton, 1,900 .... C 3
32960 Gifford, 5,772 .... F 4
32040 Glen Saint Mary, 357 .... D 1
32742 Glenwood, 400 .... E 2
33160 Golden Beach, 849 .... C 4
33940 Golden Gate, 1,410 .... E 5
† 33455 Gomez, 400 .... F 4
32560 Gonzalez, 750 .... B 6
33933 Goodland, 500 .... E 6
† 32502 Goulding, 500 .... B 6
33170 Goulds, 6,690 .... F 6
32440 Graceville, 2,560 .... D 5
32042 Graham, 150 .... D 2
32638 Grandin, 150 .... E 2
32442 Grand Ridge, 512 .... A 1
32949 Grant, 500 .... F 4
33440 Greenacres City, 1,731 .... F 5
32043 Green Cove Springs⊙, 3,857 .... E 2
32330 Greensboro, 716 .... B 1
32331 Greenville, 1,141 .... C 1
32443 Greenwood, 515 .... A 1
32332 Gretna, 883 .... B 1
33533 Grove City, 1,178 .... F 5
32736 Groveland, 1,928 .... E 3
32561 Gulf Breeze, 4,190 .... B 6
32639 Gulf Hammock, 300 .... D 2
† 33552 Gulf Harbors, 1,177 .... D 3
33737 Gulfport, 9,730 .... B 3
† 33444 Gulf Stream, 408 .... F 5
† 32601 Hague, 200 .... D 2
33844 Haines City, 8,956 .... E 3
33009 Hallandale, 23,849 .... B 4
32044 Hampton, 386 .... D 2
33440 Harlem, 2,006 .... F 5
32563 Harold, 150 .... B 6
32045 Hastings, 320 .... E 2
32333 Havana, 2,022 .... B 1
32640 Hawthorne, 1,126 .... D 2
32642 Hernando, 524 .... D 3
* 33010 Hialeah, 102,297 .... B 4
† 33010 Hialeah Gardens, 492 .... B 4
33846 Highland City, 900 .... E 4
† 33515 High Point, 800 .... B 3
32643 High Springs, 2,787 .... D 2
32401 Hiland Park, 3,691 .... C 6
† 33827 Hillcrest Heights, 154 .... E 4
32046 Hilliard, 1,205 .... E 1
† 32327 Hilliardville, 150 .... B 1
† 33060 Hillsboro Beach, 713 .... F 5
† 32333 Hinson, 250 .... B 1
33455 Hobe Sound, 2,029 .... F 4
32645 Holder, 134 .... D 3
32047 Hollister, 500 .... E 2
32017 Holly Hill, 8,191 .... E 2
* 33020 Hollywood, 106,873 .... B 4
† 33020 Hollywood Ridge Farms, 302 .... B 4
33509 Holmes Beach, 2,699 .... D 4
32564 Holt, 850 .... C 6
33030 Homestead, 13,674 .... F 6
32646 Homosassa, 850 .... D 3
32647 Homosassa Springs, 550 .... D 3
32334 Hosford, 975 .... B 1
32737 Howey In The Hills, 466 .... E 3
33568 Hudson, 2,278 .... D 3
† 33460 Hypoluxo, 336 .... F 5
33934 Immokalee, 3,764 .... E 5
32901 Indialantic, 2,685 .... F 3
32935 Indian Harbour Beach, 5,371 .... F 3
33535 Indian Rocks Beach, 2,666 .... B 3
† 33535 Indian Rocks Beach South Shore, 791 .... B 3
33456 Indiantown, 2,283 .... F 4
32649 Inglis, 449 .... D 2
33848 Intercession City, 600 .... E 3
32048 Interlachen, 478 .... E 2
32650 Inverness⊙, 2,299 .... D 3
33036 Islamorada, 1,251 .... F 7
32654 Island Grove, 200 .... D 2
* 32201 Jacksonville⊙, 528,865 .... E 1
Jacksonville, ‡528,865 .... E 1
32250 Jacksonville Beach, 12,049 .... E 1
32052 Jasper⊙, 2,221 .... D 1
32565 Jay, 646 .... B 5
32053 Jennings, 582 .... C 1
33457 Jensen Beach, 3,000 .... F 4
† 32901 June Park, 3,090 .... F 3
† 33404 Juno Beach, 747 .... F 5
33458 Jupiter, 3,136 .... F 5
† 33455 Jupiter Island, 295 .... F 4
33849 Kathleen, 900 .... D 3
32739 Kenansville, 450 .... F 4
33156 Kendall, 35,497 .... B 5
† 32670 Kendrick, 200 .... D 2
33709 Kenneth City, 3,862 .... B 3
33149 Key Biscayne, 4,563 .... B 5
33051 Key Colony Beach, 371 .... F 7
33037 Key Largo, 2,866 .... F 6
32656 Keystone Heights, 800 .... E 2
33040 Key West⊙, 27,563 .... E 7
32449 Kinard, 450 .... D 6
32741 Kissimmee⊙, 7,119 .... E 3
† 32010 Korona, 200 .... E 2
33935 La Belle⊙, 1,823 .... E 5
33537 Lacoochee, 1,380 .... D 3
32658 La Crosse, 365 .... D 2
32659 Lady Lake, 382 .... E 3
33850 Lake Alfred, 2,847 .... E 3
32054 Lake Butler⊙, 1,598 .... D 1
† 33601 Lake Carroll, 5,577 .... C 2
32055 Lake City⊙, 10,575 .... D 1
32057 Lake Como, 340 .... E 2
33459 Lake Harbor, 300 .... F 5
32744 Lake Helen, 1,303 .... E 3
32745 Lake Jem, 314 .... E 3
* 33801 Lakeland, 41,550 .... D 3
† 33601 Lake Magdalene, 9,266 .... D 3
32746 Lake Mary, 900 .... E 3
32747 Lake Monroe, 500 .... E 3
33403 Lake Park, 6,993 .... F 5
33852 Lake Placid, 656 .... E 4
† 33471 Lakeport, 375 .... E 5
33853 Lake Wales, 8,240 .... E 4
32566 Lakewood, 525 .... C 5
33460 Lake Worth, 23,714 .... G 5
32336 Lamont, 500 .... C 1
33539 Land O'Lakes, 900 .... D 3
33460 Lantana, 7,126 .... F 5
33540 Largo, 22,031 .... B 3
33308 Lauderdale-by-the-Sea, 2,879 .... C 3
† 33301 Lauderdale Lakes, 10,577 .... B 4
33313 Lauderhill, 8,465 .... B 4
32567 Laurel Hill, 418 .... C 5
33545 Laurel-Nokomis, 3,238 .... D 4
32058 Lawtey, 636 .... D 1
32661 Lecanto, 125 .... D 3
32059 Lee, 240 .... C 1
32748 Leesburg, 11,869 .... E 3
33936 Lehigh Acres, 4,394 .... E 5
33030 Leisure City, 2,900 .... F 6
† 33601 Leto, 8,458 .... C 2
33064 Lighthouse Point, 9,071 .... F 5
† 33865 Limestone, 200 .... E 4
32060 Live Oak⊙, 6,830 .... D 1
32337 Lloyd, 225 .... C 1
32662 Lochloosa, 175 .... E 2
33548 Longboat Key, 2,850 .... D 4
33001 Long Key, 150 .... F 7
32750 Longwood, 3,203 .... E 3
33857 Lorida, 950 .... E 4
33858 Loughman, 950 .... E 3
32663 Lowell, 350 .... D 2
33470 Loxahatchee, 950 .... F 5
33549 Lutz, 950 .... D 3
32444 Lynn Haven, 4,044 .... C 6
32063 Macclenny⊙, 2,733 .... D 1
33738 Madeira Beach, 4,158 .... B 3
32340 Madison⊙, 3,737 .... C 1
32751 Maitland, 7,157 .... E 3
32950 Malabar, 634 .... F 3
32445 Malone, 667 .... A 1
33550 Mango, 950 .... D 4
33050 Marathon, 4,397 .... E 7
33937 Marco, 900 .... E 6
33063 Margate, 8,867 .... F 5
32446 Marianna⊙, 6,741 .... A 1
† 32084 Marineland, 13 .... E 2
33569 Mary Esther, 3,192 .... B 6
32753 Masaryktown, 389 .... D 3
32754 Mascotte, 966 .... E 3
32066 Mayo⊙, 793 .... C 1
32068 McDavid, 500 .... B 5
32664 McIntosh, 287 .... D 2
† 33101 Medley, 351 .... B 4
32901 Melbourne, 40,236 .... F 3
32951 Melbourne Beach, 2,262 .... F 3
32666 Melrose, 950 .... D 2
† 33101 Melrose Park, 6,111 .... B 4
† 33561 Memphis, 3,207 .... D 4
32952 Merritt Island, 29,233 .... F 3
32410 Mexico Beach, 588 .... D 6
* 33101 Miami⊙, 334,859 .... B 5
Miami, ‡1,267,792 .... B 5
33139 Miami Beach, 87,072 .... C 5
† 33101 Miami Lakes, 3,500 .... B 4
33153 Miami Shores, 9,425 .... B 4
33166 Miami Springs, 13,279 .... B 5
32667 Micanopy, 759 .... D 2
† 32960 Micco, 400 .... F 4
32309 Miccosukee, 275 .... B 1
32068 Middleburg, 950 .... E 1
32343 Midway, 900 .... B 1
32537 Milligan, 950 .... C 6
32570 Milton⊙, 5,360 .... B 6
32754 Mims, 8,309 .... F 3
32755 Minneola, 878 .... E 3
33023 Miramar, 23,973 .... B 4
32577 Molino, 850 .... B 6
† 32696 Montbrook, 250 .... D 2
32344 Monticello⊙, 2,473 .... C 1
32756 Montverde, 308 .... E 3
33471 Moore Haven⊙, 974 .... E 5
32434 Mossy Head, 160 .... C 6
32757 Mount Dora, 4,543 .... E 3
32352 Mount Pleasant, 150 .... B 1
33860 Mulberry, 2,701 .... E 4
33551 Myakka City, 672 .... D 4
32506 Myrtle Grove, 16,186 .... B 6
33940 Naples⊙, 12,042 .... E 5
† 33940 Naples Park, 1,522 .... E 5
33030 Naranja, 2,900 .... F 6
32233 Neptune Beach, 2,868 .... E 1
32669 Newberry, 1,247 .... D 2
33552 New Port Richey, 6,098 .... D 3
32069 New Smyrna Beach, 10,580 .... F 2
32578 Niceville, 4,024 .... C 6
33863 Nichols, 300 .... E 4
33864 Nocatee, 950 .... E 4
33555 Nokomis-Laurel, 3,238 .... D 4
32452 Noma, 234 .... C 5
33141 North Bay Village, 4,831 .... B 4
33903 North Fort Myers, 8,798 .... E 5
33161 North Miami, 34,767 .... B 4
33161 North Miami Beach, 30,723 .... C 4
† 33940 North Naples, 3,201 .... E 5
33403 North Palm Beach, 9,035 .... F 5
33595 North Port Charlotte, 2,244 .... D 4
† 33708 North Redington Beach, 768 .... B 3
† 33054 Norwood, 14,973 .... B 4
32759 Oak Hill, 747 .... F 3
32760 Oakland, 672 .... E 3
33307 Oakland Park, 16,261 .... B 3
32071 O'Brien, 200 .... D 1
32670 Ocala⊙, 22,583 .... D 2
† 33457 Ocean Breeze, 714 .... F 4
33444 Ocean Ridge, 1,074 .... F 5
33943 Ochopee, 200 .... E 6
32761 Ocoee, 3,937 .... E 3
33556 Odessa, 500 .... D 3
33163 Ojus, 12,000 .... B 4
32762 Okahumpka, 470 .... D 3
33472 Okeechobee⊙, 3,715 .... F 4
32679 Oklawaha, 700 .... E 2
33557 Oldsmar, 1,538 .... B 2
32680 Old Town, 500 .... C 2
32072 Olustee, 400 .... D 1
33865 Ona, 236 .... E 4
33558 Oneco, 3,246 .... D 4
33054 Opa-locka, 11,902 .... B 4
32763 Orange City, 1,777 .... E 3
32681 Orange Lake, 900 .... D 2
32073 Orange Park, 7,619 .... E 1
32682 Orange Springs, 500 .... E 2
* 32801 Orlando⊙, 99,006 .... E 3
Orlando, ‡428,003 .... E 3
32074 Ormond Beach, 14,063 .... E 2
33559 Osprey, 1,115 .... D 4
32764 Osteen, 875 .... E 3
32683 Otter Creek, 400 .... D 2
32765 Oviedo, 1,870 .... E 3
32684 Oxford, 490 .... D 3
33560 Ozona, 900 .... D 3
32570 Pace, 1,776 .... B 6
33476 Pahokee, 5,663 .... F 5
32077 Palatka⊙, 9,310 .... E 2
32901 Palm Bay, 6,927 .... F 3
33480 Palm Beach, 9,086 .... G 4
† 33404 Palm Beach Shores, 1,214 .... G 5
33490 Palm City, 900 .... F 4
33561 Palmetto, 7,422 .... D 4
33563 Palm Harbor, 1,763 .... D 3
33619 Palm River-Clair Mel, 8,536 .... C 3
32935 Palm Shores, 202 .... F 3
33460 Palm Springs, 4,340 .... F 5
32346 Panacea, 950 .... B 1
32401 Panama City⊙, 32,096 .... C 6
32401 Parker, 4,212 .... C 6
33564 Parrish, 950 .... D 4
32538 Paxton, 243 .... C 5
† 33023 Pembroke Park, 2,949 .... B 4
33023 Pembroke Pines, 15,520 .... B 4
32079 Penney Farms, 561 .... E 2
* 32501 Pensacola⊙, 59,507 .... B 6
Pensacola, ‡243,075 .... B 6
33157 Perrine, 10,257 .... F 6
32347 Perry⊙, 7,701 .... C 1
33867 Pierce, 500 .... E 4
32080 Pierson, 654 .... E 2
33565 Pinellas Park, 22,287 .... B 3
32350 Pinetta, 300 .... C 1
† 33042 Pirates Cove, 150 .... E 7
33946 Placida, 250 .... D 5
33314 Plantation, 23,523 .... B 4
33566 Plant City, 15,451 .... D 3
32768 Plymouth, 950 .... E 3
33868 Polk City, 151 .... E 3
32081 Pomona Park, 578 .... E 2
* 33060 Pompano Beach, 37,724 .... F 5
32455 Ponce de Leon, 288 .... C 6
† 32019 Ponce Inlet, 328 .... F 2
32082 Ponte Vedra Beach, 2,100 .... E 1
33950 Port Charlotte, 10,769 .... D 5
† 32439 Portland, 228 .... C 6
† 33438 Port Mayaca, 400 .... F 5
32019 Port Orange, 3,781 .... F 2
33568 Port Richey, 1,259 .... D 3
32456 Port Saint Joe, 4,401 .... D 6
33450 Port Saint Lucie, 330 .... F 4
33492 Port Salerno, 1,161 .... F 4
33171 Princeton, 1,900 .... F 6
† 33619 Progress, 1,328 .... C 3
† 32061 Providence, 150 .... D 2
33950 Punta Gorda⊙, 3,879 .... E 5
32351 Quincy⊙, 8,334 .... B 1
32083 Raiford, 500 .... D 1
† 32696 Raleigh, 275 .... D 2
32455 Redbay, 150 .... C 6
32686 Reddick, 305 .... D 2
33708 Redington Beach, 1,583 .... B 3
† 33708 Redington Shores, 1,733 .... B 3
† 33599 Richland, 928 .... D 3
† 33158 Richmond Heights, 6,663 .... F 6
33569 Riverview, 2,225 .... D 4
33404 Riviera Beach, 21,401 .... G 5
32955 Rockledge, 10,523 .... F 3
32957 Roseland, 550 .... F 4
32447 Round Lake, 275 .... D 6
33570 Ruskin, 2,414 .... C 3
33572 Safety Harbor, 3,103 .... B 2
32084 Saint Augustine⊙, 12,352 .... E 2
32084 Saint Augustine Beach, 632 .... E 2
33573 Saint Catherine, 350 .... D 3
32769 Saint Cloud, 5,041 .... E 3
33956 Saint James City, 500 .... D 5
33574 Saint Leo, 1,145 .... D 3
† 33450 Saint Lucie, 428 .... F 4
† 32355 Saint Marks, 366 .... B 1
* 33701 Saint Petersburg, 216,232 .... B 3
33736 Saint Petersburg Beach, 8,024 .... B 3
32356 Salem, 150 .... C 2
33505 Samoset, 4,070 .... D 4
† 32069 Samsula, 270 .... E 2
33576 San Antonio, 473 .... D 3
32087 Sanderson, 150 .... D 1
32771 Sanford⊙, 17,393 .... E 3
33957 Sanibel, 750 .... D 5
32088 San Mateo, 975 .... E 2
† 32670 Santos, 150 .... D 2
* 33577 Sarasota⊙, 40,237 .... D 4
32935 Satellite Beach, 6,558 .... F 3
32089 Satsuma, 610 .... E 2
32775 Scottsmoor, 850 .... F 3
† 33301 Sea Ranch Lakes, 660 .... C 3
32958 Sebastian, 825 .... F 4
33870 Sebring⊙, 7,223 .... E 4
33584 Seffner, 2,000 .... D 4
33540 Seminole, 2,410 .... B 3
32090 Seville, 500 .... E 2
† 33457 Sewalls Point, 298 .... F 4
32579 Shalimar, 578 .... C 6
† 32628 Shamrock, 200 .... C 2
32959 Sharpes, 427 .... F 3
32688 Silver Springs, 500 .... D 2
32460 Sneads, 1,550 .... B 1
32358 Sopchoppy, 460 .... B 1
32776 Sorrento, 500 .... E 3
33493 South Bay, 2,958 .... F 5
32021 South Daytona, 497 .... F 2
† 36441 South Flomaton, 329 .... B 5
33143 South Miami, 19,571 .... B 5
33707 South Pasadena, 2,063 .... B 3
† 32401 Southport, 1,560 .... C 6
32690 Sparr, 450 .... D 2
32401 Springfield, 5,949 .... D 6
32091 Starke⊙, 4,848 .... D 2
32359 Steinhatchee, 800 .... C 2
33494 Stuart⊙, 4,820 .... F 4
32335 Sumatra, 150 .... B 1
32691 Summerfield, 450 .... D 2
33042 Summerland Key, 350 .... E 7
33586 Sun City, 2,143 .... D 4
† 33450 Sunland Gardens, 1,900 .... F 4
33160 Sunny Isles, 950 .... C 4
† 33577 Sunnyland, 4,900 .... D 4
32461 Sunnyside, 370 .... C 6
33313 Sunrise Golf Village, 7,403 .... B 4
33154 Surfside, 3,614 .... B 4
32692 Suwannee, 203 .... C 2
† 33144 Sweetwater, 3,307 .... B 5
† 33601 Sweetwater Creek, 19,453 .... B 2
† 32043 Switzerland, 500 .... E 1
32809 Taft, 1,183 .... E 3
* 32301 Tallahassee (cap.)⊙, 71,897 .... B 1
Tallahassee, ‡103,047 .... B 1
† 33301 Tamarac, 5,078 .... B 3
* 33601 Tampa⊙, 277,767 .... C 2
Tampa-Saint Petersburg, ‡1,012,594 .... C 2
33589 Tarpon Springs, 7,118 .... D 3
32778 Tavares⊙, 3,261 .... E 3
33070 Tavernier, 900 .... F 6
32360 Telogia, 300 .... B 1
33617 Temple Terrace, 7,347 .... C 2
33458 Tequesta, 2,642 .... F 5
33591 Terra Ceia, 450 .... D 4
33592 Thonotosassa, 900 .... D 3
33905 Tice, 7,254 .... E 5
32780 Titusville⊙, 30,515 .... F 3
33740 Treasure Island, 6,120 .... B 3
32693 Trenton⊙, 1,074 .... D 2
33593 Trilby, 930 .... D 3
32784 Umatilla, 1,600 .... E 3
32580 Valparaiso, 6,504 .... C 6
33595 Venice, 6,648 .... D 4
33960 Venus, 300 .... E 4
32462 Vernon, 691 .... C 6
32960 Vero Beach⊙, 11,908 .... F 4
† 32548 Villa Tasso, 200 .... C 6
† 33166 Virginia Gardens, 2,524 .... B 5
32970 Wabasso, 950 .... F 4
32361 Wacissa, 275 .... B 1
† 32327 Wakulla, 225 .... B 1
32694 Waldo, 800 .... D 2
32568 Walnut Hill, 500 .... B 5
32507 Warrington, 15,848 .... B 6
† 32055 Watertown, 3,624 .... D 1
33873 Wauchula⊙, 3,007 .... E 4
32463 Wausau, 288 .... D 6
33877 Waverly, 1,172 .... E 4
33597 Webster, 739 .... D 3
32695 Weirsdale, 995 .... D 3
32093 Welaka, 496 .... E 2
32094 Wellborn, 600 .... D 1
32401 Westbay, 350 .... C 6
† 32901 West Melbourne, 3,050 .... F 3
† 33101 West Miami, 5,494 .... B 5
* 33401 West Palm Beach⊙, 57,375 .... F 5
West Palm Beach, ‡348,753 .... F 5
32401 West Panama City Beach, 1,052 .... C 6
32505 West Pensacola, 20,924 .... B 6
32464 Westville, 475 .... C 6
† 33101 Westwood Lakes, 12,811 .... B 5
32465 Wewahitchka⊙, 1,733 .... D 6
† 32465 White City, 600 .... F 4
32096 White Springs, 767 .... D 1
32785 Wildwood, 2,082 .... D 3
32696 Williston, 1,939 .... D 2
33305 Wilton Manors, 10,948 .... B 3
33598 Wimauma, 650 .... D 4
32786 Windermere, 894 .... E 3
32971 Winter Beach, 350 .... F 4
32787 Winter Garden, 5,153 .... E 3
33880 Winter Haven, 16,136 .... E 3
32789 Winter Park, 21,895 .... E 3
32362 Woodville, 900 .... B 1
32697 Worthington Springs, 214 .... D 2
32797 Yalaha, 675 .... E 3
32698 Yankeetown, 490 .... D 2
32466 Youngstown, 400 .... D 6
32097 Yulee, 950 .... E 1
32798 Zellwood, 550 .... E 3
33599 Zephyrhills, 3,369 .... D 3
33890 Zolfo Springs, 1,117 .... E 4

⊙ County seat.
‡ Population of metropolitan area.
† Zip of nearest p.o.
* Multiple zips

Using local pines for pulpwood, this plant in Augusta, Georgia, is turning out paper for milk cartons.

A. D'Arazien — Shostal Associates

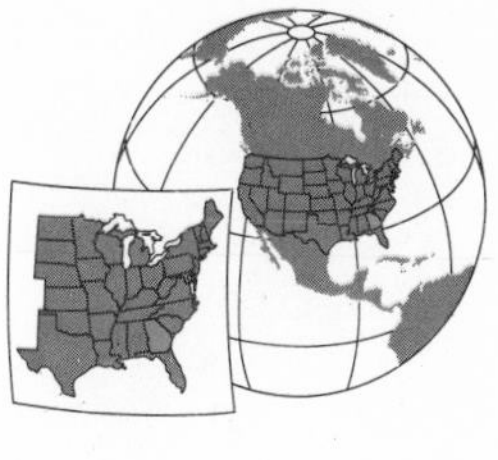

AREA 58,876 sq. mi.
POPULATION 4,589,575
CAPITAL Atlanta
LARGEST CITY Atlanta
HIGHEST POINT Brasstown Bald 4,784 ft.
SETTLED IN 1733
ADMITTED TO UNION January 2, 1788
POPULAR NAME Empire State of the South; Peach State
STATE FLOWER Cherokee Rose
STATE BIRD Brown Thrasher

COUNTIES

Appling, 12,726 H 7
Atkinson, 5,879 G 8
Bacon, 8,233 G 7
Baker, 3,875 D 8
Baldwin, 34,240 F 4
Banks, 6,833 E 2
Barrow, 16,859 E 2
Bartow, 32,663 C 2
Ben Hill, 13,171 F 7
Berrien, 11,556 F 8
Bibb, 143,418 E 5
Bleckley, 10,291 F 6
Brantley, 5,940 J 8
Brooks, 13,739 E 9
Bryan, 6,539 K 6
Bulloch, 31,585 J 6
Burke, 18,255 J 4
Butts, 10,560 E 4
Calhoun, 6,606 C 7
Camden, 11,334 J 9
Candler, 6,412 H 6
Carroll, 45,404 B 3
Catoosa, 28,271 B 1
Charlton, 5,680 H 9
Chatham, 187,767 K 6
Chattahoochee, 25,813 C 6
Chattooga, 20,541 B 1
Cherokee, 31,059 D 2
Clarke, 65,177 F 3
Clay, 3,636 B 7
Clayton, 98,043 D 3
Clinch, 6,405 G 9
Cobb, 196,793 C 3
Coffee, 22,828 G 8
Colquitt, 32,200 E 8
Columbia, 22,327 H 3
Cook, 12,129 F 8
Coweta, 32,310 C 4
Crawford, 5,748 E 5
Crisp, 18,087 E 7
Dade, 9,910 A 1
Dawson, 3,639 D 2
Decatur, 22,310 C 9
De Kalb, 415,387 D 3
Dodge, 15,658 F 6
Dooly, 10,404 E 6
Dougherty, 89,639 D 7
Douglas, 28,659 C 3
Early, 12,682 C 8
Echols, 1,924 G 9
Effingham, 13,632 K 6
Elbert, 17,262 G 2
Emanuel, 18,189 H 5
Evans, 7,290 J 6
Fannin, 13,357 D 1
Fayette, 11,364 C 4
Floyd, 73,742 B 2
Forsyth, 16,928 D 2
Franklin, 12,784 F 2
Fulton, 607,592 D 3
Gilmer, 8,956 D 1
Glascock, 2,280 G 4
Glynn, 50,528 J 8
Gordon, 23,570 C 2
Grady, 17,826 D 9
Greene, 10,212 F 3
Gwinnett, 72,349 D 2
Habersham, 20,691 E 1
Hall, 59,405 E 2
Hancock, 9,019 G 4
Haralson, 15,927 B 3
Harris, 11,520 C 5
Hart, 15,814 G 2
Heard, 5,354 B 4
Henry, 23,724 D 4
Houston, 62,924 E 6
Irwin, 8,036 F 7
Jackson, 21,093 E 2
Jasper, 5,760 E 4
Jeff Davis, 9,425 G 7
Jefferson, 17,174 H 4
Jenkins, 8,332 J 5
Johnson, 7,727 G 5
Jones, 12,218 E 5
Lamar, 10,688 D 4
Lanier, 5,031 F 8
Laurens, 32,738 G 6
Lee, 7,044 D 7
Liberty, 17,569 J 7
Lincoln, 5,895 H 3
Long, 3,746 J 7
Lowndes, 55,112 F 9
Lumpkin, 8,728 D 1
Macon, 12,933 D 6
Madison, 13,517 F 2
Marion, 5,099 C 6
McDuffie, 15,276 H 4
McIntosh, 7,371 K 7
Meriwether, 19,461 C 4
Miller, 6,397 C 8
Mitchell, 18,956 D 8
Monroe, 10,991 E 4
Montgomery, 6,099 G 6
Morgan, 9,904 F 3
Murray, 12,986 C 1
Muscogee, 167,377 C 6
Newton, 26,282 E 3
Oconee, 7,915 F 3
Oglethorpe, 7,598 F 3
Paulding, 17,520 C 3
Peach, 15,990 E 5
Pickens, 9,620 D 2
Pierce, 9,281 H 8
Pike, 7,316 D 4
Polk, 29,656 B 3
Pulaski, 8,066 E 6
Putnam, 8,394 F 4
Quitman, 2,180 B 7
Rabun, 8,327 F 1
Randolph, 8,734 C 7
Richmond, 162,437 H 4
Rockdale, 18,152 D 3
Schley, 3,097 D 6
Screven, 12,591 J 5
Seminole, 7,059 C 9
Spalding, 39,514 D 4
Stephens, 20,331 F 1
Stewart, 6,511 C 6
Sumter, 26,931 D 6
Talbot, 6,625 C 5
Taliaferro, 2,423 G 3
Tattnall, 16,557 J 6
Taylor, 7,865 D 5
Telfair, 11,381 G 7
Terrell, 11,416 D 7
Thomas, 34,515 E 9
Tift, 27,288 E 7
Toombs, 19,151 H 6
Towns, 4,565 E 1
Treutlen, 5,647 G 6
Troup, 44,466 B 4
Turner, 8,790 E 7
Twiggs, 8,222 F 5
Union, 6,811 E 1
Upson, 23,505 D 5
Walker, 50,691 B 1
Walton, 23,404 E 3
Ware, 33,525 H 8
Warren, 6,669 G 4
Washington, 17,480 G 4
Wayne, 17,858 J 7
Webster, 2,362 C 6
Wheeler, 4,596 G 6
White, 7,742 E 1
Whitfield, 55,108 B 1
Wilcox, 6,998 F 7
Wilkes, 10,184 G 3
Wilkinson, 9,393 F 5
Worth, 14,770 E 8

CITIES and TOWNS

Zip *Name/Pop.* *Key*

31001 Abbeville⊙, 781 F 7
30101 Acworth, 3,929 C 2
30103 Adairsville, 1,676 C 2
31620 Adel⊙, 4,972 F 8
31002 Adrian, 705 G 5
30410 Ailey, 487 G 6
30411 Alamo⊙, 833 G 6
31622 Alapaha, 633 F 8
* 31701 Albany⊙, 72,623 D 7
Albany, ‡89,639 D 7
† 30204 Aldora, 322 D 4
30801 Alexander, 200 J 4
31301 Allenhurst, 230 J 7
31003 Allentown, 295 F 5
31510 Alma⊙, 3,756 G 7
† 30209 Almon, 400 E 3
30201 Alpharetta, 2,455 D 2
30510 Alto, 372 E 2
† 30161 Alto Park, 2,963 B 2
31512 Ambrose, 253 G 7
31709 Americus⊙, 16,091 D 6
31711 Andersonville, 274 D 6
30802 Appling⊙, 212 H 3
31712 Arabi, 305 E 7
30104 Aragon, 850 B 2
† 30549 Arcade, 229 E 2
31520 Arco, 6,009 J 8
31623 Argyle, 206 G 8
31713 Arlington, 1,698 C 8
30105 Armuchee, 600 B 2
31714 Ashburn⊙, 4,209 E 7
† 30521 Ashland, 350 F 2
30601 Athens⊙, 44,342 F 3
* 30301 Atlanta (cap.)⊙, 496,973 D 3
Atlanta, ‡1,390,164 D 3
31715 Attapulgus, 513 D 9
30203 Auburn, 361 E 2
* 30901 Augusta⊙, 59,864 J 4
Augusta, ‡253,460 J 4
30001 Austell, 2,632 C 3
† 30557 Avalon, 204 F 1
30803 Avera, 217 G 4
30002 Avondale Estates, 1,735 D 3
31624 Axson, 250 G 8
31716 Baconton, 710 D 8
31717 Bainbridge⊙, 10,887 C 9
30511 Baldwin, 772 E 2
30107 Ball Ground, 617 D 2
30204 Barnesville⊙, 4,935 D 4
† 31601 Barretts, 275 F 8
30413 Bartow, 333 G 5
31720 Barwick, 381 E 9
31513 Baxley⊙, 3,503 H 7
† 31792 Beachton, 200 D 9
30414 Bellville, 234 H 6
† 31601 Bemiss, 325 F 9
31722 Berlin, 422 E 8
30748 Berryton, 200 B 2
30620 Bethlehem, 304 E 3
31904 Bibb City, 812 B 5
30621 Bishop, 235 F 3
31516 Blackshear⊙, 2,624 H 8
30512 Blairsville⊙, 491 E 1
31723 Blakely⊙, 5,267 C 8
† 31308 Blitchton, 256 J 6
31302 Bloomingdale, 1,588 K 6
30513 Blue Ridge⊙, 1,602 D 1
30805 Blythe, 333 H 4
30622 Bogart, 667 E 3
31626 Boston, 1,443 E 9
30623 Bostwick, 289 E 3
30108 Bowdon, 1,753 B 3
30109 Bowdon Junction, 200 B 3
30516 Bowersville, 301 G 2
30624 Bowman, 724 G 2
31801 Box Springs, 600 C 5
30517 Braselton, 386 E 2
30110 Bremen, 3,484 B 3
31701 Bridgeboro, 250 E 8
31725 Brinson, 231 C 9
31726 Bronwood, 500 D 7
31727 Brookfield, 860 F 8
30415 Brooklet, 683 J 6
31519 Broxton, 957 G 7
31520 Brunswick⊙, 19,585 K 8
30113 Buchanan⊙, 800 B 3
31803 Buena Vista⊙, 1,486 C 6
30518 Buford, 4,640 D 2
† 31020 Bullard, 230 F 5
31006 Butler⊙, 1,589 D 5
31007 Byromville, 419 E 6
31008 Byron, 1,368 E 5
31009 Cadwell, 354 G 6
31728 Cairo⊙, 8,061 D 9
30701 Calhoun⊙, 4,748 C 1
31729 Calvary, 500 D 9
30807 Camak, 224 G 4
31730 Camilla⊙, 4,987 D 8
30520 Canon, 709 F 2
30114 Canton⊙, 3,654 C 2
† 30720 Carbondale, 300 B 1
30203 Carl, 234 E 3
30627 Carlton, 294 F 2
30521 Carnesville⊙, 510 F 2
30117 Carrollton⊙, 13,520 C 3
† 30540 Cartecay, 250 D 1
30120 Cartersville⊙, 9,929 C 2
30123 Cassville, 350 C 2
31804 Cataula, 500 C 5
30124 Cave Spring, 1,305 B 2
31627 Cecil, 265 F 8
30125 Cedartown⊙, 9,253 B 2
† 30601 Center, 213 F 2
31093 Centerville, 1,725 E 5
† 31816 Chalybeate Springs, 266 C 5
30341 Chamblee, 9,127 D 3
30705 Chatsworth⊙, 2,706 C 1
31011 Chauncey, 308 F 6
31012 Chester, 409 F 6
30707 Chickamauga, 1,842 B 1
† 30512 Choestoe, 215 E 1
31733 Chula, 300 E 7
30523 Clarkesville⊙, 1,294 F 1
30021 Clarkston, 3,127 D 3
30417 Claxton⊙, 2,669 J 6
30525 Clayton⊙, 1,569 F 1
30128 Clem, 350 B 3
30527 Clermont, 290 E 2
30528 Cleveland⊙, 1,353 E 1
31734 Climax, 275 D 9
31604 Clyattville, 500 F 9
31303 Clyo, 300 K 6
30420 Cobbtown, 321 H 6
31014 Cochran⊙, 5,161 F 6
30710 Cohutta, 300 C 1
30628 Colbert, 532 F 2
30337 College Park, 18,203 C 3
30421 Collins, 574 H 6
31737 Colquitt⊙, 2,026 C 8
* 31901 Columbus⊙, 154,168 C 6
Columbus, ‡238,584 C 6
30629 Comer, 828 F 2
30529 Commerce, 3,702 E 2
30206 Concord, 312 D 4
30207 Conyers⊙, 4,890 D 3
31738 Coolidge, 717 E 8
30129 Coosa, 600 B 2
31015 Cordele⊙, 10,733 E 7
30531 Cornelia, 3,014 E 1
30209 Covington⊙, 10,267 E 3
30630 Crawford, 624 F 3
30631 Crawfordville⊙, 735 G 3
† 30105 Crystal Springs, 500 B 2
31016 Culloden, 272 D 5
30130 Cumming⊙, 2,031 D 2
31805 Cusseta⊙, 1,251 C 6
31740 Cuthbert⊙, 3,972 C 7
30211 Dacula, 782 E 3
30533 Dahlonega⊙, 2,658 D 1
30132 Dallas⊙, 2,133 C 3
30720 Dalton⊙, 18,872 C 1
31741 Damascus, 272 C 8
30633 Danielsville⊙, 378 F 2
31017 Danville, 515 F 5
31305 Darien⊙, 1,826 K 8
31601 Dasher, 452 F 9
31018 Davisboro, 476 G 5
31742 Dawson⊙, 5,383 D 7
30534 Dawsonville⊙, 288 D 2
30808 Dearing, 555 H 4
* 30030 Decatur⊙, 21,943 D 3
† 31501 Deenwood, 3,015 H 8
30535 Demorest, 1,070 F 1
31532 Denton, 244 G 7
31743 De Soto, 321 D 7
31019 Dexter, 438 G 6
† 31520 Dock Junction (Arco), 6,009 J 8
31744 Doerun, 1,157 E 8
31745 Donalsonville⊙, 2,907 C 8
30340 Doraville, 9,039 D 3
31533 Douglas⊙, 10,195 G 7
30134 Douglasville⊙, 5,472 C 3
31020 Dry Branch, 700 F 5
31021 Dublin⊙, 15,143 G 5
31022 Dudley, 423 F 5
30136 Duluth, 1,810 D 2
31630 Du Pont, 252 G 9
30538 Eastanollee, 365 F 1
31021 East Dublin, 1,986 G 5
30539 East Ellijay, 488 C 1
31023 Eastman⊙, 5,416 F 6
† 30263 East Newnan, 1,634 C 4
30344 East Point, 39,315 C 3
31024 Eatonton⊙, 4,125 F 4
31307 Eden, 300 K 6
31746 Edison, 1,210 C 7
† 31093 Elberta, 500 E 5
30635 Elberton⊙, 6,438 G 2
30060 Elizabeth, 950 C 2
31025 Elko, 450 E 6
31308 Ellabell, 400 K 6
31806 Ellaville⊙, 1,391 D 6
31747 Ellenton, 337 E 8
31807 Ellerslie, 615 C 5
30540 Ellijay⊙, 1,326 C 1
30137 Emerson, 813 C 2
31026 Empire, 325 F 6
31749 Enigma, 505 F 8
† 30217 Ephesus, 212 B 4
30541 Epworth, 300 D 1
30724 Eton, 286 C 1
† 31331 Eulonia, 500 K 7
30809 Evans, 1,500 H 3
31536 Everett, 300 J 8
30212 Experiment, 2,256 D 4
30213 Fairburn, 3,143 C 3
30139 Fairmount, 623 C 2
31631 Fargo, 800 G 9
30214 Fayetteville⊙, 2,160 C 4
30140 Felton, 300 B 3
31750 Fitzgerald⊙, 8,015 F 7
† 31313 Flemington, 265 K 7
30215 Flippen, 600 D 3
30216 Flovilla, 289 E 4
30542 Flowery Branch, 779 E 2
31537 Folkston⊙, 2,112 H 9
30050 Forest Park, 19,994 D 3
31029 Forsyth⊙, 3,736 E 4
31751 Fort Gaines⊙, 1,255 C 7
30741 Fort Oglethorpe, 3,869 B 1
31030 Fort Valley⊙, 9,251 E 5
31752 Fowlstown, 400 D 9
30217 Franklin⊙, 749 B 4
30639 Franklin Springs, 501 F 2
37317 Fry, 300 D 1
31753 Funston, 293 E 8
30501 Gainesville⊙, 15,459 E 2
31408 Garden City, 5,741 K 6
30425 Garfield, 214 H 5
31810 Geneva, 250 C 5
31754 Georgetown⊙, 578 B 7
30810 Gibson⊙, 701 G 4
30426 Girard, 241 J 4
30427 Glennville, 2,965 J 7
30428 Glenwood, 670 G 6
30641 Good Hope, 202 E 3
31031 Gordon, 2,553 F 5
30811 Gough, 300 H 4
30812 Gracewood, 1,200 H 4
30220 Grantville, 1,128 C 4
31032 Gray⊙, 2,014 F 4
30221 Grayson, 366 E 3
30642 Greensboro⊙, 2,583 F 3
30222 Greenville⊙, 1,085 C 4
† 31620 Greggs, 250 F 8
30223 Griffin⊙, 22,734 D 4
† 31036 Grovania, 300 E 6
30813 Grovetown, 3,169 H 4
31312 Guyton, 742 K 6
30544 Habersham, 225 F 1
31033 Haddock, 600 F 4
30429 Hagan, 572 J 6
31632 Hahira, 1,326 F 9
31811 Hamilton⊙, 357 C 5
30228 Hampton, 1,551 D 4
30354 Hapeville, 9,567 D 3
31034 Hardwick, 14,047 F 4
30814 Harlem, 1,540 H 4
31035 Harrison, 329 G 5
30643 Hartwell⊙, 4,865 G 2
31036 Hawkinsville⊙, 4,077 E 6
31539 Hazlehurst⊙, 4,065 G 7
30545 Helen, 252 E 1
31037 Helena, 1,230 G 6
30815 Hephzibah, 987 H 4
30546 Hiawassee⊙, 415 E 1
31038 Hillsboro, 250 E 4
30467 Hilltonia, 294 J 5
31313 Hinesville⊙, 4,115 J 7
30141 Hiram, 441 C 3
31542 Hoboken, 424 H 8
30230 Hogansville, 3,075 C 4
30142 Holly Springs, 575 D 2
30523 Hollywood, 300 E 1
† 31537 Homeland, 595 H 9
30547 Homer⊙, 365 F 2
31634 Homerville⊙, 3,025 G 8
31543 Hortense, 400 J 8
30548 Hoschton, 509 E 2
30646 Hull, 222 F 2
30561 Hurst, 216 D 1
31041 Ideal, 543 D 6
30647 Ila, 202 F 2
30231 Indian Springs, 300 E 4
30232 Inman, 475 D 4
31759 Iron City, 351 C 8
31042 Irwinton⊙, 757 F 5
31760 Irwinville, 550 F 7
31406 Isle of Hope, 975 K 7
† 31031 Ivey, 245 F 5
30233 Jackson⊙, 3,778 E 4
31544 Jacksonville, 214 G 7
30143 Jasper⊙, 1,202 D 2

(continued on following page)

GEORGIA

SCALE

0 5 10   20   30   40 MI.

0 5 10   20   30   40 KM.

State Capitals.......................⊛

County Seats........................⊛

© C. S. HAMMOND & Co., N.Y.

30549 Jefferson⊙, 1,647....F 2
31044 Jeffersonville⊙, 1,302....F 5
30234 Jenkinsburg, 382....E 4
31545 Jesup⊙, 9,091....J 7
30236 Jonesboro⊙, 4,105....D 4
31046 Juliette, 600....E 4
31812 Junction City, 269....C 5
31813 Juniper, 525....C 6
30551 Juno, 522....D 2
30144 Kennesaw, 3,548....C 2
30214 Kenwood, 500....D 3
30816 Keysville, 500....H 4
31548 Kingsland, 1,831....J 9
30145 Kingston, 714....C 2
31049 Kite, 336....G 5
31050 Knoxville, 25....E 5
30728 La Fayette⊙, 6,044....B 1
30240 La Grange⊙, 23,301....B 4
30260 Lake, 2,306....D 3
31635 Lakeland⊙, 2,569....F 8
30552 Lakemont, 295....F 1
31636 Lake Park, 361....F 9
30553 Lavonia, 2,044....F 2
30245 Lawrenceville⊙, 5,115....D 3
31650 Lax, 350....F 8
30528 Leaf, 250....E 1
30802 Leah, 210....H 3
31762 Leary, 907....C 8
30146 Lebanon, 340....D 2
31763 Leesburg⊙, 996....D 7
31637 Lenox, 860....F 8
31764 Leslie, 562....D 7
30648 Lexington⊙, 322....F 3
30247 Lilburn, 1,668....D 3
30286 Lincoln Park, 1,852....D 5
30817 Lincolnton⊙, 1,442....G 3
30147 Lindale, 2,768....B 2
30728 Linwood, 588....B 1
30057 Lithia Springs, 950....C 3
30058 Lithonia, 2,270....D 3
31052 Lizella, 975....E 5
30248 Locust Grove, 642....D 4
30741 Loganville, 1,318....E 3
30741 Lookout Mountain, 1,538....B 1
30034 Louisville⊙, 2,691....H 4
31814 Louvale, 263....C 6
31316 Ludowici⊙, 1,419....J 7
30175 Ludville, 205....C 2
30554 Lula, 736....E 2
31549 Lumber City, 1,377....G 7
31815 Lumpkin⊙, 1,431....C 6
30251 Luthersville, 400....C 4
30730 Lyerly, 426....B 1
30436 Lyons⊙, 3,739....H 6
30059 Mableton, 9,500....C 3
31201 Macon⊙, 122,423....E 5
    Macon, ‡206,342....E 5
30650 Madison⊙, 2,890....E 3
31816 Manchester, 4,779....C 5
31550 Manor, 500....G 8
30255 Mansfield, 340....D 3
30148 Marblehill, 300....D 2
30060 Marietta⊙, 27,216....C 3
†31312 Marlow, 500....K 6
31057 Marshallville, 1,376....D 6

30557 Martin, 201....F 2
30907 Martinez, 950....H 3
30671 Maxeys, 229....F 3
30558 Maysville, 553....E 2
†30908 McBean, 300....J 4
30555 McCaysville, 1,619....D 1
30253 McDonough⊙, 2,675....D 4
31054 McIntyre, 471....F 5
31055 McRae⊙, 3,151....G 6
30256 Meansville, 313....D 4
31765 Meigs, 1,226....D 8
31318 Meldrim, 500....K 6
30731 Menlo, 593....B 2
30819 Mesena, 400....G 4
†31792 Metcalf, 213....E 9
30439 Metter⊙, 2,912....H 6
31820 Midland, 250....C 5
30441 Midville, 665....H 5
31060 Milan, 1,084....G 6
31061 Milledgeville⊙, 11,601....F 4
30442 Millen⊙, 3,713....J 5
30257 Milner, 270....D 4
30207 Milstead, 1,157....D 3
30258 Molena, 389....D 4
30655 Monroe⊙, 8,071....E 3
31063 Montezuma, 4,125....E 6
31064 Monticello⊙, 2,132....E 4
30259 Moreland, 363....C 4
31766 Morgan⊙, 280....C 7
30560 Morganton, 205....D 1
31638 Morven, 449....E 9
31768 Moultrie⊙, 14,302....E 8
30562 Mountain City, 594....F 1
30563 Mount Airy, 463....F 1
30149 Mount Berry, 1,500....B 2
30445 Mount Vernon⊙, 1,579....G 6
30261 Mountville, 218....C 4
30150 Mount Zion, 264....B 3
30564 Murrayville, 550....E 2
31769 Mystic, 250....F 7
†31808 Nankipooh, 500....C 5
31639 Nashville⊙, 4,323....F 8
31641 Naylor, 244:...F 9
30151 Nelson, 613....D 2
30262 Newborn, 294....E 3
†30501 New Holland, 950....E 2
30446 Newington, 402....J 5
30263 Newnan⊙, 11,205....C 4
31770 Newton⊙, 624....D 8
31554 Nicholls, 1,150....G 7
30565 Nicholson, 397....F 2
†30728 Noble, 250....B 1
30071 Norcross, 2,755....D 3
31771 Norman Park, 912....E 8
30319 North Atlanta, 15,000....D 3
†30114 North Canton, 950....C 2
30821 Norwood, 272....G 4
31903 Oak Park, 226....H 6
30566 Oakwood, 250....E 2
31773 Ochlocknee, 611....E 8
31774 Ocilla⊙, 3,185....F 7
31067 Oconee, 262....G 5
31555 Odum, 379....H 7

31556 Offerman, 500....H 8
31406 Oglethorpe⊙, 1,286....D 6
30449 Oliver, 217....J 5
31775 Omega, 831....E 8
†30701 Oostanaula, 300....B 1
30267 Oxford, 1,373....E 3
30268 Palmetto, 2,045....C 3
31777 Parrott, 222....D 7
31557 Patterson, 788....H 8
31778 Pavo, 775....E 9
†31201 Payne, 236....E 5
30214 Peachtree City, 793....C 4
31642 Pearson⊙, 1,700....G 8
31779 Pelham, 4,539....D 8
31321 Pembroke⊙, 1,361....J 6
30567 Pendergrass, 267....E 2
30822 Perkins, 250....J 5
31069 Perry⊙, 7,771....E 6
†31794 Phillipsburg, 2,335....E 8
31629 Pidcock, 210....E 9
31071 Pinehurst, 405....E 6
30152 Pine Log, 205....C 2
31822 Pine Mountain, 862....C 5
†31312 Pineora, 266....K 6
†31728 Pine Park, 330....D 9
31071 Pineview, 528....F 6
31072 Pitts, 345....F 7
31780 Plains, 683....D 6
31322 Pooler, 1,517....L 6
30450 Portal, 643....J 5
30270 Porterdale, 1,773....E 3
31407 Port Wentworth, 3,905....K 6
31781 Poulan, 766....E 8
30073 Powder Springs, 2,559....C 3
31824 Preston⊙, 226....C 6
30451 Pulaski, 230....J 6
31782 Putney, 750....D 8
31643 Quitman⊙, 4,818....E 9
30568 Rabun Gap, 250....F 1
31645 Ray City, 617....F 8
30660 Rayle, 300....G 3
31783 Rebecca, 266....E 7
30272 Red Oak, 3,500....C 3
30452 Register, 300....J 6
30453 Reidsville⊙, 1,806....H 6
31601 Remerton, 523....F 9
31075 Rentz, 392....G 5
30735 Resaca, 500....C 1
31076 Reynolds, 1,253....D 5
31077 Rhine, 471....G 6
31323 Riceboro, 252....K 7
31825 Richland, 1,823....C 6
31324 Richmond Hill, 826....K 7
31326 Rincon, 1,854....K 6
30736 Ringgold⊙, 1,381....B 1
30738 Rising Fawn, 400....A 1
30274 Riverdale, 2,521....D 3
31204 Riverside, 1,159....B 2
31078 Roberta, 746....D 5
†30545 Robertstown, 290....E 1
31079 Rochelle, 1,380....F 7
30153 Rockmart, 3,800....B 2
30740 Rocky Face, 500....C 1
30455 Rocky Ford, 252....J 5
30161 Rome⊙, 30,759....B 2

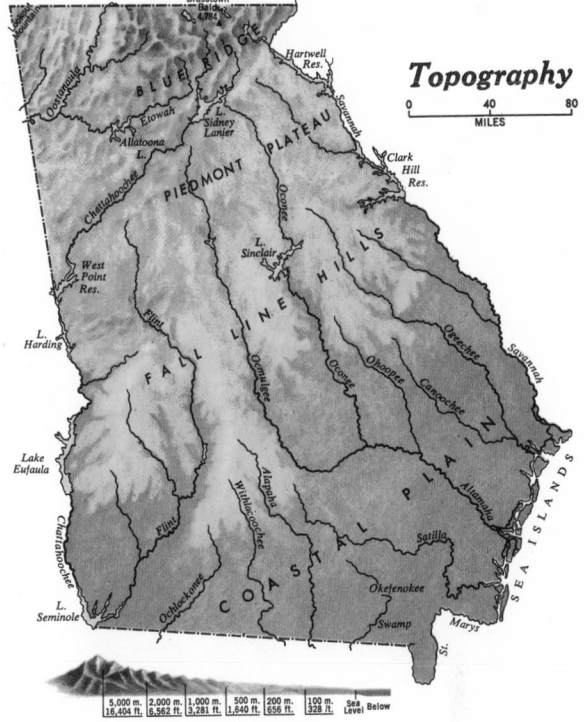

Topography

0   40   80
MILES

5,000 m. 2,000 m. 1,000 m. 500 m. 200 m. 100 m. Sea Level Below
16,404 ft. 6,562 ft. 3,281 ft. 1,640 ft. 656 ft. 328 ft.

30170 Roopville, 221....B 4
30741 Rossville, 3,869....B 1
30075 Roswell, 5,430....D 2
30662 Royston, 2,428....F 2
†30680 Russell, 378....E 3
30663 Rutledge, 628....E 3
31646 Saint George, 600....H 9
31558 Saint Marys, 3,408....J 9
31522 Saint Simons Island, 5,346....K 8
31784 Sale City, 323....D 8
31082 Sandersville⊙, 5,546....G 5
31327 Sapelo Island, 250....K 8
30456 Sardis, 643....J 5
30275 Sargent, 800....C 4
31785 Sasser, 339....D 7
30571 Sautee-Nacoochee, 350....E 1
*31401 Savannah⊙, 118,349....L 6
    Savannah, ‡187,767....L 6
31328 Savannah Beach, 1,786....L 6
31083 Scotland, 261....G 6
31095 Scott, 215....G 5
31560 Screven, 936....H 7
31561 Sea Island, 500....K 8
30276 Senoia, 910....C 4
30172 Shannon, 1,563....B 2
31786 Shellman, 1,166....C 7
31826 Shiloh, 298....C 5
†31781 Shingler, 300....E 7
30665 Siloam, 300....F 3
30173 Silver Creek, 450....B 2
31086 Smarr, 350....E 5
31787 Smithville, 713....D 7
30080 Smyrna, 19,157....D 3
30279 Social Circle, 1,961....E 3
30457 Soperton⊙, 2,596....G 6
31647 Sparks, 1,337....F 8
31087 Sparta⊙, 2,172....F 4
31329 Springfield⊙, 1,001....K 6
30705 Spring Place, 241....C 1
30823 Stapleton, 390....H 4
31648 Statenville⊙, 700....G 9
30458 Statesboro⊙, 14,616....J 6
31088 Stevens Pottery, 350....F 5
30464 Stillmore, 354....H 6
30281 Stockbridge, 1,561....D 3
30083 Stone Mountain, 1,899....D 3
30282 Stonewall, 950....C 3
†30747 Subligna, 400....B 1
30572 Suches, 300....E 1
30518 Sugar Hill, 1,745....E 2
†30747 Summerville⊙, 5,043....B 2
31789 Sumner, 207....E 7
30284 Sunny Side, 209....D 4
31563 Surrency, 600....H 7
30174 Suwanee, 615....D 2
30401 Swainsboro⊙, 7,325....H 5
31790 Sycamore, 547....E 7
30467 Sylvania⊙, 3,199....J 5
31791 Sylvester⊙, 4,226....E 7
31827 Talbotton⊙, 1,045....C 5
30176 Tallapoosa, 2,896....B 3
30573 Tallulah Falls, 255....F 1
30177 Tate, 950....D 2
30178 Taylorsville, 253....C 2
30179 Temple, 864....B 3
30751 Tennga, 300....C 1
31089 Tennille, 1,753....G 5
30286 Thomaston⊙, 10,024....D 5
31792 Thomasville⊙, 18,155....E 9

30824 Thomson⊙, 6,503....H 4
31404 Thunderbolt, 2,750....K 6
31794 Tifton⊙, 12,179....F 8
30576 Tiger, 312....F 1
30668 Tignall, 756....G 3
30577 Toccoa⊙, 6,971....F 1
31090 Toomsboro, 682....F 5
31331 Townsend, 300....J 7
30752 Trenton⊙, 1,523....A 1
30753 Trion, 1,965....B 1
30755 Tunnel Hill, 900....C 1
30289 Turin, 242....C 4
30471 Twin City, 1,119....H 5
31795 Ty Ty, 447....E 8
31091 Unadilla, 1,457....E 6
30291 Union City, 3,031....D 3
30669 Union Point, 1,624....F 3
31794 Unionville, 1,646....F 8
30473 Uvalda, 663....H 6
31601 Valdosta⊙, 32,303....F 9
30756 Varnell, 400....C 1
30474 Vidalia, 9,507....H 6
31092 Vienna⊙, 2,341....E 6
30180 Villa Rica, 3,922....C 3
30182 Waco, 431....B 3
30477 Wadley, 1,989....H 5
30183 Waleska, 487....D 2
31333 Walthourville, 300....J 7
31564 Waresboro, 350....H 8
31830 Warm Springs, 523....C 5
31093 Warner Robins, 33,491....E 5
30828 Warrenton⊙, 2,073....G 4
31796 Warwick, 466....E 7
30673 Washington⊙, 4,094....G 3
30677 Watkinsville⊙, 986....E 3
31565 Waverly, 250....J 8
31831 Waverly Hall, 621....C 5
31501 Waycross⊙, 18,996....H 8
30830 Waynesboro⊙, 5,530....J 4
31566 Waynesville, 500....J 8
31833 West Point, 4,232....B 5
31797 Whigham, 381....D 9
30184 White, 462....C 2
30603 White Hall, 400....F 2
30678 White Plains, 236....F 4
30185 Whitesburg, 720....B 4
30186 Whitestone, 450....C 1
†31833 Whitesville, 250....C 5
30581 Wiley, 300....F 1
31650 Willacoochee, 1,120....G 8
30292 Williamson, 284....D 4
31404 Wilmington Island, 3,284....L 7
30680 Winder⊙, 6,605....E 3
†30824 Winfield, 444....H 3
30187 Winston, 625....C 3
30683 Winterville, 551....F 3
31569 Woodbine⊙, 1,002....J 9
30293 Woodbury, 1,422....C 5
31836 Woodland, 689....C 5
30188 Woodstock, 870....D 2
30670 Woodville, 379....F 3
30833 Wrens, 2,204....H 4
31096 Wrightsville⊙, 2,106....G 5
31097 Yatesville, 423....D 5
30582 Young Harris, 544....E 1
30295 Zebulon⊙, 776....D 4

⊙ County seat.
‡ Population of metropolitan area.
† Zip of nearest p.o.
* Multiple zips

Agriculture, Industry and Resources

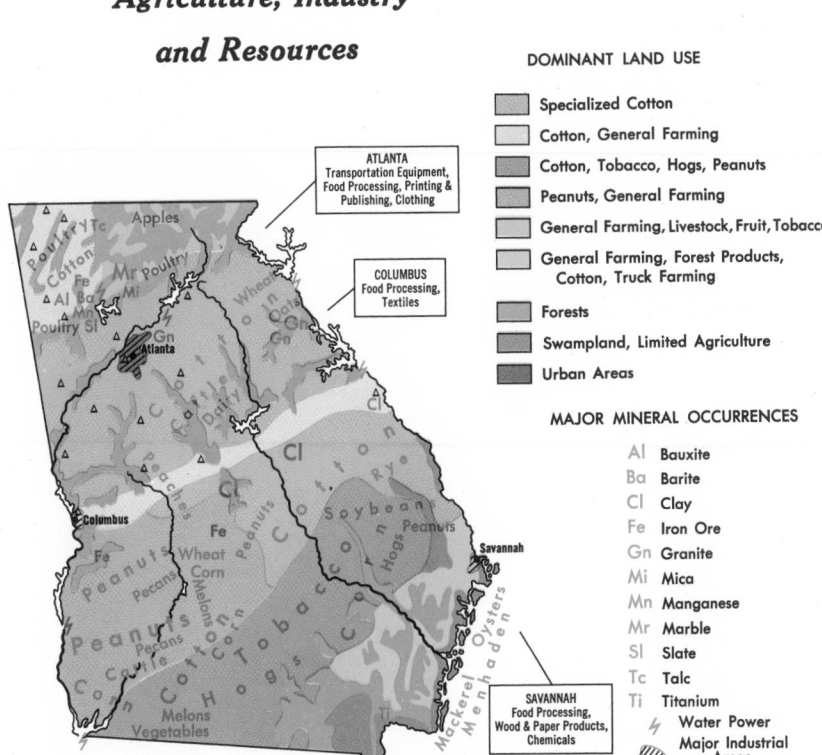

ATLANTA
Transportation Equipment, Food Processing, Printing & Publishing, Clothing

COLUMBUS
Food Processing, Textiles

SAVANNAH
Food Processing, Wood & Paper Products, Chemicals

DOMINANT LAND USE

- Specialized Cotton
- Cotton, General Farming
- Cotton, Tobacco, Hogs, Peanuts
- Peanuts, General Farming
- General Farming, Livestock, Fruit, Tobacco
- General Farming, Forest Products, Cotton, Truck Farming
- Forests
- Swampland, Limited Agriculture
- Urban Areas

MAJOR MINERAL OCCURRENCES

Al Bauxite
Ba Barite
Cl Clay
Fe Iron Ore
Gn Granite
Mi Mica
Mn Manganese
Mr Marble
Sl Slate
Tc Talc
Ti Titanium
⚡ Water Power
〰 Major Industrial Areas
△ Major Textile Manufacturing Centers

154 Hawaii

Topography

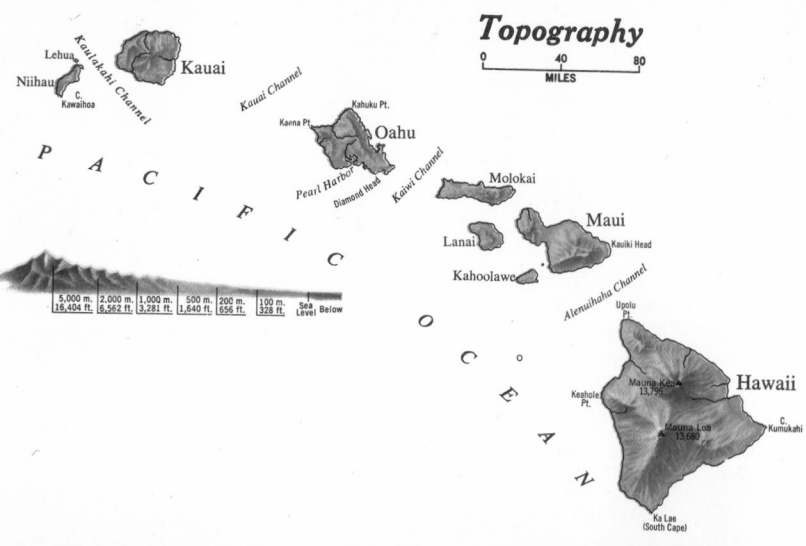

Topography

0   40   80
MILES

5,000 m. | 2,000 m. | 1,000 m. | 500 m. | 200 m. | 100 m. | Sea | Below
16,404 ft. | 6,562 ft. | 3,281 ft. | 1,640 ft. | 656 ft. | 328 ft. | Level

Agriculture, Industry and Resources

Sharp spikes bristle protectively around their precious fruit crop on Pineapple Hill, west Maui. Second only to sugarcane, pineapples rank high in Hawaii's economy.

David Muench—Shostal Associates

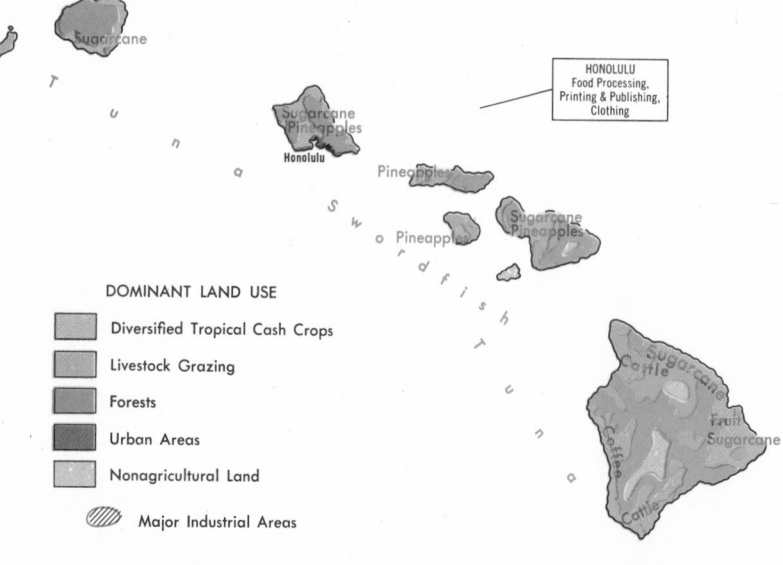

HONOLULU
Food Processing,
Printing & Publishing,
Clothing

DOMINANT LAND USE

- Diversified Tropical Cash Crops
- Livestock Grazing
- Forests
- Urban Areas
- Nonagricultural Land

/// Major Industrial Areas

KAUAI COUNTY

SCALE
0   5   10   15 MI.
0   5   10   15 KM.

160°   Longitude West of Greenwich   159

A   B   C

HONOLULU & PEARL HARBOR

SCALE
0   1   2 MI.
0   1   2 KM.

HAWAII

State Capital .... ⊛
County Seats .... ⊙

© C.S. HAMMOND & Co., N.Y.

† 96750 Kainaliu, 450 ...... G 5
96757 Kalae, 150 ...... G 1
96741 Kalaheo, 1,514 ...... C 2
96740 Kalaoa, 300 ...... G 5
† 96742 Kalaupapa⊙, 164 ...... G 1
96817 Kalihi, 32,650 ...... C 4
† 96748 Kaluaaha, 300 ...... H 1
† 96748 Kamalo, 300 ...... H 1
96743 Kamuela, 756 ...... G 3
96744 Kaneohe, 29,903 ...... F 2
96746 Kapaa, 3,794 ...... D 2
† 96778 Kapaahu, 850 ...... J 6
96755 Kapaau, 237 ...... G 3
† 96778 Kapoho, 300 ...... K 5
96758 Kapulena, 125 ...... H 4
96747 Kaumakani, 1,014 ...... C 2
96748 Kaunakakai, 1,070 ...... G 1
† 96708 Kaupakulua, 100 ...... K 2
96743 Kawaihae, 50 ...... G 4
† 96712 Kawailoa, 900 ...... E 1
96749 Keaau, 951 ...... J 5
96750 Kealakekua, 740 ...... G 5
96751 Kealia, 600 ...... D 1
96751 Kealia, 550 ...... G 6
96752 Kekaha, 2,404 ...... C 2
† 96704 Keokea, 500 ...... G 6
96790 Keokea, 750 ...... J 2
96753 Kihei, 1,450 ...... J 2
96754 Kilauea, 671 ...... C 1
† 96713 Koali, 100 ...... K 2
† 96755 Kohala (Kapaau), 237 ...... G 3

† 96708 Kokomo, 200 ...... K 2
96756 Koloa, 1,368 ...... C 2
96757 Kualapuu, 441 ...... G 1
96758 Kukuihaele, 310 ...... H 3
96790 Kula, 800 ...... J 2
96759 Kunia, 545 ...... E 2
96760 Kurtistown, 900 ...... J 5
96761 Laie, 3,009 ...... E 1
96762 Lahaina, 3,718 ...... H 2
96763 Lanai City, 2,122 ...... H 2
96764 Laupahoehoe, 452 ...... J 4
96765 Lawai, 950 ...... C 2
96766 Lihue⊙, 3,124 ...... C 2
† 96779 Lower Paia, 1,105 ...... J 1
96753 Maalaea, 80 ...... J 2
96792 Maili, 4,397 ...... D 2
96792 Makaha, 4,644 ...... D 2
96706 Makakilo City, 3,499 ...... E 2
96711 Makapala, 201 ...... G 3
96768 Makawao, 1,066 ...... K 2
96769 Makaweli, 500 ...... B 2
96770 Manaloa, 872 ...... G 1
96744 Maunawili, 5,303 ...... F 2
96786 Mililani, 2,035 ...... E 2
96704 Milolii, 100 ...... G 6
96734 Mokapu, 7,860 ...... F 2
96791 Mokuleia, 880 ...... D 1
96771 Mountainview, 419 ...... J 5
96772 Naalehu, 1,014 ...... H 7
96792 Nanakuli, 6,506 ...... D 2
96773 Ninole, 75 ...... J 4

† 96761 Olowalu, 750 ...... H 2
† 96781 Onomea, 500 ...... J 4
† 96774 Ookala, 486 ...... J 4
† 96778 Opihikao, 125 ...... K 6
96775 Paauhau, 400 ...... H 4
96776 Paauilo, 710 ...... H 4
† 96801 Pacific Heights, 5,305 ...... C 4
† 96782 Pacific Palisades, 7,846 ...... E 2
96777 Pahala, 1,507 ...... H 6
96778 Pahoa, 924 ...... J 5
96779 Paia, 541 ...... J 1
† 96801 Palama, 15,307 ...... C 4
† 96704 Papa, 100 ...... G 6
96780 Papaaloa, 319 ...... J 4
96781 Papaikou, 1,888 ...... J 5
† 96781 Paukaa, 450 ...... J 5
96708 Pauwela, 355 ...... K 2
96782 Pearl City, 19,552 ...... B 3
96783 Pepeekeo, 1,150 ...... J 4
96756 Poipu, 466 ...... C 2
96788 Puhi, 772 ...... C 2
96788 Pukalani, 1,629 ...... J 2
† 96748 Pukoo, 300 ...... H 1
96784 Punene, 1,132 ...... J 2
† 96801 Puunui, 10,082 ...... C 4
96769 Puuwai, 200 ...... A 2
96786 Schofield Barracks, 13,516 ...... E 2
96779 Spreckelsville, 350 ...... J 2
96785 Ulupalakua, 75 ...... J 2
96766 Wahiawa, 17,598 ...... E 2

† 96788 Waiakoa, 1,050 ...... J 2
96731 Waialae, 80 ...... E 1
96791 Waialua, Oahu, 4,047 ...... D 1
96792 Waianae, 3,302 ...... D 2
96793 Waihee, 346 ...... J 2
96793 Waikapu, 598 ...... J 2
96815 Waikiki, 35,000 ...... C 4
96748 Wailau, 300 ...... H 1
96710 Wailea, 315 ...... J 4
96746 Wailua, 1,379 ...... D 2
96793 Wailuku⊙, 7,979 ...... J 2
96701 Waimanalo, 2,982 ...... F 2
96795 Waimanalo Beach, 3,045 ...... F 2
96743 Waimea (Kamuela), Hawaii 756 ...... G 3
96796 Waimea, Kauai, 1,569 ...... B 2
96712 Waimea, Oahu, 200 ...... E 1
96772 Waiohinu, 200 ...... G 7
96797 Waipahu, 22,798 ...... A 3
96786 Waipio Acres, 2,146 ...... E 2
96786 Whitmore Village, 2,015 ...... E 2
† 96801 Woodlawn, 5,569 ...... D 4

MIDWAY ISLANDS
Total Population 2,356

⊙ County seat.
‡ Population of metropolitan area.
† Zip of nearest p.o.
* Multiple zips

AREA 6,450 sq. mi.
POPULATION 769,913
CAPITAL Honolulu
LARGEST CITY Honolulu
HIGHEST POINT Mauna Kea 13,796 ft.
SETTLED IN —
ADMITTED TO UNION August 21, 1959
POPULAR NAME Aloha State; Paradise of the Pacific
STATE FLOWER Red Hibiscus
STATE BIRD Nene (Hawaiian Goose)

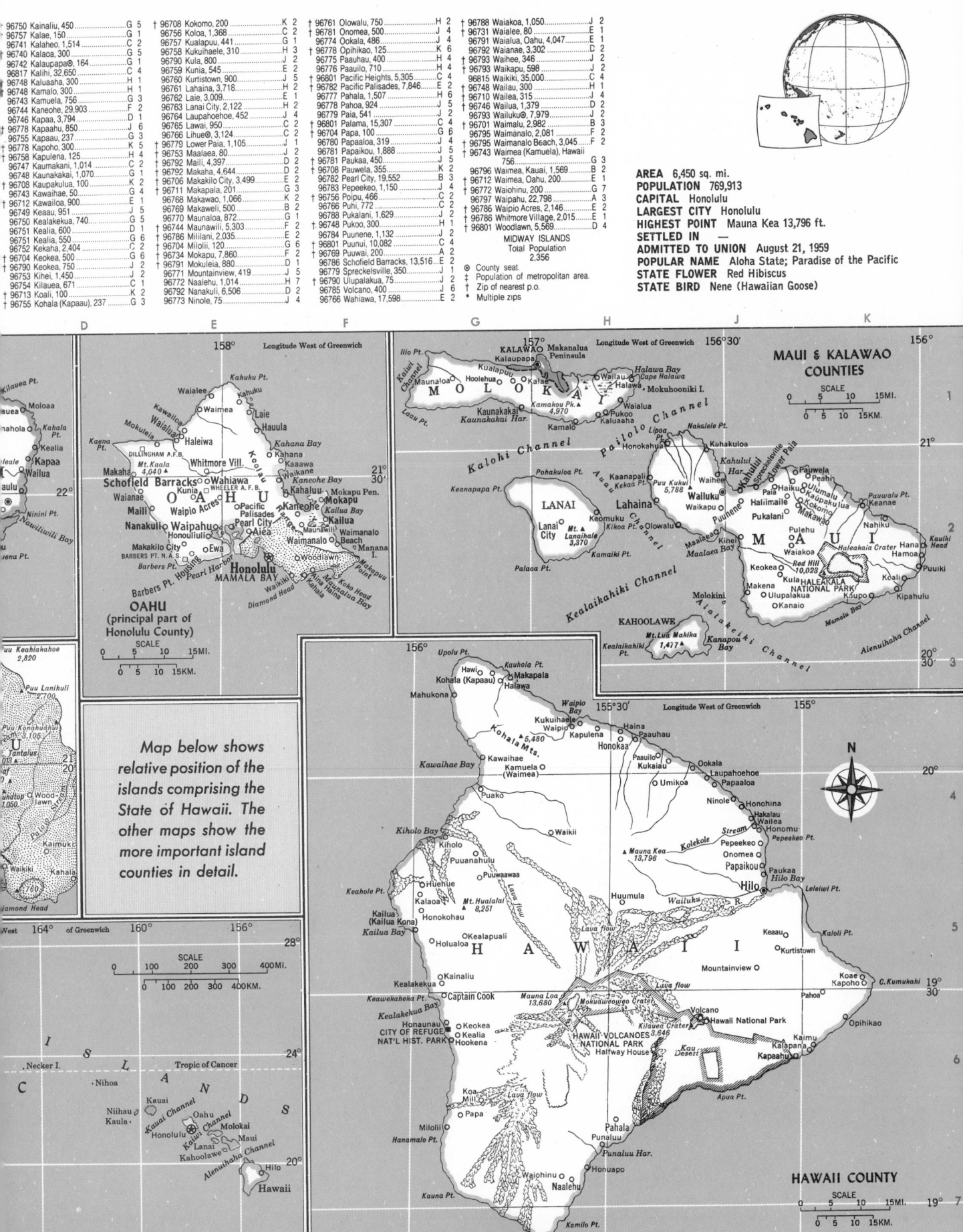

Map below shows relative position of the islands comprising the State of Hawaii. The other maps show the more important island counties in detail.

COUNTIES

Name/Pop.	Key
Ada, 112,230	B 6
Adams, 2,877	B 5
Bannock, 52,200	F 7
Bear Lake, 5,801	G 7
Benewah, 6,230	B 2
Bingham, 29,167	F 6
Blaine, 5,749	D 6
Boise, 1,763	C 6
Bonner, 15,560	B 1
Bonneville, 51,250	G 6
Boundary, 6,371	B 1
Butte, 2,925	E 6
Camas, 728	D 6
Canyon, 61,288	B 6
Caribou, 6,534	G 7
Cassia, 17,017	E 7
Clark, 741	F 5
Clearwater, 10,871	C 3
Custer, 2,967	D 5
Elmore, 17,479	C 6
Franklin, 7,373	G 7
Fremont, 8,710	G 5
Gem, 9,387	B 6
Gooding, 8,645	D 6
Idaho, 12,891	C 4
Jefferson, 11,619	F 6
Jerome, 10,253	D 7
Kootenai, 35,332	B 2
Latah, 24,891	B 3
Lemhi, 5,566	D 4
Lewis, 3,867	B 3
Lincoln, 3,057	D 6
Madison, 13,452	G 6
Minidoka, 15,731	E 7
Nez Perce, 30,376	B 3
Oneida, 2,864	F 7
Owyhee, 6,422	B 7
Payette, 12,401	B 5
Power, 4,864	F 7
Shoshone, 19,718	B 2
Teton, 2,351	G 6
Twin Falls, 41,807	D 7
Valley, 3,609	C 5
Washington, 7,633	B 5

CITIES and TOWNS

Zip	Name/Pop.	Key
83210	Aberdeen, 1,542	F 7
83310	Acequia, 107	E 7
83520	Ahsahka, 500	B 3
83311	Albion, 229	E 7
83312	Almo, 170	E 7
83211	American Falls⊙, 2,769	E 7
83401	Ammon, 1,338	G 6
83212	Arbon, 75	F 7
83213	Arco⊙, 1,244	E 6
83214	Arimo, 252	F 7
83420	Ashton, 1,187	G 5
83801	Athol, 190	B 2
83601	Atlanta, 50	C 6
83215	Atomic City, 24	F 6
83802	Avery, 250	C 2
83461	Baker, 98	E 4
83217	Bancroft, 366	G 7
83264	Banida, 76	G 7
83602	Banks, 49	B 5
83218	Basalt, 349	F 6
83803	Bayview, 300	B 2
83313	Bellevue, 537	D 6
83219	Bennington, 60	G 7
83220	Bern, 135	G 7
83221	Blackfoot⊙, 8,716	F 6
83804	Blanchard, 120	A 1
83314	Bliss, 114	D 7
83223	Bloomington, 186	G 7
* 83701	Boise (cap.)⊙, 74,990	B 6
	Boise, ‡112,230	B 6
83805	Bonners Ferry⊙, 2,796	B 1
83806	Bovill, 343	B 3
† 83651	Bowmont, 100	B 6
83315	Bridge, 140	E 7
83604	Bruneau, 150	C 7
83316	Buhl, 2,975	D 7
83807	Burke, 150	C 2
83318	Burley⊙, 8,279	E 7
† 83213	Butte City, 42	E 6
83808	Calder, 140	B 2
83605	Caldwell⊙, 14,219	B 6
83610	Cambridge, 383	B 5
83320	Carey, 750	E 6
83809	Careywood, 60	B 1
83462	Carmen, 40	E 4
83611	Cascade⊙, 833	C 5
83321	Castleford, 174	C 7
83810	Cataldo, 275	B 2
† 83241	Central, 60	G 7
83226	Challis⊙, 784	D 5
† 83851	Chatcolet, 95	B 2
83421	Chester, 206	G 5
† 83217	Chesterfield, 50	G 7
83201	Chubbuck, 2,924	F 7
83811	Clark Fork, 367	B 1
83812	Clarkia, 147	B 2
83227	Clayton, 36	D 5
83521	Clearwater, 110	C 3
† 83263	Cleveland, 60	G 7
83228	Clifton, 137	F 7
83229	Cobalt, 35	D 4
83814	Coeur d'Alene⊙, 16,228	B 2
83865	Colburn, 200	B 1
83230	Conda, 250	G 7
83821	Coolin, 110	B 1
83322	Corral, 21	D 6
83522	Cottonwood, 867	B 3
83612	Council⊙, 899	B 5
83523	Craigmont, 554	B 3
† 83622	Crouch, 71	B 5
83524	Culdesac, 211	B 3
† 83814	Dalton Gardens, 1,559	B 2
83232	Dayton, 198	F 7
83823	Deary, 411	B 3
83323	Declo, 251	E 7
83824	Desmet, 154	B 2
83324	Dietrich, 84	D 7
83233	Dingle, 300	G 7
83615	Donnelly, 114	B 5
83825	Dover, 300	B 1
83234	Downey, 586	F 7
83422	Driggs⊙, 727	G 6
83423	Dubois⊙, 400	F 5
83616	Eagle, 525	B 6
† 83836	East Hope, 175	B 1
83826	Eastport, 83	B 1
83325	Eden, 343	D 7
83326	Elba, 87	E 7
83525	Elk City, 500	C 4
83827	Elk River, 383	B 3
83235	Ellis, 75	D 5
83828	Emida, 135	B 2
83617	Emmett⊙, 3,945	B 6
83829	Enaville, 90	B 2
83327	Fairfield⊙, 157	D 6
83424	Felt, 90	G 6
83531	Fenn, 45	B 4
83526	Ferdinand, 157	B 3
83830	Fernwood, 360	B 2
83328	Filer, 1,173	D 7
83236	Firth, 362	F 6
83261	Fish Haven, 120	G 7
83203	Fort Hall, 750	F 6
83237	Franklin, 402	G 7
83619	Fruitland, 1,576	B 6
83620	Fruitvale, 90	B 5
83621	Gardena, 44	B 5
83704	Garden City, 2,368	B 6
83622	Garden Valley, 100	C 5
† 83873	Gem, 50	C 2
83832	Genesee, 619	B 3
83238	Geneva, 200	G 7
83239	Georgetown, 421	G 7
83463	Gibbonsville, 85	E 4
83623	Glenns Ferry, 1,386	C 7
83330	Gooding⊙, 2,599	D 7
83241	Grace, 826	G 7
83624	Grand View, 450	B 7
83530	Grangeville⊙, 3,636	B 4
83533	Greencreek, 72	B 3
83626	Greenleaf, 425	B 6
† 83544	Greer, 70	B 3
83332	Hagerman, 436	D 7
83333	Hailey⊙, 1,425	D 6
83425	Hamer, 81	F 6
83627	Hammett, 653	C 7
83334	Hansen, 415	D 7
† 83521	Harpster, 250	C 4
83833	Harrison, 249	B 2
83834	Harvard, 50	B 3
† 83854	Hauser, 349	A 2
† 83835	Hayden, 1,285	B 2
83835	Hayden Lake, 260	B 2
83335	Hazelton, 396	E 7
83534	Headquarters, 350	C 3
† 83443	Heise, 84	G 6
83336	Heyburn, 1,637	E 7
83337	Hill City, 30	D 6
83243	Holbrook, 100	F 7
† 83301	Hollister, 57	D 7
83628	Homedale, 1,411	A 6
83836	Hope, 63	B 1
83629	Horseshoe Bend, 511	B 6
83244	Howe, 428	F 6
† 83854	Huetter, 49	B 2
83631	Idaho City⊙, 164	C 6
83401	Idaho Falls⊙, 35,776	F 6
83632	Indian Valley, 72	B 5
83245	Inkom, 522	F 7
83427	Iona, 890	G 6
83428	Irwin, 228	G 6
83429	Island Park, 136	G 5
83338	Jerome⊙, 4,183	D 7
83535	Juliaetta, 423	B 3
83536	Kamiah, 1,307	B 3
83837	Kellogg, 3,811	B 2
83537	Kendrick, 426	B 3
83340	Ketchum, 1,454	D 6
83538	Keuterville, 26	B 3
† 83423	Kilgore, 50	G 5
83341	Kimberly, 1,557	D 7
83633	King Hill, 150	C 6
83539	Kooskia, 809	C 3
83840	Kootenai, 168	B 1
83634	Kuna, 593	B 6
83841	Laclede, 200	B 1
83635	Lake Fork, 141	B 5
83430	Lamont, 30	G 6
83540	Lapwai, 400	B 3
83246	Lava Hot Springs, 516	F 7
83464	Leadore, 111	E 5
83465	Lemhi, 36	E 5
83249	Leslie, 100	E 6
83636	Letha, 115	B 6
83501	Lewiston⊙, 26,068	A 3
83431	Lewisville, 468	F 6
83432	Lorenzo, 125	G 6
† 83242	Lost River, 58	E 6
83637	Lowman, 45	C 5
83542	Lucile, 105	B 4
† 83241	Lund, 100	G 7
83251	Mackay, 539	E 6
83433	Macks Inn, 150	G 5
83252	Malad City⊙, 1,848	F 7
83342	Malta, 196	E 7
83639	Marsing, 610	B 6
83253	May, 120	E 5
83638	McCall, 1,758	C 5
83250	McCammon, 623	F 7
83640	Meadows, 250	B 5
83641	Melba, 197	B 6
83434	Menan, 545	F 6
83642	Meridian, 2,616	B 6
83643	Mesa, 25	B 5
83644	Middleton, 739	B 6
83645	Midvale, 176	B 5
83343	Minidoka, 131	E 7
83435	Monteview, 110	F 6
83646	Montour, 138	B 6
83254	Montpelier, 2,604	G 7
83255	Moore, 156	E 6
83256	Moreland, 500	F 6
83843	Moscow⊙, 14,146	B 3
83647	Mountain Home⊙, 6,451	C 6
83845	Moyie Springs, 203	B 1
† 83450	Mud Lake, 194	F 6
83846	Mullan, 1,279	C 2
83650	Murphy⊙, 75	B 6
83874	Murray, 100	C 2
83344	Murtaugh, 124	D 7
83345	Naf, 42	E 7
83651	Nampa, 20,768	B 6
83847	Naples, 463	B 1
83436	Newdale, 267	G 6
83654	New Meadows, 605	B 4
83655	New Plymouth, 986	B 6
83543	Nezperce⊙, 555	B 3
83848	Nordman, 168	B 1
83466	North Fork, 150	D 4
83656	Notus, 304	B 6
† 83254	Nounan, 92	G 7
83346	Oakley, 656	D 7
83259	Obsidian, 22	D 6
83657	Ola, 78	B 5
† 99156	Oldtown, 161	A 1
† 83855	Onaway, 166	B 3
83659	Oreana, 115	B 6
83544	Orofino⊙, 3,883	B 3
† 83525	Orogrande, 34	C 4
83849	Osburn, 2,248	B 2
83260	Ovid, 150	G 7
† 83263	Oxford, 75	F 7
83437	Palisades, 95	G 6
83261	Paris⊙, 615	G 7
83438	Parker, 266	G 6
83660	Parma, 1,228	B 6
83347	Paul, 911	E 7
83661	Payette⊙, 4,521	B 5
83545	Peck, 238	B 3
83348	Picabo, 50	D 6
83546	Pierce, 1,218	C 3
83850	Pinehurst, 1,934	B 2
83262	Pingree, 115	F 6
83851	Plummer, 443	B 2
83201	Pocatello⊙, 40,036	F 7
83547	Pollock, 50	B 4
83852	Ponderay, 275	B 1
83853	Porthill, 39	B 1
83854	Post Falls, 2,371	A 2
83855	Potlatch, 871	A 3
83263	Preston⊙, 3,310	G 7
83856	Priest River, 1,493	A 1
83857	Princeton, 124	B 3
83858	Rathdrum, 741	A 2
† 83114	Raymond, 65	G 7
83548	Reubens, 81	B 3
83440	Rexburg⊙, 8,272	G 6
83349	Richfield, 290	D 6
† 89832	Riddle, 44	B 7
83442	Rigby⊙, 2,293	F 6
83549	Riggins, 533	B 4
83443	Ririe, 575	G 6
83444	Roberts, 393	F 6
† 83221	Rockford, 150	F 6
83271	Rockland, 209	F 7
83302	Rogerson, 45	D 7
† 83660	Roswell, 65	A 6
83350	Rupert⊙, 4,563	E 7
83860	Sagle, 100	B 1
83445	Saint Anthony⊙, 2,877	G 6
83272	Saint Charles, 200	G 7
† 83861	Saint Joe, 50	B 2
83861	Saint Maries⊙, 2,571	B 2
83467	Salmon⊙, 2,910	D 4
83252	Samaria, 137	F 7
83862	Samuels, 467	B 1
83863	Sanders, 27	B 2
83864	Sandpoint⊙, 4,144	B 1
83866	Santa, 100	B 2
83274	Shelley, 2,614	F 6
83352	Shoshone⊙, 1,233	D 7
† 83650	Silver City, 1	B 6
† 83423	Small, 35	F 5
83868	Smelterville, 967	B 2
83276	Soda Springs⊙, 2,977	G 7
83550	Southwick, 38	B 3
83446	Spencer, 45	F 5
83869	Spirit Lake, 622	A 2
83277	Springfield, 180	F 6
83447	Squirrel, 43	G 5
83278	Stanley, 47	D 5
83669	Star, 500	B 6
83279	Sterling, 73	F 6
83552	Stites, 263	C 3
83280	Stone, 114	F 7
83448	Sugar City, 617	G 6
83353	Sun Valley, 180	D 6
83281	Swanlake, 145	F 7
83449	Swan Valley, 235	G 6
83670	Sweet, 120	B 6
83468	Tendoy, 150	E 5
83870	Tensed, 151	B 2
83450	Terreton, 42	F 6
83451	Teton, 390	G 6
83452	Tetonia, 176	G 6
83283	Thatcher, 300	G 7
83453	Thornton, 177	G 6
83871	Troy, 541	B 3
83354	Tuttle, 53	D 7
83301	Twin Falls⊙, 21,914	D 7
83454	Ucon, 664	F 6
83455	Victor, 241	G 6
83872	Viola, 300	B 3
† 83234	Virginia, 100	F 7
83873	Wallace⊙, 2,206	C 2
83875	Wardner, 492	B 2
83611	Warm Lake, 200	C 5
83285	Wayan, 50	G 7
83553	Weippe, 713	C 3
83672	Weiser⊙, 4,108	B 5
83355	Wendell, 1,122	D 7
83286	Weston, 230	F 7
83554	White Bird, 185	B 4
83676	Wilder, 564	A 6
83555	Winchester, 274	B 3
83876	Worley, 235	B 2
83677	Yellow Pine, 45	C 4

⊙ County seat.
‡ Population of metropolitan area.
† Zip of nearest p.o.
* Multiple zips

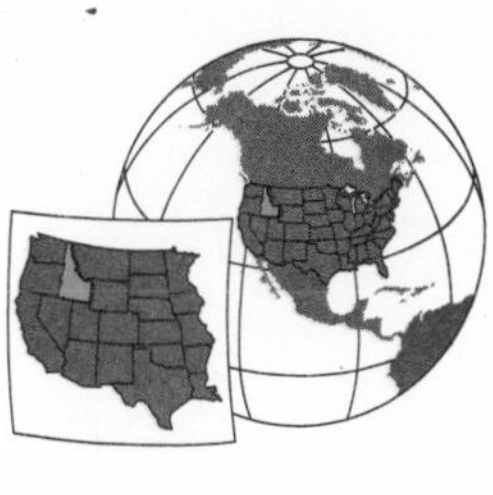

AREA 83,557 sq. mi.
POPULATION 713,008
CAPITAL Boise
LARGEST CITY Boise
HIGHEST POINT Borah Pk. 12,662 ft.
SETTLED IN 1842
ADMITTED TO UNION July 3, 1890
POPULAR NAME Gem State
STATE FLOWER Syringa
STATE BIRD Mountain Bluebird

Agriculture, Industry and Resources

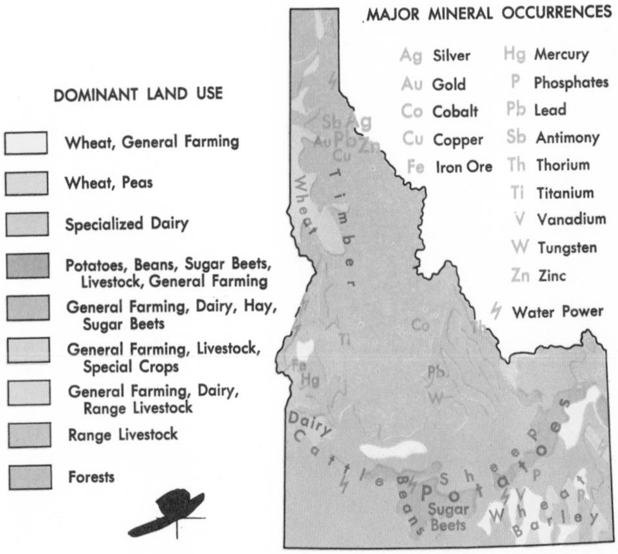
DOMINANT LAND USE
Wheat, General Farming
Wheat, Peas
Specialized Dairy
Potatoes, Beans, Sugar Beets, Livestock, General Farming
General Farming, Dairy, Hay, Sugar Beets
General Farming, Livestock, Special Crops
General Farming, Dairy, Range Livestock
Range Livestock
Forests
MAJOR MINERAL OCCURRENCES
Ag Silver
Au Gold
Co Cobalt
Cu Copper
Fe Iron Ore
Hg Mercury
P Phosphates
Pb Lead
Sb Antimony
Th Thorium
Ti Titanium
V Vanadium
W Tungsten
Zn Zinc
Water Power
Wheat
Timber
Dairy
Cattle
Sheep
Potatoes
Beans
Sugar Beets
Wheat
Barley

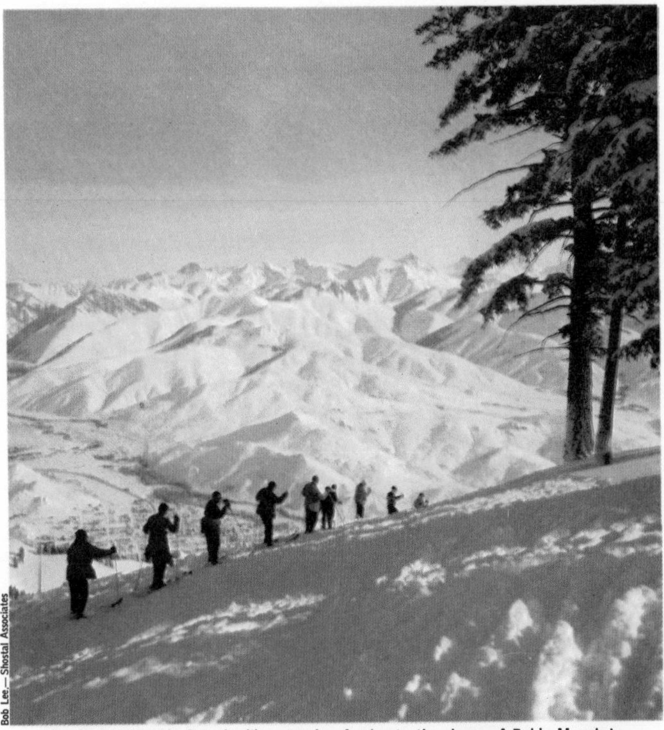

Bob Lee—Shostal Associates

The Sun Valley Ski Patrol adds a touch of color to the slopes of Baldy Mountain. Here, in one of the country's most popular resorts, visitors acquire tropical tans while swimming in heated pools, skiing, skijoring, dogsledding or just sunbathing in the glacial air.

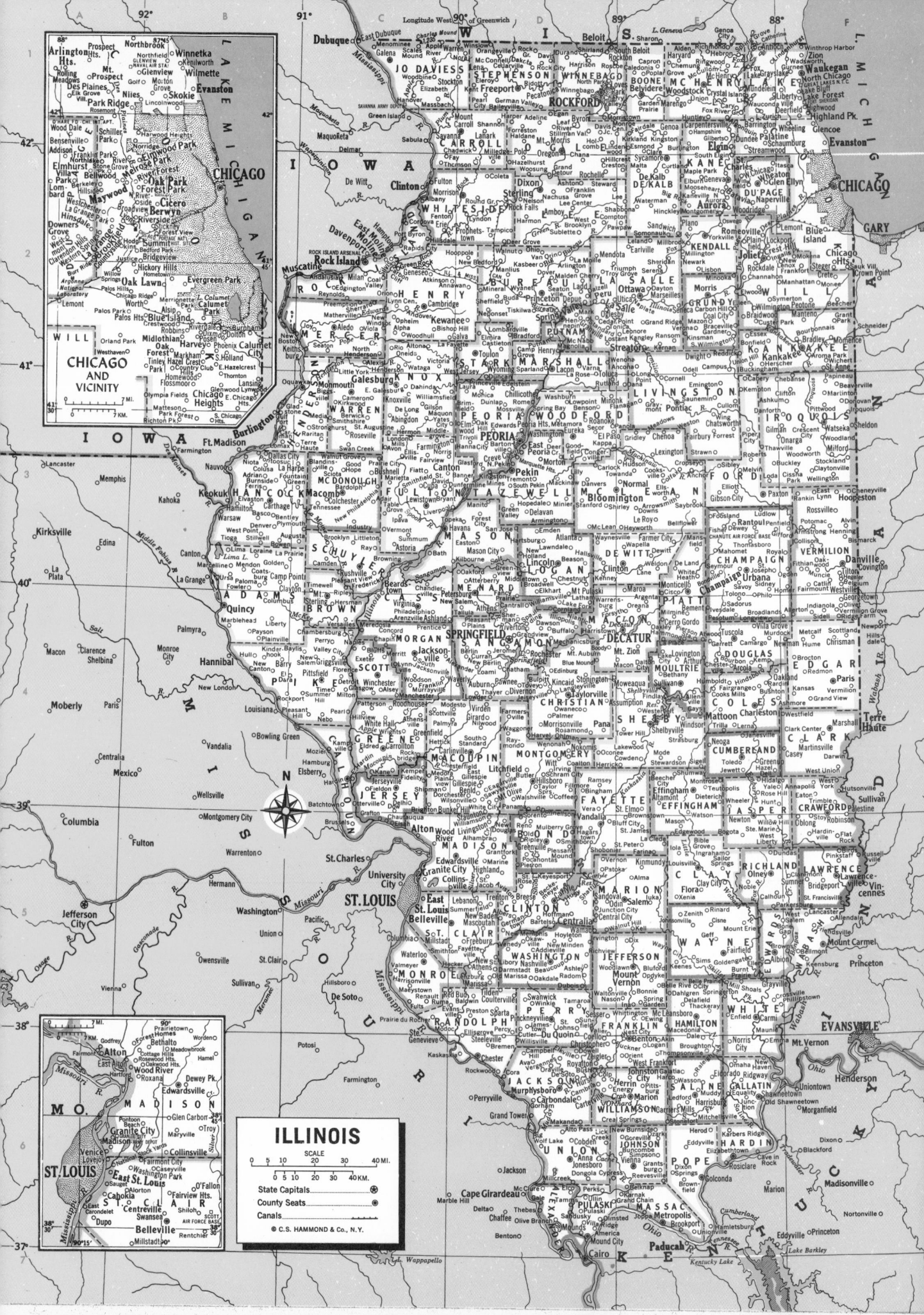

CHICAGO AND VICINITY

SCALE
0 5 10 20 30 40 MI.
0 5 10 20 30 40 KM.

ILLINOIS

State Capitals .... ⊛
County Seats .... ◉
Canals

© C.S. HAMMOND & Co., N.Y.

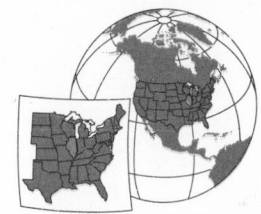

COUNTIES

County	Pop.	Key
dams, 70,861		B 4
lexander, 12,015		D 6
ond, 14,012		D 5
oone, 25,440		E 1
rown, 5,586		D 2
ureau, 38,541		D 2
alhoun, 5,675		C 4
arroll, 19,276		D 1
ass, 14,219		D 3
hampaign, 163,281		E 3
hristian, 35,948		D 4
lark, 16,216		F 4
lay, 14,735		E 5
linton, 28,315		D 5
oles, 47,815		E 4
ook, 5,492,369		F 2
rawford, 19,824		F 4
umberland, 9,772		E 4
e Kalb, 71,654		E 2
e Witt, 16,975		E 3
ouglas, 18,997		E 4
u Page, 491,882		E 2
dgar, 21,591		F 4
dwards, 7,090		E 5
ffingham, 24,608		E 4
ayette, 20,752		D 4
ord, 16,382		E 3
ranklin, 38,329		E 5
ulton, 41,890		C 3
allatin, 7,418		E 6
reene, 17,014		C 4
rundy, 26,535		E 2
amilton, 8,665		E 5
ancock, 23,645		B 3
ardin, 4,914		E 6
enderson, 8,451		C 3
enry, 53,217		C 2
roquois, 33,532		F 3
ackson, 55,008		D 6
asper, 10,741		E 4
efferson, 31,446		E 5
ersey, 18,492		C 4
o Daviess, 21,766		C 1
ohnson, 7,550		E 6
ane, 251,005		E 2
ankakee, 97,250		F 2
endall, 26,374		E 2
nox, 61,280		C 3
ake, 382,638		E 1
a Salle, 111,409		E 2
awrence, 17,522		F 5
ee, 37,947		D 2
ivingston, 40,690		E 3
ogan, 33,538		D 3
Macon, 125,010		E 4
Macoupin, 44,557		D 4
Madison, 250,934		D 5
Marion, 38,986		E 5
Marshall, 13,302		D 3
Mason, 16,161		D 3
Massac, 14,341		E 6
McDonough, 36,653		C 3
McHenry, 111,555		E 1
McLean, 104,389		E 3
Menard, 9,685		D 3
Mercer, 17,294		C 2
Monroe, 18,831		C 5
Montgomery, 30,260		D 4
Morgan, 36,174		C 4
Moultrie, 13,263		E 4
Ogle, 42,867		D 1
Peoria, 195,318		D 3
Perry, 19,757		D 5
Piatt, 15,509		E 4
Pike, 19,185		C 4
Pope, 3,857		E 6
Pulaski, 8,741		D 6
Putnam, 5,007		D 2
Randolph, 31,379		D 5
Richland, 16,829		E 5
Rock Island, 166,734		C 2
Saint Clair, 285,176		D 5
Saline, 25,721		E 6
Sangamon, 161,335		D 4
Schuyler, 8,135		C 3
Scott, 6,096		C 4
Shelby, 22,589		E 4
Stark, 7,510		D 3
Stephenson, 48,861		D 1
Tazewell, 118,649		D 3
Union, 16,071		D 6
Vermilion, 97,047		F 3
Wabash, 12,841		F 5
Warren, 21,595		C 3
Washington, 13,780		D 5
Wayne, 17,004		E 5
White, 17,312		E 5
Whiteside, 62,877		D 2
Will, 249,498		F 2
Williamson, 49,021		E 6
Winnebago, 246,623		D 1
Woodford, 28,012		D 3

CITIES and TOWNS

Zip	Name/Pop.	Key
61410	Abingdon, 3,936	C 3
60101	Addison, 24,482	A 2
61230	Albany, 942	C 2
62215	Albers, 656	D 5
62806	Albion⊙, 1,791	E 5
61231	Aledo⊙, 3,325	C 2
61412	Alexis, 946	C 2
60102	Algonquin, 3,515	E 1
62001	Alhambra, 594	D 5
† 62207	Alorton, 3,573	B 6
61413	Alpha, 771	C 2
† 60601	Alsip, 11,141	B 2
62411	Altamont, 1,929	E 4
62002	Alton, 39,700	A 6
61310	Amboy, 2,184	D 2
61232	Andalusia, 950	C 2
62906	Anna, 4,766	D 6
61234	Annawan, 787	C 2
60002	Antioch, 3,189	E 1
61910	Arcola, 2,276	E 4
62501	Argenta, 1,034	E 4
61914	Bethany, 1,235	E 4
61420	Blandinsville, 922	C 3
61701	Bloomington⊙, 39,992	D 3
	Bloomington-Normal, ‡104,389	
60406	Blue Island, 22,958	B 2
62513	Blue Mound, 1,181	D 4
62621	Bluffs, 866	C 4
60914	Bourbonnais, 5,909	F 2
60407	Braceville, 668	E 2
61421	Bradford, 885	D 2
60915	Bradley, 9,881	F 2
60408	Braidwood, 2,323	E 2
62230	Breese, 2,885	D 5
62417	Bridgeport, 2,262	F 5
60455	Bridgeview, 12,522	B 2
62012	Brighton, 1,889	C 4
61517	Brimfield, 729	D 3
60153	Broadview, 9,307	A 4
60513	Brookfield, 20,284	A 2
† 62059	Brooklyn (Lovejoy), 1,702	A 6
62910	Brookport, 1,046	E 6
62418	Brownstown, 689	E 5
60918	Buckley, 680	F 3
61314	Buda, 675	D 2
62014	Bunker Hill, 1,465	C 4
† 60601	Burnham, 3,634	B 2
60558	Burr Ridge, 1,637	A 2
61422	Bushnell, 3,703	C 3
61010	Byron, 1,749	D 1
62606	Cahokia, 20,649	B 6
62914	Cairo⊙, 6,277	D 6
60409	Calumet City, 32,956	B 2
† 60601	Calumet Park, 10,069	B 2
62915	Cambria, 798	D 6
61238	Cambridge⊙, 2,095	C 2
62320	Camp Point, 1,143	B 3
61520	Canton, 14,217	C 3
61012	Capron, 654	E 1
61239	Carbon Cliff, 1,369	C 2
62901	Carbondale, 22,816	D 6
62626	Carlinville⊙, 5,675	D 4
62231	Carlyle⊙, 3,139	D 5
62821	Carmi⊙, 6,033	E 5
60110	Carpentersville, 24,059	E 1
62917	Carriers Mills, 2,013	E 6
62016	Carrollton⊙, 2,866	C 4
62918	Carterville, 3,061	D 6
62321	Carthage⊙, 3,350	B 3
60013	Cary, 4,358	E 1
62420	Casey, 2,994	F 4
62232	Caseyville, 3,411	B 6
61817	Catlin, 2,093	F 3
62013	Cedarville, 578	D 1
† 62801	Central City, 1,377	D 5
62801	Centralia, 15,217	D 5
62206	Centreville, 11,378	B 6
61818	Cerro Gordo, 1,368	E 4
61014	Chadwick, 605	D 1
61820	Champaign, 56,532	E 3
	Champaign-Urbana, ‡163,281	E 3
62627	Chandlerville, 762	C 3
60410	Channahon, 1,505	E 2
62628	Chapin, 552	C 4
61920	Charleston⊙, 16,421	E 4
62629	Chatham, 2,788	D 4
60921	Chatsworth, 1,255	E 3
60922	Chebanse, 1,185	F 3
61726	Chenoa, 1,860	E 3
61016	Cherry Valley, 952	D 1
62233	Chester⊙, 5,310	D 6
* 60601	Chicago⊙, 3,366,957	B 2
	Chicago, ‡6,978,947	B 2
60411	Chicago Heights, 40,900	B 3
60415	Chicago Ridge, 9,187	A 2
61523	Chillicothe, 6,052	D 3
61924	Chrisman, 1,285	F 4
62822	Christopher, 2,910	D 6
60650	Cicero, 67,058	B 2
62823	Cisne, 615	E 5
60924	Cissna Park, 773	F 3
60514	Clarendon Hills, 6,750	A 2
62824	Clay City, 1,049	E 5
62324	Clayton, 727	B 3
60927	Clifton, 1,339	F 3
61727	Clinton⊙, 7,570	E 3
60416	Coal City, 3,040	E 2
61240	Coal Valley, 3,088	C 2
62920	Cobden, 1,114	D 6
62017	Coffeen, 641	D 4
62326	Colchester, 1,747	C 3
61728	Colfax, 935	E 3
62234	Collinsville, 17,773	B 6
62236	Columbia, 4,188	C 5
61242	Cordova, 589	C 2
62018	Cottage Hills, 1,261	B 6
62237	Coulterville, 1,186	D 5
60477	Country Club Hills, 6,920	A 3
* 60525	Countryside, 2,888	A 2
62922	Creal Springs, 830	E 6
60928	Crescent City, 597	F 3
60435	Crest Hill, 7,460	E 2
60113	Creston, 595	D 2
60445	Crestwood, 5,543	B 2
60417	Crete, 4,656	F 2
61611	Creve Coeur, 6,440	D 3
62827	Crossville, 860	F 5
60014	Crystal Lake, 14,541	E 1
61427	Cuba, 1,581	C 3
60929	Cullom, 572	E 3
62330	Dallas City, 1,284	B 3
61320	Dalzell, 579	D 2
61732	Danvers, 854	D 3
61832	Danville⊙, 42,570	F 3
* 62521	Decatur⊙, 90,397	E 4
	Decatur, ‡125,010	E 4

(continued on following page)

AREA 56,400 sq. mi.
POPULATION 11,113,976
CAPITAL Springfield
LARGEST CITY Chicago
HIGHEST POINT Charles Mound 1,235 ft.
SETTLED IN 1720
ADMITTED TO UNION December 3, 1818
POPULAR NAME Prairie State
STATE FLOWER Violet
STATE BIRD Cardinal

Agriculture, Industry and Resources

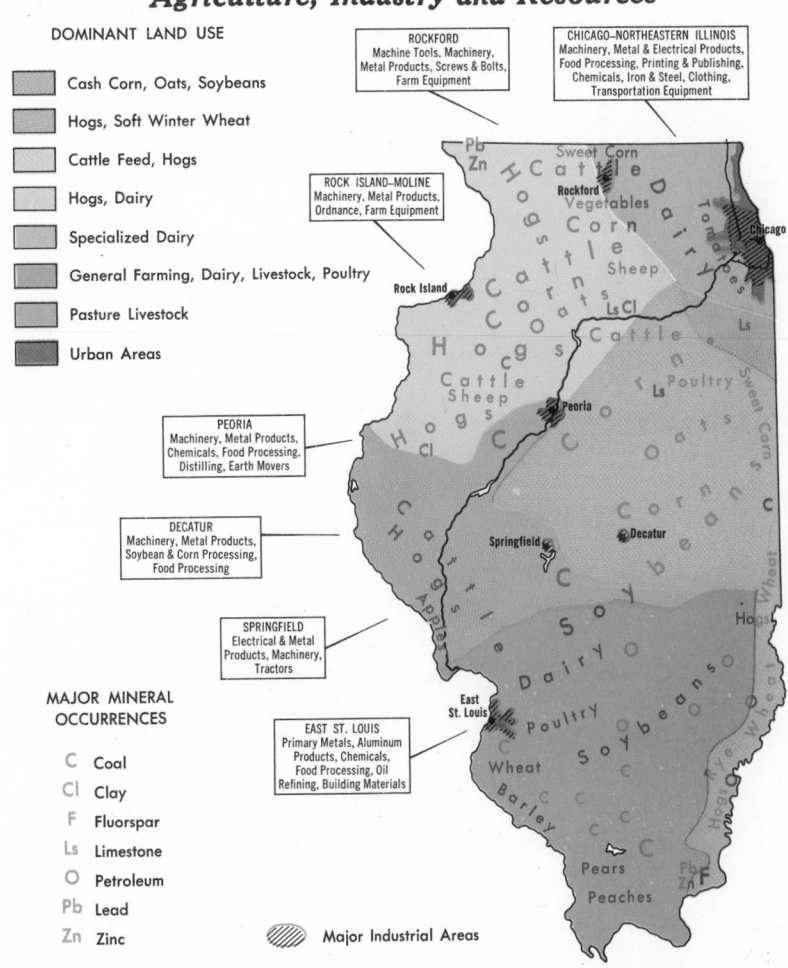

DOMINANT LAND USE

- Cash Corn, Oats, Soybeans
- Hogs, Soft Winter Wheat
- Cattle Feed, Hogs
- Hogs, Dairy
- Specialized Dairy
- General Farming, Dairy, Livestock, Poultry
- Pasture Livestock
- Urban Areas

ROCKFORD
Machine Tools, Machinery, Metal Products, Screws & Bolts, Farm Equipment

CHICAGO–NORTHEASTERN ILLINOIS
Machinery, Metal & Electrical Products, Food Processing, Printing & Publishing, Chemicals, Iron & Steel, Clothing, Transportation Equipment

ROCK ISLAND–MOLINE
Machinery, Metal Products, Ordnance, Farm Equipment

PEORIA
Machinery, Metal Products, Chemicals, Food Processing, Distilling, Earth Movers

DECATUR
Machinery, Metal Products, Soybean & Corn Processing, Food Processing

SPRINGFIELD
Electrical & Metal Products, Machinery, Tractors

EAST ST. LOUIS
Primary Metals, Aluminum Products, Chemicals, Food Processing, Oil Refining, Building Materials

MAJOR MINERAL OCCURRENCES

- C Coal
- Cl Clay
- F Fluorspar
- Ls Limestone
- O Petroleum
- Pb Lead
- Zn Zinc

Major Industrial Areas

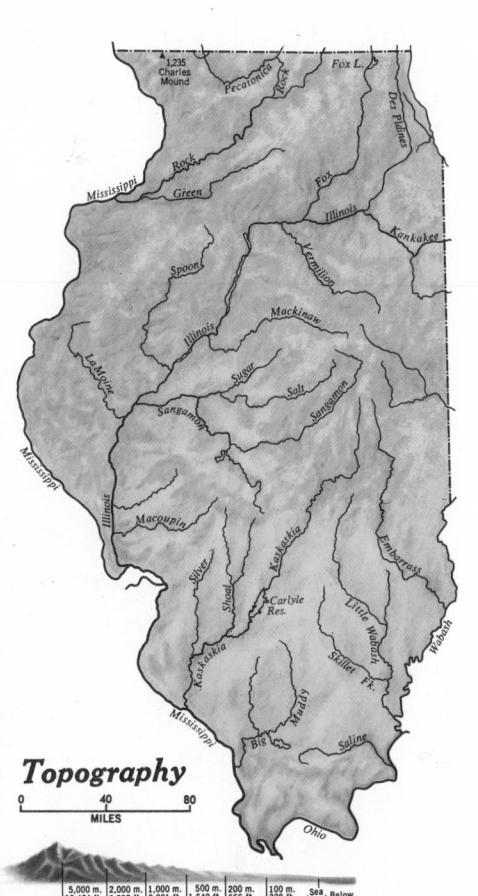

Topography

1,235
Charles Mound

0	40	80
	MILES	

| 5,000 m. 16,404 ft. | 2,000 m. 6,562 ft. | 1,000 m. 3,281 ft. | 500 m. 1,640 ft. | 200 m. 656 ft. | 100 m. 328 ft. | Sea Level | Below |

(continued)

61733 Deer Creek, 647 ....D 3
60015 Deerfield, 18,949 ....F 1
60115 De Kalb, 32,949 ....E 2
61734 Delavan, 1,844 ....D 3
61322 Depue, 1,919 ....D 2
62924 De Soto, 966 ....D 6
* 60016 Des Plaines, 57,239 ....A 1
† 62025 Dewey Park, 2,029 ....B 6
62530 Divernon, 1,010 ....D 4
† 60469 Dixmoor, 4,735 ....B 2
61021 Dixon⊙, 18,147 ....D 2
60419 Dolton, 25,937 ....B 2
62926 Dongola, 825 ....D 6
60515 Downers Grove, 32,751 ....A 2
61736 Downs, 651 ....E 3
60118 Dundee (East and West Dundee), 6,215 ....E 1
61525 Dunlap, 656 ....D 3
62239 Dupo, 2,842 ....A 6
62832 Du Quoin, 6,691 ....D 5
61024 Durand, 972 ....D 1
60420 Dwight, 3,841 ....E 2
60518 Earlville, 1,410 ....E 2
62024 East Alton, 7,309 ....B 6
† 60411 East Chicago Heights, 5,000 ....B 3
61025 East Dubuque, 2,408 ....C 1
† 60118 East Dundee (Dundee), 2,920 ....E 1
61430 East Galesburg, 706 ....C 3
† 60429 East Hazelcrest, 1,885 ....B 2
61244 East Moline, 20,832 ....C 2
61611 East Peoria, 18,455 ....D 3
* 62201 East Saint Louis, 69,996 ....B 6
62531 Edinburg, 1,153 ....D 4
62025 Edwardsville⊙, 11,070 ....B 6
62401 Effingham⊙, 9,458 ....E 4
60119 Elburn, 1,122 ....E 2
62930 Eldorado, 3,876 ....E 6
60120 Elgin, 55,691 ....E 1
61028 Elizabeth, 707 ....C 1
62931 Elizabethtown⊙, 436 ....E 6
60007 Elk Grove Village, 24,516 ....A 1
62932 Elkville, 850 ....D 6
60126 Elmhurst, 50,547 ....A 2
61529 Elmwood, 2,014 ....D 3
60635 Elmwood Park, 26,160 ....B 2
61738 El Paso, 2,291 ....D 3
60421 Elwood, 794 ....E 2
62635 Emden, 552 ....D 3
62933 Energy, 812 ....E 6
62835 Enfield, 764 ....E 5
62934 Equality, 732 ....E 6
61250 Erie, 1,566 ....C 2
61530 Eureka⊙, 3,028 ....D 3
* 60201 Evanston, 79,808 ....B 1
62242 Evansville, 838 ....D 5
60642 Evergreen Park, 25,487 ....B 2
61739 Fairbury, 3,359 ....E 3
62837 Fairfield⊙, 5,897 ....E 5
† 62002 Fairmont, 1,521 ....A 6
† 62201 Fairmont City, 2,769 ....B 6
61841 Fairmount, 785 ....F 3
61432 Fairview 601 ....C 3
62232 Fairview Heights, 8,625 ....B 6
62838 Farina, 634 ....E 5
61842 Farmer City, 2,217 ....E 3
61531 Farmington, 2,959 ....C 3
62534 Findlay, 809 ....E 4
61843 Fisher, 1,525 ....E 3
61844 Fithian, 562 ....F 3
61740 Flanagan, 878 ....E 3
62839 Flora, 5,283 ....E 5
60422 Flossmoor, 7,846 ....B 3
† 62018 Forest Homes, 1,998 ....B 6
60130 Forest Park, 15,472 ....B 2
† 60402 Forest View, 927 ....B 2
61741 Forrest, 1,219 ....E 3
61030 Forreston, 1,227 ....D 1
60020 Fox Lake, 4,511 ....E 1
60021 Fox River Grove, 2,245 ....E 1
60423 Frankfort, 2,325 ....F 2
62638 Franklin, 565 ....C 4
61031 Franklin Grove, 968 ....D 2
60131 Franklin Park, 20,497 ....A 2
62243 Freeburg, 2,495 ....D 5
61032 Freeport⊙, 27,736 ....D 1
61252 Fulton, 3,630 ....C 2
62935 Galatia, 792 ....E 6
61036 Galena⊙, 3,930 ....C 1
61401 Galesburg⊙, 36,290 ....C 3
61434 Galva, 3,061 ....D 2
60424 Gardner, 1,212 ....E 2
61254 Geneseo, 5,840 ....C 2
60134 Geneva⊙, 9,115 ....E 2
60135 Genoa, 3,003 ....E 1
61846 Georgetown, 3,984 ....F 4
62245 Germantown, 1,108 ....D 5
60936 Gibson City, 3,454 ....E 3
61847 Gifford, 814 ....E 3
62033 Gillespie, 3,457 ....D 4
60938 Gilman, 1,786 ....E 3
62640 Girard, 1,881 ....D 4
61533 Glasford, 1,066 ....D 3
62034 Glen Carbon, 1,897 ....B 6
60022 Glencoe, 10,542 ....F 1
60137 Glen Ellyn, 21,909 ....F 2
60025 Glenview, 24,880 ....B 1
60425 Glenwood, 7,416 ....B 3
62035 Godfrey, 1,225 ....A 6
62938 Golconda⊙, 922 ....E 6
62339 Golden, 571 ....B 3
62939 Goreville, 1,109 ....E 6
62037 Grafton, 1,018 ....C 5
61325 Grand Ridge, 698 ....E 2
62942 Grand Tower, 664 ....D 6
† 62701 Grandview, 2,242 ....D 4
62040 Granite City, 40,440 ....B 6
60940 Grant Park, 801 ....F 2
61326 Granville, 1,232 ....D 2
60030 Grayslake, 4,907 ....E 1
62844 Grayville, 2,035 ....E 5
62044 Greenfield, 1,179 ....C 4
† 61241 Green Rock, 2,744 ....C 2
62428 Greenup, 1,618 ....E 4
61534 Green Valley, 617 ....D 3
62045 Greenview, 740 ....D 3
62246 Greenville⊙, 4,631 ....D 5
61741 Gridley, 1,007 ....E 3
62340 Griggsville, 1,245 ....C 4
60031 Gurnee, 2,738 ....F 1
62341 Hamilton, 2,764 ....B 3
60140 Hampshire, 1,611 ....E 1
61256 Hampton, 1,612 ....C 2
61536 Hanna City, 1,282 ....D 3
61041 Hanover, 1,243 ....C 1
62047 Hardin⊙, 1,035 ....C 4
62946 Harrisburg⊙, 9,535 ....E 6
62048 Hartford, 2,243 ....B 6
60033 Harvard, 5,177 ....E 1
60426 Harvey, 34,636 ....B 2
60656 Harwood Heights, 9,060 ....B 1
62644 Havana⊙, 4,376 ....D 3
60429 Hazel Crest, 10,329 ....B 2
60034 Hebron, 781 ....E 1
† 61832 Hegeler, 1,595 ....F 3
61327 Hennepin⊙, 535 ....D 2
61537 Henry, 2,610 ....D 2
62948 Herrin, 9,623 ....E 6
60941 Herscher, 988 ....E 2
61745 Heyworth, 1,441 ....E 3
60457 Hickory Hills, 13,176 ....B 2
62249 Highland, 5,981 ....D 5
60035 Highland Park, 32,263 ....F 1
60040 Highwood, 4,973 ....F 1
61244 Hillcrest, 630 ....D 2
62049 Hillsboro⊙, 4,267 ....D 4
60162 Hillside, 8,888 ....A 2
60520 Hinckley, 1,053 ....E 2
60521 Hinsdale, 15,918 ....A 2
60525 Hodgkins, 2,270 ....A 2
61849 Homer, 1,354 ....F 3
60456 Hometown, 6,729 ....B 2
60430 Homewood, 18,871 ....B 3
60942 Hoopeston, 6,461 ....F 3
61747 Hopedale, 923 ....D 3
61748 Hudson, 802 ....E 3
62343 Hull, 585 ....B 4
60142 Huntley, 1,432 ....E 1
62949 Hurst, 934 ....D 6
62539 Illiopolis, 1,122 ....D 4
61440 Industry, 558 ....C 3
† 60431 Ingalls Park, 5,615 ....F 2
61441 Ipava, 608 ....C 3
62051 Irving, 599 ....D 4
60042 Island Lake, 1,973 ....E 1
60143 Itasca, 4,638 ....F 2
62650 Jacksonville⊙, 20,553 ....C 4
† 62701 Jerome, 1,673 ....D 4
62052 Jerseyville⊙, 7,446 ....C 4
62951 Johnston City, 3,928 ....E 6
* 60431 Joliet⊙, 80,378 ....E 2
62952 Jonesboro⊙, 1,676 ....D 6
† 60453 Justice, 9,473 ....A 2
60901 Kankakee⊙, 30,944 ....F 2
61933 Kansas, 779 ....F 4
62956 Karnak, 641 ....E 6
† 63673 Kaskaskia, 79 ....C 6
61442 Keithsburg, 836 ....B 2
60043 Kenilworth, 2,980 ....B 1
61443 Kewanee, 15,762 ....C 2
62540 Kincaid, 1,424 ....D 4
62854 Kinmundy, 759 ....E 5
60146 Kirkland, 1,138 ....E 1
61447 Kirkwood, 817 ....C 3
61448 Knoxville, 2,930 ....C 3
61540 Lacon⊙, 2,147 ....D 2
61329 Ladd, 1,328 ....D 2
60525 La Grange, 16,773 ....A 2
60525 La Grange Park, 15,626 ....A 2
61450 La Harpe, 1,240 ....C 3
60044 Lake Bluff, 4,979 ....F 1
† 60002 Lake Catherine, 1,219 ....E 1
60045 Lake Forest, 15,642 ....F 1
60047 Lake Zurich, 4,082 ....E 1
61330 La Moille, 669 ....D 2
61046 Lanark, 1,495 ....D 1
60438 Lansing, 25,805 ....B 3
61301 La Salle, 10,736 ....E 2
62439 Lawrenceville⊙, 5,863 ....F 5
61047 Leaf River, 633 ....D 1
62254 Lebanon, 3,564 ....D 5
60531 Leland, 743 ....E 2
60439 Lemont, 5,080 ....A 2
61048 Lena, 1,691 ....D 1
61752 Le Roy, 2,435 ....E 3
61542 Lewistown⊙, 2,706 ....C 3
61753 Lexington, 1,615 ....E 3
60048 Libertyville, 11,684 ....F 1
62656 Lincoln⊙, 17,582 ....D 3
† 60601 Lincolnwood, 12,929 ....B 1
60046 Lindenhurst, 3,141 ....F 1
62056 Litchfield, 7,190 ....D 4
62058 Livingston, 916 ....D 5
60441 Lockport, 9,985 ....F 2
61454 Lomax, 565 ....B 3
60148 Lombard, 35,977 ....A 2
61544 London Mills, 600 ....C 3
62858 Louisville⊙, 1,020 ....E 5
62059 Lovejoy, 1,702 ....A 6
61111 Loves Park, 12,390 ....E 1
61937 Lovington, 1,303 ....E 4
61261 Lyndon, 673 ....D 2
† 60411 Lynwood, 1,042 ....B 3
60534 Lyons, 11,124 ....B 2
61755 Mackinaw, 1,293 ....D 3
61455 Macomb⊙, 19,643 ....C 3
62544 Macon, 1,249 ....E 4
62060 Madison, 7,042 ....B 6
61853 Mahomet, 1,296 ....E 3
60150 Malta, 961 ....E 2
60442 Manhattan, 1,530 ....F 2
61546 Manito, 1,334 ....D 3
61854 Mansfield, 870 ....E 3
60950 Manteno, 2,864 ....F 2
60151 Maple Park, 660 ....E 2
60152 Marengo, 4,235 ....E 1
62061 Marine, 882 ....D 5
62959 Marion⊙, 11,724 ....E 6
62257 Marissa, 2,004 ....D 5
60426 Markham, 15,987 ....B 2
61756 Maroa, 1,467 ....E 3
† 61554 Marquette Heights, 2,758 ....D 3
61341 Marseilles, 4,320 ....E 2
62441 Marshall⊙, 3,468 ....F 4

Fred Boler,—Shostal Associates

Sailboats lie anchored in Lake Michigan while many of their owners turn the wheels of industry behind Chicago's steel and glass facade.

62442 Martinsville, 1,374 ....F 4
62062 Maryville, 809 ....B 6
62258 Mascoutah, 5,045 ....D 5
62664 Mason City, 2,611 ....D 3
61263 Matherville, 699 ....C 2
60443 Matteson, 4,741 ....B 3
61938 Mattoon, 19,681 ....E 4
60153 Maywood, 30,036 ....A 2
60444 Mazon, 727 ....E 2
62957 McClure, 800 ....D 6
† 60050 McCullom Lake, 873 ....E 1
60050 McHenry, 6,772 ....E 1
61754 McLean, 820 ....D 3
62859 McLeansboro⊙, 2,630 ....E 5
† 62010 Meadowbrook, 1,295 ....B 6
* 60160 Melrose Park, 22,706 ....A 2
62351 Mendon, 883 ....B 3
61342 Mendota, 6,902 ....D 2
62665 Meredosia, 1,178 ....C 4
† 60601 Merrionette Park, 2,303 ....B 2
61548 Metamora, 2,176 ....D 3
62960 Metropolis⊙, 6,940 ....E 6
62666 Middletown, 626 ....D 3
60445 Midlothian, 15,939 ....B 2
61264 Milan, 4,873 ....C 2
60953 Milford, 1,656 ....F 3
61051 Milledgeville, 1,130 ....D 1
62260 Millstadt, 2,168 ....B 6
61759 Minier, 986 ....D 3
61760 Minonk, 2,267 ....D 3
60447 Minooka, 768 ....E 2
60448 Mokena, 1,643 ....F 2
61265 Moline, 46,237 ....C 2
60954 Momence, 2,836 ....F 2
60449 Monee, 940 ....F 2
61462 Monmouth⊙, 11,022 ....C 3
60538 Montgomery, 3,278 ....E 2
61856 Monticello⊙, 4,130 ....E 3
60539 Mooseheart, 850 ....E 2
60450 Morris⊙, 8,194 ....E 2
61270 Morrison⊙, 4,387 ....C 2
62546 Morrisonville, 1,178 ....D 4
† 61101 Morristown, 669 ....D 1
61550 Morton, 10,419 ....D 3
60053 Morton Grove, 26,369 ....B 1
62963 Mound City⊙, 1,177 ....D 6
62964 Mounds, 1,718 ....D 6
62863 Mount Carmel⊙, 8,096 ....F 5
61053 Mount Carroll⊙, 2,143 ....D 1
61054 Mount Morris, 3,173 ....D 1
62069 Mount Olive, 2,288 ....D 4
60056 Mount Prospect, 34,995 ....A 1
62548 Mount Pulaski, 1,677 ....D 3
62353 Mount Sterling⊙, 2,182 ....C 4
62864 Mount Vernon⊙, 15,980 ....E 5
62549 Mount Zion, 2,343 ....E 4
62550 Moweaqua, 1,687 ....E 4
62262 Mulberry Grove, 697 ....D 5
60060 Mundelein, 16,128 ....E 1
62966 Murphysboro⊙, 10,013 ....D 6
62668 Murrayville, 595 ....C 4
60540 Naperville, 23,885 ....E 2
† 61350 Naplate, 686 ....E 2
62263 Nashville⊙, 3,027 ....D 5
62354 Nauvoo, 1,047 ....B 3
62447 Neoga, 1,270 ....E 4
60541 Newark, 590 ....E 2
62264 New Athens, 2,000 ....D 5
62265 New Baden, 1,953 ....D 5
62670 New Berlin, 754 ....D 4
61272 New Boston, 706 ....B 2
62867 New Haven, 606 ....E 6
60451 New Lenox, 2,855 ....F 2
61942 Newman, 1,018 ....F 4
62448 Newton⊙, 3,024 ....E 5
61465 New Windsor, 723 ....C 2
62551 Niantic, 705 ....D 4
60648 Niles, 31,432 ....A 1
62868 Noble, 719 ....E 5
62075 Nokomis, 2,532 ....D 4
61761 Normal, 26,396 ....E 3
† 60601 Norridge, 16,880 ....B 1
62869 Norris City, 1,319 ....E 6
60542 North Aurora, 4,833 ....E 2
60062 Northbrook, 27,297 ....A 1
60064 North Chicago, 47,275 ....F 1
60093 Northfield, 5,010 ....B 1
60164 Northlake, 14,212 ....A 2
† 61101 North Park, 15,679 ....D 1
† 61554 North Pekin, 1,886 ....D 3
60546 North Riverside, 8,097 ....B 2
† 61373 North Utica (Utica), 974 ....E 2
60452 Oak Forest, 17,870 ....B 2
61943 Oakland, 1,012 ....F 4
* 60453 Oak Lawn, 60,305 ....B 2
60303 Oak Park, 62,511 ....B 2
61858 Oakwood, 1,367 ....F 3
† 62095 Oakwood Heights, 3,229 ....B 6
62449 Oblong, 1,860 ....F 5
60460 Odell, 1,076 ....E 2
62870 Odin, 1,263 ....D 5
62269 O'Fallon, 7,268 ....B 6
61348 Oglesby, 4,175 ....D 2
62271 Okawville, 992 ....D 5
62969 Olive Branch, 600 ....D 6
62450 Olney⊙, 8,974 ....E 5
60461 Olympia Fields, 3,478 ....B 3
60955 Onarga, 1,436 ....F 3
61467 Oneida, 728 ....C 2
61469 Oquawka⊙, 1,352 ....C 3
62554 Oreana, 1,092 ....E 4
61061 Oregon⊙, 3,539 ....D 1
61273 Orion, 1,801 ....C 2
60462 Orland Park, 6,391 ....A 2
60543 Oswego, 1,862 ....E 2
61350 Ottawa⊙, 18,716 ....E 2
60067 Palatine, 25,904 ....E 1
62451 Palestine, 1,640 ....F 4
62674 Palmyra, 776 ....C 4
60463 Palos Heights, 9,915 ....A 2
60465 Palos Hills, 6,629 ....A 2
60464 Palos Park, 3,297 ....A 2
62557 Pana, 6,326 ....D 4
61944 Paris⊙, 9,971 ....F 4
60466 Park Forest, 30,638 ....B 3
60068 Park Ridge, 42,466 ....A 1
62875 Patoka, 562 ....D 5
62558 Pawnee, 1,936 ....D 4
61353 Pawpaw, 846 ....E 2
60957 Paxton⊙, 4,373 ....E 3
62360 Payson, 589 ....B 4
61063 Pecatonica, 1,781 ....D 1
61554 Pekin⊙, 31,375 ....D 3
* 61601 Peoria⊙, 126,963 ....D 3
Peoria, ‡341,979 ....D 3
61614 Peoria Heights, 7,943 ....D 3
60468 Peotone, 2,345 ....F 2
62272 Percy, 967 ....D 5
61354 Peru, 11,772 ....D 2
62675 Petersburg⊙, 2,632 ....D 4
61864 Philo, 1,022 ....E 3
† 60426 Phoenix, 3,596 ....B 2
62274 Pinckneyville⊙, 3,377 ....D 5
60959 Piper City, 817 ....E 3
62363 Pittsfield⊙, 4,244 ....C 4
60544 Plainfield, 2,928 ....E 2
60545 Plano, 4,664 ....E 2
62366 Pleasant Hill, 1,064 ....C 4
62677 Pleasant Plains, 644 ....D 4
62367 Plymouth, 740 ....C 3
62275 Pocahontas, 764 ....D 5
61074 Polo, 2,542 ....D 1
61764 Pontiac⊙, 9,031 ....E 3
61065 Poplar Grove, 607 ....E 1
61275 Port Byron, 1,222 ....C 2
60469 Posen, 5,498 ....B 2
61865 Potomac, 909 ....F 3
61470 Prairie City, 630 ....C 3
62277 Prairie du Rocher, 658 ....C 5
61356 Princeton⊙, 6,959 ....D 2
61559 Princeville, 1,455 ....D 3
61277 Prophetstown, 1,915 ....D 2
60070 Prospect Heights, 13,333 ....A 1
62301 Quincy⊙, 45,288 ....B 4
62080 Ramsey, 830 ....D 4
60960 Rankin, 727 ....F 3
61866 Rantoul, 25,562 ....E 3
61278 Rapids City, 656 ....C 2
62560 Raymond, 890 ....D 4
62278 Red Bud, 2,559 ....D 5
62279 Reynolds, 610 ....C 2
60071 Richmond, 1,153 ....E 1
60471 Richton Park, 2,558 ....B 3
61870 Ridge Farm, 1,015 ....F 4
62979 Ridgway, 1,160 ....E 6
60627 Riverdale, 15,806 ....B 2
60305 River Forest, 13,402 ....B 2
60171 River Grove, 11,465 ....A 2
60546 Riverside, 10,432 ....B 2
62561 Riverton, 2,090 ....D 4
61561 Roanoke, 2,040 ....D 3
60472 Robbins, 9,641 ....B 2
62454 Robinson⊙, 7,178 ....F 5
61068 Rochelle, 8,594 ....D 2
62563 Rochester, 1,667 ....D 4
60436 Rockdale, 2,085 ....E 2
61071 Rock Falls, 10,287 ....D 2
* 61101 Rockford⊙, 147,370 ....D 1
Rockford, ‡272,063 ....D 1
61201 Rock Island⊙, 50,166 ....C 2
Rock Island-Moline-Davenport, ‡362,638 ....C 2
61072 Rockton, 2,099 ....E 1
60008 Rolling Meadows, 19,178 ....A 1
61562 Rome, 1,919 ....D 3
† 60441 Romeoville, 12,674 ....E 2
62082 Roodhouse, 2,357 ....C 4
61073 Roscoe, 949 ....E 1
60018 Rosemont, 4,360 ....A 1
61473 Roseville, 1,111 ....C 3
† 62024 Rosewood Heights, 3,391 ....B 6
62982 Rosiclare, 1,421 ....E 6
60963 Rossville, 1,420 ....F 3
62084 Roxana, 1,882 ....B 6
62983 Royalton, 1,166 ....D 6
62681 Rushville⊙, 3,300 ....C 3
60964 Saint Anne, 1,271 ....F 2
60174 Saint Charles, 12,928 ....E 2
61563 Saint David, 773 ....C 3
62458 Saint Elmo, 1,676 ....E 4
62460 Saint Francisville, 997 ....F 5
62281 Saint Jacob, 659 ....D 5
61873 Saint Joseph, 1,554 ....E 3
62881 Salem⊙, 6,187 ....E 5
62882 Sandoval, 1,332 ....D 5
60548 Sandwich, 5,056 ....E 2
62682 San Jose, 681 ....D 3
60411 Sauk Village, 7,479 ....F 2
61074 Savanna, 4,942 ....C 1
61874 Savoy, 592 ....E 3
61770 Saybrook, 814 ....E 3
60172 Schaumburg, 18,730 ....E 1
60176 Schiller Park, 12,712 ....A 1
† 62049 Schram City, 657 ....D 4
61360 Seneca, 1,781 ....E 2
62884 Sesser, 2,125 ....D 5
61875 Seymour, 850 ....E 3
60550 Shabbona, 730 ....E 2
61078 Shannon, 848 ....D 1
62984 Shawneetown⊙, 1,742 ....E 6
61361 Sheffield, 1,038 ....D 2
62565 Shelbyville⊙, 4,597 ....E 4
60966 Sheldon, 1,455 ....F 3
60551 Sheridan, 724 ....E 2
61281 Sherrard, 808 ....C 2
† 62220 Shiloh, 945 ....B 6
61876 Sidell, 645 ....F 4
61877 Sidney, 915 ....E 3
61282 Silvis, 5,907 ....C 2
60076 Skokie, 68,627 ....B 1
62285 Smithton, 847 ....C 5
60552 Somonauk, 1,112 ....E 2
62086 Sorento, 625 ....D 5
61080 South Beloit, 3,804 ....E 1
60411 South Chicago Heights, 4,923 ....B 3
60177 South Elgin, 4,289 ....E 2
60473 South Holland, 23,931 ....B 2
62650 South Jacksonville, 2,950 ....C 4
61564 South Pekin, 955 ....D 3
60474 South Wilmington, 725 ....E 2
61565 Sparland, 585 ....D 2
62286 Sparta, 4,307 ....D 5
* 62701 Springfield (cap.)⊙, 91,753 ....D 4
Springfield, ‡161,335 ....D 4
61362 Spring Valley, 5,605 ....D
61774 Stanford, 657 ....D
62088 Staunton, 4,396 ....D
62288 Steeleville, 1,957 ....D
60475 Steger, 8,104 ....F
61081 Sterling, 16,113 ....D
62463 Stewardson, 729 ....E
60402 Stickney, 6,601 ....B
61084 Stillman Valley, 871 ....D
61085 Stockton, 1,930 C
60165 Stone Park, 4,451 ....A
62567 Stonington, 1,096 ....D
60103 Streamwood, 18,176 ....E
61364 Streator, 15,600 ....E
61480 Stronghurst, 836 C
61951 Sullivan⊙, 4,112 ....E
60501 Summit, 11,569 ....B
62466 Sumner, 1,201 ....F
62221 Swansea, 5,432 ....B 6
60178 Sycamore⊙, 7,843 ....E
62688 Tallula, 643 ....D
62888 Tamaroa, 799 ....D
62988 Tamms, 645 ....D 6
61283 Tampico, 838 ....D 2
62089 Taylor Springs, 620 ....D 4
62568 Taylorville⊙, 10,644 ....D 4
62467 Teutopolis, 1,249 ....E 4
62689 Thayer, 616 ....D 4
61878 Thomasboro, 806 ....E 3
61285 Thomson, 617 ....C 2
60476 Thornton, 3,714 ....B 3
62292 Tilden, 909 ....D 5
† 61832 Tilton, 2,544 ....F 3
60477 Tinley Park, 12,382 ....B 2
61368 Tiskilwa, 973 ....D 2
62468 Toledo⊙, 1,068 ....E 4
61880 Tolono, 2,027 ....E 3
61369 Toluca, 1,319 ....D 2
61370 Tonica, 821 ....E 2
61483 Toulon⊙, 1,207 ....D 2
61776 Towanda, 578 ....E 3
62571 Tower Hill, 683 ....E 4
61568 Tremont, 1,942 ....D 3
62293 Trenton, 2,328 ....D 5
62294 Troy, 2,144 ....B 6
61953 Tuscola⊙, 3,917 ....E 4
60180 Union, 579 ....E 1
61801 Urbana⊙, 32,800 ....E 3
61373 Utica, 974 ....E 2
62891 Valier, 628 ....D 5
62295 Valmeyer, 733 ....C 5
62471 Vandalia⊙, 5,160 ....D 5
62090 Venice, 4,680 ....A 6
61484 Vermont, 947 ....C 3
61485 Victoria, 782 ....C 2
62995 Vienna⊙, 1,325 ....E 6
61956 Villa Grove, 2,605 ....E 4
60181 Villa Park, 25,891 ....A 2
61486 Viola, 946 ....C 2
62690 Virden, 3,504 ....D 4
62691 Virginia⊙, 1,814 ....C 4
60083 Wadsworth, 756 ....F 1
61376 Walnut, 1,295 ....D 2
† 62801 Wamac, 1,347 ....D 5
61777 Wapella, 572 ....E 3
61087 Warren, 1,523 ....C 1
62573 Warrensburg, 738 ....D 4
62379 Warsaw, 1,758 ....B 3
61570 Washburn, 1,173 ....D 3
61571 Washington, 6,790 ....D 3
62204 Washington Park, 9,524 ....B 6
61488 Wataga, 570 ....C 2
62298 Waterloo⊙, 4,546 ....C 5
60556 Waterman, 990 ....E 2
60970 Watseka⊙, 5,294 ....F 3
60084 Wauconda, 5,460 ....E 1
60085 Waukegan⊙, 65,269 ....F 1
62692 Waverly, 1,442 ....D 4
62895 Wayne City, 985 ....E 5
61882 Weldon, 553 ....E 3
61377 Wenona, 1,080 ....E 2
60153 Westchester, 20,033 ....A 2
60185 West Chicago, 10,111 ....E 2
† 62812 West City, 637 ....E 5
† 60118 West Dundee (Dundee), 3,295 ....E 1
60558 Western Springs, 12,147 ....A 2
62474 Westfield, 678 ....F 4
62896 West Frankfort, 8,836 ....E 6
60559 Westmont, 8,482 ....A 2
62476 West Salem, 979 ....F 5
61883 Westville, 3,655 ....F 3
60187 Wheaton⊙, 31,138 ....E 2
60090 Wheeling, 14,746 ....F 1
62092 White Hall, 2,979 ....C 4
61489 Williamsfield, 552 ....C 3
62693 Williamsville, 923 ....D 4
62997 Willisville, 659 ....D 6
60480 Willow Springs, 3,318 ....A 2
60091 Wilmette, 32,134 ....B 1
60481 Wilmington, 4,335 ....E 2
62093 Wilsonville, 691 ....D 4
62694 Winchester⊙, 1,788 ....C 4
61957 Windsor, 1,126 ....E 4
† 61465 Windsor (New Windsor) 723 ....C 2
60190 Winfield, 4,285 ....E 2
61088 Winnebago, 1,285 ....D 1
60093 Winnetka, 14,131 ....B 1
60096 Winthrop Harbor, 4,794 ....F 1
62094 Witt, 1,040 ....D 4
60191 Wood Dale, 8,831 ....A 1
61490 Woodhull, 898 ....C 2
60515 Woodridge, 11,028 ....E 2
62095 Wood River, 13,186 ....B 6
60098 Woodstock⊙, 10,226 ....E 1
62097 Worden, 1,091 ....B 6
60482 Worth, 11,999 ....A 2
61379 Wyanet, 1,005 ....D 2
61491 Wyoming, 1,563 ....D 2
61572 Yates City, 840 ....C 3
60560 Yorkville⊙, 2,049 ....E 2
62999 Zeigler, 1,940 ....D 6
60099 Zion, 17,268 ....F 1

⊙ County seat.
‡ Population of metropolitan area.
† Zip of nearest p.o.
* Multiple zips

COUNTIES

Adams, 26,871 H 3
Allen, 280,455 G 2
Bartholomew, 57,022 F 6
Benton, 11,262 C 3
Blackford, 15,888 G 4
Boone, 30,870 E 4
Brown, 9,057 E 6
Carroll, 17,734 D 3
Cass, 40,456 E 3
Clark, 75,876 F 8
Clay, 23,933 C 6
Clinton, 30,547 E 4
Crawford, 8,033 E 8
Daviess, 26,602 C 7
Dearborn, 29,430 H 6
Decatur, 22,738 G 6
De Kalb, 30,837 H 2
Delaware, 129,219 G 4
Dubois, 30,934 D 8
Elkhart, 126,529 F 1
Fayette, 26,216 G 5
Floyd, 55,622 F 8
Fountain, 18,257 C 4
Franklin, 16,943 G 6
Fulton, 16,984 E 2
Gibson, 30,444 B 8
Grant, 83,955 F 3
Greene, 26,894 D 6
Hamilton, 54,532 E 4
Hancock, 35,096 F 5
Harrison, 20,423 E 8
Hendricks, 53,974 D 5
Henry, 52,603 G 5
Howard, 83,198 E 4
Huntington, 34,970 G 3
Jackson, 33,187 E 7
Jasper, 20,429 C 2
Jay, 23,575 G 4
Jefferson, 27,006 G 7
Jennings, 19,454 F 7
Johnson, 61,138 E 6
Knox, 41,546 C 7
Kosciusko, 48,127 F 2
Lagrange, 20,890 G 1
Lake, 546,253 C 2
LaPorte, 105,342 D 1
Lawrence, 38,038 E 7
Madison, 138,451 F 4
Marion, 792,299 E 5
Marshall, 34,986 E 2
Martin, 10,969 D 7
Miami, 39,246 E 3
Monroe, 84,849 D 6
Montgomery, 33,930 D 4
Morgan, 44,176 E 6
Newton, 11,606 C 3
Noble, 31,382 G 2
Ohio, 4,289 H 7
Orange, 16,968 E 7
Owen, 12,163 D 6
Parke, 14,600 C 5
Perry, 19,075 D 8
Pike, 12,281 C 8
Porter, 87,114 C 2
Posey, 21,740 B 8
Pulaski, 12,534 D 2
Putnam, 26,932 D 5
Randolph, 28,915 G 4
Ripley, 21,138 G 6
Rush, 20,352 G 5
Saint Joseph, 245,045 E 1
Scott, 17,144 F 7
Shelby, 37,797 F 5
Spencer, 17,134 C 9
Starke, 19,280 D 2
Steuben, 20,159 G 1
Sullivan, 19,889 C 6
Switzerland, 6,306 G 7
Tippecanoe, 109,378 D 4
Tipton, 16,650 E 4
Union, 6,582 H 5
Vanderburgh, 168,772 B 8
Vermillion, 16,793 C 5
Vigo, 114,528 C 6
Wabash, 35,553 F 3
Warren, 8,705 C 4
Warrick, 27,972 C 8
Washington, 19,278 E 7
Wayne, 79,109 G 5
Wells, 23,821 G 3
White, 20,995 D 3
Whitley, 23,395 F 2

CITIES and TOWNS

Zip *Name/Pop.* *Key*

47240 Adams, 300 F 6
† 46947 Adamsboro, 325 E 3
46102 Advance, 561 D 5
46910 Akron, 1,019 E 2
47320 Albany, 2,293 G 4
46701 Albion⊙, 1,498 G 2
† 47283 Alert, 210 F 6
46001 Alexandria, 5,097 F 4
† 46738 Altona, 209 G 2
47917 Ambia, 300 C 4
46911 Amboy, 473 F 3
† 46131 Amity, 400 E 6
46103 Amo, 422 D 5
* 46011 Anderson⊙, 70,787 F 4
Anderson, ‡138,451 F 4
† 47024 Andersonville, 250 G 5
46702 Andrews, 1,207 F 3
46703 Angola⊙, 5,117 G 1
46030 Arcadia, 1,338 E 4
46704 Arcola, 325 G 2
† 46624 Ardmore, 800 E 1
46501 Argos, 1,393 E 2
46104 Arlington, 550 F 5
46705 Ashley, 721 G 1
46031 Atlanta, 620 E 4
47918 Attica, 4,262 C 4
46502 Atwood, 300 F 2
46706 Auburn⊙, 7,337 G 2
47001 Aurora, 4,293 H 6
47102 Austin, 4,902 F 7
46710 Avilla, 881 G 2
47420 Avoca, 400 D 7
46105 Bainbridge, 703 D 5
46106 Bargersville, 873 E 5
47006 Batesville, 3,799 G 6
47920 Battle Ground, 818 D 3
47421 Bedford⊙, 13,087 E 7
46107 Beech Grove, 13,468 E 5
† 46526 Benton, 221 F 2
46711 Berne, 2,988 H 3
46301 Beverly Shores, 946 C 1
47512 Bicknell, 3,717 C 7
46713 Bippus, 220 F 3
47513 Birdseye, 404 D 8
† 46401 Blackoak, 9,624 C 1
47831 Blanford, 700 B 5
47170 Blocher, 350 F 7
47424 Bloomfield⊙, 2,565 D 6
47832 Bloomingdale, 391 C 5
47401 Bloomington⊙, 42,890 D 6
† 47360 Blountsville, 220 G 4
† 46176 Blue Ridge, 236 F 5
46714 Bluffton⊙, 8,297 G 3
46110 Boggstown, 200 F 5
46302 Boone Grove, 225 C 2
47601 Boonville⊙, 5,736 C 8
47106 Borden, 337 F 8
47324 Boston, 210 H 5
47921 Boswell, 998 C 3
46504 Bourbon, 1,606 E 2
47833 Bowling Green, 200 D 6
47107 Bradford, 400 E 8
47834 Brazil⊙, 8,163 C 5
46506 Bremen, 3,487 E 2
47836 Bridgeton, 350 C 5
† 45030 Bright, 450 H 6
46720 Brimfield, 258 G 2
46913 Bringhurst, 250 E 3
46507 Bristol, 1,100 F 1
† 47354 Bronson (Losantville), 212 G 4
47922 Brook, 919 C 3
46111 Brooklyn, 911 E 5
47923 Brookston, 1,232 D 3
47012 Brookville⊙, 2,864 G 6
46112 Brownsburg, 5,186 E 5
47220 Brownstown⊙, 2,376 F 7
47325 Brownsville, 285 H 5
47516 Bruceville, 627 C 7
47326 Bryant, 320 G 3
47924 Buck Creek, 260 D 4
47517 Buckskin, 275 C 8
47925 Buffalo, 350 D 3
46914 Bunker Hill, 956 E 3
46508 Burket, 210 F 2
46915 Burlington, 685 E 4
47926 Burnettsville, 510 D 3
47222 Burney, 344 F 6
† 46401 Burns Harbor, 1,284 C 1
46916 Burrows, 259 E 3
46721 Butler, 2,394 H 2
47223 Butlerville, 275 F 6
† 46371 Byron, 200 C 5
† 47362 Cadiz, 207 G 5
47327 Cambridge City, 2,481 G 5
46917 Camden, 577 D 3
47108 Campbellsburg, 678 E 7
47520 Cannelton⊙, 2,280 D 9
47837 Carbon, 344 C 5
47838 Carlisle, 714 C 7
46032 Carmel, 6,568 E 5
46114 Cartersburg, 400 E 5
46115 Carthage, 946 F 5
† 47460 Cataract, 200 D 6
47928 Cayuga, 1,090 C 5
47016 Cedar Grove, 248 H 6
46303 Cedar Lake, 7,589 C 2
47521 Celestine, 300 D 8
† 47842 Centenary, 225 B 5
46918 Center, 310 E 4
47840 Centerpoint, 275 C 6
46116 Centerton, 250 E 6
47330 Centerville, 2,380 H 5
47929 Chalmers, 544 D 3
47610 Chandler, 2,032 C 8
47111 Charlestown, 5,890 F 8
46117 Charlottesville, 500 F 5
† 47138 Chelsea, 200 F 7
46017 Chesterfield, 3,001 F 4
46304 Chesterton, 6,177 D 1
47611 Chrisney, 550 C 8
47223 Churubusco, 1,528 G 2
46034 Cicero, 1,378 E 4
47225 Clarksburg, 347 G 6
47930 Clarks Hill, 741 D 4
47130 Clarksville, 13,806 F 8
47841 Clay City, 900 C 6
46510 Claypool, 468 F 2
46118 Clayton, 736 D 5
47426 Clear Creek, 250 E 6
† 46737 Clear Lake, 271 H 1
47226 Clifford, 275 F 6
47842 Clinton, 5,340 C 5
46120 Cloverdale, 870 D 5
47427 Coal City, 300 D 6
47845 Coalmont, 400 C 6
46121 Coatesville, 453 D 5
47931 Colburn, 300 D 3
46035 Colfax, 633 D 4
47978 Collegeville, 1,700 C 3
46725 Columbia City⊙, 4,911 G 2
47201 Columbus⊙, 27,141 E 6
47331 Connersville⊙, 17,604 G 5
46919 Converse, 1,163 F 3
47228 Cortland, 200 F 7
46730 Corunna, 359 G 2
47112 Corydon⊙, 2,719 E 8
47932 Covington⊙, 2,641 C 4
† 47302 Cowan, 428 G 4
47522 Crane, 339 D 7
47933 Crawfordsville⊙, 13,842 D 4
46732 Cromwell, 475 F 2
47229 Crothersville, 1,663 F 7
46307 Crown Point⊙, 10,931 C 2
46511 Culver, 1,783 E 2
46229 Cumberland, 479 E 5
47612 Cynthiana, 793 B 8
47523 Dale, 1,113 D 8
47334 Daleville, 1,730 F 4
47847 Dana, 720 C 5
46122 Danville⊙, 3,771 D 5
47940 Darlington, 802 D 4
47941 Dayton, 840 D 4
46733 Decatur⊙, 8,445 H 3
47524 Decker, 268 B 7
† 46917 Deer Creek, 250 E 3
46923 Delphi⊙, 2,582 D 3
46310 Demotte, 1,697 C 2
46926 Denver, 566 E 3
47230 Deputy, 255 F 7
47302 Desoto, 385 G 4
47018 Dillsboro, 840 G 6
46513 Donaldson, 250 E 2
† 47118 Doolittle Mills, 200 D 8
47335 Dublin, 1,021 G 5
47525 Dubois, 500 D 8
47848 Dugger, 1,150 C 6
† 46304 Dune Acres, 301 C 1
47336 Dunkirk, 3,465 G 4
† 46514 Dunlap, 1,900 F 1
47337 Dunreith, 200 F 5
47231 Dupont, 357 G 7
46311 Dyer, 4,906 C 1
† 46074 Eagletown, 365 E 4
47942 Earl Park, 478 C 3
46312 East Chicago, 46,982 C 1
47019 East Enterprise, 250 H 7
46405 East Gary, 9,858 C 1
† 47370 East Germantown (Pershing), 447 G 5
47338 Eaton, 1,594 G 4
47116 Eckerty, 200 D 8
47339 Economy, 285 G 5
† 46011 Edgewood, 2,326 F 4
46124 Edinburg, 4,906 E 6
47528 Edwardsport, 482 C 7
† 47150 Edwardsville, 700 F 8
47613 Elberfeld, 834 C 8
47232 Elizabethtown, 519 F 6
46514 Elkhart, 43,152 F 1
47429 Ellettsville, 1,627 D 6
47529 Elnora, 873 C 7
† 47018 Elrod, 200 G 6
† 47901 Elston, 500 D 4
46036 Elwood, 11,196 F 4
46125 Eminence, 200 D 5
47118 English⊙, 664 E 8
46524 Etna Green, 516 E 2
† 47928 Eugene, 300 B 5
* 47701 Evansville⊙, 138,764 C 9
Evansville, ‡232,775 C 9
46126 Fairland, 950 F 5
46928 Fairmount, 3,427 F 4
† 47842 Fairview Park, 1,067 C 5
47850 Farmersburg, 962 C 6
47340 Farmland, 1,262 G 4
47532 Ferdinand, 1,432 D 8
46128 Fillmore, 600 D 5
46129 Finly, 350 F 5
46038 Fishers, 628 E 5
47234 Flat Rock, 289 F 6
46929 Flora, 1,877 E 3
47119 Floyds Knobs, 350 F 8
47851 Fontanet, 200 C 5
46039 Forest, 400 E 4
47533 Fort Branch, 2,535 B 8
46040 Fortville, 2,460 F 5
* 46801 Fort Wayne⊙, 177,671 G 2
Fort Wayne, ‡280,455 G 2
47341 Fountain City, 852 H 5
46130 Fountaintown, 225 F 5
47944 Fowler⊙, 2,643 C 3
46930 Fowlerton, 337 F 4
47946 Francesville, 1,015 D 3
47534 Francisco, 621 B 8
46041 Frankfort⊙, 14,956 E 4
46131 Franklin⊙, 11,477 E 6
46044 Frankton, 1,796 F 4
47120 Fredericksburg, 207 E 8
47431 Freedom, 262 D 6
47535 Freelandville, 710 C 7
47235 Freetown, 550 E 7
46737 Fremont, 1,043 H 1
47432 French Lick, 2,059 D 7
46931 Fulton, 372 E 3
† 47119 Galena, 250 F 8
46932 Galveston, 1,284 E 3
46738 Garrett, 4,715 G 2
* 46401 Gary, 175,415 C 1
Gary-Hammond-East Chicago, ‡ 633,367 C 1
46933 Gas City, 5,742 F 4
47342 Gaston, 928 G 4
46740 Geneva, 1,100 H 3
47537 Gentryville, 281 C 8
47122 Georgetown, 1,273 F 8
47343 Glenwood, 452 G 5
† 47567 Glezen, 300 C 8
46045 Goldsmith, 235 E 4
47948 Goodland, 1,176 C 3
46526 Goshen⊙, 17,171 F 1
47433 Gosport, 692 D 6
46741 Grabill, 570 H 2
47615 Grandview, 696 C 9
46530 Granger, 200 E 1
46135 Greencastle⊙, 8,852 D 5
† 47025 Greendale, 3,783 H 6
46140 Greenfield⊙, 9,986 F 5
47344 Greensboro, 225 G 5
47240 Greensburg⊙, 8,620 G 6
47345 Greens Fork, 444 H 5
46936 Greentown, 1,870 E 4
47124 Greenville, 611 F 8
46142 Greenwood, 11,408 E 5
46319 Griffith, 18,168 C 1
46144 Gwynneville, 240 F 5
47346 Hagerstown, 2,059 G 5
46742 Hamilton, 537 H 1
46532 Hamlet, 761 D 2
* 46320 Hammond, 107,790 B 1
46340 Hanna, 500 D 2
47243 Hanover, 3,018 F 7
47125 Hardinsburg, 263 E 8

AREA 36,291 sq. mi.
POPULATION 5,193,669
CAPITAL Indianapolis
LARGEST CITY Indianapolis
HIGHEST POINT 1,257 ft. (Wayne County)
SETTLED IN 1730
ADMITTED TO UNION December 11, 1816
POPULAR NAME Hoosier State
STATE FLOWER Peony
STATE BIRD Cardinal

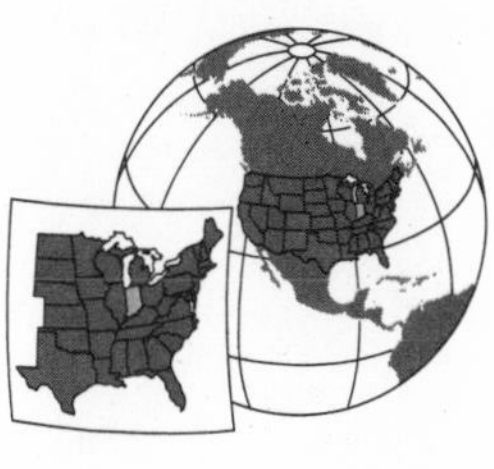

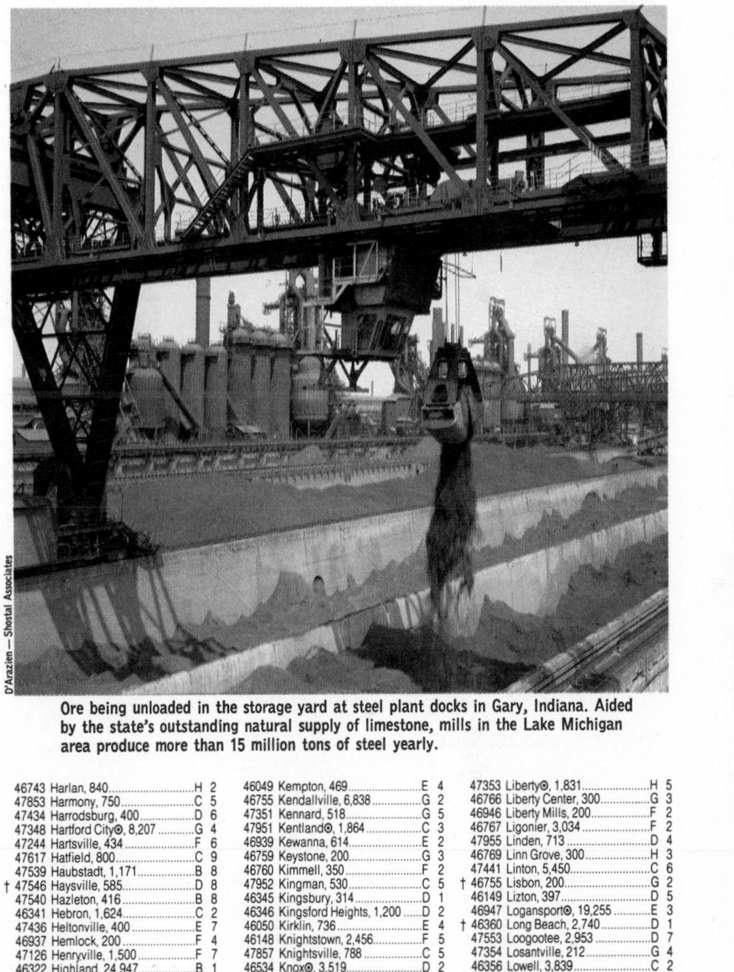

D'Arazien — Shostal Associates

Ore being unloaded in the storage yard at steel plant docks in Gary, Indiana. Aided by the state's outstanding natural supply of limestone, mills in the Lake Michigan area produce more than 15 million tons of steel yearly.

46743 Harlan, 840 H 2
47853 Harmony, 750 C 5
47434 Harrodsburg, 400 D 6
47348 Hartford City⊙, 8,207 G 4
47244 Hartsville, 434 F 6
47617 Hatfield, 800 C 9
47539 Haubstadt, 1,171 B 8
† 47546 Haysville, 585 D 8
47540 Hazleton, 416 B 8
46341 Hebron, 1,624 C 2
47436 Heltonville, 400 E 7
46937 Hemlock, 200 F 4
47126 Henryville, 1,500 F 7
46322 Highland, 24,947 B 1
46046 Hillisburg, 225 E 4
47949 Hillsboro, 505 C 4
47854 Hillsdale, 500 C 5
46745 Hoagland, 530 H 3
46342 Hobart, 21,485 C 1
46047 Hobbs, 400 F 4
47541 Holland, 662 C 8
47023 Holton, 610 G 6
46146 Homer, 245 F 5
47246 Hope, 1,603 F 6
† 46069 Hortonville, 240 E 4
46746 Howe, 800 G 1
46747 Hudson, 464 G 1
46552 Hudson Lake, 1,134 D 1
46748 Huntertown, 775 G 2
47542 Huntingburg, 4,794 D 8
46750 Huntington⊙, 16,217 G 3
† 46064 Huntsville, 450 G 4
47437 Huron, 580 D 7
47855 Hymera, 907 C 6
47950 Idaville, 600 D 3
* 46201 Indianapolis (cap.)⊙ 744,624 E 5
Indianapolis, ‡1,109,882 E 5
46048 Ingalls, 888 F 5
47545 Ireland, 527 C 8
46147 Jamestown, 938 D 5
47438 Jasonville, 2,335 C 6
47546 Jasper⊙, 8,641 D 8
47130 Jeffersonville⊙, 20,008 F 8
† 47565 Johnson, 250 B 8
† 46074 Jolietville, 265 E 4
46938 Jonesboro, 2,466 F 4
47247 Jonesville, 202 F 6
46049 Kempton, 469 E 4
46755 Kendallville, 6,838 G 2
47351 Kennard, 518 G 5
47951 Kentland⊙, 1,864 C 3
46939 Kewanna, 614 E 2
46759 Keystone, 200 G 3
46760 Kimmell, 350 F 2
47952 Kingman, 530 C 5
46345 Kingsbury, 314 D 1
46346 Kingsford Heights, 1,200 D 2
46050 Kirklin, 736 E 4
46148 Knightstown, 2,456 F 5
47857 Knightsville, 788 C 5
46534 Knox⊙, 3,519 D 2
46901 Kokomo⊙, 44,042 E 4
† 46574 Koontz Lake, 900 D 2
46347 Kouts, 1,388 C 2
46348 La Crosse, 696 D 2
47954 Ladoga, 1,099 D 5
* 47901 Lafayette⊙, 44,955 D 4
Lafayette-West Lafayette, ‡109,378 D 4
46940 La Fontaine, 793 F 3
46761 Lagrange⊙, 2,053 F 1
46941 Lagro, 552 F 3
† 46703 Lake James, 400 H 1
46943 Laketon, 500 F 3
46349 Lake Village, 600 C 2
46536 Lakeville, 712 E 1
† 46567 Lake Wawasee, 600 F 2
47136 Lanesville, 586 E 8
46763 Laotto, 312 G 2
46537 Lapaz, 604 E 2
46051 Lapel, 1,725 F 4
46350 LaPorte⊙, 22,140 D 1
46764 Larwill, 324 F 2
47024 Laurel, 753 G 6
46226 Lawrence, 16,646 E 5
47025 Lawrenceburg⊙, 4,636 H 6
47137 Leavenworth, 330 E 8
46052 Lebanon⊙, 9,766 D 4
46538 Leesburg, 561 F 2
46945 Leiters Ford, 250 E 2
46765 Leo, 500 G 2
46355 Leroy, 350 C 2
† 47240 Letts, 247 F 6
47352 Lewisville, 530 G 5
47138 Lexington, 400 F 7
47353 Liberty⊙, 1,831 H 5
46766 Liberty Center, 300 G 3
46946 Liberty Mills, 200 F 2
46767 Ligonier, 3,034 F 2
47955 Linden, 713 D 4
46769 Linn Grove, 300 H 3
47441 Linton, 5,450 C 6
† 46755 Lisbon, 200 G 2
46149 Lizton, 397 D 5
46947 Logansport⊙, 19,255 E 3
† 46360 Long Beach, 2,740 D 1
47553 Loogootee, 2,953 D 7
47354 Losantville, 212 G 4
46356 Lowell, 3,839 C 2
† 46601 Lydick, 1,341 E 1
† 47874 Lyford, 400 C 5
47355 Lynn, 1,360 H 4
47619 Lynnville, 556 C 8
47443 Lyons, 702 C 7
46951 Macy, 273 E 3
47250 Madison⊙, 13,081 G 7
† 47001 Manchester, 250 H 6
46150 Manilla, 300 F 5
† 47872 Mansfield, 200 C 5
47140 Marengo, 767 E 8
47556 Mariah Hill, 275 D 8
† 46176 Marietta, 280 F 6
46952 Marion⊙, 39,607 F 3
46770 Markle, 963 G 3
46056 Markleville, 457 F 5
47859 Marshall, 365 C 5
46151 Martinsville⊙, 9,723 D 6
46957 Matthews, 728 F 4
46154 Maxwell, 245 F 5
46055 McCordsville, 500 F 5
47860 Mecca, 800 C 5
47957 Medaryville, 732 D 2
47260 Medora, 788 E 7
47958 Mellott, 325 C 4
47143 Memphis, 324 F 8
46539 Mentone, 830 E 2
47861 Merom, 305 B 6
46410 Merrillville, 15,918 C 2
47030 Metamora, 400 G 6
† 46703 Metz, 200 H 1
46958 Mexico, 850 E 3
46959 Miami, 420 E 3
46360 Michigan City, 39,369 C 1

(continued on following page)

46057 Michigantown, 457 E 4
46540 Middlebury, 1,055 F 1
47356 Middletown, 2,046 F 4
47445 Midland, 220 C 6
47031 Milan, 1,260 G 6
46542 Milford, 1,264 F 2
46543 Millersburg, 618 F 1
47261 Millhousen, 252 G 6
47145 Milltown, 829 E 8
† 47362 Millville, 275 G 5
46156 Milroy, 750 G 6
47357 Milton, 694 G 5
46544 Mishawaka, 35,517 E 1
47446 Mitchell, 4,092 E 7
47358 Modoc, 275 G 4
46771 Mongo, 225 G 1
47959 Monon, 1,548 D 3
46772 Monroe, 622 H 3
47557 Monroe City, 603 C 7
46773 Monroeville, 1,353 H 3
46157 Monrovia, 750 E 5
46960 Monterey, 268 D 2
47862 Montezuma, 1,192 C 5
47558 Montgomery, 411 C 7
47960 Monticello⊙, 4,869 D 3
47962 Montmorenci, 350 D 4
47359 Montpelier, 2,093 G 3
47360 Mooreland, 495 G 5
47032 Moores Hill, 616 G 6
46158 Mooresville, 5,800 E 5
46160 Morgantown, 1,134 E 6
47963 Morocco, 1,285 C 3
47033 Morris, 435 G 6
46161 Morristown, 838 F 5
47361 Mount Summit, 395 G 4
47620 Mount Vernon⊙, 6,770 B 9
46058 Mulberry, 1,075 D 4
* 47302 Muncie⊙, 69,080 G 4
Muncie, ‡129,219 G 4
46321 Munster, 16,514 B 1
47147 Nabb, 204 F 7
47034 Napoleon, 282 G 6
46550 Nappanee, 4,159 F 2
47448 Nashville⊙, 527 E 6
† 47421 Needmore, 200 E 7
47150 New Albany⊙, 38,402 F 8
47449 Newberry, 295 C 7
47630 Newburgh, 2,302 C 9
46552 New Carlisle, 1,434 E 1
47362 New Castle⊙, 21,215 G 5
† 46342 New Chicago, 2,231 C 1
47863 New Goshen, 500 B 5
47631 New Harmony, 971 B 8
46774 New Haven, 5,728 H 2
47366 New Lisbon, 350 G 5
† 46979 New London, 200 E 4
47965 New Market, 640 D 5
46163 New Palestine, 863 F 5
46553 New Paris, 1,080 F 2
† 47165 New Pekin, 912 F 7
47263 New Point, 381 G 6
47966 Newport⊙, 708 C 5
† 47106 New Providence (Borden), 337 F 8
47967 New Richmond, 381 D 4
47968 New Ross, 318 D 5
† 46173 New Salem, 270 G 5
47161 New Salisbury, 350 E 8
47969 Newtown, 286 C 4
47035 New Trenton, 200 H 6
47162 New Washington, 1,100 F 7
46184 New Whiteland, 4,200 E 5
46060 Noblesville⊙, 7,548 F 4
46366 North Judson, 1,738 D 2
46554 North Liberty, 1,259 E 1
46962 North Manchester, 5,791 F 3
46165 North Salem, 601 D 5
47805 North Terre Haute, 1,400 C 5
47265 North Vernon, 4,582 F 6
46555 North Webster, 456 F 2
† 47960 Norway, 250 D 3
46556 Notre Dame, 8,400 E 1
† 47331 Nulltown, 250 G 5
46965 Oakford, 300 E 4
47560 Oakland City, 3,289 C 8
47561 Oaktown, 726 C 7
47367 Oakville, 250 G 4
47562 Odon, 1,433 C 7
† 46401 Ogden Dunes, 1,361 C 1
47036 Oldenburg, 758 G 6
47451 Oolitic, 1,155 E 7
† 47343 Orange, 200 G 5
46063 Orestes, 519 F 4
46776 Orland, 457 G 1
47452 Orleans, 1,834 D 7
46561 Osceola, 1,572 E 1
47037 Osgood, 1,346 G 6
46777 Ossian, 1,538 G 3
46367 Otis, 300 D 1
47163 Otisco, 375 F 7
47970 Otterbein, 899 C 4
47564 Otwell, 850 C 8
47453 Owensburg, 700 D 7
47565 Owensville, 1,056 B 8
47971 Oxford, 1,098 C 3
† 46508 Palestine, 200 F 2
47164 Palmyra, 483 E 8
47454 Paoli⊙, 3,281 E 7
46166 Paragon, 538 D 6
47368 Parker, 1,179 G 4
47566 Patoka, 529 B 8
47455 Patricksburg, 265 D 6
47038 Patriot, 216 H 7
47865 Paxton, 250 C 6
47165 Pekin, 950 E 7
46064 Pendleton, 2,243 F 5
47369 Pennville, 798 G 4
† 46011 Perkinsville, 300 F 4
47974 Perrysville, 510 C 4
47370 Pershing, 447 G 5
† 46975 Pershing, 425 E 2
46970 Peru⊙, 14,139 E 3
47567 Petersburg⊙, 2,697 C 7
46778 Petroleum, 200 G 3
46562 Pierceton, 1,175 F 2
47866 Pimento, 200 C 6
† 46350 Pine Lake, 1,954 D 1
47975 Pine Village, 291 C 4
46167 Pittsboro, 867 D 5
46168 Plainfield, 8,211 E 5
47568 Plainville, 538 C 7
46779 Pleasant Lake, 650 H 1
46563 Plymouth⊙, 7,661 E 2
47868 Poland, 300 C 6
46781 Poneto, 286 G 3
46368 Portage, 19,127 C 1
46304 Porter, 3,058 C 1
47371 Portland⊙, 7,115 H 4
47633 Poseyville, 1,035 B 8
† 46360 Pottawattamie Park, 374 C 1
47869 Prairie Creek, 225 C 6
47870 Prairieton, 400 B 6
† 46164 Princes Lakes, 597 E 6
47570 Princeton⊙, 7,431 B 8
46170 Putnamville, 200 D 5
47456 Quincy, 250 D 6
47573 Ragsdale, 200 C 7
46737 Ray, 200 H 1
† 47274 Reddington, 245 F 6
47373 Redkey, 1,667 G 4
46171 Reelsville, 210 D 5
47977 Remington, 1,127 C 3
47978 Rensselaer⊙, 4,688 C 3
47980 Reynolds, 641 D 3
47634 Richland, 650 C 9
47374 Richmond⊙, 43,999 H 5
47380 Ridgeville, 924 G 4
47871 Riley, 257 C 6
47040 Rising Sun⊙, 2,305 H 7
46172 Roachdale, 1,004 D 5
46974 Roann, 509 F 3
46783 Roanoke, 858 G 3
46975 Rochester⊙, 4,631 E 2
46977 Rockfield, 300 D 3
47635 Rockport⊙, 2,565 C 9
47872 Rockville⊙, 2,820 C 5
46371 Rolling Prairie, 2,500 D 1
47574 Rome, 1,354 D 9
46784 Rome City, 1,385 G 1
47981 Romney, 420 D 4
47874 Rosedale, 817 C 5
† 46601 Roseland, 895 E 1
46372 Roselawn, 200 C 2
46065 Rossville, 830 D 4
46978 Royal Center, 987 E 3
† 47302 Royerton, 411 G 4
46173 Rushville⊙, 6,686 G 5
46175 Russellville, 390 D 5
46975 Russiaville, 844 E 4
47575 Saint Anthony, 460 D 8
47875 Saint Bernice, 900 C 5
46785 Saint Joe, 564 H 2
46373 Saint John, 1,757 C 2
† 45030 Saint Leon, 435 H 6
47876 Saint Mary-of-the-Woods, 1,200 B 6
† 46556 Saint Marys, 1,600 E 1
47577 Saint Meinrad, 1,100 D 8
47272 Saint Paul, 785 F 6
† 47012 Saint Peter, 200 H 6
† 47620 Saint Philip, 400 B 9
† 47638 Saint Wendel, 250 B 8
47167 Salem⊙, 5,041 E 7
47578 Sandborn, 528 C 7
† 47401 Sanders, 200 E 6
46374 San Pierre, 300 D 2
47579 Santa Claus, 125 D 8
47382 Saratoga, 406 H 4
† 47283 Sardinia, 225 F 6
46375 Schererville, 3,663 C 2
46376 Schneider, 426 C 2
47273 Scipio, 250 F 6
47170 Scottsburg⊙, 4,791 F 7
47878 Seelyville, 1,195 C 6
47172 Sellersburg, 3,177 F 8
47383 Selma, 890 G 4
47274 Seymour, 13,352 F 7
46068 Sharpsville, 672 E 4
47879 Shelburn, 1,281 C 6
46377 Shelby, 400 C 2
46176 Shelbyville⊙, 15,094 F 6
47880 Shepardsville, 325 B 5
46069 Sheridan, 2,137 E 4
† 47338 Shideler, 275 G 4
46565 Shipshewana, 448 F 1
47384 Shirley, 958 F 5

Topography

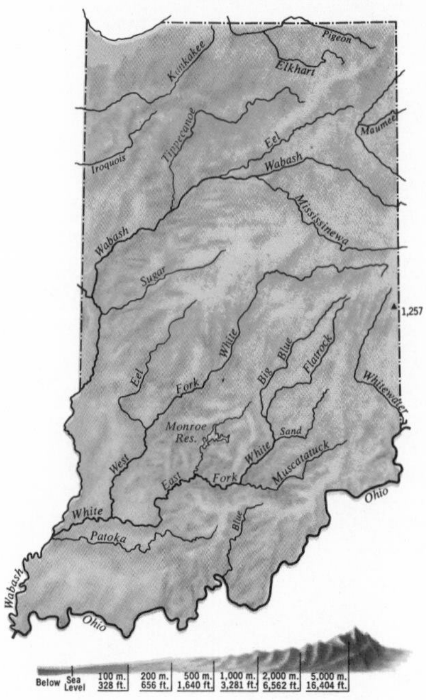

0 40 80
MILES
Pigeon
Elkhart
Kankakee
Maumee
Tippecanoe
Iroquois
Eel
Wabash
Mississinewa
Wabash
Sugar
1,257
White
Big Blue
Flatrock
Whitewater
Eel
Fork
Monroe Res.
Sand
West
White
Muscatatuck
East
Fork
Ohio
White
Patoka
Blue
Wabash
Ohio
Below Sea Level
100 m. 328 ft.
200 m. 656 ft.
500 m. 1,640 ft.
1,000 m. 3,281 ft.
2,000 m. 6,562 ft.
5,000 m. 16,404 ft.

Agriculture, Industry and Resources

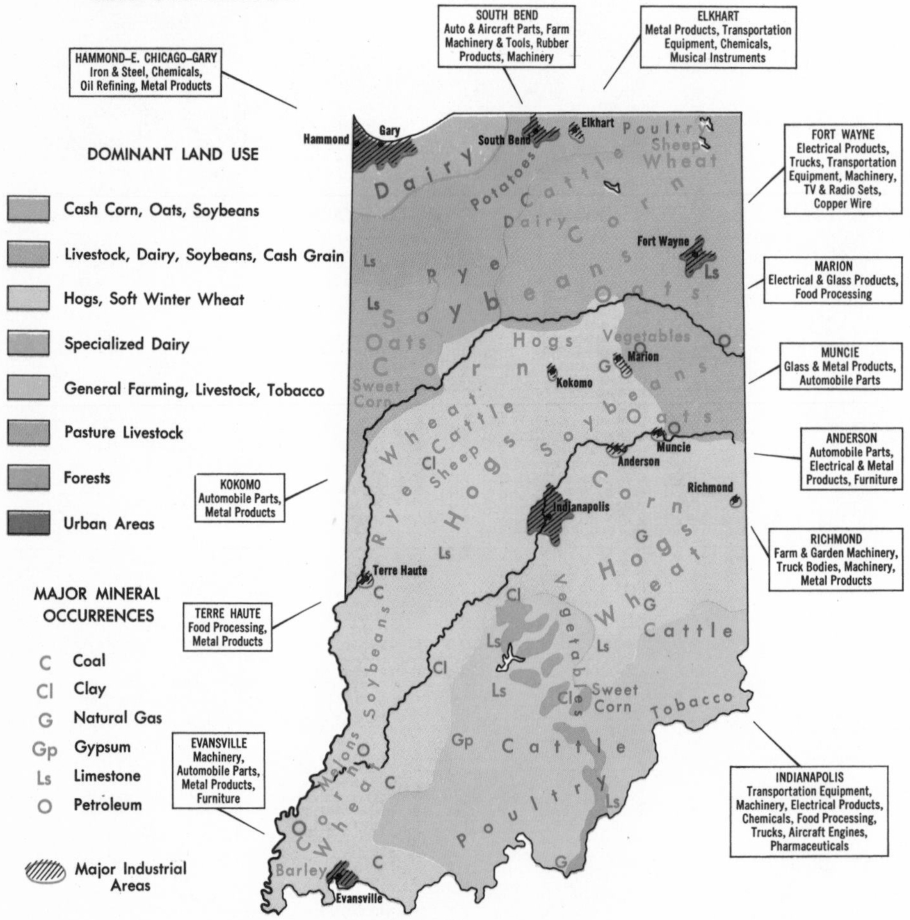

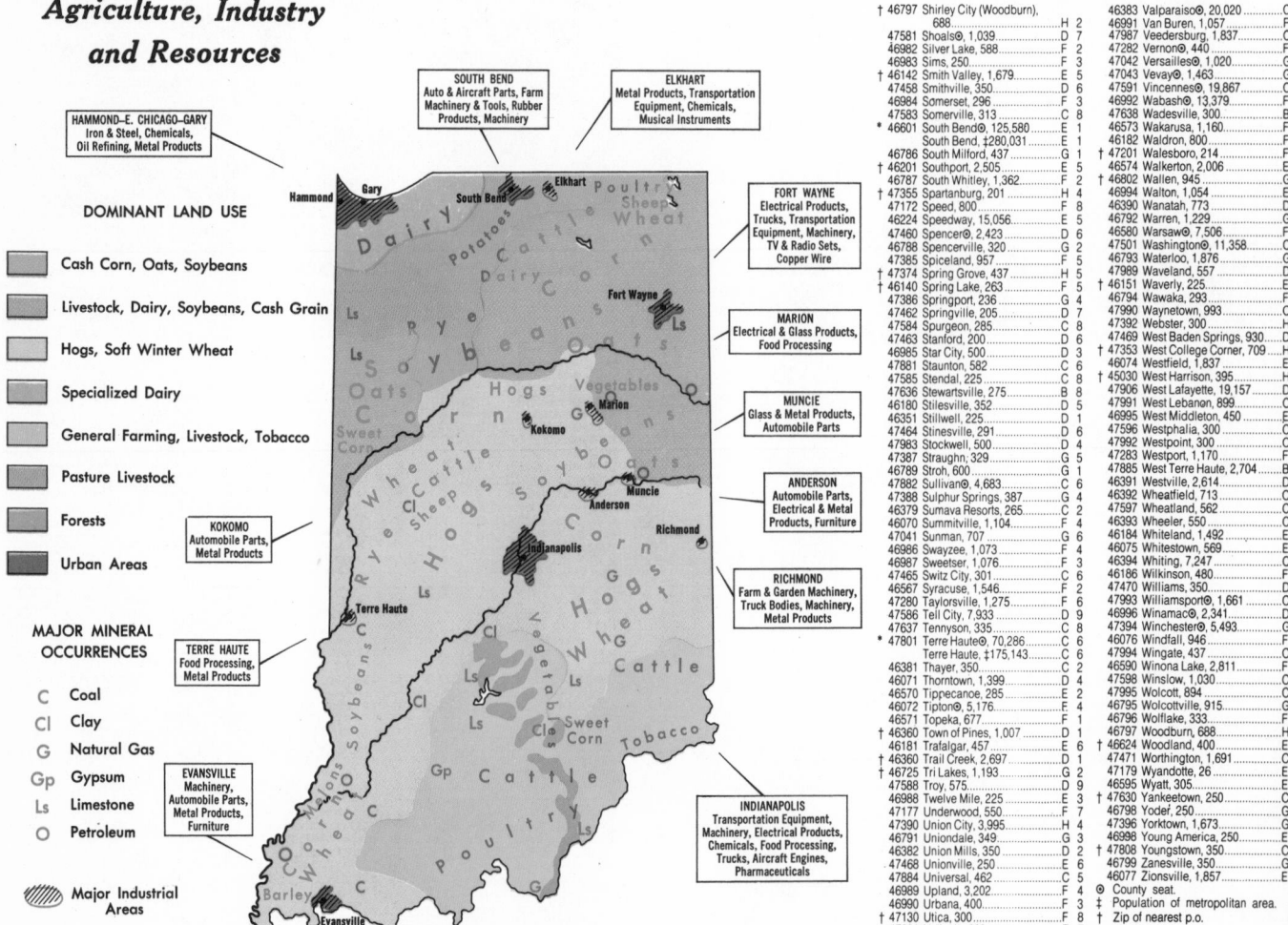

HAMMOND-E. CHICAGO-GARY
Iron & Steel, Chemicals, Oil Refining, Metal Products
SOUTH BEND
Auto & Aircraft Parts, Farm Machinery & Tools, Rubber Products, Machinery
ELKHART
Metal Products, Transportation Equipment, Chemicals, Musical Instruments
FORT WAYNE
Electrical Products, Trucks, Transportation Equipment, Machinery, TV & Radio Sets, Copper Wire
MARION
Electrical & Glass Products, Food Processing
MUNCIE
Glass & Metal Products, Automobile Parts
ANDERSON
Automobile Parts, Electrical & Metal Products, Furniture
RICHMOND
Farm & Garden Machinery, Truck Bodies, Machinery, Metal Products
INDIANAPOLIS
Transportation Equipment, Machinery, Electrical Products, Chemicals, Food Processing, Trucks, Aircraft Engines, Pharmaceuticals
KOKOMO
Automobile Parts, Metal Products
TERRE HAUTE
Food Processing, Metal Products
EVANSVILLE
Machinery, Automobile Parts, Metal Products, Furniture
DOMINANT LAND USE
Cash Corn, Oats, Soybeans
Livestock, Dairy, Soybeans, Cash Grain
Hogs, Soft Winter Wheat
Specialized Dairy
General Farming, Livestock, Tobacco
Pasture Livestock
Forests
Urban Areas
MAJOR MINERAL OCCURRENCES
C Coal
Cl Clay
G Natural Gas
Gp Gypsum
Ls Limestone
O Petroleum
Major Industrial Areas
Hammond
Gary
South Bend
Elkhart
Fort Wayne
Marion
Kokomo
Muncie
Anderson
Richmond
Indianapolis
Terre Haute
Evansville
Dairy
Potatoes
Cattle
Poultry
Sheep
Wheat
Corn
Rye
Soybeans
Oats
Hogs
Vegetables
Sweet Corn
Tobacco
Melons
Barley

† 46797 Shirley City (Woodburn), 688 H 2
47581 Shoals⊙, 1,039 D 7
46982 Silver Lake, 588 F 2
46983 Sims, 250 F 3
† 46142 Smith Valley, 1,679 E 5
47458 Smithville, 350 D 6
46984 Somerset, 296 F 3
47583 Somerville, 313 C 8
* 46601 South Bend⊙, 125,580 E 1
South Bend, ‡280,031 E 1
46786 South Milford, 437 G 1
† 46201 Southport, 2,505 E 5
46787 South Whitley, 1,362 F 2
† 47355 Spartanburg, 201 H 4
47172 Speed, 800 F 8
46224 Speedway, 15,056 E 5
47460 Spencer⊙, 2,423 D 6
46788 Spencerville, 320 G 2
47385 Spiceland, 957 F 5
† 47374 Spring Grove, 437 H 5
† 46140 Spring Lake, 263 F 5
47386 Springport, 236 G 4
47462 Springville, 205 D 7
47584 Spurgeon, 285 C 8
47463 Stanford, 200 D 6
46985 Star City, 500 D 3
47881 Staunton, 582 C 6
47585 Stendal, 225 C 8
47636 Stewartsville, 275 B 8
46180 Stilesville, 352 D 5
46351 Stillwell, 225 D 1
47464 Stinesville, 291 D 6
47983 Stockwell, 500 D 4
47387 Straughn, 329 G 5
46789 Stroh, 600 G 1
47882 Sullivan⊙, 4,683 C 6
47388 Sulphur Springs, 387 G 4
46379 Sumava Resorts, 265 C 2
46070 Summitville, 1,104 F 4
47041 Sunman, 707 G 6
46986 Swayzee, 1,073 F 4
46987 Sweetser, 1,076 F 3
47465 Switz City, 301 C 6
46567 Syracuse, 1,546 F 2
47280 Taylorsville, 1,275 F 6
47586 Tell City, 7,933 D 9
47637 Tennyson, 335 C 8
* 47801 Terre Haute⊙, 70,286 C 6
Terre Haute, ‡175,143 C 6
46381 Thayer, 350 C 2
46071 Thorntown, 1,399 D 4
46570 Tippecanoe, 285 E 2
46072 Tipton⊙, 5,176 E 4
46571 Topeka, 677 F 1
† 46360 Town of Pines, 1,007 D 1
46181 Trafalgar, 457 E 6
† 46360 Trail Creek, 2,697 D 1
† 46725 Tri Lakes, 1,193 G 2
47588 Troy, 575 D 9
46988 Twelve Mile, 225 E 3
47177 Underwood, 550 F 7
47390 Union City, 3,995 H 4
46791 Uniondale, 349 G 3
46382 Union Mills, 350 D 2
47468 Unionville, 250 E 6
47884 Universal, 462 C 5
46989 Upland, 3,202 F 4
46990 Urbana, 400 F 3
† 47130 Utica, 300 F 8
47281 Vallonia, 600 E 7
46383 Valparaiso⊙, 20,020 C
46991 Van Buren, 1,057 F
47987 Veedersburg, 1,837 C
47282 Vernon⊙, 440 F
47042 Versailles⊙, 1,020 G
47043 Vevay⊙, 1,463 G
47591 Vincennes⊙, 19,867 C
46992 Wabash⊙, 13,379 F
47638 Wadesville, 300 B
46573 Wakarusa, 1,160 F
46182 Waldron, 800 F
† 47201 Walesboro, 214 F
46574 Walkerton, 2,006 E
† 46802 Wallen, 945 G
46994 Walton, 1,054 E
46390 Wanatah, 773 D
46792 Warren, 1,229 G
46580 Warsaw⊙, 7,506 F
47501 Washington⊙, 11,358 C
46793 Waterloo, 1,876 G
47989 Waveland, 557 D
† 46151 Waverly, 225 E
46794 Wawaka, 293 F
47990 Waynetown, 993 C
47392 Webster, 300 H
47469 West Baden Springs, 930 D
† 47353 West College Corner, 709 H
46074 Westfield, 1,837 E
† 45030 West Harrison, 395 H
47906 West Lafayette, 19,157 D
47991 West Lebanon, 899 C
46995 West Middleton, 450 E
47596 Westphalia, 300 C
47992 Westpoint, 300 C
47283 Westport, 1,170 F
47885 West Terre Haute, 2,704 B
46391 Westville, 2,614 D
46392 Wheatfield, 713 C
47597 Wheatland, 562 C
46393 Wheeler, 550 C
46184 Whiteland, 1,492 E
46075 Whitestown, 569 E
46394 Whiting, 7,247 C
46186 Wilkinson, 480 F
47470 Williams, 350 D
47993 Williamsport⊙, 1,661 C
46996 Winamac⊙, 2,341 D
47394 Winchester⊙, 5,493 G
46076 Windfall, 946 F
47994 Wingate, 437 C
46590 Winona Lake, 2,811 F
47598 Winslow, 1,030 C
47995 Wolcott, 894 C
46795 Wolcottville, 915 G
46796 Wolflake, 333 F
46797 Woodburn, 688 H
† 46624 Woodland, 400 E
47471 Worthington, 1,691 C
47179 Wyandotte, 26 E
46595 Wyatt, 305 E
† 47630 Yankeetown, 250 C
46798 Yoder, 250 G
47396 Yorktown, 1,673 G
46998 Young America, 250 E
† 47808 Youngstown, 350 C
46799 Zanesville, 350 G
46077 Zionsville, 1,857 E

⊙ County seat.
‡ Population of metropolitan area.
† Zip of nearest p.o.
* Multiple zips

INDIANA

SCALE

0 5 10   20   30   40 MI.

0 5 10   20   30   40 KM.

State Capitals............⊛

County Seats.............◉

© C.S. HAMMOND & Co., N.Y.

164 Iowa

50421 Belmond, 2,358......F 3	50044 Bussey, 498......H 6	51012 Cherokee⊙, 7,272......B 3
52721 Bennett, 385......L 5	52729 Calamus, 396......M 5	50050 Churdan, 598......D 4
52722 Bettendorf, 22,126......N 5	50523 Callender, 421......E 4	52549 Cincinnati, 570......G 7
52535 Birmingham, 452......K 7	52132 Calmar, 1,941......K 2	50524 Clare, 249......E 3
50034 Blairsburg, 287......F 4	51009 Calumet, 219......B 3	52216 Clarence, 915......M 5
52209 Blairstown, 612......J 5	52730 Camanche, 3,470......N 5	51632 Clarinda⊙, 5,420......C 7
52536 Blakesburg, 403......H 7	50046 Cambridge, 661......G 5	50525 Clarion⊙, 2,972......F 3
51523 Blencoe, 255......A 5	52542 Cantril, 258......J 7	50619 Clarksville, 1,360......H 3
50836 Blockton, 273......D 7	50047 Carlisle, 2,246......G 6	50840 Clearfield, 430......D 7
52537 Bloomfield⊙, 2,718......J 7	51401 Carroll⊙, 8,716......D 4	50428 Clear Lake, 6,430......G 2
52726 Blue Grass, 1,032......M 5	51525 Carson, 756......C 6	51014 Cleghorn, 274......B 3
50519 Bode, 372......E 3	† 68101 Carter Lake, 3,268......B 6	52135 Clermont, 582......K 2
52620 Bonaparte, 517......K 7	52033 Cascade, 1,744......L 4	52732 Clinton⊙, 34,719......N 5
50035 Bondurant, 462......G 5	50048 Casey, 561......D 5	50053 Clive, 3,005......G 5
50036 Boone⊙, 12,468......F 4	52133 Castalia, 210......K 2	52217 Clutier, 275......J 4
50040 Boxholm, 242......E 4	51010 Castana, 211......B 4	† 50501 Coalville, 275......E 3
51234 Boyden, 670......B 2	50613 Cedar Falls, 29,597......H 3	52218 Coggon, 656......L 4
52210 Brandon, 432......K 4	* 52401 Cedar Rapids⊙, 110,642......K 5	51636 Coin, 294......C 7
51436 Breda, 518......C 4	Cedar Rapids, ‡163,213......K 5	52035 Colesburg, 379......L 3
52540 Brighton, 632......K 6	52213 Center Point, 1,456......K 4	50054 Colfax, 2,293......G 5
50611 Bristow, 230......H 3	52544 Centerville⊙, 6,531......H 7	50055 Collins, 404......G 5
50423 Britt, 2,069......F 2	52214 Central City, 1,116......K 4	50056 Colo, 606......G 5
52211 Brooklyn, 1,410......J 5	50049 Chariton⊙, 5,009......G 6	52737 Columbus City, 312......L 6
52728 Buffalo, 1,513......M 6	50616 Charles City⊙, 9,268......H 2	52738 Columbus Junction, 1,205......L 6
50424 Buffalo Center, 1,118......F 2	52731 Charlotte, 444......M 5	52739 Conesville, 295......L 6
52601 Burlington⊙, 32,366......L 7	51439 Charter Oak, 715......C 4	50631 Conrad, 932......H 4
50522 Burt, 608......E 2	52215 Chelsea, 381......J 5	

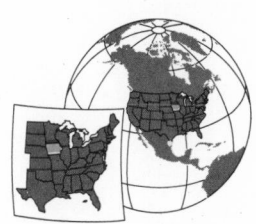

AREA 56,290 sq. mi.
POPULATION 2,825,041
CAPITAL Des Moines
LARGEST CITY Des Moines
HIGHEST POINT Ocheyedan Mound 1,675 ft.
SETTLED IN 1788
ADMITTED TO UNION December 28, 1846
POPULAR NAME Hawkeye State
STATE FLOWER Wild Rose
STATE BIRD Eastern Goldfinch

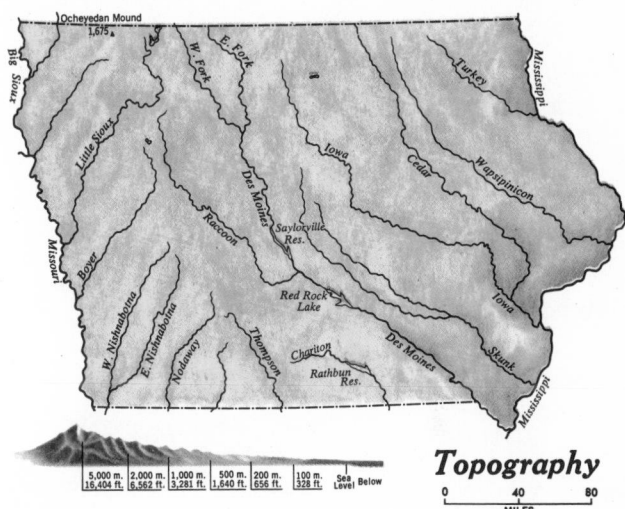

Topography

5,000 m. 2,000 m. 1,000 m. 500 m. 200 m. 100 m. Sea Level / Below
16,404 ft. 6,562 ft. 3,281 ft. 1,640 ft. 656 ft. 328 ft.
0   40   80   MILES

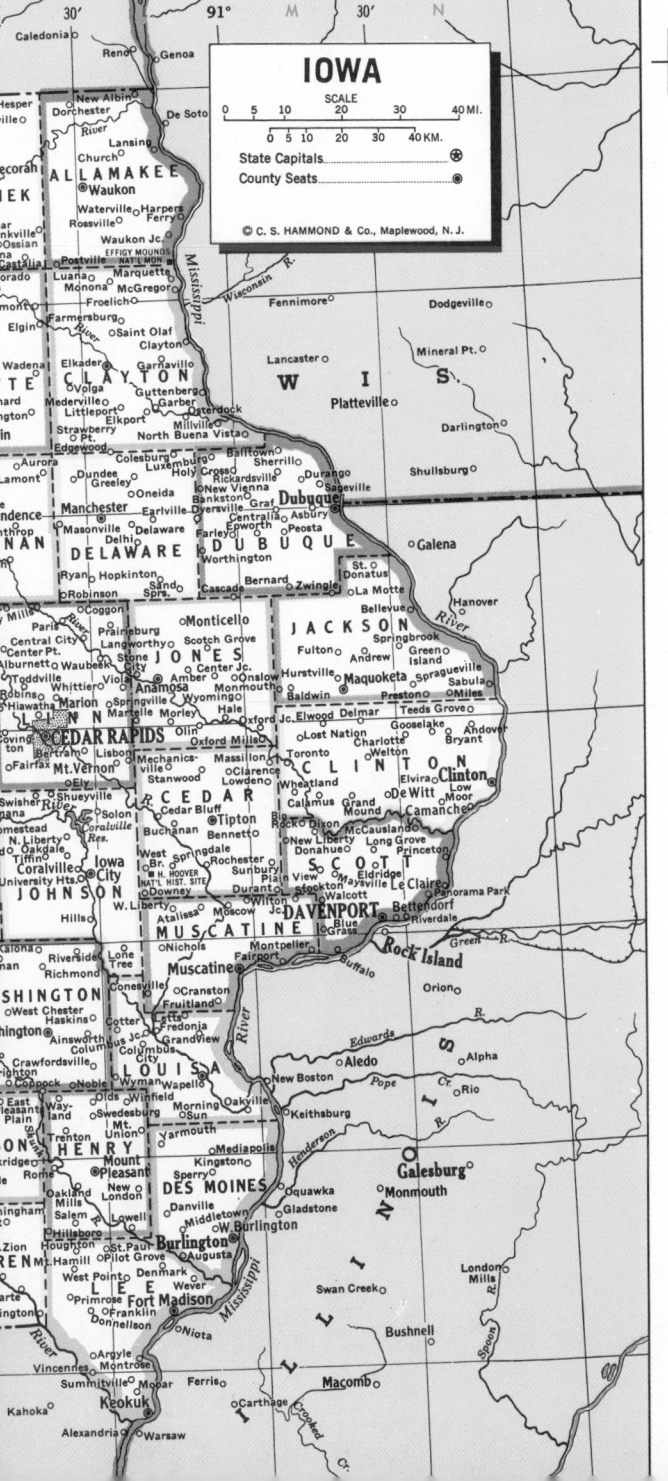

IOWA
SCALE
0 5 10 20 30 40 MI.
0 5 10 20 30 40 KM.
State Capitals........⊛
County Seats........⊙
© C. S. HAMMOND & Co., Maplewood, N.J.

50058 Coon Rapids, 1,381......D 5	52553 Eddyville, 945......H 6	50108 Grand River, 211......F 7
52240 Coralville, 6,130......K 5	52042 Edgewood, 786......K 3	52752 Grandview, 357......L 6
50841 Corning⊙, 2,095......D 7	52554 Eldon, 1,319......J 7	50109 Granger, 661......F 5
51016 Correctionville, 870......B 4	50627 Eldora⊙, 3,223......G 4	51022 Granville, 383......B 3
50430 Corwith, 407......F 3	52748 Eldridge, 1,535......M 5	50848 Gravity, 286......D 7
50060 Corydon⊙, 1,745......G 7	52141 Elgin, 613......K 3	52050 Greeley, 242......L 3
50431 Coulter, 262......G 3	52043 Elkader⊙, 1,592......L 3	50636 Greene, 1,363......H 3
51501 Council Bluffs⊙, 60,348......B 6	50073 Elkhart, 269......F 5	50849 Greenfield⊙, 2,212......D 6
52621 Crawfordsville, 288......K 6	51531 Elk Horn, 667......C 5	50111 Grimes, 834......F 5
51526 Crescent, 284......B 6	† 50700 Elk Run Heights, 1,175......J 4	50112 Grinnell⊙, 8,402......H 5
52136 Cresco⊙, 3,927......J 2	51532 Elliott, 423......C 6	51535 Griswold, 1,181......C 6
50801 Creston⊙, 8,234......E 6	50075 Ellsworth, 443......F 4	50638 Grundy Center⊙, 2,712......H 4
50432 Crystal Lake, 276......F 2	50628 Elma, 601......H 2	50115 Guthrie Center⊙, 1,834......D 5
50843 Cumberland, 385......D 6	52227 Ely, 275......K 5	52052 Guttenberg, 2,177......L 3
50529 Dakota City⊙, 746......E 3	51533 Emerson, 484......C 6	51444 Halbur, 281......D 4
50062 Dallas, 438......G 6	50536 Emmetsburg⊙, 4,150......D 2	51640 Hamburg, 1,649......B 7
50063 Dallas Center, 1,128......E 5	52045 Epworth, 1,132......M 4	50441 Hampton⊙, 4,376......G 3
51019 Danbury, 527......B 4	52047 Essex, 770......C 7	51536 Hancock, 228......C 6
52623 Danville, 948......L 7	51334 Estherville⊙, 8,108......D 2	50544 Harcourt, 365......E 4
* 52801 Davenport⊙, 98,469......M 5	50707 Evansdale, 5,038......J 4	51537 Harlan⊙, 5,049......C 5
Davenport-Rock Island-Moline, ‡362,638......M 5	52169 Everly, 699......C 2	52146 Harpers Ferry, 227......L 2
50065 Davis City, 301......F 7	50076 Exira, 966......D 5	50118 Hartford, 582......F 6
50066 Dawson, 232......E 5	52555 Exline, 224......H 7	51346 Hartley, 1,561......C 2
50530 Dayton, 909......E 4	50629 Fairbank, 810......K 3	50119 Harvey, 217......H 6
52101 Decorah⊙, 7,458......K 2	52228 Fairfax, 635......K 5	51540 Hastings, 229......C 6
52222 Deep River, 323......J 5	52556 Fairfield⊙, 8,715......J 6	50546 Havelock, 220......D 3
51527 Defiance, 392......C 5	52046 Farley, 1,096......L 4	51023 Hawarden, 2,789......A 2
52223 Delhi, 527......L 4	52047 Farmersburg, 232......L 3	52147 Hawkeye, 529......K 3
52037 Delmar, 599......M 4	52626 Farmington, 800......K 7	50641 Hazleton, 626......K 3
51441 Deloit, 279......C 4	50538 Farnhamville, 393......D 4	52563 Hedrick, 790......J 6
52550 Delta, 475......J 6	51639 Farragut, 521......C 7	51541 Henderson, 211......B 6
51442 Denison⊙, 5,882......C 5	52142 Fayette, 1,947......K 3	52233 Hiawatha, 2,416......K 5
52624 Denmark, 375......L 7	50539 Fenton, 403......E 2	52235 Hills, 507......K 5
50622 Denver, 1,169......J 3	50434 Fertile, 394......G 2	52630 Hillsboro, 252......K 7
* 50301 Des Moines (cap.)⊙, 200,587......G 5	50435 Floyd, 380......H 2	51024 Hinton, 488......A 3
Des Moines, ‡286,101......G 5	50540 Fonda, 980......D 3	50642 Holland, 258......H 4
50069 De Soto, 369......E 5	50846 Fontanelle, 752......E 6	51025 Holstein, 1,445......B 3
52742 De Witt, 3,647......N 5	50436 Forest City⊙, 3,841......F 2	52053 Holy Cross, 290......L 3
50070 Dexter, 652......E 5	52144 Fort Atkinson, 339......J 2	52237 Hopkinton, 800......L 4
50845 Diagonal, 327......E 7	50501 Fort Dodge⊙, 31,263......E 3	51026 Hornick, 250......A 4
51333 Dickens, 240......C 2	52627 Fort Madison⊙, 13,996......L 7	51238 Hospers, 646......B 2
50624 Dike, 794......H 3	51340 Fostoria, 219......C 2	50122 Hubbard, 846......G 4
52745 Dixon, 276......M 5	50630 Fredericksburg, 912......J 3	50643 Hudson, 1,535......H 4
52746 Donahue, 216......M 5	52561 Fremont, 480......H 6	51239 Hull, 1,523......A 2
52625 Donnellson, 798......K 7	51020 Galva, 319......C 3	50548 Humboldt, 4,665......E 3
51235 Doon, 437......A 2	50103 Garden Grove, 285......F 7	50123 Humeston, 673......G 7
52551 Douds, 247......J 7	52049 Garnavillo, 634......L 3	50124 Huxley, 937......F 5
51528 Dow City, 571......C 5	50438 Garner⊙, 2,217......F 2	51445 Ida Grove⊙, 2,261......B 4
50071 Dows, 777......F 3	52229 Garrison, 383......J 4	50644 Independence⊙, 5,910......K 4
52001 Dubuque⊙, 62,309......M 3	50632 Garwin, 563......H 4	50125 Indianola⊙, 8,852......F 6
Dubuque, ‡90,609......M 3	51237 George, 1,194......A 2	51240 Inwood, 644......A 2
50625 Dumont, 724......H 3	50105 Gilbert, 521......F 4	50645 Ionia, 270......H 2
50532 Duncombe, 418......E 4	50634 Gilbertville, 655......J 4	52240 Iowa City⊙, 46,850......K 5
50626 Dunkerton, 663......J 3	50106 Gilman, 513......H 5	50126 Iowa Falls, 6,454......G 3
51529 Dunlap, 1,292......B 5	50541 Gilmore City, 766......D 3	51027 Ireton, 582......A 2
52747 Durant, 1,472......M 5	50635 Gladbrook, 961......H 4	51446 Irwin, 446......C 5
52040 Dyersville, 3,437......L 3	51534 Glenwood⊙, 4,195......B 6	50128 Jamaica, 231......E 5
52224 Dysart, 1,251......J 4	51443 Glidden, 964......D 4	50647 Janesville, 741......J 3
50533 Eagle Grove, 4,489......F 3	50542 Goldfield, 722......F 3	50129 Jefferson⊙, 4,735......E 4
50072 Earlham, 916......E 6	50439 Goodell, 218......F 3	50648 Jesup, 1,662......K 4
51530 Earling, 573......C 5	52750 Gooselake, 218......N 5	50130 Jewell, 1,152......F 4
52041 Earlville, 751......L 4	50543 Gowrie, 1,225......E 4	50131 Johnston, 222......F 5
50535 Early, 727......C 4	51342 Graettinger, 907......D 2	52247 Kalona, 1,488......K 6
	50440 Grafton, 254......G 2	50132 Kamrar, 243......F 4
	50107 Grand Junction, 967......E 4	50447 Kanawha, 705......F 3
	52751 Grand Mound, 627......M 5	50133 Kellerton, 299......E 7

(continued on following page)

(continued)

Agriculture, Industry and Resources

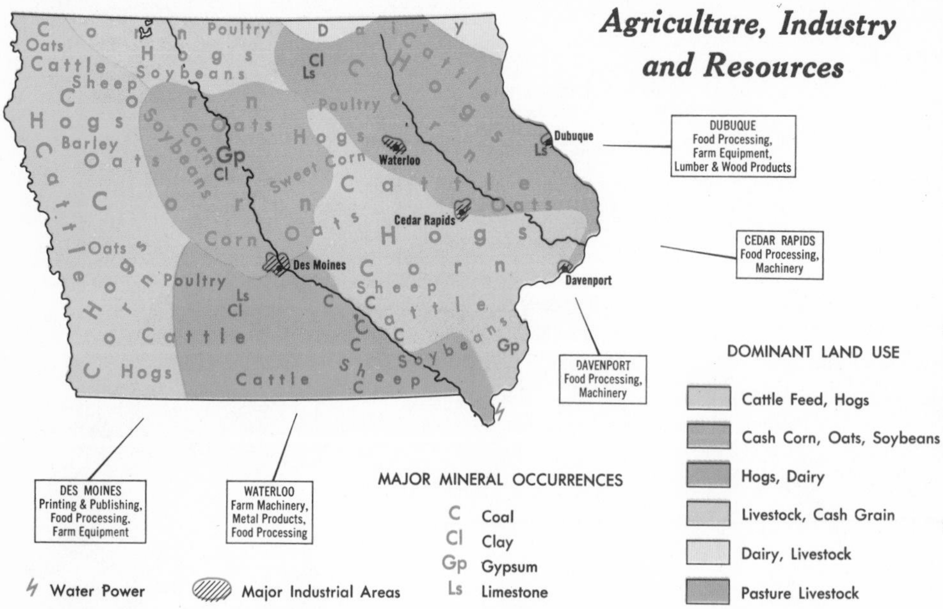

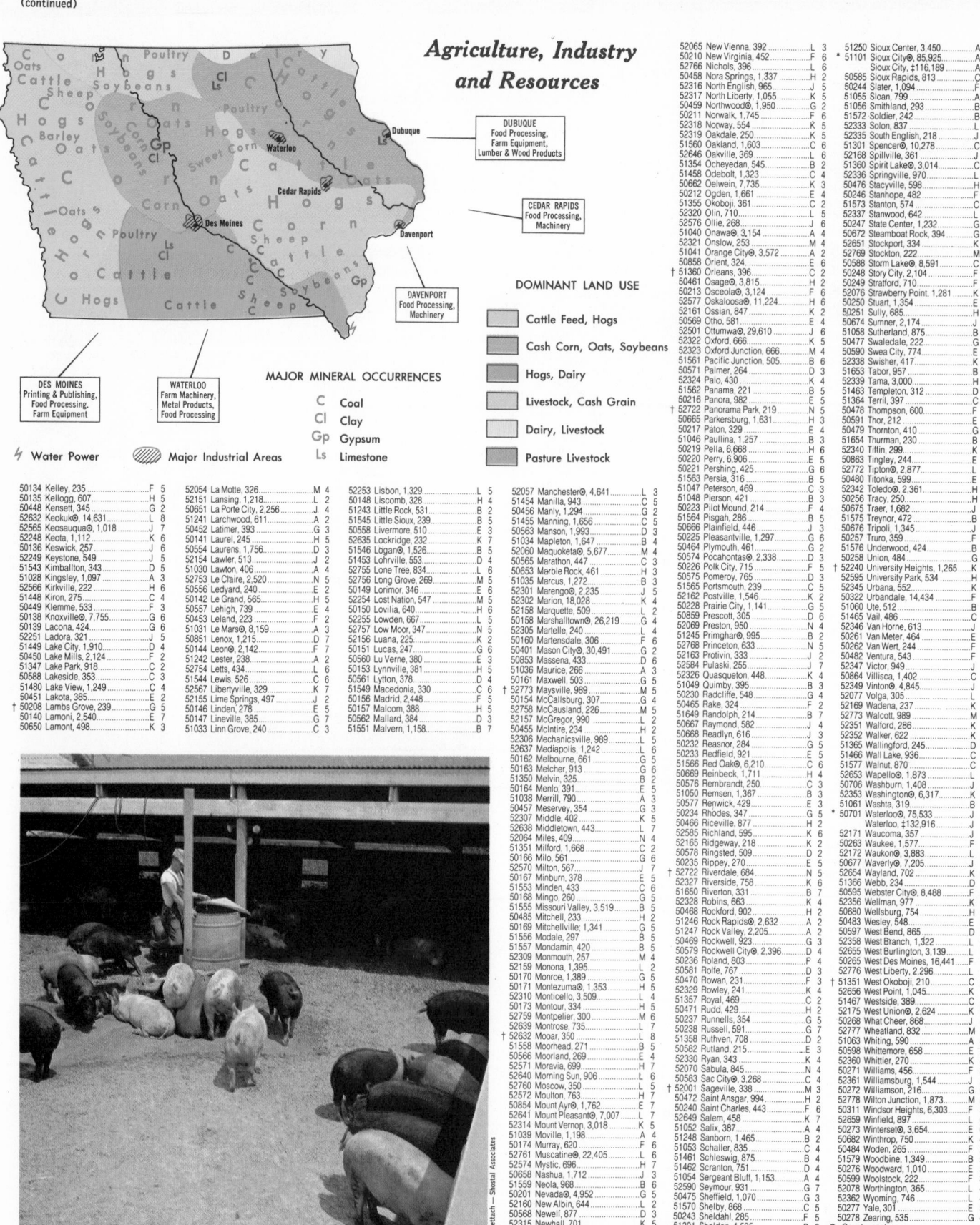

Corn
Oats
Cattle
Sheep
Hogs
Barley
Poultry
Soybeans
Dairy
Sweet Corn
Waterloo
Cedar Rapids
Dubuque
Des Moines
Davenport
C
Cl
Gp
Ls
DUBUQUE
Food Processing, Farm Equipment, Lumber & Wood Products
CEDAR RAPIDS
Food Processing, Machinery
DAVENPORT
Food Processing, Machinery
DES MOINES
Printing & Publishing, Food Processing, Farm Equipment
WATERLOO
Farm Machinery, Metal Products, Food Processing
DOMINANT LAND USE
Cattle Feed, Hogs
Cash Corn, Oats, Soybeans
Hogs, Dairy
Livestock, Cash Grain
Dairy, Livestock
Pasture Livestock
MAJOR MINERAL OCCURRENCES
C Coal
Cl Clay
Gp Gypsum
Ls Limestone
Water Power
Major Industrial Areas

50134 Kelley, 235 ....F 5
50135 Kellogg, 607 ....H 5
50448 Kensett, 345 ....G 2
52632 Keokuk⊙, 14,631 ....L 8
52565 Keosauqua⊙, 1,018 ....J 7
52248 Keota, 1,112 ....K 6
50136 Keswick, 257 ....J 6
52249 Keystone, 549 ....J 5
51543 Kimballton, 343 ....D 5
51028 Kingsley, 1,097 ....A 3
52566 Kirkville, 222 ....H 6
51448 Kiron, 275 ....C 4
50449 Klemme, 533 ....F 3
50138 Knoxville⊙, 7,755 ....G 6
50139 Lacona, 424 ....G 6
52251 Ladora, 321 ....J 5
51449 Lake City, 1,910 ....D 4
50450 Lake Mills, 2,124 ....F 2
51347 Lake Park, 918 ....C 2
50588 Lakeside, 353 ....C 3
51480 Lake View, 1,249 ....C 4
50451 Lakota, 385 ....E 2
† 50208 Lambs Grove, 239 ....G 5
50140 Lamoni, 2,540 ....E 7
50650 Lamont, 498 ....K 3
52054 La Motte, 326 ....M 4
52151 Lansing, 1,218 ....L 2
50651 La Porte City, 2,256 ....J 4
51241 Larchwood, 611 ....A 2
50452 Latimer, 393 ....G 3
50141 Laurel, 245 ....H 5
50554 Laurens, 1,756 ....D 3
52154 Lawler, 513 ....J 2
51030 Lawton, 406 ....A 4
52753 Le Claire, 2,520 ....N 5
50556 Ledyard, 240 ....E 2
50142 Le Grand, 565 ....H 5
50557 Lehigh, 739 ....E 4
50453 Leland, 223 ....F 2
51031 Le Mars⊙, 8,159 ....A 3
50851 Lenox, 1,215 ....D 7
50144 Leon⊙, 2,142 ....F 7
51242 Lester, 238 ....A 2
52754 Letts, 434 ....L 6
51544 Lewis, 526 ....C 6
52567 Libertyville, 329 ....K 7
52155 Lime Springs, 497 ....J 2
50146 Linden, 278 ....E 5
50147 Lineville, 385 ....G 7
51033 Linn Grove, 240 ....C 3
52253 Lisbon, 1,329 ....L 5
50148 Liscomb, 328 ....H 4
51243 Little Rock, 531 ....B 2
51545 Little Sioux, 239 ....B 5
50558 Livermore, 510 ....E 3
52635 Lockridge, 232 ....K 7
51546 Logan⊙, 1,526 ....B 5
51453 Lohrville, 553 ....D 4
52755 Lone Tree, 834 ....L 6
52756 Long Grove, 269 ....M 5
50149 Lorimor, 346 ....E 6
52254 Lost Nation, 547 ....M 5
50150 Lovilia, 640 ....H 6
52255 Lowden, 667 ....L 5
52757 Low Moor, 347 ....N 5
52156 Luana, 225 ....K 2
50151 Lucas, 247 ....G 6
50560 Lu Verne, 380 ....E 3
50153 Lynnville, 381 ....H 5
50561 Lytton, 378 ....D 4
51549 Macedonia, 330 ....C 6
50156 Madrid, 2,448 ....F 5
50157 Malcom, 388 ....H 5
50562 Mallard, 384 ....D 3
51551 Malvern, 1,158 ....B 7

A. M. Wettach — Shostal Associates

This Iowa farmer confines his hogs to concrete pens as a more efficient and sanitary method of raising healthy animals for market. Iowa's record-breaking hog production is due largely to the availability of corn for fodder.

52057 Manchester⊙, 4,641 ....L 3
51454 Manilla, 943 ....C 5
50456 Manly, 1,294 ....G 2
51455 Manning, 1,656 ....C 5
50563 Manson, 1,993 ....D 3
51034 Mapleton, 1,647 ....B 4
52060 Maquoketa⊙, 5,677 ....M 4
50565 Marathon, 447 ....C 3
50653 Marble Rock, 461 ....H 3
51035 Marcus, 1,272 ....B 3
52301 Marengo⊙, 2,235 ....J 5
52302 Marion, 18,028 ....K 4
52158 Marquette, 509 ....L 2
50158 Marshalltown⊙, 26,219 ....G 4
52305 Martelle, 240 ....L 4
50160 Martensdale, 306 ....F 6
50401 Mason City⊙, 30,491 ....G 2
50853 Massena, 433 ....D 6
51036 Maurice, 266 ....A 3
50161 Maxwell, 503 ....G 5
† 52773 Maysville, 989 ....M 5
50154 McCallsburg, 307 ....G 4
52758 McCausland, 226 ....M 5
52157 McGregor, 990 ....L 2
50455 McIntire, 234 ....H 2
52306 Mechanicsville, 989 ....L 5
52637 Mediapolis, 1,242 ....L 6
50162 Melbourne, 661 ....G 5
50163 Melcher, 913 ....G 6
51350 Melvin, 325 ....B 2
50164 Menlo, 391 ....E 5
51038 Merrill, 790 ....A 3
50457 Meservey, 354 ....G 3
52307 Middle, 402 ....K 5
52638 Middletown, 443 ....L 7
52064 Miles, 409 ....N 4
51351 Milford, 1,668 ....C 2
50166 Milo, 561 ....G 6
52570 Milton, 567 ....J 7
50167 Minburn, 378 ....E 5
51553 Minden, 433 ....C 6
50168 Mingo, 260 ....G 5
51555 Missouri Valley, 3,519 ....B 5
50485 Mitchell, 233 ....H 2
50169 Mitchellville, 1,341 ....G 5
51556 Modale, 297 ....B 5
51557 Mondamin, 420 ....B 5
52309 Monmouth, 257 ....M 4
52159 Monona, 1,395 ....L 2
50170 Monroe, 1,389 ....G 5
50171 Montezuma⊙, 1,353 ....H 5
52310 Monticello, 3,509 ....L 4
50173 Montour, 334 ....H 5
52759 Montpelier, 300 ....M 6
52639 Montrose, 735 ....L 7
† 52632 Mooar, 350 ....L 8
51558 Moorhead, 271 ....B 5
50566 Moorland, 269 ....E 4
52571 Moravia, 699 ....H 7
52640 Morning Sun, 906 ....L 6
52760 Moscow, 350 ....L 5
52572 Moulton, 763 ....H 7
50854 Mount Ayr⊙, 1,762 ....E 7
52641 Mount Pleasant⊙, 7,007 ....L 7
52314 Mount Vernon, 3,018 ....K 5
51039 Moville, 1,198 ....A 4
50174 Murray, 620 ....F 6
52761 Muscatine⊙, 22,405 ....L 6
52574 Mystic, 696 ....H 7
50658 Nashua, 1,712 ....J 3
51559 Neola, 968 ....B 6
50201 Nevada⊙, 4,952 ....G 5
52160 New Albin, 644 ....L 2
50568 Newell, 877 ....D 3
52315 Newhall, 701 ....K 5
50659 New Hampton⊙, 3,621 ....J 2
50660 New Hartford, 690 ....H 3
52645 New London, 1,900 ....L 7
51646 New Market, 501 ....D 7
50206 New Providence, 208 ....G 4
50207 New Sharon, 944 ....H 6
50208 Newton⊙, 15,619 ....H 5
52065 New Vienna, 392 ....L 3
50210 New Virginia, 452 ....F 6
52766 Nichols, 396 ....L 6
50458 Nora Springs, 1,337 ....H 2
52316 North English, 965 ....J 5
52317 North Liberty, 1,055 ....K 5
50459 Northwood⊙, 1,950 ....G 2
50211 Norwalk, 1,745 ....F 6
52318 Norway, 554 ....K 5
52319 Oakdale, 250 ....K 5
51560 Oakland, 1,603 ....C 6
52646 Oakville, 369 ....L 6
51354 Ocheyedan, 545 ....B 2
51458 Odebolt, 1,323 ....C 4
50662 Oelwein, 7,735 ....K 3
50212 Ogden, 1,661 ....E 4
51355 Okoboji, 361 ....C 2
52320 Olin, 710 ....L 5
52576 Ollie, 268 ....J 6
51040 Onawa⊙, 3,154 ....A 4
52321 Onslow, 253 ....M 4
51041 Orange City⊙, 3,572 ....A 2
50858 Orient, 324 ....E 6
† 51360 Orleans, 396 ....C 2
50461 Osage⊙, 3,815 ....H 2
50213 Osceola⊙, 3,124 ....F 6
52577 Oskaloosa⊙, 11,224 ....H 6
52161 Ossian, 847 ....K 2
50569 Otho, 581 ....E 4
52501 Ottumwa⊙, 29,610 ....J 6
52322 Oxford, 666 ....K 5
52323 Oxford Junction, 666 ....M 4
51561 Pacific Junction, 505 ....B 6
50571 Palmer, 264 ....D 3
52324 Palo, 430 ....K 4
51562 Panama, 221 ....B 5
50216 Panora, 982 ....E 5
† 52722 Panorama Park, 219 ....N 5
50665 Parkersburg, 1,631 ....H 3
50217 Paton, 329 ....E 4
51046 Paullina, 1,257 ....B 3
50219 Pella, 6,668 ....H 6
50220 Perry, 6,906 ....E 5
50221 Pershing, 425 ....G 6
51563 Persia, 316 ....B 5
51047 Peterson, 469 ....C 3
51048 Pierson, 421 ....B 3
50223 Pilot Mound, 214 ....F 4
51564 Pisgah, 286 ....B 5
50666 Plainfield, 446 ....J 3
50225 Pleasantville, 1,297 ....G 6
50464 Plymouth, 461 ....G 2
50574 Pocahontas⊙, 2,338 ....D 3
50226 Polk City, 715 ....F 5
50575 Pomeroy, 765 ....D 3
51565 Portsmouth, 239 ....C 5
52162 Postville, 1,546 ....K 2
50228 Prairie City, 1,141 ....G 5
50859 Prescott, 305 ....D 6
52069 Preston, 950 ....N 4
51245 Primghar⊙, 995 ....B 2
52768 Princeton, 633 ....N 5
52163 Protivin, 333 ....J 2
52584 Pulaski, 255 ....J 7
52326 Quasqueton, 448 ....K 4
51049 Quimby, 395 ....B 3
50230 Radcliffe, 548 ....G 4
50465 Rake, 324 ....F 2
51649 Randolph, 214 ....B 7
50667 Raymond, 582 ....J 4
50668 Readlyn, 616 ....J 3
50232 Reasnor, 284 ....G 5
50233 Redfield, 921 ....E 5
51566 Red Oak⊙, 6,210 ....C 6
50669 Reinbeck, 1,711 ....H 4
50576 Rembrandt, 250 ....C 3
51050 Remsen, 1,367 ....B 3
50577 Renwick, 429 ....E 3
50234 Rhodes, 347 ....G 5
50466 Riceville, 877 ....H 2
52585 Richland, 595 ....K 6
52165 Ridgeway, 218 ....K 2
50578 Ringsted, 509 ....D 2
50235 Rippey, 270 ....E 5
† 52722 Riverdale, 684 ....N 5
52327 Riverside, 758 ....K 6
51650 Riverton, 331 ....B 7
52328 Robins, 663 ....K 4
50468 Rockford, 902 ....H 2
51246 Rock Rapids⊙, 2,632 ....A 2
51247 Rock Valley, 2,205 ....A 2
50469 Rockwell, 923 ....G 3
50579 Rockwell City⊙, 2,396 ....D 4
50236 Roland, 803 ....F 4
50581 Rolfe, 767 ....D 3
50470 Rowan, 231 ....F 3
52329 Rowley, 241 ....K 4
51357 Royal, 469 ....C 2
50471 Rudd, 429 ....H 2
50237 Runnells, 354 ....G 5
50238 Russell, 591 ....G 7
51358 Ruthven, 708 ....D 2
50582 Rutland, 215 ....E 3
52330 Ryan, 343 ....K 4
52070 Sabula, 845 ....N 4
50583 Sac City⊙, 3,268 ....C 4
† 52001 Sageville, 338 ....M 3
50472 Saint Ansgar, 994 ....H 2
50240 Saint Charles, 443 ....F 6
52649 Salem, 458 ....K 7
51052 Salix, 387 ....A 4
51248 Sanborn, 1,465 ....B 2
51053 Schaller, 835 ....C 4
51461 Schleswig, 875 ....B 4
51462 Scranton, 751 ....D 4
51054 Sergeant Bluff, 1,153 ....A 4
52590 Seymour, 931 ....G 7
50475 Sheffield, 1,070 ....G 3
51570 Shelby, 868 ....C 5
50243 Sheldahl, 285 ....F 5
51201 Sheldon, 4,535 ....B 2
50670 Shell Rock, 1,159 ....H 3
52332 Shellsburg, 740 ....K 4
51601 Shenandoah, 5,968 ....C 7
51249 Sibley⊙, 2,749 ....B 2
51652 Sidney⊙, 1,061 ....B 7
52591 Sigourney⊙, 2,319 ....J 6
51571 Silver City, 272 ....B 6
51250 Sioux Center, 3,450 ....A 2
* 51101 Sioux City⊙, 85,925 ....A 3
Sioux City, ‡116,189 ....A 3
50585 Sioux Rapids, 813 ....C 3
50244 Slater, 1,094 ....F 5
51055 Sloan, 799 ....A 4
51056 Smithland, 293 ....B 4
51572 Soldier, 242 ....B 5
52333 Solon, 837 ....L 5
52335 South English, 218 ....J 6
51301 Spencer⊙, 10,278 ....C 2
52168 Spillville, 361 ....J 2
51360 Spirit Lake⊙, 3,014 ....C 2
52336 Springville, 970 ....L 4
50476 Stacyville, 598 ....H 2
50246 Stanhope, 482 ....F 4
51573 Stanton, 574 ....C 7
52337 Stanwood, 642 ....L 5
50247 State Center, 1,232 ....G 5
50672 Steamboat Rock, 394 ....G 4
52651 Stockport, 334 ....K 7
52769 Stockton, 222 ....M 5
50588 Storm Lake⊙, 8,591 ....C 3
50248 Story City, 2,104 ....F 4
50249 Stratford, 710 ....F 4
52076 Strawberry Point, 1,281 ....K 3
50250 Stuart, 1,354 ....E 6
50251 Sully, 685 ....H 5
50674 Sumner, 2,174 ....J 3
51058 Sutherland, 875 ....B 3
50477 Swaledale, 222 ....G 3
50590 Swea City, 774 ....E 2
52338 Swisher, 417 ....K 5
51653 Tabor, 957 ....B 7
52339 Tama, 3,000 ....H 5
51463 Templeton, 312 ....D 5
51364 Terril, 397 ....C 2
50478 Thompson, 600 ....F 2
50591 Thor, 212 ....E 3
50479 Thornton, 410 ....G 3
51654 Thurman, 230 ....B 7
52340 Tiffin, 299 ....K 5
50863 Tingley, 244 ....E 7
52772 Tipton⊙, 2,877 ....L 5
50480 Titonka, 599 ....E 2
52342 Toledo⊙, 2,361 ....H 4
50256 Tracy, 250 ....H 6
50675 Traer, 1,682 ....J 4
51575 Treynor, 472 ....B 6
50676 Tripoli, 1,345 ....J 3
50257 Truro, 359 ....F 6
51576 Underwood, 424 ....B 6
50258 Union, 484 ....G 4
† 52240 University Heights, 1,265 ....K 5
52595 University Park, 534 ....H 6
52345 Urbana, 552 ....K 4
50322 Urbandale, 14,434 ....F 5
51060 Ute, 512 ....B 4
51465 Vail, 486 ....C 4
52346 Van Horne, 613 ....J 4
50261 Van Meter, 464 ....E 5
50262 Van Wert, 244 ....F 7
50482 Ventura, 543 ....F 2
52347 Victor, 949 ....J 5
50864 Villisca, 1,402 ....C 7
52349 Vinton⊙, 4,845 ....J 4
52077 Volga, 305 ....L 3
52169 Wadena, 237 ....K 3
52773 Walcott, 989 ....M 5
52351 Walford, 286 ....K 5
52352 Walker, 622 ....K 4
51365 Wallingford, 245 ....D 2
51466 Wall Lake, 936 ....C 4
51577 Walnut, 870 ....C 6
52653 Wapello⊙, 1,873 ....L 6
50706 Washburn, 1,408 ....J 4
52353 Washington⊙, 6,317 ....K 6
51061 Washta, 319 ....B 3
* 50701 Waterloo⊙, 75,533 ....J 4
Waterloo, ‡132,916 ....J 4
52171 Waucoma, 357 ....J 2
50263 Waukee, 1,577 ....F 5
52172 Waukon⊙, 3,883 ....L 2
50677 Waverly⊙, 7,205 ....J 3
52654 Wayland, 702 ....K 6
51366 Webb, 234 ....D 3
50595 Webster City⊙, 8,488 ....F 4
52356 Wellman, 977 ....K 6
50680 Wellsburg, 754 ....H 4
50483 Wesley, 548 ....E 2
50597 West Bend, 865 ....D 3
52358 West Branch, 1,322 ....L 5
52655 West Burlington, 3,139 ....L 7
50265 West Des Moines, 16,441 ....F 5
52776 West Liberty, 2,296 ....L 5
† 51351 West Okoboji, 210 ....C 2
52656 West Point, 1,045 ....K 7
51467 Westside, 389 ....C 4
52175 West Union⊙, 2,624 ....K 3
50268 What Cheer, 868 ....J 6
52777 Wheatland, 832 ....M 5
51063 Whiting, 590 ....A 4
50598 Whittemore, 658 ....E 2
52360 Whittier, 270 ....K 4
50271 Williams, 456 ....F 3
52361 Williamsburg, 1,544 ....J 5
50272 Williamson, 216 ....G 6
52778 Wilton Junction, 1,873 ....M 5
50311 Windsor Heights, 6,303 ....F 5
52659 Winfield, 897 ....L 6
50273 Winterset⊙, 3,654 ....E 6
50682 Winthrop, 750 ....K 4
50484 Woden, 265 ....F 2
51579 Woodbine, 1,349 ....B 5
50276 Woodward, 1,010 ....E 5
50599 Woolstock, 222 ....F 3
52078 Worthington, 365 ....L 4
52362 Wyoming, 746 ....L 4
50277 Yale, 301 ....E 5
50278 Zearing, 535 ....G 4

⊙ County seat.
‡ Population of metropolitan area.
† Zip of nearest p.o.
* Multiple zips

Agriculture, Industry and Resources

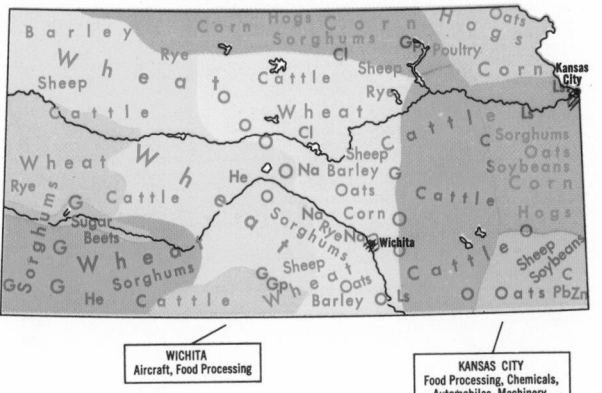

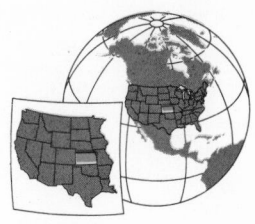

AREA 82,264 sq. mi.
POPULATION 2,249,071
CAPITAL Topeka
LARGEST CITY Wichita
HIGHEST POINT Mt. Sunflower 4,039 ft.
SETTLED IN 1831
ADMITTED TO UNION January 29, 1861
POPULAR NAME Sunflower State
STATE FLOWER Sunflower
STATE BIRD Western Meadowlark

DOMINANT LAND USE

- Specialized Wheat
- Wheat, General Farming
- Wheat, Range Livestock
- Wheat, Grain Sorghums, Range Livestock
- Cattle Feed, Hogs
- Livestock, Cash Grain
- Livestock, Cash Grain, Dairy
- General Farming, Livestock, Cash Grain
- General Farming, Livestock, Special Crops
- Range Livestock

MAJOR MINERAL OCCURRENCES

C	Coal	Ls	Limestone
Cl	Clay	Na	Salt
G	Natural Gas	O	Petroleum
Gp	Gypsum	Pb	Lead
He	Helium	Zn	Zinc

Major Industrial Areas

WICHITA Aircraft, Food Processing

KANSAS CITY Food Processing, Chemicals, Automobiles, Machinery, Metal Products

Loaded with wheat for storage, a truck pulls onto a weighing platform at the Salina grain elevators. Wheat is grown here on such a scale that Kansas is known as the Breadbasket of the World.

Robert Leahey — Shostal Associates

McPherson, 24,778	E 3
Meade, 4,912	B 4
Miami, 19,254	H 3
Mitchell, 8,010	D 2
Montgomery, 39,949	G 4
Morris, 6,432	F 3
Morton, 3,576	A 4
Nemaha, 11,825	F 2
Neosho, 18,812	G 4
Ness, 4,791	C 3
Norton, 7,279	C 2
Osage, 13,352	G 3
Osborne, 6,416	D 2
Ottawa, 6,183	E 2
Pawnee, 8,484	C 3
Phillips, 7,888	C 2
Pottawatomie, 11,755	F 2
Pratt, 10,056	D 4
Rawlins, 4,393	A 2
Reno, 60,765	D 4
Republic, 8,498	E 2
Rice, 12,320	D 3
Riley, 56,788	F 2
Rooks, 7,628	C 2
Rush, 5,117	C 3
Russell, 9,428	D 3
Saline, 46,592	E 3
Scott, 5,606	B 3
Sedgwick, 350,694	E 4
Seward, 15,744	B 4
Shawnee, 155,322	G 2
Sheridan, 3,859	B 2
Sherman, 7,792	A 2
Smith, 6,757	D 2
Stafford, 5,943	D 3
Stanton, 2,287	A 4
Stevens, 4,198	A 4
Sumner, 23,553	E 4
Thomas, 7,501	A 2
Trego, 4,436	C 3
Wabaunsee, 6,397	F 3
Wallace, 2,215	A 3
Washington, 9,249	E 2
Wichita, 3,274	A 3
Wilson, 11,317	G 4
Woodson, 4,789	G 4
Wyandotte, 186,845	H 2

COUNTIES

County	Key
Allen, 15,043	G 4
Anderson, 8,501	G 3
Atchison, 19,165	G 2
Barber, 7,016	D 4
Barton, 30,663	D 3
Bourbon, 15,215	H 4
Brown, 11,685	G 2
Butler, 38,658	F 4
Chase, 3,408	F 3
Chautauqua, 4,642	F 4
Cherokee, 21,549	H 4
Cheyenne, 4,256	A 2
Clark, 2,896	C 4
Clay, 9,890	E 2
Cloud, 13,466	E 2
Coffey, 7,397	G 3
Comanche, 2,702	C 4
Cowley, 35,012	F 4
Crawford, 37,850	H 4
Decatur, 4,988	B 2
Dickinson, 19,993	E 3
Doniphan, 9,107	G 2
Douglas, 57,932	G 2
Edwards, 4,581	C 4
Elk, 3,858	F 4
Ellis, 24,730	C 3
Ellsworth, 6,146	D 3
Finney, 18,947	B 3
Ford, 22,587	C 4
Franklin, 20,007	G 3
Geary, 28,111	F 3
Gove, 3,940	B 3
Graham, 4,751	C 2
Grant, 5,961	A 4
Gray, 4,516	B 4
Greeley, 1,819	A 3
Greenwood, 9,141	F 4
Hamilton, 2,747	A 3
Harper, 7,871	D 4
Harvey, 27,236	E 3
Haskell, 3,672	B 4
Hodgeman, 2,662	C 3
Jackson, 10,342	G 2
Jefferson, 11,945	G 2
Jewell, 6,099	D 2
Johnson, 217,662	H 3
Kearny, 3,047	A 3
Kingman, 8,886	D 4
Kiowa, 4,088	C 4
Labette, 25,775	G 4
Lane, 2,707	B 3
Leavenworth, 53,340	G 2
Lincoln, 4,582	D 2
Linn, 7,770	H 3
Logan, 3,814	A 3
Lyon, 32,071	F 3
Marion, 13,935	E 3
Marshall, 13,139	F 2

CITIES and TOWNS

Zip	Name/Pop.	Key
67510	Abbyville, 143	D 4
67410	Abilene⊙, 6,661	E 3
67414	Ada, 120	E 2
66830	Admire, 144	F 3
66930	Agenda, 107	E 2
67621	Agra, 294	C 2
67511	Albert, 235	C 3
67512	Alden, 238	D 3
67513	Alexander, 129	C 3
66833	Allen, 175	F 3
66401	Alma⊙, 905	F 2
67622	Almena, 489	C 2
67330	Altamont, 845	G 4
66834	Alta Vista, 402	F 3
67623	Alton, 214	D 2
66710	Altoona, 475	G 4
66835	Americus, 441	F 3
67001	Andale, 500	E 4
67002	Andover, 1,880	E 4
67003	Anthony⊙, 2,653	D 4
66711	Arcadia, 388	H 4
67004	Argonia, 591	E 4
67005	Arkansas City, 13,216	E 4
67514	Arlington, 503	D 4
66712	Arma, 1,348	H 4
67831	Ashland⊙, 1,244	C 4
67416	Assaria, 303	E 3
66002	Atchison⊙, 12,565	G 2
66932	Athol, 108	D 2
67008	Atlanta, 216	F 4
67009	Attica, 639	D 4
67730	Atwood⊙, 1,658	B 2
66402	Auburn, 261	G 3
67010	Augusta, 5,977	F 4
67417	Aurora, 120	E 2
66403	Axtell, 456	F 2
66404	Baileyville, 110	F 2
66006	Baldwin City, 2,520	G 3
67418	Barnard, 190	D 2
66933	Barnes, 209	F 2
67332	Bartlett, 138	G 4
66713	Baxter Springs, 4,489	H 4
67516	Bazine, 386	C 3
66406	Beattie, 288	F 2
67012	Beaumont, 135	F 4
67013	Belle Plaine, 1,553	E 4
66935	Belleville⊙, 3,063	E 2
67420	Beloit⊙, 4,121	D 2
67519	Belpre, 191	C 4
66407	Belvue, 161	F 2
67422	Bennington, 561	E 2
67016	Bentley, 260	E 4
67017	Benton, 517	E 4
66408	Bern, 191	F 2
67423	Beverly, 193	E 2
67731	Bird City, 671	A 2
67520	Bison, 285	C 3
66010	Blue Mound, 308	H 3
66411	Blue Rapids, 1,148	F 2
67018	Bluff City, 109	E 4
67625	Bogue, 257	C 2
66012	Bonner Springs, 3,662	H 2
67732	Brewster, 320	A 2
66716	Bronson, 397	H 4
67425	Brookville, 238	E 3
67834	Bucklin, 771	C 4
66013	Bucyrus, 196	H 3
66717	Buffalo, 321	G 4
67522	Buhler, 1,019	E 3
67626	Bunker Hill, 181	D 3
67019	Burden, 503	F 4
67523	Burdett, 285	C 3
66838	Burdick, 120	F 3
66413	Burlingame, 999	G 3
66839	Burlington⊙, 2,099	G 3
66840	Burns, 268	F 3
66936	Burr Oak, 426	D 2
67020	Burrton, 808	E 3
67427	Bushton, 397	D 3
67022	Caldwell, 1,540	E 4
67023	Cambridge, 110	F 4
67333	Caney, 2,192	G 4
67428	Canton, 893	E 3
66414	Carbondale, 1,041	G 3
66842	Cassoday, 123	F 3
67627	Catharine, 126	C 3
67430	Cawker City, 726	D 2
67024	Cedar Vale, 665	F 4
66415	Centralia, 511	F 2
66720	Chanute, 10,341	G 4
67431	Chapman, 1,132	E 3
67524	Chase, 800	D 3
67334	Chautauqua, 137	F 4
67025	Cheney, 1,160	E 4
66724	Cherokee, 790	H 4
67335	Cherryvale, 2,609	G 4
67336	Chetopa, 1,596	G 4
† 66762	Chicopee, 300	H 4
87835	Cimarron⊙, 1,373	B 4
66416	Circleville, 178	G 2
67525	Claflin, 887	D 3
67432	Clay Center⊙, 4,963	E 2
67629	Clayton, 127	B 2
67026	Clearwater, 1,435	E 4
66937	Clifton, 718	E 2
66938	Clyde, 946	E 2
67028	Coats, 152	D 4
67337	Coffeyville, 15,116	G 4
67701	Colby⊙, 4,658	A 2
67029	Coldwater⊙, 1,016	C 4
67631	Collyer, 182	B 2
66015	Colony, 382	G 3
66725	Columbus⊙, 3,356	H 4
67030	Colwich, 879	E 4
66901	Concordia⊙, 7,221	E 2
67031	Conway Springs, 1,153	E 4
67836	Coolidge, 102	A 3
67837	Copeland, 267	B 4
66417	Corning, 162	F 2
66845	Cottonwood Falls⊙, 987	F 3
66846	Council Grove⊙, 2,403	F 3
66939	Courtland, 403	E 2
66728	Crestline, 102	H 4
66940	Cuba, 290	E 2
† 67124	Cullison, 117	D 4
67435	Culver, 148	E 3
66016	Cummings, 826	G 2
67035	Cunningham, 483	D 4
67632	Damar, 245	C 2
67340	Dearing, 338	G 4
67838	Deerfield, 474	A 4
66418	Delia, 168	G 2
67436	Delphos, 599	E 2
66419	Denison, 248	G 2
67341	Dennis, 120	G 4
66017	Denton, 162	G 2
67037	Derby, 7,947	E 4
66018	De Soto, 1,839	H 3
67038	Dexter, 286	F 4
67839	Dighton⊙, 1,540	B 3
67801	Dodge City⊙, 14,127	B 4
67634	Dorrance, 234	D 3
67039	Douglass, 1,126	F 4
66420	Dover, 122	G 3
67437	Downs, 1,268	D 2
67635	Dresden, 103	B 2
67438	Durham, 143	E 3
66849	Dwight, 322	F 3
66731	Earlton, 102	G 4
† 67201	Eastborough, 1,141	E 4
66020	Easton, 435	G 2
66021	Edgerton, 513	H 3
67342	Edna, 418	G 4
66022	Edwardsville, 619	H 2
66023	Effingham, 605	G 2
67041	Elbing, 128	E 3
67042	El Dorado⊙, 12,308	F 4
67361	Elgin, 115	F 4
67344	Elk City, 432	G 4
67345	Elk Falls, 124	F 4
67950	Elkhart⊙, 2,089	A 4
67526	Ellinwood, 2,416	D 3
67637	Ellis, 2,137	C 3

(continued on following page)

KANSAS

SCALE

0 5 10 20 30 40 50 MI.

0 5 10 20 30 40 50 KM.

State Capitals ⊛

County Seats ⊙

ⓒ C.S. HAMMOND & Co., N.Y.

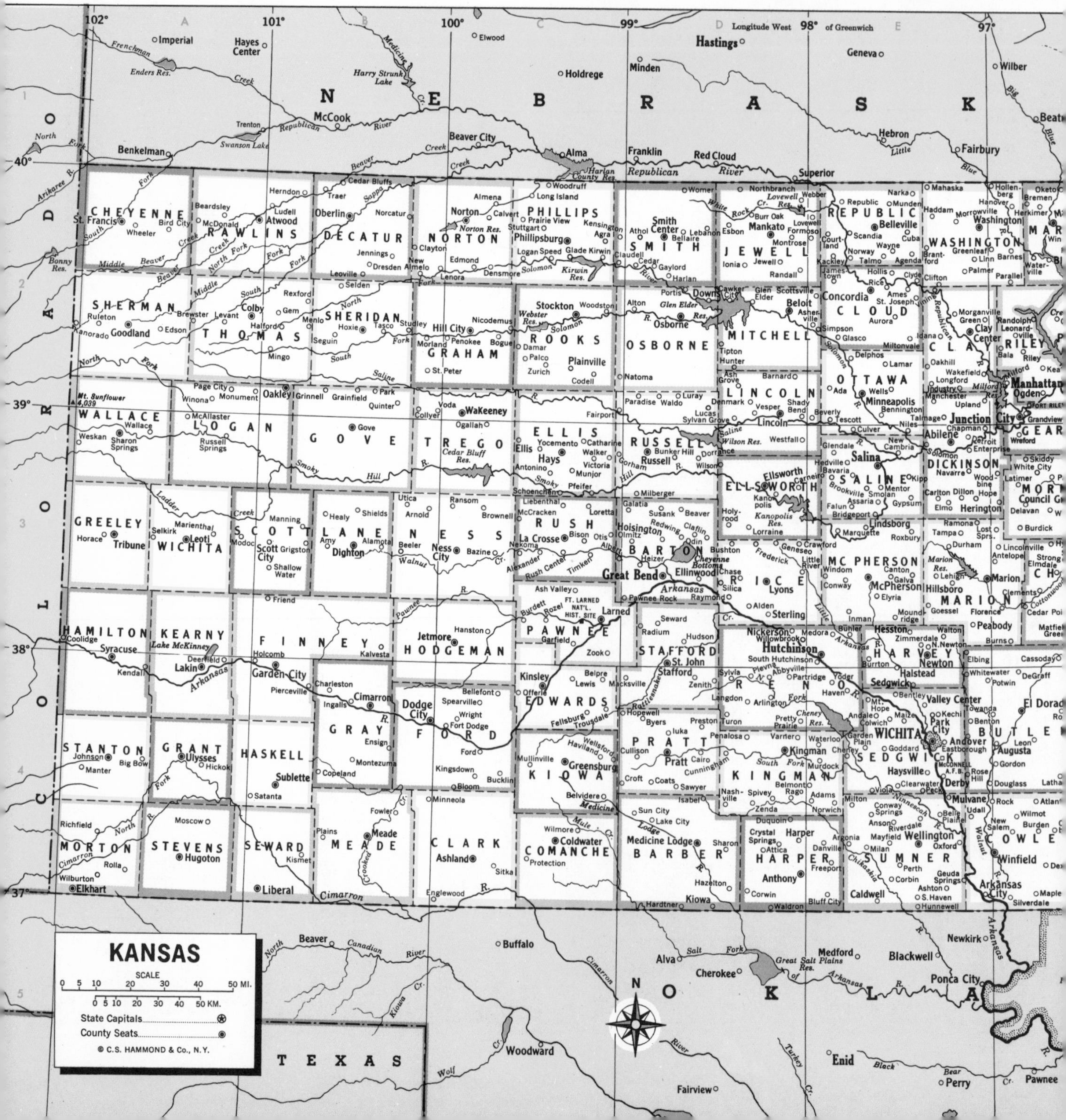

66449 Leonardville, 412...F 3
67861 Leoti⊙, 1,916...A 3
66857 Le Roy, 551...G 3
67743 Levant, 425...C 2
67552 Lewis, 525...C 4
67901 Liberal⊙, 13,471...B 4
67351 Liberty, 185...G 4
67553 Liebenthal, 169...C 3
67455 Lincoln⊙, 1,582...D 2
66858 Lincolnville, 218...F 3
67456 Lindsborg, 2,764...E 2
66953 Linn, 388...E 2
66052 Linwood, 323...G 2
67457 Little River, 493...E 3
67646 Logan, 760...C 2
67647 Long Island, 195...C 2
67352 Longton, 304...F 4
67459 Lorraine, 153...D 3
66859 Lost Springs, 103...E 3
66053 Louisburg, 1,033...H 3
66450 Louisville, 204...F 2
67648 Lucas, 524...D 2
67649 Luray, 303...D 2
66451 Lyndon⊙, 958...G 3
67554 Lyons⊙, 4,355...D 3
67557 Macksville, 484...D 4

66860 Madison, 1,061...F 3
66955 Mahaska, 122...E 2
67101 Maize, 785...E 4
66502 Manhattan⊙, 27,575...F 2
66956 Mankato⊙, 1,287...D 2
67862 Manter, 219...A 4
66507 Maple Hill, 327...F 2
66754 Mapleton, 112...H 3
67863 Marienthal, 120...A 3
66861 Marion⊙, 2,052...E 3
67464 Marquette, 578...E 3
66508 Marysville⊙, 3,588...F 2
66509 Mayetta, 246...G 2
67103 Mayfield, 110...E 4
67556 McCracken, 333...C 3
66753 McCune, 487...H 4
67745 McDonald, 269...A 2
66501 McFarland, 209...F 2
66054 McLouth, 623...G 2
67460 McPherson⊙, 10,851...E 3
67864 Meade⊙, 1,899...B 4
67104 Medicine Lodge⊙, 2,545...D 4
67558 Medora, 110...E 3
66510 Melvern, 455...G 3
66512 Meriden, 472...G 2
66203 Merriam, 10,851...H 3

Topography

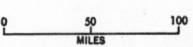

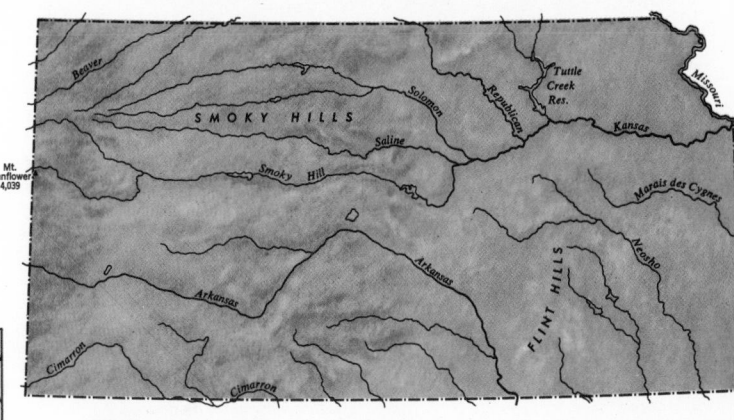

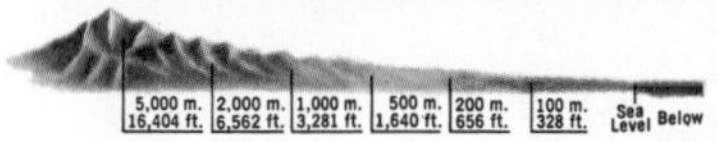

| 5,000 m. | 2,000 m. | 1,000 m. | 500 m. | 200 m. | 100 m. | Sea Level | Below |
| 16,404 ft. | 6,562 ft. | 3,281 ft. | 1,640 ft. | 656 ft. | 328 ft. | | |

67105 Milan, 162...E 4
66514 Milford, 296...F 2
67466 Miltonvale, 718...E 2
67467 Minneapolis⊙, 1,971...E 2
67865 Minneola, 630...C 4
67353 Moline, 555...F 4
67867 Montezuma, 606...B 4
66755 Moran, 550...G 3
67468 Morganville, 257...E 2
67650 Morland, 300...B 2
66515 Morrill, 308...G 2
66958 Morrowville, 201...E 2
67952 Moscow, 228...A 4
66056 Mound City⊙, 714...H 3
67107 Moundridge, 1,271...E 3
67354 Mound Valley, 467...G 4
67108 Mount Hope, 665...E 4
66758 Mulberry, 622...H 4
67109 Mullinville, 376...C 4
67110 Mulvane, 3,185...E 4
66959 Munden, 123...E 2
†67601 Munjor, 200...C 3
66058 Muscotah, 206...G 2
67112 Nashville, 107...D 4
67651 Natoma, 603...D 2
66757 Neodesha, 3,295...G 4
66758 Neosho Falls, 184...G 3
66864 Neosho Rapids, 234...F 3
67560 Ness City⊙, 1,756...C 3
66516 Netawaka, 192...G 2
67470 New Cambria, 160...E 3
67114 Newton⊙, 15,439...E 3
67561 Nickerson, 1,187...D 3
67653 Norcatur, 284...B 2
67117 North Newton, 963...E 3
67654 Norton⊙, 3,627...C 2
66060 Nortonville, 727...G 2
67118 Norwich, 414...E 4
67748 Oakley⊙, 2,327...B 2
67749 Oberlin⊙, 2,291...B 2
67562 Odin, 117...D 3
67563 Offerle, 212...C 4
67656 Ogallah, 110...C 3
66517 Ogden, 1,491...F 2
66518 Oketo, 133...F 2
66061 Olathe⊙, 17,917...H 3
67564 Olmitz, 161...D 3
66865 Olpe, 453...F 3
66520 Olsburg, 151...F 2
66521 Onaga, 761...F 2
66522 Oneida, 112...G 2
66760 Opolis, 160...H 4
66523 Osage City, 2,600...G 3
66064 Osawatomie, 4,294...H 3
67473 Osborne⊙, 1,980...D 2
66066 Oskaloosa⊙, 955...G 2
67356 Oswego⊙, 2,200...G 4
67565 Otis, 387...C 3
66067 Ottawa⊙, 11,036...G 3
66524 Overbrook, 748...G 3
66204 Overland Park, 76,623...H 3
67119 Oxford, 1,113...E 4
66070 Ozawkie, 137...G 2
66957 Palco, 398...C 2
66962 Palmer, 166...E 2
67071 Paola⊙, 4,622...H 3
67658 Paradise, 145...D 2
67751 Park, 178...B 2
67219 Park City, 2,529...E 4
66072 Parker, 255...H 3
67357 Parsons, 13,015...G 4
66619 Pauline, 800...G 3
67567 Pawnee Rock, 442...D 3
66526 Paxico, 216...F 2
66866 Peabody, 1,368...E 3
67120 Peck, 150...E 4
66073 Perry, 664...G 2
67360 Peru, 289...G 4
67661 Phillipsburg⊙, 3,241...C 2
67122 Piedmont, 116...F 4
67868 Pierceville, 175...B 4

66761 Piqua, 107...G 4
66762 Pittsburg, 20,171...H 4
67869 Plains, 857...B 4
67663 Plainville, 2,627...C 2
66075 Pleasanton, 1,216...H 3
67568 Plevna, 124...D 4
66076 Pomona, 541...G 3
67474 Portis, 178...D 2
67123 Potwin, 497...F 4
66527 Powhattan, 111...G 2
67664 Prairie View, 201...C 2
66208 Prairie Village, 28,138...H 2
67124 Pratt⊙, 6,736...D 4
66767 Prescott, 222...H 3
67569 Preston, 239...D 4
67570 Pretty Prairie, 561...D 4
66078 Princeton, 159...G 3
67127 Protection, 673...C 4
66528 Quenemo, 429...G 3
67752 Quinter, 930...B 2
67475 Ramona, 121...E 3
66963 Randall, 195...D 2
66554 Randolph, 166...F 2
67572 Ransom, 416...C 3
66079 Rantoul, 163...G 3
67573 Raymond, 133...D 3
66868 Reading, 247...F 3
66769 Redfield, 138...H 4
66964 Republic, 243...E 2
66529 Reserve, 117...G 2
67753 Rexford, 231...B 2
67560 Richmond, 464...G 3
66531 Riley, 668...F 2
66770 Riverton, 500...H 4
66532 Robinson, 278...G 2
†66205 Roeland Park, 9,974...H 2
67954 Rolla, 400...A 4
67132 Rosalia, 130...F 4
67133 Rose Hill, 387...E 4
66533 Rossville, 934...G 2
67476 Roxbury, 110...E 3
67134 Rozel, 236...C 3
67575 Rush Center, 237...C 3
67665 Russell⊙, 5,371...D 3
66534 Sabetha, 2,376...G 2
67756 Saint Francis⊙, 1,725...A 2
66535 Saint George, 241...F 2
67576 Saint John⊙, 1,377...D 3
66536 Saint Marys, 1,434...G 2
66771 Saint Paul, 804...G 4
67401 Salina⊙, 37,714...E 3
67870 Satanta, 1,161...B 4
66772 Savonburg, 109...G 4
67134 Sawyer, 164...D 4
66773 Scammon, 457...H 4
66966 Scandia, 567...E 2
67667 Schoenchen, 182...C 3
67871 Scott City⊙, 4,001...B 3
66537 Scranton, 575...G 3
67361 Sedan⊙, 1,555...F 4
67135 Sedgwick, 1,083...E 4
66538 Seneca⊙, 2,182...F 2
66081 Severance, 128...G 2
67137 Severy, 384...F 4
67872 Shallow Water, 106...B 3
67138 Sharon, 265...D 4
67758 Sharon Springs⊙, 1,012...A 3
66203 Shawnee, 20,482...H 3
67874 Shields, 110...B 3
66539 Silver Lake, 811...G 2
67478 Simpson, 101...D 2
67479 Smolan, 175...E 3
66540 Soldier, 173...G 2
67480 Solomon, 973...E 3
67140 South Haven, 413...E 4
†67501 South Hutchinson, 1,879...D 3
67876 Spearville, 738...C 4
66083 Spring Hill, 1,186...H 3
67578 Stafford, 1,414...D 4
66084 Stanley, 450...H 3
66775 Stark, 124...G 4
67579 Sterling, 2,312...D 3
66085 Stilwell, 350...H 3

67669 Stockton⊙, 1,818...C 2
66869 Strong City, 545...F 3
67877 Sublette⊙, 1,208...B 4
66541 Summerfield, 254...F 2
67143 Sun City, 119...D 4
66019 Sunflower, 1,744...H 3
67363 Sycamore, 125...G 4
67581 Sylvia, 390...D 4
67878 Syracuse⊙, 1,720...A 3
67482 Talmage, 125...E 3
67483 Tampa, 154...E 3
66542 Tecumseh, 270...G 2
67484 Tescott, 393...E 2
66776 Thayer, 430...G 4
67582 Timken, 123...C 3
67485 Tipton, 315...D 2
66086 Tonganoxie, 1,717...G 2
* 66601 Topeka (cap.)⊙, 125,011...G 2
Topeka, ‡155,322...G 2
67777 Toronto, 431...F 4
67144 Towanda, 1,190...F 4
66778 Treece, 225...H 4
67879 Tribune⊙, 1,013...A 3
66087 Troy⊙, 1,047...G 2
67583 Turon, 430...D 4
67364 Tyro, 206...G 4
67146 Udall, 668...E 4
67880 Ulysses⊙, 3,779...A 4
66779 Uniontown, 286...G 4
67584 Utica, 297...B 3
67147 Valley Center, 2,551...E 4
66088 Valley Falls, 1,169...G 2
66544 Vermillion, 191...F 2
67671 Victoria, 1,246...C 3
67149 Viola, 189...E 4
67671 Virgil, 179...F 3
67672 WaKeeney⊙, 2,334...C 2
67487 Wakefield, 583...E 2
67673 Waldo, 123...D 2
67761 Wallace, 112...A 3
66780 Walnut, 330...G 4
67151 Walton, 211...E 3
66547 Wamego, 2,507...F 2
66968 Washington⊙, 1,584...F 2
66548 Wathena, 632...G 2
66090 Wathena, 1,150...H 2
66871 Waverly, 510...G 3
66781 Weir, 740...H 4
66091 Welda, 149...G 3
67152 Wellington⊙, 8,072...E 4
66552 Wellsville, 1,183...G 3
67762 Weskan, 350...A 3
66782 West Mineral, 232...H 4
66549 Westmoreland, 485...F 2
66093 Westphalia, 185...G 3
67869 West Plains (Plains), 857...B 4
66550 Wetmore, 392...G 2
66551 Wheaton, 106...F 2
66872 White City, 458...F 3
66094 White Cloud, 210...G 2
67154 Whitewater, 520...E 4
66552 Whiting, 256...G 2
* 67201 Wichita⊙, 276,554...E 4
Wichita, ‡389,352...E 4
† 66601 Willard, 124...G 2
66095 Williamsburg, 286...G 3
66873 Wilsey, 169...F 3
67490 Wilson, 870...D 3
66097 Winchester, 492...G 2
67491 Windom, 183...E 3
67156 Winfield⊙, 11,405...F 4
67764 Winona, 293...A 2
67492 Woodbine, 170...E 3
67675 Woodston, 211...C 2
67882 Wright, 173...C 4
66783 Yates Center⊙, 1,967...G 4
67585 Yoder, 155...D 3
67159 Zenda, 109...D 4
67676 Zurich, 189...C 2

⊙ County seat.
‡ Population of metropolitan area.
† Zip of nearest p.o.
* Multiple zips

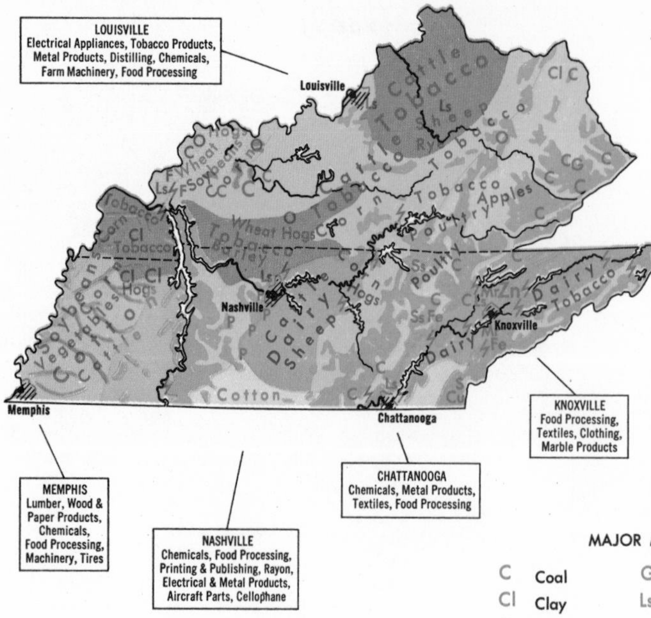
LOUISVILLE
Electrical Appliances, Tobacco Products, Metal Products, Distilling, Chemicals, Farm Machinery, Food Processing
Louisville
Nashville
Knoxville
Memphis
Chattanooga
KNOXVILLE
Food Processing, Textiles, Clothing, Marble Products
MEMPHIS
Lumber, Wood & Paper Products, Chemicals, Food Processing, Machinery, Tires
CHATTANOOGA
Chemicals, Metal Products, Textiles, Food Processing
NASHVILLE
Chemicals, Food Processing, Printing & Publishing, Rayon, Electrical & Metal Products, Aircraft Parts, Cellophane

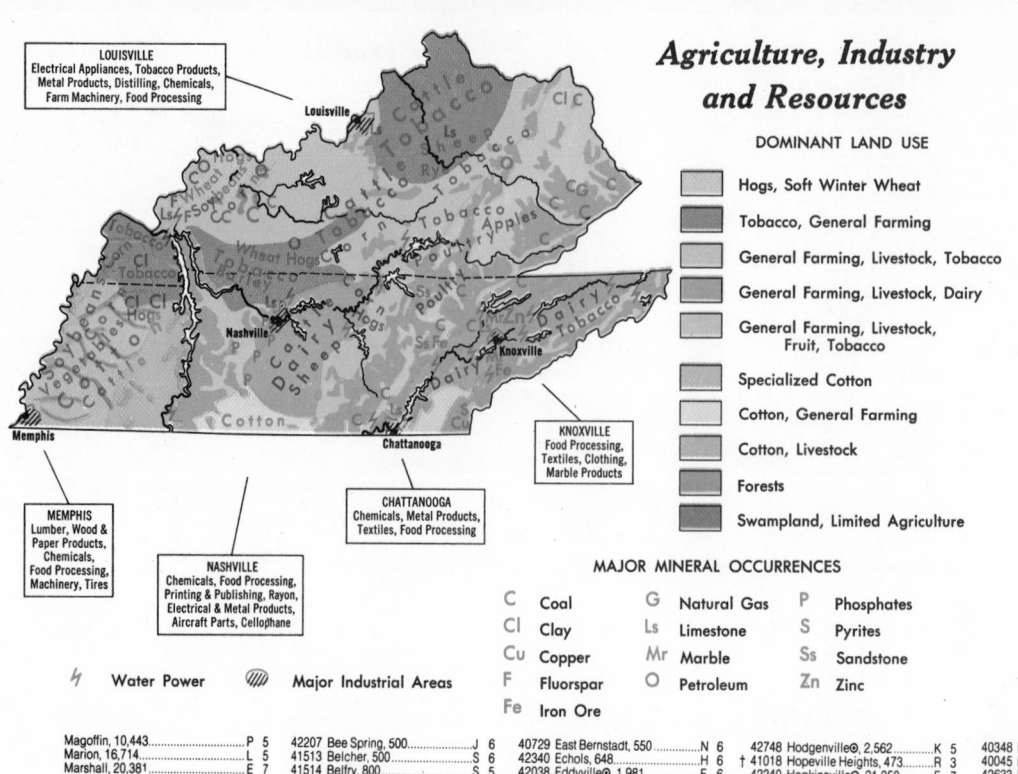

Agriculture, Industry and Resources

DOMINANT LAND USE

- Hogs, Soft Winter Wheat
- Tobacco, General Farming
- General Farming, Livestock, Tobacco
- General Farming, Livestock, Dairy
- General Farming, Livestock, Fruit, Tobacco
- Specialized Cotton
- Cotton, General Farming
- Cotton, Livestock
- Forests
- Swampland, Limited Agriculture

MAJOR MINERAL OCCURRENCES

C	Coal	G	Natural Gas	P	Phosphates
Cl	Clay	Ls	Limestone	S	Pyrites
Cu	Copper	Mr	Marble	Ss	Sandstone
F	Fluorspar	O	Petroleum	Zn	Zinc
Fe	Iron Ore				

Water Power   Major Industrial Areas

KENTUCKY

COUNTIES

Name/Pop.	Key
Adair, 13,037	L 6
Allen, 12,598	J 7
Anderson, 9,358	M 5
Ballard, 8,276	C 6
Barren, 28,677	K 7
Bath, 9,235	O 4
Bell, 31,087	O 7
Boone, 32,812	M 3
Bourbon, 18,476	N 4
Boyd, 52,376	R 4
Boyle, 21,090	M 5
Bracken, 7,227	N 3
Breathitt, 14,221	P 5
Breckinridge, 14,789	H 5
Bullitt, 26,090	K 5
Butler, 9,723	H 6
Caldwell, 13,179	F 6
Calloway, 27,692	E 7
Campbell, 88,501	N 3
Carlisle, 5,354	C 7
Carroll, 8,523	L 3
Carter, 19,850	P 4
Casey, 12,930	M 6
Christian, 56,224	F 7
Clark, 24,090	N 4
Clay, 18,481	O 6
Clinton, 8,174	L 7
Crittenden, 8,493	E 6
Cumberland, 6,850	L 7
Daviess, 79,486	G 5
Edmonson, 8,751	J 6
Elliott, 5,933	P 4
Estill, 12,752	O 5
Fayette, 174,323	N 4
Fleming, 11,366	O 4
Floyd, 35,889	R 5
Franklin, 34,481	M 4
Fulton, 10,183	C 7
Gallatin, 4,134	M 3
Garrard, 9,457	M 5
Grant, 9,999	M 3
Graves, 30,939	D 7
Grayson, 16,445	J 5
Green, 10,350	K 6
Greenup, 33,192	R 3
Hancock, 7,080	H 5
Hardin, 78,421	K 5
Harlan, 37,370	P 7
Harrison, 14,158	N 4
Hart, 13,980	K 6
Henderson, 36,031	F 5
Henry, 10,910	L 4
Hickman, 6,264	C 7
Hopkins, 38,167	F 6
Jackson, 10,005	N 6
Jefferson, 695,055	K 4
Jessamine, 17,430	M 5
Johnson, 17,539	R 5
Kenton, 129,440	M 3
Knott, 14,698	R 6
Knox, 23,689	O 7
Larue, 10,672	K 5
Laurel, 27,386	N 6
Lawrence, 10,726	R 4
Lee, 6,587	O 5
Leslie, 11,623	P 6
Letcher, 23,165	R 6
Lewis, 12,355	P 3
Lincoln, 16,663	M 6
Livingston, 7,596	E 6
Logan, 21,793	H 7
Lyon, 5,562	E 6
Madison, 42,730	N 5
Magoffin, 10,443	P 5
Marion, 16,714	L 5
Marshall, 20,381	E 7
Martin, 9,377	R 5
Mason, 17,273	O 3
McCracken, 58,281	D 6
McCreary, 12,548	N 7
McLean, 9,062	G 5
Meade, 18,796	J 5
Menifee, 4,050	O 5
Mercer, 15,960	M 5
Metcalfe, 8,177	K 7
Monroe, 11,642	K 7
Montgomery, 15,364	O 4
Morgan, 10,019	P 5
Muhlenberg, 27,537	G 6
Nelson, 23,477	K 5
Nicholas, 6,508	N 4
Ohio, 18,790	H 6
Oldham, 14,687	L 4
Owen, 7,470	M 3
Owsley, 5,023	O 6
Pendleton, 9,949	N 3
Perry, 25,714	P 6
Pike, 61,059	S 6
Powell, 7,704	O 5
Pulaski, 35,234	M 6
Robertson, 2,163	N 3
Rockcastle, 12,305	N 6
Rowan, 17,010	P 4
Russell, 10,542	L 7
Scott, 17,948	M 4
Shelby, 18,999	L 4
Simpson, 13,054	H 7
Spencer, 5,488	L 4
Taylor, 17,138	L 6
Todd, 10,823	G 7
Trigg, 8,620	F 7
Trimble, 5,349	L 3
Union, 15,882	F 5
Warren, 57,432	H 6
Washington, 10,728	L 5
Wayne, 14,268	M 7
Webster, 13,282	F 5
Whitley, 24,145	N 7
Wolfe, 5,669	O 5
Woodford, 14,434	M 4

CITIES and TOWNS

Zip	Name/Pop.	Key
42202	Adairville, 973	H 7
41510	Aflex, 475	S 5
42602	Albany⊙, 1,891	L 7
41001	Alexandria⊙, 3,844	N 3
41601	Allen, 724	R 5
40223	Anchorage, 1,477	K 4
40402	Annville, 500	O 6
40902	Arjay, 975	O 7
42021	Arlington, 549	D 7
41101	Ashland, 29,245	R 4
	Ashland-Huntington, ‡253,743	R 4
42206	Auburn, 1,160	H 7
† 40201	Audubon Park, 1,862	K 4
41002	Augusta, 1,434	N 3
41602	Auxier, 900	R 5
41603	Banner, 550	R 5
40906	Barbourville⊙, 3,549	O 7
40004	Bardstown⊙, 5,816	L 5
42023	Bardwell⊙, 1,049	D 7
42024	Barlow, 746	D 6
41311	Beattyville⊙, 923	O 5
41203	Beauty, 800	S 5
42320	Beaver Dam, 2,622	H 6
40006	Bedford⊙, 780	L 3
40359	Beechwood, 1,788	K 4
42207	Bee Spring, 500	J 6
41513	Belcher, 500	S 6
41514	Belfry, 800	S 5
41073	Bellevue, 8,847	S 2
40807	Benham, 1,000	R 7
42025	Benton⊙, 3,652	E 7
40403	Berea, 6,956	N 5
41605	Betsy Layne, 975	R 5
40914	Big Creek, 473	O 6
41804	Blackey, 500	R 6
40008	Bloomfield, 1,072	L 5
† 41501	Boldman, 500	R 5
41719	Bonnyman, 800	P 6
41314	Booneville⊙, 126	O 6
42101	Bowling Green⊙, 36,253	H 7
40108	Brandenburg⊙, 1,637	J 4
40409	Brodhead, 769	N 6
† 41016	Bromley, 1,069	S 2
40109	Brooks, 850	K 4
41004	Brooksville⊙, 609	N 3
42326	Browder, 450	H 6
42210	Brownsville⊙, 542	J 6
41125	Bruin, 500	P 4
40218	Buechel, 5,359	K 4
41722	Bulan, 800	P 6
40310	Burgin, 1,002	M 5
42717	Burkesville⊙, 1,717	L 7
41005	Burlington⊙, 500	R 3
42519	Burnside, 586	M 6
41006	Butler, 558	N 3
42211	Cadiz⊙, 1,987	F 7
42327	Calhoun⊙, 901	G 5
42029	Calvert City, 2,104	E 6
40011	Campbellsburg, 479	L 3
42718	Campbellsville⊙, 7,598	L 6
41301	Campton⊙, 419	O 5
42721	Caneyville, 530	J 6
40311	Carlisle⊙, 1,579	N 4
41008	Carrollton⊙, 3,884	L 3
41129	Catlettsburg⊙, 3,420	R 4
42127	Cave City, 1,818	K 6
40815	Cawood, 800	P 7
42724	Cecilia, 500	K 5
42330	Central City, 3,455	G 6
41727	Chavies, 500	P 6
42726	Clarkson, 660	J 6
42404	Clay, 1,426	F 6
40312	Clay City, 983	O 5
40313	Clearfield, 550	P 4
42031	Clinton⊙, 1,618	D 7
40414	Clover Bottom, 600	N 5
40111	Cloverport, 1,388	H 5
41076	Cold Spring, 5,348	T 3
42728	Columbia⊙, 3,234	L 6
41729	Combs, 900	P 6
42609	Cooper, 500	M 7
40701	Corbin, 7,317	N 7
42406	Corydon, 880	F 5
* 41011	Covington, 52,535	S 2
40419	Crab Orchard, 861	M 6
† 41016	Crescent Springs, 1,662	R 2
† 41076	Crestview, 657	S 2
† 41017	Crestview Hills, 1,114	R 3
42217	Crofton, 631	G 6
42034	Crutchfield, 500	D 7
40823	Cumberland, 3,317	R 6
42035	Cunningham, 700	D 7
41031	Cynthiana⊙, 6,356	N 4
41733	Daisy, 500	P 6
40422	Danville⊙, 11,542	M 5
42408	Dawson Springs, 2,830	F 6
41074	Dayton, 8,691	T 2
42409	Dixon⊙, 572	F 5
41520	Dorton, 750	R 6
42337	Drakesboro, 907	H 6
41035	Dry Ridge, 1,100	M 3
42410	Earlington, 2,321	F 6
40729	East Bernstadt, 550	N 6
42340	Echols, 648	H 6
42038	Eddyville⊙, 1,981	F 6
† 41017	Edgewood, 4,139	S 3
42129	Edmonton⊙, 958	K 7
42701	Elizabethtown⊙, 11,748	K 5
41522	Elkhorn City, 1,081	S 6
42220	Elkton⊙, 1,612	G 7
† 41018	Elsmere, 5,161	R 3
40019	Eminence, 2,225	L 4
40826	Eolia, 768	R 6
41018	Erlanger, 12,676	R 3
40828	Evarts, 1,182	P 7
41039	Ewing, 525	O 4
40118	Fairdale, 12,079	K 4
41426	Falcon, 450	P 5
40119	Falls of Rough, 700	J 5
41040	Falmouth⊙, 2,593	N 3
42039	Fancy Farm, 850	D 7
42532	Faubush, 496	M 6
41524	Fedscreek, 950	S 6
42533	Ferguson, 507	M 6
41427	Flat Fork, 500	P 5
41219	Flatgap, 450	R 5
40935	Flat Lick, 500	O 7
41139	Flatwoods, 7,380	R 4
41816	Fleming, 473	R 6
41041	Flemingsburg⊙, 2,483	O 4
41042	Florence, 11,457	R 3
42343	Fordsville, 489	H 5
40121	Fort Knox, 37,608	K 5
41017	Fort Mitchell, 6,982	S 3
41075	Fort Thomas, 16,338	S 2
† 41011	Fort Wright-Lookout Heights, 4,819	S 3
40601	Frankfort (cap.)⊙, 21,356	M 4
42134	Franklin⊙, 6,553	J 7
42411	Fredonia, 450	E 6
40322	Frenchburg⊙, 467	O 5
† 41175	Fullerton, 950	P 3
42041	Fulton, 3,250	D 7
41630	Garrett, 985	R 6
41141	Garrison, 800	P 3
40324	Georgetown⊙, 8,629	M 4
40943	Girdler, 500	O 7
42141	Glasgow⊙, 11,301	J 7
41046	Glencoe, 500	M 3
42232	Gracey, 450	F 7
42344	Graham, 500	G 6
41142	Grahn, 450	P 4
40734	Gray, 800	O 7
40434	Gray Hawk, 500	N 6
41143	Grayson⊙, 2,184	R 4
42743	Greensburg⊙, 1,990	K 6
41144	Greenup⊙, 1,284	R 3
42345	Greenville⊙, 3,875	G 6
41329	Guage, 450	P 5
42234	Guthrie, 1,200	G 7
41820	Hall, 500	R 6
40947	Hammond, 500	O 7
42048	Hardin, 522	E 7
40143	Hardinsburg⊙, 1,547	H 5
41531	Hardy, 950	S 5
40831	Harlan⊙, 3,318	P 7
40330	Harrodsburg⊙, 6,741	M 5
42347	Hartford⊙, 1,868	H 6
41514	Hatfield, 700	S 5
42348	Hawesville⊙, 1,262	H 5
41701	Hazard⊙, 5,459	P 6
41048	Hebron, 550	R 2
42420	Henderson⊙, 22,976	F 5
42050	Hickman⊙, 3,048	C 7
41076	Highland Heights, 460	T 3
40951	Hima, 600	O 6
† 41203	Himlerville (Beauty), 800	S 5
41822	Hindman⊙, 808	R 6
41146	Hitchins, 500	R 4
42748	Hodgenville⊙, 2,562	K 5
† 41018	Hopeville Heights, 473	R 3
42240	Hopkinsville⊙, 21,250	F 7
42749	Horse Cave, 2,068	K 6
41749	Hyden⊙, 482	P 6
† 42408	Ilsley, 500	F 6
41051	Independence⊙, 1,784	M 3
41224	Inez⊙, 469	S 5
40336	Irvine⊙, 2,918	O 5
40146	Irvington, 1,300	J 5
41339	Jackson⊙, 1,887	P 5
42629	Jamestown⊙, 1,027	L 7
41751	Jeff, 615	P 6
40299	Jeffersontown, 9,701	L 4
40337	Jeffersonville, 800	O 5
41537	Jenkins, 2,552	R 6
40440	Junction City, 1,046	M 5
40737	Keavy, 500	N 6
40847	Kenvir, 800	P 7
42053	Kevil, 504	D 6
40848	Kitts, 950	P 7
42055	Kuttawa, 453	E 6
42056	La Center, 1,044	C 6
40031	La Grange⊙, 1,713	L 4
† 41017	Lakeside Park, 2,511	R 3
40444	Lancaster⊙, 3,230	M 5
40342	Lawrenceburg⊙, 3,579	M 4
41756	Leatherwood, 750	P 6
40033	Lebanon⊙, 5,528	L 5
40150	Lebanon Junction, 1,571	K 5
41343	Leeco, 475	O 5
42754	Leitchfield⊙, 2,983	J 6
40849	Lejunior, 597	P 7
42256	Lewisburg, 651	G 6
42351	Lewisport, 1,595	H 5
* 40501	Lexington⊙, 108,137	N 4
	Lexington, ‡174,323	N 4
42539	Liberty⊙, 1,765	M 6
41646	Ligon, 500	R 6
40740	Lily, 800	N 6
41834	Littcarr, 550	R 6
42352	Livermore, 1,594	G 5
42059	Lola, 600	E 6
40741	London⊙, 4,337	N 6
42001	Lone Oak, 3,759	D 6
41542	Lookout, 600	S 6
40037	Loretto, 985	L 5
41348	Lost Creek, 500	P 6
41701	Lothair, 800	P 6
41230	Louisa⊙, 1,781	R 4
* 40201	Louisville⊙, 361,472	K 4
	Louisville, ‡826,553	K 4
41231	Lovely, 500	S 5
41232	Lowmansville, 500	R 5
40854	Loyall, 1,212	P 7
41016	Ludlow, 5,815	S 2
40855	Lynch, 800	R 7
† 40201	Lynnview, 1,165	K 4
42431	Madisonville⊙, 15,332	F 6
41547	Majestic, 600	S 5
40962	Manchester⊙, 1,664	O 6
42064	Marion⊙, 3,008	E 6
42631	Marshes Siding, 950	M 7
41649	Martin, 786	R 5
42066	Mayfield⊙, 10,724	D 7
41056	Maysville⊙, 7,411	O 3
41543	McAndrews, 975	S 5
40447	McKee⊙, 255	O 6
40448	McKinney, 475	M 6
41835	McRoberts, 1,037	R 6
41546	McVeigh, 700	S 5
41059	Melbourne, 500	T 3
41501	Meta, 600	S 5
40965	Middlesboro, 11,844	O 7
40243	Middletown, 2,500	L 4
40347	Midway, 1,278	M 4
41501	Millard. 600	S 6
40348	Millersburg, 788	N 4
40045	Milton, 756	L 3
42633	Monticello⊙, 3,618	M 7
40351	Morehead⊙, 7,191	P 4
42437	Morganfield⊙, 3,563	E 5
42261	Morgantown⊙, 1,394	H 6
42440	Mortons Gap, 1,169	F 6
41064	Mount Olivet⊙, 442	N 3
40353	Mount Sterling⊙, 5,083	N 4
40456	Mount Vernon⊙, 1,639	N 6
40047	Mount Washington, 2,020	K 4
40155	Muldraugh, 1,773	J 5
42765	Munfordville⊙, 1,233	J 6
42071	Murray⊙, 13,537	E 7
42544	Nancy, 600	M 6
41840	Neon, 705	R 6
40050	New Castle⊙, 755	L 4
40051	New Haven, 977	K 5
* 41071	Newport, 25,988	S 2
40356	Nicholasville⊙, 5,829	N 5
41357	Noctor, 500	P 5
42442	Nortonville, 699	G 6
41238	Oil Springs, 900	P 5
40219	Okolona, 17,643	K 4
41164	Olive Hill, 1,197	P 4
40972	Oneida, 700	O 6
42301	Owensboro⊙, 50,329	G 5
40359	Owenton⊙, 1,280	M 3
40360	Owingsville⊙, 1,381	O 4
42001	Paducah⊙, 31,627	D 6
41240	Paintsville⊙, 3,868	R 5
40361	Paris⊙, 7,823	N 4
42160	Park City, 567	J 6
† 41011	Park Hills, 3,999	S 2
40464	Parksville, 560	M 5
42266	Pembroke, 634	G 7
40468	Perryville, 730	M 5
40056	Pewee Valley, 950	L 4
41553	Phelps, 770	S 6
42366	Philpot, 531	H 5
41501	Pikeville⊙, 4,576	S 6
42635	Pine Knot, 950	M 7
40977	Pineville⊙, 2,817	O 7
40755	Pittsburg, 938	N 6
40258	Pleasure Ridge Park, 28,566	J 4
40057	Pleasureville, 747	L 4
42367	Powderly, 631	G 6
41845	Premium, 489	R 6
41653	Prestonsburg⊙, 3,422	R 5
42445	Princeton⊙, 6,292	F 6
40059	Prospect, 500	K 4
42450	Providence, 4,270	F 6
41169	Raceland, 1,857	R 3
40160	Radcliff, 7,881	K 5
40472	Ravenna, 784	O 5
42638	Revelo, 500	N 7
40475	Richmond⊙, 16,861	N 5
42452	Robards, 701	F 5
41169	Russell, 1,982	R 3
42642	Russell Springs, 1,641	L 6
42276	Russellville⊙, 6,456	H 7
40207	Saint Matthews, 13,152	K 4
42078	Salem, 650	E 6
40371	Salt Lick, 441	O 4
40372	Salvisa, 500	M 5
41465	Salyersville⊙, 1,196	P 5
41171	Sandy Hook⊙, 192	P 4
40982	Scalf, 500	O 7
42553	Science Hill, 470	M 6
42164	Scottsville⊙, 3,584	J 7
42455	Sebree, 1,092	F 5
† 41385	Sewell, 500	P 5
40983	Sextons Creek, 975	O 6
41562	Shelbiana, 800	R 6
40065	Shelbyville⊙, 4,182	L 4
40165	Shepherdsville⊙, 2,769	K 4

40216	Shively, 19,223	K 4
40984	Sibert, 500	O 6
41085	Silver Grove, 1,365	T 3
40067	Simpsonville, 628	L 4
41763	Slemp, 500	P 6
41764	Smilax, 856	P 6
42081	Smithland⊙, 514	E 6
42171	Smiths Grove, 756	J 6
42646	Smith Town, 500	M 7
41173	Soldier, 600	P 4
42501	Somerset⊙, 10,436	M 6
41071	Southgate, 3,212	S 2
41174	South Portsmouth, 950	P 3
41175	South Shore, 676	R 3
25661	South Williamson, 850	S 5
42458	Spottsville, 914	G 5
40069	Springfield⊙, 2,961	L 5
41256	Staffordsville, 700	R 5
40484	Stanford⊙, 2,474	M 5
40380	Stanton⊙, 2,037	O 5
42647	Stearns, 900	N 7
40170	Stephensport, 500	H 5
41567	Stone, 850	S 5
42459	Sturgis, 2,210	F 5
42558	Tateville, 680	M 7
41011	Taylor Mill, 3,253	S 3
40071	Taylorsville⊙, 897	L 4
41259	Thealka, 550	R 5
41189	Tollesboro, 500	O 3
42167	Tompkinsville⊙, 2,207	K 7
42286	Trenton, 496	G 7
40486	Tyner, 590	O 6
41091	Union, 500	M 3
42461	Uniontown, 1,255	F 5
42784	Upton, 552	K 6
40272	Valley Station, 24,471	K 4
41179	Vanceburg⊙, 1,773	P 3
41265	Van Lear, 1,033	R 5
40872	Verda, 950	P 7
41092	Verona, 500	M 3
40383	Versailles⊙, 5,679	M 4
† 41017	Villa Hills, 1,647	R 2
40175	Vine Grove, 2,987	K 5
41572	Virgie, 600	R 6
41094	Walton, 1,801	M 3
41095	Warsaw⊙, 1,232	M 3
41667	Weeksbury, 950	R 6
41472	West Liberty⊙, 1,387	P 5
40177	West Point, 1,741	J 4
42564	West Somerset, 850	M 6
41268	West Van Lear, 975	R 5
41101	Westwood, 2,900	R 4
41669	Wheelwright, 793	R 6
42464	White Plains, 729	G 6
41858	Whitesburg⊙, 1,137	R 6
42378	Whitesville, 752	H 5
42653	Whitley City⊙, 1,060	N 7
42087	Wickliffe⊙, 1,211	C 7
† 41071	Wilders, 823	S 3
40769	Williamsburg⊙, 3,687	N 7
41097	Williamstown⊙, 2,063	M 3
40390	Wilmore, 3,466	M 5
40391	Winchester⊙, 13,402	N 4
42088	Wingo, 593	D 7
† 41011	Winston Park, 578	S 3
41394	Wolverine, 500	P 5
40771	Woodbine, 700	N 7
† 42001	Woodlawn, 1,639	D 6
† 41071	Woodlawn, 525	S 2
41776	Wooton, 750	P 6
41183	Worthington, 1,364	R 3
41501	Zebulon, 800	R 5

TENNESSEE

COUNTIES

Anderson, 60,300	N 8
Bedford, 25,039	J 9
Benton, 12,126	E 8
Bledsoe, 7,643	L 9
Blount, 63,744	O 9
Bradley, 50,686	M10
Campbell, 26,045	N 8
Cannon, 8,467	J 9
Carroll, 25,741	E 9
Carter, 42,575	S 8
Cheatham, 13,199	G 8
Chester, 9,927	D 10
Claiborne, 19,420	O 8
Clay, 6,624	K 7
Cocke, 25,283	P 9
Coffee, 32,572	J 9
Crockett, 14,402	C 9
Cumberland, 20,733	L 9
Davidson, 447,877	H 8
Decatur, 9,457	E 9
De Kalb, 11,151	K 9
Dickson, 21,977	G 8
Dyer, 30,427	C 8
Fayette, 22,692	C 10
Fentress, 12,593	M 8
Franklin, 27,244	J 10
Gibson, 47,871	D 9
Giles, 22,138	G10
Grainger, 13,948	O 8
Greene, 47,630	R 8
Grundy, 10,631	K 10
Hamblen, 38,696	P 8
Hamilton, 254,236	L 10
Hancock, 6,719	P 7
Hardeman, 22,435	C 10
Hardin, 18,212	E 10
Hawkins, 33,726	P 8
Haywood, 19,596	C 9
Henderson, 17,291	E 9
Henry, 23,749	E 8
Hickman, 12,096	G 9
Houston, 5,845	F 8
Humphreys, 13,560	F 8
Jackson, 8,141	K 8
Jefferson, 24,940	P 8
Johnson, 11,569	T 7
Knox, 276,293	O 9
Lake, 7,896	B 8
Lauderdale, 20,271	B 9
Lawrence, 29,097	G10
Lewis, 6,761	F 9
Lincoln, 24,318	H10
Loudon, 24,266	N 9
Macon, 12,315	J 7
Madison, 65,727	D 9
Marion, 20,577	K 10
Marshall, 17,319	H 10
Maury, 43,376	G 9
McMinn, 35,462	M10
McNairy, 18,369	D 10
Meigs, 5,219	M 9
Monroe, 23,475	N 10
Montgomery, 62,721	G 8
Moore, 3,568	J 10
Morgan, 13,619	M 8
Obion, 29,936	C 8
Overton, 14,866	L 8
Perry, 5,238	F 9
Pickett, 3,774	M 7
Polk, 11,669	N 10
Putnam, 35,487	K 8
Rhea, 17,202	M 9
Roane, 38,881	M 9
Robertson, 29,102	H 7
Rutherford, 59,428	J 9
Scott, 14,762	M 8
Sequatchie, 6,331	L 10
Sevier, 28,241	O 9
Shelby, 722,014	B 10
Smith, 12,509	J 8
Stewart, 7,319	F 7
Sullivan, 127,329	S 7
Sumner, 56,106	J 8
Tipton, 28,001	B 9
Trousdale, 5,155	J 8
Unicoi, 15,254	S 8
Union, 9,072	O 8
Van Buren, 3,758	L 9
Warren, 26,972	K 9
Washington, 73,924	R 8
Wayne, 12,365	F 10
Weakley, 28,827	D 8
White, 17,088	L 9
Williamson, 34,330	H 9
Wilson, 36,999	J 8

KENTUCKY

AREA 40,395 sq. mi.
POPULATION 3,219,311
CAPITAL Frankfort
LARGEST CITY Louisville
HIGHEST POINT Black Mtn. 4,145 ft.
SETTLED IN 1774
ADMITTED TO UNION June 1, 1792
POPULAR NAME Blue Grass State
STATE FLOWER Goldenrod
STATE BIRD Cardinal

TENNESSEE

AREA 42,244 sq. mi.
POPULATION 3,924,164
CAPITAL Nashville
LARGEST CITY Memphis
HIGHEST POINT Clingmans Dome 6,643 ft.
SETTLED IN 1757
ADMITTED TO UNION June 1, 1796
POPULAR NAME Volunteer State
STATE FLOWER Iris
STATE BIRD Mockingbird

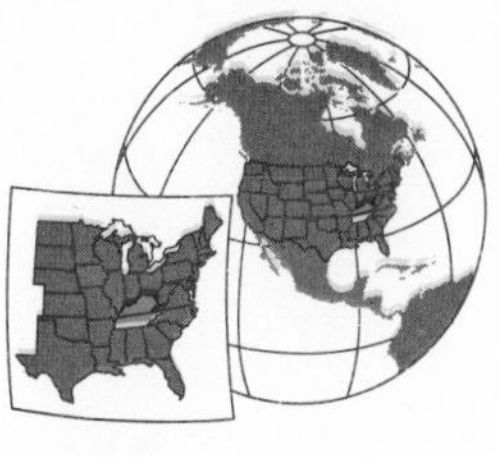

CITIES and TOWNS

Zip	*Name/Pop.*	*Key*
37010	Adams, 458	G 7
38310	Adamsville, 1,344	E 10
37616	Afton, 550	R 8
38001	Alamo⊙, 2,499	C 9
37701	Alcoa, 7,739	N 9
37012	Alexandria, 680	J 8
38501	Algood, 1,808	K 8
38504	Allardt, 610	M 8
38541	Allons, 600	L 8
37301	Altamont⊙, 546	K 10
38449	Ardmore, 601	H 10
38002	Arlington, 1,349	B 10
38506	Armathwaite, 625	M 8
37707	Arthur, 500	O 7
37015	Ashland City⊙, 2,027	G 8
37303	Athens⊙, 11,790	M10
38004	Atoka, 446	B 10
38220	Atwood, 937	D 9
37304	Bakewell, 600	L 10
† 37650	Banner Hill, 2,517	R 8
38005	Bartlett, 1,150	B 10
38311	Bath Springs, 725	E 10
38544	Baxter, 1,229	K 8
37708	Bean Station, 500	P 8
37018	Beechgrove, 600	J 9
37305	Beersheba Springs, 560	K 10
37205	Belle Meade, 3,082	H 8
38006	Bells, 1,474	C 9
38314	Bemis, 1,883	D 9
37307	Benton⊙, 749	M10
† 37201	Berry Hill, 1,551	H 8
† 37027	Berry's Chapel, 1,345	H 9
38315	Bethel Springs, 781	D 10
38221	Big Sandy, 539	E 8
37308	Birchwood, 900	M10
37709	Blaine, 650	O 8
37660	Bloomingdale, 3,120	R 7
38545	Bloomington Springs, 800	K 8
37617	Blountville⊙, 900	S 7
37618	Bluff City, 947	S 8
38008	Bolivar⊙, 6,674	C 10
38316	Bradford, 968	D 8
37658	Braemar-Hampton, 1,100	S 8
37027	Brentwood, 1,091	H 8
37710	Briceville, 850	N 8
38011	Brighton, 952	B 10
37620	Bristol, 20,064	S 7
38012	Brownsville⊙, 7,011	C 9
38317	Bruceton, 1,450	E 8
38014	Brunswick, 500	B 10
38318	Buena Vista, 500	E 9
37711	Bulls Gap, 774	P 8
37640	Butler, 500	T 8
38549	Byrdstown⊙, 582	L 7
37309	Calhoun, 624	M10
38320	Camden⊙, 3,052	E 8
38129	Capleville, 450	B 10
37030	Carthage⊙, 2,491	K 8
37714	Caryville, 648	N 8
38551	Celina⊙, 1,370	K 7
37033	Centerville⊙, 2,592	G 9
37034	Chapel Hill, 752	H 9
37310	Charleston, 792	M10
37036	Charlotte⊙, 610	G 8
* 37401	Chattanooga⊙, 119,082	K 10
	Chattanooga, ‡304,927	K 10
37642	Church Hill, 2,822	R 7
37715	Clairfield, 650	O 7
38553	Clarkrange, 675	L 8
37040	Clarksville⊙, 31,719	G 7
37311	Cleveland⊙, 20,651	M10
38425	Clifton, 737	F 10
37716	Clinton⊙, 4,794	N 8
37719	Coalfield, 712	N 8
37313	Coalmont, 518	K 10
37314	Cokercreek, 500	N 10
37315	Collegedale, 3,031	M10
38017	Collierville, 3,625	B 10
38450	Collinwood, 922	F 10
37663	Colonial Heights, 3,027	R 8
38401	Columbia⊙, 21,471	G 9
37720	Concord, 500	N 9
38501	Cookeville⊙, 14,270	L 8
37317	Copperhill, 563	N 10
38018	Cordova, 600	B 10
37047	Cornersville, 655	H 10
37721	Corryton, 500	O 8
38326	Counce, 975	E 10
38019	Covington⊙, 5,801	B 9
37318	Cowan, 1,772	K 10
37723	Crab Orchard, 900	M 9
38555	Crossville⊙, 5,381	L 9
37051	Cumberland Furnace, 800	G 8
38452	Cypress Inn, 500	F 10
37725	Dandridge⊙, 1,270	O 8
37321	Dayton⊙, 4,361	L 9
37322	Decatur⊙, 698	M 9
38329	Decaturville⊙, 958	E 9
37324	Decherd, 2,148	J 10
37055	Dickson, 5,665	G 8
37214	Donelson, 17,195	H 8
37058	Dover⊙, 1,179	F 8
38559	Doyle, 1,205	K 9
38225	Dresden⊙, 1,939	D 8
38023	Drummonds, 700	A 10
37326	Ducktown, 562	N 10
37327	Dunlap⊙, 1,672	L 10
38330	Dyer, 2,501	D 8
38024	Dyersburg⊙, 14,523	C 8
† 37801	Eagleton, 5,345	O 9
† 37311	East Cleveland, 1,870	M10
37412	East Ridge, 21,799	L 11
37732	Elgin, 500	M 8
37643	Elizabethton⊙, 12,269	S 8
37734	Elk Valley, 750	N 7
38029	Ellendale, 1,500	B 10
† 37601	Embreeville Junction, 1,293	R 8
37735	Emory Gap, 500	M 9
37329	Englewood, 1,878	M10
37061	Erin⊙, 1,157	F 8
37650	Erwin⊙, 4,715	S 8
37330	Estill Springs, 919	J 10
38456	Ethridge, 600	G10
37331	Etowah, 3,736	M10
37332	Evensville, 475	M 9
37062	Fairview, 1,630	G 9
37656	Fall Branch, 825	R 8
37334	Fayetteville⊙, 7,030	H 10
38030	Finley, 950	B 8
37335	Flintville, 500	H 10
38031	Forest Hill, 850	B 10
† 37201	Forest Hills, 2,101	H 8
38032	Fort Pillow, 700	B 9
37064	Franklin⊙, 9,404	H 9
38034	Friendship, 441	C 9
37737	Friendsville, 575	N 9
38337	Gadsden, 523	D 9
38562	Gainesboro⊙, 1,101	K 8
37066	Gallatin⊙, 13,093	H 8
38037	Gates, 523	C 9
37738	Gatlinburg, 2,329	O 9
38038	Germantown, 3,474	B 10
37071	Gladeville, 500	J 8
38229	Gleason, 1,314	D 8
37072	Goodlettsville, 3,163	H 8
38563	Gordonsville, 601	K 8
37337	Grandview, 1,250	M 9
37338	Graysville, 951	L 10
37073	Green Brier, 2,279	H 8
37743	Greeneville⊙, 13,722	R 8
38230	Greenfield, 2,050	D 8
38565	Grimsley, 500	L 2
37339	Gruetli, 910	K 10
† 37766	Habersham, 800	N 8
38040	Halls, 2,323	C 9
38461	Hampshire, 500	G 9
37658	Hampton-Braemar, 1,100	S 8
37748	Harriman, 8,734	M 9
37341	Harrison, 500	L 10
37752	Harrogate, 950	O 8
37074	Hartsville⊙, 2,243	J 8
37755	Helenwood, 675	M 8
38340	Henderson⊙, 3,581	D 10
38041	Henning, 605	B 9
37343	Hixson, 6,188	L 10
38462	Hohenwald⊙, 3,385	F 9
38342	Hollow Rock, 722	E 8
38343	Humboldt, 10,066	D 9
38344	Huntingdon⊙, 3,661	E 8
37345	Huntland, 849	J 10
37756	Huntsville⊙, 337	N 8
37079	Indian Mound, 600	F 7
† 37201	Inglewood, 26,527	H 8
38463	Iron City, 504	F 10
37757	Jacksboro⊙, 689	N 8
38301	Jackson⊙, 39,996	D 9
38556	Jamestown⊙, 1,899	M 8
37347	Jasper⊙, 1,811	K 10
37760	Jefferson City, 5,124	P 8
37762	Jellico, 2,235	N 7
37601	Johnson City, 33,770	S 8
37659	Jonesboro⊙, 1,510	R 8
37921	Karns, 1,105	N 9
38233	Kenton, 1,439	C 8
† 34347	Kimball, 807	K 10
* 37660	Kingsport, 31,938	R 7
37763	Kingston⊙, 4,142	N 9
* 37901	Knoxville⊙, 174,587	O 9
	Knoxville, ‡400,337	O 9
37349	Laager, 675	K 10
37083	Lafayette⊙, 2,583	J 7
37766	La Follette, 6,902	N 8
37769	Lake City, 1,923	N 8
37416	Lake Hills-Murray Hills, 7,806	L 10
† 37138	Lakewood, 2,500	H 8
37086	La Vergne, 2,825	H 9
38464	Lawrenceburg⊙, 8,889	G10
37087	Lebanon⊙, 12,492	J 8
37771	Lenoir City, 5,324	N 9
37091	Lewisburg⊙, 7,207	H 10
38351	Lexington⊙, 4,955	E 9
37681	Limestone, 500	R 8
37096	Linden⊙, 1,062	F 9
38570	Livingston⊙, 3,050	L 8
37097	Lobelville, 773	F 9
† 37662	Long Island, 1,352	S 7
37350	Lookout Mountain, 1,741	L 11
38469	Loretto, 1,375	G10
37774	Loudon⊙, 3,728	N 9
37777	Louisville, 500	N 9
37351	Lupton City, 750	L 10
37779	Luttrell, 819	O 8
38471	Lutts, 850	F 10

(continued on following page)

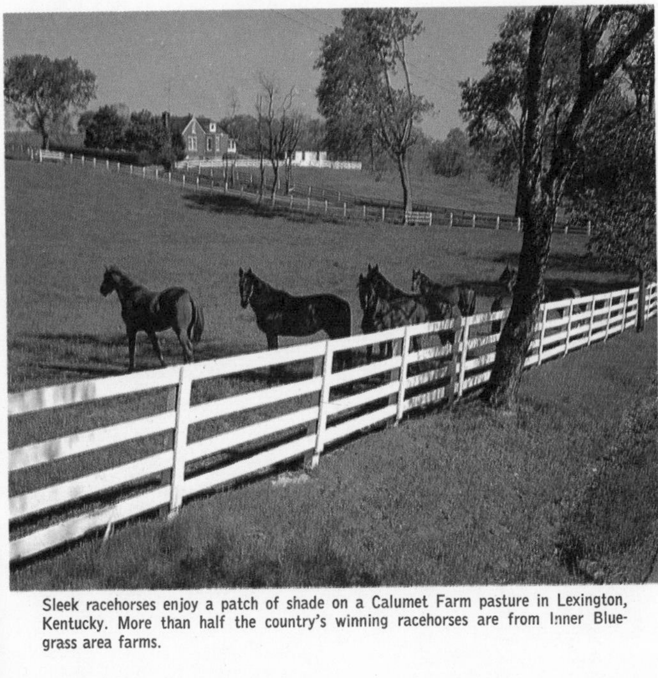

Jack Zehrt — Shostal Associates

Sleek racehorses enjoy a patch of shade on a Calumet Farm pasture in Lexington, Kentucky. More than half the country's winning racehorses are from Inner Bluegrass area farms.

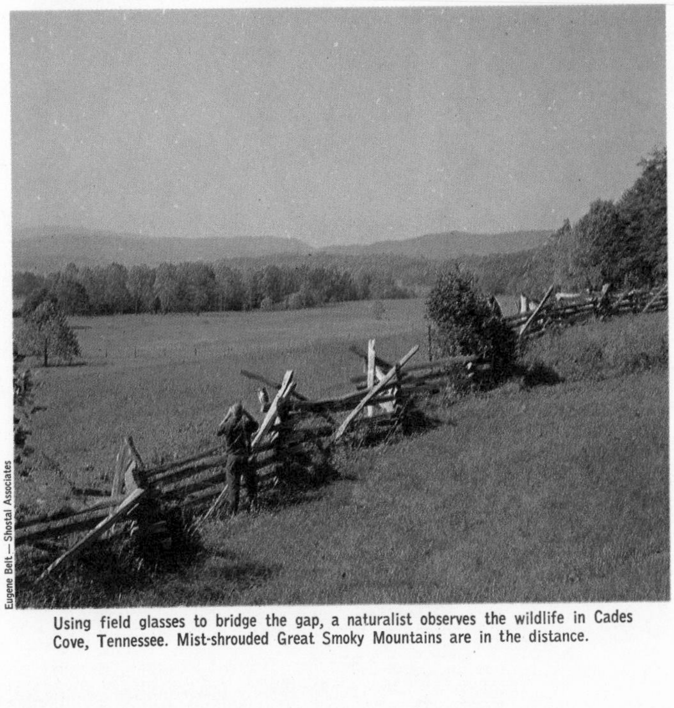

Eugene Belt — Shostal Associates

Using field glasses to bridge the gap, a naturalist observes the wildlife in Cades Cove, Tennessee. Mist-shrouded Great Smoky Mountains are in the distance.

TENNESSEE (continued)

37352 Lynchburg◉, 361 ....J 10
37115 Madison, 13,583 ....H 8
37354 Madisonville◉, 2,614 ....N 9
38354 Maleus, 600 ....D 9
37355 Manchester◉, 6,208 ....J 10
† 37771 Martel, 500 ....N 9
38237 Martin, 7,781 ....D 8
38471 Martins Mills, 440 ....F 10
37801 Maryville◉, 13,808 ....O 9
37806 Mascot, 1,050 ....O 8
38049 Mason, 443 ....B 10
38050 Maury City, 813 ....C 9
37807 Maynardville◉, 702 ....O 8
37353 McDonald, 500 ....M10
37101 McEwen, 1,237 ....F 8
38201 McKenzie, 4,873 ....E 8
37110 McMinnville◉, 10,662 ....K 9
38355 Medina, 755 ....D 9
* 38101 Memphis◉, 623,530 ....B 10
    Memphis, ‡770,120............B 10
38052 Middleton, 654 ....D 10
38358 Milan, 7,313 ....D 8
37682 Milligan College, 1,170 ...S 8
38053 Millington, 21,106 ....B 10
37356 Monteagle, 934 ....K 10
38574 Monterey, 2,351 ....L 8
† 37660 Morrison City, 2,178 ....R 7
37814 Morristown◉, 20,318 ....P 8
38057 Moscow, 448 ....C 10
37818 Mosheim, 450 ....P 8
37683 Mountain City◉, 1,883 ....T 8
37122 Mount Juliet, 800 ....H 8
38474 Mount Pleasant, 3,530 ....G 9
38058 Munford, 1,281 ....B 10
37130 Murfreesboro◉, 26,360 ...J 9
* 37201 Nashville (cap.)◉, 447,877 ..H 8
    Nashville, ‡540,982 ....H 8
† 37901 Neubert, 1,500 ....O 9
38059 Newbern, 2,124 ....C 9
38819 Newcomb, 550 ....N 7
37134 New Johnsonville, 970 ....E 8
37820 New Market, 950 ....O 8
37821 Newport◉, 7,328 ....P 9
37825 New Tazewell, 1,192 ......N 8
37826 Niota, 629 ....M 9
37828 Norris, 1,359 ....N 8
† 37201 Oak Hill, 4,490 ....H 8
37830 Oak Ridge, 28,319 ....N 8
38240 Obion, 1,010 ....C 8
37138 Old Hickory, 7,500 ....H 8
37840 Oliver Springs, 3,405 ....N 8
37841 Oneida, 2,602 ....M 7
37363 Ooltewah, 1,200 ....M10
† 37660 Orebank, 1,111 ....R 7
38577 Pall Mall, 500 ....M 7
37365 Palmer, 898 ....K 10
38242 Paris◉, 9,892 ....E 8
38363 Parsons, 2,167 ....E 9
37143 Pegram, 850 ....H 8
37144 Petersburg, 463 ....H10
37845 Petros, 800 ....M 8
37846 Philadelphia, 554 ....N 9
37862 Pigeon Forge, 1,361 ......O 9
37367 Pikeville◉, 1,454 ....L 9
37148 Portland, 2,872 ....H 7
37849 Powell, 1,200 ....N 8
† 37201 Providence, 3,830 ....H 8
38478 Pulaski◉, 6,989 ....G10
38251 Puryear, 458 ....E 8
38128 Raleigh, 2,500 ....B 10
37415 Red Bank, 12,715 ....L 10
37150 Red Boiling Springs, 726 ..K 7
37370 Riceville, 500 ....M10
38580 Rickman, 500 ....L 8
38080 Ridgely, 1,657 ....B 8
† 37401 Ridgeside, 458 ....L 10
37152 Ridgetop, 810 ....H 8
38063 Ripley◉, 4,794 ....B 9
38253 Rives, 5,259 ....C 8
37687 Roan Mountain, 950 ....S 8
37853 Rockford, 950 ....O 9
37854 Rockwood, 5,259 ....M 8
37857 Rogersville◉, 4,045 ....P 8
38053 Rosemark, 950 ....B 10
37860 Russellville, 850 ....P 8
38369 Rutherford, 1,385 ....C 8
37861 Rutledge◉, 863 ....P 8
38481 Saint Joseph, 637 ....G10
37373 Sale Creek, 900 ....L 10
38254 Samburg, 463 ....C 8
38372 Savannah◉, 5,576 ....E 10
38374 Scotts Hill, 476 ....E 10
38375 Selmer◉, 3,495 ....D 10
37374 Sequatchie, 450 ....K 10
37862 Sevierville◉, 2,661 ....P 9
37375 Sewanee, 1,886 ....K 10
37865 Seymour, 500 ....O 9
38255 Sharon, 1,188 ....D 8
37160 Shelbyville◉, 12,262 ......H10
37377 Signal Mountain, 4,839 ...L 10
37166 Smithville◉, 2,997 ....K 9
37167 Smyrna, 5,698 ....H 9
37869 Sneedville◉, 874 ....P 7
37379 Soddy-Daisy, 7,569 ....L 10
38068 Somerville◉, 1,816 ....C 10
† 37030 South Carthage, 859 ......J 8
37311 South Cleveland, 5,070 ...M10
37716 South Clinton, 1,484 .....N 8
42041 South Fulton, 3,122 ....D 8
37380 South Pittsburg, 3,613 ...K 10
37171 Southside, 800 ....G 8
38583 Sparta◉, 4,930 ....K 9
38585 Spencer◉, 1,179 ....L 9
37381 Spring City, 1,756 ....M 9
38378 Spring Creek, 500 ....D 9
37172 Springfield◉, 9,720 ....G 8
37174 Spring Hill, 685 ....H 9
37871 Strawberry Plains, 680 ...O 8
† 37660 Sullivan Gardens, 900 ....R 7
38660 Summertown, 700 ....G10
37382 Summitville, 500 ....K 9
37872 Sunbright, 500 ....M 8
37873 Surgoinsville, 1,285 ......P 8
37874 Sweetwater, 4,340 ....N 9
37877 Talbott, 975 ....P 8

37879 Tazewell◉, 1,860 ....O 8
37385 Tellico Plains, 773 ....N10
37880 Ten Mile, 700 ....M 9
37178 Tennessee Ridge, 664 ....F 8
† 37401 Tiftona, 1,750 ....L 11
38079 Tiptonville◉, 2,229 ....B 8
37387 Tracy City, 1,388 ....K 10
37883 Treadway, 712 ....P 8
37884 Trenton◉, 4,226 ....D 9
38258 Trezevant, 877 ....D 8
38259 Trimble, 675 ....C 8
38260 Troy, 826 ....C 8
37388 Tullahoma, 15,311 ....J 10
37743 Tusculum, 1,157 ....R 8
37692 Unicoi, 500 ....S 8
38261 Union City◉, 11,925 ......C 8
37393 Victoria, 800 ....K10
37885 Vonore, 524 ....N 9
37887 Wartburg◉, 541 ....M 8
37183 Wartrace, 616 ....J 9
37184 Watertown, 1,061 ....J 8
37185 Waverly◉, 3,794 ....F 8
38485 Waynesboro◉, 1,983 .....F 10
38074 Western State Hospital,
    2,900 ....C 10
37186 Westmoreland, 1,423 .....J 7
37187 White Bluff, 516 ....G 8
38116 Whitehaven, 19,000 ......A 10
37188 White House, 650 ....H 8
37890 White Pine, 1,532 ....P 8
37891 Whitesburg, 500 ....P 8
37396 Whiteside, 523 ....K 10
38075 Whiteville, 992 ....C 10
37397 Whitwell, 1,669 ....K 10
37398 Winchester◉, 5,211 ....J 10
37892 Winfield, 950 ....M 7
37190 Woodbury◉, 1,725 ....J 9
37191 Woodlawn, 500 ....G 7

◉ County seat.
‡ Population of metropolitan area.
† Zip of nearest p.o.
* Multiple zips

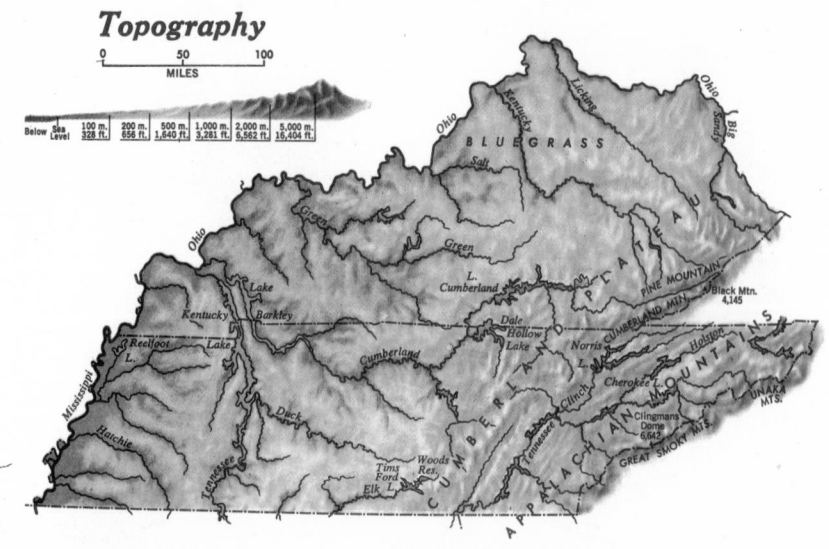

Topography

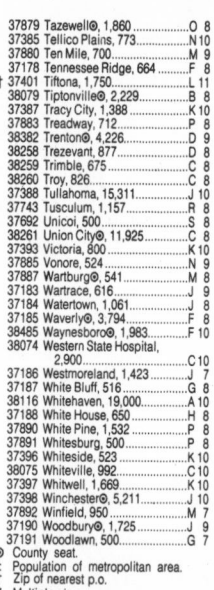

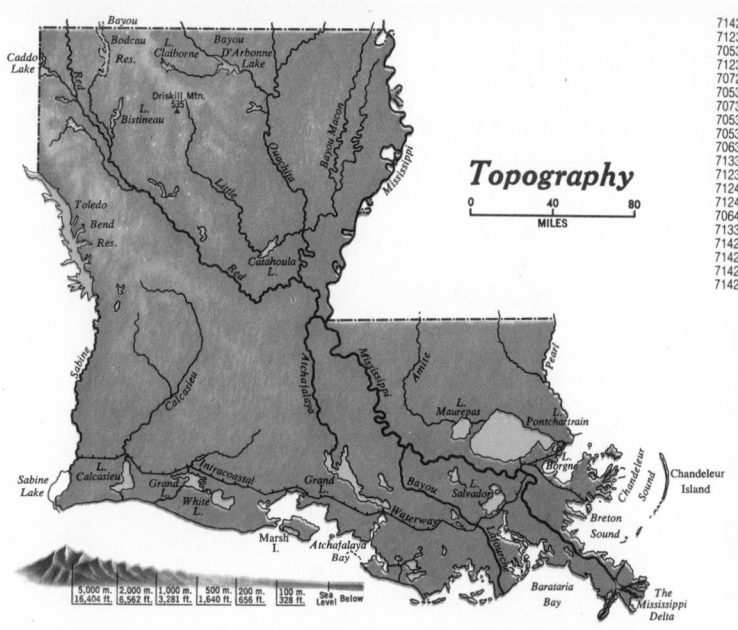

Topography

0   40   80
MILES

5,000 m. | 2,000 m. | 1,000 m. | 500 m. | 200 m. | 100 m. | Sea
16,404 ft. | 6,562 ft. | 3,281 ft. | 1,640 ft. | 656 ft. | 328 ft. | Level Below

LOUISIANA
SCALE
0 5 10 20 30 40 MI.
0 5 10 20 30 40 KM.

State Capitals..............⊛
Parish Seats..............◉
Canals..............

© C.S. HAMMOND & Co., N.Y.

PARISHES

Acadia, 52,109..............F 6
Allen, 20,794..............E 5
Ascension, 37,086..............J 6
Assumption, 19,654..............H 7
Avoyelles, 37,751..............G 4
Beauregard, 22,888..............D 5
Bienville, 16,024..............D 2
Bossier, 64,519..............C 1
Caddo, 230,184..............C 1
Calcasieu, 145,415..............D 6
Caldwell, 9,354..............F 2
Cameron, 8,194..............D 7
Catahoula, 11,769..............G 3
Claiborne, 17,024..............D 1
Concordia, 22,578..............G 4
De Soto, 22,764..............C 2
East Baton Rouge, 285,167..............K 5
East Carroll, 12,884..............H 1
East Feliciana, 17,657..............J 5
Evangeline, 31,932..............F 5
Franklin, 23,946..............G 3
Grant, 13,671..............E 3
Iberia, 57,397..............G 7
Iberville, 30,746..............H 6
Jackson, 15,963..............E 2
Jefferson, 337,568..............K 7
Jefferson Davis, 29,554..............E 6
Lafayette, 109,716..............F 6
Lafourche, 68,941..............K 7
La Salle, 13,295..............F 3
Lincoln, 33,800..............E 1
Livingston, 36,511..............L 2
Madison, 15,065..............H 2
Morehouse, 32,463..............G 1
Natchitoches, 35,219..............D 3
Orleans, 593,471..............L 6
Ouachita, 115,387..............F 2
Plaquemines, 25,225..............L 8
Pointe Coupee, 22,022..............G 5
Rapides, 118,078..............E 4
Red River, 9,226..............D 2
Richland, 21,774..............G 2
Sabine, 18,638..............C 3
Saint Bernard, 51,185..............L 7
Saint Charles, 29,550..............K 7
Saint Helena, 9,937..............J 5
Saint James, 19,733..............L 3
Saint John the Baptist, 23,813..............M 3
Saint Landry, 80,364..............F 5
Saint Martin, 32,453..............G 6
Saint Mary, 60,752..............H 7
Saint Tammany, 63,585..............L 6
Tangipahoa, 65,875..............K 5
Tensas, 9,732..............H 2
Terrebonne, 76,049..............J 8
Union, 18,447..............F 1
Vermilion, 43,071..............F 7
Vernon, 53,794..............D 4
Washington, 41,987..............K 5
Webster, 39,939..............D 1
West Baton Rouge, 16,864..............H 1
West Carroll, 13,028..............H 1
West Feliciana, 11,376..............H 5
Winn, 16,369..............E 3

CITIES and TOWNS

Zip   Name/Pop.   Key

70510 Abbeville◉, 10,996..............F 7
70420 Abita Springs, 839..............L 6
71316 Acme, 212..............G 4
† 70774 Acy, 570..............L 3
70710 Addis, 724..............J 2
† 70544 Adeline, 200..............G 7
70711 Albany, 700..............M 1
† 71016 Alberta, 300..............D 2
71301 Alexandria◉, 41,557..............E 4
70340 Amelia, 2,292..............H 7
70422 Amite◉, 3,593..............K 5

71403 Anacoco, 575..............D 4
† 71301 Anandale, 1,779..............F 4
70426 Angie, 317..............L 5
70712 Angola, 550..............G 5
70032 Arabi, 12,000..............K 7
† 70736 Arbroth, 250..............H 5
71001 Arcadia◉, 2,970..............E 1
71218 Archibald, 300..............G 2
71343 Archie, 280..............G 3
70456 Arcola, 240..............K 5
70512 Arnaudville, 1,673..............G 6
71002 Ashland, 211..............D 2
71003 Athens, 387..............E 1
71404 Atlanta, 342..............E 3
70513 Avery Island, 591..............G 7
70713 Bains, 400..............H 5
70714 Baker, 8,281..............K 1
70514 Baldwin, 2,117..............H 7
71405 Ball, 500..............F 4
† 70401 Baptist, 150..............M 1
70036 Barataria, 950..............K 7
70515 Basile, 1,779..............E 5
71219 Baskin, 177..............G 2
71220 Bastrop◉, 14,713..............G 1
† 70801 Baton Rouge (cap.)◉, 165,963..............K 2
     Baton Rouge, ‡285,167..............K 2
† 70754 Bayou Barbary, 200..............M 2
† 70360 Bayou Cane, 9,077..............J 7
70716 Bayou Goula, 850..............J 3
70380 Bayou Vista, 5,121..............H 7
71220 Beekman, 300..............G 1
70675 Bel, 150..............D 6
71004 Belcher, 400..............C 1
70630 Bell City, 350..............D 6
† 70341 Belle Alliance, 350..............K 3
70037 Belle Chasse, 950..............O 4
71330 Belledeau, 450..............F 4
70341 Belle Rose, 900..............K 3
† 71468 Bellwood, 150..............D 3
71406 Belmont, 150..............C 3
71005 Benson, 200..............C 3
71407 Bentley, 300..............E 3
71006 Benton◉, 1,493..............C 1
71222 Bernice, 1,794..............F 1
† 70040 Bertrandville, 175..............L 7
70342 Berwick, 4,168..............H 7
71007 Bethany, 250..............B 2
71008 Bienville, 287..............D 2
71009 Blanchard, 806..............C 1
70427 Bogalusa, 18,412..............L 5
† 71064 Bolinger, 250..............L 4
71223 Bonita, 533..............G 1
70038 Boothville, 300..............M 8
71320 Bordelonville, 450..............G 4
71224 Bosco, 480..............F 2
71010 Bossier City, 41,595..............C 1
70353 Boudreaux, 275..............J 8
70343 Bourg, 900..............J 8
70039 Boutte, 950..............N 4
70040 Braithwaite, 550..............P 4
70517 Breaux Bridge, 4,942..............G 6
70718 Brittany, 290..............L 3
70518 Broussard, 1,707..............G 6
70719 Brusly, 1,282..............J 2
71322 Bunkie, 5,395..............F 4
70041 Buras-Triumph, 4,113..............L 8
70738 Burnside, 500..............L 3
70431 Bush, 275..............L 5
70519 Cade, 800..............G 6
71433 Calcasieu, 400..............E 4
71225 Calhoun, 653..............F 2
71410 Calvin, 286..............E 3
70631 Cameron◉, 975..............D 7
71411 Campti, 1,078..............D 3
70584 Cankton, 260..............F 6
70520 Carencro, 2,302..............G 6
70042 Carlisle, 975..............L 7
70721 Carville, 950..............K 3
71016 Castor, 178..............D 2

71425 Enterprise, 300..............G 3
71237 Epps, 448..............G 1
70533 Erath, 2,024..............F 7
71238 Eros, 164..............F 2
70729 Erwinville, 790..............H 5
70534 Estherwood, 661..............F 6
70730 Ethel, 350..............H 5
70535 Eunice, 11,390..............F 6
70537 Evangeline, 400..............F 6
70639 Evans, 400..............D 5
71333 Evergreen, 307..............F 5
71239 Extension, 950..............G 3
71240 Fairbanks, 150..............F 1
71241 Farmerville◉, 3,416..............F 1
70640 Fenton, 404..............E 6
71334 Ferriday, 5,239..............G 3
71426 Fisher, 300..............D 4
71427 Flatwoods, 450..............E 4
71428 Flora, 200..............D 3
71429 Florien, 639..............D 4

70436 Fluker, 400..............K 5
70437 Folsom, 249..............K 5
70732 Fordoche, 488..............G 5
71242 Forest, 221..............H 1
71430 Forest Hill, 370..............E 4
71449 Fort Jesup, 950..............C 3
71243 Fort Necessity, 150..............G 2
70538 Franklin◉, 9,325..............G 7
70438 Franklinton◉, 3,562..............K 5
70733 French Settlement, 800..............L 2
71027 Frierson, 700..............C 2
† 70753 Frost, 700..............L 3
† 71039 Fryeburg, 150..............D 2
71354 Galliano, 950..............K 8
70540 Garden City, 515..............H 7
71245 Garyville, 2,474..............M 3
70734 Geismar, 300..............K 3
71432 Georgetown, 306..............F 3
71028 Gibsland, 1,380..............E 1

70356 Gibson, 950..............J 7
71336 Gilbert, 746..............G 2
71029 Gilliam, 211..............C 1
71244 Girard, 250..............G 2
† 70538 Glencoe, 200..............G 7
71433 Glenmora, 1,651..............E 5
71030 Gloster, 975..............C 2
70736 Glynn, 400..............H 5
70357 Golden Meadow, 2,681..............K 8
71031 Goldonna, 337..............D 2
70737 Gonzales, 4,512..............L 3
70079 Good Hope, 950..............N 3
71337 Good Pine, 535..............F 3
71245 Grambling, 4,407..............E 1
70052 Gramercy, 2,567..............M 3
71032 Grand Cane, 284..............C 2
70643 Grand Chenier, 710..............E 7
70541 Grand Coteau, 1,301..............G 6
70358 Grand Isle, 2,236..............L 8
† 70601 Grand Lake, 400..............D 6

(continued on following page)

AREA 48,523 sq. mi.
POPULATION 3,643,180
CAPITAL Baton Rouge
LARGEST CITY New Orleans
HIGHEST POINT Driskill Mtn. 535 ft.
SETTLED IN 1699
ADMITTED TO UNION April 30, 1812
POPULAR NAME Pelican State
STATE FLOWER Magnolia
STATE BIRD Eastern Brown Pelican

Agriculture, Industry and Resources

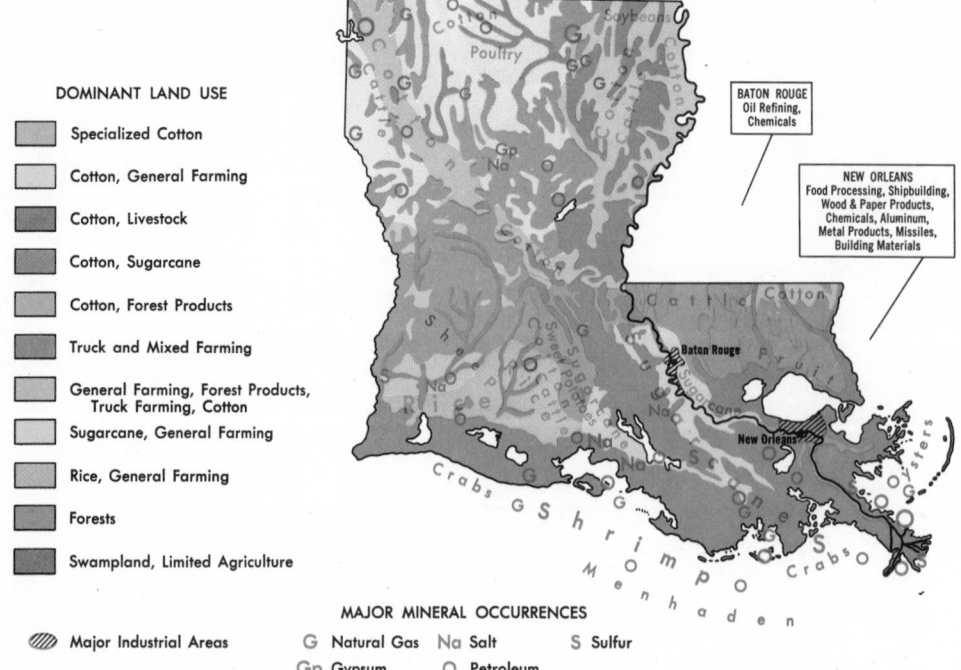

DOMINANT LAND USE

- Specialized Cotton
- Cotton, General Farming
- Cotton, Livestock
- Cotton, Sugarcane
- Cotton, Forest Products
- Truck and Mixed Farming
- General Farming, Forest Products, Truck Farming, Cotton
- Sugarcane, General Farming
- Rice, General Farming
- Forests
- Swampland, Limited Agriculture

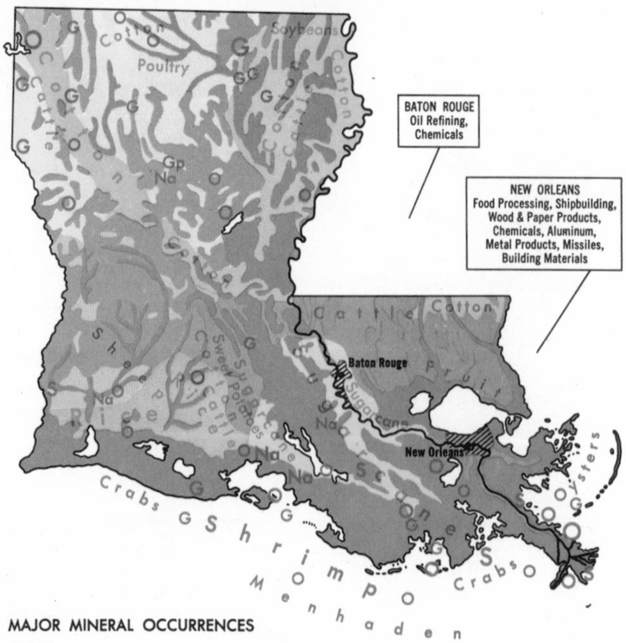

BATON ROUGE
Oil Refining, Chemicals
NEW ORLEANS
Food Processing, Shipbuilding, Wood & Paper Products, Chemicals, Aluminum, Metal Products, Missiles, Building Materials
Baton Rouge
New Orleans
Poultry
Soybeans
Cotton
Cattle
Crabs
Shrimp
Menhaden

MAJOR MINERAL OCCURRENCES

Major Industrial Areas

G Natural Gas · Na Salt · S Sulfur · Gp Gypsum · O Petroleum

71047 Keithville, 500 ..... C 2
71441 Kelly, 250 ..... F 3
70062 Kenner, 29,858 ..... N 4
70444 Kentwood, 2,736 ..... J 5
71253 Kilbourne, 370 ..... H 1
† 70462 Killian, 275 ..... M 2
70066 Killona, 600 ..... M 3
70648 Kinder, 2,307 ..... E 6
70370 Klotzville, 248 ..... K 3
70371 Kraemer, 510 ..... M 4
70750 Krotz Springs, 1,435 ..... G 5
70372 Labadieville, 700 ..... K 4
70650 Lacassine, 494 ..... E 6
70445 Lacombe, 750 ..... L 6
70501 Lafayette⊙, 68,908 ..... F 6
Lafayette, ‡109,716 ..... F 6
70067 Lafitte, 1,223 ..... K 7
† 70301 Lafourche, 200 ..... J 7
70549 Lake Arthur, 3,551 ..... E 6
70601 Lake Charles⊙, 77,998 ..... D 6
Lake Charles, ‡145,415 ..... D 6
70752 Lakeland, 400 ..... H 5
71254 Lake Providence⊙, 6,183 ..... H 1
70068 Laplace, 5,953 ..... N 3
70373 Larose, 4,267 ..... K 7
71344 Larto, 500 ..... G 4
70550 Lawtell, 600 ..... F 5
71345 Lebeau, 270 ..... F 5
71346 Lecompte, 1,518 ..... F 4
71446 Leesville⊙, 8,928 ..... D 4
71447 Lena, 250 ..... E 4
70551 Leonville, 512 ..... G 6
70753 Lettsworth, 200 ..... G 5
† 70525 Lewisburg, 265 ..... F 6
71348 Libuse, 500 ..... F 4
71256 Lillie, 160 ..... E 1
71048 Lisbon, 151 ..... E 1
† 71343 Lismore, 380 ..... G 3
† 70062 Little Farms, 15,713 ..... N 4
70754 Livingston⊙, 1,398 ..... L 1
70755 Livonia, 611 ..... G 5
70374 Lockport, 1,995 ..... K 7
71049 Logansport, 1,330 ..... C 3
† 71367 Lonepine, 850 ..... F 5
71448 Longleaf, 250 ..... E 4
71050 Longstreet, 182 ..... B 2
70652 Longville, 250 ..... D 5
70446 Loranger, 200 ..... N 1
70552 Loreauville, 728 ..... G 6
70756 Lottie, 350 ..... G 5
70069 Lucy, 825 ..... M 3
70070 Luling, 3,255 ..... N 4
70071 Lutcher, 3,911 ..... L 3
70447 Madisonville, 801 ..... K 6
70554 Mamou, 3,275 ..... F 5
70448 Mandeville, 2,282 ..... L 6
71259 Mangham, 544 ..... G 2
71052 Mansfield⊙, 6,432 ..... C 2
71350 Mansura, 1,699 ..... G 4
71449 Many⊙, 3,112 ..... C 3
70663 Maplewood, 1,900 ..... D 6
70757 Maringouin, 1,365 ..... G 6
71260 Marion, 796 ..... F 1
71351 Marksville⊙, 4,519 ..... G 4
70072 Marrero, 29,015 ..... O 4
70375 Mathews, 600 ..... J 7
70449 Maurepas, 200 ..... M 2
70555 Maurice, 476 ..... F 6
† 71433 McNary, 220 ..... E 5
71451 Melder, 200 ..... E 4
71353 Melville, 2,076 ..... G 5
70556 Mermentau, 756 ..... E 6
71261 Mer Rouge, 819 ..... G 1
70653 Merryville, 1,286 ..... D 5
* 70001 Metairie, 135,816 ..... O 4
70557 Midland, 500 ..... F 6
70558 Milton, 500 ..... F 6
71055 Minden⊙, 13,996 ..... D 1
70376 Modeste, 230 ..... K 3
71201 Monroe⊙, 56,374 ..... F 1
Monroe, ‡115,387 ..... F 1
70377 Montegut, 950 ..... J 8
71354 Monterey, 800 ..... G 4
71454 Montgomery, 923 ..... E 3
70422 Montpelier, 211 ..... M 1
† 70068 Montz, 200 ..... M 3
71060 Mooringsport, 830 ..... B 1
71455 Mora, 378 ..... E 4
71355 Moreauville, 807 ..... G 4
70380 Morgan City, 16,586 ..... H 7
70759 Morganza, 836 ..... G 5
71356 Morrow, 350 ..... F 5
70559 Morse, 759 ..... F 6
70076 Mount Airy, 700 ..... M 3
70077 Nairn, 500 ..... L 8
70390 Napoleonville⊙, 1,008 ..... K 4
70451 Natalbany, 900 ..... N 1
71456 Natchez, 600 ..... D 3
71457 Natchitoches⊙, 15,974 ..... D 3
† 71342 Nebo, 200 ..... F 3
71460 Negreet, 200 ..... C 4
71357 Newellton, 1,403 ..... H 2
† 71354 New Era, 200 ..... G 4
70560 New Iberia⊙, 30,147 ..... G 6
71461 Newllano, 1,800 ..... D 4
* 70101 New Orleans⊙, 593,471 ..... O 4
New Orleans, ‡1,045,809 ..... O 4
70760 New Roads⊙, 3,945 ..... G 5
70078 New Sarpy, 1,643 ..... N 4
71462 Noble, 209 ..... C 3
70079 Norco, 4,773 ..... N 3
† 71247 North Hodge, 640 ..... E 2
70761 Norwood, 348 ..... H 5
71463 Oakdale, 7,301 ..... E 5
71263 Oak Grove⊙, 1,980 ..... H 1
71264 Oak Ridge, 276 ..... G 1
70655 Oberlin⊙, 1,857 ..... E 5
† 71369 Odenburg, 175 ..... G 5
71061 Oil City, 907 ..... C 1
† 70560 Olivier, 300 ..... G 7
71465 Olla, 1,387 ..... F 3
70570 Opelousas⊙, 20,121 ..... G 5
70762 Oscar, 700 ..... H 5
71358 Palmetto, 312 ..... G 5
70391 Paincourtville, 600 ..... K 3
70080 Paradis, 750 ..... M 4
70582 Parks, 491 ..... G 6
† 70544 Patoutville, 230 ..... G 7
70392 Patterson, 4,409 ..... H 7
70763 Paulina, 500 ..... L 3
70452 Pearl River, 1,361 ..... L 6
† 70548 Pecan Island, 480 ..... F 7
70575 Perry, 225 ..... F 7
† 70042 Phoenix, 525 ..... L 7
70453 Pine Grove, 500 ..... J 5
70576 Pine Prairie, 515 ..... E 5
71360 Pineville, 8,951 ..... F 4
71266 Pioneer, 188 ..... H 1
70656 Pitkin, 700 ..... E 5
71064 Plain Dealing, 2,116 ..... C 1
70764 Plaquemine⊙, 7,739 ..... J 2
70393 Plattenville, 400 ..... K 4
71362 Plaucheville, 224 ..... G 5
71065 Pleasant Hill, 826 ..... C 3
70082 Pointe a la Hache⊙, 750 ..... L 7
71467 Pollock, 341 ..... F 3
70454 Ponchatoula, 4,545 ..... N 2
70767 Port Allen⊙, 5,728 ..... J 2
70577 Port Barre, 2,133 ..... G 5
† 70791 Port Hudson, 200 ..... J 1
70083 Port Sulphur, 3,022 ..... L 8
† 70726 Port Vincent, 387 ..... L 2
71066 Powhatan, 277 ..... D 3
70769 Prairieville, 500 ..... K 2
71067 Princeton, 350 ..... C 1
71468 Provencal, 530 ..... D 3
71268 Quitman, 169 ..... E 2
70394 Raceland, 4,880 ..... J 7
70578 Rayne, 9,510 ..... F 6
71269 Rayville⊙, 3,962 ..... G 2
70580 Reddell, 800 ..... F 5
70658 Reeves, 214 ..... D 5
† 70085 Reggio, 400 ..... L 7
† 70763 Remy, 850 ..... L 3
70084 Reserve, 6,381 ..... M 3
71334 Ridgecrest, 1,076 ..... G 3
71068 Ringgold, 1,731 ..... D 2
† 70427 Rio, 250 ..... L 5
70581 Roanoke, 640 ..... E 6
71469 Robeline, 274 ..... D 3
70455 Robert, 600 ..... N 1
71069 Rodessa, 273 ..... B 1
70772 Rosedale, 621 ..... G 6
70456 Roseland, 1,273 ..... J 5
70659 Rosepine, 587 ..... D 5
71365 Ruby, 350 ..... F 4
71270 Ruston⊙, 17,365 ..... E 1
70774 Saint Amant, 900 ..... L 2
70457 Saint Benedict, 200 ..... K 5
70085 Saint Bernard, 750 ..... L 7
70775 Saint Francisville⊙ 1,603 ..... H 5
70776 Saint Gabriel, 975 ..... K 2
70086 Saint James, 600 ..... L 3
71366 Saint Joseph⊙, 1,864 ..... H 3
71367 Saint Landry, 950 ..... F 5
70582 Saint Martinville⊙, 7,153 ..... G 6
71471 Saint Maurice, 650 ..... E 3
70087 Saint Rose, 2,106 ..... N 4
71070 Saline, 307 ..... E 2
71301 Samtown, 4,210 ..... F 4
71071 Sarepta, 882 ..... D 1
70395 Schriever, 700 ..... J 7
70807 Scotlandville, 22,557 ..... J 1
70583 Scott, 1,334 ..... F 6
† 70560 Segura, 200 ..... G 6
† 70764 Seymourville, 2,506 ..... J 2
71072 Shongaloo, 173 ..... D 1
* 71101 Shreveport⊙, 182,064 ..... C 1
Shreveport, ‡294,703 ..... C 1
71073 Sibley, 869 ..... D 1
71368 Sicily Island, 630 ..... G 3
71472 Sieper, 200 ..... E 4
71473 Sikes, 237 ..... F 2
71369 Simmesport, 2,027 ..... G 5
71474 Simpson, 491 ..... D 4
71275 Simsboro, 412 ..... E 1
70660 Singer, 400 ..... D 5
71475 Slagle, 200 ..... D 4
70777 Slaughter, 580 ..... H 5
70458 Slidell, 16,101 ..... L 6
† 70346 Smoke Bend, 300 ..... K 3
71276 Sondheimer, 325 ..... H 1
70778 Sorrento, 1,182 ..... L 3
† 71052 South Mansfield, 439 ..... C 3
71277 Spearsville, 197 ..... E 1
70462 Springfield, 423 ..... M 2
71075 Springhill, 6,496 ..... D 1
† 71465 Standard, 190 ..... F 3
70661 Starks, 750 ..... C 6
71279 Start, 200 ..... G 2
71280 Sterlington, 1,118 ..... F 1
71078 Stonewall, 500 ..... C 2
70663 Sulphur, 13,551 ..... D 6
71079 Summerfield, 170 ..... E 1
70463 Sun, 288 ..... L 5
70584 Sunset, 1,675 ..... F 6
70780 Sunshine, 900 ..... K 2
70396 Supreme, 617 ..... K 4
71281 Swartz, 650 ..... G 1
† 70601 Sweet Lake, 300 ..... D 7
70464 Talisheek, 292 ..... L 5
71282 Tallulah⊙, 9,643 ..... H 2
70465 Tangipahoa, 469 ..... J 5
71080 Taylor, 500 ..... D 1
† 71290 Tendal, 200 ..... H 2
† 70053 Terry Town, 13,832 ..... O 4
70397 Theriot, 950 ..... J 8
70301 Thibodaux⊙, 14,925 ..... J 7
70466 Tickfaw, 370 ..... M 1
71477 Tioga, 457 ..... F 4
71286 Transylvania, 400 ..... H 1
71081 Trees, 247 ..... B 1
† 70041 Triumph-Buras, 4,113 ..... L 8
71371 Trout, 500 ..... F 3
71479 Tullos, 600 ..... F 3
70782 Tunica, 475 ..... G 5
70585 Turkey Creek, 280 ..... F 5
70723 Union, 665 ..... L 3
71480 Urania, 950 ..... F 3
70090 Vacherie, 2,145 ..... L 3
† 70757 Valverda, 200 ..... G 5
70467 Varnado, 320 ..... L 5
70091 Venice, 900 ..... M 8
71372 Vick, 500 ..... F 4
71373 Vidalia⊙, 5,538 ..... G 3
71270 Vienna, 250 ..... E 1
70586 Ville Platte⊙, 9,692 ..... F 5
70668 Vinton, 3,454 ..... C 6
70092 Violet, 975 ..... P 4
71082 Vivian, 4,046 ..... B 1
70784 Wakefield, 200 ..... H 5
70785 Walker, 1,363 ..... L 1
† 70049 Wallace, 200 ..... M 3
71374 Walters, 500 ..... G 3
71289 Warden, 350 ..... H 1
† 71301 Wardville, 1,087 ..... F 4
70589 Washington, 1,473 ..... G 5
71375 Waterproof, 1,438 ..... H 3
70786 Watson, 700 ..... L 1
71290 Waverly, 350 ..... H 2
† 70569 Weeks, 400 ..... G 7
70093 Welcome, 450 ..... L 3
70591 Welsh, 3,203 ..... E 6
70669 Westlake, 4,082 ..... D 6
71291 West Monroe, 14,868 ..... F 1
† 70082 West Pointe a la Hache, 250 ..... L 7
70094 Westwego, 11,402 ..... O 4
70787 Weyanoke, 500 ..... H 5
70788 White Castle, 2,206 ..... J 3
† 70462 Whitehall, 380 ..... M 2
71376 Whiteville, 450 ..... F 5
71377 Wildsville, 650 ..... G 3
70789 Wilson, 606 ..... H 5
71483 Winnfield⊙, 7,142 ..... E 3
71295 Winnsboro⊙, 5,349 ..... G 2
71378 Wisner, 1,339 ..... G 3
71485 Woodworth, 409 ..... E 4
70592 Youngsville, 1,002 ..... G 6
70791 Zachary, 4,964 ..... K 1
71486 Zwolle, 2,169 ..... C 3

⊙ Parish seat.
‡ Population of metropolitan area.
† Zip of nearest p.o.
* Multiple zips

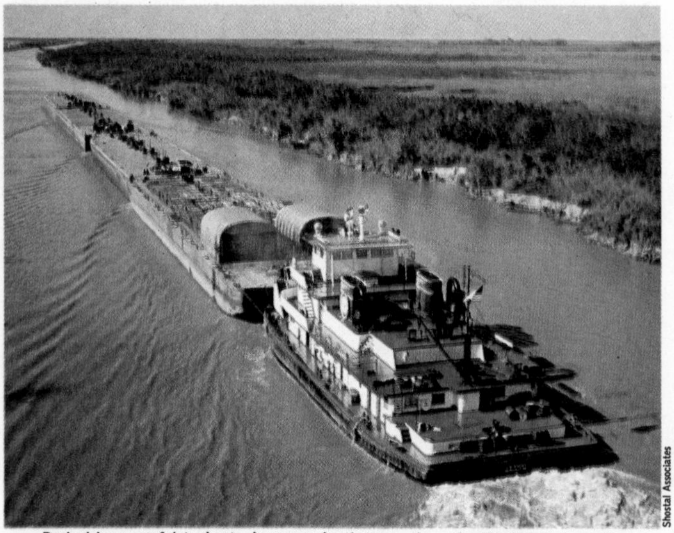

Shostal Associates

Pushed by powerful tugboats, barges make their way from the Mississippi down the shallow Gulf Intracoastal Waterway to deliver their cargoes to New Orleans, Morgan City and Lake Charles, Louisiana.

AREA 33,215 sq. mi.
POPULATION 993,663
CAPITAL Augusta
LARGEST CITY Portland
HIGHEST POINT Katahdin 5,268 ft.
SETTLED IN 1624
ADMITTED TO UNION March 15, 1820
POPULAR NAME Pine Tree State
STATE FLOWER Pine Cone & Tassel
STATE BIRD Chickadee

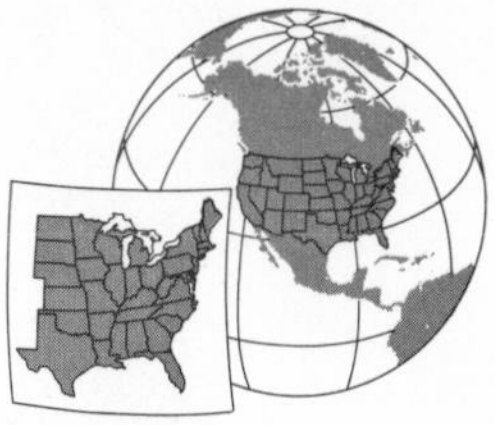

COUNTIES

Name/Pop.	Key
Androscoggin, 91,279	C 7
Aroostook, 92,463	F 2
Cumberland, 192,528	C 8
Franklin, 22,444	B 5
Hancock, 34,590	G 6
Kennebec, 95,247	D 7
Knox, 29,013	E 7
Lincoln, 20,537	D 7
Oxford, 43,457	B 7
Penobscot, 125,393	F 5
Piscataquis, 16,285	E 4
Sagadahoc, 23,452	D 7
Somerset, 40,597	C 4
Waldo, 23,328	E 6
Washington, 29,859	H 6
York, 111,576	B 9

CITIES and TOWNS

Zip	Name/Pop.	Key
04406	Abbot Village, ∆453	D 5
04001	Acton, ∆697	B 8
04606	Addison, ∆773	H 6
04910	Albion, ∆1,056	E 6
† 04610	Alexander, ∆169	H 5
04002	Alfred⊙, ∆1,211	B 9
† 04774	Allagash, ∆456	F 1
† 04938	Allens Mills, 150	C 6
04535	Alna, ∆315	D 7
† 04468	Alton, ∆340	F 5
† 04408	Amherst, ∆148	G 6
04216	Andover, ∆791	B 6
04216	Andover, 350	B 6
04911	Anson. ∆2,168	D 6
04911	Anson, 950	D 6
† 04862	Appleton, ∆628	E 7
04732	Ashland, ∆1,761	G 2
04732	Ashland, 750	G 2
04912	Athens, ∆592	D 6
04912	Athens, 200	D 6
† 04426	Atkinson, ∆213	E 5
04210	Auburn⊙, 24,151	C 7
04330	Augusta (cap.)⊙, 21,945	D 7
04408	Aurora, ∆72	G 6
04003	Bailey Island, 400	D 8
04409	Bancroft, ∆53	H 4
04401	Bangor⊙, 33,168	F 6
04609	Bar Harbor, ∆3,716	G 7
04609	Bar Harbor, 2,392	G 7
04610	Baring, 150	J 5
04004	Bar Mills, 800	C 8
04653	Bass Harbor, 413	G 7
04530	Bath⊙, 9,679	D 8
04915	Bayside, 238	F 7
04611	Beals, ∆663	H 7
† 04622	Beddington, ∆32	H 6
04915	Belfast⊙, 5,957	F 7
04917	Belgrade, ∆1,302	D 7
04917	Belgrade, 300	D 7
04918	Belgrade Lakes, 700	D 6
† 04915	Belmont, ∆349	E 7
04733	Benedicta, ∆177	G 4
† 04919	Benton, ∆1,729	D 6
03901	Berwick, ∆3,136	B 9
03901	Berwick, 1,765	B 9
† 04285	Berry Mills, 245	C 6
04217	Bethel, ∆2,220	B 7
04217	Bethel, 750	B 7
04005	Biddeford, 19,983	B 9
04006	Biddeford Pool, 500	C 9
04920	Bingham, ∆1,254	D 5
04920	Bingham, 1,184	D 5
04613	Birch Harbor, 210	H 7
04734	Blaine, ∆903	H 2
04734	Blaine-Mars Hill, 1,854	H 2
† 04406	Blanchard, ∆56	D 5
04614	Blue Hill, ∆1,367	F 7
04614	Blue Hill, 850	F 7
† 04040	Bolsters Mills, 150	B 7
04537	Boothbay, ∆1,814	D 8
04537	Boothbay, 700	D 8
04538	Boothbay Harbor, 2,320	D 8
04008	Bowdoinham, ∆1,294	D 7
04481	Bowerbank, ∆29	E 5
04410	Bradford, ∆569	F 5
04410	Bradford, 150	F 5
04411	Bradley, ∆1,010	F 6
04412	Brewer, 9,300	F 6
04735	Bridgewater, ∆895	H 3
04009	Bridgton, ∆2,967	B 7
04009	Bridgton, 1,779	B 7
† 04990	Brighton, ∆58	D 5
04539	Bristol, ∆1,721	D 8
04539	Bristol, 160	D 8
04616	Brooklin, ∆598	F 7
04921	Brooks, ∆751	E 6
04617	Brooksville, ∆673	F 7
04413	Brookton, 225	H 4
04010	Brownfield, ∆478	B 8
04010	Brownfield, 200	B 8
04414	Brownville, ∆1,490	E 5
04414	Brownville, 1,641	E 5
04415	Brownville Junction, 950	E 5
04011	Brunswick, ∆16,195	C 8
04011	Brunswick, 10,867	C 8
04219	Bryant Pond, 350	B 7
04220	Buckfield, ∆929	C 7
04618	Bucks Harbor, 161	J 6
04416	Bucksport, ∆3,756	F 6
04416	Bucksport, 2,456	F 6
04417	Burlington, ∆266	G 5
04922	Burnham, ∆802	E 6
† 04093	Buxton, ∆3,135	C 8
† 04275	Byron, ∆132	B 6
04619	Calais, 4,044	J 5
04923	Cambridge, ∆281	E 5
04843	Camden, ∆4,115	F 7
04843	Camden, 3,492	F 7
04924	Canaan, ∆904	D 6
04221	Canton, ∆742	C 7
03902	Cape Neddick, 850	B 9
04014	Cape Porpoise, 500	C 9
04925	Caratunk, ∆96	C 5
04418	Cardville, 223	F 5
04736	Caribou, 10,419	G 2
04419	Carmel, ∆1;301	E 6
04420	Carroll, ∆132	G 5
† 04224	Carthage, ∆354	C 6
† 04465	Cary, ∆184	H 4
04015	Casco, ∆1,256	B 7
04015	Casco, 250	B 7
04421	Castine, ∆1,080	F 7
† 04623	Centerville, ∆19	H 6
† 04757	Chapman, ∆328	G 2
04422	Charleston, ∆909	F 5
† 04666	Charlotte, ∆199	J 5
04017	Chebeague Island, 400	C 8
† 04345	Chelsea, ∆2,095	D 7
04622	Cherryfield, ∆771	H 6
† 04458	Chester, ∆255	F 5
† 04938	Chesterville, ∆643	C 6
04926	China, ∆1,850	E 7
04926	China, 336	E 7
04222	Chisholm, 1,530	C 7
† 04428	Clifton, ∆233	G 6
04927	Clinton, ∆1,971	D 6
04927	Clinton, 1,124	D 6
† 04623	Columbia, ∆162	H 6
04623	Columbia Falls, ∆367	H 6
† 04638	Cooper, ∆88	H 6
04341	Coopers Mills, 200	E 7
04624	Corea, 300	H 7
04928	Corinna, ∆1,700	E 6
04020	Cornish, ∆839	B 8
† 04976	Cornville, ∆623	D 6
04423	Costigan, 200	F 5
04625	Cranberry Isles, ∆186	G 7
† 04610	Crawford, ∆74	H 5
† 04015	Crescent Lake, 175	C 7
04738	Crouseville, 300	G 2
† 04747	Crystal, ∆281	G 4
04021	Cumberland Center, ∆4,096	C 8
04021	Cumberland Center, 950	C 8
04011	Cundys Harbor, 150	D 8
† 04563	Cushing, ∆522	E 7
04626	Cutler, ∆588	J 6
04626	Cutler, 153	J 6
04543	Damariscotta, ∆1,264	E 7
04543	Damariscotta-Newcastle, 1,188	E 7
04424	Danforth, ∆794	H 4
04424	Danforth, 650	H 4
† 04622	Deblois, ∆20	H 6
† 04429	Dedham, ∆522	F 6
04627	Deer Isle, ∆1,211	F 7
04627	Deer Isle, 600	F 7
04022	Denmark, ∆397	B 8
04628	Dennysville, ∆278	J 6
04425	Derby, 300	E 5
04929	Detroit, ∆663	E 6
04930	Dexter, ∆3,725	E 5
04936	Dexter, 2,732	E 5
04224	Dixfield, ∆2,188	C 6
04224	Dixfield, 1,535	C 6
04932	Dixmont, ∆559	E 6
04426	Dover-Foxcroft, ∆4,178	E 5
04426	Dover-Foxcroft⊙, 3,102	E 5
04342	Dresden, ∆787	D 7
04225	Dryden, 675	C 6
† 04039	Dry Mills, 700	C 8
† 04747	Dyer Brook, ∆165	G 3
04739	Eagle Lake, ∆908	F 1
04739	Eagle Lake, 675	F 1
04226	East Andover, 194	B 6
04024	East Baldwin, 175	B 8
04629	East Blue Hill, 150	G 7
04544	East Boothbay, 400	D 8
04427	East Corinth, 525	F 5
04227	East Dixfield, 288	C 6
04428	East Eddington, 200	F 6
04026	East Hiram, 198	B 8
04429	East Holden, 450	F 6
04027	East Lebanon, 950	B 9
† 04049	East Limington, 200	B 8
04228	East Livermore, 290	C 7
04630	East Machias, ∆1,057	J 6
04630	East Machias, 750	J 6
† 04950	East Madison, 400	D 6
04430	East Millinocket, ∆2,567	F 4
04430	East Millinocket, 2,564	F 4
04740	Easton, ∆1,305	H 2
† 04270	East Otisfield, 200	B 7
04229	East Peru, 350	C 7
04230	East Poland, 700	C 7
04631	Eastport, 1,989	K 6
04231	East Stoneham, 150	B 7
04632	East Sullivan, 300	G 6
† 04862	East Union, 220	E 7
04935	East Vassalboro, 300	D 7
04030	East Waterboro, 365	B 8
04234	East Wilton, 650	C 6
† 04428	Eddington, ∆1,358	F 6
† 04428	Eddington, 250	F 6
04545	Edgecomb, ∆549	D 8
† 04628	Edmunds, 229	J 6
03903	Eliot, ∆3,497	B 9
04605	Ellsworth⊙, 4,603	F 6
04433	Enfield, ∆1,148	F 5
04433	Enfield, 150	F 5
04434	Etna, ∆526	E 6
04936	Eustis, ∆595	B 5
04435	Exeter, ∆663	E 6
† 04938	Fairbanks, 300	C 6
04937	Fairfield, ∆5,684	D 6
04937	Fairfield, 3,694	D 6
† 04937	Fairfield Center, 975	D 6
04105	Falmouth, ∆6,291	C 8
04105	Falmouth, 1,621	C 8
† 04105	Falmouth Foreside (Falmouth), 1,621	C 8
† 04345	Farmingdale, ∆2,423	D 7
† 04345	Farmingdale, 1,832	D 7
04938	Farmington, ∆5,657	C 6
04938	Farmington⊙, 3,096	C 6
04940	Farmington Falls, 500	C 6
04344	Fayette, ∆447	C 7
04546	Five Islands, 161	D 8
04742	Fort Fairfield, ∆4,859	H 2
04742	Fort Fairfield, 2,322	H 2
04743	Fort Kent, ∆4,575	F 1
04743	Fort Kent, 2,876	F 1
04744	Fort Kent Mills, 300	F 1
04438	Frankfort, ∆620	F 6
04634	Franklin, ∆708	G 6
04634	Franklin, 350	G 6
04941	Freedom, ∆373	E 7
04032	Freeport, ∆4,781	C 8
04032	Freeport, 1,822	C 8
04745	Frenchville, ∆1,375	G 1
04745	Frenchville, 800	G 1
04547	Friendship, ∆834	E 7
04547	Friendship, 700	E 7
04037	Fryeburg, ∆2,208	A 7
04037	Fryeburg, 1,075	A 7
04345	Gardiner, 6,685	D 7
04939	Garland, ∆596	E 5
04939	Garland, 300	E 5
04548	Georgetown, ∆464	D 8
04548	Georgetown, 190	D 8
† 04217	Gilead, ∆153	B 7
† 04401	Glenburn, ∆1,196	F 6
04846	Glen Cove, 300	E 7
† 04005	Goodwins Mills, 340	B 8
† 04046	Goose Rocks Beach, 200	C 9
04038	Gorham, ∆7,839	C 8
04038	Gorham, 3,337	C 8
04636	Gouldsboro, ∆1,310	H 7
04636	Gouldsboro, 296	H 7
04746	Grand Isle, ∆797	G 1
04746	Grand Isle, 400	G 1
04637	Grand Lake Stream, ∆186	H 5
04039	Gray, ∆2,939	C 8
04039	Gray, 525	C 8
04236	Greene, ∆1,772	C 7
04441	Greenville, ∆1,894	D 5
04441	Greenville, 1,714	D 5
04442	Greenville Junction, 150	D 5
04443	Guilford, ∆1,694	E 5
04443	Guilford, 1,216	E 5
04347	Hallowell, 2,814	D 7
† 04785	Hamlin, ∆357	H 1
04444	Hampden, ∆4,693	F 6
04444	Hampden, 2,207	F 6
04445	Hampden Highlands, 950	F 6
04640	Hancock, ∆1,070	G 6
04237	Hanover, ∆275	B 7
04942	Harmony, ∆650	D 6
04942	Harmony, 350	D 6
† 04011	Harpswell, ∆2,552	D 8
04643	Harrington, ∆553	H 6
04040	Harrison, ∆1,045	B 7
† 04221	Hartford, ∆312	C 7
04943	Hartland, ∆1,414	D 6
04943	Hartland, 975	D 6
04446	Haynesville, ∆157	G 4
04238	Hebron, ∆532	C 7
† 04401	Hermon, ∆2,376	F 6
† 04082	Highland Lake, 600	C 8
04944	Hinckley, 317	D 6
04041	Hiram, ∆686	B 8
04041	Hiram, 175	B 8
04730	Hodgdon, ∆933	H 3
† 04429	Holden, ∆1,789	H 3
† 04429	Holden, 900	H 3
04042	Hollis Center, ∆1,560	B 8
04847	Hope, ∆500	E 7
04847	Hope, 175	E 7
04730	Houlton, ∆8,111	H 3
04730	Houlton⊙, 6,760	H 3
04448	Howland, ∆1,468	F 5
04448	Howland, 1,418	F 5
04449	Hudson, ∆482	F 5
04644	Hulls Cove, 200	G 7
04747	Island Falls, ∆913	G 3
04645	Isle au Haut, ∆45	F 7
04848	Islesboro, ∆421	F 7
04848	Islesboro, 200	F 7
04945	Jackman, ∆848	C 4
04945	Jackman, 700	C 4
04647	Jacksonville, 200	J 6
04239	Jay, ∆3,954	C 7
04239	Jay, 850	C 7
04348	Jefferson, ∆1,242	D 7
04648	Jonesboro, ∆448	J 6
04649	Jonesport, ∆1,326	H 6
04649	Jonesport, 1,073	H 6
04748	Keegan, 450	G 1
04450	Kenduskeag, ∆733	E 6
04043	Kennebunk, ∆5,646	B 9
04043	Kennebunk, 2,764	B 9
04046	Kennebunkport, ∆2,160	C 9
04046	Kennebunkport, 1,097	C 9
04349	Kents Hill, 250	D 7
04047	Kezar Falls, 680	B 8
04947	Kingfield, ∆877	C 6
04451	Kingman, 250	G 4
† 04990	Kingsbury, ∆7	D 5
03904	Kittery, ∆11,028	B 9
03904	Kittery, 7,363	B 9
03905	Kittery Point, 1,172	B 9
† 04986	Knox, ∆443	E 6
04453	La Grange, ∆393	F 5
04453	La Grange, 250	F 5
† 04463	Lake View, ∆16	F 5
† 04605	Lamoine, ∆615	G 7
04455	Lee, ∆599	G 5
† 04263	Leeds, ∆1,031	C 7
04456	Levant, ∆862	F 6
04240	Lewiston, 41,779	C 7
	Lewiston-Auburn, ‡72,474	C 7
04949	Liberty, ∆515	E 7
04949	Liberty, 200	E 7
04749	Lille, 300	G 1
04048	Limerick, ∆963	B 8
04750	Limestone, ∆8,745	H 2
04750	Limestone, 1,572	H 2
04049	Limington, ∆1,066	B 8
04049	Limington, 250	B 8
04457	Lincoln, ∆4,759	G 5
04457	Lincoln, 3,482	G 5
04458	Lincoln Center, 325	G 5
04849	Lincolnville, ∆955	E 7
04849	Lincolnville, 800	E 7
04755	Linneus, ∆608	H 3
04250	Lisbon, ∆6,544	C 7
* 04250	Lisbon-Lisbon Center, 1,475	C 7
04252	Lisbon Falls, 3,257	D 7
04350	Litchfield, ∆1,222	D 7
04650	Little Deer Isle, 275	F 7
† 04760	Littleton, ∆958	H 3
04253	Livermore, ∆1,610	C 7
04253	Livermore, 280	C 7
04254	Livermore Falls, ∆3,450	C 7
04254	Livermore Falls, 2,378	C 7
04255	Locke Mills, 300	B 7
04051	Lovell, ∆607	B 7
04051	Lovell, 180	B 7
† 04433	Lowell, ∆154	F 5
04652	Lubec, ∆1,949	K 6
04652	Lubec, 900	K 6
† 04730	Ludlow, ∆259	G 3
04654	Machias, ∆2,441	J 6
04654	Machias⊙, 1,368	J 6
04655	Machiasport, ∆887	H 6
04655	Machiasport, 374	H 6
† 04451	Macwahoc, ∆126	G 4
04756	Madawaska, ∆5,585	G 1
04756	Madawaska, 4,452	G 1
04950	Madison, ∆4,278	D 6
04950	Madison, 2,920	D 6
† 04966	Madrid, ∆107	B 6
04351	Manchester, ∆1,331	D 7
04757	Mapleton, ∆1,598	G 2
04758	Mars Hill, ∆1,875	H 2
04758	Mars Hill-Blaine, 1,854	H 2
04759	Masardis, ∆317	G 3
04459	Mattawamkeag, ∆988	G 5
04256	Mechanic Falls, ∆2,193	C 7
04256	Mechanic Falls, 1,872	C 7
04657	Meddybemps, ∆76	J 5
† 04453	Medford, ∆146	F 5
04460	Medway, ∆1,491	G 4
04957	Mercer, ∆313	D 6
04257	Mexico, ∆4,309	B 6
04257	Mexico, 3,325	B 6
04658	Milbridge, ∆1,154	H 6
04461	Milford, ∆1,828	F 6
04461	Milford, 1,519	F 6
04462	Millinocket, ∆7,742	F 4
04462	Millinocket, 7,558	F 4
04463	Milo, ∆2,572	F 5
04463	Milo, 1,514	F 5
04258	Minot, ∆919	C 7
04258	Minot, 250	C 7
04852	Monhegan, ∆44	E 8
04259	Monmouth. ∆2,062	D 7

(continued on following page)

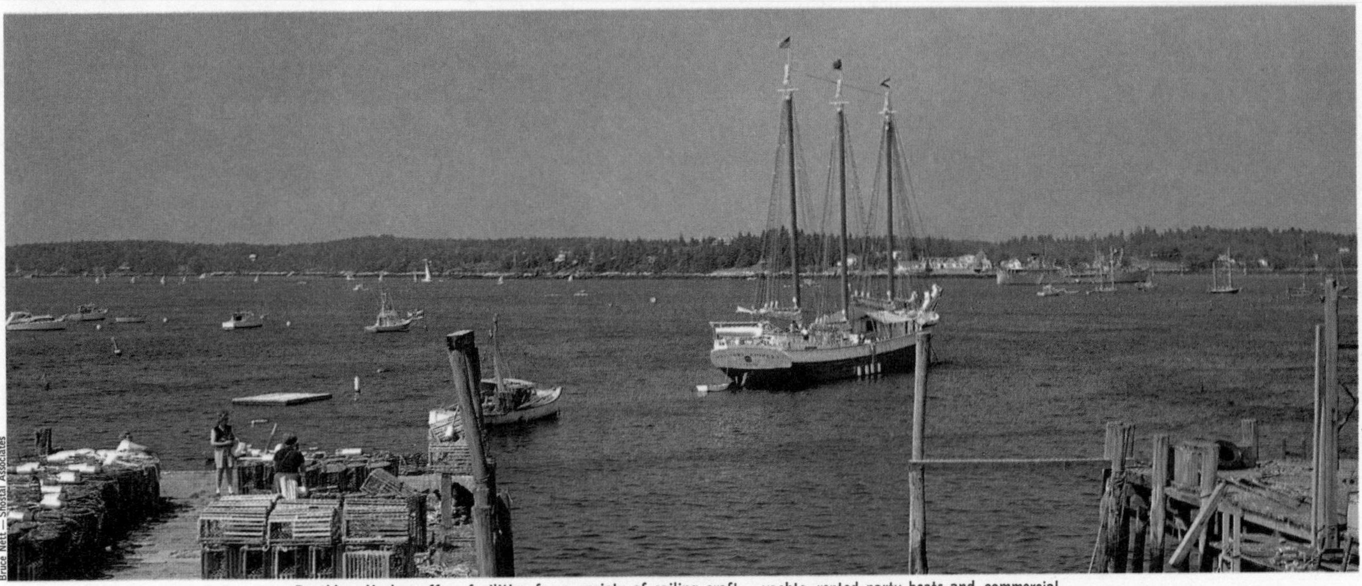

Bruce Nett — Shostal Associates

Boothbay Harbor offers facilities for a variety of sailing craft — yachts, rented party boats and commercial fishermen, all seen here at anchor. This active port rates high among Maine's popular coastal resort towns.

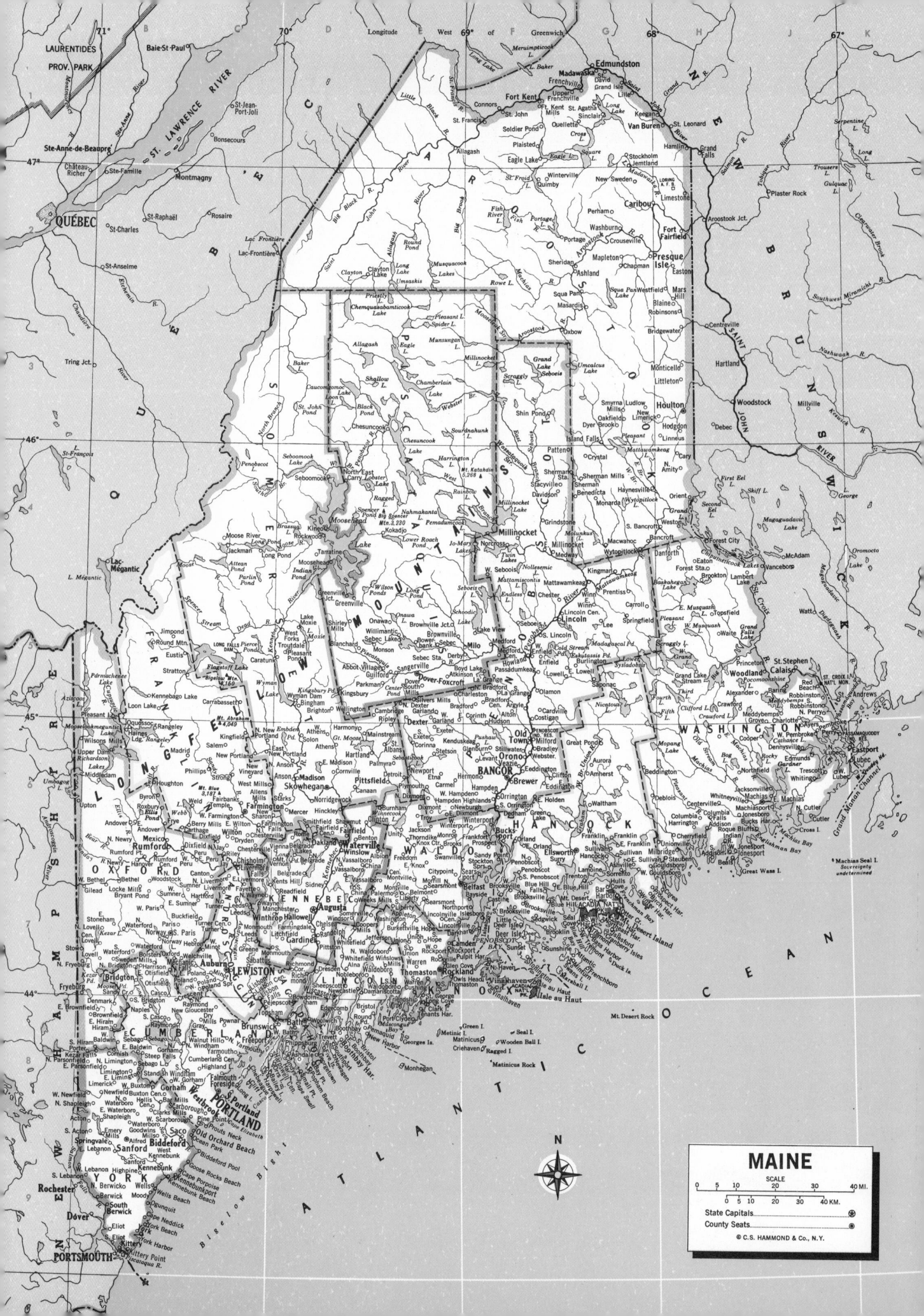

MAINE

SCALE

0 5 10   20   30   40 MI.
0 5 10 20   40 KM.

State Capitals .... ⊛
County Seats .... ⊚

© C.S. HAMMOND & Co., N.Y.

04259 Monmouth, 500 D 7
04951 Monroe, Δ478 E 6
04464 Monson, Δ669 E 5
04760 Monticello, Δ1,072 H 3
04941 Montville, Δ430 E 7
04054 Moody, 500 B 9
04945 Moose River, Δ255 C 4
04952 Morrill, Δ410 E 7
04660 Mount Desert, Δ1,659 G 7
04352 Mount Vernon, Δ680 D 7
04055 Naples, Δ956 B 8
04445 Newburgh, Δ835 F 6
04553 Newcastle, Δ1,076 D 7
04553 Newcastle-Damariscotta, 1,188 E 7
04056 Newfield, Δ458 B 8
04056 Newfield, 165 B 8
04260 New Gloucester, Δ2,811 C 8
04260 New Gloucester, 400 C 8
04554 New Harbor, 580 E 8
04761 New Limerick, Δ427 G 3
04953 Newport, Δ2,260 E 6
04953 Newport, 1,588 E 6
04954 New Portland, Δ559 C 6
04954 New Portland, 201 C 6
04261 Newry, Δ208 B 6
04955 New Sharon, Δ725 C 6
04762 New Sweden, Δ639 G 2
04762 New Sweden, 400 G 2
04956 New Vineyard, Δ444 C 6
04555 Nobleboro, Δ850 D 7
04957 Norridgewock, Δ1,964 D 6
04957 Norridgewock, 1,067 D 6
04958 North Anson 950 D 6
04959 North Belgrade, 300 D 7
03906 North Berwick, Δ2,224 B 9
03906 North Berwick, 1,449 B 9
04057 North Bridgton, 200 B 7
04626 North Cutler, 153 J 6
04662 Northeast Harbor, 700 G 7
04654 Northfield, Δ57 H 6
04058 North Fryeburg, 250 B 7
04853 North Haven, Δ399 F 7
04853 North Haven, 300 F 7
04262 North Jay, 800 C 6
04049 North Limington, 400 B 8
04254 North Livermore, 280 C 7
04663 North Lubec, 250 J 6
04961 North New Portland, 300 C 6
04849 Northport, Δ744 E 7
04664 North Sullivan, 280 G 6
04266 North Turner, 300 C 7
04962 North Vassalboro, 950 D 7
† 04572 North Waldoboro, 250 E 7
04061 North Waterboro, 200 B 8
04267 North Waterford, 217 B 7
† 04284 North Wayne, 175 C 7
04353 North Whitefield, 300 D 7
04062 North Windham, 600 C 8
† 04219 North Woodstock, 400 B 7
† 04096 North Yarmouth, Δ1,383 C 8
† 04096 North Yarmouth, 500 C 8
04268 Norway, Δ3,595 B 7
04268 Norway, 2,430 B 7
04763 Oakfield, Δ836 G 3
04963 Oakland, Δ5,273 D 6
04963 Oakland, 2,261 D 6
03907 Ogunquit, 800 B 9
04064 Old Orchard Beach, Δ5,404 C 9
04064 Old Orchard Beach, 5,273 C 9
04468 Old Town, 9,057 F 6
04964 Oquossoc, 210 B 6
04471 Orient, Δ83 H 4
04472 Orland, Δ1,307 F 6
04472 Orland, 500 F 6
04473 Orono, Δ9,989 F 6
04473 Orono, 9,146 F 6
04474 Orrington, Δ2,702 F 6
04474 Orrington, 250 F 6
04066 Orrs Island, 500 D 8
† 04270 Otisfield, Δ589 B 7
04665 Otter Creek, 350 G 7
04854 Owls Head, Δ1,281 F 7
04764 Oxbow, Δ92 G 3
04270 Oxford, Δ1,892 B 7
04270 Oxford, 550 B 7
04354 Palermo, Δ645 E 7
04965 Palmyra, Δ1,104 E 6
04271 Paris, Δ3,739 B 7
† 04443 Parkman, Δ457 D 5
04475 Passadumkeag, Δ326 F 5
04765 Patten, Δ1,266 F 4
04765 Patten, 1,068 F 4
04067 Pejepscott, 200 D 8
04558 Pemaquid, 160 E 8
04666 Pembroke, Δ700 J 6
04666 Pembroke, 300 J 6
04476 Penobscot, Δ786 F 7
04766 Perham, Δ436 G 2
04667 Perry, Δ878 J 6
04272 Peru, Δ1,345 C 6
04966 Phillips, Δ979 C 6
04562 Phippsburg, Δ1,229 D 8
04562 Phippsburg, 280 D 8
† 04064 Pine Point, 650 C 8
04967 Pittsfield, Δ4,274 E 6
04967 Pittsfield, 3,398 E 6
† 04345 Pittston, Δ1,617 D 7
04969 Plymouth, Δ542 E 6
04273 Poland, Δ2,015 C 7
04273 Poland, 300 C 7
04768 Portage, Δ477 G 2
04855 Port Clyde, 300 E 8
04068 Porter, Δ1,115 B 8
04068 Porter, 225 B 8
* 04101 Portland⊙, 65,116 C 8
Portland, ‡141,625 C 8
04069 Pownal, Δ800 C 8
04477 Prentiss, Δ159 G 5
04769 Presque Isle, 11,452 H 2
04668 Princeton, Δ956 H 5
† 04981 Prospect, Δ358 F 6
04669 Prospect Harbor, 350 H 7
† 04345 Randolph, Δ1,741 D 7
† 04345 Randolph, 1,548 D 7
04970 Rangeley, Δ941 B 6
04970 Rangeley, 600 B 6
04071 Raymond, Δ1,328 B 8
04071 Raymond, 550 B 8
04355 Readfield, Δ1,258 D 7
04355 Readfield, 300 D 7
04670 Red Beach, 210 J 5
04357 Richmond, Δ2,168 D 7
04357 Richmond, 1,449 D 7
† 04357 Richmond Corner, 200 D 7
† 04930 Ripley, Δ297 E 5
04671 Robbinston, Δ396 J 5
04671 Robbinston, 200 J 5
† 04734 Robinsons, 487 H 3
04841 Rockland⊙, 8,505 E 7
04856 Rockport, Δ2,067 F 7
04856 Rockport, 875 F 7
† 04841 Rockville, 250 E 7
04478 Rockwood, 250 D 4
† 04957 Rome, Δ362 D 6
† 04654 Roque Bluffs, Δ153 H 6
04564 Round Pond, 375 E 8
04275 Roxbury, Δ271 B 6
04276 Rumford, Δ9,363 B 6
04276 Rumford, 6,198 B 6
04278 Rumford Center, 325 B 7
04280 Sabattus, 950 C 7
04072 Saco, 11,678 C 8
04772 Saint Agatha, Δ868 G 1
04971 Saint Albans, Δ1,041 E 6
04773 Saint David, 915 G 1
04774 Saint Francis, Δ811 E 1
04857 Saint George, Δ1,639 E 7
04857 Saint George, 250 E 7
† 04743 Saint John, Δ377 F 1
† 04983 Salem, 300 C 6
04972 Sandy Point, 300 F 7
04073 Sanford, Δ10,457 B 9
04073 Sanford, 15,812 B 9
04479 Sangerville, Δ1,107 E 5
04074 Scarborough, Δ7,845 C 8
04074 Scarborough, 500 C 8
04675 Seal Harbor, 336 G 7
04973 Searsmont, Δ624 E 7
04973 Searsmont, 400 E 7
04974 Searsport, Δ1,951 F 7
04974 Searsport, 1,110 F 7
04075 Sebago Lake, 500 B 8
04481 Sebec, Δ325 E 5
04484 Seboeis, Δ63 F 5
04676 Sedgwick, Δ578 F 7
04076 Shapleigh, Δ559 B 8
04975 Shawmut, 250 D 6
04775 Sheridan, 250 F 2
† 04777 Sherman, Δ949 G 4
† 04777 Sherman, 165 G 4
04776 Sherman Mills, 600 G 4
04777 Sherman Station, 300 F 4
04485 Shirley Mills, Δ174 D 5
04485 Shirley Mills, 180 D 5
† 04330 Sidney, Δ1,319 D 7
04779 Sinclair, 260 G 1
04976 Skowhegan, Δ7,601 D 6
04976 Skowhegan⊙, 6,571 D 6
04978 Smithfield, Δ527 D 6
04780 Smyrna Mills, Δ318 G 3
04780 Smyrna Mills, 250 G 3
04781 Soldier Pond, 500 F 1
04979 Solon, Δ712 D 6
† 04341 Somerville, Δ215 D 7
04677 Sorrento, Δ199 G 7
03908 South Berwick, Δ3,488 B 9
03908 South Berwick, 1,863 B 9
04568 South Bristol, Δ664 D 8
04077 South Casco, 200 B 8
04358 South China, 225 D 7
† 03903 South Eliot, 1,635 B 9
04079 South Harpswell, 650 C 8
04080 South Hiram, 175 B 8
† 04862 South Hope, 200 E 7
† 03901 South Lebanon, 200 A 9
† 04259 South Monmouth, 168 D 7
† 04474 South Orrington, 400 F 6
04281 South Paris⊙, 2,315 C 7
† 04569 Southport, Δ473 D 8
04569 Southport, 175 D 8
04106 South Portland, 23,267 C 8
† 04073 South Sanford, 850 B 9
04858 South Thomaston, Δ831 E 7
† 04864 South Union, 180 E 7
† 04572 South Waldoboro, 300 E 7
04081 South Waterford, 320 B 7
04679 Southwest Harbor, Δ1,657 G 7
04082 South Windham, 1,453 C 8
04487 Springfield, Δ336 G 5
04083 Springvale, 2,914 B 9
04782 Stacyville, Δ547 F 4
04084 Standish, Δ3,122 B 8
04084 Standish, 700 B 8
04980 Starks, Δ323 D 6
04085 Steep Falls, 500 B 8
04488 Stetson, Δ395 E 6
04680 Steuben, Δ697 H 6
04680 Steuben, 200 H 6
04489 Stillwater, 600 F 6
04783 Stockholm, Δ388 G 1
04981 Stockton Springs, Δ1,142 F 7
04981 Stockton Springs, 500 F 7
04681 Stonington, Δ1,291 F 7
† 04058 Stow, Δ109 A 7
04982 Stratton, 450 B 5
04983 Strong, Δ1,132 C 6
04682 Sullivan, Δ824 G 6
† 04292 Sumner, Δ525 C 7
04683 Sunset, 170 F 7
† 04627 Sunshine, 175 G 7
04684 Surry, Δ623 F 7
04685 Swans Island, Δ323 G 7
† 04915 Swanville, Δ487 E 6
† 04040 Sweden, Δ110 B 7
04984 Temple, Δ367 C 6
04860 Tenants Harbor, 600 E 8
04861 Thomaston, Δ2,646 E 7
04861 Thomaston, 2,160 E 7
04986 Thorndike, Δ439 E 6
04490 Topsfield, 180 H 5
04086 Topsham, Δ5,022 D 8
04086 Topsham, 2,700 D 8
† 04653 Tremont, Δ1,003 G 7
† 04653 Tremont, 175 G 7
† 04605 Trenton, Δ392 G 7
† 04652 Trescott, 200 J 6
04571 Trevett, 275 D 8
04987 Troy, Δ543 E 6
04282 Turner, Δ2,246 C 7
04282 Turner, 400 C 7
04862 Union, Δ1,189 E 7
04862 Union, 300 E 7
04988 Unity, Δ1,280 E 6
04784 Upper Frenchville, 375 G 1
04261 Upton, Δ54 B 6
04785 Van Buren, Δ3,971 G 1
04785 Van Buren, 3,429 G 1
04491 Vanceboro, Δ263 J 4
04989 Vassalboro, Δ2,618 D 7
04401 Veazie, Δ1,556 F 6
04401 Veazie, 1,174 F 6
04360 Vienna, Δ205 D 6
04863 Vinalhaven, Δ1,135 F 7
04492 Waite, Δ70 H 5
† 04915 Waldo, Δ431 E 7
04572 Waldoboro, Δ3,146 E 7
04572 Waldoboro, 824 E 7
† 04021 Walnut Hill, 400 C 8
† 04605 Waltham, Δ167 G 6
04864 Warren, Δ1,864 E 7
04864 Warren, 770 E 7
04786 Washburn, Δ1,914 G 2
04786 Washburn, 1,098 G 2
04574 Washington, Δ723 E 7
04087 Waterboro, Δ1,208 B 8
04087 Waterboro, 400 B 8
04088 Waterford, Δ760 B 7
04901 Waterville, 18,192 D 6
04284 Wayne, Δ577 D 7
04284 Wayne, 175 D 7
04361 Weeks Mills, 235 E 7
04285 Weld, Δ360 C 6
04990 Wellington, Δ232 D 5
04090 Wells, Δ4,448 B 9
04090 Wells, 950 B 9
04090 Wells Beach, 600 B 9
04686 Wesley, Δ110 H 6
† 04530 West Bath, Δ836 D 8
04286 West Bethel, 155 B 7
04092 Westbrook, 14,444 C 8
† 04617 West Brooksville, 156 F 7
04093 West Buxton, 185 B 8
04493 West Enfield, 500 F 5
04992 West Farmington, 700 C 6
04787 Westfield, Δ517 G 2
† 04634 West Franklin, 350 G 6
† 04345 West Gardiner, Δ1,435 D 7
† 04445 West Hampden, 800 E 6
04649 West Jonesport, 400 H 6
† 04652 West Lubec, 275 J 6
04288 West Minot, 200 C 7
04095 West Newfield, 225 B 8
04494 Weston, Δ162 H 4
04289 West Paris, Δ1,171 B 7
04290 West Peru, 650 C 7
04291 West Poland, 300 C 7
04865 West Rockport, 350 E 7
04074 West Scarborough, 850 C 8
04690 West Tremont, 200 G 7
04362 Whitefield, Δ1,131 D 7
04362 Whitefield, 550 D 7
04691 Whiting, Δ269 J 6
04692 Whitneyville, Δ155 H 6
† 04443 Willimantic, Δ126 E 5
04294 Wilton, Δ3,802 C 6
04294 Wilton, 2,225 C 6
04363 Windsor, Δ1,097 D 7
04495 Winn, Δ516 G 5
04495 Winn, 250 G 5
04901 Winslow, Δ7,299 D 6
04901 Winslow, 5,389 D 6
04693 Winter Harbor, Δ1,028 G 7
04496 Winterport, Δ1,963 F 6
04496 Winterport, 900 F 6
04788 Winterville, Δ164 F 2
04364 Winthrop, Δ4,335 C 7
04364 Winthrop, 2,571 C 7
04578 Wiscasset⊙, Δ2,244 D 8
04694 Woodland, 1,534 H 5
04579 Woolwich, Δ1,710 D 8
† 04920 Wyman Dam, 300 D 5
04497 Wytopitlock, 200 G 4
04096 Yarmouth, Δ4,854 C 8
04096 Yarmouth, 2,421 C 8
03909 York, Δ5,690 B 9
03909 York, 2,912 B 9
03910 York Beach, 900 B 9
03911 York Harbor, 950 B 9

⊙ County seat.
‡ Population of metropolitan area.
Δ Population of town or township.
† Zip of nearest p.o.
* Multiple zips

Agriculture, Industry and Resources

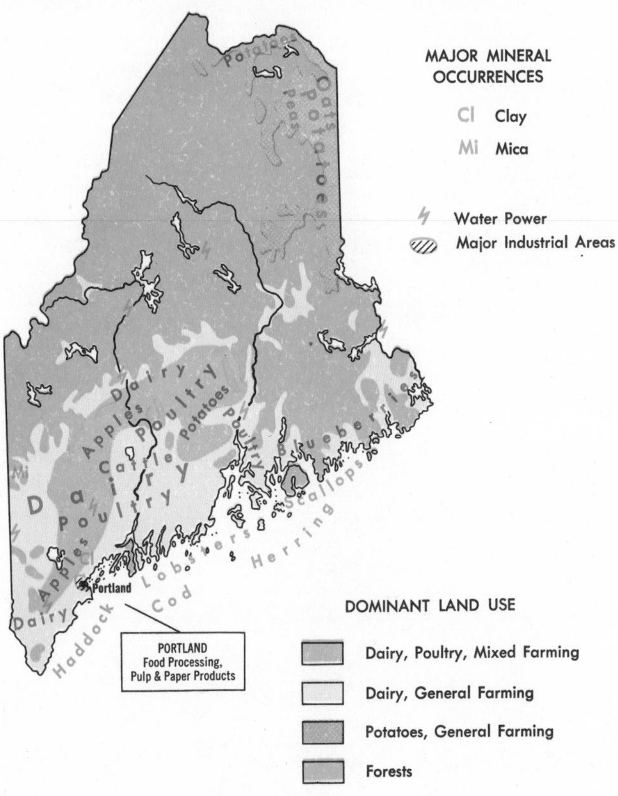
MAJOR MINERAL OCCURRENCES
Cl Clay
Mi Mica
Water Power
Major Industrial Areas
Potatoes
Oats
Potatoes
Dairy
Poultry
Potatoes
Apples
Cattle
Dairy
Poultry
Blueberries
Scallops
Lobsters
Herring
Cod
Haddock
Portland
PORTLAND
Food Processing,
Pulp & Paper Products
DOMINANT LAND USE
Dairy, Poultry, Mixed Farming
Dairy, General Farming
Potatoes, General Farming
Forests

Topography

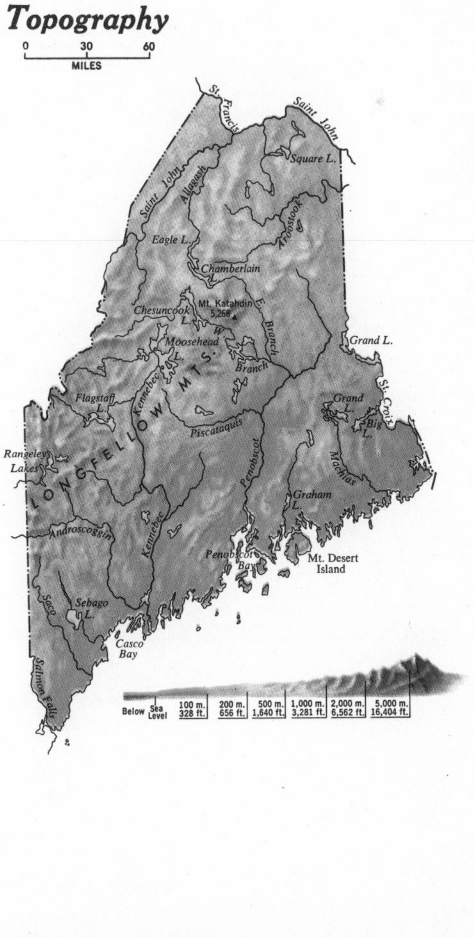
0 30 60
MILES
St. Francis
Saint John
Square L.
Saint John
Allagash
Aroostook
Eagle L.
Chamberlain
Mt. Katahdin 5,268
Chesuncook L.
Moosehead L.
E. Branch
Grand L.
St. Croix
Flagstaff
Kennebec
LONGFELLOW MTS.
Piscataquis
Grand L.
Big L.
Rangeley Lakes
Penobscot
Machias
Graham L.
Androscoggin
Kennebec
Penobscot Bay
Mt. Desert Island
Saco
Sebago L.
Casco Bay
Salmon Falls
Below Sea Level
100 m. 328 ft.
200 m. 656 ft.
500 m. 1,640 ft.
1,000 m. 3,281 ft.
2,000 m. 6,562 ft.
5,000 m. 16,404 ft.

MARYLAND
COUNTIES

Allegany, 84,044 .... C 2
Anne Arundel, 297,539 .... M 4
Baltimore, 621,077 .... M 3
Baltimore (city county), 905,759 .. M 3
Calvert, 20,682 .... M 6
Caroline, 19,781 .... P 5
Carroll, 69,006 .... K 2
Cecil, 53,291 .... P 2
Charles, 47,678 .... K 6
Dorchester, 29,405 .... O 7
Frederick, 84,927 .... J 3
Garrett, 21,476 .... A 2
Harford, 115,378 .... N 2
Howard, 61,911 .... L 4
Kent, 16,146 .... O 3
Montgomery, 522,809 .... J 4
Prince Georges, 660,567 .... L 5
Queen Annes, 18,422 .... P 4
Saint Marys, 47,388 .... M 7
Somerset, 18,924 .... R 8
Talbot, 23,682 .... O 5
Washington, 103,829 .... G 2
Wicomico, 54,236 .... R 7
Worcester, 24,442 .... S 8

CITIES and TOWNS

Zip	Name/Pop.	Key
21001	Aberdeen, 12,375	O 2
21009	Abingdon, 3,000	N 3
21520	Accident, 237	A 2
20607	Accokeek, 450	L 6
21710	Adamstown, 265	H 3
21810	Allen, 200	R 7
† 21043	Allview, 2,314	L 3
21401	Annapolis (cap.)⊙, 29,592	M 5
20701	Annapolis Junction, 775	M 4
† 21782	Antietam, 150	H 3
20608	Aquasco, 950	L 6
* 20785	Ardmore, 500	G 4
20015	Aspen Hill, 16,799	K 4
* 21201	Baltimore, 905,759	M 3
	Baltimore, ‡2,070,670	M 3
21607	Barclay, 187	P 4
20703	Barnesville, 162	J 4
20610	Barstow, 500	M 6
21521	Barton, 723	B 2
† 21901	Bayview, 250	P 2
21014	Bel Air⊙, 6,307	N 2
20611	Bel Alton, 675	L 7
† 21662	Bellevue, 300	O 6
20705	Beltsville, 8,912	G 3
20612	Benedict, 700	M 6
21811	Berlin, 1,942	T 7
† 20740	Berwyn Heights, 3,934	G 4
20014	Bethesda, 71,621	E 4
21609	Bethlehem, 200	P 6
21610	Betterton, 327	O 3
21611	Bishops Head, 250	O 7
21813	Bishopville, 300	T 7
21814	Bivalve, 450	P 7
20710	Bladensburg, 7,488	G 4
21523	Bloomington, 235	B 3
21713	Boonsboro, 1,410	H 2
† 21532	Borden Shaft, 208	B 2
21020	Boring, 283	L 2
† 20027	Boulevard Heights, 500	F 5
20678	Bowens, 250	M 6
20715	Bowie, 35,028	L 4
20720	Boyds, 300	J 4
21612	Bozman, 500	N 5
20613	Brandywine, 525	L 6
20722	Brentwood, 3,426	F 4
21715	Brownsville, 185	H 3
21716	Brunswick, 3,566	H 3
21717	Buckeystown, 400	J 3
21718	Burkittsville, 221	H 3
20730	Burtonsville, 3,000	L 4
20618	Bushwood, 675	L 7
21023	Butler, 150	M 2
20731	Cabin John, 2,500	E 4
20619	California, 350	M 7
† 20705	Calverton, 6,453	L 4
21613	Cambridge⊙, 11,595	O 6
20031	Camp Springs, 22,776	G 6
20027	Capitol Heights, 2,852	G 5
21024	Cardiff, 510	N 2
* 20780	Carrollton, 13,395	G 4
21025	Carrollton, 174	L 2
† 21034	Castleton, 675	N 2
† 21788	Catoctin Furnace, 516	J 2
21228	Catonsville, 54,812	M 3
21720	Cavetown, 325	H 2
21913	Cecilton, 581	P 3
† 20767	Cedar Grove, 300	K 4
† 20027	Cedar Heights, 6,049	G 5
21617	Centreville⊙, 1,853	O 4
21816	Chance, 500	P 8
20621	Chaptico, 300	M 7
21914	Charlestown, 721	P 2
20622	Charlotte Hall, 200	M 7
21027	Chase, 900	N 3
20623	Cheltenham, 950	L 6
† 21921	Cherry Hill, 214	P 2
20732	Chesapeake Beach, 934	N 6
21915	Chesapeake City, 1,031	P 2
21619	Chester, 950	N 5
21620	Chestertown⊙, 3,476	O 4
20785	Cheverly, 6,696	G 4
20015	Chevy Chase, 16,424	E 4
21721	Chewsville, 350	H 2
20783	Chillum, 35,656	F 4
21623	Church Hill, 247	O 4
21028	Churchville, 500	N 2
21624	Claiborne, 150	N 5
20734	Clarksburg, 400	J 4
21029	Clarksville, 500	L 4
21722	Clear Spring, 499	G 2
20624	Clements, 800	L 7
20735	Clinton, 1,900	G 6
21030	Cockeysville, 2,900	M 3
20740	College Park, 26,156	G 4
* 20722	Colmar Manor, 1,715	F 4
21917	Colora, 500	O 2

20626	Coltons Point, 310	M 8
21043	Columbia, 8,815	L 3
20627	Compton, 500	M 7
21918	Conowingo, 150	O 2
21723	Cooksville, 497	K 3
† 20027	Coral Hills, 7,105	G 5
21625	Cordova, 365	O 5
21524	Corriganville, 850	C 2
† 20722	Cottage City, 993	F 4
† 20611	Cox Station (Bel Alton), 675	L 7
† 21788	Creagerstown, 240	J 2
21525	Crellin, 500	A 3
21502	Cresaptown, 1,731	C 2
21817	Crisfield, 3,078	P 9
21627	Crocheron, 150	O 8
21113	Crofton, 4,478	M 4
21032	Crownsville, 1,900	M 4
21628	Crumpton, 375	P 4
21502	Cumberland⊙, 29,724	D 2
20750	Damascus, 2,638	K 3
20628	Dameron, 500	N 8
21820	Dames Quarter, 300	P 8
25425	Dargan, 245	H 3
21034	Darlington, 800	N 2
20760	Darnestown, 950	J 4
21035	Davidsonville, 250	M 5

20751	Deale, 1,059	M 5
21821	Deal Island, 800	P 8
21550	Deer Park, 310	A 3
† 19940	Delmar, 1,191	R 7
21629	Denton⊙, 1,561	P 5
20855	Derwood, 450	K 4
20753	Dickerson, 500	J 4
20028	District Heights, 8,424	G 5
21710	Doubs, 273	J 3
21795	Downsville, 255	G 2
20630	Drayden, 450	N 8
21154	Dublin, 366	N 2
21222	Dundalk, 85,377	N 3
20608	Eagle Harbor, 200	M 6
21146	Earleigh Heights, 1,500	M 4
21631	East New Market, 251	P 6
21601	Easton⊙, 6,809	O 5
21528	Eckhart Mines, 900	C 2
21040	Edgewood, 8,551	N 3
20781	Edmonston, 1,441	F 4
21784	Eldersburg, 1,739	L 3
21920	Elk Mills, 500	P 2
21901	Elk Neck, 700	P 2
21227	Elkridge, 4,900	M 4
21921	Elkton⊙, 5,362	P 2
21529	Ellerslie, 950	C 2

21043	Ellicott City⊙, 9,506	L 3
21727	Emmitsburg, 1,532	J 2
21221	Essex, 38,193	N 3
21824	Ewell, 350	O 9
21620	Fairlee, 300	O 4
† 20027	Fairmont Heights, 1,972	G 5
21047	Fallston, 617	N 2
21632	Federalsburg, 1,917	P 6
21061	Ferndale, 9,929	M 4
21048	Finksburg, 450	L 3
21634	Fishing Creek, 595	N 7
21530	Flintstone, 395	D 2
† 20907	Forest Glen, 1,900	F 4
† 20001	Forest Heights, 3,600	F 5
21050	Forest Hill, 450	N 2
20028	Forestville, 16,152	G 5
20013	Fort Foote, 700	F 6
20735	Fort Washington, 1,650	L 6
21740	Fountain Head, 2,029	H 2
21760	Foxville, 400	J 2
21701	Frederick⊙, 23,641	J 3
21053	Freeland, 500	M 2
21531	Friendsville, 566	A 2
21157	Frizzellburg, 300	L 3
21532	Frostburg, 7,327	C 2
21826	Fruitland, 2,315	R 7

21734	Funkstown, 1,051	H 2
20760	Gaithersburg, 8,344	K 4
21635	Galena, 361	P 3
21054	Gambrills, 460	M 4
20766	Garrett Park, 1,258	E 3
21055	Garrison, 950	L 3
20767	Germantown, 260	J 4
21829	Girdletree, 850	S 8
20801	Glenarden, 4,502	G 4
21057	Glen Arm, 350	N 3
21061	Glen Burnie, 38,608	M 4
20768	Glen Echo, 297	E 4
† 20013	Glen Echo Heights, 2,025	E 4
20737	Glenelg, 400	L 3
21071	Glyndon-Reisterstown, 14,037	L 3
21636	Goldsboro, 231	P 4
† 20715	Good Luck, 10,584	G 4
21788	Graceham, 300	J 2
21163	Granite, 950	L 3
21536	Grantsville, 517	B 2
21638	Grasonville, 1,182	O 5
20770	Greenbelt, 18,199	G 4
21122	Green Haven, 1,841	M 4
21072	Greenmount, 325	L 2
21639	Greensboro, 1,173	P 5

21740	Hagerstown⊙, 35,862	H 2
† 21740	Halfway, 6,106	G 2
20850	Halpine, 5,912	K 4
21074	Hampstead, 961	L 2
21750	Hancock, 1,832	E 2
21201	Hanover, 500	M 4
21787	Harney, 250	J 2
21078	Havre de Grace, 9,791	O 2
21830	Hebron, 705	R 7
21080	Henryton, 400	L 3
21111	Hereford, 680	M 2
21753	Highfield, 500	J 2
20901	Hillandale, 19,520	F 4
† 20001	Hillcrest Heights, 24,037	F 5
21641	Hillsboro, 177	P 5
20636	Hollywood, 500	M 7
21642	Hoopersville, 300	O 8
20637	Hughesville, 850	L 6
20639	Huntingtown, 450	M 6
21643	Hurlock, 1,056	P 6
† 21864	Hursley Station (Stockton), 500	S 8
20734	Hyattstown, 150	J 4
* 20780	Hyattsville, 14,998	F 4
20640	Indian Head, 5,000	K 6
21644	Ingleside, 180	P 4

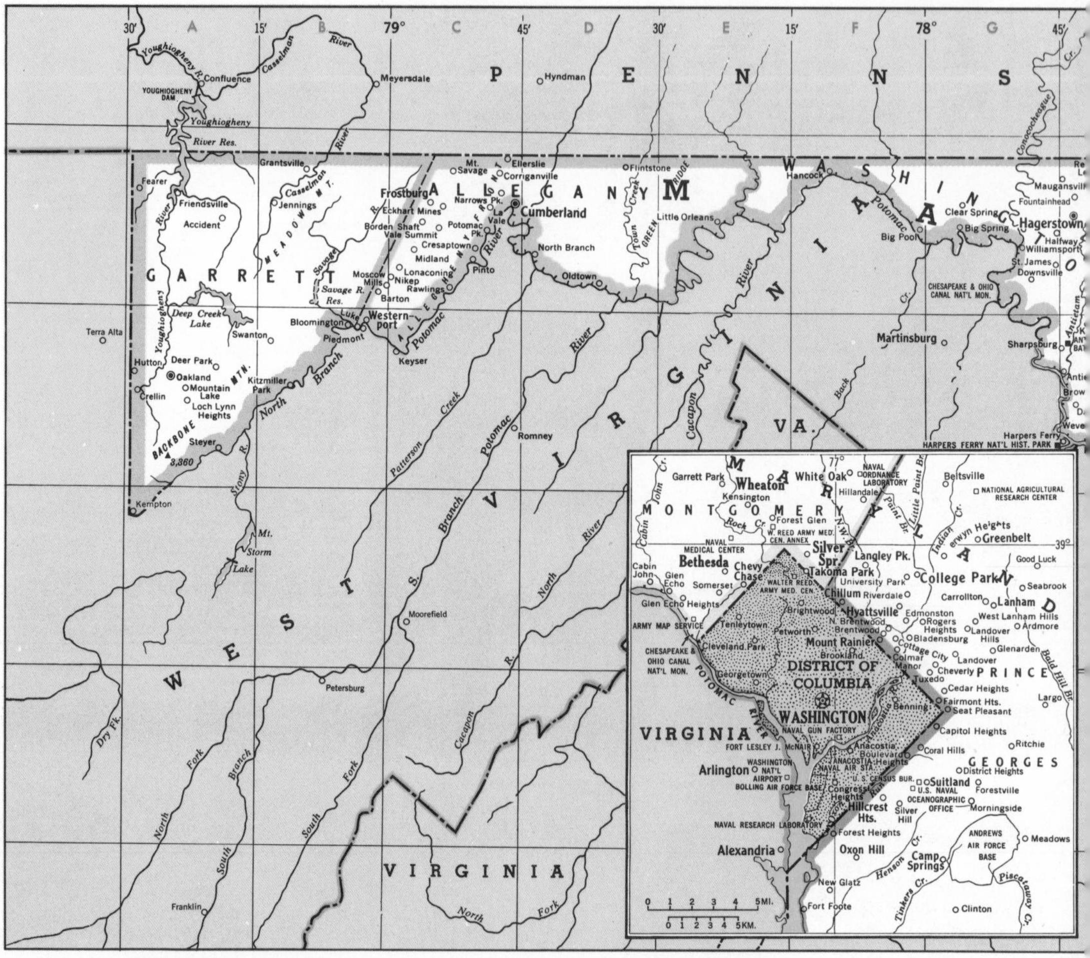

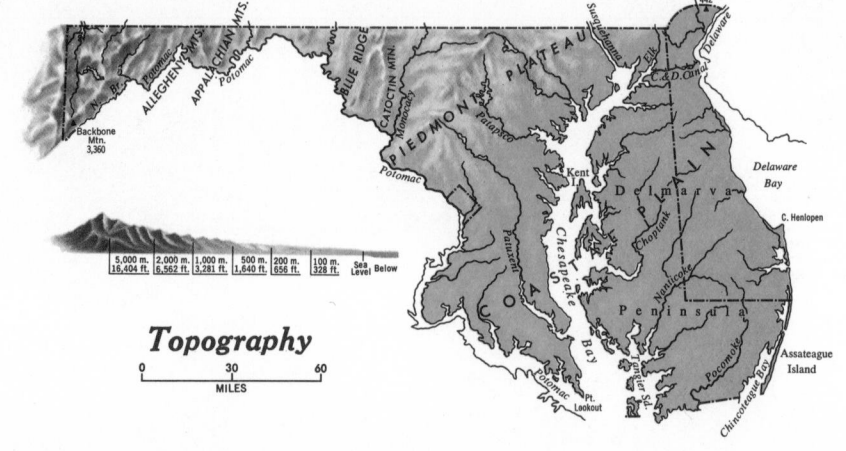

Topography

0   30   60
MILES

MARYLAND
AREA 10,577 sq. mi.
POPULATION 3,922,399
CAPITAL Annapolis
LARGEST CITY Baltimore
HIGHEST POINT Backbone Mtn. 3,360 ft.
SETTLED IN 1634
ADMITTED TO UNION April 28, 1788
POPULAR NAME Old Line State; Free State
STATE FLOWER Black-eyed Susan
STATE BIRD Baltimore Oriole

DELAWARE
AREA 2,057 sq. mi.
POPULATION 548,104
CAPITAL Dover
LARGEST CITY Wilmington
HIGHEST POINT Ebright Road 442 ft.
SETTLED IN 1627
ADMITTED TO UNION December 7, 1787
POPULAR NAME First State; Diamond State
STATE FLOWER Peach Blossom
STATE BIRD Blue Hen Chicken

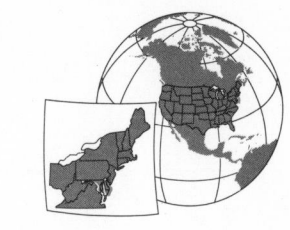

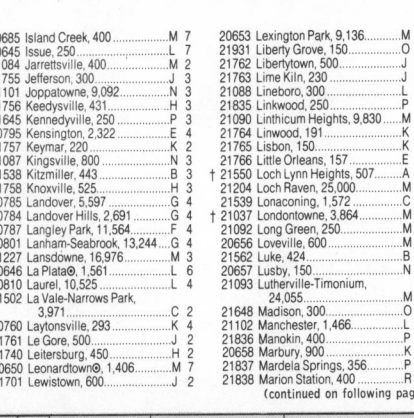

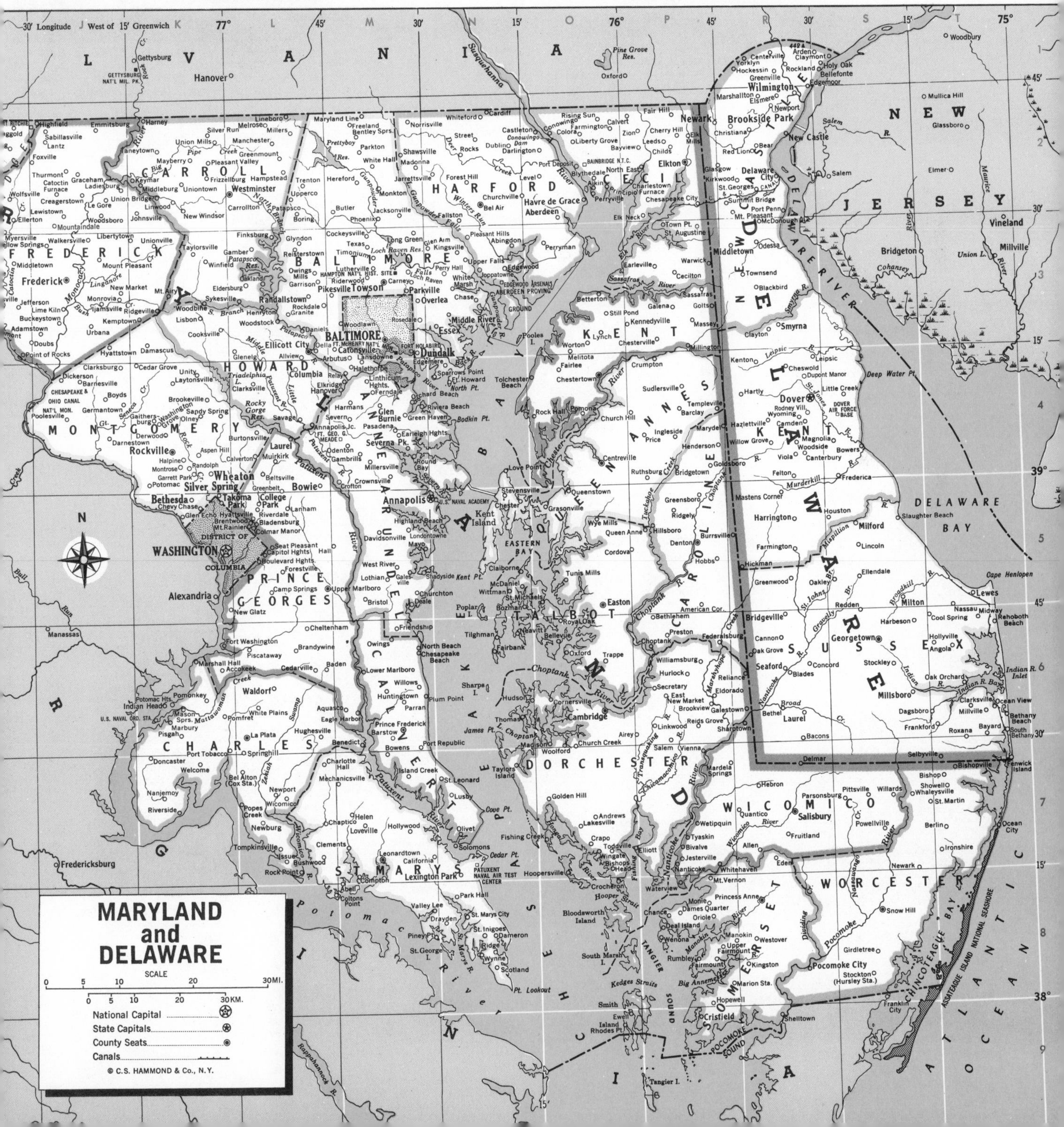

MARYLAND
and
DELAWARE

SCALE

0 5 10   20   30 MI.

0 5 10   20   30 KM.

National Capital .... ⊛
State Capitals .... ⊛
County Seats .... ◉
Canals ....

© C.S. Hammond & Co., N.Y.

MARYLAND (continued)

- † 20616 Marshall Hall, 325 ... K 6
- 21649 Marydel, 176 ... P 4
- 21105 Maryland Line, 250 ... M 2
- 21650 Massey, 220 ... P 3
- 21767 Maugansville, 1,069 ... H 2
- 21106 Mayo, 2,154 ... M 5
- 21647 McDaniel, 325 ... N 5
- † 20870 Meadows, 200 ... G 5
- 20659 Mechanicsville, 784 ... M 7
- 21768 Middleburg, 200 ... K 2
- 21220 Middle River, 19,935 ... N 3
- 21769 Middletown, 1,262 ... J 3
- 21542 Midland, 665 ... C 2
- 21108 Millersville, 380 ... M 4
- 21651 Millington, 474 ... P 3
- 21111 Monkton, 307 ... M 2
- 21770 Monrovia, 300 ... J 3
- † 20850 Montrose, 6,140 ... K 4
- † 20028 Morningside, 1,665 ... G 5
- † 21521 Moscow Mills, 275 ... B 2
- † 21701 Mountaindale, 400 ... J 2
- 21550 Mountain Lake Park, 1,263 ... A 3
- 21771 Mount Airy, 1,825 ... K 3
- † 21701 Mount Pleasant, 400 ... J 3
- 20822 Mount Rainier, 8,180 ... F 4
- 21545 Mount Savage, 1,413 ... C 2
- † 21853 Mount Vernon, 900 ... P 8
- † 20705 Muirkirk, 950 ... L 4
- 21773 Myersville, 450 ... H 3
- 20662 Nanjemoy, 238 ... K 7
- 21840 Nanticoke, 400 ... P 7
- † 21502 Narrows Park-La Vale, 3,971 ... C 2
- 21652 Neavitt, 241 ... N 6
- 21841 Newark, 800 ... S 7
- 20664 Newburg, 550 ... L 7
- † 20013 New Glatz, 950 ... F 6
- 21774 New Market, 339 ... J 3
- 21776 New Windsor, 788 ... K 2
- 21546 Nikep, 400 ... C 2
- 20831 North Beach, 761 ... N 6
- † 20722 North Brentwood, 758 ... F 4
- 21901 North East, 1,818 ... P 2
- 21550 Oakland⊙, 1,786 ... A 3
- 21550 Oakland, 1,256 ... L 3
- 21842 Ocean City, 1,493 ... T 7
- 21113 Odenton, 5,989 ... M 4
- † 21043 Oella, 600 ... L 3
- 21555 Oldtown, 400 ... D 2
- 20832 Olney, 2,138 ... K 4
- † 21122 Orchard Beach, 200 ... M 4
- 21206 Overlea, 13,086 ... N 3
- 20836 Owings, 700 ... M 6
- 21117 Owings Mills, 7,360 ... L 3
- 21654 Oxford, 750 ... O 6
- 20021 Oxon Hill, 11,974 ... F 6
- 20667 Park Hall, 600 ... N 8
- 21120 Parkton, 290 ... M 2
- 21234 Parkville, 33,897 ... M 3
- † 20639 Parran, 200 ... M 6
- 21849 Parsonsburg, 200 ... R 7
- 21122 Pasadena, 2,380 ... M 4
- 21127 Patapsco, 160 ... L 2
- 21128 Perry Hall, 5,446 ... N 3
- 21130 Perryman, 665 ... O 3
- 21903 Perryville, 2,091 ... O 2
- 21131 Phoenix, 165 ... M 2
- 21208 Pikesville, 25,395 ... M 3
- 20674 Piney Point, 950 ... M 8
- 21556 Pinto, 165 ... C 2
- 20640 Pisgah, 650 ... K 6
- 21850 Pittsville, 477 ... S 7
- † 21087 Pleasant Hills, 1,754 ... N 3
- 21851 Pocomoke City, 3,573 ... R 8
- 21777 Point of Rocks, 400 ... J 3
- 20675 Pomfret, 600 ... L 6
- 20837 Poolesville, 349 ... J 4
- 21904 Port Deposit, 906 ... O 2
- 20677 Port Tobacco, 590 ... K 6
- 20854 Potomac (Potomac Valley), 5,094 ... K 4
- 20640 Potomac Heights, 1,983 ... K 6
- † 21502 Potomac Park, 2,253 ... C 2
- 21852 Powellville, 450 ... S 7
- 21655 Preston, 509 ... P 6
- 20678 Prince Frederick⊙, 950 ... M 6
- 21853 Princess Anne⊙, 975 ... P 8
- 21856 Quantico, 200 ... R 7
- 21657 Queen Anne, 292 ... O 5
- 21658 Queenstown, 387 ... O 5
- 21133 Randallstown, 33,683 ... L 3
- † 20853 Randolph, 13,233 ... K 4
- 21557 Rawlings, 600 ... C 2
- 21136 Reisterstown-Glyndon, 14,037 ... L 3
- 21139 Riderwood, 8,000 ... M 3
- 20680 Ridge, 550 ... N 8
- 21660 Ridgely, 822 ... P 5
- 21911 Rising Sun, 956 ... O 2
- † 20013 Ritchie, 950 ... G 5
- 20840 Riverdale, 5,724 ... F 4
- 21122 Riviera Beach, 7,464 ... N 4
- 21661 Rock Hall, 1,125 ... O 4
- 20682 Rock Point, 300 ... L 7
- * 20850 Rockville⊙, 41,564 ... K 4
- † 20780 Rogers Heights, 3,000 ... G 4
- 21779 Rohrersville, 500 ... H 3
- 21237 Rosedale, 19,417 ... M 3
- 21662 Royal Oak, 600 ... O 6
- 21780 Sabillasville, 200 ... J 2
- 20684 Saint Inigoes, 750 ... N 8
- 21781 Saint James, 400 ... G 2
- 20685 Saint Leonard, 244 ... N 7
- 20686 Saint Marys City, 1,900 ... N 8
- 21663 Saint Michaels, 1,456 ... N 5
- 21801 Salisbury⊙, 15,252 ... R 7
- 20860 Sandy Spring, 500 ... K 4
- 20863 Savage, 2,116 ... L 4
- 20687 Scotland, 660 ... N 8
- 20801 Seabrook-Lanham, 13,244 ... G 4
- 20027 Seat Pleasant, 7,217 ... G 5
- 21664 Secretary, 352 ... P 6
- 21146 Severna Park, 16,358 ... M 4
- 20867 Shady Side, 1,562 ... N 5
- 21782 Sharpsburg, 833 ... G 3
- 21861 Sharptown, 660 ... R 6

J. C. Maycock — Shostal Associates

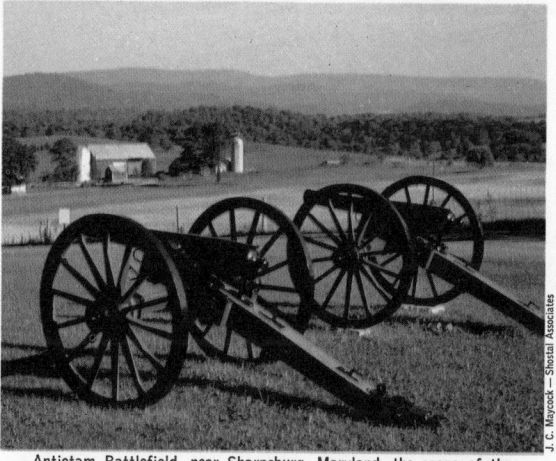

Antietam Battlefield, near Sharpsburg, Maryland, the scene of the country's bloodiest one-day battle on September 17, 1862. A national battlefield site today, it is surrounded by farms, some of whose cattle graze among the cannons and monuments.

Dorothy Bacheller

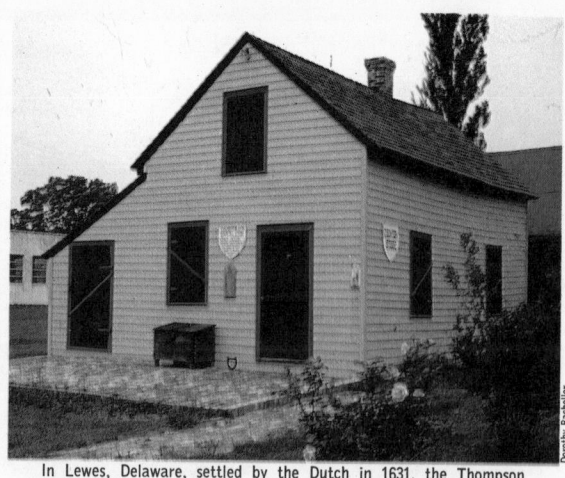

In Lewes, Delaware, settled by the Dutch in 1631, the Thompson Country Store sign establishes its origin as c.1800. The home of generations of Delaware River ship pilots, this seafaring town survives a history of shipwreck, bombardment and plundering.

- 21862 Showell, 250 ... T 7
- 20023 Silver Hill-Suitland, 30,355 ... F 5
- * 20901 Silver Spring, 77,496 ... F 4
- 21783 Smithsburg, 671 ... H 2
- 21863 Snow Hill⊙, 2,201 ... S 8
- 20688 Solomons, 250 ... N 7
- † 20015 Somerset, 1,303 ... E 4
- 21666 Stevensville, 500 ... N 5
- 21667 Still Pond, 250 ... O 3
- 21864 Stockton, 500 ... S 8
- 21154 Street, 200 ... N 2
- 21668 Sudlersville, 417 ... P 4
- 20023 Suitland-Silver Hill, 30,355 ... F 5
- 21561 Swanton, 223 ... A 3
- 21784 Sykesville, 1,399 ... K 3
- 20012 Takoma Park, 18,455 ... F 4
- 21787 Taneytown, 1,731 ... K 2
- 21669 Taylors Island, 375 ... N 7
- 21788 Thurmont, 2,359 ... J 2
- 21671 Tilghman, 950 ... N 6
- 21093 Timonium-Lutherville, 24,055 ... M 3
- 21672 Toddville, 300 ... O 7
- 21204 Towson⊙, 77,809 ... M 3
- 21673 Trappe, 426 ... O 6
- 20781 Tuxedo, 500 ... G 5
- 21791 Union Bridge, 904 ... K 2
- 21157 Uniontown, 250 ... K 2
- 21792 Unionville, 250 ... K 3
- † 20740 University Park, 2,926 ... F 4
- 21155 Upperco, 500 ... L 2
- 21867 Upper Fairmount, 300 ... P 8
- 21156 Upper Falls, 900 ... N 3
- 20870 Upper Marlboro⊙, 646 ... M 5
- 20692 Valley Lee, 600 ... M 8
- 21869 Vienna, 358 ... P 7
- 20601 Waldorf, 7,368 ... L 6
- 21793 Walkersville, 1,269 ... J 3
- 21912 Warwick, 550 ... P 3
- 20880 Washington Grove, 688 ... K 4
- 20693 Welcome, 438 ... K 7
- 21870 Wenona, 323 ... P 8
- 21562 Westernport, 3,106 ... B 3
- † 20784 West Lanham Hills, 950 ... G 4
- 21157 Westminster⊙, 7,207 ... L 2
- 21871 Westover, 450 ... R 8
- 20881 West River, 796 ... M 5
- 20902 Wheaton, 66,247 ... E 3
- 21160 Whiteford, 500 ... N 2
- 21161 White Hall, 350 ... M 2
- 21162 White Marsh, 500 ... N 3
- † 20901 White Oak, 19,769 ... F 3
- 20695 White Plains, 1,600 ... L 6
- 21874 Willards, 494 ... S 7
- 21674 Williamsburg, 300 ... P 6
- 21795 Williamsport, 2,270 ... G 2
- 21675 Wingate, 200 ... O 7
- 21676 Wittman, 500 ... N 5
- 21797 Woodbine, 872 ... K 3
- † 21201 Woodlawn, 28,811 ... M 3
- 21798 Woodsboro, 439 ... J 2
- 21163 Woodstock, 700 ... L 3
- 21677 Woolford, 295 ... O 7
- 21678 Worton, 315 ... O 3
- 21679 Wye Mills, 300 ... O 5
- † 21701 Yellow Springs, 940 ... H 3

DELAWARE

COUNTIES

- Kent, 81,892 ... R 4
- New Castle, 385,856 ... R 2
- Sussex, 80,356 ... S 6

CITIES and TOWNS

Zip *Name/Pop.* *Key*

- † 19801 Arden, 3,340 ... R 1
- 19701 Bear, 200 ... R 2
- 19809 Bellefonte, 1,442 ... S 1
- 19930 Bethany Beach, 189 ... T 6
- 19931 Bethel, 219 ... R 6
- † 19973 Blades, 632 ... R 6
- 19993 Bridgeville, 1,317 ... R 6
- 19711 Brookside Park, 7,856 ... R 2
- 19934 Camden, 1,241 ... R 4
- † 19801 Centerville, 1,260 ... R 1
- 19936 Cheswold, 286 ... R 4
- 19702 Christiana, 550 ... R 2
- 19937 Clarksville, 350 ... T 6
- 19703 Claymont, 6,584 ... S 1
- 19938 Clayton, 1,015 ... R 3
- 19930 Dagsboro, 375 ... S 6
- 19706 Delaware City, 2,024 ... R 2
- 19940 Delmar, 943 ... R 7
- 19901 Dover (cap.)⊙, 17,488 ... R 4
- † 19901 Dupont Manor, 1,256 ... R 4
- † 19801 Edgemoor, 2,100 ... S 1
- 19941 Ellendale, 399 ... S 5
- † 19801 Elsmere, 8,415 ... R 2
- 19943 Felton, 495 ... R 4
- 19945 Frankford, 635 ... S 6
- 19946 Frederica, 878 ... S 4
- 19947 Georgetown⊙, 1,844 ... S 6
- 19807 Greenville, 230 ... R 1
- 19950 Greenwood, 654 ... R 5
- 19951 Harbeson, 312 ... S 6
- 19952 Harrington, 2,407 ... R 5
- 19953 Hartly, 180 ... R 4
- 19707 Hockessin, 950 ... R 1
- † 19801 Holly Oak, 1,140 ... S 1
- 19954 Houston, 317 ... S 5
- 19955 Kenton, 205 ... R 4
- 19708 Kirkwood, 450 ... R 2
- 19956 Laurel, 2,408 ... R 6
- 19958 Lewes, 2,563 ... T 5
- 19960 Lincoln, 757 ... S 5
- 19961 Little Creek, 215 ... S 4
- 19962 Magnolia, 319 ... R 4
- 19808 Marshallton, 1,240 ... R 2
- 19709 Middletown, 2,644 ... R 3
- 19963 Milford, 5,314 ... S 5
- 19966 Millsboro, 1,073 ... S 6
- 19967 Millville, 224 ... T 6
- 19968 Milton, 1,490 ... S 5
- 19711 Newark, 20,757 ... P 2
- 19720 New Castle, 4,814 ... R 2
- 19804 Newport, 1,366 ... R 2
- 19970 Ocean View, 411 ... T 6
- 19730 Odessa, 547 ... R 3
- 19731 Port Penn, 325 ... R 2
- 19971 Rehoboth Beach, 1,614 ... T 6
- 19901 Rodney Village, 2,127 ... R 4
- 19733 Saint Georges, 450 ... R 2
- 19973 Seaford, 5,537 ... R 6
- 19975 Selbyville, 1,099 ... S 7
- 19977 Smyrna, 4,243 ... R 3
- 19734 Townsend, 505 ... R 3
- 19979 Viola, 154 ... R 4
- 19801 Wilmington⊙, 80,386 ... R 2
- Wilmington, ‡498,977 ... R 2
- 19980 Woodside, 223 ... R 4
- 19934 Wyoming, 1,062 ... R 4
- 19736 Yorklyn, 300 ... R 1

DISTRICT OF COLUMBIA

CITIES and TOWNS

Zip *Name/Pop.* *Key*

- 20007 Georgetown, ... E 5
- * 20001 Washington, D.C. (cap.), U.S. 756,510 ... F 5
- Washington, ‡2,861,123 ... F 5

⊙ County seat.
‡ Population of metropolitan area.
† Zip of nearest p.o.
* Multiple zips

Agriculture, Industry and Resources

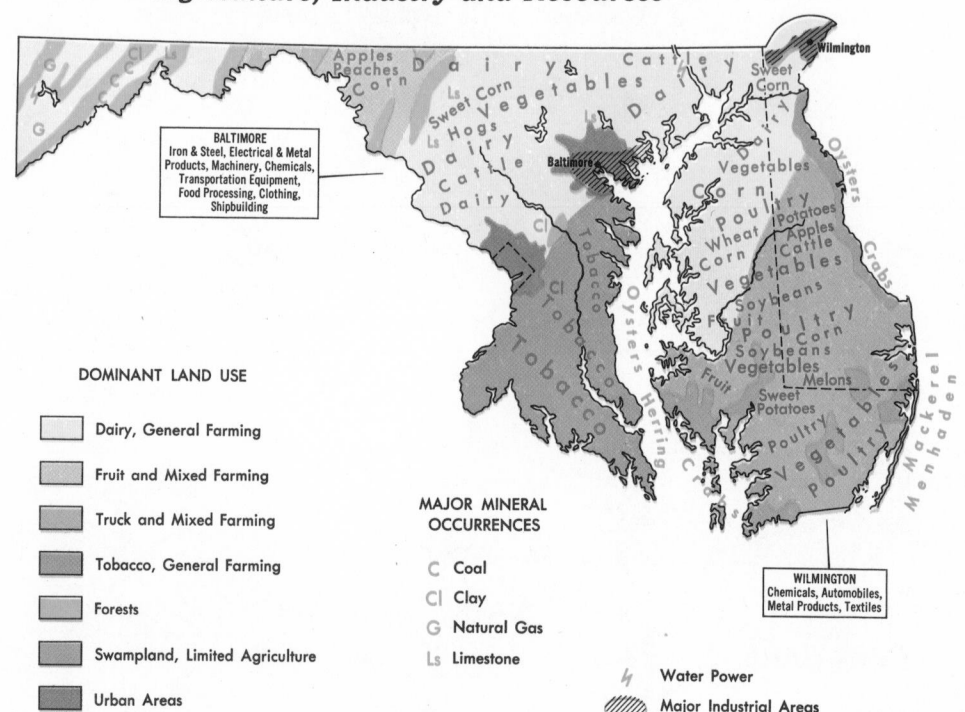

Apples
Peaches
Corn
Dairy
Cattle
Sweet Corn
Vegetables
Hogs
BALTIMORE
Iron & Steel, Electrical & Metal Products, Machinery, Chemicals, Transportation Equipment, Food Processing, Clothing, Shipbuilding
Baltimore
Wilmington
Oysters
Poultry
Wheat
Potatoes
Soybeans
Fruit
Tobacco
Crabs
Herring
Melons
Sweet Potatoes
Mackerel
Menhaden
WILMINGTON
Chemicals, Automobiles, Metal Products, Textiles

DOMINANT LAND USE

- Dairy, General Farming
- Fruit and Mixed Farming
- Truck and Mixed Farming
- Tobacco, General Farming
- Forests
- Swampland, Limited Agriculture
- Urban Areas

MAJOR MINERAL OCCURRENCES

- C Coal
- Cl Clay
- G Natural Gas
- Ls Limestone

- Water Power
- Major Industrial Areas

MASSACHUSETTS

AREA 8,257 sq. mi.
POPULATION 5,689,170
CAPITAL Boston
LARGEST CITY Boston
HIGHEST POINT Mt. Greylock 3,491 ft.
SETTLED IN 1620
ADMITTED TO UNION February 6, 1788
POPULAR NAME Bay State; Old Colony
STATE FLOWER Mayflower
STATE BIRD Chickadee

RHODE ISLAND

AREA 1,214 sq. mi.
POPULATION 949,723
CAPITAL Providence
LARGEST CITY Providence
HIGHEST POINT Jerimoth Hill 812 ft.
SETTLED IN 1636
ADMITTED TO UNION May 29, 1790
POPULAR NAME Little Rhody
STATE FLOWER Violet
STATE BIRD Rhode Island Red

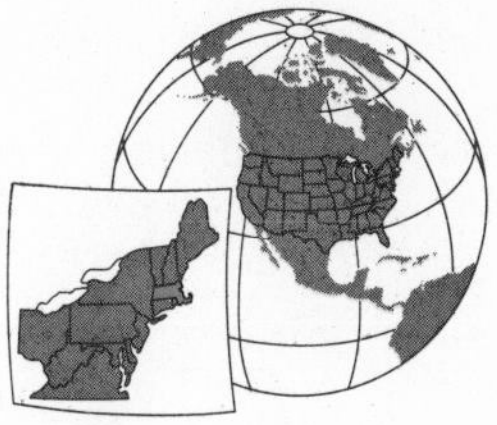

Agriculture, Industry and Resources

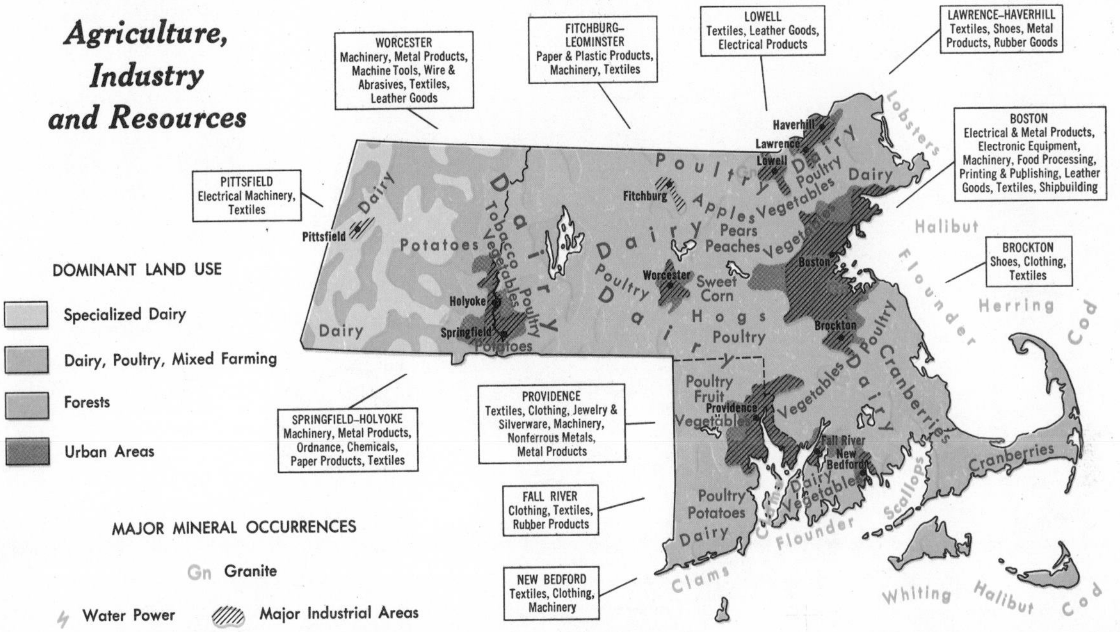
WORCESTER
Machinery, Metal Products, Machine Tools, Wire & Abrasives, Textiles, Leather Goods
FITCHBURG–LEOMINSTER
Paper & Plastic Products, Machinery, Textiles
LOWELL
Textiles, Leather Goods, Electrical Products
LAWRENCE–HAVERHILL
Textiles, Shoes, Metal Products, Rubber Goods
BOSTON
Electrical & Metal Products, Electronic Equipment, Machinery, Food Processing, Printing & Publishing, Leather Goods, Textiles, Shipbuilding
PITTSFIELD
Electrical Machinery, Textiles
BROCKTON
Shoes, Clothing, Textiles
SPRINGFIELD–HOLYOKE
Machinery, Metal Products, Ordnance, Chemicals, Paper Products, Textiles
PROVIDENCE
Textiles, Clothing, Jewelry & Silverware, Machinery, Nonferrous Metals, Metal Products
FALL RIVER
Clothing, Textiles, Rubber Products
NEW BEDFORD
Textiles, Clothing, Machinery
DOMINANT LAND USE
Specialized Dairy
Dairy, Poultry, Mixed Farming
Forests
Urban Areas
MAJOR MINERAL OCCURRENCES
Gn Granite
Water Power
Major Industrial Areas
Haverhill
Lawrence
Lowell
Fitchburg
Pittsfield
Worcester
Boston
Holyoke
Springfield
Brockton
Providence
Fall River
New Bedford
Dairy
Potatoes
Tobacco
Vegetables
Poultry
Apples
Pears
Peaches
Sweet Corn
Hogs
Fruit
Cranberries
Lobsters
Halibut
Flounder
Herring
Cod
Scallops
Clams
Whiting

MASSACHUSETTS

COUNTIES

County/Pop.	Key
Barnstable, 96,656	N 6
Berkshire, 149,402	B 3
Bristol, 444,301	K 5
Dukes, 6,117	M 7
Essex, 637,887	L 2
Franklin, 39,210	D 2
Hampden, 459,050	D 4
Hampshire, 123,981	D 3
Middlesex, 1,397,268	J 3
Nantucket, 3,774	O 7
Norfolk, 605,051	K 4
Plymouth, 333,314	L 5
Suffolk, 735,190	K 3
Worcester, 637,969	G 3

CITIES and TOWNS

	Zip	Name/Pop.	Key
	02351	Abington, ▵12,334	L 4
	02351	Abington, 5,900	L 4
	01720	Acton, ▵14,770	J 3
	01220	Adams, ▵11,772	B 2
	01220	Adams, 11,256	B 2
	01001	Agawam, ▵21,717	D 4
†	01261	Alford, ▵302	A 4
	01913	Amesbury, ▵11,388	L 1
	01913	Amesbury, 10,088	L 1
	01002	Amherst, ▵26,331	E 3
	01002	Amherst, 17,926	E 3
	01810	Andover, ▵23,695	K 2
	02174	Arlington, ▵53,524	C 6
	01430	Ashburnham, ▵3,484	G 2
	01431	Ashby, ▵2,274	G 2
	01330	Ashfield, ▵1,274	C 2
	01721	Ashland, ▵8,882	J 3
	01331	Athol, ▵11,185	F 2
	01331	Athol, 9,723	F 2
	02703	Attleboro, 32,907	J 5
	02763	Attleboro Falls, 5,000	J 5
	01501	Auburn, ▵15,347	G 4
†	02166	Auburndale, 7,235	B 7
	02322	Avon, ▵5,295	K 4
*	01432	Ayer, ▵7,393	H 2
	02630	Barnstable⊙, ▵19,842	N 6
	01005	Barre, ▵3,825	F 3
	01223	Becket, ▵929	B 3
	01730	Bedford, ▵13,513	B 6
	01007	Belchertown, ▵5,936	E 3
	02019	Bellingham, ▵13,967	J 4
	02019	Bellingham, 4,228	J 4
	02178	Belmont, ▵28,285	C 6
†	02780	Berkley, ▵2,027	K 5
	01503	Berlin, ▵2,099	H 3
	01337	Bernardston, ▵1,659	D 2
	01915	Beverly, 38,348	E 5
	01821	Billerica, ▵31,648	J 2
	01504	Blackstone, ▵6,566	H 4
	01008	Blandford, ▵863	C 4
	01740	Bolton, ▵1,905	H 3
*	02101	Boston (cap.)⊙, 641,071	D 7
		Boston, ‡2,753,700	D 7
	02532	Bourne, ▵12,636	M 6
†	01720	Boxborough, ▵1,451	H 3
	01921	Boxford, ▵4,032	L 2
	01505	Boylston, ▵2,774	H 3
	02184	Braintree, ▵35,050	D 8
	02631	Brewster, ▵1,790	O 5
	02324	Bridgewater, ▵11,829	K 5
	02324	Bridgewater, 4,032	K 5
	01010	Brimfield, ▵1,907	F 4
*	02401	Brockton, 89,040	K 4
		Brockton, ‡189,820	K 4
	01506	Brookfield, ▵2,063	F 4
	02147	Brookline, ▵58,886	C 7
	01338	Buckland, ▵1,892	C 2
	01803	Burlington, ▵21,980	C 5
†	02138	Cambridge⊙, 100,361	C 7
	02021	Canton, ▵17,100	C 8
	01741	Carlisle, ▵2,871	J 2
	02330	Carver, ▵2,420	M 5
	01339	Charlemont, ▵897	C 2
	01507	Charlton, ▵4,654	F 4
	02633	Chatham, ▵4,554	P 6
	01824	Chelmsford, ▵31,432	J 2
	02150	Chelsea, 30,625	D 6
	01225	Cheshire, ▵3,006	B 2
	01011	Chester, ▵1,025	C 3
	01012	Chesterfield, ▵704	C 3
*	01013	Chicopee, 66,676	D 4
	02535	Chilmark, ▵340	M 7
	01510	Clinton, ▵13,383	H 3
	01778	Cochituate, 6,000	A 7
	02025	Cohasset, ▵6,954	F 7
	02025	Cohasset, 3,900	F 7
†	01826	Collinsville, 4,000	J 2
	01340	Colrain, ▵1,420	D 2
	01742	Concord, ▵16,148	B 6
	01742	Concord, 5,900	B 6
	01341	Conway, ▵998	D 2
	01026	Cummington, ▵562	C 3
	01226	Dalton, ▵7,505	B 3
	01923	Danvers, ▵26,151	D 5
	02714	Dartmouth, ▵18,800	K 6
	02026	Dedham⊙, ▵26,938	C 7
	01342	Deerfield, ▵3,850	D 2
	02638	Dennis, ▵6,454	O 5
	02715	Dighton, ▵4,667	K 5
†	02122	Dorchester, 153,061	D 7
†	01516	Douglas, ▵2,947	H 4
	02030	Dover, ▵4,529	B 7
	01826	Dracut, ▵18,214	J 2
	01570	Dudley, ▵8,087	G 4
	01827	Dunstable, ▵1,292	J 2
	02332	Duxbury, ▵7,636	M 4
	02332	Duxbury, 2,477	M 4
†	02184	East Braintree, 12,000	D 8
	02333	East Bridgewater, ▵8,347	L 4
	01515	East Brookfield, ▵1,800	G 4
	02642	Eastham, ▵2,043	O 5
	01027	Easthampton, ▵13,012	D 3
	01028	East Longmeadow, ▵13,029	E 4
†	02186	East Milton, 9,500	D 7
	02334	Easton, ▵12,157	K 4
	01437	East Pepperell, 4,200	H 2
†	01906	East Saugus, 4,200	D 6
	02032	East Walpole, 4,500	C 8
†	02189	East Weymouth, 20,000	E 8
	02539	Edgartown, ▵1,481	M 7
	02539	Edgartown⊙, 1,006	M 7
	01344	Erving, ▵1,260	E 2
	02112	Essex, ▵2,670	L 2
	02149	Everett, 42,485	D 6
	02719	Fairhaven, ▵16,332	L 6
*	02720	Fall River, 96,898	K 6
		Fall River, ‡149,976	K 6
*	02540	Falmouth, ▵15,942	M 6
*	02540	Falmouth, 5,806	M 6
	01030	Feeding Hills, 9,500	D 4
	01420	Fitchburg, 43,343	G 2
		Fitchburg-Leominster, ‡97,164	G 2
†	01247	Florida, ▵672	B 2
	02035	Foxboro, ▵14,218	J 4
	02035	Foxboro, 4,090	J 4
	01701	Framingham, 64,048	A 7
	01701	Framingham Center, 16,000	J 3
	02038	Franklin, ▵17,830	J 4
	02038	Franklin, 8,863	J 4
	01440	Gardner, 19,748	G 2
†	02535	Gay Head, ▵118	L 7
	01830	Georgetown, ▵5,290	L 2
†	01376	Gill, ▵1,100	D 2
	01930	Gloucester, 27,941	M 2
	01032	Goshen, ▵483	C 3
	01519	Grafton, ▵11,659	H 4
	01033	Granby, ▵5,473	E 3
	01034	Granville, ▵1,008	C 4
	01230	Great Barrington, ▵7,537	A 4
	01301	Greenfield, ▵18,116	D 2
	01301	Greenfield⊙, 14,642	D 2
	01880	Greenwood, 7,500	D 6
	01450	Groton, ▵5,109	H 2
	01830	Groveland, ▵5,382	L 1
	01035	Hadley, ▵3,750	D 3
	02338	Halifax, ▵3,537	L 5
	01936	Hamilton, ▵6,373	L 2
	01036	Hampden, ▵4,572	E 4
	01237	Hancock, ▵675	A 2
	02339	Hanover, ▵10,107	L 4
	02341	Hanson, ▵7,148	L 4
	01037	Hardwick, ▵2,379	F 3
	01451	Harvard, ▵13,426	H 2
	02645	Harwich, ▵5,892	O 6
	02645	Harwich, 3,842	O 6
	01038	Hatfield, ▵2,825	D 3
	01830	Haverhill, 46,120	K 1
	01346	Heath, ▵383	C 2
	02043	Hingham, ▵18,845	E 8
	01235	Hinsdale, ▵1,588	B 3
	02343	Holbrook, ▵11,775	D 8
	01520	Holden, ▵12,564	G 3
†	01550	Holland, ▵931	F 4
	01746	Holliston, ▵12,069	A 8
	01746	Holliston, 3,900	A 8
	01040	Holyoke, 50,112	D 4
	01747	Hopedale, ▵4,292	H 4
	01748	Hopkinton, ▵5,981	J 4
	01452	Hubbardston, ▵1,437	F 3
	01749	Hudson, ▵16,084	H 3
	01749	Hudson, 14,283	H 3
	02045	Hull, ▵9,961	E 7
	01050	Huntington, ▵1,593	C 4
	02601	Hyannis, 6,847	N 6
	02136	Hyde Park, 25,000	C 7
	01938	Ipswich, ▵10,750	L 2
	01938	Ipswich, 5,022	L 2
	02090	Islington, 3,800	C 8
	02130	Jamaica Plain, 50,000	C 7
	02360	Kingston, ▵5,999	M 5
	02360	Kingston, 3,772	M 5
	02346	Lakeville, ▵4,376	L 5
	01523	Lancaster, ▵6,095	H 3
	01237	Lanesboro, ▵2,972	A 2
*	01840	Lawrence, 66,915	K 2
		Lawrence-Haverhill, ‡232,395	K 2
	01238	Lee, ▵6,426	B 3
	01524	Leicester, ▵9,140	G 4
	01240	Lenox, ▵5,804	A 3
	01240	Lenox, 2,208	A 3
	01453	Leominster, 32,939	G 2
	01054	Leverett, ▵1,005	E 3
	02173	Lexington, ▵31,886	B 6
†	01301	Leyden, ▵376	D 2
	01773	Lincoln, ▵7,567	B 6
	01460	Littleton, ▵6,380	H 2
	01106	Longmeadow, ▵15,630	D 4
*	01850	Lowell, 94,239	J 2
		Lowell, ‡212,860	J 2
	01056	Ludlow, ▵17,580	E 4
	02745	Lunds Corner, 7,020	L 6
	01462	Lunenburg, ▵7,419	H 2
*	01901	Lynn, 90,294	D 6
	01940	Lynnfield, ▵10,826	D 5
†	01940	Lynnfield Center (Lynnfield P.O.), 6,500	C 5
	02148	Malden, 56,127	D 6
	01944	Manchester, ▵5,151	F 5
	02048	Mansfield, ▵9,939	J 4
	02048	Mansfield, 4,778	J 4
	01945	Marblehead, ▵21,295	E 7
	02738	Marion, ▵3,466	L 6
	01752	Marlborough, 27,936	H 3
	02050	Marshfield, ▵15,223	M 4
	02649	Mashpee, ▵1,288	M 6
	02126	Mattapan, 18,500	C 7
	02739	Mattapoisett, ▵4,500	L 6
	01754	Maynard, ▵9,710	J 3
	02052	Medfield, ▵9,821	B 8
	02052	Medfield, 3,900	B 8
	02155	Medford, 64,397	C 6
	02053	Medway, ▵7,938	J 4
	02053	Medway, 3,716	J 4
	02176	Melrose, 33,180	D 6
	01756	Mendon, ▵2,524	H 4
	01860	Merrimac, ▵4,245	L 1
	01844	Methuen, 35,456	K 2
	02346	Middleboro, ▵13,607	L 5
	02346	Middleboro, 6,259	L 5
	01243	Middlefield, ▵288	B 3
	01949	Middleton, ▵4,044	K 2
	01757	Milford, ▵19,352	H 4
	01757	Milford, 13,740	H 4
	01527	Millbury, ▵11,987	H 4
	02054	Millis, ▵5,686	A 8
	01529	Millville, ▵1,764	H 4
	02186	Milton, ▵27,190	D 7
	01057	Monson, ▵7,355	E 4
	01351	Montague, ▵8,451	E 2
	01245	Monterey, ▵600	B 4
†	12517	Mount Washington, ▵52	A 4
	01908	Nahant, ▵4,119	E 6
	02554	Nantucket, ▵3,774	O 7
	02554	Nantucket⊙, 2,461	O 7
	01760	Natick, ▵31,057	A 7
	02192	Needham, ▵29,748	B 7
	02194	Needham Heights, 10,000	B 7
†	02122	Neponset, 25,000	D 7
*	02740	New Bedford, 101,777	K 6
		New Bedford, ‡152,642	K 6
	01531	New Braintree, ▵631	F 3
	01950	Newbury, ▵3,804	L 1
	01950	Newburyport, 15,807	L 1
†	01230	New Marlboro, ▵1,031	B 4
	01355	New Salem, ▵474	E 2
†	02158	Newton, 91,066	C 7
†	02159	Newton Center, 20,790	C 7
†	02161	Newton Highlands, 6,900	C 7
†	02160	Newtonville, 14,000	C 7
	02790	Noquochoke P.O. (Westport), ▵950	K 6
	02056	Norfolk, ▵4,656	J 4
	02351	North Abington, 6,200	L 4
	01247	North Adams, 19,195	B 2
	01060	Northampton⊙, 29,664	D 3
	01845	North Andover, ▵16,284	K 2
*	02760	North Attleboro, ▵18,665	J 5
	01862	North Billerica, 4,900	J 2
	01532	Northboro, ▵9,218	H 3
	01532	Northboro, 3,900	H 3
	01536	Northbridge, ▵11,795	H 4
	01535	North Brookfield, ▵3,967	F 3
	01863	North Chelmsford, 3,700	J 2
	02747	North Dartmouth, 6,000	K 6
	02356	North Easton, 6,000	K 4
	01360	Northfield, ▵2,631	E 2
	01536	North Grafton, 5,500	H 4
	01864	North Reading, ▵11,264	C 5
	02060	North Scituate, 5,507	F 8
†	02191	North Weymouth, 13,000	D 8
	01067	North Wilbraham, 5,700	E 4
	02766	Norton, ▵9,487	K 5
	02061	Norwell, ▵7,796	F 8
	02062	Norwood, ▵30,815	B 8
	02557	Oak Bluffs, ▵1,385	M 7
	01068	Oakham, ▵730	F 3
†	01566	Old Sturbridge Village, 500	F 4
	01364	Orange, ▵6,104	E 2
	01364	Orange, 3,847	E 2
	02653	Orleans, ▵3,055	O 5
	01253	Otis, ▵820	B 4
	01540	Oxford, ▵10,345	G 4
	01540	Oxford, 6,109	G 4
	01069	Palmer, ▵11,680	E 4
	01069	Palmer, 3,649	E 4
	01612	Paxton, ▵3,731	G 3
	01960	Peabody, 48,080	E 5
†	01002	Pelham, ▵937	E 3
	02359	Pembroke, ▵11,193	L 4
	01463	Pepperell, ▵5,887	H 2
	01366	Petersham, ▵1,014	F 3
†	01331	Phillipston, ▵872	F 2
	01866	Pinehurst, 5,681	B 5
	01201	Pittsfield⊙, 57,020	A 3
		Pittsfield, ‡79,727	A 3
	01070	Plainfield, ▵287	C 2
	02762	Plainville, ▵4,953	J 4
*	02360	Plymouth, ▵18,606	M 5
*	02360	Plymouth⊙, 6,940	M 5
	02367	Plympton, ▵1,224	L 5
†	02726	Pottersville, 3,722	K 6
	01541	Princeton, ▵1,681	G 3
	02657	Provincetown, ▵2,911	O 4
†	02169	Quincy, 87,966	D 7
	02368	Randolph, ▵27,035	D 8
	02767	Raynham, ▵6,705	K 5
	01867	Reading, ▵22,539	C 5
	02137	Readville, 10,000	C 8
	02769	Rehoboth, ▵6,512	K 5
	02151	Revere, 43,159	D 6
	01254	Richmond, ▵1,461	A 3
	02770	Rochester, ▵1,770	L 6
	02370	Rockland, ▵15,674	L 4
	01966	Rockport, ▵5,636	M 2
	01966	Rockport, 4,166	M 2
	01367	Rowe, ▵277	C 2
	01969	Rowley, ▵3,040	L 2
†	02119	Roxbury, 200,000	C 7
	01368	Royalston, ▵809	F 2
	01071	Russell, ▵1,382	C 4
	01543	Rutland, ▵3,198	G 3
	01970	Salem⊙, 40,556	E 5
	01950	Salisbury, ▵4,179	L 1
	01255	Sandisfield, ▵547	B 4
	02563	Sandwich, ▵5,239	N 5
	01906	Saugus, ▵25,110	D 6
	01256	Savoy, ▵322	B 2
	01701	Saxonville, 15,000	A 7
	02066	Scituate, ▵16,973	F 8
	02066	Scituate, 3,738	F 8
	02771	Seekonk, ▵11,116	J 5
	02067	Sharon, ▵12,367	K 4
	01810	Shawsheen Village, 5,200	K 2
	01257	Sheffield, ▵2,374	A 4
	01770	Sherborn, ▵3,309	A 8
	01464	Shirley, ▵4,909	H 2
	01545	Shrewsbury, ▵19,196	H 3
	01072	Shutesbury, ▵489	E 3
	02726	Somerset, ▵18,088	K 5
†	02143	Somerville, 88,779	C 6
	01073	Southampton, ▵3,069	C 4
	01772	Southborough, ▵5,798	H 3
†	02185	South Braintree, 6,000	D 8

(continued on following page)

MASSACHUSETTS (continued)

01550 Southbridge, △17,057......G 4
01550 Southbridge, 14,261......G 4
02748 South Dartmouth, 9,209......L 6
02375 South Easton, 4,400......K 4
01075 South Hadley, 17,033......D 4
01075 South Hadley Falls, 6,500......D 4
† 02190 South Weymouth, 17,500......E 8
01077 Southwick, △6,330......C 4
02664 South Yarmouth, 5,380......O 6
01562 Spencer, △8,779......F 3
01562 Spencer, 5,895......F 3
* 01101 Springfield, ▷ 163,905......D 4
    Springfield-Chicopee-
    Holyoke, ‡529,921......D 4
01564 Sterling, △4,247......G 3
01262 Stockbridge, △2,312......A 3
01262 Stockbridge, 1,147......A 3
02180 Stoneham, △20,725......C 6
02072 Stoughton, △23,459......H 6
01775 Stow, △3,984......H 3
01566 Sturbridge, △4,878......F 4

01776 Sudbury, △13,506......A 3
01375 Sunderland, △2,236......D 3
01527 Sutton, △4,590......G 4
01907 Swampscott, △13,578......E 6
02777 Swansea, △12,640......K 5
02780 Taunton◉, 43,756......K 5
01468 Templeton, △5,863......F 2
01876 Tewksbury, △22,755......K 2
01034 Tolland, △172......D 4
01983 Topsfield, △5,225......L 2
01469 Townsend, △4,281......H 2
02666 Truro, △1,234......O 5
01376 Turners Falls, 5,168......D 2
01879 Tyngsboro, △4,204......J 2
01264 Tyringham, △234......A 4
01568 Upton, △4,484......H 4
01569 Uxbridge, △8,253......H 4
01235 Vineyard Haven, 1,599......M 7
† 02168 Waban, 6,871......B 7
01880 Wakefield, △25,402......C 5
01081 Wales, △852......F 4
02154 Waltham, 61,582......B 6

01082 Ware, △8,187......E 3
01082 Ware, 6,509......E 3
02571 Wareham, △11,492......L 5
01083 Warren, △3,633......E 4
01378 Warwick, △492......E 2
† 01223 Washington, △406......B 3
02172 Watertown, △39,307......C 6
02179 Waverley, 15,000......B 6
01778 Wayland, △13,461......A 3
01570 Webster, △14,917......G 4
01570 Webster, 12,432......G 4
02181 Wellesley, △28,051......B 7
02181 Wellesley Hills, 11,800......B 7
02667 Wellfleet, △1,743......O 5
01379 Wendell, △405......E 2
01984 Wenham, △3,849......L 2
01581 Westboro, △12,594......H 3
01581 Westboro, 4,474......H 3
01583 West Boylston, △6,369......G 3
02379 West Bridgewater, △7,152......K 4
01585 West Brookfield, △2,653......F 3
01085 Westfield, 31,433......D 4
01886 Westford, △10,368......J 2

† 01027 Westhampton, △793......C 3
01473 Westminster, △4,273......G 2
01985 West Newbury, △2,254......L 1
02165 West Newton, 13,500......B 7
02193 Weston, △10,870......B 6
02790 Westport, △9,791......K 6
02790 Westport P.O. (North
    Westport), 4,000......K 6
01089 West Springfield, △28,461......D 4
01266 West Stockbridge, △1,354......A 3
02575 West Tisbury, △453......M 7
02090 Westwood, △12,750......B 7
02673 West Yarmouth, 3,699......N 6
02188 Weymouth, 54,610......D 8
01093 Whately, △1,145......D 3
01588 Whitinsville, 5,210......H 4
02382 Whitman, △13,059......J 4
01095 Wilbraham, △11,984......E 4
01095 Wilbraham, 3,540......E 4
01096 Williamsburg, △2,342......C 3
01267 Williamstown, △8,454......B 2
01267 Williamstown, 4,285......B 2
01887 Wilmington, △17,102......C 5

01887 Wilmington, 3,900......C 5
01475 Winchendon, △6,635......F 2
01475 Winchendon, 3,997......F 2
01890 Winchester, △22,269......C 6
01270 Windsor, △468......B 2
02152 Winthrop, △20,335......D 7
01801 Woburn, 37,406......C 6
02543 Woods Hole, 750......M 6
* 01601 Worcester◉, 176,572......H 3
    Worcester, ‡339,730......H 3
01098 Worthington, △712......C 3
02093 Wrentham, △7,315......J 4
† 02675 Yarmouth, △12,033......O 6

RHODE ISLAND

COUNTIES

Bristol, 45,937......J 6
Kent, 142,382......H 6
Newport, 94,559......K 6
Providence, 580,261......H 5
Washington, 83,586......H 7

CITIES and TOWNS

Zip	Name/Pop.	Key
02816	Anthony, 7,000......H 5	
† 02887	Apponaug, 6,533......J 6	
02806	Barrington, △17,554......J 6	
02806	Barrington, 13,000......J 6	
02809	Bristol, △17,860......J 6	
02809	Bristol◉, 14,000......J 6	
02911	Centerdale, 8,000......H 5	
02863	Central Falls, 18,716......H 5	
02813	Charlestown, △2,863......H 6	
02920	Cranston, 73,037......H 5	
02818	East Greenwich◉	
	△9,577......J 5	
02914	East Providence, 48,151......J 5	
02822	Exeter, △3,245......H 6	
02825	Foster, △2,626......H 5	
02828	Greenville, 3,500......H 5	
02833	Hopkinton, △5,392......H 7	
02835	Jamestown, △2,911......J 6	

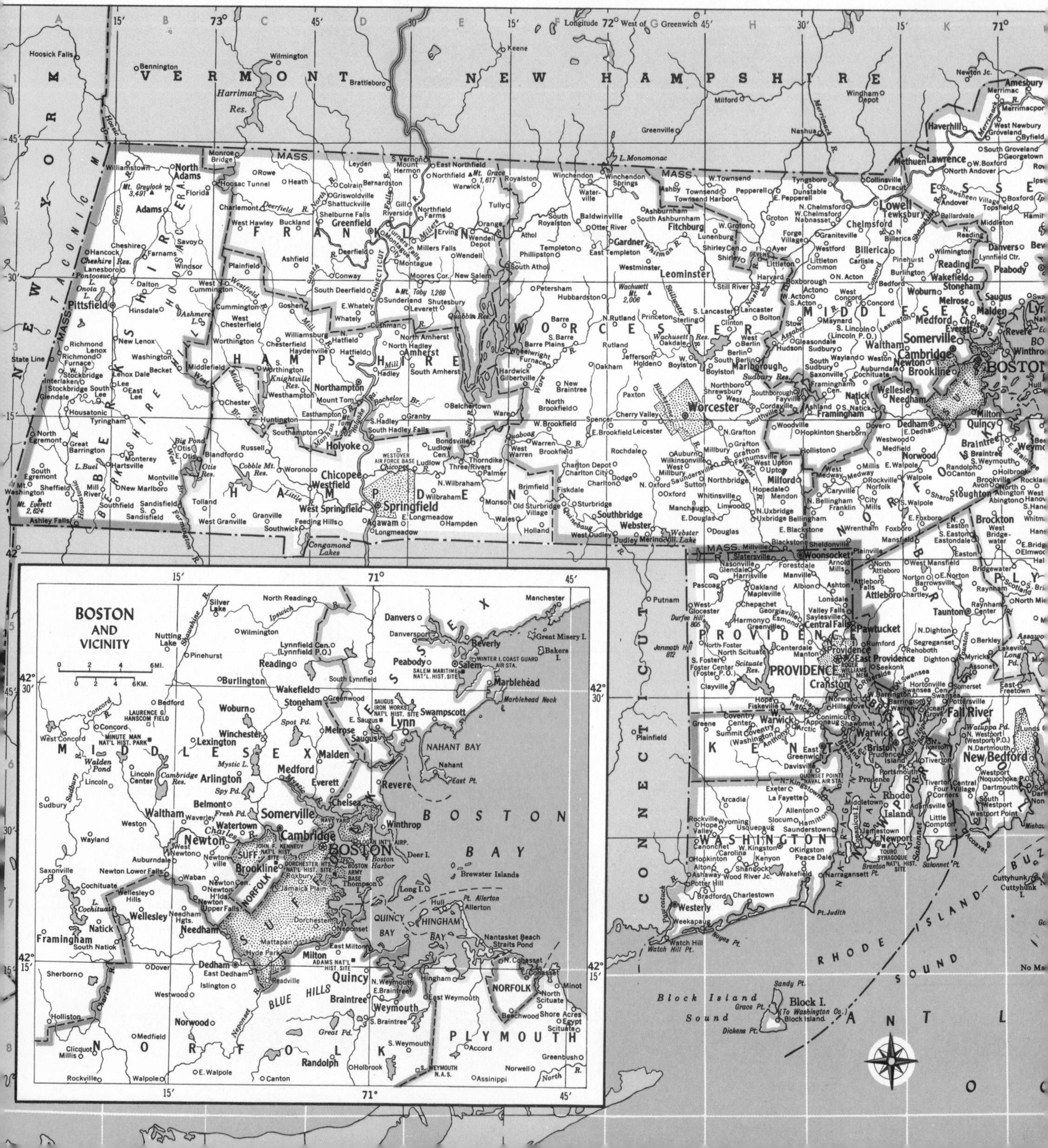

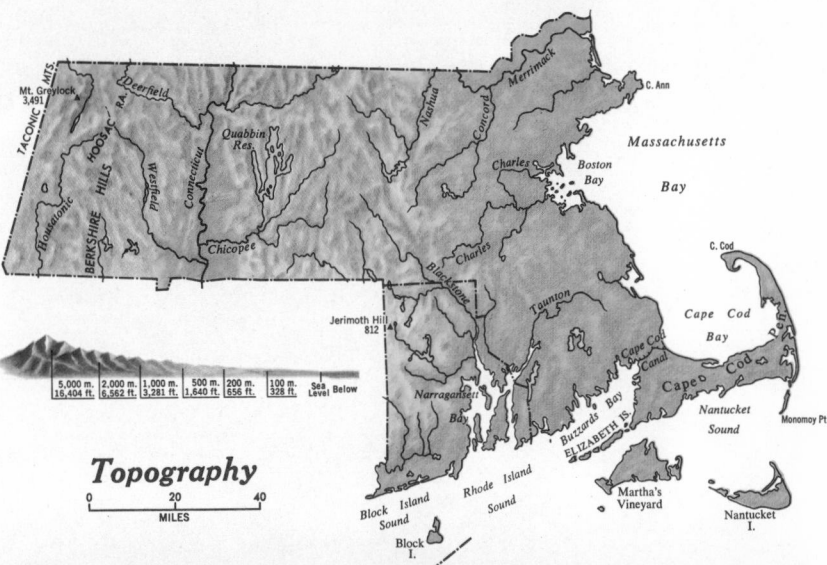

Topography

Marking the site of the first battle of the Revolutionary War on April 19, 1775, the Minuteman Statue faces the line of advancing Redcoats at Lexington, Massachusetts.

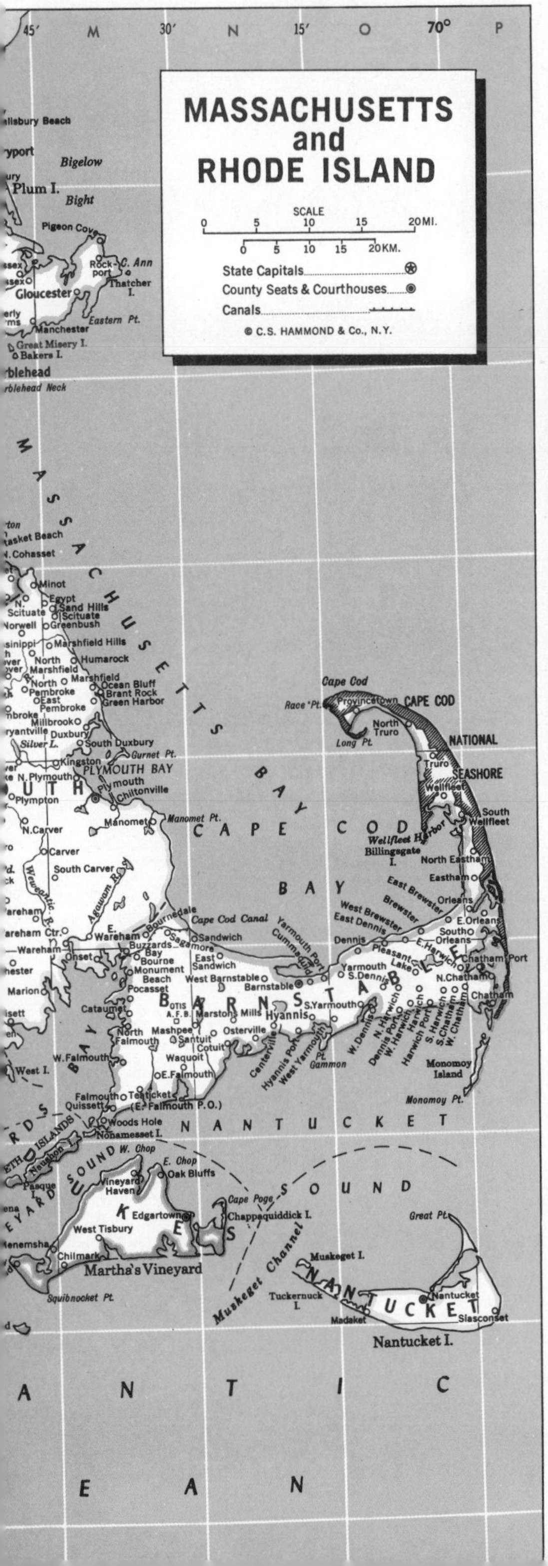

Jack Zehrt — Shostal Associates

Typical Newport turn-of-the-century grandeur in a French chalet-style mansion, with mansard roof and wrought iron gates.

Dorothy Bacheller

MASSACHUSETTS and RHODE ISLAND

SCALE
0   5   10   15   20 MI.
0   5   10   15   20 KM.

State Capitals.................⊛
County Seats & Courthouses......⊛
Canals.........................

© C.S. HAMMOND & Co., N.Y.

MICHIGAN

SCALE

State Capitals
County Seats
Canals

© C.S. HAMMOND & Co., N.Y.

AREA 58,216 sq. mi.
POPULATION 8,875,083
CAPITAL Lansing
LARGEST CITY Detroit
HIGHEST POINT Mt. Curwood 1,980 ft.
SETTLED IN 1650
ADMITTED TO UNION January 26, 1837
POPULAR NAME Wolverine State
STATE FLOWER Apple Blossom
STATE BIRD Robin

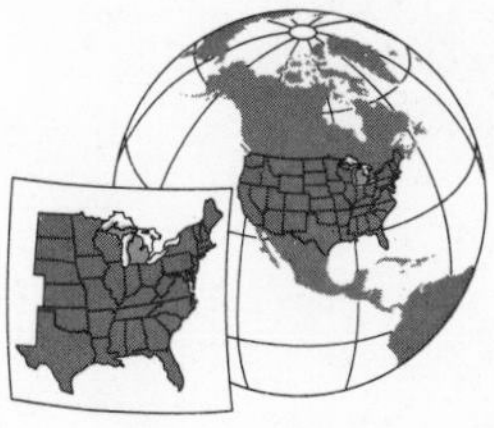

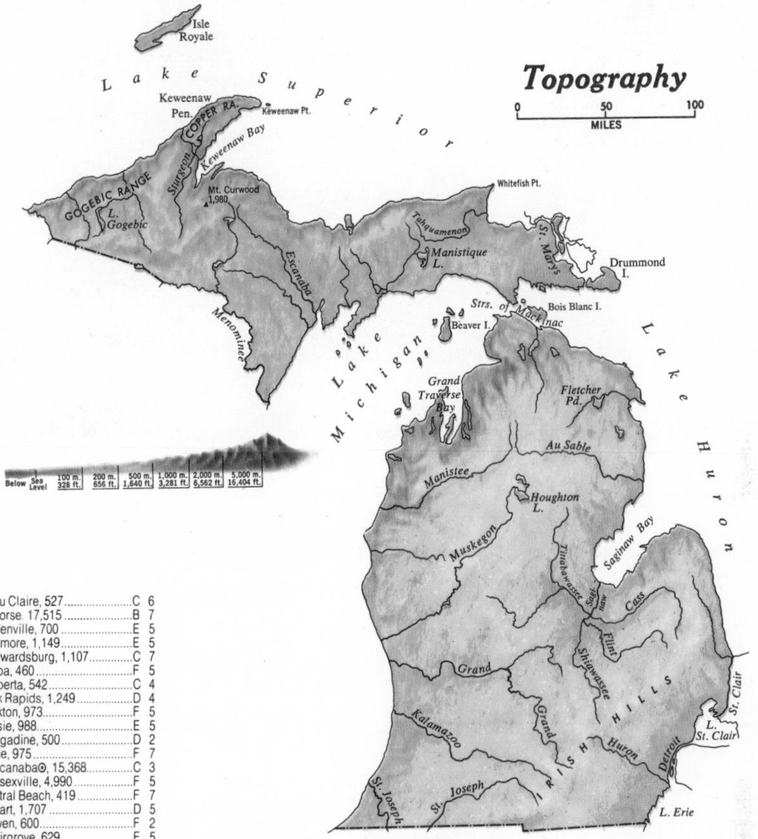

COUNTIES

County	Key
Alcona, 7,113	F 4
Alger, 8,568	C 2
Allegan, 66,575	D 6
Alpena, 30,708	F 4
Antrim, 12,612	D 3
Arenac, 11,149	F 4
Baraga, 7,789	A 2
Barry, 38,166	D 6
Bay, 117,339	E 5
Benzie, 8,593	C 4
Berrien, 163,875	C 7
Branch, 37,906	D 7
Calhoun, 141,963	D 6
Cass, 43,312	C 7
Charlevoix, 16,541	D 3
Cheboygan, 16,573	E 3
Chippewa, 32,412	E 2
Clare, 16,695	E 5
Clinton, 48,492	E 6
Crawford, 6,482	E 4
Delta, 35,924	C 2
Dickinson, 23,753	B 2
Eaton, 68,892	E 6
Emmet, 18,331	E 3
Genesee, 444,341	F 5
Gladwin, 13,471	E 4
Gogebic, 20,676	F 2
Grand Traverse, 39,175	D 4
Gratiot, 39,246	E 5
Hillsdale, 37,171	E 7
Houghton, 34,652	G 1
Huron, 34,083	F 5
Ingham, 261,039	E 6
Ionia, 45,848	D 6
Iosco, 24,905	F 4
Iron, 13,813	G 2
Isabella, 44,594	E 5
Jackson, 143,274	E 6
Kalamazoo, 201,550	D 6
Kalkaska, 5,272	D 4
Kent, 411,044	D 5
Keweenaw, 2,264	A 1
Lake, 5,661	D 5
Lapeer, 52,317	F 5
Leelanau, 10,872	D 4
Lenawee, 81,609	E 7
Livingston, 58,967	F 6
Luce, 6,789	D 2
Mackinac, 9,660	D 2
Macomb, 625,309	G 6
Manistee, 20,094	C 4
Marquette, 64,686	B 2
Mason, 22,612	C 4
Mecosta, 27,992	D 5
Menominee, 24,587	B 3
Midland, 63,769	E 5
Missaukee, 7,126	D 4
Monroe, 118,479	F 7
Montcalm, 39,660	D 5
Montmorency, 5,247	E 3
Muskegon, 157,246	C 5
Newaygo, 27,992	D 5
Oakland, 907,871	F 6
Oceana, 17,984	C 5
Ogemaw, 11,903	E 4
Ontonagon, 10,548	F 1
Osceola, 14,838	D 5
Oscoda, 4,726	E 4
Otsego, 10,422	E 3
Ottawa, 128,181	C 6
Presque Isle, 12,836	F 3
Roscommon, 9,892	E 4
Saginaw, 219,743	E 5
Saint Clair, 120,175	G 6
Saint Joseph, 47,392	D 7
Sanilac, 34,889	G 5
Schoolcraft, 8,226	C 2
Shiawassee, 63,075	E 6
Tuscola, 48,603	F 5
Van Buren, 56,173	C 6
Washtenaw, 234,103	F 6
Wayne, 2,666,751	F 6
Wexford, 19,717	D 4

CITIES and TOWNS

Zip	Name/Pop.	Key
49220	Addison, 595	E 7
49221	Adrian⊙, 20,382	F 7
48701	Akron, 525	F 5
48764	Alabaster, 46	F 4
49224	Albion, 12,112	E 6
48001	Algonac, 3,684	G 6
49010	Allegan⊙, 4,516	D 6
48101	Allen Park, 40,747	B 7
48801	Alma, 9,790	E 5
48003	Almont, 1,634	F 6
49707	Alpena⊙, 13,805	F 3
49903	Amasa, 450	G 2
48004	Anchorville, 440	G 6
* 48103	Ann Arbor⊙, 99,797	F 6
	Ann Arbor, ‡234,103	F 6
† 49659	Antrim, 475	D 4
48410	Argyle, 800	G 5
48005	Armada, 1,352	G 6
48806	Ashley, 521	E 5
49011	Athens, 996	D 6
49709	Atlanta⊙, 475	E 3
49905	Atlantic Mine, 785	G 1
48611	Auburn, 1,919	F 5
48057	Auburn Heights, 7,500	F 6
48703	Au Gres, 564	F 4
49012	Augusta, 1,025	D 6
† 48750	Au Sable-Oscoda, 3,475	F 4
† 48640	Averill, 800	E 5
48413	Bad Axe⊙, 2,999	G 5
49304	Baldwin⊙, 612	D 5
48414	Bancroft, 724	E 6
49013	Bangor, 2,050	C 6
49908	Baraga, 1,116	G 1
49807	Bark River, 550	B 3
49101	Baroda, 439	C 7
48808	Bath, 600	E 6
* 49014	Battle Creek, 38,931	D 6
48706	Bay City⊙, 49,449	F 5
	Bay City, ‡117,339	F 5
48720	Bay Port, 600	F 5
49770	Bay View, 500	E 3
48612	Beaverton, 954	E 5
49020	Bedford, 450	D 6
† 49423	Beechwood, 2,714	C 6
48809	Belding, 5,121	D 5
49615	Bellaire⊙, 897	D 4
48111	Belleville, 2,406	F 6
49021	Bellevue, 1,297	E 6
49022	Benton Harbor, 16,481	C 6
† 49022	Benton Heights, 8,067	C 6
49910	Bergland, 635	F 1
48072	Berkley, 22,618	B 6
49103	Berrien Springs, 1,951	C 7
49911	Bessemer⊙, 2,805	F 2
49617	Beulah⊙, 461	C 4
49307	Big Rapids⊙, 11,995	D 5
48415	Birch Run, 932	F 5
* 48008	Birmingham, 26,170	B 6
49228	Blissfield, 2,753	F 7
48013	Bloomfield Hills, 3,672	B 6
49026	Bloomingdale, 496	C 6
49712	Boyne City, 2,969	E 3
48615	Breckenridge, 1,257	E 5
48722	Bridgeport, 1,900	F 5
49106	Bridgman, 1,621	C 7
48116	Brighton, 2,457	F 6
49715	Brimley, 490	E 2
49229	Britton, 697	F 6
49028	Bronson, 2,390	D 7
49230	Brooklyn, 1,112	E 6
48416	Brown City, 1,142	G 5
49716	Brutus, 431	E 3
49107	Buchanan, 4,645	C 7
49314	Burnips, 725	D 6
49030	Burr Oak, 873	D 7
48418	Byron, 655	E 6
49315	Byron Center, 900	D 6
49601	Cadillac⊙, 9,990	D 4
49316	Caledonia, 716	D 6
49913	Calumet, 1,007	A 1
48014	Capac, 1,279	G 5
48117	Carleton, 1,503	F 6
48723	Caro⊙, 3,701	F 5
48724	Carrollton, 7,300	E 5
48811	Carson City, 1,217	E 5
48419	Carsonville, 621	G 5
48725	Caseville, 607	F 5
49915	Caspian, 1,165	G 2
48726	Cass City, 1,974	F 5
49031	Cassopolis⊙, 2,108	C 7
49422	Castle Park, 500	C 6
49319	Cedar Springs, 1,807	D 5
49719	Cedarville, 800	E 2
49233	Cement City, 531	E 6
48015	Center Line, 10,379	B 6
49622	Central Lake, 741	D 3
49032	Centreville⊙, 1,044	D 7
49814	Champion, 550	B 2
49815	Channing, 550	B 2
49720	Charlevoix⊙, 3,519	D 3
48813	Charlotte⊙, 8,244	E 6
49623	Chase, 534	D 5
49721	Cheboygan⊙, 5,553	E 3
48118	Chelsea, 3,858	E 6
48616	Chesaning, 2,876	E 5
48617	Clare, 2,639	E 5
49234	Clarklake, 500	E 6
48016	Clarkston, 1,034	F 6
48017	Clawson, 17,617	B 6
49235	Clayton, 505	E 7
48727	Clifford, 472	F 5
49034	Climax, 594	D 6
49236	Clinton, 1,677	F 6
48420	Clio, 2,357	F 5
49036	Coldwater⊙, 9,099	D 7
48618	Coleman, 1,295	E 5
49038	Coloma, 1,814	C 6
49040	Colon, 1,172	D 7
48421	Columbiaville, 935	F 5
49041	Comstock, 5,003	D 6
49237	Concord, 983	E 6
49042	Constantine, 1,733	D 7
49722	Conway, 560	E 3
49404	Coopersville, 2,129	C 5
49818	Cornell, 640	B 3
48817	Corunna⊙, 2,829	E 6
49043	Covert, 650	C 6
48422	Croswell, 1,954	G 5
48818	Crystal, 649	E 5
49920	Crystal Falls⊙, 2,000	A 2
† 49501	Cutlerville, 6,267	D 6
48819	Dansville, 486	E 6
48423	Davison, 5,259	F 5
* 48120	Dearborn, 104,199	B 7
48127	Dearborn Heights, 80,069	B 7
49045	Decatur, 1,764	C 6
48427	Deckerville, 817	G 5
49238	Deerfield, 834	F 7
49725	De Tour Village, 494	E 3
* 48201	Detroit⊙, 1,511,482	B 7
	Detroit, ‡4,199,931	B 7
† 48161	Detroit Beach, 2,053	F 7
48820	De Witt, 1,829	E 6
48130	Dexter, 1,729	F 6
48821	Dimondale, 970	E 6
49922	Dollar Bay, 950	G 1
49323	Dorr, 550	D 6
49406	Douglas, 813	C 6
49047	Dowagiac, 6,583	D 6
48020	Drayton Plains, 16,462	F 6
49726	Drummond Island, 700	F 3
48428	Dryden, 654	F 6
48131	Dundee, 2,472	F 7
48429	Durand, 3,678	E 6
49924	Eagle River⊙, 36	A 1
48021	East Detroit, 45,920	B 6
† 49506	East Grand Rapids, 12,565	D 6
49727	East Jordan, 2,041	D 3
† 49801	East Kingsford, 1,155	A 3
49626	Eastlake, 512	C 4
48823	East Lansing, 47,540	E 6
48730	East Tawas, 2,372	F 4
† 49001	Eastwood, 9,682	D 6
48827	Eaton Rapids, 4,494	E 6
49111	Eau Claire, 527	C 6
48229	Ecorse. 17,515	B 7
48620	Edenville, 700	E 5
48829	Edmore, 1,149	E 5
49112	Edwardsburg, 1,107	C 7
† 48446	Elba, 460	F 5
49628	Elberta, 542	C 4
49629	Elk Rapids, 1,249	D 4
48731	Elkton, 973	F 5
48831	Elsie, 988	E 5
49827	Engadine, 500	D 2
48133	Erie, 975	F 7
49829	Escanaba⊙, 15,368	C 3
48732	Essexville, 4,990	F 5
† 48166	Estral Beach, 419	F 7
49631	Evart, 1,707	D 5
49925	Ewen, 600	F 2
48733	Fairgrove, 629	F 5
48023	Fair Haven, 550	G 6
49022	Fair Plain, 3,680	C 6
48621	Fairview, 600	F 4
48024	Farmington, 13,337	F 6
48622	Farwell, 777	E 5
49408	Fennville, 811	C 6
48430	Fenton, 8,284	F 6
48220	Ferndale, 30,850	B 6
49409	Ferrysburg, 2,196	C 5
48134	Flat Rock, 5,643	F 6
* 48501	Flint⊙, 193,317	F 6
	Flint, ‡496,658	F 6
48433	Flushing, 7,190	F 5
48835	Fowler, 1,020	E 5
48836	Fowlerville, 1,978	F 6
48734	Frankenmuth, 2,834	F 5
49635	Frankfort, 1,660	C 4
48025	Franklin, 3,344	B 6
48026	Fraser, 11,868	B 6
48623	Freeland, 1,303	E 5
49325	Freeport, 501	D 6
49412	Fremont, 3,465	D 5
49415	Fruitport, 1,409	C 5
49052	Fulton, 500	D 6
49927	Gaastra, 479	G 2
49053	Galesburg, 1,355	D 6
49113	Galien, 691	C 7
49735	Gaylord⊙, 3,012	E 3
48437	Genesee, 950	F 5
49836	Germfask, 750	C 2
48173	Gibraltar, 3,325	F 6
49837	Gladstone, 5,237	C 3
48624	Gladwin⊙, 2,071	E 5
49055	Gobles, 801	D 6
49737	Good Hart, 500	D 3
48438	Goodrich, 774	F 6
48439	Grand Blanc, 5,132	F 6
49417	Grand Haven⊙, 11,884	C 5
48837	Grand Ledge, 6,032	E 6
49839	Grand Marais, 650	D 2
* 49501	Grand Rapids⊙, 197,649	D 5
	Grand Rapids, ‡539,225	D 5
49418	Grandville, 10,764	D 6
49327	Grant, 772	D 5
49240	Grass Lake, 1,061	E 6
49738	Grayling⊙, 2,143	E 4
48738	Greenbush, 650	F 4
48838	Greenville, 7,493	D 5
48138	Grosse Ile, 7,799	B 7
48236	Grosse Pointe, 6,637	B 7
† 48236	Grosse Pointe Farms, 11,701	B 6
† 48236	Grosse Pointe Park, 15,585	B 7
† 48236	Grosse Pointe Shores, 3,042	B 6
† 48236	Grosse Pointe Woods, 21,878	B 6
49840	Gulliver, 962	D 2
49841	Gwinn, 1,054	B 2
48739	Hale, 500	F 4
48139	Hamburg, 500	F 6
49419	Hamilton, 950	C 6
48212	Hamtramck, 27,245	B 6
49930	Hancock, 4,820	G 1
49241	Hanover, 513	E 6
48441	Harbor Beach, 2,134	G 5
49740	Harbor Springs, 1,662	D 3
48236	Harper Woods, 20,186	B 6
48625	Harrison⊙, 1,460	E 4
48740	Harrisville⊙, 541	F 4
48028	Harsens Island, 750	G 6
49420	Hart⊙, 2,139	C 5
49057	Hartford, 2,508	C 6
48840	Haslett, 3,492	E 6
49058	Hastings⊙, 6,501	D 6
48030	Hazel Park, 23,784	B 6
48626	Hemlock, 900	E 5
48841	Henderson, 600	E 5
49847	Hermansville, 950	B 3
49744	Herron, 950	F 3
49421	Hesperia, 877	D 5
49745	Hessel, 500	E 2
48203	Highland Park, 35,444	B 6
49242	Hillsdale⊙, 7,728	E 7
49423	Holland, 26,337	C 6
48442	Holly, 4,355	F 6
48842	Holt, 6,980	E 6
49425	Holton, 500	C 5
49245	Homer, 1,617	E 6
49328	Hopkins, 566	D 6
49931	Houghton⊙, 6,067	G 1
48629	Houghton Lake, 500	E 4
48630	Houghton Lake Heights, 1,252	E 4
49329	Howard City, 1,060	D 5
48843	Howell⊙, 5,224	E 6
49934	Hubbell, 1,251	A 1
49247	Hudson, 2,618	E 7
49426	Hudsonville, 3,523	D 6
48140	Ida, 970	F 7
49642	Idlewild, 800	D 5
48444	Imlay City, 1,980	F 5
49749	Indian River, 950	E 3
48141	Inkster, 38,595	B 7
49643	Interlochen, 800	D 4
48846	Ionia⊙, 6,361	D 6
49801	Iron Mountain⊙, 8,702	B 3
49935	Iron River, 2,684	G 2
49938	Ironwood, 8,711	F 2
49849	Ishpeming, 8,245	B 2
48847	Ithaca⊙, 2,749	E 5
* 49201	Jackson⊙, 45,484	E 6
	Jackson, ‡143,274	E 6
49428	Jenison, 11,266	D 6
49061	Jones, 420	D 7
49250	Jonesville, 2,081	E 6
* 49001	Kalamazoo⊙, 85,555	D 6
	Kalamazoo, ‡201,550	D 6
49646	Kalkaska⊙, 1,475	D 4
48631	Kawkawlin, 450	F 5
48030	Keego Harbor, 3,092	F 6
49330	Kent City, 686	D 5
49508	Kentwood, 20,310	D 6
48445	Kinde, 618	G 5
49801	Kingsford, 5,276	A 3
49649	Kingsley, 632	D 4
48741	Kingston, 464	F 5
48848	Laingsburg, 1,159	E 6
48632	Lake, 600	E 5
49651	Lake City⊙, 704	D 4
48143	Lakeland, 720	F 6
49945	Lake Linden, 1,214	A 1
† 49039	Lake Michigan Beach, 1,201	C 6
48849	Lake Odessa, 1,924	D 6
48850	Lakeview, 1,198	D 5
† 49440	Lakewood Club, 590	C 5
48144	Lambertville, 5,721	F 7
49946	L'Anse⊙, 2,538	G 1
* 48901	Lansing (cap.), 131,546	E 6
	Lansing, ‡378,423	E 6
48446	Lapeer⊙, 6,270	F 5
49913	Laurium, 2,868	A 1
49064	Lawrence, 790	C 6
49065	Lawton, 1,358	D 6
49654	Leland⊙, 776	D 3
49251	Leslie, 1,894	E 6
49755	Levering, 967	E 3
49756	Lewiston, 750	E 4
48450	Lexington, 834	G 5
48146	Lincoln Park, 52,984	B 7
48451	Linden, 1,546	F 6
48634	Linwood, 950	F 5
49252	Litchfield, 1,167	E 6
49833	Little Lake, 950	B 2
* 48150	Livonia, 110,109	F 6
48743	Long Lake, 900	F 4
49331	Lowell, 3,068	D 6
49431	Ludington⊙, 9,021	C 5
48157	Luna Pier, 1,418	F 7
48851	Lyons, 758	E 6
49757	Mackinac Island, 517	E 3
49701	Mackinaw City, 810	E 3
48071	Madison Heights, 38,599	F 6
49659	Mancelona, 1,255	E 4
48158	Manchester, 1,650	E 6
49660	Manistee⊙, 7,723	C 4
49854	Manistique⊙, 4,324	C 3
49663	Manton, 1,107	D 4
48853	Maple Rapids, 683	E 5
49067	Marcellus, 1,139	D 6
49947	Marenisco, 865	F 2
48039	Marine City, 4,567	G 6
49665	Marion, 891	D 4
48453	Marlette, 1,706	G 5
49435	Marne, 950	D 5
49855	Marquette⊙, 21,967	B 2
49068	Marshall⊙, 7,253	E 6
49070	Martin, 502	D 6
48040	Marysville, 5,610	G 6
48854	Mason⊙, 5,468	E 6
49948	Mass, 850	G 1
49071	Mattawan, 1,569	D 6
48159	Maybee, 485	F 6
48744	Mayville, 872	F 5
49657	McBain, 520	D 4
48122	Melvindale, 13,862	B 7
48041	Memphis, 1,121	G 6
49072	Mendon, 949	D 7
49858	Menominee⊙, 10,748	B 3

(continued on following page)

Turning out more than one car a minute keeps these inspectors on their toes during the final step on an assembly line in Detroit, Michigan.

A. D'Arazien – Shostal Associates

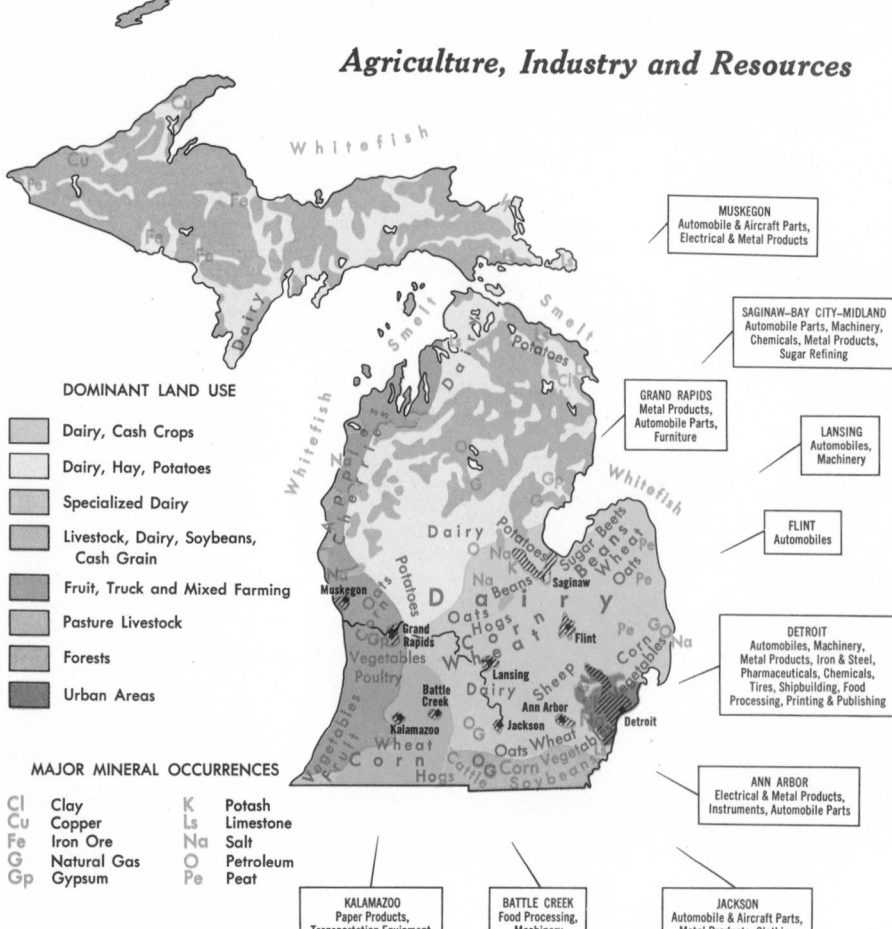

Agriculture, Industry and Resources

DOMINANT LAND USE

- Dairy, Cash Crops
- Dairy, Hay, Potatoes
- Specialized Dairy
- Livestock, Dairy, Soybeans, Cash Grain
- Fruit, Truck and Mixed Farming
- Pasture Livestock
- Forests
- Urban Areas

MAJOR MINERAL OCCURRENCES

Cl	Clay	K	Potash
Cu	Copper	Ls	Limestone
Fe	Iron Ore	Na	Salt
G	Natural Gas	O	Petroleum
Gp	Gypsum	Pe	Peat

Water Power

Major Industrial Areas

MUSKEGON Automobile & Aircraft Parts, Electrical & Metal Products

SAGINAW–BAY CITY–MIDLAND Automobile Parts, Machinery, Chemicals, Metal Products, Sugar Refining

GRAND RAPIDS Metal Products, Automobile Parts, Furniture

LANSING Automobiles, Machinery

FLINT Automobiles

DETROIT Automobiles, Machinery, Metal Products, Iron & Steel, Pharmaceuticals, Chemicals, Tires, Shipbuilding, Food Processing, Printing & Publishing

ANN ARBOR Electrical & Metal Products, Instruments, Automobile Parts

KALAMAZOO Paper Products, Transportation Equipment, Pharmaceuticals

BATTLE CREEK Food Processing, Machinery

JACKSON Automobile & Aircraft Parts, Metal Products, Clothing

COUNTIES

Aitkin, 11,403 E 4
Anoka, 154,556 E 5
Becker, 24,372 C 4
Beltrami, 26,373 C 2
Benton, 20,841 D 5
Big Stone, 7,941 B 5
Blue Earth, 52,322 D 6
Brown, 28,887 D 6
Carlton, 28,072 F 4
Carver, 28,310 E 6
Cass, 17,323 D 4
Chippewa, 15,109 C 5
Chisago, 17,492 F 5
Clay, 46,585 B 4
Clearwater, 8,013 C 3
Cook, 3,423 H 3
Cottonwood, 14,887 C 6
Crow Wing, 34,826 D 4
Dakota, 139,808 E 6
Dodge, 13,037 F 7
Douglas, 22,892 C 5
Faribault, 20,896 D 7
Fillmore, 21,916 F 7
Freeborn, 38,064 E 7
Goodhue, 34,763 F 6
Grant, 7,462 B 5
Hennepin, 960,080 E 5
Houston, 17,556 G 7
Hubbard, 10,583 D 3
Isanti, 16,560 E 5
Itasca, 35,530 E 3
Jackson, 14,352 C 7
Kanabec, 9,775 E 5
Kandiyohi, 30,548 C 5
Kittson, 6,853 B 2
Koochiching, 17,731 E 2
Lac qui Parle, 11,164 B 6
Lake, 13,351 G 3
Lake of the Woods, 3,987 D 2
Le Sueur, 21,332 E 6
Lincoln, 8,143 B 6
Lyon, 24,273 C 6
Mahnomen, 5,638 C 3
Marshall, 13,060 B 2
Martin, 24,316 D 7
McLeod, 27,662 D 6
Meeker, 18,810 D 5
Mille Lacs, 15,703 E 5
Morrison, 26,949 D 4
Mower, 43,783 F 7
Murray, 12,508 C 6
Nicollet, 24,518 D 6
Nobles, 23,208 C 7
Norman, 10,008 B 3
Olmsted, 84,104 F 7
Otter Tail, 46,097 C 4
Pennington, 13,266 B 2
Pine, 16,821 F 4
Pipestone, 12,791 B 6
Polk, 34,435 B 3
Pope, 11,107 C 5
Ramsey, 476,255 E 5
Red Lake, 5,388 B 3
Redwood, 20,024 C 6
Renville, 21,139 C 6
Rice, 41,582 E 6
Rock, 11,346 B 7
Roseau, 11,569 C 2
Saint Louis, 220,693 F 3
Scott, 32,423 E 6
Sherburne, 18,344 E 5
Sibley, 15,845 D 6
Stearns, 95,400 D 5
Steele, 26,931 E 7
Stevens, 11,218 B 5
Swift, 13,177 C 5
Todd, 22,114 D 4
Traverse, 6,254 B 5
Wabasha, 17,224 F 6
Wadena, 12,412 D 4
Waseca, 16,663 E 7
Washington, 82,948 F 5
Watonwan, 13,298 D 7
Wilkin, 9,389 B 4
Winona, 44,409 G 6
Wright, 38,933 D 5
Yellow Medicine, 14,418 B 6

CITIES and TOWNS

Zip Name/Pop. Key
56510 Ada⊙, 2,076 B 3
55909 Adams, 771 F 7
56110 Adrian, 1,350 C 7
55001 Afton, 248 F 6
56430 Ah-Gwah-Ching, 500 D 3
56431 Aitkin⊙, 1,553 E 4
56433 Akeley, 468 D 3
56307 Albany, 1,599 D 5
56207 Alberta, 140 B 5
56007 Albert Lea⊙, 19,418 E 7
55301 Albertville, 451 E 5
56009 Alden, 713 E 7
56308 Alexandria⊙, 6,973 C 5
55002 Almelund, 150 F 5
56111 Alpha, 179 D 7
55910 Altura, 334 G 6
56710 Alvarado, 302 B 2
56010 Amboy, 571 D 7
55703 Angora, 287 F 3
55302 Annandale, 1,234 D 5
55303 Anoka⊙, 13,489 E 5
56208 Appleton, 1,789 C 5
† 55378 Apple Valley, 8,502 G 6
56113 Arco, 121 B 6
56713 Argyle, 739 B 2
55307 Arlington, 1,823 D 6
† 55801 Arnold, 750 F 4
56309 Ashby, 415 C 4
55704 Askov, 287 F 4
56209 Atwater, 956 D 5
56511 Audubon, 297 C 4
55705 Aurora, 2,531 F 3
55912 Austin⊙, 25,074 E 7
56114 Avoca, 203 C 7
56310 Avon, 725 D 5
55706 Babbitt, 3,076 G 3
56435 Backus, 257 D 4
56714 Badger, 327 B 2
56621 Bagley⊙, 1,314 C 3
56115 Balaton, 649 C 6
56622 Ball Club, 150 E 3
56514 Barnesville, 1,782 B 4
55707 Barnum, 382 F 4
56311 Barrett, 342 B 5
56515 Battle Lake, 772 C 4
56623 Baudette⊙, 1,547 D 2
† 56401 Baxter, 1,556 D 4
† 56444 Bay Lake, 250 E 4
55003 Bayport, 2,987 F 5
56211 Beardsley, 366 B 5
† 55723 Bear River, 250 E 3
55601 Beaver Bay, 362 G 3
56116 Beaver Creek, 235 B 7
55308 Becker, 365 E 5
56516 Bejou, 157 B 3
56312 Belgrade, 713 C 5
† 55027 Bellechester, 199 F 6
56011 Belle Plaine, 2,328 E 6
56212 Bellingham, 263 B 5
56517 Beltrami, 171 B 3
56214 Belview, 429 C 6
56601 Bemidji⊙, 11,490 D 3
56626 Bena, 169 D 3
† 56431 Bennettville, 200 E 4
56437 Bertha, 512 C 4
56117 Bigelow, 262 C 7
56627 Big Falls, 534 E 2
56628 Bigfork, 399 E 3
55309 Big Lake, 1,015 E 5
56118 Bingham Lake, 214 C 7
55310 Bird Island, 1,309 D 6
55708 Biwabik, 1,483 F 3
56630 Blackduck, 595 D 3
† 55303 Blaine, 20,640 G 5
† 56011 Blakeley, 125 E 6
56216 Blomkest, 172 D 6
55917 Blooming Prairie, 1,804 E 7
55420 Bloomington, 81,970 G 6
56013 Blue Earth⊙, 3,965 D 7
56518 Bluffton, 195 C 4
56519 Borup, 128 B 3
55709 Bovey, 858 E 3
56314 Bowlus, 268 D 5
56218 Boyd, 311 C 6
55006 Braham, 744 E 5
56401 Brainerd⊙, 11,667 D 4
† 55056 Branch, 880 F 5
56315 Brandon, 414 C 5
56520 Breckenridge⊙, 4,200 B 4
† 56472 Breezy Point Village, 233 D 4
56119 Brewster, 563 C 7
56014 Bricelyn, 470 E 7
55710 Britt, 175 F 3
55429 Brooklyn Center, 35,173 G 5
† 55401 Brooklyn Park, 26,230 G 5
56715 Brooks, 163 B 3
55711 Brookston, 137 F 4
56316 Brooten, 615 C 5
56438 Browerville, 665 D 4
55918 Brownsdale, 625 F 7
56219 Browns Valley, 906 B 5
55919 Brownsville, 417 G 7
55312 Brownton, 688 D 6
55712 Bruno, 130 F 4
† 55051 Brunswick, 144 E 5
56317 Buckman, 158 D 5
55313 Buffalo⊙, 3,275 E 5
55314 Buffalo Lake, 758 D 6
55713 Buhl, 1,303 F 3
55378 Burnsville, 19,940 E 6
56318 Burtrum, 135 D 5
56120 Butterfield, 619 D 7
† 56723 Bygland, 475 B 3
55920 Byron, 1,419 F 6
55921 Caledonia⊙, 2,619 G 7
56521 Callaway, 233 C 3
55716 Calumet, 460 E 3
55008 Cambridge⊙, 3,467 E 5
56222 Campbell, 339 B 4
56220 Canby, 2,081 B 6
55009 Cannon Falls, 2,072 F 6
55922 Canton, 391 F 7
55717 Canyon, 125 F 3
56319 Carlos, 260 C 5
55718 Carlton⊙, 884 F 4
55315 Carver, 669 E 6
56633 Cass Lake, 1,317 D 3
55010 Castle Rock, 150 E 6
55012 Center City⊙, 324 F 5
† 55038 Centerville, 534 E 5
56121 Ceylon, 487 D 7
55316 Champlin, 2,275 G 5
56122 Chandler, 319 C 7
55317 Chanhassen, 4,879 F 6
55318 Chaska⊙, 4,352 F 6
55923 Chatfield, 1,885 F 7
55013 Chisago City, 1,068 E 5
55719 Chisholm, 5,913 E 3
56221 Chokio, 455 B 5
55014 Circle Pines, 3,918 G 5
56222 Clara City, 1,491 C 6
55924 Claremont, 520 E 6
56440 Clarissa, 599 C 4
56223 Clarkfield, 1,084 C 6
56016 Clarks Grove, 480 E 7
56634 Clearbrook, 599 C 3
55319 Clear Lake, 280 E 5
55320 Clearwater, 282 D 5
56224 Clements, 252 D 6
56017 Cleveland, 492 E 6
56523 Climax, 255 B 3
56225 Clinton, 608 B 5
56524 Clitherall, 131 C 4
56226 Clontarf, 147 C 5
55720 Cloquet, 8,699 F 4
55015 Cloverton, 150 F 4
55721 Cohasset, 536 E 3
55321 Cokato, 1,735 D 5
56320 Cold Spring, 2,006 D 5
55722 Coleraine, 1,086 E 3
56321 Collegeville, 1,600 D 5
55322 Cologne, 518 E 6
55421 Columbia Heights, 23,997 G 5
56019 Comfrey, 525 D 6
56525 Comstock, 135 B 4
56020 Conger, 167 E 7
55723 Cook, 687 F 3
55433 Coon Rapids, 30,505 G 5
† 55340 Corcoran, 1,656 F 5
56228 Cosmos, 570 D 6
55016 Cottage Grove, 13,419 F 6
55724 Cotton, 350 F 3
56229 Cottonwood, 794 C 6
56021 Courtland, 360 D 6
55725 Crane Lake, 350 F 2
55726 Cromwell, 181 F 4
56716 Crookston⊙, 8,312 B 3
56441 Crosby, 2,241 D 4
56442 Crosslake, 358 E 4
† 55005 Crown, 200 E 5
† 55401 Crystal, 30,925 G 5
55323 Crystal Bay, 6,787 F 5
56123 Currie, 368 C 6
56323 Cyrus, 289 C 5
55925 Dakota, 369 G 7
56324 Dalton, 221 C 4
56230 Danube, 497 C 6
56231 Danvers, 136 C 5
56022 Darfur, 179 D 6
55324 Darwin, 224 D 5
55325 Dassel, 1,058 D 5
56232 Dawson, 1,699 B 6
55327 Dayton, 517 E 5
55391 Deephaven, 3,853 G 5
56527 Deer Creek, 287 C 4
56636 Deer River, 815 E 3
56444 Deerwood, 448 E 4
56233 De Graff, 195 C 5
55328 Delano, 1,851 E 5
56023 Delavan, 281 D 7
56234 Delhi, 154 C 6
† 55110 Dellwood, 514 F 5
55018 Dennison, 162 E 6
56528 Dent, 156 C 4
56501 Detroit Lakes⊙, 5,797 C 4
55926 Dexter, 252 F 7
56529 Dilworth, 2,321 B 4
55927 Dodge Center, 1,603 F 6
56235 Donnelly, 252 B 5
55929 Dover, 321 F 7
55930 Dresbach, 250 G 7
* 55801 Duluth⊙, 100,578 F 4
Duluth-Superior, ‡265,350 F 4
56236 Dumont, 204 B 5
55019 Dundas, 460 E 6
56126 Dundee, 138 C 7
56127 Dunnell, 237 D 7
56446 Eagle Bend, 557 D 4
† 55005 East Bethel, 2,586 E 5
56024 Eagle Lake, 839 E 6
† 56031 East Chain, 171 D 7
56721 East Grand Forks, 7,607 B 3
† 56401 East Gull Lake, 440 D 4
56025 Easton, 352 E 7
56237 Echo, 356 C 6
55343 Eden Prairie, 6,938 G 6
55329 Eden Valley, 776 D 5
56128 Edgerton, 1,119 B 7
55424 Edina, 44,046 G 5
56639 Effie, 165 E 3
55931 Eitzen, 208 G 7
† 55910 Elba, 158 F 6
56531 Elbow Lake⊙, 1,484 B 5
55932 Elgin, 580 F 6
56533 Elizabeth, 188 B 4
55330 Elk River⊙, 2,252 E 5
55933 Elkton, 134 F 7
56026 Ellendale, 569 E 7
56129 Ellsworth, 588 C 7
56027 Elmore, 910 D 7
56325 Elrosa, 203 C 5
55731 Ely, 4,904 G 3
56028 Elysian, 445 E 6
55732 Embarrass, 195 F 3
56447 Emily, 386 E 4
56029 Emmons, 412 E 7
56534 Erhard, 748 B 4
56640 Ericsburg, 300 E 2
56535 Erskine, 571 B 3
55733 Esko, 500 F 4
56722 Euclid, 130 B 3
56238 Evan, 126 D 6
56326 Evansville, 553 C 4
55734 Eveleth, 4,721 F 3
55331 Excelsior, 2,563 E 6
55934 Eyota, 639 F 7
55332 Fairfax, 1,432 D 6
55383 Fairhaven, 129 D 5
56031 Fairmont⊙, 10,751 D 7
55113 Falcon Heights, 5,507 G 5
55021 Faribault⊙, 16,595 E 6
55024 Farmington, 3,104 E 6
56641 Federal Dam, 147 D 3
56536 Felton, 232 B 3
56537 Fergus Falls⊙, 12,443 B 4
56540 Fertile, 955 B 3
56448 Fifty Lakes, 143 D 4
55603 Finland, 300 G 3
55735 Finlayson, 192 F 4
56723 Fisher, 383 B 3
56328 Flensburg, 259 D 5
55736 Floodwood, 650 E 4
† 55792 Florenton, 635 F 3
56329 Foley⊙, 1,271 D 5
† 56308 Forada, 158 C 5
55738 Forbes, 225 F 3
55025 Forest Lake, 3,207 F 5
56330 Foreston, 273 E 5
56542 Fosston, 1,684 C 3
55935 Fountain, 347 F 7
56543 Foxhome, 185 B 4
55333 Franklin, 557 D 6
56544 Frazee, 1,015 C 4
56032 Freeborn, 296 E 7
56331 Freeport, 593 D 5
† 55801 French River, 200 G 4
55421 Fridley, 29,233 G 5
55026 Frontenac, 223 F 6

AREA 84,068 sq. mi.
POPULATION 3,805,069
CAPITAL St. Paul
LARGEST CITY Minneapolis
HIGHEST POINT Eagle Mtn. 2,301 ft.
SETTLED IN 1805
ADMITTED TO UNION May 11, 1858
POPULAR NAME North Star State; Gopher State
STATE FLOWER Lady-slipper
STATE BIRD Loon

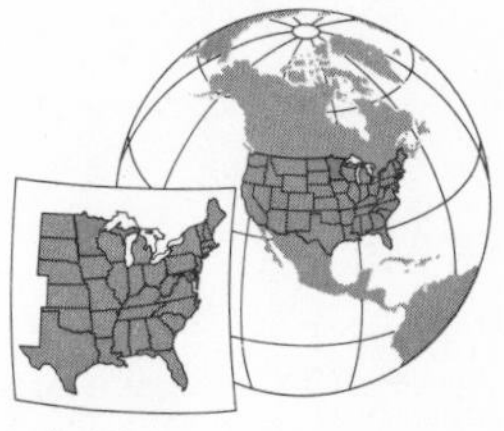

56033 Frost, 290 D 7
56131 Fulda, 1,226 C 7
56034 Garden City, 270 D 6
56332 Garfield, 198 C 5
56450 Garrison, 125 E 4
56132 Garvin, 201 C 6
56545 Gary, 265 B 3
55334 Gaylord⊙, 1,720 D 6
56035 Geneva, 358 E 7
56717 Gentilly, 179 B 3
56546 Georgetown, 141 B 3
55740 Gheen, 145 F 3
56239 Ghent, 301 C 6
55335 Gibbon, 877 D 6
55741 Gilbert, 2,287 F 3
† 56431 Glen, 125 E 4
55336 Glencoe⊙, 4,217 D 6
56036 Glenville, 740 E 7
56334 Glenwood⊙, 2,584 C 5
56547 Glyndon, 674 B 4
55427 Golden Valley, 24,246 G 5
56644 Gonvick, 344 C 3
55027 Goodhue, 539 F 6
55742 Goodland, 175 E 3
56725 Goodridge, 144 C 2
56037 Good Thunder, 489 D 6
55027 Goodview, 1,829 G 6
56240 Graceville, 735 B 5
56039 Granada, 381 D 7
55604 Grand Marais⊙, 1,301 G 2
55936 Grand Meadow, 869 F 7
55744 Grand Rapids⊙, 7,247 E 3
55029 Grandy, 155 E 5
56241 Granite Falls⊙, 3,225 C 6
55030 Grasston, 132 E 5
56726 Greenbush, 787 B 2
† 55373 Greenfield, 977 G 6
55338 Green Isle, 363 E 6
56242 Green Valley, 129 C 6
56335 Greenwald, 244 D 5
56336 Grey Eagle, 325 D 5
56243 Grove City, 502 D 5
56727 Grygla, 211 C 2
56452 Hackensack, 220 D 4
56133 Hadley, 119 C 7
56728 Hallock⊙, 1,477 A 2
56548 Halstad, 598 B 3
55339 Hamburg, 377 D 6
55340 Hamel, 2,396 F 5
55938 Hammond, 179 F 6
55031 Hampton, 369 E 6
56244 Hancock, 806 C 5
56245 Hanley Falls, 265 C 6
55341 Hanover, 365 E 5
56041 Hanska, 442 D 6
56364 Harding, 119 E 4
56134 Hardwick, 274 B 7
55939 Harmony, 1,130 F 7
55032 Harris, 559 F 5
56042 Hartland, 331 E 7
† 55374 Hassan, 778 E 5
55033 Hastings⊙, 12,195 F 6
56549 Hawley, 1,371 B 4
55940 Hayfield, 939 F 7
56043 Hayward, 261 E 7
55342 Hector, 1,178 D 6
56044 Henderson, 730 E 6
56136 Hendricks, 712 B 6
56550 Hendrum, 311 B 3
56551 Henning, 850 C 4
56248 Herman, 619 B 5
56137 Heron Lake, 777 C 7
56453 Hewitt, 198 C 4
55746 Hibbing, 16,104 F 3
55748 Hill City, 357 E 4
56138 Hills, 571 B 7
55037 Hinckley, 885 E 4
56552 Hitterdal, 178 B 4
56339 Hoffman, 627 C 5
55941 Hokah, 697 G 7
56340 Holdingford, 551 D 5
56139 Holland, 263 B 6
56045 Hollandale, 287 E 7
56249 Holloway, 146 C 5
55749 Holyoke, 190 F 4
55942 Homer, 150 G 6
56045 Hope, 125 E 7
55343 Hopkins, 13,428 G 5
55943 Houston, 1,090 G 7
55606 Hovland, 150 G 2
55349 Howard Lake, 1,162 D 5
55750 Hoyt Lakes, 3,634 F 3
55038 Hugo, 751 E 5
56047 Huntley, 139 D 7
55350 Hutchinson, 8,031 D 6
56140 Ihlen, 132 B 7
† 55359 Independence, 1,993 F 5
56649 International Falls⊙, 6,439 E 2
55075 Inver Grove Heights, 12,148 E 6
56141 Iona, 260 C 7
55751 Iron, 150 F 3
56455 Ironton, 562 D 4
55040 Isanti, 679 E 5
56342 Isle, 551 E 4
56142 Ivanhoe⊙, 738 B 6
56143 Jackson⊙, 3,550 C 7
55752 Jacobson, 225 E 4
56048 Janesville, 1,557 E 6
56144 Jasper, 754 B 7
56145 Jeffers, 436 C 6
56456 Jenkins, 148 D 4
55352 Jordan, 1,836 E 6
† 56669 Kabetogama, 150 F 2
56251 Kandiyohi, 295 D 5
56732 Karlstad, 727 B 2
56050 Kasota, 732 D 6
55944 Kasson, 1,883 F 6
55753 Keewatin, 1,382 E 3
56650 Kelliher, 289 D 3
55945 Kellogg, 403 G 6
55754 Kelly Lake, 950 F 3
55755 Kelsey, 151 F 3
56733 Kennedy, 424 B 2
56343 Kensington, 308 C 5
56553 Kent, 139 B 4
55946 Kenyon, 1,575 E 6
56252 Kerkhoven, 641 C 5
55757 Kettle River, 173 E 4
56051 Kiester, 681 E 7
56052 Kilkenny, 182 E 6
55353 Kimball, 567 D 5
55758 Kinney, 325 F 3
55609 Knife River, 350 G 4
55947 La Crescent, 3,142 G 7
56054 Lafayette, 498 D 6
56149 Lake Benton, 759 B 6
56734 Lake Bronson, 325 B 2
55041 Lake City, 3,594 F 6
56055 Lake Crystal, 1,807 D 6
55042 Lake Elmo, 4,032 F 6
56150 Lakefield, 1,820 C 7
† 55398 Lake Fremont (Zimmerman), 495 E 5
56458 Lake George, 200 D 3
55043 Lakeland, 962 F 6
56253 Lake Lillian, 316 C 6
56554 Lake Park, 658 B 4
† 55043 Lake Saint Croix Beach, 1,111 F 6
† 56401 Lake Shore, 410 D 4
55044 Lakeville, 7,556 E 6
56151 Lake Wilson, 378 B 7
56152 Lamberton, 962 C 6
56735 Lancaster, 382 B 2
55949 Lanesboro, 850 G 7
55950 Lansing, 300 F 7
56461 Laporte, 154 D 3
† 55744 La Prairie, 413 E 3
56056 La Salle, 132 D 6

(continued on following page)

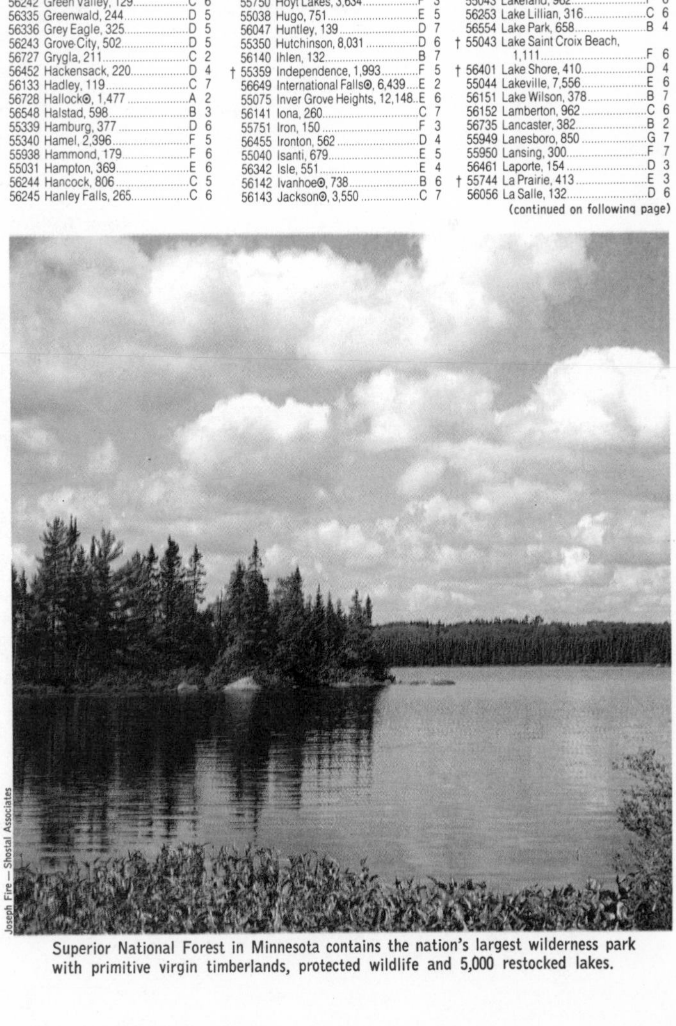

Joseph Fire — Shostal Associates

Superior National Forest in Minnesota contains the nation's largest wilderness park with primitive virgin timberlands, protected wildlife and 5,000 restocked lakes.

56344 Lastrup, 161 .... D 4
55101 Lauderdale, 2,419 .... G 5
56057 Le Center⊙, 1,890 .... E 6
56651 Lengby, 140 .... C 3
55734 Leonidas, 157 .... F 3
56153 Leota, 285 .... C 7
55951 Le Roy, 870 .... F 7
55354 Lester Prairie, 1,162 .... D 6
56058 Le Sueur, 3,745 .... E 6
55952 Lewiston, 1,000 .... G 7
56060 Lewisville, 291 .... D 7
55014 Lexington, 1,926 .... G 5
55050 Lilydale, 664 .... G 5
55045 Lindstrom, 1,260 .... F 5
55038 Lino Lakes, 3,692 .... G 5
56155 Lismore, 323 .... B 7
55355 Litchfield⊙, 5,262 .... D 5
56345 Little Falls⊙, 7,467 .... D 5
56653 Littlefork, 824 .... E 2
55611 Little Marais, 175 .... G 3
56334 Long Beach, 219 .... C 5
55356 Long Lake, 1,506 .... F 5
56347 Long Prairie⊙, 2,416 .... D 5
56655 Longville, 171 .... D 4
55046 Lonsdale, 622 .... E 6
55357 Loretto, 340 .... F 5
56349 Lowry, 257 .... C 5
56255 Lucan, 254 .... C 6
55612 Lutsen, 620 .... F 2
56156 Luverne⊙, 4,703 .... B 7
55953 Lyle, 522 .... F 7
56157 Lynd, 267 .... C 6
55954 Mabel, 888 .... G 7
56062 Madelia, 2,316 .... D 6
56256 Madison⊙, 2,242 .... B 5
56063 Madison Lake, 587 .... E 6
56158 Magnolia, 233 .... B 7
56557 Mahnomen⊙, 1,313 .... C 3
55115 Mahtomedi, 2,640 .... F 5
55762 Mahtowa, 167 .... F 4
56001 Mankato⊙, 30,895 .... E 6
55955 Mantorville⊙, 479 .... F 6
† 55369 Maple Grove, 6,275 .... F 5
55358 Maple Lake, 1,124 .... D 5
55359 Maple Plain, 1,169 .... F 5
56065 Mapleton, 1,307 .... E 7
† 55912 Mapleview, 328 .... E 7
55109 Maplewood, 25,222 .... G 5
55764 Marble, 682 .... E 3
56657 Marcell, 350 .... E 3
56257 Marietta, 264 .... B 5
55047 Marine on Saint Croix, 513 .... F 5
56258 Marshall⊙, 9,886 .... C 6
55360 Mayer, 325 .... E 6
56260 Maynard, 455 .... C 6
55956 Mazeppa, 498 .... F 6
55760 McGregor, 331 .... E 4
56556 McIntosh, 753 .... C 3
55761 McKinley, 317 .... F 3
55765 Meadowlands, 128 .... F 3
55049 Medford, 690 .... E 6
55427 Medicine Lake, 930 .... G 5
† 55340 Medina (Hamel), 2,396 .... F 5
† 56352 Meire Grove, 171 .... C 5
56352 Melrose, 2,273 .... D 5
56464 Menahga, 835 .... C 4
55050 Mendota, 327 .... G 5
† 55050 Mendota Heights, 6,165 .... G 6
56736 Mentor, 236 .... B 3
56465 Merrifield, 300 .... D 4
56737 Middle River, 369 .... B 2
† 55033 Miesville, 192 .... F 6
56353 Milaca⊙, 1,940 .... E 5
56262 Milan, 427 .... C 5
55957 Millville, 139 .... F 6
56263 Milroy, 247 .... C 6
56354 Miltona, 172 .... C 4
* 55401 Minneapolis⊙, 434,400 .... G 5
Minneapolis-Saint Paul, ‡1,813,647 .... G 5
56264 Minneota, 1,320 .... C 6
55959 Minnesota City, 301 .... G 6
56068 Minnesota Lake, 738 .... E 7
55343 Minnetonka, 35,776 .... G 5
† 55364 Minnetrista, 2,878 .... F 5
56265 Montevideo⊙, 5,661 .... C 6
56069 Montgomery, 2,281 .... E 6
55362 Monticello, 1,636 .... E 5
55363 Montrose, 379 .... E 5
56560 Moorhead⊙, 29,687 .... B 4
Moorhead-Fargo, ‡120,238 .... B 4
55767 Moose Lake, 1,400 .... F 4
56266 Mora⊙, 972 .... E 5
56266 Morgan, 972 .... D 6
56267 Morris⊙, 5,366 .... C 5
55052 Morristown, 659 .... E 6
56270 Morton, 591 .... C 6
56466 Motley, 351 .... D 4
55364 Mound, 7,572 .... E 6
† 55112 Mounds View, 9,988 .... G 5
55768 Mountain Iron, 1,698 .... F 3
56159 Mountain Lake, 1,986 .... D 7
56271 Murdock, 358 .... C 5
55769 Nashwauk, 1,341 .... E 3
56272 Nassau, 126 .... B 5
56566 Naytahwaush, 350 .... C 3
56355 Nelson, 175 .... C 5
55053 Nerstrand, 231 .... E 6
55772 Nett Lake, 470 .... E 2
56467 Nevis, 308 .... D 4
55366 New Auburn, 274 .... D 6
55112 New Brighton, 19,507 .... G 5
56738 Newfolden, 390 .... B 2
55367 New Germany, 303 .... E 6
56273 New London, 736 .... C 5
55054 New Market, 215 .... E 6
56356 New Munich, 307 .... D 5
55055 Newport, 2,922 .... F 6
56071 New Prague, 2,680 .... F 6
56072 New Richland, 1,113 .... E 7
† 55031 New Trier, 153 .... F 6
56073 New Ulm⊙, 13,051 .... D 6
56567 New York Mills, 791 .... C 4
† 56431 Nichols, 125 .... E 4
56074 Nicollet, 618 .... D 6
56568 Nielsville, 156 .... B 3
56468 Nisswa, 1,011 .... D 4
55770 Nopeming, 268 .... F 4
56274 Norcross, 137 .... B 5
55056 North Branch, 1,106 .... F 5
† 56442 North Crosslake, 362 .... D 4
55057 Northfield, 10,235 .... E 6
56001 North Mankato, 7,347 .... D 6
56661 Northome, 351 .... D 3
56275 North Redwood, 155 .... D 6
56075 Northrop, 188 .... D 7
55109 North Saint Paul, 11,950 .... E 5
55368 Norwood, 1,058 .... E 6
56276 Odessa, 194 .... B 5
56160 Odin, 166 .... D 7
56569 Ogema, 236 .... C 3
56358 Ogilvie, 384 .... E 5
56161 Okabena, 237 .... C 7
56742 Oklee, 536 .... C 3
56277 Olivia⊙, 2,553 .... C 6
56359 Onamia, 670 .... E 4
† 55044 Orchard Lake, 200 .... E 6
56162 Ormsby, 199 .... D 7
† 55323 Orono (Crystal Bay), 6,787 .... F 5
55960 Oronoco, 564 .... F 6
55771 Orr, 315 .... F 2
56278 Ortonville⊙, 2,665 .... B 5
56570 Osage, 175 .... C 4
56360 Osakis, 1,306 .... C 5
56744 Oslo, 417 .... A 2
55369 Osseo, 2,908 .... G 5
55961 Ostrander, 216 .... F 7
† 56058 Ottawa, 125 .... E 6
56571 Ottertail, 180 .... C 4
56662 Outing, 425 .... E 4
55060 Owatonna⊙, 15,341 .... E 6
56469 Palisade, 149 .... E 4
† 55801 Palmers, 150 .... G 4
† 55705 Palo, 158 .... F 3
56361 Parkers Prairie, 882 .... C 4
56470 Park Rapids⊙, 2,772 .... D 4
56362 Paynesville, 1,920 .... D 5
56363 Pease, 187 .... E 5
† 56472 Pelican Lakes (Breezy Point Village), 233 .... D 4
56572 Pelican Rapids, 1,835 .... B 4
56078 Pemberton, 128 .... E 7
55775 Pengilly, 625 .... E 3
56279 Pennock, 255 .... C 5
56472 Pequot Lakes, 499 .... D 4
56573 Perham, 1,933 .... C 4
56574 Perley, 149 .... B 3
55962 Peterson, 269 .... G 7
† 55948 Pickwick, 150 .... G 7
56364 Pierz, 893 .... D 5
56473 Pillager, 374 .... D 4
55063 Pine City⊙, 2,143 .... F 5
55963 Pine Island, 1,640 .... F 6
56474 Pine River, 803 .... D 4
56164 Pipestone⊙, 5,328 .... B 7
55964 Plainview, 2,093 .... F 6
55370 Plato, 303 .... D 6
56748 Plummer, 285 .... B 3
† 55401 Plymouth, 17,593 .... G 5
56666 Ponemah, 531 .... D 2
56280 Porter, 207 .... B 6
55965 Preston⊙, 1,413 .... F 7
55371 Princeton, 2,531 .... E 5
56281 Prinsburg, 448 .... C 6
55372 Prior Lake, 1,114 .... E 6
55810 Proctor, 3,123 .... F 4
† 55752 Rabey, 125 .... E 4
55967 Racine, 197 .... F 7
56475 Randall, 536 .... D 4
55065 Randolph, 350 .... E 6
56668 Ranier, 255 .... E 2
56669 Ray, 200 .... E 2
56282 Raymond, 589 .... C 5
56165 Reading, 150 .... C 7
55968 Reads Landing, 150 .... F 6
56670 Redby, 475 .... D 3
56671 Redlake, 300 .... C 3
56750 Red Lake Falls⊙, 1,740 .... B 3
55066 Red Wing⊙, 10,441 .... F 6
56283 Redwood Falls⊙, 4,774 .... C 6
56672 Remer, 403 .... E 3
56284 Renville, 1,252 .... C 6
56166 Revere, 166 .... C 6
56367 Rice, 366 .... D 5
55423 Richfield, 47,231 .... G 6
56368 Richmond, 866 .... D 5
55422 Robbinsdale, 16,845 .... G 5
55901 Rochester⊙, 53,766 .... F 6
55067 Rock Creek, 805 .... F 5
55373 Rockford, 730 .... F 5
56369 Rockville, 302 .... D 5
55374 Rogers, 544 .... F 5
55969 Rollingstone, 450 .... G 6
56371 Roscoe, 195 .... D 5
56751 Roseau⊙, 2,552 .... C 2
55970 Rose Creek, 390 .... F 7
† 56216 Roseland, 123 .... C 6
55068 Rosemount, 1,337 .... E 6
55113 Roseville, 34,518 .... G 5
56579 Rothsay, 448 .... B 4
56167 Round Lake, 506 .... C 7
56373 Royalton, 534 .... D 5
55069 Rush City, 1,130 .... F 5
55971 Rushford, 1,318 .... G 7
56168 Rushmore, 394 .... C 7
56169 Russell, 398 .... C 6
56170 Ruthton, 405 .... B 6
55778 Rutledge, 123 .... F 4
56580 Sabin, 333 .... B 4
56285 Sacred Heart, 707 .... C 6
55779 Saginaw, 407 .... F 4
55414 Saint Anthony Falls, 9,239 .... G 5
55375 Saint Bonifacius, 685 .... F 5
55972 Saint Charles, 1,942 .... F 7
56080 Saint Clair, 488 .... E 6
56301 Saint Cloud⊙, 39,691 .... D 5
55070 Saint Francis, 897 .... E 5
56554 Saint Hilaire, 337 .... B 2
56081 Saint James⊙, 4,027 .... D 7
56374 Saint Joseph, 1,786 .... D 5
55426 Saint Louis Park, 48,883 .... G 5
56376 Saint Martin, 188 .... D 5
56376 Saint Michael, 1,021 .... E 5
* 55101 Saint Paul (cap.)⊙, 309,980 .... G 6
55071 Saint Paul Park, 5,587 .... G 6
56082 Saint Peter⊙, 8,339 .... E 6
56375 Saint Stephen, 331 .... D 5
56755 Saint Vincent, 171 .... A 2
56083 Sanborn, 505 .... C 6
55072 Sandstone, 1,641 .... F 4
56377 Sartell, 1,323 .... D 5
56378 Sauk Centre, 3,750 .... C 5
56379 Sauk Rapids, 5,051 .... D 5
55378 Savage, 3,611 .... G 6
55780 Sawyer, 200 .... F 4
55073 Scandia, 200 .... F 5
† 55720 Scanlon, 1,132 .... F 4
55613 Schroeder, 550 .... G 3
56287 Seaforth, 132 .... C 6
56084 Searles, 160 .... D 6
56477 Sebeka, 668 .... C 4
55074 Shafer, 149 .... F 5
55379 Shakopee⊙, 6,876 .... F 6
56581 Shelly, 260 .... B 3
56171 Sherburn, 1,190 .... D 7
56676 Shevlin, 185 .... C 3
† 55021 Shieldsville, 150 .... E 6
† 55331 Shorewood, 4,223 .... F 5
55614 Silver Bay, 3,504 .... G 3
55380 Silver Creek, 125 .... D 5
55381 Silver Lake, 694 .... D 6
† 56001 Skyline, 400 .... D 6
56172 Slayton⊙, 2,351 .... C 7
56085 Sleepy Eye, 3,461 .... D 6
† 56345 Sobieski, 189 .... D 5
55782 Soudan, 900 .... F 3
55382 South Haven, 238 .... D 5
56679 South International Falls, 2,116 .... E 2
55075 South Saint Paul, 25,016 .... G 6
56288 Spicer, 586 .... C 5
56087 Springfield, 2,530 .... C 6
55974 Spring Grove, 1,290 .... G 7
55432 Spring Lake Park, 6,417 .... E 5
55384 Spring Park, 1,087 .... F 5
55975 Spring Valley, 2,572 .... F 7
55079 Stacy, 278 .... E 5
55080 Stanchfield, 155 .... E 5
56479 Staples, 2,657 .... D 4
56381 Starbuck, 1,138 .... C 5
56173 Steen, 191 .... B 7
56757 Stephen, 904 .... A 2
55385 Stewart, 666 .... D 6
55976 Stewartville, 2,802 .... F 7
55082 Stillwater⊙, 10,191 .... F 5
55988 Stockton, 346 .... G 6
56174 Storden, 364 .... C 6
56758 Strandquist, 138 .... B 2
55783 Sturgeon Lake, 167 .... F 4
56289 Sunburg, 144 .... C 5
† 55075 Sunfish Lake, 269 .... E 6
56290 Svea, 125 .... C 6
56382 Swanville, 300 .... D 5
55785 Swatara, 250 .... E 4
55786 Taconite, 352 .... E 3
56291 Taunton, 195 .... B 6
55084 Taylors Falls, 587 .... F 5
56683 Tenstrike, 138 .... D 3
56701 Thief River Falls⊙, 8,618 .... B 2
† 56319 Thomson, 159 .... F 4
56583 Tintah, 167 .... B 5
55615 Tofte, 400 .... H 3
55789 Toivola, 185 .... F 3
† 55331 Tonka Bay, 1,397 .... F 5
55790 Tower, 699 .... F 3
56175 Tracy, 2,516 .... C 6
56176 Trimont, 835 .... D 7
56088 Truman, 1,137 .... D 7
55791 Twig, 165 .... F 4
56089 Twin Lakes, 230 .... E 7
56584 Twin Valley, 868 .... B 3
55616 Two Harbors⊙, 4,437 .... G 3
56178 Tyler, 1,069 .... B 6
56585 Ulen, 486 .... B 3
56586 Underwood, 278 .... C 4
56384 Upsala, 312 .... D 5
† 56361 Urbank, 125 .... C 4
55979 Utica, 240 .... G 7
† 55101 Vadnais Heights, 3,391 .... G 5
56587 Vergas, 281 .... C 4
55085 Vermillion, 359 .... F 6
56481 Verndale, 570 .... C 4
† 55752 Verndon, 135 .... E 4
56090 Vernon Center, 347 .... D 7
55086 Veseli, 150 .... E 6
56292 Vesta, 330 .... C 6
55386 Victoria, 850 .... F 6
56385 Villard, 221 .... C 5
56588 Vining, 121 .... C 4
55792 Virginia, 12,450 .... F 3
55981 Wabasha⊙, 2,371 .... G 6
56293 Wabasso, 738 .... C 6
55387 Waconia, 2,445 .... E 6
56482 Wadena⊙, 4,640 .... C 4
56386 Wahkon, 208 .... E 4
56387 Waite Park, 2,824 .... D 5
56091 Waldorf, 285 .... E 7
56484 Walker⊙, 2,073 .... D 3
56180 Walnut Grove, 756 .... C 6
56092 Walters, 152 .... E 7
55982 Waltham, 189 .... F 7
55983 Wanamingo, 574 .... F 6
56294 Wanda, 124 .... C 6
55743 Warba, 148 .... E 3
56762 Warren⊙, 1,999 .... B 2
56763 Warroad, 1,086 .... C 2
55087 Warsaw, 200 .... E 6
56093 Waseca⊙, 6,789 .... E 6
55388 Watertown, 1,390 .... E 6
56096 Waterville, 1,539 .... E 6
55389 Watkins, 785 .... D 5
56295 Watson, 228 .... C 5
56589 Waubun, 345 .... C 3
55390 Waverly, 546 .... E 5
55391 Wayzata, 3,700 .... G 5
55088 Webster, 175 .... E 6
56181 Welcome, 694 .... D 7
56097 Wells, 2,791 .... E 7
56590 Wendell, 247 .... B 4
56183 Westbrook, 990 .... C 6
55985 West Concord, 718 .... F 6
55118 West Saint Paul, 18,799 .... G 5
56296 Wheaton⊙, 2,029 .... B 5
56485 Whipholt, 142 .... D 3
55110 White Bear Lake, 23,313 .... G 5
56591 White Earth, 150 .... C 3
56184 Wilder, 132 .... C 7
55090 Willernie, 697 .... G 5
56686 Williams, 220 .... D 2
56201 Willmar⊙, 12,869 .... C 5
55795 Willow River, 331 .... F 4
56185 Wilmont, 390 .... C 7
56687 Wilton, 119 .... C 3
56101 Windom⊙, 3,952 .... C 7
56592 Winger, 228 .... B 3
56098 Winnebago, 1,791 .... D 7
55987 Winona⊙, 26,438 .... G 6
55395 Winsted, 1,266 .... D 6
55396 Winthrop, 1,391 .... D 6
55796 Winton, 193 .... G 3
56594 Wolverton, 171 .... B 4
† 55798 Woodbury, 6,184 .... F 6
56297 Wood Lake, 418 .... C 6
56186 Woodstock, 217 .... B 7
56187 Worthington⊙, 9,825 .... C 7
55797 Wrenshall, 147 .... F 4
55798 Wright, 132 .... E 4
55990 Wykoff, 450 .... F 7
55092 Wyoming, 695 .... F 5
55397 Young America, 611 .... E 6
55799 Zim, 608 .... F 3
55398 Zimmerman, 495 .... E 5
55991 Zumbro Falls, 203 .... F 6
55992 Zumbrota, 1,929 .... F 6

⊙ County seat.
‡ Population of metropolitan area.
† Zip of nearest p.o.
* Multiple zips

Agriculture, Industry and Resources

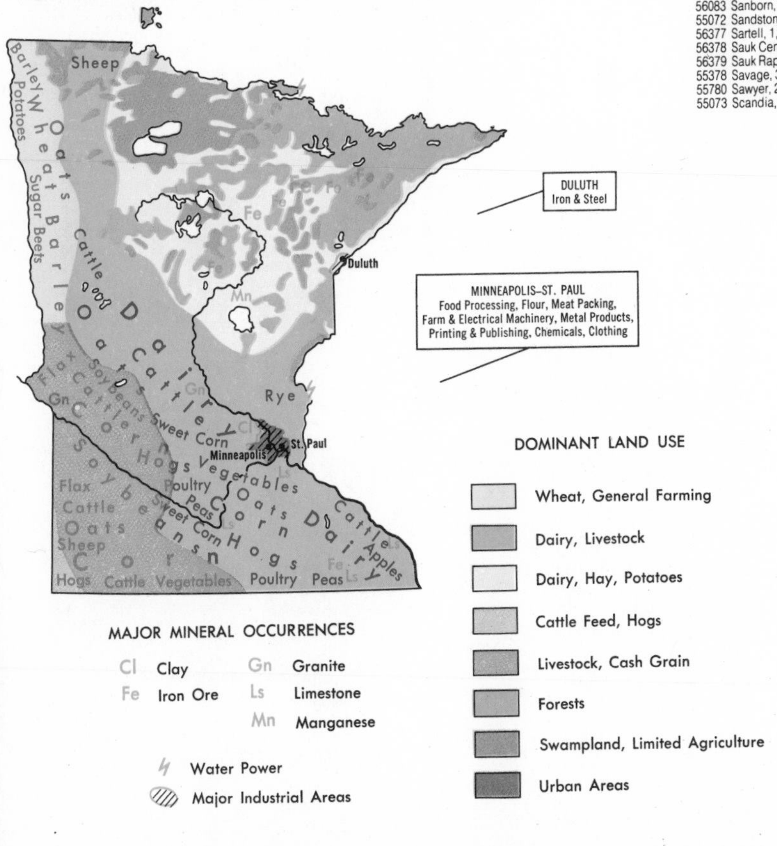
Sheep
Barley
Potatoes
Wheat
Oats
Barley
Sugar Beets
Cattle
Dairy
Oats
Cattle
Flax
Soybeans
Sweet Corn
Hogs
Vegetables
Poultry
Peas
Corn
Rye
Fe
Mn
Gn
Cl
Ls
Duluth
St. Paul
Minneapolis
Apples
DULUTH
Iron & Steel
MINNEAPOLIS–ST. PAUL
Food Processing, Flour, Meat Packing, Farm & Electrical Machinery, Metal Products, Printing & Publishing, Chemicals, Clothing
DOMINANT LAND USE
Wheat, General Farming
Dairy, Livestock
Dairy, Hay, Potatoes
Cattle Feed, Hogs
Livestock, Cash Grain
Forests
Swampland, Limited Agriculture
Urban Areas
MAJOR MINERAL OCCURRENCES
Cl Clay
Fe Iron Ore
Gn Granite
Ls Limestone
Mn Manganese
Water Power
Major Industrial Areas

Topography

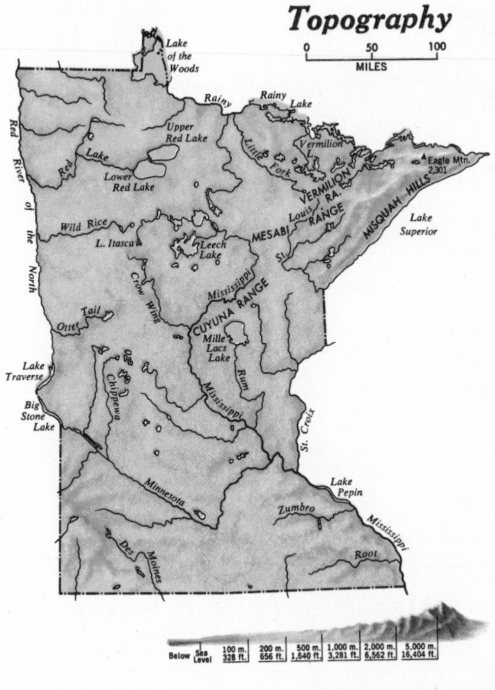
0 50 100
MILES
Lake of the Woods
Rainy
Rainy Lake
Red River of the North
Upper Red Lake
Lower Red Lake
Red Lake
Little Fork
Vermilion
VERMILION RA.
Eagle Mtn. 2,301
MESABI RANGE
MISQUAH HILLS
Lake Superior
St. Louis
Wild Rice
L. Itasca
Leech Lake
Mississippi
Crow Wing
CUYUNA RANGE
Mille Lacs Lake
Otter Tail
Lake Traverse
Big Stone Lake
Chippewa
Rum
St. Croix
Minnesota
Lake Pepin
Zumbro
Des Moines
Root
Below Sea Level
100 m. 328 ft.
200 m. 656 ft.
500 m. 1,640 ft.
1,000 m. 3,281 ft.
2,000 m. 6,562 ft.
5,000 m. 16,404 ft.

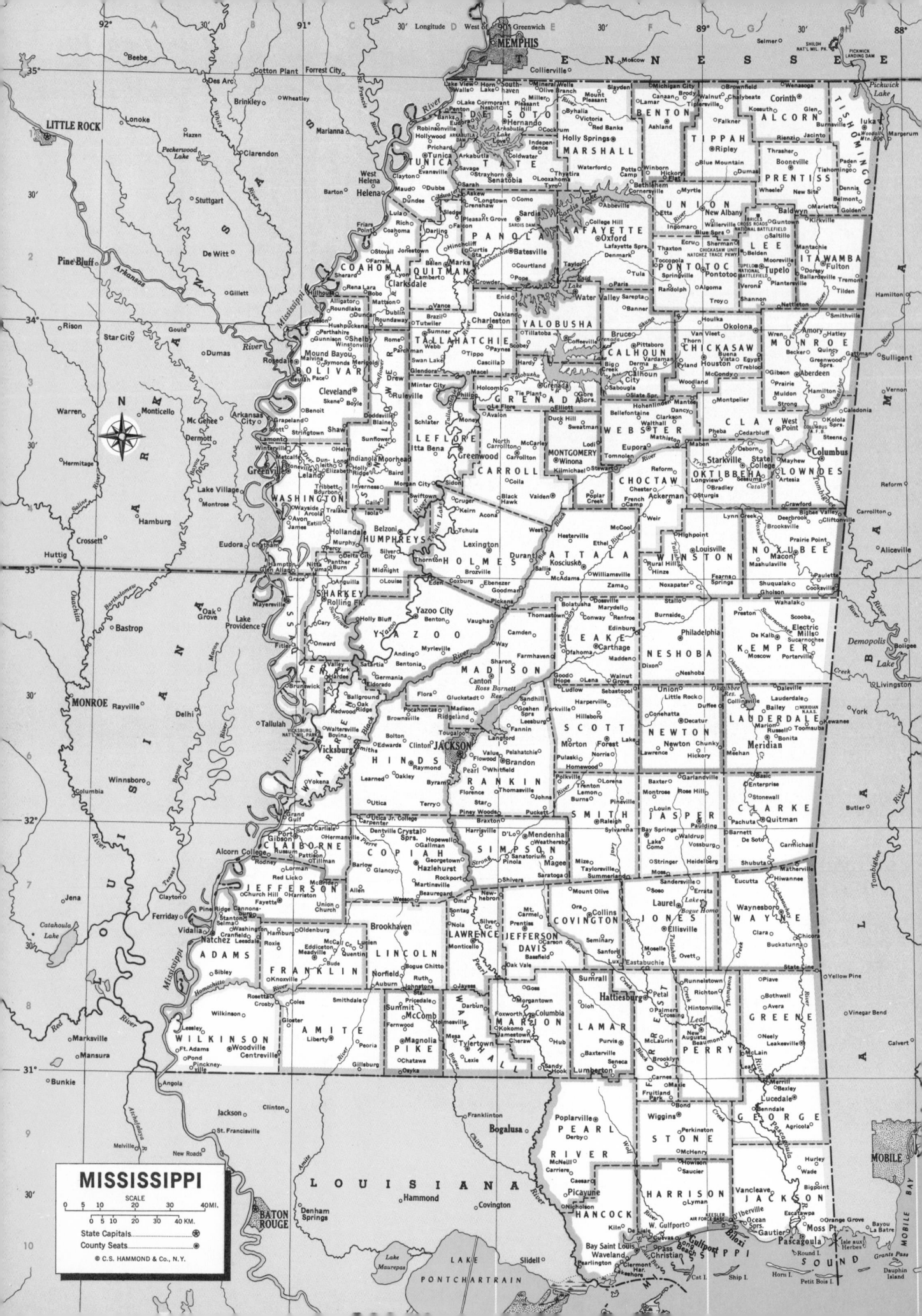

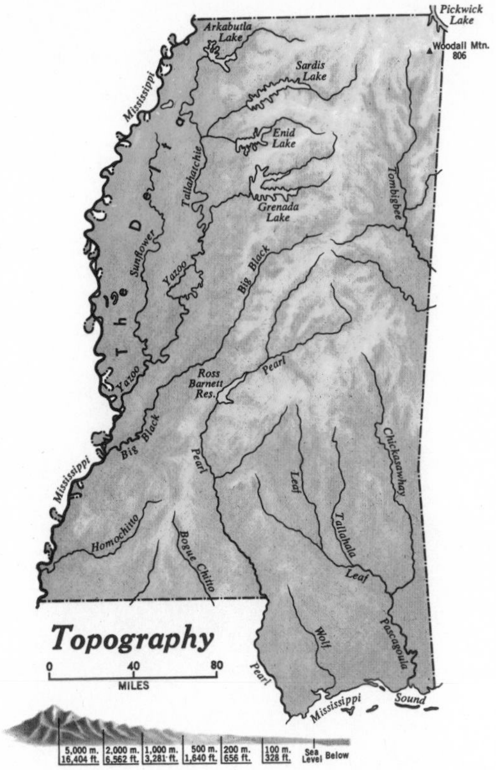
Pickwick Lake
Woodall Mtn. 806
Arkabutla Lake
Sardis Lake
Enid Lake
Grenada Lake
Mississippi
Tallahatchie
Sunflower
Yazoo
Big Black
Tombigbee
Ross Barnett Res.
Pearl
Chickasawhay
Leaf
Tallahala
Homochitto
Bogue Chitto
Wolf
Pascagoula
Mississippi Sound
The Delta
Topography
0 40 80
MILES
5,000 m. 16,404 ft.
2,000 m. 6,562 ft.
1,000 m. 3,281 ft.
500 m. 1,640 ft.
200 m. 656 ft.
100 m. 328 ft.
Sea Level
Below

AREA 47,716 sq. mi.
POPULATION 2,216,912
CAPITAL Jackson
LARGEST CITY Jackson
HIGHEST POINT Woodall Mtn. 806 ft.
SETTLED IN 1716
ADMITTED TO UNION December 10, 1817
POPULAR NAME Magnolia State
STATE FLOWER Magnolia
STATE BIRD Mockingbird

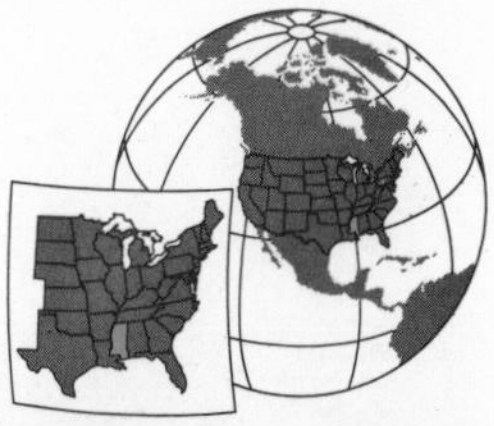

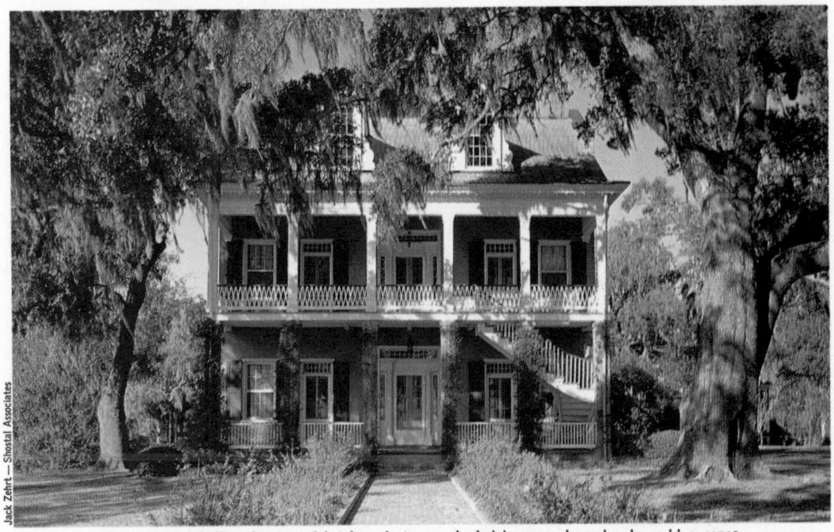

Jack Zehrt—Shostal Associates

Gracious antebellum houses of brick and stucco, shaded by moss-draped oaks, add a sense of permanence to the older section of Biloxi, Mississippi.

COUNTIES

County	Key
Adams, 37,293	B 8
Alcorn, 27,179	G 1
Amite, 13,763	C 8
Attala, 19,570	E 4
Benton, 7,505	F 1
Bolivar, 49,409	C 3
Calhoun, 14,623	F 3
Carroll, 9,397	E 4
Chickasaw, 16,805	G 3
Choctaw, 8,440	F 4
Claiborne, 10,086	C 7
Clarke, 15,049	G 6
Clay, 18,840	G 3
Coahoma, 40,447	C 2
Copiah, 24,749	D 7
Covington, 14,002	E 7
De Soto, 35,885	E 1
Forrest, 57,849	F 8
Franklin, 8,011	C 8
George, 12,459	G 9
Greene, 8,545	G 8
Grenada, 19,854	E 3
Hancock, 17,387	E 10
Harrison, 134,582	F 10
Hinds, 214,973	D 6
Holmes, 23,120	D 4
Humphreys, 14,601	C 4
Issaquena, 2,737	B 5
Itawamba, 16,847	H 2
Jackson, 87,975	G 9
Jasper, 15,994	F 6
Jefferson, 9,295	B 7
Jefferson Davis, 12,936	E 7
Jones, 56,357	F 7
Kemper, 10,233	G 5
Lafayette, 24,181	E 2
Lamar, 15,209	E 8
Lauderdale, 67,087	G 6
Lawrence, 11,137	D 7
Leake, 17,085	E 5
Lee, 46,148	G 2
Leflore, 42,111	D 3
Lincoln, 26,198	D 8
Lowndes, 49,700	H 4
Madison, 29,737	D 5
Marion, 22,871	E 8
Marshall, 24,027	E 1
Monroe, 34,043	H 3
Montgomery, 12,918	E 4
Neshoba, 20,802	F 5
Newton, 18,983	F 6
Noxubee, 14,288	G 4
Oktibbeha, 28,752	G 4
Panola, 26,829	E 2
Pearl River, 27,802	E 9
Perry, 9,065	G 8
Pike, 31,756	D 8
Pontotoc, 17,363	F 2
Prentiss, 20,133	G 1
Quitman, 15,888	D 2
Rankin, 43,933	E 6
Scott, 21,369	E 6
Sharkey, 8,937	C 5
Simpson, 19,947	E 7
Smith, 13,561	E 6
Stone, 8,101	F 9
Sunflower, 37,047	C 3
Tallahatchie, 19,338	D 3
Tate, 18,544	E 1
Tippah, 15,852	G 1
Tishomingo, 14,940	H 1
Tunica, 11,854	D 1
Union, 19,096	F 2
Walthall, 12,500	D 8
Warren, 44,981	C 6
Washington, 70,581	C 4
Wayne, 16,650	G 7
Webster, 10,047	F 3
Wilkinson, 11,099	B 8
Winston, 18,406	F 4
Yalobusha, 11,915	E 2
Yazoo, 27,304	D 5

CITIES and TOWNS

	Zip	*Name/Pop.*	*Key*
	38601	Abbeville, 600	F 2
	39730	Aberdeen⊙, 6,157	H 3
	39735	Ackerman⊙, 1,502	F 4
†	39095	Acona, 200	D 4
†	39452	Agricola, 200	G 9
	39096	Alcorn College, 2,380	B 7
	38820	Algoma, 150	G 2
	38720	Alligator, 280	C 2
	38821	Amory, 7,236	H 3
	38721	Anguilla, 612	C 5
	38722	Arcola, 517	C 4
	38602	Arkabutla, 195	D 1
	39736	Artesia, 444	G 4
	38603	Ashland⊙, 348	F 1
	38604	Askew, 200	D 1
†	39664	Auburn, 500	C 8
	38912	Avalon, 275	D 3
†	39456	Avera, 150	G 8
	38723	Avon, 400	B 4
	39320	Bailey, 320	G 6
	38724	Baird, 212	C 4
	38824	Baldwyn, 2,366	G 2
†	38801	Ballardsville, 105	H 2
†	38664	Banks, 100	D 1
	38913	Banner, 200	F 2
	39421	Bassfield, 354	E 8
	38606	Batesville⊙, 3,796	E 2
†	39343	Baxter, 225	F 6
†	39455	Baxterville, 100	E 8
	39520	Bay Saint Louis⊙, 6,752	F 10
	39422	Bay Springs⊙, 1,801	F 7
	39423	Beaumont, 1,061	G 8
†	39191	Beauregard, 199	D 7
	38825	Becker, 450	G 3
	38826	Belden, 241	G 2
	38609	Belen, 500	D 2
	39737	Bellefontaine, 360	F 3
	38827	Belmont, 968	H 1
	39038	Belzoni⊙, 3,146	C 4
†	39450	Benndale, 500	G 9
	38725	Benoit, 473	C 3
	39039	Benton, 500	D 5
	39040	Bentonia, 544	D 5
†	38659	Bethlehem, 210	F 1
	38726	Beulah, 443	B 3
	39453	Bexley, 130	G 9
	39738	Bigbee Valley, 370	H 4
	38914	Big Creek, 148	F 3
†	39567	Bigpoint, 100	H 9
*	39530	Biloxi, 48,486	G 10
		Biloxi-Gulfport, ‡134,582	G 10
	38918	Black Hawk, 100	E 4
	38610	Blue Mountain, 677	G 1
	38828	Blue Springs, 125	G 2
	38728	Bobo, 200	C 2
	39629	Bogue Chitto, 658	D 8
	39041	Bolton, 787	D 6
	39550	Bond, 350	F 9
	39321	Bonita, 300	G 6
	38829	Booneville⊙, 5,895	G 1
†	39456	Bothwell, 100	G 8
	38729	Bourbon, 350	C 4
	38730	Boyle, 861	C 3
	39042	Brandon⊙, 2,685	E 6
	39044	Braxton, 180	D 6
	38956	Brazil, 229	D 2
	39601	Brookhaven⊙, 10,700	C 7
	39425	Brooklyn, 750	F 8
	39739	Brooksville, 978	G 4
†	38683	Brownfield, 300	G 1
†	39041	Brownsville, 200	D 6
†	39095	Brozville, 150	D 4
	38915	Bruce, 2,033	F 3
†	39180	Brunswick, 90	C 5
	39322	Buckatunna, 500	G 7
	39630	Bude, 1,146	C 8
†	39153	Burns, 100	E 6
	38833	Burnsville, 435	H 1
	38611	Byhalia, 702	E 1
†	39205	Byram, 250	D 6
†	38754	Caile, 350	C 4
	39740	Caledonia, 245	H 3
	38916	Calhoun City, 1,847	F 3
	39045	Camden, 248	E 5
	38612	Canaan, 200	F 1
†	39120	Cannonsburg, 240	B 7
	39046	Canton⊙, 10,503	D 5
	39049	Carlisle, 350	C 7
†	39360	Carmichael, 150	G 7
	39426	Carriere, 900	E 9
	38917	Carrollton⊙, 295	E 4
	39427	Carson, 285	E 7
	39051	Carthage⊙, 3,031	E 5
	39054	Cary, 517	C 5
	38920	Cascilla, 150	D 3
	39741	Cedarbluff, 180	G 3
	39631	Centreville, 1,819	B 8
	38684	Chalybeate, 350	G 1
	38921	Charleston⊙, 2,821	D 2
	39632	Chatawa, 300	D 8
†	39483	Cheraw, 100	E 8
	39323	Chunky, 280	G 6
	39324	Clara, 400	G 7
	38614	Clarksdale⊙, 21,673	D 2
†	39752	Clarkson, 100	F 3
	39551	Clermont Harbor, 200	F 10
	38732	Cleveland⊙, 13,327	C 3
	39742	Cliftonville, 280	H 4
	39056	Clinton, 7,246	D 6
	38617	Coahoma, 350	C 2
	38922	Coffeeville⊙, 1,024	E 3
	38618	Coldwater, 1,450	E 1
	39639	Coles, 195	C 8
†	38655	College Hill, 175	E 2
	39428	Collins⊙, 1,934	E 7
	39325	Collinsville, 700	G 6
	39429	Columbia⊙, 7,587	E 8
	39701	Columbus⊙, 25,795	H 3
	38619	Como, 1,003	E 1
†	39051	Conway, 125	E 5
	38834	Corinth⊙, 11,581	G 1
†	38659	Cornersville, 235	F 1
	38620	Courtland, 316	E 2
†	39095	Coxburg, 300	D 5
†	39120	Cranfield, 100	B 7
	39743	Crawford, 391	G 4
	38621	Crenshaw, 1,271	D 2
	39633	Crosby, 491	B 8
	38622	Crowder, 815	D 2
	38924	Cruger, 415	D 4
	39059	Crystal Springs, 4,180	D 7
†	39571	Cuevas, 200	F 10
†	38606	Curtis Station, 200	D 2
†	39751	Dancy, 116	F 3
†	39643	Darbun, 100	D 8
	38623	Darling, 250	D 2
	39327	Decatur⊙, 1,311	F 6
	39328	De Kalb⊙, 1,072	G 5
†	39571	De Lisle, 450	F 10
	39061	Delta City, 300	C 4
	38838	Dennis, 175	H 1
†	39470	Derby, 189	E 9
	38839	Derma, 660	F 3
	39360	De Soto, 150	G 7
	39532	D'Iberville, 7,288	G 10
†	39350	Dixon, 125	F 5
	39062	D'Lo, 485	E 7
	38736	Doddsville, 276	C 3
	38840	Dorsey, 100	H 2
	38737	Drew, 2,574	C 3
	38739	Dublin, 385	C 2
	38925	Duck Hill, 809	E 3
†	39337	Duffee, 100	G 6
	38625	Dumas, 200	G 1
	38740	Duncan, 599	C 2
†	38756	Dunleith, 140	C 4
	39063	Durant, 2,752	E 4
	39436	Eastabuchie, 200	F 8
	39064	Ebenezer, 150	D 5
	38841	Ecru, 417	F 2
	39634	Eddiceton, 175	C 8
	39065	Eden, 152	D 5
†	39051	Edinburg, 200	F 5
	39066	Edwards, 1,236	C 6
	38842	Egypt, 100	G 3
	39329	Electric Mills, 200	G 5
	38742	Elizabeth, 540	C 4
	38926	Elliott, 200	E 3
	39437	Ellisville⊙, 4,643	F 7
	39330	Enterprise, 458	G 6
	39552	Escatawpa, 1,579	G 10
†	38748	Estill, 100	C 4
	39067	Ethel, 560	F 4
	38627	Etta, 100	F 2
†	38632	Eudora, 200	D 1
	39744	Eupora, 1,792	F 3
	38628	Falcon, 230	D 2
	38629	Falkner, 500	G 1
†	39042	Fannin, 250	E 6
	38630	Farrell, 400	C 2
	39069	Fayette⊙, 1,725	B 7
	39635	Fernwood, 600	D 8
	39070	Fitler, 800	B 5
	39071	Flora, 987	D 5
	39073	Florence, 404	D 6
†	39201	Flowood, 352	D 6
	39074	Forest⊙, 4,085	F 6
	39076	Forkville, 180	E 6
	39636	Fort Adams, 129	B 8
	39483	Foxworth, 950	E 8
	39745	French Camp, 174	F 4
	38631	Friars Point, 1,177	C 2
	38843	Fulton⊙, 2,899	H 2
†	39345	Garlandville, 150	F 6
	38844	Gattman, 175	H 3
	39553	Gautier, 2,087	G 10
	39078	Georgetown, 339	D 7
†	39083	Glancy, 120	C 7
	38846	Glen, 250	H 1
	38744	Glen Allan, 400	B 4
	38928	Glendora, 201	D 3
	39638	Gloster, 1,401	B 8
†	39110	Gluckstadt, 150	D 5
	38847	Golden, 115	H 2
†	39094	Good Hope, 125	E 5
	39079	Goodman, 1,194	E 5
	38929	Gore Springs, 120	E 3
†	39042	Goshen Springs, 100	E 6
†	39429	Goss, 100	E 8
	38745	Grace, 325	C 5
†	38725	Grapeland, 200	B 3
	38701	Greenville⊙, 39,648	B 4
	38930	Greenwood⊙, 22,400	D 4
	38848	Greenwood Springs, 170	H 3
	38901	Grenada⊙, 9,944	E 3
	39501	Gulfport⊙, 40,791	F 10
	38746	Gunnison, 545	C 3
	38849	Guntown, 304	G 2
	39746	Hamilton, 350	H 3
†	38744	Hampton, 200	B 4
†	39177	Hardee, 100	C 5
	39080	Harperville, 260	E 6
	39081	Harriston, 500	C 7
	39082	Harrisville, 500	D 7
†	38821	Hatley, 500	H 3
	39401	Hattiesburg⊙, 38,277	F 8
	39083	Hazlehurst⊙, 4,577	D 7
	39439	Heidelberg, 1,112	F 7
	39086	Hermanville, 500	C 7
	38632	Hernando⊙, 2,499	E 1
†	39192	Hesterville, 100	E 4
	39332	Hickory, 570	F 6
	38633	Hickory Flat, 354	F 1
	39087	Hillsboro, 350	E 6
†	38646	Hinchcliff, 125	D 2
†	39462	Hintonville, 100	F 8
†	39108	Hinze, 140	F 4
	39333	Hiwannee, 250	G 7
†	39751	Hohenlinden, 96	F 3
	38748	Hollandale, 3,260	C 4
	39088	Holly Bluff, 250	C 5
	38749	Holly Ridge, 375	C 4
	38635	Holly Springs⊙, 5,728	E 1
†	38676	Hollywood, 125	D 1
†	39648	Holmesville, 200	D 8
†	39059	Hopewell, 300	D 7
	38637	Horn Lake, 850	D 1
	38850	Houlka, 646	G 2
	38851	Houston⊙, 2,720	G 3
	39555	Hurley, 500	H 9
†	38774	Hushpuckena, 100	C 2
	38638	Independence, 150	E 1
	38751	Indianola⊙, 8,947	C 4
†	38652	Ingomar, 150	F 2
	38753	Inverness, 1,119	C 4
	38754	Isola, 458	C 4
	38941	Itta Bena, 2,489	D 4
	38852	Iuka⊙, 2,389	H 1
†	38865	Jacinto, 150	H 1
*	39201	Jackson (cap.)⊙, 153,968	D 6
		Jackson, ‡258,906	D 6
†	38748	James, 100	B 4
	39641	Jayess, 150	D 8
†	39042	Johns, 90	E 6
	38639	Jonestown, 1,110	D 2
	39334	Kewanee, 100	H 6
	39747	Kilmichael, 543	E 4
	39556	Kiln, 750	F 10
†	38856	Kirkville, 200	H 2
†	39661	Knoxville, 100	B 8
	39643	Kokomo, 150	E 8
†	39740	Kolola Springs, 150	H 3
	39090	Kosciusko⊙, 7,266	E 4
	38834	Kossuth, 227	G 1
	39092	Lake, 441	F 6
†	39422	Lake Como, 150	F 7
	38641	Lake Cormorant, 300	D 1
	39558	Lakeshore, 550	F 10
†	38680	Lake View, 125	D 1
	38642	Lamar, 135	F 1
	38643	Lambert, 1,511	D 2
	38755	Lamont, 450	B 3
†	39042	Langford, 100	E 6
	39335	Lauderdale, 600	G 5
	39440	Laurel⊙, 24,145	F 7
	39336	Lawrence, 200	F 6
	39450	Leaf, 350	G 8
	39451	Leakesville⊙, 1,090	G 8
	39093	Learned, 116	C 6
	38942	Le Flore, 99	D 3
	38756	Leland, 6,000	C 4
†	39074	Lemon, 90	E 6
	39094	Lena, 233	E 5
	39644	Lessley, 100	B 8
†	39667	Lexie, 270	D 8
	39095	Lexington⊙, 2,756	D 4
	39645	Liberty⊙, 612	C 8
	39337	Little Rock, 130	F 5
†	38828	Long, 110	C 4
	39560	Long Beach, 6,170	F 10
†	38665	Longtown, 150	D 1
	39749	Longview, 800	G 4
†	38668	Looxahoma, 200	E 1
†	39153	Lorena, 90	F 6
	39096	Lorman, 500	B 7
	39338	Louin, 382	F 6
	39097	Louise, 444	C 5
	39339	Louisville⊙, 6,626	G 4
	39452	Lucedale⊙, 2,083	G 9
	39098	Ludlow, 300	E 5
	38644	Lula, 445	C 2
	39455	Lumberton, 2,084	E 8
†	39501	Lyman, 500	F 10
	38645	Lyon, 383	D 2
	39750	Maben, 862	F 3
	39341	Macon⊙, 2,612	G 4
	39109	Madden, 450	F 5
	39110	Madison, 853	D 6
	39111	Magee, 2,973	E 7
	39652	Magnolia⊙, 1,913	D 8

(continued on following page)

† 38769 Malvina, 100.....C 3
38855 Mantachie, 200.....H 2
39751 Mantee, 142.....F 3
38856 Marietta, 250.....H 2
39342 Marion, 550.....G 6
38646 Marks◉, 2,609.....D 2
† 39083 Martinsville, 250.....D 7
39051 Marydell, 125.....F 5
† 39341 Mashulaville, 227.....G 4
† 39360 Matherville, 150.....G 7
39752 Mathiston, 570.....F 3
38758 Mattson, 200.....C 2
† 39425 Maxie, 100.....F 9
39113 Mayersville◉, 500.....B 5
39753 Mayhew, 200.....G 4
39107 McAdams, 240.....E 4
39647 McCall Creek, 250.....C 7
38943 McCarley, 250.....E 3
39648 McComb, 11,969.....D 8
38854 McCondy, 150.....G 3
39108 McCool, 225.....F 4
39561 McHenry, 550.....F 9
39456 McLain, 632.....G 8
† 39401 McLaurin, 100.....F 8
39457 McNeill, 800.....E 9
39653 Meadville◉, 594.....C 8
† 39301 Meehan, 100.....G 6
39114 Mendenhall◉, 2,402.....E 7
39301 Meridian◉, 45,083.....G 6
38759 Merigold, 772.....C 3
† 39452 Merrill, 100.....G 9
38760 Metcalfe, 600.....B 4
38647 Michigan City, 350.....F 1
39115 Midnight, 450.....C 4
38648 Mineral Wells, 250.....E 1
38944 Minter City, 300.....D 3
39116 Mize, 372.....E 7
38945 Money, 350.....D 3
39654 Monticello◉, 1,790.....D 7
39754 Montpelier, 200.....G 3
39343 Montrose, 160.....F 6
38857 Mooreville, 200.....G 2
38761 Moorhead, 2,284.....C 4
38946 Morgan City, 300.....D 4
39484 Morgantown, 305.....C 8
39117 Morton, 2,672.....E 6
39459 Moselle, 525.....F 8
39460 Moss, 150.....F 7
39563 Moss Point, 19,321.....G10
38762 Mound Bayou, 2,134.....C 3
39119 Mount Olive, 923.....E 7
38649 Mount Pleasant, 250.....E 1
† 38748 Murphy, 100.....C 4
38650 Myrtle, 308.....F 1
39120 Natchez◉, 19,704.....B 7
39461 Neely, 200.....G 8
38651 Nesbit, 300.....D 1
39344 Neshoba, 250.....F 5
38858 Nettleton, 1,591.....G 2
38652 New Albany◉, 6,426.....G 2
39462 New Augusta◉, 511.....F 8
39140 Newhebron, 456.....D 7
39345 Newton, 3,556.....F 6
39463 Nicholson, 400.....E 10
38763 Nitta Yuma, 150.....C 4
† 39665 Nola, 120.....D 7
† 39629 Norfield, 225.....C 8
38947 North Carrollton, 611.....E 3

39346 Noxapater, 554.....F 5
38948 Oakland, 493.....E 2
† 39154 Oakley, 420.....D 6
† 39180 Oak Ridge, 350.....C 6
39656 Oak Vale, 166.....E 8
39564 Ocean Springs, 9,580.....G10
39141 Ofahoma, 850.....E 5
38860 Okolona◉, 3,002.....G 2
38654 Olive Branch, 1,513.....E 1
† 39482 Oloh, 100.....E 8
39142 Oma, 100.....D 7
39428 Ora, 140.....E 7
39501 Orange Grove, 200.....H10
39657 Osyka, 628.....D 8
39464 Ovett, 250.....F 8
38655 Oxford◉, 13,846.....F 2
38764 Pace, 629.....C 3
39347 Pachuta, 271.....G 6
38861 Paden, 97.....H 1
† 39401 Palmers Crossing, 250.....F 8
38765 Panther Burn, 400.....C 4
38738 Parchman, 200.....D 3
38949 Paris, 253.....F 2
39567 Pascagoula◉, 27,264.....G10
39571 Pass Christian, 2,979.....F 10
39144 Pattison, 540.....C 7
39348 Paulding, 769.....F 6
39349 Paulette, 230.....H 4
38920 Paynes, 100.....D 3
39208 Pearl, 9,623.....D 6
39572 Pearlington, 500.....E 10
39145 Pelahatchie, 1,306.....E 6
† 38664 Penton, 175.....D 1
† 39645 Peoria, 100.....C 8
39573 Perkinston, 950.....F 9
39465 Petal, 6,986.....F 8
39755 Pheba, 280.....G 3
39350 Philadelphia◉, 6,274.....F 5
38950 Philipp, 975.....D 3
† 39476 Piave, 250.....G 8
39466 Picayune, 10,467.....E 9
39146 Pickens, 1,012.....E 5
† 39120 Pine Ridge, 175.....B 7
39148 Piney Woods, 300.....D 6
39149 Pinola, 102.....E 7
38951 Pittsboro◉, 188.....F 3
38862 Plantersville, 910.....G 2
38657 Pleasant Grove, 150.....D 2
† 38651 Pleasant Hill, 400.....E 1
39118 Polkville, 500.....E 6
38863 Pontotoc◉, 3,453.....G 2
38568 Pope, 210.....E 2
† 39747 Poplar Creek, 100.....E 4
39470 Poplarville◉, 2,312.....E 9
39352 Porterville, 150.....G 5
39150 Port Gibson◉, 2,589.....B 7
38659 Potts Camp, 459.....F 1
39353 Prairie Point, 150.....H 4
39474 Prentiss◉, 1,789.....E 7
39354 Preston, 120.....G 5
† 39666 Pricedale, 400.....D 8
38660 Prichard, 150.....D 1
39151 Puckett, 333.....E 6
39152 Pulaski, 108.....E 6
39475 Purvis◉, 1,860.....F 8
38851 Pyland, 75.....F 3
39660 Quentin, 150.....C 8
39355 Quitman◉, 2,702.....G 6

Agriculture, Industry and Resources

DOMINANT LAND USE

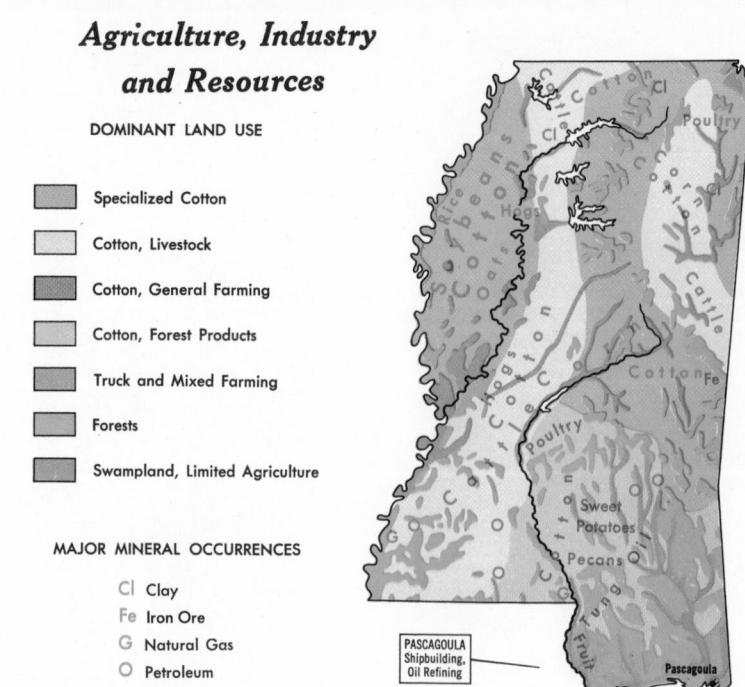

- Specialized Cotton
- Cotton, Livestock
- Cotton, General Farming
- Cotton, Forest Products
- Truck and Mixed Farming
- Forests
- Swampland, Limited Agriculture

MAJOR MINERAL OCCURRENCES

Cl Clay
Fe Iron Ore
G   Natural Gas
O   Petroleum
//// Major Industrial Areas

PASCAGOULA
Shipbuilding,
Oil Refining

39153 Raleigh◉, 1,018.....F 6
38864 Randolph, 205.....F 2
39154 Raymond◉, 1,620.....D 6
38661 Red Banks, 350.....F 1
† 39096 Red Lick, 250.....B 7
39156 Redwood, 400.....C 6
39757 Reform, 150.....F 4
38767 Rena Lara, 400.....C 2
† 39051 Renfroe, 100.....F 5
39476 Richton, 1,110.....F 8
39157 Ridgeland, 1,650.....D 6
38865 Rienzi, 363.....G 1
38663 Ripley◉, 3,482.....G 1
38664 Robinsonville, 285.....D 1

† 39083 Rockport, 100.....D 7
† 39096 Rodney, 200.....B 7
39159 Rolling Fork◉, 2,034.....C 5
38768 Rome, 171.....C 3
38769 Rosedale◉, 2,599.....B 3
39356 Rose Hill, 300.....F 6
† 38614 Roundaway, 175.....C 2
38740 Roundlake, 105.....C 2
39661 Roxie, 662.....C 8
38771 Ruleville, 2,351.....D 3
† 39401 Runnelstown, 200.....F 8
39108 Rural Hill, 125.....F 4
39357 Russell, 300.....G 6
39662 Ruth, 150.....D 8

38955 Sabougla, 100.....F 3
39160 Sallis, 213.....E 4
38866 Saltillo, 836.....G 2
39112 Sanatorium, 400.....E 7
39477 Sandersville, 694.....F 7
38962 Sandhill, 392.....E 5
39478 Sandy Hook, 108.....E 8
39479 Sanford, 150.....F 8
38665 Sarah, 300.....D 1
38666 Sardis◉, 2,391.....E 2
38867 Sarepta, 650.....F 2
39554 Saucier, 100.....F 9
38667 Savage, 100.....D 1
38952 Schlater, 398.....D 3
38953 Scobey, 100.....E 3
39358 Scooba, 626.....G 5
38772 Scott, 500.....B 3
39359 Sebastopol, 268.....F 5
39479 Seminary, 269.....E 7
38668 Senatobia◉, 4,247.....E 1
39758 Sessums, 100.....G 4
38868 Shannon, 575.....G 2
38773 Shaw, 2,513.....C 3
38774 Shelby, 2,645.....C 3
38669 Sherard, 160.....C 2
38869 Sherman, 468.....G 2
39164 Shivers, 100.....E 7
39360 Shubuta, 602.....G 7
39361 Shuqualak, 591.....G 5
39165 Sibley, 250.....B 8
38954 Sidon, 348.....D 4
39166 Silver City, 370.....C 4
39663 Silver Creek, 257.....D 7
38775 Skene, 300.....C 3
38955 Slate Spring, 105.....F 3
† 38642 Slayden, 310.....F 1
38670 Sledge, 516.....D 2
39664 Smithdale, 200.....C 8
38870 Smithville, 552.....H 2
39665 Sontag, 200.....D 7
39480 Soso, 230.....F 7
38871 Southhaven, 8,931.....E 1
† 38863 Springville, 100.....F 5
† 39350 Stallo, 100.....F 5
39167 Star, 175.....D 6
39759 Starkville◉, 11,369.....G 4
39762 State College, 4,595.....G 4
39362 State Line, 598.....G 8
39766 Steens, 125.....H 3
39767 Stewart, 150.....F 4
38776 Stoneville, 700.....C 4
39363 Stonewall, 1,161.....G 6
38672 Stovall, 260.....C 2
† 38665 Strayhorn, 800.....D 1
39481 Stringer, 340.....F 7
38777 Stringtown, 300.....C 3
39769 Sturgis, 321.....G 4
† 39168 Summerland, 150.....F 7
39666 Summit, 1,640.....D 8
38957 Sumner◉, 533.....D 3
39482 Sumrall, 955.....E 8
38778 Sunflower, 983.....C 3
38958 Swan Lake, 250.....D 3
38959 Swiftown, 400.....D 4
39153 Sylvarena, 205.....F 6
† 38929 Symonds, 200.....C 3
38673 Taylor, 92.....E 2
39168 Taylorsville, 1,299.....F 7
39169 Tchula, 1,729.....E 5
39170 Terry, 546.....D 6
38871 Thaxton, 250.....F 1
39171 Thomastown, 350.....E 5
38872 Thorn, 125.....F 3
39172 Thornton, 120.....D 4

38829 Thrasher, 800.....G 1
† 38668 Thyatira, 100.....E 1
38960 Tie Plant, 950.....E 3
† 38843 Tilden, 250.....H 2
38961 Tillatoba, 102.....E 3
38674 Tiplersville, 120.....G 1
38962 Tippo, 200.....D 3
38873 Tishomingo, 410.....H 1
38674 Toccopola, 175.....F 2
39770 Tomnolen, 225.....F 4
39364 Toomsuba, 500.....G 6
39174 Tougaloo, 1,720.....D 6
38757 Tralake, 200.....C 4
38875 Trebloc, 750.....G 3
38876 Tremont, 250.....H 2
38779 Tribbett, 200.....C 4
† 38863 Troy, 150.....G 2
38675 Tula, 100.....F 2
38676 Tunica◉, 1,685.....D 1
38801 Tupelo◉, 20,471.....G 2
38963 Tutwiler, 1,103.....D 2
39667 Tylertown◉, 1,736.....D 8
39365 Union, 1,856.....F 5
39668 Union Church, 194.....C 7
39175 Utica, 1,019.....C 6
39175 Utica Junior College, 700.....C 6
39176 Vaiden◉, 716.....E 4
39177 Valley Park, 350.....C 6
39178 Value, 327.....D 6
38964 Vance, 500.....D 2
† 39564 Vancleave, 500.....G 9
38851 Van Vleet, 300.....G 3
38878 Vardaman, 777.....F 3
38879 Verona, 1,877.....G 2
39180 Vicksburg◉, 25,478.....C 6
38679 Victoria, 400.....E 1
39366 Vossburg, 250.....F 7
39575 Wade, 800.....G 9
† 39422 Waldrup, 125.....F 7
38680 Walls, 850.....D 1
38683 Walnut, 458.....G 1
39189 Walnut Grove, 398.....F 5
38863 Waltersville, 150.....C 6
39771 Walthall◉, 161.....F 4
39190 Washington, 250.....B 7
38685 Waterford, 375.....F 2
38965 Water Valley◉, 3,285.....F 2
39576 Waveland, 3,108.....F 10
39367 Waynesboro◉, 4,368.....G 7
38780 Wayside, 150.....C 4
38966 Webb, 751.....D 3
39772 Weir, 573.....F 4
39191 Wenasoga, 150.....G 1
39191 Wesson, 1,253.....D 7
39192 West, 305.....E 4
† 39501 West Gulfport, 6,996.....F 10
39773 West Point◉, 8,714.....G 3
38880 Wheeler, 600.....G 1
39193 Whitfield, 6,200.....D 6
39577 Wiggins◉, 2,995.....F 9
38659 Winborn, 122.....F 1
39090 Williamsville, 250.....F 4
38781 Winstonville, 536.....C 3
39782 Winterville, 500.....B 4
39776 Woodland, 130.....F 3
39669 Woodville◉, 1,734.....B 8
† 39730 Wren, 150.....G 3
39194 Yazoo City◉, 10,796.....D 5
39090 Zama, 125.....D 5

◉ County seat.
‡ Population of metropolitan area.
† Zip of nearest p.o.
* Multiple zips

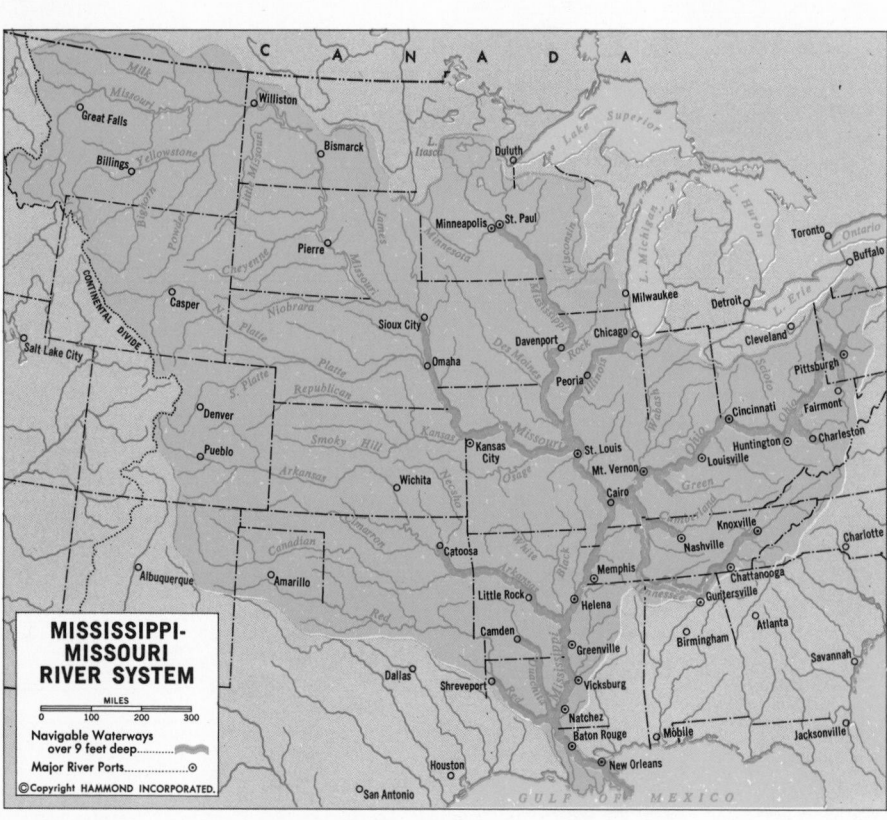

MISSISSIPPI-
MISSOURI
RIVER SYSTEM

MILES
0   100   200   300

Navigable Waterways
over 9 feet deep.
Major River Ports.....◉
© Copyright HAMMOND INCORPORATED.

AREA 69,686 sq. mi.
POPULATION 4,677,399
CAPITAL Jefferson City
LARGEST CITY St. Louis
HIGHEST POINT Taum Sauk Mtn. 1,772 ft.
SETTLED IN 1764
ADMITTED TO UNION August 10, 1821
POPULAR NAME Show Me State
STATE FLOWER Hawthorn
STATE BIRD Bluebird

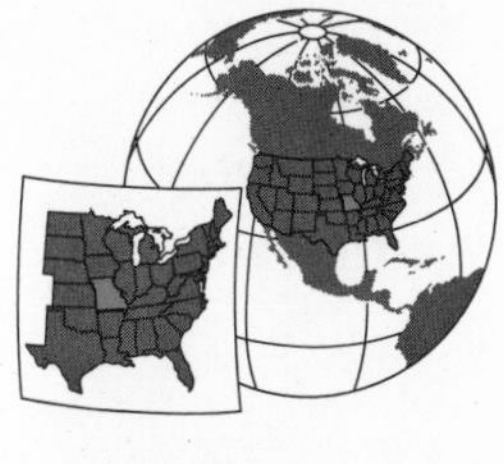

COUNTIES

County	Key
Adair, 22,472	G 2
Andrew, 11,913	C 3
Atchison, 9,240	B 2
Audrain, 25,362	J 4
Barry, 19,597	E 9
Barton, 10,431	D 7
Bates, 15,468	D 6
Benton, 9,695	F 6
Bollinger, 8,820	M 8
Boone, 80,911	H 4
Buchanan, 86,915	C 3
Butler, 33,529	M 9
Caldwell, 8,351	E 3
Callaway, 25,850	J 5
Camden, 13,315	G 6
Cape Girardeau, 49,350	N 8
Carroll, 12,565	F 4
Carter, 3,878	L 9
Cass, 39,448	D 5
Cedar, 9,424	E 7
Chariton, 11,084	F 3
Christian, 15,124	F 9
Clark, 8,260	J 2
Clay, 123,322	D 4
Clinton, 12,462	D 3
Cole, 46,228	H 6
Cooper, 14,732	G 5
Crawford, 14,828	K 7
Dade, 6,850	E 8
Dallas, 10,054	F 7
Daviess, 8,420	E 3
De Kalb, 7,305	D 3
Dent, 11,457	J 7
Douglas, 9,268	G 9
Dunklin, 33,742	M10
Franklin, 55,116	K 6
Gasconade, 11,878	J 6
Gentry, 8,060	D 2
Greene, 152,929	F 8
Grundy, 11,819	E 2
Harrison, 10,257	E 2
Henry, 18,451	E 6
Hickory, 4,481	F 7
Holt, 6,654	B 2
Howard, 10,561	G 4
Howell, 23,521	J 9
Iron, 9,529	L 7
Jackson, 654,558	D 5
Jasper, 79,852	D 8
Jefferson, 105,248	L 6
Johnson, 34,172	E 5
Knox, 5,692	H 2
Laclede, 19,944	G 7
Lafayette, 26,626	E 4
Lawrence, 24,585	E 8
Lewis, 10,993	J 2
Lincoln, 18,041	L 4
Linn, 15,125	F 3
Livingston, 15,368	E 3
Macon, 15,432	G 3
Madison, 8,641	M 8
Maries, 6,851	J 6
Marion, 28,121	J 3
McDonald, 12,357	D 9
Mercer, 4,910	E 2
Miller, 15,026	H 6
Mississippi, 16,647	O 9
Moniteau, 10,742	G 5
Monroe, 9,542	H 3
Montgomery, 11,000	K 5
Morgan, 10,068	G 6
New Madrid, 23,420	N 9
Newton, 32,901	D 9
Nodaway, 22,467	C 2
Oregon, 9,180	K 9
Osage, 10,994	J 6
Ozark, 6,226	H 9
Pemiscot, 26,373	N10
Perry, 14,393	N 7
Pettis, 34,137	F 5
Phelps, 29,481	J 7
Pike, 16,928	K 4
Platte, 32,081	C 4
Polk, 15,415	F 7
Pulaski, 53,781	H 7
Putnam, 5,916	F 2
Ralls, 7,764	J 3
Randolph, 22,434	G 3
Ray, 17,599	E 4
Reynolds, 6,106	L 8
Ripley, 9,803	L 9
Saint Charles, 92,954	L 5
Saint Clair, 7,667	E 6
Sainte Genevieve, 12,867	M 7
Saint Francois, 36,818	M 7
Saint Louis, 951,353	M 5
Saint Louis (city county), 622,236	M 5
Saline, 24,633	F 4
Schuyler, 4,665	G 2
Scotland, 5,499	H 2
Scott, 33,250	N 8
Shannon, 7,196	K 8
Shelby, 7,906	H 3
Stoddard, 25,771	N 9
Stone, 9,921	F 9
Sullivan, 7,572	F 2
Taney, 13,023	F 9
Texas, 18,320	J 8
Vernon, 19,065	D 7
Warren, 9,699	K 5
Washington, 15,086	L 7
Wayne, 8,546	L 8
Webster, 15,562	G 8
Worth, 3,359	D 2
Wright, 13,667	H 8

CITIES and TOWNS

Zip	*Name/Pop.*	*Key*
64720	Adrian, 1,259	D 6
63730	Advance, 903	N 8
63123	Affton, 24,067	P 3
† 64836	Airport Drive, 300	C 8
64830	Alba, 365	D 8
64402	Albany⊙, 1,804	D 2
63430	Alexandria, 453	K 2
63001	Allenton, 800	N 3
64001	Alma, 380	E 4
64620	Altamont, 225	D 3
63732	Altenburg, 277	O 7
65606	Alton⊙, 715	K 9
64421	Amazonia, 326	C 3
64722	Amoret, 219	C 6
64831	Anderson, 1,065	D 9
63620	Annapolis, 330	L 8
63820	Anniston, 515	O 9
64724	Appleton City, 1,058	D 6
63821	Arbyrd, 575	M10
63621	Arcadia, 627	L 7
64725	Archie, 525	D 5
65001	Argyle, 262	J 6
65230	Armstrong, 354	G 4
63010	Arnold, 11,994	P 4
65604	Ash Grove, 934	E 8
65010	Ashland, 769	H 5
63530	Atlanta, 377	H 3
63332	Augusta, 259	M 3
65605	Aurora, 5,359	E 9
65231	Auxvasse, 808	J 4
65608	Ava⊙, 2,504	G 9
64010	Avondale, 748	P 5
63011	Ballwin, 10,656	O 3
63531	Baring, 206	H 2
64423	Barnard, 206	C 2
64011	Bates City, 229	E 5
† 65619	Battlefield, 291	F 8
63622	Belgrade, 349	L 7
63735	Bell City, 424	N 8
65013	Belle, 1,133	J 6
† 63101	Bellefontaine Neighbors, 13,987	R 2
63623	Belleview, 225	L 7
63333	Bellflower, 360	K 4
64012	Belton, 9,783	C 5
63736	Benton⊙, 640	O 8
63014	Berger, 226	K 5
63134	Berkeley, 19,743	P 2
63822	Bernie, 1,641	M 9
63823	Bertrand, 604	O 9
64424	Bethany⊙, 2,914	E 2
63532	Bevier, 806	G 3
65610	Billings, 760	F 8
65438	Birch Tree, 573	K 9
† 64068	Birmingham, 266	P 5
63624	Bismarck, 1,387	L 7
65321	Blackburn, 294	F 4
† 63031	Black Jack, 3,500	P 2
65322	Blackwater, 249	G 5
65014	Bland, 621	J 6
63824	Blodgett, 220	O 8
63825	Bloomfield⊙, 1,584	M 9
63627	Bloomsdale, 411	M 6
64015	Blue Springs, 6,779	R 6
† 64101	Blue Summit, 1,283	R 5
64426	Blythedale, 213	E 2
64622	Bogard, 294	E 4
65612	Bois D'Arc, 250	F 8
64427	Bolckow, 225	C 2
65613	Bolivar⊙, 4,769	F 7
63628	Bonne Terre, 3,622	L 7
65016	Bonnots Mill, 210	J 5
65233	Boonville⊙, 7,514	G 5
64723	Bosworth, 386	F 4
65441	Bourbon, 955	K 6
63334	Bowling Green⊙, 2,936	K 4
63826	Braggadocio, 285	N10
63827	Bragg City, 210	N10
65616	Branson, 2,175	F 9
63533	Brashear, 316	H 2
64624	Braymer, 919	E 3
64625	Breckenridge, 598	E 3
† 63101	Breckenridge Hills, 7,011	O 2
63144	Brentwood, 11,248	P 3
63044	Bridgeton, 19,992	O 2
64728	Bronaugh, 203	C 7
64628	Brookfield, 5,491	F 3
64630	Browning, 412	F 2
65236	Brunswick, 1,870	F 4
64631	Bucklin, 654	G 3
64016	Buckner, 1,695	R 5
65622	Buffalo⊙, 1,915	F 7
65237	Bunceton, 437	G 5
63629	Bunker, 447	K 8
64428	Burlington Junction, 634	B 2
64730	Butler⊙, 3,984	D 6
65689	Cabool, 1,848	H 8
63630	Cadet, 300	L 6
64632	Cainsville, 454	E 2
65239	Cairo, 248	H 4
65323	Calhoun, 360	E 6
65018	California⊙, 3,105	H 5
63534	Callao, 373	G 3
64017	Camden, 286	D 4
65020	Camdenton⊙, 1,636	G 6
64429	Cameron, 3,960	D 3
63933	Campbell, 1,979	M 9
63828	Canalou, 358	N 9
63435	Canton, 2,680	J 2
63701	Cape Girardeau, 31,282	O 8
63829	Cardwell, 859	M10
64834	Carl Junction, 1,661	C 8
64633	Carrollton⊙, 4,847	E 4
64835	Carterville, 1,716	D 8
64836	Carthage⊙, 11,035	D 8
63830	Caruthersville⊙, 7,350	N10
65625	Cassville⊙, 1,910	E 9
63015	Catawissa, 250	N 4
65022	Cedar City, 454	H 5
63016	Cedar Hill, 500	L 6
63436	Center, 588	J 3
65023	Centertown, 277	H 5
64019	Centerview, 234	E 5
63633	Centerville⊙, 209	L 8
65240	Centralia, 3,618	H 4
63740	Chaffee, 2,793	N 8
65024	Chamois, 615	J 5
63834	Charleston⊙, 5,131	O 9
63017	Chesterfield, 13,000	O 3
64733	Chilhowee, 297	E 5
64601	Chillicothe⊙, 9,519	E 3
64635	Chula, 244	F 3
63437	Clarence, 1,050	H 3
65243	Clark, 271	H 4
65025	Clarksburg, 343	G 5
64430	Clarksdale, 248	D 3
63336	Clarksville, 668	K 4
63837	Clarkton, 1,177	M10
64119	Claycomo, 1,841	P 5
63105	Clayton⊙, 16,222	P 3
64431	Clearmont, 226	C 1
64734	Cleveland, 256	C 5
65631	Clever, 430	F 8
64735	Clinton⊙, 7,504	E 6
65325	Cole Camp, 1,038	F 6
65201	Columbia⊙, 58,804	H 5
63742	Commerce, 234	O 8
64434	Conception Junction, 237	C 2
64020	Concordia, 1,854	E 5
65632	Conway, 547	G 7
63839	Cooter, 414	N10
64021	Corder, 476	E 4
63338	Cottleville, 275	N 2
† 64501	Country Club Village, 221	C 3
64637	Cowgill, 232	E 3
64437	Craig, 369	B 2
65633	Crane, 1,003	E 9
64739	Creighton, 294	D 6
63018	Crescent, 425	N 3
† 63101	Crestwood, 15,398	O 3
63141	Creve Coeur, 8,967	O 3
65452	Crocker, 814	H 7
65634	Cross Timbers, 204	F 6
63019	Crystal City, 3,898	M 6
65453	Cuba, 2,070	K 6
63339	Curryville, 337	K 4
64439	Dearborn, 543	C 3
64740	Deepwater, 565	E 6
64440	De Kalb, 287	C 3
63744	Delta, 462	N 8
63636	Des Arc, 222	L 8
63601	Desloge, 2,818	M 7
63020	De Soto, 5,984	M 6
63131	Des Peres, 5,333	O 3
63841	Dexter, 6,024	N 9
64840	Diamond, 554	D 9
65459	Dixon, 1,387	H 6
63637	Doe Run, 900	M 7
63935	Doniphan⊙, 1,850	L 9
† 65550	Doolittle, 509	J 7
63844	Dorena, 500	O 9
63536	Downing, 406	H 2
64742	Drexel, 723	C 6
63936	Dudley, 248	M 9
64841	Duenweg, 656	D 8
† 64801	Duquesne, 738	D 8
64442	Eagleville, 388	D 2
64743	East Lynne, 255	D 5
63845	East Prairie, 3,275	O 9
65462	Edgar Springs, 450	J 7
64444	Edgerton, 477	C 4
63537	Edina⊙, 1,574	H 2
65026	Eldon, 3,520	G 6
64744	El Dorado Springs, 3,300	E 7
63638	Ellington, 1,094	L 8
63011	Ellisville, 4,681	N 3
63937	Ellsinore, 342	L 9
63343	Elsberry, 1,398	L 4
63639	Elvins, 1,603	L 7
65466	Eminence⊙, 520	K 8
65327	Emma, 224	F 5
63344	Eolia, 321	L 4
63846	Essex, 493	N 9
† 63601	Esther, 1,040	M 7
63025	Eureka, 2,384	N 3
65646	Everton, 264	E 8
63440	Ewing, 330	J 2
64024	Excelsior Springs, 9,411	R 4
65647	Exeter, 434	D 9
64446	Fairfax, 835	B 2
65648	Fair Grove, 431	F 8
65649	Fair Play, 328	E 7
64842	Fairview, 263	D 9
63345	Farber, 470	J 4
63640	Farmington⊙, 6,590	M 7
65248	Fayette⊙, 3,520	G 4
63026	Fenton, 2,275	P 3
63135	Ferguson, 28,915	P 2
63028	Festus, 7,530	M 6
64449	Fillmore, 251	C 2
63940	Fisk, 503	M 9
63601	Flat River, 4,550	M 7
* 63031	Florissant, 65,908	P 2
63347	Foley, 224	L 4
65652	Fordland, 399	G 8
64451	Forest City, 365	B 3
63348	Foristell, 273	M 2
65653	Forsyth⊙, 803	F 9
63441	Frankford, 472	K 4
65250	Franklin, 252	G 4
63645	Fredericktown⊙, 3,799	M 7
65035	Freeburg, 577	J 6
64746	Freeman, 417	C 5
63748	Frohna, 225	N 7
† 63101	Frontenac, 3,920	O 3
65251	Fulton⊙, 12,148	J 5
65655	Gainesville⊙, 627	G 9
65656	Galena⊙, 391	F 9
64640	Gallatin⊙, 1,833	E 3
64641	Galt, 261	F 2
64747	Garden City, 633	D 5
65036	Gasconade, 235	J 5
63037	Gerald, 762	K 6
63848	Gideon, 1,112	N10
65330	Gilliam, 248	F 4
64642	Gilman City, 376	D 2
64118	Gladstone, 23,128	P 5
65254	Glasgow, 1,336	G 4
† 64068	Glenaire, 505	R 5
63038	Glencoe, 2,500	N 3
63122	Glendale, 6,891	P 3
64748	Golden City, 810	D 8
63843	Goodman, 565	C 9
63543	Gorin, 220	H 2
64454	Gower, 758	C 3
64455	Graham, 213	C 2
64029	Grain Valley, 709	S 6
64844	Granby, 1,678	D 9
63943	Grandin, 243	L 9
64030	Grandview, 17,456	P 6
63650	Graniteville, 375	L 7
64456	Grant City⊙, 1,095	D 2
65037	Gravois Mills, 994	G 6
63850	Grayridge, 300	N 9
63039	Gray Summit, 950	M 3
63544	Green Castle, 235	G 2
63545	Green City, 629	F 2
65661	Greenfield⊙, 1,172	E 8
65332	Green Ridge, 403	F 5
63546	Greentop, 351	H 2
63944	Greenville⊙, 328	M 8
64034	Greenwood, 925	R 6
63040	Grover, 550	O 3
64643	Hale, 461	F 3
65255	Hallsville, 790	H 4
64644	Hamilton, 1,645	E 3
63401	Hannibal, 18,609	K 3
64035	Hardin, 683	E 4
64701	Harrisonville⊙, 4,928	D 5
65667	Hartville⊙, 524	G 8
63349	Hawk Point, 354	K 5
63851	Hayti, 3,841	N10
* 63042	Hazelwood, 14,082	P 2
63047	Hematite, 300	L 6
64460	Hemple, 350	D 3
64036	Henrietta, 466	E 4
63048	Herculaneum, 1,885	M 6
65041	Hermann⊙, 2,658	K 5
65668	Hermitage⊙, 284	F 7
65257	Higbee, 641	H 4
64037	Higginsville, 4,318	E 4
63049	High Ridge, 350	O 4
63050	Hillsboro⊙, 432	L 6
63852	Holcomb, 593	N10
64040	Holden, 2,089	E 5
63853	Holland, 329	N10
65672	Hollister, 906	F 9
64048	Holt, 319	D 4
64461	Hopkins, 656	C 1
† 63070	Horine, 850	M 6
63855	Hornersville, 693	M10
63051	House Springs, 500	O 4
65483	Houston⊙, 2,178	J 8
65333	Houstonia, 312	F 5
65674	Humansville, 825	E 7
64752	Hume, 350	C 6
63443	Hunnewell, 304	J 3
65259	Huntsville⊙, 1,442	H 4
63547	Hurdland, 225	H 2
65486	Iberia, 741	H 6
63754	Illmo, 1.232	O 8
63052	Imperial, 900	P 4
* 64050	Independence⊙, 111,662	R 5
63648	Irondale, 319	L 7
63650	Ironton⊙, 1,452	L 7
63755	Jackson⊙, 5,896	N 8
64648	Jamesport, 614	E 3
65046	Jamestown, 243	G 5
64755	Jasper, 796	D 8
65101	Jefferson City (cap.)⊙, 32,407	H 5
63136	Jennings, 19,379	P 2
63351	Jonesburg, 479	K 5
64801	Joplin, 39,256	C 8
† 63385	Josephville, 250	N 2
63445	Kahoka⊙, 2,207	J 2
* 64101	Kansas City, 507,087	P 5
	Kansas City, ‡1,253,916	P 5
64060	Kearney, 984	D 4
63758	Kelso, 401	O 8
63857	Kennett⊙, 9,852	M10
65261	Keytesville⊙, 730	G 4
64649	Kidder, 231	D 3
63053	Kimmswick, 268	M 6
64463	King City, 1,023	D 2
64650	Kingston⊙, 291	E 3
64061	Kingsville, 284	D 5
63140	Kinloch, 5,629	P 2
63501	Kirksville⊙, 15,560	H 2
63122	Kirkwood, 31,890	O 3
65336	Knob Noster, 2,264	E 5
63446	Knox City, 284	H 2
63054	Koch, 600	P 4
65692	Koshkonong, 216	J 9
† 63090	Krakow, 300	K 6
63055	Labadie, 350	N 3
63447	La Belle, 848	J 2
64651	Laclede, 430	F 3
63352	Laddonia, 745	J 4
† 64758	Ladue, 10,491	P 3
63448	La Grange, 1,237	K 2
64063	Lake Lotawana, 1,786	R 6
65049	Lake Ozark, 507	G 6
† 64015	Lake Tapawingo, 867	R 6
† 64034	Lake Winnebago, 432	R 6
64759	Lamar⊙, 3,760	D 8
65337	La Monte, 814	F 5
64847	Lanagan, 374	C 9
63548	Lancaster⊙, 821	H 1
63549	La Plata, 1,377	H 2
64652	Laredo, 383	E 2
64465	Lathrop, 1,268	D 3
64062	Lawson, 1,034	D 4
† 63640	Leadington, 299	M 7
63653	Leadwood, 1,397	L 7
65535	Leasburg, 218	K 6
65536	Lebanon⊙, 8,616	G 7
64063	Lee's Summit, 16,230	R 6
64761	Leeton, 425	E 5
63125	Lemay, 40,115	P 3
63654	Lesterville, 275	L 8
64066	Levasy, 283	S 5
63452	Lewistown, 615	J 2
64067	Lexington⊙, 5,388	E 4
64762	Liberal, 644	D 7
64068	Liberty⊙, 13,679	R 5
65542	Licking, 1,002	J 8
63862	Lilbourn, 1,152	N 9
65338	Lincoln, 574	F 6
65051	Linn⊙, 1,289	J 5
65052	Linn Creek, 268	G 6
64653	Linneus⊙, 400	F 3
65682	Lockwood, 887	E 8
65054	Loose Creek, 370	J 5
63353	Louisiana, 4,533	K 4
64763	Lowry City, 520	E 6
63762	Lutesville, 626	M 8
63552	Macon⊙, 5,301	H 3
65263	Madison, 540	H 4
64466	Maitland, 319	B 2
63863	Malden, 5,374	M 9
65339	Malta Bend, 342	F 4
65704	Mansfield, 1,056	G 8
63143	Maplewood, 12,785	P 3
63764	Marble Hill⊙, 589	N 8
64658	Marceline, 2,622	F 3
65705	Marionville, 1,496	E 8
63655	Marquand, 400	M 8
65340	Marshall⊙, 11,847	F 4
65706	Marshfield⊙, 2,961	G 8
63866	Marston, 666	N 9
63357	Marthasville, 415	L 5
65264	Martinsburg, 318	J 4
64468	Maryville⊙, 9,970	C 2
63857	Matthews, 538	N 9
64469	Maysville⊙, 1,045	D 3
64071	Mayview, 330	E 4
64657	McFall, 203	D 2
64659	Meadville, 409	F 3
63555	Memphis⊙, 2,081	H 2
64660	Mendon, 289	F 3
64661	Mercer, 364	F 2
65058	Meta, 387	H 6
65265	Mexico⊙, 11,807	J 4
65344	Miami, 205	F 4
63359	Middletown, 235	J 4
63556	Milan⊙, 1,794	F 2
65707	Miller, 676	E 8
63952	Mill Spring, 207	L 8
64769	Mindenmines, 279	D 8
63659	Mine La Motte, 200	M 7
† 63801	Miner, 640	N 9
63660	Mineral Point, 369	L 7
64072	Missouri City, 375	R 5
65270	Moberly, 12,988	G 4

(continued on following page)

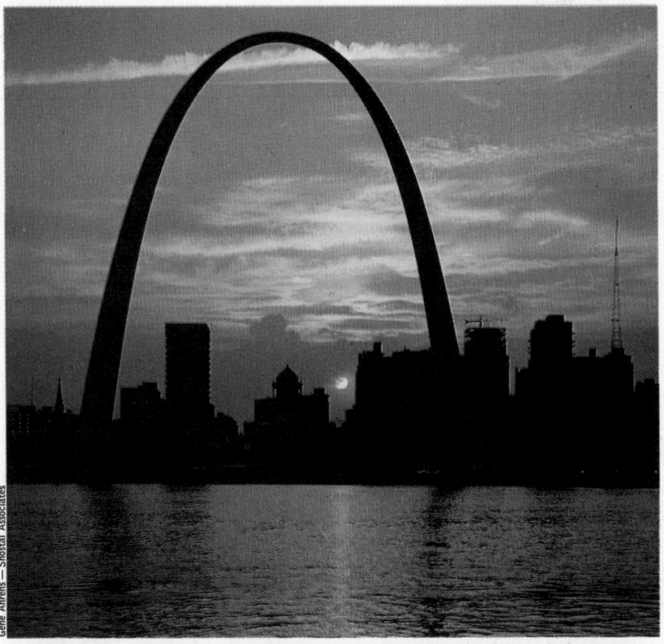
Gene Ahrens — Shostal Associates

The Gateway Arch soars in silhouette against the St. Louis skyline. A Saarinen design, the monument is the centerpiece of the Jefferson National Expansion Memorial. Internal passenger trains carry sightseers up either leg to the long observation room.

Agriculture, Industry and Resources

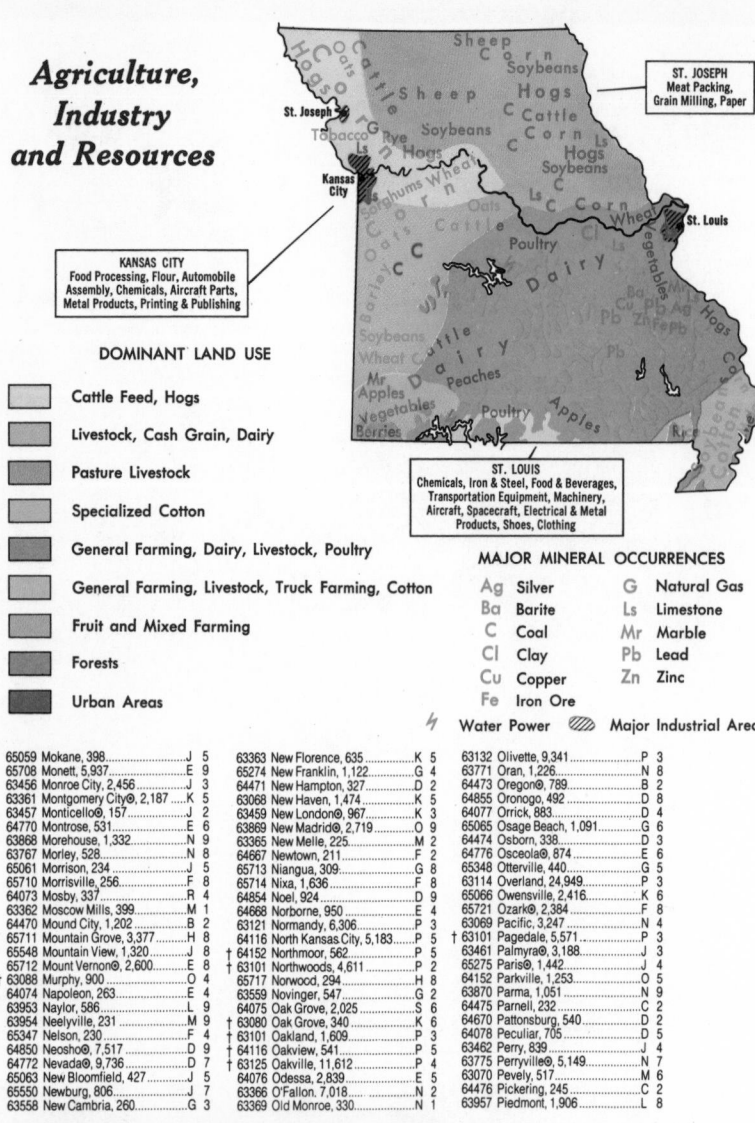

ST. JOSEPH
Meat Packing, Grain Milling, Paper

KANSAS CITY
Food Processing, Flour, Automobile Assembly, Chemicals, Aircraft Parts, Metal Products, Printing & Publishing

ST. LOUIS
Chemicals, Iron & Steel, Food & Beverages, Transportation Equipment, Machinery, Aircraft, Spacecraft, Electrical & Metal Products, Shoes, Clothing

DOMINANT LAND USE

- Cattle Feed, Hogs
- Livestock, Cash Grain, Dairy
- Pasture Livestock
- Specialized Cotton
- General Farming, Dairy, Livestock, Poultry
- General Farming, Livestock, Truck Farming, Cotton
- Fruit and Mixed Farming
- Forests
- Urban Areas

MAJOR MINERAL OCCURRENCES

Ag	Silver	G	Natural Gas
Ba	Barite	Ls	Limestone
C	Coal	Mr	Marble
Cl	Clay	Pb	Lead
Cu	Copper	Zn	Zinc
Fe	Iron Ore		

Water Power   Major Industrial Areas

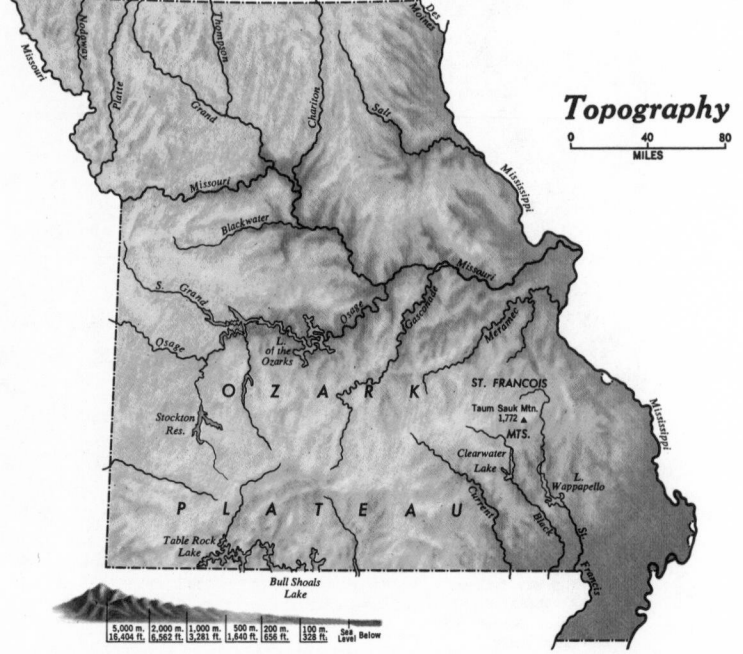

Topography

0   40   80
MILES

5,000 m. 2,000 m. 1,000 m. 500 m. 200 m. 100 m. Sea
16,404 ft. 6,562 ft. 3,281 ft. 1,640 ft. 656 ft. 328 ft. Level Below

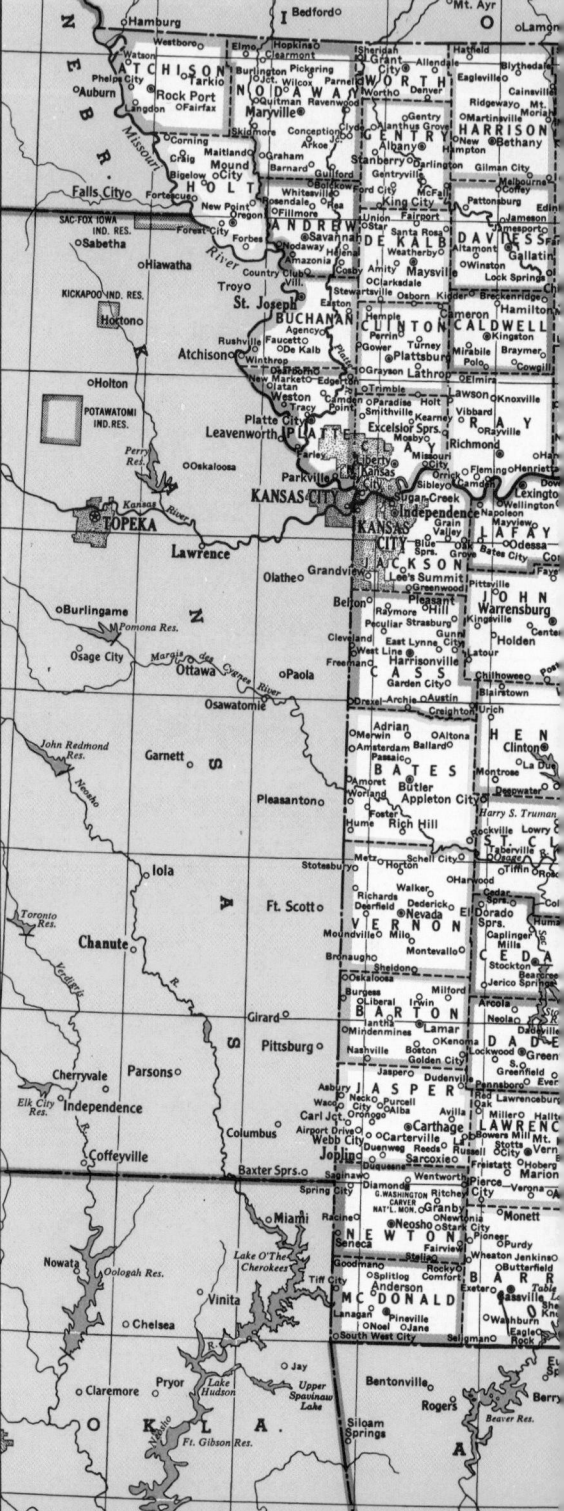

64780 Rockville, 203............D 6
65742 Rogersville, 574.........G 8
65401 Rolla◉, 13,245...........K 6
63091 Rosebud, 305.............K 6
64483 Rosendale, 245...........C 2
65074 Rushville, 300............B 3
65074 Russellville, 557.........H 6
63074 Saint Ann, 18,215........O 2
63301 Saint Charles◉, 31,834...O 2
63077 Saint Clair, 2,978........N 6
63670 Sainte Genevieve◉, 4,468...M 6
65075 Saint Elizabeth, 287......J 6
63101 Saint George, 1,806......P 3
65559 Saint James, 2,787.......J 6
63114 Saint John, 8,960........P 2
64501 Saint Joseph◉, 72,691....C 3
      Saint Joseph, ‡86,915.....C 3
63101 Saint Louis◉ 622,236.....P 3
      Saint Louis, ‡2,363,017....P 3
63673 Saint Marys, 645.........M 7
63376 Saint Peters, 486.........N 2
65560 Salem◉, 4,363.............J 7
65281 Salisbury, 1,960..........G 4

64862 Sarcoxie, 1,175..........D 8
64485 Savannah◉, 3,324........C 3
64783 Schell City, 367..........D 6
63780 Scott City, 2,464.........O 8
65301 Sedalia◉, 22,847.........F 5
65745 Seligman, 424............D 9
63876 Senath, 1,484............M10
64865 Seneca, 1,577............C 9
65746 Seymour, 1,208..........G 8
63468 Shelbina, 2,060..........H 3
63469 Shelbyville◉, 601.........H 3
64784 Sheldon, 498.............D 7
64486 Sheridan, 251............C 1
† 63101 Shrewsbury, 5,896.......P 3
63861 Sikeston, 14,699.........N 9
63377 Silex, 306................K 4
64487 Skidmore, 440...........B 2
65349 Slater, 2,576.............G 4
63530 Smithton, 402...........F 5
64089 Smithville, 1,785.........D 4
64863 South West City, 453.....D 9
63101 Spanish Lake, 15,647.....O 3

65753 Sparta, 380..............F 9
64679 Spickard, 408............F 2
65801 Springfield◉, 120,096....F 8
      Springfield, ‡152,929.....F 8
64489 Stanberry, 1,479.........C 2
63079 Stanton, 350.............K 6
63877 Steele, 2,107............N10
65565 Steelville◉, 1,392........K 7
64490 Stewartsville, 634........C 3
65785 Stockton◉, 1,063........E 7
65567 Stoutland, 205...........G 6
65078 Stover, 849...............G 6
65757 Strafford, 491............F 8
65284 Sturgeon, 872............H 4
64054 Sugar Creek, 4,755.......D 5
63080 Sullivan, 5,100...........K 6
65571 Summersville, 435........J 8
† 63101 Sunset Hills, 3,728......P 3
65351 Sweet Springs, 1,716.....G 4
64491 Tarkio, 2,517.............B 1
64063 Tarsney Lakes, 401.......D 5
65791 Thayer, 1,609............J 9
63025 Times Beach, 1,265......O 3

65081 Tipton, 1,914............G 5
64091 Tracy, 252...............C 4
64683 Trenton◉, 6,063.........E 2
64492 Trimble, 206.............D 4
63379 Troy◉, 2,538............K 5
63080 Truesdail, 262...........K 5
63082 Tuscumbia◉, 256........H 6
63084 Union◉, 5,183...........L 6
64494 Union Star, 417..........C 3
63565 Unionville◉, 2,075.......K 5
64063 Unity, 242...............R 6
63130 University City, 46,309....P 3
65767 Urbana, 369.............F 7
64788 Urich, 433...............E 6
64686 Utica, 275...............D 3
65079 Valley Park, 3,662........O 3
63965 Van Buren◉, 714........J 8
63784 Vanduser, 306...........N 9
65769 Verona, 515.............E 8
63383 Versailles◉, 2,244.......G 6
65566 Viburnum, 520..........K 7
65580 Vichy, 250...............J 6

† 63020 Victoria, 250............M 6
65581 Vida, 300................J 7
65582 Vienna◉, 505...........H 6
64790 Walker, 227.............D 7
65770 Walnut Grove, 442.......E 7
63966 Wappapello, 254.........M 8
63879 Wardell, 275.............N10
65101 Wardsville, 460.........H 5
64093 Warrensburg◉, 13,125...E 5
63383 Warrenton◉, 2,057.....K 5
65355 Warsaw◉, 1,423........F 6
65772 Washburn, 250..........D 9
63090 Washington, 8,499......K 5
64096 Waverly, 827............F 4
65583 Waynesville◉, 3,375....H 7
† 64152 Weatherby Lake, 832....O 5
65774 Weaubleau, 343........F 7
64870 Webb City, 6,811........C 8
63119 Webster Groves, 26,995...P 3
64097 Wellington, 720..........E 5
63112 Wellston, 7,050..........P 3
63384 Wellsville, 1,565.........K 4

65385 Wentzville, 3,223........M 2
63386 Westalton, 435..........R 2
64498 Westboro, 234...........B 1
64098 Weston, 1,267...........C 4
65085 Westphalia, 332.........H 6
65775 West Plains◉, 6,893.....J 9
65779 Wheatland, 317.........F 7
64874 Wheaton, 360...........E 9
64688 Wheeling, 5,040.........F 3
65781 Willard, 1,018...........F 8
63977 Williamsville, 398........L 9
65793 Willow Springs, 2,045....H 9
65360 Windsor, 2,734..........E 5
63389 Winfield, 620............L 5
65588 Winona, 973............K 8
† 63101 Woodson Terrace, 5,936...P 2
63390 Wright City, 943.........K 5
63474 Wyaconda, 356.........J 2
63882 Wyatt, 562..............O 9

◉ County seat.
★ Population of metropolitan area.
† Zip of nearest p.o.
‡ Multiple zips.

198 Montana

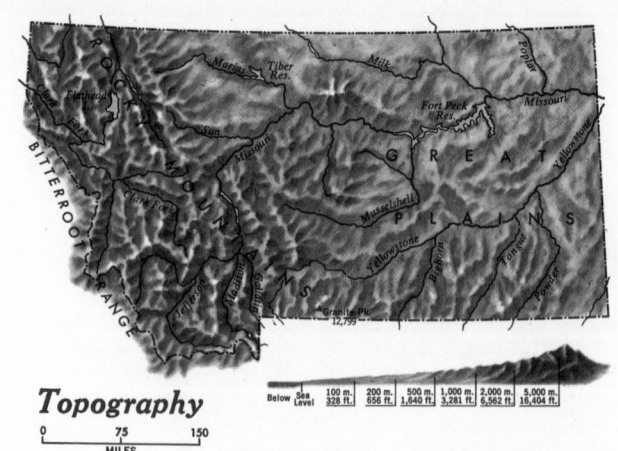

Topography

Below Sea Level | 100 m. 328 ft. | 200 m. 656 ft. | 500 m. 1,640 ft. | 1,000 m. 3,281 ft. | 2,000 m. 6,562 ft. | 5,000 m. 16,404 ft.

0   75   150
MILES

MONTANA

SCALE

0 5 10   20   40   60 MI.

0 5 10 20   40   60KM.

State Capitals .... ⊛
County Seats .... ⊙

© C.S. HAMMOND & Co., N.Y.

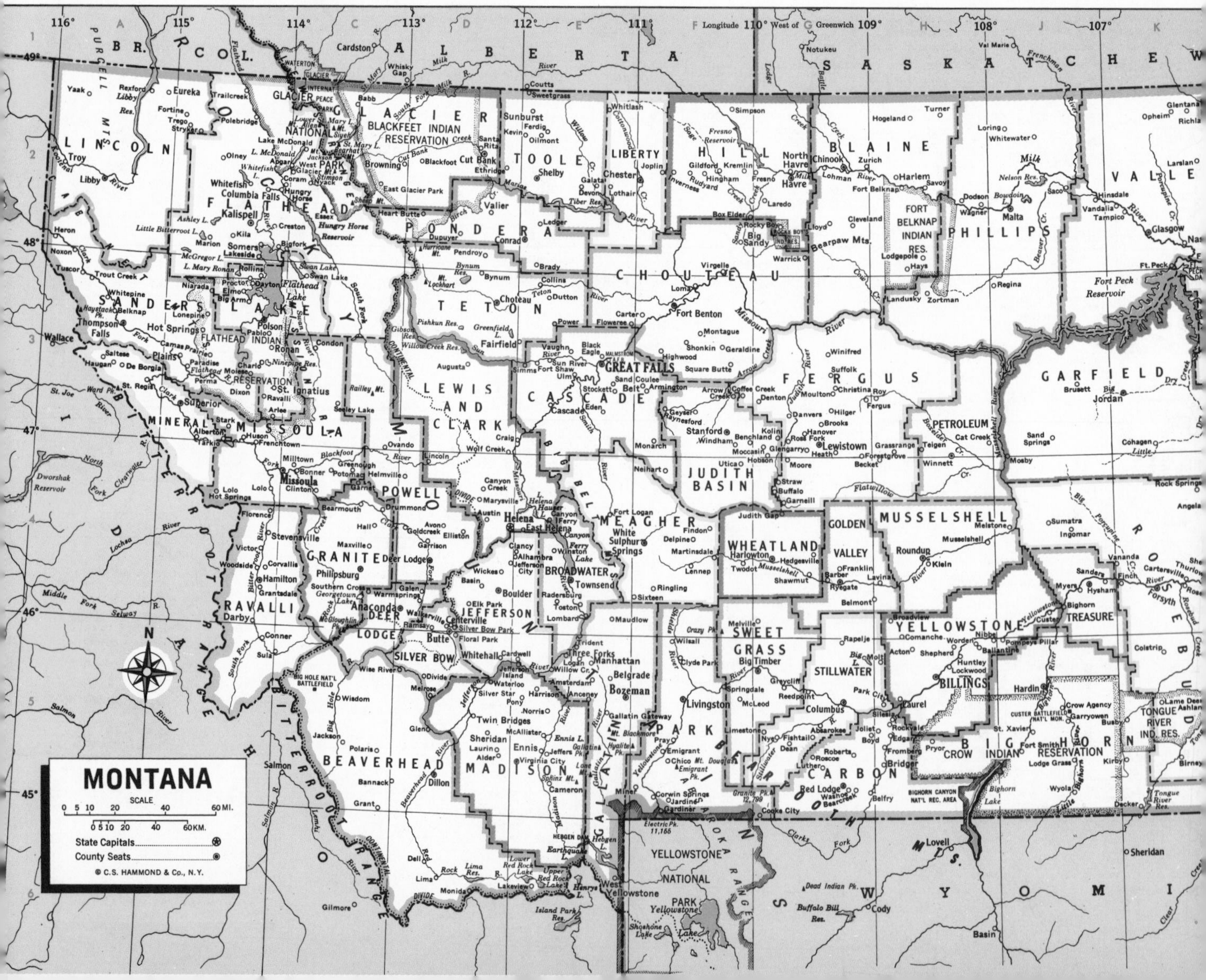

Surrounded by the wide open spaces, a Montana ranch basks in the reflected glory of the Rocky Mountains while it awaits cattle returning from the range. Ranches accommodate so many head of cattle that the state's residents are outnumbered six to one.

AREA 147,138 sq. mi.
POPULATION 694,409
CAPITAL Helena
LARGEST CITY Billings
HIGHEST POINT Granite Pk. 12,799 ft.
SETTLED IN 1809
ADMITTED TO UNION November 8, 1889
POPULAR NAME Treasure State
STATE FLOWER Bitterroot
STATE BIRD Western Meadowlark

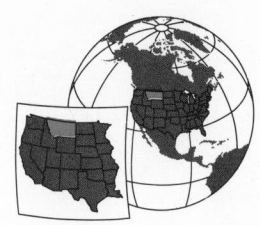

Agriculture, Industry and Resources

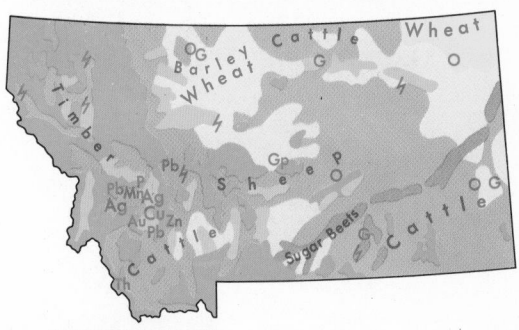

DOMINANT LAND USE

- Specialized Wheat
- Wheat, Range Livestock
- General Farming, Dairy, Range Livestock
- General Farming, Livestock, Special Crops
- Range Livestock
- Sugar Beets, Beans, Livestock, General Farming
- Forests

MAJOR MINERAL OCCURRENCES

Ag	Silver	O	Petroleum
Au	Gold	P	Phosphates
Cu	Copper	Pb	Lead
G	Natural Gas	Th	Thorium
Gp	Gypsum	Zn	Zinc
Mn	Manganese	⚡	Water Power

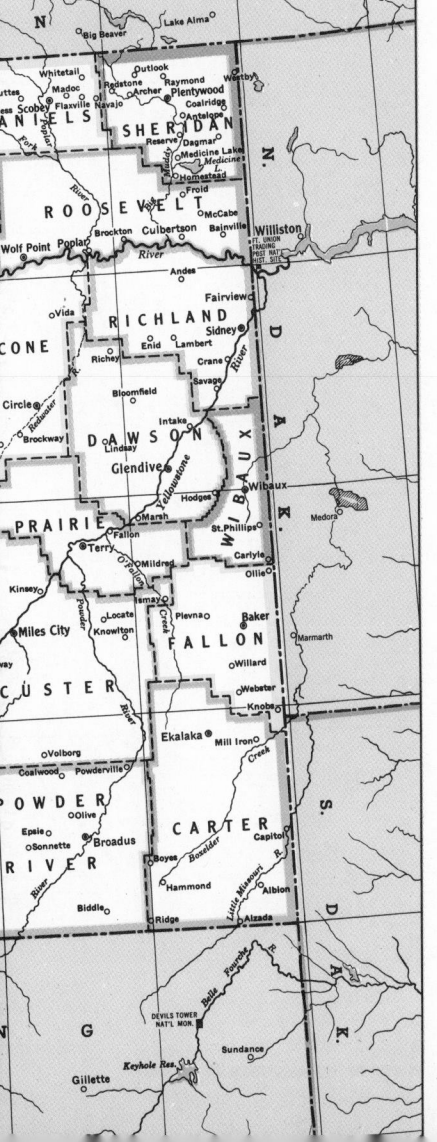

59230 Glasgow⊙, 4,700	K 2
† 59725 Glen, 100	D 5
59330 Glendive⊙, 6,305	M 3
59240 Glentana, 40	K 2
59733 Goldcreek, 76	D 4
59835 Grantsdale, 250	B 4
59032 Grassrange, 181	H 3
59401 Great Falls⊙, 60,091	E 3
Great Falls, ‡81,804	E 3
59836 Greenough, 100	C 4
59837 Hall, 95	C 4
59840 Hamilton⊙, 2,499	B 4
59034 Hardin⊙, 2,733	J 5
59526 Harlem, 1,094	H 2
59036 Harlowton⊙, 1,375	F 4
59735 Harrison, 275	E 5
59333 Hathaway, 45	K 4
59842 Haugan, 40	A 3
59501 Havre⊙, 10,558	G 2
59527 Hays, 950	H 2
59448 Heart Butte, 450	C 2
59601 Helena (cap.)⊙, 22,730	E 4
59843 Helmville, 76	D 4
59844 Heron, 185	A 2
59450 Highwood, 360	F 3
59451 Hilger, 40	G 3
59528 Hingham, 262	F 2
59241 Hinsdale, 500	K 2
59452 Hobson, 192	G 4
† 59353 Hodges, 50	M 4
59529 Hogeland, 68	H 2
59242 Homestead, 75	M 2
59845 Hot Springs, 664	C 3
59919 Hungry Horse, 700	C 2
59037 Huntley, 225	H 5
59846 Huson, 40	B 3
59038 Hysham⊙, 373	J 4
59039 Ingomar, 55	J 4
59335 Intake, 40	M 3
59530 Inverness, 150	F 2
59336 Ismay, 40	M 4
59736 Jackson, 196	C 5
59737 Jeffers, 70	E 5
59638 Jefferson City, 99	E 4
† 59721 Jefferson Island, 31	D 5
59041 Joliet, 412	G 5
59531 Joplin, 350	F 2
59337 Jordan⊙, 529	J 3
59453 Judith Gap, 160	G 4
59901 Kalispell⊙, 10,526	B 2
59454 Kevin, 250	D 2
59920 Kila, 44	B 2
† 59072 Klein, 40	H 4
59532 Kremlin, 347	F 2
59922 Lakeside, 663	B 2
59243 Lambert, 141	M 3
59043 Lame Deer, 460	K 5
59533 Landusky, 50	H 2
59244 Larslan, 140	K 2
59044 Laurel, 4,454	H 5

59738 Laurin, 60	D 5
59046 Lavina, 169	H 4
59457 Lewistown⊙, 6,437	G 3
59923 Libby⊙, 3,286	A 2
59739 Lima, 351	D 6
59639 Lincoln, 473	D 4
59339 Lindsay, 40	L 3
59047 Livingston⊙, 6,883	F 5
59535 Lloyd, 70	G 2
59048 Locate, 49	L 4
† 59101 Lockwood, 950	H 5
59050 Lodge Grass, 806	J 5
† 59524 Lodgepole, 39	H 2
59763 Logan, 53	E 5
59847 Lolo, 300	B 4
59460 Loma, 172	F 3
59461 Lothair, 35	E 2
59538 Malta⊙, 2,195	J 2
59741 Manhattan, 816	E 5
59925 Marion, 120	B 2
59053 Martinsdale, 203	F 4
59640 Marysville, 42	D 4
59742 Maudlow, 75	E 4
59844 Maxville, 44	C 4
59740 McAllister, 62	E 5
59247 Medicine Lake, 393	M 2
59743 Melrose, 350	D 5
59055 Melstone, 227	H 4
59054 Melville, 150	F 4
59301 Miles City⊙, 9,023	L 4
59851 Milltown, 500	C 4
59801 Missoula⊙, 29,497	C 4
59462 Moccasin, 100	F 3
59463 Monarch, 80	F 3
59464 Moore, 219	G 4
59059 Musselshell, 32	H 4
59248 Nashua, 513	K 2
59465 Neihart, 109	F 4
59745 Norris, 37	E 5
† 59501 North Havre, 1,073	G 2
59853 Noxon, 250	A 3
59936 Nyack, 31	C 2
59061 Nye, 65	G 5
59466 Oilmont, 75	E 2
59927 Olney, 250	B 2
59250 Opheim, 306	K 2
59251 Oswego, 75	L 2
59252 Outlook, 153	M 2
59854 Ovando, 102	C 3
59855 Pablo, 350	B 3
59856 Paradise, 500	B 3
59063 Park City, 400	H 5
59467 Pendroy, 35	D 2
59858 Philipsburg⊙, 1,128	C 4
59859 Plains, 1,046	B 3
59254 Plentywood⊙, 2,381	M 2
59344 Plevna, 189	M 4
59860 Polson⊙, 2,464	B 3
59064 Pompeys Pillar, 69	J 5

59747 Pony, 111	E 5
59255 Poplar, 1,389	L 2
59862 Potomac, 58	C 4
59468 Power, 91	E 3
59929 Proctor, 108	B 3
59066 Pryor, 150	H 5
59639 Radersburg, 65	E 4
59748 Ramsay, 140	D 4
59067 Rapelje, 295	G 5
59863 Ravalli, 150	B 3
59256 Raymond, 34	M 2
59469 Raynesford, 100	F 3
59068 Red Lodge⊙, 1,844	G 5
59257 Redstone, 77	M 2
59069 Reedpoint, 125	G 5
59258 Reserve, 90	M 2
59930 Rexford, 243	A 2
59259 Richey, 389	L 3
59260 Richland, 37	K 2
59642 Ringling, 51	F 4
59070 Roberts, 291	G 5
† 59521 Rocky Boy, 150	G 2
59831 Rollins, 200	B 3
59864 Ronan, 1,347	C 3
59347 Rosebud, 120	K 4
59072 Roundup⊙, 2,116	H 4
59471 Roy, 175	H 3
59540 Rudyard, 550	F 2
59074 Ryegate⊙, 261	G 4
59261 Saco, 356	J 2
59865 Saint Ignatius, 925	C 3
59866 Saint Regis, 500	A 3
59075 Saint Xavier, 110	J 5
59867 Saltese, 95	A 3
59472 Sand Coulee, 500	E 3
59076 Sanders, 50	J 4
59473 Santa Rita, 125	D 2
59262 Savage, 300	M 3
59263 Scobey⊙, 1,486	L 2
59868 Seeley Lake, 400	C 3
59078 Shawmut, 60	G 4
59347 Sheffield, 40	K 4
59474 Shelby⊙, 3,111	E 2
59079 Shepherd, 100	H 5
59749 Sheridan, 636	D 5
59270 Sidney⊙, 4,543	M 3
59080 Silesia, 90	H 5
59701 Silver Bow Park, 5,524	D 4
59751 Silver Star, 100	D 5
59477 Simms, 299	E 3
59541 Simpson, 70	F 2
59932 Somers, 950	B 2
59348 Sonnette, 44	L 5
59442 Square Butte, 48	F 3
59479 Stanford⊙, 505	F 3
59846 Stark, 51	C 4
59870 Stevensville, 829	C 4
59480 Stockett, 500	E 3
59933 Stryker, 60	B 2
59481 Suffolk, 45	G 3

59482 Sunburst, 604	E 2
59483 Sun River, 190	E 3
59872 Superior⊙, 993	B 3
59911 Swan Lake, 200	C 3
59484 Sweetgrass, 120	E 2
59349 Terry⊙, 870	L 4
59873 Thompson Falls⊙, 1,356	A 3
59752 Three Forks, 1,188	E 5
59347 Thurlow, 40	K 4
59643 Toston, 75	E 4
59644 Townsend⊙, 1,371	E 4
59934 Trego, 50	B 2
59753 Trident, 50	E 5
59874 Trout Creek, 200	A 3
59935 Troy, 1,046	A 2
59542 Turner, 175	H 2
59754 Twin Bridges, 613	D 5
59085 Twodot, 118	F 4
59485 Ulm, 450	E 3
59452 Utica, 40	F 4
59486 Valier, 651	D 2
59237 Vananda, 50	K 4
59487 Vaughn, 345	E 3
59875 Victor, 500	B 4
59274 Vida, 52	L 3
59755 Virginia City⊙, 149	E 5
59701 Walkerville, 1,097	D 4
59756 Warmsprings, 1,600	D 4
59757 Waterloo, 102	D 5
59214 Watkins, 40	K 3
59275 Westby, 287	M 2
59936 West Glacier, 348	C 2
59758 West Yellowstone, 756	E 6
59937 Whitefish, 3,349	B 2
59759 Whitehall, 1,035	D 5
59784 Whitepine, 50	A 3
59645 White Sulphur Springs⊙, 1,200	E 4
59276 Whitetail, 125	L 2
59544 Whitewater, 100	J 2
59353 Wibaux⊙, 644	M 3
59760 Willow Creek, 325	E 5
59086 Wilsall, 200	F 5
59488 Windham, 60	F 3
59489 Winifred, 190	G 3
59087 Winnett⊙, 271	H 4
59647 Winston, 115	E 4
59761 Wisdom, 155	C 5
59762 Wise River, 125	C 5
59648 Wolf Creek, 200	D 3
59201 Wolf Point⊙, 3,095	L 2
59875 Woodside, 80	B 4
59088 Worden, 350	H 5
59089 Wyola, 110	J 5
59935 Yaak, 75	A 2
59547 Zurich, 89	G 2

⊙ County seat.
‡ Population of metropolitan area.
† Zip of nearest p.o.
* Multiple zips

COUNTIES

Adams, 30,553 ....F 4
Antelope, 9,047 ....F 2
Arthur, 606 ....C 3
Banner, 1,034 ....A 3
Blaine, 847 ....E 3
Boone, 8,190 ....F 3
Box Butte, 10,094 ....A 2
Boyd, 3,752 ....F 2
Brown, 4,021 ....E 2
Buffalo, 31,222 ....E 4
Burt, 9,247 ....H 3
Butler, 9,461 ....G 3
Cass, 18,076 ....H 4
Cedar, 12,192 ....G 2
Chase, 4,129 ....C 4
Cherry, 6,846 ....C 2
Cheyenne, 10,778 ....A 3
Clay, 8,266 ....F 4
Colfax, 9,498 ....G 3
Cuming, 12,034 ....H 3
Custer, 14,092 ....E 3
Dakota, 13,137 ....H 2
Dawes, 9,693 ....A 2
Dawson, 19,467 ....E 4
Deuel, 2,717 ....B 3
Dixon, 7,453 ....H 2
Dodge, 34,782 ....H 3
Douglas, 389,455 ....H 3
Dundy, 2,926 ....C 4
Fillmore, 8,137 ....G 4
Franklin, 4,566 ....F 4
Frontier, 3,982 ....D 4
Furnas, 6,897 ....E 4
Gage, 25,719 ....H 4
Garden, 2,929 ....B 3
Garfield, 2,411 ....F 3
Gosper, 2,178 ....E 4
Grant, 1,019 ....C 3
Greeley, 4,000 ....F 3
Hall, 42,851 ....F 4
Hamilton, 8,867 ....F 4
Harlan, 4,357 ....E 4
Hayes, 1,530 ....D 4
Hitchcock, 4,051 ....D 4
Holt, 12,933 ....F 2
Hooker, 939 ....C 3
Howard, 6,807 ....F 4
Jefferson, 10,436 ....H 4
Johnson, 5,743 ....H 4
Kearney, 6,707 ....F 4
Keith, 8,487 ....C 3
Keya Paha, 1,340 ....E 2
Kimball, 6,009 ....A 3
Knox, 11,723 ....G 2
Lancaster, 167,972 ....H 4
Lincoln, 29,538 ....D 4
Logan, 991 ....D 3
Loup, 854 ....E 3
Madison, 27,402 ....G 3
McPherson, 623 ....C 3
Merrick, 8,751 ....F 3
Morrill, 5,813 ....A 3
Nance, 5,142 ....F 3
Nemaha, 8,976 ....J 4
Nuckolls, 7,404 ....F 4
Otoe, 15,576 ....H 4
Pawnee, 4,473 ....H 4
Perkins, 3,423 ....C 4
Phelps, 9,553 ....E 4
Pierce, 8,493 ....G 2
Platte, 26,508 ....G 3
Polk, 6,468 ....G 3
Red Willow, 12,191 ....D 4
Richardson, 12,277 ....J 4
Rock, 2,231 ....E 2
Saline, 12,809 ....G 4
Sarpy, 63,696 ....H 3
Saunders, 17,018 ....H 3
Scotts Bluff, 36,432 ......A 3
Seward, 14,460 ....G 4
Sheridan, 7,285 ....B 2
Sherman, 4,725 ....F 3

Sioux, 2,034 ....A 2
Stanton, 5,758 ....G 3
Thayer, 7,779 ....G 4
Thomas, 954 ....D 3
Thurston, 6,942 ....H 2
Valley, 5,783 ....E 3
Washington, 13,310 ....H 3
Wayne, 10,400 ....G 2
Webster, 6,477 ....F 4
Wheeler, 1,054 ....F 3
York, 13,685 ....G 4

CITIES and TOWNS

Zip	Name/Pop.	Key
68301	Adams, 463	H 4
69210	Ainsworth⊙, 2,073	D 2
68620	Albion⊙, 2,074	F 3
68810	Alda, 456	F 4
68710	Allen, 309	H 2
69301	Alliance⊙, 6,862	A 2
68920	Alma⊙, 1,299	E 4
68814	Ansley, 631	E 3
68922	Arapahoe, 1,147	E 4
68815	Arcadia, 418	F 3
68002	Arlington, 910	H 3
69120	Arnold, 752	D 3
69121	Arthur⊙, 175	C 3
68003	Ashland, 2,176	H 3
68713	Atkinson, 1,406	E 2
68305	Auburn⊙, 3,650	J 4
68818	Aurora⊙, 3,180	G 4
68924	Axtell, 500	E 4
68004	Bancroft, 545	H 2
68622	Bartlett⊙, 193	F 3
69020	Bartley, 283	D 4
68714	Bassett⊙, 983	E 2
68715	Battle Creek, 1,158	G 3
69334	Bayard, 1,338	A 3
68310	Beatrice⊙, 12,389	H 4
68926	Beaver City⊙, 802	E 4
68313	Beaver Crossing, 400	G 4
68716	Beemer, 699	H 3
68005	Bellevue, 19,449	J 3
68624	Bellwood, 361	G 3
69021	Benkelman⊙, 1,349	C 4
68317	Bennet, 489	H 4
68007	Bennington, 683	H 3
68927	Bertrand, 662	E 4
69122	Big Springs, 472	B 3
68928	Bladen, 293	F 4
68008	Blair⊙, 6,106	H 3
68718	Bloomfield, 1,287	G 2
68930	Blue Hill, 1,201	F 4
68318	Blue Springs, 494	H 4
68010	Boys Town, 989	H 3
68319	Bradshaw, 347	G 4
69123	Brady, 311	D 3
68626	Brainard, 309	G 3
68821	Brewster⊙, 54	D 3
69336	Bridgeport⊙, 1,490	A 3
68822	Broken Bow⊙, 3,734	E 3
68321	Brownville, 174	J 4
69127	Brule, 423	C 3
68322	Bruning, 315	G 4
68823	Burwell⊙, 1,341	E 3
68722	Butte⊙, 575	F 2
68824	Cairo, 686	F 4
68825	Callaway, 523	D 3
69022	Cambridge, 1,145	D 4
68932	Campbell, 447	F 4
68015	Cedar Bluffs, 616	H 3
68627	Cedar Rapids, 449	F 3
68724	Center⊙, 111	G 2
68826	Central City⊙, 2,803	F 3
68017	Ceresco, 474	H 3
69337	Chadron⊙, 5,853	B 2
68725	Chambers, 321	F 2
68827	Chapman, 73	F 3
69129	Chappell⊙, 1,204	B 3
68327	Chester, 459	G 4
68628	Clarks, 480	G 3
68629	Clarkson, 805	G 3

Zip	Name/Pop.	Key
68933	Clay Center⊙, 952	F 4
68726	Clearwater, 398	F 2
68727	Coleridge, 608	G 2
68601	Columbus⊙, 15,471	G 3
68329	Cook, 328	H 4
68331	Cortland, 326	H 4
69130	Cozad, 4,219	E 4
68019	Craig, 295	H 3
69339	Crawford, 1,291	A 2
68729	Creighton, 1,461	G 2
68333	Crete, 4,444	G 4
68730	Crofton, 677	G 2
69024	Culbertson, 801	C 4
69025	Curtis, 1,166	D 4
68731	Dakota City⊙, 1,057	H 2
69131	Dalton, 354	B 3
68831	Dannebrog, 384	F 3
68335	Davenport, 427	G 4
68632	David City⊙, 2,380	G 3
68020	Decatur, 679	H 2
68340	Deshler, 937	G 4
68341	De Witt, 651	G 4
68342	Diller, 287	H 4
69133	Dix, 342	A 3
68633	Dodge, 704	H 3
68832	Doniphan, 542	F 4
68343	Dorchester, 492	G 4
68634	Duncan, 298	G 3
68347	Eagle, 441	H 4
68935	Edgar, 707	F 4
68636	Elgin, 917	F 3
68022	Elkhorn, 1,184	H 3
68836	Elm Creek, 798	E 4
68349	Elmwood, 548	H 4
68937	Elwood⊙, 601	E 4
68733	Emerson, 850	H 2
69028	Eustis, 400	D 4
68735	Ewing, 552	F 2
68351	Exeter, 759	G 4
68352	Fairbury⊙, 5,265	G 4
68938	Fairfield, 487	G 4
68354	Fairmont, 761	G 4
68355	Falls City⊙, 5,444	J 4
68358	Firth, 328	H 4
68023	Fort Calhoun, 642	J 3
68939	Franklin⊙, 1,193	E 4
68025	Fremont⊙, 22,962	H 3
68359	Friend, 1,126	G 4
68638	Fullerton⊙, 1,444	F 3
68361	Geneva⊙, 2,275	G 4
68640	Genoa, 1,174	G 3
69341	Gering⊙, 5,639	A 3
68840	Gibbon, 1,388	E 4
68841	Giltner, 408	F 4
68941	Glenvil, 332	F 4
69343	Gordon, 2,106	B 2
69138	Gothenburg, 3,154	D 4
68801	Grand Island⊙, 31,269	F 4
68140	Grant⊙, 1,099	C 4
68842	Greeley⊙, 580	F 3
68366	Greenwood, 506	H 3
68028	Gretna, 1,557	H 3
68942	Guide Rock, 318	F 4
68843	Hampton, 387	G 4
69345	Harrisburg⊙, 80	A 3
69346	Harrison⊙, 377	A 2
68739	Hartington, 1,581	G 2
68944	Harvard, 1,230	F 4
68901	Hastings⊙, 23,580	F 4
69032	Hayes Center⊙, 237	C 4
69347	Hay Springs, 682	B 2
68370	Hebron⊙, 1,667	G 4
69348	Hemingford, 734	A 2
68371	Henderson, 901	G 4
68029	Herman, 323	H 3
69143	Hershey, 526	D 3
68372	Hickman, 415	H 4
68947	Hildreth, 352	E 4
68948	Holbrook, 307	D 4
68949	Holdrege⊙, 5,635	E 4
68030	Homer, 457	H 2
68031	Hooper, 895	H 3
68641	Howells, 682	H 3
68376	Humboldt, 1,194	J 4

Miles of pens hold thousands of head of cattle in the Union Stockyards, Omaha. Next stop — the meat packers' plant.

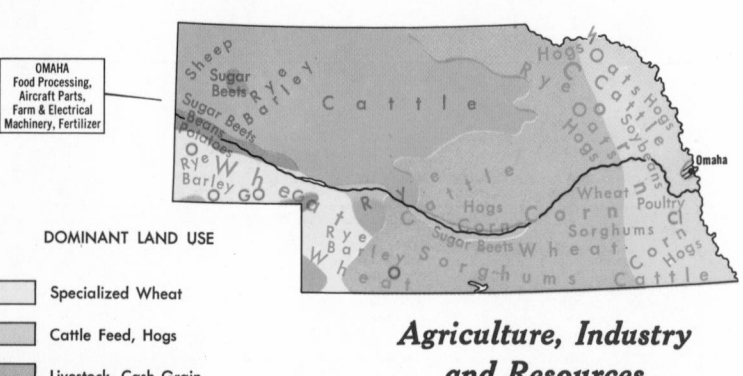

OMAHA
Food Processing, Aircraft Parts, Farm & Electrical Machinery, Fertilizer

Agriculture, Industry and Resources

DOMINANT LAND USE

- Specialized Wheat
- Cattle Feed, Hogs
- Livestock, Cash Grain
- General Farming, Livestock, Special Crops
- Sugar Beets, Dry Beans, Livestock, General Farming
- Range Livestock
- Major Industrial Areas

MAJOR MINERAL OCCURRENCES

- Cl Clay
- G   Natural Gas
- O   Petroleum
- ⚡ Water Power

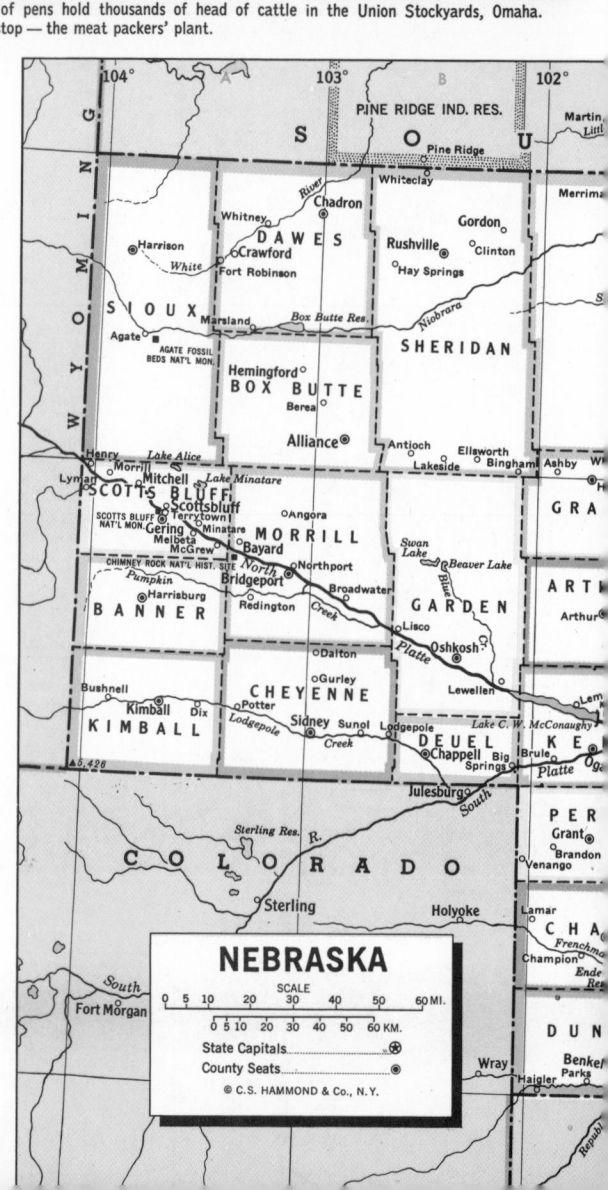

NEBRASKA

SCALE
0 5 10 20 30 40 50 60 MI.
0 5 10 20 30 40 50 60 KM.

State Capitals .... ⊛
County Seats .... ⊙

© C.S. HAMMOND & Co., N.Y.

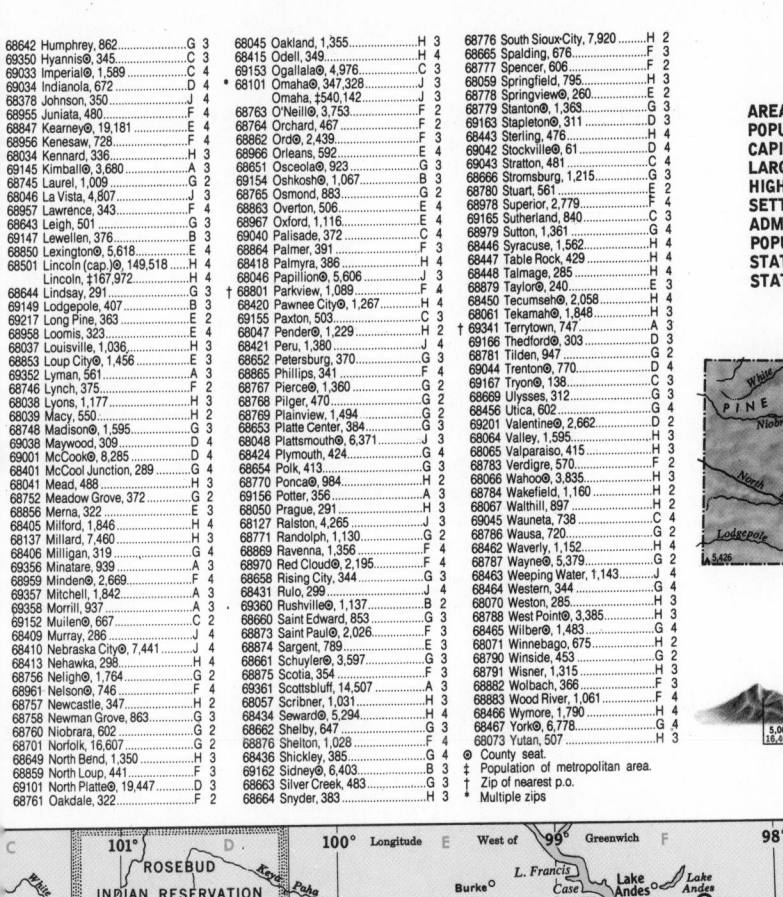

Zip	Place		Zip	Place		Zip	Place	
68642	Humphrey, 862	G 3	68045	Oakland, 1,355	H 3	68776	South Sioux City, 7,920	H 2
69350	Hyannis◉, 345	C 3	68415	Odell, 349	H 4	68665	Spalding, 676	F 3
69033	Imperial◉, 1,589	C 3	69153	Ogallala◉, 4,976	C 3	68777	Spencer, 606	F 2
69034	Indianola, 672	D 4	* 68101	Omaha◉, 347,328	J 3	68059	Springfield, 795	H 3
68378	Johnson, 350	J 4		Omaha, ‡540,142	J 3	68778	Springview◉, 260	E 2
68955	Juniata, 480	F 4	68763	O'Neill◉, 3,753	F 2	68779	Stanton◉, 1,368	G 3
68847	Kearney◉, 19,181	E 4	68764	Orchard, 467	F 2	69163	Stapleton◉, 311	D 3
68956	Kenesaw, 728	F 4	68862	Ord◉, 2,439	F 3	68443	Sterling, 476	H 4
68034	Kennard, 336	H 3	68966	Orleans, 592	E 4	69042	Stockville◉, 61	D 4
69145	Kimball◉, 3,680	A 3	68651	Osceola◉, 923	G 3	69043	Stratton, 481	C 4
68745	Laurel, 1,009	G 2	69154	Oshkosh◉, 1,067	B 3	68666	Stromsburg, 1,215	G 3
68404	La Vista, 4,807	J 2	68765	Osmond, 883	G 2	68780	Stuart, 561	E 2
68957	Lawrence, 343	F 4	68863	Overton, 506	E 4	68978	Superior, 2,779	F 4
68643	Leigh, 501	G 3	68967	Oxford, 1,116	E 4	69165	Sutherland, 840	C 3
69147	Lewellen, 376	B 3	69040	Palisade, 372	C 4	68899	Sutton, 1,361	G 4
68850	Lexington◉, 5,618	E 4	68864	Palmer, 391	F 3	68446	Syracuse, 1,562	H 4
68501	Lincoln (cap.)◉, 149,518	H 4	68418	Palmyra, 386	H 4	68447	Table Rock, 429	H 4
	Lincoln, ‡167,972	H 4	68046	Papillion◉, 5,606	J 3	68448	Talmage, 285	H 4
68644	Lindsay, 291	G 3	68420	Pawnee City◉, 1,267	H 4	68061	Tekamah◉, 1,848	H 3
69149	Lodgepole, 407	B 3	69155	Paxton, 503	C 3	68879	Taylor◉, 240	F 3
69217	Long Pine, 363	E 2	68047	Pender◉, 1,229	H 2	68450	Tecumseh◉, 2,058	H 4
68958	Loomis, 323	E 4	68421	Peru, 1,380	J 4	† 69341	Terrytown, 747	A 3
68037	Louisville, 1,036	J 3	68652	Petersburg, 370	G 3	69166	Thedford◉, 303	D 3
68853	Loup City◉, 1,456	F 3	68865	Phillips, 341	F 4	68781	Tilden, 947	G 2
69352	Lyman, 561	A 3	68767	Pierce◉, 1,360	G 2	69044	Trenton◉, 770	D 4
68746	Lynch, 375	H 3	68768	Pilger, 470	G 2	69167	Tryon◉, 138	C 3
68038	Lyons, 1,177	H 3	68769	Plainview, 1,494	G 2	68669	Ulysses, 312	G 3
68039	Macy, 550	H 2	68653	Platte Center, 384	G 3	68456	Utica, 602	G 4
68748	Madison◉, 1,595	G 3	68048	Plattsmouth◉, 6,371	J 3	69201	Valentine◉, 2,662	D 2
69038	Maywood, 309	D 4	68424	Plymouth, 424	G 4	68064	Valley, 1,595	H 3
69001	McCook◉, 8,285	D 4	68654	Polk, 413	G 3	68065	Valparaiso, 415	H 3
68401	McCool Junction, 289	G 4	69770	Ponca◉, 984	H 2	68783	Verdigre, 570	F 2
68041	Mead, 408	H 3	69156	Potter, 356	A 3	69066	Wahoo◉, 3,835	H 3
68752	Meadow Grove, 372	G 2	68127	Ralston, 4,265	J 2	68784	Wakefield, 1,160	H 2
68856	Merna, 322	E 3	68771	Randolph, 1,130	G 2	68067	Walthill, 897	H 2
68405	Milford, 1,846	H 4	68869	Ravenna, 1,356	F 4	69045	Wauneta, 738	C 4
68137	Millard, 7,460	H 3	68970	Red Cloud◉, 2,195	F 4	68786	Wausa, 720	G 2
68406	Milligan, 319	G 4	68658	Rising City, 344	G 3	68462	Waverly, 1,952	H 4
69356	Minatare, 939	A 3	68431	Rulo, 299	J 4	68787	Wayne◉, 5,379	G 2
68959	Minden◉, 2,669	E 4	69360	Rushville◉, 1,137	C 2	68463	Weeping Water, 1,143	J 4
69357	Mitchell, 1,842	A 3	68660	Saint Edward, 853	G 3	68464	Western, 344	G 4
69358	Morrill, 937	A 3	68873	Saint Paul◉, 2,026	F 3	68070	Weston, 285	H 3
69152	Mullen◉, 667	C 2	68874	Sargent, 789	E 3	68788	West Point◉, 3,385	H 3
68409	Murray, 286	J 4	68661	Schuyler◉, 3,597	G 3	68465	Wilber◉, 1,483	H 4
68410	Nebraska City◉, 7,441	J 4	68875	Scotia, 354	F 3	68071	Winnebago, 675	H 2
68413	Nehawka, 298	H 4	69361	Scottsbluff, 14,507	A 3	68790	Winside, 453	G 2
68756	Neligh◉, 1,764	G 2	68057	Scribner, 1,031	H 3	68791	Wisner, 1,315	G 2
68961	Nelson◉, 746	H 2	68434	Seward◉, 5,294	H 4	68882	Wolbach, 366	F 3
68757	Newcastle, 347	H 2	68662	Shelby, 647	G 3	68883	Wood River, 1,061	F 4
68758	Newman Grove, 863	G 3	68876	Shelton, 1,028	F 4	68466	Wymore, 1,790	H 4
68760	Niobrara, 602	H 2	68436	Shickley, 385	G 4	68467	York◉, 6,778	G 4
68701	Norfolk, 16,607	G 2	69162	Sidney◉, 6,403	B 3	68073	Yutan, 507	H 3
68649	North Bend, 1,350	H 3	68663	Silver Creek, 483	G 3			
68859	North Loup, 441	F 3	68664	Snyder, 383	H 3			
69101	North Platte◉, 19,447	D 3						
68761	Oakdale, 382	F 2						

◉ County seat.
‡ Population of metropolitan area.
† Zip of nearest p.o.
* Multiple zips

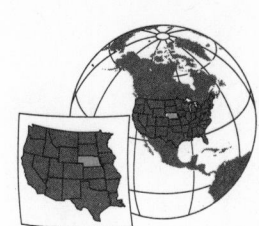

AREA 77,227 sq. mi.
POPULATION 1,483,791
CAPITAL Lincoln
LARGEST CITY Omaha
HIGHEST POINT 5,426 ft. (Kimball Co.)
SETTLED IN 1847
ADMITTED TO UNION March 1, 1867
POPULAR NAME Cornhusker State
STATE FLOWER Goldenrod
STATE BIRD Western Meadowlark

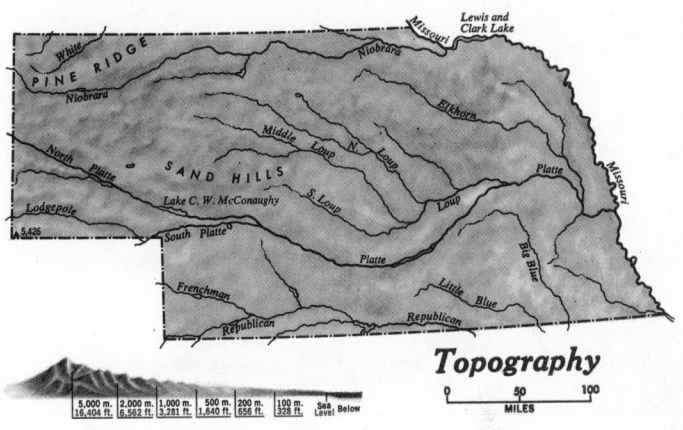

Topography

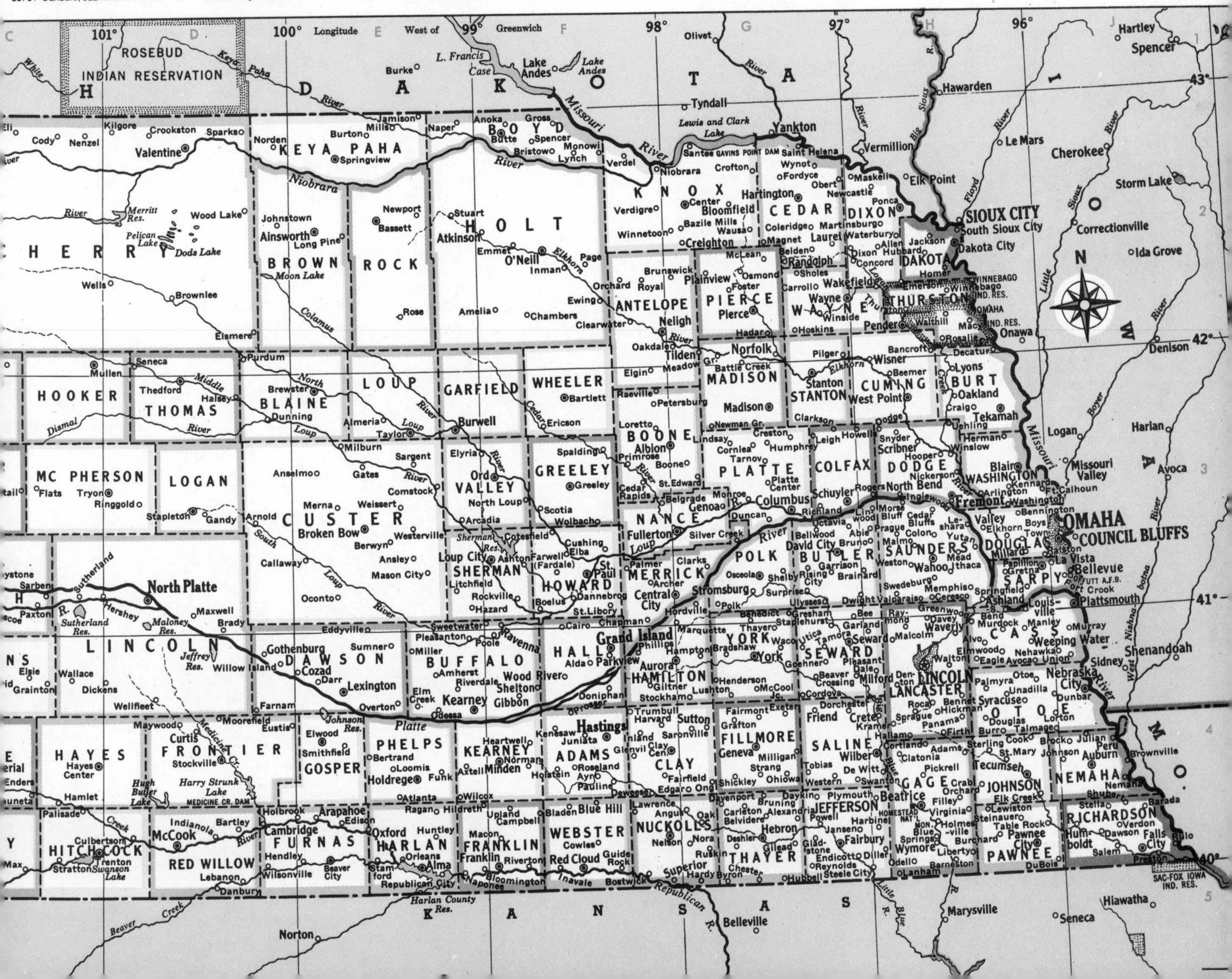

5,000 m.	2,000 m.	1,000 m.	500 m.	200 m.	100 m.	Sea
16,404 ft.	6,562 ft.	3,281 ft.	1,640 ft.	656 ft.	328 ft.	Level Below

0   50   100
MILES

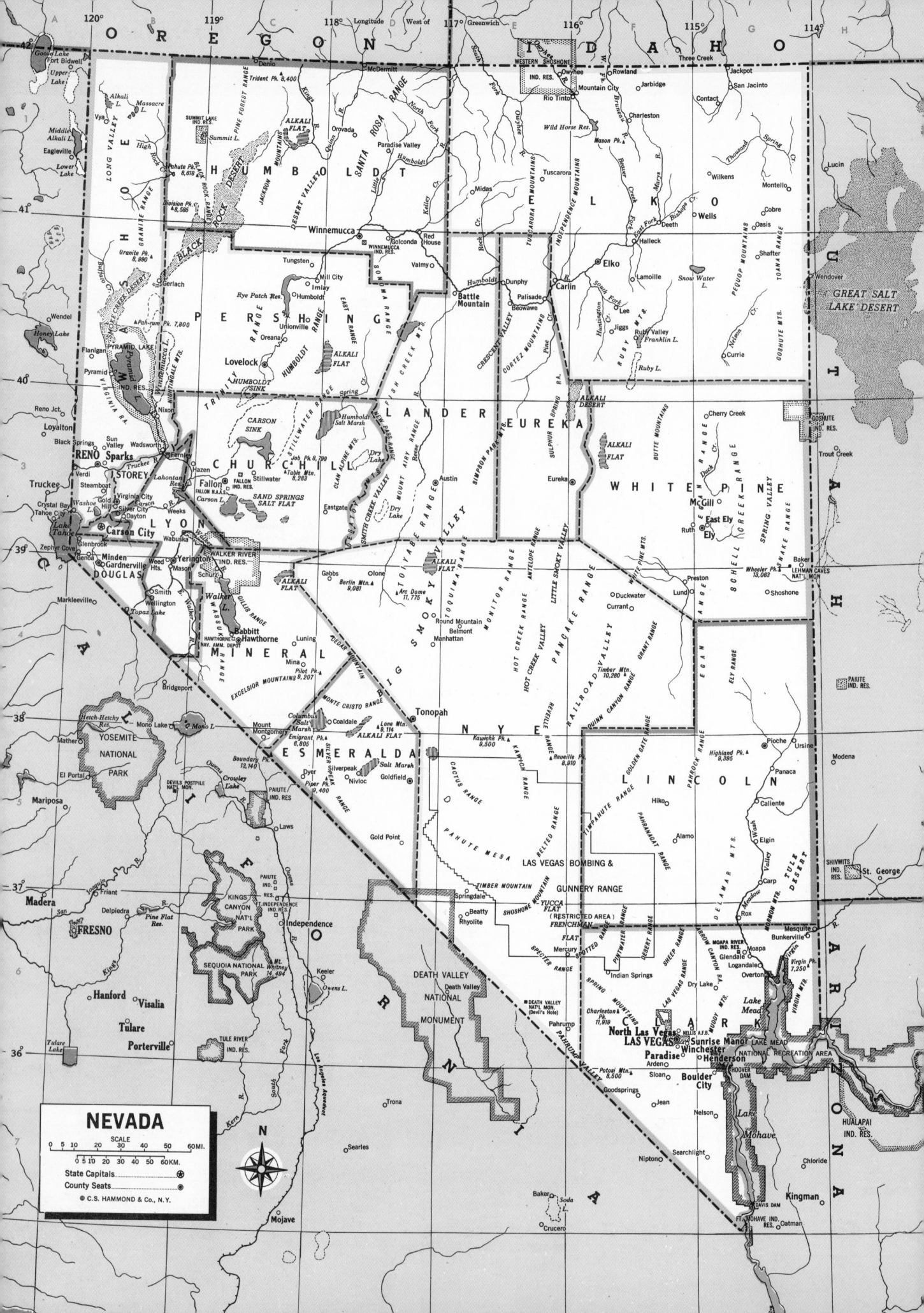

NEVADA

SCALE
0 5 10   20   30   40   50   60 MI.
0 5 10 20 30 40 50 60 KM.

State Capitals
County Seats
© C.S. HAMMOND & Co., N.Y.

COUNTIES

Carson City (city), 15,468 ....D 3
Churchill, 10,513 ....C 3
Clark, 273,288 ....F 6
Douglas, 6,882 ....B 4
Elko, 13,958 ....F 1
Esmeralda, 629 ....D 5
Eureka, 948 ....E 3
Humboldt, 6,375 ....C 1
Lander, 2,666 ....D 3
Lincoln, 2,557 ....F 5
Lyon, 8,221 ....B 3
Mineral, 7,051 ....C 4
Nye, 5,599 ....E 4
Pershing, 2,670 ....C 2
Storey, 695 ....B 3
Washoe, 121,068 ....B 2
White Pine, 10,150 ....F 3

CITIES and TOWNS

Zip Name/Pop. Key

89001 Alamo, 300 ....F 5
89310 Austin⊙, 300 ....E 3
89416 Babbitt, 1,579 ....C 4
89311 Baker, 75 ....G 3
89820 Battle Mountain, 1,856 ....E 2
89003 Beatty, 570 ....E 6
89045 Belmont, 25 ....E 4
89821 Beowawe, 104 ....E 2
89508 Black Springs, 2,500 ....B 3
89005 Boulder City, 5,223 ....G 7
89007 Bunkerville, 150 ....G 6
89008 Caliente, 916 ....G 5
89822 Carlin, 1,313 ....E 2
89009 Carp, 32 ....G 5
89701 Carson City (cap.)⊙, 15,468 ..B 3
89801 Charleston, 14 ....F 1
89312 Cherry Creek, 75 ....D 3
89049 Coaldale, 31 ....D 4
89830 Cobre, 14 ....G 1
89825 Contact, 9 ....G 1
89402 Crystal Bay, 950 ....A 3
89314 Currant, 30 ....F 4
89313 Currie, 15 ....G 2
89403 Dayton, 350 ....B 3
89823 Deeth, 27 ....F 1
89404 Denio, 28 ....C 1
89040 Dry Lake, 5 ....G 6
89314 Duckwater, 85 ....F 4
89821 Dunphy, 20 ....C 2
89010 Dyer, 65 ....G 5
89315 East Ely, 1,992 ....G 3
89406 Eastgate, 17 ....D 3
89112 East Las Vegas, 6,501 ....F 6
89009 Elgin, 8 ....G 5
89801 Elko⊙, 7,621 ....F 2
89301 Ely⊙, 4,176 ....G 3
89316 Eureka⊙, 300 ....E 3
89406 Fallon⊙, 2,959 ....C 3
89408 Fernley, 750 ....B 3
89409 Gabbs, 874 ....D 4
89410 Gardnerville, 800 ....B 4
89411 Genoa, 170 ....B 4
89412 Gerlach, 150 ....B 2
89413 Glenbrook, 80 ....B 3
89025 Glendale, 20 ....G 6
89414 Golconda, 150 ....D 2
89013 Goldfield⊙, 213 ....D 5
89440 Gold Hill, 50 ....B 3
89013 Gold Point, 10 ....D 5
89019 Goodsprings, 120 ....F 7
89824 Halleck, 50 ....F 2
89415 Hawthorne⊙, 3,539 ....C 4
89417 Hazen, 60 ....C 3

89015 Henderson, 16,395 ....G 6
89017 Hiko, 150 ....F 5
† 89418 Humboldt, 12 ....C 2
89418 Humboldt, 12 ....C 2
89411 Imlay, 150 ....C 2
89018 Indian Springs, 500 ....F 6
89310 Ione, 15 ....D 4
89825 Jackpot, 400 ....G 1
89826 Jarbidge, 25 ....F 1
89019 Jean, 100 ....F 7
89827 Jiggs, 6 ....F 2
89828 Lamoille, 51 ....F 2
* 89101 Las Vegas⊙, 125,787 ....F 6
         Las Vegas‡, ‡273,288 ......F 6
89829 Lee, 180 ....F 2
89021 Logandale, 410 ....G 6
89419 Lovelock⊙, 1,571 ....C 2
89317 Lund, 300 ....F 4
89420 Luning, 55 ....C 4
89022 Manhattan, 28 ....E 4
† 89447 Mason, 200 ....B 4
89421 McDermitt, 300 ....D 1
89023 McGill, 2,164 ....G 3
89024 Mercury, 2,200 ....E 6
89024 Mesquite, 500 ....G 6
89414 Midas, 6 ....E 1
† 89418 Mill City, 4 ....D 2
89422 Mina, 375 ....C 4
89423 Minden⊙, 520 ....B 4
89025 Moapa, 250 ....G 6
89830 Montello, 150 ....G 1
89831 Mountain City, 80 ....F 1
† 89422 Mount Montgomery, 10 ....C 5
† 89046 Nelson, 67 ....G 7
89424 Nixon, 300 ....B 3
89030 North Las Vegas, 36,216 ......F 6
† 89830 Oasis, 5 ....G 1
† 89419 Oreana, 18 ....C 2
89425 Orovada, 250 ....D 1
89040 Overton, 900 ....G 6
89832 Owyhee, 100 ....F 1
89041 Pahrump, 400 ....E 6
† 89822 Palisade, 5 ....E 2
89042 Paraca, 500 ....G 5
89101 Paradise, 24,477 ....F 6
89426 Paradise Valley, 110 ....D 1
89043 Pioche⊙, 525 ....G 5
† 89301 Preston, 44 ....G 4
89414 Red House, 4 ....D 2
* 89501 Reno⊙, 72,863 ....B 3
         Reno, ‡121,068 ....B 3
89003 Rhyolite, 8 ....E 6
89831 Rio Tinto, 5 ....E 1
89045 Round Mountain, 100 ....E 4
89831 Rowland, 10 ....F 1
† 89009 Rox, 12 ....G 6
89833 Ruby Valley, 225 ....F 2
89319 Ruth, 750 ....F 3
† 89825 San Jacinto, 8 ....G 1
89427 Schurz, 8 ....C 4
89046 Searchlight, 279 ....F 7
† 89835 Shafter, 7 ....G 2
89428 Silver City, 100 ....B 3
89047 Silverpeak, 80 ....D 5
† 89114 Sloan, 25 ....F 7
89430 Smith, 300 ....B 4
89431 Sparks, 24,187 ....B 3
89436 Steamboat, 560 ....B 3
89406 Stillwater, 30 ....C 3
† 89101 Sunrise Manor, 10,886 ......F 6
89431 Sun Valley, 2,414 ....B 3
89049 Tonopah⊙, 1,716 ....D 4
89834 Tuscarora, 15 ....E 1
† 89418 Unionville, 18 ....C 2
† 89043 Ursine, 40 ....G 5
89438 Valmy, 50 ....D 2

89439 Verdi, 100 ....B 3
89440 Virginia City⊙, 300 ....B 3
96104 Vya, 12 ....B 1
† 89447 Wabuska, 50 ....B 3
89442 Wadsworth, 375 ....B 3
89443 Weed Heights, 750 ....B 4
† 89447 Weeks, 15 ....B 4
89444 Wellington, 100 ....B 4
89835 Wells, 1,081 ....G 1
† 89835 Wilkins, 6 ....G 1
† 89101 Winchester, 13,981 ....F 6
89445 Winnemucca⊙, 3,587 ....D 2
89447 Yerington⊙, 2,010 ....B 4
89448 Zephyr Cove, 400 ....A 3

⊙ County seat.
‡ Population of metropolitan area.
† Zip of nearest p.o.
* Multiple zips

AREA 110,540 sq. mi.
POPULATION 488,738
CAPITAL Carson City
LARGEST CITY Las Vegas
HIGHEST POINT Boundary Pk. 13,140 ft.
SETTLED IN 1850
ADMITTED TO UNION October 31, 1864
POPULAR NAME Silver State
STATE FLOWER Sagebrush
STATE BIRD Mountain Bluebird

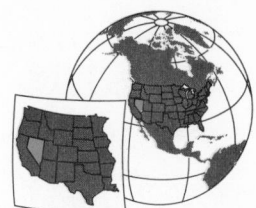

Bill McKinney — Shostal Associates

An incandescent oasis in the Nevada desert, Reno beckons travelers to its varied diversions — from games of chance and nightclub entertainment to annual rodeos and skiing in the Sierra Nevada.

Agriculture, Industry and Resources

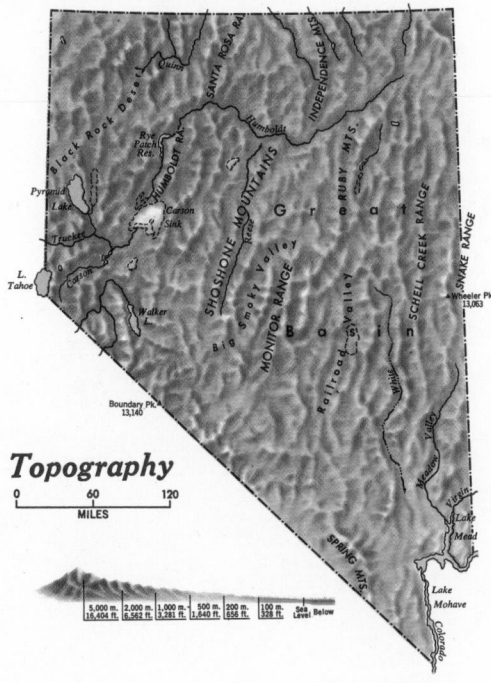

Topography

0   60   120
MILES

5,000 m. | 2,000 m. | 1,000 m. | 500 m. | 200 m. | 100 m. | Sea
16,404 ft. | 6,562 ft. | 3,281 ft. | 1,640 ft. | 656 ft. | 328 ft. | Level Below

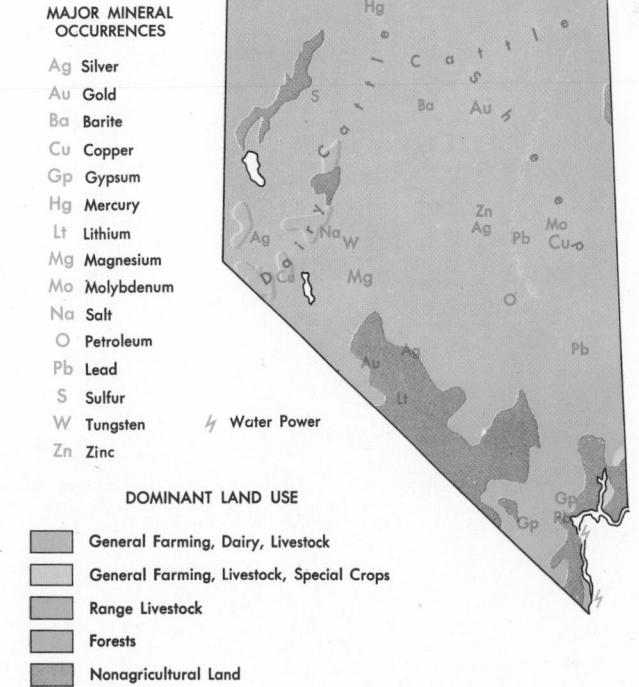

MAJOR MINERAL OCCURRENCES

Ag Silver
Au Gold
Ba Barite
Cu Copper
Gp Gypsum
Hg Mercury
Lt Lithium
Mg Magnesium
Mo Molybdenum
Na Salt
O   Petroleum
Pb Lead
S   Sulfur
W   Tungsten   ϟ Water Power
Zn Zinc

DOMINANT LAND USE

General Farming, Dairy, Livestock
General Farming, Livestock, Special Crops
Range Livestock
Forests
Nonagricultural Land

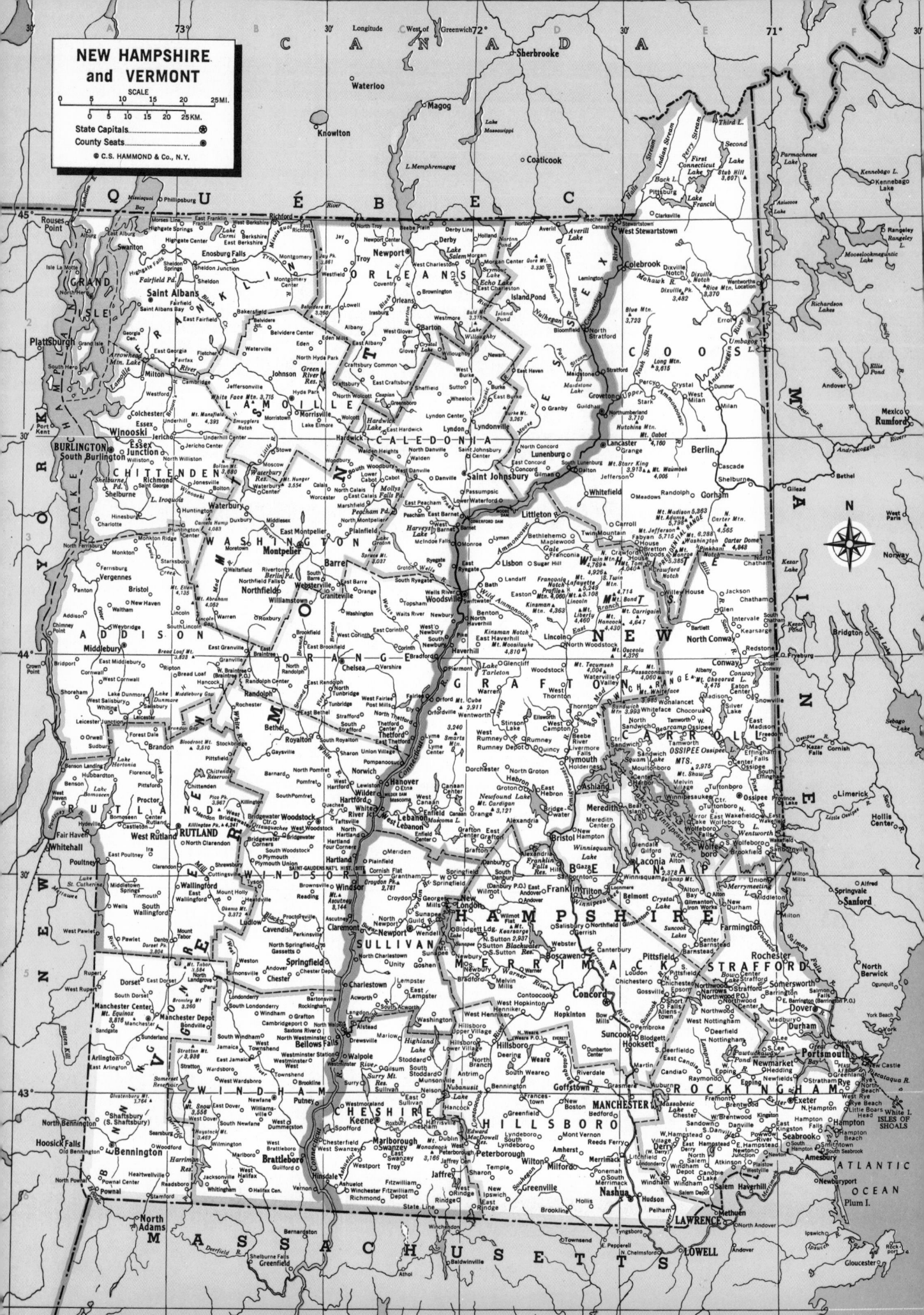

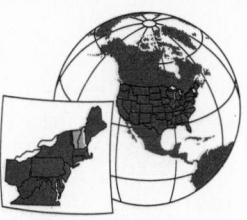

NEW HAMPSHIRE
COUNTIES

Name/Pop.	Key
Belknap, 32,367	D 4
Carroll, 18,548	E 4
Cheshire, 52,364	C 6
Coos, 34,291	E 2
Grafton, 54,914	D 4
Hillsboro, 223,941	D 6
Merrimack, 80,925	D 5
Rockingham, 138,951	E 5
Strafford, 70,431	E 5
Sullivan, 30,949	C 5

CITIES and TOWNS

Zip	Name/Pop.	Key
03601	Acworth, ▲459	C 5
03864	Albany, ▲259	E 4
† 03222	Alexandria, ▲466	D 4
† 03275	Allenstown, ▲2,732	E 5
03602	Alstead, ▲1,185	C 5
03602	Alstead, 450	C 5
03809	Alton, ▲1,647	E 5
03809	Alton, 450	E 5
03031	Amherst, ▲4,605	D 6
03810	Amherst, 600	D 6
03216	Andover, ▲1,138	D 5
03216	Andover, 500	D 5
03440	Antrim, ▲2,122	D 5
03440	Antrim, 750	D 5
03217	Ashland, ▲1,599	D 4
03217	Ashland, 1,391	D 4
03441	Ashuelot, 750	C 6
03811	Atkinson, ▲2,291	E 6
03032	Auburn, ▲2,035	E 5
03218	Barnstead, ▲1,119	E 5
03218	Barnstead, 400	E 5
† 03825	Barrington, ▲1,865	F 5
03812	Bartlett, ▲1,098	E 3
03812	Bartlett, 600	E 3
03740	Bath, ▲607	D 3
03102	Bedford, ▲5,859	D 6
03220	Belmont, ▲2,493	E 5
03220	Belmont, 900	E 5
03442	Bennington, ▲639	D 5

Zip	Name/Pop.	Key
† 03785	Benton, ▲194	D 3
03570	Berlin, 15,256	E 3
03574	Bethlehem, ▲1,142	D 3
03574	Bethlehem, 500	D 3
03301	Boscawen, ▲3,162	D 5
03301	Bow Mills, ▲600	D 5
03221	Bradford, ▲679	D 5
† 03833	Brentwood, ▲1,468	E 6
03575	Bretton Woods, 6	E 3
† 03222	Bridgewater, ▲398	D 4
03222	Bristol, ▲1,670	D 4
03222	Bristol, 1,080	D 4
03872	Brookfield, ▲198	E 4
03033	Brookline, ▲1,167	D 6
03223	Campton, ▲1,171	D 4
03741	Canaan, ▲1,923	C 4
03741	Canaan, 500	C 4
03034	Candia, ▲1,997	E 5
† 03079	Canobie Lake, 500	E 6
03224	Canterbury, ▲895	D 5
03595	Carroll, ▲310	D 3
03813	Center Conway, 450	E 4
03226	Center Harbor, ▲540	E 4
03814	Center Ossipee, 550	E 4
03603	Charlestown, ▲3,274	C 5
03603	Charlestown, 1,285	C 5
† 04037	Chatham, ▲134	E 4
03036	Chester, ▲1,382	E 5
03443	Chesterfield, ▲1,817	C 5
03443	Chesterfield, 450	C 5
03258	Chichester, ▲1,083	E 5
03743	Claremont, 14,221	C 5
05902	Clarksville, ▲166	E 1
03576	Colebrook, ▲2,094	E 2
03576	Colebrook, 1,070	E 2
03301	Concord (cap.)◉, 30,022	D 5
03229	Contoocook, 975	D 5
03818	Conway, ▲4,865	E 4
03818	Conway, 1,489	E 4
† 03753	Croydon, ▲396	C 5
03598	Dalton, ▲425	D 3
03230	Danbury, ▲489	D 4
03819	Danville, ▲924	E 5
03037	Deerfield, ▲1,178	E 5
† 03244	Deering, ▲578	D 5
03038	Derry, ▲11,712	E 6
03038	Derry, 6,090	E 5

Zip	Name/Pop.	Key
03266	Dorchester, ▲141	D 4
03820	Dover◉, 20,850	F 5
03444	Dublin, ▲837	C 6
03588	Dummer, ▲225	E 2
03301	Dunbarton, ▲825	D 5
03824	Durham, ▲8,869	F 5
03824	Durham, 7,221	F 5
03231	East Andover, 450	D 5
03041	East Derry, 600	E 6
03827	East Kingston, ▲838	F 6
† 03580	Easton, ▲92	D 3
03446	East Swanzey, 500	C 6
† 03894	East Wolfeboro, 400	E 4
03832	Eaton Center, ▲221	E 4
03264	Ellsworth, ▲13	D 4
03748	Enfield, ▲2,345	C 4
03748	Enfield, 1,408	C 4
03042	Epping, ▲2,356	E 5
03042	Epping, 1,097	E 5
03234	Epsom, ▲1,469	E 5
03579	Errol, ▲199	E 2
03750	Etna, 550	C 4
03833	Exeter, ▲8,892	F 6
03833	Exeter◉, 6,439	F 6
03835	Farmington, ▲3,588	E 5
03835	Farmington, 2,884	E 5
03447	Fitzwilliam, ▲1,362	C 6
03447	Fitzwilliam, 750	C 6
03043	Francestown, ▲525	D 6
03580	Franconia, ▲655	D 3
03235	Franklin, 7,292	D 5
03836	Freedom, ▲387	E 4

NEW HAMPSHIRE
AREA 9,304 sq. mi.
POPULATION 737,681
CAPITAL Concord
LARGEST CITY Manchester
HIGHEST POINT Mt. Washington 6,288 ft.
SETTLED IN 1623
ADMITTED TO UNION June 21, 1788
POPULAR NAME Granite State
STATE FLOWER Purple Lilac
STATE BIRD Purple Finch

VERMONT
AREA 9,609 sq. mi.
POPULATION 444,732
CAPITAL Montpelier
LARGEST CITY Burlington
HIGHEST POINT Mt. Mansfield 4,393 ft.
SETTLED IN 1764
ADMITTED TO UNION March 4, 1791
POPULAR NAME Green Mountain State
STATE FLOWER Red Clover
STATE BIRD Hermit Thrush

Topography

```
0        20        40
|_____|_____|
      MILES
```

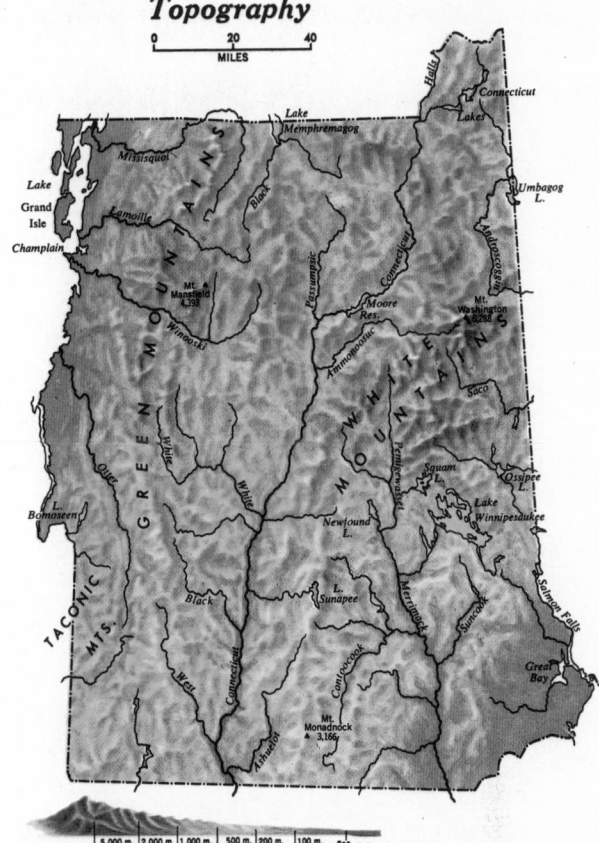

```
5,000 m.  2,000 m.  1,000 m.  500 m.  200 m.  100 m.  Sea
16,404 ft. 6,562 ft. 3,281 ft. 1,640 ft. 656 ft. 328 ft. Level  Below
```

Agriculture, Industry and Resources

DOMINANT LAND USE

- Specialized Dairy
- Dairy, General Farming
- Dairy, Poultry, Mixed Farming
- Forests
- ⚡ Water Power
- Major Industrial Areas

MANCHESTER
Leather Goods, Textiles, Electrical Products

MAJOR MINERAL OCCURRENCES

Ab	Asbestos	Mr	Marble
Be	Beryl	Sl	Slate
Gn	Granite	Tc	Talc
Mi	Mica	Th	Thorium

Zip	Name/Pop.	Key
03044	Fremont, ▲993	E 6
† 03246	Gilford, ▲3,219	E 4
03237	Gilmanton, ▲1,010	E 5
03448	Gilsum, ▲570	C 5
03045	Goffstown, ▲9,284	D 5
03045	Goffstown, 2,272	D 5
03581	Gorham, ▲2,998	E 3
03581	Gorham, 2,020	E 3
03752	Goshen, ▲395	C 5
03239	Gossville, 800	E 5
03240	Grafton, ▲370	D 4
03753	Grantham, ▲366	C 5
03045	Grasmere, 513	D 5
03047	Greenfield, ▲1,058	D 6
03840	Greenland, ▲1,784	F 5
03048	Greenville, ▲1,587	D 6
03048	Greenville, 1,332	D 6
† 03241	Groton, ▲120	D 4
03582	Groveton, 1,597	D 2
03841	Hampstead, ▲2,401	E 6
03841	Hampstead, 500	E 6
03842	Hampton, ▲8,011	F 6
03842	Hampton, 5,407	F 6
03842	Hampton Beach, 975	F 6
03844	Hampton Falls, ▲1,254	F 6
03449	Hancock, ▲909	C 6
03755	Hanover, ▲8,494	C 4
03755	Hanover, 6,147	C 4
03450	Harrisville, ▲584	C 6
03765	Haverhill, ▲3,090	C 3
03765	Haverhill, 400	C 3
03241	Hebron, ▲234	D 4
03242	Henniker, ▲2,348	D 5
03242	Henniker, 950	D 5
03243	Hill, ▲450	D 4
03244	Hillsboro, ▲2,775	D 5
03244	Hillsboro, 1,784	D 5
03451	Hinsdale, ▲3,276	C 6
03451	Hinsdale, 1,059	C 6
03245	Holderness, ▲1,048	D 4
03049	Hollis, ▲2,616	D 6
03049	Hollis, 500	D 6
03106	Hooksett, ▲5,564	E 5
03106	Hooksett, 1,303	E 5
03054	Merrimack, ▲8,595	D 6

Zip	Name/Pop.	Key
03301	Hopkinton, ▲3,007	D 5
03301	Hopkinton, 500	D 5
03051	Hudson, ▲10,638	E 6
03051	Hudson, 4,900	E 6
03845	Intervale, 500	E 3
03846	Jackson, ▲404	E 3
03452	Jaffrey, ▲3,353	C 6
03452	Jaffrey, 1,922	C 6
03583	Jefferson, ▲714	D 3
03431	Keene◉, 20,467	C 6
03848	Kingston, ▲2,882	E 6
03246	Laconia◉, 14,888	E 4
03584	Lancaster, ▲3,166	D 3
03584	Lancaster◉, 2,120	D 3
03585	Landaff, ▲292	D 3
† 03602	Langdon, ▲337	C 5
03766	Lebanon, 9,725	C 4
† 03241	Lee, ▲1,481	F 5
03606	Lempster, ▲360	C 5
03251	Lincoln, ▲1,341	D 3
03251	Lincoln, 900	D 3
03585	Lisbon, ▲1,480	D 3
03585	Lisbon, 1,247	D 3
† 03051	Litchfield, ▲1,420	E 6
03561	Littleton, ▲5,290	D 3
03561	Littleton, 4,180	D 3
03252	Lochmere, 500	D 5
03053	Londonderry, ▲5,346	E 6
03301	Loudon, ▲1,707	E 5
† 03585	Lyman, ▲213	D 3
03768	Lyme, ▲1,112	C 4
03768	Lyme, 400	C 4
03082	Lyndeboro, ▲789	D 6
† 03820	Madbury, ▲704	F 5
03849	Madison, ▲572	E 4
* 03101	Manchester, 87,754	E 6
	Manchester, ‡108,461	E 6
03455	Marlborough, ▲1,671	C 6
03455	Marlborough, 1,231	C 6
03456	Marlow, ▲390	C 5
03253	Meredith, ▲2,904	D 4
03253	Meredith, 1,017	D 4
03770	Meriden, 495	C 4
03054	Merrimack, 850	D 6

Zip	Name/Pop.	Key
03054	Merrimack, 850	D 6
† 03887	Middleton, ▲430	E 5
03588	Milan, ▲713	E 2
03055	Milford, ▲6,622	D 6
03055	Milford, 4,997	D 6
03851	Milton, ▲1,859	F 5
03851	Milton, 750	F 5
03771	Monroe, ▲385	C 3
03057	Mont Vernon, ▲906	D 6
03254	Moultonboro, ▲1,310	E 4
03060	Nashua◉, 55,820	D 6
† 03457	Nelson, ▲304	C 5
03070	New Boston, ▲1,390	D 6
03070	New Boston, 450	D 6
03255	Newbury, ▲509	C 5
03854	New Castle, ▲975	F 5
03855	New Durham, ▲583	E 5
03856	Newfields, ▲843	F 5
03256	New Hampton, ▲946	D 4
† 03801	Newington, ▲798	F 5
03071	New Ipswich, ▲1,803	C 6
03257	New London, ▲2,236	D 5
03257	New London, 1,347	D 5
03857	Newmarket, ▲3,361	F 5
03857	Newmarket, 2,645	F 5
03773	Newport, ▲5,899	C 5
03773	Newport◉, 3,296	C 5
03858	Newton, ▲1,920	E 6
03858	Newton, 483	E 6
03859	Newton Junction, 500	E 6
03258	North Chichester, 450	E 5
03860	North Conway, 1,723	E 3
† 03276	Northfield, ▲2,193	D 5
† 03276	Northfield-Tilton, 2,420	D 5
03862	North Hampton, ▲3,259	F 6
03862	North Hampton, 750	F 6
03774	North Haverhill, 750	C 3
† 03773	North Newport, 500	C 5
03073	North Salem, 950	E 6
03590	North Stratford, 650	D 2
03582	Northumberland, ▲2,493	D 2
† 03608	North Walpole, 950	C 5
03281	North Weare, 600	D 5
03261	Northwood, ▲1,526	E 5

(continued on following page)

Designed to protect wooden structures from the ravages of weather, a few early covered bridges are still standing in New Hampshire. This barn-red relic is in Jackson.

Located in the heart of Vermont, Barre rightfully boasts of its granite quarries which provide a sculptured panorama set off by surrounding green hills.

COUNTIES

Atlantic, 175,043 ....D 5
Bergen, 898,012 ....E 2
Burlington, 323,132 ....D 4
Camden, 456,291 ....D 4
Cape May, 59,554 ....D 5
Cumberland, 121,374 ....C 5
Essex, 929,986 ....E 2
Gloucester, 172,681 ....C 4
Hudson, 609,266 ....E 2
Hunterdon, 69,718 ....D 2
Mercer, 303,968 ....D 3
Middlesex, 583,813 ....E 3
Monmouth, 459,379 ....E 3
Morris, 383,454 ....D 2
Ocean, 208,470 ....E 4
Passaic, 460,782 ....E 1
Salem, 60,346 ....C 4
Somerset, 198,372 ....D 2
Sussex, 77,528 ....D 1
Union, 543,116 ....E 2
Warren, 73,879 ....C 2

CITIES and TOWNS

Zip	Name/Pop.	Key
08201	Absecon, 6,094	D 5
07820	Allamuchy, 600	D 2
07401	Allendale, 6,240	B 1
07711	Allenhurst, 1,012	F 3
08501	Allentown, 1,603	D 3
08720	Allenwood, 2,200	E 3
08001	Alloway, 850	C 4
08865	Alpha, 2,829	C 2
07620	Alpine, 1,344	C 1
07821	Andover, 813	D 2
08801	Annandale, 675	D 2
07712	Asbury Park, 16,533	F 3
† 08033	Ashland, 2,500	B 3
08004	Atco, 2,980	D 4
* 08401	Atlantic City, 47,859	E 5
	Atlantic City, 175,043	E 5
07716	Atlantic Highlands, 5,102	F 3
08106	Audubon, 10,802	B 3
† 08106	Audubon Park, 1,492	B 3
08202	Avalon, 1,283	D 5
07001	Avenel, 10,250	E 2
07717	Avon by the Sea, 2,163	F 3
08005	Barnegat, 900	E 4
08006	Barnegat Light, 554	F 4
08007	Barrington, 8,409	B 3
07920	Basking Ridge, 2,500	D 2
08742	Bay Head, 1,083	E 3
07002	Bayonne, 72,743	B 2
08721	Bayville, 6,000	E 4
08008	Beach Haven, 1,488	F 4
08722	Beachwood, 4,390	E 4
07921	Bedminster, 1,250	D 2
07718	Belford, 7,000	E 3
08502	Belle Mead, 1,950	D 2
08030	Bellmawr, 15,618	A 3
07719	Belmar, 5,782	E 3
07823	Belvidere☉, 2,641	C 2
07621	Bergenfield, 33,131	C 1
07922	Berkeley Heights, ▲13,078	E 2
08009	Berlin, 4,997	D 4
07924	Bernardsville, 6,652	D 2
08010	Beverly, 3,105	D 3
08012	Blackwood, 9,500	C 4
07825	Blairstown, 1,900	C 2
07003	Bloomfield, 52,029	B 2
07403	Bloomingdale, 7,797	E 1
08804	Bloomsbury, 879	C 2
07603	Bogota, 8,125	B 2
07005	Boonton, 9,261	E 2
08505	Bordentown, 4,490	D 3
08805	Bound Brook, 10,450	D 2
07720	Bradley Beach, 4,163	F 3
07826	Branchville, 911	D 1
08723	Breton Woods, 1,900	E 3
08723	Brick Town, ▲35,057	E 3
08014	Bridgeport, 950	C 4
08302	Bridgeton☉, 20,435	C 5
08730	Brielle, 3,594	E 3
08203	Brigantine, 6,741	E 5
08030	Brooklawn, 2,870	A 3
07926	Brookside, 1,300	D 2
08015	Browns Mills, 7,144	D 4
07405	Butler, 7,051	E 2
08016	Burlington, 11,991	D 3
08310	Buena, 3,283	D 5
08068	Budd Lake, 3,168	D 2
07830	Califon, 970	D 2
* 08101	Camden☉, 102,551	B 3
† 08701	Candlewood, 5,629	E 4
08204	Cape May, 4,392	D 6
08210	Cape May Court House☉, 2,062	D 5
07072	Carlstadt, 7,947	B 2
08069	Carneys Point, 3,900	C 4
07008	Carteret, 23,137	E 2
08018	Cedar Brook, 600	D 4
07009	Cedar Grove, ▲15,582	B 2
07927	Cedar Knolls, 3,900	C 2
08311	Cedarville, 900	C 5
† 08723	Cedarwood Park, 1,400	E 3
07928	Chatham, 9,566	E 2
08019	Chatsworth, 700	D 4
08879	Cheesequake, 2,900	E 3
08034	Cherry Hill, ▲64,395	B 3
08089	Chesilhurst, 801	D 4
07930	Chester, 1,299	D 2
08505	Chesterfield, ▲3,190	D 3
07066	Clark, ▲18,829	A 3
08020	Clarksboro, 1,500	C 4
08510	Clarksburg, 800	E 3
08312	Clayton, 5,193	C 4
08021	Clementon, 4,492	D 4
07010	Cliffside Park, 14,387	C 2
07721	Cliffwood, 7,056	E 3
07011	Clifton, 82,437	B 2
08809	Clinton, 1,742	D 2
07624	Closter, 8,604	C 1
08108	Collingswood, 17,422	B 3
08213	Cologne, 800	D 4
07067	Colonia, 12,000	E 2
07722	Colts Neck, 950	E 3
08022	Columbus, 800	D 3
07961	Convent Station, 6,587	C 2
08512	Cranbury, 1,253	E 2
07016	Cranford, ▲27,391	E 2
07626	Cresskill, 7,164	C 1
08515	Crosswicks, 700	D 3
07723	Deal, 2,401	F 3
08023	Deepwater, 800	C 4
08110	Delair, 2,800	B 3
08075	Delanco, ▲4,157	D 3
08075	Delran, 675	D 3
07627	Demarest, 6,262	C 1
08214	Dennisville, 990	D 5
07834	Denville, 12,200	E 2
08096	Deptford, ▲24,232	B 4
08317	Dorothy, 850	D 5
07801	Dover, 15,039	D 2

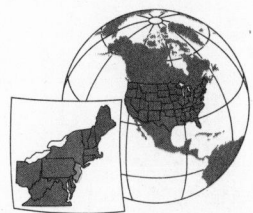

AREA 7,836 sq. mi.
POPULATION 7,168,164
CAPITAL Trenton
LARGEST CITY Newark
HIGHEST POINT High Point 1,803 ft.
SETTLED IN 1617
ADMITTED TO UNION December 18, 1787
POPULAR NAME Garden State
STATE FLOWER Violet
STATE BIRD Eastern Goldfinch

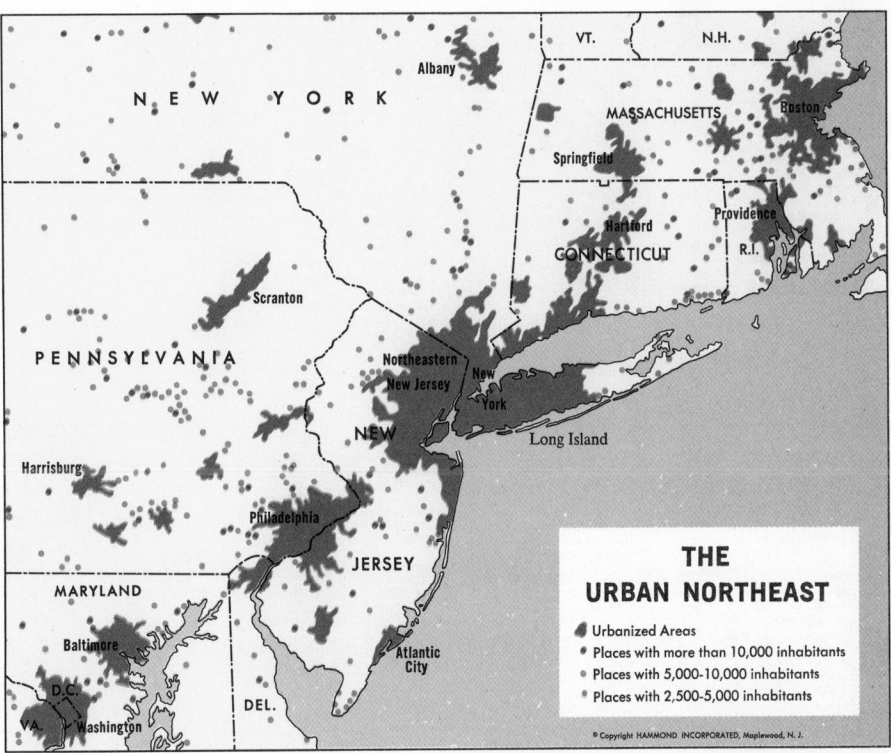

THE URBAN NORTHEAST

◢ Urbanized Areas
● Places with more than 10,000 inhabitants
• Places with 5,000-10,000 inhabitants
· Places with 2,500-5,000 inhabitants

© Copyright HAMMOND INCORPORATED, Maplewood, N. J.

Agriculture, Industry and Resources

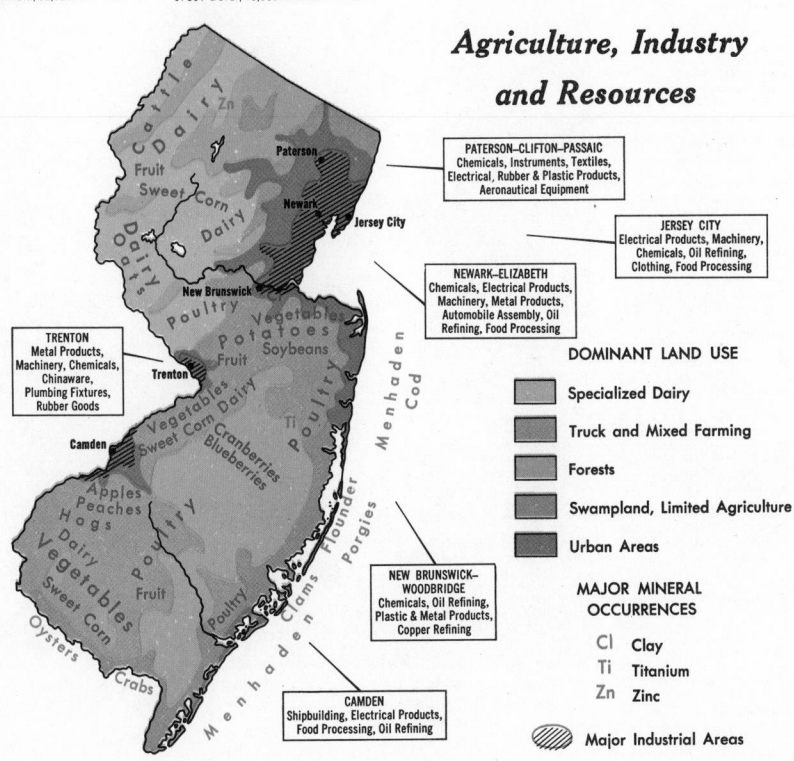

PATERSON–CLIFTON–PASSAIC
Chemicals, Instruments, Textiles,
Electrical, Rubber & Plastic Products,
Aeronautical Equipment

JERSEY CITY
Electrical Products, Machinery,
Chemicals, Oil Refining,
Clothing, Food Processing

NEWARK–ELIZABETH
Chemicals, Electrical Products,
Machinery, Metal Products,
Automobile Assembly, Oil
Refining, Food Processing

TRENTON
Metal Products,
Machinery, Chemicals,
Chinaware,
Plumbing Fixtures,
Rubber Goods

NEW BRUNSWICK–WOODBRIDGE
Chemicals, Oil Refining,
Plastic & Metal Products,
Copper Refining

CAMDEN
Shipbuilding, Electrical Products,
Food Processing, Oil Refining

DOMINANT LAND USE

Specialized Dairy
Truck and Mixed Farming
Forests
Swampland, Limited Agriculture
Urban Areas

MAJOR MINERAL OCCURRENCES

Cl Clay
Ti Titanium
Zn Zinc

▨ Major Industrial Areas

07628	Dumont, 17,534	C 1
08812	Dunellen, 7,072	D 2
08816	East Brunswick, ▲34,166	E 3
07936	East Hanover, ▲7,734	E 2
07734	East Keansburg, 5,000	E 3
08873	East Millstone, 950	D 3
† 07100	East Newark, 1,922	B 2
07017	East Orange, 75,471	B 2
07407	East Paterson, 22,749	B 2
07073	East Rutherford, 8,536	B 2
07724	Eatontown, 14,619	E 3
07020	Edgewater, 4,849	C 2
† 08010	Edgewater Park, ▲7,412	D 3
08817	Edison, ▲67,120	E 2
08215	Egg Harbor City, 4,304	D 4
07740	Elberon, 2,900	F 3
* 07201	Elizabeth☉, 112,654	B 2
08318	Elmer, 1,592	C 4
07630	Emerson, 8,428	B 1
* 07631	Englewood, 24,985	C 2
07632	Englewood Cliffs, 5,938	C 2
† 08330	English Creek, 950	D 5
07726	Englishtown, 1,048	E 3
07849	Espanong (Lake Hopatcong), 1,941	D 2
07021	Essex Fells, 2,541	B 2
07006	Fairfield, 6,731	A 2
07701	Fair Haven, 6,142	E 3
07410	Fair Lawn, 37,975	B 1
08320	Fairton, 600	C 5
07022	Fairview, 10,698	C 2
07023	Fanwood, 8,920	E 2
07931	Far Hills, 780	D 2
07727	Farmingdale, 1,148	E 3
* 08505	Fieldsboro, 615	D 3
08821	Flagtown, 800	D 2
07836	Flanders, 3,875	D 2
08822	Flemington☉, 3,917	D 2
08518	Florence-Roebling, 7,551	D 3
07932	Florham Park, 8,094	E 2
† 08037	Folsom, 1,767	D 4
08863	Fords, 14,000	E 2
08731	Forked River, 1,422	E 4
07024	Fort Lee, 30,631	C 2
07416	Franklin, ▲30,389	D 1
07416	Franklin, 4,236	D 1
07417	Franklin Lakes, 7,550	B 1
08322	Franklinville, 2,500	C 4
07728	Freehold☉, 10,545	E 3
08825	Frenchtown, 1,459	C 2
07026	Garfield, 30,722	B 2
07027	Garwood, 5,260	E 2
08026	Gibbsboro, 2,634	B 4
08027	Gibbstown, 3,400	C 4
† 08753	Gilford Park, 4,007	E 4

07933	Gillette, 2,950	E 2
08028	Glassboro, 12,938	C 4
08029	Glendora, 10,280	B 4
08826	Glen Gardner, 874	D 2
07028	Glen Ridge, 8,518	B 2
07452	Glen Rock, 13,011	B 1
08030	Gloucester City, 14,707	B 3
08219	Green Creek, 975	D 5
07435	Green Pond, 800	E 1
07935	Green Village, 800	D 2
08323	Greenwich, ▲963	C 5
08032	Grenloch, 950	C 4
07950	Greystone Park, 5,500	D 2
08620	Groveville, 2,800	D 3
07093	Guttenberg, 5,754	C 2
* 07601	Hackensack☉, 35,911	B 2
07840	Hackettstown, 9,472	D 2
08033	Haddonfield, 13,118	B 3
08035	Haddon Heights, 9,365	B 3
08036	Hainesport, ▲2,990	D 4
07508	Haledon, 6,767	B 2
07419	Hamburg, 1,820	D 1
08690	Hamilton Square, 11,300	D 3
08037	Hammonton, 11,464	D 4
08827	Hampton, 1,386	D 2
07640	Harrington Park, 4,841	C 1
07029	Harrison, 11,811	B 2
08039	Harrisonville, 950	C 4
† 08057	Hartford, 650	D 4
07604	Hasbrouck Heights, 13,651	B 2
07641	Haworth, 3,760	C 1
07507	Hawthorne, 19,173	B 2
07730	Hazlet, 15,000	E 3
08828	Helmetta, 955	E 3
07421	Hewitt, 950	E 1
08829	High Bridge, 2,606	D 2
08904	Highland Park, 14,385	D 2
07732	Highlands, 3,916	F 3
08520	Hightstown, 5,431	D 3
07502	Hillcrest, 1,975	C 2
07642	Hillsdale, 11,768	B 1
07205	Hillside, ▲21,636	B 2
† 08083	Hi-Nella, 1,195	B 4
07030	Hoboken, 45,380	C 2
07423	Ho-ho-kus, 4,348	B 1
07733	Holmdel, 5,500	E 3
07843	Hopatcong, 9,052	D 2
07844	Hope, 950	D 2
08525	Hopewell, 2,271	D 3
07727	Howell, ▲21,756	E 3
† 08865	Huntington, 1,900	C 2
07712	Interlaken, 1,182	F 3
07845	Ironia, 1,500	D 2
07111	Irvington, 59,743	B 2
08830	Iselin, 19,000	E 2

(continued on following page)

(continued)

	Zip	Place	Key
	08732	Island Heights, 1,397	E 4
	08527	Jackson, ▵18,276	E 3
	08831	Jamesburg, 4,584	E 3
*	07301	Jersey City⊙, 260,545	B 2
		Jersey City, ‡609,266	B 2
	07734	Keansburg, 9,720	E 3
	07032	Kearny, 37,585	B 2
	08832	Keasbey, 1,200	E 2
	08824	Kendall Park, 7,412	D 3
	07033	Kenilworth, 9,165	E 2
	07735	Keyport, 7,205	E 3
	08528	Kingston, 1,200	D 3
	07405	Kinnelon, 7,600	E 2
	08043	Kirkwood, 800	B 4
	07848	Lafayette, 900	D 1
	07034	Lake Hiawatha, 11,389	E 2
	07849	Lake Hopatcong, 1,941	D 2
	08733	Lakehurst, 2,641	E 3
†	07871	Lake Mohawk, 6,262	D 1
	08701	Lakewood, 17,874	E 3
	08530	Lambertville, 4,359	D 3
	07850	Landing, 2,370	D 2
	08734	Lanoka Harbor, 1,066	E 4
	08021	Laurel Springs, 2,566	B 4
	08879	Laurence Harbor, 6,715	E 3
	08735	Lavallette, 1,509	E 4
	08045	Lawnside, 2,757	B 3
	08648	Lawrenceville, 1,464	D 3
	08833	Lebanon, 885	D 2
	07852	Ledgewood, 2,800	D 2
	08327	Leesburg, 800	D 5
	07737	Leonardo, 4,000	E 3
	07605	Leonia, 8,847	C 2
	07938	Liberty Corner, 1,900	D 2
	07035	Lincoln Park, 9,034	A 1
	07738	Lincroft, 4,900	E 3
	07036	Linden, 41,409	A 3
	08021	Lindenwold, 12,199	B 4
	08221	Linwood, 6,159	D 5
	07424	Little Falls, ▵11,727	B 2
	07643	Little Ferry, 9,042	B 2
	07739	Little Silver, 6,010	F 3
	07039	Livingston, ▵30,127	E 2
	07644	Lodi, 25,213	B 2
	08008	Long Branch, 31,774	F 3
	08403	Longport, 1,225	D 5
	07853	Long Valley, 1,645	D 2
	08048	Lumberton, 600	D 4
	07071	Lyndhurst, ▵22,729	B 2
	07939	Lyons, 3,900	D 2
	07940	Madison, 16,710	E 2
	08049	Magnolia, 5,893	B 3
	07430	Mahwah, ▵10,539	E 1
	08328	Malaga, 950	C 4
	08050	Manahawkin, 1,278	E 4
	08736	Manasquan, 4,971	E 3
	08051	Mantua, 5,530	C 4
	08835	Manville, 13,029	D 2
	08052	Maple Shade, ▵16,464	B 3
	07040	Maplewood, ▵24,932	E 2
†	07866	Marcella, 540	E 2
	08402	Margate City, 10,576	E 5
	07746	Marlboro, 2,380	E 3
	08053	Marlton, 10,180	D 4
	08223	Marmora, 650	D 5
	08836	Martinsville, 3,500	D 2
	08054	Masonville, 900	D 4
	07747	Matawan, 9,136	E 3
	08330	Mays Landing⊙, 1,272	D 5
	07607	Maywood, 11,087	B 2
	07428	McAfee, 800	D 1
†	08232	McKee City, 950	D 5
	08055	Medford, 1,448	D 4
	08055	Medford Lakes, 4,792	D 4
	07945	Mendham, 3,729	D 2
	08817	Menlo Park, 10,000	E 2
	08619	Mercerville, 5,456	D 3
	08109	Merchantville, 4,425	B 3
	08840	Metuchen, 16,031	E 2
	08056	Mickleton, 950	C 4
	08846	Middlesex, 15,038	E 2
	07748	Middletown, ▵54,623	E 3
	07432	Midland Park, 8,159	B 1
	08848	Milford, 1,230	C 2
	07041	Millburn, ▵21,307	E 2
	07946	Millington, 975	D 2
	08849	Millstone, 630	D 2
	08850	Milltown, 6,470	E 3
	08332	Millville, 21,366	C 5
	07438	Milton, 2,220	D 1
†	07801	Mine Hill, ▵3,557	D 2
	08342	Mizpah, 900	D 5
	07750	Monmouth Beach, 2,042	F 3
	08852	Monmouth Junction, 1,900	D 3
	07434	Monroe, ▵9,138	E 3
†	12771	Montague, 750	D 1
*	07042	Montclair, 44,043	B 2
	07645	Montvale, 7,327	B 1
	07045	Montville, 4,900	E 2
	07074	Moonachie, 2,937	B 2
	08057	Moorestown, 14,179	B 3
	07950	Morris Plains, 5,540	D 2
	07960	Morristown⊙, 17,662	D 2
	07046	Mountain Lakes, 4,739	E 2
	07092	Mountainside, 7,520	E 2
†	07470	Mountain View, 9,000	B 2
	07856	Mount Arlington, 3,590	D 2
	08059	Mount Ephraim, 5,625	B 3
	07970	Mount Freedom, 1,621	D 2
	08060	Mount Holly⊙, ▵12,713	D 4
†	07885	Mount Hope, 1,510	D 2
	08061	Mount Royal, 850	C 4
	08062	Mullica Hill, 800	C 4
†	08087	Mystic Islands, 900	E 4
	08063	National Park, 3,730	B 3
	07752	Navesink, 2,400	E 3
	07753	Neptune, ▵27,863	E 3
	07753	Neptune City, 5,502	E 3
†	08853	Neshanic, 752	D 3
	07857	Netcong, 2,858	D 2
*	07101	Newark⊙, 382,417	B 2
		Newark, ‡2,056,556	B 2
*	08901	New Brunswick⊙, 41,885	E 3
	08533	New Egypt, 1,769	E 3
	08344	Newfield, 1,487	D 4
	07435	Newfoundland, 900	D 1
	08224	New Gretna, 700	E 4
	07646	New Milford, 20,201	B 1
	08345	Newport, 700	C 5
	07974	New Providence, 13,796	E 2
	07724	New Shrewsbury, 5,925	E 3
	07860	Newton⊙, 7,297	D 1
	08346	Newtonville, 750	D 4
	07976	New Vernon, 1,900	D 2
	08817	Nixon, 12,000	E 2
	08347	Norma, 1,200	C 4
	07032	North Arlington, 18,096	B 2
	07047	North Bergen, ▵47,751	B 2
	08876	North Branch, 610	D 2
	08902	North Brunswick, ▵16,691	E 3
†	07006	North Caldwell, 6,425	B 2
	08204	North Cape May, 3,812	C 6
	08225	Northfield, 8,875	D 5
	07508	North Haledon, 7,614	B 1
	07060	North Plainfield, 21,796	E 2
	07647	Northvale, 5,177	F 1
	08260	North Wildwood, 3,914	D 6
	07648	Norwood, 4,398	C 1
	07110	Nutley, 32,099	B 2
	07755	Oakhurst, 5,558	E 3
	07436	Oakland, 14,420	B 1
	08107	Oaklyn, 4,626	B 3
	07438	Oak Ridge, 750	E 1
	08226	Ocean City, 10,575	D 5
	08740	Ocean Gate, 1,081	E 4
	07756	Ocean Grove, 7,000	F 3
	07757	Oceanport, 7,503	F 3
	08230	Ocean View, 950	D 5
	08231	Oceanville, 600	D 5
	07439	Ogdensburg, 2,222	D 1
	08857	Old Bridge, 25,176	E 3
	07675	Old Tappan, 3,917	C 1
	08858	Oldwick, 600	D 2
	07649	Oradell, 8,903	B 1
*	07050	Orange, 32,566	B 2
	08723	Osbornsville, 3,900	E 3
	07863	Oxford, 1,411	C 2
	07470	Packanack Lake, 4,000	B 1
†	08226	Palermo, 600	D 5
	07650	Palisades Park, 13,351	C 2
	08065	Palmyra, 6,969	B 3
	07652	Paramus, 29,495	B 1
†	08087	Parkertown, 600	E 4
	07656	Park Ridge, 8,709	B 1
	07054	Parsippany, ▵55,112	E 2
*	07055	Passaic, 55,124	E 2
*	07501	Paterson⊙, 144,824	B 2
		Paterson-Clifton-Passaic, ‡1,358,794	B 2
	08066	Paulsboro, 8,084	C 4
	07977	Peapack-Gladstone, 1,924	D 2
	08067	Pedricktown, 1,500	C 4
	08068	Pemberton, 1,344	D 4
	08534	Pennington, 2,151	D 3
	08110	Pennsauken, ▵36,394	B 3
	08069	Penns Grove, 5,727	C 4
	08070	Pennsville, 11,014	C 4
	07440	Pequannock, 4,900	B 1
*	08861	Perth Amboy, 38,798	E 2
	08865	Phillipsburg, 17,849	C 2
	08741	Pine Beach, 1,395	E 4
	07058	Pine Brook, 3,500	E 2
	08021	Pine Hill, 5,132	D 4
	08854	Piscataway, ▵36,418	D 2
	08071	Pitman, 10,257	C 4
*	07060	Plainfield, 46,862	E 2
	08536	Plainsboro, 1,200	D 3
	08232	Pleasantville, 13,778	D 5
	08742	Point Pleasant, 4,882	E 3
	08742	Point Pleasant Beach, 15,968	E 3
	08240	Pomona, 900	D 5
	07442	Pompton Lakes, 11,397	A 1
	07444	Pompton Plains, 9,500	B 1
	07758	Port Monmouth, 4,556	E 3
†	07850	Port Morris, 950	D 2
	07865	Port Murray, 800	D 2
	08349	Port Norris, 1,955	C 5
	07064	Port Reading, 4,900	E 2
	08241	Port Republic, 586	D 4
	08540	Princeton, 12,311	D 3
	08550	Princeton Junction, 950	D 3
†	07885	Prospect Park, 5,176	B 1
	08072	Quinton, 575	C 4
*	07065	Rahway, 29,114	E 2
†	07945	Ralston, 650	D 2
†	08057	Ramblewood, 5,556	D 4
	07446	Ramsey, 12,571	B 1
	08869	Raritan, 6,691	D 2
	07701	Red Bank, 12,847	E 3
	08350	Richland, 950	D 5
	07657	Ridgefield, 11,308	B 2
	07660	Ridgefield Park, 14,453	B 2
*	07450	Ridgewood, 27,547	B 1
	08551	Ringoes, 682	D 3
	07456	Ringwood, 10,393	E 1
	08242	Rio Grande, 1,203	D 5
	07457	Riverdale, 2,729	A 1
	07661	River Edge, 12,850	B 1
	08075	Riverside, ▵8,616	B 3
	08077	Riverton, 3,412	B 3
	08691	Robbinsville, 650	D 3
	07662	Rochelle Park, ▵6,380	B 2
	07866	Rockaway, ▵18,955	D 2
	07866	Rockaway, 6,383	D 2
	08553	Rocky Hill, 917	D 3
	08554	Roebling-Florence, 7,551	D 3
	08555	Roosevelt, 814	E 3
	07068	Roseland, 4,453	A 2
	07203	Roselle, 22,585	B 2
	07204	Roselle Park, 14,277	A 2
	08352	Rosenhayn, 950	C 5
†	07876	Roxbury, ▵15,754	D 2
	07760	Rumson, 7,421	F 3
	08078	Runnemede, 10,475	B 3
*	07070	Rutherford, 20,802	B 2
	07662	Saddle Brook, ▵15,098	B 1
	07458	Saddle River, 2,437	B 1
	08079	Salem⊙, 7,648	C 4
	08872	Sayreville, 32,508	E 3
	07076	Scotch Plains, ▵22,279	E 2
	07760	Sea Bright, 1,339	F 3
	08302	Seabrook, 1,569	C 5
	08750	Sea Girt, 2,207	E 3
	08243	Sea Isle City, 1,712	D 5
	08751	Seaside Heights, 1,248	E 4
	08752	Seaside Park, 1,432	E 4
	07094	Secaucus, 13,228	B 2
	07077	Sewaren, 3,200	E 2
	08080	Sewell, 2,210	C 4
	08353	Shiloh, 573	C 5
	08008	Ship Bottom, 1,079	E 4
	07078	Short Hills, 14,000	E 2
	07701	Shrewsbury, 3,315	E 3
	08081	Sicklerville, 1,700	D 4
†	07424	Singac, 3,942	B 2
	08558	Skillman, 1,955	D 3
†	07728	Smithburg, 750	E 3
	08083	Somerdale, 6,510	B 4
	08244	Somers Point, 7,919	D 5
	08876	Somerville⊙, 13,652	D 2
	08879	South Amboy, 9,338	E 3
†	07719	South Belmar, 1,490	E 3
	08880	South Bound Brook, 4,525	E 2
†	08852	South Brunswick, ▵14,058	E 3
	07079	South Orange, 16,971	A 2
	07080	South Plainfield, 21,142	E 2
	08882	South River, 15,428	E 3
	08246	South Seaville, 600	D 5
	08753	South Toms River, 3,981	E 4
	07871	Sparta, 3,000	D 1
	08884	Spotswood, 7,891	E 3
	07081	Springfield, ▵15,740	E 2
	07762	Spring Lake, 3,896	F 3
	07762	Spring Lake Heights, 4,602	E 3
	07874	Stanhope, 3,040	D 2
	08885	Stanton, 700	D 2
	08886	Stewartsville, 950	C 2
	07980	Stirling, 1,450	E 2
	07460	Stockholm, 1,477	D 1
	08559	Stockton, 619	D 3
	08247	Stone Harbor, 1,089	D 5
	08084	Stratford, 9,801	B 4
†	07747	Strathmore, 7,674	E 3
	07876	Succasunna, 5,000	D 2
	07901	Summit, 23,620	E 2
	08008	Surf City, 1,129	E 4
	07461	Sussex, 2,038	D 1
	08085	Swedesboro, 2,287	C 4
	07878	Tabor, 1,500	E 2
	07666	Teaneck, ▵42,355	B 2
	07670	Tenafly, 14,827	C 1
	07608	Teterboro, 14	B 2
	08086	Thorofare, 4,200	B 4
	08887	Three Bridges, 750	D 2
	08560	Titusville, 900	D 3
	08753	Toms River⊙, 7,303	E 4
	07511	Totowa, 11,580	B 1
	07082	Towaco, 2,500	E 2
*	08601	Trenton (cap.)⊙, 104,638	D 3
		Trenton, ‡303,968	D 3
	08087	Tuckerton, 1,926	E 4
	07083	Union, ▵53,077	A 2
	07735	Union Beach, 6,472	E 3
	07087	Union City, 58,537	C 2
†	07421	Upper Greenwood Lake 1,505	E 1
†	07458	Upper Saddle River, 7,949	B 1
†	07724	Vail Homes, 1,164	E 3
	07088	Vauxhall, 9,245	A 2
	08406	Ventnor City, 10,385	E 5
	07462	Vernon, 800	E 1
	07044	Verona, 15,067	B 2
	08251	Villas, 3,155	D 5
	08088	Vincentown, 900	D 4
	08360	Vineland, 47,399	C 5
		Vineland-Millville-Bridgeton, ‡121,374	C 5
	07463	Waldwick, 12,313	B 1
	07719	Wall, ▵16,498	E 3
	07055	Wallington, 10,284	B 2
†	07712	Wanamassa, 4,600	E 3
	07465	Wanaque, 8,636	B 1
	08758	Waretown, 1,800	E 4
	07882	Washington, 5,943	D 2
	07060	Watchung, 4,750	E 2
	08089	Waterford Works, 950	D 4
	07470	Wayne, ▵49,141	A 1
	07087	Weehawken, ▵13,383	C 2
	08090	Wenonah, 2,364	C 4
	07006	West Caldwell, 11,887	A 2
†	08204	West Cape May, 1,005	D 6
	08092	West Creek, 630	E 4
*	07090	Westfield, 33,720	E 2
	07764	West Long Branch, 6,845	F 3
	07480	West Milford, 950	E 1
	07093	West New York, 40,627	C 2
	07052	West Orange, 43,715	A 2
	07424	West Paterson, 11,692	B 2
	08628	West Trenton, 5,900	D 3
	08093	Westville, 5,170	B 3
	07675	Westwood, 11,105	B 1
	07885	Wharton, 5,535	D 2
	07981	Whippany, 7,500	E 2
	08888	Whitehouse, 800	D 2
	08889	White House Station, 1,019	D 2
	08252	Whitesboro, 700	D 5
†	08701	Whitesville, 600	E 3
	08759	Whiting, 750	E 4
	07765	Wickatunk, 950	E 3
	08260	Wildwood, 4,110	D 6
	08260	Wildwood Crest, 3,483	D 6
	08094	Williamstown, 4,075	D 4
	08046	Willingboro, ▵43,414	D 3
†	07036	Winfield, ▵2,184	B 2
	08270	Woodbine, 2,625	D 5
	07095	Woodbridge, ▵98,944	E 2
	08096	Woodbury⊙, 12,408	B 4
	08097	Woodbury Heights, 3,621	B 4
	07675	Woodcliff Lake, 5,506	B 1
	08107	Wood-Lynne, 3,101	B 3
†	07885	Woodport, 2,100	D 2
	07075	Wood-Ridge, 8,311	B 2
	08098	Woodstown, 3,137	C 4
	08562	Wrightstown, 2,719	D 3
	07481	Wyckoff, ▵16,039	B 1
	08620	Yardville, 9,500	D 3

⊙ County seat.
‡ Population of metropolitan area.
▵ Population of town or township.
† Zip of nearest p.o.
* Multiple zips

Topography

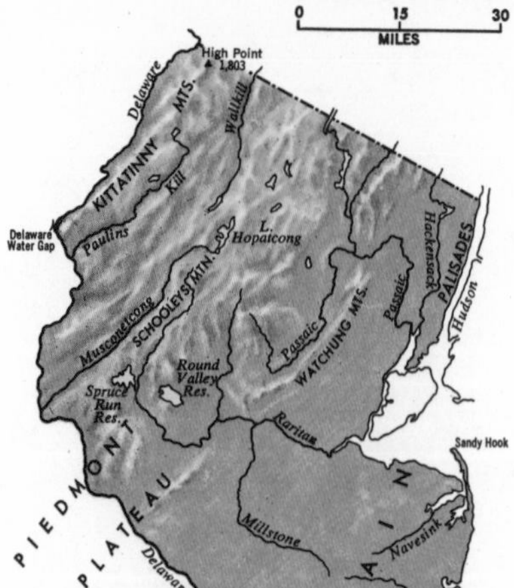

0 15 30
MILES
High Point 1,803
Delaware
Kittatinny Mts.
Wallkill
Kill
Paulins
Delaware Water Gap
L. Hopatcong
Musconetcong
Schooleys Mtn.
Spruce Run Res.
Round Valley Res.
Watchung Mts.
Passaic
Hackensack
Palisades
Hudson
Raritan
Sandy Hook
Piedmont Plateau
Millstone
Navesink
Coastal Plain
Rancocas
Pine Barrens
Toms
Barnegat B.
Long Beach
Mullica
Gt. Egg Harbor
Great Bay
Maurice
Cohansey
Delaware Bay
C. May
Below Sea Level
100 m. 328 ft.
200 m. 656 ft.
500 m. 1,640 ft.
1,000 m. 3,281 ft.
2,000 m. 6,562 ft.
5,000 m. 16,404 ft.

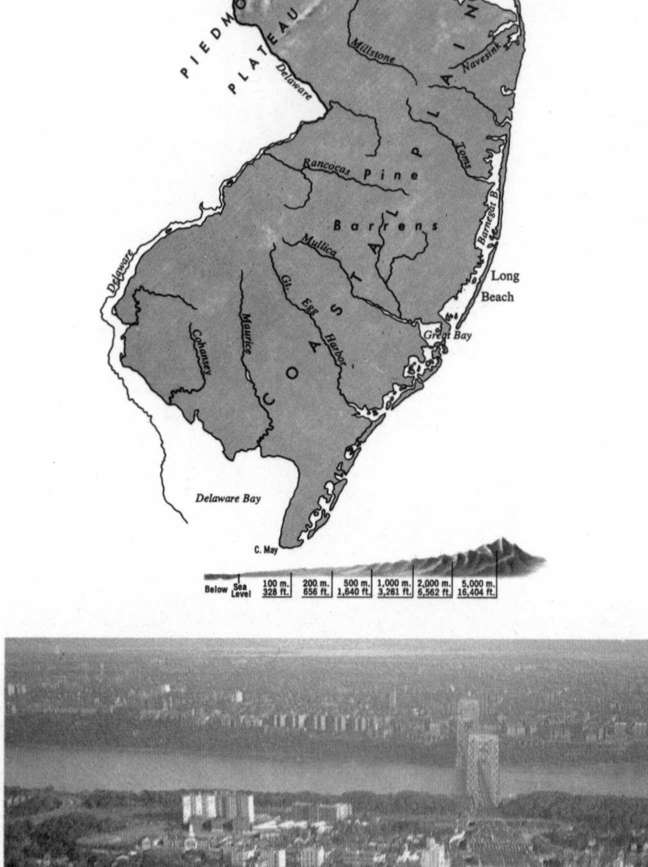
Michael Lewy—Shostal Associates

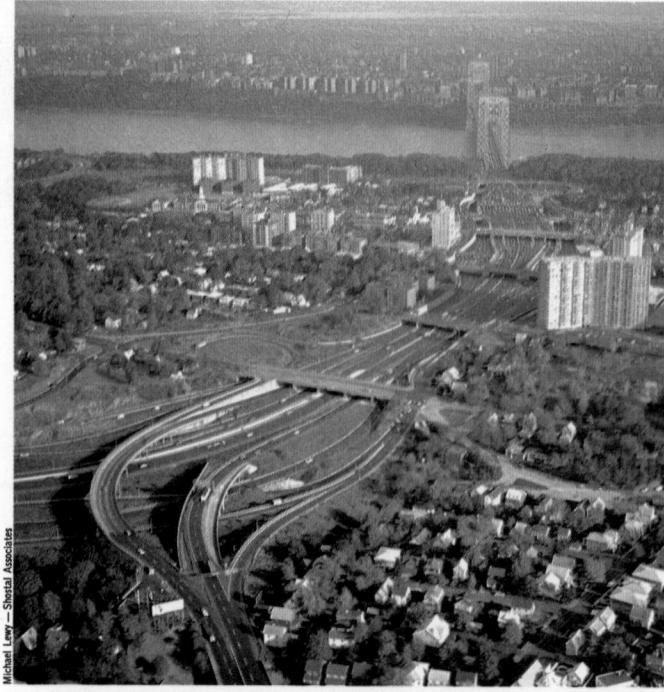

New Jersey towns become suburbs of Manhattan, thanks to connecting links like the Holland and Lincoln Tunnels and the George Washington Bridge. Scene above is the Fort Lee approach to the Bridge.

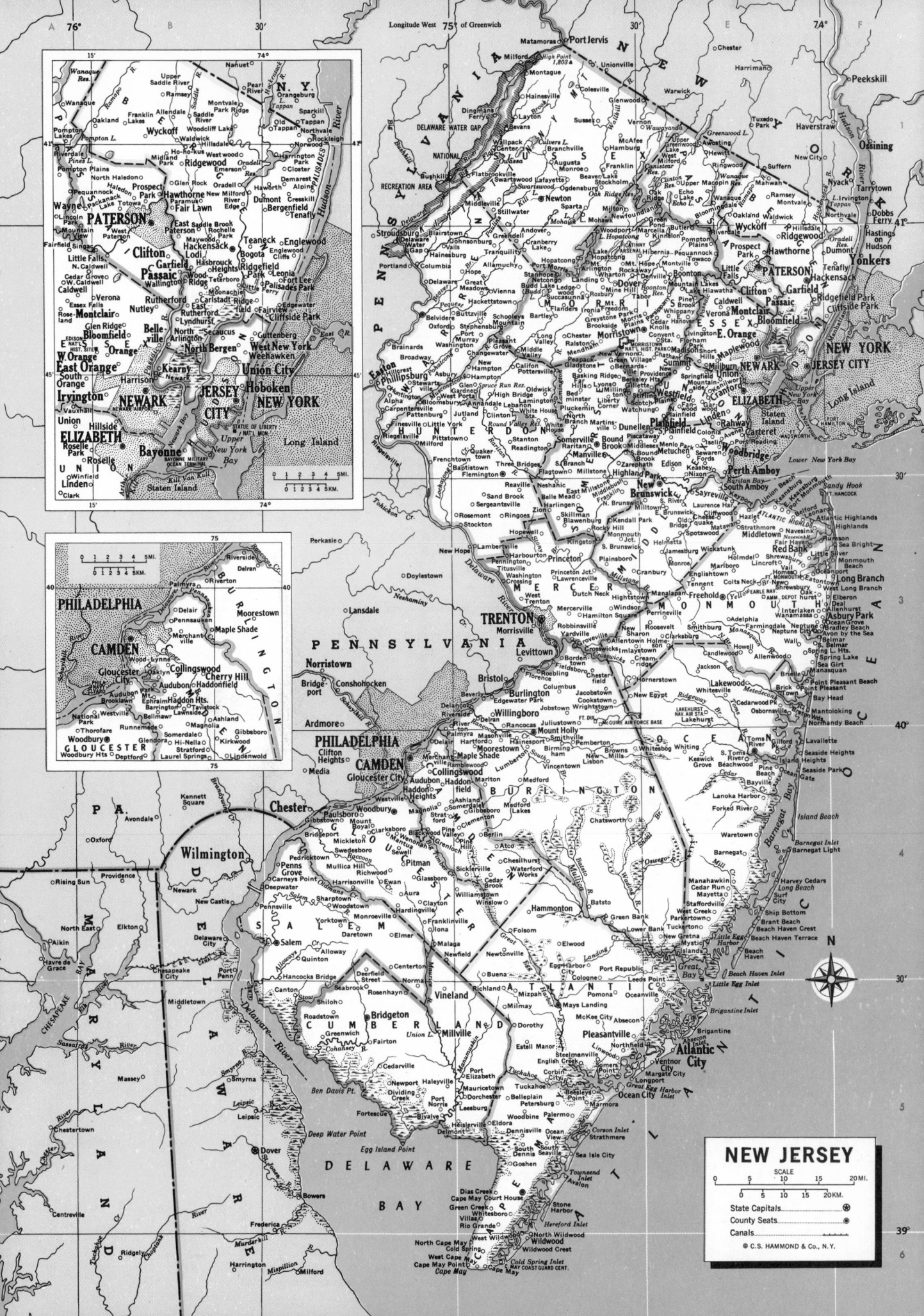

COUNTIES

Bernalillo, 315,774 .... C 4
Catron, 2,198 .... A 4
Chaves, 43,335 .... E 5
Colfax, 12,170 .... E 2
Curry, 39,517 .... F 4
De Baca, 2,547 .... E 4
Dona Ana, 69,773 .... C 6
Eddy, 41,119 .... E 6
Grant, 22,030 .... A 5
Guadalupe, 4,969 .... E 4
Harding, 1,348 .... F 3
Hidalgo, 4,734 .... A 6
Lea, 49,554 .... F 6
Lincoln, 7,560 .... D 5
Los Alamos, 15,198 .... C 3
Luna, 11,706 .... B 6
McKinley, 43,208 .... A 3
Mora, 4,673 .... D 3
Otero, 41,097 .... D 6
Quay, 10,903 .... F 3
Rio Arriba, 25,170 .... B 2
Roosevelt, 16,479 .... F 4
Sandoval, 17,492 .... C 3
San Juan, 52,517 .... A 2
San Miguel, 21,951 .... D 3
Santa Fe, 53,756 .... C 3
Sierra, 7,189 .... B 5
Socorro, 9,763 .... C 5
Taos, 17,516 .... D 2
Torrance, 5,290 .... D 4
Union, 4,925 .... F 2
Valencia, 40,539 .... A 4

CITIES and TOWNS

Zip	Name/Pop.	Key
87510	Abiquiu, 310	C 2
† 87049	Acoma, 150	B 4
† 87049	Acomita, 975	B 3
87114	Alameda, 5,000	C 3
88310	Alamogordo⊛, 23,035	C 6
† 87101	Albuquerque⊛, 243,751	C 3
	Alburquerque, ‡315,774	C 3
87511	Alcalde, 975	C 2
87001	Algodones, 195	C 3
88312	Alto, 104	D 5
87512	Amalia, 200	D 2
88020	Animas, 75	A 7
88021	Anthony, 1,728	C 6
87711	Anton Chico, 600	D 3
87004	Bernalillo⊛, 2,016	C 3
87815	Bingham, 300	C 5
87412	Blanco, 300	B 2
87413	Bloomfield, 1,574	A 2
87005	Bluewater, 300	A 3
87006	Bosque, 300	C 4
87712	Buena Vista, 178	D 3
87515	Canjilon, 300	C 2
87516	Canones, 200	C 2
88316	Capitan, 439	D 5
88414	Capulin, 100	F 2
88220	Carlsbad⊛, 21,297	E 6
88301	Carrizozo⊛, 1,123	D 5
87007	Casa Blanca, 560	B 4
88113	Causey, 150	F 4
87518	Cebolla, 150	C 2
87008	Cedar Crest, 600	C 3
† 87410	Cedar Hill, 145	B 2
88026	Central, 1,864	A 6
87010	Cerrillos, 118	C 3
87519	Cerro, 400	D 2
87713	Chacon, 200	D 3
87520	Chama, 899	C 2
88027	Chamberino, 400	C 6
87521	Chamisal, 637	D 2
† 87059	Chilili, 80	C 4
87522	Chimayo, 900	C 2
87714	Cimarron, 927	E 2
88415	Clayton⊛, 2,931	F 2
87715	Cleveland, 500	D 3
88028	Cliff, 350	A 6
88317	Cloudcroft, 525	D 6
88101	Clovis⊛, 28,495	F 4
† 87041	Cochiti, 300	C 3
88029	Columbus, 241	B 7
88416	Conchas Dam, 192	E 3
87523	Cordova, 400	D 2
88318	Corona, 262	D 4
87048	Corrales, 975	C 3
87524	Costilla, 400	D 2
87012	Coyote, 125	C 2
87313	Crownpoint, 876	A 3
† 86500	Crystal, 200	A 2
87013	Cuba, 300	B 2
87014	Cubero, 300	B 4
88417	Cuervo, 150	E 3
87522	Cundiyo, 98	C 2
87821	Datil, 150	B 4
88030	Deming⊛, 8,343	B 6
87933	Derry, 350	B 5
88418	Des Moines, 204	F 2
88230	Dexter, 746	E 5
† 87711	Dilia, 125	D 3
88527	Dixon, 640	D 2
88032	Dona Ana, 800	C 6
88115	Dora, 196	F 4
87528	Dulce, 450	B 2
88319	Duran, 100	D 4
87718	Eagle Nest, 300	D 2
87015	Edgewood, 75	C 3
87935	Elephant Butte, 75	B 5
88116	Elida, 233	F 5
† 87731	El Porvenir, 90	D 3
87529	El Prado, 200	D 2
87530	El Rito, 475	C 2
87531	Embudo, 400	C 2
88321	Encino, 250	D 4
87532	Espanola, 4,528	C 2
87016	Estancia⊛, 721	C 4
88231	Eunice, 2,641	F 6
88033	Fairacres, 400	C 6
87720	Farley, 81	F 2
87401	Farmington, 21,979	A 2
88034	Faywood, 75	A 6
† 88041	Fierro, 200	A 6

New Mexico state map with scale in miles and kilometers. State Capitals ⊛. County Seats ⊛.
© C.S. HAMMOND & Co., N.Y.

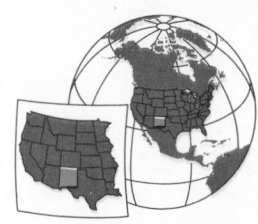

87415 Flora Vista, 500 ....A 2
88118 Floyd, 248 ....F 4
88322 Flying H, 61 ....E 5
88419 Folsom, 75 ....F 2
88036 Fort Bayard, 390 ....A 6
88323 Fort Stanton, 389 ....D 5
88119 Fort Sumner⊙, 1,615 ...E 4
87316 Fort Wingate, 800 ....A 3
87416 Fruitland, 600 ....A 2
† 87540 Galisteo, 125 ....D 3
87017 Gallina, 500 ....C 2
87301 Gallup⊙, 14,596 ....A 3
87317 Gamerco, 800 ....A 3
87936 Garfield, 600 ....B 6
88421 Garita, 154 ....E 3
88038 Gila, 300 ....A 6
88324 Glencoe, 140 ....D 5
88039 Glenwood, 175 ....A 6
87535 Glorieta, 300 ....D 3
88120 Grady, 104 ....F 4
87020 Grants, 8,768 ....B 3
87722 Guadalupita, 305 ....D 2
88232 Hagerman, 953 ....E 5
88041 Hanover, 350 ....A 6
87937 Hatch, 867 ....B 6
87537 Hernandez, 600 ....C 2
88325 High Rolls Mountain Park, 650 ....D 5
88042 Hillsboro, 125 ....B 6
88240 Hobbs, 26,025 ....F 6
88723 Holman, 510 ....D 2
88336 Hondo, 200 ....D 5
88250 Hope, 90 ....E 6
87901 Hot Springs (Truth or Consequences), 4,656 .....B 5
88121 House, 119 ....F 4
88251 Humble City, 65 ....F 6
88043 Hurley, 1,796 ....A 6
87538 Ilfeld, 68 ....D 3
87022 Isleta, 1,080 ....C 4
88252 Jal, 2,602 ....F 6
87023 Jarales, 525 ....C 4
87024 Jemez Pueblo, 1,197 ....C 3
87025 Jemez Springs, 356 ......C 3
87417 Kirtland, 800 ....A 2
† 87712 La Cueva, 200 ....D 3
87026 Laguna, 900 ....B 3
87027 La Jara, 210 ....B 2
87028 Lajoya, 97 ....C 4
88253 Lake Arthur, 306 ....E 5
88337 La Luz, 800 ....C 6
87539 La Madera, 200 ....C 2
88044 La Mesa, 900 ....C 6
87540 Lamy, 66 ....D 3
87418 La Plata, 150 ....A 2
88001 Las Cruces⊙, 37,857 ...C 6
87541 Las Tablas, 65 ....C 2
88701 Las Vegas (city)⊙, 7,528 ..D 3
† 88021 La Union, 200 ....C 7
87725 Ledoux, 400 ....D 3
87823 Lemitar, 400 ....B 4
88338 Lincoln, 100 ....D 5
87543 Llano, 270 ....D 2
88255 Loco Hills, 350 ....F 6
88426 Logan, 386 ....F 3
88045 Lordsburg⊙, 3,429 ......A 6
87544 Los Alamos⊙, 11,310 ...C 3
87031 Los Lunas⊙, 973 ....C 4
† 87101 Los Ranchos de Albuquerque, 1,900 ..C 3
88256 Loving, 1,192 ....E 6
88260 Lovington⊙, 8,915 ......F 6
87547 Lumberton, 190 ....C 2
87824 Luna, 175 ....A 5
87825 Magdalena, 652 ....B 4
88263 Malaga, 250 ....E 6
87318 Manuelito, 200 ....A 3
† 87016 Manzano, 110 ....C 4
87728 Maxwell, 393 ....E 2
88339 Mayhill, 200 ....D 5

38262 McDonald, 170 ....F 5
† 79901 Meadow Vista, 1,402 .....C 7
88124 Melrose, 636 ....F 4
87319 Mentmore, 315 ....A 3
88340 Mescalero, 950 ....D 5
88046 Mesilla, 1,713 ....C 6
88047 Mesilla Park, 1,500 .....C 6
88048 Mesquite, 950 ....C 6
87320 Mexican Springs, 150 ...A 3
87729 Miami, 200 ....E 2
87020 Milan, 2,185 ....B 3
88049 Mimbres, 155 ....B 6
87731 Montezuma, 110 ....D 3
87939 Monticello, 125 ....B 5
88265 Monument, 250 ....F 6
87732 Mora⊙, 1,400 ....D 2
87035 Moriarty, 758 ....D 4
87733 Mosquero⊙, 244 ....F 3
87036 Mountainair, 1,022 .....C 4
† 87501 Nambe, 100 ....D 3
88430 Nara Visa, 400 ....F 3
87328 Navajo, 920 ....A 3
† 87325 Newcomb, 300 ....A 2
88431 Newkirk, 75 ....E 3
87038 New Laguna, 450 ....B 4
88341 Nogal, 80 ....D 5
87734 Ocate, 288 ....E 2
88266 Oil Center, 300 ....F 6
87549 Ojo Caliente, 500 ....D 2
87735 Ojo Feliz, 146 ....E 2
87550 Ojo Sarco, 184 ....D 2
88052 Organ, 500 ....C 6
88342 Orogrande, 80 ....D 6
† 88220 Otis, 200 ....E 6
87040 Paguate, 775 ....B 3
87551 Park View, 788 ....C 2
87552 Pecos, 598 ....D 3
87041 Penablanca, 320 ....C 3
88553 Penasco, 1,169 ....D 2
87042 Peralta, 400 ....C 4
87576 Petaca, 84 ....C 2
88343 Picacho, 120 ....D 5
87827 Pie Town, 99 ....A 4
88053 Pinos Altos, 200 ....A 6
87043 Placitas, 88 ....C 3
87044 Ponderosa, 400 ....C 3
88130 Portales⊙, 10,554 ......F 4
87045 Prewitt, 300 ....B 3
88432 Puerto de Luna, 180 ....E 4
88433 Quay, 75 ....F 4
87829 Quemado, 520 ....A 4
87556 Questa, 1,095 ....D 2
88054 Radium Springs, 150 ....B 6
87736 Rainsville, 300 ....D 2
87321 Ramah, 574 ....A 3
87557 Ranches of Taos, 2,900 ...D 2
87740 Raton⊙, 6,962 ....E 2
87558 Red River, 125 ....D 2
87046 Regina, 65 ....B 2
87322 Rehoboth, 300 ....A 3
87830 Reserve⊙, 800 ....A 5
87560 Ribera, 400 ....D 3
87940 Rincon, 300 ....C 6
87742 Rociada, 164 ....D 2
88056 Rodarte, 650 ....D 2
87743 Rodeo, 100 ....A 7
87562 Rowe, 150 ....D 3
87743 Roy, 476 ....E 3
88345 Ruidoso, 2,216 ....D 5
88346 Ruidoso Downs, 702 ....D 5
87563 Rutheron, 90 ....C 2
87941 Salem, 400 ....B 6
87831 San Acacia, 150 ....B 4
87232 San Antonio, 359 ....B 5
87564 San Cristobal, 275 ......D 2
87047 Sandia Park, 200 ....C 3
† 87001 San Felipe, 1,187 .....C 3
† 87049 San Fidel, 150 ....B 3
† 87501 San Ildefonso, 140 .....C 3

88434 San Jon, 308 ....F 3
87565 San Jose, 115 ....D 3
87566 San Juan Pueblo, 900 ...C 2
88057 San Lorenzo, 264 ....B 6
87050 San Mateo, 200 ....B 3
88058 San Miguel, 400 ....C 6
88348 San Patricio, 250 ....D 5
87051 San Rafael, 300 ....A 3
87567 Santa Cruz, 754 ....D 2
87501 Santa Fe (cap.)⊙, 41,167 ...C 3
88059 Santa Rita, 600 ....A 6
88435 Santa Rosa⊙, 2,485 ....E 4
87052 Santo Domingo Pueblo, 1,662 ....C 3
87053 San Ysidro, 280 ....C 3
87745 Sapello, 144 ....D 3
87055 Seboyeta, 125 ....B 3
87568 Sena, 150 ....D 3
87569 Serafina, 280 ....D 3
87420 Shiprock, 800 ....A 2
88061 Silver City⊙, 7,751 .....A 6
87801 Socorro⊙, 4,687 ....C 4
† 87565 Soham, 104 ....D 3
87746 Solano, 70 ....E 3
87747 Springer, 1,574 ....E 2
87056 Stanley, 60 ....D 3
87057 Tajique, 150 ....C 4
87571 Taos⊙, 2,475 ....D 2
† 87571 Taos Pueblo, 1,030 ...D 2
88267 Tatum, 982 ....F 5
87574 Tesuque, 800 ....C 3
88135 Texico, 772 ....F 4
87323 Thoreau, 550 ....A 3
87575 Tierra Amarilla⊙, 850 ...C 2
87059 Tijeras, 500 ....C 3
88351 Tinnie, 95 ....D 5
87324 Toadlena, 200 ....A 2
87325 Tohatchi, 500 ....A 3
87060 Torreon, 100 ....C 4
87061 Torreon, 100 ....C 4
87576 Trampas, 76 ....D 2
88439 Trementina, 80 ....E 3
87577 Tres Piedras, 200 ....D 2
87578 Truchas, 275 ....D 2
87748 Trujillo, 148 ....E 3
87901 Truth or Consequences⊙, 4,656 ....B 5
88401 Tucumcari⊙, 7,189 .....F 3
88352 Tularosa, 2,851 ....C 5
88065 Tyrone, 100 ....A 6
88001 University Park, 4,165 ...C 6
87749 Ute Park, 75 ....D 2
87579 Vadito, 335 ....D 2
88072 Vado, 350 ....C 6
87580 Vadner, 190 ....D 2
† 87031 Valencia, 500 ....C 4
87581 Vallecitos, 450 ....C 2
88073 Vanadium, 300 ....A 6
88353 Vaughn, 867 ....D 4
87582 Velarde, 365 ....C 2
† 81091 Vermejo Park, 85 ......D 2
87583 Villanueva, 300 ....D 3
† 88055 Virden, 151 ....A 6
87752 Wagon Mound, 630 .....E 2
87421 Waterflow, 475 ....A 2
87753 Watrous, 250 ....D 3
87544 White Rock, 3,861 ......C 3
88002 White Sands Missile Range, 4,167 ....C 6
88268 Whites City, 300 ....E 6
87063 Willard, 209 ....D 4
87942 Williamsburg, 367 ......B 5
88136 Yeso, 200 ....E 4
87064 Youngsville, 130 ....C 2
† 87053 Zia Pueblo, 600 ....C 3
87327 Zuni, 3,958 ....A 3

⊙ County seat.
† Population of metropolitan area.
‡ Zip of nearest p.o.
* Multiple zips

AREA 121,666 sq. mi.
POPULATION 1,016,000
CAPITAL Santa Fe
LARGEST CITY Albuquerque
HIGHEST POINT Wheeler Pk. 13,161 ft.
SETTLED IN 1605
ADMITTED TO UNION January 6, 1912
POPULAR NAME Land of Enchantment
STATE FLOWER Yucca
STATE BIRD Road Runner

Stephen Voynick – Shostal Associates

Golden adobe against the blue Sangre de Cristo Mountains. Clear, pure colors, magnificent surroundings and congenial atmosphere combine to draw artists and writers to Taos, New Mexico.

Topography

0   50   100
MILES

Below Sea Level | 100 m. 328 ft. | 200 m. 656 ft. | 500 m. 1,640 ft. | 1,000 m. 3,281 ft. | 2,000 m. 6,562 ft. | 5,000 m. 16,404 ft.

Agriculture, Industry and Resources

DOMINANT LAND USE

- Wheat, Grain Sorghums, Range Livestock
- General Farming, Livestock, Special Crops
- General Farming, Livestock, Cash Grain
- Dry Beans, General Farming
- Cotton, Forest Products
- Range Livestock
- Forests
- Nonagricultural Land

MAJOR MINERAL OCCURRENCES

Ag Silver
Au Gold
C Coal
Cu Copper
G Natural Gas
Gp Gypsum
K Potash
Mo Molybdenum
Mr Marble
Na Salt
O Petroleum
Pb Lead
U Uranium
V Vanadium
Zn Zinc
⚡ Water Power

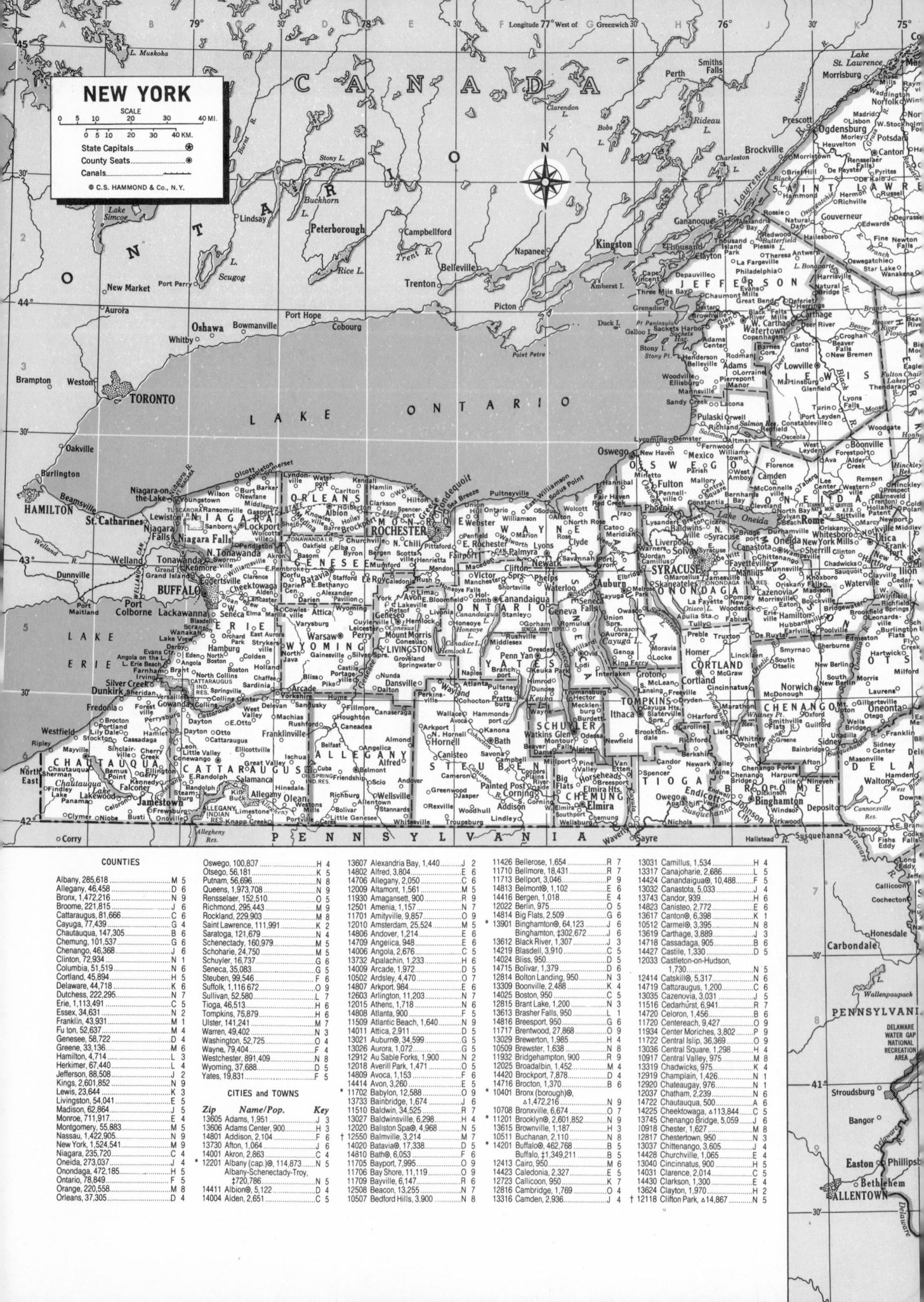

NEW YORK

SCALE
0 5 10 20 30 40 MI.
0 5 10 20 30 40 KM.

State Capitals .... ⊛
County Seats .... ◉
Canals ....

© C.S. HAMMOND & Co., N.Y.

COUNTIES

County	Pop.	Key
Albany	285,618	M 5
Allegany	46,458	D 6
Bronx	1,472,216	N 9
Broome	221,815	J 6
Cattaraugus	81,666	C 6
Cayuga	77,439	G 4
Chautauqua	147,305	A 6
Chemung	101,537	G 6
Chenango	46,368	J 5
Clinton	72,934	N 1
Columbia	51,519	N 5
Cortland	45,894	H 5
Delaware	44,718	K 6
Dutchess	222,295	N 7
Erie	1,113,491	C 5
Essex	34,631	M 2
Franklin	43,931	M 1
Fu ton	52,637	M 4
Genesee	58,722	D 4
Greene	33,136	M 6
Hamilton	4,714	L 3
Herkimer	67,440	L 3
Jefferson	88,508	J 2
Kings	2,601,852	N 9
Lewis	23,644	K 3
Livingston	54,041	E 5
Madison	62,864	J 4
Monroe	711,917	E 4
Montgomery	55,883	L 4
Nassau	1,422,905	N 9
New York	1,524,541	N 9
Niagara	235,720	C 4
Oneida	273,037	J 4
Onondaga	472,185	H 5
Ontario	78,849	F 5
Orange	220,558	M 8
Orleans	37,305	D 4
Oswego	100,807	H 4
Otsego	56,181	K 5
Putnam	56,696	N 8
Queens	1,973,708	N 9
Rensselaer	152,510	O 5
Richmond	295,443	M 9
Rockland	229,903	M 8
Saint Lawrence	111,991	K 2
Saratoga	121,679	N 4
Schenectady	160,979	M 5
Schoharie	24,750	M 5
Schuyler	16,737	G 6
Seneca	35,083	G 5
Steuben	99,546	F 6
Suffolk	1,116 672	O 9
Sullivan	52,580	L 7
Tioga	46,513	H 6
Tompkins	75,879	H 6
Ulster	141,241	M 7
Warren	49,402	N 3
Washington	52,725	O 4
Wayne	79,404	F 4
Westchester	891,409	N 8
Wyoming	37,688	D 5
Yates	19,831	F 5

CITIES and TOWNS

Zip	Name/Pop.	Key
13605	Adams, 1,951	J 3
13606	Adams Center, 900	H 3
14801	Addison, 2,104	F 6 †
13730	Afton, 1,064	J 6
14001	Akron, 2,863	C 4
*12201	Albany (cap.)◉, 114,873	N 5
	Albany-Schenectady-Troy, †720,786	N 5
14411	Albion◉, 5,122	D 4
14004	Alden, 2,651	C 5
13607	Alexandria Bay, 1,440	J 2
14802	Alfred, 3,804	E 6
14706	Allegany, 2,050	C 6
12009	Altamont, 1,561	M 5
11930	Amagansett, 900	R 9
12501	Amenia, 1,157	N 7
11701	Amityville, 9,857	O 9
12010	Amsterdam, 25,524	M 5
14806	Andover, 1,214	E 6
14709	Angelica, 948	E 6
14006	Angola, 2,676	C 5
13732	Apalachin, 1,233	H 6
14009	Arcade, 1,972	D 5
10502	Ardsley, 4,470	O 7
14807	Arkport, 984	E 6
12603	Arlington, 11,203	N 7
12015	Athens, 1,718	N 6
14808	Atlanta, 900	F 5
11509	Atlantic Beach, 1,640	N 9
14011	Attica, 2,911	D 5
13021	Auburn◉, 34,599	G 5
13026	Aurora, 1,072	G 5
12912	Au Sable Forks, 1,900	N 2
12018	Averill Park, 1,471	O 5
14809	Avoca, 1,153	F 6
14710	Avon, 3,260	E 5
11426	Bellerose, 1,654	R 7
11710	Bellmore, 18,431	R 7
11713	Bellport, 3,046	P 9
14813	Belmont◉, 1,102	E 6
14416	Bergen, 1,018	E 4
12022	Berlin, 975	O 5
14814	Big Flats, 2,509	G 6
*13901	Binghamton◉, 64,123	J 6
	Binghamton, †302,672	J 6
13612	Black River, 1,307	J 3
14219	Blasdell, 3,910	C 5
14024	Bliss, 950	D 5
14715	Bolivar, 1,379	D 6
12814	Bolton Landing, 950	N 3
13309	Boonville, 2,488	K 4
14025	Boston, 950	C 5
12815	Brant Lake, 1,200	N 3
13613	Brasher Falls, 950	L 1
14816	Breesport, 950	G 6
11717	Brentwood, 27,868	O 9
13029	Brewerton, 1,985	H 4
10509	Brewster, 1,638	N 8
11932	Bridgehampton, 900	R 9
12025	Broadalbin, 1,452	M 4
14420	Brockport, 7,878	E 4
14716	Brocton, 1,370	B 6
10401	Bronx (borough)◉, ∆1,472,216	N 9
10708	Bronxville, 6,674	O 7
*11201	Brooklyn◉, 2,601,852	N 9
13615	Brownville, 1,187	H 3
10511	Buchanan, 2,110	N 8
*14201	Buffalo◉, 462,768	B 5
	Buffalo, †1,349,211	B 5
12413	Cairo, 950	M 6
14423	Caledonia, 2,327	E 5
12723	Callicoon, 950	K 7
12816	Cambridge, 1,769	O 4
13316	Camden, 2,936	J 4
13031	Camillus, 1,534	H 4
13317	Canajoharie, 2,686	L 5
14424	Canandaigua◉, 10,488	F 5
13032	Canastota, 5,033	J 4
13743	Candor, 939	H 6
14823	Canisteo, 2,772	E 6
13617	Canton◉, 6,398	K 1
10512	Carmel◉, 3,395	N 8
13619	Carthage, 3,889	J 3
14718	Cassadaga, 905	B 6
14427	Castile, 1,330	D 5
12033	Castleton-on-Hudson, 1,730	N 5
12414	Catskill◉, 5,317	N 6
14719	Cattaraugus, 1,200	C 6
13035	Cazenovia, 3,031	J 5
11516	Cedarhurst, 6,941	N 9
14720	Celoron, 1,456	B 6
11720	Centereach, 9,427	O 9
11934	Center Moriches, 3,802	P 9
11722	Central Islip, 36,369	O 9
13036	Central Square, 1,298	H 4
10917	Central Valley, 975	M 8
13319	Chadwicks, 975	K 4
12919	Champlain, 1,426	N 1
12920	Chateaugay, 976	N 1
12037	Chatham, 2,239	N 5
14722	Chautauqua, 950	A 6
14225	Cheektowaga, ∆113,844	C 5
13745	Chenango Bridge, 5,059	J 6
10918	Chester, 1,627	M 8
12817	Chestertown, 950	N 3
13037	Chittenango, 3,605	J 4
14428	Churchville, 1,065	E 4
13040	Cincinnatus, 900	J 5
14031	Clarence, 2,014	C 5
14430	Clarkson, 1,300	E 4
13624	Clayton, 1,970	H 2
†12118	Clifton Park, ∆14,867	N 5

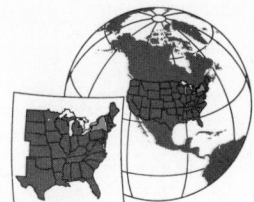

AREA 49,576 sq. mi.
POPULATION 18,190,740
CAPITAL Albany
LARGEST CITY New York
HIGHEST POINT Mt. Marcy 5,344 ft.
SETTLED IN 1614
ADMITTED TO UNION July 26, 1788
POPULAR NAME Empire State
STATE FLOWER Rose
STATE BIRD Bluebird

Topography

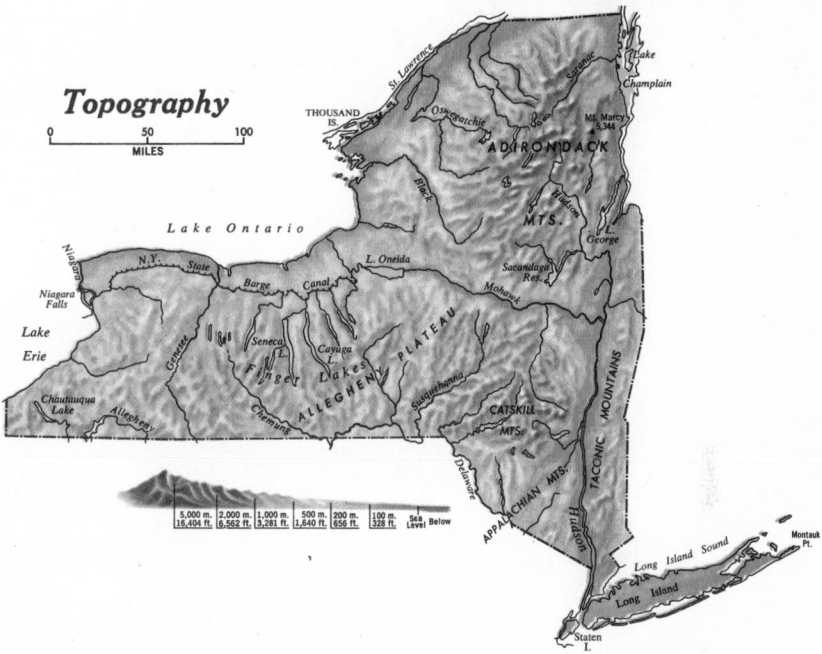

0   50   100
MILES

5,000 m.   2,000 m.   1,000 m.   500 m.   200 m.   100 m.   Sea
16,404 ft. 6,562 ft. 3,281 ft. 1,640 ft. 656 ft. 328 ft. Level Below

14432 Clifton Springs, 2,058........F 4	† 12601 Fairview, 8,517................N 7	
14323 Clinton, 2,271..................K 4	14733 Falconer, 2,983................B 6	
14433 Clyde, 2,828....................G 4	11735 Farmingdale, 9,297...........N 9	
12043 Cobleskill, 4,368..............L 5	13066 Fayetteville, 4,996............J 4	
12045 Coeymans, 975.................N 6	12524 Fishkill, 913....................N 8	
12047 Cohoes, 18,613................N 5	11001 Floral Park, 18,422...........R 7	
14033 Colden, 950....................C 5	10921 Florida, 1,674.................M 8	
10516 Cold Spring, 2,083............N 8	13337 Fly Creek, 910.................K 5	
† 12201 Colonie, 8,701................N 5	12068 Fonda⊙, 1,120................M 5	
13326 Cooperstown⊙, 2,403........L 5	14062 Forestville, 908...............B 6	
12822 Corinth, 3,267................N 4	12937 Fort Covington, 983..........H 1	
14830 Corning, 15,792..............F 6	12828 Fort Edward, 3,733...........O 4	
12518 Cornwall, 2,032..............M 8	13339 Fort Plain, 2,809.............L 5	
13045 Cortland⊙, 19,621...........H 5	13340 Frankfort, 3,305..............K 4	
12051 Coxsackie, 2,399.............N 6	14737 Franklinville, 1,948...........C 6	
10519 Croton Falls, 950.............N 8	14063 Fredonia, 10,326.............B 6	
10520 Croton-on-Hudson, 7,523....N 8	11520 Freeport, 40,374.............R 7	
14727 Cuba, 1,735..................D 6	14738 Frewsburg, 1,772.............B 7	
12929 Dannemora, 3,735............N 1	14739 Friendship, 1,285............D 6	
14437 Dansville, 5,436..............E 5	13069 Fulton, 14,003................H 4	
11729 Deer Park, 31,120...........O 9	11530 Garden City, 25,373.........R 7	
14042 Delevan, 994..................D 6	10524 Garrison, 975................N 8	
13753 Delhi⊙, 3,017...............L 6	14067 Gasport, 950................C 4	
12054 Delmar, 7,500................N 5	14454 Geneseo⊙, 5,714............E 5	
13043 Depew, 22,158................C 5	14456 Geneva, 16,793.............G 5	
13754 Deposit, 2,061................K 6	14740 Gerry, 950..................B 6	
14047 Derby, 4,900..................B 5	12432 Glasco, 1,169...............M 6	
13214 DeWitt, 10,032...............H 4	11542 Glen Cove, 25,770...........R 7	
13634 Dexter, 1,061.................H 2	11545 Glen Head, 4,000............R 7	
10522 Dobbs Ferry, 10,353..........O 6	12801 Glens Falls, 17,222..........N 4	
13329 Dolgeville, 2,872.............L 4	12078 Gloversville, 19,677.........M 4	
12522 Dover Plains, 975.............O 7	10526 Golden's Bridge, 1,101.......N 8	
13053 Dryden, 1,490................H 6	10924 Goshen⊙, 4,342............M 8	
14837 Dundee, 1,539................F 5	13642 Gouverneur, 4,574...........K 2	
14048 Dunkirk, 16,855..............B 5	14070 Gowanda, 3,110.............C 6	
13054 Durhamville, 975.............J 4	12434 Grand Gorge, 950...........L 6	
13332 Earlville, 1,050...............J 5	14072 Grand Island, 900...........B 5	
14052 East Aurora, 7,033............C 5	12832 Granville, 2,784.............O 4	
12061 East Greenbush, 985..........N 5	* 11020 Great Neck, 10,724.........N 8	
11937 East Hampton, 1,753.........R 9	14616 Greece, ▲75,136............E 4	
11554 East Meadow, 46,252.........P 7	13778 Greene, 1,874..............J 6	
11940 East Moriches, 1,702.........P 9	12183 Green Island, 3,297..........N 5	
11731 East Northport, 12,392.......O 9	11944 Greenport, 2,481...........P 8	
11941 Eastport, 1,308...............P 9	12834 Greenwich, 2,092...........O 4	
14445 East Rochester, 8,347.........F 4	10925 Greenwood Lake, 2,262......M 8	
11518 East Rockaway, 10,323.......R 7	13073 Groton, 2,112...............H 5	
13057 East Syracuse, 4,333.........H 4	13780 Guilford, 995..............J 6	
14057 Eden, 2,962..................C 5	12086 Hagaman, 1,410............M 5	
† 14226 Eggertsville, 55,000.........C 5	14075 Hamburg, 10,215...........C 5	
13060 Elbridge, 1,040..............G 5	13346 Hamilton, 3,636...........J 5	
12932 Elizabethtown⊙, 607........N 2	14840 Hammondsport, 1,066......F 6	
12428 Ellenville, 4,482.............M 7	11946 Hampton Bays, 1,862.......P 9	
14731 Ellicottville, 955.............C 6	13783 Hancock, 1,688............K 6	
14059 Elma, 2,784..................C 5	10926 Harriman, 955.............M 8	
* 14901 Elmira⊙, 39,945............G 6	10528 Harrison, 9,250............O 7	
14903 Elmira Heights, 4,906........G 6	10706 Hastings on Hudson, 9,479...O 6	
11003 Elmont, 29,363..............R 7	10927 Haverstraw, 8,198..........M 8	
10523 Elmsford, 3,911.............P 6	10532 Hawthorne, 5,000...........O 6	
13760 Endicott, 16,556.............H 6	* 11550 Hempstead, 39,411........R 7	
13760 Endwell, 15,999.............H 6	13650 Henderson, 900............H 3	
14450 Fairport, 6,474..............F 4	13350 Herkimer⊙, 8,960..........L 4	

(continued on following page)

(continued)

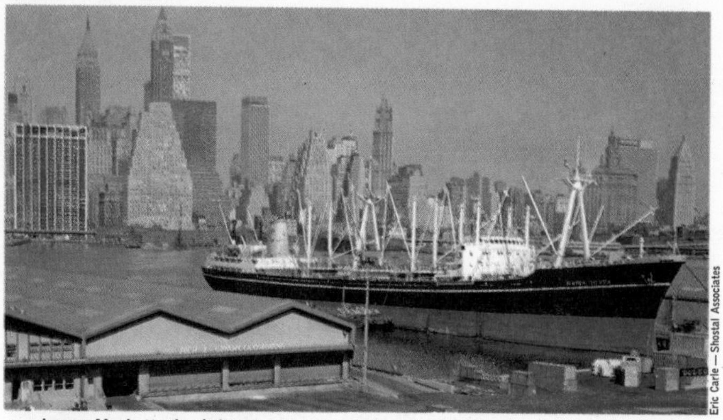

Eric Carle — Shostal Associates

Lower Manhattan's skyline in an unusual view from a pier at the Brooklyn Port Authority Marine Terminal.

11557 Hewlett, 6,796 R 7
* 11801 Hicksville, 48,075 R 7
12440 High Falls, 950 M 7
12528 Highland, 2,184 M 7
10928 Highland Falls, 4,638 M 8
10931 Hillburn, 1,058 M 8
14468 Hilton, 2,440 E 4
14080 Holland, 950 C 5
14470 Holley, 1,868 D 4
13077 Homer, 4,143 H 5
14472 Honeoye Falls, 2,248 F 5
12090 Hoosick Falls, 3,897 O 5
12533 Hopewell Junction, 2,055 N 7
14843 Hornell, 12,144 E 6
14845 Horseheads, 7,989 G 6
14744 Houghton, 1,620 D 6
12534 Hudson⊙, 8,940 N 6
12839 Hudson Falls⊙, 7,917 O 4
11743 Huntington, 12,130 O 9
11746 Huntington Station, 28,817 O 9
12443 Hurley, 4,081 M 7
12538 Hyde Park, 2,805 N 6
13357 Ilion, 9,808 K 5
12842 Indian Lake, 950 M 3
11696 Inwood, 8,433 R 7
14617 Irondequoit, ▵63,675 E 4
10533 Irvington, 5,878 O 6
11558 Island Park, 5,396 R 8
11751 Islip, ▵7,692 O 9
14850 Ithaca⊙, 26,226 G 6
* 11401 Jamaica⊙, 765,078 N 9
14701 Jamestown, 39,795 B 6
13078 Jamesville, 900 H 5
11753 Jericho, 14,010 S 7
13790 Johnson City, 18,025 J 6
12095 Johnstown⊙, 10,045 M 4
13080 Jordan, 1,493 H 4
10536 Katonah, 4,189 N 8
12944 Keeseville, 2,122 O 2
14271 Kenmore, 20,980 C 5
14747 Kennedy, 950 B 6
12446 Kerhonkson, 1,243 M 7
14478 Keuka Park, 990 F 5
12106 Kinderhook, 1,233 N 6
* 11201 Kings (Brooklyn) (borough), ▵2,601,852 N 9
11754 Kings Park, 5,555 O 9
11024 Kings Point, 5,525 R 7
12401 Kingston⊙, 25,544 M 7
14218 Lackawanna, 28,657 B 5
10512 Lake Carmel, 4,796 N 8
12845 Lake George⊙, 1,046 N 4
12449 Lake Katrine, 1,092 M 7
12846 Lake Luzerne, 900 N 4
12946 Lake Placid, 2,731 N 2
12108 Lake Pleasant⊙, 364 M 4
11040 Lake Success, 3,254 R 7
14085 Lake View, 6,000 B 5
14750 Lakewood, 3,864 B 6
14086 Lancaster, 13,365 C 5
10538 Larchmont, 7,203 P 7
11559 Lawrence, 6,566 R 7
14482 Le Roy, 5,118 E 5
11756 Levittown, 65,440 S 7
14092 Lewiston, 3,292 B 4
12754 Liberty, 4,293 L 7
14485 Lima, 1,686 E 5
11757 Lindenhurst, 28,338 O 9
13365 Little Falls, 7,629 L 4
14755 Little Valley⊙, 1,340 C 6
13088 Liverpool, 3,307 H 4
12758 Livingston Manor, 1,522 L 7
14487 Livonia, 1,278 E 5
14094 Lockport⊙, 25,399 C 4
11561 Long Beach, 33,127 R 8
13367 Lowville, 3,671 J 3
11563 Lynbrook, 23,776 R 7
12952 Lyon Mountain, 1,200 N 1
14489 Lyons⊙, 4,496 F 4
14502 Macedon, 1,168 F 4
13660 Madrid, 950 K 1
10541 Mahopac, 5,265 N 8
13103 Mallory, 900 H 4
12953 Malone⊙, 8,048 M 1
11565 Malverne, 10,036 R 7
10543 Mamaroneck, 18,909 P 7
14504 Manchester, 1,305 F 5
11030 Manhasset, 8,541 R 7
* 10001 Manhattan (borough), ▵1,524,541 M 9
13104 Manlius, 4,295 J 5
13803 Marathon, 1,053 J 6
13108 Marcellus, 1,456 H 5
13403 Marcy, 2,417 K 4
14505 Marion, 925 F 4
12542 Marlboro, 1,580 M 7
11758 Massapequa, 26,951 O 9
11762 Massapequa Park, 22,112 O 9
13662 Massena, 14,042 L 1
11950 Mastic Beach, 4,870 P 9
11952 Mattituck, 1,995 P 9
12543 Maybrook, 1,536 M 8
12117 Mayfield, 981 M 4
14757 Mayville⊙, 1,567 A 6
13101 McGraw, 1,319 H 5
12118 Mechanicville, 6,247 N 5
14103 Medina, 6,415 D 4
† 13021 Melrose Park, 2,189 G 5
† 12201 Menands, 3,449 N 5
11566 Merrick, 25,904 S 7
13114 Mexico, 1,555 H 4
12122 Middleburg, 1,410 M 5
12550 Middle Hope, 2,327 M 7
14105 Middleport, 2,132 C 4
10940 Middletown, 22,607 L 8
12545 Millbrook, 1,735 N 7
12546 Millerton, 1,042 O 7
11765 Mill Neck, 982 R 6
12547 Milton, 1,900 M 7
12547 Milton, 1,861 N 4
11501 Mineola⊙, 21,845 R 7
13115 Minetto, 950 H 4
12956 Mineville-Witherbee, 1,967 O 2
13407 Mohawk, 3,301 L 4
10950 Monroe, 4,439 M 8
12549 Montgomery, 1,533 M 7
12701 Monticello⊙, 5,991 L 7
14865 Montour Falls, 1,534 G 6
13118 Moravia, 1,642 H 5
12960 Moriah, 953 N 2
12962 Morrisonville, 1,276 N 1
13408 Morrisville, 2,296 J 5
12763 Mountain Dale, 950 L 7
10549 Mount Kisco, 8,172 N 8
14510 Mount Morris, 3,417 E 5
* 10550 Mount Vernon, 72,778 O 7
12458 Napanoch, 975 M 7
14512 Naples, 1,324 F 5
12123 Nassau, 1,466 N 5
14513 Newark, 11,644 G 4
13811 Newark Valley, 1,286 H 6
13411 New Berlin, 1,369 K 5
12550 Newburgh, 26,219 M 7
10956 New City⊙, 27,344 N 8
14108 Newfane, 2,588 C 4
13413 New Hartford, 2,433 K 4
11040 New Hyde Park, 10,116 R 7
12561 New Paltz, 6,058 M 7
13416 Newport, 908 K 4
* 10801 New Rochelle, 75,385 P 7
12550 New Windsor, 8,803 N 8
* 10001 New York (5 boroughs)⊙, 7,867,760 M 9
New York, ‡11,517,483 M 9
13417 New York Mills, 3,805 K 4
* 14301 Niagara Falls, 85,615 C 4
12309 Niskayuna, 6,186 N 5
13667 Norfolk, 1,379 K 1
14110 North Boston, 1,635 C 5
14514 North Chili, 3,163 E 4
14111 North Collins, 1,675 C 5
15853 North Creek, 950 M 3
14113 North Java, 950 D 5
11768 Northport, 7,440 O 9
13212 North Syracuse, 8,687 H 4
10591 North Tarrytown, 8,334 O 6
14120 North Tonawanda, 36,012 C 4
12134 Northville, 1,192 M 4
13815 Norwich⊙, 8,843 J 5
13668 Norwood, 2,098 L 1
14517 Nunda, 1,254 E 5
10960 Nyack, 6,659 N 8
14125 Oakfield, 1,964 D 4
11572 Oceanside, 35,028 R 7
13669 Ogdensburg, 14,554 K 1
14126 Olcott, 1,592 C 4
13420 Old Forge, 950 L 3
14760 Olean, 19,169 D 6
13421 Oneida, 11,658 J 4
13820 Oneonta, 16,030 K 6
14127 Orchard Park, 3,732 C 5
13424 Oriskany, 1,627 K 4
13425 Oriskany Falls, 927 J 5
10562 Ossining, 21,659 N 8
13126 Oswego⊙, 23,844 G 4
13825 Otego, 956 K 6
10963 Otisville, 933 L 8
14521 Ovid⊙, 779 G 5
13827 Owego⊙, 5,152 H 6
13830 Oxford, 1,944 J 6
11771 Oyster Bay, 14,330 S 6
14870 Painted Post, 2,496 F 6
14522 Palmyra, 3,776 F 4
12768 Parksville, 950 L 7
11772 Patchogue, 11,582 P 9
12563 Patterson, 975 N 7
12137 Pattersonville, 950 M 5
12564 Pawling, 1,914 N 7
10965 Pearl River, 17,146 M 8
10566 Peekskill, 18,881 N 8
† 10803 Pelham Manor, 6,673 O 7
14526 Penfield, 8,904 F 4
14527 Penn Yan⊙, 5,168 F 5
14530 Perry, 4,538 D 5
12972 Peru, 1,261 N 1
14532 Phelps, 1,989 F 5
12565 Philmont, 1,674 N 6
13135 Phoenix, 2,617 H 4
10968 Piermont, 2,386 M 8
12566 Pine Bush, 1,183 M 7
10969 Pine Island, 925 L 8
12567 Pine Plains, 950 N 7
14534 Pittsford, 1,755 E 4
11803 Plainview, 32,195 O 9
12901 Plattsburgh⊙, 18,715 O 1
10570 Pleasantville, 7,110 N 8
13140 Port Byron, 1,330 G 4
10573 Port Chester, 25,803 P 7
12466 Port Ewen, 2,882 N 7
12974 Port Henry, 1,532 O 2
11777 Port Jefferson, 5,515 P 9
12771 Port Jervis, 8,852 L 8
14770 Portville, 1,304 D 6
11050 Port Washington, 15,923 R 6
13676 Potsdam, 9,985 K 1
* 12601 Poughkeepsie⊙, 32,029 N 7
13142 Pulaski, 2,480 H 3
10577 Purchase, 2,900 P 7
10579 Putnam Valley, ▵975 N 8
* 11101 Queens (borough), ▵1,973,708 N 9
11429 Queens Village, 72,000 R 7
14772 Randolph, 1,498 C 6
14131 Ransomville, 1,034 C 4
12143 Ravena, 2,797 N 6
12571 Red Hook, 1,680 N 7
12144 Rensselaer, 10,136 N 5
12572 Rhinebeck, 2,336 N 7
13439 Richfield Springs, 1,540 K 5
14775 Ripley, 1,173 A 6
11901 Riverhead⊙, 7,585 P 9
† 14830 Riverside, 911 F 6
* 14601 Rochester⊙, 296,233 E 4
Rochester, ‡882,667 E 4
* 11570 Rockville Centre, 27,444 R 7
13440 Rome, 50,148 J 4
11779 Ronkonkoma, 7,284 O 9
11575 Roosevelt, 15,008 R 7
12776 Roscoe, 1,300 L 7
12472 Rosendale, 1,220 M 7
11576 Roslyn, 2,546 R 7
12979 Rouses Point, 2,250 O 1
10580 Rye, 15,869 P 7
13685 Sackets Harbor, 1,202 H 3
11963 Sag Harbor, 2,363 R 8
10301 Saint George⊙, 13,000 M 9
13452 Saint Johnsville, 2,089 L 5
14779 Salamanca, 7,877 C 6
12865 Salem, 1,025 O 4
† 11050 Sands Point, 2,916 N 9
12983 Saranac Lake, 6,086 M 2
12866 Saratoga Springs, 18,845 N 4
12477 Saugerties, 4,190 M 6
13456 Sauquoit, 1,900 K 5
14879 Savona, 933 F 6
11782 Sayville, 11,680 O 9
10583 Scarsdale, 19,229 P 7
* 12301 Schenectady⊙, 77,859 M 5
12157 Schoharie⊙, 1,125 M 5
12870 Schroon Lake, 950 N 3
12871 Schuylerville, 1,402 N 4
12302 Scotia, 8,224 N 5
14546 Scottsville, 1,967 E 4
† 14075 Scranton, 925 C 5
† 14617 Sea Breeze, 1,200 F 4
11579 Sea Cliff, 5,890 R 6
13148 Seneca Falls, 7,794 G 5
13460 Sherburne, 1,613 K 5
13461 Sherrill, 2,986 J 4
14548 Shortsville, 1,516 F 5
13838 Sidney, 4,789 K 6
14136 Silver Creek, 3,182 B 5
13152 Skaneateles, 3,055 H 5
† 14201 Sloan, 5,216 C 5
10974 Sloatsburg, 3,134 M 8
11787 Smithtown, 15,000 O 9
14551 Sodus, 1,813 G 4
14555 Sodus Point, 1,172 G 4
13209 Solvay, 8,280 H 4
11968 Southampton, 4,904 R 9
14830 South Corning, 1,414 F 6
12779 South Fallsburg, 1,590 L 7
† 12801 South Glens Falls, 4,013 N 4
11971 Southold, 2,030 P 8
† 14901 Southport, 8,685 G 6
14559 Spencerport, 2,929 E 4
10977 Spring Valley, 18,112 M 8
14141 Springville, 4,350 C 5
12167 Stamford, 1,286 L 6
* 10301 Staten Island (borough), ▵295,443 M 9
12170 Stillwater, 1,428 N 5
11790 Stony Brook, 6,391 O 9
10980 Stony Point, 8,270 M 8
12172 Stottville, 1,106 N 6
10901 Suffern, 8,273 M 8
11791 Syosset, 9,970 S 7
* 13201 Syracuse⊙, 197,208 H 4
Syracuse, ‡635,946 H 4
10591 Tarrytown, 11,115 O 6
13691 Theresa, 985 J 2
† 11020 Thomaston, 2,486 R 7
12883 Ticonderoga, 3,268 N 3
12486 Tillson, 1,256 M 7
14150 Tonawanda, 21,898 B 4
* 12180 Troy⊙, 62,918 N 5
14886 Trumansburg, 1,618 G 5
10707 Tuckahoe, 6,236 O 7
12986 Tupper Lake, 4,854 M 2
13849 Unadilla, 1,489 K 6
13160 Union Springs, 1,183 G 5
* 13501 Utica⊙, 91,611 K 4
Utica-Rome, ‡337,477 K 4
12184 Valatie, 1,288 N 6
10595 Valhalla, 6,000 P 6
* 11580 Valley Stream, 40,413 N 9
13850 Vestal, 8,303 H 6
14564 Victor, 2,187 F 5
12186 Voorheesville, 2,826 M 5
13694 Waddington, 955 K 1
11792 Wading River, 975 P 9
12586 Walden, 5,277 M 7
12589 Wallkill, 1,849 M 7
13856 Walton, 3,744 K 6
13163 Wampsville⊙, 586 J 4
† 14075 Wanakah, 1,600 C 5
11793 Wantagh, 21,873 N 9
12590 Wappingers Falls, 5,607 N 7
12885 Warrensburg, 2,743 N 3
14569 Warsaw⊙, 3,619 D 5
10990 Warwick, 3,604 M 8
12188 Waterford, 2,879 N 5
13165 Waterloo⊙, 5,418 G 5
13601 Watertown⊙, 30,787 J 3
13480 Waterville, 1,808 K 5
12189 Watervliet, 12,404 N 5
14891 Watkins Glen⊙, 2,716 G 6
14892 Waverley, 5,261 G 7
14572 Wayland, 2,022 E 5
14580 Webster, 5,037 F 4
13166 Weedsport, 1,900 G 4
14895 Wellsville, 5,815 E 6
11590 Westbury, 15,362 R 7
† 13619 West Carthage, 2,047 J 3
† 14901 West Elmira, 5,901 G 6
14787 Westfield, 3,651 A 6
† 12801 West Glens Falls, 3,363 N 4
11977 Westhampton, 1,156 P 9
11978 Westhampton Beach, 1,926 P 9
10996 West Point, 8,100 M 8
11796 West Sayville, 7,386 O 9
14224 West Seneca, ▵48,404 C 5
13491 West Winfield, 1,018 K 5
12887 Whitehall, 3,764 O 3
* 10601 White Plains⊙, 50,220 P 6
13492 Whitesboro, 4,805 K 4
13862 Whitney Point, 1,058 J 6
14589 Williamson, 1,991 F 4
14221 Williamsville, 6,835 C 5
11596 Williston Park, 9,154 R 7
12996 Willsboro, 950 N 2
14172 Wilson, 1,284 C 4
13865 Windsor, 1,098 J 6
12998 Witherbee-Mineville, 1,967 N 2
14590 Wolcott, 1,617 G 4
12788 Woodbourne, 1,155 M 7
11598 Woodmere, 19,831 R 7
12789 Woodridge, 1,071 L 7
12498 Woodstock, 1,073 M 6
* 10701 Yonkers, 204,370 O 7
† 10598 Yorktown, 9,008 N 8
13495 Yorkville, 3,425 K 4
14174 Youngstown, 2,169 C 4

⊙ County seat.
‡ Population of metropolitan area.
▵ Population of town or township.
† Zip of nearest p.o.
* Multiple zips

Agriculture, Industry and Resources

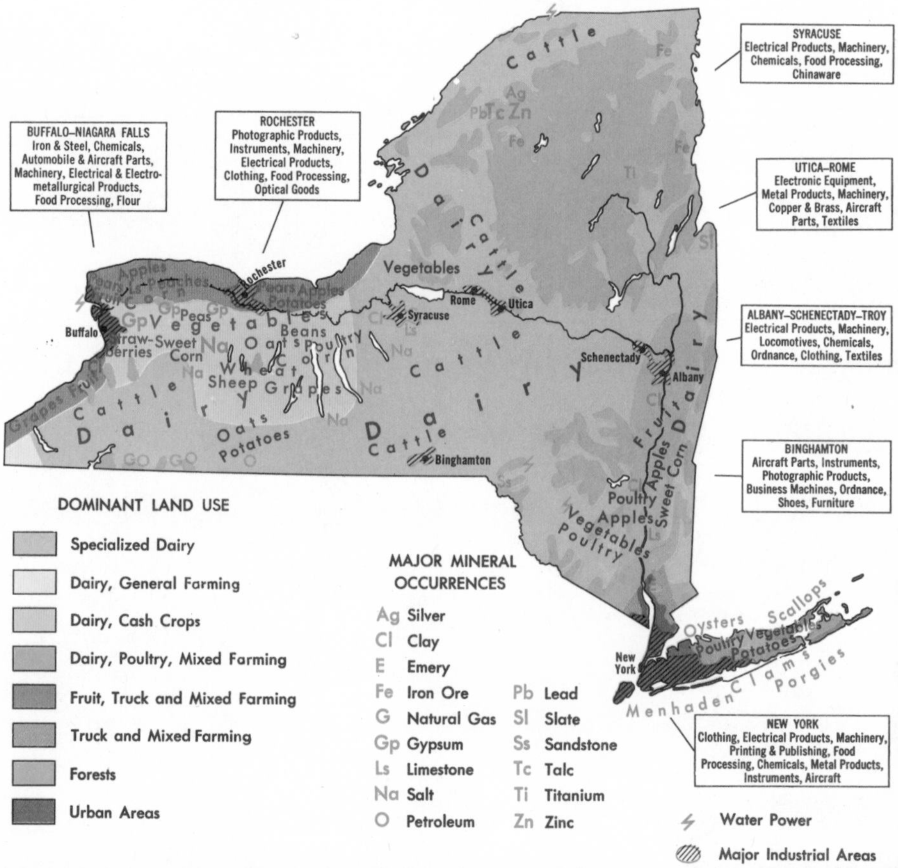
SYRACUSE
Electrical Products, Machinery, Chemicals, Food Processing, Chinaware
BUFFALO–NIAGARA FALLS
Iron & Steel, Chemicals, Automobile & Aircraft Parts, Machinery, Electrical & Electro-metallurgical Products, Food Processing, Flour
ROCHESTER
Photographic Products, Instruments, Machinery, Electrical Products, Clothing, Food Processing, Optical Goods
UTICA–ROME
Electronic Equipment, Metal Products, Machinery, Copper & Brass, Aircraft Parts, Textiles
ALBANY–SCHENECTADY–TROY
Electrical Products, Machinery, Locomotives, Chemicals, Ordnance, Clothing, Textiles
BINGHAMTON
Aircraft Parts, Instruments, Photographic Products, Business Machines, Ordnance, Shoes, Furniture
NEW YORK
Clothing, Electrical Products, Machinery, Printing & Publishing, Food Processing, Chemicals, Metal Products, Instruments, Aircraft
Cattle
Dairy
Vegetables
Rochester
Rome
Utica
Syracuse
Buffalo
Schenectady
Albany
Binghamton
New York
Apples
Pears
Peaches
Grapes
Sweet Corn
Strawberries
Beans
Oats
Wheat
Sheep
Potatoes
Poultry
Fruit
Oysters
Scallops
Clams
Porgies
Menhaden
DOMINANT LAND USE
Specialized Dairy
Dairy, General Farming
Dairy, Cash Crops
Dairy, Poultry, Mixed Farming
Fruit, Truck and Mixed Farming
Truck and Mixed Farming
Forests
Urban Areas
MAJOR MINERAL OCCURRENCES
Ag Silver
Cl Clay
E Emery
Fe Iron Ore
G Natural Gas
Gp Gypsum
Ls Limestone
Na Salt
O Petroleum
Pb Lead
Sl Slate
Ss Sandstone
Tc Talc
Ti Titanium
Zn Zinc
Water Power
Major Industrial Areas

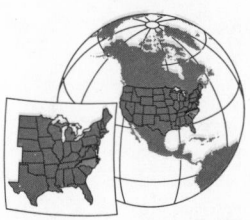

COUNTIES

Alamance, 96,362 .... L 3
Alexander, 19,466 .... G 3
Alleghany, 8,134 .... G 1
Anson, 23,488 .... J 4
Ashe, 19,571 .... F 2
Avery, 12,655 .... F 2
Beaufort, 35,980 .... R 4
Bertie, 20,528 .... P 2
Bladen, 26,477 .... M 5
Brunswick, 24,223 .... N 6
Buncombe, 145,056 .... D 3
Burke, 60,364 .... F 3
Cabarrus, 74,629 .... H 4
Caldwell, 56,699 .... F 3
Camden, 5,453 .... S 2
Carteret, 31,603 .... R 5
Caswell, 19,055 .... L 2
Catawba, 90,873 .... G 3
Chatham, 29,554 .... L 3
Cherokee, 16,330 .... A 4
Chowan, 10,764 .... R 2
Clay, 5,180 .... B 4
Cleveland, 72,556 .... F 4
Columbus, 46,937 .... M 6
Craven, 62,554 .... P 4
Cumberland, 212,042 .... M 4
Currituck, 6,976 .... S 2
Dare, 6,995 .... T 3
Davidson, 95,627 .... J 3
Davie, 18,855 .... H 3
Duplin, 38,015 .... O 5
Durham, 132,681 .... M 3
Edgecombe, 52,341 .... O 3
Forsyth, 214,348 .... J 2
Franklin, 26,820 .... N 2
Gaston, 148,415 .... G 4
Gates, 8,524 .... R 2
Graham, 6,562 .... B 4
Granville, 32,762 .... M 2
Greene, 14,967 .... O 3
Guilford, 288,590 .... K 3
Halifax, 53,884 .... O 2
Harnett, 49,667 .... M 4
Haywood, 41,710 .... C 3
Henderson, 42,804 .... D 3
Hertford, 23,529 .... P 2
Hoke, 16,436 .... L 4
Hyde, 5,571 .... S 3
Iredell, 72,197 .... H 3
Jackson, 21,593 .... C 4
Johnston, 61,737 .... N 4
Jones, 9,779 .... P 4
Lee, 30,467 .... L 4
Lenoir, 55,204 .... O 4
Lincoln, 32,682 .... G 3
Macon, 15,788 .... B 4
Madison, 16,003 .... D 3
Martin, 24,730 .... P 3
McDowell, 30,648 .... E 3
Mecklenburg, 354,656 .... H 4
Mitchell, 13,447 .... E 2
Montgomery, 19,267 .... K 4
Moore, 39,048 .... L 4
Nash, 59,122 .... O 2
New Hanover, 82,996 .... O 6
Northampton, 24,009 .... P 2
Onslow, 103,126 .... P 5
Orange, 57,707 .... L 2
Pamlico, 9,467 .... R 4
Pasquotank, 26,824 .... S 2
Pender, 18,149 .... O 5
Perquimans, 8,351 .... S 2
Person, 25,914 .... M 2

Pitt, 73,900 .... P 3
Polk, 11,735 .... E 4
Randolph, 76,358 .... K 3
Richmond, 39,889 .... K 4
Robeson, 84,842 .... L 5
Rockingham, 72,402 .... K 2
Rowan, 90,035 .... H 3
Rutherford, 47,337 .... E 4
Sampson, 44,954 .... N 4
Scotland, 26,929 .... L 5
Stanly, 42,822 .... J 4
Stokes, 23,782 .... J 2
Surry, 51,415 .... H 2
Swain, 7,861 .... B 3
Transylvania, 19,713 .... D 4
Tyrrell, 3,806 .... S 3
Union, 54,714 .... H 4
Vance, 32,691 .... N 2
Wake, 228,453 .... M 3
Warren, 15,810 .... N 2
Washington, 14,038 .... R 3
Watauga, 23,404 .... F 2
Wayne, 85,408 .... N 4
Wilkes, 49,524 .... G 2
Wilson, 57,486 .... O 3
Yadkin, 24,599 .... H 2
Yancey, 12,629 .... E 3

CITIES and TOWNS

Zip	Name/Pop.	Key
28321	Abbottsburg, 425	M 5
28315	Aberdeen, 1,592	L 4
27006	Advance, 206	J 3
27910	Ahoskie, 5,105	P 2
27201	Alamance, 450	K 2
† 28713	Alarka, 900	C 4
28001	Albemarle⊙, 11,126	J 4
† 27589	Alert, 200	N 2
28701	Alexander, 200	D 3
28509	Alliance, 577	R 4
† 28364	Alma, 200	L 5
28702	Almond, 200	B 4
27202	Altamahaw, 900	L 2
28901	Andrews, 1,384	B 4
27501	Angier, 1,431	M 4
28007	Ansonville, 694	J 4
27502	Apex, 2,192	M 3
28510	Arapahoe, 212	R 4
27589	Arcola, 300	N 2
27263	Archdale, 6,103	K 3
28704	Arden, 850	D 3
† 28642	Arlington, 711	H 2
28420	Ash, 250	N 6
27203	Asheboro⊙, 10,797	K 3
* 28801	Asheville⊙, 57,681	D 3
	Asheville, ‡145,056	D 3
28603	Ashford, 225	—
† 27983	Askewville, 247	N 5
28421	Atkinson, 325	M 5
27207	Bear Creek, 500	L 3
28516	Beaufort⊙, 3,368	R 5
27807	Bailey, 724	N 3
27812	Bethel, 1,514	P 3
28518	Beulaville, 1,156	O 5
† 28803	Biltmore Forest, 1,298	E 3
27209	Biscoe, 1,244	K 4
28512	Atlantic Beach, 300	R 5
27805	Aulander, 947	P 2
27806	Aurora, 620	R 4
28318	Autryville, 213	M 4
27915	Avon, 400	U 4
† 28704	Avondale-Henrietta, 1,307	F 4
28513	Ayden, 3,450	P 3
28009	Badin, 1,626	J 4
27503	Bahama, 280	M 2
28705	Bakersville⊙, 409	E 2
28706	Balfour, 2,014	E 3
27203	Balfours, 4,836	K 3
28707	Balsam, 300	C 4
† 27030	Bannertown, 1,138	H 1
27917	Barco, 325	T 2
† 28739	Barker Heights, 2,933	D 3
28710	Bat Cave, 400	E 4
27808	Bath, 231	R 4
27809	Battleboro, 688	O 2
28515	Bayboro⊙, 665	R 4
27207	Bear Creek, 500	L 3
27810	Belhaven, 2,259	R 3
28012	Belmont, 4,814	H 4
27919	Belvidere, 275	S 2
† 28621	Benham, 400	G 2
27208	Bennett, 200	K 3
27504	Benson, 2,267	N 4
† 27565	Berea, 200	M 2
28016	Bessemer City, 5,217	G 4
† 28779	Beta, 500	C 4

27813	Black Creek, 449	O 3
28711	Black Mountain, 3,204	E 3
28320	Bladenboro, 783	M 5
27212	Blanch, 210	L 2
28605	Blowing Rock, 801	F 2
28323	Bunnlevel, 200	M 4
28092	Boger City, 2,203	G 4
† 28760	Bogue, 600	—
28461	Boiling Spring Lakes, 245	N 7
28017	Boiling Springs, 2,284	F 4
28423	Bolton, 534	N 6
27213	Bonlee, 275	L 3
28606	Boomer, 212	G 2
28607	Boone⊙, 8,754	F 2
27011	Boonville, 687	H 2
28322	Bowdens, 250	N 4
28712	Brevard⊙, 5,243	D 4
28519	Bridgeton, 520	R 4
27505	Broadway, 694	L 4
28607	Brookford, 590	G 3
27214	Browns Summit, 500	K 2
28424	Brunswick, 206	M 6
28713	Bryson City⊙, 1,290	C 4
† 28377	Buies, 275	L 5
27506	Buies Creek, 2,024	M 4
27507	Bullock, 550	M 2
27508	Bunn, 284	N 3
28425	Burgaw⊙, 1,744	N 5
27215	Burlington, 35,930	K 2
28714	Burnsville⊙, 1,348	E 3
27509	Butner, 3,538	M 2
28324	Butters, 225	M 5
27920	Buxton, 700	U 4
27228	Bynum, 400	L 3
28325	Calypso, 462	N 4
27921	Camden⊙, 300	S 2
28326	Cameron, 204	L 4
28715	Candler, 950	D 3
27229	Candor, 561	K 4
28716	Canton, 5,158	D 3
28019	Caroleen, 975	F 4
28428	Carolina Beach, 1,663	O 6
27510	Carrboro, 3,472	L 3
28327	Carthage⊙, 1,034	M 3
27511	Cary, 7,430	M 3
28020	Casar, 350	F 4
28717	Cashiers, 230	C 4
27816	Castalia, 265	O 2
28429	Castle Hayne, 900	O 6
28609	Catawba, 565	G 3
† 28754	Catharine Lake, 500	O 5
27230	Cedar Falls, 500	K 3
28520	Cedar Island, 250	S 5
28718	Cedar Mountain, 250	D 4
28323	Chadbourn, 2,213	M 6
27514	Chapel Hill, 25,537	M 3
* 28201	Charlotte⊙, 241,178	H 4
	Charlotte, ‡409,370	H 4
28719	Cherokee, 975	C 4
28021	Cherryville, 5,258	G 4
28023	China Grove, 1,788	H 3
28521	Chinquapin, 350	O 5
27817	Chocowinity, 566	P 4
28610	Claremont, 788	G 3
28432	Clarendon, 300	M 6
28433	Clarkton, 662	M 6
27520	Clayton, 3,103	N 3
27268	Clemmons, 4,900	J 2
27013	Cleveland, 614	H 3
28438	Cliffside, 950	F 4
27233	Climax, 475	K 3
28328	Clinton⊙, 7,157	N 5
28721	Clyde, 900	D 3
27521	Coats, 1,051	M 4
27922	Cofield, 422	R 2
27923	Coinjock, 655	S 2
27924	Colerain, 373	R 2
28234	Coleridge, 600	K 3
28611	Collettsville, 275	F 3
27925	Columbia⊙, 900	S 3
28722	Columbus⊙, 731	E 4
28522	Comfort, 340	O 5
27818	Como, 211	P 1
28025	Concord⊙, 18,464	H 4
28612	Connellys Springs, 500	F 3
28613	Conover, 3,355	G 3
27820	Conway, 694	P 2
27014	Cooleemee, 1,115	H 3
28031	Cornelius, 1,296	H 4
28523	Cove City, 485	P 4
28032	Cramerton, 2,142	G 4
27522	Creedmoor, 1,405	M 2
28033	Crouse, 850	G 4
† 28716	Cruso, 800	D 4
28723	Cullowhee, 6,300	C 4
28331	Cumberland, 800	M 5
28435	Currie, 294	N 6
27929	Currituck⊙, 500	T 2
27015	Cycle, 210	H 2
28034	Dallas, 4,059	G 4
† 27043	Dalton, 400	J 2
27016	Danbury⊙, 152	J 2
28036	Davidson, 2,931	H 4
28524	Davis, 600	R 5
28436	Delco, 450	N 6
27239	Denton, 1,017	J 3
28725	Dillsboro, 215	C 4
27017	Dobson⊙, 933	H 2
† 28685	Dockery, 300	G 2
28526	Dover, 585	P 4
28619	Drexel, 1,431	F 3
28332	Dublin, 283	M 5
28334	Dunn, 8,302	M 4
* 27701	Durham⊙, 95,438	M 2
	Durham, ‡190,388	M 2
† 28761	Dysartsville, 950	F 3
27242	Eagle Springs, 500	K 4
28038	Earl, 300	—
27018	East Bend, 485	H 2
28726	East Flat Rock, 2,627	E 4
28352	East Laurinburg, 487	L 5
† 28752	East Marion, 3,015	F 3
28039	East Spencer, 2,217	J 3
27288	Eden, 15,871	K 1
27932	Edenton⊙, 4,766	R 2
27243	Efland, 600	L 2
27909	Elizabeth City⊙, 14,069	S 2
28337	Elizabethtown⊙, 1,418	M 5
28621	Elkin, 2,899	H 2
28622	Elk Park, 503	F 2
28040	Ellenboro, 465	F 4
28338	Ellerbe, 913	K 4
27822	Elm City, 1,201	O 3
27244	Elon College, 2,150	L 2
27823	Enfield, 3,272	O 2
27824	Engelhard, 500	T 3
28728	Enka, 500	D 3
28527	Ernul, 350	P 4
28339	Erwin, 2,852	M 4
27247	Ether, 375	K 4
28729	Etowah, 700	D 4
27830	Eureka, 263	O 3
28438	Evergreen, 250	M 6
28439	Fair Bluff, 1,039	M 6
27826	Fairfield, 954	S 3
28340	Fairmont, 2,827	L 5
28730	Fairview, 800	D 3
28341	Faison, 598	N 4
28041	Faith, 506	J 3
28342	Falcon, 357	M 4
† 27028	Farmington, 300	H 3
28442	Farmville, 4,424	O 3
* 28301	Fayetteville⊙, 53,510	M 4
	Fayetteville, ‡212,042	M 4
28731	Flat Rock, 650	E 4
28732	Fletcher, 950	E 4
28043	Forest City, 7,179	E 4
† 27028	Fork, 250	—
27829	Fountain, 434	O 3
27524	Four Oaks, 1,057	N 4
28734	Franklin⊙, 2,336	C 4
27525	Franklinton, 1,459	N 2
27248	Franklinville, 794	K 3
28440	Freeland, 500	N 6
27830	Fremont, 1,596	N 3
27936	Frisco, 205	T 4
27526	Fuquay-Varina, 3,576	M 3
28441	Garland, 656	M 5
27529	Garner, 4,923	M 3
27831	Garysburg, 231	O 2

(continued on following page)

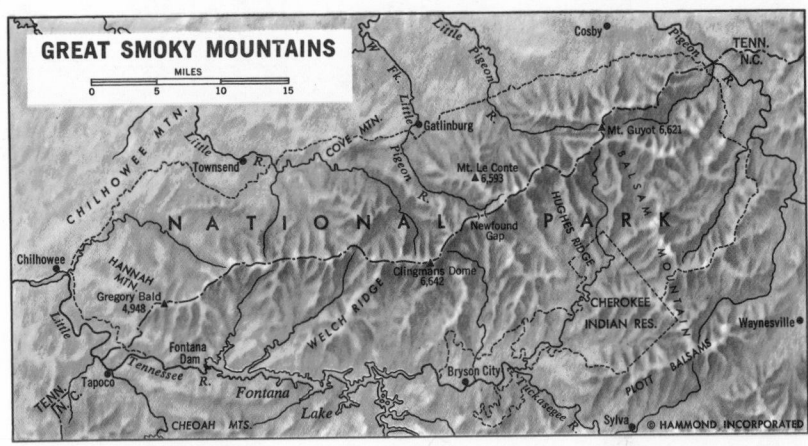

GREAT SMOKY MOUNTAINS

AREA 52,586 sq. mi.
POPULATION 5,082,059
CAPITAL Raleigh
LARGEST CITY Charlotte
HIGHEST POINT Mt. Mitchell 6,684 ft.
SETTLED IN 1650
ADMITTED TO UNION November 21, 1789
POPULAR NAME Tarheel State
STATE FLOWER Flowering Dogwood
STATE BIRD Cardinal

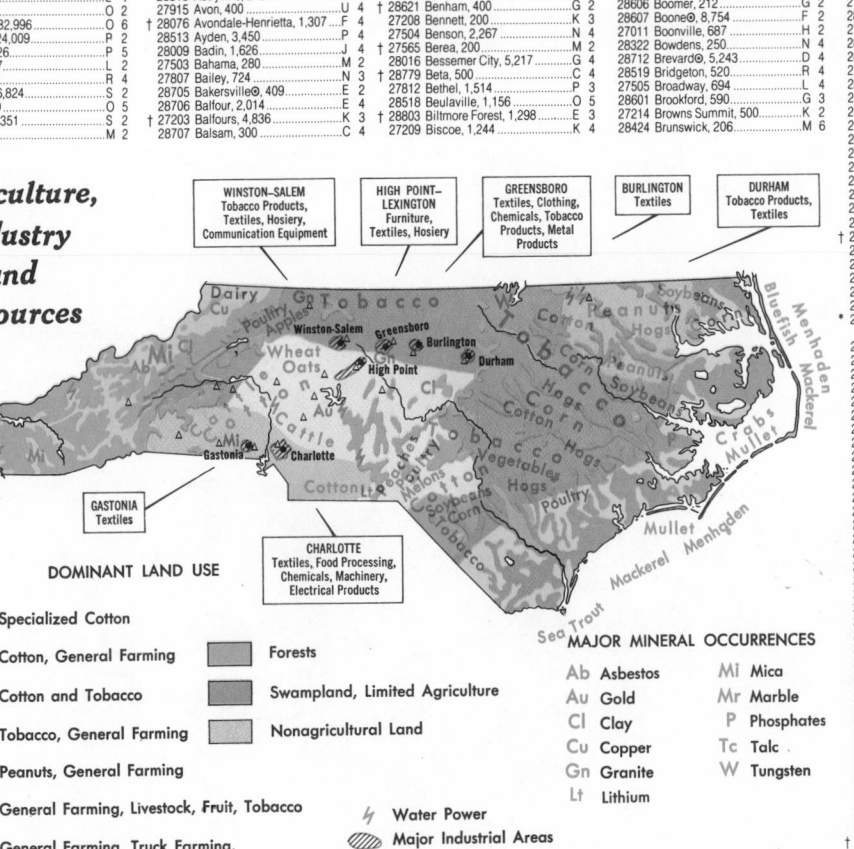

Agriculture, Industry and Resources

WINSTON–SALEM
Tobacco Products, Textiles, Hosiery, Communication Equipment

HIGH POINT–LEXINGTON
Furniture, Textiles, Hosiery

GREENSBORO
Textiles, Clothing, Chemicals, Tobacco Products, Metal Products

BURLINGTON
Textiles

DURHAM
Tobacco Products, Textiles

GASTONIA
Textiles

CHARLOTTE
Textiles, Food Processing, Chemicals, Machinery, Electrical Products

DOMINANT LAND USE

- Specialized Cotton
- Cotton, General Farming
- Cotton and Tobacco
- Tobacco, General Farming
- Peanuts, General Farming
- General Farming, Livestock, Fruit, Tobacco
- General Farming, Truck Farming, Tobacco, Livestock
- Forests
- Swampland, Limited Agriculture
- Nonagricultural Land

⚡ Water Power
▨ Major Industrial Areas
△ Major Textile Manufacturing Centers

MAJOR MINERAL OCCURRENCES

Ab Asbestos
Au Gold
Cl Clay
Cu Copper
Gn Granite
Lt Lithium
Mi Mica
Mr Marble
P Phosphates
Tc Talc
W Tungsten

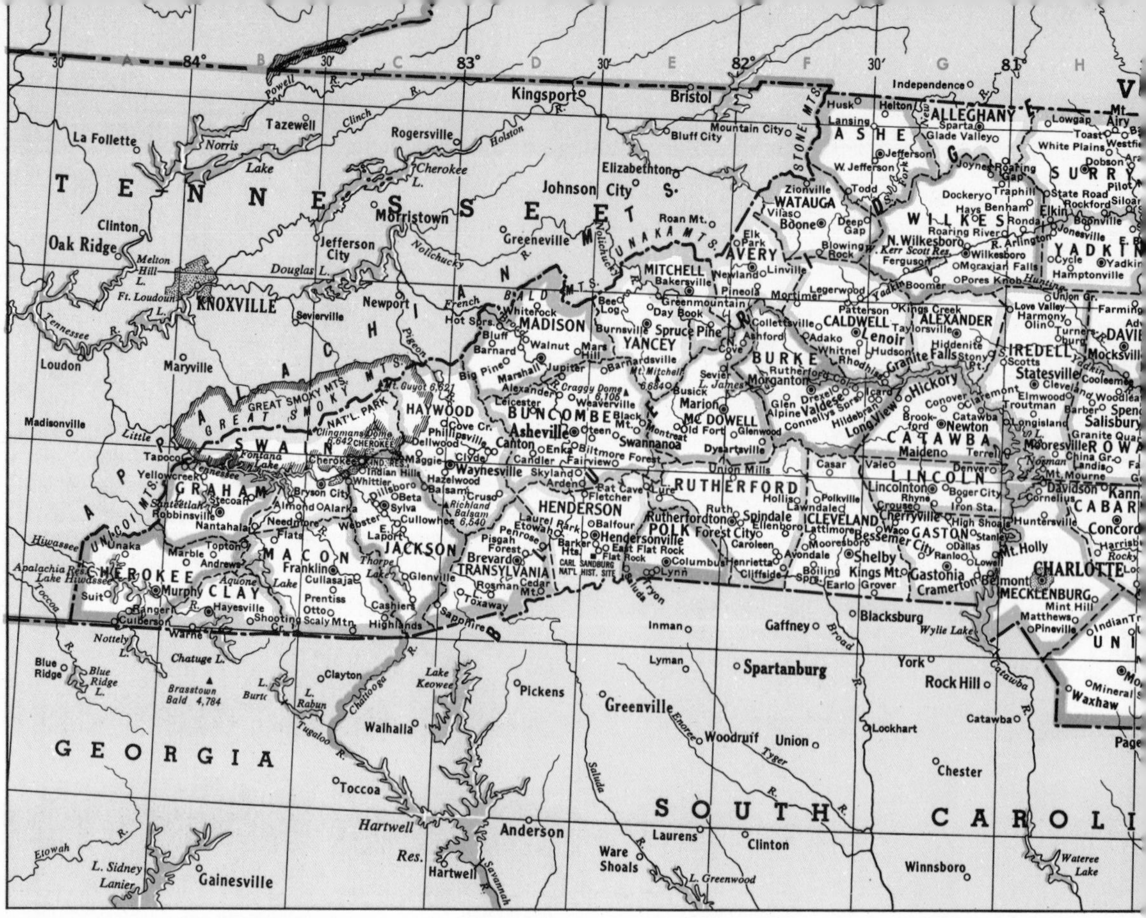

Topography

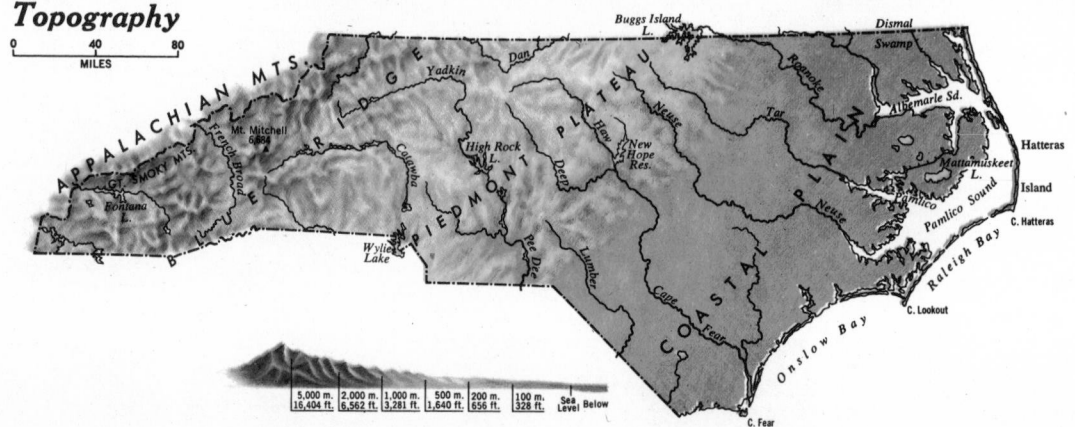

0   40   80
MILES

| 5,000 m. | 2,000 m. | 1,000 m. | 500 m. | 200 m. | 100 m. | Sea | Below |
| 16,404 ft. | 6,562 ft. | 3,281 ft. | 1,640 ft. | 656 ft. | 328 ft. | Level | |

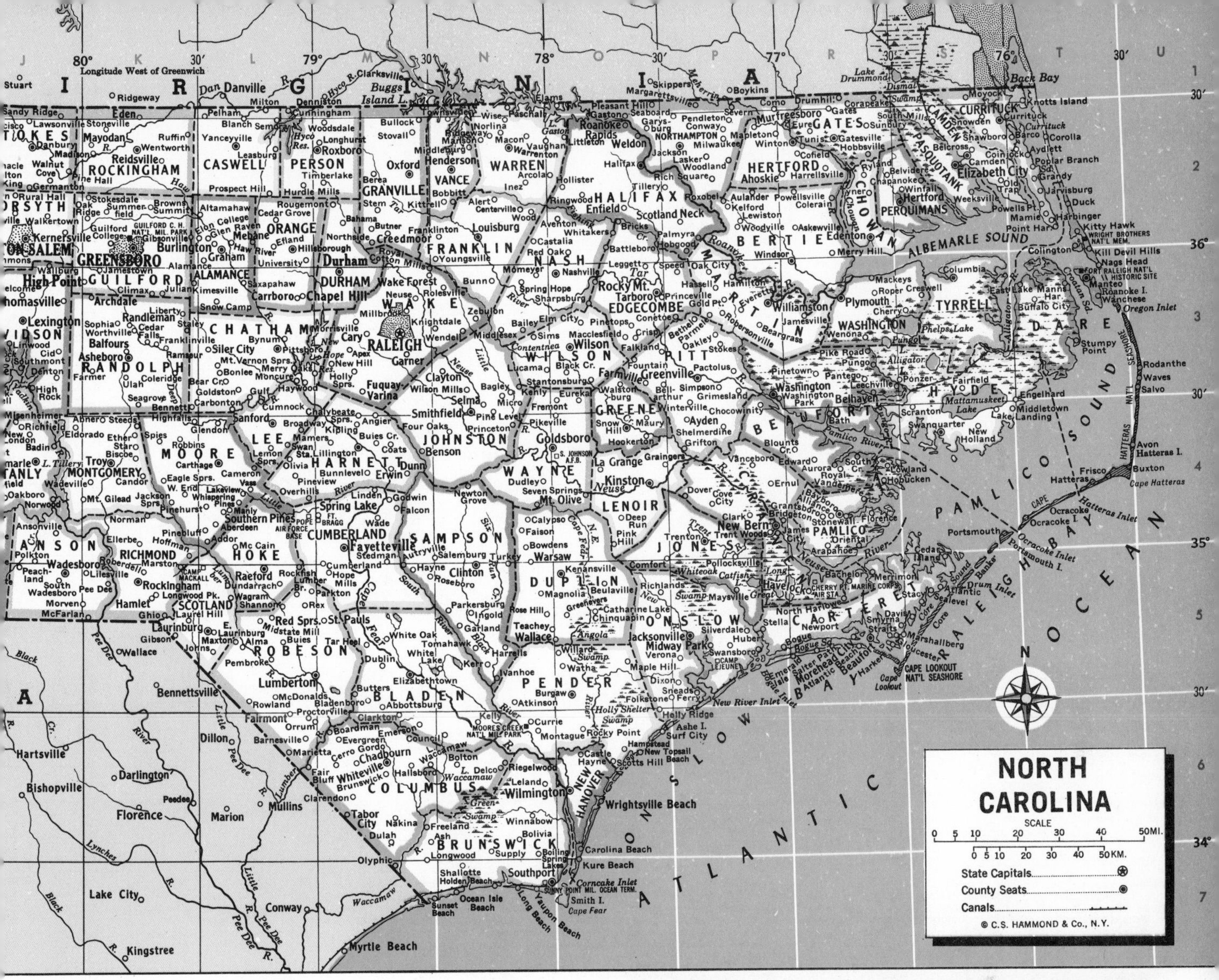

NORTH CAROLINA

SCALE
0 5 10   20   30   40   50 MI.
0 5 10   20   30   40 50 KM.

State Capitals...............................⊛
County Seats.................................⊙
Canals.................................

© C.S. HAMMOND & Co., N.Y.

28384	Saint Pauls, 2,011	M 5	† 28771	Stecoah, 250	B 4	27981	Wanchese, 975	T 3

28384 Saint Pauls, 2,011......M 5
28385 Salemburg, 669......N 4
28144 Salisbury⊙, 22,515......H 3
28575 Salter Path, 500......R 5
28773 Saluda, 546......E 4
27046 Sandy Ridge, 500......J 1
27330 Sanford⊙, 11,716......L 4
27340 Saxapahaw, 950......L 3
28775 Scaly Mountain, 250......C 4
27874 Scotland Neck, 2,869......P 2
27875 Scranton, 220......S 4
27876 Seaboard, 611......O 1
27341 Seagrove, 354......K 3
28577 Sealevel, 600......S 5
27576 Selma, 4,356......N 3
27343 Semora, 250......L 2
27877 Severn, 356......P 2
† 28752 Sevier, 302......E 3
28459 Shallotte, 597......N 7
27878 Sharpsburg, 789......O 3
27973 Shawboro, 300......S 2
28150 Shelby⊙, 16,328......F 3
† 27043 Shoals, 350......J 2
† 28904 Shooting Creek, 250......B 4
27344 Siler City, 4,689......L 3
† 28539 Silverdale, 250......P 5
27880 Sims, 205......N 3
27879 Simpson, 300......P 3
28776 Skyland, 2,177......D 4
27577 Smithfield⊙, 6,677......N 3
28579 Smyrna, 225......R 5
28460 Sneads Ferry, 700......P 5
28580 Snow Hill⊙, 1,359......O 4
27350 Sophia, 700......K 3
28387 Southern Pines, 5,937......L 4
27976 South Mills, 950......S 2
27351 Southmont, 900......J 3
28461 Southport⊙, 2,220......N 7
28675 Sparta⊙, 1,304......G 1
28159 Spencer, 3,075......H 3
28160 Spindale, 3,848......F 4
27882 Spring Hope, 1,334......N 3
28390 Spring Lake, 3,968......M 4
28777 Spruce Pine, 2,333......C 4
28581 Stacy, 410......S 5
27355 Staley, 239......J 4
28163 Stanfield, 458......J 4
28164 Stanley, 2,336......G 4
† 27045 Stantonsburg, 2,362......O 3
27883 Stantonsburg, 869......O 3
27356 Star, 892......K 4
28676 State Road, 800......H 2
28677 Statesville⊙, 19,996......H 3

† 28771 Stecoah, 250......B 4
28391 Stedman, 505......M 4
† 27341 Steeds, 300......K 4
28582 Stella, 300......P 5
27581 Stem, 242......M 2
27357 Stokesdale, 800......K 2
27048 Stoneville, 1,030......K 2
28583 Stonewall, 335......R 4
28678 Stony Point, 1,001......G 3
27582 Stovall, 405......M 2
27358 Summerfield, 900......K 2
27979 Sunbury, 350......R 2
28462 Supply, 300......N 6
28778 Swannanoa, 1,966......E 3
27885 Swanquarter⊙, 175......S 4
28584 Swansboro, 1,207......P 5
28779 Sylva⊙, 1,561......C 4
28463 Tabor City, 2,400......M 6
27886 Tarboro⊙, 9,425......O 3
28681 Taylorsville⊙, 1,231......G 3
28464 Teachey, 219......N 5
28682 Terrell, 319......G 3
27360 Thomasville, 15,230......J 3
27887 Tillery, 300......O 2
28781 Topton, 240......B 4
27584 Townsville, 250......N 1
28685 Traphill, 350......H 2
† 28560 Trent Woods, 719......P 4
28166 Troutman, 797......H 3
27371 Troy⊙, 2,429......K 4
28782 Tryon, 1,951......E 4
28393 Turkey, 329......N 4
27980 Tyner, 252......R 2
27203 Ulah, 500......K 3
28908 Unaka, 300......A 4
28167 Union Mills, 500......F 3
28690 Valdese, 3,182......F 3
28586 Vanceboro, 758......P 4
28587 Vandemere, 379......R 4
28394 Vass, 885......L 4
28540 Verona, 300......O 5
28692 Vilas, 250......F 2
28169 Waco, 245......G 4
28395 Wade, 315......M 4
28170 Wadesboro⊙, 3,977......J 5
28396 Wagram, 718......L 5
27587 Wake Forest, 3,148......M 3
27051 Walkertown, 1,652......J 2
28466 Wallace, 2,905......N 5
27373 Wallburg, 225......J 3
27052 Walnut Cove, 1,213......J 2

27981 Wanchese, 975......T 3
28909 Warne, 305......B 5
27589 Warrenton⊙, 1,035......N 2
28398 Warsaw, 2,701......N 4
27889 Washington⊙, 8,961......R 3
† 27889 Washington Park, 517......R 3
28173 Waxhaw, 1,248......H 5
28786 Waynesville⊙, 6,488......D 4
28787 Weaverville, 1,280......D 3
27909 Weeksville, 300......S 2
27374 Welcome, 975......J 3
27890 Weldon⊙, 2,304......O 2
27591 Wendell, 1,929......N 3
27375 Wentworth⊙, 150......K 2
27376 West End, 950......K 4
27053 Westfield, 500......J 2
28694 West Jefferson, 889......F 2
28327 Whispering Pines, 362......L 4
27891 Whitakers, 926......O 2
28337 White Lake, 232......M 5
27031 White Plains, 350......H 2
28472 Whiteville⊙, 4,195......M 6
28645 Whitnel, 975......F 3
28789 Whittier, 325......C 4
28697 Wilkesboro⊙, 1,974......G 2
28478 Willard, 300......N 5
27892 Williamston⊙, 6,570......R 3
28401 Wilmington⊙, 46,169......N 6
    Wilmington,‡107,219......N 6
27893 Wilson⊙, 29,347......O 3
27593 Wilson Mills, 283......M 3
27983 Windsor⊙, 2,199......P 2
27985 Winfall, 581......S 2
28174 Wingate, 2,569......J 5
27101 Winston-Salem⊙, 132,913......J 2
28590 Winterville, 1,437......P 3
27986 Winton⊙, 917......P 2
27594 Wise, 500......N 2
27897 Woodland, 744......P 2
27054 Woodleaf, 750......H 3
† 27849 Woodville, 253......P 2
28480 Wrightsville Beach, 1,701......O 6
27055 Yadkinville⊙, 2,232......H 2
27379 Yanceyville⊙, 1,274......L 2
28461 Yaupon Beach, 334......N 7
28771 Yellowcreek, 204......A 4
27596 Youngsville, 555......N 3
27597 Zebulon, 1,839......N 3
26698 Zionville, 350......F 2

⊙ County seat.
† Population of metropolitan area.
‡ Zip of nearest p.o.
∗ Multiple zips.

Weeding "green gold" — tobacco is North Carolina's money crop.

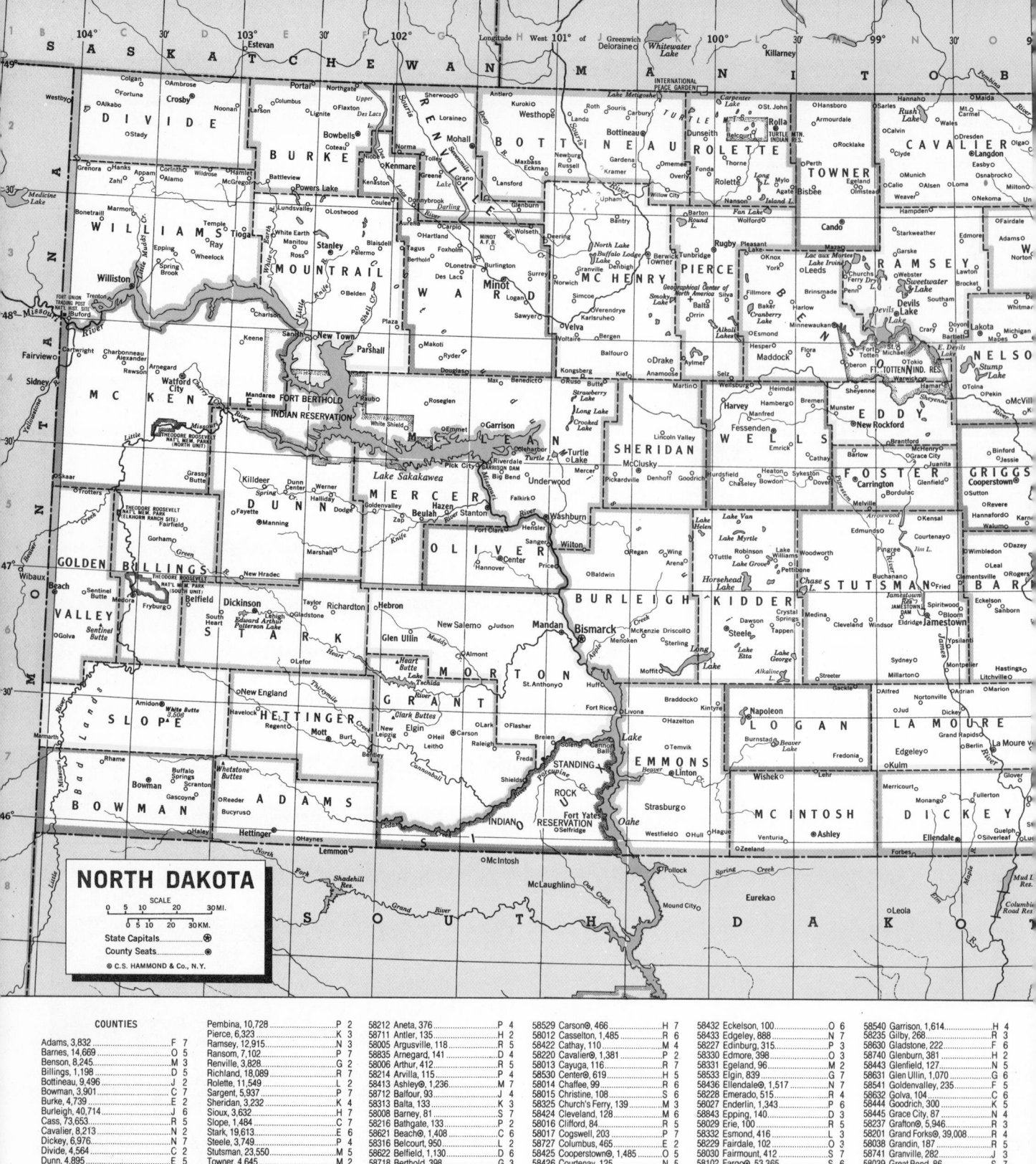

NORTH DAKOTA

SCALE
0 5 10 20 30 MI.
0 5 10 20 30 KM.

State Capitals................⊛
County Seats................⊙

© C.S. HAMMOND & Co., N.Y.

COUNTIES

Adams, 3,832	F 7
Barnes, 14,669	O 5
Benson, 8,245	M 3
Billings, 1,198	D 5
Bottineau, 9,496	J 2
Bowman, 3,901	C 7
Burke, 4,739	E 2
Burleigh, 40,714	J 6
Cass, 73,653	R 5
Cavalier, 8,213	N 2
Dickey, 6,976	N 7
Divide, 4,564	C 2
Dunn, 4,895	E 5
Eddy, 4,103	N 4
Emmons, 7,200	K 7
Foster, 4,832	N 5
Golden Valley, 2,611	C 5
Grand Forks, 69,102	P 3
Grant, 5,009	G 6
Griggs, 4,184	O 5
Hettinger, 5,075	E 6
Kidder, 4,362	L 6
La Moure, 7,117	N 7
Logan, 4,245	L 7
McHenry, 8,977	J 3
McIntosh, 5,545	L 7
McKenzie, 6,127	D 4
McLean, 11,251	G 4
Mercer, 6,175	F 5
Morton, 20,310	H 6
Mountrail, 8,437	E 3
Nelson, 5,776	O 4
Oliver, 2,322	H 5

CITIES and TOWNS

Zip	Name/Pop.	Key
58001	Abercrombie, 262	S 7
58210	Adams, 284	O 3
58830	Alamo, 124	D 2
58831	Alexander, 208	C 4
58003	Alice, 83	P 6
58520	Almont, 109	H 6
58311	Alsen, 201	N 2
58833	Ambrose, 108	D 2
58620	Amidon⊙, 54	D 7
58710	Anamoose, 401	K 4

58212	Aneta, 376	P 4
58711	Antler, 135	J 2
58005	Argusville, 118	R 5
58835	Arnegard, 141	D 4
58006	Arthur, 412	R 5
58214	Arvilla, 115	P 4
58413	Ashley⊙, 1,236	M 7
58712	Balfour, 93	J 4
58313	Balta, 133	K 3
58008	Barney, 81	S 7
58216	Bathgate, 133	P 2
58621	Beach⊙, 1,408	C 6
58316	Belcourt, 950	L 2
58622	Belfield, 1,130	D 6
58718	Berthold, 398	G 3
58523	Beulah, 1,344	G 5
58416	Binford, 242	N 4
58317	Bisbee, 305	M 2
58501	Bismarck (cap.)⊛, 34,703	J 6
58318	Bottineau⊙, 2,760	J 2
58721	Bowbells⊙, 584	F 2
58418	Bowdon, 229	L 5
58623	Bowman⊙, 1,762	D 7
58524	Braddock, 106	K 6
58321	Brocket, 95	O 3
58420	Buchanan, 100	N 5
58011	Buffalo, 241	R 6
58722	Burlington, 247	H 3
58723	Butte, 193	J 4
58218	Buxton, 235	R 4
58324	Cando⊙, 1,512	M 3
58528	Cannon Ball, 550	J 7
† 58241	Canton (Hensel), 81	P 2
58725	Carpio, 215	G 3
58421	Carrington⊙, 2,491	M 5

58529	Carson⊙, 466	H 7
58012	Casselton, 1,485	R 6
58422	Cathay, 110	M 4
58220	Cavalier⊙, 1,381	P 2
58013	Cayuga, 116	P 7
58530	Center⊙, 619	H 5
58014	Chaffee, 99	R 6
58015	Christine, 108	S 6
58325	Church's Ferry, 139	M 3
58424	Cleveland, 128	M 6
58016	Clifford, 84	R 5
58017	Cogswell, 203	P 7
58727	Columbus, 365	E 2
58425	Cooperstown⊙, 1,485	O 5
58426	Courtenay, 125	N 5
58327	Crary, 150	N 3
58730	Crosby⊙, 1,545	D 2
58222	Crystal, 272	P 2
58021	Davenport, 191	R 6
58428	Dawson, 131	L 6
58429	Dazey, 128	O 5
58430	Denhoff, 95	K 5
58733	Des Lacs, 197	G 3
58301	Devils Lake⊙, 7,078	N 3
58431	Dickey, 146	N 6
58601	Dickinson⊙, 12,405	E 6
58625	Dodge, 121	F 5
58734	Donnybrook, 163	G 2
58735	Douglas, 144	H 4
58736	Drake, 636	K 4
58225	Drayton, 1,095	P 2
58532	Driscoll, 128	K 6
58626	Dunn Center, 107	E 5
58329	Dunseith, 811	K 2
58024	Dwight, 93	S 7

58432	Eckelson, 100	O 6
58433	Edgeley, 888	N 7
58227	Edinburg, 315	P 3
58330	Edmore, 398	O 3
58331	Egeland, 96	M 2
58533	Elgin, 839	G 7
58436	Ellendale⊙, 1,517	N 7
58228	Emerado, 515	P 4
58027	Enderlin, 1,343	P 6
58843	Epping, 140	D 3
58029	Erie, 100	R 5
58332	Esmond, 416	L 4
58229	Fairdale, 102	O 3
58030	Fairmount, 412	S 7
58102	Fargo⊙, 53,365	S 6
	Fargo-Moorhead, ‡120,238	S 6
58438	Fessenden⊙, 815	L 4
58031	Fingal, 166	P 6
58230	Finley⊙, 809	P 4
58535	Flasher, 467	H 6
58737	Flaxton, 286	F 2
58439	Forbes, 88	N 8
58231	Fordville, 360	P 3
58233	Forest River, 169	P 3
58032	Forman⊙, 596	P 7
58033	Fort Ransom, 121	P 6
58335	Fort Totten, 550	N 4
58844	Fortuna, 216	C 2
58538	Fort Yates⊙, 1,153	J 7
58440	Fredonia, 100	M 7
58441	Fullerton, 117	O 7
58442	Gackle, 470	M 6
58035	Galesburg, 134	R 5
58739	Gardena, 84	J 2
58036	Gardner, 96	R 5

58540	Garrison⊙, 1,614	H 4
58235	Gilby, 268	R 3
58630	Gladstone, 222	F 6
58740	Glenburn, 381	H 2
58443	Glenfield, 127	N 5
58631	Glen Ullin, 1,070	G 6
58541	Goldenvalley, 235	F 5
58632	Golva, 104	C 6
58444	Goodrich, 300	K 5
58445	Grace City, 87	N 4
58237	Grafton⊙, 5,946	R 3
58201	Grand Forks⊙, 39,008	R 3
58038	Grandin, 187	R 5
58741	Granville, 282	J 3
58039	Great Bend, 86	S 7
58845	Grenora, 401	C 2
58040	Gwinner, 623	P 7
58542	Hague, 146	L 7
58636	Halliday, 413	F 5
58238	Hamilton, 110	P 2
58338	Hampden, 114	N 2
58041	Hankinson, 1,125	S 7
58448	Hannaford, 244	O 5
58239	Hannah, 145	N 2
58340	Harlow, 85	M 3
58341	Harvey, 2,361	L 4
58042	Harwood, 267	R 5
58240	Hatton, 808	R 4
58043	Havana, 156	P 7
58544	Hazelton, 374	K 7
58545	Hazen, 1,240	G 5
58638	Hebron, 1,103	G 6
58342	Heimdal, 101	L 4
58547	Hensler, 100	H 5
58639	Hettinger⊙, 1,655	E 8

COUNTIES (continued)

Pembina, 10,728	P 2
Pierce, 6,323	K 3
Ramsey, 12,915	N 3
Ransom, 7,102	P 7
Renville, 3,828	G 2
Richland, 18,089	R 7
Rolette, 11,549	L 2
Sargent, 5,937	P 7
Sheridan, 3,232	K 4
Sioux, 3,632	H 7
Slope, 1,484	C 7
Stark, 19,613	E 6
Steele, 3,749	P 4
Stutsman, 23,550	M 5
Towner, 4,645	M 2
Traill, 9,571	R 5
Walsh, 16,251	P 3
Ward, 58,560	G 3
Wells, 7,847	L 4
Williams, 19,301	C 3

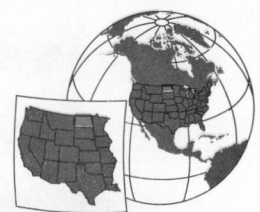

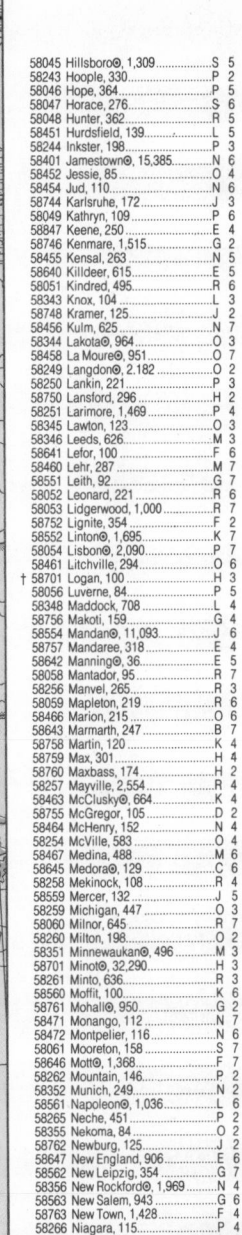

58045 Hillsboro⊙, 1,309.............S 5
58243 Hoople, 330.......................P 2
58046 Hope, 364.........................P 5
58047 Horace, 276.......................S 6
58048 Hunter, 362........................R 5
58451 Hurdsfield, 139....................L 5
58244 Inkster, 198.......................P 3
58401 Jamestown⊙, 15,385............N 6
58452 Jessie, 85..........................O 4
58454 Jud, 110............................N 6
58744 Karlsruhe, 172.....................J 3
58049 Kathryn, 109........................P 6
58847 Keene, 250..........................E 4
58746 Kenmare, 1,515....................G 2
58455 Kensal, 295.........................N 5
58640 Killdeer, 615........................E 5
58051 Kindred, 495.......................S 6
58343 Knox, 104...........................L 3
58748 Kramer, 125.........................J 2
58456 Kulm, 625............................N 7
58344 Lakota⊙, 964.......................O 3
58458 La Moure⊙, 951....................O 7
58249 Langdon⊙, 2,182..................O 2
58250 Lankin, 221..........................P 3
58750 Lansford, 296......................H 2
58251 Larimore, 1,469....................P 4
58345 Lawton, 123.........................O 3
58346 Leeds, 626...........................M 3
58641 Lefor, 100............................F 6
58460 Lehr, 287..............................M 7
58551 Leith, 92..............................G 7
58052 Leonard, 221........................R 6
58053 Lidgerwood, 1,000................R 7
58752 Lignite, 354...........................F 2
58552 Linton⊙, 1,695.....................K 7
58054 Lisbon⊙, 2,090....................R 6
58461 Litchville, 294......................O 6
† 58701 Logan, 100...........................H 3
58056 Luverne, 84..........................P 5
58348 Maddock, 708......................L 4
58756 Makoti, 159..........................G 4
58554 Mandan⊙, 11,093..................H 6
58757 Mandaree, 318.....................E 4
58642 Manning⊙, 36.......................E 5
58058 Mantador, 95........................R 7
58256 Marvel, 265..........................R 4
58059 Mapleton, 219......................R 6
58466 Marion, 215..........................O 6
58643 Marmarth, 247......................B 7
58758 Martin, 120...........................K 4
58759 Max, 301.............................H 4
58760 Maxbass, 174.......................H 2
58257 Mayville, 2,554.....................P 4
58463 McClusky⊙, 664...................K 4
58755 McGregor, 105......................D 2
58464 McHenry, 152.......................N 4
58254 McVille, 583.........................O 4
58467 Medina, 488.........................M 6
58645 Medora⊙, 129......................C 6
58258 Mekinock, 185......................P 4
58559 Mercer, 132..........................J 5
58259 Michigan, 447.......................O 3
58060 Milnor, 645...........................R 7
58260 Milton, 196...........................O 3
58351 Minnewaukan⊙, 496.............M 3
58701 Minot⊙, 32,290....................H 3
58261 Minto, 636............................P 4
58560 Moffit, 100............................K 6
58761 Mohall⊙, 950........................G 2
58471 Monango, 112.......................N 7
58472 Montpelier, 116......................N 6
58061 Mooreton, 158......................S 7
58646 Mott⊙, 1,368........................F 7
58262 Mountain, 146.......................P 3
58352 Munich, 249...........................N 2
58561 Napoleon⊙, 1,036................L 6
58265 Neche, 451............................O 2
58355 Nekoma, 84...........................O 3
58762 Newburg, 125........................J 2
58647 New England, 906.................E 7
58562 New Leipzig, 354....................G 7
58356 New Rockford⊙, 1,969..........N 4
58563 New Salem, 943....................G 6
58763 New Town, 1,428..................E 4
58266 Niagara, 115.........................P 4
58062 Nome, 103.............................P 6

AREA 70,665 sq. mi.
POPULATION 617,761
CAPITAL Bismarck
LARGEST CITY Fargo
HIGHEST POINT White Butte 3,506 ft.
SETTLED IN 1780
ADMITTED TO UNION November 2, 1889
POPULAR NAME Flickertail State; Sioux State
STATE FLOWER Prairie Rose
STATE BIRD Meadowlark

Topography

5,000 m. 2,000 m. 1,000 m. 500 m. 200 m. 100 m. Sea
16,404 ft. 6,562 ft. 3,281 ft. 1,640 ft. 656 ft. 328 ft. Level / Below

MILES
0   50   100

58765 Noonan, 403........................D 2
58267 Northwood, 1,189.................P 4
58473 Nortonville, 90......................N 6
58474 Oakes, 1,742........................O 7
† 58237 Oakwood, 91........................R 3
58357 Oberon, 151.........................M 4
58063 Oriska, 128...........................P 6
58269 Osnabrock, 255....................O 2
58064 Page, 247............................P 5
58769 Palermo, 146........................H 3
58270 Park River, 1,680..................P 3
58770 Parshall, 1,246.....................H 4
58361 Pekin, 120...........................O 4
58271 Pembina, 741.......................R 2
58272 Petersburg, 266....................P 3
58475 Pettibone, 173.......................L 5
† 58545 Pick City, 119.......................G 5
58273 Pisek, 154...........................P 3
58771 Plaza, 291............................G 3
58772 Portal, 251............................R 5
58274 Portland, 534........................P 5
58773 Powers Lake, 523..................F 3
58849 Ray, 776..............................D 3
58649 Reeder, 306.........................E 7
58650 Regent, 344..........................F 7
58275 Reynolds, 236........................R 4
58651 Rhame, 206..........................C 7
58652 Richardton, 799.....................F 6
58565 Riverdale, 600.......................H 4
58478 Robinson, 125.......................L 5
58365 Rocklake, 270........................M 2
58479 Rogers, 96............................O 5
58366 Rolette, 579..........................L 2
58367 Rolla⊙, 1,458........................L 2
58776 Ross, 125.............................E 3
58368 Rugby⊙, 2,889.......................L 3
58067 Rutland, 225.........................P 7

58779 Ryder, 211...........................G 4
58369 Saint John, 367.....................L 2
58276 Saint Thomas, 508................R 2
58480 Sanborn, 255........................O 6
58780 Sanish, 25............................E 4
58372 Sarles, 148...........................N 2
58781 Sawyer, 373.........................H 3
58653 Scranton, 360........................D 7
58568 Selfridge, 346........................J 7
58373 Selz, 110..............................L 4
58654 Sentinel Butte, 125.................C 6
58277 Sharon, 201..........................P 4
58068 Sheldon, 192..........................P 6
58782 Sherwood, 369......................H 2
58374 Sheyenne, 362......................M 4
58569 Shields, 125...........................H 7
58570 Solen, 180..............................J 7
58783 Souris, 151.............................J 2
58655 South Heart, 132...................D 6
58481 Spiritwood, 100.......................N 6
58784 Stanley⊙, 1,581.....................F 3
58571 Stanton⊙, 517......................H 5
58377 Starkweather, 193..................N 3
58482 Steele⊙, 696........................K 6
58573 Strasburg, 642........................K 7
58483 Streeter, 324.........................M 6
58785 Surrey, 361...........................H 3
58484 Sutton, 87............................O 5
58486 Sykeston, 232.......................M 5
58487 Tappen, 294..........................L 6
58656 Taylor, 162............................E 6
58278 Thompson, 291......................R 4
58852 Tioga, 1,667.........................E 3
58379 Tokio, 130............................N 4
58787 Tolley, 163............................G 2
58380 Tolna, 247............................O 4
58071 Tower City, 289.......................P 6

58788 Towner⊙, 870......................K 3
58853 Trenton, 150.........................C 3
58575 Turtle Lake, 712......................J 4
58488 Tuttle, 216.............................L 5
58576 Underwood, 781....................H 5
58789 Upham, 272..........................J 2
58072 Valley City⊙, 7,843...............P 6
58790 Velva, 1,241..........................J 3
58490 Verona, 140...........................O 7
58075 Wahpeton⊙, 7,076...............S 7
58077 Walcott, 175..........................R 6
58281 Wales, 116...........................N 2
58282 Walhalla, 1,471......................P 2
58577 Washburn⊙, 804...................J 5
58854 Watford City⊙, 1,768.............D 4
58078 West Fargo, 5,161.................S 6
‡ 58078 West Fargo Industrial Park,
          104...............................S 6
58793 Westhope, 705......................H 2
58794 White Earth, 128....................E 3
58795 Wildrose, 235.........................D 2
58801 Williston⊙, 11,280................C 3
58384 Willow City, 403......................K 2
58579 Wilton, 695............................J 5
58492 Wimbledon, 337....................O 5
58494 Wing, 223.............................K 5
58495 Wishek, 1,275........................L 7
58496 Woodworth, 139....................M 5
58081 Wyndmere, 516.....................R 7
58386 York, 102.............................L 3
58497 Ypsilanti, 139.........................N 6
58580 Zap, 271...............................G 5
58581 Zeeland, 313..........................L 8

⊙ County seat.
‡ Population of metropolitan area.
† Zip of nearest p.o.
• Multiple zips

North Dakota's wealth springs from her soil. The state has the largest
farms and leads in production of barley, wheat and flaxseed.

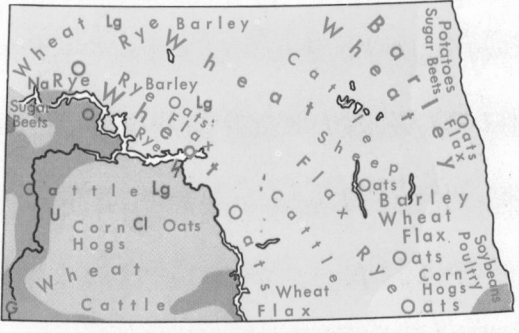

DOMINANT LAND USE

Agriculture,
Industry
and Resources

MAJOR MINERAL
OCCURRENCES

Specialized Wheat

Wheat, General Farming

Wheat, Range Livestock

Livestock, Cash Grain

Sugar Beets, Dry Beans,
Livestock, General Farming

Range Livestock

Water Power

Cl   Clay
G   Natural Gas
Lg   Lignite
Na   Salt
O   Petroleum
U   Uranium

OHIO

SCALE

0   5   10   20   30   40 MI.

0 5 10   20   30   40KM.

State Capitals .... ⊛

County Seats .... ◉

© C.S. HAMMOND & Co., N.Y.

COUNTIES

Adams, 18,957 ... D 8
Allen, 111,144 ... B 4
Ashland, 43,303 ... F 4
Ashtabula, 98,237 ... J 2
Athens, 54,889 ... F 7
Auglaize, 38,602 ... B 4
Belmont, 80,917 ... J 5
Brown, 26,635 ... C 8
Butler, 226,207 ... A 7
Carroll, 21,579 ... H 4
Champaign, 30,491 ... C 5
Clark, 137,115 ... C 6
Clermont, 95,725 ... B 7
Clinton, 31,464 ... C 7
Columbiana, 108,310 ... J 4
Coshocton, 33,486 ... G 5
Crawford, 50,364 ... E 4
Cuyahoga, 1,721,300 ... G 3
Darke, 49,141 ... A 5
Defiance, 36,949 ... A 3
Delaware, 42,908 ... D 5
Erie, 75,909 ... E 3
Fairfield, 73,301 ... E 6
Fayette, 25,461 ... D 6
Franklin, 833,249 ... E 5
Fulton, 33,071 ... B 2
Gallia, 25,239 ... F 8
Geauga, 62,977 ... H 3
Greene, 125,057 ... C 6
Guernsey, 37,665 ... H 5
Hamilton, 924,018 ... A 7
Hancock, 61,217 ... C 3
Hardin, 30,813 ... C 4
Harrison, 17,013 ... H 5
Henry, 27,058 ... B 3
Highland, 28,996 ... C 7
Hocking, 20,322 ... F 6
Holmes, 23,024 ... G 4
Huron, 49,587 ... E 3
Jackson, 27,174 ... E 7
Jefferson, 96,193 ... J 5
Knox, 41,795 ... F 5
Lake, 197,200 ... H 2
Lawrence, 56,868 ... E 8
Licking, 107,799 ... F 5
Logan, 35,072 ... C 5
Lorain, 256,843 ... F 3
Lucas, 484,370 ... C 2
Madison, 28,318 ... D 6
Mahoning, 303,424 ... J 4
Marion, 64,724 ... D 4
Medina, 82,717 ... G 3
Meigs, 19,799 ... F 7
Mercer, 35,265 ... A 4
Miami, 84,342 ... B 5
Monroe, 15,739 ... H 6
Montgomery, 606,148 ... B 6
Morgan, 12,375 ... G 6
Morrow, 21,348 ... E 4
Muskingum, 77,826 ... G 5
Noble, 10,428 ... G 6
Ottawa, 37,099 ... D 2
Paulding, 19,329 ... A 3
Perry, 27,434 ... F 6
Pickaway, 40,071 ... D 6
Pike, 19,114 ... D 7
Portage, 125,868 ... H 3
Preble, 34,719 ... A 6
Putnam, 31,134 ... B 3
Richland, 129,997 ... E 4
Ross, 61,211 ... D 7
Sandusky, 60,983 ... D 3
Scioto, 76,951 ... D 8
Seneca, 60,696 ... D 3
Shelby, 37,748 ... B 5
Stark, 372,210 ... H 4
Summit, 553,371 ... G 3
Trumbull, 232,579 ... J 3
Tuscarawas, 77,211 ... H 5
Union, 23,786 ... D 5
Van Wert, 29,194 ... A 4
Vinton, 9,420 ... E 7
Warren, 84,925 ... B 7
Washington, 57,160 ... H 7
Wayne, 87,123 ... G 4
Williams, 33,669 ... A 2
Wood, 89,722 ... C 3
Wyandot, 21,826 ... D 4

CITIES and TOWNS

Zip *Name/Pop.* *Key*

45101 Aberdeen, 1,165 ... C 8
45810 Ada, 5,309 ... C 4
45001 Addyston, 1,336 ... B 9
43901 Adena, 1,134 ... J 5
* 44301 Akron⊙, 275,425 ... G 3
Akron⊙, ‡679,239 ... G 3
45710 Albany, 899 ... F 7
43001 Alexandria, 588 ... E 5
45812 Alger, 1,071 ... C 4
44601 Alliance, 26,547 ... H 4
43102 Amanda, 788 ... E 6
† 45201 Amberley, 5,574 ... C 9
45102 Amelia, 820 ... D 10
44001 Amherst, 9,902 ... F 3
43903 Amsterdam, 882 ... J 5
44003 Andover, 1,179 ... J 2
45302 Anna, 792 ... B 5
45303 Ansonia, 1,044 ... A 5
45813 Antwerp, 1,735 ... A 3
44606 Apple Creek, 784 ... G 4
44804 Arcadia, 689 ... D 3
45304 Arcanum, 1,993 ... A 6
43502 Archbold, 3,047 ... B 2
45814 Arlington, 1,066 ... C 4
† 45201 Arlington Heights, 1,476 ... C 9
44805 Ashland⊙, 19,872 ... F 4
43003 Ashley, 1,034 ... E 5
44004 Ashtabula, 24,313 ... J 2
43103 Ashville, 1,772 ... E 6
45701 Athens⊙, 23,310 ... F 7
44807 Attica, 1,005 ... E 3
44201 Atwater, 975 ... H 3
44202 Aurora, 6,549 ... H 3
44010 Austinburg, 900 ... J 2
44515 Austintown, 29,393 ... J 3
44011 Avon, 7,214 ... F 3
44012 Avon Lake, 12,261 ... F 2
† 43512 Ayersville, 950 ... B 3
45612 Bainbridge, 1,057 ... D 7
† 43420 Ballville, 1,652 ... D 3
43804 Baltic, 571 ... G 5
43105 Baltimore, 2,418 ... E 6
44203 Barberton, 33,052 ... G 4
43713 Barnesville, 4,292 ... H 6
43905 Barton, 975 ... J 5
45103 Batavia⊙, 1,894 ... B 7
† 44870 Bay View, 798 ... E 3
44140 Bay Village, 18,163 ... G 9
44608 Beach City, 1,133 ... G 4
† 44101 Beachwood, 9,631 ... J 9
45808 Beaverdam, 525 ... C 4
44146 Bedford, 17,552 ... H 9
† 44146 Bedford Heights, 13,063 ... J 9
43906 Bellaire, 9,655 ... J 5
45305 Bellbrook, 1,268 ... C 6
43310 Belle Center, 985 ... C 4
43311 Bellefontaine⊙, 11,255 ... C 5
44811 Bellevue, 8,604 ... E 3
44813 Bellville, 1,685 ... E 4
43718 Belmont, 666 ... J 5
44609 Beloit, 921 ... J 4
45714 Belpre, 7,189 ... G 7
44017 Berea, 22,396 ... G 10
43908 Bergholz, 914 ... J 4
44814 Berlin Heights, 828 ... F 3
45106 Bethel, 2,214 ... B 8
43719 Bethesda, 1,157 ... H 5
44815 Bettsville, 833 ... D 3
45715 Beverly, 1,396 ... G 6
43209 Bexley, 14,888 ... E 6
45107 Blanchester, 3,080 ... B 7
44817 Bloomdale, 727 ... D 3
43106 Bloomingburg, 895 ... D 6
44818 Bloomville, 884 ... D 3
† 45201 Blue Ash, 8,324 ... C 9
45817 Bluffton, 2,935 ... C 4
44512 Boardman, 30,852 ... J 3
44612 Bolivar, 1,084 ... G 4
† 44264 Boston Heights, 846 ... J 10
45306 Botkins, 1,057 ... B 5
43402 Bowling Green⊙, 21,760 ... C 3
45308 Bradford, 2,163 ... B 5
43406 Bradner, 1,140 ... C 3
† 44101 Bratenahl, 1,613 ... H 9
44141 Brecksville, 9,137 ... H 10
43107 Bremen, 1,413 ... F 6
44613 Brewster, 2,020 ... G 4
† 44215 Briarwood Beach, 508 ... G 3
43912 Bridgeport, 3,001 ... J 5
† 45201 Bridgetown, 13,352 ... B 9
43913 Brilliant, 2,178 ... J 5
44240 Brimfield, 950 ... H 3
44402 Bristolville, 900 ... J 3
† 44141 Broadview Heights, 11,463 ... H 10
44403 Brookfield, 1,200 ... J 3
44144 Brooklyn, 13,142 ... H 9
† 44131 Brooklyn Heights, 1,527 ... H 9
44142 Brook Park, 30.774 ... G 9
† 43912 Brookside, 939 ... J 5
45309 Brookville, 4,403 ... B 6
44212 Brunswick, 15,852 ... G 3
43506 Bryan⊙, 7,008 ... A 3
45716 Buchtel, 592 ... F 7
43008 Buckeye Lake, 2,961 ... F 6
44820 Bucyrus⊙, 13,111 ... E 4
43722 Buffalo, 710 ... G 6
† 45680 Burlington, 900 ... F 9
44021 Burton, 1,214 ... H 3
44822 Butler, 1,052 ... F 4
43723 Byesville, 2,097 ... G 6
43907 Cadiz⊙, 3,060 ... J 5
45820 Cairo, 587 ... B 4
43920 Calcutta, 2,900 ... J 4
43724 Caldwell⊙, 2,082 ... G 6
43314 Caledonia, 792 ... D 4
43725 Cambridge⊙, 13,656 ... G 5
45311 Camden, 1,507 ... A 6
44405 Campbell, 12,577 ... J 3
45111 Camp Dennison, 550 ... D 9
44614 Canal Fulton, 2,367 ... H 4
43110 Canal Winchester, 2,412 ... E 6
44406 Canfield, 4,997 ... J 3
* 44701 Canton⊙, 110,053 ... H 4
Canton, ‡372,210 ... H 4
43315 Cardington, 1,730 ... E 5
43316 Carey, 3,523 ... D 4
45005 Carlisle, 3,821 ... B 6
43112 Carroll, 614 ... E 6
44615 Carrollton⊙, 2,817 ... J 4
44824 Castalia, 1,045 ... E 3
45314 Cedarville, 2,342 ... C 6
45822 Celina⊙, 7,779 ... A 4
43011 Centerburg, 1,038 ... E 5
45459 Centerville, 10,333 ... B 6
44022 Chagrin Falls, 4,848 ... J 9
44024 Chardon⊙, 3,991 ... H 2
45719 Chauncey, 1,117 ... F 7
† 45202 Cherry Grove, 850 ... C 10
45619 Chesapeake, 1,364 ... E 9
44026 Chesterland, 11,500 ... H 2
† 45211 Cheviot, 11,135 ... B 9
45601 Chillicothe⊙, 24,842 ... E 7
45389 Christiansburg, 724 ... C 5
* 45201 Cincinnati⊙, 452,524 ... B 9
Cincinnati, ‡1,384,851 ... B 9
43113 Circleville⊙, 11,687 ... D 6
45113 Clarksville, 574 ... C 7
45315 Clayton, 773 ... B 6
* 44101 Cleveland⊙, 750,903 ... H 9
Cleveland, ‡2,074,194 ... H 9
44118 Cleveland Heights, 60,767 ... H 9
45002 Cleves, 2,044 ... B 9
44216 Clinton, 1,335 ... G 4
43410 Clyde, 5,503 ... E 3
† 45638 Coal Grove, 2,759 ... E 9
45621 Coalton, 550 ... E 7
45828 Coldwater, 3,533 ... A 5
† 44034 Colebrook, 700 ... J 2
44028 Columbia Station, 518 ... G 10
44408 Columbiana, 4,959 ... J 4
* 43201 Columbus (cap.)⊙, 539,677 ... E 6
Columbus, ‡916,228 ... E 6
45830 Columbus Grove, 2,290 ... B 4

(continued on following page)

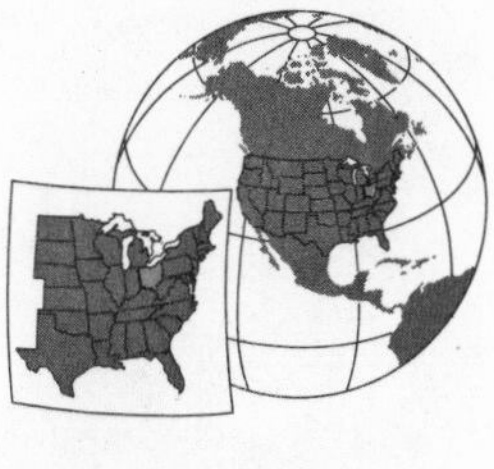

AREA 41,222 sq. mi.
POPULATION 10,652,017
CAPITAL Columbus
LARGEST CITY Cleveland
HIGHEST POINT Campbell Hill 1,550 ft.
SETTLED IN 1788
ADMITTED TO UNION March 1, 1803
POPULAR NAME Buckeye State
STATE FLOWER Scarlet Carnation
STATE BIRD Cardinal

Topography

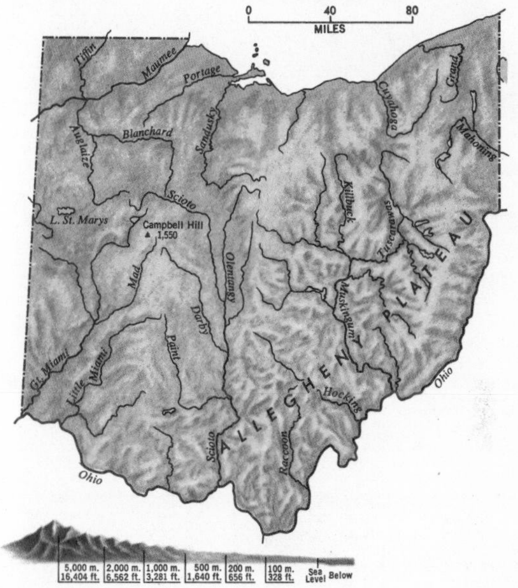
0
40
80
MILES
Tiffin
Maumee
Portage
Sandusky
Cuyahoga
Grand
Mahoning
Auglaize
Blanchard
Scioto
L. St. Marys
Campbell Hill
1,550
Killbuck
Tuscarawas
Olentangy
Mad
Darby
Muskingum
Paint
Gt. Miami
Little Miami
Hocking
Scioto
Raccoon
Ohio
Ohio
ALLEGHENY PLATEAU
5,000 m. 16,404 ft.
2,000 m. 6,562 ft.
1,000 m. 3,281 ft.
500 m. 1,640 ft.
200 m. 656 ft.
100 m. 328 ft.
Sea Level
Below

Agriculture, Industry and Resources

DOMINANT LAND USE

- Hogs, Soft Winter Wheat
- Livestock, Dairy, Soybeans, Cash Grain
- Dairy, General Farming
- General Farming, Livestock, Tobacco
- Fruit, Truck and Mixed Farming
- Forests
- Urban Areas

MAJOR MINERAL OCCURRENCES

- C Coal
- Cl Clay
- G Natural Gas
- Gp Gypsum
- Ls Limestone
- Na Salt
- O Petroleum
- Ss Sandstone

Major Industrial Areas

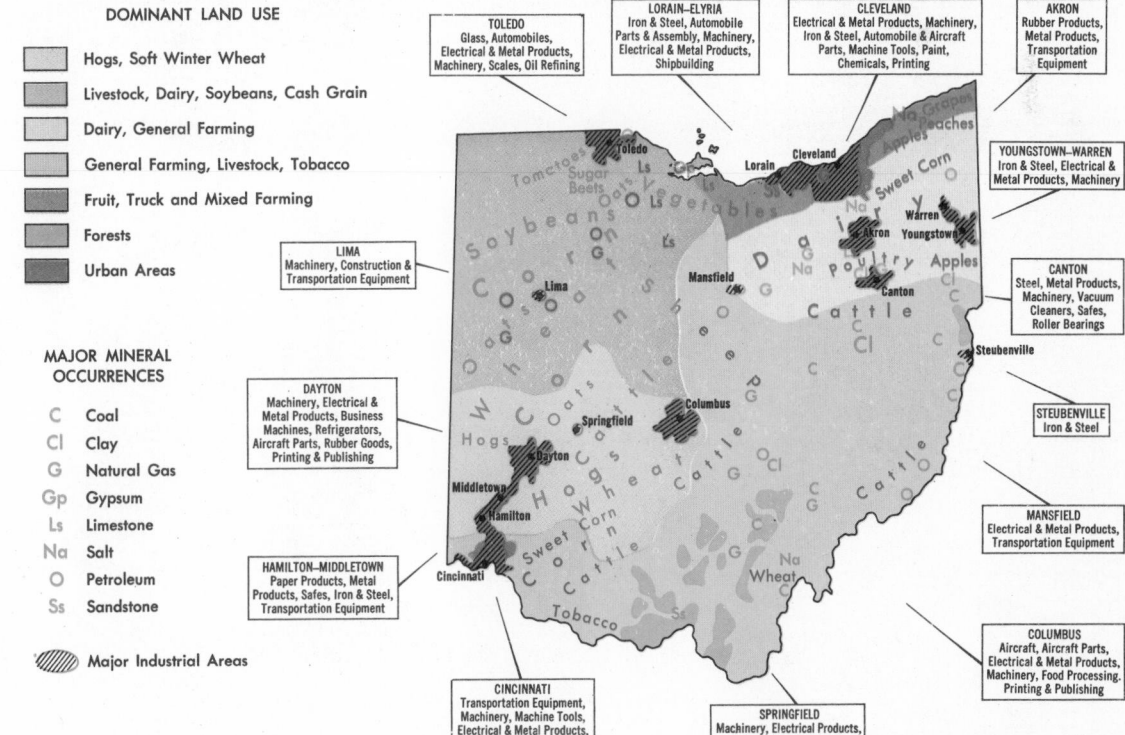

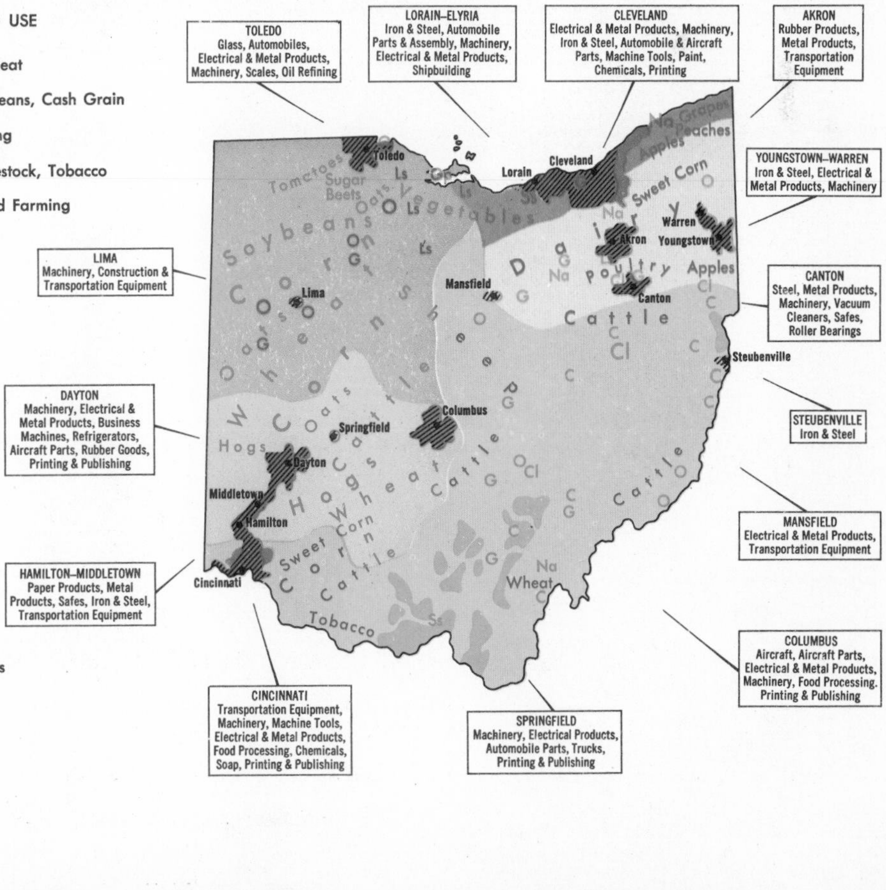
TOLEDO
Glass, Automobiles, Electrical & Metal Products, Machinery, Scales, Oil Refining
LORAIN–ELYRIA
Iron & Steel, Automobile Parts & Assembly, Machinery, Electrical & Metal Products, Shipbuilding
CLEVELAND
Electrical & Metal Products, Machinery, Iron & Steel, Automobile & Aircraft Parts, Machine Tools, Paint, Chemicals, Printing
AKRON
Rubber Products, Metal Products, Transportation Equipment
YOUNGSTOWN–WARREN
Iron & Steel, Electrical & Metal Products, Machinery
LIMA
Machinery, Construction & Transportation Equipment
CANTON
Steel, Metal Products, Machinery, Vacuum Cleaners, Safes, Roller Bearings
DAYTON
Machinery, Electrical & Metal Products, Business Machines, Refrigerators, Aircraft Parts, Rubber Goods, Printing & Publishing
STEUBENVILLE
Iron & Steel
MANSFIELD
Electrical & Metal Products, Transportation Equipment
HAMILTON–MIDDLETOWN
Paper Products, Metal Products, Safes, Iron & Steel, Transportation Equipment
COLUMBUS
Aircraft, Aircraft Parts, Electrical & Metal Products, Machinery, Food Processing. Printing & Publishing
CINCINNATI
Transportation Equipment, Machinery, Machine Tools, Electrical & Metal Products, Food Processing, Chemicals, Soap, Printing & Publishing
SPRINGFIELD
Machinery, Electrical Products, Automobile Parts, Trucks, Printing & Publishing
Toledo
Lorain
Cleveland
Akron
Warren
Youngstown
Canton
Lima
Mansfield
Steubenville
Columbus
Springfield
Dayton
Middletown
Hamilton
Cincinnati
Tomatoes
Sugar Beets
Soybeans
Oats
Vegetables
Sweet Corn
Apples
Peaches
Grapes
Dairy
Poultry
Cattle
Hogs
Wheat
Tobacco

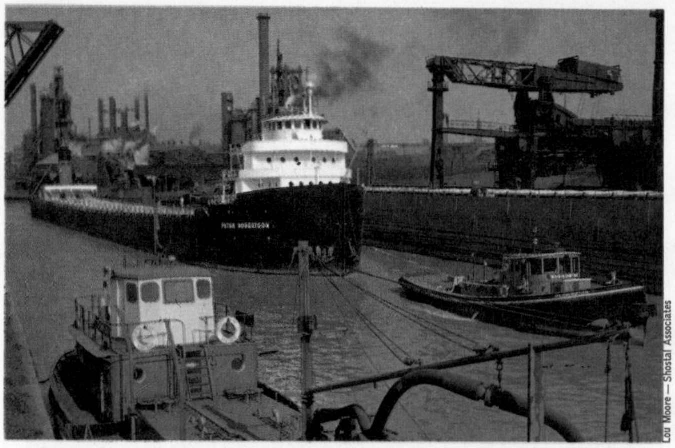

Reminiscent of children's book illustrations, the tugboat "Washington" guides ore-carrier "Peter Robertson" through Cleveland's Industrial Flats, past a Milwaukee fuel tanker.

Lou Moore — Shostal Associates

44030 Conneaut, 14,552 J 2
45831 Continental, 1,185 B 3
45832 Convoy, 991 A 4
45723 Coolville, 672 G 7
43730 Corning, 838 F 6
44410 Cortland, 2,525 J 3
43812 Coshocton⊙, 13,747 G 5
† 45201 Covedale, 6,639 B 10
45318 Covington, 2,575 B 5
† 44429 Craig Beach, 1,451 H 3
44827 Crestline, 5,947 E 4
44217 Creston, 1,632 G 3
45806 Cridersville, 1,103 B 4
43731 Crooksville, 2,828 F 6
† 45341 Crystal Lakes, 5,851 C 6
* 44221 Cuyahoga Falls, 49,678 G 3
† 44101 Cuyahoga Heights, 866 H 9
43413 Cygnet, 629 C 3
44618 Dalton, 1,177 G 4
43014 Danville, 1,025 F 5
43123 Darbydale, 743 D 6
* 45401 Dayton⊙, 243,601 B 6
Dayton, ‡850,266 B 6
44411 Deerfield, 800 H 3
45236 Deer Park, 7,415 C 9
43512 Defiance⊙, 16,281 B 3
43318 Degraff, 1,117 C 5
43015 Delaware⊙, 15,008 E 5
45833 Delphos, 7,608 B 4
43515 Delta, 2,544 B 2
44621 Dennison, 3,506 H 5
† 45202 Dent, 800 B 9
43516 Deshler, 1,938 C 3
45750 Devola, 1,989 H 7
43917 Dillonvale, 1,095 J 5
44622 Dover, 11,516 G 4
44230 Doylestown, 2,373 G 4
43821 Dresden, 1,516 G 5
43017 Dublin, 681 D 5
43734 Duncan Falls, 900 G 6
45836 Dunkirk, 1,036 C 4
44730 East Canton, 1,631 H 4
44112 East Cleveland, 39,600 H 9
44094 Eastlake, 19,690 J 8
43920 East Liverpool, 20,020 J 4
44413 East Palestine, 5,604 J 4
44626 East Sparta, 959 H 4
45320 Eaton⊙, 6,020 A 6
† 44035 Eaton Estates, 2,076 G 3
43517 Edgerton, 2,126 A 3
44004 Edgewood, 3,437 J 2
43320 Edison, 569 E 4
43518 Edon, 803 A 2
45807 Elida, 1,211 B 4
43416 Elmore, 1,316 D 3
45216 Elmwood Place, 3,525 B 9
* 44035 Elyria⊙, 53,427 F 3
45322 Englewood, 7,885 B 6
45323 Enon, 1,929 C 6
44117 Euclid, 71,552 J 9
† 45201 Evendale, 1,967 C 9
45042 Excello, 900 B 7
45324 Fairborn, 32,267 B 6
† 45201 Fairfax, 2,705 C 9
45014 Fairfield, 14,680 A 7
44313 Fairlawn, 6,102 G 3
44077 Fairport Harbor, 3,665 H 2
44126 Fairview Park, 21,681 G 9
45325 Farmersville, 865 A 6
43521 Fayette, 1,175 B 2
45120 Felicity, 786 B 8
45840 Findlay⊙, 35,800 C 3
45326 Fletcher, 539 B 5
43977 Flushing, 1,207 J 5
45843 Forest, 1,535 C 4
45405 Forest Park, 15,139 B 9
† 45202 Forestville, 950 C 10
45844 Fort Jennings, 533 B 4
45845 Fort Loramie, 744 B 5
† 45401 Fort McKinley, 11,536 B 6
45846 Fort Recovery, 1,348 A 5
† 45801 Fort Shawnee, 3,436 B 4
44830 Fostoria, 16,037 D 3
45628 Frankfort, 949 D 7
45005 Franklin, 10,075 B 6
45629 Franklin Furnace, 975 E 8
43822 Frazeysburg, 941 F 5
44627 Fredericksburg, 601 G 4
43019 Fredericktown, 1,935 F 5
43420 Fremont⊙, 18,490 D 3
45630 Friendship, 600 D 8
43230 Gahanna, 12,400 E 5
44833 Galion, 13,123 E 4
45631 Gallipolis⊙, 7,490 F 8
43022 Gambier, 1,571 F 5
44125 Garfield Heights, 41,417 J 9
44231 Garrettsville, 1,718 H 3
44040 Gates Mills, 2,378 J 9
44041 Geneva, 6,449 J 2
44043 Geneva-on-the-Lake, 877 H 2
43430 Genoa, 2,139 D 2
45121 Georgetown⊙, 2,949 C 8
45327 Germantown, 4,088 B 6
45328 Gettysburg, 526 A 5
43431 Gibsonburg, 2,585 D 3
44420 Girard, 14,119 J 3
45848 Glandorf, 732 B 3
45246 Glendale, 2,690 C 9
† 44139 Glenwillow, 526 J 10
45732 Glouster, 2,121 F 6
44629 Gnadenhutten, 1,466 G 5
† 45201 Golf Manor, 5,170 C 9
45122 Goshen, 1,174 B 7
44044 Grafton, 1,771 F 3
43522 Grand Rapids, 976 C 3
44045 Grand River, 613 H 2
† 43201 Grandview Heights, 8,460 D 6
43023 Granville, 3,963 E 5
45330 Gratis, 621 A 6
43322 Green Camp, 537 D 4
45123 Greenfield, 4,780 D 7
45218 Greenhills, 6,092 B 9
44232 Greensburg, 950 G 4
44836 Green Springs, 1,279 E 3
44630 Greentown, 1,150 H 4
45331 Greenville⊙, 12,380 A 5
44837 Greenwich, 1,473 E 3
45239 Groesbeck, 5,000 B 9
43123 Grove City, 13,911 D 6
43125 Groveport, 2,490 E 6
45849 Grover Hill, 536 B 3
45634 Hamden, 953 F 7
45130 Hamersville, 567 C 8
* 45011 Hamilton⊙, 67,865 A 7
Hamilton-Middletown, ‡226,207 A 7
43524 Hamler, 681 B 3
43931 Hannibal, 550 J 6
† 43055 Hanover, 626 F 5
43126 Harrisburg, 556 D 6
45030 Harrison, 4,408 A 9
45850 Harrod, 533 C 4
† 44085 Hartsgrove, 775 J 2
44632 Hartville, 1,752 H 4
43525 Haskins, 549 C 3
43127 Haydenville, 650 F 7
43055 Heath, 6,768 F 5
43025 Hebron, 1,699 E 6
43526 Hicksville, 3,461 A 3
† 44143 Highland Heights, 5,926 J 9
43026 Hilliard, 8,369 D 5
45133 Hillsboro⊙, 5,584 C 7
44234 Hiram, 1,484 H 3
43527 Holgate, 1,541 B 3
43528 Holland, 1,108 C 2
45033 Hooven, 550 A 9
43976 Hopedale, 916 J 5
44425 Hubbard, 8,583 J 3
45424 Huber Heights, 18,943 B 6
44236 Hudson, 3,933 H 3
† 44022 Hunting Valley, 797 J 9
44839 Huron, 6,896 E 3
44131 Independence, 7,034 H 9
† 45201 Indian Hill, 5,651 C 9
43932 Irondale, 602 J 4
45638 Ironton⊙, 15,030 E 8
45640 Jackson⊙, 6,843 E 7
45334 Jackson Center, 1,119 B 5
45740 Jacksonville, 545 F 7
45335 Jamestown, 1,790 C 6
44047 Jefferson⊙, 2,472 J 2
† 43162 Jefferson (West Jefferson), 3,664 D 6
43128 Jeffersonville, 1,031 C 6
44840 Jeromesville, 559 F 4
43986 Jewett, 901 H 5
43031 Johnstown, 3,208 E 5
43748 Junction City, 732 F 6
45853 Kalida, 900 B 4
44240 Kent, 28,183 H 3
43326 Kenton⊙, 8,315 C 4
45429 Kettering, 69,599 B 6
44637 Killbuck, 893 G 5
45034 Kings Mills, 800 B 7
45644 Kingston, 1,157 E 7
44048 Kingsville, 1,129 J 2
44428 Kinsman, 900 J 3
43033 Kirkersville, 578 E 6
44094 Kirtland, 5,530 H 2
43951 Lafferty, 900 H 5
44050 Lagrange, 1,074 F 3
44250 Lakemore, 2,708 H 3
43440 Lakeside, 850 E 2
43331 Lakeview, 1,026 C 4
44107 Lakewood, 70,173 G 9
43130 Lancaster⊙, 32,911 E 6
43934 Lansing, 950 J 5
43332 La Rue, 867 D 4
43135 Laurelville, 624 E 7
† 45501 Lawrenceville, 687 C 6
44430 Leavittsburg, 4,979 J 3
45036 Lebanon⊙, 7,934 B 7
45135 Leesburg, 984 D 7
44431 Leetonia, 2,342 J 4
45856 Leipsic, 2,072 C 3
44251 Leroy, 715 G 3
45338 Lewisburg, 1,553 A 6
44904 Lexington, 2,972 E 4
43532 Liberty Center, 1,007 B 3
* 45801 Lima⊙, 53,734 B 4
Lima, ‡171,472 B 4
† 45201 Lincoln Heights, 6,099 C 9
43442 Lindsey, 652 D 3
44432 Lisbon⊙, 3,521 J 4
44253 Litchfield, 650 F 3
43136 Lithopolis, 705 E 6
45742 Little Hocking, 520 G 7
45215 Lockland, 5,288 C 9
44254 Lodi, 2,399 F 3
43138 Logan⊙, 6,269 F 6
43140 London⊙, 6,481 C 6
* 44052 Lorain, 78,185 F 3
Lorain-Elyria, ‡256,843 F 3
44842 Loudonville, 2,865 F 4
44641 Louisville, 6,298 H 4
45140 Loveland, 7,144 D 9
45744 Lowell, 852 H 6
44436 Lowellville, 1,836 J 3
44843 Lucas, 771 F 4
45648 Lucasville, 900 E 8
43443 Luckey, 996 D 3
45142 Lynchburg, 1,186 C 7
44124 Lyndhurst, 19,749 J 9
43533 Lyons, 630 B 2
44056 Macedonia, 6,375 J 10
† 45202 Mack, 5,000 B 9
45243 Madeira, 6,713 C 9
44057 Madison, 1,678 H 2
44643 Magnolia, 1,064 H 4
43758 Malta, 1,017 G 6
44644 Malvern, 1,256 H 4
45144 Manchester, 2,195 C 8
* 44901 Mansfield⊙, 55,047 F 4
Mansfield, ‡129,997 F 4
44255 Mantua, 1,199 H 3
44137 Maple Heights, 34,093 H 9
† 43440 Marblehead, 726 E 2
45860 Maria Stein, 950 A 5
45227 Mariemont, 4,540 C 9
45750 Marietta⊙, 16,861 G 7
43302 Marion⊙, 38,646 D 4
44645 Marshallville, 693 G 4
43935 Martins Ferry, 10,757 J 5
43040 Marysville⊙, 5,744 D 5
45040 Mason, 5,677 B 7
44646 Massillon, 32,539 H 4
44438 Masury, 2,060 J 3
45069 Maud, 550 B 7
43537 Maumee, 15,937 C 2
† 44121 Mayfield, 3,548 J 9
† 44101 Mayfield Heights, 22,139 J 9
45651 McArthur⊙, 1,543 F 7
43534 McClure, 699 C 3
45858 McComb, 1,329 C 3
43756 McConnelsville⊙, 2,107 G 6
44437 McDonald, 3,177 J 3
45859 McGuffey, 704 C 4
43044 Mechanicsburg, 1,686 D 5
44256 Medina⊙, 10,913 G 3
45862 Mendon, 672 A 4
44060 Mentor, 36,912 H 2
44060 Mentor-on-the-Lake, 6,517 G 2
43540 Metamora, 594 C 2
45342 Miamisburg, 14,797 B 6
45041 Miamitown, 800 A 9
44652 Middlebranch, 600 H 4
† 44017 Middleburg Heights, 12,367 G 10
44062 Middlefield, 1,726 H 3
45863 Middle Point, 543 B 4
45760 Middleport, 2,784 F 7
45042 Middletown, 48,767 A 6
44653 Midvale, 636 H 5
44846 Milan, 1,405 E 3
45150 Milford, 4,828 D 9
43045 Milford Center, 753 D 5
43447 Millbury, 771 D 2
44654 Millersburg⊙, 2,979 F 4
43046 Millersport, 777 E 6
45013 Millville, 697 A 7
44656 Mineral City, 860 H 4
44440 Mineral Ridge, 1,500 J 3
44657 Minerva, 4,359 H 4
† 43201 Minerva Park, 1,402 E 5
43938 Mingo Junction, 5,278 J 5
45865 Minster, 2,405 B 5
44260 Mogadore, 3,858 H 3
45050 Monroe, 3,492 B 7
44847 Monroeville, 1,455 E 3
45242 Montgomery, 5,683 C 9
43543 Montpelier, 4,184 A 2
45439 Moraine, 4,898 B 6
† 44022 Moreland Hills, 3,000 J 9
45152 Morrow, 1,486 B 7
43338 Mount Gilead⊙, 2,971 E 4
45231 Mount Healthy, 7,446 B 9
45154 Mount Orab, 1,306 C 7
43939 Mount Pleasant, 635 J 5
43143 Mount Sterling, 1,536 D 6
43050 Mount Vernon⊙, 13,373 E 5
43340 Mount Victory, 633 D 4
44262 Munroe Falls, 3,794 H 3
43144 Murray City, 562 F 6
43545 Napoleon⊙, 7,791 B 3
44662 Navarre, 1,607 H 4
43940 Neffs, 900 J 5
44441 Negley, 600 J 4
45764 Nelsonville, 4,812 F 7
44849 Nevada, 917 D 4
43054 New Albany, 513 E 5
43055 Newark⊙, 41,836 F 5
45662 New Boston, 3,325 E 8
45869 New Bremen, 2,185 B 5
† 44101 Newburgh Heights, 3,396 H 9
† 45201 New Burlington, 900 B 9
45344 New Carlisle, 6,112 C 6
43832 Newcomerstown, 4,155 G 5
43762 New Concord, 2,318 G 6
43145 New Holland, 796 D 6
45871 New Knoxville, 852 B 5
45345 New Lebanon, 4,248 B 6
43764 New Lexington⊙, 4,921 F 6
44851 New London, 2,336 F 3
45346 New Madison, 959 A 6
45767 New Matamoras, 940 J 6
45011 New Miami, 3,273 A 7
44442 New Middletown, 1,664 J 4
45347 New Paris, 1,692 A 6
44663 New Philadelphia⊙, 15,184 G 5
45768 Newport, 975 H 7
45157 New Richmond, 2,650 B 8
43766 New Straitsville, 947 F 6
44444 Newton Falls, 5,378 J 3
45244 Newtown, 2,047 C 10
45159 New Vienna, 849 C 7
44854 New Washington, 1,251 E 4
44445 New Waterford, 735 J 4
44446 Niles, 21,581 J 3
45872 North Baltimore, 3,143 C 3
45052 North Bend, 638 B 9
44450 North Bloomfield, 650 J 3
44720 North Canton, 15,228 H 4
45239 North College Hill, 12,363 B 9
44855 North Fairfield, 540 E 3
44067 Northfield, 1,089 J 10
44707 North Industry, 2,000 H 4
44068 North Kingsville, 2,458 J 2
43060 North Lewisburg, 840 C 5
44452 North Lima, 800 J 4
44070 North Olmsted, 34,861 G 9
† 44081 North Perry, 851 H 2
† 44101 North Randall, 1,212 H 9
44035 North Ridgeville, 13,152 F 3
44133 North Royalton, 12,807 H 10
† 43601 Northwood, 4,222 D 2
† 43701 North Zanesville, 3,399 G 6
44203 Norton, 12,308 G 4
44857 Norwalk⊙, 13,386 E 3
45212 Norwood, 30,420 C 9
43449 Oak Harbor, 2,807 D 2
45656 Oak Hill, 1,642 E 8
45873 Oakwood, 10,095 B 6
45873 Oakwood, 3,127 H 9
45873 Oakwood, 804 B 3
44074 Oberlin, 8,761 F 3
43207 Obetz, 2,248 E 6
45874 Ohio City, 816 A 4
44138 Olmsted Falls, 2,504 G 9
44862 Ontario, 4,345 E 4
† 44101 Orange, 2,112 J 9
43616 Oregon, 16,563 D 2
44667 Orrville, 7,408 G 4
44076 Orwell, 965 J 2
45875 Ottawa⊙, 3,622 B 3
† 43601 Ottawa Hills, 4,270 C 2
45876 Ottoville, 914 B 4
45160 Owensville, 707 B 7
45056 Oxford, 15,868 A 6
44077 Painesville⊙, 16,536 H 2
45877 Pandora, 857 C 4
44080 Parkman, 750 H 3
44129 Parma, 100,216 H 9
† 44129 Parma Heights, 27,192 G 9
43062 Pataskala, 1,831 E 5
45879 Paulding⊙, 2,983 A 3
45880 Payne, 1,351 A 3
45660 Peebles, 1,629 D 8
43450 Pemberville, 1,301 C 3
44264 Peninsula, 692 G 3
44124 Pepper Pike, 5,933 J 9
44081 Perry, 917 H 2
43551 Perrysburg, 7,693 C 2
44864 Perrysville, 752 F 4
45354 Phillipsburg, 831 B 6
43771 Philo, 846 G 6
43147 Pickerington, 696 E 6
45661 Piketon, 1,347 E 7
43554 Pioneer, 968 A 2
45356 Piqua, 20,741 B 5
43064 Plain City, 2,254 D 5
45359 Pleasant Hill, 1,025 B 5
43148 Pleasantville, 754 F 6
44865 Plymouth, 1,993 E 4
† 45042 Poasttown, 650 B 6
44514 Poland, 3,097 J 3
45769 Pomeroy⊙, 2,672 G 7
43452 Port Clinton⊙, 7,202 E 2
45770 Portland, 550 G 7
45662 Portsmouth⊙, 27,633 D 8
43837 Port Washington, 550 G 5
43942 Powhatan Point, 2,167 J 6
45669 Proctorville, 881 F 9
43342 Prospect, 1,031 D 5
43456 Put-in-Bay, 135 E 2
43773 Quaker City, 510 H 6
43343 Quincy, 686 C 5
45771 Racine, 583 G 8
43066 Radnor, 950 D 5
44265 Randolph, 900 H 3
44266 Ravenna⊙, 11,780 H 3
43943 Rayland, 617 J 5
45215 Reading, 14,303 C 9
† 45202 Remington, 600 C 9
45773 Reno, 576 H 7
† 43412 Reno Beach, 1,049 D 2
44867 Republic, 705 D 3
43068 Reynoldsburg, 13,921 E 6
44286 Richfield, 3,228 G 3
43944 Richmond, 777 J 5
† 44045 Richmond (Grand River), 613 H 2
45673 Richmond Dale, 950 E 7
44143 Richmond Heights, 9,220 H 9
43344 Richwood, 2,072 D 5
45674 Rio Grande, 814 F 8
45167 Ripley, 2,745 C 8
43457 Risingsun, 730 C 3
44270 Rittman, 6,308 G 4
† 43085 Riverlea, 558 D 5
44670 Robertsville, 600 H 4
44084 Rock Creek, 731 J 2
45882 Rockford, 1,207 A 4
44116 Rocky River, 22,958 G 9
44085 Rome, 648 J 2
44272 Rootstown, 900 H 3
† 45662 Rosemount, 1,786 D 8
43777 Roseville, 1,767 F 6
45061 Ross (Venice), 1,661 B 9
43460 Rossford, 5,302 C 2
45236 Rossmoyne, 2,900 C 9
† 43943 Rush Run, 560 J 5
43347 Rushsylvania, 526 C 5
43348 Russells Point, 1,104 C 5
45775 Rutland, 663 F 7
45169 Sabina, 2,160 C 7
† 44067 Sagamore Hills, 4,100 J 10
45217 Saint Bernard, 6,080 B 9
43950 Saint Clairsville⊙, 4,754 J 5
45883 Saint Henry, 1,276 A 5
45885 Saint Marys, 7,699 B 4
43072 Saint Paris, 1,646 C 5
44460 Salem, 14,186 J 4
43945 Salineville, 1,686 J 4
44870 Sandusky⊙, 32,674 E 3
44671 Sandyville, 543 H 4
45171 Sardinia, 824 C 7
43946 Sardis, 700 J 6
43988 Scio, 1,002 H 5
† 45662 Sciotodale, 950 E 8
45679 Seaman, 866 C 8
44672 Sebring, 4,954 H 4
† 44101 Seven Hills, 12,700 H 9
45062 Seven Mile, 699 A 7
44273 Seville, 1,402 G 3
43947 Shadyside, 5,070 J 6
44120 Shaker Heights, 36,306 H 9
45241 Sharonville, 10,985 C 9
43782 Shawnee, 914 F 6
† 44052 Sheffield, 1,730 F 3
44054 Sheffield Lake, 8,734 F 3
44875 Shelby, 9,847 E 4
43556 Sherwood, 784 A 3
44878 Shiloh, 817 E 4
44676 Shreve, 1,635 F 4
45365 Sidney⊙, 16,332 B 5
† 44221 Silver Lake, 3,637 G 3
† 45201 Silverton, 6,588 C 9
43948 Smithfield, 1,245 J 5
44677 Smithville, 1,278 G 4
44139 Solon, 11,519 J 9
43783 Somerset, 1,417 F 6
† 44001 South Amherst, 2,913 F 3
† 43103 South Bloomfield, 610 D 6
45368 South Charleston, 1,500 C 6
44121 South Euclid, 29,579 H 9
45065 South Lebanon, 3,014 B 7
45680 South Point, 2,243 E 9
† 44022 South Russell, 2,673 H 3
45369 South Vienna, 545 C 6
45682 South Webster, 825 E 8
43701 South Zanesville, 1,436 F 6
44275 Spencer, 758 F 3
45887 Spencerville, 2,241 B 4
45066 Springboro, 2,799 B 6
45246 Springdale, 8,127 B 9
* 45501 Springfield⊙, 81,926 C 6
Springfield, ‡157,115 C 6
45370 Spring Valley, 667 C 6
44276 Sterling, 550 G 4
43952 Steubenville⊙, 30,771 J 5
Steubenville-Weirton, ‡165,627 J 5
43154 Stoutsville, 573 E 6
44224 Stow, 19,847 H 3
44680 Strasburg, 1,874 G 4
44240 Streetsboro, 7,966 H 3
44136 Strongsville, 15,182 G 10
44471 Struthers, 15,343 J 3
43557 Stryker, 1,296 B 3
† 44260 Suffield, 650 H 3
44681 Sugarcreek, 1,771 G 5
43074 Sunbury, 2,512 E 5
43558 Swanton, 2,927 C 2
44882 Sycamore, 1,096 D 4
43560 Sylvania, 12,031 C 2
45779 Syracuse, 684 G 7
44278 Tallmadge, 15,274 H 3
† 43771 Taylorsville (Philo), 846 G 6
45174 Terrace Park, 2,266 D 9
45780 The Plains, 1,568 F 7
43076 Thornville, 679 F 6
44883 Tiffin⊙, 21,596 D 3
43963 Tiltonsville, 2,123 J 5
† 44094 Timberlake, 964 J 8
45371 Tipp City, 5,090 B 6
† 45245 Tobasco, 950 C 10
* 43601 Toledo⊙, 383,818 D 2
Toledo, ‡692,571 D 2
43964 Toronto, 7,705 J 5
45067 Trenton, 5,278 B 7
45782 Trimble, 542 F 7
45373 Troy⊙, 17,186 B 5
44682 Tuscarawas, 830 H 5
44087 Twinsburg, 6,432 J 10
44683 Uhrichsville, 5,731 H 5
45322 Union, 3,654 B 6
† 47390 Union City, 1,808 A 5
44685 Uniontown, 875 H 4
44118 University Heights, 17,055 H 9
43221 Upper Arlington, 38,630 D 6
43351 Upper Sandusky⊙, 5,645 D 4
43078 Urbana⊙, 11,237 C 5
† 43123 Urbancrest, 754 D 6
43080 Utica, 1,977 F 5
† 43201 Valley View, 909 D 6
† 44101 Valley View, 1,422 H 9
45377 Vandalia, 10,796 B 6
45890 Vanlue, 539 C 4
45891 Van Wert⊙, 11,320 A 4
44870 Venice, 1,661 B 9
44089 Vermilion, 9,872 F 3
45378 Verona, 593 A 6
45380 Versailles, 2,441 A 5
44473 Vienna, 1,200 J 3
† 44473 Vienna (South Vienna), 545 C 6
44281 Wadsworth, 13,142 G 3
† 44094 Waite Hill, 514 H 8
44889 Wakeman, 514 F 3
43465 Walbridge, 3,208 C 2
44687 Walnut Creek, 550 G 4
† 44146 Walton Hills, 2,508 J 10
45895 Wapakoneta⊙, 7,324 B 4
* 44481 Warren⊙, 63,494 J 3
† 44100 Warrensville Heights, 18,925 H 9
43844 Warsaw, 725 G 5
43160 Washington Court House⊙, 12,495 D 6
44490 Washingtonville, 747 J 4
45786 Waterford, 600 G 6
43566 Waterville, 2,940 C 3
43567 Wauseon⊙, 4,932 B 2
45690 Waverly⊙, 4,858 D 7
43466 Wayne, 921 C 3
44688 Waynesburg, 1,337 H 4
45896 Waynesfield, 704 C 4
45068 Waynesville, 1,638 B 6
44090 Wellington, 4,137 F 3
45692 Wellston, 5,410 F 7
43968 Wellsville, 5,891 J 4
45381 West Alexandria, 1,553 A 6
45449 West Carrollton, 10,748 B 6
43081 Westerville, 12,530 D 5
44491 West Farmington, 650 J 3
43162 West Jefferson, 3,664 D 6
43845 West Lafayette, 1,719 G 5
44145 Westlake, 15,689 G 9
43357 West Liberty, 1,580 C 5
43358 West Mansfield, 753 C 5
45383 West Milton, 3,696 B 6
43569 Weston, 1,269 C 3
† 45662 West Portsmouth, 3,396 D 8
44287 West Salem, 1,058 F 4
45693 West Union⊙, 1,951 C 8
43570 West Unity, 1,589 B 2
† 44138 Westview, 2,523 G 10
45694 Wheelersburg, 3,709 E 8
43213 Whitehall, 25,263 E 6
43571 Whitehouse, 1,542 C 2
44092 Wickliffe, 21,354 J 9
44890 Willard, 5,510 E 3
45176 Williamsburg, 2,054 B 7
44093 Williamsfield, 950 J 2
43164 Williamsport, 857 D 6
44094 Willoughby, 18,634 J 8
† 44094 Willoughby Hills, 5,247 J 9
44094 Willowick, 21,237 J 8
45898 Willshire, 623 A 4
45177 Wilmington⊙, 10,051 C 7
45697 Winchester, 760 C 8
44288 Windham, 3,360 H 3
43952 Wintersville, 4,921 J 5
45245 Withamsville, 975 C 10
† 45201 Woodlawn, 3,251 C 9
† 44101 Woodmere, 976 J 9
43793 Woodsfield⊙, 3,239 H 6
43469 Woodville, 1,834 D 3
44691 Wooster⊙, 18,703 G 4
43085 Worthington, 15,326 E 5
45215 Wyoming, 9,089 C 9
45385 Xenia⊙, 25,373 C 6
45387 Yellow Springs, 4,624 C 6
43971 Yorkville, 1,656 J 5
* 44501 Youngstown⊙, 139,788 J 3
Youngstown-Warren, ‡536,003 J 3
43701 Zanesville⊙, 33,045 G 6

⊙ County seat.
‡ Population of metropolitan area.
† Zip of nearest p.o.
* Multiple zips

COUNTIES

County, Pop.	Key
Adair, 15,141	S 3
Alfalfa, 7,224	K 1
Atoka, 10,972	O 6
Beaver, 6,282	E 1
Beckham, 15,754	G 4
Blaine, 11,794	K 3
Bryan, 25,552	O 7
Caddo, 28,931	K 4
Canadian, 32,245	K 3
Carter, 37,349	M 6
Cherokee, 23,174	R 3
Choctaw, 15,141	P 6
Cimarron, 4,145	A 1
Cleveland, 81,839	M 4
Coal, 5,525	O 5
Comanche, 108,144	K 5
Cotton, 6,832	K 6
Craig, 14,722	R 1
Creek, 45,532	O 3
Custer, 22,665	H 3
Delaware, 17,767	S 2
Dewey, 5,656	H 2
Ellis, 5,129	G 2
Garfield, 55,365	L 2
Garvin, 24,874	M 5
Grady, 29,354	L 5
Grant, 7,117	L 1
Greer, 7,979	G 5
Harmon, 5,136	G 5
Harper, 5,151	G 1
Haskell, 9,578	R 4
Hughes, 13,228	O 4
Jackson, 30,902	H 5
Jefferson, 7,125	L 6
Johnston, 7,870	N 6
Kay, 48,791	M 1
Kingfisher, 12,857	L 3
Kiowa, 12,532	J 5
Latimer, 8,601	R 5
Le Flore, 32,137	S 5
Lincoln, 19,482	N 3
Logan, 19,645	M 3
Love, 5,637	M 7
Major, 7,529	K 2
Marshall, 7,682	N 6
Mayes, 23,302	R 2
McClain, 14,157	M 5
McCurtain, 28,642	S 6
McIntosh, 12,472	P 4
Murray, 10,669	M 6
Muskogee, 59,542	R 3
Noble, 10,043	M 2
Nowata, 9,773	P 1
Okfuskee, 10,683	O 3
Oklahoma, 526,805	M 3
Okmulgee, 35,358	P 3
Osage, 29,750	O 1
Ottawa, 29,800	S 1
Pawnee, 11,338	N 2
Payne, 50,654	N 2
Pittsburg, 37,521	P 5
Pontotoc, 27,867	N 5
Pottawatomie, 43,134	N 4
Pushmataha, 9,385	R 6
Roger Mills, 4,452	G 3
Rogers, 28,425	P 2
Seminole, 25,144	N 4
Sequoyah, 23,370	S 3
Stephens, 35,902	L 6
Texas, 16,352	C 1
Tillman, 12,901	J 6
Tulsa, 401,663	P 2
Wagoner, 22,163	P 3
Washington, 42,277	P 1
Washita, 12,141	J 4
Woods, 11,920	J 1
Woodward, 15,537	H 2

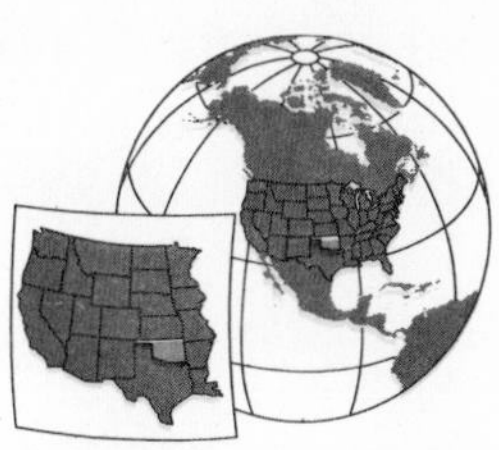

AREA 69,919 sq. mi.
POPULATION 2,559,253
CAPITAL Oklahoma City
LARGEST CITY Oklahoma City
HIGHEST POINT Black Mesa 4,973 ft.
SETTLED IN 1889
ADMITTED TO UNION November 16, 1907
POPULAR NAME Sooner State
STATE FLOWER Mistletoe
STATE BIRD Scissor-tailed Flycatcher

CITIES and TOWNS

Zip	Name/Pop.	Key
74720	Achille, 382	O 7
74820	Ada⊙, 14,859	N 5
74330	Adair, 459	R 2
73901	Adams, 175	D 1
74520	Adamson, 150	P 5
73520	Addington, 123	L 6
74331	Afton, 1,022	S 1
74824	Agra, 335	N 3
† 74955	Akins, 250	S 3
74721	Albany, 100	O 7
73001	Albert, 110	K 4
74521	Albion, 186	R 5
74522	Alderson, 215	P 5
73002	Alex, 492	L 5
† 73015	Alfalfa, 70	J 4
73716	Aline, 260	K 1
74825	Allen, 974	O 5
73521	Altus⊙, 23,302	H 5
73717	Alva⊙, 7,440	J 1
73004	Amber, 300	L 4
73718	Ames, 227	K 2
† 73723	Amorita, 63	K 1
73719	Anadarko⊙, 6,682	K 4
74523	Antlers⊙, 2,685	P 6
73006	Apache, 1,421	K 5
† 74633	Apperson, 40	N 1
73620	Arapaho⊙, 531	H 3
73007	Arcadia, 500	M 3
73401	Ardmore⊙, 20,881	M 6
74901	Arkoma, 2,098	T 4
73832	Arnett⊙, 711	G 2
74826	Asher, 437	N 5
74524	Ashland, 73	O 5
74525	Atoka⊙, 3,346	O 6
74827	Atwood, 200	O 5
74001	Avant, 439	O 2
73833	Avard, 59	J 1
74526	Bache, 100	P 5
74420	Bacone, 786	R 3
73930	Baker, 63	D 1
73931	Balko, 100	E 1
74002	Barnsdall, 1,579	O 1
† 74965	Baron, 100	S 3
74003	Bartlesville⊙, 29,683	O 1
74722	Battiest, 150	S 6
74828	Bearden, 260	O 4
73932	Beaver⊙, 1,853	F 1
74421	Beggs, 1,107	P 3
† 74523	Belzoni, 50	R 6
74929	Bengal, 75	R 5
74723	Bennington, 288	P 7
74527	Bentley, 125	O 6
† 73662	Berlin, 50	G 4
74331	Bernice, 189	S 1
73622	Bessie, 210	H 4
73008	Bethany, 21,785	L 3
74724	Bethel, 297	S 6
† 74801	Bethel Acres, 1,083	M 4
74332	Big Cabin, 198	R 1
74630	Billings, 618	M 1
73009	Binger, 730	K 4
73720	Bison, 80	L 2
74008	Bixby, 3,973	P 3
74058	Blackburn, 88	N 2
† 74962	Blackgum, 258	S 3
74631	Blackwell, 8,645	M 1
73526	Blair, 1,114	H 5
73010	Blanchard, 1,580	L 4
74528	Blanco, 200	P 5
74529	Blocker, 151	P 4
74725	Blue, 150	O 7
74333	Bluejacket, 234	R 1
† 74525	Boggy Depot, 100	O 6
73933	Boise City⊙, 1,993	B 1
74726	Bokchito, 607	O 6
74930	Bokoshe, 588	S 4
74829	Boley, 514	O 4
74727	Boswell, 755	P 6
74830	Bowlegs, 540	N 4
74009	Bowring, 100	O 1
74422	Boynton, 522	P 3
73011	Bradley, 247	L 5
74423	Braggs, 325	R 3
74632	Braman, 295	M 1
73012	Bray, 90	L 5
73721	Breckinridge, 70	L 2
74424	Briartown, 100	R 4
73013	Bridgeport, 142	K 3
74010	Bristow, 4,653	O 3
74012	Broken Arrow, 11,787	P 2
74728	Broken Bow, 2,980	S 7
74530	Bromide, 231	N 6
† 74873	Brooksville, 80	M 4
† 74437	Bryant, 86	P 4
73834	Buffalo⊙, 1,579	G 1
74931	Bunch, 90	S 3
74633	Burbank, 188	N 1
73722	Burlington, 165	K 1
73430	Burneyville, 106	M 7
73624	Burns Flat, 988	H 4
73625	Butler, 315	H 3
74831	Byars, 247	N 5
† 74820	Byng, 50	N 5
73723	Byron, 72	K 1
73527	Cache, 1,106	J 5
74729	Caddo, 886	O 6
74730	Calera, 1,063	O 7
73014	Calumet, 386	K 3
74531	Calvin, 359	O 5
73835	Camargo, 236	H 2
74932	Cameron, 311	T 4
74425	Canadian, 304	P 4
74533	Caney, 200	O 6
73724	Canton, 844	J 2
73626	Canute, 420	H 4
73725	Capron, 80	J 1
74335	Cardin, 950	S 1
73726	Carmen, 519	J 1
73015	Carnegie, 1,723	J 4
74832	Carney, 396	N 3
73727	Carrier, 125	K 2
73627	Carter, 311	H 4
† 74633	Carter Nine, 50	N 1
74934	Cartersville, 119	S 4
73016	Cashion, 329	L 3
74833	Castle, 212	O 4
74015	Catoosa, 970	P 2
73017	Cement, 892	K 5
† 74820	Center, 100	N 5
74534	Centrahoma, 155	O 5
74336	Centralia, 43	R 1
74834	Chandler⊙, 2,529	N 3
73528	Chattanooga, 302	J 6
74426	Checotah, 3,074	R 4
74016	Chelsea, 1,622	P 1
73728	Cherokee⊙, 2,119	K 1
73838	Chester, 135	J 2
73628	Cheyenne⊙, 892	G 3
73018	Chickasha⊙, 14,194	L 4
74635	Chilocco, 712	M 1
73020	Choctaw, 4,750	M 3
74337	Chouteau, 1,046	R 2
† 74965	Christie, 70	S 3
74017	Claremore⊙, 9,084	R 2
74535	Clarita, 90	O 6
74536	Clayton, 718	R 5
74835	Clearview, 350	O 4
† 73437	Clemscot, 150	L 6
† 74331	Cleora, 87	S 1
73729	Cleo Springs, 344	K 2
74020	Cleveland, 2,573	O 2
73601	Clinton, 8,513	H 3
73632	Cloud Chief, 40	J 4
74537	Cloudy, 175	R 6
74538	Coalgate⊙, 1,859	O 5
† 73059	Cogar, 40	K 4
74733	Colbert, 814	O 7
74338	Colcord, 438	S 2
† 73010	Cole, 75	L 4
73432	Coleman, 125	O 6
74021	Collinsville, 3,009	P 2
73021	Colony, 250	J 4
73529	Comanche, 1,862	L 6
74339	Commerce, 2,593	R 1
73022	Concho, 500	L 3
74836	Connerville, 150	N 6
73023	Cooperton, 55	J 5
74022	Copan, 558	P 1
73632	Cordell⊙, 3,261	H 4
† 74751	Corinne, 100	R 6
73024	Corn, 409	J 4
† 73456	Cornish, 90	L 6
74428	Council Hill, 135	P 3
73025	Countyline, 500	L 6
73730	Covington, 605	L 2
74429	Coweta, 2,457	P 3
† 74934	Cowlington, 751	S 4
73082	Cox City, 285	L 5
73027	Coyle, 303	M 3
73028	Crescent, 1,568	L 3
74837	Cromwell, 287	N 4
74430	Crowder, 339	P 4
73433	Cumberland, 150	N 6
74023	Cushing, 7,529	N 3
73639	Custer, 486	J 3
73029	Cyril, 1,302	K 5
73731	Dacoma, 226	J 1
74540	Daisy, 250	P 5
74838	Dale, 155	M 4
† 74523	Darwin, 50	P 6
74026	Davenport, 831	N 3
73530	Davidson, 515	J 6
73030	Davis, 2,223	M 5
74636	Deer Creek, 203	L 1
74027	Delaware, 534	P 1
73115	Del City, 27,133	L 4
73640	Delhi, 41	G 4
74028	Depew, 739	O 3
73531	Devol, 129	J 6
74431	Dewar, 933	P 4
74029	Dewey, 3,958	P 1
† 74868	Dewright, 100	N 4
73031	Dibble, 184	L 4
† 73401	Dickson, 798	M 6
73641	Dill City, 578	H 4
74340	Disney, 303	S 2
73032	Dougherty, 211	M 6
73733	Douglas, 79	L 2
73734	Dover, 566	L 3
74541	Dow, 300	P 5
73735	Drummond, 326	L 2
74030	Drumright, 2,931	O 3
73532	Duke, 486	G 5
73533	Duncan⊙, 19,718	L 5
74701	Durant⊙, 11,118	O 6
73642	Durham, 43	G 3
74839	Dustin, 502	O 4
73643	Eagle City, 56	J 3
74734	Eagletown, 850	S 6
73033	Eakly, 228	K 4
74840	Earlsboro, 248	N 4
† 73532	East Duke, 250	H 5
73034	Edmond, 16,633	M 3
73537	Eldorado, 737	G 6
73538	Elgin, 840	K 5
73644	Elk City, 7,323	G 4
73539	Elmer, 138	H 6
73035	Elmore City, 653	M 5
73036	El Reno⊙, 14,510	K 3
73701	Enid⊙, 44,008	L 2
† 74561	Enterprise, 130	R 4
73645	Erick, 1,285	G 4
74342	Eucha, 66	S 2
74432	Eufaula⊙, 2,355	P 4
74637	Fairfax, 1,889	N 1
74343	Fairland, 814	S 1
73736	Fairmont, 154	L 2
73737	Fairview⊙, 2,894	J 2
74935	Fanshawe, 199	S 5
73840	Fargo, 262	G 2
74542	Farris, 100	P 6
73540	Faxon, 121	J 6
73646	Fay, 75	J 3
† 74561	Featherston, 75	P 4
73937	Felt, 105	A 1
73434	Fillmore, 250	N 6
74543	Finley, 400	R 6
74842	Fittstown, 325	N 5
74843	Fitzhugh, 212	N 5
73541	Fletcher, 950	K 5
74638	Foraker, 52	Q 1
† 73101	Forest Park, 835	M 3
73938	Forgan, 496	E 1
73038	Fort Cobb, 722	K 4
74434	Fort Gibson, 1,418	R 3
73841	Fort Supply, 550	G 1
74735	Fort Towson, 430	R 7
73647	Foss, 150	H 4
73039	Foster, 50	M 5
73435	Fox, 400	M 6
74031	Foyil, 164	R 2
74844	Francis, 283	N 5
73542	Frederick⊙, 6,132	H 6
73842	Freedom, 292	H 1
73843	Gage, 536	G 2
74936	Gans, 238	S 4
73738	Garber, 1,011	M 2
74736	Garvin, 117	S 7
73844	Gate, 151	F 1
73040	Geary, 1,380	K 3
73436	Gene Autry, 120	N 6
73543	Geronimo, 587	K 6
74544	Gerty, 139	O 5
74032	Glencoe, 421	M 2
74033	Glenpool, 770	P 3
74728	Glover, 244	S 6
74737	Golden, 275	S 6
† 73093	Goldsby, 298	M 4
73739	Goltry, 282	K 1
† 74740	Goodwater, 100	S 7
73939	Goodwell, 1,467	C 1
74435	Gore, 478	R 3
73041	Gotebo, 376	J 4

(continued on following page)

Agriculture, Industry and Resources

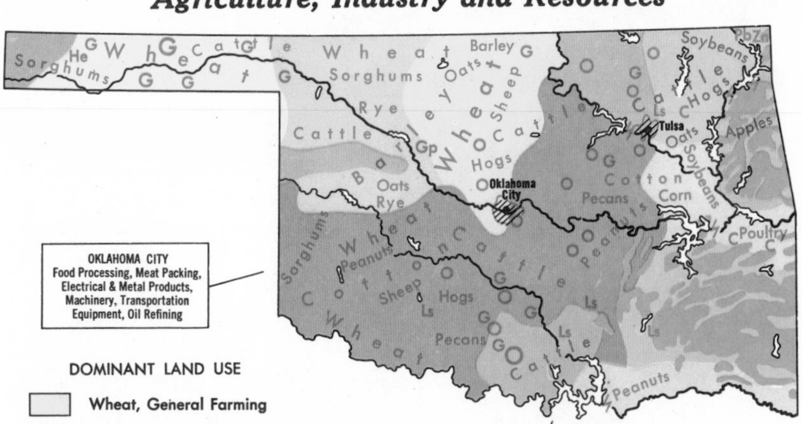

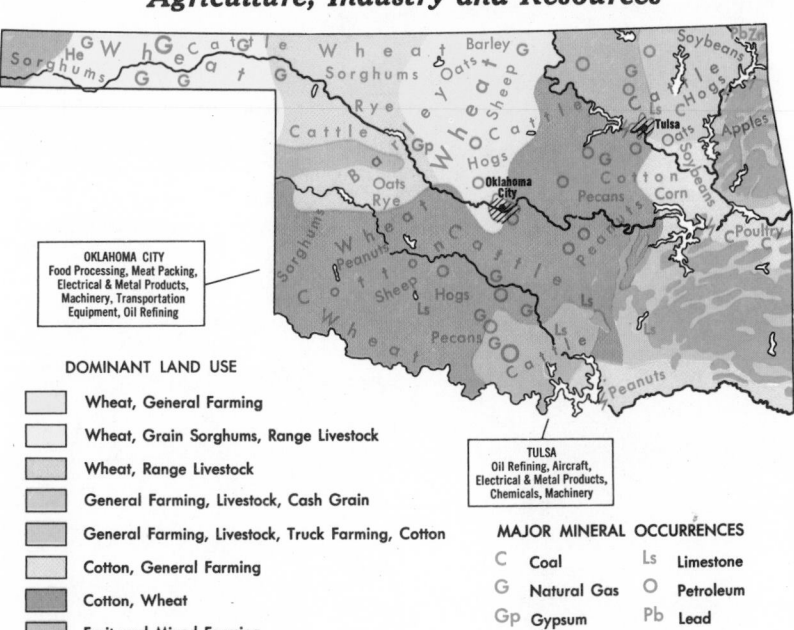

Tulsa
Oklahoma City
OKLAHOMA CITY
Food Processing, Meat Packing, Electrical & Metal Products, Machinery, Transportation Equipment, Oil Refining
TULSA
Oil Refining, Aircraft, Electrical & Metal Products, Chemicals, Machinery

DOMINANT LAND USE

- Wheat, General Farming
- Wheat, Grain Sorghums, Range Livestock
- Wheat, Range Livestock
- General Farming, Livestock, Cash Grain
- General Farming, Livestock, Truck Farming, Cotton
- Cotton, General Farming
- Cotton, Wheat
- Fruit and Mixed Farming
- Range Livestock
- Forests

Water Power

MAJOR MINERAL OCCURRENCES

- C Coal
- G Natural Gas
- Gp Gypsum
- He Helium
- Ls Limestone
- O Petroleum
- Pb Lead
- Zn Zinc

Major Industrial Areas

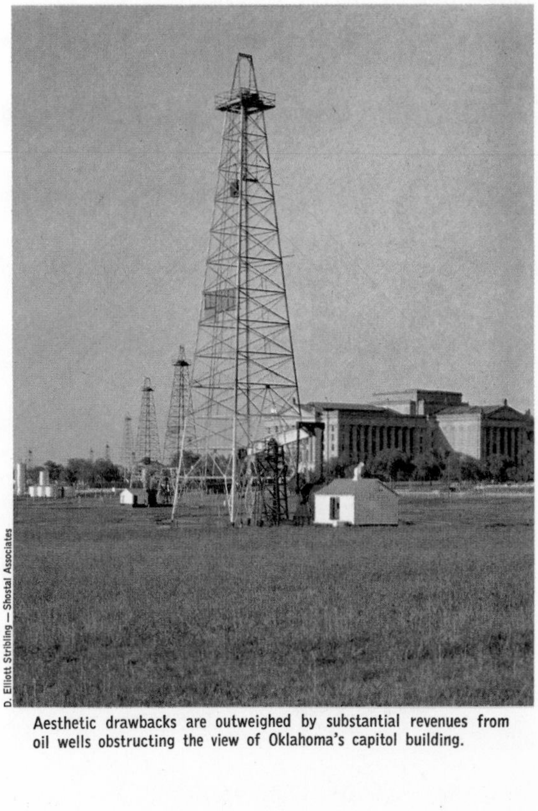

D. Elliott Stribling — Shostal Associates

Aesthetic drawbacks are outweighed by substantial revenues from oil wells obstructing the view of Oklahoma's capitol building.

73544 Gould, 368.....G 5
74545 Gowen, 350.....R 5
73042 Gracemont, 424.....K 4
73437 Graham, 250.....M 6
74639 Grainola, 66.....N 1
73546 Grandfield, 1,524.....J 6
73547 Granite, 1,808.....H 5
74738 Grant, 273.....R 7
† 74437 Grayson (Wildcat), 142.....P 4
73043 Greenfield, 143.....K 3
74344 Grove, 2,000.....S 1
73044 Guthrie⊙, 9,575.....M 3
73942 Guymon⊙, 7,674.....D 1
74546 Halleyville, 928.....P 5
74034 Hallett, 125.....N 2
73650 Hammon, 677.....H 3
74845 Hanna, 181.....P 4
† 74955 Hanson, 250.....S 4
74846 Harden City, 150.....N 5
73944 Hardesty, 223.....D 1
73045 Harrah, 1,931.....M 4
74739 Harris, 200.....S 7
74437 Hartshorne, 2,121.....R 5
74436 Haskell, 2,063.....P 3
73548 Hastings, 184.....K 6
74740 Haworth, 293.....S 7
73438 Healdton, 2,324.....M 6
74937 Heavener, 2,566.....S 5
73741 Helena, 769.....K 1
74741 Hendrix, 117.....O 7
73046 Hennepin, 306.....M 5
73742 Hennessey, 2,181.....L 2
74437 Henryetta, 6,430.....P 4
† 73539 Hess, 65.....H 4
† 73086 Hickory, 62.....N 5
73743 Hillsdale, 77.....K 1
73047 Hinton, 889.....K 4
73744 Hitchcock, 160.....K 3
74438 Hitchita, 160.....P 3
73651 Hobart⊙, 4,638.....J 5
74345 Hockerville, 125.....S 1
74939 Hodgen, 150.....S 5
74439 Hoffman, 262.....P 4
74848 Holdenville⊙, 5,181.....O 5
73550 Hollis⊙, 3,150.....G 5
73551 Hollister, 105.....J 6
73745 Homestead, 75.....K 2
74035 Hominy, 2,274.....O 2
74549 Honobia, 250.....R 5
73945 Hooker, 1,615.....D 1
73746 Hopeton, 75.....J 1
74940 Howe, 403.....S 5
74440 Hoyt, 110.....R 4
74743 Hugo⊙, 6,585.....R 6
† 67333 Hulah, 50.....O 1
74441 Hulbert, 505.....R 3
† 73521 Humphreys, 44.....H 4
74640 Hunter, 274.....L 1
73048 Hydro, 805.....J 3
74745 Idabel⊙, 5,946.....S 7
73552 Indiahoma, 434.....J 5
74442 Indianola, 205.....P 4
74036 Inola, 948.....P 2
73747 Isabella, 89.....K 2
74346 Jay⊙, 1,594.....S 2
73748 Jefferson, 128.....L 1
74037 Jenks, 1,997.....P 2
74038 Jennings, 338.....N 2
73749 Jet, 317.....K 1
73049 Jones, 1,666.....M 3
74551 Jumbo, 40.....P 6
74347 Kansas, 317.....S 2
74641 Kaw, 283.....N 1
† 74401 Keefeton, 70.....R 3
74039 Kellyville, 685.....O 3
74747 Kemp, 153.....O 7
† 74741 Kemp City (Hendrix), 117.....O 7
74040 Kendrick, 126.....N 3
74748 Kenefic, 153.....O 6
74348 Kenwood, 125.....S 4
74941 Keota, 685.....S 4
74349 Ketchum, 238.....R 1
73947 Keyes, 569.....B 1
† 74574 Kiamichi, 100.....R 5
74041 Kiefer, 803.....O 3
74642 Kildare, 79.....M 1
73750 Kingfisher⊙, 4,042.....L 3
73439 Kingston, 710.....N 6
74552 Kinta, 247.....P 5
74553 Kiowa, 754.....P 5

73847 Knowles, 52.....F 1
74849 Konawa, 1,719.....N 5
† 74557 Kosoma, 50.....P 6
74554 Krebs, 1,515.....P 5
73753 Kremlin, 200.....L 1
73754 Lahoma, 299.....K 2
74850 Lamar, 153.....O 4
74643 Lamont, 478.....L 1
74555 Lane, 218.....O 6
74350 Langley, 481.....R 2
73050 Langston, 486.....M 3
73848 Laverne, 1,373.....G 1
73501 Lawton⊙, 74,470.....K 5
　　　Lawton, ‡108,144.....K 5
74351 Leach, 75.....S 2
73440 Lebanon, 240.....N 7
73654 Leedey, 465.....H 3
74942 Leflore, 175.....S 5
74556 Lehigh, 296.....O 6
74042 Lenapah, 325.....P 1
73441 Leon, 112.....M 7
74043 Leonard, 115.....P 3
74943 Lequire, 100.....R 4
73051 Lexington, 1,516.....M 4
74858 Lima (New Lima), 238.....D 4
73052 Lindsay, 3,705.....L 5
74637 Little Chief, 40.....N 1
73446 Little City, 80.....N 6
73442 Loco, 193.....L 6
74352 Locust Grove, 1,090.....R 2
73443 Lone Grove, 1,240.....M 6
73655 Lone Wolf, 584.....H 5
73755 Longdale, 331.....K 2
73053 Lookeba, 165.....K 4
73756 Loyal, 107.....K 3

73757 Lucien, 150.....M 2
† 74825 Lula, 40.....O 5
† 74578 Lutie, 250.....R 5
74852 Macomb, 41.....M 4
73446 Madill⊙, 2,875.....N 6
73758 Manchester, 165.....L 1
73554 Mangum⊙, 4,066.....G 5
73555 Manitou, 308.....J 5
74044 Mannford, 892.....N 6
73447 Mannsville, 364.....N 6
74045 Maramec, 128.....N 2
74945 Marble City, 299.....S 3
73448 Marietta⊙, 2,013.....M 7
74644 Markland, 236.....M 1
73055 Marlow, 3,995.....K 5
73056 Marshall, 420.....L 2
73556 Martha, 268.....H 5
74853 Mason, 75.....O 3
74854 Maud, 1,143.....N 4
73851 May, 91.....G 1
73057 Maysville, 1,380.....L 5
74353 Mazie, 300.....R 2
74501 McAlester⊙, 18,802.....P 5
74944 McCurtain, 575.....R 4
74851 McLoud, 2,159.....M 4
73449 Mead, 210.....O 7
73759 Medford⊙, 1,304.....L 1
73557 Medicine Park, 562.....J 5
74855 Meeker, 683.....N 4
74074 Meno, 119.....K 2
73760 Meno, 119.....M 3
73058 Meridian, 104.....M 3
74354 Miami⊙, 13,880.....S 1
† 74882 Micawber, 41.....N 3

73110 Midwest City, 48,114.....M 4
73450 Milburn, 275.....O 6
74046 Milfay, 150.....N 3
74856 Mill Creek, 234.....N 6
74750 Millerton, 350.....S 7
73451 Milo, 85.....M 6
† 74944 Milton, 90.....S 4
73059 Minco, 1,129.....L 4
74946 Moffett, 312.....S 4
74947 Monroe, 300.....S 4
74444 Moodys, 200.....S 2
† 71821 Moon, 50.....S 7
73060 Moore, 18,761.....M 4
73852 Mooreland, 1,196.....H 2
74445 Morris, 1,119.....P 3
73061 Morrison, 421.....M 2
74047 Mounds, 766.....O 3
73559 Mountain Park, 458.....J 5
73062 Mountain View, 1,110.....J 4
74557 Moyers, 125.....P 6
74948 Muldrow, 1,680.....S 4
73063 Mulhall, 250.....M 3
74949 Muse, 75.....S 5
74401 Muskogee⊙, 37,331.....R 3
73064 Mustang, 2,637.....L 4
73853 Mutual, 94.....H 2
74646 Nardin, 135.....M 1
73761 Nash, 294.....K 1
74558 Nashoba, 100.....R 6
74056 Nelagoney, 62.....O 1
74857 Newalla, 350.....M 4
74049 New Alluwe, 116.....R 1
† 73632 New Cordell (Cordell)⊙, 3,261.....H 4

74647 Newkirk⊙, 2,173.....N 1
74858 New Lima, 238.....O 4
† 74060 New Prue (Prue), 202.....O 2
† 73466 New Woodville (Woodville), 118.....N 7
† 73101 Nichols Hills, 4,478.....L 3
73066 Nicoma Park, 2,560.....M 4
73067 Ninnekah, 300.....L 5
73068 Noble, 2,241.....M 4
73069 Norman⊙, 52,117.....M 4
73701 North Enid, 730.....L 2
74358 North Miami, 503.....R 1
74048 Nowata⊙, 3,679.....P 1
73452 Oakhurst, 500.....P 2
73452 Oakland, 317.....N 6
74359 Oaks, 219.....S 2
73658 Oakwood, 129.....J 3
74050 Ochelata, 330.....P 1
74958 Octavia, 40.....S 5
74557 Oilton, 1,087.....N 2
73762 Okarche, 826.....L 3
74446 Okay, 419.....R 3
73763 Okeene, 1,421.....K 2
74859 Okemah⊙, 2,913.....O 4
74003 Okesa, 165.....O 1
† 73101 Oklahoma City (cap.)⊙, 366,481.....L 4
　　　Oklahoma City, ‡640,889.....L 4
74403 Okmulgee⊙, 15,180.....O 3
74450 Oktaha, 193.....R 3
74751 Oleta, 50.....R 6
74030 Olive, 100.....O 3
† 74538 Olney, 42.....O 5
73560 Olustee, 819.....H 5
74053 Oologah, 458.....P 2

73948 Optima, 103.....D 1
73073 Orlando, 202.....M 3
74054 Osage, 170.....O 2
73561 Oscar, 61.....M 6
73453 Overbrook, 120.....M 6
74055 Owasso, 3,491.....P 2
74860 Paden, 442.....N 4
74951 Panama, 1,121.....S 4
74559 Panola, 100.....S 1
73074 Paoli, 480.....M 5
74451 Park Hill, 125.....S 3
73824 Parkland, 55.....N 3
73075 Pauls Valley⊙, 5,769.....M 5
74056 Pawhuska⊙, 4,238.....O 1
74058 Pawnee⊙, 2,443.....N 2
74861 Pearson, 60.....N 4
74648 Peckham, 65.....M 1
74452 Peggs, 82.....R 2
74452 Pensacola, 56.....S 1
66713 Peoria, 179.....S 1
74059 Perkins, 1,029.....M 3
73076 Pernell, 117.....M 5
73077 Perry⊙, 5,341.....M 2
74862 Pharoah, 100.....O 4
74538 Phillips, 106.....O 5
74360 Picher, 2,363.....S 1
74752 Pickens, 350.....S 6
73078 Piedmont, 269.....L 3
74560 Pittsburg, 282.....P 5
74753 Platter, 275.....O 7
74952 Plunkettville, 125.....S 6
73079 Pocasset, 200.....L 4
74902 Pocola, 1,840.....T 4
74601 Ponca City, 25,940.....M 1
73766 Pondcreek, 903.....L 1

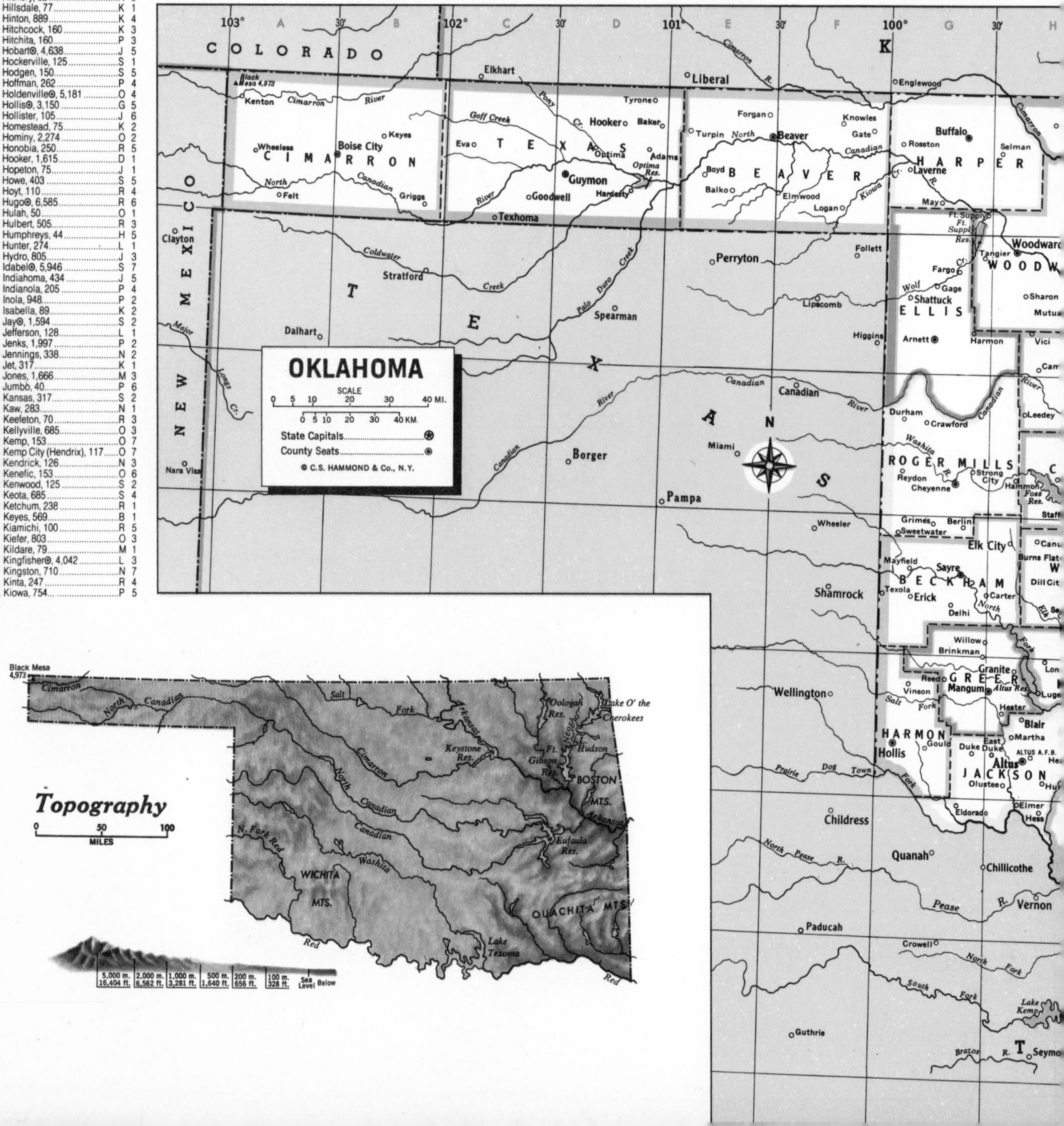

OKLAHOMA

SCALE
0 5 10 20 30 40 MI.
0 5 10 20 30 40 KM.
State Capitals .....⊛
County Seats .....⊙
© C.S. HAMMOND & Co., N.Y.

Topography

Black Mesa 4,973

MILES
0 50 100

5,000 m. | 2,000 m. | 1,000 m. | 500 m. | 200 m. | 100 m. | Sea Level | Below
16,404 ft. | 6,562 ft. | 3,281 ft. | 1,640 ft. | 656 ft. | 328 ft.

74863 Pontotoc, 150 ....N 6
73454 Pooleville, 75 ....M 6
74454 Porter, 624 ....R 3
74455 Porum, 658 ....R 4
74953 Poteau◉, 5,500 ....S 4
74864 Prague, 1,802 ....N 4
74456 Preston, 300 ....P 3
74457 Proctor, 175 ....S 3
74060 Prue, 202 ....O 2
74361 Pryor◉, 7,057 ....R 2
73080 Purcell◉, 4,076 ....M 4
73659 Putnam, 84 ....J 3
74363 Quapaw, 967 ....S 1
† 74085 Quay, 41 ....N 2
† 73852 Quinlan, 81 ....J 2
74561 Quinton, 1,262 ....R 4
74650 Ralston, 443 ....N 2
74061 Ramona, 600 ....P 1
73562 Randlett, 384 ....K 6
73081 Ratliff City, 250 ....M 5
74562 Rattan, 350 ....R 6
73455 Ravia, 373 ....N 6
† 73460 Reagan, 175 ....N 6
74458 Redbird, 230 ....P 3
74563 Red Oak, 609 ....R 5
74651 Redrock, 233 ....M 2
73563 Reed, 64 ....G 5
74459 Rentiesville, 96 ....R 4
73660 Reydon, 215 ....G 3
73456 Ringling, 1,206 ....L 6
73768 Ripley, 241 ....N 4
74062 Ripley, 307 ....N 2
† 74701 Roberta, 45 ....O 7
74933 Rock Island, 97 ....T 4
73661 Rocky, 260 ....J 4

74865 Roff, 632 ....N 5
74954 Roland, 827 ....S 4
73564 Roosevelt, 353 ....J 5
74364 Rose, 120 ....R 3
74831 Rosedale, 98 ....M 5
73855 Rosston, 56 ....G 1
73457 Rubottom, 110 ....M 6
74755 Rufe, 54 ....R 6
73082 Rush Springs, 1,381 ....L 5
73565 Ryan, 1,011 ....L 6
† 74017 Sageeyah, 49 ....P 2
74866 Saint Louis, 207 ....N 4
74365 Salina, 1,024 ....R 2
74955 Sallisaw◉, 4,888 ....S 4
74063 Sand Springs, 11,519 ....O 3
74066 Sapulpa◉, 15,159 ....O 3
74564 Sardis, 58 ....R 5
74867 Sasakwa, 321 ....N 5
74565 Savanna, 948 ....R 5
74756 Sawyer, 210 ....R 6
73662 Sayre◉, 2,712 ....G 4
74460 Schulter, 210 ....P 4
74566 Scipio, 100 ....P 4
73663 Seiling, 1,033 ....H 3
73856 Selman, 93 ....H 1
74868 Seminole, 7,878 ....H 4
73664 Sentinel, 984 ....H 4
74956 Shady Point, 350 ....S 4
74068 Shamrock, 204 ....P 3
73857 Sharon, 155 ....H 2
73858 Shattuck, 1,546 ....G 2
74801 Shawnee◉, 25,075 ....N 4
74757 Sherwood, 60 ....R 6
74652 Shidler, 717 ....N 1
† 72955 Short, 200 ....S 3

74069 Skedee, 117 ....N 2
74070 Skiatook, 2,930 ....O 2
74071 Slick, 171 ....O 3
74957 Smithville, 144 ....S 6
74567 Snow, 150 ....R 5
73566 Snyder, 1,671 ....J 5
74759 Soper, 322 ....R 6
73770 Southard, 130 ....K 2
74072 South Coffeyville, 646 ....P 1
74869 Sparks, 183 ....N 3
74366 Spavinaw, 470 ....R 2
73084 Spencer, 3,603 ....M 3
74760 Spencerville, 275 ....R 6
74073 Sperry, 1,123 ....O 2
74959 Spiro, 2,057 ....S 4
73458 Springer, 256 ....M 5
73557 Sterling, 675 ....K 5
74461 Stidham, 53 ....P 4
74462 Stigler◉, 2,347 ....R 4
74074 Stillwater◉, 31,126 ....N 3
74075 Stilwell◉, 2,134 ....S 3
† 74436 Stonebluff, 52 ....P 3
74871 Stonewall, 653 ....O 5
74367 Strang, 164 ....R 2
74872 Stratford, 1,278 ....M 5
74569 Stringtown, 397 ....P 5
73459 Stroud, 2,502 ....N 3
74570 Stuart, 294 ....O 5
† 73565 Sugden, 54 ....L 6
73086 Sulphur◉, 5,158 ....N 5
74966 Summerfield, 210 ....S 5
74761 Swink, 88 ....R 6
74463 Taft, 525 ....R 3
74464 Tahlequah◉, 9,254 ....S 3
74080 Talala, 163 ....P 1

74571 Talihina, 1,227 ....S 5
74876 Taloga◉, 363 ....J 2
73087 Tatums, 502 ....M 6
74873 Tecumseh, 4,451 ....N 4
73568 Temple, 1,354 ....K 6
74081 Terlton, 111 ....O 2
73569 Terral, 636 ....L 7
73949 Texhoma, 921 ....C 1
73668 Texola, 144 ....G 4
73459 Thackerville, 257 ....M 7
73120 The Village, 13,695 ....L 3
73669 Thomas, 1,336 ....J 3
† 74017 Tiawah, 119 ....P 2
73570 Tipton, 1,206 ....H 6
73460 Tishomingo◉, 2,663 ....N 6
74762 Tom, 600 ....S 7
74653 Tonkawa, 3,337 ....M 1
† 74852 Tribbey, 60 ....M 4
74856 Troy, 92 ....L 6
74875 Tryon, 301 ....N 4
74466 Tullahassee, 183 ....P 3
* 74101 Tulsa◉, 331,638 ....O 2
         Tulsa, ±476,945 ....O 2
74572 Turpin, 485 ....E 1
73950 Turpin, 295 ....E 1
74573 Tushka, 400 ....O 6
74572 Tuskahoma, 200 ....R 5
73088 Tussy, 150 ....L 6
73089 Tuttle, 1,640 ....L 4
73951 Tyrone, 588 ....D 1
74601 Uncas, 53 ....M 1
73090 Union, 306 ....L 4
74763 Utica, 177 ....O 7
† 73101 Valley Brook, 2,869 ....L 3

74764 Valliant, 840 ....R 6
74876 Vanoss, 130 ....N 5
73091 Velma, 611 ....L 5
74082 Vera, 215 ....P 2
73092 Verden, 439 ....K 4
† 74017 Verdigris, 307 ....P 2
74877 Vernon, 84 ....P 4
74962 Vian, 1,131 ....S 4
73859 Vici, 694 ....H 2
74301 Vinita◉, 5,847 ....R 1
73571 Vinson, 51 ....G 5
74765 Wade, 50 ....O 7
74467 Wagoner◉, 4,959 ....R 3
74468 Wainwright, 135 ....R 3
73771 Wakita, 426 ....L 1
73572 Walters◉, 2,611 ....K 6
74878 Wanette, 303 ....M 5
73092 Wann, 135 ....P 1
73461 Wapanucka, 425 ....N 6
74576 Wardville, 100 ....P 5
74469 Warner, 1,217 ....R 4
73123 Warr Acres, 9,887 ....L 3
74879 Warwick, 146 ....M 3
73093 Washington, 322 ....M 4
73094 Washita, 160 ....K 4
73772 Watonga◉, 3,696 ....K 3
74963 Watson, 48 ....S 6
74964 Watts, 326 ....S 2
73773 Waukomis, 241 ....K 2
73573 Waurika◉, 1,833 ....L 6
73095 Wayne, 618 ....M 4
73860 Waynoka, 1,444 ....J 1
73096 Weatherford, 7,959 ....J 4
74560 Weathers, 100 ....P 5
74654 Webb City, 186 ....N 1

74470 Webbers Falls, 485 ....R 3
74369 Welch, 651 ....R 1
74880 Weleetka, 1,199 ....O 4
74471 Welling, 50 ....S 3
74881 Wellston, 789 ....M 3
74882 Welty, 89 ....O 4
* 72761 West Siloam Springs, 210 ....S 2
74965 Westville, 934 ....S 3
74883 Wetumka, 1,687 ....O 4
74884 Wewoka◉, 5,284 ....O 4
74472 Whitefield, 250 ....R 4
74301 Whiteoak, 200 ....R 1
74577 Whitesboro, 355 ....S 5
74578 Wilburton◉, 2,280 ....R 5
74437 Wildcat, 142 ....P 3
73462 Willis, 250 ....N 7
73673 Willow, 188 ....G 4
73463 Wilson, 1,569 ....M 6
73464 Wirt, 350 ....L 6
74966 Wister, 927 ....S 5
73466 Woodville, 118 ....N 7
73801 Woodward◉, 8,710 ....H 2
74766 Wright City, 1,068 ....R 6
74370 Wyandotte, 297 ....S 1
73098 Wynnewood, 2,374 ....M 5
74084 Wynona, 547 ....O 1
74085 Yale, 1,239 ....N 3
74574 Yanush, 350 ....R 5
74885 Yeager, 107 ....O 4
74767 Yuba, 63 ....O 7
74884 Yukon, 8,411 ....L 3

◉ County seat.
● Population of metropolitan area.
† Zip of nearest p.o.
✶ Multiple zips

COUNTIES

Baker, 14,919 .... K 3
Benton, 53,776 .... D 3
Clackamas, 166,088 .... E 2
Clatsop, 28,473 .... D 1
Columbia, 28,790 .... D 2
Coos, 56,515 .... C 4
Crook, 9,985 .... G 3
Curry, 13,006 .... C 5
Deschutes, 30,442 .... F 4
Douglas, 71,743 .... D 4
Gilliam, 2,342 .... G 2
Grant, 6,996 .... J 3
Harney, 7,215 .... H 4
Hood River, 13,187 .... E 5
Jackson, 94,533 .... E 5
Jefferson, 8,548 .... F 3
Josephine, 35,746 .... D 5
Klamath, 50,021 .... F 5
Lake, 6,343 .... G 5
Lane, 213,358 .... E 4
Lincoln, 25,755 .... C 3
Linn, 71,914 .... E 3
Malheur, 23,169 .... K 4

Marion, 151,309 .... E 3
Morrow, 4,465 .... H 2
Multnomah, 556,667 .... E 2
Polk, 35,349 .... D 3
Sherman, 2,139 .... G 2
Tillamook, 17,930 .... D 2
Umatilla, 44,923 .... J 2
Union, 19,377 .... J 2
Wallowa, 6,247 .... K 2
Wasco, 20,133 .... F 2
Washington, 157,920 .... D 2
Wheeler, 1,849 .... G 3
Yamhill, 40,213 .... D 2

CITIES and TOWNS

Zip	Name/Pop.	Key
97810	Adams, 219	J 2
97620	Adel, 200	H 5
97901	Adrian, 200	K 4
97320	Agate Beach, 975	C 3
97406	Agness, 120	C 5
† 97361	Airlie, 45	D 3
† 97321	Albany⊙, 18,181	D 3
† 97601	Algoma, 77	F 5
97811	Alicel, 30	J 2
97407	Allegany, 200	D 4
97006	Aloha, 6,000	A 2
97408	Alpine, 80	C 2
† 97324	Alsea, 600	D 3
† 97601	Altamont, 15,746	F 5
97409	Alvadore, 350	D 3
97101	Amity, 708	D 2
97001	Antelope, 51	G 3
97530	Applegate, 125	D 5
97458	Arago, 200	C 4
97812	Arlington, 375	G 2
† 97473	Ash, 80	D 4
97520	Ashland, 12,342	E 5
97103	Astoria⊙, 10,244	D 1
97813	Athena, 872	J 2
97325	Aumsville, 590	E 3
97002	Aurora, 306	B 2
† 97817	Austin, 170	J 3
97410	Azalea, 40	D 5
97814	Baker⊙, 9,354	K 3
97378	Ballston, 120	D 2
97459	Bancroft, 25	D 3
97411	Bandon, 1,832	C 4
97106	Banks, 430	A 1

Zip	Name/Pop.	Key
97003	Barlow, 105	B 2
97009	Barton, 100	B 2
† 97136	Bar View, 75	C 2
97817	Bates, 430	J 3
97107	Bay City, 898	D 2
97621	Beatty, 50	F 5
97108	Beaver, 450	D 2
97004	Beavercreek, 708	B 2
97005	Beaverton, 18,577	A 2
97456	Bellfountain, 50	D 3
97701	Bend⊙, 13,710	F 3
97058	Biggs, 50	G 2
97016	Birkenfeld, 45	D 1
97412	Blachly, 425	D 3
97108	Blaine, 150	D 2
97326	Blodgett, 150	D 3
97413	Blue River, 350	E 3
97622	Bly, 500	F 5
97818	Boardman, 192	H 2
97623	Bonanza, 230	F 5
97008	Bonneville, 130	E 2
97009	Boring, 150	E 2
97021	Boyd, 26	F 2
97010	Bridal Veil, 155	E 2
97458	Bridge, 250	D 4
97819	Bridgeport, 45	K 3
† 97136	Brighton, 52	C 2
97001	Brightwood, 420	E 2
† 97032	Broadacres, 80	A 3
97414	Broadbent, 265	C 4
97903	Brogan, 140	K 3
97415	Brookings, 2,720	C 5
97305	Brooks, 490	A 3
97840	Brownlee, 50	L 3
97524	Brownsboro, 150	E 5
97327	Brownsville, 1,034	E 3
97351	Buena Vista, 90	D 3
97420	Bunker Hill, 1,549	C 4
97720	Burns⊙, 3,293	H 4
97522	Butte Falls, 358	E 5
† 97002	Butteville, 385	A 2
97109	Buxton, 163	D 1
97416	Camas Valley, 665	D 4
97730	Camp Sherman, 87	F 3
† 97493	Canary, 50	D 3
97013	Canby, 3,813	B 2
97110	Cannon Beach, 779	C 2
97820	Canyon City⊙, 600	J 3
97417	Canyonville, 940	D 5

Zip	Name/Pop.	Key
97111	Carlton, 1,126	D 2
† 97415	Carpenterville, 30	C 5
† 97415	Carver, 500	B 2
97014	Cascade Locks, 574	E 2
97329	Cascadia, 150	E 3
97523	Cave Junction, 415	D 5
97821	Cayuse, 300	J 2
97822	Cecil, 75	H 2
97225	Cedar Hills, 2,900	A 2
97005	Cedar Mill, 50	A 2
97058	Celilo, 50	F 2
97501	Central Point, 4,004	D 5
97420	Charleston, 500	C 4
97306	Chemawa, 900	A 3
97731	Chemult, 580	F 4
97058	Chenoweth, 2,329	F 2
97119	Cherry Grove, 280	A 2
97055	Cherryville, 280	D 3
97419	Cheshire, 750	D 3
97624	Chiloquin, 826	F 5
97015	Clackamas, 6,000	D 5
97016	Clatskanie, 1,286	D 1
97112	Cloverdale, 151	D 2
97401	Coburg, 665	D 3
97017	Colton, 305	B 3

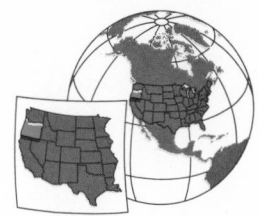

97018 Columbia City, 537........E 2	97429 Days Creek, 602..........D 5	97343 Eddyville, 50................D 3
97823 Condon◉, 973..............G 2	97114 Dayton, 949................A 3	97827 Elgin, 1,375................K 2
97420 Coos Bay, 13,466........C 4	97825 Dayville, 197..............H 3	97391 Elk City, 30.................D 3
97423 Coquille◉, 4,437..........C 4	97054 Deer Island, 120.........E 2	97436 Elkton, 176.................D 4
97113 Cornelius, 1,903..........A 2	97341 Depoe Bay, 450..........C 3	97437 Elmira, 950.................D 4
97330 Corvallis◉, 35,153........D 3	97342 Detroit, 328...............E 3	† 97138 Elsie, 30..................D 2
97424 Cottage Grove, 6,004...D 4	97431 Dexter, 450...............E 4	97828 Enterprise◉, 1,680.......K 2
97824 Cove, 363..................K 2	97731 Diamond Lake, 56.......E 4	97023 Estacada, 1,164..........D 3
† 97148 Cove Orchard, 50.......D 2	97432 Dillard, 602...............D 4	† 97401 Eugene◉, 76,346.......D 3
97335 Crabtree, 350.............D 3	97116 Dilley, 250.................A 2	Eugene, ‡213,358
97732 Crane, 63..................J 4	97020 Donald, 231...............A 3	97024 Fairview, 1,045..........B 2
† 97601 Crater Lake, 30.........E 5	† 97458 Dora, 30..................D 4	97601 Falcon Heights, 1,389...F 5
97336 Crawfordsville, 350......E 3	97434 Dorena, 550..............E 4	97438 Fall Creek, 58............E 4
97733 Crescent, 850............F 4	97435 Drain, 1,204..............D 4	97344 Falls City, 745............D 3
97425 Crescent Lake, 70.......F 4	97484 Drew, 60..................E 5	97710 Fields, 150................J 5
97426 Creswell, 1,199...........D 4	97021 Dufur, 493................F 2	† 97828 Flora, 25.................K 2
† 97401 Crow, 200................D 4	97115 Dundee, 588.............A 2	97439 Florence, 2,246..........C 4
97427 Culp Creek, 194..........E 4	† 97493 Dunes (Westlake), 976..C 4	97116 Forest Grove, 8,275.....A 2
97734 Culver, 407................F 3	† 97233 Durham, 410............A 2	97626 Fort Klamath, 150........E 5
97428 Curtin, 300................D 4	97905 Durkee, 140..............K 3	97735 Fort Rock, 75............F 4
† 97439 Cushman, 175...........C 4	97022 Eagle Creek, 98.........D 2	97830 Fossil◉, 511..............G 2
97625 Dairy, 74..................F 5	97524 Eagle Point, 1,241.......E 5	97345 Foster, 850...............E 3
97880 Dale, 25...................J 3	97420 Eastside, 1,331..........C 4	97301 Four Corners, 6,199.....A 3
97338 Dallas◉, 6,361...........D 3	97826 Echo, 479................H 2	97831 Fox, 75..................H 3
† 97910 Danner, 40..............K 5		97736 Frenchglen, 45..........H 4

AREA 96,981 sq. mi.
POPULATION 2,091,385
CAPITAL Salem
LARGEST CITY Portland
HIGHEST POINT Mt. Hood 11,235 ft.
SETTLED IN 1810
ADMITTED TO UNION February 14, 1859
POPULAR NAME Beaver State
STATE FLOWER Oregon Grape
STATE BIRD Western Meadowlark

Topography

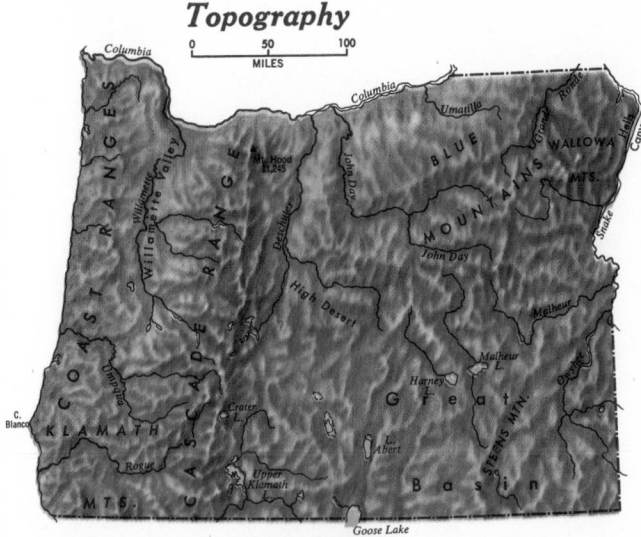

Below Sea Level	100 m. 328 ft.	200 m. 656 ft.	500 m. 1,640 ft.	1,000 m. 3,281 ft.	2,000 m. 6,562 ft.	5,000 m. 16,404 ft.

† 97526 Fruitdale, 2,655.........D 5	97351 Independence, 2,594.....D 3	† 97850 May Park, 1,466........J 2
97117 Gales Creek, 500........D 2	97843 Ione, 355.................H 2	† 97201 Maywood Park, 1,230..B 2
† 97532 Galice, 30...............D 5	97908 Ironside, 36..............K 3	† 97338 McCoy, 40..............D 2
97223 Garden Home, 2,900.....A 2	97844 Irrigon, 261..............H 2	97401 McKenzie Bridge, 100...E 3
97441 Gardiner, 500............C 4	97851 Island City, 202..........K 2	97128 McMinnville◉, 10,125.....D 2
97118 Garibaldi, 1,083..........D 2	97530 Jacksonville, 1,611.......D 5	97858 McNary, 330.............H 2
97119 Gaston, 429..............D 2	97909 Jamieson, 103...........K 3	97859 Meacham, 130............J 2
97346 Gates, 250................E 3	97401 Jasper, 231...............E 3	97501 Medford◉, 28,454......E 5
† 97741 Gateway, 95............F 3	97352 Jefferson, 936............D 3	97860 Medical Springs, 45.....K 2
97458 Gaylord, 125.............C 4	97267 Jennings Lodge, 3,500...B 2	† 97844 Mehama, 250...........E 3
97138 Gearhart, 829............C 1	97845 John Day, 1,566.........J 3	† 97470 Melrose, 30............D 4
97026 Gervais, 746.............A 3	97910 Jordan Valley, 196........K 5	97532 Merlin, 500..............D 5
† 97810 Gibbon, 100.............J 2	97846 Joseph, 839.............K 2	97633 Merrill, 722..............F 5
97027 Gladstone, 6,237.........B 2	97448 Junction City, 2,373......D 3	97622 Metolius, 270...........F 3
† 97439 Glenada, 75.............C 4	97911 Juntura, 56...............J 4	† 97223 Metzger, 2,900.........A 2
97442 Glendale, 709............D 5	† 97761 Kah-Nee-Ta, 50.........F 3	97634 Midland, 205............F 5
97388 Gleneden Beach, 400....C 3	97303 Keizer, 11,405...........A 3	97861 Mikkalo, 40..............G 2
97120 Glenwood, 500...........D 2	97627 Keno, 650...............F 5	97360 Mill City, 1,451..........E 3
97443 Glide, 470................D 4	97033 Kent, 58................G 2	97455 Milo, 600................E 4
97048 Goble, 108................E 1	97531 Kerby, 650..............D 5	97862 Milton-Freewater, 4,105..J 2
97444 Gold Beach◉, 1,554.....C 5	97367 Kernville, 50.............D 3	97222 Milwaukie, 16,379......B 2
97525 Gold Hill, 603.............D 5	† 97848 Kimberly, 30............H 3	97016 Mist, 40.................D 1
97401 Goshen, 98..............D 4	† 97123 King City, 1,427.........A 2	† 97750 Mitchell, 196...........G 3
97028 Government Camp, 175...F 2	97353 Kings Valley, 100.........D 3	† 97624 Modoc Point, 65........F 5
97347 Grand Ronde, 289........D 2	97849 Kinzua, 400..............H 3	97477 Mohawk, 50............E 3
97526 Grants Pass◉, 12,455....D 5	97601 Klamath Falls◉, 15,775...F 5	97038 Molalla, 2,005...........B 3
97029 Grass Valley, 153.........G 2	† 97103 Knappa, 950............D 1	97072 Monitor, 82.............B 3
† 97470 Green, 1,612............D 4	97354 Lacomb, 450............E 3	97361 Monmouth, 5,237......D 3
97445 Greenleaf, 47............D 3	97127 Lafayette, 786...........A 2	97456 Monroe, 443............D 3
97030 Gresham, 9,875..........B 2	† 97850 La Grande◉, 9,645......J 2	97864 Monument, 161.........H 3
97833 Haines, 212...............J 3	† 97524 Lakecreek, 160..........E 5	97039 Moro◉, 290.............G 2
97834 Halfway, 317.............K 3	97034 Lake Oswego, 14,573....B 2	97040 Mosier, 217.............F 2
97348 Halsey, 467..............D 3	97449 Lakeside, 150............C 4	† 97106 Mountaindale, 50.......A 1
97121 Hammond, 709..........C 1	97630 Lakeview◉, 2,705........G 5	97362 Mount Angel, 1,973.....B 3
† 97222 Happy Valley, 1,392.....B 2	97450 Langlois, 150............C 5	97041 Mount Hood, 215.......F-2
97415 Harbor, 750..............C 5	97739 La Pine, 1,500...........F 4	97865 Mount Vernon, 423......H 3
† 97760 Latourell Falls, 40........E 2	97042 Mulino, 600.............D 3
† 97343 Harlan, 35...............C 3	97740 Lawen, 95...............J 4	97533 Murphy, 300............D 5
97906 Harper, 102..............K 4	97401 Leaburg, 630............E 3	97457 Myrtle Creek, 2,733.....D 4
† 97601 Harriman, 50............E 5	97355 Lebanon, 6,636.........E 3	97458 Myrtle Point, 2,511......C 4
97446 Harrisburg, 1,311.........D 3	† 97478 Leland, 70..............D 5	97131 Nehalem, 241...........D 2
97459 Hauser, 400..............C 4	97839 Lexington, 230...........H 2	97364 Neotsu, 259............C 3
† 97301 Hayesville, 5,518.......A 3	97042 Liberal, 60...............B 3	97149 Neskowin, 500..........C 2
97122 Hebo, 350...............D 2	97341 Lincoln Beach, 275.......C 3	97143 Netarts, 975............C 2
97835 Helix, 152................J 2	97367 Lincoln City, 4,198.......C 3	97132 Newberg, 6,507.........A 2
97836 Heppner◉, 1,429.........H 2	97405 Logan, 450..............B 2	† 97870 New Bridge, 50.........K 3
97837 Hereford, 50.............K 3	97357 Logsden, 55.............D 3	97013 New Era, 50.............B 2
97838 Hermiston, 4,893.........H 2	97856 Long Creek, 196........H 3	97956 New Pine Creek, 260....G 5
† 97625 Hildebrand, 50...........F 5	97857 Lostine, 196.............K 2	97365 Newport◉, 5,188........C 3
97123 Hillsboro◉, 14,675.......A 2	97452 Lowell, 567..............E 4	97459 North Bend, 8,553......C 4
97738 Hines, 1,407.............H 4	97358 Lyons, 645...............E 3	97133 North Plains, 800........A 2
† 97208 Holbrook, 494..........A 1	97741 Madras◉, 1,689.........F 3	97043 North Portland, 950.....B 1
97031 Holley, 250...............E 3	97632 Malin, 486...............F 5	97867 North Powder, 304......K 2
97031 Hood River◉, 3,991.......F 2	97136 Manhattan Beach, 70....D 2	97460 Norway, 115............C 4
† 97448 Horton, 188.............D 3	97130 Manzanita, 261..........C 2	97913 Nyssa, 2,620............K 4
† 97850 Hot Lake, 60............K 2	97453 Mapleton, 950...........C 3	97268 Oak Grove, 6,300.......B 2
97032 Hubbard, 975............A 3	97454 Marcola, 900............E 3	97462 Oakland, 1,010.........D 4
97907 Huntington, 507.........K 3	97359 Marion, 450..............B 3	97463 Oakridge, 3,422........E 4
97350 Idanha, 382.............E 3	97362 Marquam, 40............B 3	97134 Oceanside, 165.........C 2
97447 Idleyld Park, 150.........D 4	97016 Marshland, 30...........D 1	97044 Odell, 450..............F 2
† 97016 Ilahe, 30................C 5	97037 Maupin, 428.............F 2	97812 Olex, 40................G 2
97841 Imbler, 139..............J 2	† 97016 Mayger, 35.............D 1	
97842 Imnaha, 37..............L 2		(continued on following page)

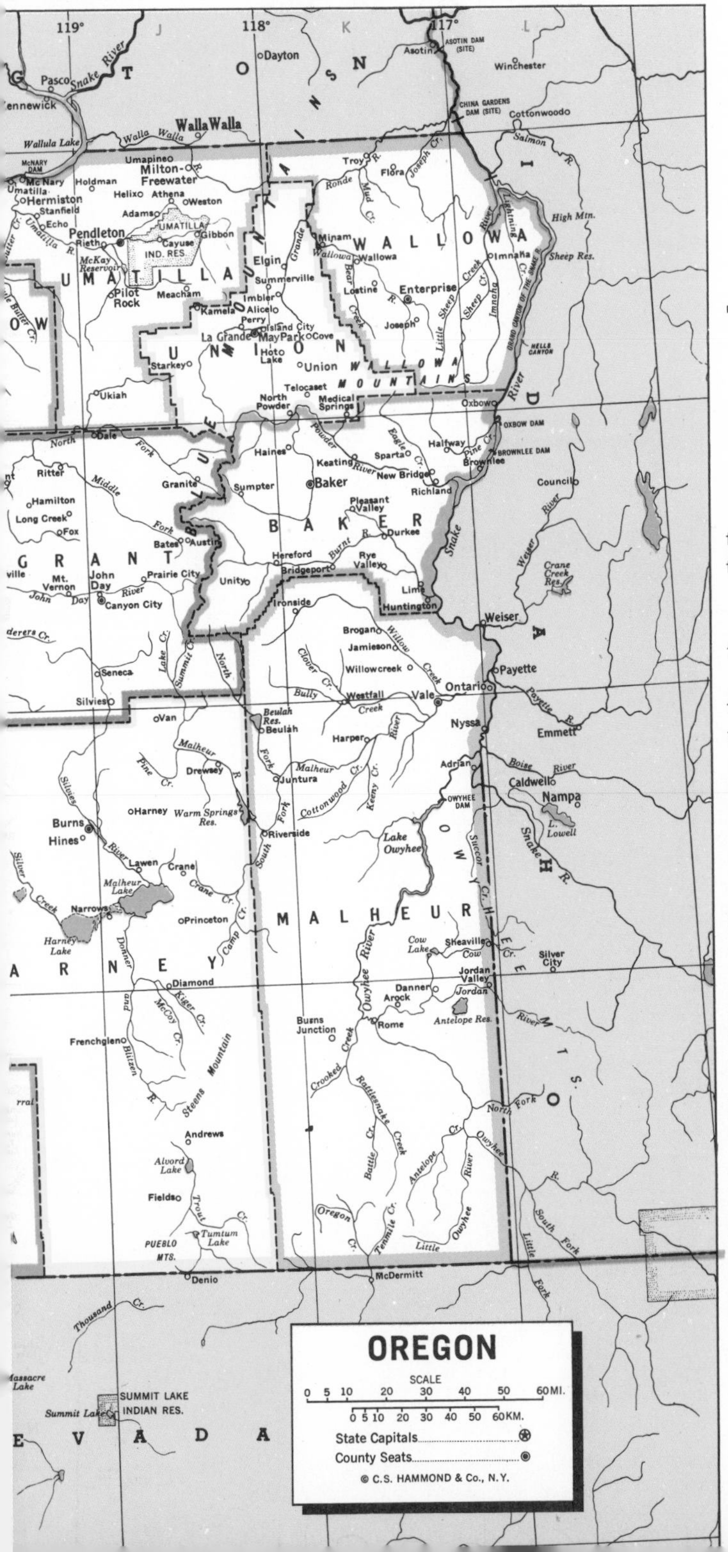

OREGON

SCALE
0 5 10   20   30   40   50   60 MI.

0 5 10 20 30 40 50 60 KM.

State Capitals............................⊛
County Seats.............................◉

◉ C.S. HAMMOND & Co., N.Y.

Agriculture, Industry and Resources

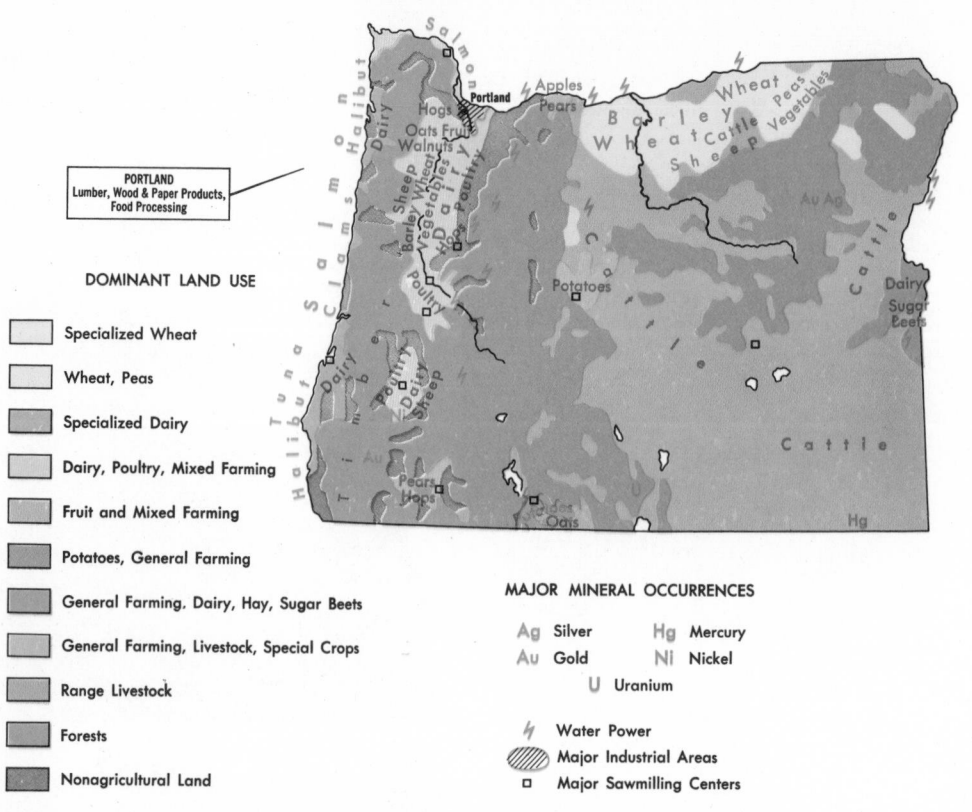

PORTLAND
Lumber, Wood & Paper Products,
Food Processing

DOMINANT LAND USE

- Specialized Wheat
- Wheat, Peas
- Specialized Dairy
- Dairy, Poultry, Mixed Farming
- Fruit and Mixed Farming
- Potatoes, General Farming
- General Farming, Dairy, Hay, Sugar Beets
- General Farming, Livestock, Special Crops
- Range Livestock
- Forests
- Nonagricultural Land

MAJOR MINERAL OCCURRENCES

Ag Silver   Hg Mercury
Au Gold   Ni Nickel
U Uranium

⚡ Water Power
▨ Major Industrial Areas
▫ Major Sawmilling Centers

Oregon's magnificently rugged coastline — sandy beaches interspersed with rock fragments ("stacks") torn from the cliffs.

Oregon State Highway Department

Agriculture, Industry and Resources

DOMINANT LAND USE

- Specialized Dairy
- Dairy, General Farming
- Fruit and Mixed Farming
- Fruit, Truck and Mixed Farming
- General Farming, Livestock, Tobacco
- General Farming, Livestock, Fruit, Tobacco
- Forests
- Urban Areas

AREA 45,333 sq. mi.
POPULATION 11,793,909
CAPITAL Harrisburg
LARGEST CITY Philadelphia
HIGHEST POINT Mt. Davis 3,213 ft.
SETTLED IN 1682
ADMITTED TO UNION December 12, 1787
POPULAR NAME Keystone State
STATE FLOWER Mountain Laurel
STATE BIRD Ruffed Grouse

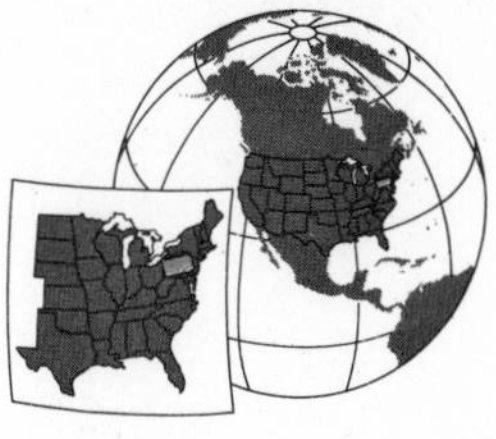

MAJOR MINERAL OCCURRENCES

C Coal — Cl Clay — Co Cobalt — Fe Iron Ore — G Natural Gas — Ls Limestone — O Petroleum — Sl Slate — Ss Sandstone — Zn Zinc

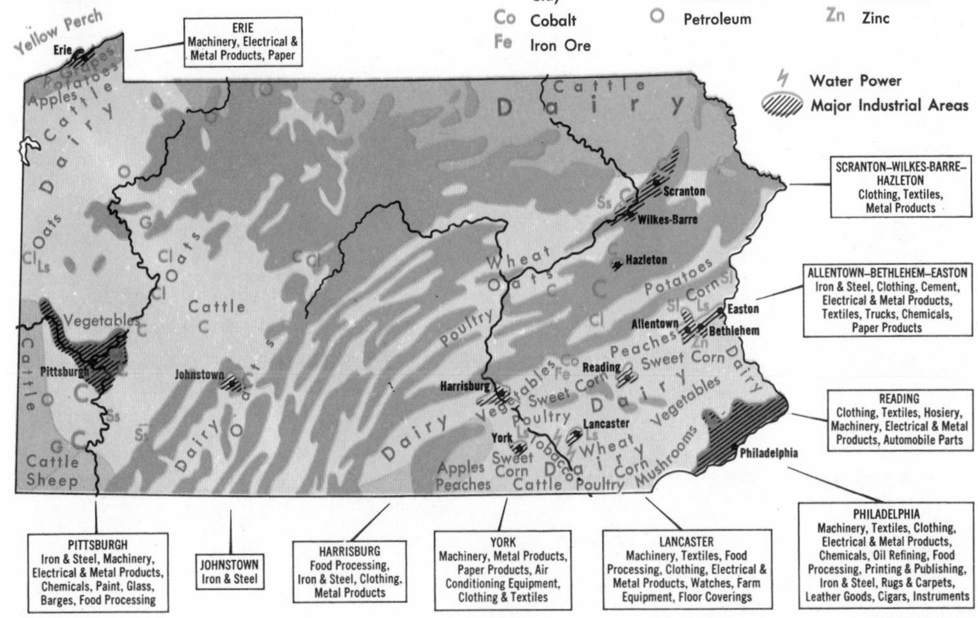
Water Power
Major Industrial Areas
Yellow Perch
Erie
ERIE
Machinery, Electrical & Metal Products, Paper
Grapes
Potatoes
Apples
Cattle
Dairy
Oats
Wheat
Vegetables
Poultry
Potatoes
Corn
Peaches
Sweet Corn
Tobacco
Mushrooms
Sheep
Scranton
Wilkes-Barre
Hazleton
Easton
Allentown
Bethlehem
Reading
Harrisburg
Lancaster
York
Philadelphia
Pittsburgh
Johnstown
SCRANTON–WILKES-BARRE–HAZLETON
Clothing, Textiles, Metal Products
ALLENTOWN–BETHLEHEM–EASTON
Iron & Steel, Clothing, Cement, Electrical & Metal Products, Textiles, Trucks, Chemicals, Paper Products
READING
Clothing, Textiles, Hosiery, Machinery, Electrical & Metal Products, Automobile Parts
PHILADELPHIA
Machinery, Textiles, Clothing, Electrical & Metal Products, Chemicals, Oil Refining, Food Processing, Printing & Publishing, Iron & Steel, Rugs & Carpets, Leather Goods, Cigars, Instruments
PITTSBURGH
Iron & Steel, Machinery, Electrical & Metal Products, Chemicals, Paint, Glass, Barges, Food Processing
JOHNSTOWN
Iron & Steel
HARRISBURG
Food Processing, Iron & Steel, Clothing, Metal Products
YORK
Machinery, Metal Products, Paper Products, Air Conditioning Equipment, Clothing & Textiles
LANCASTER
Machinery, Textiles, Food Processing, Clothing, Electrical & Metal Products, Watches, Farm Equipment, Floor Coverings

COUNTIES

Adams, 56,937 .... H 6
Allegheny, 1,605,016 .... B 5
Armstrong, 75,590 .... D 4
Beaver, 208,418 .... B 4
Bedford, 42,353 .... E 6
Berks, 296,382 .... K 5
Blair, 135,356 .... F 4
Bradford, 57,962 .... J 2
Bucks, 415,056 .... M 5
Butler, 127,941 .... C 4
Cambria, 186,785 .... E 4
Cameron, 7,096 .... F 3
Carbon, 50,573 .... L 4
Centre, 99,267 .... G 4
Chester, 278,311 .... L 6
Clarion, 38,414 .... D 3
Clearfield, 74,619 .... F 3
Clinton, 37,721 .... G 3
Columbia, 55,114 .... K 3
Crawford, 81,342 .... B 2
Cumberland, 158,177 .... H 5
Dauphin, 223,834 .... J 5
Delaware, 600,035 .... M 6
Elk, 37,770 .... E 3
Erie, 263,654 .... B 2
Fayette, 154,667 .... C 6
Forest, 4,926 .... D 2
Franklin, 100,833 .... G 6
Fulton, 10,776 .... F 6
Greene, 36,090 .... B 6
Huntingdon, 39,108 .... F 5
Indiana, 79,451 .... D 4
Jefferson, 43,695 .... D 3
Juniata, 16,712 .... H 4
Lackawanna, 234,107 .... L 3
Lancaster, 319,693 .... K 5
Lawrence, 107,374 .... B 4
Lebanon, 99,665 .... K 5
Lehigh, 255,304 .... L 4
Luzerne, 342,301 .... L 3
Lycoming, 113,296 .... H 3
McKean, 51,915 .... E 2
Mercer, 127,175 .... B 3
Mifflin, 45,268 .... G 4
Monroe, 45,422 .... M 3
Montgomery, 623,799 .... M 5
Montour, 16,508 .... J 3
Northampton, 214,368 .... M 4
Northumberland, 99,190 .... J 4
Perry, 28,615 .... H 5
Philadelphia (city county), 1,948,609 .... M 6
Pike, 11,818 .... M 3
Potter, 16,395 .... G 2
Schuylkill, 160,089 .... K 4
Snyder, 29,269 .... H 4
Somerset, 76,037 .... D 6
Sullivan, 5,961 .... J 3
Susquehanna, 34,344 .... L 2
Tioga, 39,691 .... H 2
Union, 28,603 .... H 4
Venango, 62,353 .... C 3
Warren, 47,682 .... D 2
Washington, 210,876 .... B 5
Wayne, 29,581 .... M 2
Westmoreland, 376,935 .... D 5
Wyoming, 19,082 .... K 2
York, 272,603 .... J 6

CITIES and TOWNS

Zip *Name/Pop.* *Key*

19001 Abington, 8,594 .... M 5
19501 Adamstown, 1,202 .... K 5
17501 Akron, 3,149 .... K 5
16401 Albion, 1,768 .... B 2
18011 Alburtis, 1,142 .... L 5
19018 Aldan, 5,001 .... M 7
15001 Aliquippa, 22,277 .... B 4
* 18101 Allentown⊙, 109,527 .... L 4
Allentown-Bethlehem-Easton, ‡543,551 .... L 4
15101 Allison Park, 7,500 .... C 4
* 16601 Altoona, 62,900 .... F 4
Altoona, ‡135,356 .... F 4
19002 Ambler, 7,800 .... M 5
15003 Ambridge, 11,324 .... B 4
19020 Andalusia, 8,169 .... N 5
17003 Annville, 4,704 .... J 5
15613 Apollo, 2,308 .... C 4
18403 Archbald, 6,118 .... M 2
19003 Ardmore, 5,801 .... M 6
15068 Arnold, 8,174 .... C 4
17921 Ashland, 4,737 .... K 4
18706 Ashley, 4,095 .... L 3
15215 Aspinwall, 3,541 .... C 6
18810 Athens, 4,173 .... K 2
17851 Atlas, 1,527 .... K 4
15202 Avalon, 7,065 .... B 6
15312 Avella, 1,109 .... B 5
17721 Avis, 1,749 .... H 3
18641 Avoca, 3,543 .... L 3
19311 Avondale, 1,025 .... L 6
15618 Avonmore, 1,267 .... C 4
15005 Baden, 5,536 .... B 4
17502 Bainbridge, 950 .... J 5
19004 Bala-Cynwyd, 6,483 .... N 6
† 15201 Baldwin, 26,729 .... B 7
19503 Bally, 1,197 .... L 5
18013 Bangor, 5,425 .... M 4
15714 Barnesboro, 2,708 .... E 4
18014 Bath, 1,829 .... M 4
15009 Beaver⊙, 6,100 .... B 4
15921 Beaverdale, 1,579 .... E 5
15010 Beaver Falls, 14,375 .... B 4
18216 Beaver Meadows, 1,274 .... L 4
15522 Bedford⊙, 3,302 .... F 5
16823 Bellefonte⊙, 6,828 .... G 4
15012 Belle Vernon, 1,496 .... C 5
17004 Belleville, 1,817 .... G 4
15202 Bellevue, 11,586 .... B 6
16617 Bellwood, 2,395 .... F 4
† 15201 Ben Avon, 2,713 .... B 6
15314 Bentleyville, 2,714 .... B 5
17814 Benton, 1,027 .... K 3
15530 Berlin, 1,766 .... E 6
18603 Berwick, 12,274 .... K 3
19312 Berwyn, 14,000 .... L 5
16112 Bessemer, 1,427 .... B 4
19507 Bethel, 950 .... K 5
15102 Bethel Park, 34,791 .... B 7
* 18015 Bethlehem, 72,686 .... M 4
17307 Biglerville, 977 .... H 6
19508 Birdsboro, 3,196 .... L 5
15716 Black Lick, 1,074 .... D 4
15717 Blairsville, 4,411 .... D 5
18447 Blakely, 6,391 .... L 2
15238 Blawnox, 1,907 .... C 6
15224 Bloomfield (New Bloomfield)⊙, 1,032 .... H 5
17815 Bloomsburg⊙, 11,652 .... J 3
16912 Blossburg, 1,753 .... H 2
17214 Blue Ridge Summit, 950 .... G 6
16827 Boalsburg, 950 .... G 4
15315 Bobtown, 1,055 .... B 6
17007 Boiling Springs, 1,521 .... H 5
19061 Boothwyn, 8,900 .... L 7
15135 Boston, 2,500 .... C 7
15531 Boswell, 1,529 .... E 5
19512 Boyertown, 4,428 .... L 5
15014 Brackenridge, 4,796 .... C 4
15104 Braddock, 8,682 .... C 7
16701 Bradford, 12,672 .... E 2
15227 Brentwood, 13,732 .... B 7
19405 Bridgeport, 5,630 .... M 5
15017 Bridgeville, 6,717 .... B 5
15009 Bridgewater, 966 .... B 4
19007 Bristol (borough), 12,085 .... N 5
19007 Bristol (urban township), 67,498 .... N 5
15824 Brockway, 2,529 .... E 3
19015 Brookhaven, 7,370 .... M 7
15825 Brookville⊙, 4,314 .... D 3
19008 Broomall, 20,000 .... M 6
15236 Broughton, 3,276 .... B 7
15417 Brownsville, 4,856 .... C 5
19009 Bryn Athyn, 970 .... M 5
19010 Bryn Mawr, 5,737 .... M 5
15021 Burgettstown, 2,118 .... A 5
17009 Burnham, 2,607 .... H 4
16001 Butler⊙, 18,691 .... C 4
16212 Cadogan, ∆563 .... C 4
15419 California, 6,635 .... C 5
16403 Cambridge Springs, 1,998 .... C 2
17011 Camp Hill, 9,931 .... H 5
18325 Canadensis, 950 .... M 3
15317 Canonsburg, 11,439 .... B 5
17724 Canton, 2,037 .... J 2
18407 Carbondale, 12,808 .... L 2
17013 Carlisle⊙, 18,079 .... H 5
15106 Carnegie, 10,864 .... B 7
15722 Carrolltown, 1,507 .... E 4
15234 Castle Shannon, 11,899 .... B 7
18032 Catasauqua, 5,702 .... M 4
17820 Catawissa, 1,701 .... K 4
15321 Cecil, 1,900 .... B 5
16404 Centerville, 4,175 .... B 6
15926 Central City, 1,547 .... E 5
17927 Centralia, 1,165 .... K 4
16828 Centre Hall, 1,282 .... G 4
18914 Chalfont, 2,366 .... M 5
17201 Chambersburg⊙, 17,315 .... G 6
15022 Charleroi, 6,723 .... C 5
† 19380 Chatwood, 7,168 .... L 6
19012 Cheltenham, ∆40,238 .... M 5
* 19013 Chester, 56,331 .... L 7
19017 Chester Heights, 1,277 .... L 7
15024 Cheswick, 2,580 .... C 6
16025 Chicora, 1,166 .... C 4
17509 Christiana, 1,132 .... K 6
† 15201 Churchill, 4,690 .... C 7
15025 Clairton, 15,051 .... C 7
16214 Clarion⊙, 6,095 .... D 3
18411 Clarks Summit, 5,376 .... L 3
16625 Claysburg, 1,516 .... F 5
15323 Claysville, 951 .... B 5
16830 Clearfield⊙, 8,176 .... F 3
19018 Clifton Heights, 8,348 .... M 7
15728 Clymer, 2,054 .... E 4
18218 Coaldale, 3,023 .... L 4
19320 Coatesville, 12,331 .... L 5
16314 Cochranton, 1,229 .... B 2
19426 Collegeville, 3,191 .... M 5
19023 Collingdale, 10,605 .... N 7
18915 Colmar, 950 .... M 5
17512 Columbia, 11,237 .... K 5
16405 Columbus, 950 .... C 2
15927 Colver, 1,175 .... E 4
† 19023 Colwyn, 3,169 .... N 7
15424 Confluence, 954 .... D 6
16406 Conneautville, 1,032 .... A 2
15425 Connellsville, 11,643 .... C 5
19428 Conshohocken, 10,195 .... M 5
15027 Conway, 2,822 .... B 4
18219 Conyngham, 1,850 .... K 3
18036 Coopersburg, 2,326 .... M 5
18037 Coplay, 3,642 .... L 4
15108 Coraopolis, 8,435 .... B 4
17016 Cornwall, 2,111 .... K 5
16407 Corry, 7,435 .... C 2
16915 Coudersport⊙, 2,831 .... G 2
15624 Crabtree, 1,021 .... D 5
15205 Crafton, 8,233 .... B 7
16630 Cresson, 2,446 .... E 5
17929 Cressona, 1,814 .... K 4
19022 Crum Lynne, 3,700 .... M 7
15031 Cuddy, 2,500 .... B 5
16833 Curwensville, 3,189 .... E 4
† 15901 Dale, 2,274 .... E 5
18612 Dallas, 2,913 .... K 3
17313 Dallastown, 3,560 .... J 6
18414 Dalton, 1,282 .... L 2
17821 Danville⊙, 6,176 .... J 4
19023 Darby, 13,729 .... M 7
17018 Dauphin, 998 .... J 5
15626 Delmont, 1,934 .... D 5
17517 Denver, 2,248 .... K 5
15627 Derry, 3,338 .... D 5
18519 Dickson City, 7,698 .... L 3
17019 Dillsburg, 1,441 .... J 5
15734 Dixonville, 950 .... D 4
15033 Donora, 8,825 .... C 5
15216 Dormont, 12,856 .... B 7
19518 Douglassville, 975 .... L 5
17315 Dover, 1,168 .... J 6
19335 Downingtown, 7,437 .... L 5
18901 Doylestown⊙, 8,270 .... M 5
15034 Dravosburg, 2,916 .... C 7
19026 Drexel Hill, 50,000 .... M 6
18221 Drifton, 1,295 .... L 3
15801 DuBois, 10,112 .... E 3
† 17701 Duboistown, 1,468 .... H 3
15431 Dunbar, 1,499 .... C 6
17020 Duncannon, 1,739 .... H 5
16635 Duncansville, 2,210 .... F 5
18512 Dunmore, 17,300 .... L 3
15110 Duquesne, 11,410 .... C 7
18642 Duryea, 5,264 .... L 3
17316 East Berlin, 1.086 .... J 6
† 18603 East Berwick, 2,090 .... K 3
16028 East Brady, 1,218 .... C 3
15909 East Conemaugh, 2,710 .... E 5
† 17701 East Faxon, 4,175 .... J 3
18041 East Greenville, 2,003 .... L 5
† 19050 East Lansdowne, 3,186 .... M 7
18042 Easton⊙, 30,256 .... M 4
17520 East Petersburg, 3,407 .... K 5
18301 East Stroudsburg, 7,894 .... M 4
† 15301 East Washington, 2,198 .... B 5
15931 Ebensburg⊙, 4,318 .... E 5
† 15005 Economy, 7,176 .... B 4
19020 Eddington, 20,517 .... N 5
19013 Eddystone, 2,706 .... M 7
† 15201 Edgewood, 5,101 .... B 7
† 15143 Edgeworth, 2,200 .... B 4
16412 Edinboro, 4,871 .... B 2
16731 Eldred, 1,092 .... F 2
15037 Elizabeth, 2,206 .... C 5
17022 Elizabethtown, 8,072 .... J 5
17023 Elizabethville, 1,629 .... J 4
16920 Elkland, 1,942 .... H 1
15331 Ellsworth, 1,268 .... B 5
16117 Ellwood City, 10,857 .... B 4
15038 Elrama, 950 .... C 5
17824 Elysburg, 1,337 .... K 4
18049 Emmaus, 11,511 .... M 4
15834 Emporium⊙, 3,074 .... F 2
15202 Emsworth, 3,332 .... B 6
17025 Enola, 4,900 .... J 5
17522 Ephrata, 9,662 .... K 5
* 16501 Erie⊙, 129,231 .... B 1
Erie, ‡263,654 .... B 1
17815 Espy, 1,652 .... K 4
19029 Essington, 3,100 .... M 7
15223 Etna, 5,819 .... B 6
16033 Evans City, 2,144 .... B 4
15537 Everett, 2,243 .... F 5
15631 Everson, 1,143 .... C 5
15632 Export, 1,402 .... C 5
15436 Fairchance, 1,906 .... C 6
19030 Fairless Hills, 16,000 .... N 5
16415 Fairview, 1,707 .... B 1
15840 Falls Creek, 1,255 .... E 3
16121 Farrell, 11,022 .... A 3
15438 Fayette City, 968 .... C 5
17222 Fayetteville, 2,449 .... G 6
18921 Ferndale, 2,482 .... E 5
19522 Fleetwood, 3,064 .... L 5
17745 Flemington, 1,519 .... G 3
† 17552 Florin, 975 .... J 5
19032 Folcroft, 9,610 .... M 7
19033 Folsom, 7,815 .... M 7
16226 Ford City, 4,749 .... D 4
18421 Forest City, 2,322 .... L 2
15221 Forest Hills, 9,561 .... C 7
18704 Forty Fort, 6,114 .... L 3
† 18015 Fountain Hill, 5,384 .... L 4
15238 Fox Chapel, 4,684 .... C 6
17931 Frackville, 5,445 .... K 4
16323 Franklin⊙, 8,629 .... C 3
17026 Fredericksburg, 1,073 .... B 2
17026 Fredericksburg, 950 .... J 5
15333 Fredericktown, 1,067 .... C 6
15042 Freedom, 2,643 .... B 4
18224 Freeland, 4,784 .... L 3
18017 Freemansburg, 1,681 .... M 4
16229 Freeport, 2,375 .... C 4
† 16117 Frisco, 950 .... B 4
16922 Galeton, 1,552 .... G 2
16641 Gallitzin, 2,496 .... E 4
17527 Gap, 1,022 .... L 6
† 17701 Garden View, 2,662 .... H 3
15904 Geistown, 3,633 .... E 5
17325 Gettysburg⊙, 7,275 .... H 6
17934 Gilberton, 1,293 .... K 4
16417 Girard, 2,613 .... B 2
17935 Girardville, 2,450 .... K 4
15045 Glassport, 7,450 .... C 7
18617 Glen Lyon, 3,408 .... K 3
19036 Glenolden, 8,697 .... M 7
19037 Glen Riddle, 950 .... L 7
17327 Glen Rock, 1,600 .... J 6
15116 Glenshaw, 19,500 .... C 6
19038 Glenside, 17,353 .... M 5
15634 Grapeville, 1,600 .... C 5
17225 Greencastle, 3,293 .... G 6
15601 Greensburg⊙, 15,870 .... D 5
† 15201 Greentree, 6,441 .... B 7
16125 Greenville, 8,704 .... B 3
16127 Grove City, 8,312 .... B 3
18822 Hallstead, 1,447 .... L 2
19526 Hamburg, 3,909 .... L 4
17331 Hanover, 15,623 .... J 6
† 15201 Harmarville, 1,900 .... C 6
16037 Harmony, 1,207 .... B 4
* 17101 Harrisburg (cap.)⊙, 68,061 .... H 5
Harrisburg, ‡410,626 .... H 5
18618 Harveys Lake, 1,693 .... K 3
16646 Hastings, 1,791 .... E 4
19040 Hatboro, 8,880 .... M 5
19440 Hatfield, 2,385 .... M 5
19041 Haverford, ∆55,132 .... M 6
19083 Havertown, 42,500 .... M 6
16840 Hawk Run, 1,020 .... F 4
18428 Hawley, 1,331 .... M 3
18201 Hazleton, 30,426 .... L 4
15106 Heidelberg, 2,034 .... B 7
17406 Hellam, 1,825 .... J 6
18055 Hellertown, 6,613 .... M 4
15637 Herminie, 975 .... C 5
17033 Hershey, 7,407 .... J 5
† 17044 Highland Park, 1,704 .... H 4
17034 High Spire, 2,947 .... J 5
16132 Hillsville, 950 .... A 4
16648 Hollidaysburg⊙, 6,262 .... F 5
15748 Homer City, 2,465 .... D 4
15120 Homestead, 6,309 .... B 7
18431 Honesdale⊙, 5,224 .... M 2
19344 Honey Brook, 1,115 .... L 5
15936 Hooversville, 962 .... E 5
15445 Hopwood, 2,190 .... C 6

(continued on following page)

PENNSYLVANIA

SCALE
0 5 10 20 30 40 MI.
0 5 10 20 30 40KM.

State Capitals.............✦
County Seats..............⊙
Canals

Ⓒ C. S. HAMMOND & Co., N.Y.

15342 Houston, 1,812	B 5	16501 Kearsarge, 7,300	B 1
16651 Houtzdale, 1,193	F 4	† 19601 Kenhorst, 3,482	K 5
17737 Hughesville, 2,249	J 3	19348 Kennett Square, 4,876	L 6
17036 Hummelstown, 4,723	K 5	18704 Kingston, 18,325	K 3
16652 Huntingdon⊙, 6,987	G 5	16201 Kittanning⊙, 6,231	D 4
16843 Hyde, 1,264	F 4	16232 Knox, 1,306	C 3
15545 Hyndman, 1,151	E 6	16136 Koppel, 1,312	B 4
19345 Immaculata, 1,200	L 6	17834 Kulpmont, 4,026	J 4
15126 Imperial, 2,385	A 5	19530 Kutztown, 6,017	L 5
15701 Indiana⊙, 16,100	D 4	16423 Lake City, 2,117	B 1
15052 Industry, 2,442	B 4	16602 Lakemont, 1,350	F 5
15205 Ingram, 4,902	B 7	* 17601 Lancaster⊙, 57,690	K 5
15642 Irwin, 4,059	C 5	Lancaster, †319,693	K 5
17407 Jacobus, 1,368	J 6	17538 Landisville, 1,900	K 5
15644 Jeannette, 15,209	C 5	19047 Langhorne, 1,889	N 5
15344 Jefferson, 8,512	B 7	19446 Lansdale, 18,451	M 5
19046 Jenkintown, 5,990	M 5	19050 Lansdowne, 14,090	M 7
18433 Jermyn, 2,435	L 2	18232 Lansford, 5,168	L 4
15937 Jerome, 1,158	D 5	18626 Laporte⊙, 207	K 3
17740 Jersey Shore, 5,322	H 3	15647 Larimer, 2,500	C 5
18229 Jim Thorpe⊙, 5,456	L 4	15650 Latrobe, 11,749	D 5
15845 Johnsonburg, 4,304	E 3	19605 Laureldale, 4,519	L 5
* 15901 Johnstown, 42,476	D 5	15229 Laurel Gardens, 1,830	B 6
Johnstown, †262,822	D 5	16511 Lawrence Park, ▲4,517	C 1
17038 Jonestown, 954	K 5	17042 Lebanon⊙, 28,572	K 5
16735 Kane, 5,001	E 2	15656 Leechburg, 2,999	C 4

19533 Leesport, 1,158	K 5	15754 Lucernemines, 1,380	D 4
15056 Leetsdale, 1,862	A 5	18709 Luzerne, 4,504	L 3
18235 Lehighton, 6,095	L 4	17048 Lykens, 2,506	J 4
16851 Lemont, 2,547	G 4	16045 Lyndora, 8,415	B 4
17043 Lemoyne, 4,625	J 5	18062 Macungie, 1,414	L 5
19113 Lester, 1,700	M 7	16661 Madera, 950	F 4
19053 Levittown, 21,000	N 5	17948 Mahanoy City, 7,257	K 4
17837 Lewisburg⊙, 5,620	J 4	19355 Malvern, 2,583	L 5
17044 Lewistown⊙, 11,098	G 4	17345 Manchester, 2,391	J 5
16930 Liberty, 3,594	C 7	17545 Manheim, 5,434	K 5
15129 Library, 4,900	C 6	18057 Manor, 2,276	C 5
15658 Ligonier, 2,258	D 5	16933 Mansfield, 4,114	H 2
15938 Lilly, 1,429	D 5	19061 Marcus Hook, 3,041	L 7
15037 Lincoln, 1,885	C 7	17547 Marietta, 2,838	J 5
19352 Lincoln University, 1,400	L 6	17235 Marion, 950	G 6
16424 Linesville, 1,265	A 2	16046 Mars, 1,488	B 4
19468 Linfield, 975	L 5	16662 Martinsburg, 2,088	F 5
17112 Linglestown, 3,500	J 4	18063 Martins Creek, 950	M 4
† 17837 Linntown, 1,851	J 4	17053 Marysville, 2,328	J 5
19061 Linwood, 2,900	L 7	15461 Masontown, 4,226	C 6
17543 Lititz, 7,072	K 5	18336 Matamoras, 2,244	N 3
17340 Littlestown, 3,026	H 6	18229 Mauch Chunk (Jim Thorpe)⊙, 5,456	L 4
17745 Lock Haven⊙, 11,427	H 3	18433 Mayfield, 2,176	L 2
15940 Loretto, 1,661	L 2	18237 McAdoo, 3,326	L 4
15068 Lower Burrell, 13,654	C 4	17841 McClure, 1,094	H 4
15661 Loyalhanna, 4,283	D 5	15348 Millsboro, 980	B 5

17233 McConnellsburg⊙, 1,228	F 6	15209 Millvale, 5,815	B 7
15057 McDonald, 2,879	B 5	19033 Milmont Park, 2,891	M 7
* 15130 McKeesport, 37,977	C 7	17063 Milroy, 1,575	G 4
15136 McKees Rocks, 11,901	B 7	17847 Milton, 7,723	J 3
17344 McSherrystown, 2,773	H 6	17954 Minersville, 6,012	K 4
15347 Meadow Lands, 3,609	B 5	18655 Monaca, 950	L 5
16335 Meadville⊙, 16,573	B 2	19540 Mohnton, 2,153	L 5
17055 Mechanicsburg, 9,385	H 5	15061 Monaca, 7,486	B 4
* 19063 Media⊙, 6,444	L 7	15062 Monessen, 15,216	C 5
16137 Mercer⊙, 2,654	B 3	15063 Monongahela, 7,113	C 5
17236 Mercersburg, 1,727	G 6	15146 Monroeville, 29,011	C 7
19066 Merion Station, 5,686	M 6	17237 Mont Alto, 1,532	G 6
15552 Meyersdale, 2,648	E 6	17752 Montgomery, 1,902	H 3
17842 Middleburg⊙, 1,369	H 4	17754 Montoursville, 5,985	J 3
17057 Middletown, 9,080	J 5	18801 Montrose⊙, 2,058	L 2
15059 Midland, 5,271	A 4	18507 Moosic, 4,273	L 3
15060 Midway, 1,188	B 5	19067 Morrisville, 11,309	N 5
16853 Milesburg, 1,196	G 4	19070 Morton, 2,602	M 7
17751 Mill Hall, 1,838	H 3	18444 Moscow, 1,430	L 3
16853 Millersburg, 3,074	J 4	17851 Mount Carmel, 9,317	J 4
17551 Millersville, 6,396	K 6	17065 Mount Holly Springs, 2,009	H 5
17751 Mill Hall, 1,838	G 3	16740 Mount Jewett, 1,060	E 2
15228 Mount Lebanon, ▲39,596	B 7	17552 Mount Joy, 5,041	J 5
		15228 Mount Lebanon, ▲39,596	B 7
		15210 Mount Oliver, 5,487	C 7
		19606 Mount Penn, 3,465	L 5

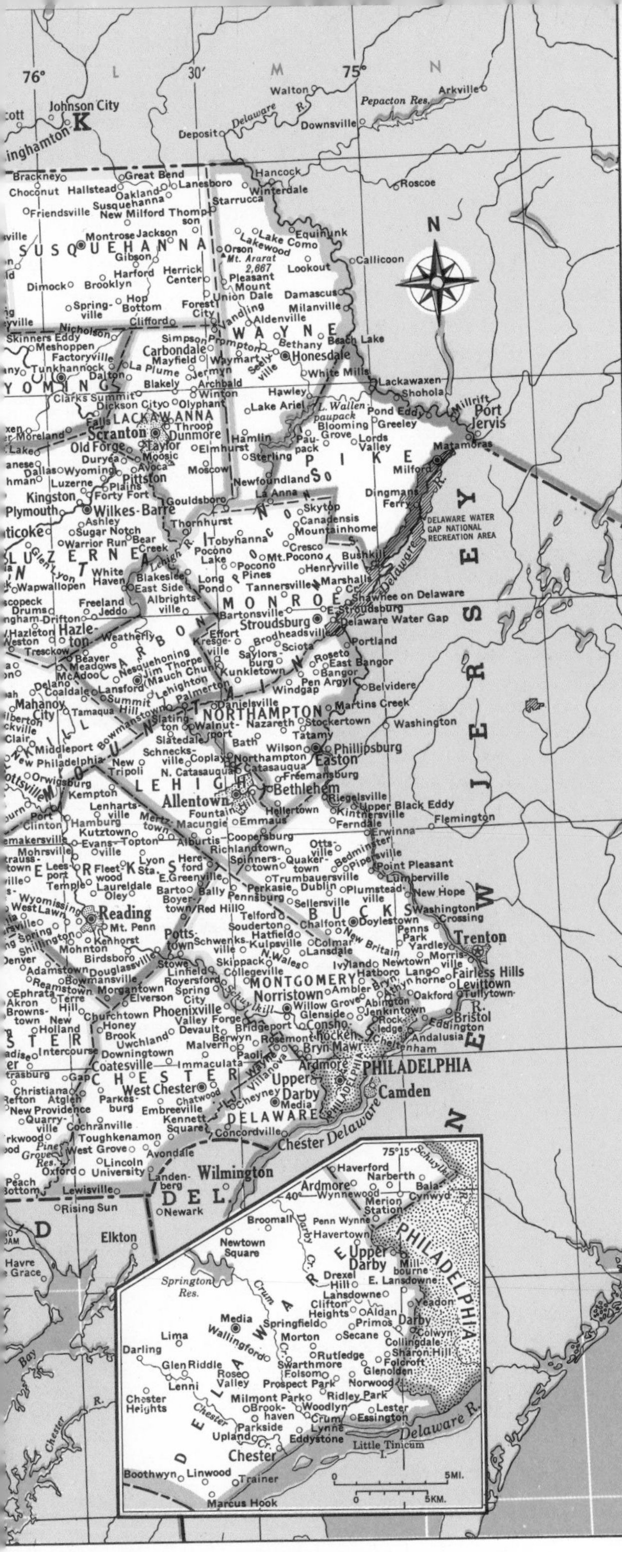

Johnson City
Walton
Pepacton Res.
Arkville
Downsville
Deposit
Delaware R.
Great Bend
Hancock
Roscoe
Hallstead
Oakland
Lanesboro
Susquehanna
Starrucca
Winterdale
Friendsville
New Milford
Equinunk
Montrose
SUSQUEHANNA
Lake Como
Callicoon
Mt. Ararat 2,667
Harford
Herrick Center
Lookout
Dimock
Brooklyn
Pleasant Mount
Union Dale
Damascus
Forest City
Milanville
WAYNE
Clifford
Nicholson
Aldenville
Carbondale
Beach Lake
Meshoppen
Factoryville
Mayfield
Honesdale
Tunkhannock
La Plume
Jermyn
White Mills
Blakely
Archbald
Lackawaxen
Shohola
Clarks Summit
Hawley
Winton
Lake Ariel
L. Wallenpaupack
Milford
Port Jervis
Dickson City
Olyphant
Throop
LACKAWANNA
Scranton
Dunmore
Old Forge
Taylor
Moosic
Greeley
Lords Valley
Matamoras
Dallas
Wyoming
Avoca
Pittston
Elmhurst
Moscow
PIKE
Kingston
Forty Fort
Plymouth
Wilkes-Barre
Newfoundland
Dingmans Ferry
Ashley
Sugar Notch
Warrior Run
Gouldsboro
Thornhurst
Skytop
Canadensis
Mountainhome
DELAWARE WATER GAP NATIONAL RECREATION AREA
Bear Creek
Tobyhanna
Pocono Lake
Mt. Pocono
Cresco
Bushkill
White Haven
Blakeslee
Long Pond
Pocono Pines
Henryville
Tannersville
Marshalls Creek
Freeland
Jeddo
Albrightsville
MONROE
Shawnee on Delaware
East Stroudsburg
Stroudsburg
Delaware Water Gap
Hazleton
Weatherly
Effort
Brodheadsville
Portland
Sciota
Nesquehoning
Jim Thorpe
Saylorsburg
Kunkletown
Roseto
Bangor
East Bangor
Pen Argyl
Belvidere
Lansford
Summit Hill
Lehighton
Palmerton
Windgap
Martins Creek
Tamaqua
NORTHAMPTON
Nazareth
Stockertown
Washington
Slatington
Walnut-port
Tatamy
Bath
Wilson
Phillipsburg
Northampton
Easton
Catasauqua
Coplay
Schnecksville
Fremansburg
Bethlehem
LEHIGH
Allentown
Riegelsville
Black Eddy
Fountain Hill
Kintnersville
Hellertown
Emmaus
Macungie
Ferndale
Flemington
Coopersburg
Richlandtown
Quakertown
Trumbauersville
Perkasie
Dublin
Plumsteadville
New Hope
Washington Crossing
BUCKS
Doylestown
Chalfont
Sellersville
Pennsburg
Telford
Souderton
Hatfield
Lansdale
Colmar
New Britain
Yardley
Trenton
Reading
Mt. Penn
Kenhorst
Shillington
Mohnton
Birdsboro
Pottstown
Schwenksville
Skippack
Collegeville
Norristown
Ambler
MONTGOMERY
Willow Grove
Levittown
Fairless Hills
Bristol
Tullytown
Oakford
Phoenixville
Royersford
Spring City
Valley Forge
Jenkintown
Abington
Glenside
Conshohocken
Rosemont
Bryn Mawr
Malvern
Berwyn
Paoli
Coatesville
Downingtown
CHESTER
West Chester
Ardmore
Upper Darby
Media
PHILADELPHIA
Camden
Kennett Square
Chester
DELAWARE
Concordville
Avondale
West Grove
Toughkenamon
Lincoln University
Oxford
Wilmington
DEL.
Newark
Rising Sun
Elkton
Havre de Grace
Delaware R.
JERSEY
NEW

15666 Mount Pleasant, 5,895	D 5
18344 Mount Pocono, 1,019	M 3
17066 Mount Union, 3,662	G 5
17554 Mountville, 1,454	K 5
17347 Mount Wolf, 1,811	J 5
17756 Muncy, 2,872	H 4
15120 Munhall, 16,674	C 7
15668 Murrysville, 3,900	C 5
17067 Myerstown, 3,645	K 5
18634 Nanticoke, 14,632	K 3
15943 Nanty Glo, 4,298	E 5
19072 Narberth, 5,151	M 6
15065 Natrona Heights, 15,000	C 4
18064 Nazareth, 5,815	M 4
15351 Nemacolin, 1,273	B 6
18635 Nescopeck, 1,897	K 3
18240 Nesquehoning, 3,338	L 4
† 16141 New Beaver, 1,426	B 4
16140 New Bedford, 950	A 3
16242 New Bethlehem, 1,406	D 3
17068 New Bloomfield⊙, 1,032	H 5
15066 New Brighton, 7,637	B 4
18901 New Britain, 2,428	M 5
* 16101 New Castle⊙, 38,559	B 3
17070 New Cumberland, 9,803	J 5
15067 New Eagle, 2,497	B 5
17349 New Freedom, 1,495	J 6
17557 New Holland, 3,971	K 5
18938 New Hope, 978	N 5
15068 New Kensington, 20,312	C 4
18834 New Milford, 1,143	L 2
17350 New Oxford, 1,495	H 6
17959 New Philadelphia, 1,528	K 4
17074 Newport, 1,747	H 5
15468 New Salem, 1,337	C 6
15626 New Salem (Delmont), 1,934	D 5
18940 Newtown, 2,216	N 5
19073 Newtown Square, 16,000	L 6
17241 Newville, 1,631	H 5
16142 New Wilmington, 2,721	B 3
17759 Nisbet, 950	H 3
* 19401 Norristown⊙, 38,169	M 5
18067 Northampton, 8,389	M 4
15673 North Apollo, 1,618	D 4
15104 North Braddock, 10,838	C 7
† 18032 North Catasauqua, 2,941	L 4
16428 North East, 3,846	C 1
17857 Northumberland, 4,102	J 4
19454 North Wales, 3,911	M 5
16365 North Warren, 1,360	D 2
15674 Norvelt, 2,588	C 5
19074 Norwood, 7,229	M 7
18636 Noxen, 950	K 3
18241 Nuremberg, 950	K 4
15071 Oakdale, 1,614	B 5
† 19047 Oakford, 3,800	N 5
15139 Oakmont, 7,550	C 6
† 15059 Ohioville, 3,918	B 4
16301 Oil City, 15,033	C 3
18518 Old Forge, 9,522	L 3
15472 Oliver, 3,091	C 6
18447 Olyphant, 5,422	L 3
17961 Orwigsburg, 2,661	K 4
16666 Osceola Mills, 1,671	F 4
19363 Oxford, 3,658	K 6
† 15963 Paint, 1,233	E 5
18071 Palmerton, 5,620	L 4
17078 Palmyra, 7,615	J 5
19301 Paoli, 5,835	M 5
17562 Paradise, 975	K 5
19365 Parkesburg, 2,701	L 6
† 19013 Parkside, 2,343	M 7
† 17331 Parkville, 5,120	J 6
16668 Patton, 2,762	E 4
17111 Paxtang, 2,160	J 5
18072 Pen Argyl, 3,668	M 4
17103 Penbrook, 3,379	J 5
18073 Pennsburg, 2,260	M 5
† 19003 Penn Wynne, 6,038	M 6
18944 Perkasie, 5,451	M 5
15473 Perryopolis, 2,043	C 5
* 19101 Philadelphia⊙, 1,948,609	N 6
Philadelphia, ‡4,817,914	N 6
16866 Philipsburg, 3,700	F 4
19460 Phoenixville, 14,823	L 5
17963 Pine Grove, 2,197	K 4
16868 Pine Grove Mills, 950	G 4
15140 Pitcairn, 4,741	C 5
* 15201 Pittsburgh⊙, 520,117	B 7
Pittsburgh, ‡2,401,245	B 7
* 18640 Pittston, 11,113	L 3
18705 Plains, 6,606	L 3
16823 Pleasant Gap, 1,773	G 4
15236 Pleasant Hills, 10,409	B 7
16341 Pleasantville, 1,005	C 2
15239 Plum, 21,932	C 5
18651 Plymouth, 9,536	K 3
† 16830 Plymptonville, 1,040	F 3
15474 Point Marion, 1,750	C 6
16342 Polk, 3,673	C 3
15946 Portage, 4,151	E 5
16743 Port Allegany, 2,703	F 2
17965 Port Carbon, 2,717	K 4
15133 Port Vue, 5,862	C 7
19464 Pottstown, 25,355	L 5
17901 Pottsville⊙, 19,715	K 4
19018 Primos, 3,900	M 7
16052 Prospect, 973	B 4
19076 Prospect Park, 7,250	M 7
15767 Punxsutawney, 7,792	E 4
18951 Quakertown, 7,276	M 5
17566 Quarryville, 1,571	K 6
† 15104 Rankin, 3,817	C 7
* 19601 Reading⊙, 87,643	L 5
Reading, ‡415,056	L 5
17567 Reamstown, 1,050	K 5
18076 Red Hill, 1,201	L 5
17356 Red Lion, 5,645	J 6
17084 Reedsville, 950	G 4
17764 Renovo, 2,620	G 3
15851 Reynoldsville, 2,771	D 3
17087 Richland, 1,444	K 5
15853 Ridgway⊙, 6,022	E 3
19078 Ridley Park, 9,025	M 7
18077 Riegelsville, 1,050	M 4
15678 Rillton, 975	C 5
16248 Rimersburg, 1,146	D 3
17868 Riverside, 1,905	J 4
16673 Roaring Spring, 2,811	F 5
19551 Robesonia, 1,685	K 5
15949 Robinson, 975	D 5
15074 Rochester, 4,819	B 4
19111 Rockledge, 2,564	M 5
15557 Rockwood, 1,051	D 6
15477 Roscoe, 1,176	C 5
19010 Rosemont, 4,900	M 5
18013 Roseto, 1,538	M 4
17250 Rouzerville, 1,419	G 6
† 17067 Royalton, 1,040	J 5
19468 Royersford, 4,235	L 5
16249 Rural Valley, 962	D 4
16345 Russell, 950	D 2
15076 Russellton, 1,597	C 4
19070 Rutledge, 1,167	M 7
16433 Saegertown, 1,348	B 2
17970 Saint Clair, 4,576	K 4
15857 Saint Marys, 7,470	E 3
15951 Saint Michael, 1,248	E 5
15681 Saltsburg, 1,037	C 4
† 15801 Sandy, 2,000	E 3
16056 Saxonburg, 1,191	C 4
18840 Sayre, 7,473	K 2
15963 Scalp Level, 1,353	E 5
17088 Schaefferstown, 1,027	K 5
18078 Schnecksville, 1,550	L 4
17972 Schuylkill Haven, 6,125	K 4
18354 Sciota, 950	M 4
15683 Scottdale, 5,818	C 5
* 18501 Scranton⊙, 103,564	L 3
Scranton, ‡234,107	L 3
19018 Secane, 5,700	M 7
17870 Selinsgrove, 5,116	J 4
18960 Sellersville, 2,829	M 5
15143 Sewickley, 5,660	B 4
17872 Shamokin, 11,719	J 4
17876 Shamokin Dam, 1,562	J 4
16146 Sharon, 22,653	B 3
19079 Sharon Hill, 7,464	N 7
15215 Sharpsburg, 5,499	B 6
16150 Sharpsville, 6,126	A 3
16347 Sheffield, 1,564	D 2
17976 Shenandoah, 8,287	K 4
18655 Shickshinny, 1,685	K 3
19607 Shillington, 6,249	K 5
16748 Shinglehouse, 1,320	F 2
17257 Shippensburg, 6,536	H 5
19555 Shoemakersville, 1,427	K 4
17361 Shrewsbury, 1,716	J 6
18407 Simpson, 1,900	L 2
19608 Sinking Spring, 2,862	K 5
19474 Skippack, 975	M 5
18080 Slatington, 4,687	L 4
15684 Slickville, 1,066	C 5
16057 Slippery Rock, 4,949	B 3
16749 Smethport⊙, 1,883	F 2
15478 Smithfield, 969	C 6
15501 Somerset⊙, 6,269	D 6
18964 Souderton, 6,366	M 5
15425 South Connellsville, 2,385	C 6
15956 South Fork, 1,661	E 5
† 14892 South Waverly, 1,307	J 2
17701 South Williamsport, 7,153	J 3
15775 Spangler, 3,109	E 4
19475 Spring City, 3,578	L 5
15144 Springdale, 5,202	C 4
19064 Springfield, ▵2,446	M 7
17362 Spring Grove, 1,669	J 6
16801 State College, 33,778	G 4
17113 Steelton, 8,556	J 5
17363 Stewartstown, 1,157	K 6
16153 Stoneboro, 1,129	B 3
19464 Stowe, 3,596	L 5
17579 Strasburg, 1,897	K 6
18360 Stroudsburg⊙, 5,451	M 4
† 16323 Sugarcreek, 5,944	C 3
18706 Sugar Notch, 1,333	L 3
18250 Summit Hill, 3,811	L 4
17801 Sunbury⊙, 13,025	J 4
18847 Susquehanna, 2,319	L 2
19081 Swarthmore, 6,156	M 7
15218 Swissvale, 13,821	C 7
15865 Sykesville, 1,311	E 3
18252 Tamaqua, 9,246	L 4
15084 Tarentum, 7,379	C 4
18517 Taylor, 6,977	L 3
18969 Telford, 3,409	M 5
19560 Temple, 1,667	L 5
16259 Templeton, 950	C 4
17581 Terre Hill, 1,129	L 5
18512 Throop, 4,307	L 3
16353 Tionesta⊙, 711	C 2
16354 Titusville, 7,331	C 2
19562 Topton, 1,744	L 5
19374 Toughkenamon, 1,233	L 6
18848 Towanda⊙, 4,224	J 2
17980 Tower City, 1,774	J 4
15085 Trafford, 4,383	C 5
† 19013 Trainer, 2,336	L 7
17981 Tremont, 1,833	K 4
18254 Tresckow, 1,146	K 4
17881 Trevorton, 2,196	J 4
16947 Troy, 1,315	J 2
19007 Tullytown, 2,194	N 5
18657 Tunkhannock⊙, 2,251	L 2
15145 Turtle Creek, 8,308	C 7
15960 Twin Rocks, 975	E 4
16686 Tyrone, 7,072	F 4
16438 Union City, 3,631	C 2
15401 Uniontown⊙, 16,282	C 6
15689 United, 975	D 5
15235 Universal, 1,900	C 7
† 19013 Upland, 3,930	L 7
* 19082 Upper Darby, ▵95,910	M 6
19481 Valley Forge, 400	L 5
17983 Valley View, 1,585	J 4
15690 Vandergrift, 7,873	D 4
15147 Verona, 3,737	C 6
15132 Versailles, 2,754	C 7
19085 Villanova, 5,250	M 6
† 15148 Wall, 1,265	C 5
19086 Wallingford, 3,500	L 7
18088 Walnutport, 1,942	L 4
16157 Wampum, 1,189	B 4
16365 Warren⊙, 12,998	D 2
15301 Washington⊙, 19,827	B 5
16441 Waterford, 1,468	B 2
17777 Watsontown, 2,514	J 3
18472 Waymart, 1,122	M 2
19087 Wayne, 12,500	M 6
17268 Waynesboro, 10,011	G 6
15370 Waynesburg⊙, 5,152	B 6
18255 Weatherly, 2,554	L 4
16901 Wellsboro⊙, 4,003	H 2
19565 Wernersville, 1,761	K 5
16510 Wesleyville, 3,920	C 1
15417 West Brownsville, 1,426	C 5
19380 West Chester⊙, 19,301	L 6
16950 Westfield, 1,273	H 2
19390 West Grove, 1,870	L 6
18201 West Hazleton, 6,059	K 4
† 16201 West Kittanning, 956	C 4
19609 West Lawn, 1,973	K 5
† 15656 West Leechburg, 1,422	C 4
16159 West Middlesex, 1,293	B 3
15122 West Mifflin, 28,070	C 7
† 15901 Westmont, 6,673	D 5
15089 West Newton, 3,648	C 5
15229 West View, 8,312	B 6
† 17401 West York, 5,314	J 6
16161 Wheatland, 1,421	B 3
15120 Whitaker, 1,697	C 7
18052 Whitehall, 16,551	B 7
18661 White Haven, 2,134	L 3
15131 White Oak, 9,304	C 7
17097 Wiconisco, 1,236	J 4
15870 Wilcox, 950	E 2
* 18701 Wilkes-Barre⊙, 58,856	L 3
Wilkes-Barre-Hazleton, ‡342,301	L 3
15221 Wilkinsburg, 26,780	C 7
16693 Williamsburg, 1,704	F 5
17701 Williamsport⊙, 37,918	H 3
17098 Williamstown, 1,919	J 4
19090 Willow Grove, 16,494	M 5
15148 Wilmerding, 3,218	C 7
15025 Wilson, 8,482	M 4
15963 Windber, 6,332	E 5
18091 Windgap, 2,270	M 4
17366 Windsor, 1,298	J 6
† 18434 Winton, 4,948	M 3
† 15301 Wolfdale, 1,202	B 5
19567 Womelsdorf, 1,551	K 5
19094 Woodlyn, 6,500	M 7
17368 Wrightsville, 2,668	J 5
19096 Wynnewood, 9,200	M 6
18644 Wyoming, 4,195	L 3
19610 Wyomissing, 7,136	K 5
19067 Yardley, 2,616	N 5
19050 Yeadon, 12,136	N 7
17099 Yeagertown, 1,363	G 4
* 17401 York⊙, 50,335	J 6
York, ‡329,540	J 6
16371 Youngsville, 2,158	D 2
15697 Youngwood, 3,057	D 5
16063 Zelienople, 3,602	B 4

⊙ County seat.
‡ Population of metropolitan area.
▵ Population of town of township.
† Zip of nearest p.o.
* Multiple zips

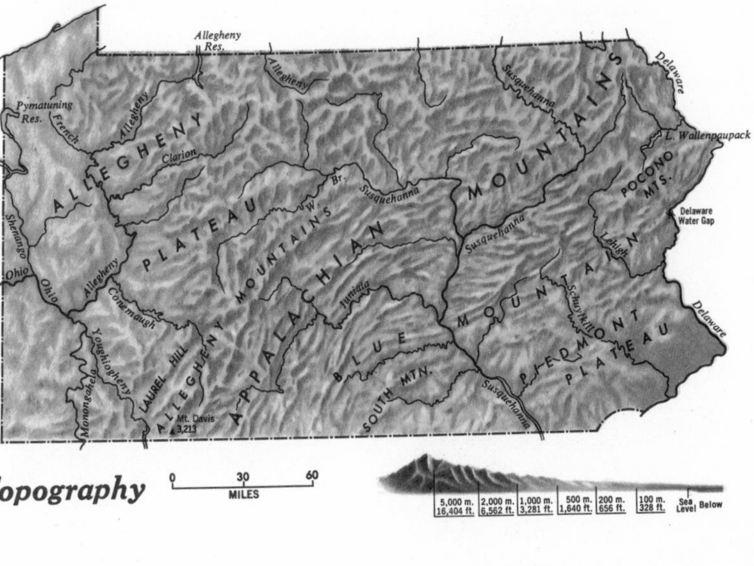

Allegheny Res.
Allegheny
Pymatuning Res.
French
ALLEGHENY
Clarion
Susquehanna
L. Wallenpaupack
MOUNTAINS
POCONO MTS.
Delaware Water Gap
Delaware
PLATEAU
W. Br. Susquehanna
APPALACHIAN MOUNTAINS
Juniata
Lehigh
Schuylkill
BLUE MOUNTAIN
PIEDMONT PLATEAU
SOUTH MTN.
Ohio
Shenango
Conemaugh
Youghiogheny
Monongahela
LAUREL HILL
Mt. Davis 3,213
0 30 60
MILES
5,000 m. 16,404 ft.
2,000 m. 6,562 ft.
1,000 m. 3,281 ft.
500 m. 1,640 ft.
200 m. 656 ft.
100 m. 328 ft.
Sea Level
Below

Topography

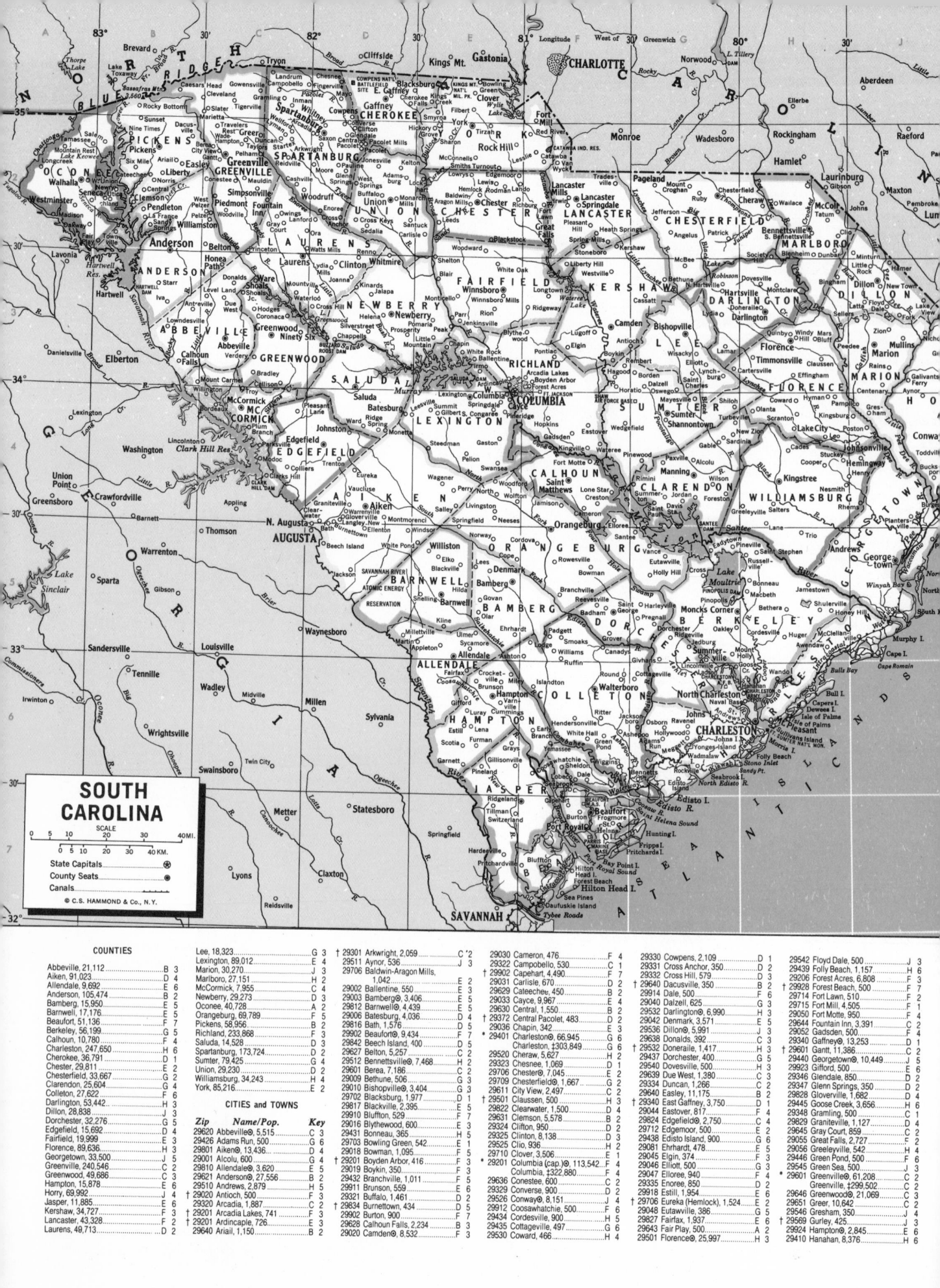

SOUTH CAROLINA

SCALE
0 5 10   20   30   40MI.
0 5 10   20   30   40 KM.

State Capitals .... ⊛
County Seats .... ◉
Canals ....

© C.S. HAMMOND & Co., N.Y.

COUNTIES

Abbeville, 21,112 .... B 3
Aiken, 91,023 .... D 4
Allendale, 9,692 .... E 6
Anderson, 105,474 .... B 2
Bamberg, 15,950 .... E 5
Barnwell, 17,176 .... E 5
Beaufort, 51,136 .... F 7
Berkeley, 56,199 .... G 5
Calhoun, 10,780 .... F 4
Charleston, 247,650 .... H 6
Cherokee, 36,791 .... D 1
Chester, 29,811 .... E 2
Chesterfield, 33,667 .... G 2
Clarendon, 25,604 .... G 4
Colleton, 27,622 .... F 6
Darlington, 53,442 .... H 3
Dillon, 28,838 .... J 3
Dorchester, 32,276 .... G 5
Edgefield, 15,692 .... D 4
Fairfield, 19,999 .... E 3
Florence, 89,636 .... H 3
Georgetown, 33,500 .... J 5
Greenville, 240,546 .... C 2
Greenwood, 49,686 .... C 3
Hampton, 15,878 .... E 6
Horry, 69,992 .... J 4
Jasper, 11,885 .... E 6
Kershaw, 34,727 .... F 3
Lancaster, 43,328 .... F 2
Laurens, 49,713 .... D 2

Lee, 18,323 .... G 3
Lexington, 89,012 .... E 4
Marion, 30,270 .... J 3
Marlboro, 27,151 .... H 2
McCormick, 7,955 .... C 4
Newberry, 29,273 .... D 3
Oconee, 40,728 .... A 2
Orangeburg, 69,789 .... F 5
Pickens, 58,956 .... B 2
Richland, 233,868 .... F 3
Saluda, 14,528 .... D 3
Spartanburg, 173,724 .... D 2
Sumter, 79,425 .... F 3
Union, 29,230 .... D 2
Williamsburg, 34,243 .... H 4
York, 85,216 .... E 2

CITIES and TOWNS

Zip   Name/Pop.   Key
29620 Abbeville◉, 5,515 ...... C 3
29426 Adams Run, 500 .... G 6
29801 Aiken◉, 13,436 .... D 4
29001 Alcolu, 600 .... G 4
29810 Allendale◉, 3,620 ...... E 5
29621 Anderson◉, 27,556 ... B 2
29510 Andrews, 2,879 .... H 5
† 29020 Antioch, 500 .... F 3
29320 Arcadia, 1,887 .... C 2
† 29201 Arcadia Lakes, 741 ... F 3
29902 Burton, 1,095 .... F 7
29628 Calhoun Falls, 2,234 .. B 3
29640 Ariail, 1,150 .... B 2
29020 Camden◉, 8,532 .... F 3

† 29301 Arkwright, 2,059 .... C *2
29511 Aynor, 536 .... J 3
29706 Baldwin-Aragon Mills,
         1,042 .... D 1
29002 Ballentine, 550 .... E 3
29003 Bamberg◉, 3,406 ...... E 5
29812 Barnwell◉, 4,439 ...... E 5
29006 Batesburg, 4,036 ...... D 4
29816 Bath, 1,576 .... D 5
29902 Beaufort◉, 9,434 ...... F 7
29842 Beech Island, 400 ..... D 5
29627 Belton, 5,257 .... C 2
29512 Bennettsville◉, 7,468 . H 2
29009 Berea, 7,186 .... C 2
29009 Bethune, 506 .... G 3
29010 Bishopville◉, 3,404 ... G 3
29702 Blacksburg, 1,977 ..... D 1
29817 Blackville, 2,395 .... E 5
29910 Bluffton, 529 .... F 7
29016 Blythewood, 600 .... F 3
29431 Bonneau, 365 .... H 5
29703 Bowling Green, 542 ... E 1
29018 Bowman, 1,095 .... F 5
† 29201 Boyden Arbor, 416 ..... F 3
29019 Boykin, 350 .... F 3
29432 Branchville, 1,011 ..... F 5
29911 Brunson, 599 .... E 6
29321 Buffalo, 1,461 .... D 2
29834 Burnettown, 434 .... D 5

29030 Cameron, 476 .... F 4
29322 Campobello, 530 .... C 1
29902 Capehart, 4,490 .... F 7
29031 Carlisle, 670 .... D 2
29629 Cateechee, 450 .... B 2
29033 Cayce, 9,967 .... E 4
29532 Central, 1,550 .... B 2
† 29372 Central Pacolet, 483 ... D 2
* 29036 Chapin, 342 .... E 3
* 29401 Charleston◉, 66,945 ... G 6
         Charleston, ‡303,849 . G 6
29520 Cheraw, 5,627 .... H 2
29323 Chesnee, 1,069 .... D 1
29706 Chester◉, 7,045 .... E 2
29611 Chesterfield◉, 1,667 ... G 2
29611 City View, 2,497 .... C 2
† 29401 Claussen, 500 .... H 3
29622 Clearwater, 1,500 ...... D 4
29631 Clemson, 5,578 .... B 2
29324 Clifton, 950 .... D 2
29325 Clinton, 8,138 .... D 3
29525 Clio, 936 .... J 2
29710 Clover, 3,506 .... E 1
* 29201 Columbia (cap)◉, 113,542 . F 4
         Columbia, ‡322,880 ... F 4
29636 Converse, 600 .... D 2
29329 Converse, 900 .... D 2
29526 Conway◉, 8,151 .... J 4
29912 Cooshawatchie, 500 ... E 6
29434 Cordesville, 900 .... H 5
29435 Cottageville, 497 .... G 6
29530 Coward, 466 .... H 4

29330 Cowpens, 2,109 .... D 1
29331 Cross Anchor, 350 ..... D 2
29332 Cross Hill, 579 .... D 3
† 29640 Dacusville, 350 .... B 2
29914 Dale, 500 .... F 6
29040 Dalzell, 625 .... G 3
29532 Darlington◉, 6,990 .... H 3
29042 Denmark, 3,571 .... E 5
29536 Dillon◉, 5,991 .... J 3
29638 Donalds, 392 .... C 3
† 29532 Doneraile, 1,417 .... H 3
29437 Dorchester, 400 .... G 5
29540 Dovesville, 500 .... H 3
29639 Due West, 1,360 .... C 3
29334 Duncan, 1,266 .... C 2
29640 Easley, 11,175 .... B 2
29044 Eastover, 817 .... F 4
29824 Edgefield◉, 2,750 ..... C 4
29712 Edgemoor, 500 .... E 2
29438 Edisto Island, 900 ..... G 6
29081 Ehrhardt, 478 .... E 5
29045 Elgin, 374 .... F 3
29046 Elliott, 500 .... G 3
29047 Elloree, 940 .... F 4
29335 Enoree, 850 .... D 2
29918 Estill, 1,954 .... E 6
* 29601 Eureka (Hemlock), 1,524 . C 2
29708 Eutawville, 386 .... G 5
29827 Fairfax, 1,937 .... E 6
29643 Fair Play, 500 .... A 2
29501 Florence◉, 25,997 ..... H 3

29542 Floyd Dale, 500 .... J 3
29439 Folly Beach, 1,157 .... H 6
29206 Forest Acres, 6,808 ... F 3
† 29928 Forest Beach, 500 ..... F 7
29714 Fort Lawn, 510 .... F 2
29715 Fort Mill, 4,505 .... F 1
29050 Fort Motte, 950 .... F 4
29644 Fountain Inn, 3,391 ... C 2
29052 Gadsden, 500 .... F 4
29340 Gaffney◉, 13,253 ...... D 1
† 29601 Gantt, 11,386 .... C 2
29440 Georgetown◉, 10,449 . J 5
29923 Gifford, 500 .... E 6
29346 Glendale, 850 .... D 2
29347 Glenn Springs, 350 ... D 2
29828 Gloverville, 1,682 ...... D 5
29445 Goose Creek, 3,656 ... H 6
29348 Gramling, 500 .... C 2
29829 Graniteville, 1,127 .... D 5
29645 Gray Court, 859 .... C 2
29055 Great Falls, 2,727 ..... E 2
29056 Greeleyville, 542 ...... H 4
29446 Green Pond, 500 .... F 6
29545 Green Sea, 500 .... J 3
* 29601 Greenville◉, 61,208 .... C 2
         Greenville, ‡299,502 .. C 2
29646 Greenwood◉, 21,069 . C 3
29651 Greer, 10,642 .... C 2
29546 Gresham, 350 .... J 3
29645 Gurley, 425 .... J 3
29569 Hamlet, 500 .... J 3
29924 Hampton◉, 2,845 ...... E 6
29410 Hanahan, 8,376 .... H 6

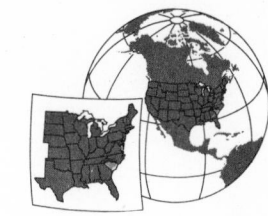

Agriculture, Industry and Resources

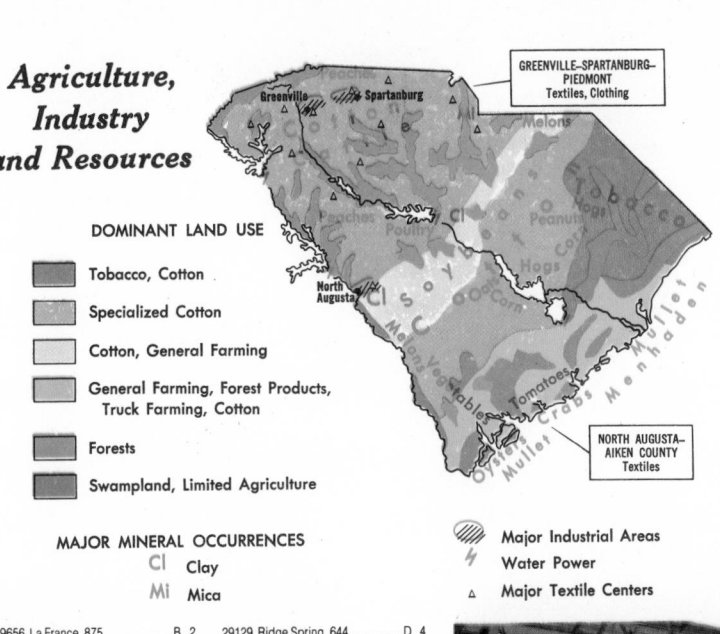

GREENVILLE–SPARTANBURG–PIEDMONT
Textiles, Clothing

NORTH AUGUSTA–AIKEN COUNTY
Textiles

DOMINANT LAND USE

- Tobacco, Cotton
- Specialized Cotton
- Cotton, General Farming
- General Farming, Forest Products, Truck Farming, Cotton
- Forests
- Swampland, Limited Agriculture

MAJOR MINERAL OCCURRENCES

- Cl Clay
- Mi Mica

- ⧄ Major Industrial Areas
- ⚡ Water Power
- △ Major Textile Centers

AREA 31,055 sq. mi.
POPULATION 2,590,516
CAPITAL Columbia
LARGEST CITY Columbia
HIGHEST POINT Sassafras Mtn. 3,560 ft.
SETTLED IN 1670
ADMITTED TO UNION May 23, 1788
POPULAR NAME Palmetto State
STATE FLOWER Yellow Jessamine
STATE BIRD Carolina Wren

Colorful materials being Sanforized in a South Carolina textile mill. Textiles are by far the most important of the state's industries.

D'Arazien – Shostal Associates

Topography

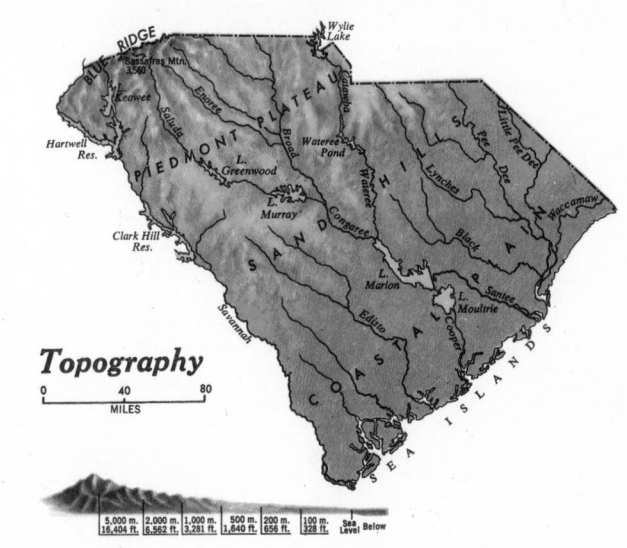

BLUE RIDGE
PIEDMONT PLATEAU
SAND HILLS
COASTAL PLAIN
SEA ISLANDS

0   40   80
MILES

5,000 m. / 2,000 m. / 1,000 m. / 500 m. / 200 m. / 100 m. / Sea Level
16,404 ft. / 6,562 ft. / 3,281 ft. / 1,640 ft. / 656 ft. / 328 ft. / Below

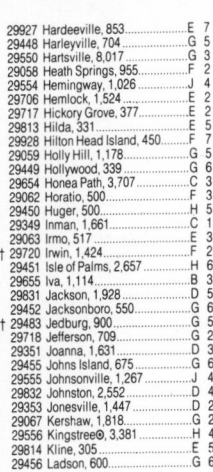

234 South Dakota

COUNTIES

County	Pop.	Key
Aurora, 4,183	M 6
Beadle, 20,877	N 5
Bennett, 3,088	F 7
Bon Homme, 8,577	O 7
Brookings, 22,158	R 5
Brown, 36,920	N 2
Brule, 5,870	L 6
Buffalo, 1,739	L 5
Butte, 7,825	B 4
Campbell, 2,866	J 2
Charles Mix, 9,994	M 7
Clark, 5,515	O 4
Clay, 12,923	P 7
Codington, 19,140	P 4
Corson, 4,994	G 2
Custer, 4,698	B 6
Davison, 17,319	N 6
Day, 8,713	O 3
Deuel, 5,686	R 4
Dewey, 5,170	G 3
Douglas, 4,569	N 7
Edmunds, 5,548	L 3
Fall River, 7,505	B 7
Faulk, 3,893	L 3
Grant, 9,005	R 3
Gregory, 6,710	L 7
Haakon, 2,802	F 5
Hamlin, 5,172	Q 4
Hand, 5,883	L 4
Hanson, 3,781	O 6
Harding, 1,855	B 2
Hughes, 11,632	J 5
Hutchinson, 10,379	O 7
Hyde, 2,515	K 4
Jackson, 1,531	F 6
Jerauld, 3,310	M 5
Jones, 1,882	H 6
Kingsbury, 7,657	O 5
Lake, 11,456	P 5
Lawrence, 17,453	B 5
Lincoln, 11,761	R 7
Lyman, 4,060	J 6
Marshall, 5,965	O 2
McCook, 7,246	P 6
McPherson, 5,022	L 2
Meade, 16,618	D 5
Mellette, 2,420	H 6
Miner, 4,454	O 5
Minnehaha, 95,209	R 6
Moody, 7,622	R 5

County	Pop.	Key
Pennington, 59,349	C 6
Perkins, 4,769	D 3
Potter, 4,449	J 3
Roberts, 11,678	P 2
Sanborn, 3,697	N 5
Shannon, 8,198	D 7
Spink, 10,595	N 4
Stanley, 2,457	H 5
Sully, 2,362	J 4
Todd, 6,606	H 7
Tripp, 8,171	K 7
Turner, 9,872	P 7
Union, 9,643	R 8
Walworth, 7,842	J 3
Washabaugh, 1,389	F 6
Yankton, 19,039	P 7
Ziebach, 2,221	F 4

CITIES and TOWNS

Zip	Name/Pop.	Key
57401 Aberdeen⊙, 26,476	M 3
57310 Academy, 17	M 7
57520 Agar, 156	J 4
57420 Akaska, 46	J 3
57210 Albee, 26	S 3

Zip	Name/Pop.	Key
57001 Alcester, 627	R 7
57311 Alexandria⊙, 598	O 6
57714 Allen, 150	F 7
57312 Alpena, 307	N 5
57211 Altamont, 54	R 4
57421 Amherst, 75	O 2
57422 Andover, 138	O 3
57715 Ardmore, 14	B 7
57212 Arlington, 954	P 5
57313 Armour⊙, 925	N 7
57423 Artas, 73	K 2
57314 Artesian, 277	O 6
57424 Ashton, 137	N 3
57213 Astoria, 153	S 4
57425 Athol, 50	M 3
57002 Aurora, 237	R 5
57315 Avon, 610	N 8
57214 Badger, 122	P 5
57003 Baltic, 364	R 6
57316 Bancroft, 48	O 4
57426 Barnard, 72	N 2
57428 Batesland, 135	E 7
57427 Bath, 150	N 3
57717 Belle Fourche⊙, 4,236	B 4
57521 Belvidere, 96	G 6

Zip	Name/Pop.	Key
57215 Bemis, 28	R 4
57004 Beresford, 1,655	R 7
57216 Big Stone City, 631	S 3
† 57310 Bijou Hills, 12	L 6
57620 Bison⊙, 406	E 2
57718 Black Hawk, 550	C 5
57522 Blunt, 445	J 4
57317 Bonesteel, 354	M 7
57318 Bonilla, 33	N 4
57428 Bowdle, 667	K 3
57719 Box Elder, 607	D 5
57217 Bradley, 157	O 3
57005 Brandon, 1,431	R 6
57218 Brandt, 132	R 4
57429 Brentford, 94	N 3
57319 Bridgewater, 633	P 6
57219 Bristol, 470	O 3
57430 Britton⊙, 1,465	O 2
† 57350 Broadland, 45	N 4
57006 Brookings⊙, 13,717	R 5
57220 Bruce, 217	R 5
57221 Bryant, 502	P 4
57720 Buffalo⊙, 393	B 2
57722 Buffalo Gap, 155	C 6
57621 Bullhead, 449	G 2
57010 Burbank, 96	R 8

Zip	Name/Pop.	Key
57523 Burke⊙, 892	L 7
57011 Bushnell, 65	R 5
57222 Butler, 38	O 3
57724 Camp Crook, 150	A 2
57012 Canistota, 636	P 6
57321 Canova, 204	P 6
57013 Canton⊙, 2,665	R 7
57725 Caputa, 43	D 6
† 57533 Carlock, 13	L 7
57322 Carpenter, 50	O 4
57526 Carter, 17	J 7
57323 Carthage, 362	O 5
57223 Castlewood, 523	P 4
57324 Cavour, 134	N 5
† 57058 Center, 18	P 6
57014 Centerville, 910	R 7
57727 Central City, 188	B 5
57325 Chamberlain⊙, 2,626	L 6
57015 Chancellor, 220	R 7
57431 Chelsea, 45	M 3
57622 Cherry Creek, 275	F 4
57016 Chester, 260	R 6
57224 Claire City, 100	P 2
57432 Claremont, 214	N 2
57225 Clark⊙, 1,356	O 4

(continued on following page)

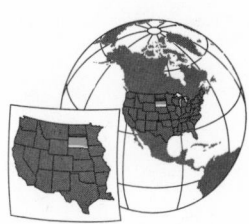

AREA 77,047 sq. mi.
POPULATION 666,257
CAPITAL Pierre
LARGEST CITY Sioux Falls
HIGHEST POINT Harney Pk. 7,242 ft.
SETTLED IN 1856
ADMITTED TO UNION November 2, 1889
POPULAR NAME Coyote State; Sunshine State
STATE FLOWER Pasqueflower
STATE BIRD Ring-necked Pheasant

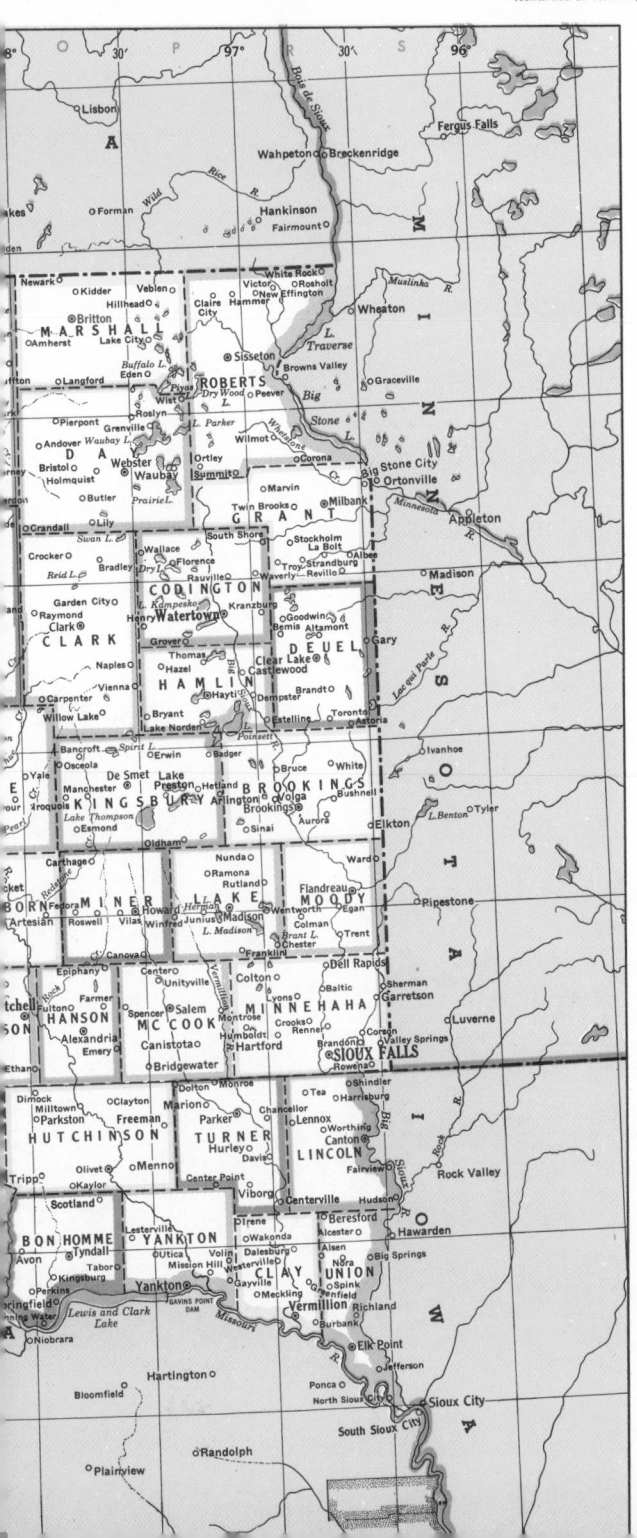

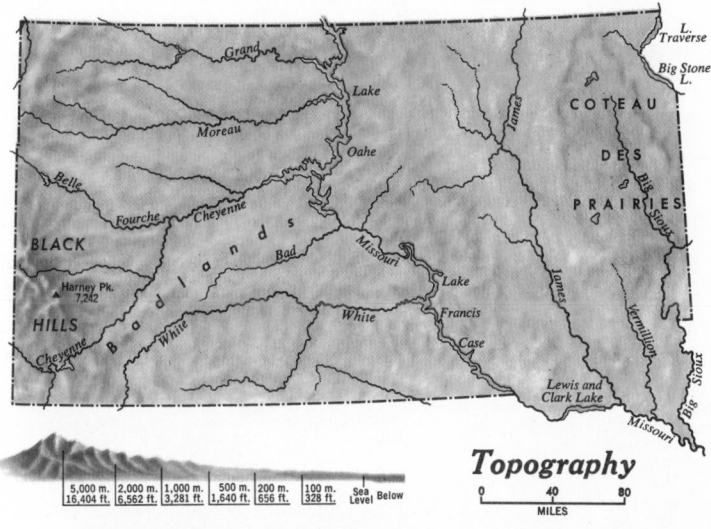

Topography

5,000 m.	2,000 m.	1,000 m.	500 m.	200 m.	100 m.	Sea Level	Below
16,404 ft.	6,562 ft.	3,281 ft.	1,640 ft.	656 ft.	328 ft.		

0   40   80
MILES

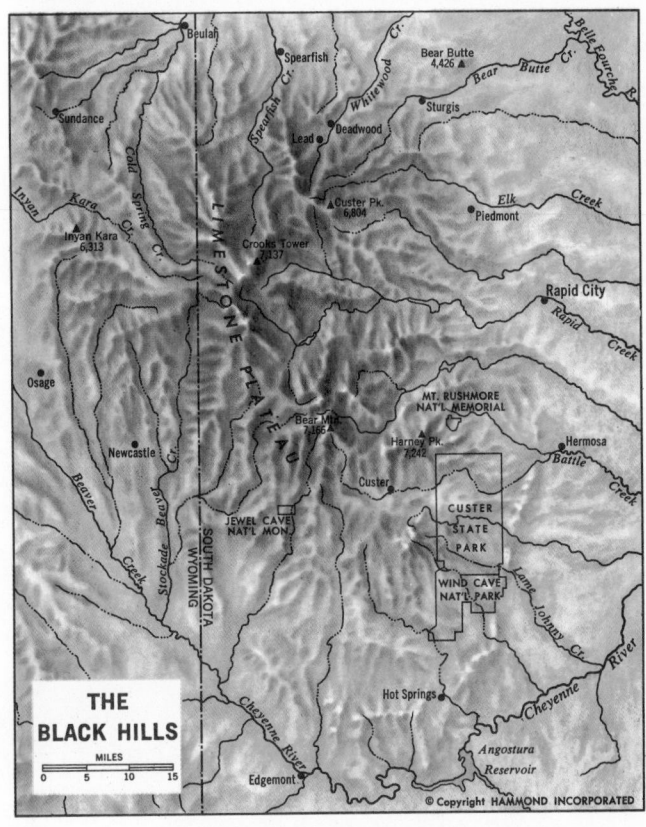

THE BLACK HILLS

MILES
0   5   10   15

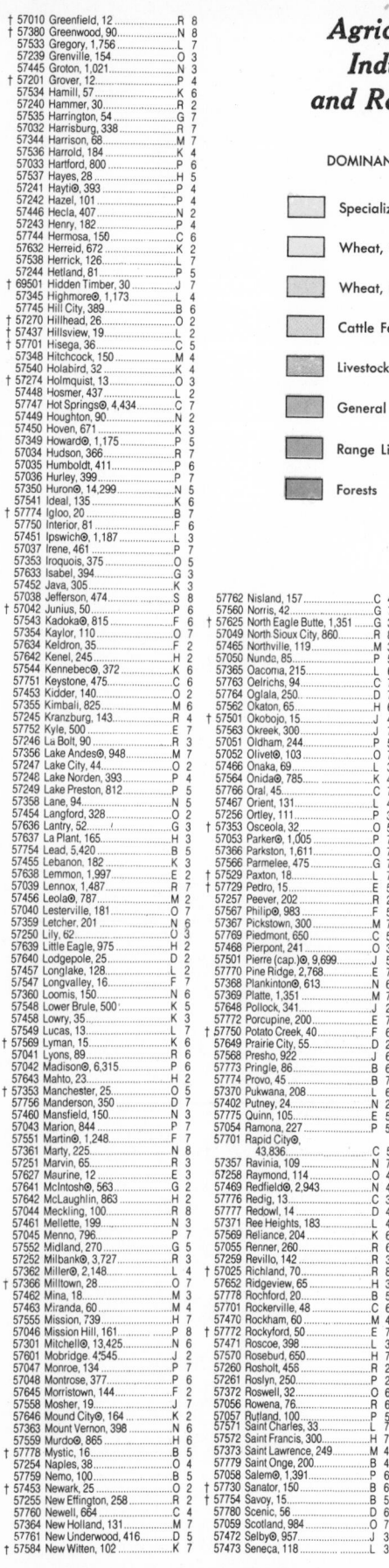

Agriculture,
Industry
and Resources

DOMINANT LAND USE

Specialized Wheat

Wheat, General Farming

Wheat, Range Livestock

Cattle Feed, Hogs

Livestock, Cash Grain

General Farming, Livestock, Special Crops

Range Livestock

Forests

⚡ Water Power

MAJOR MINERAL OCCURRENCES

Ag	Silver	Mi	Mica
Au	Gold	O	Petroleum
Be	Beryl	U	Uranium
Gn	Granite	V	Vanadium

E. C. Werner—Shostal Associates

Beds of fossils await paleontologists in the vast, semi-arid buttes of the Badlands, east of the Black Hills of South Dakota.

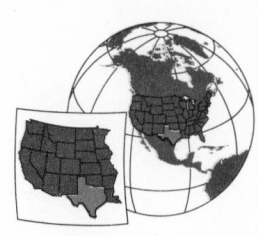

COUNTIES

AREA 267,339 sq. mi.
POPULATION 11,196,730
CAPITAL Austin
LARGEST CITY Houston
HIGHEST POINT Guadalupe Pk. 8,751 ft.
SETTLED IN 1686
ADMITTED TO UNION December 29, 1845
POPULAR NAME Lone Star State
STATE FLOWER Bluebonnet
STATE BIRD Mockingbird

CITIES and TOWNS

(continued on following page)

Agriculture, Industry and Resources

DOMINANT LAND USE

- Wheat, Grain Sorghums, Range Livestock
- Cotton, Wheat
- Specialized Cotton
- Cotton, General Farming
- Cotton, Forest Products
- Cotton, Range Livestock
- Rice, General Farming
- Peanuts, General Farming
- General Farming, Livestock, Cash Grain
- General Farming, Forest Products, Truck Farming, Cotton
- Fruit, Truck and Mixed Farming
- Range Livestock
- Forests
- Swampland, Limited Agriculture
- Nonagricultural Land
- Urban Areas

MAJOR MINERAL OCCURRENCES

At	Asphalt
Cl	Clay
Fe	Iron Ore
G	Natural Gas
Gn	Granite
Gp	Gypsum
Gr	Graphite
He	Helium
Ls	Limestone
Na	Salt
O	Petroleum
S	Sulfur
Tc	Talc
U	Uranium

⚡ Water Power
Major Industrial Areas

DALLAS
Aircraft, Food Processing, Machinery, Electrical & Metal Products, Automobile Assembly, Chemicals, Clothing

FORT WORTH
Aircraft, Automobile Assembly, Meat Packing, Food Processing

BEAUMONT–PORT ARTHUR
Oil Refining, Chemicals

EL PASO
Copper, Lead & Zinc Refining, Oil Refining, Clothing, Food Processing

SAN ANTONIO
Food Processing, Building Materials, Clothing, Chemicals

HOUSTON
Chemicals, Oil Refining, Machinery, Oil Field Equipment, Metal Products, Iron & Steel, Paper, Food Processing

CORPUS CHRISTI
Oil Refining, Aluminum

GALVESTON–TEXAS CITY
Chemicals, Oil Refining, Machinery, Metal Products

TEXAS

State Capitals .... ⊛
County Seats .... ⊙

© C.S. HAMMOND & Co., N.Y.

78834 Carrizo Springs⊙, 5,374 E 9
75006 Carrollton, 13,855 G 1
75633 Carthage⊙, 5,392 K 5
78009 Castroville, 1,893 E 8
75104 Cedar Hill, 2,610 G 2
75009 Celina, 1,272 H 4
75935 Center⊙, 4,989 K 6
75833 Centerville⊙, 831 H 6
77530 Channelview, 9,000 K 1
79018 Channing⊙, 336 B 2
78011 Charlotte, 1,329 F 9
79201 Childress⊙, 5,408 D 3
79225 Chillicothe, 1,116 E 3
76437 Cisco, 4,160 E 5
79226 Clarendon⊙, 1,974 C 3
75426 Clarksville⊙, 3,346 K 4
79019 Claude⊙, 992 C 2
† 77565 Clear Lake Shores, 500 K 2
76031 Cleburne⊙, 16,015 G 5
77327 Cleveland, 5,627 K 7
76634 Clifton, 2,578 G 6
77531 Clute, 6,023 J 9
79510 Clyde, 1,635 E 5
79511 Coahoma, 1,158 C 5
75211 Cockrell Hill, 3,515 G 2
77331 Coldspring⊙, 500 J 7
76834 Coleman⊙, 5,608 E 6
77840 College Station, 17,676 H 7
76034 Colleyville, 3,368 F 1
79512 Colorado City⊙, 5,227 C 5
78934 Columbus⊙, 3,342 H 8
76442 Comanche⊙, 3,933 F 6
75428 Commerce, 9,534 J 4
77301 Conroe⊙, 11,969 J 7
75432 Cooper⊙, 2,258 J 4
75019 Coppell, 1,728 F 1
76522 Copperas Cove, 10,818 G 6
* 78401 Corpus Christi⊙, 204,525 G 10
Corpus Christi, ‡284,832 G 10
75939 Corrigan, 1,304 K 7
75110 Corsicana⊙, 19,972 H 5
78014 Cotulla⊙, 3,415 E 9
79731 Crane⊙, 3,427 B 6
75835 Crockett⊙, 6,616 J 6
77532 Crosby, 1,118 J 8
79322 Crosbyton⊙, 2,251 C 4
76443 Cross Plains, 1,192 E 5
79227 Crowell⊙, 1,399 E 4
76036 Crowley, 2,662 E 2
78839 Crystal City⊙, 8,104 E 9
77954 Cuero⊙, 6,956 G 8
75638 Daingerfield⊙, 2,630 K 4
77533 Daisetta, 1,084 K 7
79022 Dalhart⊙, 5,705 B 1
* 75201 Dallas⊙, 844,401 H 2
Dallas, ‡1,555,950 H 2
77535 Dayton, 3,804 J 7
76234 Decatur⊙, 3,240 G 4
77536 Deer Park, 12,773 K 2
75559 De Kalb, 2,197 K 4
76444 De Leon, 2,170 F 5
78840 Del Rio⊙, 21,330 D 8
75020 Denison, 24,923 H 4
76201 Denton⊙, 39,874 G 4
79323 Denver City, 4,133 B 4
75115 De Soto, 6,617 G 2
78016 Devine, 3,311 E 8
75941 Diboll, 3,557 K 6
79229 Dickens⊙, 295 D 4
77539 Dickinson, 10,776 K 3
78017 Dilley, 2,362 E 9
79027 Dimmitt⊙, 4,327 B 3
78537 Donna, 7,365 F 11
76446 Dublin, 2,810 F 5
79029 Dumas⊙, 9,771 C 2
75116 Duncanville, 14,105 G 2
77434 Eagle Lake, 3,587 H 8
78852 Eagle Pass⊙, 15,364 D 9
79031 Earth, 1,152 B 3
77435 East Bernard, 1,159 H 8
76448 Eastland⊙, 3,178 F 5
76837 Eden, 1,291 E 6
78539 Edinburg⊙, 17,163 F 11
77957 Edna⊙, 5,332 H 9
77437 El Campo, 8,563 H 8
76936 Eldorado⊙, 1,446 D 7
76360 Electra, 3,895 F 4
78621 Elgin, 3,832 G 7
* 79901 El Paso⊙, 322,261 A 10
El Paso, ‡359,291 A 10
78543 Elsa, 4,400 G 11
75440 Emory⊙, 693 J 5
75119 Ennis, 11,046 H 5
76039 Euless, 19,316 F 2
76140 Everman, 4,570 F 2
79838 Fabens, 3,241 B 10
75840 Fairfield⊙, 2,074 H 6
78355 Falfurrias⊙, 6,355 F 10
75234 Farmers Branch, 27,492 G 1
75031 Farmersville, 2,311 H 4
79325 Farwell⊙, 1,185 A 3
75125 Ferris, 2,180 H 2
78941 Flatonia, 1,108 G 8
78114 Floresville⊙, 3,707 F 8
79235 Floydada⊙, 4,109 C 3
75701 Forest Hill, 8,236 F 2
75126 Forney, 1,745 H 5
79734 Fort Davis⊙, 900 D 11
79735 Fort Stockton⊙, 8,283 A 7
* 76101 Fort Worth⊙, 393,476 E 2
Fort Worth, ‡762,086 E 2
77856 Franklin⊙, 1,063 H 7
75763 Frankston, 1,056 J 5
78624 Fredericksburg⊙, 5,326 E 7
76842 Fredonia, 50 E 7
77541 Freeport, 11,997 J 9
78357 Freer, 2,804 F 10
77546 Friendswood, 5,675 J 2
79035 Friona, 3,111 B 3
75034 Frisco, 1,845 H 4
79036 Fritch, 1,778 C 2
79738 Gail⊙, 150 C 5
76240 Gainesville⊙, 13,830 G 4
77547 Galena Park, 10,479 J 1
77550 Galveston⊙, 61,809 L 3
Galveston-Texas City, ‡169,812 L 3
77962 Ganado, 1,640 H 8

79739 Garden City⊙, 300 C 6
75040 Garland, 81,437 H 1
75946 Garrison, 1,082 K 6
76528 Gatesville⊙, 4,683 G 6
78626 Georgetown⊙, 6,395 G 7
78022 George West⊙, 2,022 F 9
78942 Giddings⊙, 2,783 H 7
75644 Gilmer⊙, 4,196 J 5
75647 Gladewater, 5,574 K 5
76043 Glen Rose⊙, 1,554 G 5
76844 Goldthwaite⊙, 1,693 F 6
77963 Goliad⊙, 1,709 G 9
78629 Gonzales⊙, 5,854 G 8
76454 Gorman, 1,236 F 5
76046 Graham⊙, 7,477 F 4
76048 Granbury⊙, 2,473 G 5
75050 Grand Prairie, 50,904 G 2
75140 Grand Saline, 2,257 J 5
76530 Granger, 1,256 G 7
75844 Grapeland, 1,211 J 6
76051 Grapevine, 7,023 F 1
75401 Greenville⊙, 22,043 H 4
76642 Groesbeck⊙, 2,396 H 6
77619 Groves, 18,067 L 8
75845 Groveton⊙, 1,219 J 7
78548 Grulla, 1,194 F 11
79040 Gruver, 1,265 C 1
79236 Guthrie⊙, 150 D 4
79041 Hale Center, 1,964 C 3
77964 Hallettsville⊙, 2,712 G 8
75650 Hallsville, 1,038 K 5
76117 Haltom City, 28,127 F 2
76531 Hamilton⊙, 2,760 G 6
79520 Hamlin, 3,325 E 5
78550 Harlingen, 33,503 G 11
79521 Haskell⊙, 3,655 E 4
77859 Hearne, 4,982 H 7
78361 Hebbronville⊙, 4,079 F 10
75948 Hemphill⊙, 1,005 L 6
77445 Hempstead⊙, 1,891 J 7
75652 Henderson⊙, 10,187 K 5
76365 Henrietta⊙, 2,897 F 4
79045 Hereford⊙, 13,414 B 3
78557 Hidalgo, 1,289 F 11
† 75201 Highland Park, 10,133 G 2
77562 Highlands, 3,462 K 1
76645 Hillsboro⊙, 7,224 G 5
77563 Hitchcock, 5,565 K 3
76366 Holliday, 1,048 F 4
78861 Hondo⊙, 5,487 E 8
75446 Honey Grove, 1,853 J 4
75561 Hooks, 2,545 K 4
* 77001 Houston⊙, 1,232,802 J 2
Houston, ‡1,985,031 J 2
76648 Hubbard, 1,572 H 6
75656 Hughes Springs, 1,701 K 5
77338 Humble, 3,278 J 7
† 77001 Hunters Creek Village, 3,959 J 1
75949 Huntington, 1,192 K 6
77340 Huntsville⊙, 17,610 J 7
76053 Hurst, 27,215 F 2
75141 Hutchins, 1,755 G 2
79329 Idalou, 1,729 C 4
76367 Iowa Park, 5,796 F 4
75060 Irving, 97,260 G 2
76651 Italy, 1,309 H 5
76055 Itasca, 1,483 G 5
77029 Jacinto City, 9,563 J 1
76056 Jacksboro⊙, 3,554 F 4
75766 Jacksonville, 9,734 J 5
75951 Jasper⊙, 6,251 L 7
79528 Jayton⊙, 703 D 4
75657 Jefferson⊙, 2,866 K 5
78636 Johnson City⊙, 767 F 7
† 77541 Jones Creek, 1,268 J 9
78026 Jourdanton⊙, 1,841 F 9
76849 Junction⊙, 2,654 E 7
78118 Karnes City⊙, 2,926 G 9
77450 Katy, 2,923 J 8
75142 Kaufman⊙, 4,012 H 5
76059 Keene, 2,440 G 5
76248 Keller, 1,474 F 1
77565 Kemah, 1,144 K 2
78119 Kenedy, 4,156 G 9
76060 Kennedale, 3,076 F 2
79745 Kermit⊙, 7,884 B 6
78028 Kerrville⊙, 12,672 E 7
75662 Kilgore, 9,495 K 5
76541 Killeen, 35,507 G 6
78363 Kingsville⊙, 28,711 G 10
† 78109 Kirby, 2,558 F 8
75956 Kirbyville, 1,869 K 7
75145 Kleberg, 4,768 H 2
79529 Knox City, 1,536 E 4
77625 Kountze⊙, 1,703 K 7
78640 Kyle, 1,629 G 8
78559 La Feria, 2,642 G 11
78945 La Grange⊙, 3,092 G 8
78560 La Joya, 1,217 F 11
77566 Lake Jackson, 13,376 J 8
76135 Lake Worth, 4,958 E 2
77568 La Marque, 16,131 K 3
79331 Lamesa⊙, 11,559 C 5
76550 Lampasas⊙, 5,922 F 6
75146 Lancaster, 10,522 G 2
77571 La Porte, 7,149 K 2
78040 Laredo⊙, 69,024 E 10
Laredo, ‡72,859 E 10
77573 League City, 10,818 K 2
78873 Leakey⊙, 393 E 8
75452 Leonard, 1,423 H 4
79336 Levelland⊙, 11,445 B 4
75067 Lewisville, 9,264 G 5
77575 Liberty⊙, 5,591 K 7
75771 Lindale, 1,631 J 5
75563 Linden⊙, 2,264 K 4
79356 Lipscomb⊙, 100 D 1
79339 Littlefield⊙, 6,738 B 4
77351 Livingston⊙, 3,925 K 7
78643 Llano⊙, 2,608 F 7
78644 Lockhart⊙, 6,489 G 8
79241 Lockney, 2,094 C 3
75601 Longview⊙, 45,547 K 5
79343 Lorenzo, 1,206 C 4
78566 Los Fresnos, 1,297 G 11
* 79401 Lubbock⊙, 149,101 C 4
Lubbock, ‡179,295 C 4

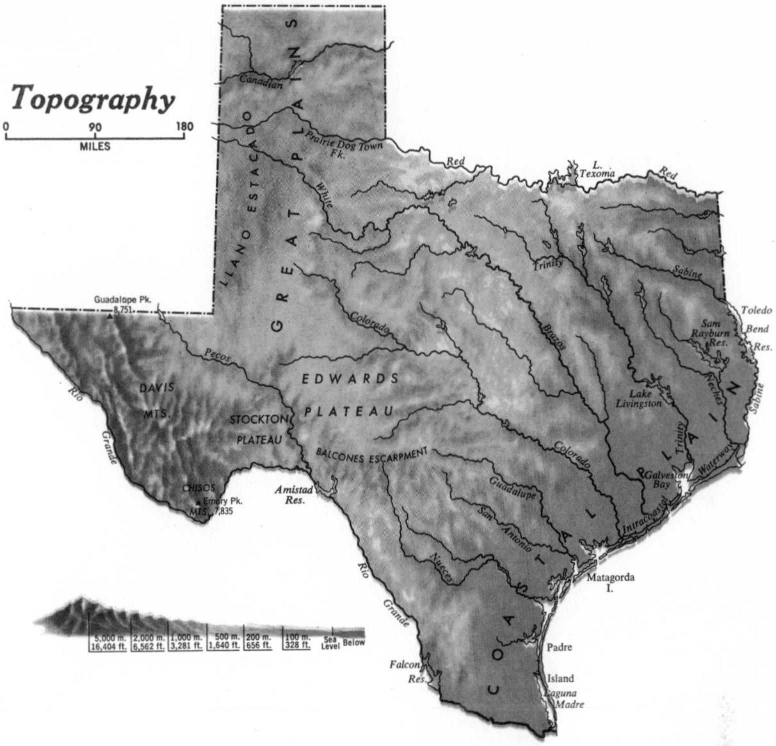
Topography
0 90 180
MILES
Canadian
Prairie Dog Town Fk.
Red
L. Texoma
LLANO ESTACADO
GREAT PLAINS
White
Trinity
Sabine
Toledo Bend Res.
Sam Rayburn Res.
Guadalupe Pk. 8,751
Colorado
Brazos
Pecos
EDWARDS PLATEAU
DAVIS MTS.
STOCKTON PLATEAU
BALCONES ESCARPMENT
Lake Livingston
Neches
Rio Grande
CHISOS MTS.
Emory Pk. 7,835
Amistad Res.
Guadalupe
San Antonio
Nueces
Galveston Bay
Intracoastal Waterway
Matagorda I.
Padre Island
Laguna Madre
Falcon Res.
COASTAL PLAIN
5,000 m. 16,404 ft.
2,000 m. 6,562 ft.
1,000 m. 3,281 ft.
500 m. 1,640 ft.
200 m. 656 ft.
100 m. 328 ft.
Sea Level
Below

75901 Lufkin⊙, 23,049 K 6
78648 Luling, 4,719 G 8
78569 Lyford, 1,425 G 11
78052 Lytle, 1,271 F 8
75147 Mabank, 1,239 H 5
77864 Madisonville⊙, 2,881 J 7
75148 Malakoff, 2,045 H 5
76063 Mansfield, 3,658 F 2
78654 Marble Falls, 2,209 F 7
79843 Marfa⊙, 2,647 C 12
76661 Marlin⊙, 6,351 H 6
75670 Marshall⊙, 22,937 K 5
76664 Mart, 2,183 H 6
76856 Mason⊙, 1,806 E 7
79244 Matador⊙, 1,091 D 3
78368 Mathis, 5,351 G 9
75957 Maud, 1,107 K 4
78501 McAllen, 37,636 F 11
McAllen-Pharr-Edinburg, ‡181,535 F 11
79752 McCamey, 2,647 B 6
76657 McGregor, 4,365 G 6
75069 McKinney⊙, 15,193 H 4
79057 McLean, 1,183 D 2
77520 McNair, 2,039 K 1
79245 Memphis⊙, 3,227 D 3
76859 Menard⊙, 1,740 E 7
79754 Mentone⊙, 50 D 10
78570 Mercedes, 9,355 F 12
76665 Meridian⊙, 1,162 G 6
79536 Merkel, 2,163 E 5
76941 Mertzon⊙, 513 C 6
75149 Mesquite, 55,131 H 2
76667 Mexia, 5,943 H 6
79059 Miami⊙, 611 D 2
79701 Midland⊙, 59,463 C 6
Midland, ‡65,433 C 6
76065 Midlothian, 2,322 G 5
75773 Mineola, 3,926 J 5
76067 Mineral Wells, 18,411 F 5
78572 Mission, 13,043 F 11
77459 Missouri City, 4,136 J 2
79756 Monahans⊙, 8,333 B 6
76251 Montague⊙, 490 G 4
77580 Mont Belvieu, 1,144 L 1
76557 Moody, 1,286 G 6
79346 Morton⊙, 2,738 B 4
75455 Mount Pleasant⊙, 8,877 K 4
75457 Mount Vernon⊙, 1,806 J 4
76252 Muenster, 1,411 G 4
79347 Muleshoe⊙, 4,525 B 3
76371 Munday, 1,726 E 4
75961 Nacogdoches⊙, 22,544 J 6
75568 Naples, 1,726 K 4
75569 Nash, 1,961 K 4
78059 Natalia, 1,296 F 8
77868 Navasota, 5,111 J 7
77627 Nederland, 16,810 K 8
77461 Needville, 1,024 J 8
75570 New Boston, 3,699 K 4
78130 New Braunfels⊙, 17,859 F 8
75966 Newton⊙, 1,529 L 7
78140 Nixon, 1,925 G 8
76255 Nocona, 2,871 G 4
† 76118 North Richland Hills, 16,514 F 1
79760 Odessa⊙, 78,380 B 6
Odessa, ‡91,805 B 6
79351 O'Donnell, 1,148 C 6
76374 Olney, 3,624 F 4
79064 Olton, 1,782 B 3
77630 Orange⊙, 24,457 L 7
78372 Orange Grove, 1,075 F 10
75684 Overton, 2,084 K 5

76943 Ozona⊙, 2,864 C 7
79248 Paducah⊙, 2,052 D 4
76866 Paint Rock⊙, 193 E 6
77465 Palacios, 3,642 H 9
75801 Palestine⊙, 14,525 J 6
76072 Palo Pinto⊙, 350 F 5
79065 Pampa⊙, 21,726 D 2
79068 Panhandle⊙, 2,141 C 2
75460 Paris⊙, 23,441 J 4
* 77501 Pasadena, 89,277 J 2
77581 Pearland, 6,444 J 2
78061 Pearsall⊙, 5,545 E 9
79772 Pecos⊙, 12,682 D 10
79070 Perryton⊙, 7,810 D 1
79250 Petersburg, 1,300 C 4
78577 Pharr, 15,829 F 11
79071 Phillips, 2,515 C 2
76258 Pilot Point, 1,663 H 4
75968 Pineland, 1,127 L 6
† 77001 Piney Point Village, 2,548 J 1
75686 Pittsburg⊙, 3,844 J 4
79355 Plains⊙, 1,087 B 4
79072 Plainview⊙, 19,096 C 3
75074 Plano, 17,872 H 4
78064 Pleasanton, 5,407 F 9
77978 Point Comfort, 1,446 H 9
78373 Port Aransas, 1,218 H 10
77640 Port Arthur, 57,371 K 8
77365 Porter, 1,900 J 7
78578 Port Isabel, 3,067 G 11
78374 Portland, 7,302 G 10
77979 Port Lavaca⊙, 10,491 H 9
77651 Port Neches, 10,894 K 7
79356 Post⊙, 3,854 C 4
78065 Poteet, 3,013 F 8
78147 Poth, 1,296 F 8
77445 Prairie View, 3,589 J 7
78375 Premont, 3,282 F 10
79845 Presidio, 850 C 12
79252 Quanah⊙, 3,948 E 3
75572 Queen City, 1,227 L 4
75783 Quitman, 1,494 J 5
79357 Ralls, 1,962 C 4
76470 Ranger, 3,094 F 5
79778 Rankin⊙, 1,105 B 6
78580 Raymondville⊙, 7,987 G 11
78377 Refugio⊙, 4,340 G 9
75080 Richardson, 48,582 G 1
76118 Richland Hills, 8,865 F 2
77469 Richmond⊙, 5,777 J 8
78582 Rio Grande City⊙, 5,676 F 11
78583 Rio Hondo, 1,167 G 11
77019 River Oaks, 8,193 E 2
76945 Robert Lee⊙, 1,119 D 6
78380 Robstown, 11,217 G 10
79543 Roby⊙, 784 D 5
76567 Rockdale, 4,655 G 7
78382 Rockport⊙, 3,879 H 9
78880 Rocksprings⊙, 1,221 D 8
75087 Rockwall⊙, 3,121 H 5
76569 Rogers, 1,030 G 7
78584 Roma-Los Saenz, 2,154 E 11
79545 Roscoe, 1,580 D 5
76570 Rosebud, 1,597 G 7
77471 Rosenberg, 12,098 J 8
79546 Rotan, 2,404 D 5
78664 Round Rock, 2,811 G 7
75088 Rowlett, 1,696 H 1
75089 Royse City, 1,535 H 4
78151 Runge, 1,147 G 9
75785 Rusk⊙, 4,914 J 6
78881 Sabinal, 1,554 E 8
76079 Saginaw, 2,382 E 1

76265 Saint Jo, 1,054 G 4
76901 San Angelo⊙, 63,884 D 6
San Angelo, ‡71,047 D 6
* 78201 San Antonio⊙, 654,153 F 8
San Antonio, ‡864,014 F 8
75972 San Augustine⊙, 2,539 K 6
78586 San Benito, 15,176 G 12
79848 Sanderson⊙, 1,229 B 7
78384 San Diego⊙, 4,490 F 10
76266 Sanger, 1,603 G 4
78289 San Juan, 5,070 F 11
77539 San Leon, 1,500 L 2
78666 San Marcos⊙, 18,860 F 8
76877 San Saba⊙, 2,555 F 6
† 76101 Sansom Park Village, 4,771 E 2
76878 Santa Anna, 1,310 E 6
78385 Sarita⊙, 250 G 10
78154 Schertz, 4,061 F 8
78956 Schulenburg, 2,294 H 8
77586 Seabrook, 3,811 K 2
77983 Seadrift, 1,092 H 9
75159 Seagoville, 4,390 H 2
79359 Seagraves, 2,440 B 5
77474 Sealy, 2,685 H 8
78155 Seguin⊙, 15,934 G 8
79360 Seminole⊙, 5,007 B 5
76380 Seymour⊙, 3,469 E 4
79363 Shallowater, 1,339 B 4
79079 Shamrock, 2,644 D 2
† 77001 Sheldon, 1,665 K 1
75090 Sherman⊙, 29,061 H 4
Sherman-Denison, ‡83,225 H 4
77984 Shiner, 2,102 G 8
† 77571 Shore Acres, 1,872 K 2
79851 Sierra Blanca⊙, 900 B 11
77656 Silsbee, 7,271 K 7
79257 Silverton⊙, 1,026 C 3
78387 Sinton⊙, 5,563 G 9
79364 Slaton, 6,583 C 4
78957 Smithville, 2,959 G 7
79549 Snyder⊙, 11,171 D 5
77879 Somerville, 1,250 H 7
76950 Sonora⊙, 2,149 D 7
77659 Sourlake, 1,694 K 7
77587 South Houston, 11,527 J 2
76051 Southlake, 2,031 F 1
† 77001 Southside Place, 1,466 J 2
79081 Spearman⊙, 3,435 C 1
77373 Spring, 1,900 J 7
76082 Springtown, 1,194 G 5
† 77001 Spring Valley, 3,170 J 1
79370 Spur, 1,747 D 4
77477 Stafford, 2,906 J 2
79553 Stamford, 4,558 E 5
79782 Stanton⊙, 2,117 C 5
76401 Stephenville⊙, 9,277 F 5
76951 Sterling City⊙, 780 D 6
79083 Stinnett⊙, 2,014 C 2
78160 Stockdale, 1,132 G 8
79084 Stratford⊙, 2,139 C 1
77478 Sugar Land, 3,318 J 8
75482 Sulphur Springs⊙, 10,642 J 4
79372 Sundown, 1,129 B 4
79086 Sunray, 1,854 C 1
77480 Sweeny, 3,191 J 8
79556 Sweetwater⊙, 12,020 D 5
78390 Taft, 3,274 G 9
79373 Tahoka⊙, 2,956 C 4
76574 Taylor, 9,616 G 7
75860 Teague, 2,867 H 6
76501 Temple, 33,431 G 6
75974 Tenaha, 1,094 K 6
79852 Terlingua, 100 D 12

75160 Terrell, 14,182 H 5
† 78201 Terrell Hills, 5,225 F 8
75501 Texarkana, 30,497 L 4
Texarkana, ‡101,198 L 4
77590 Texas City, 38,908 K 3
73949 Texhoma, 356 C 1
76577 Thorndale, 1,031 G 7
78071 Three Rivers, 1,761 F 9
76083 Throckmorton⊙, 1,105 F 4
78072 Tilden⊙, 600 F 9
75975 Timpson, 1,254 K 6
77375 Tomball, 2,734 J 7
75163 Trinidad, 1,079 J 5
75862 Trinity, 2,512 J 7
75789 Troup, 1,668 J 5
79088 Tulia⊙, 5,294 C 3
75701 Tyler⊙, 57,770 J 5
Tyler, ‡97,096 J 5
78228 University Park, 23,498 H 2
78801 Uvalde⊙, 10,764 E 8
75790 Van, 1,593 J 5
75095 Van Alstyne, 1,981 H 4
79855 Van Horn⊙, 2,240 C 11
79092 Vega⊙, 839 B 2
76384 Vernon⊙, 11,454 E 3
77901 Victoria⊙, 41,349 H 9
77662 Vidor, 9,738 L 7
* 76701 Waco⊙, 95,326 G 6
Waco, ‡147,553 G 6
78959 Waelder, 1,138 G 8
75501 Wake Village, 2,408 K 4
77485 Wallis, 1,028 H 8
75692 Waskom, 1,460 L 5
75165 Waxahachie⊙, 13,452 H 5
76086 Weatherford⊙, 11,750 G 5
77598 Webster, 2,231 K 2
78962 Weimar, 2,104 H 8
79095 Wellington⊙, 2,884 D 3
78596 Weslaco, 15,313 G 11
76691 West, 2,406 G 6
77486 West Columbia, 3,335 J 8
77630 West Orange, 4,787 L 7
† 77001 West University Place, 13,317 J 2
† 76101 Westworth, 4,578 E 2
77488 Wharton⊙, 7,881 J 8
79096 Wheeler⊙, 1,116 D 2
79097 White Deer, 1,092 C 2
76273 Whitesboro, 2,927 H 4
76108 White Settlement, 13,449 E 2
75491 Whitewright, 1,742 H 4
76692 Whitney, 1,371 G 6
* 76301 Wichita Falls⊙, 97,564 F 4
Wichita Falls, ‡127,621 F 4
77378 Willis, 1,577 J 7
75169 Wills Point, 2,636 J 5
75172 Wilmer, 1,922 H 2
77665 Winnie, 1,543 K 8
75494 Winnsboro, 3,064 J 5
79567 Winters, 2,907 E 6
75496 Wolfe City, 1,433 J 4
79382 Wolfforth, 1,090 C 4
78393 Woodsboro, 1,839 G 9
75979 Woodville⊙, 2,662 K 7
76693 Wortham, 1,036 H 6
75098 Wylie, 2,675 H 5
77995 Yoakum, 5,755 G 8
78164 Yorktown, 2,411 G 9
78076 Zapata⊙, 2,102 E 11

⊙ County seat.
‡ Population of metropolitan area.
† Zip of nearest p.o.
* Multiple zips

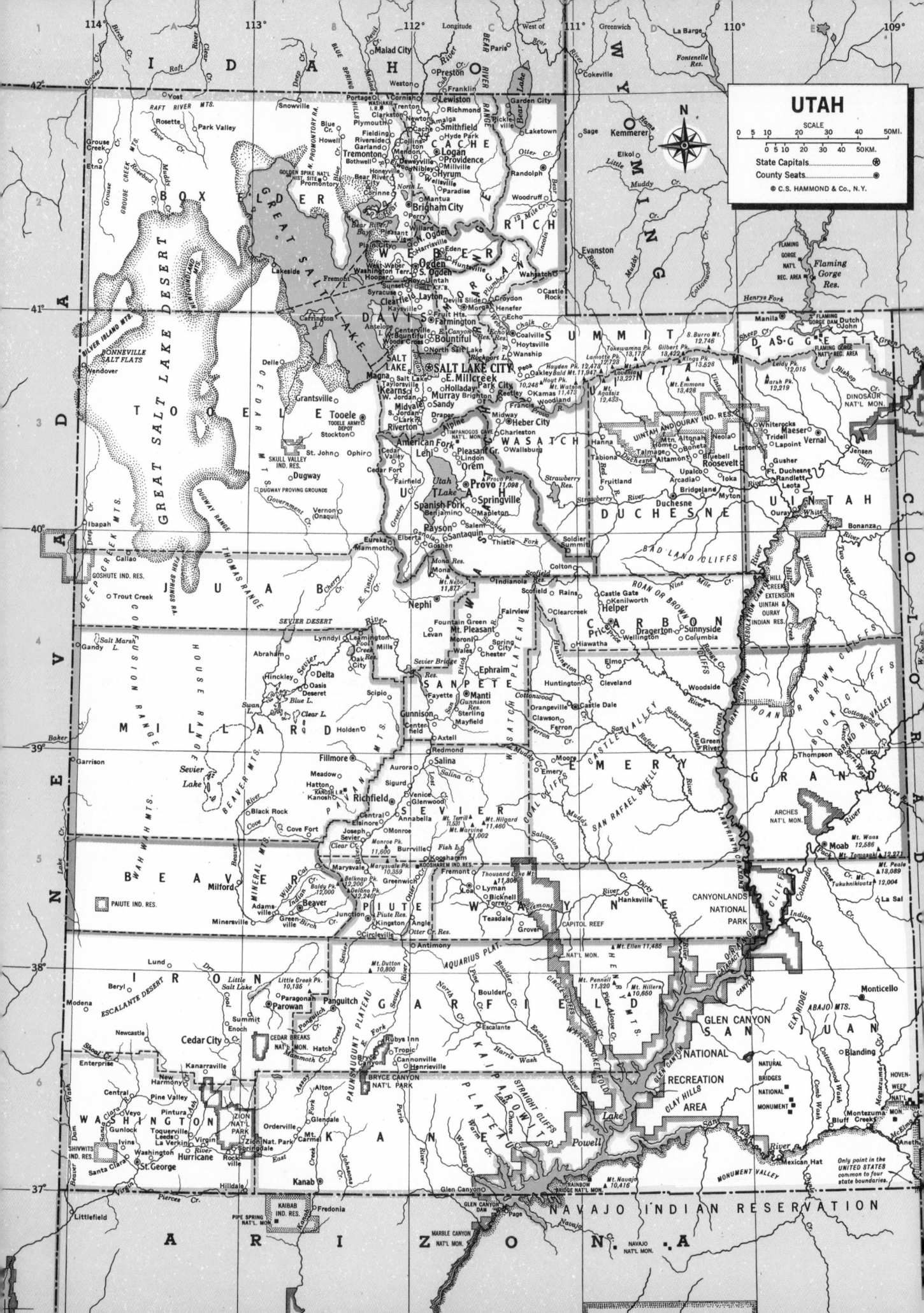

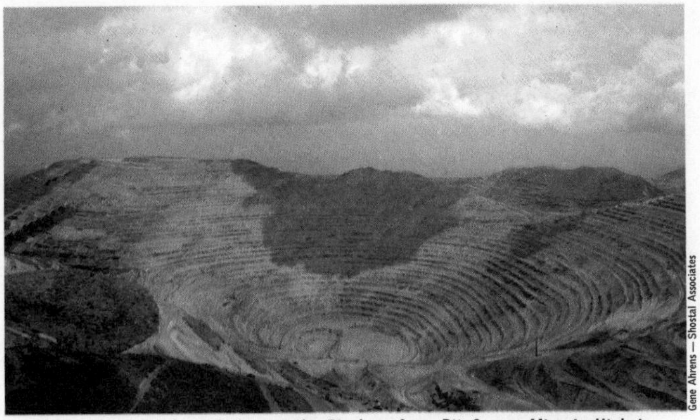

Gene Ahrens — Shostal Associates

Rising like a Greek amphitheater, the Bingham Open Pit Copper Mine in Utah is constantly changing as giant electric shovels remove seven tons of earth at a time.

AREA 84,916 sq. mi.
POPULATION 1,059,273
CAPITAL Salt Lake City
LARGEST CITY Salt Lake City
HIGHEST POINT Kings Pk. 13,528 ft.
SETTLED IN 1847
ADMITTED TO UNION January 4, 1896
POPULAR NAME Beehive State
STATE FLOWER Sego Lily
STATE BIRD Sea Gull

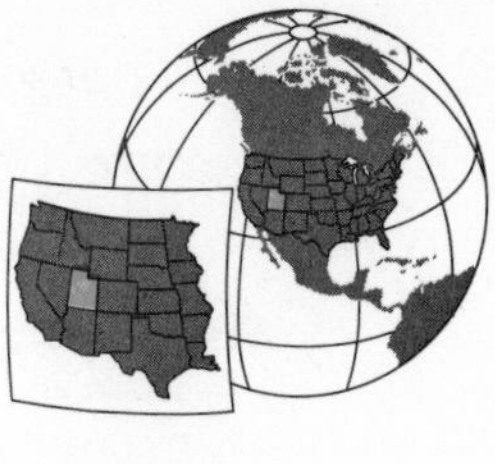

COUNTIES

Name/Pop.	Key
Beaver, 3,800	A 5
Box Elder, 28,129	A 2
Cache, 42,331	C 2
Carbon, 15,647	D 4
Daggett, 666	E 3
Davis, 99,028	B 3
Duchesne, 7,299	D 3
Emery, 5,137	D 4
Garfield, 3,157	C 6
Grand, 6,688	E 5
Iron, 12,177	A 6
Juab, 4,574	A 4
Kane, 2,421	B 6
Millard, 6,988	A 4
Morgan, 3,983	C 2
Piute, 1,164	B 5
Rich, 1,615	C 2
Salt Lake, 458,607	B 3
San Juan, 9,606	E 6
Sanpete, 10,976	C 4
Sevier, 10,103	C 5
Summit, 5,879	D 3
Tooele, 21,545	A 3
Uintah, 12,684	E 3
Utah, 137,776	C 3
Wasatch, 5,863	C 3
Washington, 13,669	A 6
Wayne, 1,483	C 5
Weber, 126,278	B 2

CITIES and TOWNS

Zip	Name/Pop.	Key
† 84003	Alpine, 1,047	C 3
84001	Altamont, 129	D 3
84002	Altonah, 225	D 3
† 84335	Amalga, 207	C 2
84003	American Fork, 7,713	C 3
84510	Aneth, 250	E 6
84711	Annabella, 221	B 5
84712	Antimony, 113	C 5
84005	Arcadia, 150	D 3
84620	Aurora, 493	B 5
84621	Axtell, 150	C 4
84301	Bear River City, 445	B 2
84713	Beaver⊙, 1,453	B 5
† 84660	Benjamin, 503	C 3
84715	Bicknell, 264	C 5
84511	Blanding, 2,250	E 6
84007	Bluebell, 210	D 3
84512	Bluff, 300	E 6
84008	Bonanza, 150	E 3
† 84337	Bothwell, 300	B 2
84716	Boulder, 93	C 6
84010	Bountiful, 27,853	C 3
84012	Bridgeland, 150	D 3
84302	Brigham City⊙, 14,007	C 2
84117	Brighton, 150	C 3
84717	Bryce Canyon, 229	B 6
84718	Cannonville, 113	B 6
84513	Castle Dale⊙, 541	D 4
84514	Castle Gate, 205	D 4
84720	Cedar City, 8,946	A 6
† 84013	Cedar Fort, 188	B 3
84013	Cedar Valley, 290	B 3
84622	Centerfield, 419	C 4
84014	Centerville, 3,268	C 3
84722	Central, 154	B 5
† 84032	Charleston, 196	C 3
84623	Chester, 130	C 4
84723	Circleville, 443	B 5
84305	Clarkston, 420	B 2
84516	Clawson, 95	C 4
84015	Clearfield, 13,316	B 2
84518	Cleveland, 244	D 4
84017	Coalville⊙, 864	C 3
84519	Columbia, 380	D 4
84307	Corinne, 471	B 2
84308	Cornish, 173	B 2
84018	Croydon, 90	C 2
84624	Delta, 1,610	B 4
84625	Deseret, 215	B 4
84309	Deweyville, 248	B 2
84520	Dragerton, 1,614	D 4
84020	Draper, 4,000	C 3
84021	Duchesne⊙, 1,094	D 3
84022	Dugway, 2,357	B 3
84023	Dutch John, 263	E 3
† 84101	East Millcreek, 26,579	C 3
84310	Eden, 421	C 2
84626	Elberta, 325	B 4
84521	Elmo, 141	D 4
84724	Elsinore, 357	B 5
† 84337	Elwood, 294	B 2
84522	Emery, 216	C 5
† 84720	Enoch, 120	A 6
84725	Enterprise, 844	A 6
84627	Ephraim, 2,127	C 4
84726	Escalante, 638	C 6
84628	Eureka, 753	B 4
84629	Fairview, 696	C 4
84025	Farmington⊙, 2,526	C 3
84630	Fayette, 93	C 4
84523	Ferron, 663	C 4
84311	Fielding, 254	B 2
84631	Fillmore⊙, 1,411	B 5
84026	Fort Duchesne, 300	E 3
84632	Fountain Green, 467	C 4
† 84036	Francis, 268	C 3
84727	Fremont, 160	C 5
† 84037	Fruit Heights, 800	C 2
84028	Garden City, 134	C 2
84312	Garland, 1,187	B 2
† 84655	Genola, 424	C 4
84729	Glendale, 200	B 6
84730	Glenwood, 212	C 5
84633	Goshen, 459	C 4
84029	Grantsville, 2,931	B 3
84525	Green River, 1,033	D 4
84731	Greenville, 97	B 5
84313	Grouse Creek, 100	A 2
84733	Gunlock, 93	A 6
84634	Gunnison, 1,073	C 4
84030	Gusher, 125	E 3
84734	Hanksville, 224	D 5
84031	Hanna, 135	D 3
† 84401	Harrisville, 603	C 2
84735	Hatch, 139	B 6
84032	Heber City⊙, 3,245	C 3
84526	Helper, 1,964	D 4
84033	Henefer, 446	C 2
84736	Henrieville, 145	C 6
84527	Hiawatha, 166	D 4
† 84767	Hilldale, 480	B 6
84635	Hinckley, 400	B 4
84636	Holden, 351	B 4
84117	Holladay, 23,014	C 3
84314	Honeyville, 640	B 2
84315	Hooper, 1,705	B 2
84316	Howell, 146	B 2
† 84017	Hoytsville, 500	C 3
84528	Huntington, 857	C 4
84317	Huntsville, 553	C 2
84737	Hurricane, 1,408	A 6
84318	Hyde Park, 1,025	C 2
84319	Hyrum, 2,340	C 2
84034	Ibapah, 135	A 3
† 84052	Ioka, 115	D 3
84738	Ivins, 137	A 6
84035	Jensen, 360	E 3
84739	Joseph, 125	B 5
84740	Junction⊙, 135	B 5
84036	Kamas, 806	C 3
84741	Kanab⊙, 1,381	B 6
84742	Kanarraville, 204	A 6
84637	Kanosh, 319	B 5
84037	Kaysville, 6,192	B 2
84118	Kearns, 17,071	B 3
84529	Kenilworth, 500	D 4
84743	Kingston, 114	B 5
84744	Koosharem, 141	C 5
84038	Laketown, 208	C 2
84039	Lapoint, 335	E 3
84040	Lark, 728	B 3
84530	La Sal, 200	E 5
84745	La Verkin, 463	A 6
84041	Layton, 13,603	C 2
84638	Leamington, 112	B 4
84746	Leeds, 151	A 6
84043	Lehi, 4,659	C 3
84639	Levan, 376	C 4
84320	Lewiston, 1,244	C 2
† 84062	Lindon, 1,644	C 3
84747	Loa⊙, 324	C 5
84321	Logan⊙, 22,333	C 2
84749	Lyman, 180	C 5
84640	Lynndyl, 111	B 4
† 84078	Maeser, 1,248	E 3
84044	Magna, 5,509	B 3
84046	Manila⊙, 226	E 3
84642	Manti⊙, 1,803	C 4
† 84302	Mantua, 413	C 2
† 84663	Mapleton, 1,980	C 3
84750	Marysvale, 289	B 5
84643	Mayfield, 267	C 4
84644	Meadow, 238	B 5
84325	Mendon, 345	B 2
84531	Mexican Hat, 100	E 6
84047	Midvale, 7,840	B 3
84049	Midway, 804	C 3
84751	Milford, 1,304	A 5
84326	Millville, 441	C 2
84752	Minersville, 448	A 5
84532	Moab⊙, 4,793	E 5
84645	Mona, 309	C 4
84754	Monroe, 918	B 5
84534	Montezuma Creek, 500	E 6
84535	Monticello⊙, 1,431	E 6
84050	Morgan⊙, 1,586	C 2
84646	Moroni, 894	C 4
84051	Mountain Home, 140	D 3
84647	Mount Pleasant, 1,516	C 4
84107	Murray, 21,206	C 3
84052	Myton, 322	D 3
84053	Neola, 600	D 3
84648	Nephi⊙, 2,699	C 4
84756	Newcastle, 150	A 6
84327	Newton, 444	C 2
† 84321	Nibley, 367	C 2
† 84401	North Ogden, 5,257	C 2
84054	North Salt Lake, 2,143	C 3
84649	Oak City, 278	B 4
84055	Oakley, 265	C 3
84650	Oasis, 150	B 4
* 84401	Ogden⊙, 69,478	C 2
	Ogden, ‡126,278	C 4
† 84080	Onaqui (Vernon), 541	B 3
84537	Orangeville, 511	C 4
84758	Orderville, 399	B 6
84057	Orem, 25,729	C 3
84059	Ouray, 100	E 3
84759	Panguitch⊙, 1,318	B 6
84328	Paradise, 399	C 2
84760	Paragonah, 275	B 6
84060	Park City, 1,193	C 3
84329	Park Valley, 100	A 2
84761	Parowan⊙, 1,423	B 6
84651	Payson, 4,501	C 3
84061	Peoa, 230	C 3
† 84302	Perry, 909	C 2
† 84028	Pickleville, 106	C 2
† 84401	Plain City, 1,543	B 2
84062	Pleasant Grove, 5,327	C 3
† 84401	Pleasant View, 2,028	B 2
84330	Plymouth, 203	B 2
84331	Portage, 144	B 2
84501	Price⊙, 6,218	D 4
84332	Providence, 1,608	C 2
84601	Provo⊙, 53,131	C 3
	Provo-Orem, ‡137,776	C 3
84063	Randlett, 350	E 3
84064	Randolph⊙, 500	C 2
84652	Redmond, 409	C 4
84701	Richfield⊙, 4,471	B 5
84333	Richmond, 1,000	C 2
84334	Riverside, 290	B 2
84065	Riverton, 2,820	B 3
84763	Rockville, 110	A 6
84066	Roosevelt, 2,005	D 3
84067	Roy, 14,356	C 2
84770	Saint George⊙, 7,097	A 6
84069	Saint John, 200	B 3
84653	Salem, 1,081	C 3
84654	Salina, 1,494	C 5
* 84101	Salt Lake City (cap.)⊙, 175,885	B 3
	Salt Lake City, ‡557,635	B 3
84070	Sandy, 6,438	C 3
84765	Santa Clara, 271	A 6
84655	Santaquin, 1,236	C 4
84656	Scipio, 264	B 4
84657	Sigurd, 291	B 5
84335	Smithfield, 3,342	C 2
84336	Snowville, 174	B 2
† 84065	South Jordan, 2,942	B 3
† 84401	South Ogden, 9,991	C 2
84115	South Salt Lake, 7,810	C 3
84660	Spanish Fork, 7,284	C 3
84662	Spring City, 456	C 4
84767	Springdale, 172	B 6
84663	Springville, 8,790	C 3
84665	Sterling, 144	C 4
84071	Stockton, 469	B 3
84772	Summit, 150	B 6
84539	Sunnyside, 485	D 4
† 84015	Sunset, 6,268	B 2
† 84041	Syracuse, 1,843	B 2
84072	Tabiona, 125	D 3
84073	Talmage, 140	D 3
† 84101	Taylorsville, 12,522	B 3
84773	Teasdale, 160	C 5
84074	Tooele⊙, 12,539	B 3
84774	Toquerville, 185	A 6
84337	Tremonton, 2,794	B 2
84338	Trenton, 390	B 2
84076	Tridell, 212	E 3
84776	Tropic, 329	B 6
† 84401	Uintah, 400	C 2
† 84007	Upalco, 150	D 3
84777	Venice, 220	C 5
84078	Vernal⊙, 3,908	E 3
84080	Vernon, 541	B 3
† 84722	Veyo, 144	A 6
84779	Virgin, 119	A 6
84082	Wallsburg, 211	C 3
† 84017	Wanship, 175	C 3
84780	Washington, 750	A 6
† 84401	Washington Terrace, 7,241	B 2
84542	Wellington, 922	D 4
84339	Wellsville, 1,267	C 2
84083	Wendover, 781	A 3
† 84087	West Bountiful, 1,246	B 3
84084	West Jordan, 4,221	B 3
† 84401	West Weber, 750	B 2
84085	Whiterocks, 600	E 3
84340	Willard, 1,045	C 2
† 84036	Woodland, 190	C 3
84086	Woodruff, 173	C 2
84087	Woods Cross, 3,124	B 3

⊙ County seat.
‡ Population of metropolitan area.
† Zip of nearest p.o.
* Multiple zips

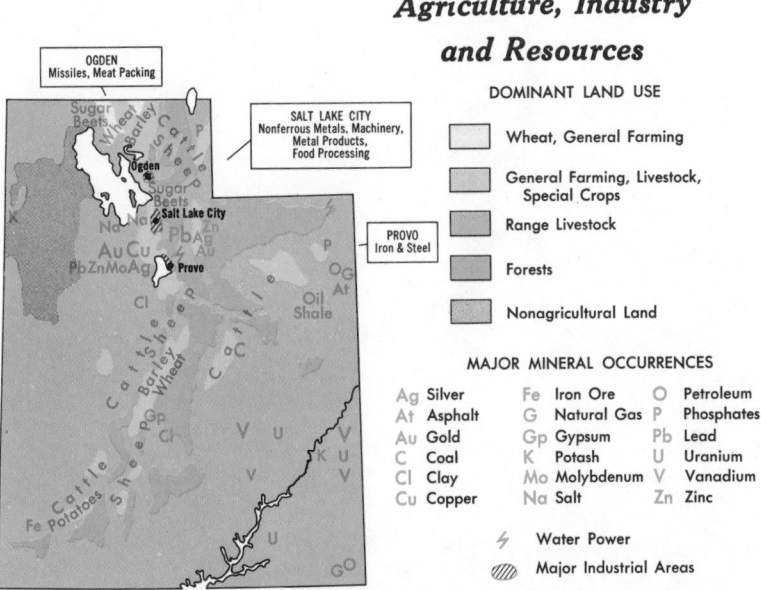

Agriculture, Industry and Resources

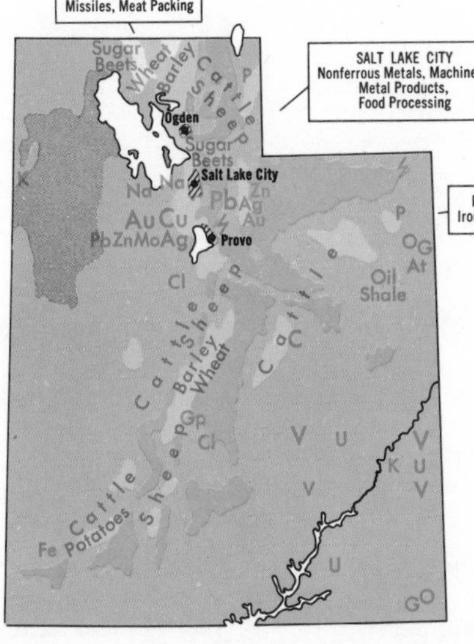

OGDEN
Missiles, Meat Packing
SALT LAKE CITY
Nonferrous Metals, Machinery, Metal Products, Food Processing
PROVO
Iron & Steel
Ogden
Salt Lake City
Provo
Sugar Beets
Wheat
Barley
Cattle
Sheep
Oil Shale
Potatoes

DOMINANT LAND USE

- Wheat, General Farming
- General Farming, Livestock, Special Crops
- Range Livestock
- Forests
- Nonagricultural Land

MAJOR MINERAL OCCURRENCES

Ag	Silver	Fe	Iron Ore	O	Petroleum
At	Asphalt	G	Natural Gas	P	Phosphates
Au	Gold	Gp	Gypsum	Pb	Lead
C	Coal	K	Potash	U	Uranium
Cl	Clay	Mo	Molybdenum	V	Vanadium
Cu	Copper	Na	Salt	Zn	Zinc

Water Power

Major Industrial Areas

Topography

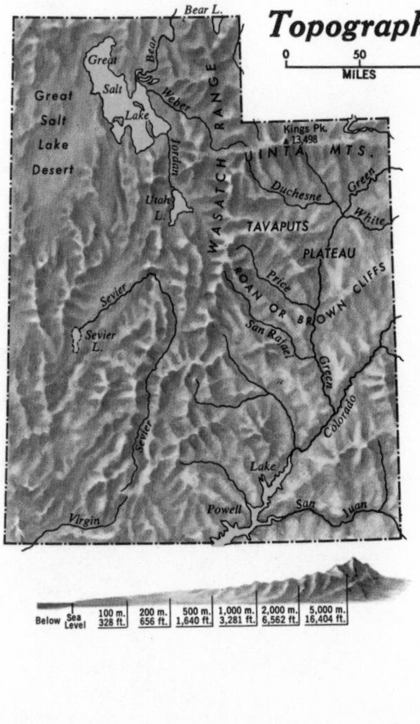

0 50 100
MILES
Bear L.
Great Salt Lake
Great Salt Lake Desert
Weber
Jordan
Utah L.
WASATCH RANGE
Kings Pk. 13,498
UINTA MTS.
Duchesne
Green
White
TAVAPUTS PLATEAU
Price
ROAN OR BROWN CLIFFS
San Rafael
Sevier
Sevier L.
Colorado
Lake Powell
Virgin
San Juan
Below Sea Level
100 m. 328 ft.
200 m. 656 ft.
500 m. 1,640 ft.
1,000 m. 3,281 ft.
2,000 m. 6,562 ft.
5,000 m. 16,404 ft.

Topography

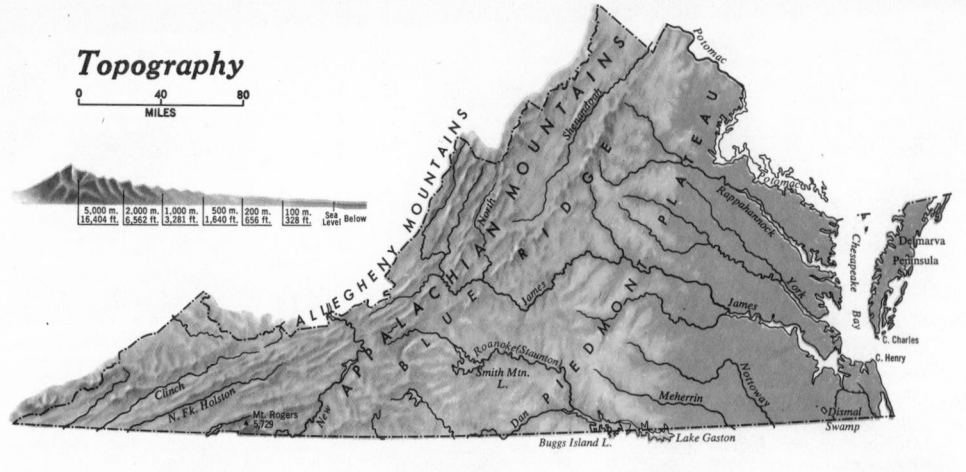

MILES
0 40 80

5,000 m.	2,000 m.	1,000 m.	500 m.	200 m.	100 m.	Sea
16,404 ft.	6,562 ft.	3,281 ft.	1,640 ft.	656 ft.	328 ft.	Level Below

COUNTIES

Accomack, 29,004................S 5
Albemarle, 37,780................L 5
Alleghany, 12,461................H 5
Amelia, 7,592................M 6
Amherst, 26,072................K 5
Appomattox, 9,784................L 6
Arlington, 174,284................O 3
Augusta, 44,220................K 4
Bath, 5,192................J 4
Bedford, 26,728................J 6
Bland, 5,423................F 6
Botetourt, 18,193................J 5
Brunswick, 16,172................N 7
Buchanan, 32,071................D 6
Buckingham, 10,597................L 6
Campbell, 43,319................K 6
Caroline, 13,925................O 4
Carroll, 23,092................G 7
Charles City, 6,158................O 6
Charlotte, 11,551................L 6
Chesterfield, 76,855................N 6
Clarke, 8,102................M 2
Craig, 3,524................H 6
Culpeper, 18,218................M 4
Cumberland, 6,179................M 6
Dickenson, 16,077................D 6
Dinwiddie, 25,046................N 6
Essex, 7,099................P 5
Fairfax, 455,021................O 3
Fauquier, 26,375................N 3
Floyd, 9,775................H 7
Fluvanna, 7,621................M 5
Franklin, 26,858................J 6
Frederick, 28,893................M 2
Giles, 16,741................G 6
Gloucester, 14,059................P 6
Goochland, 10,069................N 5
Grayson, 15,439................F 7
Greene, 5,248................M 4
Greensville, 9,604................N 7
Halifax, 30,076................L 7
Hanover, 37,479................N 5
Henrico, 154,364................O 5
Henry, 50,901................J 7
Highland, 2,529................J 4
Isle of Wight, 18,285................P 7
James City, 17,853................P 6
King and Queen, 5,491................P 5
King George, 8,039................O 4
King William, 7,497................O 5
Lancaster, 9,126................P 5
Lee, 20,321................B 7
Loudoun, 37,150................N 2
Louisa, 14,004................N 5
Lunenburg, 11,687................M 7
Madison, 8,638................M 4
Mathews, 7,168................R 6
Mecklenburg, 29,426................M 7
Middlesex, 6,295................R 5
Montgomery, 47,157................H 6
Nansemond, 35,166................P 7
Nelson, 11,702................L 5
New Kent, 5,300................P 5
Northampton, 14,442................S 6
Northumberland, 9,239................R 5
Nottoway, 14,260................M 6
Orange, 13,792................M 4
Page, 16,581................M 3
Patrick, 15,282................H 7
Pittsylvania, 58,789................K 7
Powhatan, 7,696................N 5
Prince Edward, 14,379................M 6
Prince George, 29,092................O 6
Prince William, 111,102................O 3
Pulaski, 29,564................G 6
Rappahannock, 5,199................M 3
Richmond, 5,841................P 5
Roanoke, 67,339................H 6
Rockbridge, 16,637................K 5
Rockingham, 47,890................L 4
Russell, 24,533................D 7
Scott, 24,376................C 7
Shenandoah, 22,852................L 3
Smyth, 31,349................E 7
Southampton, 18,582................O 7
Spotsylvania, 16,424................N 4
Stafford, 24,587................O 4
Surry, 5,882................P 6
Sussex, 11,464................O 7
Tazewell, 39,816................E 6
Warren, 15,301................M 3
Washington, 40,835................D 7
Westmoreland, 12,142................P 4

Wise, 35,947................C 6
Wythe, 22,139................F 7
York, 33,203................P 6

INDEPENDENT CITIES

Zip	Name/Pop.	Key
* 22301	Alexandria, 110,938	P 3
24523	Bedford⊙, 6,011	J 6
24201	Bristol, 14,857	D 7
24416	Buena Vista, 6,425	K 5
* 22901	Charlottesville⊙, 38,880	M 4
23320	Chesapeake, 89,580	R 7
24422	Clifton Forge, 5,501	J 5
23834	Colonial Heights, 15,097	O 6
24541	Danville, 46,391	J 7
23847	Emporia⊙, 5,300	N 7
22030	Fairfax⊙, 21,970	O 3
22040	Falls Church, 10,772	O 3
23851	Franklin, 6,880	P 7
22401	Fredericksburg, 14,450	N 4
24333	Galax, 6,278	G 7
* 23360	Hampton, 120,779	R 6
22801	Harrisonburg⊙, 14,605	K 4
23860	Hopewell, 23,471	O 6
24450	Lexington⊙, 7,597	J 5
24501	Lynchburg, 54,083	K 6
24112	Martinsville⊙, 19,653	J 7
23601	Newport News, 138,177	P 6

23501	Norfolk, 307,951	R 7
24273	Norton, 4,001	C 7
23803	Petersburg, 36,103	N 6
23701	Portsmouth⊙, 110,963	R 7
24141	Radford, 11,596	G 6
23201	Richmond (cap.)⊙, 249,621	O 5
24001	Roanoke, 92,115	H 6
24153	Salem, 21,982	H 6
24592	South Boston, 6,889	L 7
24401	Staunton⊙, 24,504	K 4
23434	Suffolk⊙, 9,858	P 7
23450	Virginia Beach, 172,106	S 7
22980	Waynesboro, 16,707	L 4
23185	Williamsburg⊙, 9,069	P 6
22601	Winchester⊙, 14,643	M 2

CITIES and TOWNS

24210	Abingdon⊙, 4,376	D 7
23301	Accomac⊙, 373	S 5
23001	Achilles, 525	R 6
22920	Afton, 325	L 4
22959	Alberene, 200	L 5
23821	Alberta, 466	N 7
24310	Allisonia, 325	G 7
24517	Altavista, 2,708	K 6
24520	Alton, 250	K 7
23002	Amelia Court House⊙, 537	N 6
24521	Amherst⊙, 1,108	K 5
22002	Amissville, 150	M 3

24601	Amonate, 500	E 6
24215	Andover, 300	C 7
22003	Annandale, 27,428	O 3
24216	Appalachia, 2,161	C 7
24522	Appomattox⊙, 1,400	L 6
24053	Ararat, 500	H 7
22201	Arlington⊙, 174,284	P 3
22922	Arrington, 350	L 5
23004	Arvonia, 300	M 5
22011	Ashburn, 345	O 2
23005	Ashland, 2,934	N 5
24311	Atkins, 500	F 7
24411	Augusta Springs, 400	K 4
24312	Austinville, 750	F 7
24054	Axton, 540	J 7
23009	Aylett, 300	O 5
24602	Bandy, 500	E 6
24231	Banner, 350	D 7
22923	Barboursville, 207	L 4
24313	Barren Springs, 150	G 7
24055	Bassett, 3,058	J 7
24314	Bastian, 450	F 6
22924	Batesville, 450	L 5
23016	Beaverlett, 178	R 6
† 23201	Bellbluff, 3,900	N 6
23306	Belle Haven, 504	S 5
22307	Belleview, 8,299	O 3
24218	Ben Hur, 300	B 7
24059	Bent Mountain, 140	H 6
22610	Bentonville, 700	M 3

22811	Bergton, 150	L 3
22611	Berryville⊙, 1,569	M 2
24526	Big Island, 500	K 5
24603	Big Rock, 350	D 6
24219	Big Stone Gap, 4,153	C 7
24220	Birchleaf, 650	D 6
23307	Birdsnest, 250	S 6
24604	Bishop, 400	E 6
23916	Blackridge, 140	M 7
24060	Blacksburg, 9,384	H 6
23824	Blackstone, 3,412	N 6
24221	Blackwater, 205	B 7
24527	Blairs, 500	J 7
24315	Bland⊙, 950	F 6
23308	Bloxom, 391	S 5
24605	Bluefield, 5,286	F 6
22012	Bluemont, 310	N 2
24064	Blue Ridge, 926	J 6
24606	Boissevain, 975	F 6
23235	Bon Air, 10,562	N 5
24065	Boones Mill, 363	J 6
24427	Bowling Green⊙, 528	O 4
22620	Boyce, 378	M 2
23917	Boydton⊙, 541	M 7
23827	Boykins, 742	O 7
23828	Branchville, 189	O 7
22714	Brandy Station, 530	N 3
24607	Breaks, 500	D 6
23022	Bremo Bluff, 200	M 5
22812	Bridgewater, 2,828	K 4

22715	Brightwood, 250	M 4
24316	Broadford, 850	E 7
22815	Broadway, 887	L 3
23920	Brodnax, 569	N 7
22430	Brooke, 275	O 4
24528	Brookneal, 1,037	L 6
24415	Brownsburg, 200	K 5
22610	Browntown, 175	M 3
22622	Brucetown, 150	M 2
† 22810	Bryce Mountain, 205	L 3
24066	Buchanan, 1,326	J 5
23921	Buckingham⊙, 200	L 5
22432	Burgess, 300	R 5
24608	Burkes Garden, 275	F 6
23922	Burkeville, 703	M 6
24420	Burnsville, 138	J 4
22435	Callao, 500	P 5
24067	Callaway, 191	H 7
22016	Calverton, 200	N 3
24317	Cana, 168	G 7
23310	Cape Charles, 1,689	S 6
23313	Capeville, 300	R 6
23829	Capron, 314	O 7
† 23039	Cardwell, 200	N 5
23315	Carrsville, 375	P 7
23830	Carson, 200	O 6
22017	Casanova, 200	N 3
24069	Cascade, 835	J 7
24224	Castlewood, 799	D 7
22019	Catlett, 500	N 3
24609	Cedar Bluff, 1,050	E 6
† 22630	Cedar Springs, 200	F 7
22630	Cedarville, 150	M 3
22437	Center Cross, 360	P 5
24438	Champlain, 160	O 4
22021	Chantilly, 620	O 3
23030	Charles City⊙, 5	O 6
23923	Charlotte Court House⊙, 539	L 6
23924	Chase City, 2,909	M 7
24531	Chatham⊙, 1,801	K 7
23316	Cheriton, 655	R 6
23831	Chester, 5,556	O 6
23832	Chesterfield⊙, 950	N 6
22623	Chester Gap, 450	M 3
24319	Chilhowie, 1,317	E 7
23336	Chincoteague, 1,867	T 5
24073	Christiansburg⊙, 7,857	H 6
23339	Chuckatuck, 500	P 7
23032	Church View, 200	P 5
24421	Churchville, 250	K 4
22928	Cismont, 400	M 4
23899	Claremont, 383	O 6
23927	Clarksville, 1,641	M 7
24076	Claudville, 180	H 7
† 23061	Clay Bank, 200	P 6
24225	Cleveland, 357	D 7
24533	Clifford, 160	K 5
24321	Clinchburg, 250	E 7
24226	Clinchco, 900	D 6
24227	Clinchport, 286	C 7
24228	Clintwood⊙, 1,320	D 6

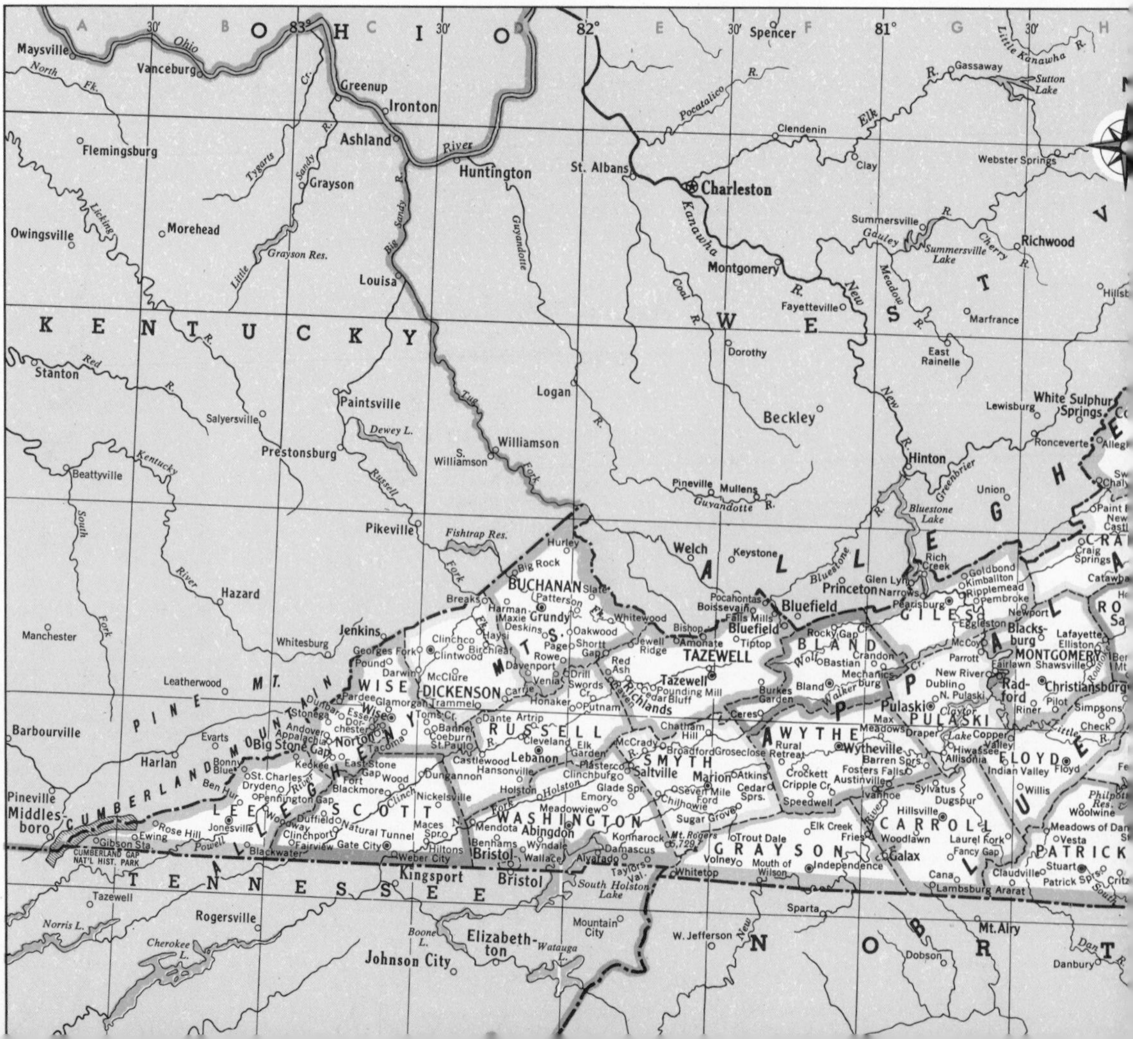

24534 Clover, 227 .... L 7
24077 Cloverdale, 850 .... J 6
24535 Cluster Springs, 500 .... L 7
23035 Cobbs Creek, 600 .... R 6
24230 Coeburn, 2,362 .... D 7
24536 Coleman Falls, 250 .... K 6
22442 Coles Point, 200 .... P 4
† 24450 Collierstown, 125 .... J 5
24078 Collinsville, 6,015 .... J 7
22443 Colonial Beach, 2,058 .... P 4
23038 Columbia, 125 .... M 5
24538 Concord, 400 .... K 6
24080 Copper Valley, 425 .... G 7
23837 Courtland⊙, 899 .... O 7
22931 Covesville, 500 .... L 5
24430 Craigsville, 988 .... J 4
† 24315 Crandon, 250 .... G 6
23930 Crewe, 1,433 .... M 6
24431 Crimora, 450 .... L 4
24322 Cripple Creek, 200 .... F 7
24082 Critz, 150 .... H 7
24323 Crockett, 300 .... F 7
22625 Cross Junction, 200 .... M 2
22932 Crozet, 1,433 .... L 4
23039 Crozier, 300 .... N 5
24539 Crystal Hill, 475 .... L 7
23934 Cullen, 140 .... L 6
22701 Culpeper⊙, 6,056 .... M 4
23040 Cumberland⊙, 500 .... M 6
22448 Dahlgren, 950 .... O 4
† 22172 Dale City, 13,857 .... O 3
24083 Daleville, 450 .... J 6
24236 Damascus, 1,230 .... E 7
24237 Dante, 1,153 .... D 7
24239 Davenport, 300 .... D 6
22821 Dayton, 978 .... L 4
24432 Deerfield, 200 .... K 4
22025 Delaplane, 164 .... N 3
23043 Deltaville, 950 .... R 5
23839 Dendron, 336 .... P 6
23840 De Witt, 140 .... N 6
23936 Dillwyn, 497 .... M 5
23841 Dinwiddie⊙, 500 .... N 6
23842 Disputanta, 500 .... O 6
23047 Doswell, 200 .... N 5
23937 Drakes Branch, 702 .... L 7
24324 Draper, 276 .... G 7
23844 Drewryville, 250 .... O 7
24242 Drill, 192 .... E 6
23346 Driver, 250 .... P 7
24243 Dryden, 400 .... B 7
24084 Dublin, 1,653 .... G 6
22026 Dumfries, 1,890 .... O 3
23938 Dundas, 200 .... M 7
24245 Dungannon, 282 .... D 7
22454 Dunnsville, 312 .... P 5
24085 Eagle Rock, 750 .... J 5
22936 Earleysville, 210 .... M 4
24246 East Stone Gap, 500 .... C 7
23347 Eastville⊙, 203 .... R 6
23845 Ebony, 150 .... N 7
23349 Eclipse, 295 .... R 7
† 22485 Edgehill, 225 .... O 4
22824 Edinburg, 766 .... M 3
24086 Eggleston, 500 .... G 6
23846 Elberon, 200 .... P 6
22827 Elkton, 1,511 .... L 4
24087 Elliston, 700 .... H 6
24327 Emory, 458 .... E 7
22937 Esmont, 950 .... L 5
24274 Esserville, 975 .... G 2
23803 Ettrick, 3,950 .... O 6
23939 Evergreen, 300 .... L 6
24550 Evington, 175 .... K 6
24248 Ewing, 700 .... B 7
23350 Exmore, 1,421 .... S 5
24435 Fairfield, 465 .... K 5
24141 Fairlawn, 1,767 .... G 6
† 22539 Fairport, 175 .... R 5
24613 Falls Mills, 500 .... F 6
22401 Falmouth, 2,139 .... O 4
23901 Farmville⊙, 4,331 .... M 6
22460 Farnham, 150 .... P 5
24088 Ferrum, 200 .... H 7
24089 Fieldale, 1,337 .... H 7
24090 Fincastle⊙, 397 .... J 6
22939 Fishersville, 975 .... K 4
22627 Flint Hill, 200 .... M 3
24091 Floyd⊙, 474 .... H 7
24551 Forest, 497 .... K 6
23055 Fork Union, 350 .... M 5
24250 Fort Blackmore, 600 .... C 7
22578 Foxwells, 400 .... R 5
24330 Fries, 885 .... F 7
22630 Front Royal⊙, 8,211 .... M 3
22830 Fulks Run, 130 .... L 3
22065 Gainesville, 600 .... N 3
22463 Garrisonville, 200 .... N 4
23857 Gasburg, 150 .... N 7
24251 Gate City⊙, 1,914 .... C 7
† 24228 Georges Fork, 500 .... C 6
† 24248 Gibson Station, 200 .... A 7
24340 Glade Spring, 1,615 .... E 7
24554 Gladys, 312 .... K 6
24555 Glasgow, 1,304 .... K 5
23060 Glen Allen, 985 .... N 5
24093 Glen Lyn, 191 .... G 6
24438 Glen Wilton, 280 .... J 5
† 24541 Glenwood, 1,295 .... K 7
23061 Gloucester⊙, 700 .... P 6
23062 Gloucester Point, 850 .... R 6
24094 Goldbond, 250 .... G 6
22720 Goldvein, 350 .... N 4
23063 Goochland⊙, 800 .... N 5
24556 Goode, 200 .... K 6
22942 Gordonsville, 1,253 .... M 4
22637 Gore, 150 .... M 2
23490 Grafton, 500 .... P 6
23356 Greenbackville, 300 .... T 5
23942 Green Bay, 150 .... M 6

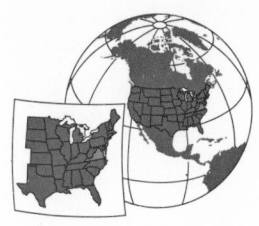

(continued on following page)

AREA 40,817 sq. mi.
POPULATION 4,648,494
CAPITAL Richmond
LARGEST CITY Norfolk
HIGHEST POINT Mt. Rogers 5,729 ft.
SETTLED IN 1607
ADMITTED TO UNION June 26, 1788
POPULAR NAME Old Dominion
STATE FLOWER Dogwood
STATE BIRD Cardinal

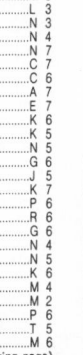

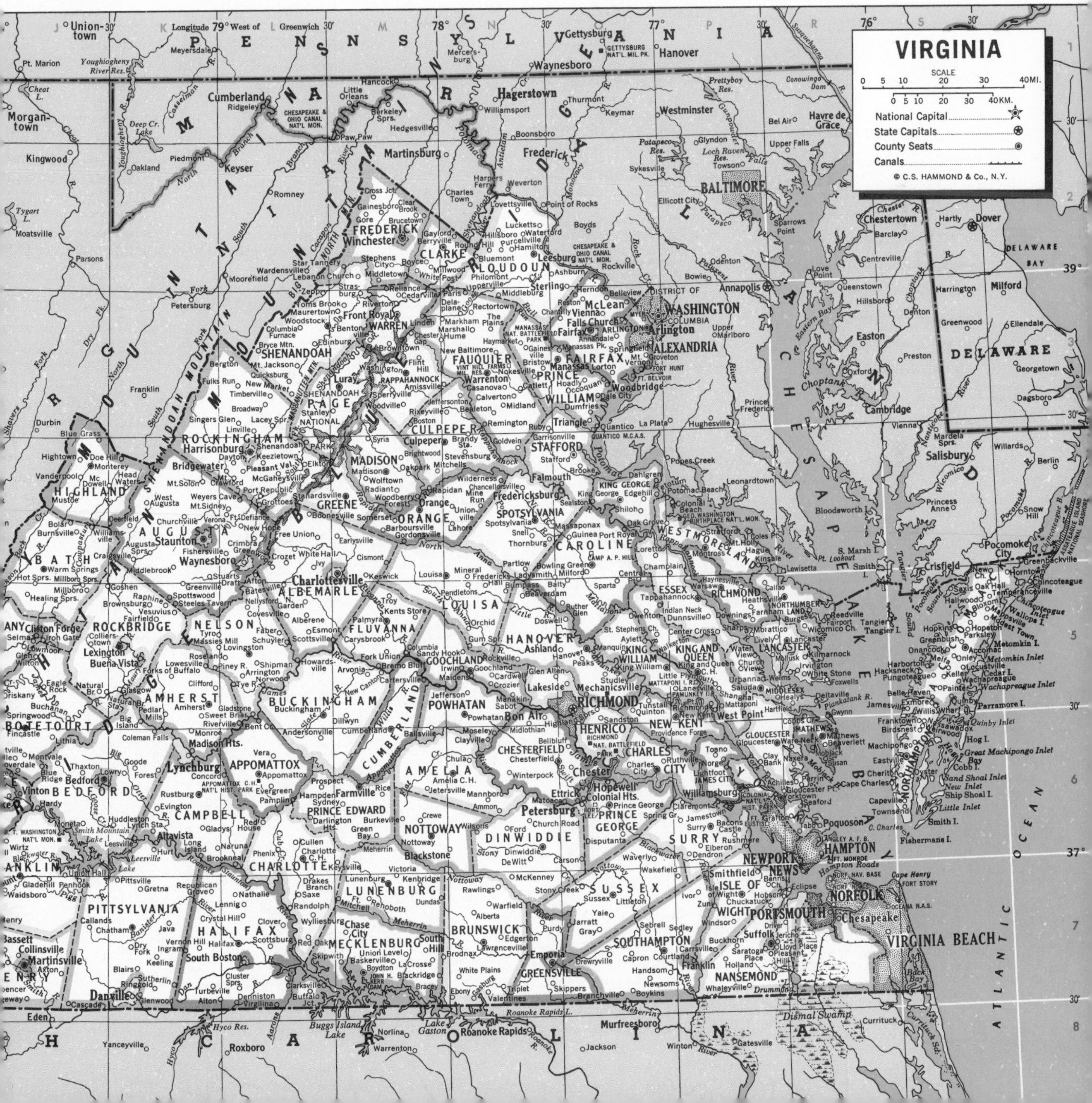

Agriculture, Industry and Resources

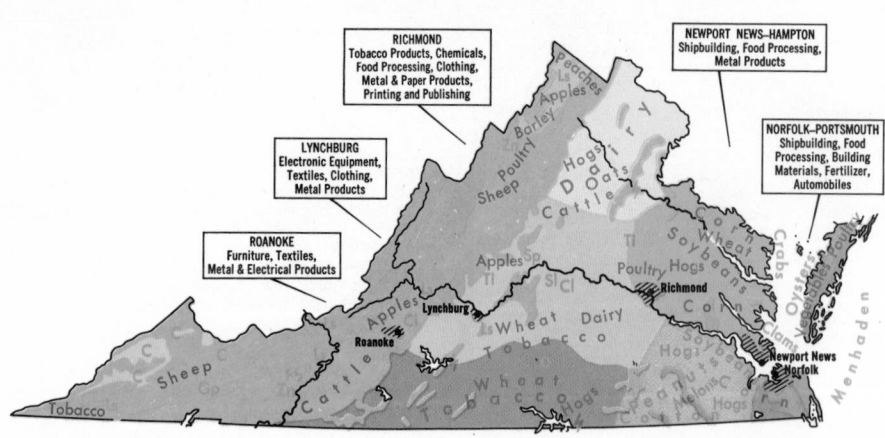

RICHMOND
Tobacco Products, Chemicals,
Food Processing, Clothing,
Metal & Paper Products,
Printing and Publishing

LYNCHBURG
Electronic Equipment,
Textiles, Clothing,
Metal Products

ROANOKE
Furniture, Textiles,
Metal & Electrical Products

NEWPORT NEWS–HAMPTON
Shipbuilding, Food Processing,
Metal Products

NORFOLK–PORTSMOUTH
Shipbuilding, Food
Processing, Building
Materials, Fertilizer,
Automobiles

DOMINANT LAND USE

- Dairy, General Farming
- General Farming, Livestock, Dairy
- General Farming, Livestock, Tobacco
- General Farming, Livestock, Fruit, Tobacco
- General Farming, Truck Farming, Tobacco, Livestock
- Tobacco, General Farming
- Peanuts, General Farming
- Fruit and Mixed Farming
- Truck and Mixed Farming
- Forests
- Swampland, Limited Agriculture

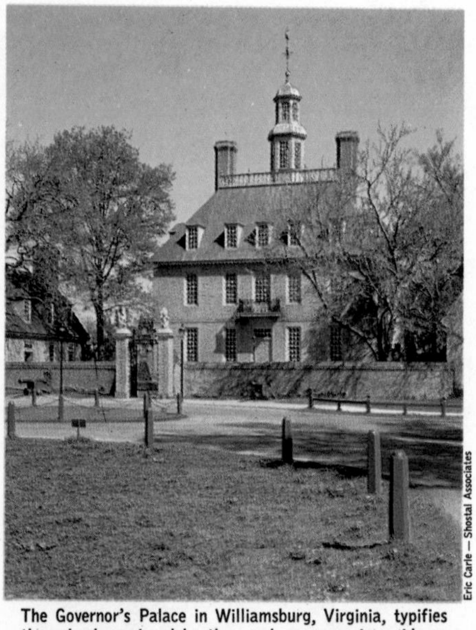

MAJOR MINERAL OCCURRENCES

C	Coal	Sl	Slate
Cl	Clay	Sp	Soapstone
Gp	Gypsum	Ti	Titanium
Ls	Limestone	Zn	Zinc
Pb	Lead		

⚡ Water Power
▨ Major Industrial Areas

The Governor's Palace in Williamsburg, Virginia, typifies the splendor enjoyed by the royal governors in residence from 1720 to 1780.

Eric Carle — Shostal Associates

Agriculture, Industry and Resources

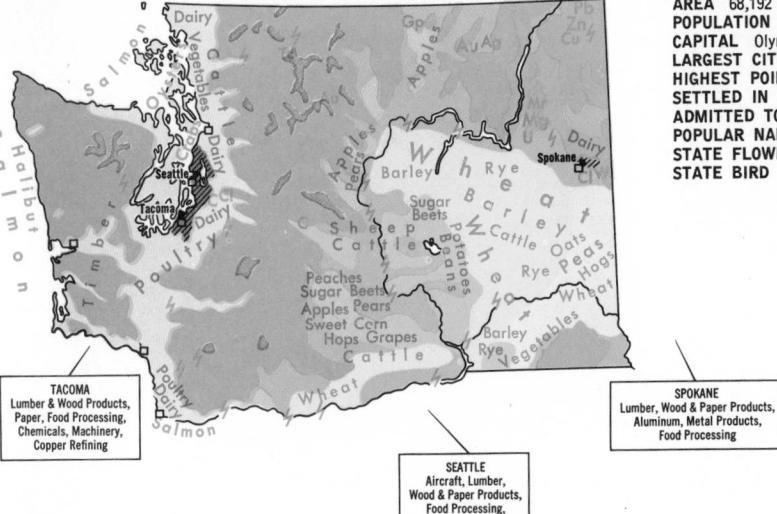

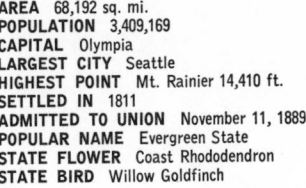

AREA 68,192 sq. mi.
POPULATION 3,409,169
CAPITAL Olympia
LARGEST CITY Seattle
HIGHEST POINT Mt. Rainier 14,410 ft.
SETTLED IN 1811
ADMITTED TO UNION November 11, 1889
POPULAR NAME Evergreen State
STATE FLOWER Coast Rhododendron
STATE BIRD Willow Goldfinch

TACOMA
Lumber & Wood Products,
Paper, Food Processing,
Chemicals, Machinery,
Copper Refining

SEATTLE
Aircraft, Lumber,
Wood & Paper Products,
Food Processing,
Metal Products

SPOKANE
Lumber, Wood & Paper Products,
Aluminum, Metal Products,
Food Processing

DOMINANT LAND USE

- Specialized Wheat
- Wheat, Peas
- Dairy, Poultry, Mixed Farming
- Fruit and Mixed Farming
- General Farming, Dairy, Range Livestock
- General Farming, Livestock, Special Crops
- Range Livestock
- Forests
- Urban Areas
- Nonagricultural Land

MAJOR MINERAL OCCURRENCES

Ag	Silver	Mr	Marble
Au	Gold	Pb	Lead
C	Coal	Tc	Talc
Cl	Clay	U	Uranium
Cu	Copper	W	Tungsten
Gp	Gypsum	Zn	Zinc
Mg	Magnesium		

- ⚡ Water Power
- Major Industrial Areas
- ▫ Major Sawmilling Centers

Pulpwood being rafted to the mills is a familiar sight in the Northwest, the region which leads the country in lumber production.

Warren Dick — Shostal Associates

COUNTIES

County	Pop.	Key
Adams, 12,014	G	3
Asotin, 13,799	H	4
Benton, 67,540	F	4
Chelan, 41,355	E	3
Clallam, 34,770	B	2
Clark, 128,454	C	5
Columbia, 4,439	H	4
Cowlitz, 68,616	C	4
Douglas, 16,787	F	3
Ferry, 3,655	G	2
Franklin, 25,816	G	4
Garfield, 2,911	H	4
Grant, 41,881	F	3
Grays Harbor, 59,533	B	3
Island, 27,011	C	2
Jefferson, 10,661	B	3
King, 1,156,633	D	3
Kitsap, 101,732	C	3
Kittitas, 25,039	E	3
Klickitat, 12,138	E	5
Lewis, 45,467	C	4
Lincoln, 9,572	G	3
Mason, 20,918	B	3
Okanogan, 25,867	F	2
Pacific, 15,796	B	4
Pend Oreille, 6,025	H	2
Pierce, 411,027	C	3
San Juan, 3,856	C	2
Skagit, 52,381	D	2
Skamania, 5,845	D	5
Snohomish, 265,236	D	2
Spokane, 287,487	H	3
Stevens, 17,405	H	2
Thurston, 76,894	C	4
Wahkiakum, 3,592	B	4
Walla Walla, 42,176	G	4
Whatcom, 81,950	D	2
Whitman, 37,900	H	4
Yakima, 144,971	E	4

CITIES and TOWNS

Zip	Name/Pop.	Key
98520	Aberdeen, 18,489	B 3
98220	Acme, 170	C 2
99101	Addy, 141	H 2
98522	Adna, 150	B 4
98810	Aeneas, 85	F 2
99001	Airway Heights, 744	H 3
99102	Albion, 687	H 4
98301	Alder, 300	C 4
98002	Algona, 1,276	C 3
98524	Allyn, 850	C 3
99103	Almira, 376	G 3
98525	Aloha, 140	A 3
† 98643	Altoona, 66	B 4
98526	Amanda Park, 495	A 3
99002	Amber, 32	H 3
98601	Amboy, 480	C 5
98221	Anacortes, 7,701	C 2
98330	Anatone, 70	H 4
98602	Appleton, 40	D 5
† 99114	Arden, 30	H 2
98811	Ardenvoir, 350	E 3
98603	Ariel, 386	C 5
98223	Arlington, 2,261	C 2
98304	Ashford, 415	C 4
99402	Asotin⊙, 637	H 4
98002	Auburn, 21,817	C 3
† 99348	Ayer, 70	G 4
98816	Azwell, 152	F 3
98110	Bainbridge Island-Winslow, 1,461	A 2
98224	Baring, 75	D 3
98604	Battle Ground, 1,438	C 5
98527	Bay Center, 350	A 4
† 98520	Bay City, 58	B 4
† 98004	Beaux Arts, 475	B 2
98305	Beaver, 450	A 2
98528	Belfair, 500	C 3
* 98004	Bellevue, 61,102	B 2
98225	Bellingham⊙, 39,375	C 2
98104	Belmont, 59	H 3
99105	Benge, 45	G 4
99320	Benton City, 1,070	F 4
99321	Beverly, 86	F 4
99322	Bickleton, 200	E 5
† 98273	Biglake, 105	C 2
98605	Bingen, 671	D 5
98010	Black Diamond, 1,160	D 3
98230	Blaine, 1,955	C 2
98231	Blanchard, 200	C 2
98106	Bluecreek, 40	H 2
† 98382	Blyn, 350	B 3
98532	Boistfort, 55	B 4
† 98390	Bonney Lake, 2,313	C 3
99126	Bossburg, 66	H 2
98011	Bothell, 4,883	B 1
98232	Bow, 975	C 2
99107	Boyds, 68	G 2
98310	Bremerton, 35,307	A 2
98812	Brewster, 1,059	F 2
98813	Bridgeport, 952	F 3
98036	Brier, 3,093	C 3
98320	Brinnon, 500	B 3
† 98537	Brooklyn, 50	B 4
98920	Brownstown, 80	E 4
† 98310	Brownsville, 50	A 2
98606	Brush Prairie, 200	C 5
† 98101	Bryn Mawr, 4,589	B 2
98321	Buckley, 3,446	C 3
98530	Bucoda, 421	C 4
98921	Buena, 590	E 4
99323	Burbank, 800	G 4
98166	Burien, 2,000	A 2
98322	Burley, 200	C 3
98233	Burlington, 3,138	C 2
98013	Burton, 650	C 3
98607	Camas, 5,790	C 5
98323	Carbonado, 394	D 3
98324	Carlsborg, 500	B 2
98814	Carlton, 120	F 2
98014	Carnation, 530	D 3
98609	Carrolls, 400	C 4
98610	Carson, 500	D 5
98815	Cashmere, 1,976	E 3
98611	Castle Rock, 1,647	B 4
98612	Cathlamet⊙, 647	B 4
† 98045	Cedar Falls, 200	D 3
98613	Centerville, 100	D 5
98531	Centralia, 10,054	C 4
98520	Central Park, 2,720	B 3
99003	Chattaroy, 250	H 3
98532	Chehalis⊙, 5,727	C 4
98816	Chelan, 2,430	E 3
98817	Chelan Falls, 200	E 3
99004	Cheney, 6,358	H 3
98818	Chesaw, 32	G 2
99109	Chewelah, 1,365	H 2
98325	Chimacum, 275	C 3
98614	Chinook, 445	A 4
98533	Cinebar, 35	C 4
98826	Clallam Bay, 750	A 2
99403	Clarkston, 6,312	H 4
99110	Clayton, 204	H 3
98235	Clearlake, 750	C 2
98399	Clearwater, 155	A 3
98922	Cle Elum, 1,725	E 3
† 98937	Cliffdell, 50	E 4
98236	Clinton, 500	C 3
† 99402	Cloverland, 80	H 4
† 98004	Clyde Hill, 2,987	B 2
† 98055	Coalfield, 500	B 2
99005	Colbert, 225	H 3
† 98366	Colby, 150	A 2
99111	Colfax⊙, 2,664	H 4
99324	College Place, 4,510	G 4
99113	Colton, 279	H 4
† 98632	Columbia Heights, 1,572	C 4
99114	Colville⊙, 3,742	H 2
98819	Conconully, 122	F 2
98237	Concrete, 573	D 2
99326	Connell, 1,161	G 4
98238	Conway, 120	C 2
98605	Cook, 240	D 5
98535	Copalis Beach, 481	A 3
98536	Copalis Crossing, 200	B 3
98537	Cosmopolis, 1,599	B 4
99616	Cougar, 76	C 4
99115	Coulee City, 558	F 3
99116	Coulee Dam, 1,425	G 3
98239	Coupeville⊙, 678	C 2
98923	Cowiche, 150	E 4
99117	Creston, 325	G 3
98015	Cumberland, 250	D 3
99118	Curlew, 200	G 2
98538	Curtis, 200	B 4
99119	Cusick, 257	H 2
98240	Custer, 315	C 2
98617	Dallesport, 400	D 5
99121	Danville, 108	G 2
98241	Darrington, 1,094	D 2
99122	Davenport⊙, 1,363	G 3
99328	Dayton⊙, 2,596	H 4
† 99010	Deepcreek, 73	H 3
98618	Deep River, 500	B 4
98243	Deer Harbor, 200	B 2
99006	Deer Park, 1,295	H 3
98244	Deming, 250	C 2
† 99006	Denison, 100	H 3
98188	Des Moines, 3,871	B 2
† 98283	Diablo, 200	D 2
† 99111	Diamond, 49	H 4
99213	Dishman, 9,079	H 3
99329	Dixie, 200	C 2
† 98279	Doebay, 100	C 2
98951	Donald, 100	E 4
98539	Doty, 210	B 4
98858	Douglas, 27	F 3
† 98532	Dryad, 184	B 4
98821	Dryden, 550	E 3
† 98382	Dungeness, 675	B 3
98327	Du Pont, 384	C 3
98019	Duvall, 607	C 3
98540	East Olympia, 300	B 4
98925	Easton, 300	D 3
98245	Eastsound, 800	B 2
98801	East Wenatchee, 913	E 3
98328	Eatonville, 2,446	C 4
98246	Edison, 250	C 2
98020	Edmonds, 23,998	C 3

(continued on following page)

WASHINGTON

SCALE
0 5 10 20 30 40 MI.
0 5 10 20 30 40 KM.

State Capitals..............✹
County Seats..............◉

© C.S. HAMMOND & Co., N.Y.

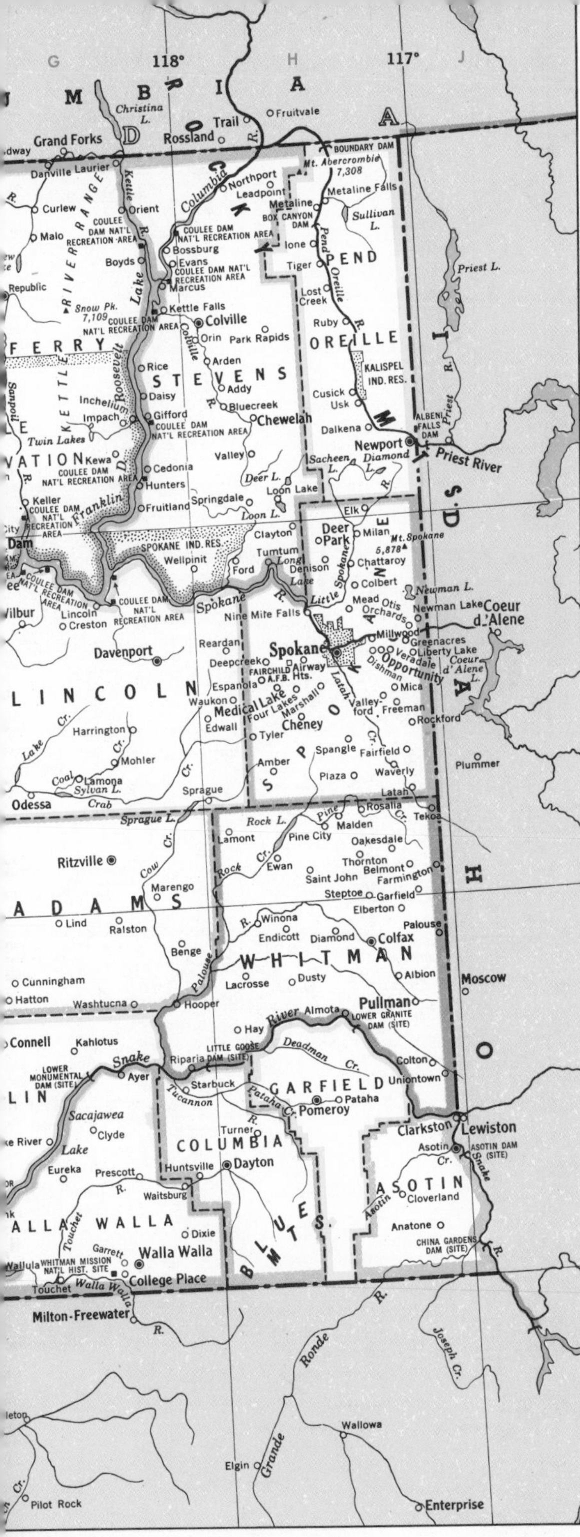
118°
117°
Grand Forks
Rossland
Trail
Fruitvale
Colville
Chewelah
Newport
Priest River
STEVENS
PEND OREILLE
FERRY
LINCOLN
SPOKANE
Spokane
Coeur d'Alene
Davenport
Ritzville
ADAMS
WHITMAN
Colfax
Pullman
Moscow
GARFIELD
Pomeroy
COLUMBIA
Dayton
Clarkston
Lewiston
ASOTIN
WALLA WALLA
Walla Walla
College Place
Milton-Freewater
Pilot Rock
Elgin
Wallowa
Enterprise

Topography

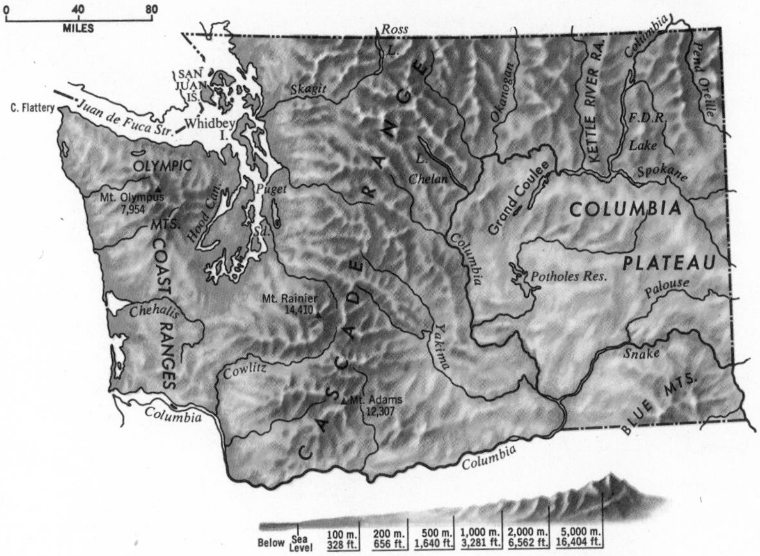
0 40 80
MILES
Ross L.
SAN JUAN IS.
C. Flattery
Juan de Fuca Str.
Whidbey I.
Skagit
Okanogan
KETTLE RIVER RA.
Columbia
Pend Oreille
F.D.R. Lake
Spokane
OLYMPIC MTS.
Mt. Olympus 7,954
Puget Sd.
Hood Can.
CASCADE RANGE
Chelan L.
Grand Coulee
COLUMBIA PLATEAU
Potholes Res.
Palouse
Mt. Rainier 14,410
Chehalis
COAST RANGES
Cowlitz
Yakima
Snake
BLUE MTS.
Mt. Adams 12,307
Columbia
Below Sea Level
100 m. 328 ft.
200 m. 656 ft.
500 m. 1,640 ft.
1,000 m. 3,281 ft.
2,000 m. 6,562 ft.
5,000 m. 16,404 ft.

98559 Malone, 175 .... B 4
98829 Malott, 350 .... F 2
98353 Manchester, 400 .... A 2
98830 Mansfield, 273 .... F 3
98831 Manson, 220 .... E 3
98266 Maple Falls, 90 .... D 2
98038 Maple Valley, 2,900 .... C 3
98267 Marblemount, 387 .... D 2
99151 Marcus, 142 .... H 2
98268 Marietta, 300 .... C 2
† 98520 Markham, 180 .... B 4
98832 Marlin, 52 .... F 3
99020 Marshall, 150 .... H 3
† 98620 Maryhill, 90 .... E 5
98270 Marysville, 4,343 .... C 2
98560 Matlock, 250 .... B 3
99344 Mattawa, 180 .... F 4
98557 McCleary, 1,265 .... B 3
98558 McKenna, 250 .... C 4
† 98273 McMurray, 62 .... C 2
99021 Mead, 1,099 .... H 3
99022 Medical Lake, 3,529 .... H 3
98039 Medina, 3,455 .... B 2
† 98563 Melbourne, 200 .... B 4
98561 Menlo, 200 .... B 4
98040 Mercer Island (city), 19,047 .. B 2
† 98826 Merritt, 150 .... E 3
99343 Mesa, 274 .... G 4
99152 Metaline, 197 .... H 2
99153 Metaline Falls, 307 .... H 2
98834 Methow, 84 .... E 2
99023 Mica, 130 .... H 3
99024 Milan, 90 .... H 3
99212 Millwood, 1,770 .... H 3
98354 Milton, 2,607 .... C 3
98355 Mineral, 500 .... C 4
98562 Moclips, 650 .... A 3
98836 Monitor, 75 .... E 3
98272 Monroe, 2,687 .... D 3
† 98812 Monse, 29 .... F 2
98563 Montesano⊙, 2,847 .... B 4
98356 Morton, 1,134 .... C 4
98837 Moses Lake, 10,310 .... F 3
98564 Mossyrock, 409 .... C 4
98043 Mountlake Terrace, 16,600 .... B 1
98273 Mount Vernon⊙, 8,804 .... C 2
98936 Moxee City, 600 .... E 4
98275 Mukilteo, 1,369 .... C 3
98937 Naches, 666 .... E 4
98537 Nahcotta, 200 .... A 4
98565 Napavine, 377 .... C 4
98638 Naselle, 500 .... B 4
† 98310 Navy Yard City, 2,827 .... A 2
98357 Neah Bay, 750 .... A 2
98566 Neilton, 250 .... B 3
99155 Nespelem, 323 .... G 2
† 98283 Newhalem, 350 .... D 2
99025 Newman Lake, 102 .... J 3
99156 Newport⊙, 1,418 .... H 2
99026 Nine Mile Falls, 150 .... H 3
† 98501 Nisqually, 500 .... C 3
98276 Nooksack, 322 .... C 2
98358 Nordland, 500 .... C 2
† 98100 Normandy Park, 4,208 .... A 2
98045 North Bend, 1,625 .... D 3
98639 North Bonneville, 459 .... C 5
† 98590 North Cove, 50 .... A 4
99157 Northport, 423 .... H 2
99158 Oakesdale, 447 .... H 3
98277 Oak Harbor, 9,167 .... C 2
98568 Oakville, 460 .... B 4
98569 Ocean City, 350 .... A 3
98640 Ocean Park, 918 .... A 4
† 98520 Ocosta, 300 .... B 4
99159 Odessa, 1,074 .... G 3
98840 Okanogan⊙, 2,015 .... F 2
98359 Olalla, 800 .... A 2
98279 Olga, 150 .... C 2
98501 Olympia (cap.)⊙, 23,111 .... C 3
98841 Omak, 4,164 .... F 2
98570 Onalaska, 288 .... C 4
99214 Opportunity, 16,604 .... H 3
98662 Orchards, 800 .... C 5
99160 Orient, 200 .... G 2
98843 Orondo, 130 .... E 3
98844 Oroville, 1,555 .... F 2
98360 Orting, 1,643 .... C 3
98223 Oso, 150 .... D 2
99344 Othello, 4,122 .... F 4
99027 Otis Orchards, 900 .... H 3
98938 Outlook, 300 .... E 4
98641 Oysterville, 86 .... A 4
† 98326 Ozette, 50 .... A 2
98047 Pacific, 1,831 .... C 3
98571 Pacific Beach, 975 .... A 3
98361 Packwood, 800 .... D 4
98845 Palisades, 90 .... E 3
98048 Palmer, 250 .... D 3
99161 Palouse, 948 .... H 4
98398 Paradise Inn, 200 .... D 4
98939 Parker, 700 .... E 4
98444 Parkland, 21,012 .... C 3
99301 Pasco⊙, 13,920 .... F 4
† 99347 Pataha, 97 .... H 4
98846 Pateros, 472 .... E 2
99345 Paterson, 50 .... F 5
98572 Pe Ell, 582 .... B 4
98847 Peshastin, 200 .... E 3
99162 Pine City, 48 .... H 3
† 98826 Plain, 75 .... E 3
99028 Plaza, 50 .... H 3
99346 Plymouth, 89 .... F 5
98281 Point Roberts, 400 .... B 2
99347 Pomeroy⊙, 1,823 .... H 4
98362 Port Angeles⊙, 16,367 .... B 2
98110 Port Blakely, 600 .... A 2
98573 Porter, 200 .... B 4
98364 Port Gamble, 425 .... C 3
98365 Port Ludlow, 200 .... C 3
98366 Port Orchard⊙, 3,904 .... A 2
98368 Port Townsend⊙, 5,241 .... C 2
98574 Potlatch, 350 .... B 3
98370 Poulsbo, 1,856 .... A 1
99348 Prescott, 242 .... G 4
98050 Preston, 500 .... D 3
† 98250 Prevost, 25 .... B 2
99350 Prosser⊙, 2,954 .... F 4
99163 Pullman, 20,509 .... H 4
98371 Puyallup, 14,742 .... C 3
† 98399 Queets, 180 .... A 3
98376 Quilcene, 900 .... B 3
98575 Quinault, 340 .... B 3
98848 Quincy, 3,237 .... F 3
98576 Rainier, 382 .... C 4
99165 Ralston, 35 .... G 4
98377 Randle, 950 .... D 4
98051 Ravensdale, 400 .... D 3
98577 Raymond, 3,126 .... B 4
99029 Reardan, 389 .... H 3
98052 Redmond, 11,031 .... B 1
98054 Redondo, 950 .... C 3
98055 Renton, 25,258 .... B 2
99166 Republic⊙, 862 .... G 2
98378 Retsil, 419 .... A 2
99352 Richland, 26,290 .... F 4
98160 Richmond Beach, 2,550 .... A 1
† 98133 Richmond Highlands, 6,854 .... A 1
98642 Ridgefield, 1,004 .... C 5
99169 Ritzville⊙, 1,876 .... G 3
98849 Riverside, 228 .... F 2
† 98188 Riverton, 23,160 .... B 2
98188 Riverton Heights, 34,800 .... B 2
† 98252 Robe, 175 .... D 2
98250 Roche Harbor, 175 .... B 2
98579 Rochester, 325 .... C 4
99030 Rockford, 327 .... H 3
† 98801 Rock Island, 191 .... E 3
98283 Rockport, 350 .... D 2
† 98626 Rocky Point, 1,733 .... A 2
98061 Rollingbay, 950 .... A 2
98940 Ronald, 200 .... E 3
99356 Roosevelt, 60 .... E 5
99170 Rosalia, 569 .... H 3
98643 Rosburg, 250 .... B 4
98941 Roslyn, 1,031 .... E 3
98580 Roy, 381 .... C 4
99357 Royal City, 477 .... F 4
† 98832 Ruff, 40 .... F 3
† 98401 Ruston, 668 .... C 3
98581 Ryderwood, 345 .... B 4
99171 Saint John, 575 .... H 3
98582 Salkum, 298 .... C 4
† 98239 San de Fuca, 80 .... C 2
98379 Sappho, 200 .... A 2
98583 Satsop, 300 .... B 3
† 98283 Sauk, 50 .... D 2
† 98370 Scandia, 75 .... A 1
† 99321 Schawana, 100 .... F 4
98380 Seabeck, 200 .... C 3
† 98110 Seabold, 250 .... A 1
98062 Seahurst, 3,000 .... A 2
* 98101 Seattle⊙, 530,831 .... A 2
Seattle-Everett, ‡1,421,869 ... A 2
98644 Seaview, 950 .... A 4
98284 Sedro-Woolley, 4,598 .... C 2
98381 Sekiu, 500 .... A 2
98942 Selah, 3,070 .... E 4
98064 Selleck, 300 .... D 3
98382 Sequim, 1,549 .... B 2
98286 Shaw Island, 95 .... B 2
98584 Shelton⊙, 6,515 .... B 3
† 98270 Shoultes, 4,754 .... C 2
98287 Silvana, 300 .... C 2
98585 Silver Creek, 382 .... C 4
98383 Silverdale, 950 .... A 2
98645 Silverlake, 42 .... C 4
† 98252 Silverton, 65 .... D 2
98646 Skamania, 250 .... C 5
98647 Skamokawa, 500 .... B 4
98288 Skykomish, 283 .... D 3
† 99357 Smyrna, 70 .... F 4
98290 Snohomish, 5,174 .... D 3
98065 Snoqualmie, 1,260 .... D 3
98066 Snoqualmie Falls, 250 .... D 3
98851 Soap Lake, 1,064 .... F 3
98586 South Bend⊙, 1,795 .... B 4
† 98901 South Broadway, 3,298 .... E 4
98943 South Cle Elum, 374 .... D 3
98384 South Colby, 450 .... A 2
98385 South Prairie, 206 .... D 3
98386 Southworth, 425 .... A 2
98387 Spanaway, 5,768 .... C 3
99031 Spangle, 179 .... H 3
* 99201 Spokane⊙, 170,516 .... H 3
Spokane, ‡287,487 .... H 3
99032 Sprague, 550 .... G 3
99173 Springdale, 215 .... H 2
98292 Stanwood, 1,347 .... C 2
99359 Starbuck, 216 .... G 4
98293 Startup, 450 .... D 3
98852 Stehekin, 40 .... E 2
98388 Steilacoom, 2,850 .... C 3
99174 Steptoe, 200 .... H 3
98648 Stevenson⊙, 916 .... C 5
98853 Stratford, 160 .... F 3
98294 Sultan, 1,119 .... D 3
98295 Sumas, 689 .... C 2
98390 Sumner, 4,325 .... C 3
† 98101 Sunnydale, 1,850 .... B 2
98944 Sunnyside, 6,751 .... F 4
98392 Suquamish, 950 .... A 1
* 98401 Tacoma⊙, 154,581 .... C 3
Tacoma, ‡411,027 .... C 3
98587 Taholah, 550 .... A 3
98588 Tahuya, 260 .... B 3
99033 Tekoa, 808 .... H 3
† 98826 Telma, 150 .... E 3
98589 Tenino, 962 .... C 4
98901 Terrace Heights, 1,033 .... E 4
99176 Thornton, 97 .... H 3
98946 Thorp, 350 .... E 3
98947 Tieton, 415 .... E 4
99177 Tiger, 69 .... H 2
98492 Tillicum, 1,900 .... C 3
98590 Tokeland, 300 .... A 4
98591 Toledo, 654 .... C 4
98855 Tonasket, 951 .... F 2
98948 Toppenish, 5,744 .... E 4
99360 Touchet, 250 .... G 4
98649 Toutle, 813 .... C 4
98393 Tracyton, 1,413 .... A 2
† 98848 Trinidad, 30 .... F 3
98650 Trout Lake, 500 .... D 5
98188 Tukwila, 3,496 .... B 2
† 98270 Tulalip, 325 .... C 2
99034 Tumtum, 100 .... H 3
98501 Tumwater, 5,373 .... B 3
† 99328 Turner, 25 .... H 4
98856 Twisp, 756 .... E 2
99035 Tyler, 69 .... H 3
98651 Underwood, 500 .... D 5
98592 Union, 380 .... B 3
98903 Union Gap, 2,040 .... E 4
99179 Uniontown, 310 .... H 4
99180 Usk, 250 .... H 2
98593 Vader, 387 .... B 4
99181 Valley, 156 .... H 2
99036 Valleyford, 250 .... H 3
* 98660 Vancouver⊙, 42,493 .... C 5
98950 Vantage, 125 .... E 4
98244 Van Zandt, 25 .... C 2
98070 Vashon, 350 .... A 2
98394 Vaughn, 600 .... C 3
99037 Veradale, 5,320 .... H 3
98670 Wahkiacus, 65 .... D 5
99361 Waitsburg, 953 .... G 4
98297 Waldron, 75 .... B 2
99362 Walla Walla⊙, 23,619 .... G 4
99363 Wallula, 89 .... G 4
98951 Wapato, 2,841 .... E 4
98857 Warden, 1,254 .... F 4
† 98292 Warm Beach, 225 .... C 2
98671 Washougal, 3,388 .... C 5
99371 Washtucna, 316 .... G 4
98858 Waterville⊙, 919 .... E 3
99038 Waukon, 41 .... H 3
98395 Wauna, 300 .... C 3
99039 Waverly, 48 .... H 3
99040 Wellpinit, 125 .... G 3
98801 Wenatchee⊙, 16,912 .... E 3
† 98837 Westlake, 258 .... F 3
98595 Westport, 1,364 .... A 4
99352 West Richland, 1,107 .... F 4
† 98801 West Wenatchee, 2,134 .... E 3
† 98837 Wheeler, 75 .... F 3
98146 White Center, 17,300 .... A 2
† 98541 Whites, 70 .... B 3
98672 White Salmon, 1,585 .... D 5
98952 White Swan, 270 .... E 4
98285 Wickersham, 200 .... C 2
99185 Wilbur, 1,074 .... G 3
98906 Wiley City, 250 .... E 4
98396 Wilkeson, 317 .... D 3
† 98577 Willapa, 300 .... B 4
98860 Wilson Creek, 184 .... F 3
† 98848 Winchester, 70 .... F 3
98596 Winlock, 890 .... C 4
99186 Winona, 51 .... H 4
† 98110 Winslow (Bainbridge Island-Winslow), 1,461 .... A 2
98862 Winthrop, 371 .... E 2
98673 Wishram, 575 .... D 5
98863 Withrow, 30 .... F 3
98072 Woodinville, 2,900 .... B 1
98674 Woodland, 1,622 .... C 5
† 98020 Woodway, 879 .... C 3
98675 Yacolt, 488 .... C 5
* 98901 Yakima⊙, 45,588 .... E 4
† 98004 Yarrow Point, 1,103 .... B 2
98597 Yelm, 628 .... C 4
98188 Zenith, 1,900 .... C 3
98953 Zillah, 1,138 .... E 4

⊙ County seat.
‡ Population of metropolitan area.
† Zip of nearest p.o.
* Multiple zips

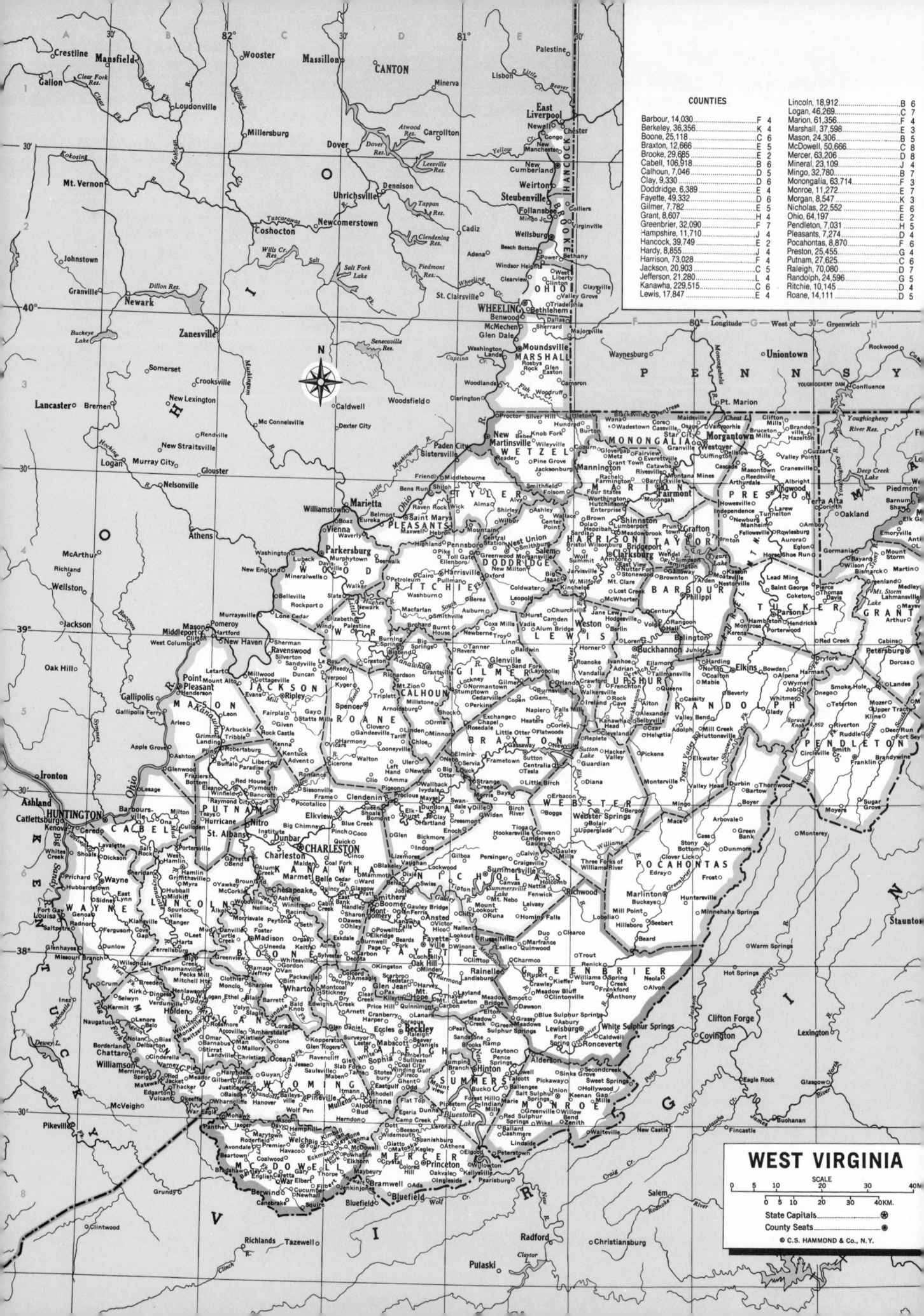

COUNTIES

Barbour, 14,030	F 4	Lincoln, 18,912	B 6
Berkeley, 36,356	K 4	Logan, 46,269	C 7
Boone, 25,118	C 6	Marion, 61,356	F 3
Braxton, 12,666	E 5	Marshall, 37,598	E 3
Brooke, 29,685	E 2	Mason, 24,306	A 5
Cabell, 106,918	A 6	McDowell, 50,666	C 8
Calhoun, 7,046	D 5	Mercer, 63,206	D 8
Clay, 9,330	D 6	Mineral, 23,109	J 4
Doddridge, 6,389	E 4	Mingo, 32,780	B 7
Fayette, 49,332	D 6	Monongalia, 63,714	F 3
Gilmer, 7,782	E 5	Monroe, 11,272	E 8
Grant, 8,607	H 4	Morgan, 8,547	J 4
Greenbrier, 32,090	F 7	Nicholas, 22,552	E 6
Hampshire, 11,710	J 4	Ohio, 64,197	D 3
Hancock, 39,749	E 2	Pendleton, 7,031	H 5
Hardy, 8,855	J 4	Pleasants, 7,274	D 4
Harrison, 73,028	E 4	Pocahontas, 8,870	F 6
Jackson, 20,903	C 5	Preston, 25,455	G 3
Jefferson, 21,280	L 4	Putnam, 27,625	C 6
Kanawha, 229,515	C 6	Raleigh, 70,080	D 7
Lewis, 17,847	E 4	Randolph, 24,596	G 5
		Ritchie, 10,145	D 4
		Roane, 14,111	D 5

WEST VIRGINIA

SCALE

0 5 10   20   30   40MI.

0 5 10   20   30   40KM.

State Capitals .... ⊛

County Seats .... ◉

© C.S. HAMMOND & Co., N.Y.

Summers, 13,213 E 7
Taylor, 13,878 F 4
Tucker, 7,447 G 4
Tyler, 9,929 E 4
Upshur, 19,092 F 5
Wayne, 37,581 B 6
Webster, 9,809 F 6
Wetzel, 20,314 E 3
Wirt, 4,154 D 4
Wood, 86,818 D 4
Wyoming, 30,095 C 7

AREA 24,181 sq. mi.
POPULATION 1,744,237
CAPITAL Charleston
LARGEST CITY Huntington
HIGHEST POINT Spruce Knob 4,862 ft.
SETTLED IN 1774
ADMITTED TO UNION June 20, 1863
POPULAR NAME Mountain State
STATE FLOWER Rhododendron
STATE BIRD Cardinal

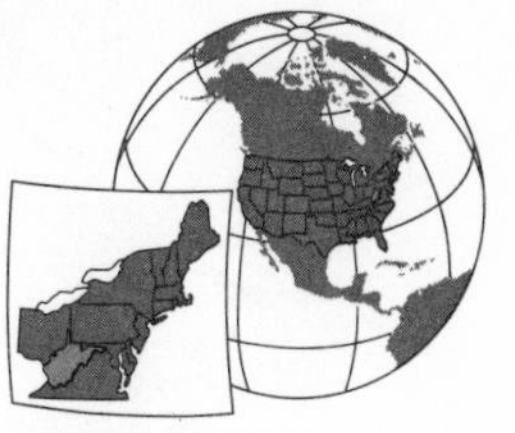

CITIES and TOWNS

Zip	Name/Pop.	Key
25606	Accoville, 975	C 7
† 24701	Ada, 250	D 8
† 26288	Addison (Webster Springs)⊙, 1,038	F 6
26210	Adrian, 500	F 5
26519	Albright, 319	G 3
24910	Alderson, 1,278	E 7
24807	Algoma, 400	D 8
25501	Alkol, 500	C 6
26320	Alma, 296	E 4
24710	Alpoca, 200	D 7
25003	Alum Creek, 900	C 6
25004	Ameagle, 210	D 7
25607	Amherstdale, 1,602	C 4
24808	Anawalt, 801	D 8
26323	Anmoore, 944	F 4
25812	Ansted, 1,511	D 6
24915	Arbovale, 300	G 6
25006	Arbuckle, 300	C 5
26324	Arden, 200	G 4
25007	Arnett, 300	D 7
25234	Arnoldsburg, 175	D 5
26816	Arthur, 200	H 4
26520	Arthurdale, 950	G 3
24916	Asbury, 280	E 7
24809	Asco, 200	C 8
25009	Ashford, 400	C 6
24712	Athens, 967	E 8
26704	Augusta, 550	J 4
26705	Aurora, 275	G 4
24811	Avondale, 250	C 8
24812	Baileysville, 800	C 7
25608	Baisden, 500	C 7
26801	Baker, 200	J 4
25410	Bakerton, 250	L 4
25010	Bald Knob, 356	C 7
24918	Ballard, 220	E 8
25011	Bancroft, 446	C 5
25504	Barboursville, 2,279	B 6
25609	Barnabus, 750	C 7
26559	Barrackville, 1,596	F 3
25013	Barrett, 950	C 7
24813	Bartley, 600	C 8
† 25411	Bath, 944	K 3
26707	Bayard, 475	H 4
† 26629	Bays, 186	E 5
25014	Beards Fork, 350	D 6
24814	Beartown, 500	C 8
25813	Beaver (Glen Hedrick), 1,711	D 7
25801	Beckley⊙, 19,884	D 7
26030	Beech Bottom, 544	E 2
24714	Beeson, 250	D 8
26250	Belington, 1,567	F 4
25015	Belle, 1,786	C 6
26134	Belmont, 802	D 4
26656	Belva, 550	D 6
26031	Benwood, 2,737	E 2
26298	Bergoo, 260	F 6
† 25401	Berkeley, 600	L 4
25411	Berkeley Springs⊙, 2,200	K 3
24815	Berwind, 675	C 8
26032	Bethany, 602	E 2
† 26003	Bethlehem, 2,461	E 2
26253	Beverly, 470	G 5
25019	Bickmore, 375	D 6
25302	Big Chimney, 450	C 6
25505	Big Creek, 500	B 7
† 24853	Big Four, 200	C 8
25021	Bim, 395	C 7
26610	Birch River, 650	E 6
26521	Blacksville, 264	F 3
25022	Blair, 700	C 7
25023	Blakeley, 260	D 6
25026	Blue Creek, 300	D 6
24701	Bluefield, 15,921	D 8
26288	Bolair, 450	F 6
25426	Bolivar, 943	L 4
25030	Bomont, 412	D 6
25031	Boomer, 1,261	D 6
25665	Borderland, 250	B 7
24817	Bradshaw, 1,048	C 8
24715	Bramwell, 1,125	D 8
26802	Brandywine, 188	H 5
25666	Breeden, 300	B 7
26330	Bridgeport, 4,777	F 4
† 25314	Brounland, 900	C 6
26334	Brownton, 700	F 4
26525	Bruceton Mills, 209	G 3
26201	Buckhannon⊙, 7,261	F 5
24716	Bud, 400	D 7
25033	Buffalo, 831	C 5
25413	Bunker Hill, 500	K 4
26710	Burlington, 338	J 4
26335	Burnsville, 591	E 5
26562	Burton, 250	F 3
25035	Cabin Creek, 900	C 6
26855	Cabins, 300	H 4
26337	Cairo, 412	D 4
24925	Caldwell, 425	F 7
26660	Calvin, 200	E 6
26208	Camden on Gauley, 243	E 6
26033	Cameron, 1,537	E 3
25820	Camp Creek, 200	D 7
24819	Canebrake, 250	C 8
26662	Canvas, 300	E 6
26711	Capon Bridge, 211	K 4
26823	Capon Springs, 250	K 4
25037	Carbon, 200	D 6
24821	Caretta, 650	C 8
26527	Cassville, 800	F 3
26564	Catawba, 186	F 3
25039	Cedar Grove, 1,275	D 6
26340	Central Station, 275	E 4
26214	Century, 239	F 4
25507	Ceredo, 1,583	B 6
25508	Chapmanville, 1,175	B 7
* 25301	Charleston (cap.)⊙, 71,505	C 6
	Charleston, ‡229,515	C 6
25414	Charles Town⊙, 3,023	L 4
25958	Charmco, 900	E 6
25667	Chattaroy, 1,145	B 7
25315	Chesapeake, 2,428	C 6
26034	Chester, 3,614	E 1
25306	Cinco, 500	D 6
26804	Circleville, 180	H 5
26301	Clarksburg⊙, 24,864	F 4
25043	Clay⊙, 479	D 6
25044	Clear Creek, 300	D 7
† 26003	Clearview, 512	E 2
25045	Clendenin, 1,438	D 5
25237	Clifton, 358	B 5
† 25854	Clifty, 250	E 6
† 26058	Clinton, 350	E 2
25046	Clio, 300	D 5
25047	Clothier, 950	C 7
25238	Clover, 350	D 5
24929	Clover Lick, 250	F 6
25823	Coal City, 1,089	D 7
25306	Coal Fork, 950	D 6
26257	Coalton, 234	G 5
24824	Coalwood, 650	C 8
26565	Coburn, 230	F 3
25048	Colcord, 600	D 7
26035	Colliers, 500	E 2
† 24740	Colored Hill, 1,031	D 8
26615	Copen, 312	E 5
25826	Corinne, 1,090	D 7
26713	Corinth, 195	H 4
25051	Costa, 500	C 6
25239	Cottageville, 500	C 5
25509	Cove Gap, 650	B 6
26206	Cowen, 467	E 6
26205	Craigsville, 300	E 6
25828	Cranberry, 297	D 7
25669	Crum, 300	B 7
24826	Cucumber, 275	C 8
25510	Culloden, 1,033	B 6
24827	Cyclone, 500	C 7
25832	Daniels, 950	D 7
25053	Danville, 580	C 6
† 25428	Darkesville, 375	L 4
26260	Davis, 868	H 4
26142	Davisville, 200	C 4
24828	Davy, 993	C 8
25054	Dawes, 800	D 6
24932	Dawson, 200	E 7
25055	Decota, 800	D 6
25670	Delbarton, 903	B 7
26531	Dellslow, 500	G 3
26217	Diana, 600	F 5
† 25535	Dickson, 200	B 6
26617	Dille, 300	E 6
25671	Dingess, 600	B 7
25059	Dixie, 800	D 6
† 26386	Dola, 200	F 4
26835	Dorcas, 250	H 5
25060	Dorothy, 400	D 7
25062	Dry Creek, 290	D 7
26263	Dryfork, 208	H 5
25063	Duck, 500	E 5
25064	Dunbar, 9,151	C 6
24934	Dunmore, 200	G 6
26264	Durbin, 347	G 5
25067	East Bank, 1,025	D 6
25835	Eastgulf, 300	D 7
25512	East Lynn, 500	B 6
† 26301	East View, 1,618	F 4
25836	Eccles, 1,105	D 7
24829	Eckman, 850	C 8
25672	Edgarton, 415	B 7
† 24954	Edray, 175	F 6
24830	Elbert, 400	C 8
25070	Eleanor, 1,035	C 5
26143	Elizabeth⊙, 821	D 4
26717	Elk Garden, 291	H 4
26241	Elkins⊙, 8,287	G 5
† 24868	Elkridge, 500	D 6
25071	Elkview, 1,486	C 6
26267	Ellamore, 400	F 5
26346	Ellenboro, 267	D 4
25965	Elton, 320	E 7
24832	English, 500	C 8
26568	Enterprise, 975	F 4
26203	Erbacon, 350	E 5
25075	Eskdale, 500	D 6
25076	Ethel, 450	C 7
25241	Evans, 400	C 5
26533	Everettville, 200	F 3
26554	Fairmont, 26,093	F 4
† 25271	Fairplain, 200	C 5
26570	Fairview, 640	F 3
† 24966	Falling Springs (Renick), 255	F 6
26571	Farmington, 595	F 3
25840	Fayetteville⊙, 1,712	D 6
26202	Fenwick, 500	E 6
25513	Ferrellsburg, 300	B 6
25823	Fireco, 300	D 7
26818	Fisher, 250	H 4
25841	Flat Top, 550	D 7
26621	Flatwoods, 220	E 5
26347	Flemington, 458	F 4
26037	Follansbee, 3,883	E 2
26348	Folsom, 325	E 4
24935	Forest Hill, 314	E 7
26719	Fort Ashby, 1,225	J 4
25514	Fort Gay, 792	A 6
26806	Fort Seybert, 208	H 5
24936	Fort Spring, 250	E 7
26572	Four States, 300	F 4
25071	Frame, 200	C 5
26623	Frametown, 600	E 5
24938	Frankford, 200	F 7
26807	Franklin⊙, 695	H 5
26218	French Creek, 200	F 5
26219	Frenchton, 212	F 5
26146	Friendly, 190	D 3
25515	Gallipolis Ferry, 325	B 5
26349	Galloway, 289	F 4
25243	Gandeeville, 271	D 5
24836	Gary, 850	C 8
26624	Gassaway, 1,253	E 5
25085	Gauley Bridge, 1,800	D 6
25420	Gerrardstown, 258	K 4
25843	Ghent, 450	D 7
† 24736	Giatto, 400	D 8
25621	Gilbert, 778	C 7
26671	Gilboa, 375	E 6
25086	Glasgow, 904	D 6
26038	Glen Dale, 2,150	E 3
25844	Glen Daniel, 300	D 7
25090	Glen Ferris, 275	D 6
† 25813	Glen Hedrick (Beaver), 1,711	D 7
25846	Glen Jean, 1,510	D 7
25848	Glen Rogers, 500	D 7
26351	Glenville⊙, 2,183	E 5
25849	Glen White, 600	D 7
25520	Glenwood, 400	B 5
25093	Gordon, 500	C 7
26720	Gormania, 250	H 4
26354	Grafton⊙, 6,433	G 4
26147	Grantsville⊙, 795	D 5
26574	Grant Town, 946	F 3
26534	Granville, 1,027	F 3
25422	Great Cacapon, 750	K 3
25966	Green Sulphur Springs, 300	E 7
† 25166	Greenview, 250	C 6
26360	Greenwood, 460	E 4
25521	Griffithsville, 300	B 6
25095	Grimms Landing, 350	B 5
26221	Guardian, 200	F 5
24838	Guyan, 250	C 7
25423	Halltown, 325	L 4
26269	Hambleton, 328	G 4
25523	Hamlin⊙, 1,024	B 6
25623	Hampden, 251	C 7
25102	Handley, 500	D 6
24839	Hanover, 300	C 7
† 26250	Harding, 200	G 5
25851	Harper, 300	D 7
25425	Harpers Ferry, 423	L 4
26362	Harrisville⊙, 1,464	E 4
25247	Hartford, 527	C 4
25852	Harvey, 500	D 7
24841	Havaco, 329	C 8
26627	Heaters, 343	E 5
25427	Hedgesville, 274	K 3
26224	Helvetia, 269	F 5
24842	Hemphill, 785	C 8
25106	Henderson, 496	B 5
26271	Hendricks, 317	G 4
25624	Henlawson, 900	B 7
26369	Hepzibah, 600	F 4
24726	Herndon, 500	D 7
25854	Hico, 750	D 6
24946	Hillsboro, 267	F 6
25951	Hinton⊙, 4,503	E 7
26262	Holcomb, 200	E 6
25625	Holden, 2,325	B 7
† 26651	Hookersville, 250	E 6
26575	Hundred, 475	E 3
* 25701	Huntington⊙, 74,315	A 6
	Huntington-Ashland, ‡253,743	A 6
25526	Hurricane, 3,491	C 6
24844	Iaeger, 822	C 8
25111	Indore, 200	D 6
25112	Institute, 3,100	C 6
25428	Inwood, 600	K 4
24847	Itmann, 500	D 7
25113	Ivydale, 700	D 5
26377	Jacksonburg, 735	E 3
26378	Jane Lew, 397	F 4
† 26462	Jarvisville, 250	F 4
25114	Jeffrey, 900	C 7
24848	Jenkinjones, 800	D 8
26674	Jodie, 300	D 6
25969	Jumping Branch, 297	E 7
26275	Junior, 513	G 5
24851	Justice, 600	C 7
25430	Kearneysville, 250	L 4
24731	Kegley, 450	D 8
24732	Kellysville, 200	E 8
25248	Kenna, 380	C 5
25530	Kenova, 4,860	A 6
25674	Kermit, 716	B 7
26726	Keyser⊙, 6,586	J 4
24852	Keystone, 1,008	D 8
25859	Kilsyth, 450	D 7
24853	Kimball, 962	C 8
26537	Kingwood⊙, 2,550	G 4
† 25671	Kirk, 400	B 7
25628	Kistler, 750	C 7
24854	Kopperston, 900	C 7
25860	Lanark, 375	D 7
† 25831	Landisburg, 250	E 7
25629	Landville, 250	C 7
25535	Lavalette, 600	B 6
25864	Layland, 455	E 7
† 26430	Layopolis (Sand Fork), 252	E 5
25251	Left Hand, 200	D 5
26676	Leivasy, 450	E 6
25676	Lenore, 800	B 7
25123	Leon, 192	C 5
25971	Lerona, 350	D 8
25537	Lesage, 600	B 5
25972	Leslie, 500	E 6
25865	Lester, 507	D 7
25253	Letart, 250	C 5
24901	Lewisburg⊙, 2,407	E 7
24951	Lindside, 225	E 8
26384	Linn, 212	E 4
26629	Little Birch, 180	E 5
† 26624	Little Otter, 250	E 5
26581	Littleton, 333	F 3
25125	Lizemores, 400	D 6
26677	Lockwood, 300	D 6
25601	Logan⊙, 3,311	B 7
25868	Lookout, 200	E 6
25630	Lorado, 400	C 7
26385	Lost Creek, 571	F 4
† 26101	Lubeck, 500	C 4
26386	Lumberport, 957	F 4
25631	Lundale, 700	C 7
25870	Maben, 200	D 7
26278	Mabie, 366	G 5
25871	Mabscott, 1,254	D 7
25873	MacArthur, 1,614	D 7
25130	Madison⊙, 2,342	C 6
26541	Maidsville, 485	F 3
25306	Malden, 900	C 6
25634	Mallory, 1,240	C 7
25132	Mammoth, 576	D 6
25635	Man, 1,201	C 7
26582	Mannington, 2,747	F 3
25975	Marfrance, 240	E 6
24954	Marlinton⊙, 1,286	F 6
25315	Marmet, 2,339	C 6
25401	Martinsburg⊙, 14,626	K 4
25260	Mason, 1,319	B 4
26542	Masontown, 868	G 3
25678	Matewan, 651	B 7
24736	Matoaka, 608	D 8
24861	Maybeury, 850	D 8

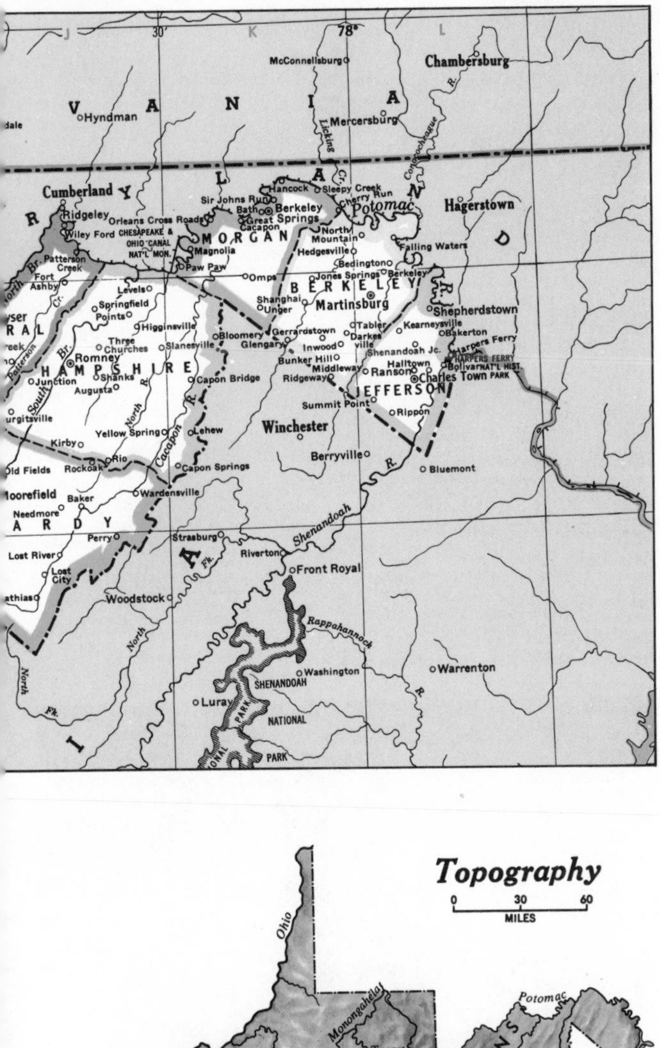

Chambersburg
McConnellsburg
Hyndman
Mercersburg
Hagerstown
Cumberland
Ridgeley
Hancock
Berkeley Springs
MORGAN
Hedgesville
Martinsburg
BERKELEY
Shepherdstown
Kearneysville
Romney
HAMPSHIRE
Capon Bridge
Charles Town
JEFFERSON
Winchester
Berryville
Bluemont
Moorefield
Wardensville
Strasburg
Front Royal
Woodstock
Washington
Warrenton
Luray
Shenandoah
Rappahannock
Potomac
SHENANDOAH NATIONAL PARK

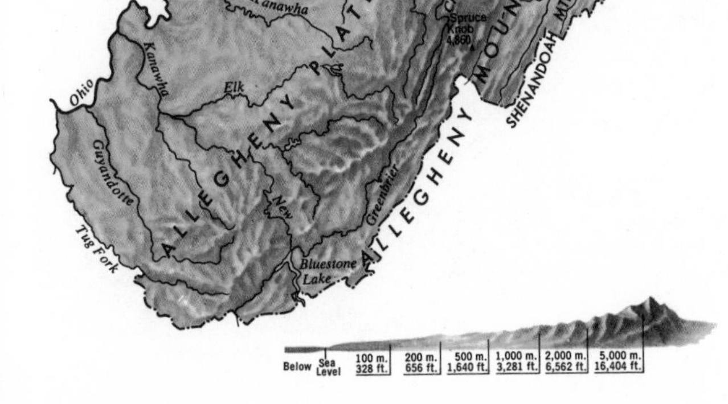

Topography
0 30 60
MILES
Ohio
Monongahela
Potomac
Tygart L.
Little Kanawha
ALLEGHENY PLATEAU
ALLEGHENY MOUNTAINS
SHENANDOAH MTN.
Cheat
Spruce Knob 4,860
Kanawha
Elk
Guyandotte
Tug Fork
New
Greenbrier
Bluestone Lake
Below Sea Level
100 m. 328 ft.
200 m. 656 ft.
500 m. 1,640 ft.
1,000 m. 3,281 ft.
2,000 m. 6,562 ft.
5,000 m. 16,404 ft.

(continued on following page)

(continued)

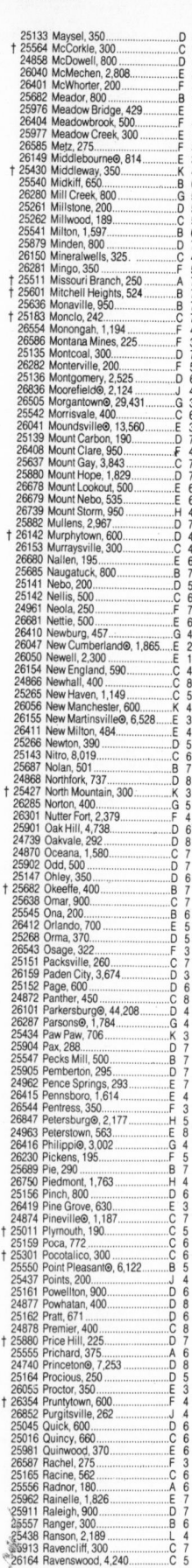

25133 Maysel, 350 .... D 5
† 25564 McCorkle, 300 .... C 6
24858 McDowell, 800 .... D 8
26040 McMechen, 2,808 .... E 3
26401 McWhorter, 200 .... F 4
25682 Meador, 800 .... B 7
25976 Meadow Bridge, 429 .... E 7
26404 Meadowbrook, 500 .... F 4
25977 Meadow Creek, 300 .... E 7
26585 Metz, 275 .... F 3
26149 Middlebourne⊙, 814 .... E 3
† 25430 Middleway, 350 .... K 4
25540 Midkiff, 650 .... B 6
26280 Mill Creek, 800 .... G 5
25261 Millstone, 200 .... D 5
25262 Millwood, 189 .... C 5
25541 Milton, 1,597 .... B 6
25879 Minden, 800 .... D 7
26150 Mineralwells, 325 .... C 4
26281 Mingo, 350 .... F 5
† 25511 Missouri Branch, 250 .... A 7
† 25601 Mitchell Heights, 524 .... B 7
25636 Monaville, 950 .... B 7
† 25183 Monclo, 242 .... C 7
26554 Monongah, 1,194 .... F 4
26586 Montana Mines, 225 .... F 3
25135 Montcoal, 300 .... D 7
26282 Monterville, 200 .... F 5
25136 Montgomery, 2,525 .... D 6
26836 Moorefield⊙, 2,124 .... J 4
26505 Morgantown⊙, 29,431 .... G 3
25542 Morrisvale, 400 .... C 6
26041 Moundsville⊙, 13,560 .... E 3
25139 Mount Carbon, 190 .... D 7
26408 Mount Clare, 950 .... F 4
25637 Mount Gay, 3,843 .... C 7
25880 Mount Hope, 1,829 .... D 7
26678 Mount Lookout, 500 .... E 6
26679 Mount Nebo, 535 .... E 6
26739 Mount Storm, 950 .... H 4
25882 Mullens, 2,967 .... D 7
† 26142 Murphytown, 600 .... D 4
26153 Murraysville, 300 .... C 4
26680 Nallen, 195 .... E 6
25685 Naugatuck, 800 .... B 7
25141 Nebo, 200 .... D 5
25142 Nellis, 500 .... C 6
24961 Neola, 250 .... F 7
26681 Nettie, 500 .... E 6
26410 Newburg, 457 .... G 4
26047 New Cumberland⊙, 1,865 .... E 2
26050 Newell, 2,300 .... E 1
26154 New England, 590 .... C 4
24866 Newhall, 400 .... C 8
25265 New Haven, 1,149 .... C 5
26056 New Manchester, 600 .... K 4
26155 New Martinsville⊙, 6,528 .... E 3
26411 New Milton, 484 .... E 4
25266 Newton, 390 .... D 5
25143 Nitro, 8,019 .... C 6
25687 Nolan, 501 .... B 7
24868 Northfork, 737 .... D 8
† 25427 North Mountain, 300 .... K 3
26285 Norton, 400 .... G 5
26301 Nutter Fort, 2,379 .... F 4
25901 Oak Hill, 4,738 .... D 6
24739 Oakvale, 292 .... D 8
24870 Oceana, 1,580 .... C 7
25902 Odd, 500 .... D 7
25147 Ohley, 350 .... D 6
† 25682 Okeeffe, 400 .... B 7
25638 Omar, 900 .... C 7
25545 Ona, 200 .... B 6
26412 Orlando, 700 .... E 5
25268 Orma, 370 .... D 5
26543 Osage, 322 .... F 3
25151 Packsville, 260 .... C 7
26159 Paden City, 3,674 .... D 3
25152 Page, 600 .... D 6
24872 Panther, 450 .... C 8
26101 Parkersburg⊙, 44,208 .... D 4
26287 Parsons⊙, 1,784 .... G 4
25434 Paw Paw, 706 .... K 3
25904 Pax, 288 .... D 7
25547 Pecks Mill, 500 .... B 7
25905 Pemberton, 295 .... D 7
24962 Pence Springs, 293 .... E 7
26415 Pennsboro, 1,614 .... E 4
26544 Pentress, 350 .... F 3
26847 Petersburg⊙, 2,177 .... H 5
24963 Peterstown, 563 .... E 8
26416 Philippi⊙, 3,002 .... G 4
26230 Pickens, 195 .... F 5
25689 Pie, 290 .... B 7
26750 Piedmont, 1,763 .... H 4
25156 Pinch, 800 .... D 6
26419 Pine Grove, 630 .... E 3
24874 Pineville⊙, 1,187 .... C 7
† 25011 Plymouth, 190 .... C 5
25159 Poca, 772 .... C 6
† 25301 Pocotalico, 300 .... C 6
25550 Point Pleasant⊙, 6,122 .... B 5
25437 Points, 200 .... J 4
25161 Powellton, 900 .... D 6
24877 Powhatan, 400 .... D 8
25162 Pratt, 671 .... D 6
24878 Premier, 400 .... C 8
† 25880 Price Hill, 225 .... D 7
25555 Prichard, 375 .... A 6
24740 Princeton⊙, 7,253 .... D 8
25164 Procious, 250 .... D 5
26055 Proctor, 350 .... E 3
† 26354 Pruntytown, 600 .... F 4
26852 Purgitsville, 262 .... J 4
25045 Quick, 600 .... D 6
25016 Quincy, 660 .... C 6
25981 Quinwood, 370 .... E 6
26587 Rachel, 275 .... F 3
25165 Racine, 562 .... C 6
25556 Radnor, 180 .... A 6
25962 Rainelle, 1,826 .... E 7
25911 Raleigh, 900 .... D 7
25557 Ranger, 300 .... B 6
25438 Ranson, 2,189 .... L 4
25913 Ravencliff, 300 .... C 7
26164 Ravenswood, 4,240 .... C 5

Agriculture, Industry and Resources

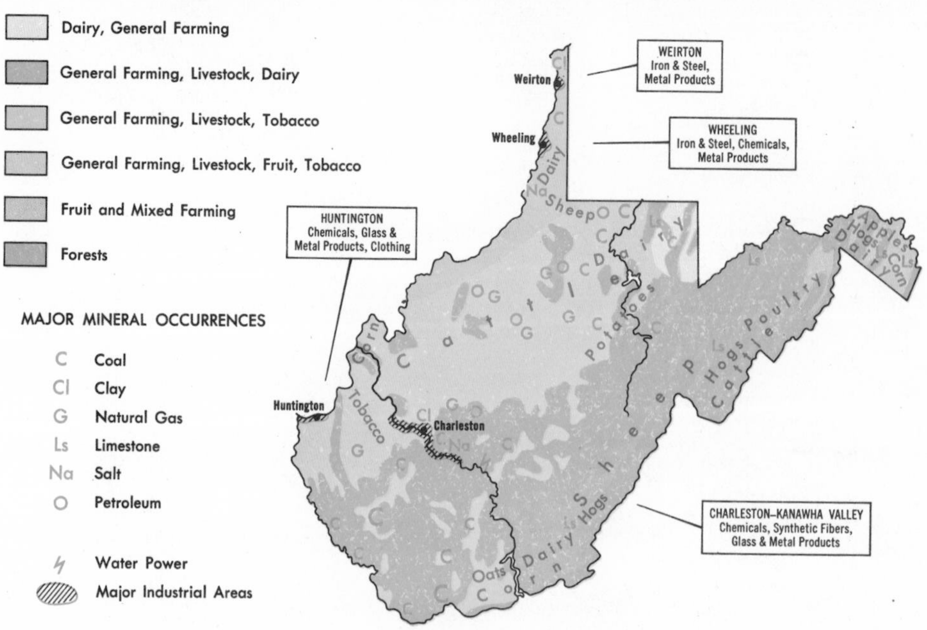
DOMINANT LAND USE
Dairy, General Farming
General Farming, Livestock, Dairy
General Farming, Livestock, Tobacco
General Farming, Livestock, Fruit, Tobacco
Fruit and Mixed Farming
Forests
MAJOR MINERAL OCCURRENCES
C Coal
Cl Clay
G Natural Gas
Ls Limestone
Na Salt
O Petroleum
Water Power
Major Industrial Areas
WEIRTON
Iron & Steel, Metal Products
WHEELING
Iron & Steel, Chemicals, Metal Products
HUNTINGTON
Chemicals, Glass & Metal Products, Clothing
CHARLESTON–KANAWHA VALLEY
Chemicals, Synthetic Fibers, Glass & Metal Products
Weirton
Wheeling
Huntington
Charleston
Dairy
Sheep
Apples
Hogs
Poultry
Cattle
Potatoes
Corn
Tobacco
Oats

† 25159 Raymond City, 370 .... C 6
26167 Reader, 822 .... E 3
25168 Red House, 600 .... C 5
25692 Red Jacket, 800 .... B 7
25914 Redstar, 200 .... D 7
26547 Reedsville, 379 .... G 3
25270 Reedy, 351 .... D 5
24966 Renick, 255 .... F 6
25915 Rhodell, 500 .... D 7
26261 Richwood, 3,717 .... F 6
26753 Ridgeley, 1,112 .... J 3
25271 Ripley⊙, 3,244 .... C 5
25441 Rippon, 500 .... L 4
26588 Rivesville, 1,108 .... F 3
26234 Rock Cave, 300 .... F 5
24881 Roderfield, 1,161 .... C 8
26757 Romney⊙, 2,364 .... J 4
24970 Ronceverte, 1,981 .... F 7
26636 Rosedale, 234 .... E 5
25643 Rossmore, 400 .... C 7
26425 Rowlesburg, 829 .... G 4
25984 Rupert, 1,027 .... E 7
26689 Russellville, 240 .... E 6
25177 Saint Albans, 14,356 .... C 6
26170 Saint Marys⊙, 2,348 .... D 4
26426 Salem, 2,597 .... E 4
25559 Salt Rock, 350 .... B 6
26430 Sand Fork, 252 .... E 5
25985 Sandstone, 350 .... E 7
25275 Sandyville, 500 .... C 5
25917 Scarbro, 800 .... D 7
† 25674 Selwyn, 500 .... B 7
25181 Seth, 950 .... C 6
† 25427 Shanghai, 200 .... K 4
25182 Sharon, 700 .... D 6
25183 Sharples, 450 .... C 7
25442 Shenandoah Junction, 600 .... L 4
25443 Shepherdstown, 1,688 .... L 4
26057 Sherrard, 400 .... E 3
26431 Shinnston, 2,576 .... F 4
26435 Simpson, 250 .... F 4
25320 Sissonville, 450 .... C 5
26175 Sistersville, 2,246 .... D 3
25920 Slab Fork, 300 .... D 7
† 25654 Slagle, 450 .... C 7
† 26143 Slate, 200 .... D 4
25186 Smithers, 2,020 .... D 6
26437 Smithfield, 294 .... E 4
26178 Smithville, 500 .... D 4
24977 Smoot, 300 .... E 7
25921 Sophia, 1,303 .... D 7
25303 South Charleston, 16,333 .... C 6
25922 Spanishburg, 425 .... D 8
25276 Spencer⊙, 2,271 .... D 5
26763 Springfield, 250 .... J 4
24884 Squire, 900 .... C 8
26505 Star City, 1,312 .... F 3
25188 Stickney, 240 .... D 7
25645 Stirrat, 250 .... C 7
26301 Stonewood, 1,950 .... F 4
25929 Stotesbury, 199 .... D 7
26651 Summersville⊙, 2,429 .... E 6
25446 Summit Point, 455 .... K 4
26601 Sutton⊙, 1,031 .... E 5
24980 Sweet Springs, 500 .... F 7
26690 Swiss, 500 .... D 6
25647 Switzer, 850 .... B 7
25193 Sylvester, 245 .... C 6
† 25428 Tabler, 300 .... L 4
24981 Talcott, 700 .... E 7
26237 Tallmansville, 260 .... F 5
25569 Teays, 200 .... B 6
26764 Terra Alta, 1,474 .... H 4
26640 Tesla, 300 .... E 5
25694 Thacker, 325 .... B 7
26292 Thomas, 713 .... H 4
26440 Thornton, 300 .... G 4
24888 Thorpe, 600 .... D 8
† 26206 Three Forks of Williams River, 375 .... F 6
26691 Tioga, 320 .... E 6
26059 Triadelphia, 547 .... E 2
† 25095 Tribble, 350 .... C 5
26444 Tunnelton, 369 .... G 4
25203 Turtle Creek, 566 .... C 6
25205 Uneeda, 850 .... C 6
24983 Union⊙, 566 .... E 7
26266 Upperglade, 500 .... F 6
26293 Valley Bend, 950 .... F 5
26060 Valley Grove, 509 .... E 2
26294 Valley Head, 600 .... G 5
25206 Van, 800 .... C 7
25696 Varney, 750 .... B 7
25649 Verdunville, 950 .... B 7
26101 Vienna, 11,549 .... D 4
24891 Vivian, 500 .... D 8
26238 Volga, 350 .... F 4
26589 Wadestown, 210 .... F 3
24984 Waiteville, 252 .... F 8
26448 Wallace, 325 .... E 4
25286 Walton, 250 .... D 5
24892 War, 2,004 .... C 8
† 25039 Ward, 850 .... D 6
26851 Wardensville, 288 .... J 4
26181 Washington, 450 .... C 4
† 26041 Washington Lands, 500 .... E 3
26184 Waverly, 407 .... D 4
25570 Wayne⊙, 1,385 .... B 6
26288 Webster Springs⊙, 1,038 .... F 6
26062 Weirton, 27,131 .... E 2
Weirton-Steubenville, ‡165,627 .... E 2
24801 Welch⊙, 4,149 .... C 8
26070 Wellsburg⊙, 4,600 .... E 2
25287 West Columbia, 245 .... B 5
25571 West Hamlin, 715 .... B 6
26074 West Liberty, 975 .... E 2
25601 West Logan, 685 .... C 7
26451 West Milford, 356 .... F 4
26452 Weston⊙, 7,323 .... F 4
26505 Westover, 5,086 .... G 3
26456 West Union⊙, 1,141 .... E 4
25651 Wharncliffe, 1,012 .... C 7
25208 Wharton, 900 .... C 7
26003 Wheeling⊙, 48,188 .... E 2
Wheeling, ‡182,712 .... E 2
24986 White Sulphur Springs, 2,396 .... F 7
25209 Whitesville, 781 .... C 6
26296 Whitmer, 411 .... G 5
25211 Widen, 230 .... E 6
26767 Wiley Ford, 750 .... J 3
26186 Wileyville, 190 .... E 3
25653 Wilkinson, 975 .... B 7
24991 Williamsburg, 225 .... F 7
25661 Williamson⊙, 5,831 .... B 7
26187 Williamstown, 2,743 .... C 4
26461 Wilsonburg, 200 .... F 4
25699 Wilsondale, 200 .... B 7
26075 Windsor Heights, 850 .... E 2
25213 Winfield⊙, 328 .... C 5
25214 Winifrede, 750 .... C 6
25942 Winona, 250 .... E 6
26462 Wolf Summit, 750 .... F 4
† 26257 Womelsdorf (Coalton), 234 .... G 5
† 26055 Woodlands, 200 .... E 3
26591 Worthington, 288 .... F 4
25573 Yawkey, 985 .... C 6
26865 Yellow Spring, 250 .... J 4
25654 Yolyn, 750 .... C 7

⊙ County seat.
‡ Population of metropolitan area
† Zip of nearest p.o.
* Multiple zips

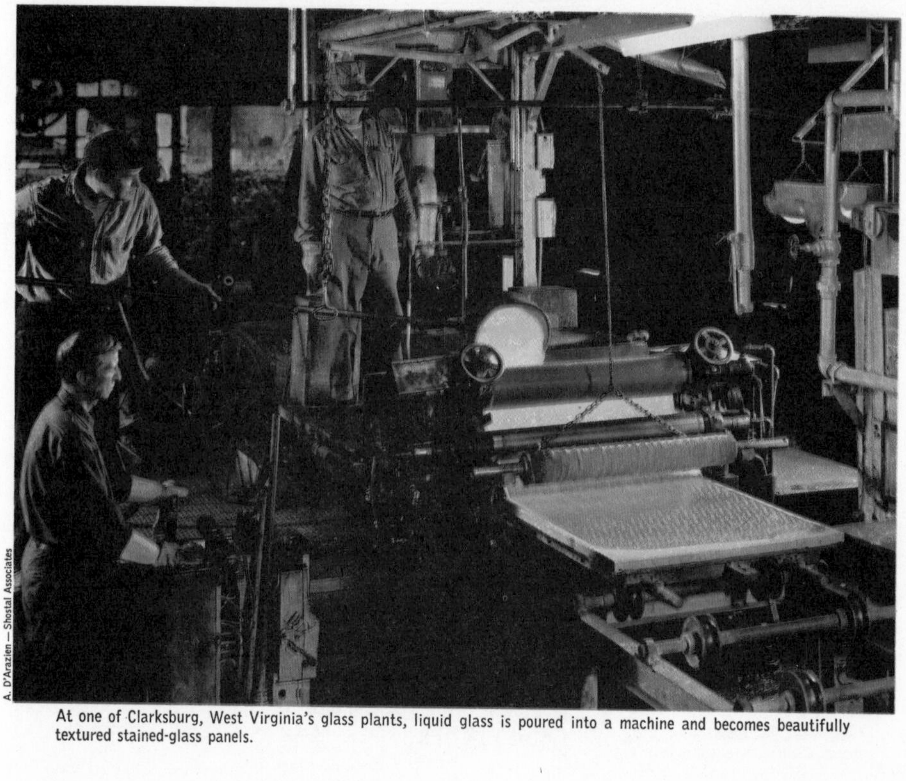

A. D'Arazien — Shostal Associates

At one of Clarksburg, West Virginia's glass plants, liquid glass is poured into a machine and becomes beautifully textured stained-glass panels.

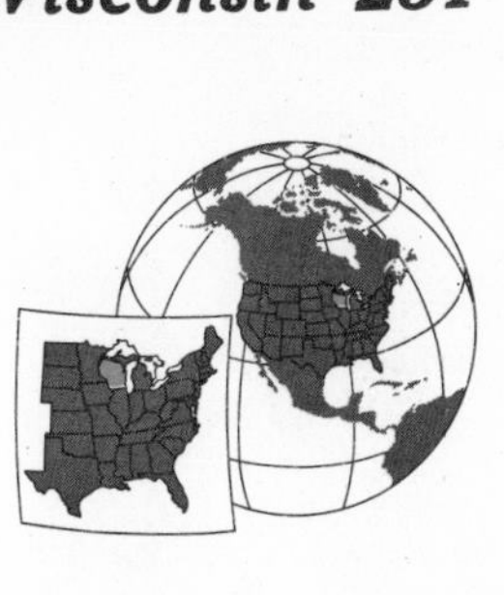

AREA 56,154 sq. mi.
POPULATION 4,417,933
CAPITAL Madison
LARGEST CITY Milwaukee
HIGHEST POINT Timms Hill 1,952 ft.
SETTLED IN 1670
ADMITTED TO UNION May 29, 1848
POPULAR NAME Badger State
STATE FLOWER Wood Violet
STATE BIRD Robin

COUNTIES

Adams, 9,234 G 8
Ashland, 16,743 E 3
Barron, 33,955 C 5
Bayfield, 11,683 D 3
Brown, 158,244 L 7
Buffalo, 13,743 C 7
Burnett, 9,276 B 4
Calumet, 27,604 K 7
Chippewa, 47,717 D 5
Clark, 30,361 E 6
Columbia, 40,150 H 9
Crawford, 15,252 E 9
Dane, 290,272 H 9
Dodge, 69,004 J 9
Door, 20,106 M 6
Douglas, 44,657 C 3
Dunn, 29,154 C 6
Eau Claire, 67,219 D 6
Florence, 3,298 K 4
Fond du Lac, 84,567 K 8
Forest, 7,691 J 4
Grant, 48,398 E 10
Green, 26,714 G 10
Green Lake, 16,878 H 8
Iowa, 19,306 F 9
Iron, 6,533 F 3
Jackson, 15,325 E 7
Jefferson, 60,060 J 9
Juneau, 18,455 F 8
Kenosha, 117,917 K 10
Kewaunee, 18,961 L 6
La Crosse, 80,468 D 8
Lafayette, 17,456 F 10
Langlade, 19,220 H 5
Lincoln, 23,499 G 5
Manitowoc, 82,294 L 7
Marathon, 97,457 G 6
Marinette, 35,810 K 5
Marquette, 8,865 H 8
Menominee, 2,607 J 5
Milwaukee, 1,054,063 L 9
Monroe, 31,610 E 8
Oconto, 25,553 K 6
Oneida, 24,427 G 4
Outagamie, 119,356 K 7
Ozaukee, 54,421 L 9
Pepin, 7,319 C 6
Pierce, 26,652 B 6
Polk, 26,666 B 5
Portage, 47,541 G 6
Price, 14,520 F 4
Racine, 170,838 K 10
Richland, 17,079 F 9
Rock, 131,970 H 10
Rusk, 14,238 D 5
Saint Croix, 34,354 B 5
Sauk, 39,057 G 9
Sawyer, 9,670 D 4
Shawano, 32,650 J 6
Sheboygan, 96,660 L 8
Taylor, 16,958 E 5
Trempealeau, 23,344 D 7
Vernon, 24,557 E 8
Vilas, 10,958 G 3
Walworth, 63,444 J 10
Washburn, 10,601 C 4
Washington, 63,839 K 9
Waukesha, 231,365 K 9
Waupaca, 37,780 J 6
Waushara, 14,795 H 7
Winnebago, 129,931 J 7
Wood, 65,362 F 7

CITIES and TOWNS

Zip	Name/Pop.	Key
54405	Abbotsford, 1,375	F 6
54101	Abrams, 300	L 6
53910	Adams, 1,440	G 8
53001	Adell, 380	L 8
53501	Afton, 250	H 10
53502	Albany, 875	G 10
† 53534	Albion, 250	H 10
54201	Algoma, 4,023	M 6
53002	Allenton, 584	K 9
† 54301	Allouez, 13,753	L 7
54610	Alma⊙, 956	C 7
54611	Alma Center, 495	E 7
54805	Almena, 423	B 5
54909	Almond, 440	G 7
54720	Altoona, 2,842	C 6
49936	Alvin, 160	J 4
54102	Amberg, 711	K 5
54001	Amery, 2,126	B 5
54406	Amherst, 585	H 7
† 54162	Angelica, 200	K 6
54408	Aniwa, 233	H 6
54409	Antigo⊙, 9,005	H 5
54911	Appleton⊙, 57,143	J 7
	Appleton-Oshkosh, ‡276,893	J 7
54510	Arbor Vitae, 950	G 4
54612	Arcadia, 2,159	D 7
53503	Arena, 377	G 9
54511	Argonne, 400	J 4
53504	Argyle, 673	G 10
54721	Arkansaw, 350	B 6
53911	Arlington, 379	H 9
54103	Armstrong Creek, 555	K 4
54410	Arpin, 355	G 6
53003	Ashippun, 400	H 1
54806	Ashland⊙, 9,615	E 2
54304	Ashwaubenon, 9,323	K 7
54411	Athens, 856	G 5
54412	Auburndale, 468	F 6
54722	Augusta, 1,242	D 6
54920	Auroraville, 250	H 7
53506	Avoca, 421	F 9
† 53520	Avon, 600	H 10
54413	Babcock, 260	F 7
53801	Bagley, 271	D 10
54202	Baileys Harbor, 900	M 5
54002	Baldwin, 1,399	B 6
54810	Balsam Lake⊙, 648	B 5
54921	Bancroft, 150	G 7
54614	Bangor, 974	E 8
53913	Baraboo⊙, 7,931	G 9
† 54873	Barnes, 450	D 3
53507	Barneveld, 528	F 10
54812	Barron⊙, 2,337	C 5
† 53001	Batavia, 160	K 8
54723	Bay City, 317	B 6
54814	Bayfield, 874	E 2
† 53201	Bayside, 4,461	M 1
54922	Bear Creek, 520	J 6
53916	Beaver Dam, 14,265	J 9
53802	Beetown, 170	E 10
53004	Belgium, 809	L 8
53508	Belleville, 1,063	G 10
53510	Belmont, 688	F 10
53511	Beloit, 35,729	H 10
54815	Bennett, 350	C 3
53803	Benton, 873	F 10
54923	Berlin, 5,338	H 8
† 53401	Berryville, 150	M 3
† 54410	Bethel, 210	F 6
† 54440	Bevent, 200	H 6
53103	Big Bend, 1,148	K 2
54817	Birchwood, 394	C 4
54414	Birnamwood, 632	H 6
† 54494	Biron, 771	G 7
54106	Black Creek, 921	K 7
53515	Black Earth, 1,114	G 9
54615	Black River Falls⊙, 3,273	E 7
† 54541	Blackwell, 350	J 4
54616	Blair, 1,036	D 7
53516	Blanchardville, 671	G 10
54724	Bloomer, 3,143	D 5
53804	Bloomington, 719	E 10
53517	Blue Mounds, 261	G 9
53518	Blue River, 369	E 9
54107	Bonduel, 995	K 6
53805	Boscobel, 2,510	E 9
54512	Boulder Junction, 500	G 3
54416	Bowler, 272	J 6
54725	Boyceville, 725	C 5
54726	Boyd, 574	E 6
54203	Branch, 225	L 7
53919	Brandon, 872	J 8
54513	Brantwood, 500	F 4
53920	Briggsville, 250	H 8
54110	Brillion, 2,588	L 7
53520	Brodhead, 2,515	G 10
54417	Brokaw, 312	G 5
53005	Brookfield, 32,140	K 1
53521	Brooklyn, 565	H 10
† 53201	Brown Deer, 12,622	L 1
† 53105	Browns Lake, 1,669	K 3
53006	Brownsville, 374	J 8
53522	Browntown, 253	G 10
54819	Bruce, 799	D 5
54820	Brule, 675	C 2
54204	Brussels, 306	L 6
† 54622	Buffalo, 671	C 7
53105	Burlington, 7,479	K 10
53922	Burnett, 241	J 9
53007	Butler, 2,261	K 1
54514	Butternut, 453	E 3
54821	Cable, 281	D 3
54727	Cadott, 977	D 6
53923	Cambria, 631	H 8
53523	Cambridge, 689	H 9
54822	Cameron, 893	C 5
† 53019	Campbellsport, 1,681	K 8
54618	Camp Douglas, 547	F 8
53109	Camp Lake, 1,898	K 10
54928	Caroline, 450	J 6
53011	Cascade, 603	K 8
54205	Casco, 481	L 6
54619	Cashton, 824	E 8
53806	Cassville, 1,343	E 10
54515	Catawba, 215	E 4
53924	Cazenovia, 335	F 8
54111	Cecil, 369	K 6
53012	Cedarburg, 7,697	L 9
53013	Cedar Grove, 1,276	L 8
54824	Centuria, 632	A 5
54621	Chaseburg, 224	D 8
† 53029	Chenequa, 642	J 1
54728	Chetek, 1,630	C 5
54420	Chili, 205	F 6
53014	Chilton⊙, 3,030	K 7
54729	Chippewa Falls⊙, 12,351	D 6
54004	Clayton, 306	B 5
54005	Clear Lake, 721	B 5
54518	Clearwater Lake, 200	H 4
53015	Cleveland, 761	L 8
53525	Clinton, 1,333	J 10
54929	Clintonville, 4,600	J 6
53016	Clyman, 328	J 9
53526	Cobb, 410	F 10
54622	Cochrane, 506	C 7
54421	Colby, 1,178	F 6
54112	Coleman, 683	L 5
54730	Colfax, 1,026	C 6
54930	Coloma, 336	H 7
53925	Columbus, 3,789	H 9
54113	Combined Locks, 2,734	K 7
† 53147	Como, 1,132	K 10
† 53066	Concord, 200	H 1
54519	Conover, 500	H 3
54623	Coon Valley, 596	E 8
54732	Cornell, 1,616	D 5
54827	Cornucopia, 250	D 2
54520	Crandon⊙, 1,582	H 4
54114	Crivitz, 985	L 5
53528	Cross Plains, 1,478	G 9
53807	Cuba City, 1,993	F 10
53110	Cudahy, 22,078	M 2
54829	Cumberland, 1,839	C 4
54931	Dale, 410	J 7
54733	Dallas, 359	C 5
53926	Dalton, 320	H 8
54830	Danbury, 350	B 3
53529	Dane, 486	G 9
53114	Darien, 839	J 10
53530	Darlington⊙, 2,351	F 10
53531	Deerfield, 1,067	H 9
54007	Deer Park, 217	B 5
53532	De Forest, 1,911	H 9
53018	Delafield, 3,182	J 1
53115	Delavan, 5,526	J 10
† 53115	Delavan Lake, 2,124	J 10
54856	Delta, 180	D 3
54208	Denmark, 1,364	L 7
54115	De Pere, 13,309	K 7
† 54663	De Soto, 295	D 9
53808	Dickeyville, 1,057	E 10
54625	Dodge, 204	D 7
53533	Dodgeville⊙, 3,255	F 10
54425	Dorchester, 491	F 5
53118	Dousman, 451	J 1
54734	Downing, 215	B 5
53928	Doylestown, 265	H 9
54009	Dresser, 533	A 5
54736	Durand⊙, 2,103	C 6
† 54217	Dyckesville, 300	L 6
53119	Eagle, 745	H 2
54521	Eagle River⊙, 1,326	H 4
54626	Eastman, 319	D 9
53120	East Troy, 1,711	J 2
54701	Eau Claire⊙, 44,619	D 6
53019	Eden, 376	K 8
54426	Edgar, 928	G 6
53534	Edgerton, 4,118	H 10
54209	Egg Harbor, 184	M 5
54427	Eland, 229	H 6
54428	Elcho, 500	H 5
54429	Elderon, 185	H 6
54932	Eldorado, 200	J 8
54738	Eleva, 574	D 6
53020	Elkhart Lake, 787	L 8
53121	Elkhorn⊙, 3,992	J 10
54739	Elk Mound, 471	C 6
54011	Ellsworth⊙, 1,983	A 6
53122	Elm Grove, 7,201	K 1
54740	Elmwood, 737	B 6
† 53401	Elmwood Park, 456	M 3
53929	Elroy, 1,513	F 8
54430	Elton, 250	J 5
54933	Embarrass, 472	J 6
53930	Endeavor, 328	G 8
54211	Ephraim, 236	M 5
54627	Ettrick, 463	D 7
54934	Eureka, 300	J 7
53536	Evansville, 2,992	H 10
54835	Exeland, 189	D 4
54741	Fairchild, 562	D 6
53931	Fair Water, 373	J 8
54742	Fall Creek, 825	D 6
53932	Fall River, 633	H 9
54120	Fence, 187	K 4
53809	Fennimore, 1,861	E 9
54628	Ferryville, 183	D 9
54524	Fifield, 287	F 4
54212	Fish Creek, 275	M 5
54121	Florence⊙, 800	K 4
54935	Fond du Lac⊙, 35,515	K 8
53125	Fontana, 1,464	J 10
53537	Footville, 698	H 10
54123	Forest Junction, 255	K 7
54213	Forestville, 349	L 6
53538	Fort Atkinson, 9,164	J 10
54629	Fountain City, 1,017	C 7
54836	Foxboro, 950	B 2
53933	Fox Lake, 1,242	J 8
53217	Fox Point, 7,937	M 1
54214	Francis Creek, 492	L 7
53132	Franklin, 12,247	L 2
53126	Franksville, 375	M 3
54837	Frederic, 908	B 4
53021	Fredonia, 1,045	L 8
54940	Fremont, 598	J 7
53934	Friendship⊙, 641	G 8
53935	Friesland, 301	H 8
54630	Galesville, 1,162	D 7
54631	Gays Mills, 623	E 9
† 53127	Genesee, 375	J 2
53127	Genesee Depot, 425	J 2
54632	Genoa, 305	D 8
53128	Genoa City, 1,085	K 11
53022	Germantown, 6,974	K 1
† 53085	Gibbsville, 408	L 8
54525	Gile, 450	F 3
54124	Gillett, 1,288	K 6
54433	Gilman, 328	E 5
54743	Gilmanton, 200	C 7
54435	Gleason, 300	G 5
53023	Glenbeulah, 496	L 8
† 53201	Glendale, 13,436	M 1
53810	Glen Haven, 250	E 10
54013	Glenwood City, 822	B 5
54527	Glidden, 860	E 3
54125	Goodman, 800	K 4
54838	Gordon, 350	C 3
53540	Gotham, 175	F 9
53024	Grafton, 5,998	L 9
53936	Grand Marsh, 200	G 8
53939	Grand View, 350	D 3
54436	Granton, 288	E 6
54840	Grantsburg⊙, 930	A 4
53541	Gratiot, 249	F 10
* 54301	Green Bay⊙, 87,809	K 6
	Green Bay, ‡158,244	K 6
53129	Greendale, 15,089	L 2
53220	Greenfield, 24,424	L 2
54941	Green Lake⊙, 1,109	H 8
54126	Greenleaf, 350	L 7
54942	Greenville, 900	J 7
54437	Greenwood, 1,036	E 6
54128	Gresham, 448	J 6
53130	Hales Corners, 7,771	K 2
† 54729	Hallie, 1,223	D 6
54438	Hamburg, 170	G 5
54015	Hammond, 768	A 6
54943	Hancock, 404	G 7
54529	Harshaw, 200	G 4
53027	Hartford, 6,499	K 9
53029	Hartland, 2,763	J 1
54440	Hatley, 315	H 6
54841	Haugen, 246	C 4
54530	Hawkins, 385	E 4
54843	Hayward⊙, 1,457	D 3
53811	Hazel Green, 982	F 11
54531	Hazelhurst, 334	G 4
† 53538	Hebron, 190	J 10
53137	Helenville, 230	J 10
54844	Herbster, 250	D 2
54441	Hewitt, 300	F 6
53543	Highland, 785	F 9
54129	Hilbert, 896	K 7
54533	Hiles, 260	J 4
54634	Hillsboro, 1,231	F 8
53031	Hingham, 210	K 8
54635	Hixton, 300	E 7
54745	Holcombe, 200	D 5
53544	Hollandale, 256	G 10
54636	Holmen, 1,081	D 8
53138	Honey Creek, 350	J 3
53032	Horicon, 3,356	J 9
54944	Hortonville, 1,524	J 7
† 55082	Houlton, 400	A 5
54303	Howard, 4,911	K 6
† 53081	Howards Grove-Millersville, 998	L 8
53033	Hubertus, 600	K 1
54016	Hudson⊙, 5,049	A 6
54746	Humbird, 219	E 6
54534	Hurley⊙, 2,418	F 3
53034	Hustisford, 789	J 9
54637	Hustler, 190	F 8
† 54450	Hutchins, 409	H 6
54747	Independence, 1,036	D 7
54945	Iola, 900	H 6
54536	Iron Belt, 425	F 3
53035	Iron Ridge, 480	K 9
54847	Iron River, 800	D 2
53938	Ironton, 195	F 8
† 53177	Ives Grove, 250	L 3
53036	Ixonia, 300	H 1
53037	Jackson, 561	K 9
54236	Jacksonport, 180	M 6
53545	Janesville⊙, 46,426	J 10
53549	Jefferson⊙, 5,429	J 10
54748	Jim Falls, 310	D 5
53038	Johnson Creek, 790	J 9
53550	Juda, 500	H 10
54443	Junction City, 396	G 6
53039	Juneau⊙, 2,043	J 9
53139	Kansasville, 300	L 3
54130	Kaukauna, 11,292	K 7
† 53050	Kekoskee, 233	J 8
54215	Kellnersville, 250	L 7
54638	Kendall, 468	F 8
54537	Kennan, 167	E 5
53140	Kenosha⊙, 78,805	M 3
	Kenosha, ‡117,917	M 3
54135	Keshena⊙, 980	J 6
53040	Kewaskum, 1,926	K 8
54216	Kewaunee⊙, 2,901	M 7
53042	Kiel, 2,848	L 8
53812	Kieler, 653	E 10
54136	Kimberly, 6,131	K 7
54946	King, 1,040	H 7
53939	Kingston, 343	H 8
54749	Knapp, 369	B 6
53044	Kohler, 1,738	L 8
53147	Krakow, 315	K 6
54538	Lac du Flambeau, 500	G 4
† 53066	Lac La Belle, 227	H 1
54601	La Crosse⊙, 51,153	D 8
	La Crosse, ‡80,468	D 8
54848	Ladysmith⊙, 3,674	D 5
54639	La Farge, 748	E 8
53940	Lake Delton, 1,059	G 8
53147	Lake Geneva, 4,890	K 10
53551	Lake Mills, 3,556	H 9
54849	Lake Nebagamon, 523	C 3
54539	Lake Tomahawk, 555	H 4
† 54494	Lake Wazeecha, 1,285	G 7
† 54729	Lake Wissota, 1,419	D 6
54138	Lakewood, 300	K 5
† 53065	Lamartine, 190	J 8
53813	Lancaster⊙, 3,756	E 10
54540	Land O'Lakes, 786	H 3
53046	Lannon, 1,056	K 1
54541	Laona, 1,500	J 4
54850	La Pointe, 300	E 2
53941	La Valle, 411	F 8
53047	Lebanon, 250	H 1
54139	Lena, 569	K 6
† 54656	Leon, 160	E 8
† 53190	Lima Center, 175	J 10
53942	Limeridge, 203	F 9
53553	Linden, 408	F 10
54140	Little Chute, 5,365	K 7
54141	Little Suamico, 190	L 6
53554	Livingston, 503	E 10
53555	Lodi, 1,831	G 9
53943	Loganville, 199	F 9
† 54970	Lohrville, 195	H 7
53048	Lomira, 1,084	J 8
† 53523	London, 317	H 9
53556	Lone Rock, 506	F 9
54852	Loretta, 200	E 4
53557	Lowell, 322	J 9
54446	Loyal, 1,126	E 6
54853	Luck, 848	B 4
54217	Luxemburg, 853	L 6
53944	Lyndon Station, 533	F 8
53148	Lyons, 550	K 10
* 53701	Madison (cap.)⊙, 173,258	H 9
	Madison, ‡290,272	H 9
54750	Maiden Rock, 172	B 6
54949	Manawa, 1,105	J 7
54220	Manitowoc⊙, 33,430	L 7
54226	Maplewood, 192	M 6
54448	Marathon, 1,214	G 6
54855	Marengo, 350	E 3
54227	Maribel, 316	L 7
54143	Marinette⊙, 12,696	L 5
54950	Marion, 1,218	J 6
53946	Markesan, 1,378	J 8
53947	Marquette, 161	H 8
53559	Marshall, 1,043	H 9
54449	Marshfield, 15,619	F 6
54450	Mattoon, 377	J 5
53948	Mauston⊙, 3,466	F 8
53050	Mayville, 4,139	K 9
53560	Mazomanie, 1,217	G 9
53558	McFarland, 2,386	H 10
54543	McNaughton, 350	H 4
54451	Medford⊙, 3,454	F 5
54546	Mellen, 1,168	E 3
54642	Melrose, 505	E 7
54952	Menasha, 14,905	J 7
53051	Menomonee Falls, 31,697	K 1
54751	Menomonie⊙, 11,275	C 6
53092	Mequon, 12,110	L 1
54547	Mercer, 1,100	F 3
54452	Merrill⊙, 9,502	G 5
54754	Merrillan, 612	E 7
53561	Merrimac, 376	G 9
53056	Merton, 646	K 1
54148	Middle Inlet, 200	K 5
53562	Middleton, 8,286	G 9
54857	Mikana, 215	C 4
54454	Milladore, 229	G 6
54643	Millston, 200	E 7
54858	Milltown, 634	B 4
53563	Milton, 3,699	J 10
* 53201	Milwaukee⊙, 717,099	M 1
	Milwaukee, ‡1,403,887	M 1
54644	Mindoro, 230	D 7
53565	Mineral Point, 2,305	F 10
54548	Minocqua, 950	G 4
54859	Minong, 420	C 3
54228	Mishicot, 938	L 7
54755	Mondovi, 2,338	C 6
54549	Monico, 285	H 4
53716	Monona, 10,420	H 9
53566	Monroe⊙, 8,654	G 10
53949	Montello⊙, 1,082	H 8
53569	Montfort, 518	E 10
53570	Monticello, 870	G 10
54550	Montreal, 877	F 3

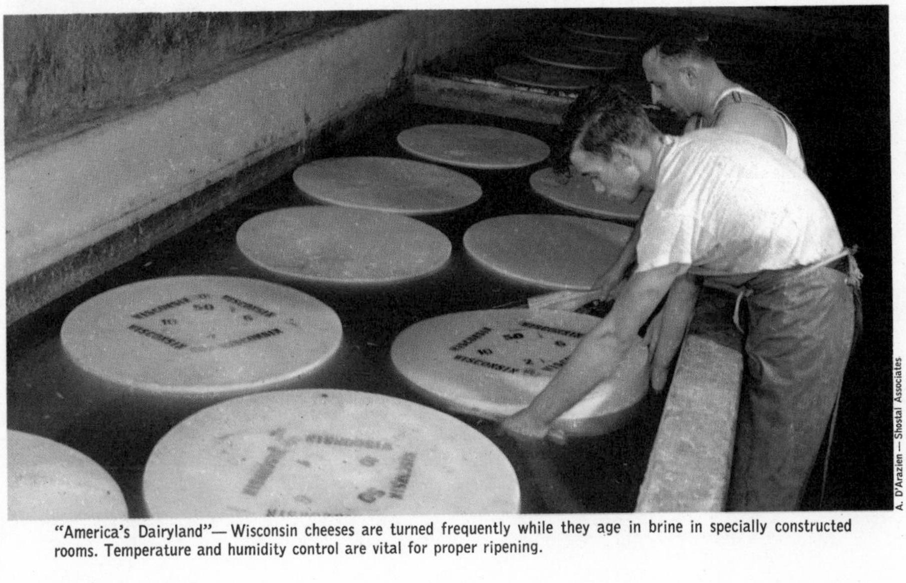

A. D'Arazien—Shostal Associates

"America's Dairyland"—Wisconsin cheeses are turned frequently while they age in brine in specially constructed rooms. Temperature and humidity control are vital for proper ripening.

(continued on following page)

53571 Morrisonville, 350	G 9	54901 Oshkosh⊙, 53,221	J 8	53579 Reeseville, 566	J 9
54455 Mosinee, 2,395	G 6	54758 Osseo, 1,356	D 6	53580 Rewey, 232	F 10
54149 Mountain, 298	K 5	54460 Owen, 1,031	F 6	54501 Rhinelander⊙, 8,218	H 4
53057 Mount Calvary, 942	K 8	53952 Oxford, 453	H 8	54470 Rib Lake, 782	F 5
53816 Mount Hope, 176	D 10	53953 Packwaukee, 250	G 8	54868 Rice Lake, 7,278	C 5
53572 Mount Horeb, 2,402	G 10	† 53168 Paddock Lake, 1,470	K 10	53076 Richfield, 247	K 1
54645 Mount Sterling, 181	D 9	53156 Palmyra, 1,341	H 2	53581 Richland Center⊙, 5,086	F 9
† 54565 Mount Vernon, 250	G 10	53954 Pardeeville, 1,507	H 8	54763 Ridgeland, 266	B 5
53149 Mukwonago, 2,367	J 2	54552 Park Falls, 2,953	F 4	53582 Ridgeway, 463	F 10
53573 Muscoda, 1,099	F 9	† 54481 Park Ridge, 817	H 6	53960 Rio, 792	H 9
53150 Muskego, 11,573	K 2	53817 Patch Grove, 187	D 10	54231 Rio Creek, 200	L 6
53058 Nashotah, 410	J 1	54514 Peeksville, 250	E 3	54971 Ripon, 7,053	J 8
54646 Necedah, 740	F 7	54156 Pembine, 500	L 4	54022 River Falls, 7,238	A 6
54956 Neenah, 22,892	J 7	54553 Pence, 315	F 3	† 53201 River Hills, 1,561	M 1
54456 Neillsville⊙, 2,750	E 6	54153 Pensaukee, 225	L 6	54023 Roberts, 484	A 6
54457 Nekoosa, 2,409	G 7	54759 Pepin, 747	B 7	53167 Rochester, 436	K 3
54756 Nelson, 272	C 7	† 53511 Perrygo Place, 5,912	J 10	† 53523 Rockdale, 172	J 10
54458 Nelsonville, 152	H 7	53072 Pewaukee, 3,271	K 1	54764 Rock Falls, 200	C 6
54150 Neopit, 1,122	J 6	54554 Phelps, 1,100	H 3	53077 Rockfield, 340	L 1
53059 Neosho, 400	J 9	54555 Phillips⊙, 1,511	E 4	54653 Rockland, 278	D 8
54960 Neshkoro, 385	H 8	54464 Phlox, 235	J 5	53961 Rock Springs, 432	F 8
54551 Newald, 180	J 4	54465 Pickerel, 400	J 5	† 53178 Rome, 250	H 1
54757 New Auburn, 368	D 5	54760 Pigeon Falls, 198	D 7	54974 Rosendale, 464	J 8
53151 New Berlin, 26,937	K 2	54466 Pittsville, 708	F 7	54473 Rosholt, 466	H 6
53060 Newburg, 425	K 9	53577 Plain, 688	F 9	54474 Rothschild, 3,141	G 6
† 61075 New Diggings, 224	F 10	54966 Plainfield, 642	G 7	† 53583 Roxbury, 220	G 9
54229 New Franken, 250	L 6	53818 Platteville, 9,599	F 10	54975 Royalton, 200	J 7
53574 New Glarus, 1,454	G 10	53158 Pleasant Prairie, 950	L 10	54475 Rubicon, 261	K 9
53061 New Holstein, 3,012	K 8	54467 Plover, 1,900	G 7	54475 Rudolph, 349	G 7
53950 New Lisbon, 1,361	F 8	54761 Plum City, 451	B 6	53079 Saint Cloud, 550	K 8
54961 New London, 5,801	J 7	53073 Plymouth, 5,810	L 8	54024 Saint Croix Falls, 1,425	A 5
54017 New Richmond, 3,707	A 5	54864 Poplar, 455	C 2	54761 Saint Francis, 10,489	M 2
54151 Niagara, 2,347	K 4	53901 Portage⊙, 7,821	G 8	† 54601 Saint Joseph Ridge, 250	D 8
54152 Nichols, 250	K 6	54469 Port Edwards, 2,126	G 7	54232 Saint Nazianz, 718	L 7
† 53401 North Bay, 263	M 3	53074 Port Washington⊙, 8,752	L 9	54765 Sand Creek, 200	C 5
54935 North Fond du Lac, 3,286	J 8	54865 Port Wing, 486	D 2	53583 Sauk City, 2,385	G 9
53951 North Freedom, 596	G 9	53820 Potosi, 713	E 10	53080 Saukville, 1,389	L 9
† 54016 North Hudson, 1,547	A 5	54160 Potter, 320	K 7	54559 Saxon, 600	F 3
53064 North Lake, 525	J 1	54161 Pound, 284	L 5	54560 Sayner, 300	H 4
53153 North Prairie, 669	J 2	53955 Poynette, 1,118	G 9	54977 Scandinavia, 268	H 7
54648 Norwalk, 432	E 8	54967 Poy Sippi, 500	J 7	54476 Schofield, 2,577	H 6
53154 Oak Creek, 13,901	M 2	53821 Prairie du Chien⊙, 5,540	D 9	53042 School Hill, 228	L 8
54649 Oakdale, 300	F 8	53578 Prairie du Sac, 1,902	G 9	† 54843 Seeley, 213	D 3
53065 Oakfield, 918	J 8	54762 Prairie Farm, 426	C 5	54654 Seneca, 250	E 9
53066 Oconomowoc, 8,741	H 1	54556 Prentice, 519	F 4	53584 Sextonville, 325	F 9
† 53066 Oconomowoc Lake, 599	H 1	54021 Prescott, 2,331	A 6	54165 Seymour, 2,194	K 6
54153 Oconto⊙, 4,667	L 6	54557 Presque Isle, 251	G 3	53585 Sharon, 1,216	J 11
54154 Oconto Falls, 2,517	K 6	54968 Princeton, 1,446	H 8	54166 Shawano⊙, 6,488	J 6
54861 Odanah, 442	E 2	54162 Pulaski, 1,717	K 6	53081 Sheboygan⊙, 48,484	L 8
54962 Ogdensburg, 206	J 7	* 53401 Racine⊙, 95,162	M 3	53085 Sheboygan Falls, 4,771	L 8
54459 Ogema, 280	F 5	Racine, ‡170,838	M 3	54766 Sheldon, 218	D 5
53069 Okauchee, 3,134	J 1	54867 Radisson, 206	D 4	54871 Shell Lake⊙, 928	C 4
† 53555 Okee, 300	H 9	53956 Randolph, 1,582	H 8	54169 Sherwood, 350	K 7
† 54880 Oliver, 210	B 2	53075 Random Lake, 1,068	K 8	54170 Shiocton, 830	K 7
54963 Omro, 2,341	J 7	† 53126 Raymond, 300	L 2	† 53525 Shiopiere, 350	H 10
54650 Onalaska, 4,909	D 8	54969 Readfield, 200	J 7	54843 Shorewood, 15,576	M 1
54155 Oneida, 900	K 7	54652 Readstown, 395	E 9	† 53701 Shorewood Hills, 2,206	G 9
54651 Ontario, 392	E 8	54814 Red Cliff, 250	E 2	53586 Shullsburg, 1,376	F 10
53070 Oostburg, 1,309	L 8	54970 Redgranite, 645	J 7	53170 Silver Lake, 1,210	K 10
53575 Oregon, 2,553	H 10	53959 Reedsburg, 4,585	G 8	54872 Siren, 639	B 4
53576 Orfordville, 888	H 10	54230 Reedsville, 994	L 7	54234 Sister Bay, 483	M 5
54020 Osceola, 1,152	A 5			53086 Slinger, 1,022	K 9

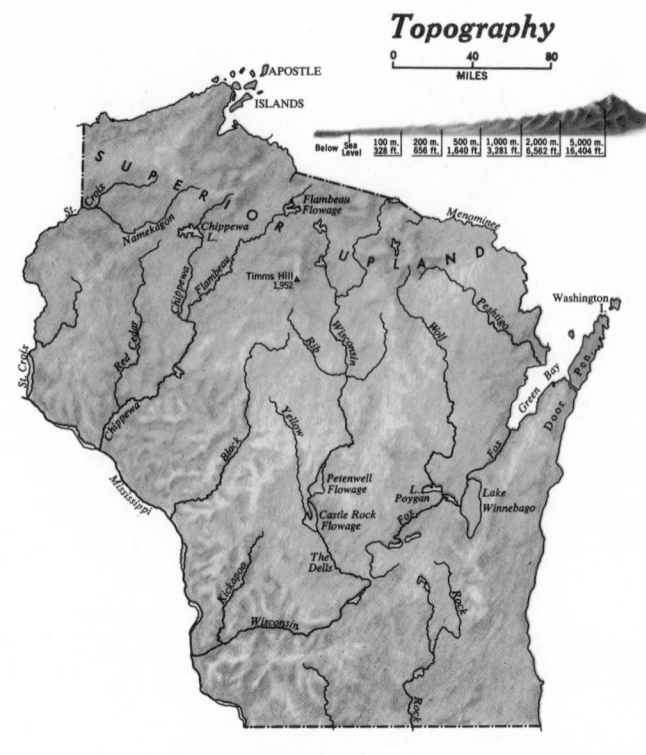

Topography

Below Sea Level	100 m. 328 ft.	200 m. 656 ft.	500 m. 1,640 ft.	1,000 m. 3,281 ft.	2,000 m. 6,562 ft.	5,000 m. 16,404 ft.	

0   40   80
MILES

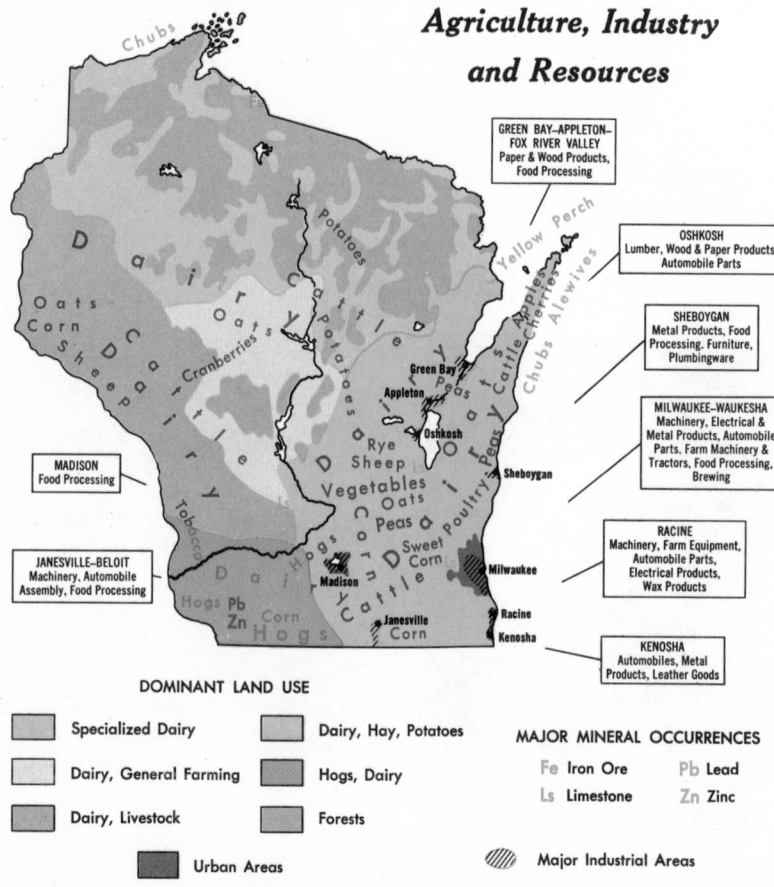

Agriculture, Industry and Resources

GREEN BAY–APPLETON–FOX RIVER VALLEY
Paper & Wood Products, Food Processing

OSHKOSH
Lumber, Wood & Paper Products, Automobile Parts

SHEBOYGAN
Metal Products, Food Processing. Furniture, Plumbingware

MILWAUKEE–WAUKESHA
Machinery, Electrical & Metal Products, Automobile Parts, Farm Machinery & Tractors, Food Processing, Brewing

MADISON
Food Processing

RACINE
Machinery, Farm Equipment, Automobile Parts, Electrical Products, Wax Products

JANESVILLE–BELOIT
Machinery, Automobile Assembly, Food Processing

KENOSHA
Automobiles, Metal Products, Leather Goods

DOMINANT LAND USE

- Specialized Dairy
- Dairy, General Farming
- Dairy, Livestock
- Urban Areas
- Dairy, Hay, Potatoes
- Hogs, Dairy
- Forests

MAJOR MINERAL OCCURRENCES

- Fe Iron Ore
- Ls Limestone
- Pb Lead
- Zn Zinc

///// Major Industrial Areas

54655 Soldiers Grove, 514	E 9	53183 Wales, 691	J 1
54873 Solon Springs, 598	C 3	53184 Walworth, 1,637	J 10
53171 Somers, 400	M 3	54666 Warrens, 300	E 7
54025 Somerset, 778	A 5	54890 Wascott, 200	C 3
53172 South Milwaukee, 23,297	M 2	54891 Washburn⊙, 1,957	D 2
53587 South Wayne, 436	G 10	54246 Washington Island, 550	M 5
54656 Sparta⊙, 6,258	E 8	53185 Waterford, 1,922	J 2
54479 Spencer, 1,181	F 6	53594 Waterloo, 2,253	J 9
54801 Spooner, 2,444	B 4	53094 Watertown, 15,683	J 9
53588 Spring Green, 1,199	G 9	53021 Waubeka, 300	L 9
54767 Spring Valley, 995	B 6	54980 Waukau, 245	J 8
54768 Stanley, 2,049	E 6	53186 Waukesha⊙, 40,258	K 1
54026 Star Prairie, 362	A 5	53597 Waunakee, 2,181	G 9
54480 Stetsonville, 305	F 5	54981 Waupaca⊙, 4,342	H 7
54657 Steuben, 179	E 9	53963 Waupun, 7,946	J 8
54481 Stevens Point⊙, 23,479	G 7	54401 Wausau⊙, 32,806	G 6
54172 Stiles, 300	L 6	54177 Wausaukee, 557	K 5
53825 Stitzer, 295	E 10	54982 Wautoma⊙, 1,624	H 7
53088 Stockbridge, 582	K 7	53226 Wauwatosa, 58,676	L 1
54876 Stone Lake, 190	C 4	53826 Wauzeka, 437	E 9
† 53066 Stone Bank, 390	J 1	54893 Webster, 502	B 4
53589 Stoughton, 6,081	H 10	53214 West Allis, 71,723	L 1
54484 Stratford, 1,239	F 6	† 53913 West Baraboo, 563	G 8
54770 Strum, 738	D 6	53095 West Bend⊙, 16,555	K 9
54235 Sturgeon Bay⊙, 6,776	M 6	54490 Westboro, 950	F 5
53177 Sturtevant, 3,376	M 3	54667 Westby, 1,568	E 8
54173 Suamico, 900	K 6	53964 Westfield, 884	H 8
53178 Sullivan, 467	H 1	† 54601 West La Crosse, 950	D 8
54485 Summit Lake, 200	H 5	53201 West Milwaukee, 4,405	L 1
53590 Sun Prairie, 9,935	H 9	† 54476 Weston, 3,375	G 6
54880 Superior (city)⊙, 32,237	C 2	54669 West Salem, 2,180	D 8
Superior-Duluth, ‡265,350	C 2	54983 Weyauwega, 1,377	H 7
† 54880 Superior Village, 476	B 2	54895 Weyerhauser, 285	D 5
54174 Suring, 499	K 5	54772 Wheeler, 212	C 5
53089 Sussex, 2,758	K 1	53217 Whitefish Bay, 17,394	M 1
53090 Taycheedah, 600	K 8	54773 Whitehall⊙, 1,486	D 7
54659 Taylor, 322	E 7	54491 White Lake, 309	J 5
† 53820 Tennyson, 402	E 10	54247 Whitelaw, 557	L 7
53091 Theresa, 611	K 8	53190 Whitewater, 12,038	J 10
53092 Thiensville, 3,182	L 1	† 54481 Whiting, 1,782	H 7
54771 Thorp, 1,469	E 6	54984 Wild Rose, 585	H 7
54562 Three Lakes, 950	H 4	53191 Williams Bay, 1,554	J 10
† 53088 Tichigan, 500	K 2	54670 Wilton, 516	F 8
54486 Tigerton, 742	H 6	54567 Winchester, 230	G 3
54240 Tisch Mills, 259	L 7	53185 Wind Lake, 900	K 2
54660 Tomah, 5,647	F 8	† 53401 Wind Point, 1,251	M 2
54487 Tomahawk, 3,419	G 5	53598 Windsor, 827	H 9
54175 Townsend, 450	K 5	54985 Winnebago, 1,550	J 7
54888 Trego, 200	C 4	54986 Winneconne, 1,608	J 7
54661 Trempealeau, 743	C 8	54896 Winter, 450	E 4
53180 Troy Center, 250	J 2	53965 Wisconsin Dells, 2,401	G 8
54662 Tunnel City, 226	E 7	54494 Wisconsin Rapids⊙, 18,587	G 7
54889 Turtle Lake, 807	B 5	54498 Withee, 480	E 6
53181 Twin Lakes, 2,276	K 11	54499 Wittenberg, 895	H 6
54241 Two Rivers, 13,553	M 7	53968 Wonewoc, 835	F 8
53962 Union Center, 205	F 8	54568 Woodruff, 800	G 4
53182 Union Grove, 2,703	L 3	54028 Woodville, 522	B 6
54488 Unity, 363	F 6	54180 Wrightstown, 1,020	K 7
54245 Valders, 821	L 7	54671 Wyeville, 203	F 7
53593 Verona, 2,334	G 9	53969 Wyocena, 809	H 9
54489 Vesper, 355	F 7	54182 Zachow, 160	K 6
54664 Viola, 659	E 8		
54665 Viroqua⊙, 3,739	D 8	⊙ County seat.	
54566 Wabeno, 800	J 5	‡ Population of metropolitan area.	
53093 Waldo, 408	L 8	† Zip of nearest p.o.	
		* Multiple zips	

WISCONSIN

SCALE

0 5 10   20   30   40 MI.

0 5 10 20   30   40 KM.

State Capitals..............⊛
County Seats..............⊙
Canals........................

© C.S. HAMMOND & Co., N.Y.

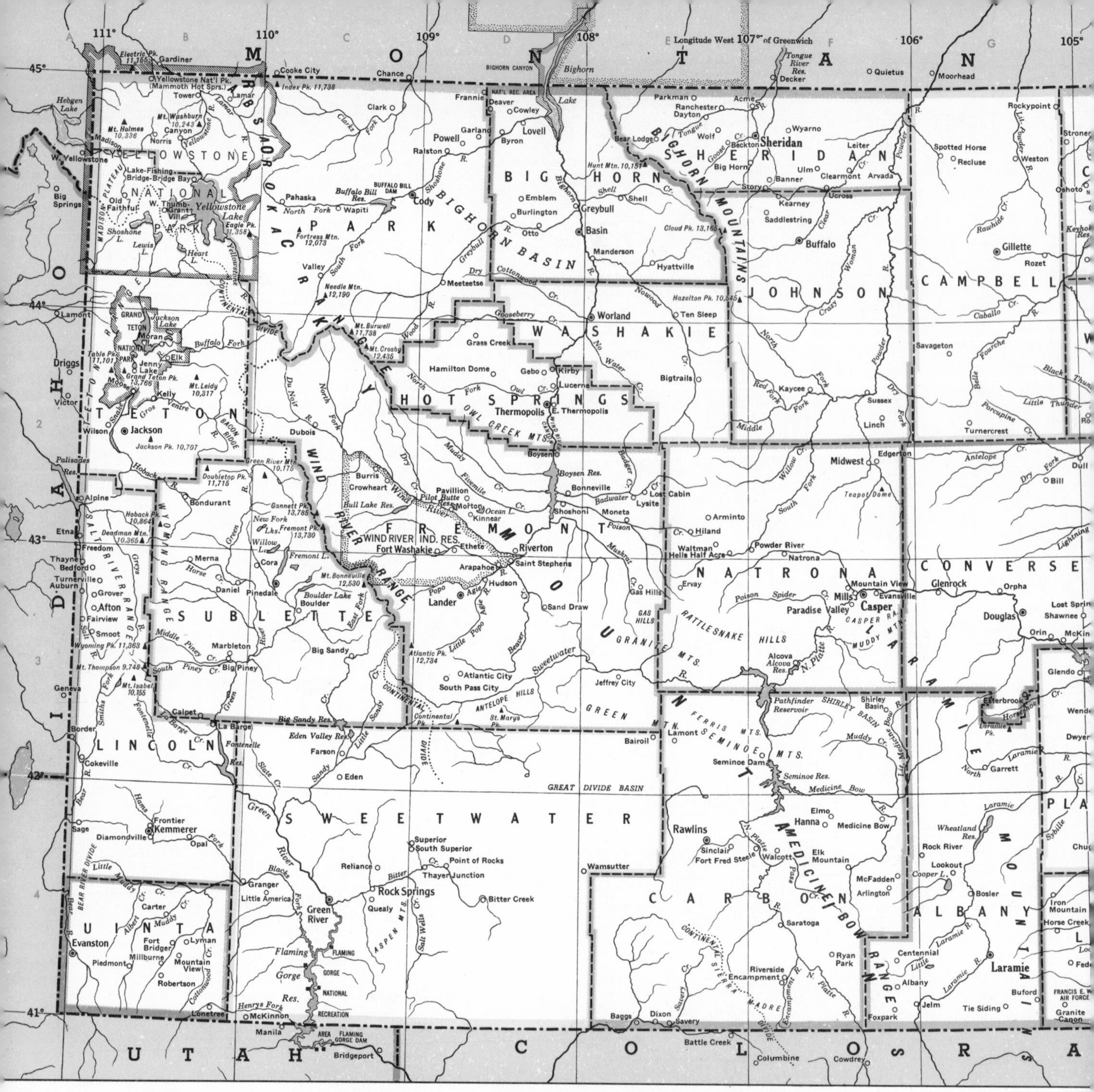

Agriculture, Industry and Resources

DOMINANT LAND USE

- Specialized Wheat
- Range Livestock
- Specialized Dairy
- Forests
- General Farming, Livestock, Special Crops
- Nonagricultural Land
- Sugar Beets, Dry Beans, Livestock, General Farming

MAJOR MINERAL OCCURRENCES

- C Coal
- Cl Clay
- Fe Iron Ore
- G Natural Gas
- O Petroleum
- P Phosphates
- U Uranium
- V Vanadium
- Water Power

COUNTIES

Albany, 26,431	G 4
Big Horn, 10,202	E 1
Campbell, 12,957	G 1
Carbon, 13,354	F 4
Converse, 5,938	G 3
Crook, 4,535	H 1
Fremont, 28,352	D 2
Goshen, 10,885	H 4
Hot Springs, 4,952	D 2
Johnson, 5,587	F 1
Laramie, 56,360	H 4
Lincoln, 8,640	B 3
Natrona, 51,264	F 3
Niobrara, 2,924	H 2
Park, 17,752	C 1
Platte, 6,486	H 4
Sheridan, 17,852	F 1
Sublette, 3,755	C 3
Sweetwater, 18,391	D 4
Teton, 4,823	B 2
Uinta, 7,100	B 4
Washakie, 7,569	E 2
Weston, 6,307	H 2

CITIES and TOWNS

Zip	*Name/Pop.*	*Key*
82830	Acme, 98	E 1
83110	Afton, 1,290	B 3

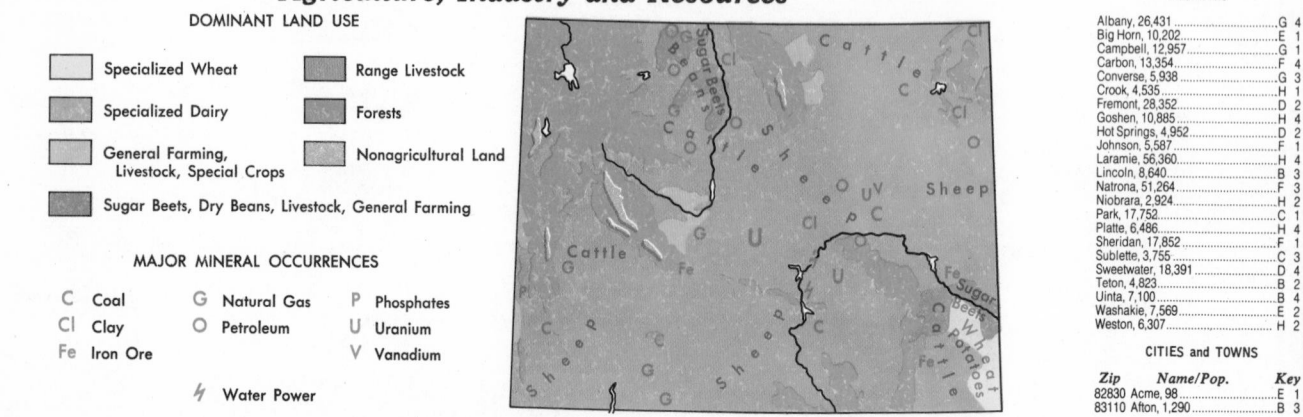

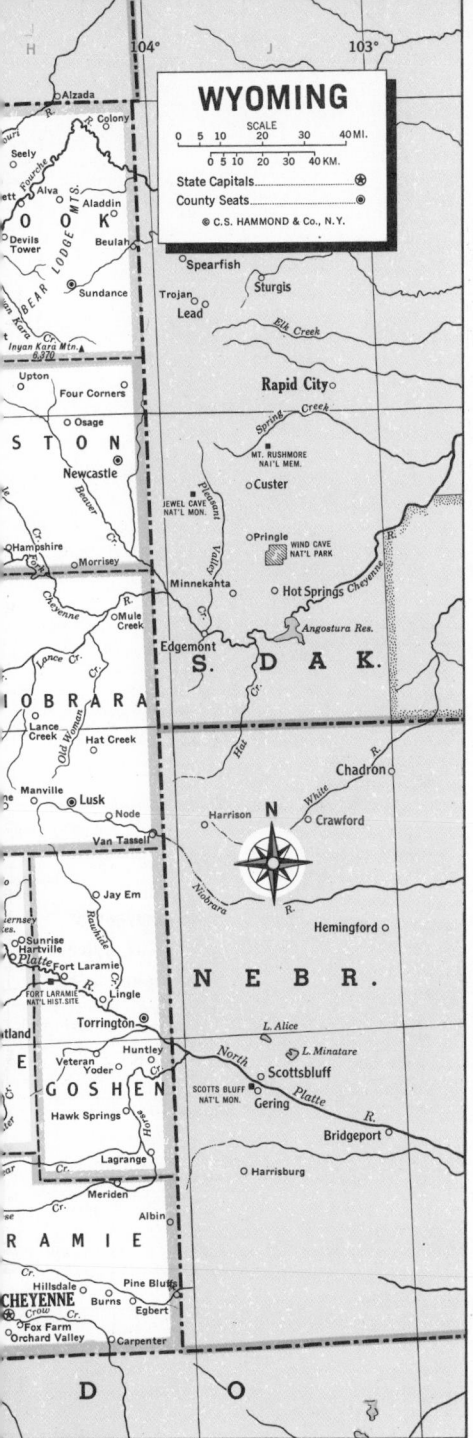

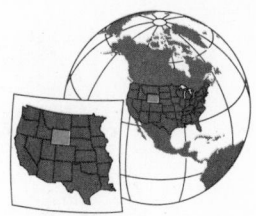

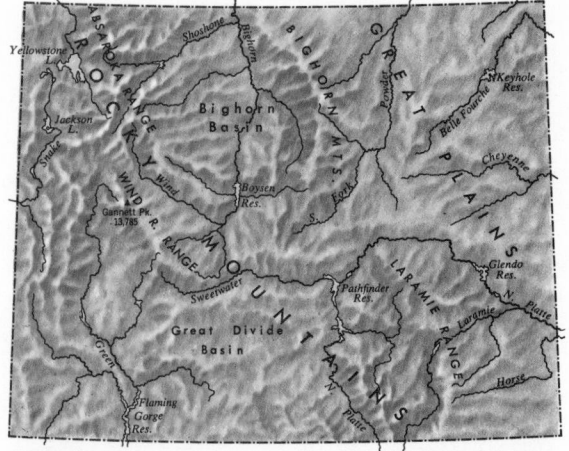

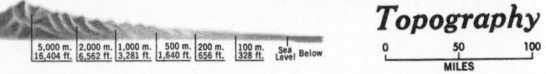

Topography

5,000 m. 16,404 ft.	2,000 m. 6,562 ft.	1,000 m. 3,281 ft.	500 m. 1,640 ft.	200 m. 656 ft.	100 m. 328 ft.	Sea Level Below

MILES
0   50   100

AREA 97,914 sq. mi.
POPULATION 332,416
CAPITAL Cheyenne
LARGEST CITY Cheyenne
HIGHEST POINT Gannett Pk. 13,785 ft.
SETTLED IN 1834
ADMITTED TO UNION July 10, 1890
POPULAR NAME Equality State
STATE FLOWER Indian Paintbrush
STATE BIRD Meadowlark

Intrepid mountain climbers are challenged by the sheer granite cliffs of Wyoming's Teton Range. Lowland meadows and trails attract less ambitious sportsmen.

Jack Zehrt — Shostal Associates

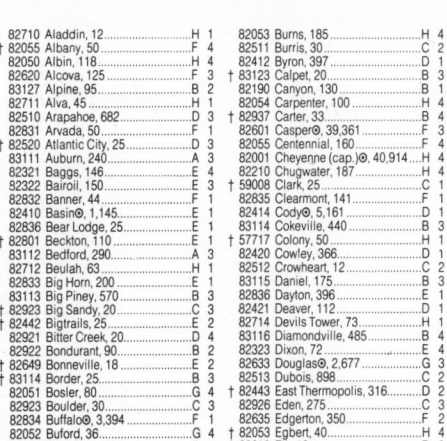

82710 Aladdin, 12..................H 1
† 82055 Albany, 50..................F 4
82050 Albin, 118..................H 4
82620 Alcova, 125..................F 3
83127 Alpine, 95..................B 2
82711 Alva, 45..................H 1
82510 Arapahoe, 682..................D 3
82831 Arvada, 50..................F 2
† 82520 Atlantic City, 25..................D 3
83111 Auburn, 240..................A 3
82321 Baggs, 146..................E 4
82322 Bairoil, 150..................E 3
82832 Banner, 40..................F 1
82410 Basin⊙, 1,145..................E 1
82836 Bear Lodge, 25..................E 1
† 82801 Beckton, 110..................E 1
83112 Bedford, 290..................A 3
82712 Beulah, 63..................H 1
82833 Big Horn, 200..................F 1
83113 Big Piney, 570..................B 3
† 82923 Big Sandy, 20..................C 3
† 82442 Bigtrails, 25..................E 2
82921 Bitter Creek, 20..................D 4
82922 Bondurant, 90..................B 2
82649 Boomerang, 18..................E 2
† 83114 Border, 25..................A 3
82501 Bosler, 80..................G 4
82923 Boulder, 30..................C 3
82834 Buffalo⊙, 3,394..................F 1
82052 Buford, 36..................G 4
82411 Burlington, 300..................D 1

82053 Burns, 185..................H 4
82511 Burris, 30..................C 2
82412 Byron, 397..................D 1
† 83123 Calpet, 25..................B 3
82190 Canyon, 130..................B 1
82054 Carpenter, 100..................H 4
† 82937 Carter, 33..................B 4
82601 Casper⊙, 39,361..................F 3
82055 Centennial, 160..................F 4
82001 Cheyenne (cap.)⊙, 40,914..................H 4
82716 Gillette⊙, 7,194..................G 1
82213 Glendo, 210..................G 3
82637 Glenrock, 1,515..................G 3
82934 Granger, 137..................B 4
82059 Granite Canon, 72..................G 4
82425 Grass Creek, 125..................D 2
83114 Cokeville, 440..................B 3
† 57717 Colony, 50..................H 1
82420 Cowley, 366..................D 1
82512 Crowheart, 12..................C 2
83115 Daniel, 175..................B 3
82836 Dayton, 396..................E 1
82421 Deaver, 112..................D 1
82714 Devils Tower, 73..................H 1
82327 Hanna, 460..................F 4
83116 Diamondville, 485..................B 4
82323 Dixon, 72..................E 4
82633 Douglas⊙, 2,677..................G 3
82513 Dubois, 898..................C 2
† 82443 East Thermopolis, 316..................D 2
82926 Eden, 275..................C 3
82635 Edgerton, 350..................F 2
† 82053 Egbert, 40..................H 4
83013 Elk, 10..................B 2

82324 Elk Mountain, 127..................F 4
† 82327 Elmo, 53..................F 4
82422 Emblem, 250..................D 1
82325 Encampment, 321..................F 4
82520 Ethete, 30..................D 2
83118 Etna, 400..................A 2
82930 Evanston⊙, 4,462..................B 4
82636 Evansville, 832..................F 3
83119 Fairview, 245..................B 3
82932 Farson, 210..................C 3
† 82001 Federal, 15..................G 4
82933 Fort Bridger, 150..................B 4
82301 Fort Fred Steele, 15..................E 4
82212 Fort Laramie, 197..................H 3
82514 Fort Washakie, 140..................C 2
† 82001 Fox Farm, 1,329..................H 4
82057 Foxpark, 110..................F 4
82423 Frannie, 139..................D 1
83120 Freedom, 497..................B 3
83121 Frontier, 246..................B 3
82424 Garland, 57..................D 1
82058 Garrett, 10..................G 3
82501 Gas Hills, 200..................E 3
82430 Gebo, 15..................D 2
82214 Guernsey, 793..................H 3
82427 Hamilton Dome, 106..................D 2
82735 Hampshire, 23..................H 2
82215 Hartville, 246..................H 3
82217 Hawk Springs, 125..................H 4
82060 Hillsdale, 160..................H 4
82061 Horse Creek, 225..................G 4
82515 Hudson, 381..................D 3
82720 Hulett, 318..................H 1
82218 Huntley, 50..................H 4
82428 Hyattville, 73..................E 1
82062 Iron Mountain, 12..................G 4

83001 Jackson⊙, 2,101..................B 2
82219 Jay Em, 25..................H 3
82310 Jeffrey City, 702..................E 3
82063 Jelm, 29..................G 4
83012 Jenny Lake, 10..................B 2
82639 Kaycee, 272..................F 2
82832 Kearney, 49..................F 1
82220 Keeline, 30..................H 3
83011 Kelly, 35..................B 2
83101 Kemmerer⊙, 2,292..................B 3
82516 Kinnear, 44..................D 2
82430 Kirby, 75..................D 2
83123 La Barge, 375..................B 3
82212 Lagrange, 189..................H 4
† 82190 Lake-Fishing Bridge-Bridge Bay, 167..................B 1
† 82190 Lamar, 27..................B 1
82328 Lamont, 30..................E 3
82222 Lance Creek, 175..................H 2
82520 Lander⊙, 7,125..................D 3
82070 Laramie⊙, 23,143..................G 4
82837 Leiter, 100..................F 1
82640 Linch, 185..................F 2
82223 Lingle, 446..................H 4
82929 Little America, 47..................C 4
† 82051 Lookout, 20..................G 4
82642 Lost Cabin, 25..................E 2
82431 Lovell, 2,371..................D 1
82443 Lucerne, 240..................D 2
82225 Lusk⊙, 1,495..................H 3
82937 Lyman, 643..................B 4
82642 Lysite, 25..................E 2
† 82190 Madison, 42..................B 1
† 82190 Mammoth Hot Springs (Yellowstone Nat'l Park), 162..................B 1
82432 Manderson, 117..................E 1
82227 Manville, 92..................H 3
† 83113 Marbleton, 223..................B 3
82080 McFadden, 150..................F 4
82938 McKinnon, 135..................C 4
82329 Medicine Bow, 455..................F 4
82433 Meeteetse, 459..................D 1
83115 Merna, 25..................B 3
82643 Midwest, 743..................F 2
† 82933 Millburne, 54..................B 4

82644 Mills, 1,724..................F 3
82721 Moorcroft, 981..................H 1
83012 Moose, 115..................B 2
83013 Moran, 600..................B 2
† 82701 Morrisey, 28..................H 2
82522 Morton, 35..................D 2
82939 Mountain View, 1,641..................F 3
82939 Mountain View, 500..................B 4
† 57735 Mule Creek, 10..................H 2
82701 Newcastle⊙, 3,432..................H 2
82722 New Haven, 35..................H 1
† 82190 Norris, 20..................B 1
82190 Old Faithful, 134..................B 1
83124 Opal, 34..................B 3
82001 Orchard Valley, 1,015..................H 4
82652 Orin, 20..................G 3
82633 Orpha, 12..................G 3
82723 Osage, 346..................H 1
82434 Otto, 75..................D 1
82414 Pahaska, 75..................C 1
† 82601 Paradise Valley, 1,764..................F 3
82838 Parkman, 30..................E 1
82523 Pavillion, 181..................D 2
† 82933 Piedmont, 25..................B 4
82082 Pine Bluffs, 937..................H 4
82941 Pinedale⊙, 948..................C 3
82942 Point of Rocks, 20..................D 4
82648 Powder River, 75..................F 2
82435 Powell, 4,807..................D 1
82440 Ralston, 85..................D 1
82839 Ranchester, 208..................E 1
82301 Rawlins⊙, 7,855..................E 4
82725 Recluse, 25..................G 1
82943 Reliance, 425..................C 4
82325 Riverside, 46..................F 4
82501 Riverton, 7,995..................D 2
82944 Robertson, 39..................B 4
† 82701 Rochelle, 23..................H 2
82083 Rock River, 344..................G 4
82901 Rock Springs, 11,657..................C 4
82726 Rockypoint, 22..................G 1
82727 Rozet, 50..................G 1
82330 Ryan Park, 18..................F 4
82840 Saddlestring, 100..................F 1
83125 Sage, 45..................B 4
82524 Saint Stephens, 100..................D 3

82501 Sand Draw, 40..................D 3
† 82331 Saratoga, 1,181..................F 4
† 82716 Savageton, 30..................G 2
82332 Savery, 29..................E 4
† 82720 Seely, 50..................H 1
82333 Seminoe Dam, 40..................E 3
82229 Shawnee, 11..................G 3
82441 Shell, 50..................E 1
82801 Sheridan⊙, 10,856..................F 1
82601 Shirley Basin, 700..................F 3
82649 Shoshoni, 562..................D 2
82334 Sinclair, 445..................E 4
83126 Smoot, 200..................B 3
† 82945 South Superior, 197..................D 4
82842 Story, 637..................F 1
82729 Sundance⊙, 1,056..................H 1
† 82215 Sunrise, 80..................H 3
82945 Superior, 2..................D 4
82639 Sussex, 200..................F 2
82442 Ten Sleep, 320..................E 1
† 82901 Thayer Junction, 15..................D 4
83127 Thayne, 195..................A 3
82443 Thermopolis⊙, 3,063..................D 2
82240 Torrington⊙, 4,237..................H 4
† 82190 Tower, 24..................B 1
83112 Turnerville, 25..................A 3
82835 Ucross, 17..................F 1
82835 Ulm, 25..................F 1
82730 Upton, 987..................H 1
† 82242 Van Tassell, 21..................H 3
82243 Veteran, 35..................H 4
82335 Walcott, 20..................E 4
† 82648 Waltman, 20..................E 2
82336 Wamsutter, 139..................D 4
82450 Wapiti, 92..................C 1
† 82190 West Thumb-Grant Village, 64..................B 1
82201 Wheatland⊙, 2,498..................H 3
83014 Wilson, 550..................B 2
82844 Wolf, 85..................E 1
82401 Worland⊙, 5,055..................E 1
82845 Wyarno, 12..................F 1
† 82190 Yellowstone Nat'l Park, 162..................B 1
82244 Yoder, 101..................H 4

⊙ County seat.
† Zip of nearest p.o.

ACQUISITIONS OF TERRITORY

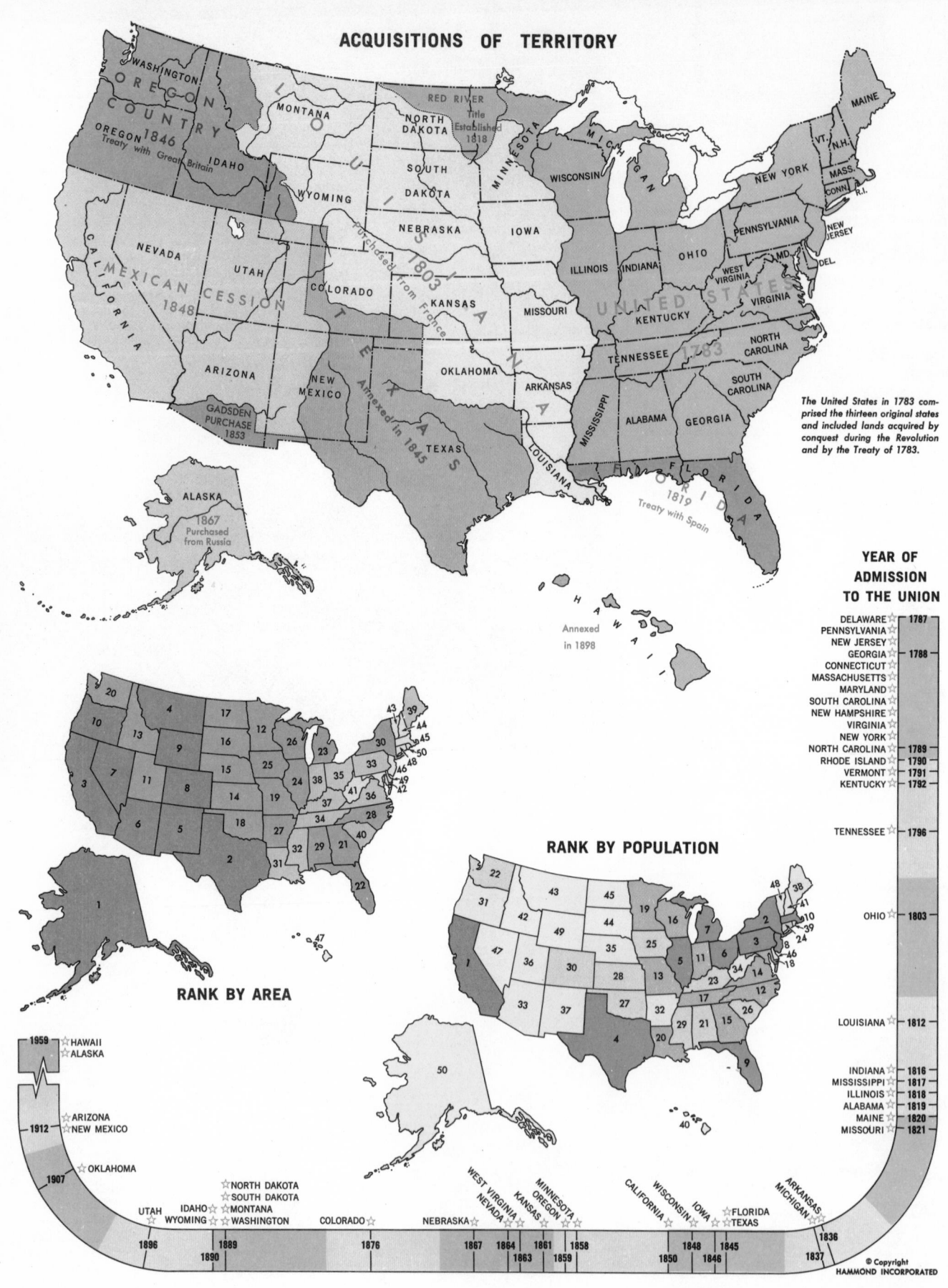

The United States in 1783 comprised the thirteen original states and included lands acquired by conquest during the Revolution and by the Treaty of 1783.

RANK BY AREA

RANK BY POPULATION

YEAR OF ADMISSION TO THE UNION

DELAWARE ☆	1787
PENNSYLVANIA ☆	1788
NEW JERSEY ☆	1788
GEORGIA ☆	1788
CONNECTICUT ☆	1788
MASSACHUSETTS ☆	1788
MARYLAND ☆	1788
SOUTH CAROLINA ☆	1788
NEW HAMPSHIRE ☆	1788
VIRGINIA ☆	1788
NEW YORK ☆	1788
NORTH CAROLINA ☆	1789
RHODE ISLAND ☆	1790
VERMONT ☆	1791
KENTUCKY ☆	1792
TENNESSEE ☆	1796
OHIO ☆	1803
LOUISIANA ☆	1812
INDIANA ☆	1816
MISSISSIPPI ☆	1817
ILLINOIS ☆	1818
ALABAMA ☆	1819
MAINE ☆	1820
MISSOURI ☆	1821

1959 ☆HAWAII ☆ALASKA

1912 ☆ARIZONA ☆NEW MEXICO

1907 ☆OKLAHOMA

☆NORTH DAKOTA
☆SOUTH DAKOTA

☆ARIZONA
☆NEW MEXICO

☆OKLAHOMA

UTAH ☆ IDAHO ☆ ☆MONTANA
☆WYOMING ☆ ☆WASHINGTON COLORADO ☆ NEBRASKA ☆

WEST VIRGINIA
NEVADA ☆ KANSAS ☆ MINNESOTA ☆ OREGON ☆ CALIFORNIA ☆ WISCONSIN ☆ IOWA ☆ ☆FLORIDA ARKANSAS ☆ MICHIGAN ☆
☆ TEXAS

| 1896 | 1889 | 1876 | 1867 | 1864 | 1861 | 1858 | 1848 | 1845 | 1836 |
| 1890 | | | | 1863 | 1859 | | 1850 | 1846 | 1837 |

© Copyright
HAMMOND INCORPORATED

Environment and Life

The Sun: ENERGY SOURCE OF THE SOLAR SYSTEM

For longer than the memory of man, a glowing furnace of nuclear activity has held our solar system within its gravitational orbit and, deep within its interior, fused the nuclei of hydrogen and helium, dispensing them as heat, light and the other forms of radiation which nurture the very elements of life on earth. The sun — with radiant energy so fierce that it was deified by ancient man — still dominates the lives of laymen and the minds of scientists who seek to comprehend its nature and utilize its mighty force.

The Earth:
ITS PERSPECTIVE IN SPACE

Tilted and spinning on its invisible axis, revolving with measured pace in orbit around the sun, moving with the sun and the other members of its solar system as it works its way through space toward the constellation Hercules, the earth in "perpetual motion" defines day and night and the seasons of the year with all their variations.

Like a giant gyroscope, the base of its axis rooted in the atmosphere, it tips its rounded surface to catch the direct rays of sun which begin to warm the Northern Hemisphere in March, as the earth angles its southern surface away from the source of heat and light. The 365¼-day procession of the seasons begins once more.

With more rapid motion the earth rotates from west to east, turning first one face and then the other toward the sun, measuring out the hours of day and night — man's labor and man's rest.

Neither flat nor completely round, our almost spherical planet is itself a gravitational force attracting all things toward itself and is subject to the effects of its rotations. Where the speed is greatest at the center of its mass it bulges out at the Equator and flattens somewhat in the slower moving polar areas.

Wrapped in a protective blanket of atmosphere which shields it from destruction by bombardment of high energy atomic particles released by the sun's giant magnetic storms, the earth in an otherwise hostile universe provides the only known environment capable of nurturing intelligent life or, as far as we know, any life at all.

But man has never been content with safety in his quest for understanding and now seeks beyond the atmosphere and beyond the stars to know — perhaps to conquer — all of his environment and find perhaps another, stranger universe.

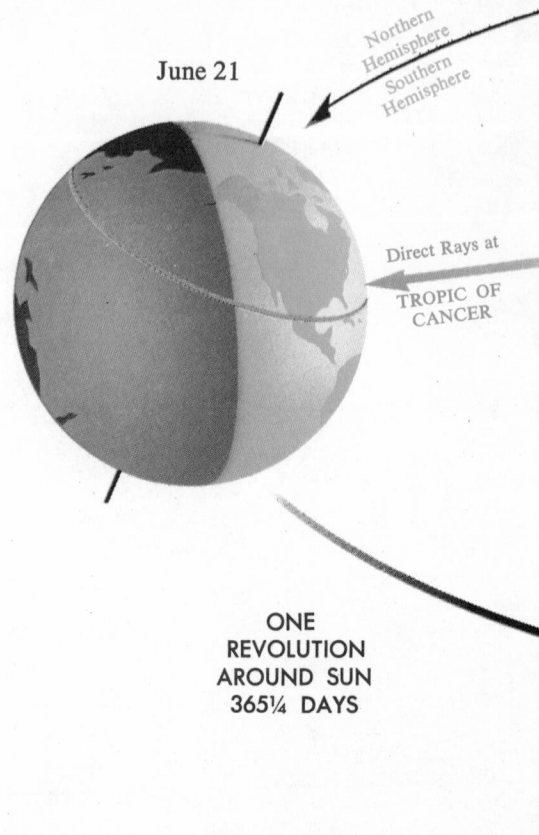

June 21

Northern Hemisphere
Southern Hemisphere

Direct Rays at
TROPIC OF CANCER

ONE
REVOLUTION
AROUND SUN
365¼ DAYS

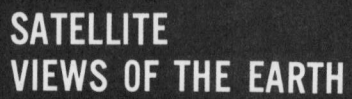

SATELLITE VIEWS OF THE EARTH

From Sunrise to Sunset

7:30 A.M.

10:30 A.M.

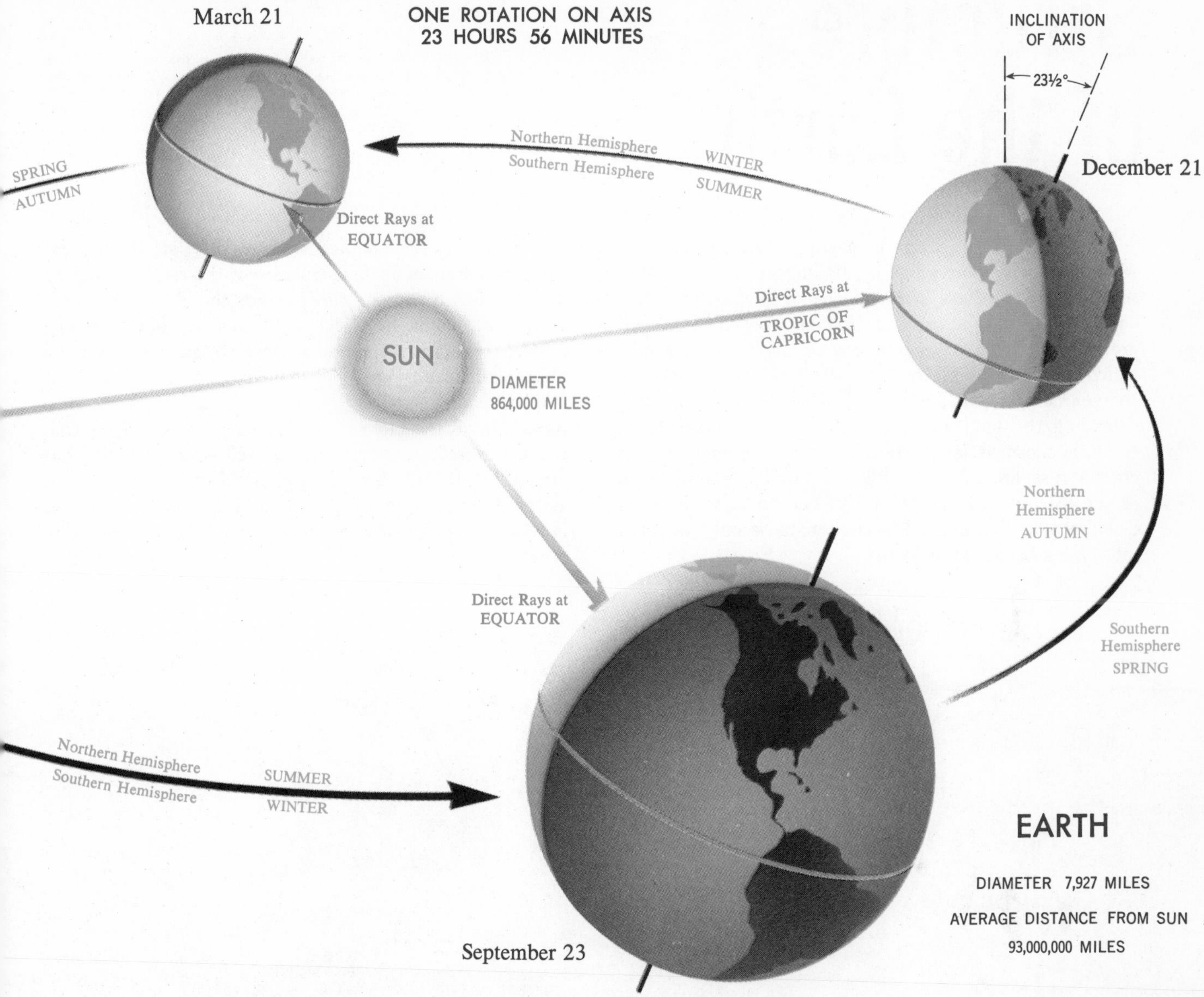

March 21

**ONE ROTATION ON AXIS
23 HOURS 56 MINUTES**

INCLINATION
OF AXIS

23½°

SPRING
AUTUMN

Northern Hemisphere   WINTER
Southern Hemisphere   SUMMER

December 21

Direct Rays at
EQUATOR

SUN

Direct Rays at
TROPIC OF
CAPRICORN

DIAMETER
864,000 MILES

Northern
Hemisphere
AUTUMN

Direct Rays at
EQUATOR

Southern
Hemisphere
SPRING

Northern Hemisphere   SUMMER
Southern Hemisphere   WINTER

EARTH

DIAMETER   7,927 MILES

AVERAGE DISTANCE FROM SUN

93,000,000 MILES

September 23

NASA

NOON   3:30 P.M.   7:30 P.M.

Structure of the Earth

The photographs (opposite) reveal views of the world seen only since the advent of satellites and space vehicles. Pictures such as these greatly increase man's understanding of the earth's structure and the visible forces which act upon it.

If man were big enough he could peel the earth somewhat like a complicated grape, finding at its heart what some scientists believe is the remains of its most primitive beginnings — a solid core of iron and nickel. Wrapped around this solid mass is a second, molten outer core which, set in motion by the earth's rotations, may be the source of its magnetic field. The solid rock mantle, extending to about 1,800 miles from the surface of the earth, is the next layer which in turn is covered by the crust and separated from it by a distinct boundary known as the Mohorovicic discontinuity. The crust, which is as deep as 40 miles under the continents, is only about 5 miles thick beneath the oceans.

To simplify the complex layerings of solids, liquids and gases which make up the structure of the earth, geologists have divided them into three zones: the lithosphere, containing all solids from the land surface to the earth's center; the hydrosphere, all surface water areas; and the atmosphere, the layered gaseous envelope extending about 600 miles above the earth's surface. From each of these three spheres the biologist has selected those parts which contain organic matter, plant as well as animal, and has grouped them together into a comprehensive zone known as the Biosphere. Here, in this world of life, man survives in relationship, however indirectly, with every other living organism.

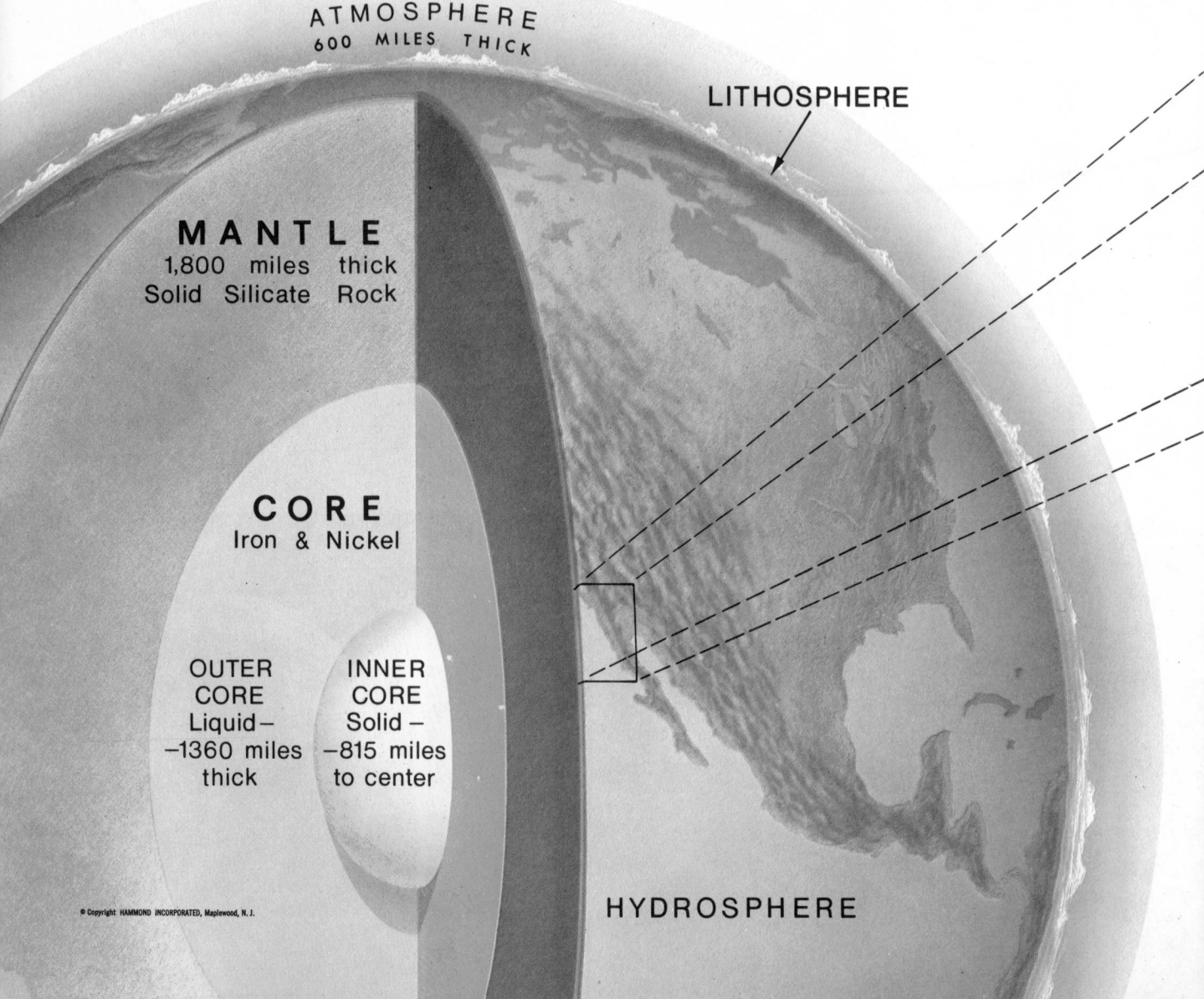

ATMOSPHERE
600 MILES THICK

LITHOSPHERE

MANTLE
1,800 miles thick
Solid Silicate Rock

CORE
Iron & Nickel

OUTER CORE
Liquid —
—1360 miles thick

INNER CORE
Solid —
—815 miles to center

HYDROSPHERE

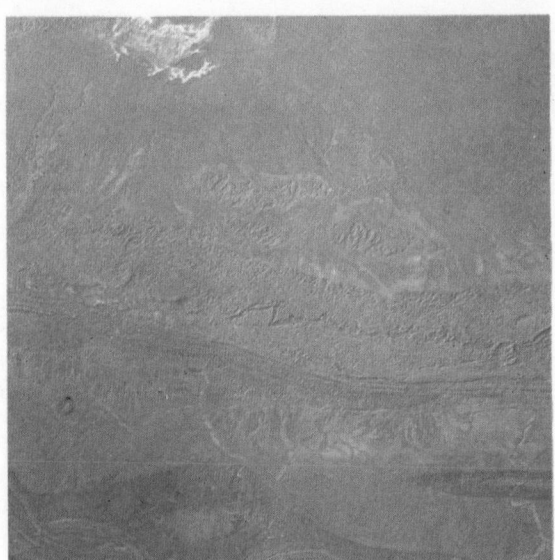

Complex geologic structures, Northern Territory, Australia   NASA

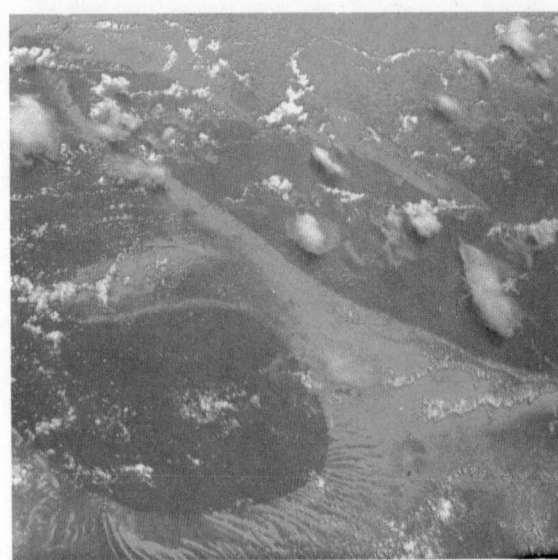

Ocean-bottom topography of the Great Bahama Bank   NASA

CRUST
Average – 25 miles thick

SIAL (Granitic)
SIMA (Basaltic)

Classic dendritic drainage patterns, Saudi Arabia   NASA

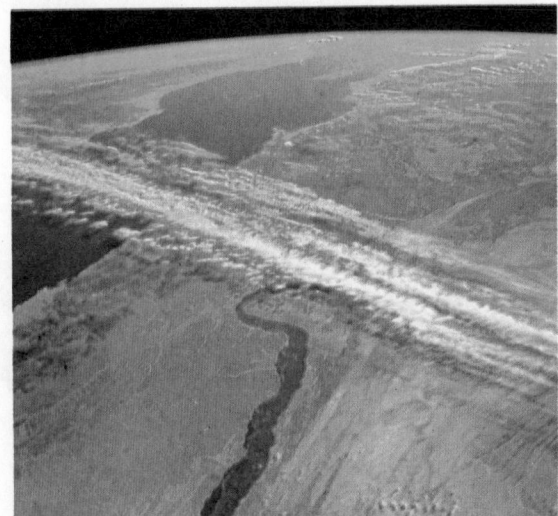

Jet stream over the Red Sea and Nile Valley   NASA

Cloud formations affecting the Indian Subcontinent   NASA

Development of Continents and Oceans

If we can envision the continents of the world as seated firmly on massive rafts of rock and moving across the surface of the earth at a rate of about 6 feet every 60 years we have a basic notion of what is meant by continental drift and the manner in which land and sea masses have been formed.

The original concept of continental drift was proposed in the 1920s, but only during the past three years or so have geologists and geophysicists accepted as fact the seemingly preposterous notion that the surface of the earth is constantly in motion.

The making of the continents began more than 200 million years ago during the Permian period with the splitting of a gigantic landmass known as Pangaea. Two con-

tinents, Laurasia to the north and Gondwana to the south, were formed by the initial division. Over a period of many millions of years these landmasses subdivided into smaller parts approximately the shapes of Africa, Eurasia, North and South America, Australia, and Antarctica as we know them today.

Although, if he could go back in time, a 20th century cartographer would recognize these landmasses by their profiles, their positions relative to each other would probably seem like a puzzle maker's bad joke. New York would rest on the Equator; Japan would be in the Arctic; and Australia and India would touch the Antarctic.

Earth's traditional timetable — rock — has provided much of the scientific basis for the theory of continental

(continued)

CRUSTAL STRUCTURE AND MOVEMENT

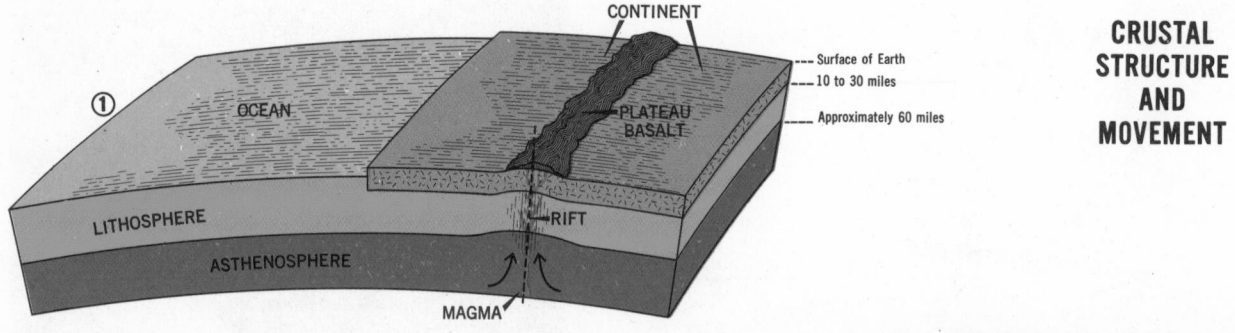

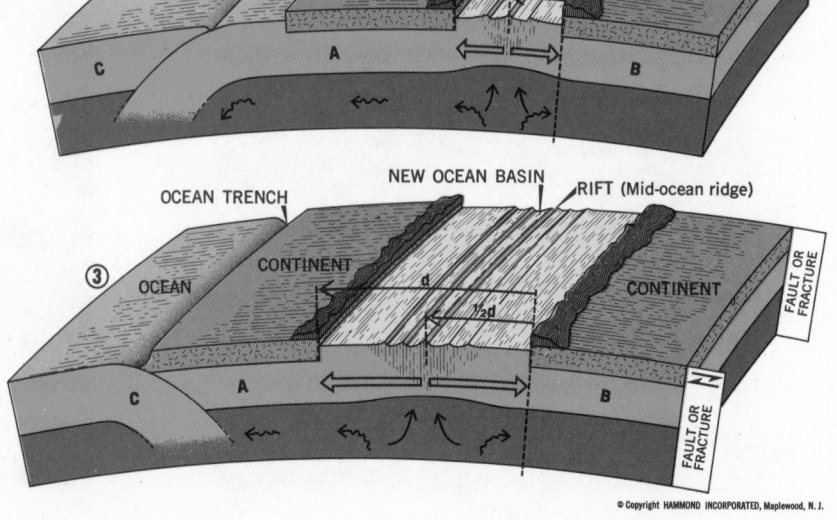

The concept of movement within the earth's crust assumes that the earth's outer layer has a firm lithosphere divided up into individual pieces called plates. These plates "float" above a weaker interior layer, the **asthenosphere**, and over vast periods of time noticeably change position, shape, size and direction depending upon forces exerted from within the earth.

① A rift or split in a lithosphere plate has caused a break in the overlying continental landmass. The pressure exerted by the outpouring of magma onto the earth's surface results in a spreading apart of the lithosphere plates.

② Continued pressure from the rift area forces plates A and B to separate and "raft" with them their accompanying continental areas. As the continents move away from each other, an ever-widening new ocean basin (d) is formed.

③ A neighboring plate, C, separated from plate A by a trench, is confronted by the rafted continental mass. The continent could be absorbed directly down into the trench or, as this diagram shows, collide with the edge of the trench, causing its downward slope angle to be reversed in direction.

PERMIAN
225 Million Years Ago

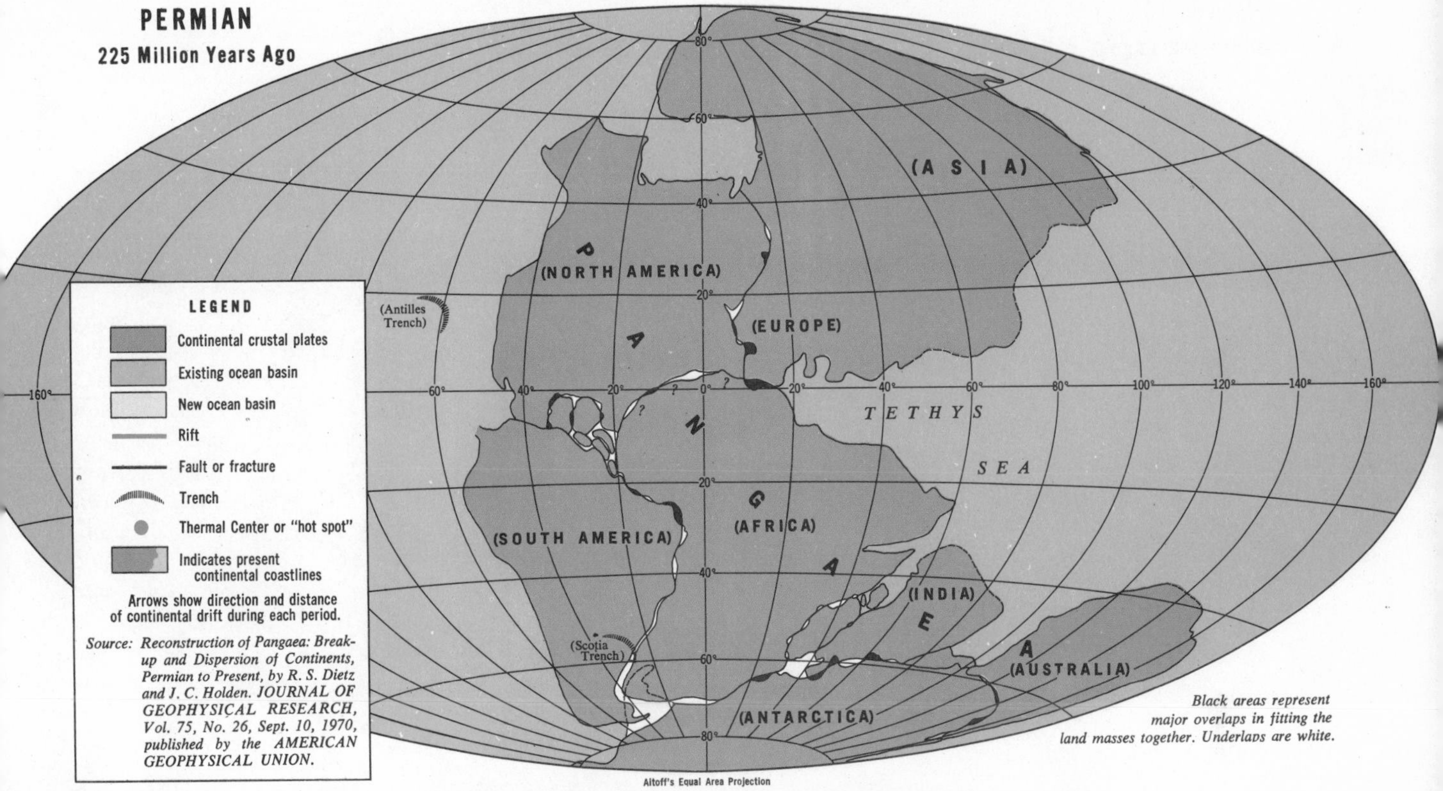

LEGEND

- Continental crustal plates
- Existing ocean basin
- New ocean basin
- Rift
- Fault or fracture
- Trench
- Thermal Center or "hot spot"
- Indicates present continental coastlines

Arrows show direction and distance of continental drift during each period.

Source: Reconstruction of Pangaea: Break-up and Dispersion of Continents, Permian to Present, by R. S. Dietz and J. C. Holden. JOURNAL OF GEOPHYSICAL RESEARCH, Vol. 75, No. 26, Sept. 10, 1970, published by the AMERICAN GEOPHYSICAL UNION.

Black areas represent major overlaps in fitting the land masses together. Underlaps are white.

Altoff's Equal Area Projection

A single earth landmass, Pangaea, is reconstructed by fitting together present-day continents at their offshore slope depths of about 2,000 meters. This line is believed to approximate the location of the original continental breaks.

TRIASSIC
180 Million Years Ago

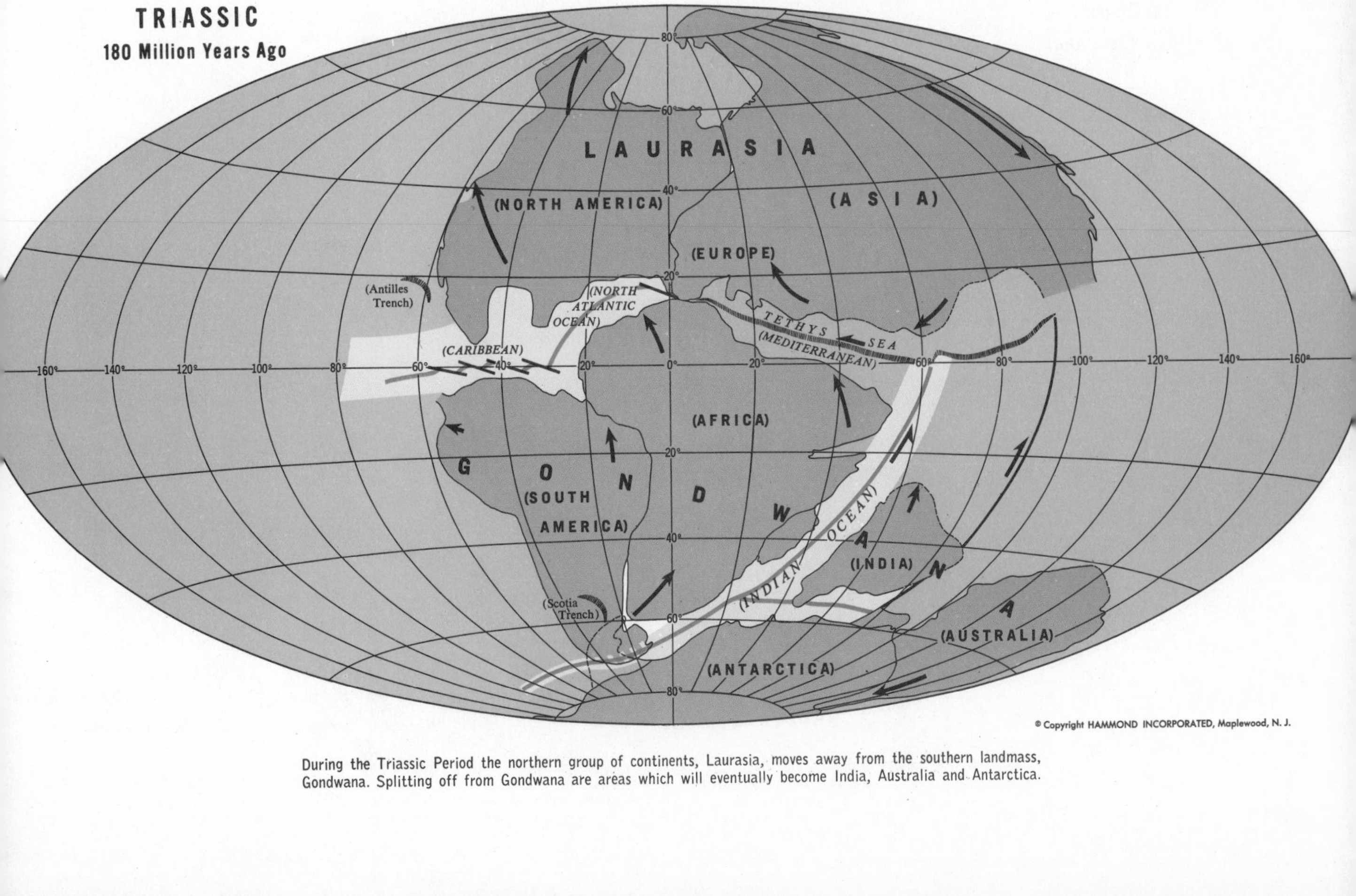

© Copyright HAMMOND INCORPORATED, Maplewood, N. J.

During the Triassic Period the northern group of continents, Laurasia, moves away from the southern landmass, Gondwana. Splitting off from Gondwana are areas which will eventually become India, Australia and Antarctica.

JURASSIC
135 Million Years Ago

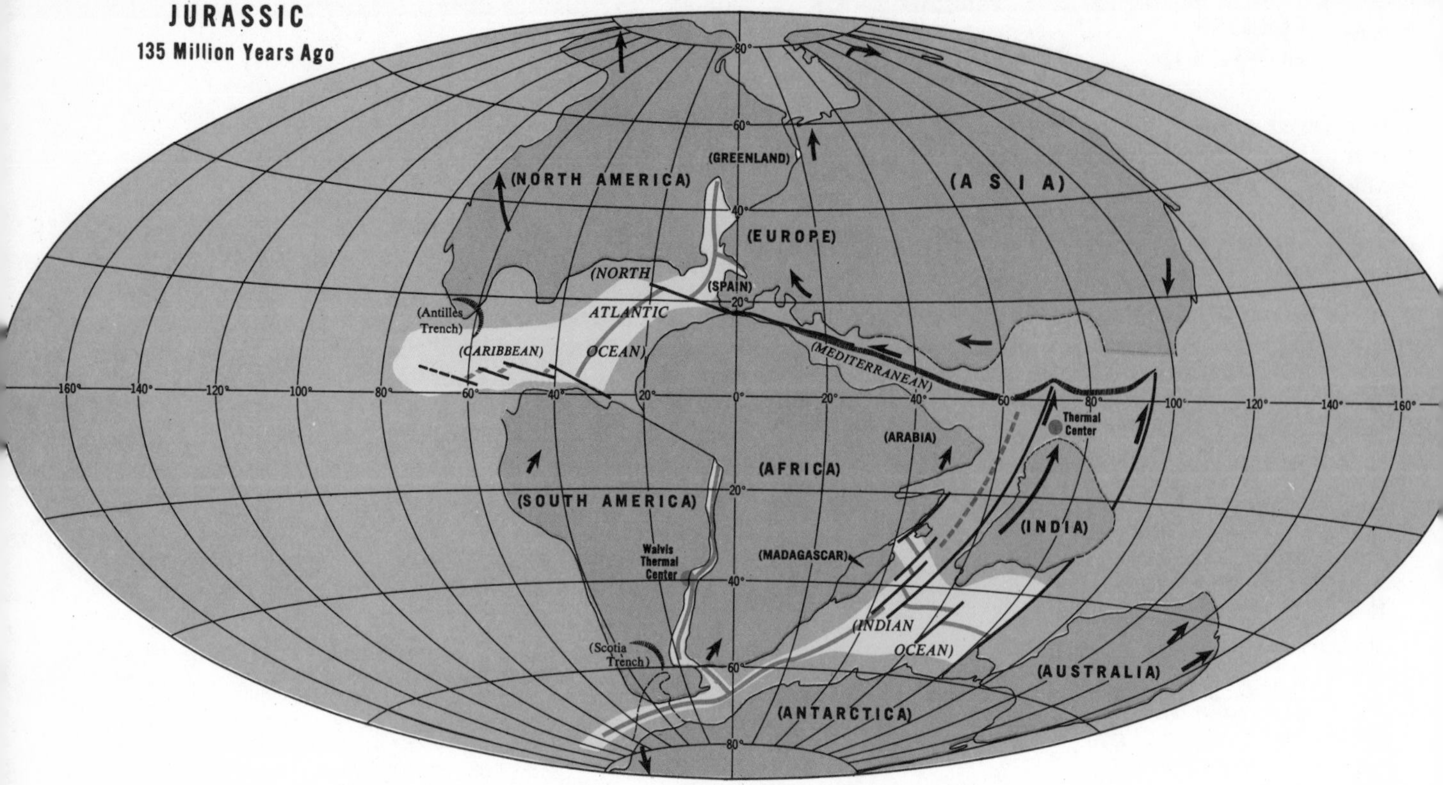

(NORTH AMERICA) (GREENLAND) (A S I A)

(EUROPE)

(NORTH ATLANTIC OCEAN) (SPAIN)

(Antilles Trench)

(CARIBBEAN)

(MEDITERRANEAN)

(ARABIA)

(AFRICA)

Thermal Center

(SOUTH AMERICA)

(INDIA)

Walvis Thermal Center (MADAGASCAR)

(INDIAN OCEAN)

(Scotia Trench)

(AUSTRALIA)

(ANTARCTICA)

Further drifting opens up the North Atlantic Ocean and creates a wide break between South America and Africa. The India landmass continues its rapid movement toward Asia.

CRETACEOUS
70 Million Years Ago

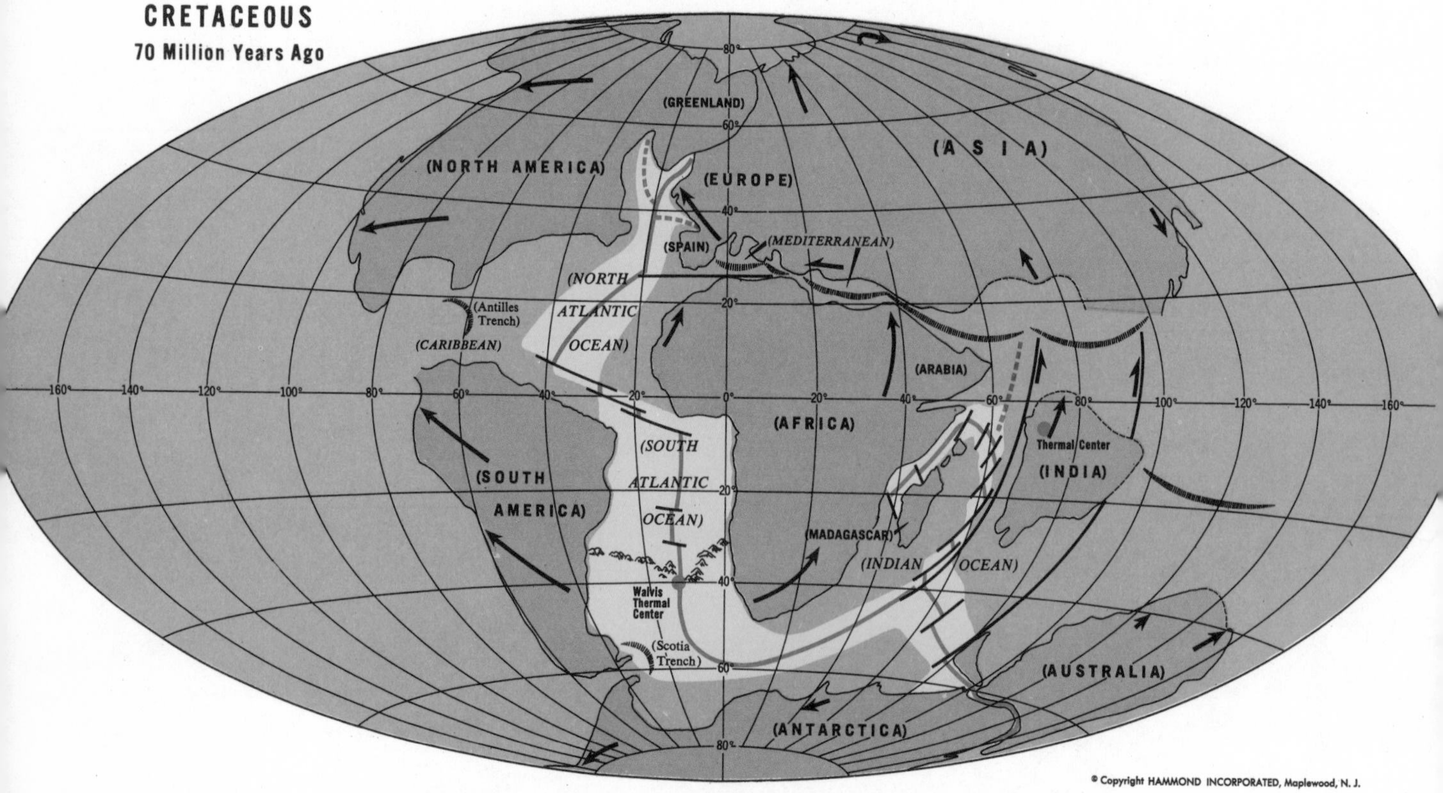

(GREENLAND) (A S I A)

(NORTH AMERICA) (EUROPE)

(MEDITERRANEAN)

(SPAIN)

(NORTH ATLANTIC OCEAN)

(Antilles Trench)

(CARIBBEAN)

(ARABIA)

(AFRICA)

(SOUTH ATLANTIC OCEAN)

Thermal Center

(INDIA)

(SOUTH AMERICA)

Walvis Thermal Center

(MADAGASCAR)

(INDIAN OCEAN)

(Scotia Trench)

(AUSTRALIA)

(ANTARCTICA)

Highlights of the Cretaceous Period are the development of the South Atlantic Ocean, further closing of the Mediterranean Sea and the breaking off of Madagascar from the African mainland.

(continued)

movement and the formation of land and sea masses. When it was in a molten state, rock captured and preserved the minerals and the primitive life of millions of years ago. In a similar fashion, it has retained the magnetic orientation present in the various geologic periods during which it became solid and stratified.

Through a study of ancient rocks, scientists are able to discover the locations of the magnetic poles at stages of the earth's development. By comparing the magnetic orientation of rock found on different continents but solidified during the same geologic periods, they have determined that magnetic pole locations vary from continent to continent. If continents had retained their original positions without shifting in their relationships, the direction of their magnetic poles would be the same.

But how do continents move? The concept of tremendous masses of land floating across the face of the earth staggers the imagination. One explanation of the continental drift mechanism can be made in terms of plate tectonics and seafloor spreading.

The lithosphere, or outer surface of the earth, is composed of rock about 60 miles thick. Beneath the lithosphere lies the relatively weak upper layer of the earth's mantle called the asthenosphere. For reasons which are not com-

pletely clear, forces generated in the asthenosphere during the Permian period caused the earth's outer surface to break into 10 major and a number of minor sections called plates. It is on these plates that the continents rest.

The rifts between the plates filled with molten material from the mantle, pushing the plates to either side and farther and farther apart as the material continued to seep through. Since material from the mantle is heavier than lithospheric rock, it leveled off below sea level forming ocean floors as water from the Pacific, or "mother" ocean, flowed in. Study of the floors of the Atlantic and Indian oceans reveal a ridge or rift running almost directly north to south at their centers indicating that they developed in this fashion.

During the past 65 million years (the Cenozoic era)—a relatively short period of geological time—nearly half of the ocean floors were created and the continents continued to move in a generally westward direction into their present positions.

Sea bottoms continue to be shoved away from the sides of rifts and continents continue in their monolithic movements. In 50 million years, if our cartographer could return, he would have to begin again to plot his pictures of the changing world.

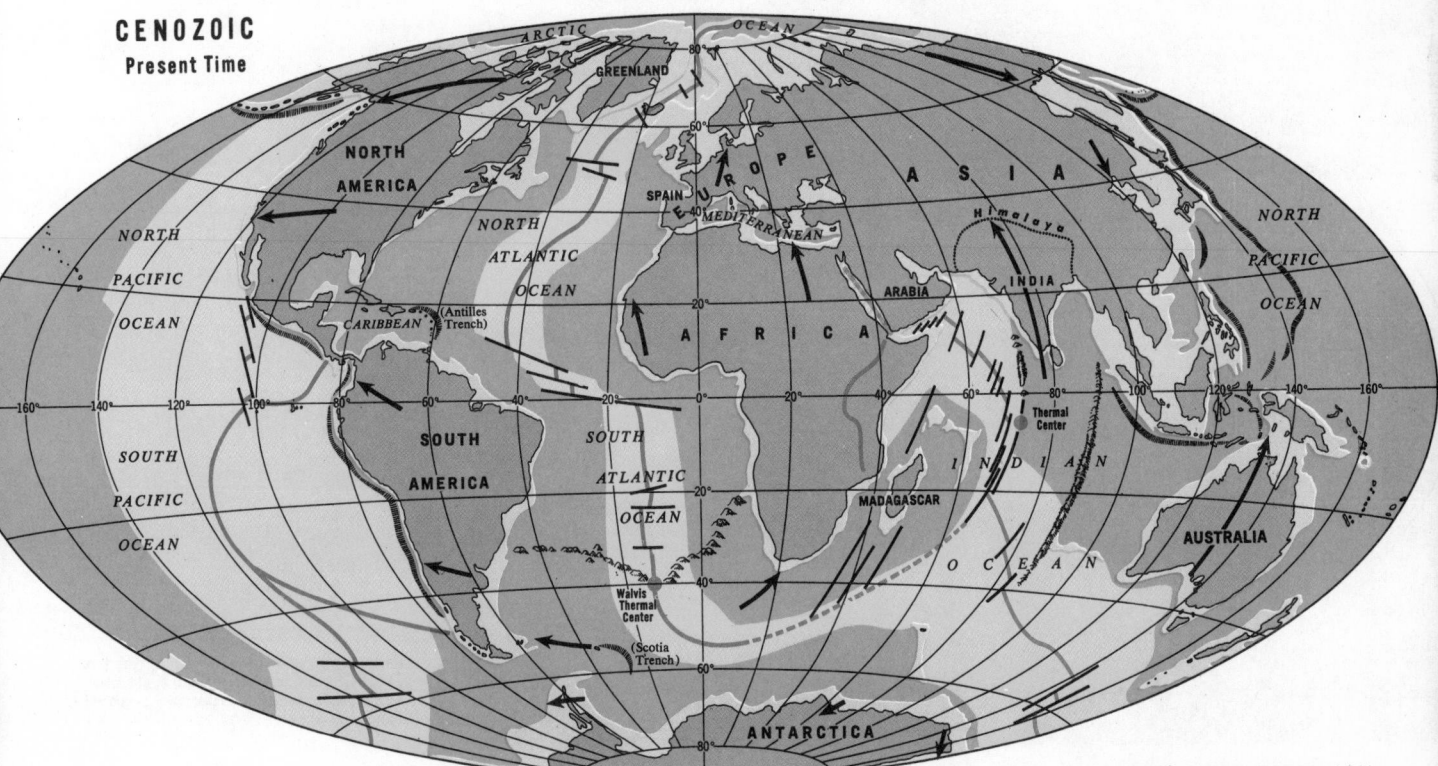

CENOZOIC
Present Time

© Copyright HAMMOND INCORPORATED, Maplewood, N. J.

The work of the past 70 million years has shaped the world as it appears today. India has collided with Asia, and Laurasia has been split apart in the North Atlantic. Movements on and within the earth's crust continue to alter the face of our planet.

The Ice Ages

Far from being an isolated instance, the movement of glaciers over the face of the earth has been a natural phenomenon for many thousands of years. Stimulated by changes in climate and resulting changes in sea level — perhaps induced by shifts in the earth's axis — glaciers have followed a rather unpredictable course of advance and retreat continuing into the 20th century.

At some point in unrecorded history during the greatest ice age, or the Pleistocene epoch, as much as 27 percent of the earth's surface was covered by glacial ice to a depth of up to 10,000 feet. The icy masses moved across the earth as far south as New York City and the Missouri River in North America, burying much of Europe and blanketing vast areas in northern Asia.

Many of the great ice sheets retreated as the climate became warmer, leaving deposits of soil and rock picked up as they traveled southward in the Northern Hemisphere. The landscape changed as the glaciers left behind their typical U-shaped valleys, amphitheater-like hollows and jagged mountain ridges, altering to a large extent the former ecological zones which changed again and again as the ice reformed and melted.

Although not enough is known about glaciers to predict accurately their future behavior, we do know that they react to climatic changes. Glaciers were advancing in Alpine regions during the 19th century until a global warm up in the beginning of this century caused their retreat. Recently the trend has been toward cooler and moister climate and, on a limited scale, glaciers are beginning to advance once more.

An imaginary scene during the Pleistocene Epoch shows an advancing continental glacier virtually covering all terrain in its path. (Courtesy of The American Museum of Natural History)

During an interglacial period of the Pleistocene, the retreating glaciers left a scoured landscape laden with ice-transported deposits. (Courtesy of The American Museum of Natural History)

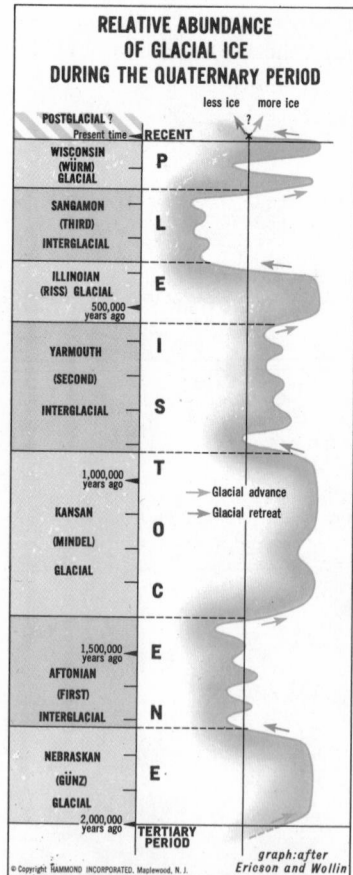

RELATIVE ABUNDANCE OF GLACIAL ICE DURING THE QUATERNARY PERIOD

less ice   more ice

POSTGLACIAL ?
Present time — RECENT

WISCONSIN (WÜRM) GLACIAL — P

SANGAMON (THIRD) INTERGLACIAL — L

ILLINOIAN (RISS) GLACIAL — E
500,000 years ago

YARMOUTH (SECOND) INTERGLACIAL — I
S

1,000,000 years ago
→ Glacial advance
→ Glacial retreat

KANSAN (MINDEL) GLACIAL — T O C

1,500,000 years ago
AFTONIAN (FIRST) INTERGLACIAL — E N

NEBRASKAN (GÜNZ) GLACIAL — E
2,000,000 years ago

TERTIARY PERIOD

© Copyright HAMMOND INCORPORATED, Maplewood, N. J.

graph: after Ericson and Wollin

Four major glacial periods highlight the last 2,000,000 years of history. Future glaciation will depend upon those factors which control the earth's climate.

EXTENT OF GLACIATION IN THE NORTHERN HEMISPHERE DURING THE ICE AGES

America's first inhabitants probably walked over a broad land bridge that once connected Asia with North America. During the last major episode of continental glaciation, large amounts of seawater became locked in glacial ice caps, continuous masses of ice several miles thick. As the sea level was hundreds of feet below its present level, a dry land corridor, the Bering Land Bridge, appeared, connecting Alaska and Siberia. About 26,000 years ago Paleolithic hunters crossed this bridge and later moved southward into present-day United States through a temporary ice-free passageway in the ice cap.

Changing the Face of the Earth

The face of the earth, like man himself, is continually changing — the victim of stress and counterstress, thrust and counterthrust from within and from without. The opposing forces of uplift, and weathering and erosion are constantly at work sculpturing the face of the land. The forces to which a given landscape is subject can be read on the surface at various stages in much the same way that a man's character can be traced in his face.

The infant's skin is relatively smooth and unbroken; as he grows toward manhood, the structure of his facial bones becomes more apparent as the jawline and cheekbones assume their clear-cut definition. So too an "infant landscape" — the consequence of the raising of land for whatever reason — is smooth. Gradually small streams and rivers develop and their narrow valleys begin to deepen

and widen as water makes its way toward the sea.

With maturity, laugh lines or the markings of innumerable frowns begin to furrow a man's skin. As he grows older and muscles weaken, much of the underlying structure disappears as the skin is smoothed down by the continual tugs of gravity. When valleys have reached their base limit their straightforward routes are ended and they begin to dissect the landscape with lateral cuts. Broad valleys result and eventually widen until old age, when the entire landscape has been flattened to an almost uninterrupted valley called a floodplain. If this flattening process, the result of weathering and erosion, were to go unchecked for several thousands of years, the earth's surface would be uninterestingly flat and covered by shallow water. But the nature of the earth is to rebuild itself.

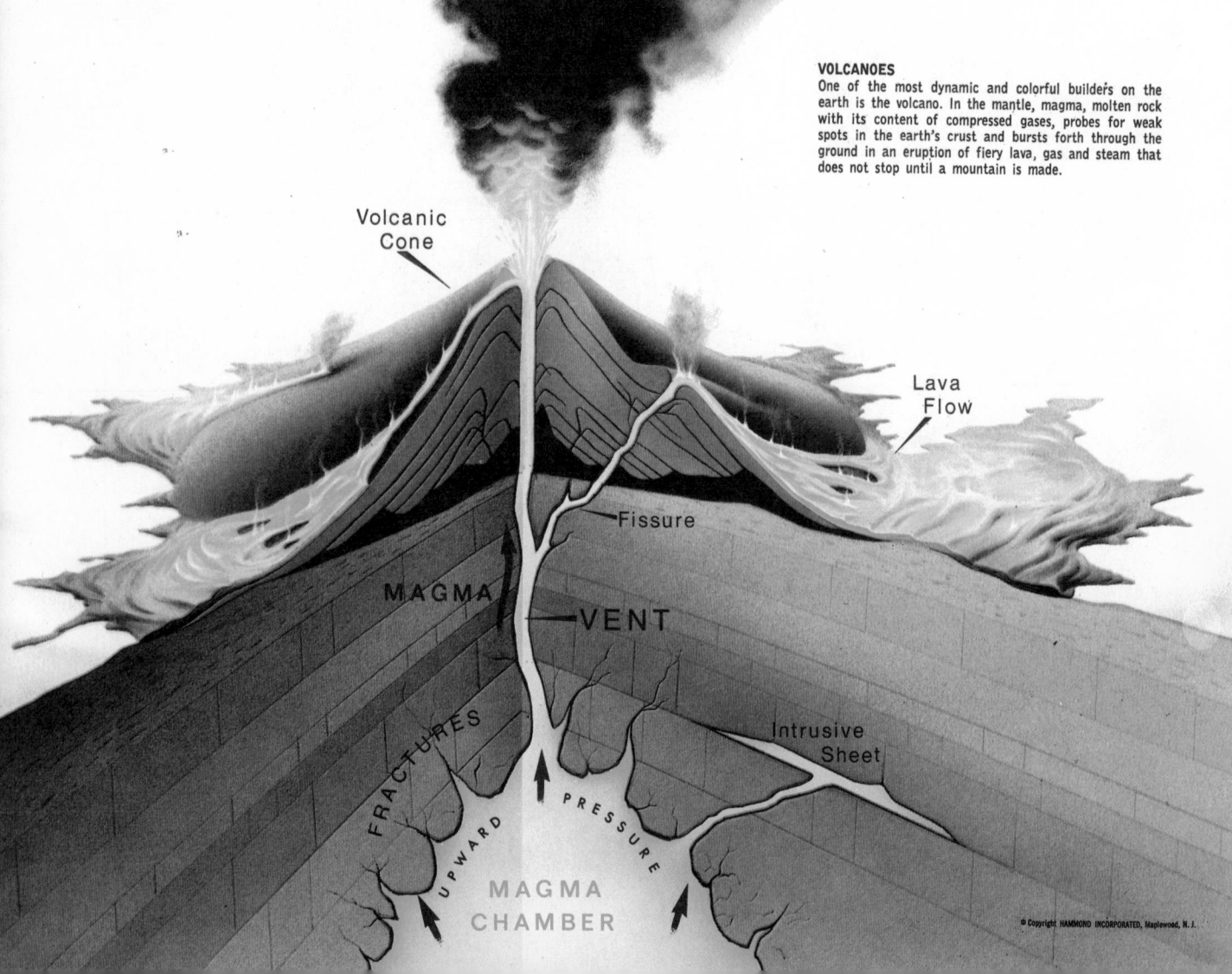

VOLCANOES
One of the most dynamic and colorful builders on the earth is the volcano. In the mantle, magma, molten rock with its content of compressed gases, probes for weak spots in the earth's crust and bursts forth through the ground in an eruption of fiery lava, gas and steam that does not stop until a mountain is made.

Volcanic Cone

Lava Flow

Fissure

MAGMA

VENT

FRACTURES

Intrusive Sheet

UPWARD PRESSURE

MAGMA CHAMBER

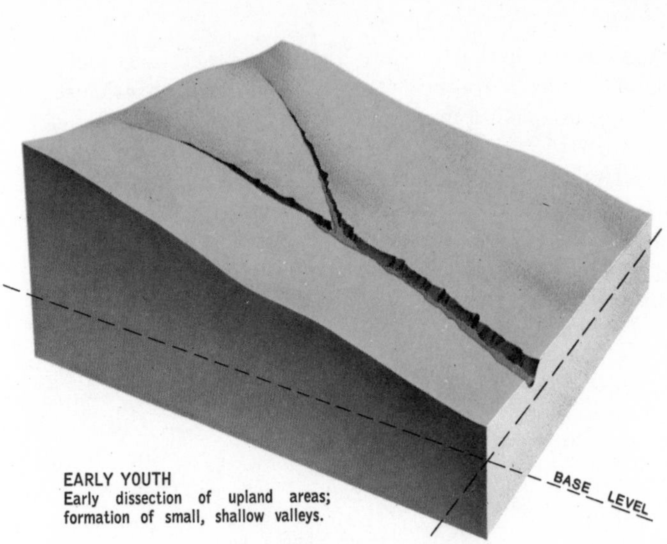

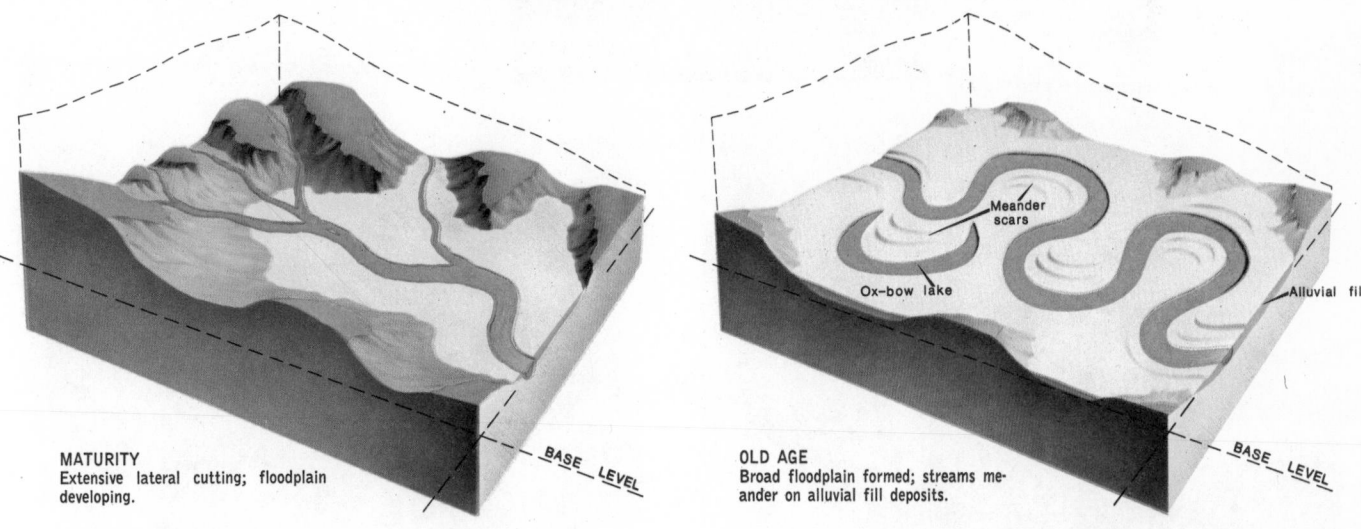

EARLY YOUTH
Early dissection of upland areas; formation of small, shallow valleys.

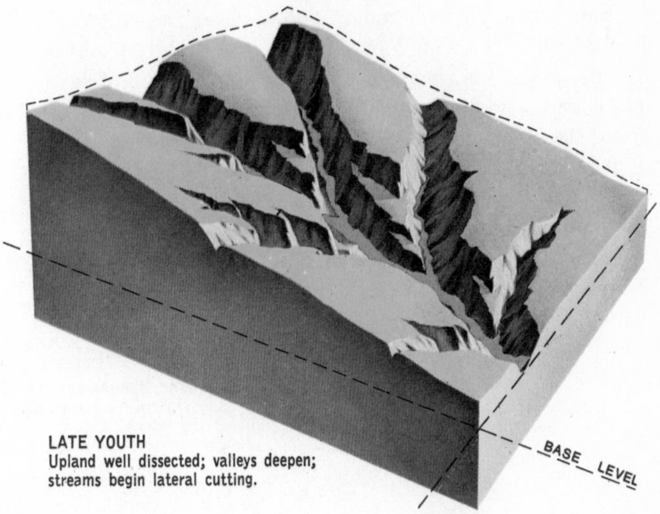

LATE YOUTH
Upland well dissected; valleys deepen; streams begin lateral cutting.

RUNNING WATER
Beginning as rainfall, running water is a prolific sculptor of the face of the land. Laden with picked-up abrasive materials, it flows downhill to the sea, carving and widening valleys until ultimately it reduces all the terrain in its path to near base level.

MATURITY
Extensive lateral cutting; floodplain developing.

OLD AGE
Broad floodplain formed; streams meander on alluvial fill deposits.

Meander scars

Ox-bow lake

Alluvial fill

Uplift, or the building process, can be as violent as erosion is passive. Uplift is the result of unbearable forces or stresses within the depths of the earth which demand to be loosed on the surface. We do not know for certain whether the energy results from cooling of the earth's core, from movement within the mantle, or from the pressures of accumulating silt deposits on the ocean floors. We do know that when the tremendous energy of a volcano or an earthquake is released, the growing pains of earth can become a disaster to mankind.

The volcano "blows its stack" when it can no longer contain the pressure of steam and other gases within the sealed chamber of its interior. As these materials seek to expand, they exert unbearable forces on the rocks overlying the chamber. Fissures are created. As the pressure continues, one of the fissures breaks through to the surface and an eruption occurs, spewing gases and molten rock — material from the magma chamber — through the main vent and through subsidiary fissures. With each subsequent eruption the volcanic cone — or the sides of the "mountain" — increase in height and depth until the volcano ceases its external activity and becomes dormant.

Sometimes volcanic mountains, such as the enigmatic Fonuafoou in the Kingdom of Tonga, rise rapidly from the depths of the sea, belch forth their complement of lava, gases and ash, and then mysteriously disappear. More often the volcanic mountain rises slowly, growing larger as it feeds on its own eruptions. Eventually the mountain quiets and supports new life until it wears away through the process of weathering and erosion.

For scientists the volcanic builders of the earth are interesting because they extend our knowledge of the workings of the earth's interior. In some instances life caught in death has been preserved for the archaeologist and anthropologist in historic cities like Pompeii, whose swift destruction was preserved by an airless blanket of lava and ash. Nothing survived the satanic blast when the top blew off the volcanic island of Krakatoa in 1882. However, the very lack of a single living organism gave us an opportunity to observe the island's recolonization and study the beginnings of life in a "primeval" territory.

Fortunately not all mountains or mountain ranges are

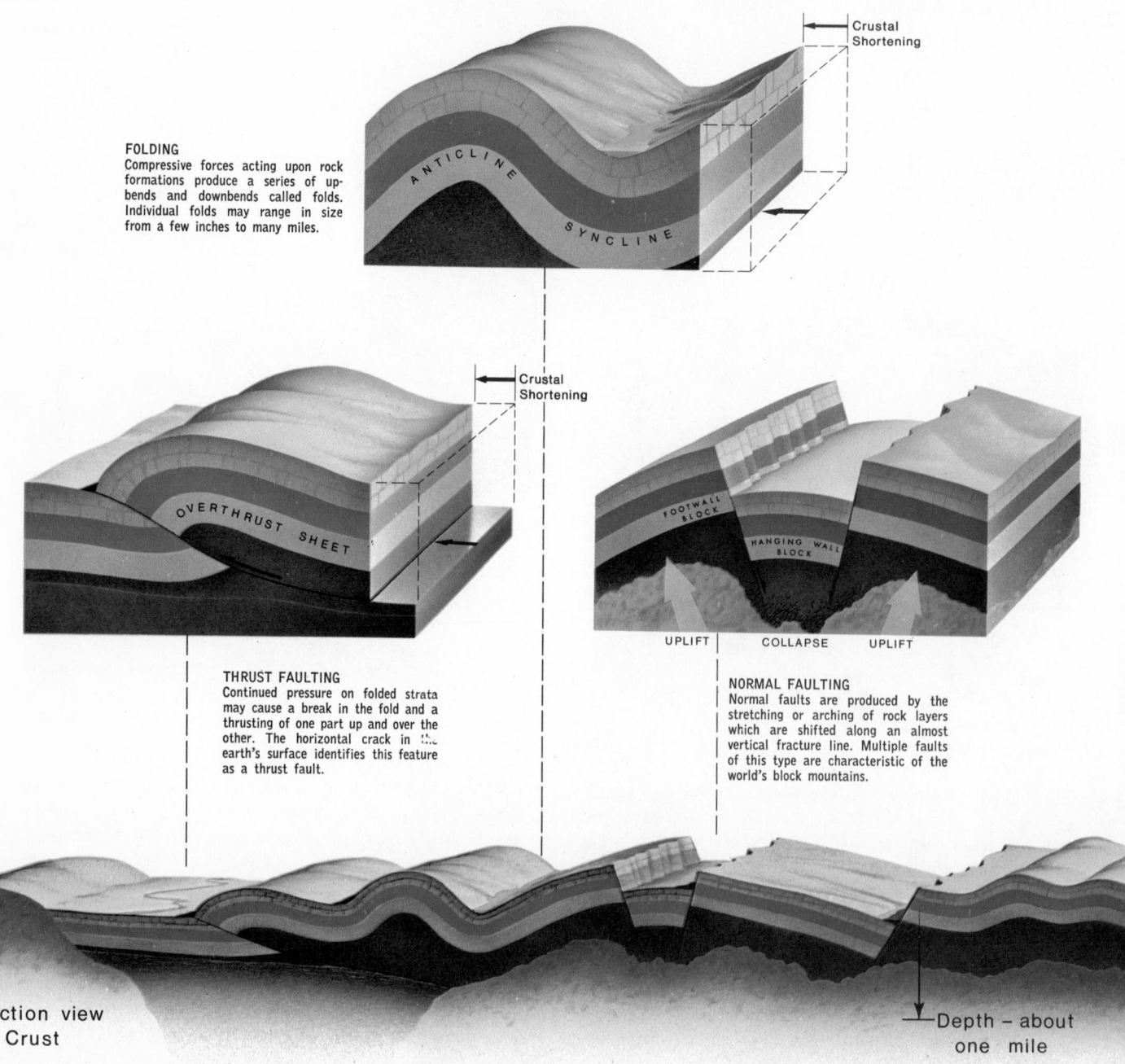

CRUSTAL DEFORMATION
Stress within the earth manifests itself in a variety of ways on the earth's crust. Most typical of these are the warped and cracked features seen on the earth's surface.

Crustal Shortening

FOLDING
Compressive forces acting upon rock formations produce a series of up-bends and downbends called folds. Individual folds may range in size from a few inches to many miles.

ANTICLINE

SYNCLINE

Crustal Shortening

OVERTHRUST SHEET

FOOTWALL BLOCK

HANGING WALL BLOCK

UPLIFT   COLLAPSE   UPLIFT

THRUST FAULTING
Continued pressure on folded strata may cause a break in the fold and a thrusting of one part up and over the other. The horizontal crack in the earth's surface identifies this feature as a thrust fault.

NORMAL FAULTING
Normal faults are produced by the stretching or arching of rock layers which are shifted along an almost vertical fracture line. Multiple faults of this type are characteristic of the world's block mountains.

Section view of Crust

Depth – about one mile

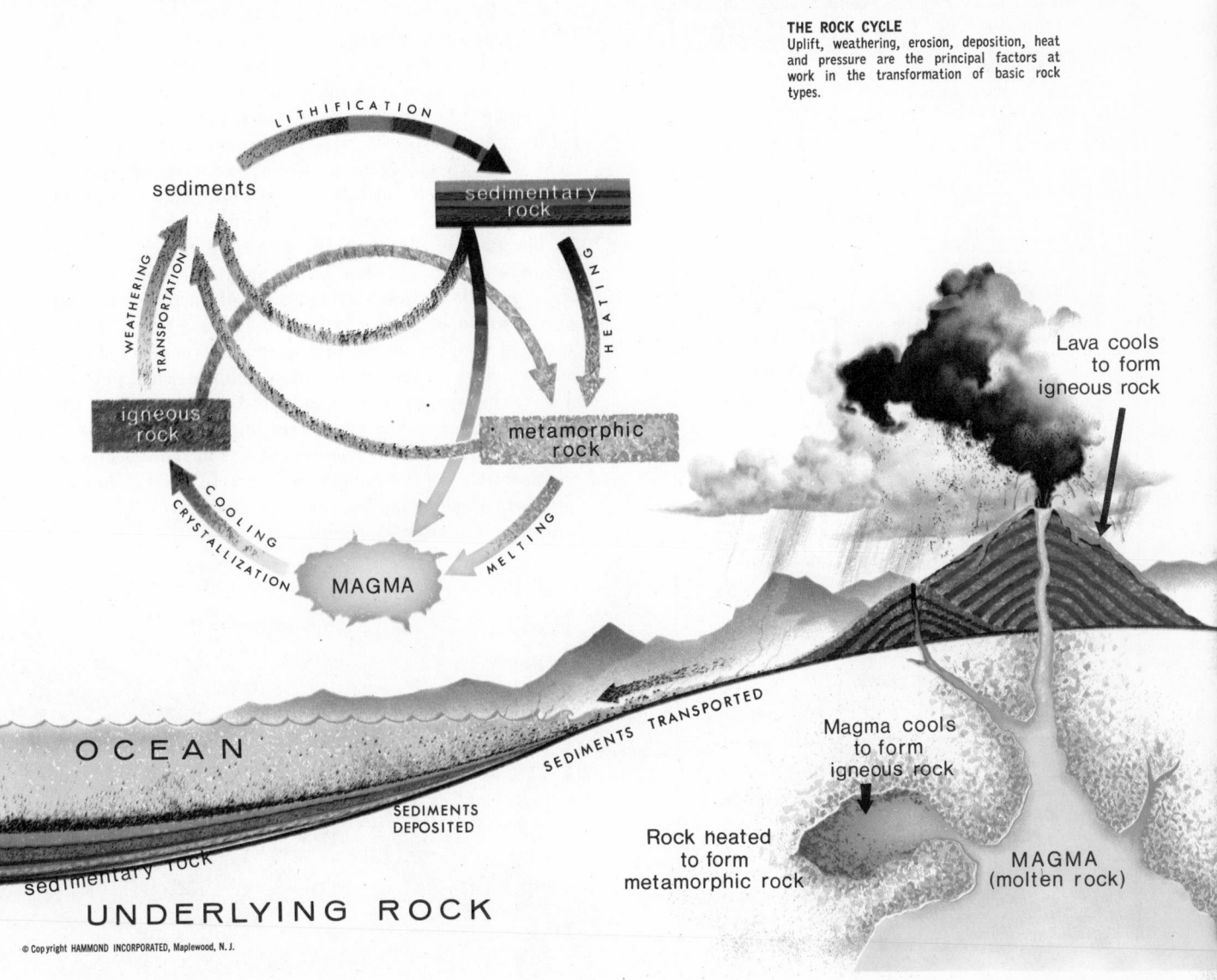

THE ROCK CYCLE
Uplift, weathering, erosion, deposition, heat and pressure are the principal factors at work in the transformation of basic rock types.

built with so much haste and violence. Often flat lands, reacting to compressive forces, grow into mountains or mountain ranges almost imperceptibly over a period of millions of years. The tides of the mantle, the layer of still-molten rock under the earth's surface, continue to flow under tremendous pressure. Sometimes this pressure creates folds or faults in the crustal rock. As pressure increases wave-like formations called folds are produced. If the underlying stress becomes too great the rock fractures or breaks creating a fault.

In recorded history as many as 100,000 people have lost their lives in a single incident as the rock on one or both sides of a fault shifted, creating an earthquake. Fracture or fault zones occur throughout the world, but the Pacific area, where most volcanoes are located, also contains the greatest concentration of major fracture zones, many connected with structures on the North American continent. Movement along the San Andreas Fault, extending more than 600 miles in California, destroyed San Francisco in 1906 and was responsible for the damage in Los Angeles during early 1971.

Clearly, men who say there is nothing new on the face of the earth have never watched it open up beneath their feet or lived long enough to see a mountain grow and wash away again. They cannot understand that time will turn the barren rock beneath their feet to soil as, often gently, sometimes violently, the face of the earth is continually altered.

GEOLOGIC TIME

TIME DIVISION			YEARS AGO	MAJOR GEOLOGIC DEVELOPMENTS
CENOZOIC ERA	QUATERNARY PERIOD	RECENT	10,000	GREAT LAKES
		PLEISTOCENE		NORWEGIAN FJORDS
			1-2 million	ICE AGES
	TERTIARY PERIOD	PLIOCENE		BLACK SEA
			11 million	CASPIAN SEA
		MIOCENE		HIMALAYAS
			25 million	
		OLIGOCENE		ALPS
			40 million	
		EOCENE		
			60 million	
		PALEOCENE		ANDES MOUNTAINS
			70 million	ROCKY MOUNTAINS
MESOZOIC ERA		CRETACEOUS PERIOD		CHALK DEPOSITS
			135 million	COAST RANGES
		JURASSIC PERIOD		SIERRA NEVADA
				JURA MOUNTAINS
			180 million	NEW JERSEY PALISADES
		TRIASSIC PERIOD		
			225 million	CAUCASUS
PALEOZOIC ERA		PERMIAN PERIOD		URAL MOUNTAINS
				APPALACHIAN MOUNTAINS
			270 million	POTASH DEPOSITS
		PENNSYLVANIAN PERIOD		
			300 million	COAL DEPOSITS
		MISSISSIPPIAN PERIOD		
			350 million	ACADIAN MOUNTAINS
		DEVONIAN PERIOD		
			400 million	
		SILURIAN PERIOD		NIAGARA FALLS CAPROCK
			440 million	TACONIC MOUNTAINS
		ORDOVICIAN PERIOD		LIMESTONE DEPOSITS
			500 million	VERMONT MOUNTAINS
		CAMBRIAN PERIOD		
			600 million	ARIZONA MOUNTAINS
		PRE-CAMBRIAN		METALLIC ORE DEPOSITS
				LAURENTIAN MOUNTAINS
				ADIRONDACK MOUNTAINS

© Copyright HAMMOND INCORPORATED, Maplewood, N. J.

Like a giant Rosetta stone the secrets of the earth's creation lie spread in strata beneath our feet, revealing their hieroglyphic message to a few of the initiated.

For billions of years layers of rock — the sedimentary deposits of ages — have piled up on the earth's surface, entrapping the characteristics of time. Time when a lifeless nature prepared for the first microscopic living organisms; time when these organisms were destroyed or became extinct; time when, through endless subtle mutations, they evolved into new forms of life.

The Paleozoic, ancient era; Mesozoic, middle era; and Cenozoic, recent era, are the designations used for the broad periods of time during which life evolved. Locked within strata of rock, vestiges of life are found in the fossilized remains of creatures over a billion years old. In succeeding layers geologists and anthropologists find other clues to the mystery of time and life: the appearance of the lowest forms of animal life; the evolution of fish, amphibians, reptiles, birds and mammals. Late in the schedule of creation traces of a strange and wonderful animal appear, for it was only one million years ago that man left his first imprint on the geologic record.

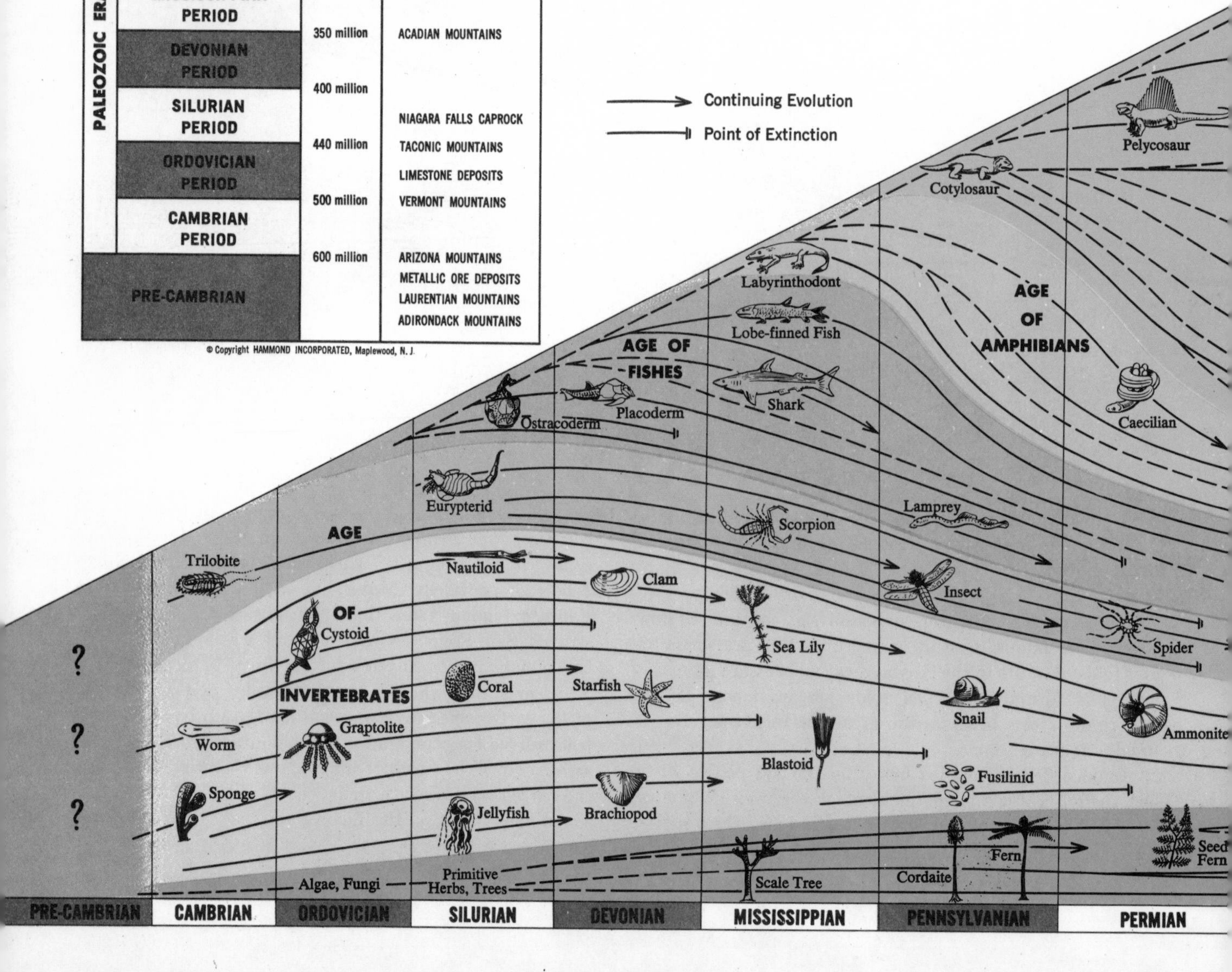

The Geologic Record

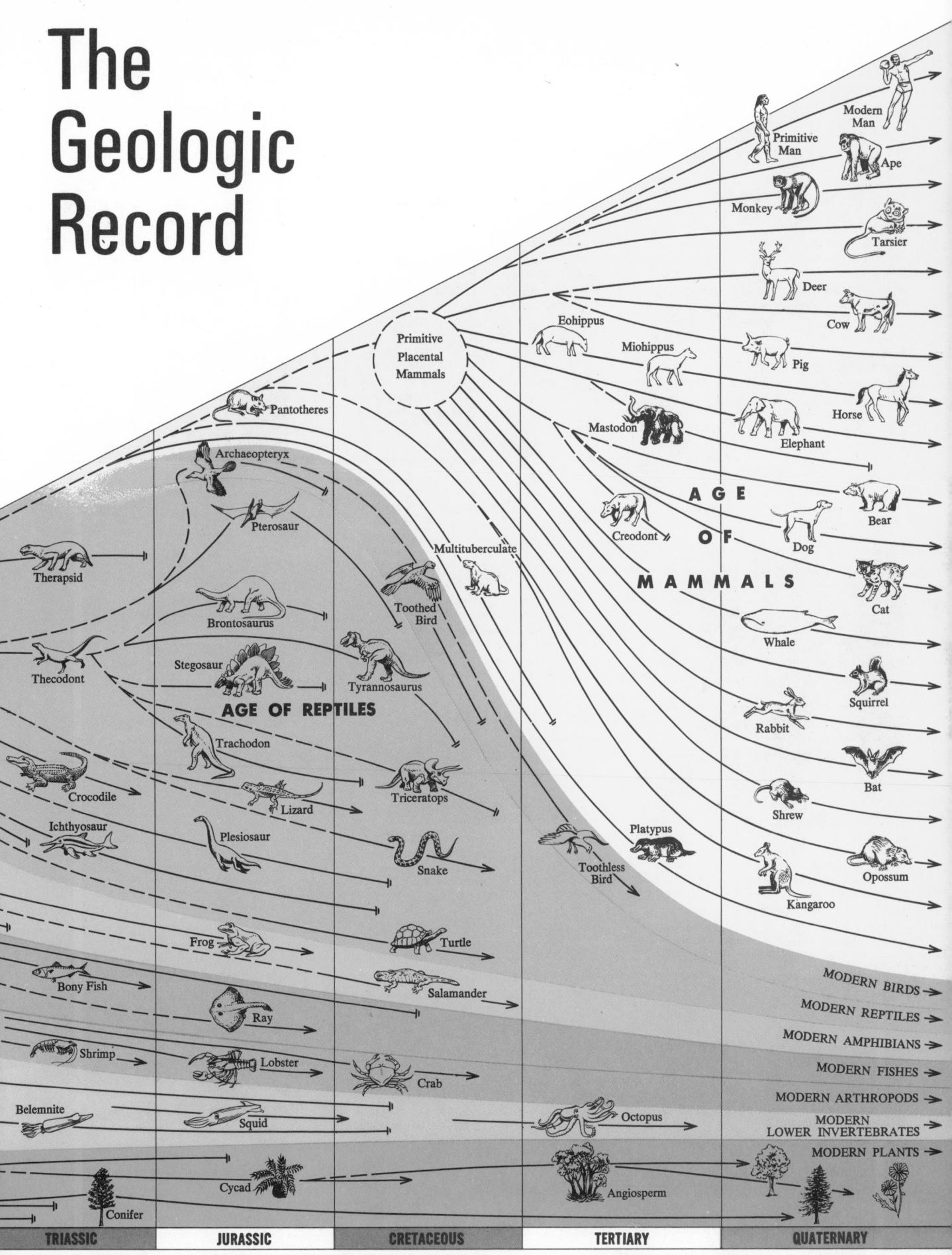

Primitive Man

Modern Man

Ape

Monkey

Tarsier

Deer

Cow

Eohippus

Miohippus

Pig

Horse

Mastodon

Elephant

Primitive Placental Mammals

AGE OF MAMMALS

Creodont

Bear

Dog

Pantotheres

Cat

Whale

Archaeopteryx

Pterosaur

Squirrel

Multituberculate

Rabbit

Therapsid

Bat

Toothed Bird

Brontosaurus

Shrew

Platypus

Stegosaur

Tyrannosaurus

Opossum

Thecodont

AGE OF REPTILES

Toothless Bird

Kangaroo

Trachodon

Lizard

Triceratops

Crocodile

Ichthyosaur

Plesiosaur

Snake

Frog

Turtle

MODERN BIRDS

Bony Fish

Salamander

MODERN REPTILES

Ray

MODERN AMPHIBIANS

MODERN FISHES

Shrimp

Lobster

Crab

MODERN ARTHROPODS

Belemnite

MODERN LOWER INVERTEBRATES

Squid

Octopus

MODERN PLANTS

Cycad

Angiosperm

Conifer

TRIASSIC | **JURASSIC** | **CRETACEOUS** | **TERTIARY** | **QUATERNARY**

The Biosphere: Realm of Living Things

Polar and mountainous regions of perpetual **ice and snow** cover one-tenth of the earth's land areas. Windswept, always below freezing, it can support life only peripherally, if at all.

A place of mosses, lichens and stunted flowering plants and trees, the **tundra** is an area so marginal that only specially adapted life-forms, such as reindeer, can live there.

As favorable climates produce and sustain an abundance of vegetation, the **mid-latitude forest** regions of the world continue to serve as home for a majority of the world's population.

Ranging from the luxuriant vegetation of the rainforest to scrub-like woodlands in drier areas, the **tropical forest** is noted for containing a wide variety of insects, birds and small animals.

The **savanna** or tropical grassland is a land of tall grass interspersed with trees. A place of winter droughts and summer rainfall, it is the true jungle home of big-game animals.

On the **mid-latitude grasslands** are found many of the sheep and cattle ranches of the earth, and, where the land has been successfully cultivated, the great grain fields.

Except in scattered oases and irrigated lands, the **deserts** of the world are inhabited only by livestock-herding nomads and wildlife capable of surviving in moisture-deficient areas.

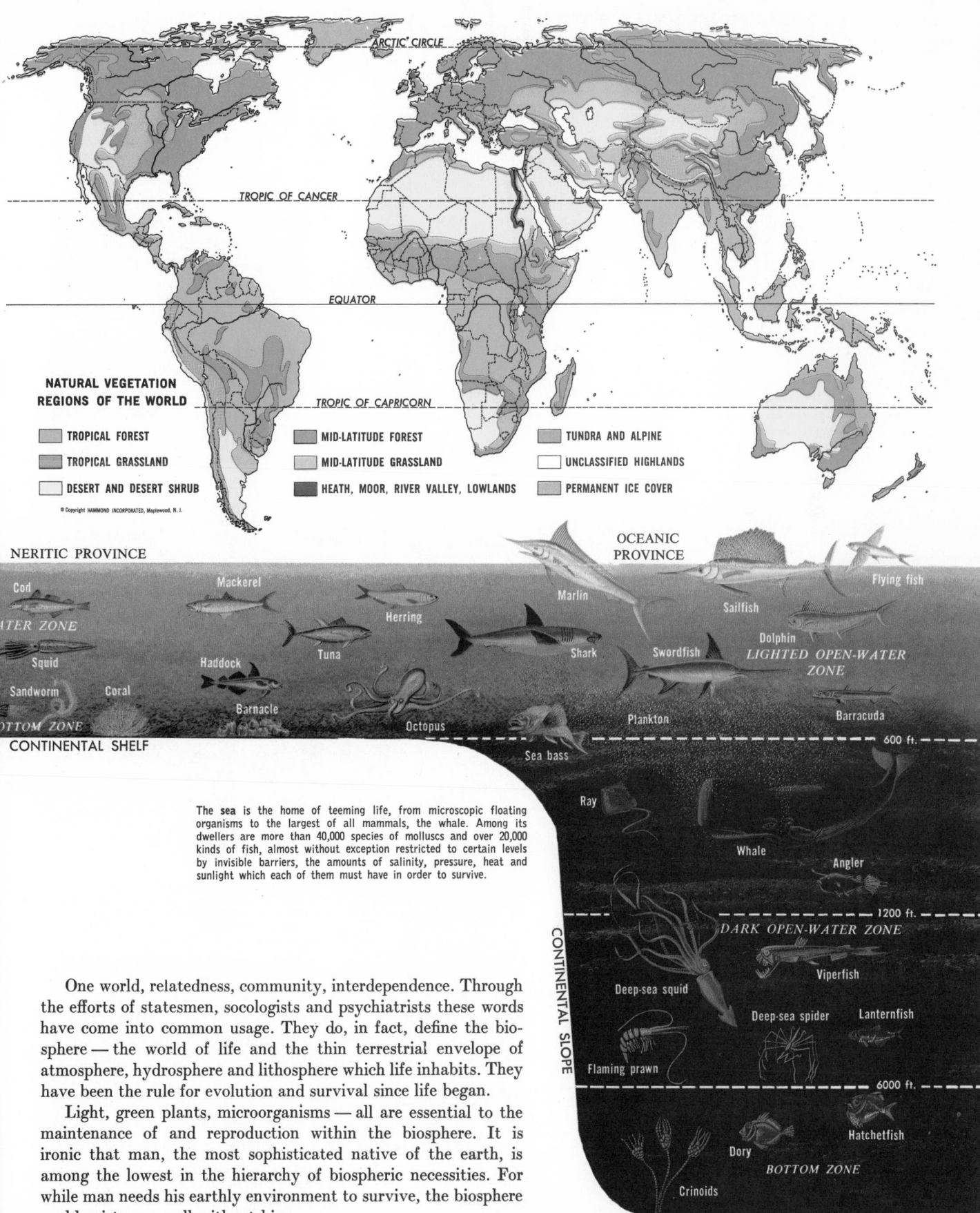

NATURAL VEGETATION
REGIONS OF THE WORLD

TROPICAL FOREST MID-LATITUDE FOREST TUNDRA AND ALPINE
TROPICAL GRASSLAND MID-LATITUDE GRASSLAND UNCLASSIFIED HIGHLANDS
DESERT AND DESERT SHRUB HEATH, MOOR, RIVER VALLEY, LOWLANDS PERMANENT ICE COVER

The **sea** is the home of teeming life, from microscopic floating organisms to the largest of all mammals, the whale. Among its dwellers are more than 40,000 species of molluscs and over 20,000 kinds of fish, almost without exception restricted to certain levels by invisible barriers, the amounts of salinity, pressure, heat and sunlight which each of them must have in order to survive.

One world, relatedness, community, interdependence. Through the efforts of statesmen, socologists and psychiatrists these words have come into common usage. They do, in fact, define the biosphere — the world of life and the thin terrestrial envelope of atmosphere, hydrosphere and lithosphere which life inhabits. They have been the rule for evolution and survival since life began.

Light, green plants, microorganisms — all are essential to the maintenance of and reproduction within the biosphere. It is ironic that man, the most sophisticated native of the earth, is among the lowest in the hierarchy of biospheric necessities. For while man needs his earthly environment to survive, the biosphere could exist very well without him.

Environmental Controls

Primitive man worshiped the sun, danced for rain, and trembled when the angry gods unleashed the force of hurricane or hid the face of the sun in clouds. Modern man curses the drought, hides from the wind and snow and builds walls against the onslaught of flood.

Little has changed in the impact of climate and environment on the life of man. There are no vegetarians in the desert or in the ice-bound regions of the far north. Houses exposing vast expanses of glass to the burning fingers of the sun are not found in the Sahara, at the Equator or near the Poles. Man does not die of malaria in regions too dry or too cold to support the larvae of mosquitoes; swollen goiterous necks are never seen in areas where local water is naturally supplied with iodine.

Men who live near lakes or seas build boats while those near mountains climb or ski. The plainsman nurtures cattle or grain; the farmer in the valley cultivates tomatoes or legumes. In work, in play, in sickness and varying degrees of health — even in the formation of national traditions — the world of man is subject to the force of nature.

By a variety of adaptations man wrestles with the problems of his environment. He can air-condition or heat his home, refrigerate his food, quench parts of the thirsty deserts with irrigated water, drain the swamps and navigate the seas. He has developed intricate technologies to forecast earthquakes, blizzards, floods and hurricanes.

But the ancient sun still governs the movements of the earth within its orbit, determining heat and cold, the progress of the winds and ocean currents, the levels of the seas — the glacier's trail. Man continues to bow before the "god of day."

The interactions of sun, rain and wind are so closely related that they function as a single entity which is, perhaps, the most dominant force in creating man's environment.

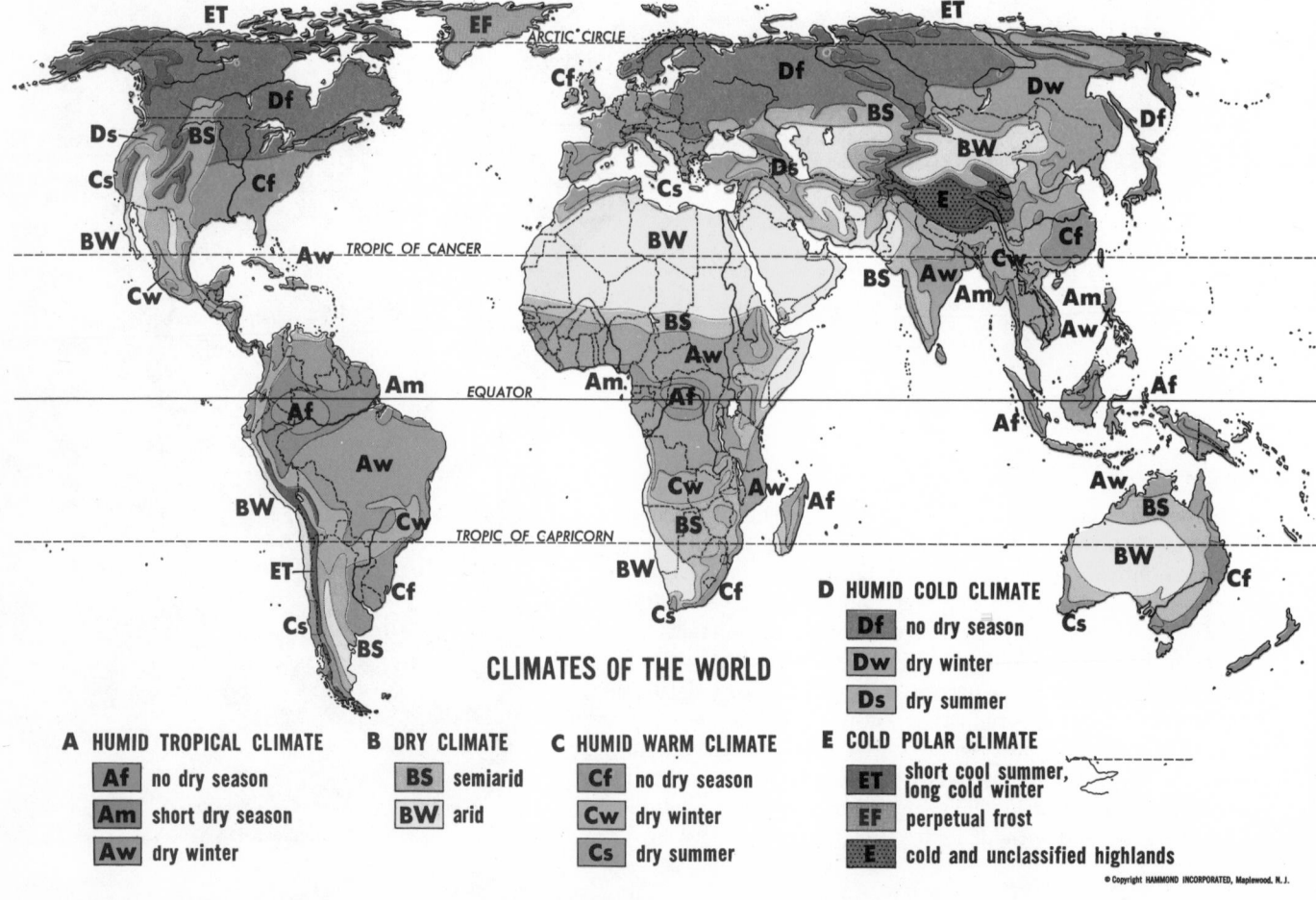

CLIMATES OF THE WORLD

A HUMID TROPICAL CLIMATE
- Af — no dry season
- Am — short dry season
- Aw — dry winter

B DRY CLIMATE
- BS — semiarid
- BW — arid

C HUMID WARM CLIMATE
- Cf — no dry season
- Cw — dry winter
- Cs — dry summer

D HUMID COLD CLIMATE
- Df — no dry season
- Dw — dry winter
- Ds — dry summer

E COLD POLAR CLIMATE
- ET — short cool summer, long cold winter
- EF — perpetual frost
- E — cold and unclassified highlands

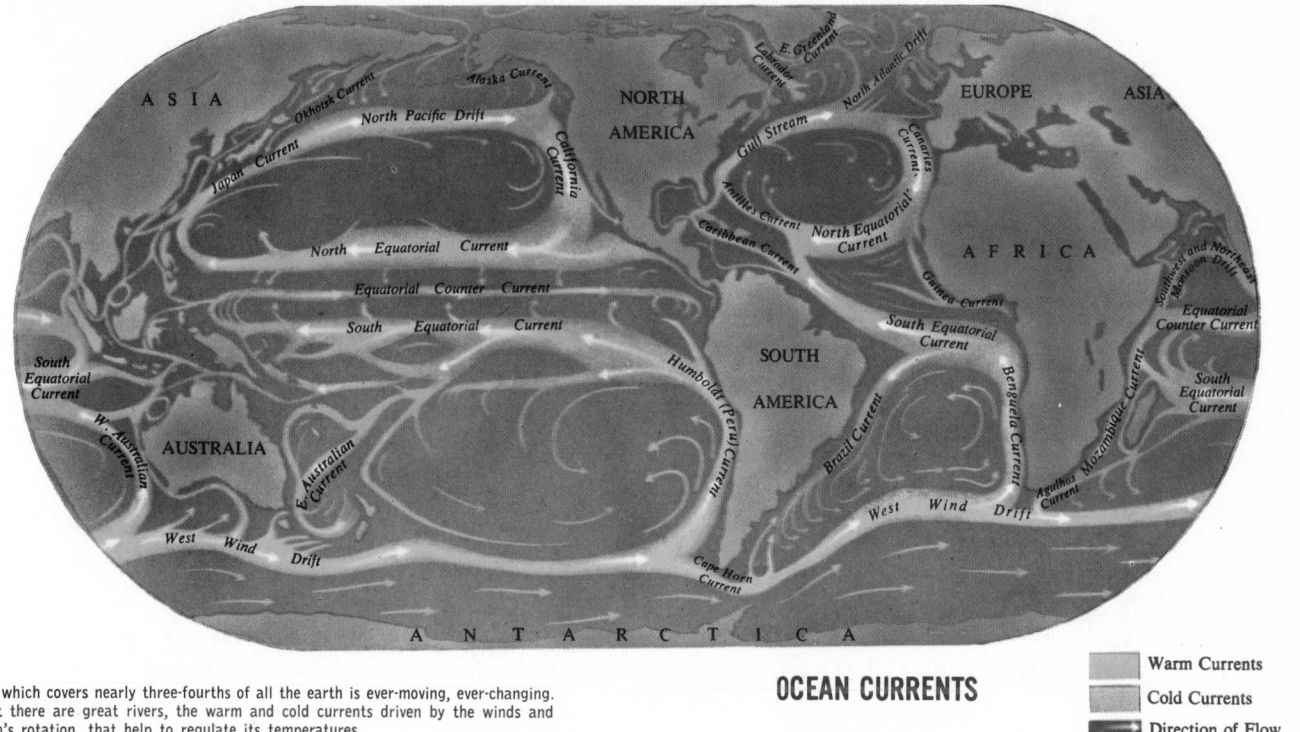

The sea, which covers nearly three-fourths of all the earth is ever-moving, ever-changing. Within it there are great rivers, the warm and cold currents driven by the winds and the earth's rotation, that help to regulate its temperatures.

OCEAN CURRENTS

Warm Currents
Cold Currents
Direction of Flow

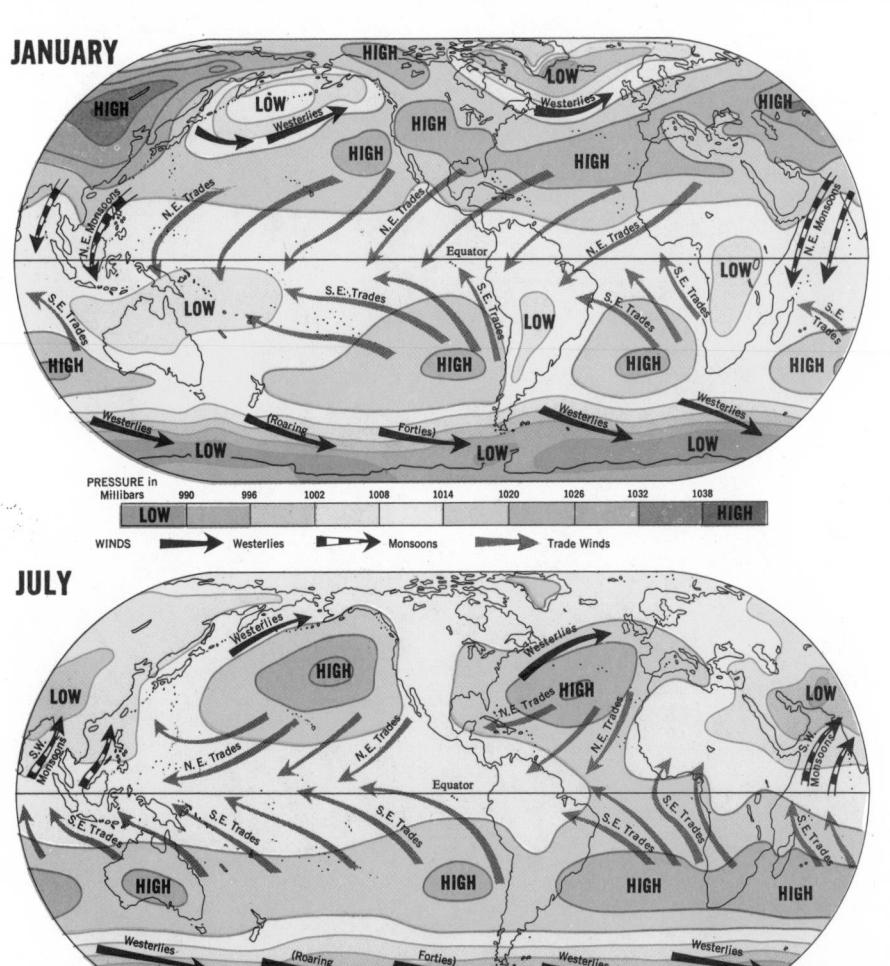

AIR PRESSURE AND WINDS

Just as the atmosphere tends to equalize heat distribution, it tends to maintain equal pressure over the earth. Whenever this equilibrium, or balance, is disturbed, air flows from areas of higher pressure to areas of lower pressure. In the Northern Hemisphere winds flow clockwise around a high pressure area (high) and counterclockwise around the center of a low pressure area (low). These movements are reversed in the Southern Hemisphere.

Life Support Cycles

With an intuition clearly beyond their scientific knowledge, the ancients of India developed a theory of reincarnation which, in some philosophic ways, parallels what science has learned of the workings of the biosphere. In the remarkable thrift of nature nothing is lost — in tremendous complex cycles atoms from the first life on earth still move through the biosphere.

The miracle of energy is constantly performed in the cycles of the "life-giving" elements. Carbon, hydrogen, oxygen, nitrogen, sulfur and phosphorus act together to produce all living matter. While many other elements such as calcium, iodine and iron are also found in living things, they are not absolute essentials in all cases. Carbon, hydrogen and oxygen are vital for photosynthesis and are the components of the basic food substances — carbohydrates and fats. Carbon, in its common gaseous form, carbon dioxide, is absorbed by green plants and triggers

the production of carbohydrate compounds by reacting with molecules of water.

Some "energy" is stored within the plant in the form of new tissue; other "energy," in the form of oxygen is released into the air to be used by other organisms. The seemingly inexhaustible supply of carbon dioxide available for use is replenished in the atmosphere through the respiration of all living things, and in the soil as bacteria and fungi break down plant and animal cells,

Nitrogen, sulfur and phosphorus are essential to animals and plants for the production and maintenance of protein. Nitrogen, with carbon, hydrogen and oxygen, is used for the growth and repair of tissue. Sulfur acts as a "stiffening" agent in all protein. To perform their functions proteins must be folded and shaped in a particular way, and their structure is maintained by bonds between sulfur atoms. While phosphorus is not a constituent of protein,

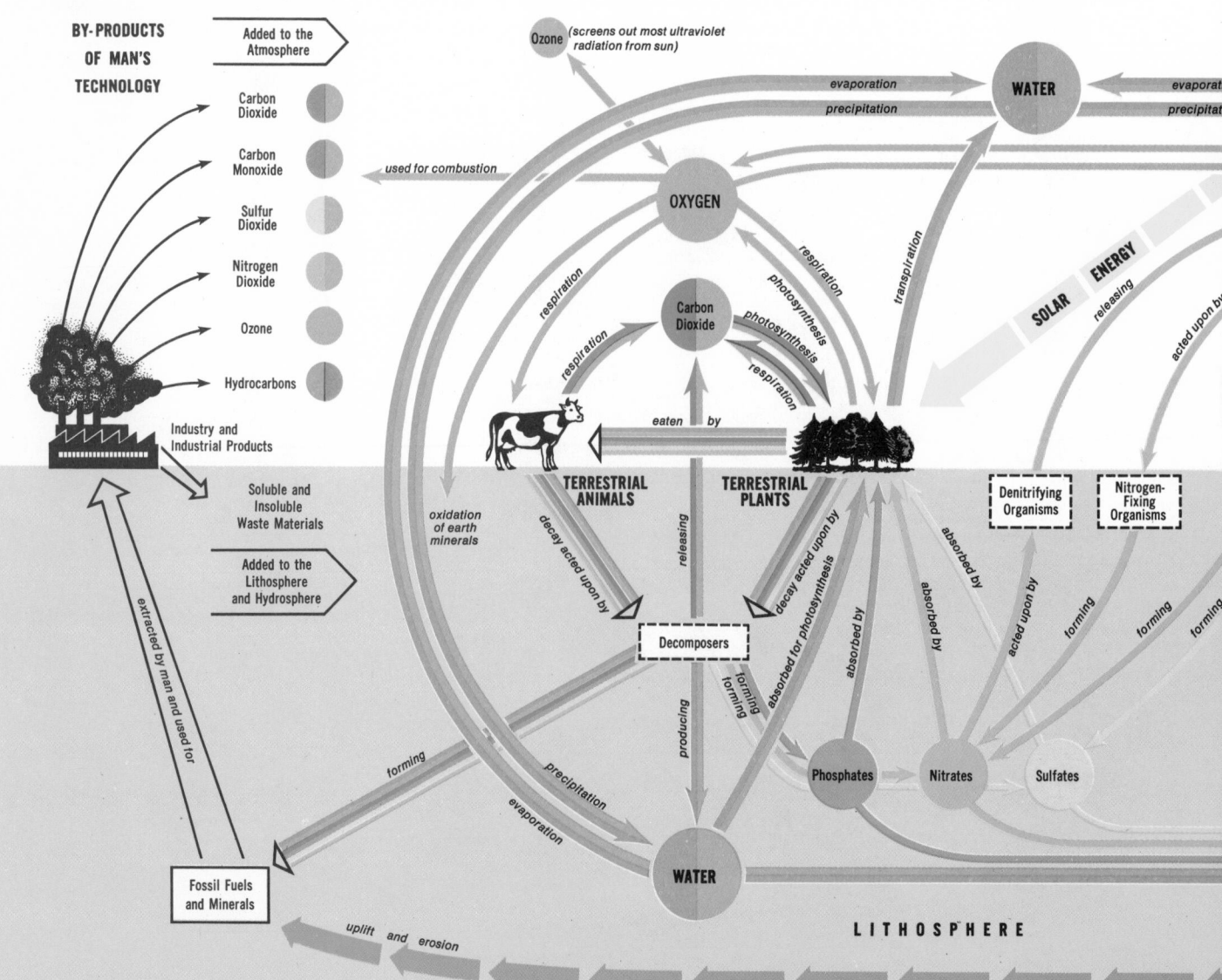

no protein can be made without it. Special phosphate compounds are the "fuel" for all biochemical work within the cell.

Although about four-fifths of the atmosphere is nitrogen, higher forms of life cannot make use of it in its "free" state and must absorb it at one or more points in its biospheric cycle. The decomposers — bacteria and fungi — act on waste matter, breaking down complex compounds into simpler usable forms including nitrogen. Some nitrogen-fixing bacteria are able to utilize atmospheric nitrogen in their own metabolism, while others convert it to those nitrogen-enriched substances necessary for all plant growth.

In nature, no part is greater than the whole and almost every element is dependent on another for some essential part of its cycle. Water, which is incorporated into every organism, is essential in the formation of free oxygen which in turn sustains the life of that organism. Water is also the principal "carrier" in the cycling of all elements. When it evaporates, water returns certain elements to the atmosphere; when it seeps through the soil on its return to the sea, water distributes nutrients to plant roots.

Carbon monoxide, sulfur and nitrogen oxides, hydrocarbons — by-products of man's industry — are being injected into the biosphere in ever-increasing amounts. There, as the "new compounds," they must in some way co-exist with the life-support cycles established throughout millions of years of evolution. Their compatability with these cycles and the organisms they nurture will determine the future of life on our planet.

Already man has learned one thing. Although the question of reincarnation or any form of life after death remains unanswered for many, science has proved that there is no natural end to the raw materials of nature or to the "new compounds" man has made from them.

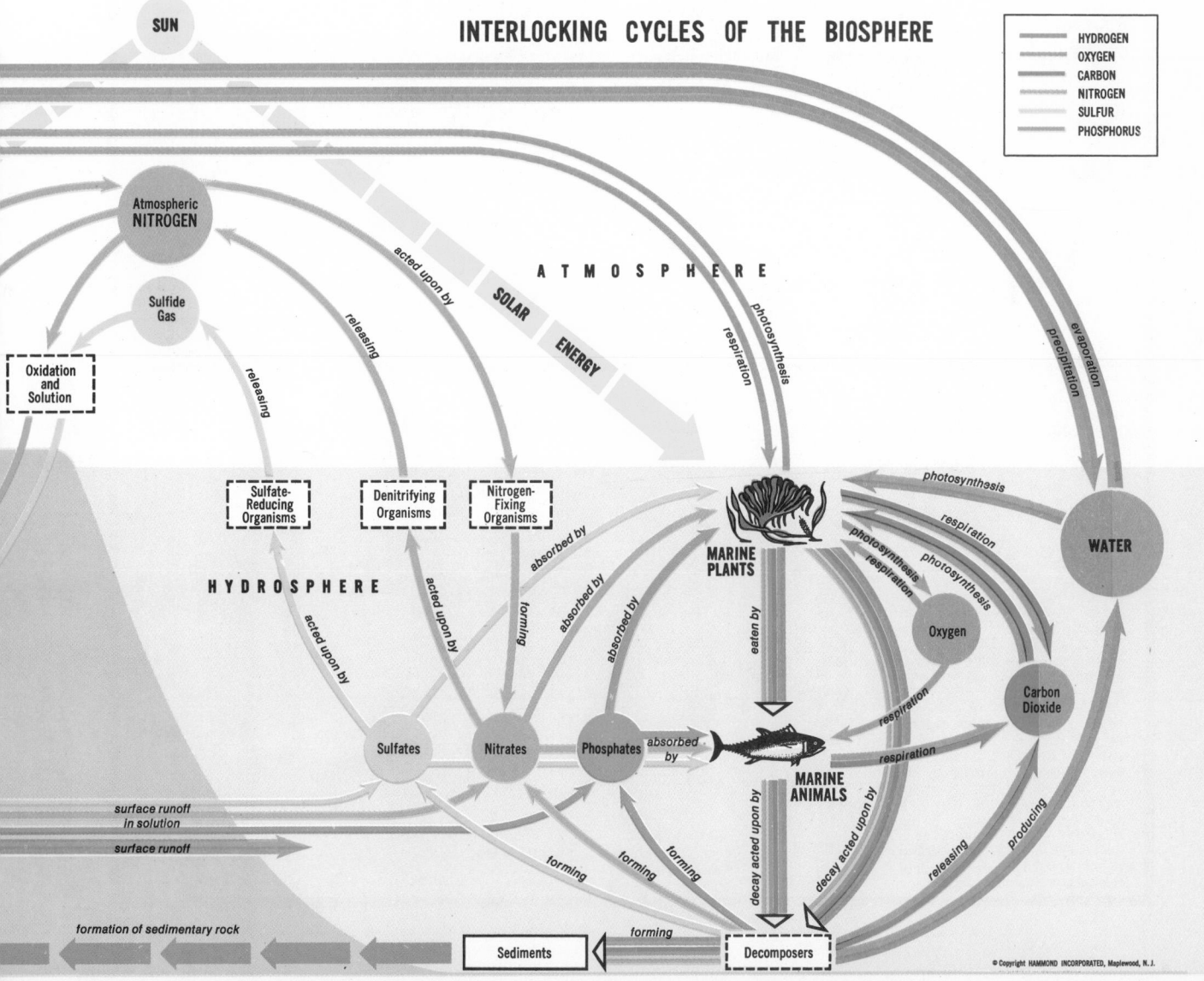

INTERLOCKING CYCLES OF THE BIOSPHERE

© Copyright HAMMOND INCORPORATED, Maplewood, N. J.

PHOTOSYNTHESIS : Converting the sun's energy

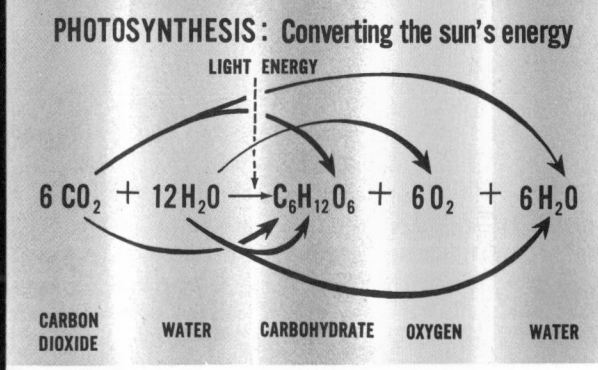

LIGHT ENERGY

$$6\ CO_2\ +\ 12\ H_2O\ \longrightarrow\ C_6H_{12}O_6\ +\ 6\ O_2\ +\ 6\ H_2O$$

| CARBON DIOXIDE | WATER | CARBOHYDRATE | OXYGEN | WATER |

Using light energy, green plants build up organic foods such as carbohydrates — stored chemical energy to be used by the entire community — from the simple inorganic substances of carbon dioxide and water. The important by-product of this reaction is the release of oxygen, an element vital to the respiration of all living things.

THE LEAF : An organ of photosynthesis
CROSS SECTION

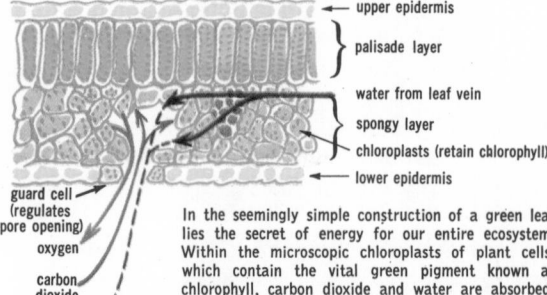

- upper epidermis
- palisade layer
- water from leaf vein
- spongy layer
- chloroplasts (retain chlorophyll)
- lower epidermis

guard cell (regulates pore opening)
oxygen
carbon dioxide
water vapor

In the seemingly simple construction of a green leaf lies the secret of energy for our entire ecosystem. Within the microscopic chloroplasts of plant cells, which contain the vital green pigment known as chlorophyll, carbon dioxide and water are absorbed, decomposed and converted into carbohydrate and oxygen molecules. Special "guard cells" control the surface pore openings to regulate the intake and output of materials.

PRODUCER - CONSUMER FOOD WEB

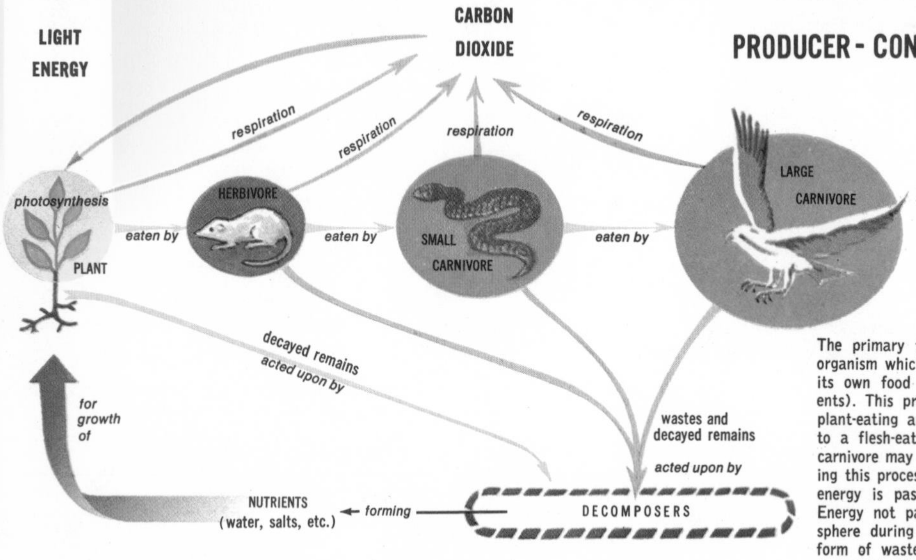

LIGHT ENERGY

CARBON DIOXIDE

respiration   respiration   respiration   respiration

photosynthesis

PLANT   HERBIVORE   SMALL CARNIVORE   LARGE CARNIVORE

eaten by   eaten by   eaten by

decayed remains acted upon by

for growth of

wastes and decayed remains

acted upon by

NUTRIENTS (water, salts, etc.) ← forming ← DECOMPOSERS

Some of the complex relationships of life in an ecological system can be described by tracing the passage of energy through a simplified community in what is called a food chain or web.

The primary food source is the producer, that organism which uses light energy to manufacture its own food from inorganic substances (nutrients). This producer or plant is consumed by a plant-eating animal which in turn may fall prey to a flesh-eating animal or carnivore. A larger carnivore may extend the food chain further. During this process part of the consumed organism's energy is passed on to the consuming animal. Energy not passed on is released to the atmosphere during respiration or to the soil in the form of waste materials. Eventually, death and decay of all organisms lead to a recycling of nutrient compounds to be used by the producers.

CHAIN OF LIFE IN THE SEA

Although community members are constructed to adapt to their watery habitat, the chain of life in the sea is quite similar to the chain of life on land.

The most important members of the oceanic community are those that contain chlorophyll or a chlorophyll-like substance and thus are able to make organic matter from inorganic ingredients. Algae and phytoplankton are the ocean's principal producers. In the open seas the initial consumers are tiny crustacea only a few centimeters long, while in coastal waters these consumers include the more familiar starfish, sea urchins, molluscs and some worms.

Just as on land, where the smaller or weaker animal is consumed by the larger and stronger, members of the oceanic community feed upon each other. Nutrients are returned to the atmosphere through respiration and to the hydrosphere through a breakdown of complex organisms by the work of decomposing organisms.

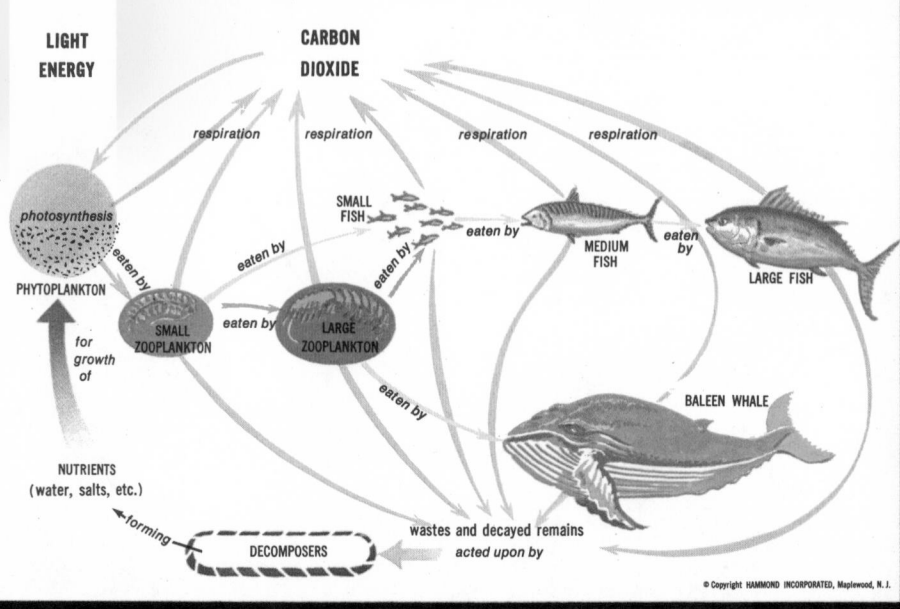

LIGHT ENERGY

CARBON DIOXIDE

respiration   respiration   respiration   respiration

photosynthesis

PHYTOPLANKTON

SMALL ZOOPLANKTON   LARGE ZOOPLANKTON

SMALL FISH   MEDIUM FISH   LARGE FISH

BALEEN WHALE

eaten by   eaten by   eaten by   eaten by   eaten by

eaten by

for growth of

NUTRIENTS (water, salts, etc.)

forming   DECOMPOSERS

wastes and decayed remains acted upon by

Ecology:
INTERRELATION OF LIVING THINGS AND THEIR SURROUNDINGS

Freedom and independence do not exist in the universe except in the creative reaches of man's intellect which distinguishes him from the other living organisms with which he shares a portion of the biosphere.

Dependent on the sun for its creation, the earth is dependent on it still for solar energy to sustain and move all living things. The amount and types of earthly life are determined by the amounts and patterns of flow of this energy which is fixed by green plants and converted into the organic compounds to maintain the plants themselves and every other organism.

In a seemingly tangled web of forces — in competition, cooperation, neutrality — in a constantly changing and more or less suitable climate, and in the processes of evolution continually in flux throughout the thin layers of atmosphere, earth and sea, strands of mutual dependence have been woven. Each form of life, from the simple one-celled organism to the complexity of man, is subject to the same laws of nature, depending one upon the other for energy and food — creating it as they destroy it and are destroyed themselves.

The word "ecology" comes from two Greek words meaning "the study of the home," and in modern times has signified the study of all living things in relation to their environments — or homes — and to each other. Western man, particularly, has romanticised his notion of a home and often chose to think of it as a solitary fortress snug against intrusion by other men and the forces of nature. But the making and maintaining of a home for man as for other forms of life is a subtle combination and balance of light, heat, moisture and food any one of which may be disturbed or destroyed by natural calamity or inadvertent act.

Through a closer study of ecology and ecological systems man is learning, hopefully not too late, that even the "lilies of the field," which neither sow nor reap, are as essential to him as are the insects clinging to their leaves, the rodents burrowing at their feet, and the soil and air that they enrich.

A TYPICAL FOOD CHAIN

1. Through the process of photosynthesis a green plant or primary producer begins the food chain.

2. A cricket, feeding upon the plant, becomes a primary consumer.

3. A secondary consumer is the frog who devours the cricket.

4. It is the fate of the frog to turn into a meal for the snake, the third or tertiary consumer.

5. The food chain ends with a snake-eating hawk, the fourth consumer, who has no predator other than man.

Photos: Ernst G. Hofmann

Man's Impact Upon Nature

Since he could think man has been at war with death. He has fought his battles against destruction with science and technology as his weapons, virtually eliminating his own annihilation by predatory animals and from diseases such as leprosy, tuberculosis and diphtheria. He has walked into many valleys of death to fight malaria and yellow fever, and he has resolved that each year more of his own kind will live to finish out their threescore years and ten.

However, the victory over nature, which had balanced population with food supply and space, is bitter, for the population has "exploded" leaving man with the seemingly insolvable problem of providing more food and space for himself or reducing his numbers by starvation or by war.

Man outsmarted himself in many ways as he worked toward creating a more perfect world for himself without understanding that natural laws go beyond human manipulation. He has destroyed forests and meadows, polluted the water and air, eliminated organisms that tried to share his bread. However, he has yet to learn to recreate the wood and brush or the interdependent communities of bacteria, insects and animals that he learned — too late — enrich the air, the soil and the water and without which he cannot function.

Modern man knows how to manufacture "miraculous" materials to work for his pleasure or his seemingly insatiable needs, but the sophistications of technology have yet to control effectively the by-products. These new materials, still subject to the order of nature's cycles, penetrate the biosphere and eventually come to roost in his own vulnerable body.

New battles are being fought throughout the world and new standards bearing the slogans of ecology float in the "unsafe" air. It is somehow ironic to find that many people now believe that man has been fighting the wrong fight in his gigantic struggle with nature. That, after all, nature never was his enemy.

Man cannot turn back to his beginnings when he lived with, and not against, the natural world. But a compromise between technology and nature must take place for our "plundered planet" cries out for the day of reckoning.

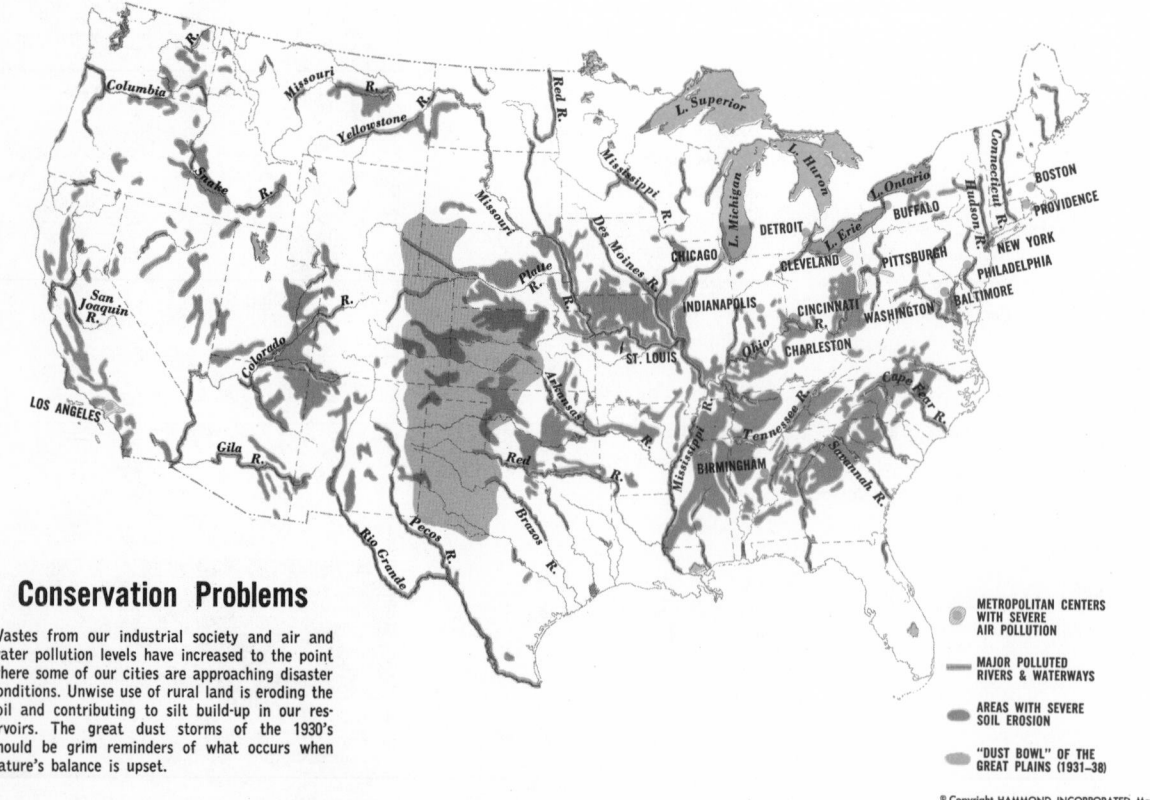

Conservation Problems

Wastes from our industrial society and air and water pollution levels have increased to the point where some of our cities are approaching disaster conditions. Unwise use of rural land is eroding the soil and contributing to silt build-up in our reservoirs. The great dust storms of the 1930's should be grim reminders of what occurs when nature's balance is upset.

METROPOLITAN CENTERS WITH SEVERE AIR POLLUTION

MAJOR POLLUTED RIVERS & WATERWAYS

AREAS WITH SEVERE SOIL EROSION

"DUST BOWL" OF THE GREAT PLAINS (1931–38)

A sloping barnyard provides a convenient runoff for chemical and organic fertilizers, causing overenrichment (eutrophication) of the pond.

Trash burning billows clouds of air pollution over the nation's capital.

A forest stripped of trees reduces the supply of oxygen-producing greenery and inhibits good soil development and maintenance.

Poor drainage procedures near a housing development produce unstable soil, resulting in earth slides.

Unauthorized dumping affects the beauty of the countryside and later will pollute the nearby river.

Photos: U.S. Department of Agriculture

This stream is rapidly becoming polluted because of the direct discharge of soap and detergent suds into it.

POLLUTION CIRCLE
TYPES OF POLLUTION AND THEIR EFFECT ON THE TOTAL ENVIRONMENT

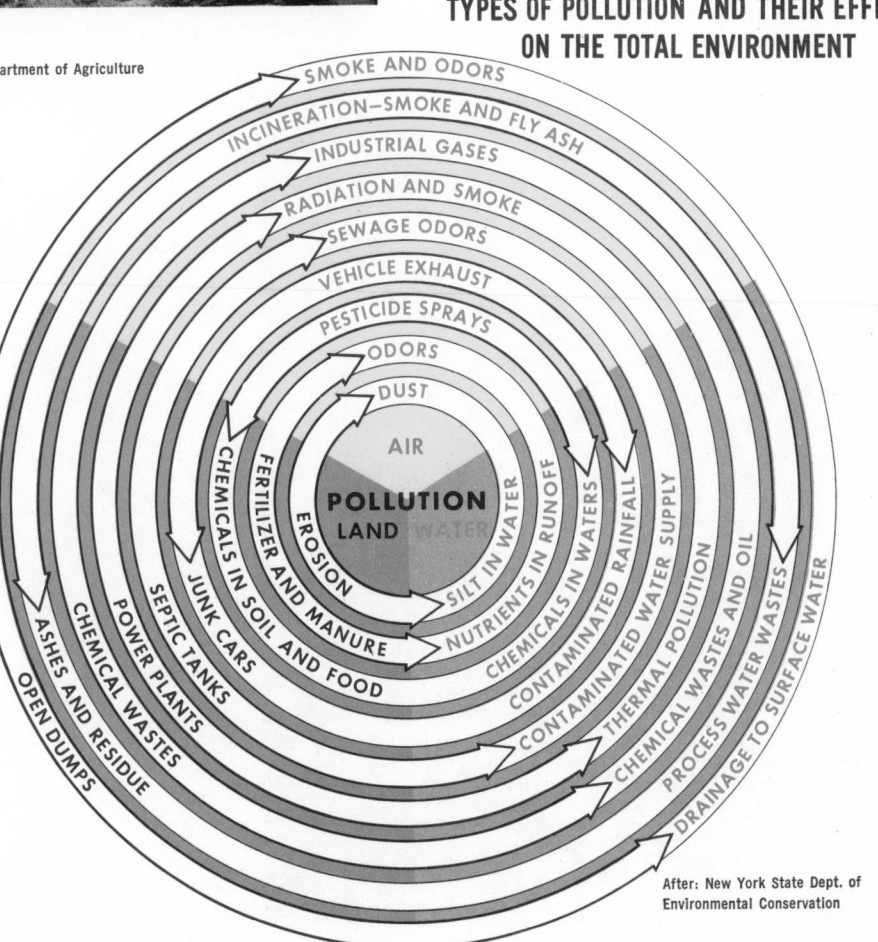

After: New York State Dept. of Environmental Conservation

The Moon:
MAN'S FIRST SPACE ODYSSEY

From the physicist to the clothes designer, from the astronomer to the welder, working in close cooperation or in isolated laboratories on almost every continent of the world, men have been involved in a mighty labor to secure their first steps into outer space.

Tantalizing and always beyond reach, the sun, the moon, the stars and the planets had been examined only by instruments, unmanned spacecraft and the earthbound imagination. For no man could live in the hazardous environment of space. The heat of friction, the deadly cold of the outer skies and the destructive girdles of radiation surrounding the earth maintained an atmosphere where no earthly organism could survive. But with the enigmatic world of space always before his eyes and prodding his imagination, man had determined to recreate and maintain his earthly environment for life beyond his normal realm.

The mysterious and "inconstant" moon, for centuries the territory of lovers and poets, became the target of technology. On July 20, 1969, two men, bundled beyond recognition in their protective lunar skins, wandered over the airless, waterless wastes of the moon's surface. They picked up rocks as they might have done as children while people the world over waited and prayed, thinking of different poems to be written in the vocabulary of the new age of enlightenment.

Bits of lunar soil, samples of rock and dust returned to earth with the lunar voyagers. As they were studied and analyzed new questions waited to be answered.

Man returned again to the lunar steppes, proving beyond doubt that he can carry his environment beyond terrestrial boundaries — proving perhaps that he will carry out his dream to live among the stars.

FAR SIDE MOON HEMISPHERE
Artist's rendering based on Lunar Orbiter photographs by NASA

A spacecraft's view of the moon shows portions of both the near and far sides. While appearing almost "full" to a visiting astronaut, the moon would only be entering its first-quarter phase to an observer on earth.

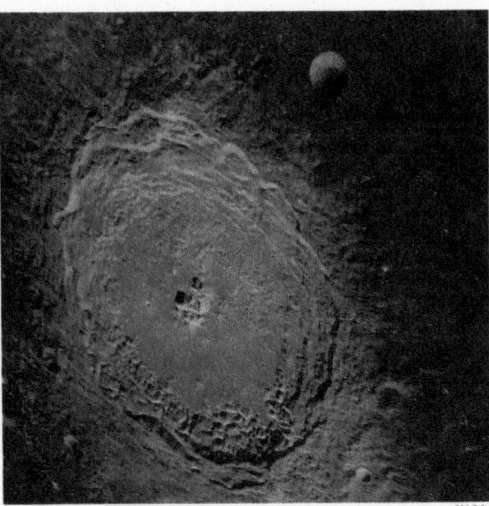

NASA

An oblique view depicts the forbidding rugged terrain encountered on the moon. A crescent earth is seen just above the horizon.

NASA

The crater Langrenus is pictured from an altitude of about 170 miles. Note the conspicuous terrace features visible on the inner crater wall.

NASA

A closeup of lunar surface material is seen. Chemical analysis of samples shows a resemblance to terrestrial igneous rocks, although percentages of specific elements may vary considerably.

NEAR SIDE MOON HEMISPHERE
Base photo mosaic supplied by Aeronautical Chart and Information Service, U.S. Air Force

NORTH

SOUTH

Widening Horizons

Luminous sirens of space — the ancient Loreleis of night — still beckon modern man with mysteries unsolved since the beginning of human thought. Steadfastly, first through observation, later with the aid of sophisticated mathematics and technology, astronomers have pursued the elusive inhabitants of space to the 20th century only to find that the more they learn the less they seem to know. It was not long ago that man believed that if he was not yet master of all he saw, at least he saw all there was to master. Now he knows that the earthly solar system, extending about three and a half billion miles in space, is but a tiny part of a universe only dimly perceived during the last few years.

Some 5,000 stars can be seen with the naked eye on a clear night. The perceptive lens of the Palomar telescope discloses billions of other heavenly bodies at distances be-

yond all but the wildest imaginings of most earthlings. And beyond them? Again some millions more stretching out in space yet undisclosed to human measurement.

The terms of time and space with which the earth scientist is familiar have no meaning as the horizons of the expanding universe retreat. With what perspective can he view the distant galaxies as they rush away from his at speeds proportionate to their distance from earth's solar system? How far will they travel and where? How can he judge their place in time when their light already has traveled millions of years to reach his eyes?

Today's cosmologist has learned to deal with speculations and assumptions as he gropes through the twilight of uncharted worlds, returning again and again to the unsolved puzzle of infinity.

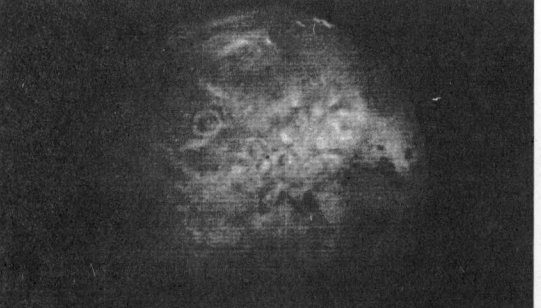

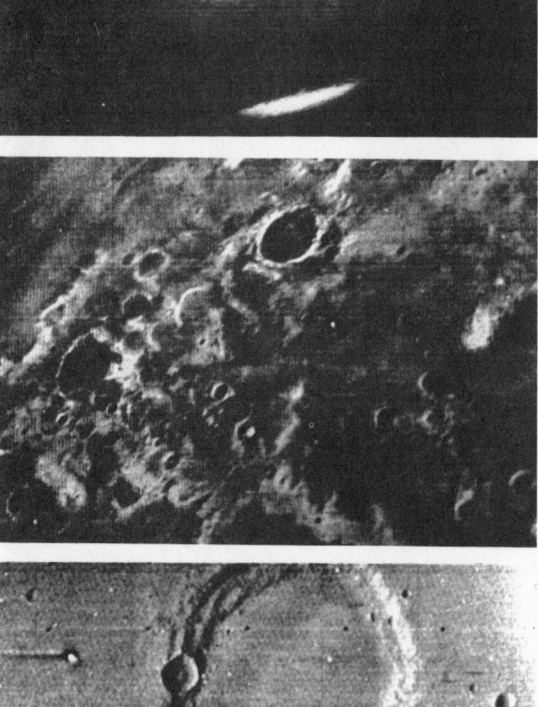

CLOSEUP VIEWS OF MARS
Except for its familiar white south polar cap, Mars has surface features strikingly similar to lunar topography.

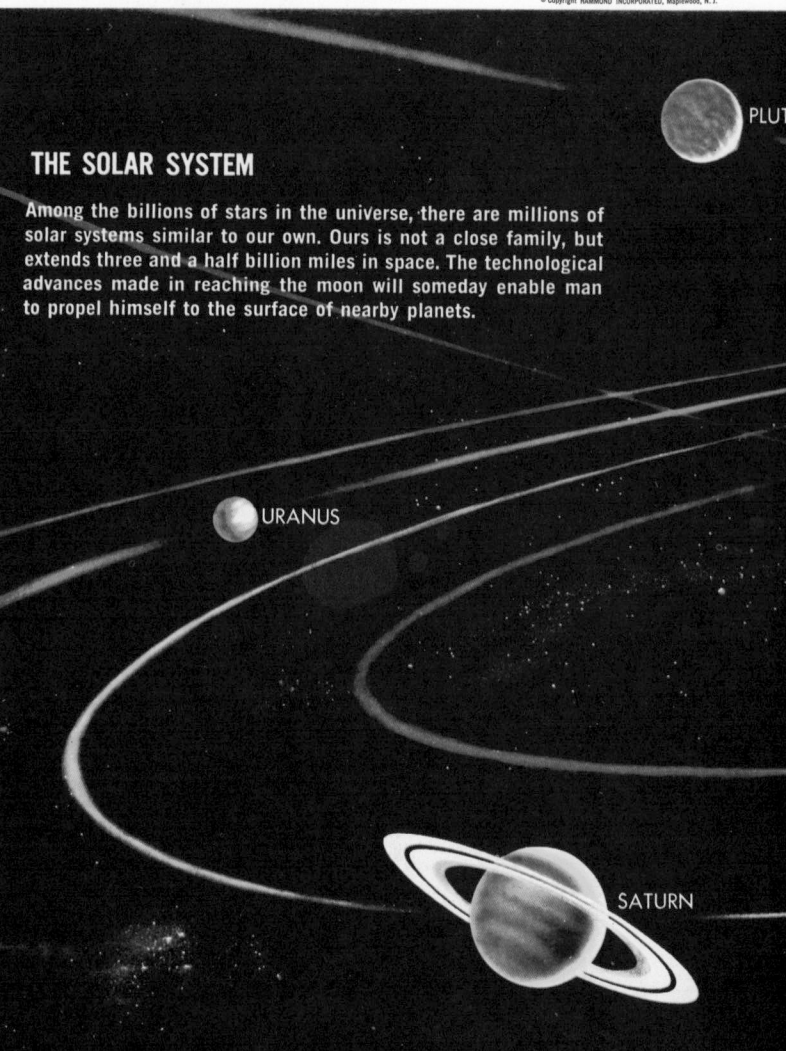

THE SOLAR SYSTEM

Among the billions of stars in the universe, there are millions of solar systems similar to our own. Ours is not a close family, but extends three and a half billion miles in space. The technological advances made in reaching the moon will someday enable man to propel himself to the surface of nearby planets.

PLUTO

URANUS

SATURN

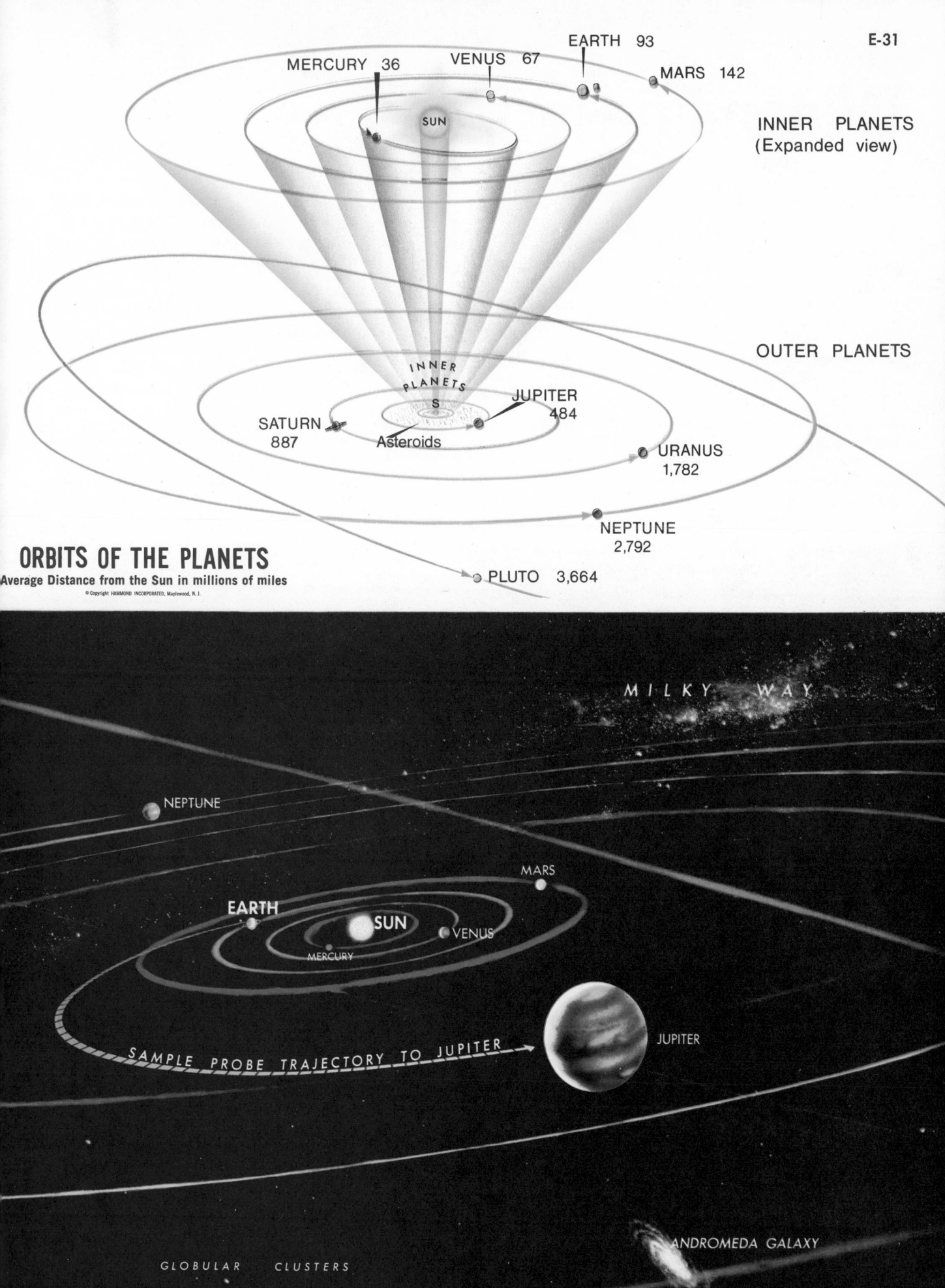

MERCURY 36   VENUS 67   EARTH 93   MARS 142

SUN

INNER PLANETS
(Expanded view)

OUTER PLANETS

INNER
PLANETS

S

JUPITER
484

SATURN
887

Asteroids

URANUS
1,782

NEPTUNE
2,792

PLUTO 3,664

ORBITS OF THE PLANETS
Average Distance from the Sun in millions of miles

© Copyright HAMMOND INCORPORATED, Maplewood, N.J.

MILKY WAY

NEPTUNE

MARS

EARTH

SUN

VENUS

MERCURY

SAMPLE PROBE TRAJECTORY TO JUPITER →

JUPITER

GLOBULAR CLUSTERS

ANDROMEDA GALAXY

In soaring cities, in golden plains of wheat, in the meanderings of highways, in the warmth of firesides — in homes, factories, forests, farms and seasides — we see the tracings of man's intellect and imagination. Unlike other creatures man's energies are not directed merely toward survival but to the challenge of creating his own environment.

For too many years man has played games with his environment without knowing nature's ground rules and it has become apparent, even to children, that the tools that mold the stuffs of nature to man's liking are double-edged.

It is unlikely that man will turn his wits and his technology toward a return to a simple and primitive way of life. It is also unlikely that man can stand still and survive.

Now man must begin to grapple with causes that have more than one effect. It is time for man to meditate on his heritage and to act, remembering that "knowledge is a fountain of life to him who possesses it."